STUDENT LOAN LAW

Collections, Intercepts, Deferments, Discharges, Repayment Plans, and Trade School Abuses

Third Edition

With CD-Rom

Deanne Loonin

Contributing Author: John Rao

National Consumer Law Center

77 Summer Street, 10th Floor   Boston, MA 02110

www.consumerlaw.org

About NCLC

The National Consumer Law Center, a nonprofit corporation founded in 1969, assists consumers, advocates, and public policy makers nationwide who use the powerful and complex tools of consumer law to ensure justice and fair treatment for all, particularly those whose poverty renders them powerless to demand accountability from the economic marketplace. For more information, go to www.consumerlaw.org.

Ordering NCLC Publications

Order securely online at www.consumerlaw.org, or contact Publications Department, National Consumer Law Center, 77 Summer Street, Boston, MA 02110, (617) 542-9595, FAX: (617) 542-8028, e-mail: publications@nclc.org.

Training and Conferences

NCLC participates in numerous national, regional, and local consumer law trainings. Its annual fall conference is a forum for consumer rights attorneys from legal services programs, private practice, government, and nonprofit organizations to share insights into common problems and explore novel and tested approaches that promote consumer justice in the marketplace. Contact NCLC for more information or see our web site.

Case Consulting

Case analysis, consulting and co-counseling for lawyers representing vulnerable consumers are among NCLC's important activities. Administration on Aging funds allow us to provide free consulting to legal services advocates representing elderly consumers on many types of cases. Massachusetts Legal Assistance Corporation funds permit case assistance to advocates representing low-income Massachusetts consumers. Other funding may allow NCLC to provide very brief consultations to other advocates without charge. More comprehensive case analysis and research is available for a reasonable fee. See our web site for more information at www.consumerlaw.org.

Charitable Donations and Cy Pres Awards

NCLC's work depends in part on the support of private donors. Tax-deductible donations should be made payable to National Consumer Law Center, Inc. For more information, contact Suzanne Cutler of NCLC's Development Office at (617) 542-8010 or scutler@nclc.org. NCLC has also received generous court-approved *cy pres* awards arising from consumer class actions to advance the interests of class members. For more information, contact Robert Hobbs (rhobbs@nclc.org) or Rich Dubois (rdubois@nclc.org) at (617) 542-8010.

Comments and Corrections

Write to the above address to the attention of the Editorial Department or e-mail consumerlaw@nclc.org.

About This Volume

This is the Third Edition of *Student Loan Law* with a 2006 companion CD-Rom. The Third Edition and 2006 CD-Rom supersede all prior editions, supplements, and CDs, which should all be discarded. Continuing developments can be found in periodic updates to this volume and in NCLC REPORTS.

Cite This Volume As

National Consumer Law Center, Student Loan Law (3d ed. 2006).

Attention

This publication is designed to provide authoritative information concerning the subject matter covered. Always use the most current edition and supplement, and use other sources for more recent developments or for special rules for individual jurisdictions. This publication cannot substitute for the independent judgment and skills of an attorney or other professional. Non-attorneys are cautioned against using these materials to conduct a lawsuit without advice from an attorney and are cautioned against engaging in the unauthorized practice of law.

About the Authors

Deanne Loonin is an NCLC staff attorney focusing on student loan law. She also works more generally in the areas of credit discrimination and consumer credit law, with an emphasis on issues affecting the elderly and new immigrants. She was formerly a legal services attorney in Los Angeles specializing in consumer fraud cases. She is the author of the first and second editions of this volume and co-author of *Credit Discrimination* (4th ed. 2005) and *Surviving Debt* (2006).

John Rao is an NCLC attorney focusing on consumer bankruptcy and credit law. He is the editor of *Consumer Bankruptcy Law and Practice* (8th ed. 2006), co-author of *Foreclosures* (2005), and a contributing author to *Student Loan Law* (2d ed. 2002) and *Repossessions* (6th ed. 2005). He is also a contributing author to *Collier on Bankruptcy* and the *Collier Bankruptcy Practice Guide*. For 18 years, he had a bankruptcy and consumer law focus at Rhode Island Legal Services and was a managing attorney there. He is a member of the board of directors of the National Association of Consumer Bankruptcy Attorneys and the American Bankruptcy Institute.

Acknowledgments: We are particularly grateful to Dorothy Tan for editorial supervision; Nathan Day for editorial assistance; Allen Agnitti, Gillian Feiner and Hellen Papavizas for research assistance; Mary Kingsley, Kurt Terwilliger, and Shirlron Williams for assistance with cite checking; Shannon Halbrook for production assistance; Mary McLean for indexing, Xylutions for typesetting services; and Neil Fogarty of Law Disks for developing the CD-Rom.

Thanks also to Geoff Walsh and Tara Twomey for their work on chapter 7, and to the following people for contributing pleadings and other information to this and prior editions: Elena Ackel, Irv Ackelsberg, Peter Barry, Tom Domonoske, Stephen Gardner, George Gingo, Kathryn Harlow, Walter Oney, Dale Pittman, James Smith, Jane Stevens, Jennifer Stoller, Alan White, and Brian Wolfman. We would also like to thank a number of Department of Education staff who have generously answered questions and clarified department policies, especially Gary Hopkins, Denise Leifeste, Susan Szabo and Debra Wiley. Special thanks to Jon Sheldon for authoring the student loan chapters in *Unfair and Deceptive Acts and Practices*, which provided the springboard for this volume.

What Your Library Should Contain

The Consumer Credit and Sales Legal Practice Series contains 17 titles, updated annually, arranged into four libraries, and designed to be an attorney's primary practice guide and legal resource in all 50 states. Each manual includes a CD-Rom allowing pinpoint searches and the pasting of text into a word processor.

Debtor Rights Library

2006 Eighth Edition (Two Volumes) with CD-Rom, Including Law Disks' 2006 Bankruptcy Forms

Consumer Bankruptcy Law and Practice: the definitive personal bankruptcy manual, from the initial interview to final discharge, including consumer rights as creditors when a company files for bankruptcy. This revised edition fully incorporates the 2005 Act in the text and includes such practice aids as a redlined Code, Interim Rules, a date calculator, over 150 pleadings and forms, initial forms software, means test data, and a client questionnaire and handout.

2004 Fifth Edition, 2006 Supplement, and 2006 CD-Rom

Fair Debt Collection: the basic reference, covering the Fair Debt Collection Practices Act and common law, state statutory and other federal debt collection protections. Appendices and companion CD-Rom contain sample pleadings and discovery, the FTC Commentary, *all* FTC staff opinion letters, and summaries of reported and unreported cases.

2005 First Edition, 2006 Supplement, and 2006 CD-Rom

Foreclosures: a new volume covering VA, FHA and other types of home foreclosures, workout agreements, servicer obligations, and tax liens. The CD-Rom reprints key federal statutes, regulations, interpretations, and handbooks, and contains numerous pleadings.

2005 Sixth Edition, 2006 Supplement, and 2006 CD-Rom

Repossessions: a unique guide to motor vehicle and mobile home repossessions, threatened seizures of household goods, statutory liens, and automobile lease and rent-to-own default remedies. The CD-Rom reprints relevant UCC provisions, summarizes many other state statutes, and includes many pleadings covering a wide variety of cases.

2006 Third Edition with CD-Rom

Student Loan Law: student loan debt collection; closed school, false certification, disability, and other discharges; tax intercepts, wage garnishment, and offset of social security benefits; and repayment plans, consolidation loans, deferments, and non-payment of loan based on school fraud. CD-Rom and appendices contain numerous forms, pleadings, letters and regulations.

2004 Third Edition, 2006 Supplement, and 2006 CD-Rom

Access to Utility Service: the only examination of consumer rights when dealing with regulated, de-regulated, and unregulated utilities, including telecommunications, terminations, billing errors, low-income payment plans, utility allowances in subsidized housing, LIHEAP, and weatherization. Includes summaries of state utility regulations.

Credit and Banking Library

2003 Fifth Edition, 2006 Supplement, and 2006 CD-Rom

Truth in Lending: detailed analysis of *all* aspects of TILA, the Consumer Leasing Act, and the Home Ownership and Equity Protection Act (HOEPA). Appendices and the CD-Rom contain the Acts, Reg. Z, Reg. M, and their Official Staff Commentaries, numerous sample pleadings, rescission notices, and two programs to compute APRs.

National Consumer Law Center ▪ **77 Summer Street** ▪ **10ᵗʰ Floor** ▪ **Boston MA** ▪ **02110**
(617) 542-9595 ▪ **FAX (617) 542-8028** ▪ **publications@nclc.org**
Order securely online at www.consumerlaw.org

2006 Sixth Edition with CD-Rom	**Fair Credit Reporting:** the cleaning up blemished credit . reports. Covers credit scoring, the Credit Repair Organizations A law claims.
2005 Third Edition, 2006 Supplement, and 2006 CD-Rom	**Consumer Banking and Payments La** rules) as to checks, money orders, credit, d setoff. Also extensive treatment of electronic food stamps, and direct deposits of federal pay relevant agency interpretations and pleadings.
2005 Third Edition, 2006 Supplement, and 2006 CD-Rom	**The Cost of Credit: Regulation, Preemption, and Ind** detailing state and federal regulation of consumer credit in . emp-tion, explaining credit math, and how to challenge excessive c . surance. The CD-Rom includes a credit math program and hard-to-find a s.
2005 Fourth Edition, 2006 Supplement, and 2006 CD-Rom	**Credit Discrimination:** analysis of the Equal Credit Opportuni , Fair Housing Act, Civil Rights Acts, and state credit discrimination statutes, including reprints of all relevant federal interpretations, government enforcement actions, and numerous sample pleadings.

Consumer Litigation Library

2004 Fourth Edition, 2006 Supplement, and 2006 CD-Rom	**Consumer Arbitration Agreements:** numerous successful approaches to challenge the enforceability of a binding arbitration agreement, the interrelation of the Federal Arbitration Act and state law, class actions in arbitration, collections via arbitration, the right to discovery, and other topics. Appendices and CD-Rom include sample discovery, numerous briefs, arbitration service provider rules and affidavits as to arbitrator costs and bias.
2006 Sixth Edition with CD-Rom	**Consumer Class Actions:** makes class action litigation manageable even for small offices, including numerous sample pleadings, class certification memoranda, discovery, class notices, settlement materials, and much more. Includes a detailed analysis of the Class Action Fairness Act of 2005, recent changes to Rule 23, class arbitration, and other contributions from experienced consumer class action litigators around the country.
2006 CD-Rom with Index Guide: ALL pleadings from ALL NCLC Manuals, including Consumer Law Pleadings Numbers One through Twelve	**Consumer Law Pleadings on CD-Rom:** Over 1200 notable recent pleadings from all types of consumer cases, including predatory lending, foreclosures, automobile fraud, lemon laws, debt collection, fair credit reporting, home improvement fraud, rent to own, student loans, and lender liability. Finding aids pinpoint the desired pleading in seconds, ready to paste into a word processing program.

Deception and Warranties Library

2004 Sixth Edition, 2006 Supplement, and 2006 CD-Rom	**Unfair and Deceptive Acts and Practices:** the only practice manual covering all aspects of a deceptive practices case in every state. Special sections on automobile sales, the federal racketeering (RICO) statute, unfair insurance practices, and the FTC Holder Rule.
2003 Second Edition, 2006 Supplement, and 2006 CD-Rom	**Automobile Fraud:** examination of title law, odometer tampering, lemon laundering, sale of salvage and wrecked cars, undisclosed prior use, prior damage to new cars, numerous sample pleadings, and title search techniques.
2006 Third Edition with CD-Rom	**Consumer Warranty Law:** comprehensive treatment of new and used car lemon laws, the Magnuson-Moss Warranty Act, UCC Articles 2 and 2A, mobile home, new home, and assistive device warranty laws, FTC Used Car Rule, tort theories, car repair and home improvement statutes, service contract and lease laws, with numerous sample pleadings.

National Consumer Law Center ■ **77 Summer Street** ■ **10th Floor** ■ **Boston MA** ■ **02110**
(617) 542-9595 ■ **FAX (617) 542-8028** ■ **publications@nclc.org**
Order securely online at www.consumerlaw.org

CD-Roms

Every NCLC manual comes with a companion CD-Rom featuring pop-up menus, PDF-format, Internet-style navigation of appendices, indices, and bonus pleadings, hard-to-find agency interpretations and other practice aids. Documents can be copied into a word processing program. Of special note is *Consumer Law in a Box*:

December 2006 CD-Rom

Consumer Law in a Box: a double CD-Rom combining *all* documents and software from 17 other NCLC CD-Roms. Quickly pinpoint a document from thousands found on the CD through keyword searches and Internet-style navigation, links, bookmarks, and other finding aids.

Other NCLC Publications for Lawyers

issued 24 times a year

NCLC REPORTS covers the latest developments and ideas in the practice of consumer law.

2006 Second Edition with CD-Rom

The Practice of Consumer Law: Seeking Economic Justice: contains an essential overview to consumer law and explains how to get started in a private or legal services consumer practice. Packed with invaluable sample pleadings and practice pointers for even experienced consumer attorneys.

First Edition with CD-Rom

STOP Predatory Lending: A Guide for Legal Advocates: provides a roadmap and practical legal strategy for litigating predatory lending abuses, from small loans to mortgage loans. The CD-Rom contains a credit math program, pleadings, legislative and administrative materials, and underwriting guidelines.

National Consumer Law Center Guide Series are books designed for consumers, counselors, and attorneys new to consumer law:

2006 Edition

NCLC Guide to Surviving Debt: a great overview of consumer law. Everything a paralegal, new attorney, or client needs to know about debt collectors, managing credit card debt, whether to refinance, credit card problems, home foreclosures, evictions, repossessions, credit reporting, utility terminations, student loans, budgeting, and bankruptcy.

2006 Edition

NCLC Guide to the Rights of Utility Consumers: explains consumer rights concerning electric, gas, and other utility services: shut off protections, rights to restore terminated service, bill payment options, weatherization tips, rights to government assistance, and much more.

2006 Edition

NCLC Guide to the Consumer Rights for Domestic Violence Survivors: provides practical advice to help survivors get back on their feet financially and safely establish their economic independence.

First Edition

NCLC Guide to Mobile Homes: what consumers and their advocates need to know about mobile home dealer sales practices and an in-depth look at mobile home quality and defects, with 35 photographs and construction details.

First Edition

Return to Sender: Getting a Refund or Replacement for Your Lemon Car: find how lemon laws work, what consumers and their lawyers should know to evaluate each other, investigative techniques and discovery tips, how to handle both informal dispute resolution and trials, and more.

> Visit **www.consumerlaw.org** to order securely online or for more information on all NCLC manuals and CD-Roms, including the full tables of contents, indices, listings of CD-Rom contents, and **web-based searches of the manuals' full text**.

National Consumer Law Center ■ **77 Summer Street** ■ **10th Floor** ■ **Boston MA** ■ **02110**
(617) 542-9595 ■ **FAX (617) 542-8028** ■ **publications@nclc.org**
Order securely online at www.consumerlaw.org

Finding Aids and Search Tips

The Consumer Credit and Sales Legal Practice Series presently contains seventeen volumes, twelve supplements, and seventeen companion CD-Roms—all constantly being updated. The Series includes over 10,000 pages, 100 chapters, 100 appendices, and over 1000 pleadings, as well as hundreds of documents found on the CD-Roms, but not found in the books. Here are a number of ways to pinpoint in seconds what you need from this array of materials.

Internet-Based Searches

www.consumerlaw.org

Electronically search every chapter and appendix of all seventeen manuals and their supplements: go to www.consumerlaw.org/keyword and enter a case name, regulation cite, or other search term. You are instantly given the book names and page numbers of any of the NCLC manuals containing that term, with those hits shown in context.

www.consumerlaw.org

Current indexes, tables of contents, and CD-Rom contents for all seventeen volumes are found at www.consumerlaw.org. Just click on *The Consumer Credit and Sales Legal Practice Series* and scroll down to the book you want. Then click on that volume's index, contents, or CD-Rom contents.

Finding Material on NCLC's CD-Roms

Consumer Law in a Box CD-Rom

Electronically search all seventeen NCLC CD-Roms, including thousands of agency interpretations, all NCLC appendices and over 1000 pleadings: use Acrobat's search button* in NCLC's *Consumer Law in a Box CD-Rom* (this CD-Rom is free to set subscribers) to find every instance that a keyword appears on any of our seventeen CD-Roms. Then, with one click, go to that location to see the full text of the document.

CD-Rom accompanying this volume

Electronically search the CD-Rom accompanying this volume, including pleadings, agency interpretations, and regulations. Use Acrobat's search button* to find every instance that a keyword appears on the CD-Rom, and then, with one click, go to that location on the CD-Rom. Or just click on subject buttons until you navigate to the document you need.

Finding Pleadings

Consumer Law Pleadings on CD-Rom and Index Guide

Search five different ways for the right pleading from over 1000 choices: use the *Index Guide* accompanying *Consumer Law Pleadings on CD-Rom* to search for pleadings by type, subject, publication title, name of contributor, or contributor's jurisdiction. The guide also provides a summary of the pleading once the right pleading is located. *Consumer Law Pleadings on CD-Rom* and the *Consumer Law in a Box CD-Rom* also let you search for all pleadings electronically by subject, type of pleading, and by publication title, giving you instant access to the full pleading in Word and/or PDF format once you find the pleading you need.

Using This Volume to Find Material in All Seventeen Volumes

This volume

The Quick Reference at the back of this volume lets you pinpoint manual sections or appendices where over 1000 different subject areas are covered.

---

* Users of NCLC CD-Roms should become familiar with "search," a powerful Acrobat tool, distinguished from "find," another Acrobat feature that is less powerful than "search." The Acrobat 5 "search" icon is a pair of binoculars with paper in the background, while the "find" icon is a pair of binoculars without the paper. Acrobat 6 and 7 use one icon, a pair of binoculars labeled "Search," that opens a dialog box with search options.

Summary Contents

Contents

Chapter 3   Deferments and Forbearances

Chapter 4   Student Loan Collection

Chapter 5   **Property and Asset Seizures**

Chapter 7   Discharging Student Loans in Bankruptcy

Chapter 8   Repayment Strategies for Getting Out of Default

Chapter 9 — Defending Student Loan Collection Actions and Challenging Trade School Abuses

Appendix A   Federal Student Loan Statutes

CD-Rom Contents

How to Use/Help
CD-Rom Text Search (Adobe Acrobat 5 and 6)
Searching NCLC Manuals
Ten-Second Tutorial on Adobe Acrobat 5
Two-Minute Tutorials on Adobe Acrobat 5 and 6
  Navigation: Bookmarks
  Disappearing Bookmarks?
  Navigation Links
  Navigation Arrows
  Navigation: "Back" Arrow
  Adobe Acrobat Articles
  View-Zoom-Magnification: Making Text Larger
  Full Screen vs. Bookmark View
  Copying Text in Adobe Acrobat
  How to Copy Only One Column
  Printing
  Other Sources of Help
Microsoft Word Files
About This CD-Rom
How to Install Adobe Acrobat Reader, with Search
Finding Aids for NCLC Manuals: What Is Available in the Books

Acrobat 6.0 Problem

Map of CD Contents

Federal Statutes
FFEL Authority (selected): 20 U.S.C. §§ 1071-1087-4
Direct Loan Authority (selected): 20 U.S.C. §§ 1087a–1087j
Perkins Authority (selected): 20 U.S.C. §§ 1087aa–1087ii
General Provisions (selected): 20 U.S.C. §§ 1088–1095a
Federal Debt Collection Act (selected): 31 U.S.C. § 3716, 31 U.S.C. § 3720A, 31
  U.S.C. § 3720D (Appendix A.1.5)

Federal Regulations
Debt Collection Regulations
  Administrative Offset: 34 C.F.R. §§ 30.20–30.31 (Appendix B.1.1)
  Tax Refund Offset: 34 C.F.R. § 30.33 (Appendix B.1.2)
  Administrative Wage Garnishment
    34 C.F.R. § 34 (Appendix B.1.3)

Policy Guidance Letters

Student Assistance Forms

Pleadings, Demand Letters

Reports, Other Information

Info for Students

Frequently Asked Questions (Appendix I)
Funding Education Beyond High School: The Guide to Federal Student Aid (English and Spanish)
Repaying Your Student Loans (English and Spanish)
Myths About Financial Aid
What Is a U.S. Department of Education PIN and Why Do I Need One?

Student Loan Law Appendices on CD-Rom

Table of Contents
Appendix A, Federal Student Loan Statutes
Appendix B, Federal Regulations
Appendix C, Department of Education Policy Guidance Letters
Appendix D, Student Assistance Forms
Appendix E, Sample Pleadings and Letters
Appendix F, Sample Discovery and Freedom of Information Act Requests
Appendix G, Directory of Guaranty Agencies
Appendix H, Student Loan Collection Agencies
Appendix I, Federal Student Financial Assistance: Frequently Asked Questions
Index
Word Processing Pleadings on CD-Rom
Quick Reference to the Consumer Credit and Sales Legal Practice Series
What Your Library Should Contain

Word Pleadings on CD-Rom

Request for Reasonable and Affordable Repayment Agreement (Appendix E.1.1)
Request for Hardship Reduction (Appendix E.1.2)
Trial Memorandum to Support Borrower's Claim for Discharge of Student Loan Based on Undue Hardship (Appendix E.6.3)
Complaint to Enjoin Discriminatory Denial of Guaranteed Student Loan in Bankruptcy (Appendix E.6.2)
False-Certification Discharge
Disability Discharges
Challenges to Collection Letters, Garnishment
Federal Benefits Offsets
Discovery in Student Loan Collection Abuse Cases
Cases Involving Trade School Abuses
Discovery Directed to Trade Schools
Discovery in Bankruptcy Proceeding to Determine Dischargeability of Student Loan (Appendix F.3)
Freedom of Information Act Requests (Appendix F.4)

Search This Manual

Search This Manual's Appendices, Plus All Other Documents on This CD-Rom
Limit Search Only to the Current File You Are Using on the CD-Rom
Search Chapters and Appendices of This Manual
Summary Contents of This Manual
Table of Contents of This Manual
Index of This Manual
CD-Rom Contents for This Manual
Contents of Other NCLC Manuals

Contents of NCLC Publications

Internet-Based Keyword Search of All NCLC Manuals
Detailed and Summary Tables of Contents for Each Manual
Short Description of Each Manual's Features with Link to Manual's Detailed Index
Short Index to Major Topics Covered in the 17-Volume Series
Descriptions of Other NCLC Books for Lawyers and Consumers
Features of *Consumer Law in a Box* (17 CD-Roms Combined into Two-CD-Rom Set)
Printer-Friendly 3-Page Description of All NCLC Publications, Latest Supplements
Printer-Friendly 25-Page Brochure Describing All NCLC Publications
Printer-Friendly Order Form for All NCLC Publications
Order Securely On-Line

Consumer Education Brochures, Books

Legal and General Audience Books Available to Order from NCLC
    The Practice of Consumer Law, Seeking Economic Justice
    STOP Predatory Lending, A Guide for Legal Advocates, with CD-Rom
    Return to Sender: Getting a Refund or Replacement for Your Lemon Car
    The NCLC Guide to Surviving Debt (2006 ed.)
    The NCLC Guide to the Rights of Utility Consumers
    The NCLC Guide to Consumer Rights for Domestic Violence Survivors
    The NCLC Guide to Consumer Rights for Immigrants
    The NCLC Guide to Mobile Homes
    Printer-Friendly Order Form
    Order Securely On-Line
Brochures for Consumers on This CD-Rom
    General Consumer Education Brochures
    Consumer Concerns for Older Americans
    Immigrant Justice in the Consumer Marketplace

Order NCLC Publications, CD-Roms

NCLC Manuals and CD-Roms
Order Publications On-Line
Printer-Friendly Order Form
Consumer Law in a Box CD-Rom
Credit Math, Bankruptcy Forms Software
Printer-Friendly Publications Brochure
NCLC Newsletters
Case Assistance
Conferences, Training
Books for Lawyers, Consumers
Consumer Education Pamphlets
Consumer Web Links

About NCLC, About This CD-Rom

National Consumer Law Center
    Mission Statement
    Contact Information: Boston, Washington Offices
    Go to NCLC Website
    What Your Library Should Contain
    Order NCLC Publications On-Line
    Learn More About NCLC Manuals, CD-Roms,
    Order Form: Order NCLC Publications via Mail, Phone, Fax

Acrobat Reader 5.0.5 and 7.0.7

Chapter 1   Getting Started

1.1 Introduction

As the cost of financing our nation's higher education system falls increasingly on students and families, student loan debt is rising at alarming rates. By the time they graduate, nearly two-thirds of students at four-year colleges and universities have student loan debt. In contrast, In 1993 less than one-half of four-year graduates had student loans.[1] Debt levels for graduating seniors with student loans more than doubled over the past decade, from $9250 to $19,200.[2] An additional factor fueling the problem is the growth of private student loan products. Companies such as Sallie Mae offer an increasing number of private loans to supplement or even replace federal education assistance.

Student loan debt is different than other types of debt on one hand because individuals incur the debt to purchase education, a truly unique commodity. If all goes well, education leads to economic rewards. College graduates earn significantly more money than those with high school degrees.[3] There is also evidence of public benefits to a more educated population, lower crime rates among more highly educated individuals and less reliance on public assistance.[4] However, this is not always the result. In the current economic environment, a bachelor's degree may be just the beginning of a student's educational journey. In addition, some college graduates may find that their professions are not as lucrative as they hoped or may lose their jobs as the economy changes. Others will confront unexpected life traumas such as disability, divorce, or death of a family member. Still others will choose career paths—such as teaching and social work—wherein success is not measured in dollars but in satisfaction and promoting social good.

Other students, including many lower-income individuals, fall victim to unscrupulous trade school practices. Unfair and deceptive vocational and correspondence school practices are a tremendous source of frustration, financial loss, and loss of opportunity for consumers, particularly low-income consumers hoping to break out of poverty. Attracted by the financing provided by government student loan and grant programs, many vocational school scams and ill-conceived schools have exploited federally-funded student assistance programs.[5]

Although the situation has improved significantly, the abuses of the past are still relevant. Many clients still need help dealing with past student loan debt that may be preventing them from going back to school, from getting good credit, or even from buying a house. Unless addressed through loan cancellation, repayment, or other remedies, these problems can literally last forever due to the elimination of a statute of limitations for most student loan collection.

Education is particularly critical for people entering the job force for the first time. This group includes many welfare-to-work clients, domestic violence survivors, and new immigrants. In addition, those re-entering the job force after lay-offs or hoping to transition into other types of work because of unemployment or disability also often look to education to move ahead. Although student loan debt is a problem that crosses class lines, low-income students tend to graduate with the highest levels of debt.[6] In general, independent low-income students are significantly more dependent on debt financing than are more traditional students.[7]

In many cases, borrowers experiencing problems with student loan debt will also have problems with other types of debt, particularly credit card debt. Many students use credit cards to cover some tuition and fees. Non-traditional students are most likely to fall into this category, with

---

1. The Project on Student Debt, *Quick Facts About Student Debt*, *available at* http://projectonstudentdebt.org/files/File/Debt_Facts_and_Sources_4_4_06.pdf.

2. *Id.*

3. *See, e.g.*, Sandy Baum, Ph.D., The Role of Student Loans in College Access (Jan. 2003) (people with college degrees earn 80% to 90% more than those with only a high school education); NEA Higher Educ. Research Ctr., *Higher Education: Who Benefits?*, Update Vol. 9 No. 3 (May 2003).

4. NEA Higher Educ. Research Ctr., *Higher Education: Who Benefits?*, Update Vol. 9 No. 3 (May 2003).

5. The scope of the problem and legal claims are discussed in Chapter 9, *infra*.

6. *See* Tracey King & Ivan Frishberg, *Big Loans, Bigger Problems: A Report on the Sticker Shock of Student Loans* (State PIRGs Mar. 2001); Tracey King & Ellynne Bannon, Higher Educ. Project, *The Burden of Borrowing: A Report on the Rising Rates of Student Loan Debt* (Mar. 2002). Both reports are available on-line at www.pirg.org/highered. *See also* Patricia M. Scherschel, *Student Debt Levels Continue to Rise* (Lumina Found. June 2000), *available at* www.luminafoundation.org.

7. Sandy Baum, The College Bd., *Research Report 5: The Role of Student Loans in College Access* (Jan. 2003).

independent students, those attending part-time, and those enrolled in two-year institutions most likely to use credit cards.[8] A 2003 study found that the median balance was $3400 for those individuals who used credit cards to help finance undergraduate education.[9] Almost 40% of this group had balances exceeding $5000 when they left school.

It is critical for advocates to understand how best to counsel and represent student loan borrowers. An important first step is to learn about local educational options, particularly low-cost community colleges and other affordable programs. Advocates should also familiarize themselves with the range of government and private financing available.

Unfortunately, most clients do not seek legal help until long after they attended schools, took out loans, and defaulted on those loans. This manual focuses on assisting these clients, reviewing in detail the primary cancellation, repayment, bankruptcy, and other options available to challenge government collection efforts and help borrowers get out of default.

The good news is that there is almost always something that borrowers can do to challenge student loan collection actions and either cancel a loan or set up an affordable monthly payment plan. Understanding borrower cancellation and repayment rights is the key to assisting clients with student loan problems. Resolving these problems is often a critical step in helping clients get back on their feet financially.

1.2 The Consequences of Student Loan Defaults

Throughout the late 1980s and early 1990s, vocational school abuses led to tremendous increases in student loan default rates. In 1968, the government paid $2 million to cover loan defaults; in 1987, default payments exceeded $1 billion; and, by 1991, default claim payments reached $3.2 billion.[10] The overall default rate peaked at 22.4% in fiscal year 1990.[11] This rate decreased all the way to 5.6% in 1999. The overall default rate has continued to decline, falling to 4.5% for all schools in fiscal year 2003.[12] The rate has even

declined among less-than-two-year proprietary schools. By fiscal year 2003, this rate was 7.9%.[13]

There has been real progress based on the cohort default rate measurement, but the problem is far from resolved. First, the cohort rate is a misleading indicator. It tracks borrowers for just the first two years after they go into repayment. This is a mere snapshot in time that does not give a full picture of default trends.[14]

In addition, the dollar amounts of loans in default remain high. The cumulative student loans in default doubled from fiscal year 1990 to fiscal year 2001.[15] This is a system-wide problem. Looking at total dollar amounts, most of the lost money in defaulted student loans comes from four-year schools (about 70%) despite their lower rates of default.[16]

The consequences of student loan defaults have grown enormously over time as the government's collection powers have steadily increased. The government has collection powers far beyond those of most unsecured creditors. As discussed in detail in Chapter 5, the government can garnish a borrower's wages without a judgment, seize the borrower's tax refund (even an earned income tax credit), seize portions of federal benefits such as Social Security, and deny the borrower eligibility for new education grants or loans. Even in bankruptcy, most student loans must be paid.[17] Unlike any other type of debt, there is no statute of limitations. The government can pursue borrowers to the grave.

For borrowers in default, education, initially seen as a way out of poverty, has led them into a cycle of endless debt. They find themselves in a trap. Student loan debt from the past keeps them from going back to school and moving into higher-paying jobs. On the other hand, they cannot afford to go back to school and get additional training without some type of financial assistance.

1.3 Using This Manual

1.3.1 Road Map

This manual is designed to help advocates negotiate the world of federal student financial assistance, specifically

---

8 *Id.*

9 Sandy Baum, Marie O'Malley, National Student Loans Survey, *College on Credit: How Borrowers Perceive Their Education Debt* (Feb. 6, 2003).

10 U.S. Gen. Accounting Office, Higher Education: Ensuring Quality Education from Proprietary Institutions, GAO/T-HEHS-96-158 (June 1996).

11 Information on default rates is available on the Department of Education's website at www.ed.gov/offices/OSFAP/defaultmanagement/cdr.html. Default rates are defined as the percentage of borrowers who entered repayment in a certain year and defaulted before the end of the next year.

12 Press Release, U.S. Dep't of Educ., Secretary Spellings Announces New Low Student Loan Default Rate (Sept. 14, 2005).

13 *Id.*

14 *See, e.g.,* Office of Inspector General, U.S. Dep't of Educ., *Final Audit Report: Audit to Determine if Cohort Default Rates Provide Sufficient Information on Defaults in the Title IV Loan Program,* ED-OIG/A03-C0017 (Dec. 2003); U.S. Gen. Accounting Office, Student Loans: Default Rates Need to Be Computed More Appropriately, GAO/HEHS-99-135 (July 1999). *See § 9.2.5, infra.*

15 *See* U.S. Gen Accounting Office, Federal Student Aid: Timely Performance Plans and Reports Would Help Guide and Assess Achievement of Default Management Goals, GAO-03-348 (Feb. 2003).

16 Office of Student Fin. Assistance, U.S. Dep't of Educ., Ensuring Loan Repayment: A National Handbook of Best Practices (2000).

17 *See* Chapter 7, *infra.*

federal student loan programs. Although geared toward advocates representing lower-income clients, many of the same programs and remedies will apply to middle- and upper-income borrowers as well.

The primary focus of this manual is on federal loan programs. However, due to the increased importance of private student lending, general information about private student loans can be found in Chapter 1. An analysis of legal remedies to challenge problems with private student loans is included in Chapter 9.[18]

Chapter 1 of this manual reviews the primary types of federal student assistance and how to help clients find out what types of loans they have. This chapter also reviews basic eligibility criteria for federal loans. It includes a checklist for advocates to follow in assisting clients with student loan problems.

Chapter 2 covers basic terms of government loans, including interest rates and origination fees. Disclosure requirements are also discussed as well as pre-default repayment options. Chapter 3 includes detailed information about deferment and forbearance rights.

Chapters 4 and 5 focus on student loan collection issues. Chapter 4 summarizes the collection process during delinquency and after default. The consequences of default, discussed briefly in Chapter 1, are covered in greater detail in this chapter. This includes a discussion of collection fees. Chapter 4 also covers common collection abuses and possible legal claims, including fair debt collection practices laws, to challenge these abuses. Chapter 5 discusses property and asset seizures, including tax refund intercepts, administrative wage garnishments, and federal benefits offsets.

Chapter 6 presents the primary cancellation options available for borrowers, including closed-school, false-certification, unpaid-refund, disability, and death cancellations. Cancellation of student loans may also be pursued in bankruptcy. The ways in which student loans can be discharged in bankruptcy are discussed in Chapter 7.

Chapter 8 includes information on repayment options, focusing on repayment strategies for low-income clients including loan consolidation, rehabilitation, and reasonable and affordable payment plans. Chapter 8 also discusses the government's compromise and write-off authority.

Chapter 9 includes information about trade school abuses and how to challenge them. The chapter also reviews general legal claims borrowers may bring to defend student loan collection actions, including contract defenses and affirmative legal claims to address student loan problems. Legal claims in private student loan cases are discussed in Chapter 9 as well.

The appendices to this manual reprint key student loan statutes and regulations and contain various practice aids. Appendix A includes critical federal student loan statutes.

---

18 *See* § 9.7, *infra.*

Key regulations can be found in Appendix B. Selected Department of Education policy guidance letters are included in Appendix C.

Appendices D, E, and F contain a number of useful forms and pleadings for practitioners. Appendix G includes a current list of state guaranty agencies along with addresses and telephone numbers. Appendix H contains a current list of collection agencies that contract with the Department of Education, and Appendix I includes basic consumer education information.

This manual also includes a CD-Rom containing the statutes, regulations, forms, and pleadings from the appendices, the index to this volume, and the quick reference to the entire National Consumer Law Center's Consumer Credit and Sales Legal Practices Series. The CD-Rom has numerous student loan-related pleadings as well as the latest regulations and proposed regulations issued by the Department of Education. See "About the CD-Rom" at the back of this volume for more information.

This manual will be supplemented, usually on an annual basis. Between supplements, new developments are reported in NCLC REPORTS, *Deceptive Practices and Warranties Edition*, published bimonthly. For subscription information, contact Publications Department, National Consumer Law Center, 77 Summer Street, 10th Floor, Boston, MA 02110, (617) 542-9595.

1.3.2 Clearinghouse Documents

Certain documents included in this manual are cited by a "Clearinghouse" number. Cases of special interest to low-income advocates, including unpublished cases, are also frequently cited by a "Clearinghouse" number. Unreported cases cited in NCLC manuals are available through the Sargent Shriver National Center on Poverty Law. Those unreported cases and other documents are cited by a "Clearinghouse" number. The Sargent Shriver National Center on Poverty (formerly the National Clearinghouse for Legal Services, Inc.) retains copies of these documents, organized by Clearinghouse number. Clearinghouse cases may be ordered from the Sargent Shriver National Center on Poverty Law after paying a per copy fee (currently $10.00 plus shipping) by writing the Sargent Shriver National Center on Poverty Law, Inc., 50 East Washington St., Suite 500, Chicago, IL 60602, by telephoning (312) 263-3830, by faxing (312) 263-3846, or e-mail: support@povertylaw.org.

1.3.3 Web-Based Text Search Feature

NCLC offers a unique web-based text search feature for this manual and all its other manuals. The search engine is located at www.consumerlaw.org. Clicking on "Keyword Search" brings up a screen that allows the user to search for any term or phrase in this or any other NCLC manual. The search can be confined to a single manual or can extend to all of NCLC's manuals. The search engine will indicate the pages in the manual where the term or phrase appears. The user can then refer to the applicable book in hard copy.

This function is not only the best way to locate the discussion of a particular topic, but it is also an excellent way to find out where a particular case, statute, or regulation is discussed in NCLC's manuals. The search instructions explain how to use wildcards, how to search for phrases and the proximity of one term to another term (for either of the two terms), and how to search for one term that is not on the same page as another term.

1.4 Introduction to Federal Student Assistance

1.4.1 Brief History

The Servicemen's Readjustment Act of 1944 (the GI Bill) and the National Defense Student Loan Program (which later became the Perkins Loan Program) were the precursors to the current federal aid programs. Many states also developed their own guaranteed loan programs.[19]

The Federal Guaranteed Student Loan Program (GSL, later renamed Stafford) was established in the Higher Education Act of 1965. The 1965 legislation also created the Federal Insured Student Loan (FISL) program, which provided federal insurance for loans. The FISL was eventually phased out. The Higher Education Act Amendments of 1992 created a new generic name, Federal Family Education Loans (FFELs) for the major forms of federal student loans.[20]

Lenders have incentives to participate in the guaranteed loan programs because the government reimburses them when borrowers default. Before getting reimbursed, lenders are required to make certain efforts to collect the loans.[21] The loans are guaranteed by the federal government against default, death, disability, or bankruptcy. For qualifying families, the government also pays interest while the students remain enrolled.

Often the original lender will sell the loan to another lender specializing in student loans, such as the Student Loan Marketing Association ("Sallie Mae"). Either the original or the subsequent lender can also contract with a servicing company to service the loan for the lender. In many cases, a loan servicing company such as Sallie Mae will also sell its own private loan products.

Although the FFEL student loan program is federal, it is mostly administered through state or private nonprofit agencies called guaranty agencies. Guaranty agencies pay off the lenders when borrowers default and, in turn, are reinsured by the Department of Education. When a loan held by a lender or other servicer goes into default, it is typically turned over to a guaranty agency for collection.[22] At a later date, the United States, as an insurer on the loan, can take over the collection effort.[23]

The Student Loan Reform Act of 1993 significantly changed the student loan landscape by creating a new Federal Direct Loan program.[24] Federal Direct Loans (referred to throughout this manual as Direct Loans) are loans directly from the federal government to the student, with the assistance of the school or other entity that originates the loan. Lenders and guaranty agencies are cut out of the process.

Private lenders provide the funds for FFEL loans, while the Department provides the funds for Direct loans. There may be multiple holders of FFEL loans but only one holder, the Department, of Direct Loans.

1.4.2 Types of Federal Student Assistance

1.4.2.1 FFEL and Direct Loans

1.4.2.1.1 General

Federal Stafford loans are made to students through the Direct Loan program and the FFEL program. Direct Stafford and FFEL Stafford loans have identical loan limits and identical deferment and cancellation provisions. The major difference is that Direct Loans are originated by the government and FFEL loans by private lenders. There are also some differences in repayment options.[25] Most important, Direct loan borrowers have access to the more favorable income contingent repayment plan.[26] Stafford loans are either subsidized or unsubsidized. Students can receive a subsidized and an unsubsidized loan for the same enrollment period.

---

19   For a concise history of these programs, see The Institute for Higher Education Policy's *Private Loans and Choice in Financing in Higher Education* (2003), which is available at www.ihep.com/Pubs/PDF/PvtLoans.pdf. The report is also available on the companion CD-Rom to the manual.

20   Pub. L. No. 102-325, 106 Stat. 448 (July 23, 1992).

21   *See* § 4.3.3, *infra.*

22   Legislation passed in 2005 amended the lender insurance provisions so that guaranty agencies must reduce the amount of insurance to a lender to 97% of a loan's unpaid principal. Previously it was 98%. *See* Pub. L. No. 109-171, 120 Stat. 4 (Feb. 8, 2006), *amending* 20 U.S.C. § 1078. *See also* 34 C.F.R. § 682.401(b)(14). In addition, the 2005 legislation requires guaranty agencies to file a reinsurance claim with the Department within thirty days after paying a lender's claim. Previously, guaranty agencies had forty-five days to file claims.

23   A list of state guaranty agencies can be found at Appendix G, *infra.*

24   Student Loan Reform Act of 1993, 107 Stat. 340, *enacted as* § 4021 of the Omnibus Budget Reconciliation Act of 1993, Pub. L. No. 103-66, 107 Stat. 312 (Aug. 10 1993).

25   §§ 2.7.3, 8.2, *infra.*

26   *See* § 2.7.3.2, *infra.*

A subsidized loan is awarded on the basis of financial need. The key difference between the two types of Stafford loans is that, for subsidized loans, borrowers are not charged any interest before the repayment period begins or during authorized periods of deferment. In essence, the government "subsidizes" the interest during these periods.

Unsubsidized loans are not awarded on the basis of financial need. Interest is charged from the time the loan is disbursed until it is paid in full. Annual and aggregate loan limits are set out in the Department of Education regulations.[27]

Both Direct and FFEL offer PLUS loans. PLUS Loans allow parents to borrow to pay for the education of dependent undergraduate children enrolled in school at least half time. To be eligible for PLUS, parents are generally required to pass a credit check.[28]

As of July 1, 2006, PLUS loans are also available for graduate and professional students. The application process is slightly different, but student PLUS borrowers are also required to pass a credit check.[29]

PLUS borrowers with adverse credit histories may still get loans if they enlist an endorser who has been determined not to have an adverse credit history.[30] The lender must find that an adverse credit history exists based on a credit report if the applicant is considered ninety or more days delinquent on the repayment of a debt or if the applicant has been the subject of a default determination, bankruptcy discharge, foreclosure, repossession, tax lien, wage garnishment, or write-off of a student loan debt during the five years preceding the date of the credit report.[31] Creditors may establish more restrictive standards.[32] However, the absence of any credit history cannot be considered an indication of an adverse credit history and is not to be used as a reason for denial.[33] The lender may waive these requirements if extenuating circumstances exist.[34]

Consolidation loans are also available through both the FFEL and Direct Loan programs. As of July 1, 2006, the terms of the two consolidation programs are similar. However, there are still some important differences, as discussed in detail in Chapter 8.

Pre-default repayment options for FFEL and Direct loans are discussed in Chapter 2. Post-default repayment is covered in Chapter 8. Selected sample loan documents are available on the companion CD-Rom to this manual.

1.4.2.1.2 Competition between FFEL and Direct Loans

The relationship between the government and private lenders participating in the FFEL program is often strained. Particularly since around 2000, Congress and the Bush Administration have expressed concern about the Direct Lending program. The Direct Loan program's Income Contingent Repayment Plan (ICRP) and the Direct Loan Consolidation program have been the target of much of this criticism.[35]

There has also been considerable controversy with respect to the Departmental authority to give Direct loan borrowers certain financial incentives to repay loans on time.[36] To date, Congress has not passed legislation to eliminate this discretion. In 2006, the Department decided to exercise its authority and continue to provide Direct loan borrowers financial incentives to repay on time.[37]

The "school as lender" program has also threatened the viability of direct lending. Schools have been allowed to act as lenders since the inception of the Higher Education Act in 1965. More recently, private lenders have fostered unprecedented expansion in this program by guaranteeing huge sums of money for schools that enter into exclusive relationships with the lenders. In many cases, as part of these deals, schools agree to stop providing federal direct loans. Instead, the university lends money to the students, with the help of the lender, and then sells the loans to the lender for a profit.[38] These "school as lender" programs generally apply only to graduate students because of limits on schools acting as lenders for undergraduates. However, many lenders sweeten the deal if the schools agree to also drop their participation in the Direct Loan program for undergraduates.[39] The GAO found that, between fiscal year 1993/1994 and fiscal year 2003/2004, the "school as lender" program increased significantly from twenty-two school lenders dis-

---

27 34 C.F.R. §§ 682.204(a) (FFEL), 685.203 (Direct Loan). *See* § 2.2, *infra*.

28 34 C.F.R. §§ 682.201(b) (applies to FFEL PLUS loans made on or after July 1, 1993), 685.200 (Direct Loans).

29 34 C.F.R. § 682.102(c)(1),(2); 34 C.F.R. § 682.201(b),(c).

30 34 C.F.R. § 682.201(b)(1)(vii); 34 C.F.R. § 685.200(b)(1)(vii).

31 34 C.F.R. § 682.201(c)(2)(ii)(A), (B) (FFEL); 34 C.F.R. § 685.200(b)(1)(vii)(B)(Direct).

32 34 C.F.R. § 682.201(c)(2)(iii).

33 34 C.F.R. § 682.201(c)(2)(iv) (FFEL); 34 C.F.R. § 685.200(b)(1)(vii)(C)(Direct).

34 34 C.F.R. § 682.201(b)(2)(ii), (v) (FFEL); 34 C.F.R. § 685.200(b)(1)(vii)(A) (Direct).

35 Much of the controversy, particularly in the Direct Loan consolidation program, began after Congress amended the law in 1998 to allow borrowers with loans from different lenders to consolidate their loans with any eligible consolidation lender. 34 C.F.R. § 682.201(c)(iv)(B). This change stimulated competition and led to the growth of many new companies seeking to lure borrowers away from Sallie Mae (the largest FFEL consolidator) and the Direct Loan program. *See* § 8.2, *infra*.

36 20 U.S.C. § 1087e(b)(7).

37 *See* Stephen Burd, *Education Secretary Takes Action to Keep Direct Loans Competitive*, Chron. of Higher Educ., Mar. 24, 2006, at A29.

38 *See* Stephen Burd, *Direct Lending in Distress*, The Chron. of Higher Educ, July 8, 2005.

39 *See also* U.S. Government Accountability Office, *Federal Family Education Loan Program: More Oversight Is Needed for Schools That Are Lenders*, GAO-05-184 (Jan. 2005).

bursing about $155 million to sixty-four schools disbursing about $1.5 billion in FFEL loans.[40]

Congressional changes in 2005 are aimed at limiting the scope of the "school as lender" program. Effective April 1, 2006, to be a school lender, a school must have met the "school as lender" requirements as they existed on February 7, 2006, and must have made FFEL loans as a lender on or before April 1, 2006.[41] Under new regulations, the school must not

- be a home study school;
- make a loan to any undergraduate student;
- make a loan other than Federal Stafford loans to a graduate or professional student; or
- make a loan to a borrower who is not enrolled at the school.[42]

There are also new regulations that, among other provisions, require the schools participating in this program to maintain a cohort default rate that is not greater than 10% and offer loans with an origination fee and/or interest rate that is less than the applicable statutory fee or rate for any loan first disbursed on or after July 1, 2006.[43] In addition, schools must use payments they receive (exclusive of return of principal and certain costs) for need-based grants.[44] They may also use some funds for reasonable administrative expenses. The funds for need-based grants must supplement, not supplant, non-federal funds the school would otherwise use for need-based grants.

In addition to the "school as lender" program, many private lenders have succeeded in persuading schools to drop out of direct lending in exchange for improved service and generous rebates. As a result, participation in direct lending peaked at more than 1300 colleges in 1996–97, when it accounted for about one-third of the total student-loan market. It has since decreased to 25%, with about 1100 participating schools.[45]

In an effort to bolster the Direct Loan program, policy-makers have introduced various bills that would reward with extra federal financial aid funds those colleges that participate in direct lending.[46] Proponents cite government estimates showing that direct lending is a less expensive alter-native to the FFEL program because it eliminates the federal subsidies lenders receive in the guaranteed program. Opponents argue that these estimates are inaccurate.[47]

1.4.2.2 Perkins Loans

Perkins Loans (formerly called National Direct Student Loans and, before that, National Defense Student Loans) are not FFELs.[48] These are low-interest loans for both undergraduate and graduate students with exceptional financial need.

Perkins Loans are originated and serviced by participating schools and repaid to the school. The government does not insure the loans but instead provides initial contributions to eligible institutions to partially capitalize a loan fund. Perkins Loans are administered by the school itself, at interest rates below those for Stafford loans.

If the student defaults, the school can seek collection through a lawsuit or otherwise. Perkins schools may assign loans to the United States when they cannot collect.[49] The United States will then seek collection from the defaulted borrower, using the full range of collection tools available.[50] However, the schools can no longer receive any of the funds collected after assignment.[51] In a few cases, such as in reviews of disability discharges, schools are required to assign loans to the Department.[52]

Since Perkins Loans have different regulations than FFELs and Direct Loans, student rights and obligations are often different. However, the 1998 Higher Education Act contained a number of provisions that made the Perkins regulations much more similar to the FFEL and Direct Loan regulations. In particular, the closed-school discharge for loans made on or after January 1, 1986, now applies to Perkins Loans as well.[53] Perkins Loan borrowers who make

---

40 *Id.*

41 Pub. L. No. 109-171, 120 Stat. 4 (Feb. 8, 2006), *amending* 20 U.S.C. § 1085.

42 34 C.F.R. § 682.601(a).

43 34 C.F.R. § 682.601(a)(5),(6).

44 34 C.F.R. § 682.601(a)(8).

45 *See* Stephen Burd, *Direct Lending in Distress*, The Chron. of Higher Educ., July 8, 2005.

46 *See, e.g.*, S. 371, 109th Cong. (introduced Feb. 14, 2005). According to the Chronicle of Higher Education, Salle Mae, the largest student loan provider in the country, has taken a leading role in fighting this legislation. *See* Stephen Burd, *Lenders Misled in Battle over Cost of Direct Lending, Budget Experts Say*, The Chron. of Higher Educ., July 8, 2005.

47 *See* Stephen Burd, *Lenders Misled in Battle over Cost of Direct Lending, Budget Experts Say*, The Chron. of Higher Educ., July 8, 2005.

48 Statutory authority can be found at 20 U.S.C. §§ 1087aa–1087*ii*.

49 34 C.F.R. § 674.50.

50 The Department claims to have collection tools, such as administrative wage garnishment, federal offset, and Department of Justice litigation, that are not available to schools. It is unclear whether this statement accurately reflects current practice. Perkins schools can presumably refer accounts to the government for tax refund intercepts. They would seem to have authority to also refer accounts for federal benefits offset. However, the Department claims this is not current practice. *See* U.S. Dep't of Educ., Dear Colleague Letter CB-02-05 (Apr. 2002). *See also* 34 C.F.R. § 674.41 (Perkins lender due diligence requirements). The situation is clearer for FFEL loans when guaranty agencies, in most cases, have specific authority to collect on behalf of the Department prior to assignment. *See generally* Ch. 5, *infra*.

51 *See* U.S. Dep't of Educ., Dear Colleague Letter CB-02-05 (Apr. 2002).

52 *See* § 6.6 (disability discharges), *infra*.

53 34 C.F.R. § 674.33(g). *See* § 6.2, *infra*.

twelve consecutive monthly payments are also now allowed to rehabilitate defaulted loans.[54]

1.4.2.3 Older Loans

Prior to 1994, borrowers could also receive Supplemental Loans for Students (SLS). Effective July 1, 1994, SLS loans were no longer issued. The SLS program was merged into the unsubsidized component of the Stafford loan program. However, many students obtained SLS loans before that date, and the conditions and benefits of those earlier loans remain unchanged.[55]

Many older loans are insured directly by the federal government, with no guaranty agency acting as intermediary. These loans are called Federally Insured Student Loans (FISLs). FISLs were made from 1966 to 1984. Unless specified otherwise, the term FFEL in this section includes FISLs.

1.4.2.4 Federal Grants

A Basic Educational Opportunity Grant (BEOG)—also called a Pell Grant[56]—and a Supplemental Educational Opportunity Grant (FSEOG)[57] are not loans and require no repayment (unless there is an overpayment).[58] The College Work Study program (CWS) provides salaries for students in exchange for work.[59] All of these assistance programs are administered by the school. Students can have more than one form of student assistance so that, for example, a student may participate in work-study, have a Pell Grant, a Stafford loan, and a PLUS Loan signed by his or her parents.

Grants do not usually have to be repaid. Two main exceptions to this general rule are for grantees who (1) received more than they were eligible to receive or (2) withdrew early from the program for which the grant was given.[60] Once a grantee is notified of a grant repayment, he or she must either pay the grant back in full or enter into a satisfactory repayment arrangement.[61] Failure to respond will lead to lost eligibility for further federal financial aid, and the school will assign the debt to the Department for collection.[62] However, the school is liable for an overpayment if it occurred because the school failed to follow proper procedures.[63] Grant overpayment debts are not eligible for either consolidation or rehabilitation.

In addition, the amount of a grant overpayment due from a student is limited to the amount by which the original overpayment exceeds 50% of the total grant funds received by the student for the payment period or period of enrollment. In addition, a student does not have to repay a grant overpayment of $50 or less for grant overpayments resulting from a student's withdrawal.[64]

The requirement to repay is waived for students who withdraw from a school because of their status as an "affected individual," defined to include those serving on active duty during a war or other military operation or during a national emergency, performing qualifying National Guard duty during a war or other military operation or during a national emergency, residing or employed in an area that is declared a disaster area by any federal, state, or local official in connection with a national emergency, or suffering direct economic hardship as a result of a war or other military operation or a national emergency, as determined by the Secretary.[65]

The Secretary is also permitted to waive a student's Title IV grant repayment if the student withdrew from an institution because of a major disaster.[66]

1.4.3 Individual Eligibility for Government Loans

There are general eligibility criteria that apply to most loan programs. In most cases, students must show financial need. The expected family contribution (EFC) is a measure of the borrower's family's financial situation and indicates how much of the borrower's (and family's, if the borrower is a dependent) resources should be available to help pay for education.

The EFC formula is calculated according to a statutory formula.[67] There is some flexibility to consider special circumstances. In addition, financial aid administrators have the discretion to use their professional judgment to make adjustments on a case-by-case basis to the data items that are used in determining a student's eligibility.[68]

Individuals who wish to apply on-line for aid must first get a personal identification number (PIN) that allows them to apply on-line. They must then complete the free application for federal student aid (FAFSA).[69] As a result of the information provided on the FAFSA, a student aid report

---

54 34 C.F.R. § 674.39.

55 SLSs were considered a part of the FFEL category of loans. Therefore FFEL regulations should apply to these loans as well.

56 20 U.S.C. § 1070a; 34 C.F.R. § 690.

57 20 U.S.C. § 1070b; 34 C.F.R. § 676.

58 *Id.*

59 42 U.S.C. §§ 2751–2756b; 34 C.F.R. § 675.

60 34 C.F.R. § 690.79(a)(1).

61 34 C.F.R. § 690.79(b),(c).

62 34 C.F.R. § 690.79(c); 34 C.F.R. § 668.32(g)(4).

63 34 C.F.R. § 690.79(a)(2).

64 34 C.F.R. § 668.22(h)(3).

65 68 Fed. Reg. 69312 (Dec. 12, 2003).

66 *See* Pub. L. No. 109-66, 119 Stat. 1999 (Sept. 21, 2005) (The Pell Grant Hurricane and Disaster Relief Act); Pub. L. No. 109-67, 119 Stat. 2001 (Sept. 21, 2005) (The Student Grant Hurricane and Disaster Relief Act). *See also* 34 C.F.R. § 668.22(h)(5).

67 20 U.S.C. § 1087nn.

68 20 U.S.C. § 1087tt.

69 A copy of the FAFSA form is reprinted at Appendix D and on the companion CD-Rom to this manual.

(SAR) is generated. The SAR includes the expected family contribution (EFC), the number used to determine federal student aid eligibility.

There has been a great deal of debate over how to improve the EFC, particularly with respect to assessing the financial position of independent students.[70] In general, a borrower's responses on the application for federal assistance will determine whether he or she is considered dependent or independent. The main difference is that dependents must also report parents' income and assets, and parents are expected to contribute to their childrens' education.

Among other provisions, borrowers are considered independent if they

- are 24 years old or older by December of the award year,
- will be enrolled in a masters or doctoral degree program,
- are married on the day of application,
- have children who receive more than half their support from them,
- have dependents other than children or spouse who live with them and receive more than half their support from them at the time of application,
- have both parents who are deceased, or
- are veterans of the U.S. Armed Forces.[71]

Not living with parents or not being claimed by them on tax forms does not determine dependency status.

Potential borrowers must also have a high school diploma or General Education certificate (GED), complete an approved home school education, or pass a test approved by the Department of Education. These tests are known as "ability to benefit" tests.[72]

Students must be enrolled in a degree, certificate, or other approved program at an eligible school.[73] In addition, prospective borrowers must be United States citizens or eligible non-citizens. Eligible non-citizens primarily include permanent residents, refugees, and asylees.[74] All borrowers must have valid Social Security numbers and must register with the Selective Service if required.[75]

Students convicted under federal or state law of sale or possession of illegal drugs are suspended from federal financial assistance programs.[76] Eligibility may be suspended for one year from the date of a first conviction on a drug possession charge, two years from the date of a second conviction, and indefinitely for a third.[77] Students convicted of selling drugs lose eligibility for two years from the date of a first conviction and indefinitely for a second.[78] Eligibility can be restored if the student satisfactorily completes a drug rehabilitation program or if the conviction is reversed or set aside.[79]

In 2002, more than 45,000 students lost their federal financial aid because of the "drug conviction" provision.[80] A 2006 study found that, overall, nearly 200,000 would-be college students have been declared ineligible to receive financial aid because of drug convictions.[81]

A key area of controversy is related to the broad scope of the drug-related prohibition. Prior to July 1, 2006, borrowers were denied aid not only if they were convicted while in school but also if they were convicted of drug offenses prior to enrolling in higher education. As of July 1, 2006, however, a student will become ineligible for aid only if the conviction is for conduct that occurred during a period of enrollment for which the student was receiving Title IV program assistance.[82]

A new eligibility requirement was added effective July 1, 2006.[83] The new requirement provides that students who have been convicted of, or have pleaded *nolo contendere* or guilty to, a crime involving fraud in obtaining Title IV HEA

---

70 *See* Sandy Baum, Lumina Found. for Educ., National Ass'n of Student Fin. Aid Administrators, *Fixing the Formula: A New Approach to Determining Independent Students' Ability to Pay for College* (May 2006).

71 20 U.S.C. § 1087vv(d).

72 20 U.S.C. § 1091(d). For more on ability-to-benefit tests and false-certification discharges, see § 6.3.2, *infra*.

73 20 U.S.C. § 1091(a)(1), (2). See § 1.4.4, *infra*.

74 20 U.S.C. § 1091(a)(5). Other eligible immigration categories include those on indefinite parole and/or humanitarian parole, Cuban-Haitian entrants with status pending, and conditional entrants (only if authorization was issued before April 1, 1980). Students in the United States with student visas only are not eligible for federal aid.

75 *See generally* U.S. Dep't of Educ., *Funding Education Beyond High*

School: The Guide to Federal Student Aid. The English version is available at http://studentaid.ed.gov/students/attachments/siteresources/StudentGuide.pdf and on the companion CD-Rom to this manual.

76 20 U.S.C. § 1091(r); 34 C.F.R. § 668.40.

77 34 C.F.R. § 668.40(b)(1).

78 34 C.F.R. § 668.40(b)(2).

79 34 C.F.R. § 668.40(c) (rehabilitation programs); 34 C.F.R. § 668.40(a)(2) (definition of "conviction").

80 Stephen Burd, *Seeking Redemption for a Drug Law*, The Chron. of Higher Educ., Apr. 5, 2002, at A17.

81 Students for Sensible Drug Policy, *Harmful Drug Law Hits Home, How Many College Students in Each State Lost Financial Aid Due to Drug Convictions?* (Apr. 17, 2006). The Advisory Committee on Student Financial Assistance has also recommended elimination of the requirement. *See* Advisory Comm. on Student Fin. Assistance, *The Student Aid Gauntlet: Making Access to College Simple and Certain* 16 (Jan. 23, 2005), *available at* www.ed.gov/about/bdscomm/list/acsfa/gauntletcorrected.pdf. In addition, the GAO was unable to find any evidence that the provision actually helped to deter drug use. *See* General Accountability Office, *Drug Offenders: Various Factors May Limit the Impact of Federal Laws that Provide for Denial of Selected Benefits*, GAO-05-238 (Sept. 26, 2005). There is also a lawsuit against the Department of Education filed by Students for Sensible Drug Policy and ACLU. For more information, see www.ssdp.org/lawsuit.

82 20 U.S.C. § 1091(r); 34 C.F.R. § 668.40(a)(1).

83 Pub. L. No. 109-171, 120 Stat. 4 (Feb. 8, 2006), *amending* 20 U.S.C. § 1091.

program assistance are not eligible for additional Title IV assistance unless they have repaid the fraudulently obtained funds.[84]

1.4.4 Institutional Eligibility

Only students that are enrolled at an "eligible institution" may receive federal aid.[85] There are different eligibility requirements for public or private nonprofit institutions and proprietary institutions.[86]

Among other requirements, all institutions must admit students who have high school diplomas or recognized equivalents. Proprietary schools must also provide eligible training programs to prepare students for gainful employment in a recognized occupation.[87] There are minimum-duration requirements that these courses must meet.[88]

There are a number of additional regulatory requirements that, at a minimum, mandate that schools collect and retain data on completions and job placement and in some cases require this information to be disclosed to prospective students including the following:

Minimum Placement and Completion Standards: Proprietary schools offering educational programs of at least 300 clock hours of instruction (but less than 600 hours), offered during a minimum of 10 weeks, are not eligible to participate in the main federal student loan programs unless they have a verified completion rate for those programs of at least 70% and a verified job placement rate of at least 70%.[89]

Disclosure Requirements for Completion and Placement. Institutions must sign agreements with the Secretary of Education in order to participate in federal student assistance programs. Institutions that advertise job placement rates as a means of attracting students to enroll must make available to prospective students, at or before the time that those students apply for enrollment, the most recent available data concerning employment statistics, graduation statistics, and any other information necessary to substantiate the truthfulness of the advertisements.[90]

Completion Disclosure Requirements. All institutions must make available to any enrolled student or prospective student, on request—through appropriate publications, mailings, or electronic media—information concerning financial assistance and the institution's completion or graduation rate and, if applicable, its transfer-out rate. In the case of a prospective student, the information must be made available

prior to the student's enrolling or entering into any financial obligation with the institution.[91]

Annual Reporting of Completion Rates. Institutions must make completion or graduation rates available annually.[92]

Proprietary schools are also subject to other rules. For example, the 85/15 (now 90/10) rule, enacted as part of the 1992 Higher Education Act reauthorization, requires each school to limit the percentage of revenues it receives from federal financial assistance.[93] Schools are required to use, in their calculations, the federal student assistance dollars its students receive as the numerator, and total revenues from educational programs as the denominator. The maximum result (equaling the school's federal student assistance dollars as a percentage of total revenues) was initially set at 85% and then increased to 90%.[94]

Prior to July 1, 2006, there were also limits on participation in the financial aid programs by "distance education" schools. Prior to that date, institutions offering more than 50% of their courses by correspondence, or a combination of correspondence and telecommunications, or enrolling 50% or more of their students in correspondence courses were generally ineligible for Title IV.[95] Many schools received waivers from these requirements through a Distance Education pilot program, passed as part of the 1998 Higher Education Act (HEA) Amendments.[96]

After July 1, 2006, the "50% rule" will no longer apply to many institutions. Domestic institutions that are accredited by an accrediting agency recognized by the Secretary for accreditation of distance education are now eligible for federal assistance if these institutions offer programs that are provided in whole or in part through telecommunications.[97] This provides considerably more flexibility to schools that offer these courses. Regulatory changes were also made, as discussed in Chapter 9, to differentiate between courses offered via telecommunications and correspondence.[98]

In extreme cases, such as natural disasters, the Department may waive certain eligibility requirements, such as the requirement that a proprietary institution derive at least 10% of its revenues from non-Title IV sources.[99]

84 *See* 34 C.F.R. § 668.32(m); 34 C.F.R. § 668.35(*i*).
85 20 U.S.C. §§ 1091(a), 1094.
86 34 C.F.R. § 600.4 (public or private nonprofit institutions); § 600.5 (proprietary institutions).
87 20 U.S.C. § 1002(b); 34 C.F.R. § 600.5(a)(5).
88 34 C.F.R. 668.8(d).
89 20 U.S.C. § 1088(b)(2)(A).
90 34 C.F.R. § 668.14.
91 34 C.F.R. § 668.41.
92 34 C.F.R. § 668.45.
93 34 C.F.R. § 600.5(a)(8). *See* U.S. Dep't of Educ., Dear Colleague Letter Gen-99-33 (Oct. 1999).
94 34 C.F.R. §§ 600.5(a)(8), 600.5(d).
95 20 U.S.C. § 1091(l). For more detail about problems related to distance education and the applicable regulations, see § 9.2.3, *infra*.
96 20 U.S.C. § 1093.
97 34 C.F.R. § 668.8.
98 *See* § 9.2.3, *infra*. The amended definition of a telecommunications course acknowledges the importance of interactivity in electronically delivered instruction and clearly distinguishes telecommunications from correspondence. 71 Fed. Reg. 45666 (Aug. 9, 2006).
99 *See, e.g.*, Dear Colleague GEN-06-07 (May 2006) (Notification and Extension of Guidance to Assist Title IV participants

1.5 Private Student Loans

1.5.1 General

Banks and other financial institutions make private student loans without any direct financial backing from the federal government. They are not subsidized, meaning that interest starts to accrue at the time the loans are obtained. There are many different types of private loans, each program with specific rules and requirements. Private loans are also known as private-label or alternative loans.

The private student loan business has experienced tremendous growth in recent years. Despite the boom in private lending, the vast majority of students still borrow primarily federal loan products. However, private loan products are coming on strong. Private borrowing by students rose to about $5 billion in 2001–2002, up from about $1 billion in 1995–1996.[100] The total volume of private loans has surpassed the amounts awarded annually under the Federal Student Education Opportunity Grant, Work-Study, and Perkins Loan programs combined.[101]

A 2003 report found that private loans comprise about 10% of total student loan volume. The percentage is much higher among professional students, approximately 16% of whom borrowed private loans in 1999–2000.[102] Overall, the number of private loan products grew from 79 in March 1997 to 272 in March 2003, an increase of 244%.[103]

There are growing concerns that schools may be steering some borrowers into private loan products and away from federal loans. This may occur for a number of reasons. First, some schools may be concerned about high cohort default rates. Schools with rates beyond prescribed limits are subject to the Department of Education's sanction powers.[104] Since private loan default statistics are not included in these calculations, less credit-worthy borrowers may be pressured to take out private loans instead.[105] Other schools may be ineligible to participate in federal programs, in some cases due to previous disqualification. Yet many schools are able to stay in business by encouraging or pressuring borrowers to take out private loans.

The groups most likely to borrow private loans include (1) traditional undergraduates at relatively high-priced private four-year institutions; (2) undergraduates who face very high non-tuition costs; and (3) professional students.[106] However, students at proprietary schools are increasingly using private loans.[107]

A high proportion of private loan borrowers also obtain federal loans and, in many cases, borrow up to the federal loan limits. In 1999–2000, 77% of professional students, 50% of undergraduates, and 32% of graduate students who borrowed private loans had also borrowed the maximum total Stafford Loan amounts for which they were eligible.[108]

However, a 2003 study by the State PIRGs Higher Education Project found that nearly 75% of private loan borrowers took on private loans without first exhausting federal grant, work-study, and loan options and/or available family contributions.[109] Concentrations of such borrowers among lower-income dependent and independent students make the problem even more severe. The State PIRGs found that lower-income students are the most likely to borrow private loans before they exhaust other options.[110]

There are many explanations for this trend. In some cases, a students' family may not actually make the expected family contribution that is built into the federal assistance calculations.[111] In these circumstances, students may have no choice but to turn to private lenders. In other cases, a student may choose to borrow beyond his or her student budget (costs of tuition and estimated living expenses) to cover higher living expenses. In many cases, however, it appears that borrowers turn to private loans because of lack of information and/or sophistication about the different government and private programs. This lack of information is particularly problematic in cases in which schools aggressively sell private loan products.

1.5.2 Comparing Private Loans and Federal Loans

Private loan terms and conditions, including interest rates and fees, are generally determined by an individual's or a co-signer's credit history. Thus, low-income students and/or those with negative credit histories are more likely to receive loans on less favorable terms. Federal student loan borrowers, in contrast, must meet eligibility requirements

---

affected by Hurricanes Katrina and Rita).

100 Kate Rube, State PIRGS' Higher Educ. Project, *Private Loans: Who's Borrowing and Why* (Apr. 2003). The study also found that private borrowing at for-profit institutions was higher than at public institutions. At less-than-two-year institutions, the average private loan was $6095.

101 The Inst. for Higher Educ. Policy, *Private Loans and Choice in Financing in Higher Education* (2003), *available at* www.ihep.com/Pubs/PDF/PvtLoans.pdf. The report is also available on the companion CD-Rom to this manual.

102 *Id.* at 33.

103 *Id.* at 14.

104 *See* § 9.2.5, *infra*.

105 *See id.*

106 The Inst. for Higher Educ. Policy, *Private Loans and Choice in Financing in Higher Education* 35 (2003).

107 *See generally* The Inst. for Higher Educ. Policy, *Private Loans and Choice in Financing in Higher Education* (2003), *available at* www.ihep.com/Pubs/PDF/PvtLoans.pdf. The report is also available on the companion CD-Rom to this manual.

108 *Id.* at 34.

109 Kate Rube, State PIRGs' Higher Educ. Project, *Private Loans: Who's Borrowing and Why?* (Apr. 2003). The study is available at www.uspirg.org and is also included on the companion CD-Rom to this manual.

110 *Id.*

111 *See* § 1.4.3, *supra*.

but do not have to prove creditworthiness.[112] All eligible federal loan borrowers are subject to the same rules regarding interest rates and other terms.

Both can be used only to help finance postsecondary educations and can be certified only up to a certain amount. For private loans, this amount often is either a set dollar amount or the cost of attendance minus aid, whichever is less. Federal loans have loan limits.[113]

The three most compelling differences relate to flexibility, the level of risk and associated interest rates, and the services and rewards attached.[114]

Private loans have traditionally had higher interest rates than government loans. There are reports of private loans with interest rates of at least 15% but are often much higher.[115] Some reports claim that the gap has narrowed in recent years.[116]

Private lenders generally assess interest risks based on credit scores. In a 2002 study, only two of 259 private student lenders offered "credit blind" loans (that is, those available without credit checks).[117] These loans often require co-signers. Those that do not require co-signers typically have very high origination fees and higher interest rates.

Private loans allow greater flexibility with regard to origination fees, interest rates, and repayment terms. This primarily benefits generally higher-income borrowers with favorable credit scores or those who can secure a "credit-worthy" co-signer. Private loans are also more flexible in allowing borrowers to obtain loans throughout the year as opposed to the limited time during each semester when federal loans are available.

A critical difference is the lack of certain protections for private loan borrowers. For example, students with private loans are not eligible for the same types of discharge options discussed in Chapter 6. The same is true with regard to deferment and forbearance rights, all of which depend on the lender's policies and the terms of the loan contracts rather than on federal regulations.

On the other hand, there are certain advantages for private loan borrowers. Unlike federal loan collections, there should be a statute of limitations for collection of private loans.[118] Private lenders have fewer collection tools. Previously, private loan borrowers were generally able to discharge their loans in bankruptcy. Due to changes in the bankruptcy law effective October 2005, the bankruptcy rules are now generally just as restrictive for private loans as for government loans.[119]

1.6 Determining What Type of Loan a Client Has

The most efficient way to find out about a client's government loan is through the National Student Loan Data System (NSLDS). The NSLDS is the Department's central database for student aid. It receives data from schools, agencies that guarantee loans, the Direct Loan program, the Pell Grant program, and other United States Department of Education programs. This information is available on the Internet at www.nslds.ed.gov.

Borrowers can use the NSLDS to make inquiries about loans and grants using a personal identification number (PIN). The site displays information on loan and/or grant amounts, outstanding balances, loan statuses, and disbursements.

A September 2004 Dear Colleague letter clarifies the requirements for requesting and using a PIN for use in the federal student aid programs. First, the person initiating a request for a PIN must be the person identified in the submission who then becomes the owner of the PIN. Second, the person to whom the PIN is sent (either by e-mail or regular mail) must be this same person. Third, the person using the PIN, for any purpose, must be the PIN owner. Finally, the owner of the PIN must not share it with any other person or transfer any of his or her rights or responsibilities to another person or entity. Advocates should note that the Department states that it is contrary to the requirements of the process for anyone to use another person's PIN, even in an attempt to provide assistance. This is true regardless of whether the PIN owner has been informed of the activity or even if he or she voluntarily agrees to provide the PIN to the other party.[120]

In April 2005, the Department issued a Dear Colleague letter reminding members of the financial aid community who have access to information contained in the NSLDS that they are responsible for using their access properly and for protecting the sensitive data contained in the system. The information is made available only for the general purpose of helping to determine the eligibility of an applicant for federal student aid and in the collection of federal student loans and grant overpayments. Most importantly, the Department emphasized that the information may not be used

---

112 *See* § 1.4.3, *supra* (federal loan eligibility requirements). Parent PLUS loan borrowers, in contrast, are required to meet certain creditworthiness standards.

113 *See* § 2.2, *infra*.

114 *See generally* The Inst. for Higher Educ. Policy, *Private Loans and Choice in Financing in Higher Education* (2003), *available at* www.ihep.com/Pubs/PDF/PvtLoans.pdf. The report is also available on the companion CD-Rom to this manual.

115 *See, e.g.,* Sam Kennedy, *School Steers Students to Backbreaking Loans*, The Morning Call, May 22, 2005, at A1.

116 *See, e.g.,* The Inst. for Higher Educ. Policy, *Private Loans and Choice in Financing in Higher Education* (2003).

117 *Id.* at 15.

118 *See* § 4.2, *infra*. The elimination of the statute of limitations in

the Higher Education Act applies only to federal loans. 20 U.S.C. § 1091a.

119 *See* § 7.2.2, *infra*.

120 U.S. Dep't of Educ., Dear Colleague Letter GEN-04-10 (Sept. 2004).

for marketing of student loans or other products. Failure to comply may result in loss of access to the NSLDS or in other sanctions. These sanctions may apply to any organization that, by sharing its program identifiers, has provided other entities or individuals the ability to access the NSLDS information. The Department expressed specific concern with the use of FFEL Lender IDs by organizations—such as collection agencies and loan brokerage or marketing firms—only minimally related to the lender of record.[121]

Borrowers can also call the Federal Student Aid Information Center, 1-800-4-FED-AID, TDD 1-800-730-8913. The Center's counselors can help borrowers, over the phone, to figure out what types of loans they have. There is a Direct Loan service center specifically for Direct Loan borrowers. Borrowers should call 1-800-848-0979 (1-800-557-7392 for Direct Consolidation Loans). The collection process, including the major collection players, is discussed in more detail in Chapter 4, *infra*.

1.7 Student Loan and Income Tax Issues

Beginning in 1998, taxpayers with qualified loans to pay certain costs of attending higher education have been allowed to take tax deductions from gross income for the interest they pay on these loans.[122] Qualified loans are loans taken out solely to pay qualified education expenses for an individual, his or her spouse, or a dependent. The loans must also be for education provided during an academic period for an eligible student. Loans from related persons and qualified employer plans do not qualify.

The maximum deductible interest on a qualified student loan is $2500 per return. Married taxpayers filing jointly are allowed to deduct the full amount only when their modified adjusted gross income is $105,000 or less. For those with incomes between $105,000 and $135,000, the deduction is gradually reduced. Taxpayers filing as single, head of household, or qualifying widow(er) may take the full $2500 deduction as long as their adjusted gross income is $50,000 or less. The deduction is phased out for those with incomes between $50,000 and $65,000. Parents may also deduct interest for loans taken out to pay their children's education as long as the children was dependents when the parents received the loan.

There are additional tax benefits for education, including (1) certain tax-free scholarships and fellowships; (2) non-refundable Hope and Lifetime Learning Credits of up to $1500 for qualified education expenses paid for each eligible student;[123] (3) limited deductions for tuition and related expenses; and (4) deductions for work-related education. It is unclear how effective these programs have been in increasing access to higher education, particularly for the neediest students.[124]

1.8 Checklist for Handling Student Loan Issues

1.8.1 Loan Cancellation

Regardless of whether the client is in default, loan cancellation is the first option to consider. Cancellation provides the most complete remedy for student loan borrowers. Advocates should always review all of the various cancellation remedies for all clients. Clients may be eligible for more than one type of cancellation, but they can recover only once.

If eligible, the client's loan will not only be canceled, but also all payments made to date including monies seized will be returned and the client's credit report should be cleared. Cancellation options are discussed in detail in Chapter 6, *infra*.

Before reviewing cancellation options, it is important to know what type of loan the client has. Cancellation and other rights vary depending on the type of loan. Some clients will have more than one type of loan. The next step is to determine when the loan was originated. Again, borrower rights differ depending on the date of origination.

In summary, before reviewing the cancellation and repayment options below, advocates should first determine

- the type of loan;
- loan origination date;
- whether the client is already in default (if not in default, deferment should also be considered, particularly while the cancellation application is pending);
- whether collection has begun (and, if so, what time deadlines are for responding to the collection action);[125] and

---

121 The explicit allowable uses of the data can be found at 64 Fed. Reg. 72384 (Dec. 27, 1999). *See* U.S. Dep't of Educ., Dear Colleague Letter GEN-05-06 (Apr. 2005).

122 For more information, see Internal Revenue Serv., Publication 970, *Tax Benefits for Education* (2005); Internal Revenue Serv., Tax Topic 456, *Student Loan Interest Deduction. See generally* Vincent G. Kalafat, *Rethinking Treasury Regulation § 1.162-5 and Slaying the Monster in the Education Tax Maze*, 80 Notre Dame L. Rev. 1985 (May 2005).

123 The Hope Credit is a non-refundable credit per student per year equal to 100% of the first $1000 of qualified tuition and related expenses and 50% of the next $1000 paid for a student's education for the first two years of post-secondary education. The Lifetime Learning Credit is a non-refundable credit but is calculated per taxpayer per year for an unlimited number of years and equals 20% of qualified tuition and related expenses not exceeding $10,000. Both are phased out for higher-income taxpayers. *See* Internal Revenue Serv., Publication 970, *Tax Benefits for Education* (2004).

124 *See, e.g.,* Michael Arnone, *Education Tax Credits Fall Short, Study Finds*, The Chron. of Higher Educ. (Oct. 24, 2003), at A27.

125 *See* Chapters 4 (possible fair debt violations), 5 (defenses to tax

- the client's goals and financial situation.

After considering these issues, advocates should determine whether the client is eligible for loan cancellation. The following are the main cancellation programs:

(1) Closed school. The closed-school cancellation applies to FFELs, federal Direct Loans, and Perkins Loans (including NDSLs) received at least in part on or after January 1, 1986.[126]

(2) False Certification. Borrowers are entitled to a loan cancellation if they received at least part of an FFEL or Direct Loan after January 1, 1986, and if their eligibility to borrow was falsely certified by the school.[127] The cancellation does not apply to Perkins Loans, but students should be able to raise the school's misconduct as a defense to loan repayment because the school is the original lender.[128]

The Department recognizes four bases for a false-certification discharge:

- the school falsifies a non-high-school graduate's ability to benefit from the program;[129]
- the school enrolls a student unable to meet minimum state employment requirements for the job for which the student is being trained;[130]
- the school forges or alters the student loan note or check endorsements;[131] or
- the borrower is a victim of identity theft.[132]

(3) Disability cancellation. The borrower's permanent and total disability is grounds for a student loan discharge.[133]

(4) Death. The borrower's death is a defense to collection actions on Stafford, SLS, Perkins, and Federal Direct Loans.[134] The deaths of both parents (assuming both parents are obligated) or the death of the student discharges PLUS loans.[135]

(5) Unpaid Refund. Provides for discharge based on the school's failure to make an owed refund to the student.[136] State tuition recovery funds should also be considered.[137]

(6) Bankruptcy. Some student loans may be discharged in bankruptcy.[138]

Obtaining a loan cancellation can take a long time. In the meantime, advocates should request administrative forbearances to stop the collection efforts pending a decision.[139] If the client wants to go back to school before a decision on the cancellation is made, advocates should consider reviewing the repayment, loan rehabilitation, and consolidation options discussed in Chapter 8, *infra*, and summarized below. It may best serve the client's goals to move forward with repayment, at least temporarily, while the cancellation application is pending.

1.8.2 Steps to Take If Cancellation Is Not Available

The next step depends on whether the client is already in default. Borrowers who are not yet in default are eligible for deferments. The various deferment programs detailed in Chapter 3, *infra*, should be reviewed at this point. Forbearance, available both before and after default, should also be considered. Both deferment and forbearance options are discussed in Chapter 3.

If the client is not eligible for a deferment or is already in default, the next step depends on whether collection has begun and, if so, what type of collection. This is important because many defenses can be raised specifically in response to certain types of collection such as tax refund intercepts or administrative wage garnishments. Timing for these challenges is critical. At this point, advocates should be sure to check all notices and determine whether it is still possible to file a response to a collection action.

For tax refund intercepts, borrowers must make a written request to inspect a loan file within twenty days of the notice of offset.[140] To obtain a review, the borrower must file a request for review at the address specified in the notice by the *later* of sixty-five days after the date of the notice or fifteen days after the borrower's loan file is provided, if requested.[141] A borrower can request a later hearing, but only a timely hearing request will stop the intercept pending the hearing. These issues are discussed in § 5.2, *infra*.

refund intercepts, wage garnishments, and federal benefits offsets), 9 (defenses to collection lawsuits), *infra*.

126 34 C.F.R. §§ 682.402(d) (FFEL), 685.214 (Direct Loans), 674.33(g) (Perkins). *See* § 6.2, *infra*.

127 34 C.F.R. §§ 682.402(e) (FFEL), 685.215 (Direct Loans).

128 *See* § 9.6.2.1, *infra*.

129 *See* § 6.3.2, *infra*.

130 *See* § 6.3.3, *infra*.

131 *See* § 6.3.4, *infra*.

132 *See* § 6.3, *infra*.

133 34 C.F.R. §§ 682.402(c) (FFEL), 685.213 (Direct Loans), 674.61 (Perkins). *See* § 6.6, *infra*. For a PLUS loan on which both parents are obligated, the disability of only one parent does not discharge the loan. 34 C.F.R. § 682.402(a)(2). *See* § 6.6.1, *infra*.

134 34 C.F.R. §§ 674.61 (Perkins), 682.402 (FFEL), 685.212(a) (Direct Loans).

135 34 C.F.R. § 682.402(b)(1). *See* § 6.7, *infra*. Assuming the parents are co-borrowers, the death of only one of the two obligated parents does not discharge a PLUS loan. 34 C.F.R.

§ 682.402(a)(2). *See* § 6.7, *infra*.

136 *See* § 6.4, *infra*.

137 *See* § 9.8.1, *infra*.

138 *See* Chapter 7, *infra*.

139 Forbearances are discussed at Chapter 3, *infra*.

140 34 C.F.R. § 30.33(c)(1).

141 34 C.F.R. § 30.33(d).

Administrative wage garnishments cannot go forward if the borrower requests a hearing within fifteen days of the borrower's receipt of the garnishment notice (receipt is presumed within five days of mailing of the notice).[142] Administrative wage garnishment is discussed in detail at § 5.3, *infra*.

Clients may also have notices of federal benefits offsets. Borrower rights to challenge offsets are discussed at § 5.4, *infra*.

The response date for lawsuits can be found on the summons. Possible defenses to student loan collection lawsuits are discussed in Chapter 9, *infra*.

Throughout this analysis, it is important to speak with clients about their goals. Do they want to go back to school? If so, getting out of default as soon as possible is critical. If instead they are primarily interested in stopping the collection efforts, it is then important to focus on challenging collection efforts as discussed in Chapters 5 and 9, *infra*. In addition, possible fair debt collection violations, discussed in Chapter 4, *infra*, should also be considered.

It is important to get a sense of the client's overall budget and in particular to determine whether the client is collection proof. A client is collection proof if he or she does not have any money or property that can legally be taken to pay the debt.

It is difficult, although not impossible, for a client to be completely protected from government student loan collection. Clients without significant federal benefits, without wages, without tax refunds, and with no other significant assets will most likely be safe from student loan collection, at least temporarily. However, as discussed in Chapter 4, *infra*, the elimination of a statute of limitations for student loan collections means that the debt may come back to haunt the client in the future.

1.8.3 *Repayment Options*

If a client is not eligible for a cancellation or cannot wait for a decision to get out of default, the next step is to consider the various repayment options. The following are primary strategies:

- Loan Consolidation. Particularly for low-income clients, a Direct Loan consolidation with an Income Contingent Repayment Plan is an excellent strategy to get out of default and pay only minimal (or even no) payments each month.[143]
- Reasonable and Affordable Payment Plans. Borrowers can renew eligibility by setting up reasonable and affordable payment plans. Six consecutive on-time monthly payments will renew eligibility. However, this option is a one-time deal. If a client sets up a reasonable

and affordable plan and stops making payments, he or she will not be eligible again for a reasonable and affordable plan.[144]
- Loan Rehabilitation. After making nine payments within twenty days of the due date during a period of ten consecutive months, a borrower can get out of default by rehabilitating a loan.[145]

Once out of default, clients are not only eligible to return to school but are also eligible for the deferment programs discussed in Chapter 3, *infra*.

1.9 Assistance for Student Loan Borrowers

1.9.1 *Assistance Within the Department of Education*

1.9.1.1 Student Loan Ombudsman

An ombudsman office has been established in the Department of Education specifically to help borrowers with difficult problems. The student loan ombudsman has a website, and borrowers can submit problems on-line at www.fsahelp.ed.gov or www.ombudsman.ed.gov. The toll-free phone number is 877-557-2575. The e-mail address is fsaombudsmanoffice@ed.gov; the fax number is 202-275-0549; and the mail address is U.S. Department of Education, FSA Ombudsman, 830 First Street, N.E., Washington, D.C. 20202-5144.[146]

The ombudsman's stated goal is to facilitate and provide creative options for borrowers needing assistance with federal loans, Direct, FFEL, SLS, and Perkins Loans. The ombudsman will research problems and determine if borrowers have been treated fairly. They will also contact other offices within the DOE, private lenders, and guaranty agencies to assist borrowers. However, the Ombudsman office strongly emphasizes that it serves as a last resort, to be consulted only after a borrower has tried to resolve a problem on his or her own.

1.9.1.2 Additional Resources

The Department of Education's website is extensive and contains a great deal of useful information. In particular, the Direct Loan page allows borrowers to calculate monthly payments under the various repayment plans, including Income Contingent Repayment Plans. The site also contains

---

142 34 C.F.R. § 682.410(b)(9)(10)(i)(K).
143 *See* § 8.2, *infra*.
144 *See* § 8.3, *infra*.
145 *See* § 8.4, *infra*.
146 *See* U.S. Dep't of Educ., Dear Colleague Letter GEN-04-07 (July 2004).

useful addresses and phone numbers within the Department as well as collection agency and guaranty agency information.

The Department of Education also publishes very useful guides, including *Funding Education Beyond High School* and *Repaying Your Student Loans*. The Guides are updated each year and are available in English and Spanish on-line or by calling the Federal Student Aid Information Center at 1-800-4-FED-AID.[147]

1.9.2 Potential Problems with For-Profit Counselors

There is a growing industry of for-profit companies claiming to help student loan borrowers stay out of default and successfully repay student loans.

In some cases, these counselors appear to act mainly as brokers, claiming that they can help arrange loan consolidation for a borrower. The companies may require the borrower to sign a statement indicating awareness that these sources may be available without the use of the company's services but that the borrower has determined it is in his or her best interest to hire the company. Generally, these companies make no guarantees. In some cases, they will assist only with federal loans and in some cases will not assist borrowers if their loans were previously in default.

These companies often charge high fees. In many cases, they are only offering to do work that the borrower could do on his or her own. Despite disclaimers to the contrary, these non-attorney counselors may very well be crossing over the line and engaging in unauthorized practice of law.[148]

---

147 The two guides are available on the companion CD-Rom to this manual.

148 *See generally* National Consumer Law Center, Unfair and Deceptive Acts and Practices § 5.12.2 (6th ed. 2004 and Supp.).

Chapter 2

Taking Out a Student Loan: Basic Terms and Pre-Default Repayment Options

2.1 Student Loan Interest Rates

2.1.1 General

The Higher Education Act (HEA) sets interest rate limits for FFELs, Direct Loans, and Perkins Loans. Prior to July 1, 2006, the rates for most student loans were variable with an upper limit of 8.25%.[1] Since around 2000, variable rates were beneficial to borrowers because of a period of historically low rates. In 2003 and 2004, most student loan interest rates were just above 3%. By 2005, interest rates had begun to climb, up to 5.3% for Stafford loans. Borrowers with variable rate loans will likely continue to see increases in the foreseeable future. In 2006, for example, Stafford loan rates were just over 7%.

PLUS loan interest rates for most loans incurred before July 1, 2006, are variable and capped at 9%.[2] Perkins loan interest rates are fixed, currently at 5%.[3] There are no limits in the Higher Education Act on private student loan interest rates.

The variable rate era ended, at least for now, on July 1, 2006. As of July 1, 2006, and for loans for which disbursement is made on or after July 1, 2006, Stafford loans will have a fixed 6.8% interest rate. PLUS loans incurred after July 1, 2006, will also have fixed interest rates. Probably due to Congressional error, there is a difference in the maximum fixed rates between the FFEL and Direct Loan programs. The fixed rate for Direct PLUS after July 1, 2006, is 7.9%[4] while the fixed rate for FFEL PLUS is 8.5%.[5]

Each program has various repayment incentives that allow lenders to reduce interest rates for borrowers who make payments electronically and under other circumstances.[6] In addition, lenders have the discretion to make loans with lower rates.[7]

There are also separate standards for consolidation loan interest rates. Interest rates for consolidation loans were fixed prior to July 1, 2006, and will remain fixed. The fixed rate is based on the weighted average of the interest rates on the loans at the time of consolidation, rounded up to the nearest one-eighth of a percentage point. The interest rate must not exceed 8.25%.[8]

Congress debated using a variable rate for consolidation loans but decided to retain the fixed rate. Policymakers were attempting to address the staggering growth in the consolidation loan programs and the corresponding costs. Direct and FFEL consolidation loans combined accounted for about 48% of the $87.4 billion in total new student loan dollars that originated during fiscal year 2003.[9] This growth is due mainly to an unprecedented period of low interest rates and aggressive marketing of consolidation loans.[10]

During periods of low interest rates, borrowers have sought to consolidate their variable rate loans and obtain low fixed-rate consolidation loans. A major cost of this trend, associated with FFEL consolidation only, is attributable to government subsidies to lenders. These are special allowances paid by the government to lenders to provide them a guaranteed rate of return on the student loans they make.[11] For example, subsidy costs for FFEL consolidation grew from $0.651 billion for loans made in fiscal year 2002 to $2.135 billion for loans made in fiscal year 2003.[12] Low

---

1 20 U.S.C. § 1077a (FFEL); 20 U.S.C. § 1087e (Direct Loans). For any twelve-month period beginning on July 1 and ending on June 30, the variable rate is determined on the preceding June 1 and is equal to the bond equivalent rate of ninety-one-day Treasury bills auctioned at the final auction held prior to June 1 plus an additional amount. For Stafford loans incurred after October 1, 1998, and before July 1, 2006, the additional amount is 2.3%.

2 20 U.S.C. §§ 1077a (FFEL), § 1087e (Direct Loans); 34 C.F.R. §§ 682.202(a)(2)(v) (FFEL), 685.202(a)(2) (Direct).

3 20 U.S.C. § 1087dd(c)(1)(D); 34 C.F.R. § 674.31(b)(1).

4 20 U.S.C. § 1087e(b)(7)(B).

5 20 U.S.C. § 1077a(l)(2), 34 C.F.R. §§ 682.202 (FFEL); 685.202 (Direct).

6 See, e.g., 34 C.F.R. §§ 685.211(b), 674.33(f) (Perkins program allows reduction of interest rates for borrowers who make forty-eight consecutive monthly repayments and reductions on balances for loans paid before end of repayment period).

7 20 U.S.C. § 1077a(m).

8 20 U.S.C. § 1077a(k)(4); 34 C.F.R. §§ 682.202(a)(4)(iv) (FFEL), 685.202(a)(3)(i)(E) (Direct).

9 U.S. Gen Accounting Office, Student Loan Programs: Lower Interest Rates and Higher Loan Volume Have Increased Federal Consolidation Loan Costs, GAO-04-568T (Mar. 17, 2004).

10 See generally § 8.2, infra.

11 Id.

12 Id.

interest rates increase these costs because FFEL consolidation loans carry a government-guaranteed rate of return to lenders that is higher than the fixed interest rate paid by consolidation loan borrowers. When the interest rate paid by borrowers does not provide the full guarantee rate to lenders, the federal government pays the difference to the lenders. Direct loans, in contrast, are made by the government and thus carry no interest rate guarantee to lenders.[13]

The switch to fixed interest rates for Stafford and PLUS loans means that consolidation loan rates will become more standardized over time. This is because the underlying loans to be consolidated will eventually have the same or similar rates. Since the consolidation loan interest rate is based on an average of the underlying loans, the consolidation rate will eventually be close to the fixed rates of the underlying loans. Presumably, consolidation will become less popular as the interest rate advantages decline. However, this will not occur overnight. Many borrowers will consolidate loans incurred before July 1, 2006, which still have variable interest rates that will rise and fall with Treasury bill rates.

2.1.2 Usury Limits

Most government student loan interest rates, as discussed in the previous sections, are fixed below the limits generally found in any state usury limits. Regardless, the HEA expressly preempts state usury laws.[14]

Private loans, in contrast, may have interest rates that approach any state usury limits. It is not uncommon to see private student loans with interest rates well above 10% and even closer to 15% or 20%. Unlike government loans, interest rates for private loans are set based on consumer credit scores.[15] State usury limits may apply in these cases unless preempted on other grounds.[16]

2.2 Loan Limits

The Department establishes limits for the various federal loan programs. Stafford loan limits vary depending on whether the borrower is financially dependent or independent. If a borrower is considered dependent, the borrower's parents' as well as his or her own income and assets will be considered in determining the level of financial aid.

Under current regulations, the total debt an independent, undergraduate borrower can accumulate from all Stafford loans combined is $46,000.[17] The limits vary for each year

of study, depending on the length of the program and the student's year of study.[18] These maximum borrowing limits are for both subsidized and unsubsidized loans.

Perkins loan limits depend on when the borrower applies, the level of need, and the school's funding level. Undergraduate students can borrow up to $4000 for each year of undergraduate study up to a total of $20,000.[19] The yearly limit on PLUS loans is equal to the student's cost of attendance minus any other financial aid received.[20]

In the Higher Education Reconciliation Act of 2005, Congress passed slight increases in loan limits for students during the first two years of study. Combined annual loan limits (for subsidized and unsubsidized loans) were not increased beyond the first two years of undergraduate study. The annual unsubsidized annual loan limit for graduate or professional students was increased.[21]

Federal loan limits have remained low for many years. Student groups and some college and university associations, on one side, generally oppose increases in loan limits. They argue that higher limits will only exacerbate students' unmanageable debt burdens. The real problem, opponents of increased loan limits argue, is skyrocketing tuition costs. They also point to the federal trend toward funding loans rather than grants for needy students.

Advocates for higher limits point to the increases in educational costs as well, arguing that this is exactly why loan limits should be raised. The current limits are simply too low, they claim, to fund most higher education programs. These advocates also caution that, without increases in loan limits, more and more students will turn to private loan products, which carry fewer consumer protections than federal loans.[22]

2.3 Origination Fees and Other Up-Front Charges

There are no origination or other fees or charges for Perkins loans. There are, however, fees for Direct and FFEL Stafford loans. Currently, origination fees can be up to 3% for FFEL Stafford loans and up to 4% for Direct Stafford loans, deducted proportionately from each loan disbursement.[23] Stafford loans also include a 1% insurance premium so that borrowers in both programs are charged no more than

---

13 *Id.*

14 20 U.S.C. § 1078(d).

15 *See generally* Sam Kennedy, *School Steers Students to Backbreaking Loans*, The Morning Call, May 22, 2005, at A1.

16 *See generally* National Consumer Law Center, The Cost of Credit: Regulation, Preemption, and Industry Abuses (3d ed. 2005 and Supp.).

17 34 C.F.R. §§ 682.204(e) (FFEL), 685.203(e) (Direct Loans).

---

18 *Id.*

19 34 C.F.R. § 674.12.

20 34 C.F.R. § 682.204(h).

21 Pub. L. No. 109-171, 120 Stat. 4 (Feb. 8, 2006). For a summary of changes in this Act, see Department of Education's Dear Colleague Letter GEN-06-02, *Enactment of the Higher Education Reconciliation Act of 2005* (Mar. 2006). The letter is available on the Department of Education website and on the companion CD-Rom to this manual.

22 *See* Stephen Burd, *Public Colleges Are At Odds over Raising Limits on Student Loans*, Chron. of Higher Educ., July 18, 2003, at A22–23. *See also* § 1.5, *supra* (Private Loans).

23 20 U.S.C. §§ 1087-1(c)(2) (FFEL), 1087e(c) (Direct Loans).

4% in fees. There are also origination fees for PLUS loans, up to 4%.[24] Consolidation loan borrowers are not charged these fees.

The Higher Education Reconciliation Act of 2005 made changes to reduce and eventually eliminate Stafford loan origination fees. Beginning with FFEL loans for which the first disbursement of principal is made on or after July 1, 2006, and before July 1, 2007, the maximum origination fee that can be charged will be 2%. The maximum fee drops to 1.5% on July 1, 2007, 1.0% on July 1, 2008, and 0.5% on July 1, 2009. The fee will be eliminated as of July 1, 2010.[25] Similar changes will be made to Direct Stafford loans, beginning with loans for which the first disbursement of principal is made on or after February 8, 2006, and before July 1, 2007. The origination fee for these loans can be more than 3%.[26] This fee drops to 2.5% on July 1, 2007, 2.0% on July 1, 2008, 1.5% on July 1, 2009, and 1.0% on July 1, 2010.[27]

Lenders are required to disclose the amount and method of calculating the origination fee.[28] In addition, borrowers should not be charged for any costs related to processing or handling of any applications or data required to determine a student's eligibility to borrow.[29]

2.4 Disclosures

2.4.1 Government Loans

Federal student loan lenders are not subject to Truth in Lending Act disclosure requirements.[30] The HEA also explicitly preempts any loan disclosure requirements of state laws.[31]

Presumably as a substitute for the lack of state and federal loan disclosure requirements, the Higher Education Act requires lenders to make certain disclosures to borrowers. There are also required disclosures before repayment begins.[32]

The HEA requirements are different from those in Truth in Lending in important ways. First, HEA disclosures must be given before or at the time of first disbursement. Truth in Lending disclosures, in contrast, must be given before the credit is extended.[33]

Similar to borrower rights in the Truth in Lending Act (TILA), student loan borrowers have the right to cancel their obligations after receiving disclosures. Borrowers have the right to cancel all or a portion of a loan if they inform the school within fourteen days after the date that the school notifies the borrower that it has credited the borrower's account with loan funds or by the first day of the payment period, whichever is later.[34]

In contrast to TILA, remedies for violations of HEA disclosures rules are severely limited. The HEA explicitly states that failure to comply with its loan disclosure requirements does *not* provide a basis for a claim for civil damages.[35] Failure to provide the required information also does not relieve a borrower of the obligation to repay the loan.[36]

The HEA requires lenders to disclose information to borrowers in "simple and understandable" terms before or at the time of the first disbursement.[37] The information that must be provided includes

- the lender's name;
- a toll-free telephone number accessible from within the U.S. that the borrower can use to obtain additional information;
- the principal amount of the loan;
- the amount of any charges, including the origination fee and the insurance premium if applicable, and an explanation of whether those charges are to be deducted from the proceeds of the loan or paid separately by the borrower;
- the actual interest rate;
- the annual and aggregate maximum amounts that may be borrowed;
- a statement that information concerning the loan, including the date of disbursement and the amount of the loan, will be reported to a national credit bureau;
- an explanation of when repayment is required and when the borrower is required to pay the interest that accrues;
- the minimum and maximum number of years in which the loan must be repaid and the minimum amount of required annual payments;
- an explanation for any special options the borrower may have for consolidating or refinancing;
- a statement that the borrower has the right to prepay all or part of the loan at any time, without penalty;
- deferment rights;
- consequences of default and the definition of "default";
- possible collection costs; and
- a statement of the total cumulative balance, including the loan applied for and owed to that lender, and an estimate of, or information that will allow the borrower to estimate, the projected monthly payment amount.[38]

---

24 20 U.S.C. § 1087-1(c)(6).

25 20 U.S.C. § 1087-1(c), 34 C.F.R. §§ 682.202(c) (FFEL), 685.202(c)(Direct).

26 The Department already provides this one percentage point origination fee reduction administratively and will continue to do so. 20 U.S.C. § 1087e(b)(8).

27 20 U.S.C. § 1087e(c).

28 20 U.S.C. § 1087-1(c)(4).

29 20 U.S.C. § 1094(a)(2).

30 20 U.S.C. § 1083(c).

31 20 U.S.C. § 1099. *See, e.g.,* Washkoviak v. Student Loan Mktg. Ass'n, 900 A.2d 168 (D.D.C. 2006).

32 20 U.S.C. § 1083(b).

33 15 U.S.C. § 1638(b)(1).

---

34 34 C.F.R. § 668.165(a).

35 20 U.S.C. § 1083(c).

36 *Id.*

37 20 U.S.C. § 1083(a); 34 C.F.R. § 682.205(a).

38 *Id.*

There are similar provisions for Perkins and Direct loans.[39]

2.4.2 Private Loans

The Higher Education Act disclosure provisions discussed in the previous section do not apply to private student loans. The Truth in Lending Act, however, should apply in most cases.

As long as the credit extended is less than $25,000, the TILA should apply.[40] Special rules exist for "interim student credit extensions."[41] Under interim student credit plans, a creditor does not know the specific terms of repayment at the time credit is advanced and therefore does not have to include in the initial disclosures the finance charge, payment schedule, total of payments, or total sale price. However, complete disclosures must be made at the time the creditor and consumer agree upon a repayment schedule for the entire obligation.[42]

2.5 Entrance and Exit Counseling Requirements

The HEA includes counseling requirements when borrowers first incur loans and after they withdraw or graduate. Initial counseling is supposed to occur prior to the release of the first loan disbursement.[43] The counseling may be in person, by audiovisual presentation, or by interactive electronic means. Schools are also supposed to ensure that an individual with expertise in financial aid is reasonably available shortly after the counseling to answer questions. Schools are not required to personally conduct entrance and exit counseling. Other entities may fulfill this responsibility on the school's behalf.[44]

The Direct Loan program allows schools to adopt alternative approaches for initial counseling. These alternatives must be designed to target borrowers who are most likely to default on repayment and to provide them more intensive counseling and support services.[45]

Among other provisions, the entrance counselor is supposed to emphasize to the borrower the seriousness and importance of the repayment obligation being assumed by the student borrower.[46] Borrowers must also receive sample monthly repayment amounts based on a range of indebtedness, the average indebtedness of borrowers at that school, or the average indebtedness of borrowers in that program of study at that school.[47]

The requirements for exit counseling are slightly different. Among other information, borrowers must be told the average anticipated monthly repayment amount based on the borrower's indebtedness or on the average indebtedness of student borrowers who have obtained Stafford or SLS loans for attendance at the same school or in the same program of study at the same school.[48]

In addition, the exit counseling must include

- a review of available repayment options, including standard, graduated, extended, and income-sensitive repayment plans and loan consolidation;
- a review of deferment, forbearance, and discharge options; and
- information about the Student Loan Ombudsman's office.[49]

By most accounts, counseling is no more than a formality, one of many hoops students jump through to get their student aid checks. Some guaranty agencies and schools have attempted to develop models to predict which borrowers are most at risk of defaulting and target more intensive efforts at these borrowers. Many focus on reaching borrowers immediately after drop-out since this is clearly a predictor of default.[50]

2.6 Return of Funds and How Loans Are Disbursed

Schools either pay borrowers directly, usually by check, or by crediting the borrower's account. In general, borrowers receive at least two payments during the academic year. For Stafford loans, no installment can be greater than half of the amount of the loan. For first-year undergraduate and

---

39   34 C.F.R. §§ 674.16(a) (Perkins), 685.206 (Direct).

40   15 U.S.C. § 1603(3); Reg. Z § 226.3(b). *See* National Consumer Law Center, Truth in Lending § 2.4 (5th ed. 2003 and Supp.).

41   12 C.F.R. § 226.17(*i*).

42   Official Staff Commentary § 226.17(*i*)-1. *See generally* § 9.7, *infra* (discussion of claims, including TILA, against private student loan creditors).

43   34 C.F.R. §§ 682.604(f) (FFEL), 685.304 (Direct).

44   34 C.F.R. § 682.604(f)(1), (g)(1) (FFEL)); 34 C.F.R. § 685.304 (Direct Loans).

45   34 C.F.R. § 685.304(a)(4).

46   34 C.F.R 682.604(f).

47   34 C.F.R. § 682.604(f)(2).

48   34 C.F.R. § 682.604(g).

49   34 C.F.R. § 682.604(g).

50   *See* Texas Guar. Student Loan Corp., *Predicting Which Borrowers Are Most Likely to Default* (1998), *available at* www.tgslc.org/publications/reports/defaults_texas/ins_intro.cfm; Lawrence Gladieux & Laura Perna, National Ctr. for Pub. Policy and Higher Educ., *Borrowers Who Drop Out: A Neglected Aspect of the College Student Loan Trend* (May 2005), *available at* www.highereducation.org/reports/borrowing/borrowers.pdf; Deanne Loonin, National Consumer Law Center, *No Way Out: Student Loans, Financial Distress, and The Need for Policy Reform* (June 2006), *available at* www.nclc.org/news/content/nowayout.pdf.

first-time borrowers, the first disbursement cannot be made until thirty days after the first day of enrollment.[51]

Student loan funds must first be used to pay for tuition, fees, and room and board. If funds remain, the borrower will receive them by check or in cash, unless the borrower gives the school written permission to hold the funds until later in the enrollment period.[52]

Borrowers have the right to cancel all or a portion of a loan if they inform the school within fourteen days after the date that the school notifies the borrower that it has credited the borrower's account with loan funds or by the first day of the payment period, whichever is later.[53]

If a borrower officially withdraws, drops out, or is expelled before the first day of class during a payment period, all funds paid to the borrower for that period are an overpayment and must be returned to the government. No additional disbursements may be made.[54]

2.7 Repayment Prior to Default

2.7.1 Disclosures Prior to Repayment

The HEA requires lenders to disclose certain information in simple and understandable terms at or prior to the beginning of the repayment period.[55] Stafford loan disclosures must be made not less than thirty days nor more than 240 days before the first payment on the loan is due.

The information that must be disclosed includes

- the lender's name and toll-free telephone number and mail address;
- the scheduled date repayment is to begin;
- the estimated balance, including the estimated amount of interest to be capitalized, owed by the borrower as of the date that the repayment period is to begin, or the date of the disclosure, whichever is later;
- the actual interest rate on the loan;
- an explanation of any fees that may accrue or be charged during the repayment period;
- the repayment schedule, including the due date of the first installment and the number, amount, and frequency of payments;
- special options the borrower may have to consolidate or refinance;
- the estimated total amount of interest to be paid on the

loan, assuming that payments are made in accordance with the repayment schedule; and
- a statement that the borrower may prepay at any time without penalty.[56]

A separate provision requires lenders, at the time they offer the borrower a loan and at the time of offering repayment options, to provide a notice informing the borrower of the availability of income-sensitive repayment.[57] Disclosures may be through written or electronic means.

2.7.2 Grace Periods

Repayment for Stafford loans begins after graduation or after a student leaves school or drops below half-time enrollment. After one of these events, a borrower has six months to begin repayment.[58] Repayment on PLUS loans generally must begin within sixty days after the final loan disbursement for the period of enrollment for which the loan was borrowed.[59] The grace period for Perkins loans is nine months.[60]

These "grace periods" do not include any period, not to exceed three years, during which a borrower who is a member of an Armed Forces reserve component is called or ordered to active duty for a period of more than thirty days.[61] Any single excluded period may not exceed three years and must include the time necessary for the borrower to resume enrollment at the next available regular enrollment period. Borrowers are entitled to another full six- or nine-month grace period, as applicable, upon completion of the excluded period of service.[62]

2.7.3 Repayment Options Prior to Default

2.7.3.1 Standard, Graduated, and Extended Repayment Plans

As of July 1, 2006, the rules for Direct Loan repayment plans are the same as for FFEL, except for the Direct Loan Income Contingent Repayment Plan (ICR). Income-sensitive and income-contingent repayment plans are discussed in the next section.

Standard repayment plans are the typical repayment plans that borrowers will get if they fail to choose another option. FFEL borrowers will automatically be assigned this plan if

---

51 34 C.F.R. § 682.207.
52 *See* U.S. Dep't of Educ., *Funding Education Beyond High School: 2006–07* at 12 (2006–07). This publication is available on the Department of Education website, www.ed.gov, and on the companion CD-Rom to this manual. *See also* 34 C.F.R. § 682.604(d).
53 34 C.F.R. § 668.165(a)(4).
54 34 C.F.R. § 668.22.
55 34 C.F.R. § 682.205(c) (FFEL).

56 *Id.*
57 34 C.F.R. § 682.205(h).
58 34 C.F.R. §§ 682.209 (FFEL), 685.207 (Direct).
59 34 C.F.R. §§ 682.209(a)(2)(i)(FFEL), 685.207(d) (Direct Loans).
60 34 C.F.R. §§ 674.2, 674.31.
61 34 C.F.R. §§ 682.209(a)(6) (FFEL), 685.207 (Direct), 674.31 (Perkins).
62 *Id.*

they do not select a different option within forty-five days of being notified by the lender to choose a repayment plan.[63] If a Direct loan borrower does not select a plan, the Department may choose either a standard, graduated, or extended plan.[64]

Standard plans carry the highest monthly payments and borrowers generally pay the same amount for each installment period. The monthly amount may vary if there is a variable loan rate. Borrowers have a minimum of five years, but not more than ten years, to repay with a standard plan.[65]

Graduated repayment plans are also available. Under these plans, payments start out low and increase during the course of the repayment period. Although payments vary over time, the loan still must be paid over a period of ten years.[66] This ten-year limit should not apply to Direct loan borrowers who entered repayment prior to July 1, 2006.[67] Graduated plans tend to work best for borrowers who are just starting out and are likely to see relatively quick increases in earnings over time.

Extended repayment plans are another option. They are available to borrowers with total outstanding principal and interest exceeding $30,000. In these cases, borrowers may repay on a fixed or graduated payment schedule for a period not to exceed twenty-five years.[68] Prior to July 1, 2006, the Direct Loan program allowed repayment for up to thirty years, depending on the amount owed.[69] Unlike FFEL, prior to July 2006, Direct borrowers owing less than $30,000 could also select extended plans.[70] The new rules should apply only to borrowers who enter repayment on or after July 1, 2006.[71]

Extended plan monthly payments usually will be less than under the standard repayment plan. However, borrowers will also usually pay more interest because the repayment period is longer.

Unless the borrower and lenders otherwise agree, FFEL borrowers must pay at least $600 annually.[72] However, the plans in all instances must cover at least the amount of interest due and payable.[73]

The Direct Loan program also allows some discretion to create alternative plans to accommodate a borrower's "exceptional circumstances."[74]

FFEL lenders must permit borrowers to change plans at least once a year, although they may allow it more frequently at their discretion.[75] Direct Loan borrowers may change repayment plans at any time after the loan has entered repayment.[76] However, Direct loan borrowers may not change to a repayment plan that has a maximum repayment period of less than the number of years the loan has already been in repayment, except that borrowers may switch to an income contingent repayment plan at any time.[77] There are different rules for Direct Loan borrowers repaying through the income contingent repayment plan.[78]

2.7.3.2 Repayment Plans Tied to Borrower's Income

The FFEL program offers borrowers Income Sensitive Repayment Plans (ISRP).[79] With these plans, the amount of the borrower's installment payment is adjusted annually based on the borrower's expected total monthly gross income.

Borrowers are required to submit income information to the lender in order to establish an Income Sensitive Repayment Plan. If the documentation shows that the borrower will be unable to repay the loan within the maximum ten-year repayment period, the lender is required to grant forbearance to the borrower for up to five years.[80]

The ISRP plans with FFELs are generally less affordable than the Income Contingent Repayment Plan (ICRP) available for Direct Loans and discussed below. This is because monthly payments under an ISRP, unlike an ICRP, must cover at least accruing interest.[81]

The more generous provisions of the Direct Loan Income Contingent Repayment Plan are particularly useful for low-income borrowers.[82] As with an FFEL Income Sensitive Plan, the ICRP allows borrowers to submit income documentation that is used to derive an affordable monthly payment. Unlike an ISRP, monthly payments under an ICRP do not need to cover monthly accruing interest. Monthly payments can be very low, even zero for borrowers with households incomes below the poverty level.[83]

---

63 34 C.F.R. § 682.209(a)(7)(v).

64 20 U.S.C. § 1087e(d)(2).

65 34 C.F.R. §§ 682.209(a)(8)(i) (FFEL), 685.208(b) (Direct). Borrowers may request to repay in less than five years.

66 20 U.S.C. § 1078(b)(9)(A)(ii); 34 C.F.R. § 682.209.

67 *See* 71 Fed. Reg. 45666 (Aug. 9, 2006), *amending* 34 C.F.R. § 685.208(f).

68 20 U.S.C. § 1078(b)(9)(A)(iv); 34 C.F.R. § 682.209(a)(7)(ix). The FFEL regulations provide that only borrowers who have no outstanding principal or interest balance on an FFEL loan as of October 7, 1998, or on the date they obtain an FFEL loan after October 7, 1998, are eligible for extended repayment plans.

69 34 C.F.R. § 685.208(e).

70 *Id.*

71 *See* 71 Fed. Reg. 45666 (Aug. 9, 2006), *amending* 34 C.F.R. § 685.208(d), (e).

72 20 U.S.C. § 1078(b)(1)(L)(i).

73 *Id.*

74 20 U.S.C. § 1087e(d)(4); 34 C.F.R. § 685.208(g).

75 34 C.F.R. § 682.209(a)(7)(x).

76 34 C.F.R. § 685.210(b).

77 34 C.F.R. § 685.210(b)(2)(i).

78 See § 2.7.3.2.

79 34 C.F.R. § 682.209(a)(7)(viii).

80 34 C.F.R. § 682.209(a)(7)(viii)(D).

81 20 U.S.C. § 1078(b)(9)(A)(iii); 34 C.F.R. § 682.209(a)(7)(iv). ISRP and ICRP payments plans are discussed in detail at § 8.2.3.1, *infra.*

82 34 C.F.R. §§ 685.208(f), 685.209.

83 *See* § 8.2.2.5, *infra.*

Under the ICRP, borrowers make minimal payments if they are below poverty income, taking family size into account. Payments increase incrementally as income increases. The required payments are capped at 20% of any earnings above the poverty level.[84] If borrowers continue making payments for twenty-five years, any debt that remains is forgiven.[85] However, this forgiven amount may be taxable income.[86]

Borrowers with ICRPs cannot change plans unless they were required to and made payments under the plan in each of the prior three months or were not required to make payments but made three reasonable and affordable payments in the prior three months.[87] The borrower must also request the change to ICRP.

Interestingly, the ICRP was not designed to benefit only low-income borrowers. The bill that was introduced by Senator Kennedy in 1993 stated that one of its purposes was to "provide borrowers with a variety of repayment plans, including an income-contingent repayment plan, so that borrowers['] . . . obligations do not foreclose community service-oriented career choices."[88] The drafters believed that a payment plan linked to income could be best administered through the direct lending program. For various reasons, including the efforts by FFEL lenders to push schools out of the Direct Loan program, the ICRP has never caught on as expected. Fewer than 1% of new borrowers at schools that offer direct federal loans choose income-contingent repayment.[89]

2.7.3.3 Perkins Loan Repayment

Perkins repayment plans vary from FFEL and Direct loan repayment plans in several significant ways. The regulations set out minimum monthly repayment rates. For example, the rate is $30 for an NDSL loan or a Perkins Loan made before October 1, 1992, and $40 after that date.[90] Schools are allowed to extend the repayment period due to a borrower's prolonged illness or unemployment.[91] This extension can be up to an additional ten years if the borrower qualifies as a low-income individual.[92] Interest continues to accrue during any extension of a repayment period.

2.7.4 How Payments Are Applied

Borrowers who are able to make partial monthly payments are often discouraged that those payments are rarely applied to principal. This is because loan holders are allowed to credit any payment received first to accrued late charges or collection costs, then to any outstanding interest, and then to outstanding principal.[93] There are similar provisions for schools collecting Perkins loans.[94]

This means, for example, that, if the collection rate for a particular year is 24%, then 24% of each payment made by a borrower is applied to collection costs, the balance to interest and then, if the payment is sufficient, to the reduction in the principal.[95]

Borrowers may repay the entire loan or any part of a loan at any time without penalty.[96] If the prepayment amounts equals or exceeds the monthly payment amount, the lender must apply the prepayment to future installments by advancing the next payment due date, unless the borrower requests otherwise. The lender must inform the borrower that any additional full payments submitted without instructions to the lender as to their handling will be applied to the borrower's future scheduled payments.[97]

---

84 34 C.F.R. § 685.209(a)(2).

85 34 C.F.R. § 685.209(c)(4)(iv).

86 *See generally* § 8.2.2.6, *infra.*

87 34 C.F.R. § 685.210(b).

88 Staff of S. Comm. on the Budget, 103d Cong., Reconciliation Submissions of the Instructed Committee Pursuant to the Concurrent Resolution on the Budget (H.R. Con. Res. 64) 453 (Comm. Print 1993) (reprinting report by Senate Committee on Labor and Human Resources to accompany Title XII of the Budget Reconciliation Act).

89 *See* U.S. Gen. Accounting Office, Direct Student Loans: Analyses of Borrowers' Use of the Income Contingent Repayment Option App. II, GAO/HEHS-97-155 at 30 (1997).

---

90 34 C.F.R. § 674.33(b)(6)(ii), (iii).

91 34 C.F.R. § 674.33(c).

92 34 C.F.R. § 674.33(c)(2).

93 34 C.F.R. § 682.209(b).

94 34 C.F.R. § 674.33(a)(4).

95 *See, e.g., In re* Evans, 322 B.R. 429 (Bankr. W.D. Wash. 2005).

96 34 C.F.R. § 682.209(b)(2) (FFEL).

97 34 C.F.R. § 682.209(b)(2)(ii). *See, e.g.,* Bomhoff v. Nelnet Loan Servs., Inc., 109 P. 3d 1241 (Kan. 2005) (rejecting plaintiff's UDAP, conversion, and fraud claims that lender failed to properly apply partial student loan payments).

Chapter 3　　　　　Deferments and Forbearances

3.1　Introduction

This chapter covers the primary deferment and forbearance programs for federally guaranteed student loans. Deferments allow eligible borrowers to postpone paying back their loans under certain circumstances. This is an extremely useful option, particularly since, in most cases, interest does not accrue on the loan during the deferment period. However, only borrowers who have not yet defaulted on their loans are eligible for deferments.

Also discussed in this chapter are forbearances. Like deferments, forbearances allow borrowers to temporarily postpone repayment. They are less optimal than deferments because interest continues to accrue during the forbearance period. Unlike deferments, forbearances may be granted to borrowers already in default.

Forbearances can be used to help borrowers avoid default in the first place. Borrowers may be able to get forbearances in order to postpone payments during periods of financial difficulty. Administrative forbearances are also available for borrowers who are waiting for decisions on cancellations, consolidation loan applications, or other matters pending with the Department or guaranty agencies.

3.2　Deferments

3.2.1　Benefits of Deferment

Student loan borrowers are legally entitled to defer payments in certain situations. Deferment rights vary depending on the type of loan and when the loan obligation was incurred. For example, deferment rights are different for Federal Family Education Loans (FFELs) issued before July 1, 1993, than FFELs issued after that date. Perkins loans also have different rights than FFELs.[1]

For all of these types of loans, the right to a deferment is an important one. For "subsidized" student loans (when the United States pays the interest while the student is enrolled in school), a deferment not only postpones when a student must make payments, but interest obligations do not accrue

during the deferment period. Instead, the federal government pays the interest portion of the loan and the student's payments on the principal are postponed until after the deferment expires.

For unsubsidized loans, on which borrowers are responsible for interest accrued while they are in school, borrowers remain obligated for accrued interest during the deferment period. In this situation, lenders may forbear and capitalize interest payments until after the deferment period.[2]

Deferments are designed to help borrowers who are financially unable to make loan payments, and thus deferments are useful for borrowers who are unemployed or back in school. If a loan is being deferred, the loan is not in default, and the borrower will not be subject to debt collection attempts or lawsuits and will be eligible for additional educational assistance.

3.2.2　Borrower's Default Limits Eligibility for Deferment

An important limitation to the usefulness of the borrower's deferment right is that the right exists only when borrowers are "delinquent" on the loan obligation, not when they are in "default."[3] If a borrower cannot qualify for a deferment because the loan is in default, the borrower can re-establish eligibility for a deferment by consolidating the loan into a new loan or by rehabilitating the defaulted loan.[4] The borrower can then apply for a deferment under the new loan. The borrower may also be eligible if he or she makes acceptable payments to the lender before the guaranty agency pays off a default claim.[5]

As a result, the borrower should first argue that a loan is only delinquent and not technically in default. Default occurs when the Secretary or guarantee agency finds it reasonable to conclude that the borrower no longer intends to

---

1　For more information on how to figure out what kind of a loan a borrower has, see § 1.6, *supra*.

2　20 U.S.C. §§ 1077, 1078; 34 C.F.R. § 682.211(a)(4). *See also* 34 C.F.R. § 682.202(b). Capitalization refers to the adding of accrued interest and unpaid insurance premiums to the borrower's unpaid principal balance.

3　34 C.F.R. § 682.210(a)(7), (8).

4　Consolidation and rehabilitation are discussed in §§ 8.2 (consolidation), 8.4 (rehabilitation), *infra*.

5　34 C.F.R. § 682.210(a)(8).

honor the obligation to repay *and* when the failure to pay persists for 270 days for loans repayable in monthly installments.[6]

The 270-day period is based on the number of days the borrower has been delinquent until the date that the condition entitling the borrower to the deferment first began.[7] For example, if the borrower had been delinquent since January 1 and applied for a deferment on December 1, the 270 days would *not* have run if the condition justifying the deferment (for example, economic hardship) occurred in June. It is the onset date of the condition and not the application date that is critical.

There is an exception to this general rule for FFEL unemployment deferments. An initial unemployment deferment cannot begin more than six months before the date the loan holder receives a request and supporting documentation for the deferment.[8]

3.2.3 General Eligibility Requirements for Deferments

The various student loan programs have different rules about when the borrower qualifies for a deferment. Rules differ not only by the type of loan (for example, Perkins or FFEL) but also by when the loan was extended. In particular, "economic hardship," an important deferment ground for low-income borrowers, is only available for Direct loans or FFELs disbursed after July 1, 1993, and then only if the borrower had no outstanding FFEL balance on the date the borrower obtained the new loan.[9] Borrowers with earlier FFELs can usually qualify for this economic hardship deferment by consolidating the earlier FFEL into a new consolidation loan and then applying for a deferment based on the post-July 1, 1993, deferment rules.[10] Consolidation loans are discussed in detail in Chapter 8, *infra*.

Most deferments carry maximum time limits, and each deferment has recertification requirements, generally every six months, for the borrower to remain eligible.[11]

The Department takes the position that the maximum length for deferments applies to the borrower and not just to the specific loan. Consequently, borrowers may not receive more than the maximum deferment time under any given deferment category regardless of how many different types of loans they have or how much time has elapsed since they last sought a deferment.[12] For example, if a borrower is entitled to a two-year unemployment deferment and uses that time up, the borrower may not later take out new loans and seek an additional unemployment deferment on those new loans.

3.2.4 Grounds for Direct Loans, FFELs, and Consolidation Loans Extended After July 1, 1993

3.2.4.1 General

One set of criteria for deferment applies to Direct loans, FFELs, and most consolidation loans first disbursed on or after July 1, 1993. With respect to FFEL consolidation loans, the post-July-1993 rules apply to borrowers who obtain an FFEL consolidation loan on or after July 1, 1993, and have no other outstanding FFEL loan at that time.[13] The following are available deferments for these loans:

- Student deferments for at least half-time study[14]
- Graduate fellowship deferments[15]
- Rehabilitation training program deferment[16]
- Unemployment deferment not to exceed three years[17]
- Economic hardship deferment, granted one year at a time for a maximum of three years[18]
- Military deferment for loans disbursed on or after July 1, 2001, for a maximum of three years[19]

---

6 34 C.F.R. § 682.200(b). The period is 330 days for loans repayable less frequently than in monthly installments. 34 C.F.R. § 682.200(b) (FFEL); 34 C.F.R. § 685.102(b) (Direct loans).

7 34 C.F.R. §§ 682.210(a)(5).

8 34 C.F.R. § 682.210(a)(5).

9 34 C.F.R. § 682.210(s)(1) (FFEL); 34 C.F.R. § 685.204(b)(iii)(B)(3)(i) (Direct Loans).

10 The "new" deferment rules apply to consolidation loans taken out after July 1, 1993, if the borrower has no other outstanding FFEL loans when the consolidation was made. 34 C.F.R. § 682.210(s)(1).

11 Deferment forms are available at the Department of Education's website, www.ed.gov. Selected forms are also available on the companion CD-Rom to this manual. The FFEL economic hardship and unemployment deferment forms are also reprinted at Appendix D, *infra*.

12 34 C.F.R. § 682.210(a)(1)(ii).

13 34 C.F.R. § 682.210(s)(1).

14 34 C.F.R. §§ 682.210(s)(2) (FFELs), 685.204(b)(1)(i)(A) (Direct Loans). The rules for this deferment are set out at 34 C.F.R. § 682.210(c).

15 34 C.F.R. §§ 682.210(s)(3) (FFELs), 685.204(b)(1)(i)(B) (Direct Loans). The rules for this deferment are set out at 34 C.F.R. § 682.210(d).

16 34 C.F.R. §§ 682.210(s)(4) (FFELs), 685.204(b)(1)(i)(C) (Direct Loans). The rules for this deferment are set out at 34 C.F.R. § 682.210(e).

17 34 C.F.R. §§ 682.210(s)(5) (FFELs), 685.204(b)(2)(i) (Direct Loans). The rules for this deferment are set out at 34 C.F.R. § 682.210(h). *See* § 3.2.4.3, *infra*.

18 34 C.F.R. §§ 682.210(s)(6) (FFELs), 685.204(b)(3)(i) (Direct Loans). The economic hardship category includes deferments for Peace Corps volunteers. 34 C.F.R. § 682.210(s)(6)(vi). The rules for economic hardship deferments are set out at 34 C.F.R. § 682.210(s)(6). *See* § 3.2.4.2.1, *infra*.

19 This deferment was added as part of the Deficit Reduction Act, P.L. 109-171 § 8007, amending 20 U.S.C. § 1078(b)(1)(M). *See* § 3.2.4.4, *infra*.

3.2.4.2 FFEL and Direct Loan Economic Hardship Deferments

3.2.4.2.1 Eligibility for economic hardship deferments

The economic hardship deferment is the most complicated and usually the most important for low-income borrowers. The first three qualification categories are "automatic" as long as the borrower can provide supporting documentation. These are the three categories:

1. Previous qualification for economic hardship deferment under another federal loan program.[20]
2. Receipt of federal or state public assistance benefits.[21] This includes anyone receiving payments under a federal or state public assistance program, such as TANF, SSI, Food Stamps, or state general public assistance.[22]
3. Peace Corps. The borrower qualifies if he or she is serving as a Peace Corps volunteer[23]

The other categories to qualify for an economic hardship deferment require additional calculations. Individuals qualify for this deferment if they can pass any one of three tests relating to income:

1. *Full-time workers making less than a stated income level.* An individual qualifies for an economic hardship deferment if he or she is working full-time and the earnings from this full-time job (not including other sources of income) do not exceed the greater of the minimum wage or the federal poverty level for a family of two (regardless of actual family size).[24]
2. *Full-time workers with high student loan debt burdens.* A borrower working full-time also qualifies for a deferment if (1) the "federal education debt burden" is at least 20% of the borrower's total monthly gross income *and* (2) the borrower's income subtracted from the "federal education debt burden" is less than 220% of either the minimum wage or federal poverty level for a family of two, whichever is greater.[25] A borrower is assumed to be working full-time if the borrower is expected to be employed for at least three consecutive months at thirty hours per week.[26]

Lenders must use the actual monthly payment amount to calculate the debt burden if the loan is scheduled to be repaid in ten years or less.[27] If the loan is scheduled to be repaid in more than ten years, the lender must continue to use the previous formula based on the monthly payment amount that would have been due if the loan had been scheduled to be repaid in ten years.[28]

For example, an individual qualifies for a deferment with an income of $25,000 if the "federal education debt burden" on an annual basis is $5000. The difference between the two ($20,000) is less than 220% of the poverty level for a family of two.[29]

3. *Those not working full-time with high student loan debt burdens.* This test applies only to a borrower whose *total* monthly gross income from all sources does not exceed twice the minimum wage or twice the poverty level for a family of two (whichever is higher).[30] Eligibility is determined by deducting the "federal education debt burden"[31] from income. The individual qualifies for a deferment if that difference does not exceed the greater of the minimum wage or the poverty level for a family of two.

An individual who is unemployed or only occasionally employed part-time will qualify for this deferment as long as that individual does not have significant sources of other income. An economic hardship deferment is thus a viable option for those who are unemployed but not eligible for the unemployment deferment because they are unable or not ready to seek employment.[32]

For example:

Borrower A is not working but is not eligible for unemployment benefits and is not seeking new employment. The first test to determine eligibility for an economic hardship deferment is whether her monthly income is less than two

---

20 34 C.F.R. §§ 682.210(s)(6)(i) (FFEL), 685.204(b)(3)(i) (Direct Loan). The Direct Loan program economic hardship deferment regulations specifically refer to the requirements in the FFEL regulations. The standards are the same for both loan programs.

21 34 C.F.R. § 682.210(s)(6)(ii).

22 34 C.F.R. §§ 682.210(s)(6)(ii) (FFELs), 685.204(b)(3)(ii) (Direct Loans).

23 34 C.F.R. § 682.210(s)(6)(vi).

24 34 C.F.R. §§ 682.210(s)(6)(iii) (FFELs), 685.204(b)(3)(ii) (Direct Loans).

25 34 C.F.R. §§ 682.210(s)(6)(iv) (FFELs), 685.204(b)(3)(ii) (Direct Loans). The poverty level for a family of two is used regardless of actual family size.

26 34 C.F.R. § 682.210(s)(6)(xi).

27 34 C.F.R. § 682.210(s)(6)(vii)(A). Previously, the Department calculated the "federal education debt burden" assuming that the loan would be paid out over ten years, regardless of the actual length of the payment schedule. *See* 67 Fed. Reg. 51039 (Aug. 6, 2002) (proposed rules); 67 Fed. Reg. 67048 (Nov. 1, 2002) (final rules).

28 34 C.F.R. § 682.210(s)(6)(vii)(B).

29 $13,200 is the 2006 poverty guideline for a family of two living in the contiguous states and D.C. The latest HHS poverty guidelines are found at 71 Fed. Reg. 3848 (Jan. 24, 2006). These guidelines are adjusted annually.

30 34 C.F.R. §§ 682.210(s)(6)(v) (FFELs), 685.204(b)(3)(ii) (Direct Loans). The poverty level for a family of two is used regardless of actual family size.

31 See test number 2, "Full-time workers with high student loan debt burdens," above.

32 There are also special rules to simplify the economic hardship deferment process for Peace Corps volunteers. 34 C.F.R. §§ 682.210(s)(vi) (FFEL), 674.34(6) (Perkins Loans).

times the minimum wage or two times the poverty level for a family of two (whichever is higher). Borrower A receives a monthly SSDI payment of $800. Her annual income of $9600 is less than the two times the 2006 annual poverty level of $13,200.

The next step is to subtract her debt burden—her monthly loan payment amount (assuming that she is on a ten-year repayment plan)—from her monthly income. Borrower A has a ten-year repayment plan requiring payments of $150 per month. This leaves her with $650 per month. This is less than the monthly minimum wage and less than the poverty level for a family of two. Therefore, Borrower A is eligible for an economic hardship deferment.

3.2.4.2.2 Economic hardship deferment policy issues

A problem with the way in which economic hardship deferments are calculated is that they are "all or nothing." Either the borrower qualifies and the government pays all of the interest during the hardship period, or the borrower gets no relief.[33] In addition, the formulas create situations in which borrowers with similar incomes and debt can have very different outcomes with respect to deferment eligibility.

The Project on Student Debt gives the following examples:

- A borrower works 40 hours a week and earns $12,000 a year. He does not qualify for hardship because he is barely above the poverty line and his loan payments do not exceed 20% of his income. If he worked 25 hours and had the same total income, he would qualify (because his income minus the payments would put him above the poverty line using a different test that applies only to part-time workers).
- A borrower has $25,000 in loans and a salary of $17,275. The student loan payments are nearly 20% of his income and more than she can afford. She does not qualify for the deferment. If she earned $25 less, she would qualify because her loan payments would exceed 20% of her income (assuming a 6.8% interest rate).[34]

The Project on Student Debt has proposed alternative formulas to calculate economic hardship that would allow borrowers in similar situations to qualify. Instead of an all-or-nothing approach, eligibility would be phased out as income increases or debt levels decrease.[35]

3.2.4.3 Unemployment Deferment

There are two ways to qualify for an unemployment deferment: the simpler route is for a borrower to provide proof of eligibility to receive unemployment benefits;[36] alternatively, the borrower must show that he or she is conscientiously searching for full-time employment (defined as at least thirty hours per week and expected to last at least three months). Borrowers may qualify for this deferment whether or not they have been previously employed.[37]

If the borrower is not eligible for the simpler route, the borrower will have to certify that he or she is diligently seeking but unable to find full-time employment and is registered with a public or private employment agency.[38] The employment agency registration requirement applies only if an agency is available within a fifty mile radius of the borrower's current address.[39] Evidence of registration may be submitted in writing or in an equivalent format.[40] The borrower will not qualify if the borrower refuses to seek or accept employment in kinds of positions or at salary and responsibility levels for which he or she feels overqualified.[41]

The initial period of deferment can be granted for a period of unemployment that begins up to six months before the lender receives the borrower's request and can be granted for up to six months after that date.[42] To continue an unemployment deferment beyond the initial period, the borrower must also certify that he or she has made at least six diligent attempts during the preceding six-month period to secure full-time employment.[43]

3.2.4.4 Military Deferment

The 2005 Deficit Reduction Act created a new military deferment for all three loan programs, FFEL, Direct Loans, and Perkins Loans.[44] The deferment applies to loans for which the first disbursement is made on or after July 1, 2001.

The deferment may be granted for a total of three years. It applies only to periods during which borrowers are serving on active duty during a war or other military operation,

---

33 *See generally* The Project on Student Debt, *White Paper: Addressing Student Loan Repayment Burdens* (Feb. 2006), *available at* http://projectonstudentdebt.org/files/pub/WHITE_PAPER_FINAL_PDF.pdf.

34 *Id.*

35 On May 4, 2006, the Project and other groups submitted a petition requesting that the U.S. Secretary of Education engage in rulemaking to amend the economic hardship deferment eligibility provisions. The petition is available at http://projectonstudentdebt.org/

files/File/Petition_to_ED_5.2.06.pdf.

36 34 C.F.R. §§ 682.210(h)(1) (FFEL), 685.204(b)(2)(i),(ii) (Direct Loans). The Direct Loan regulations specifically refer to the standards in the FFEL deferment regulations.

37 34 C.F.R. § 682.210(h)(3)(i).

38 34 C.F.R. § 682.210(h)(2).

39 34 C.F.R. § 682.210(h)(2)(i).

40 34 C.F.R. § 682.210(h)(2). The Secretary must approve this "equivalent" proof. The Department is leaving open the possibility that borrowers will have registered, for example, by phone or on-line. *See* 67 Fed. Reg. 51036 (Aug. 6, 2002).

41 34 C.F.R. § 682.210(h)(3)(ii).

42 34 C.F.R. § 682.210(h)(2)(iv).

43 34 C.F.R. § 682.210(h)(2)(ii).

44 Pub. L. No. 109-171 § 8007, 120 Stat. 4 (Feb. 8, 2006), *amending* 20 U.S.C. § 1078(b)(1)(M).

serving during a national emergency, or performing qualifying National Guard duty during a war or other military operation or national emergency.[45] Refunds for any payments already made are not authorized under this new deferment program.

There may be some cases in which a borrower is eligible for a military deferment on loans first disbursed on or after July 1, 2001, but ineligible for the deferment on older loans. A borrower consolidating loans first disbursed on or after July 1, 2001, is eligible for the new deferment on the entire consolidation loan, but only if all of the borrower's government loans included in the consolidation loan were first disbursed on or after July 1, 2001.[46]

Documentation establishing eligible active duty service may include a copy of the borrower's military orders or a written statement from the borrower's commanding officer or personnel officer that the borrower is serving on active duty during a war or other military operation, serving during a national emergency, or performing qualifying National Guard duty.

3.2.5 Grounds for FFEL Deferments Extended Before July 1, 1993

A different set of rules applies to those with FFELs extended before July 1, 1993. Although loans incurred in 1993 and before are now quite old, advocates will still see many clients with these loans. The elimination of the statute of limitations for student loan collections makes it very difficult to escape a student loan, no matter how old it is.[47]

The grounds for deferment under these loans include

- unemployment for up to two years;
- full-time student at a participating school;[48]
- active-duty status in the United States Armed Forces;[49]

- the receipt of or the scheduled receipt of service under a program designed to rehabilitate disabled individuals;
- temporary total disability for up to three years;
- the provision of nursing or similar services to a spouse who is temporarily totally disabled;
- parental leave; and
- mothers of pre-school children starting work at no more than one dollar above the minimum wage.[50]

The regulations set out detailed standards as to when a student is eligible for a deferment based on these grounds, particularly for unemployment, rehabilitation, temporary total disability, and spouse's temporary total disability.[51] Maximum deferment periods vary for each type of deferment.[52] Some can last indefinitely so long as the qualifying conditions or circumstances still apply.

The temporary total disability deferment can be especially critical for borrowers with disabilities that are not sufficiently permanent or severe to meet the requirements for a disability discharge.[53] In fact, advocates have proposed that the Department reinstate this deferment now that it is taking such a restrictive stance toward disability discharge applicants. The Department to date has refused to consider this possibility. The temporary disability deferment is still available only for pre-1993 loans.

Although disabled borrowers with older loans may apply for the temporary disability deferment, they are not entitled to the more comprehensive economic hardship deferment. The hardship deferment is available only for borrowers with loans incurred after July 1, 1993. The economic hardship deferment is broad enough to include low-income borrowers, whether disabled or not.[54] The temporary disability deferment, in contrast, applies only to those borrowers who can certify a temporary total disability or, in some cases, certify that a dependent is disabled.[55]

---

45 *Id. See also* U.S. Dep't of Educ., Dear Colleague Letter, GEN-06-02, Enactment of the Higher Education Reconciliation Act of 2005 (Mar. 2006). A copy is available at the Department's website, www.ed.gov, and on the companion CD-Rom to this manual. "Active duty" is defined at 10 U.S.C. § 101(d)(1).

46 *Id.*

47 *See* § 3.2, *supra. See, e.g.,* Williams v. New York State Higher Educ. Servs. Corp., 296 B.R. 298 (S.D.N.Y. 2003) (debtor was ineligible for deferment under student loan deferment program for teachers in teacher-shortage area, where debtor had an outstanding Stafford loan predating the institution of the program), *aff'd without opinion,* 84 Fed. Appx. 158 (S.D.N.Y. Mar. 26, 2004).

48 A borrower whose loan was obtained on or after July 1, 1987, and who has no outstanding FFEL balance on that date may obtain an in-school deferment for half-time study if the borrower also received or will receive a Stafford or SLS loan for the period during which deferment is sought. 34 C.F.R. § 682.210(c)(iii).

49 34 C.F.R. § 682.210(i). Borrowers on active duty in the United States Armed Forces are eligible for this deferment. "Armed

Forces" is defined as the Army, Navy, Air Force, Marine Corps, and the Coast Guard. 34 C.F.R. § 682.210(i)(2). Borrowers enlisted in the reserves may qualify for the military deferment only for service on a full-time basis that is expected to last for a period of at least one year in length. Borrowers enlisted in the National Guard qualify for this deferment only while they are on active-duty status as a member of the U.S. Army or Air Force Reserves and meet the other requirements of § 682.210(i). There is also a military deferment for newer loans. *See* § 3.2.4.4, *supra.*

50 20 U.S.C. § 1077(a)(2)(c); 34 C.F.R. § 682.210(b), (c), (e), (f), (g), (h), (i), (o), (r).

51 *See* 34 C.F.R. § 682.210(e), (f), (g), (h).

52 34 C.F.R. § 682.210(b).

53 *See* § 6.6 (disability discharges), *infra.*

54 *See* § 3.2.4.2.1, *supra.*

55 "Temporary total disability" is defined at 34 C.F.R. § 682.200(b). *See also* 34 C.F.R. § 682.210(b)(1)(iv).

3.2.6 Grounds for Perkins Loans Deferments

Borrowers are entitled to defer Perkins Loan principal payments with interest not accruing in certain situations. As with FFELs, the specific qualifying circumstances depend on when the loan was made. For Perkins loans made after July 1, 1993, deferments are available based on a number of grounds, including

- qualifying in-school status;[56]
- full-time teaching in certain schools and in Head Start;[57]
- full-time service in law enforcement or as correction officers under certain circumstances;[58]
- certain military service;[59]
- certain volunteer service such as the Peace Corps;[60]
- inability to find, despite seeking, full-time employment for a period not to exceed three years;[61] and
- qualifying economic hardship conditions for a period not to exceed three years.[62] The Perkins economic hardship requirements are similar to those for FFEL and Direct loans.[63]

There are different criteria for Perkins Loans made before July 1, 1993.[64] Borrowers with these older loans are not eligible for economic hardship or unemployment deferments but are eligible for temporary disability deferments, among others.

3.3 Forbearances

3.3.1 General

The Department of Education encourages the granting of forbearances to prevent borrowers from defaulting on their loans or to permit borrowers in default to resume "honoring" their loan obligations. Forbearance involves a loan holder agreeing to a temporary stoppage of payments, an extension of time for making payments, or acceptance of smaller payments.[65]

Forbearance is not as helpful for a borrower as a deferment because interest will continue to accrue while the loan

payments are reduced or postponed. Consequently, the size of the outstanding obligation may actually increase during a forbearance period. A borrower not yet in default can use a forbearance agreement to delay going into default. The 270-day period before a delinquency is transformed into a default does not include periods of time when payments are subject to forbearance.

Forbearance is available even if the borrower is in default.[66] According to the regulations, the Secretary is encouraged to grant forbearance in order to prevent the borrower from defaulting on a repayment obligation or to permit the borrower to resume honoring that obligation after default.[67] This is important because loan holders and collection agencies will often erroneously tell borrowers that they are not eligible for forbearances after default.

Although the regulations clearly provide for forbearances after default, many lenders, guaranty agencies, and state agencies will insist that borrowers are only eligible prior to default. In some cases, this is a matter of semantics. These agencies will grant "cessations of payment" as opposed to "forbearances." This is even though, as noted above, forbearances may involve an extension of time for making payments or acceptance of smaller payments in addition to temporary cessations of payments. Regardless, there should be no practical difference between a "cessation" and "forbearance."

The critical point is whether the forbearance is categorized as discretionary or mandatory. If discretionary, many agencies have developed policies against granting forbearances. However, this discretion should not be allowed in cases in which forbearances are mandatory.

In general, forbearances will not remove students from default status. They will, however, grant a temporary halt to collection actions such as tax refund intercepts, collection contacts, and garnishments during the forbearance period.

3.3.2 Discretionary Forbearances

The FFEL regulations make a distinction between discretionary and mandatory forbearances. The Direct Loan program does not make this distinction. If a Direct Loan borrower qualifies for forbearance, the regulations provide that the Secretary will grant forbearance, with no reference to discretion on the Secretary's part.[68] The grounds for forbearance vary between the two programs in some respects.

---

56 34 C.F.R. § 674.34(b)(1)(i).

57 34 C.F.R. § 674.34(c).

58 *Id.*

59 *Id.*

60 34 C.F.R. § 674.34(e).

61 34 C.F.R. § 674.34(d). The Perkins unemployment deferment does not have the same documentation requirements as FFEL and Direct Loans. However, Perkins holders will require borrowers to provide certification supporting their applications.

62 34 C.F.R. § 674.34(e).

63 *See* § 3.2.4.2.1, *supra.*

64 34 C.F.R. § 674.35.

65 34 C.F.R. §§ 682.211(a)(1) (FFELs), 685.205(a) (Direct Loans), 674.33(d) (Perkins).

66 20 U.S.C. § 1078(c)(3) (FFEL); 34 C.F.R. § 682.211(a)(1). For a description of Perkins forbearance provisions, see § 3.3.4, *infra.*

67 34 C.F.R. § 682.211(a)(1). *See generally* Derek V. Price, Lumina Found., *Student Loan Forbearance and Its Relationship to Default* (Nov. 2001), *available at* www.luminafoundation.org/publications/synopsis/loanforbearance01.pdf.

68 34 C.F.R. § 685.205(a).

Both the FFEL and Direct Loan regulations provide for forbearances if borrowers are in poor health or have other personal problems that affect the ability of the borrower to make the scheduled payments.[69] Forbearance for these reasons is discretionary under FFEL regulations.[70] The forbearance is granted up to a year at a time, but there are no limits to the number of years this type of forbearance may be granted.[71]

Both FFEL and Direct Loan regulations provide for administrative forbearances under various circumstances, such as while the lender is resolving a change in the loan's status or pending the resolution of a discharge application.[72] With a few limited exceptions such as local or national emergencies, the FFEL administrative forbearances are discretionary.[73]

Both programs provide for forbearances during:

- A properly granted period of deferment for which the lender learns the borrower did not qualify.[74]
- At the beginning of an authorized deferment period or an administrative forbearance period for FFEL loans.[75]
- For Direct Loans, the period in which payments are overdue at the beginning of an authorized deferment period.[76]
- The period beginning when the borrower entered repayment until the first payment due date was established.[77]
- The period prior to the borrower's filing of a bankruptcy petition.[78]
- For FFEL loans, a period not to exceed an additional sixty days after the lender has suspended collection for the initial sixty-day period and receives reliable information that the borrower (or student in the case of a PLUS loan) has died.[79]
- For FFEL loans, the periods described in the disability discharge regulations in regard to the borrower's total and permanent disability.[80]
- For Direct Loans, a period after the Secretary receives reliable information indicating that the borrower (or the student, in the case of a Direct PLUS Loan) has died or

the borrower has become totally and permanently disabled, until the Secretary receives documentation of death or total and permanent disability.[81]
- Periods necessary for the Secretary or the guaranty agency to determine the borrower's eligibility for discharge of the loan because of an unpaid refund, attendance at a closed school, or false certification of loan eligibility or the borrower's or, if applicable, endorser's bankruptcy.[82] The Direct Loan regulations specifically include teacher loan forgiveness programs.[83] The FFEL regulations also allow for forbearances for borrower who are performing the type of service that would qualify the borrower for loan forgiveness and associated forbearance under the requirements of the teacher loan forgiveness program. However, these forbearances are mandatory rather than discretionary.[84]
- Periods not to exceed sixty days while the lender collects and processes documentation supporting the borrower's request for a deferment, forbearance, change in repayment plan, or consolidation loan.[85]

Administrative forbearances are particularly important to request when a borrower has applied for a consolidation loan or loan discharge and it is likely that considerable time will pass before the application is resolved. In some cases, the loan holder may agree to cease collection while applications are pending but may prefer to call this cessation something other than a forbearance. It is important to advocate aggressively in these cases since the Department clearly has the discretion to grant forbearances in these circumstances.

If the forbearance agreement is made orally, the lender must confirm the oral agreement by sending a notice to the borrower and by recording the terms of the agreement in the borrower's file.[86] If the request is made in writing, it is a good idea to use the general forbearance request form issued by the Department and by many loan holders.[87]

In addition, there are a number of regulatory requirements imposed on lenders and loan holders to inform borrowers periodically about the status of their loans in forbearance. Specifically, if a forbearance involves the postponement of all payments, the lender must contact the borrower at least

---

69 34 C.F.R. §§ 682.211(a)(2)(i) (FFEL), 685.205(a)(1) (Direct Loans).

70 34 C.F.R. § 682.211(a)(2)(i).

71 34 C.F.R. §§ 682.211(c) (FFEL), 685.205(c) (Direct Loans).

72 34 C.F.R. §§ 682.211(f) (FFEL), 685.205(b) (Direct Loans).

73 The regulations for mandatory administrative forbearances are set out at 34 C.F.R. § 682.211(i). *See* § 3.3.3, *infra*.

74 34 C.F.R. §§ 682.211(f)(1), 685.205(b)(1).

75 34 C.F.R. § 682.211(f)(2).

76 34 C.F.R. § 685.205(b)(2).

77 34 C.F.R. §§ 682.211(f)(3) (FFELs), 685.205(b)(3) (Direct Loans).

78 34 C.F.R. §§ 682.211(f)(4) (FFELs), 685.205(b)(4) (Direct Loans).

79 34 C.F.R. § 682.211(f)(6).

80 34 C.F.R. § 682.211(f)(5). A similar provision for Direct Loans can be found at 34 C.F.R. § 685.205(b)(5).

81 34 C.F.R. § 685.205(b)(5) (Direct Loans).

82 34 C.F.R. §§ 682.211(f)(7) (FFELs), 685.205(b)(6).

83 34 C.F.R. § 685.205(b)(6)(iv).

84 34 C.F.R. § 682.211(h)(2)(ii)(C).

85 34 C.F.R. §§ 682.211(f)(10) (FFELs), 685.205(b)(9) (Direct Loans).

86 Prior to July 1, 2006, the statute required that oral forbearance agreements had to be approved in writing. However, the regulations permitted this practice. *See* 34 C.F.R. 682.211(b)(1). The statutory provision was amended as part of the Deficit Reduction Act, P.L. 109-171.

87 The form is available at the Department's website, www.ed.gov. A sample form can also be found at Appendix D, *infra*.

once every six months to inform the borrower of the outstanding obligation to repay, the amount of unpaid principal balance, any unpaid interest that has accrued, the fact that interest will accrue on the loan for the full term of the forbearance, and the borrower's option to discontinue the forbearance at any time.[88]

If two individuals are jointly liable for repayment of a PLUS loan or a consolidation loan, the lender may grant forbearance on repayment only if both individuals cannot make the scheduled payments based on the same or different conditions.[89]

3.3.3 Mandatory Forbearances

The FFEL program provides for mandatory forbearances based on a statutory right.[90] This right to forbearance should be available even if a student is in default.[91] To obtain mandatory forbearance, the borrower must request a forbearance from the holder of the loan and provide sufficient supporting documentation.[92]

Most relevant for low-income borrowers are mandatory administrative forbearances for up to five years in cases in which the borrower will not be able to repay the loan within the maximum repayment term.[93] For example, FFEL Standard, Graduated, and Income Sensitive Plans all generally require that the loan be repaid in not more than ten years.[94] If the documentation shows that the borrower will be unable to repay the loan within the maximum ten-year repayment period, the lender is required to grant forbearance to the borrower for up to five years.[95]

In addition, FFEL and Direct Loan forbearances are mandatory in increments of up to one year for periods that collectively do not exceed three years if the amount of the borrower's monthly student loan payments collectively is equal to or greater than 20% of the borrower's total monthly income.[96] Borrowers are required to submit documentation of income and other relevant information. Forbearances are also mandatory for teachers who are performing teaching service that would qualify them for teacher loan forgiveness.[97]

The Department may also issue special forbearance guidance in disaster situations, such as after the September 11 terrorist attacks or after natural disasters. In general, the Department may grant discretionary administrative forbearances for up to three months to borrowers affected by military mobilizations.[98] Extensions beyond the three-month limit require supporting documentation and a written agreement. For example, the Department provided for automatic administrative forbearances on loan repayments for a limited period for victims of Hurricanes Katrina and Rita.[99] The Department was specifically allowed flexibility to grant forbearances to borrowers on a case-by-case basis after the period for automatic forbearance eligibility ended.

3.3.4 Perkins Provisions

Forbearances must be granted for Perkins borrowers under the following circumstances:

1. If the amount of the borrower's loan payments (for all Title IV loans) are equal to or greater than 20% of the borrower's total monthly income;[100]
2. The borrower qualifies for a forbearance due to poor health or other "acceptable reasons";[101] or
3. The Secretary authorizes forbearances due to a national military mobilization or other national emergency.[102]

To qualify for the first category, a borrower is required to submit documentation of his or her most recent total monthly gross income and evidence of the amount of the monthly loan payments.[103]

There is generally a three-year cumulative limit on the length of Perkins forbearances.[104] The Department has waived this limit for forbearances based on military service.[105] For qualified borrowers in the military, the Department has also waived the requirement that a borrower must send a written request and supporting documentation to apply for a Perkins forbearance. Instead, the school must grant a forbearance based on the borrower's status as an "affected individual"[106] for a one-year period, including a

---

88 34 C.F.R. § 682.211(e). These rules do not apply in the case of forbearance of interest payments during a deferment.
89 34 C.F.R. § 682.211(a)(3).
90 20 U.S.C. § 1078(c)(3).
91 *Id.*
92 34 C.F.R. § 682.211(h)(2).
93 34 C.F.R. § 682.211(i)(5)(ii).
94 *See* § 2.7.3 (pre-default repayment plans), *supra*.
95 34 C.F.R. §§ 682.211(i)(5), 682.209(a)(7)(viii)(D).
96 34 C.F.R. §§ 682.211(h)(2)(i) (FFEL), 685.205(a)(6)(ii) (Direct Loans).
97 34 C.F.R. § 682.211(h)(2)(ii)(B). Partial teacher loan forgiveness is available for FFEL and Direct Loan borrowers. Full and partial forgiveness is available for Perkins borrowers. *See* § 6.8 (teacher loan forgiveness), *infra*. The teacher loan forgiveness forbearance form and forgiveness application was released as an

attachment to Dear Colleague Letter, G-01-333 (Nov. 2001).
98 Dear Colleague Letter, GEN-03-06 (Mar. 2003).
99 *See* U.S. Dep't of Educ., Dear Colleague Letter, GEN-06-07 (May 2006), *Notification and Extension of Guidance to Assist Title IV Participants Affected by Hurricanes Katrina and Rita* (May 2006).
100 34 C.F.R. § 674.33(d)(5)(i).
101 34 C.F.R. § 674.33(d)(5)(ii).
102 34 C.F.R. § 674.33(d)(5)(iii).
103 34 C.F.R. § 674.33(d)(6).
104 34 C.F.R. § 674.33(d)(2).
105 *See* 68 Fed. Reg. 25821 (May 14, 2003); 68 Fed. Reg. 69312 (Dec. 12, 2003).
106 "Affected individuals" are those who are serving on active duty during a war or other military operation or national emergency;

three-month "transition period" that immediately follows that period. These forbearances may be granted without supporting documentation or a written agreement, based on the written or oral request of the borrower, a member of the borrower's family, or another reliable source. The purpose of the three-month transition period is to assist borrowers so that they will not be required to reenter repayment imme-

are performing qualifying National Guard duty during a war or other military operation or national emergency; reside or are employed in an area that is declared a disaster area by any federal, state, or local official in connection with a national emergency; or suffered direct economic hardship as a direct result of a war or other military operation or national emergency, as determined by the Secretary.

diately after they are no longer "affected individuals." In order for the borrower to receive forbearance beyond the initial period, supporting documentation from the borrower, a member of the borrower's family, or another reliable source is required. In addition, affected individuals do not have to provide the loan holder with documentation showing that they are subject to a military mobilization. The borrower, a member of his or her family, or another reliable source may request the forbearance for one year, including a three-month transition period, without providing the loan holder with documentation. Documentation must be submitted to support a forbearance beyond this period.[107]

107 68 Fed. Reg. 69312 (Dec. 12, 2003).

Chapter 4

Student Loan Collection

4.1 Introduction to Student Loan Collections

In recent years, the Department of Education has significantly increased both its efforts to lower student loan default rates and to collect defaulted student loans. In fiscal year 2002, according to the Government Accountability Office (GAO), the Department collected $4.87 billion in defaulted student loans compared to the $2.7 billion that went into default.[1]

The growth in student loan recoveries can be attributed in large part to legislative changes giving student loan collectors enhanced collection powers. These powerful student loan collection tools, combined with aggressive government enforcement, make it increasingly difficult for borrowers to ignore student loan debt.

Congress increased the government's collection powers in large part due to tremendous increases in student loan default rates throughout the 1980s and early 1990s. In addition to increased collection powers, Congress also set up a program to sanction schools with very high default rates. Under this program, the Department has the authority to remove high-default schools from the federal student aid programs.[2]

The consequences of student loan defaults have grown enormously over time as the government's collection powers have steadily increased. The government has collection powers far beyond those of most unsecured creditors. As discussed in detail in Chapter 5, the government can garnish a borrower's wages without a judgment; seize the borrower's tax refund, even an earned income tax credit; seize portions of federal benefits such as Social Security; and deny eligibility for new education grants or loans. Even in bankruptcy, most student loans must be paid.[3] Unlike any other type of debt, there is no statute of limitations.[4] The government can pursue borrowers to the grave.

A Federal Student Aid Resource guide from 1999 to 2004 indicates that the Department collected 32% of student loan debt through rehabilitations, 25% through "regular" collections, 21% through treasury offset, 10% through wage garnishment, 10% through Direct consolidations, and 2% through FFEL consolidations.[5]

Consolidation has historically comprised an even greater portion of guaranty agency recoveries. Data from 2003, for example, show that the Department reported about 16% of its collections from consolidations. Guaranty agencies, in contrast, reported nearly 57% of total recoveries from consolidations. Reports of recoveries by the guaranty agency USA Funds from 1999–2004 confirm this trend. Fifty percent of USA's collections were through Direct Loan consolidation.[6] Thirty-three percent were from loan rehabilitations.

The Department has also enhanced its powers by using a data match system with the Department of Health and Human Services National Directory of New Hires, a database of all persons employed in the U.S. The most recent version of this system became effective on May 16, 2006.[7]

4.2 Statute of Limitations Is Not a Defense to Student Loan Collection Action

4.2.1 Statute of Limitations Generally Eliminated

The Higher Education Technical Amendments of 1991 (HEA) eliminated all statutes of limitations for any collection action by a school, guaranty agency, or the United States under a federal loan program.[8] These amendments

---

1 *See* U.S. Gen. Accounting Office, Federal Student Aid: Timely Performance Plans and Reports Would Help Guide and Assess Achievement of Default Management Goals, GAO-03-348 (Feb. 2003).

2 20 U.S.C. § 1085. A brief description of this default management program is included in Chapter 9, *infra*.

3 *See* Chapter 7, *infra*.

4 *See* § 4.2, *infra*.

5 U.S. Dep't of Educ., Federal Student Aid, *Guaranty Agency Resource Guide, FFELP Default Collections, 1999–2004*.

6 *Id.* USA Funds is administered by Sallie Mae.

7 *See* 71 Fed. Reg. 26934 (May 9, 2006) (notice of computer matching program). The legal authority cited for this collection is from the Social Security Act. 42 U.S.C. § 653(j)(6).

8 Pub. L. No. 102-26 eliminated the statute of limitations set out in 20 U.S.C. § 1091a(a). While the elimination of the limitations period was to have sunset on November 15, 1992, the Higher Education Amendments of 1992 § 1551, codified at 20 U.S.C.

also eliminated all limitation periods for tax intercepts, wage garnishments, and other collection efforts.[9] A lingering argument to apply a time limit to Social Security offsets was finally put to rest, unfortunately for borrowers, by the U.S. Supreme Court in 2005.[10]

The lack of a statute of limitations for student loan collections places student borrowers in the unenviable company of murderers, traitors, and only a few violators of civil laws. Despite the governmental and social interest in pursuing criminals, statutes of limitation apply to nearly all federal criminal actions. The rare exceptions exist for those crimes that are punishable by death, including espionage and treason.[11] Other exceptions apply to the prosecution of persons charged with absence without leave or missing in time of war and for individuals fleeing from justice.[12]

The legislative history for this unprecedented retroactive elimination of the statute of limitations is sparse, but it appears to have been derived at least in part from the unsubstantiated premise that student loan defaulters' ability to repay increases over time.[13] Furthermore, because student loans are made without considerations of creditworthiness, some in Congress argued that the benefit for the borrower far outweighs any burden resulting from the government's right to collect *forever*. Savings in the student loan program were also mentioned.

The provision eliminating the statute of limitations applies retroactively, so loans whose limitations period had expired even before 1991 are revived.[14] Courts have repeatedly rejected borrowers' due process and equal protection challenges to this retroactive change, finding that statutes of limitations are legislatively created defenses and not constitutionally protected property rights.[15] Courts have also

rejected claims based on lack of consideration or because of the *ex post facto* effect of the elimination of the statute of limitations.[16]

In a 2002 decision, a North Carolina district court noted the "obvious difficulty" that the retroactive application of the statutory change causes for students.[17] The borrower in this case was sued in 1998 for a student loan she had incurred between 1970 and 1972 and that she claimed to have repaid in 1973. The court initially granted summary judgment for the borrower but reversed itself in response to the government's motion to alter or amend the judgment. The problem, as discussed by the court, is that "people do not keep records indefinitely, especially when there is no apparent purpose to do so."[18] Even so, the court found that the borrower needed to show more than a bare assertion of payment in order to present sufficient evidence that her due process rights had been violated. This case at least leaves open the possibility that a borrower with a better memory of the circumstances surrounding payment and a more credible explanation of repayment might be able to present sufficient evidence to prove a due process violation.

4.2.2 Scope of Elimination of Statute of Limitations

The elimination of the statute of limitations applies to collection by government agencies and their agents. The statute specifically applies to institutions collecting federal grant or work assistance refunds; guaranty agencies that have agreements with the Department and are collecting federal loans; institutions that have agreements with the Department and are collecting government loans; and the Secretary of Education, Attorney General, or administrative head of another federal agency to collect government grants and loans.[19]

Collection of private student loans is not covered. Thus, statutes of limitations should apply in these cases. It also does not specifically apply to state agencies or state loans. However, state entities suing to collect student loans may also be able to avoid statutes of limitations if state law or state constitutions provide such protection. A state entity may not be able to escape time limits if it is merely

---

§ 1091a, extended indefinitely the abolition of the statute of limitations for student loan collections.

9 *Id.*

10 *See* Lockhart v. United States, 126 S. Ct. 699 (2005). *See* § 5.4.3.3, *infra*.

11 18 U.S.C. § 3281; 18 U.S.C. § 794(a), 2381.

12 10 U.S.C. § 843; 18 U.S.C. § 3290.

13 137 Cong. Reg. S7291-02, 1991 WL 95486 (June 6, 1991).

14 *See, e.g.*, United States v. Distefano, 279 F.3d 1241 (10th Cir. 2002); United States v. Phillips, 20 F.3d 1005 (9th Cir. 1994); United States v. Hodges, 999 F.2d 341 (8th Cir. 1993); Chatmon v. United States Dep't of Educ., 2003 WL 21501919 (N.D. Tex. June 24, 2003); United States v. McLaughlin, 7 F. Supp. 2d 90 (D. Mass. 1998).

15 *See, e.g.*, United States v. Phillips, 20 F.3d 1005 (9th Cir. 1994); United States v. Hodges, 999 F.2d 341 (8th Cir. 1993); United States v. Glockson, 998 F.2d 896 (11th Cir. 1993); Johnson v. United States Dep't of Educ., 2005 WL 2266109 (W.D. Pa. Sept. 13, 2005); United States v. Dwelley, 59 F. Supp. 2d 115 (D. Me. 1999); United States v. McLaughlin, 7 F. Supp. 2d 90 (D. Mass. 1998); Sibley v. United States Dep't of Educ., 913 F. Supp. 1181 (N.D. Ill. 1995), *aff'd without opinion*, 111 F.3d 133 (7th Cir. 1997), *reprinted in full at* 1997 U.S. App. LEXIS 6395 (7th Cir. 1997); United States v. Davis, 817 F. Supp. 926 (M.D. Ala. 1993).

16 *See, e.g.*, United States v. Brown, 7 Fed. Appx. 353, 354 (6th Cir. 2001); United States v. Gould, 2006 WL 1522071 (E.D. Mich. May 30, 2006); United States v. Durbin, 64 F. Supp. 2d 635, 637 (S.D. Tex. 1999); United States v. Dwelley, 59 F. Supp. 2d 115 (D. Me. 1999) (*ex post facto* clause applies only to criminal or penal measures that are applied retroactively); United States v. Davis, 817 F. Supp. 926 (M.D. Ala. 1993), *aff'd*, 17 F.3d 1439 (11th Cir. 1994) (table).

17 United States v. Charles, 240 F. Supp. 2d 488 (M.D.N.C. 2002).

18 *Id.* at 490.

19 20 U.S.C. § 1091a(a).

administering a private loan fund rather than collecting a public debt.[20]

At least one court has held that a borrower's action against the government remains covered by the applicable six-year time limit specified in 28 U.S.C. § 2401(a).[21] Thus, according to this court, only the government gets the benefit of bringing actions without time limits.

4.2.3 Laches

4.2.3.1 Barriers to Applying the Laches Doctrine in Student Loan Cases

One possible defense to a collection action instituted many years after a default is that the equitable doctrine of laches applies. There are a number of barriers to applying this doctrine in the student loan context.

First, it is possible that Congress eliminated equitable defenses when it eliminated the statute of limitations in student loan collections.[22] This is unclear. The Congressional amendments eliminating the statute of limitations state that Congress' purpose was to ensure that obligations to repay loans would be enforced without regard to any "statutory, regulatory, or administrative limitations."[23] Equitable defenses are not specifically mentioned. However, a number of courts have found that Congress did in fact intend to eliminate equitable defenses as well.[24]

Even if a court were to decide that Congress did not eliminate equitable defenses when it eliminated the statute of limitations, a second barrier is that the laches doctrine is generally inapplicable against the United States on the grounds of sovereign immunity.[25] Many courts hold to this rule absent a clear manifestation of congressional intent to the contrary. In student loan cases, these courts have found not only that there was no congressional intent to the contrary but also that Congress' retroactive elimination of all statutes of limitations appears to indicate the opposite intent.[26]

4.2.3.2 Exceptions to the Rule Barring Laches

A few courts have been willing to look beyond the traditional rule that the doctrine of laches is inapplicable against the United States. In a 1985 non-student-loan case, *S.E.R. Jobs for Progress, Inc.*, the court noted that some relaxation of the principle that laches is not a defense against the government may be developing and that exceptions to the rule might be approved in certain cases.[27]

To invoke the doctrine of laches, a borrower must show (1) a delay in asserting a right or claim; (2) that the delay was not excusable; and (3) that there was undue prejudice to the party against whom the claim is asserted.[28] Most courts that have considered this issue in the student loan context have found that the facts did not justify invoking an exception to the rule.[29]

Courts have rejected borrowers' claims for a variety of reasons. At least one court relied on the fact that, prior to 1991, the government was bound by a six-year statute of limitations for student loan collections.[30] This court speculated that, prior to the complete elimination of the statute, it was possible that the government was not actively collecting certain loans because they were barred by the existing statute of limitations. This argument should be considerably weaker now that more time has passed since the elimination of the student loan statute of limitations.

Even if borrowers can successfully persuade a court that the government was neglectful, they must also show that they were materially prejudiced by the delay. Borrowers have argued that they were prejudiced by years of inactivity on their student loan accounts, which allowed interest, penalties, and collection fees to pile up. Unfortunately for

---

20 *See* The Board of Regents for the Univ. of Okla. v. Livingston, 111 P. 3d 734 (Okla. Civ. App. 2005) (although state constitution provides that no statute of limitations applies when state is collecting a debt, court held that university was merely administering a private loan fund, not enforcing a public right and was thus subject to a statute-of-limitations defense).

21 Corum v. Paige, 2005 WL 1214598 (W.D. Tenn. May 20, 2005).

22 *See* § 4.2.1, *supra*.

23 20 U.S.C. § 1091a(a)(1).

24 *See, e.g.*, United States v. Sullivan, 68 Fed. Appx. 811 (9th Cir. 2003); United States v. Lawrence, 276 F.3d 193 (5th Cir. 2001) (citing Millard v. U.S. Funds, 66 F.3d 252 (9th Cir. 1995)); United States v. Phillips, 20 F.3d 1005, 1007 (9th Cir. 1994); United States v. Glockson, 998 F.2d 896, 897 (11th Cir. 1993); United States v. Hodges, 999 F.2d 341 (8th Cir. 1993); Chatmon v. United States Dep't of Educ., 2003 WL 21501919 (N.D. Tex. June 24, 2003). *See also* United States v. Robbins, 819 F. Supp. 672 (E.D. Mich. 1993). The *Robbins* court also speculated that, in eliminating equitable defenses, Congress might have been swayed by the fact that student loans are not collectable after a borrower's disability or death. The court noted that this may have been sufficient to assuage any Congressional fears of a completely open-ended student loan collection process. *Id.* at 676. This is ironic given the restrictive stance taken by the Department toward disability, and even death, cancellations in recent years. *See* §§ 6.6 (disability), 6.7 (death), *infra*.

25 United States v. Summerlin, 310 U.S. 414, 60 S. Ct. 1019, 84 L. Ed. 2d 1283 (1940).

26 *See, e.g.*, United States v. McLaughlin, 7 F. Supp. 90 (D. Mass. 1998); United States v. Davis, 817 F. Supp. 926 (M.D. Ala. 1993); United States v. Robbins, 819 F. Supp. 672 (E.D. Mich. 1993).

27 S.E.R., Jobs for Progress, Inc. v. United States, 759 F.2d 1, 7 (Fed. Cir. 1985).

28 United States v. Davis, 817 F. Supp. 926, 929 (M.D. Ala. 1993) (citing Envtl. Defense Fund. V. Alexander, 614 F.2d 474, 477–78 (5th Cir.), *cert. denied*, 449 U.S. 919 (1980).

29 *See, e.g.*, United States v. Durbin, 64 F. Supp. 2d 635 (S.D. Tex. 1999); United States v. Smith, 862 F. Supp. 257 (D. Haw. 1994); United States v. Davis, 817 F. Supp. 926 (M.D. Ala. 1993); United States v. Robbins, 819 F. Supp. 672 (E.D. Mich. 1993).

30 United States v. Davis, 817 F. Supp. 926 (M.D. Ala. 1993).

borrowers, most courts that have examined these arguments have found a lack of prejudice to borrowers.[31]

On a bright note for borrowers, at least one court, in *United States v. Rhodes*, found the doctrine of laches applicable in a student loan case.[32] The loan in this case was due in 1974. The government began collection seventeen years later. The court found this to be a "blatant and unreasonable delay on the part of the lender and its assignees."[33] The court found further prejudice to the borrower as the school had closed during the seventeen-year period of inactivity and the borrower no longer had access to any school records. The borrower had long since destroyed his own records.

Other courts have tended to distinguish the facts in *Rhodes*. A key distinction noted by other courts is that the borrower in *Rhodes* was defending the collection action on the grounds that he had already paid back the loan in full. Courts have tended to find this more sympathetic than "shakier" defenses such as lack of consideration or breach of contract.[34] Courts have also found it notable that, because of the government's delay in collecting the loan in *Rhodes*, records were no longer available from the school or from the borrower, making it impossible for either side to show whether the debt was still owed.[35] At least one court simply referred to the *Rhodes* case as an anomaly.[36]

4.2.3.3 FISL Collection

Another possible use of the doctrine of laches involves Department of Education attempts to collect Federally Insured Student Loans (FISLs). Congress' elimination of the statute of limitations for student loan collections has resulted in collection attempts for some very old FISL loans, going back to the early 1970s. Many students subjected to such collection attempts will have a solid defense—that federal law at the time allowed students to raise school-related claims.[37]

4.3 The Collection Process

4.3.1 The Difference Between Default and Delinquency

Borrowers are in default on Federal Family Education Loans (FFEL) or Direct loans if they fail to make required payments for 270 days for loans repayable in monthly installments or 330 days for loans repayable less frequently than monthly.[38] This nine-month period is a relatively long time for borrowers to seek alternatives to default, such as more affordable repayment plans, cancellation, deferment, and/or forbearance.[39]

During this period, the borrower is merely delinquent and not in default. This is an important distinction because, as long as the borrower is not in default, the borrower is still eligible for deferments and for flexible pre-default repayment options.

4.3.2 The Various Collection Entities: Figuring Out Who Is Collecting the Loan

The Department of Education has two major roles concerning collection of student loans. The Department sets standards and supervises the collection of student loans held by other entities such as guarantors, schools, lenders, and secondary market lenders. The Department also directly collects on loans that it holds.

The Department directly holds and thus directly collects on Direct loans, Perkins loans after the school assigns the note to the Department, and certain Stafford (GSL) loans after the guaranty agency has assigned those loans to the Department.

Guaranty agencies or schools hold other defaulted student loans.[40] The Department generally does not collect on these loans, and it is important to distinguish between the Department collecting on a loan or supervising a guarantor or school's collection on the loan.

---

31 United States v. Durbin, 64 F. Supp. 2d 635 (S.D. Tex. 1999) (laches requires reliance on failure to enforce the right; in student loan cases, borrowers do all their relying shortly after signing the note; in the years government has not collected the debt, borrower has done nothing with money or about debt); United States v. Dwelley, 59 F. Supp. 2d 115 (D. Me. 1999); United States v. McLaughlin, 7 F. Supp. 2d 90 (D. Mass. 1998) (no special hardship demonstrated sufficient to relax the laches rule); United States v. Robbins, 819 F. Supp. 672 (E.D. Mich. 1993).

32 United States v. Rhodes, 788 F. Supp. 339 (E.D. Mich. 1992).

33 *Id.* at 343.

34 *See, e.g.*, United States v. Davis, 817 F. Supp. 926, 930 (M.D. Ala. 1993) (distinguishing between the borrower's defense of lack of consideration and the borrower in *Rhodes* who alleged he had already repaid the loan).

35 *Id.*

36 Hamilton v. U.S.A., 2005 WL 2671373 (S.D. Ohio Oct. 19, 2005).

37 *See* § 9.6.2.3, *infra.* It may also be possible to argue that the statute of limitations should not be eliminated for FFELs that

have lost their guaranteed status, since neither a school, guaranty agency, nor the United States will be collecting on such a loan. *See also* § 9.6.3.2, *infra.*

38 34 C.F.R. §§ 682.200 (FFEL definition of default), 685.102(b) (Direct Loans). The rules are different for Perkins loans when default is defined as the failure of a borrower to make an installment payment when due or to comply with other terms of the promissory note or written repayment agreement. 34 C.F.R. § 674.2. The collection process and due diligence requirements for Perkins loans are set out at 34 C.F.R. §§ 674.41–.50. The collection procedures described in this section, unless otherwise noted, refer to FFEL and Direct Loans.

39 *See* § 2.7.3, *supra* (pre-default repayment plans); Ch. 3, *supra* (deferments and forbearances); Ch. 6, *infra* (loan cancellations).

40 For a list of guaranty agencies and addresses, see Appendix G, *infra.*

The Department and state guaranty agencies also contract with private collection agencies to fulfill many of their collection responsibilities.[41] The widespread use of private collection agencies to pursue student loan defaulters, combined with significant expansions in the government's arsenal of collection tools, has completely changed the landscape of student loan collections. Because the Department and its agents routinely send defaulted loan portfolios to these agencies, many borrowers seeking to get out of default or otherwise address student loan problems end up dealing with the least sympathetic of all actors, a private collection agency.[42]

The types of activities third parties can engage in to collect student loans are different for different types of loans. The rules also vary depending on which collection tool they are using. For example, third parties acting as agents for the federal government are explicitly covered by the tax intercept statute.[43]

The HEA wage garnishment statute also specifically applies to guaranty agencies.[44] However, in 2002, the Department was granted authority to garnish wages pursuant to the Debt Collection Improvement Act (DCIA) authority rather than the HEA.[45] The DCIA, unlike the HEA, applies only to garnishment by the "heads" of executive, judicial, or legislative agencies.[46] Thus, guaranty agencies have continued to garnish under HEA authority while the Department garnishes under the DCIA.[47] This issue is less important after July 1, 2006, as both the DCIA and HEA now allow garnishment of up to 15% of disposable income.[48] Previously, the HEA limit was only 10%.

Similar to the DCIA wage garnishment provisions, the federal benefits-offset statute grants offset authority only to heads of agencies.[49] Despite this language, the Department's current policy is to allow guaranty agencies to refer debts to the Department of Treasury for offset after paying the lender but before assigning loans.

The picture is less clear for Perkins Loans. Perkins schools are encouraged to assign defaulted loans to the Department.[50] The United States will then seek collection from the defaulted borrower, using the full range of collection tools available. The Department claims to have collection tools, such as wage garnishment, federal offset, and Department of Justice litigation, that are not available to schools.[51] It is unclear to what extent this statement reflects actual practice.[52]

When the Department holds a defaulted loan, collection is by the Department's Debt Collection Service. That service has a small Washington office that establishes policy and three large regional offices that handle actual consumer files. However, as discussed above, most responsibilities for debt collection on Department-held loans are delegated to private debt collection agencies hired by the Department on a commission basis.

If the Department is not holding a loan, it is generally *not* appropriate to initiate inquiries or make applications to the Department. Instead, borrowers should contact the party holding the loan—usually a guaranty agency on an FFEL and the school itself on a Perkins Loan. The guaranty agency or school may have hired a collector or servicer to deal with the loan.

Even though it is best to contact the holder directly, if problems arise, borrowers should also consider contacting the Department. The Department has the responsibility for supervising the actions of guaranty agencies and setting standards for their conduct. Much of what guarantors do has first been approved by the Department.

The federal student aid information center, 1-800-4-FED-AID (800-433-3243), is a good place for borrowers to start the process of finding out which entity is collecting. The information center staff should be able to give borrowers the address and telephone number of the agency holding a defaulted loan. The information is also available on-line through the national student loan data system.[53] Borrowers with Direct loans should contact the Direct Loan Servicing

---

41 The Department of Education website (www.ed.gov) lists the collection agencies with Department contracts. This list is also reprinted at Appendix H. All guidance from the Department to private collection agencies can be found at www.fsacollections.ed.gov/contractors/pca2004/index.html. *See* § 4.5.1, *infra*.

42 § 4.5.3.2, *infra*.

43 31 U.S.C. § 3720A. This is significant because, prior to the legislative change allowing interception of debts owed to agents of the federal government, authorization to intercept loans held by guaranty agencies was accomplished by the guarantors assigning the loans to the U.S. prior to interception. This posed practical problems for obligations that guarantors had already reduced to judgments, particularly since the interception program was not used to collect loans post-judgment. The interception program is now utilized to recover on debts pre- and post-judgment. *See* § 5.2, *infra*.

44 20 U.S.C. § 1095a(a).

45 *See* § 5.3.3, *infra*.

46 31 U.S.C. § 3720D(a).

47 *See generally* § 5.3.3, *infra*.

48 § 5.3.2.2, *infra*.

49 31 U.S.C. § 3716. *See* § 5.4, *infra*.

50 34 C.F.R. § 674.50 (assignment regulations). *See also* U.S. Dep't of Educ., Dear Colleague Letter, CB-02-05 (Apr. 2002). In August 2003, the Department issued a revised assignment form and procedures for assigning Perkins loans. *See* Letter, U.S. Dep't of Educ., Dear Colleague Letter, #CB-03-12 (Aug. 2003).

51 *See* U.S. Dep't of Educ., Dear Colleague Letter, CB-02-05 (Apr. 2002).

52 By many accounts, Perkins schools do in fact refer debts to the Department of Treasury for tax intercept. Presumably they could do the same for federal benefits offsets. However, the Department claims, at least with respect to benefits offsets, that this is not current practice.

53 For information about using the national student loan data base to find out how many loans and what types of loans a borrower has, see § 1.6, *supra*. Borrowers may also use the LoanLocator service managed by the nonprofit National Student Clearing-

Center at 1-800-848-0979. The number for information about Department-held loans is 1-800-621-3115. More information is also available at the Department's website at www.ed.gov.

It is best to contact the student loan ombudsman for help only after these other avenues have been exhausted. The toll-free phone number for the ombudsman is 1-877-557-2575.[54]

4.3.3 Pre-Default Collection (Delinquency)

Delinquency begins on the first day after the due date of the first missed payment.[55] Once a loan becomes delinquent, lenders are required to provide the borrower with information about the availability of the Student Loan Ombudsman's office.[56]

Lenders are also required to engage in at least the following collection activities, depending on how long the borrower has been delinquent:

- 1–15 days delinquent: The lender must send at least one written notice or collection letter during this period informing the borrower of the delinquency and urging the borrower to make payments.[57] The notice or collection letter must at a minimum include a lender or servicer contact, a telephone number, and a prominent statement informing borrowers that assistance may be available if they are experiencing difficulty in making scheduled payments.[58]
- 16–180 days delinquent: During this period, the lender must make at least four diligent efforts to contact the borrower by telephone and send at least four collection letters.[59] At least one attempt to contact the borrower by phone must occur on or before, and another attempt must occur after, the 90th day of delinquency. Collection letters sent during this period must include, at a minimum, information regarding deferment, forbearance, income-sensitive repayment, loan consolidation, and other available options to avoid default.[60]

At least two of the collection letters during this period must warn the borrower that, if the loan is not paid, the lender will assign the loan to the guaranty

agency. These letters must also inform the borrower that, if assigned to a guaranty agency, a defaulted loan will be reported to all national credit bureaus and that the agency may institute tax refund offsets, offsets of other federal payments, wage garnishment, or assignment of the loan to the federal government for litigation.[61] Receipt of any payments from the borrower during this period allows the lender to hold off on some of the required collection activity.[62]

- 181–270 days delinquent: At a minimum, the lender during this period must provide information to the borrower regarding options to avoid default and the consequences of default.[63] On or after the 241st day of delinquency, the lender must send a final demand letter to the borrower.[64] The lender must give the borrower at least thirty days after the date the letter is mailed to respond and to bring the loan out of default.[65]

The lender is required to ensure that there is no gap in collection activity of more than forty-five days at any point during this delinquency period.[66]

In many cases, lenders and guaranty agencies fail to provide targeted services to assist borrowers in delinquency. The main problem is that, for lenders, delinquent loans often have less value than loans in default because the government guarantees close to full payment when default claims are filed. A 2002 GAO report described the problem in greater detail. The traditional payments for guaranty agencies, according to the GAO, make it more financially beneficial for an agency to allow borrowers to default and then to try to collect rather than prevent default.[67]

Congress responded in part by giving the Department of Education the authority to develop and sign voluntary flexible agreements (VFAs) with guaranty agencies. These agreements exempt agencies from many regulatory requirements, such as the prescribed contacts with borrowers described above. They are also encouraged to set up new types of incentive payment agreements, in many cases rewarding agencies for preventing defaults rather than tying compensation to collection.[68] Some agencies claim that they can pursue these goals without a VFA because their missions

---

house. Only loans from participating schools are listed. *See* www.studentclearinghouse.org.

54   For more information about the ombudsman program, see § 1.9.9.1, *supra*.

55   34 C.F.R. § 682.411(b). For general Perkins due diligence requirements, see 34 C.F.R. § 674.41.

56   34 C.F.R. § 682.411(b)(3).

57   34 C.F.R. § 682.411(c).

58   *Id.*

59   34 C.F.R. § 682.411(d). Lenders are excused from further telephone efforts if, after making diligent efforts, they are unable to obtain the correct telephone number of a borrower. 34 C.F.R. § 682.411(g).

60   *Id.*

61   34 C.F.R. § 682.411(d)(2). These collection methods are discussed in detail in Chapter 5, *infra*.

62   34 C.F.R. § 682.411(d)(3). The obligations differ if the lender receives a payment on the loan. 34 C.F.R. § 682.411(d)(3), (4).

63   34 C.F.R. § 682.411(e).

64   34 C.F.R. § 682.411(f).

65   *Id.*

66   34 C.F.R. § 682.411(b)(2). In 2004, the Department clarified that the forty-five-day rule includes any gap between previously required collection activities and the final demand letter. U.S. Dep't of Educ., *Dear Colleague Letter*, FP-04-08, *Application of the Lender Due Diligence 45-Day Gap Rule* (Nov. 2004).

67   U.S. Gen. Accounting Office, *Federal Student Loans: Flexible Agreements with Guaranty Agencies Warrant Careful Evaluation*, GAO-02-254 (Jan. 2002).

68   *Id.*

provide sufficient motivation to increase efforts to prevent defaults and that innovations in customer service can be accomplished under current regulations.[69]

4.3.4 Post-Default Collections

4.3.4.1 Due Diligence and Notice Requirements

The regulations specify the efforts guaranty agencies must make to collect defaulted FFEL loans. These options include tax refund offsets, federal benefit offsets, wage garnishment, and litigation.[70] There are similar regulations that apply when the Department is collecting loans that it holds.[71] The Perkins program has its own set of regulations.[72]

Until 2001, the regulations prescribed specific behavior that guaranty agencies were required to follow. The rules were very detailed, listing specific collection activities for the first forty-five days through 181 days after default. The rules also restricted a guaranty agency's use of litigation in collecting defaulted loans.

Effective in 2001, the Department made a number of significant changes to these rules. In particular, guaranty agencies were no longer required to perform routine collection activities such as collection letters and phone calls.[73] Instead, the agencies are given discretion to design their own collection strategies as long as they perform at least one activity every 180 days to collect the debt, locate the borrower (if necessary), or determine if the borrower has the means to repay the debt.[74] The 2001 regulatory changes also eliminated the general prohibition against guaranty agencies suing borrowers.[75]

The changes followed previous amendments to the HEA placing greater financial responsibility for collection on guaranty agencies. As a result, guaranty agencies are now required to pay for collection activities using money in their own operating funds. Previously, agencies funded their collection efforts with federal reserves. Congress hoped to decrease costs, assuming that agencies using their own funds would develop more cost-efficient collection methods.[76] The Department argued that these financial incentives eliminated the need for prescriptive regulations.[77]

Although guaranty agencies have more freedom to develop collection strategies, certain requirements are still in place.

Prior to reporting the default and prior to assessing any collection costs, the agency must provide written notice containing the information described below. Although agencies have sixty days to report the default claim to the credit bureaus, they only have forty-five days after paying a lender's default claim to send this notice.[78]

The notice must

- advise the borrower that the agency has paid a default claim filed by the lender and has taken assignment of the loan;
- identify the lender that made the loan and the school at which the loan was made;
- list the outstanding principal, accrued interest, and any other charges owing on the loan;
- demand that the borrower immediately repay the loan;
- explain the rate of interest that will accrue on the loan, that all costs incurred to collect the loan will be charged to the borrower, the authority for assessing these costs, and the manner in which the agency will calculate the amount of these costs;
- notify the borrower that the agency will report the default to all national credit bureaus; and
- explain the opportunities available to the borrower to request access to the agency's records on the loan, to request an administrative review of the legal enforceability or past-due status of the loan and to reach a satisfactory repayment agreement, and the methods for requesting this relief.[79]

Unless the agency uses a separate notice to advise the borrower of proposed enforcement actions, the notice with the information discussed above must also describe any other enforcement action, such as tax offsets or wage garnishment, that the agency intends to use to collect the debt, and explain the procedures available to the borrower prior to these actions to access records, request administrative review, or set up a payment plan.[80]

The initial notice must also describe the grounds on which the borrower may object that the loan obligation is not a legally enforceable debt and describe any appeal and judicial rights available to the borrower from an adverse decision regarding the legal enforceability or past-due status of the loan.[81] In addition, the notice must describe collection actions the agency may take in the future, including the filing of a lawsuit by the agency or by the Department of Education.[82]

During the first forty-five days after filing a default claim, agencies have the option of including even more information in the notice described above or sending a separate notice explaining that, if the borrower does not make ac-

---

69 *Id.* at 15.

70 These collection methods are all discussed in detail in Chapter 5.

71 34 C.F.R. § 685.211(d)(3).

72 34 C.F.R. § 674.45.

73 *See* 65 Fed. Reg. 46316, 46318 (July 27, 2000).

74 34 C.F.R. § 682.410(b)(6)(i).

75 *See generally* 65 Fed. Reg. 65621, 65650 (Nov. 1, 2000) (final rules).

76 65 Fed. Reg. 46316, 46318 (July 27, 2000) (proposed rules).

77 *Id.*

---

78 34 C.F.R. § 682.410(b)(6)(v).

79 34 C.F.R. § 682.410(b)(5)(vi). *See* § 4.3.4.2, *infra.*

80 34 C.F.R. § 682.410(b)(5)(vi)(H).

81 34 C.F.R. § 682.410(b)(5)(vi)(I), (J), (K).

82 34 C.F.R. § 682.410(b)(5)(vi)(L).

ceptable repayment arrangements, the agency will promptly initiate collection procedures.[83] The various scenarios such as wage garnishment or civil suits must be listed.[84]

Given the volume of information in these collection notices, it is not surprising that borrowers are often confused about their rights. Recognizing this problem (although not necessarily solving it), the Department requires that the agency notify the borrower within forty-five days of paying a default claim that "borrowers may have certain rights in the collection of debts, and that borrowers may wish to contact counselors or lawyers regarding those rights."[85] Within a reasonable time after all of this information is sent, the agency is also required to send borrowers at least one additional notice informing the borrower that the default has been reported to all national credit bureaus (if that is the case) and that the borrower's credit rating may thereby have been damaged.[86]

During the initial sixty-day period before the agency reports the claim to credit bureaus, borrowers must also be given an opportunity to inspect and copy agency records pertaining to the loan obligation, an opportunity for an administrative review of the legal enforceability of the debt, and an opportunity to enter into a repayment agreement on terms "satisfactory to the agency."[87]

A collection agency's failure to follow these collection rules may violate the FDCPA.[88] Violations by guaranty agencies may also be actionable under the FDCPA.[89]

Agencies are required to attempt an annual federal offset, including tax refund offsets as well as offsets of other federal payments.[90] However, before attempting offset, agencies must wait at least sixty days after sending the required collection notices described above.

The agencies are also required to initiate administrative wage garnishment against all eligible borrowers.[91] The only exception to this requirement arises if the agency determines that litigation would be more effective in collecting the debt. In these circumstances, the agency may instead file a lawsuit against a borrower.[92] The regulations clarify that agencies have the discretion to file lawsuits instead of wage garnishment only if the borrower has no wages that can be garnished or if the agency determines that the borrower has sufficient attachable assets or income that is not subject to administrative wage garnishment.[93] The regulations therefore reflect the Department's growing preference for extrajudicial collection methods.

Garnishment procedures are set out separately.[94] These procedures, including administrative review and hearing rights, are discussed in detail in Chapter 5, *infra*. For purposes of possible fair debt collection violations, it is important to note that the garnishment regulations require that guaranty agencies send notice of proposed garnishment to the borrower at least thirty days before initiating proceedings.[95]

4.3.4.2　Credit Bureau Reporting

4.3.4.2.1 General

The HEA requires that guaranty agencies, lenders, and the Secretary of Education regularly exchange information with credit reporting agencies about outstanding student loans.[96] The statute provides that the Department, guaranty agencies, and lenders must enter into agreements with credit bureau organizations to exchange information concerning student borrowers.[97] There has been considerable controversy over whether the agencies must report to all national credit bureaus. Although the regulations explicitly specify that student loan default information must be reported to all national credit bureaus, there is no similar requirement with respect to the reporting of all repayment information.[98]

This issue has generated a great deal of attention. Salle Mae in particular was criticized for deciding to report loan repayment information only to a small credit bureau and to Equifax. In response to the criticism, Salle Mae reversed its policy and began reporting to Experian and TransUnion as well. Legislation has been introduced to address this issue, proposing to require lenders and other furnishers of credit information to report loan repayment information to "each national credit bureau organization."[99]

The regulations specify the information to be supplied. The guaranty agency supplies—for that borrower—the total amount of loans extended, the remaining balance, the date of default, information concerning collection of the loan, including the repayment status of the loan, changes and corrections based on information after the initial report, and the date the loan is fully repaid or discharged by reason of death, bankruptcy, or disability.[100]

83　34 C.F.R. § 682.410(b)(6)(v).

84　*Id.*

85　34 C.F.R. § 682.210(b)(6)(v).

86　34 C.F.R. § 682.410(b)(6)(vi).

87　34 C.F.R. § 682.410(b)(5)(ii).

88　*See* §§ 4.5.2, 4.5.3, *infra*.

89　*See* § 4.5.3.5, *infra*.

90　34 C.F.R. § 682.410(b)(6)(ii). *See* §§ 5.2, 5.4, *infra*.

91　34 C.F.R. § 682.410(b)(6)(iii). *See* § 5.3, *infra*.

92　34 C.F.R. § 682.410(b)(6)(iv).

93　*Id.*

94　34 C.F.R. § 682.410(b)(9).

95　34 C.F.R. § 682.410(b)(9)(i)(B). *See* § 4.3.2.1, *supra*.

96　20 U.S.C. § 1080a.

97　20 U.S.C. § 1080a(a).

98　No later than sixty days after defaulting, the guaranty agency is required to report default claims to all national credit bureaus. 34 C.F.R. § 682.410(b)(5) (reporting of defaulted student loans).

99　*See, e.g.,* The Borrower Bill of Rights, S. 3255, 109th Cong. (introduced May 26, 2006). For general information on adding positive information to credit reports, see National Consumer Law Center, Fair Credit Reporting § 13.6.4 (5th ed. 2002 and Supp.).

100　34 C.F.R. § 682.410(b)(5)(i).

Schools that are holding loans (particularly true in Perkins loan cases) are required to report any updated information to the original credit bureau to which it reported the account.[101] A March 1999 Federal Trade Commission staff letter clarified that, pursuant to the Fair Credit Reporting Act, schools must report information to the original credit bureau even if the school no longer has a contractual relationship with that bureau.[102]

A defaulted student loan will be listed as a current debt that is in default. The default will also be listed in the historical section of the report, specifying the length of the default. If the borrower repays the debt in full, the debt will no longer be listed as a current debt in default, but the debt will still be listed on the report (for up to seven years) as a debt that was at one time in default. Perkins loan defaults, however, can now be reported indefinitely.[103]

Because of the unique treatment often required for student loans, some standardized ways of furnishing information to consumer reporting agencies have been established. Below is a brief description of how student loan information is reported to the credit bureaus using the Metro 2 reporting format. Metro 2 is a software program used by student loan creditors (and other creditors) to provide information about consumer accounts to consumer reporting agencies.[104]

No distinction is made in Metro 2 between different types of student loans; they are all reported as education loans. A student loan may be reported in good status when payments are being made and also when payments are deferred with a future payment obligation. Deferred payment loans are further distinguished between those on which repayment has never (or not yet) been made and those on which the account was previously being repaid. When payments are deferred, the start date for making payments should be included in a specific segment of the program (called the K-4 segment) for specialized payments.

Student loans that are disbursed over a period of time are treated as a single account. The date opened is the date of the first disbursement, but the original loan amount, balance, and scheduled payment amounts increase appropriately as disbursements are made. If the loans are truly multiple loans, then each one is treated as a separate account. If multiple loans are consolidated, it is considered a new loan initially in good standing. The consolidated loans should be recorded as paid or closed with zero balances, although a payment rating will reveal accounts that were not in good standing.

Status code 88 cases are those that have been referred to the Department of Education for payment of the insured balance on the loan. If the claim is denied, the lender or servicer must delete the account and furnish new information about the debt, using the original date opened, status, and other attributes. As is often the case, potential errors may result in the same student loan debt being reported twice.

Student loans can be cancelled for a variety of reasons, as discussed throughout this manual.[105] If the loan is cancelled due to a school closing, it should be deleted.[106] Similarly, in a false-certification case, the loan report should also be deleted.[107] Cancellation for student disability may be reported one of two ways. If the loan never reached the repayment period, it too should be deleted.[108] However, if repayments had begun, the loan should be designated as paid or closed and the balance or amount due recorded as zero. Teacher forgiveness is treated in the same manner.[109]

Student loans, like other debts, may be sold or transferred to others for collection. In general, the Metro 2 system relies upon the transferring creditor to delete the accounts from agency files and the new creditor or servicing agent to begin furnishing information about the account. The new furnisher does not start with a new open date, payment history, or status or date of first delinquency but should retain prior information as furnished earlier on the account. A servicer, one who does not itself hold the note, must also continue to use the identification number of the holder. Mistakes when accounts are transferred can result in false or misleading information in consumer reports.[110]

If a student loan is transferred to a student loan guaranty agency, the agency is supposed to record the loan as seriously past due. If the consumer is nonetheless making payments, the debt is still coded as seriously past due, but the balance due should decline. A code also exists for accounts paid off by the government or insurer, or forgiven because the student has become totally and permanently disabled. If the guaranty agency itself transfers the account to a debt collection agency or the United States government, it should use a code "(DA)" to delete the account from the records reported to the consumer reporting agencies. The collection agency or the government will then include the debt in its own Metro 2 submissions to the reporting agencies.

---

101 34 C.F.R. § 674.45(b)(1).

102 Staff Letter from David Medine to Lee S. Harris, U.S. Dep't of Educ., Clearinghouse No. 52,490 (Mar. 22, 1999).

103 *See* § 4.3.4.2.2, *infra*.

104 *See generally* National Consumer Law Center, Fair Credit Reporting (5th ed. 2002 and Supp.).

105 *See* Ch. 6 (loan cancellations), *infra*.

106 *See* § 6.2 (closed-school discharges), *infra*.

107 *See* § 6.3 (false-certification discharges), *infra*.

108 *See* § 6.6 (disability discharges), *infra*.

109 *See* § 6.8 (teacher loan forgiveness), *infra*.

110 In general, student loan holders are furnishers of information to credit bureaus and in some circumstances can be separately liable for submitting erroneous information. *See* National Consumer Law Center, Fair Credit Reporting (5th ed. 2002 and Supp.). *See* § 4.3.4.2.3, *infra*.

4.3.4.2.2 *How long does information remain in the consumer's file?*

The HEA sets out special rules as to when reports on student loans become obsolete. With the notable exception of Perkins loans, reports for most student loan defaults may be included in consumer reports for seven years from the later of three dates:

(1) when the Secretary or the guaranty agency pays a claim to the loan holder on the guaranty;

(2) when the Secretary, guaranty agency, lender, or any other loan holder first reported the account to the consumer reporting agency; or

(3) if a borrower re-enters repayment after defaulting on a loan, from the date the student subsequently goes into default again on the loan.[111]

Due to a change in the 1998 HEA, Perkins loans, in contrast, may be reported indefinitely.[112] A small consolation for borrowers, passed at the same time, requires Perkins institutions to report to credit bureaus when a borrower has made six consecutive monthly payments on a defaulted loan and to disclose promptly any changes to information previously disclosed.[113]

4.3.4.2.3 *Cleaning up the consumer's credit record*

Consumers can use various tactics to clean up credit files containing reports of defaulted student loans. As discussed above, a defaulted student loan will be listed as a current debt that is in default. The default will also be listed in the historical section of the report, specifying the length of the default. If the borrower repays the debt in full, the debt will no longer be listed as a current debt in default, but the debt will still be listed on the report (for up to seven years) as a debt that was at one time in default. Perkins loan defaults, however, can be reported indefinitely.[114]

Most creditors (such as mortgage companies or banks) will look more carefully at the current status of debts than the historical information in a file. For example, some mortgage lenders will not make loans to applicants that have any current loan defaults. Nevertheless, the historical information is reported to creditors and others authorized to see the consumer's file, and derogatory information there can prove harmful to the consumer.[115]

If the borrower is eligible, the clearest way to remove the student loan default from *both* the current account information and the historical portion of the report is to obtain a closed-school, false-certification, or unpaid-refund discharge.[116] The regulations state that the discharge should be reported to all credit reporting agencies to which the holder previously reported the status of the loan "so as to delete all adverse credit history assigned to the loan."[117] Consequently, the guarantor or Department should tell the reporting agency not only that the loan is no longer in default but that the reporting of the loan as ever being in default was in error.

Borrowers can follow up a discharge by obtaining a copy of their credit report and determining if the current and historical information on the loan has been corrected.[118] If it has not been corrected, the borrower should first request the guarantor or the Department to report the debt's correct status to the reporting agency. They should also dispute the accuracy of the default with the reporting agency. The reporting agency will be required to verify the default with the loan holder.[119] The loan holder, in turn, should refuse to verify to the reporting agency that a default ever existed.

Loan rehabilitation is another useful tool to clear up both the current and historical status sections of a borrower's credit report.[120] In order to rehabilitate a loan, a borrower must first make nine payments within twenty days of each due date during a period of ten consecutive months, accompanied by the re-sale of the loan.[121] For FFEL loans, guaranty agencies must report to all national credit bureaus within ninety days of rehabilitation that the loan is no longer in a default status and that the default is to be removed from the borrower's credit history.[122] Under the Perkins loan

---

sumer Law Center, Guide to Surviving Debt Ch. 3 (2006); National Consumer Law Center, Fair Credit Reporting (5th ed. 2002 and Supp.).

116 For unpaid-refund discharges, it is possible that only a portion of the loan may be paid off. The credit report therefore may still show that the borrower is delinquent on a portion of the loan. *See* § 6.4, *infra.*

117 34 C.F.R. §§ 682.402(d)(2)(iv), 682.402(e)(2)(iv). A March 1999 Federal Trade Commission staff letter clarified that, pursuant to the Fair Credit Reporting Act, schools must report information to the original credit bureau even if the school no longer has a contractual relationship with that bureau. *See* FTC Staff Letter from David Medine to Lee S. Harris, U.S. Dep't of Educ., Clearinghouse No. 52,490 (Mar. 22, 1999).

118 For detailed information on how to obtain a copy of a credit report, see National Consumer Law Center, Fair Credit Reporting (5th ed. 2002 and Supp.).

119 For detailed information on how to dispute the accuracy of a credit report, and the reporting agency's responsibilities, see National Consumer Law Center, Fair Credit Reporting (5th ed. 2002 and Supp.).

120 *See* § 8.4, *infra.*

121 Prior to July 1, 2006, twelve consecutive payments were required. The longer requirement still applies to Perkins rehabilitations. *See* § 8.4.3, *infra.*

122 34 C.F.R. § 682.405(b)(3).

---

111 20 U.S.C. § 1080a(f).

112 Pub. L. No. 105-244 § 463(b) (Oct. 7, 1998), *amending* 20 U.S.C. § 1087cc(c)(3). The Secretary was given specific statutory authority to promulgate regulations establishing criteria under which a school can cease reporting the information before the loan is paid in full. 20 U.S.C. § 1087cc(c)(4)(B).

113 Pub. L. No. 105-244 § 463(b) (Oct. 7, 1998), *adding* 20 U.S.C. § 1087cc(c)(5); 34 C.F.R. § 674.45(b)(1).

114 *See* § 4.3.4.2.2, *supra.*

115 For more on clearing up credit, see generally National Con-

rehabilitation program, schools have thirty days after receiving the borrower's last on-time monthly payment to instruct any credit bureau to which the default was reported to remove the default from the borrower's credit history.[123]

An alternative method of removing both the current and historical information on a student loan default is to dispute whether the debt is owed, using as a basis forgery, fraud, school-related claims, or other defenses that go to the loan's enforceability.[124] As part of a settlement of such a claim, the loan holder may be willing to request that the reporting agency correct both the current and historical status of the debt.[125]

It is easier to improve only the current status section of a credit report. By taking any of the following steps, a borrower can have the loan's current status changed so that it no longer indicates a default:

- repay the debt;
- obtain a consolidation loan;[126] or
- obtain a discharge based on total and permanent disability.[127]

The current status of the debt on a credit report will *not* be changed if the borrower merely enters into a reasonable and affordable payment plan, even after making six payments to renew eligibility for new loans. A payment agreement with a note holder will *not* remove a default from a student's credit record unless the loan holder explicitly agrees that it will take the loan out of default.

If a student loan is discharged in bankruptcy, the debt will no longer be treated as currently in default in the consumer's credit file. On the other hand, the fact that the consumer filed bankruptcy will be on the consumer's credit record for ten years.[128] Nevertheless, many experts believe that filing for bankruptcy will generally help a consumer's credit record in the long run. Certainly, the possibility of bankruptcy should not be rejected solely because of potential damage to the debtor's credit record.[129]

Borrowers may also want to consider legal action in cases in which a lender or other furnisher of student loan payment information provides inaccurate or obsolete information to a credit reporting agency.[130] Claims under state laws, however, may be preempted by the HEA or the FCRA.[131]

4.4 Collection Fees and Penalties

4.4.1 General

In June 2003, the Department's Chief Operating Officer for Federal Student Aid (FSA), Theresa Shaw, testified about collection fees and other issues before the House Subcommittee on Government Efficiency and Financial Management.[132] Ms. Shaw testified that the Department's contracts with collection agencies have several performance-based evaluation measures. Agencies are evaluated and rated according to the overall service they perform, as well as their ability to collect defaulted debt. The agencies that perform best across all these categories receive additional incentives—both monetary rewards and new account placements. She testified further that the collection contracts rely on a contingent-fee method of compensating collection agencies. Ms. Shaw also claimed that the Department's use of collectors has reduced costs. According to her testimony, in fiscal year 1993, the contractors were paid roughly 33 cents for every dollar collected. By fiscal year 1997, costs were reduced to 23 cents per dollar collected. For existing contracts in 2003, costs were down to only 16 cents per dollar and were expected to go down further.[133]

A 2005 Department of Education Inspector General (IG) report focused on the Department's incentive payments to third-party collection agencies. The IG found that the De-

---

123 34 C.F.R. § 674.39(b)(3).

124 *See* § 9.5.3, *infra*.

125 For detailed information on how to handle credit reporting issues as part of a settlement, including sample creditor letters to a reporting agency, see National Consumer Law Center, Fair Credit Reporting (5th ed. 2002 and Supp.).

126 *See* § 8.2, *infra*.

127 *See* § 6.6, *infra*.

128 *See* National Consumer Law Center, Fair Credit Reporting (5th ed. 2002 and Supp.).

129 For a discussion of bankruptcy's positive and negative impacts on a consumer's credit rating, see National Consumer Law Center, Fair Credit Reporting (5th ed. 2002 and Supp.). For a discussion of the dischargeability of student loans in bankruptcy, see generally Chapter 7, *infra*.

130 *See generally* National Consumer Law Center, Fair Credit Reporting Ch. 10 (5th ed. 2002 and Supp.). *See also* Jordan v. Equifax Info. Servs. et al., 410 F. Supp. 2d 1349 (N.D. Ga. 2006) (FCRA claim against loan servicer SLM for improper furnishing of information about student loans in identity theft case allowed to proceed); Pirouzian v. SLM Corp., 396 F. Supp. 2d 1124 (S.D. Cal. 2005) (student loan borrower's FCRA claims partially preempted, but claim under § 1681s-2(b) allowed to proceed); Hinton v. USA Funds, 2005 WL 730963 (N.D. Ill. Mar. 20, 2005) (summary judgment granted in part and denied in part in case brought by student loan borrower raising FCRA claims); Potter v. Illinois Student Assistance Comm'n, 2004 WL 1203156 (Cal. App. 4 Dist. June 2, 2004) (unpublished decision) (borrower's state credit reporting act claims preempted by the HEA and FCRA).

131 *See, e.g.*, Pirouzian v. SLM Corp., 396 F. Supp. 2d 1124 (S.D. Cal. 2005)

132 *Hearing on the Debt Collection Improvement Act of 1996: How Well Is It Working?: Testimony to the Subcomm. on Government Efficiency and Financial Management, House Committee on Government Reform*, 108th Cong. (June 17, 2003) (testimony of Theresa S. Shaw, Chief Operating Officer, Fed. Student Aid, U.S. Dep't of Educ.).

133 *Id.* For a discussion of problems with the Department's oversight of private collection agencies, see U.S. Dep't of Educ., Office of Inspector Gen., Final Audit Report, Control #ED-OIG/A19-D0002, Dec. 23, 2003. *See* § 4.5.1, *supra*.

partment made incentive payments totaling almost $950,000 that were not consistent with the terms of the task orders. The IG also noted that FSA needed to improve its internal controls.[134]

In addition to the "special" incentives for good performance described above, the collector receives a commission on a payment as long as the collector has been assigned the file, whether or not the student's payment was instigated by that collector's actions. The Department then deducts an amount roughly equal to the commission it has paid its collector from the consumer's payment. Only the amount left over after the commission is paid is applied to interest and then principal, in that order.[135]

The collector cannot assess an amount in advance for collection fees but must instead apportion a percentage of each payment toward collection fees.[136] In an effort to prevent up-front loading of collection costs, the Department has clarified that the borrower is not legally obligated to pay costs that have not been incurred. The Department has recognized that the practice of loading fees up-front can actually discourage repayment and in any case does not reflect actual costs.[137]

Consider the following example. Assume a borrower's current obligation, including principal and interest, on a loan is $10,000 and that the commission paid to collectors is 30% of the amount collected. Even if the borrower immediately pays the full $10,000, the Department will first apply the funds to pay the collection commission, leaving only $7000 to apply to the outstanding balance. The borrower's obligation is thus lowered only to $3000. To pay off the $10,000 balance, the borrower must immediately pay $14,285.71. The Department will apply 30% of that amount (30% of $14,285.71 is $4285.71) to collection costs. The remainder ($10,000) pays off the loan.

Collection costs should be recalculated each year after a loan goes into default. As to each loan in default, the amount of the previous year's collection costs should be removed from the balance of the loan and the newly calculated rate should be applied. Rates should also be recalculated each time the loan is transferred from one entity to another.[138]

The Department's regulations require guaranty agencies to charge collection fees, whether or not provided for in the borrower's promissory note. The method of allocating students' payments to the fees must be the same as for Department-held loans.[139] Agencies must only charge amounts equal to reasonable costs incurred in collecting.[140]

The rules for lenders are different. The FFEL regulations set out what collection costs the lender can seek (that is, before the loan is turned over to the guarantor).[141] The lender can seek no collection costs unless such charges are authorized in the promissory note and such costs are actually incurred by the lender or its agent.[142] Even if incurred and authorized by contract, the regulation prohibits assessment of charges for "normal collection costs associated with preparing letters or notices or with making personal contacts with the borrower."[143]

There are distinct collection fee provisions for schools collecting Perkins loans. These schools must charge all reasonable costs with regard to a loan obligation.[144] The amount of collection costs charged must be based on either the actual costs incurred for collection actions with regard to the individual borrower's loan or average costs incurred for similar actions taken to collect loans in similar stages of delinquency.[145]

Before filing suit on a loan, the school may waive collection costs as follows:

1. The school may waive the percentage of collection costs applicable to the amount then past due on a loan equal to the percentage of that past-due balance that the borrower pays within thirty days after the date on which the borrower and the school enter into a written repayment agreement, or

2. The school may waive all collection costs in return for a lump-sum payment of the full amount of principal and interest outstanding.[146]

Schools are required to apply payments on loans in the following order: (i) collection costs; (ii) late charges; (iii) accrued interest; and (iv) principal.[147]

---

134   U.S. Dep't of Educ., Office of Inspector Gen., Final Audit Report, Control Number ED-OIG/A19-D0005 (Feb. 18, 2005).

135   34 C.F.R. § 682.404(f) (payments are applied first to collection costs and then to other incidental charges such as late charges, then to interest and principal). *See* Padilla v. Payco Gen. Am. Credits, Inc., 161 F. Supp. 2d 264 (S.D.N.Y. 2001) (defendant's summary judgment motion denied on plaintiff's claim that debt collector induced borrower to make a down payment by agreeing to apply, in violation of federal law, the payment toward principal only).

136   The Department has taken the position that a borrower is not legally obligated to pay costs that have not been incurred. Memorandum of Points and Authorities Supporting Motion to Dismiss, Hutchins v. United States Dep't of Educ., CV-F-02-6256-OWW-DLB, at 31 (E.D. Cal. filed Apr. 25, 2003) (citing H.R. Res. 300, 99th Cong. (1986), at 396, *reprinted in* 1986 U.S.C.C.A.N. 977). The agencies can charge the borrower only those costs that have been incurred as allocated to the particular payment.

137   *See* 61 Fed. Reg. 60482 (Nov. 27, 1996).

138   *See generally In re* Evans, 322 B.R. 429 (Bankr. W.D. Wash. 2005).

139   34 C.F.R. § 682.410(b)(2).

140   *Id.*

141   34 C.F.R. § 682.202(g).

142   34 C.F.R. § 682.202(g)(1).

143   34 C.F.R. § 682.202(g)(2).

144   34 C.F.R. § 674.45(e)(1). *See* College v. Turner, 844 N.E.2d 99 (Ind. Ct. App. 2006) (the regulations set out at 34 C.F.R. § 30.60 do not apply if school is collecting Perkins loan and loan has not been assigned to the Department).

145   34 C.F.R. § 674.45(e)(2).

146   34 C.F.R. § 674.47(d).

147   34 C.F.R. § 674.33(a)(4). *See* § 2.7.4, *supra*.

4.4.2 Amount of Collection Fees and How Fees Are Calculated

As described in greater detail below, there are some ceilings on the amounts of collection fees that can be charged. Fees are limited to 18.5% at the time of sale for rehabilitation, and the same limit applies to consolidated loans. Otherwise, the limit is that fees must be "reasonable."[148] Guaranty agencies cannot charge more than what the Department would charge for collection fees.[149]

In determining what is "reasonable," the regulations allow collection charges equaling the costs associated with the collection of a *particular* debt. These costs may include salaries for employees, costs for computer operations and records maintenance, court costs, and attorney costs.

The regulations also set out a formula for computing collection fees as a percentage of the debt *if* a collection agency is hired, based on the contingency fee arrangement contracted with that collection agency. The regulation does *not* authorize a percentage formula if the Department or guaranty agency does not hire an independent collection agency.

If a contingency fee arrangement is used, the regulations allow the Department to compensate collection agencies based on the average cost per borrower rather than the actual fees incurred in collecting from any particular borrower.[150] This percentage or average approach often leads to unfair results since the small number of defaulting consumers from whom recovery is made bear the brunt of all of a creditor's collection expenses. The Department has argued that the "make whole" (making the collection agencies whole) approach is fair because it allows agencies to charge enough to sustain both successful and unsuccessful collections.

A number of recent bankruptcy cases provide additional insight into student loan collection fee calculations.[151] According to a guaranty agency official's testimony in this case, the Department has taken the position that it is more efficient for guaranty agencies to assess percentage-based collection costs than to keep track of every letter and other collection contacts. According to the guaranty agency official, the Secretary of Education has determined that tracking costs of collection of each defaulted loan would create too onerous a system, such a level of specificity would be untenable and inefficient, and such detailed record-keeping would result in far higher collection costs for debtors than percentage-based collection costs. Each dollar recovered by the agency, according to the testimony, is divided between the agency's operating fund and the reserve fund of the federal government. The amounts in the reserve fund are remitted on a regular basis back to the Secretary to fund additional student loans.[152]

The Department of Education has provided a rationale for its collection costs computation methods. The Department argues that "reasonable" collection costs mean an amount that covers all federal collection costs, recovered by a flat rate charge to all paying defaulters.[153] The "make whole" collection method defended by the Department directs guaranty agencies to charge enough for collection costs to sustain both successful and unsuccessful collection activities on all the loans held by the agency.[154] Furthermore, the Department argues that the regulations are reasonable because they impose costs only on borrowers who require effort to collect.[155] According to the Department, borrowers can avoid collection costs by entering into repayment or applying for deferments or forbearances.

In general, the Department argues that estimating costs based on "analyses establishing an average of actual additional costs incurred by the agency in processing and handling claims against other debtors in similar states of delinquency" is a time-honored and reasonable way to determine those estimated costs.[156] According to the Department, averaging eliminates expense tracking and the billing of specific costs to individual debts thus reducing costs for all debtors.[157] The Department acknowledges that averaging may still result in some charges that may exceed the actual costs incurred to collect a debt owed by a particular individual. However, the Department claims that this does not make averaging unreasonable. According to the Department, some differences are *de minimis*. In other cases, below-average costs incurred for some payments will be offset by above-average costs incurred by other recoveries.[158] In sum, the Department argues that the make-whole method solves a very practical problem: "collection action costs money; many debtors are not paying now, and may never pay. The GA cannot cover costs for these non-payers unless it charges those costs to paying debtors. Unless the GA recovers enough to meet its collection costs *and* the principal and interest on the debt, the taxpayer ends up

---

148 20 U.S.C. § 1091a(b)(1); 34 C.F.R. § 682.410(b)(2).

149 34 C.F.R. § 682.410(b)(2).

150 34 C.F.R. § 30.60(d).

151 *In re* Schlehr, 290 B.R. 387 (Bankr. D. Mont. 2003). *See also In re* Evans, 322 B.R. 429 (Bankr. W.D. Wash. 2005); Educational Credit Mgmt. Corp. v. Barnes, 318 B.R. 482 (S.D. Ind. 2004), *aff'd*, Black v. Educational Credit Mgmt., 2006 WL 2358171 (7th Cir. Aug. 16, 2006).

152 *Id.*

153 Memorandum of Points and Authorities Supporting Motion to Dismiss, Hutchins v. United States Dep't of Educ., CV-F-02-6256-OWW-DLB (E.D. Cal. filed Apr. 25, 2003) (citing H.R. Res. 300 99th Cong. (1986), at 396, *reprinted in* 1986 U.S.C.C.A.N. 977). *See also* H.R. 146, 99th Cong. (1986), at 494, *reprinted in* 1986 U.S.C.C.A.N. 453. This document can be found on the companion CD-Rom to this manual.

154 Hutchins v. United States Dep't of Educ., CV-F-02-6256-OWW-DLB, at 22–23 (E.D. Cal. filed Apr. 25, 2003).

155 *Id.* at 25.

156 *Id.* at 27.

157 *Id.* at 29.

158 *Id.*

bearing those costs."[159] This rationale and the Department's approach seem ripe for legal challenge. In particular, a number of bankruptcy trustees have brought actions claiming that student loan collection costs are unreasonable because they are not related to actual costs incurred in the particular borrower's case. To date, these cases have been unsuccessful and the courts have upheld the Department's regulations.[160] One court concluded that Congress intended that borrowers, not taxpayers, should foot student loan collection bills.[161]

State laws that prohibit or limit calculating fees based on an entire portfolio of debts rather than fees incurred in each case may be useful for comparison purposes.[162] For example, Iowa allows a collection agency to collect a fee from the debtor only if the fee is reasonably related to the actions taken by the collector and the collector is legally authorized to collect it.[163]

Assuming that the Department continues to use the "make whole" method, at least until legal challenges are successful, there is still a question as to how much is reasonable for collection agencies to charge. As noted above, there is no numerical limit on collection fees outside of consolidation and rehabilitation. As of 2006, the Department's policy is to charge no more than 25% of outstanding principal and interest as collection fees.

As of 2006, this policy was affirmed on the Department's website:

> Pursuant to the Higher Education Act and the terms of most borrowers' promissory notes, you are liable for the costs of collecting your defaulted Federally-financed student loans. The largest of these costs is usually the cost of contingent fees that may be incurred to collect the loan. The Department gives you repeated warnings before it refers a debt to a collection contractor. If those warnings do not persuade you to reach repayment terms on defaulted loans, the Department refers those loans to collection contractors. The contractors earn a commission, or contingent fee, for any payments then made on those loans. The Department charges each borrower the cost of the commission earned by the contractor, and applies payments from that borrower first to defray the contingent fee earned for that payment, and then to interest and principal owed on the debt. As a result, the amount needed to satisfy a student loan

debt collected by the Department's contractors will be up to 25 percent more than the principal and interest repaid by the borrower. On each billing statement, the Department projects an estimate of the total amount needed to satisfy the debt on the date of the statement, including collection costs that would be incurred by payment in full of that amount.[164]

The 25% ceiling is not a limit set by statute but a result of a settlement in a case, *Gibbons v. Riley*, in which the Department was sued for charging fees beyond those stated in promissory notes.[165] In 1995, borrowers sued the Department for assessing up to 43% collection fees on certain student loan borrowers whose loan notes specified 25% collection fees.[166] The Department admitted that it was in error to systematically charge the higher collection costs to those with the 25% provision in their notes.[167] It also admitted that it had no method for easily distinguishing those with the 25% collection provision from other borrowers.

Under the terms of the settlement agreement, the Department agreed to temporarily assess no more than 25% collection fees on all student loan payments. The agreement specified that this system would stay in place until the Department developed a way of distinguishing between collection fee limits in different loans.

The settlement agreement does not directly bind state guaranty agencies in their assessment of collection fees. However, federal regulations provide that guaranty agencies cannot charge more in collection fees than the Department can charge.[168]

To date, the Department has abided by the *Gibbons* settlement and has not publicly announced or implemented an alternative system.

Regardless of the settlement agreement, the information posted on the Department's website, described above, and testimony of Department officials indicate that the Department sets a collection fee ceiling at 25%.[169]

---

159 *Id.* at 32.

160 *See, e.g., In re* Evans, 322 B.R. 429 (Bankr. W.D. Wash. 2005); Educational Credit Mgmt. Corp. v. Barnes, 318 B.R. 482 (S.D. Ind. 2004), *aff'd*, Black v. Educational Credit Mgmt., 2006 WL 2358171 (7th Cir. Aug. 16, 2006).

161 Educational Credit Mgmt. Corp. v. Barnes, 318 B.R. 482 (S.D. Ind. 2004), *aff'd*, Black v. Educational Credit Mgmt., 2006 WL 2358171 (7th Cir. Aug. 16, 2006).

162 These are discussed in detail in National Consumer Law Center, Fair Debt Collection § 15.2.1 (5th ed. 2004 and Supp.).

163 Iowa Code § 537.7103(5)(c).

164 *Available at* www.ed.gov/offices/OSFAP/DCS/collection.costs.html (last accessed in September 2006).

165 Gibbons v. Riley, (E.D.N.Y. Nov. 9, 1994) (complaint filed).

166 Clearinghouse No. 50,432C (E.D.N.Y. Nov. 9, 1994) (complaint filed).

167 Gibbons v. Riley, Clearinghouse No. 50,432 (E.D.N.Y. 1995) (stipulated extension of time for defendants to respond to complaint). *See also* Letter of Fred J. Marinucci, Deputy Assistant General Counsel, to Andrew J. Cohen, Legal Assistance Foundation of Chicago, Clearinghouse No. 50,423 (Oct. 18, 1994) (Department does not intend to collect any amount in excess of what is allowed by the loan agreement).

168 34 C.F.R. § 682.410(b)(2).

169 *See, e.g., In re* Schlehr, 290 B.R. 387 (Bankr. D. Mont. 2003) (guaranty agency official testified that DOE has set market for contracting out collection to private collection agencies at rate of 25%; according to official, 25% rate is ceiling under regulations at 34 C.F.R. § 30.60, against which all other guaranty agencies are capped; each guaranty agency has to come up with

The limits should be lower than 25% in certain circumstances. When originating a consolidation loan consisting of underlying loans in default, collection costs may be charged in an amount not to exceed 18.5% of the outstanding principal and interest.[170] Lenders automatically add the 18.5% fee to the consolidation. It is theoretically possible to request a waiver of collection fees before consolidation, but a waiver is very unlikely to occur in practice. After the consolidation, the fees become part of the amount due on the new loan.

In an effort to minimize the pressure many collection agencies were placing on borrowers to consolidate, Congress in 2005 set new standards to ensure that consolidation loans are not an excessive proportion of a guaranty agency's recoveries on defaulted loans.[171]

Under the new rules, if a borrower repays a defaulted loan through an FFEL consolidation loan on or after October 1, 2006, collection fees are still capped at 18.5%. However, when returning proceeds to the Department after consolidation, a guaranty agency that charged the borrower collection costs after October 1, 2006, must remit an amount that equals the lesser of the actual collection costs charged or 8.5% of the outstanding principal and interest.[172] By Oct. 1, 2009, guaranty agencies will have to remit the entire collection cost charged when returning proceeds from the consolidation of a defaulted loan that is paid off with excess consolidation proceeds. Excess proceeds means the amount of proceeds from the consolidation of defaulted loans under FFEL that exceed 45% of the agency's total collections on defaulted loans in that fiscal year.[173]

With respect to rehabilitation, collection fees of up to 18.5% of the unpaid principal and accrued interest at the time of sale are added to the new loan.[174] Collection costs should be added to the unpaid principal at the time of sale. The implication is that collection costs should not be added

prior to the sale while the borrower is making the required consecutive monthly payments.[175] However, the Department has claimed that its commission rate on those programs is such that they do not charge the full 18.5%.

Advocates should carefully scrutinize calculation of collection fees. Under current methodology used by at least some guarantors, it is also critical to determine how the guarantor applies the student's payment between collection fees, interest, and principal. If more than the pro-rata share goes to collection fees, then the amount the student must pay in interest for the exact same loan will be greater than if the Department holds the loan.[176]

4.4.3 Avoiding Collection Fees

There is no easy way to take an account away from a collection agency and avoid the collection fees. The fees will be assessed even if a borrower attempts to pay the Department directly. One exception is that no collection fees are assessed on amounts seized from tax refunds. Consequently, a borrower may be better off arranging to have a large tax refund due, and having that amount intercepted, rather than paying off the loan directly to a collection agency.

In general, funds from tax intercepts should be applied to principal and interest, not to collection fees.[177] Thus, the balance will decrease more rapidly through tax intercepts than through low monthly payment plans. Borrowers choosing this strategy should wait until the funds taken from the tax intercepts leave them with a small balance left on their loans. Once the borrower has paid down to a small balance, exclusive of collection fees, the Department will frequently agree at this point to compromise the remaining balance and accept a lump sum payment.[178] The Department will usually waive the collection fees when the principal and interest is paid in full. This strategy saves borrowers from paying the

own percentage-based collection costs based on actual expenses, which cannot exceed Department's own 25% ceiling). *See also* Educational Credit Mgmt. Corp. v. Barnes, 318 B.R. 482 (S.D. Ind. 2004), *aff'd*, Black v. Educational Credit Mgmt., 2006 WL 2358171 (7th Cir. Aug. 16, 2006); *In re* Evans, 322 B.R. 429 (Bankr. W.D. Wash. 2005); 61 Fed. Reg. 47398 (Sept. 6, 1996). The Department affirmed in a January 2006 letter that it is continuing to allow no more than 25%. U.S. Dep't of Educ., Federal Student Aid, Borrower Services-Collection Group, FY 06 Collection Costs on Defaulted Loans held by Department of Education and Managed by Borrower Services-Collections Group" (Jan. 2006) (the letter is on file with NCLC).

170 34 C.F.R. § 685.220(f)(iii) (authorizes collection costs to be charged in the same way as in the FFEL program). *See* 34 C.F.R. § 682.401(b)(27) (FFEL); George W. v. United States Dep't of Educ., 149 F. Supp. 2d 1195 (E.D. Cal. 2000) (plaintiff's claim that even the 18.5% limit may be unreasonable was dismissed on procedural grounds).

171 Pub. L. No. 109-171, 120 Stat. 4 (Feb. 8, 2006), *amending* 20 U.S.C. § 1078.

172 34 C.F.R. § 682.401(b)(27).

173 *Id.*

174 34 C.F.R. § 682.405(b)(1)(iv).

175 *See generally* § 8.4, *infra*.

176 Greater amounts violate 34 C.F.R. § 682.410(b)(2).

177 The Department of Treasury regulations on tax intercepts specify only that offsets can be allocated for past due debts, less fees charged under 31 C.F.R. § 285.2(i). This section allows fees charged by the Financial Management Service (FMS) of the Department of Treasury and the IRS to be deducted from the amount collected. To the extent allowed by law, federal agencies may add these fees to the debt. Still, the fees deducted, if any, should be less than those charged by collection agencies. *See generally* § 5.2, *infra*.

178 *See* §§ 4.4.1, 4.4.2, *supra*. *See also* U.S. Dep't of Educ., *Amendment to Agreement Pursuant to Section 428(b) of the Higher Education Act of 1965, as amended, with a State or Private Non-Profit Institution or Organization for Coverage of its Student Loan Insurance Program under the Interest Benefits Provision of Section 428(a) of the Act*, Appendix I § 5.1, Clearinghouse No. 51,926 (July 11, 1994) (if borrower agrees to pay principal within thirty days, agency may enter into a repayment agreement that includes the compromise of interest owed).

huge collection fees that accrue once an account is turned over to a collection agency.[179]

However, collection fees may even show up in offset notices. In fact, only minimal administrative fees should be charged in connection with offsets. The Department may, however, continue to seek voluntary payments by assigning files to collection agencies even when involuntary collection methods, such as offset, are in place.

There are a number of potential challenges to this practice. First, at least as a policy matter, the Department should not continue to send accounts to private collection agencies when involuntary collection methods are in place. This is particularly true for low-income borrowers who have no other assets or income. Second, even if the account is placed with a private agency, the collection fees should not show up on an offset notice because collection fees are not applied to the offset amount.

There are at least three other strategies a borrower can use to avoid paying collection costs once a loan has been turned over to a collection agency. The most complete remedy is to try to cancel the borrower's obligation on the loan. This can be done through a false-certification, unpaid-refund, or closed-school discharge; through a bankruptcy discharge; through raising school-related defenses on the loan; or if the student is totally and permanently disabled.[180] Making payments through a chapter 13 bankruptcy plan may also avoid collection fees.[181]

If the borrower is not eligible for cancellation, another possible solution is to consolidate the defaulted loan into a new Direct or FFEL loan. The consolidation loan will include an 18.5% collection fee from the old loan, but no further amounts will go to collection fees unless the consolidated loan goes into default.[182]

Third, the borrower can complain about the collection agency's illegal or improper conduct to the Department. The Department will sometimes take the loan away from the collector.[183]

4.4.4 United States Collection of Other Fees and Penalties

In some cases, the United States or private attorneys hired by the United States to collect on student loans attempt to collect court filing fees and penalties in addition to attorney fees and collection costs.[184] Because such collection actions are usually uncontested, those fees are rarely questioned. The reality is that the United States may lack statutory authority to collect these amounts. For example, the United States need not pay filing fees, so any attempt to collect this amount, even by a private attorney collecting on behalf of the government, should be improper.[185]

Another dubious fee is a 6%-per-year penalty. Authority for this fee is explicitly found in federal regulations that allow the Secretary to impose a 6%-per-year penalty on the amount delinquent if the debtor does not make at least a partial payment on a debt within ninety days of the Secretary's demand for payment.[186]

However, the 6% penalty should not be a factor in the student loan context because it does not apply to obligations when either federal regulations or the loan agreement explicitly fixes the interest.[187] Since student loans charge interest while they are in default, the 6% penalty does not apply.[188] In addition, the penalty does not apply to loans executed before October 25, 1982.[189]

The Department appears to agree that it does not have authority to seek this fee because the promissory note limits the fees that may be charged the student. Nevertheless, certain pre-1986 NDSLs (now termed Perkins loans) did specify a certain penalty or late charge in the promissory note.

Another federal statute, the Federal Debt Collection Procedures Act authorizes the United States to recover a surcharge of 10% of the amount of the debt when collecting on the debt using pre-judgment remedies (such as attachment) or post-judgment remedies (such as writs of execution).[190] However, the statute does not apply to litigation to obtain a judgment on the debt, and the United States cannot assess the surcharge based on such litigation.[191]

179 See §§ 4.4.1, 4.4.2, supra.
180 See generally Chs. 6 (loan cancellations), 7 (bankruptcy), infra.
181 See § 7.4, infra.
182 34 C.F.R. § 685.220(f)(iii), using amount in 34 C.F.R. § 682.401(b)(27) (FFEL). See §§ 8.2.3.2, 8.2.4, infra.
183 See § 4.5.5.2, supra.
184 See United States v. Singer, 943 F. Supp. 9 (D.D.C. 1996), aff'd in part, rev'd in part, 132 F.3d 1482 (D.C. Cir. 1997) (Department confessed error and the district court's ordering of 10% surcharge to Department as fees was reversed on appeal);
United States v. Smith, 862 F. Supp. 257 (D. Haw. 1994); United States v. Spann, 797 F. Supp. 980 (S.D. Fla. 1992).
185 United States v. Spann, 797 F. Supp. 980 (S.D. Fla. 1992).
186 34 C.F.R. § 30.61(a). The authority for this regulation is 31 U.S.C. § 3717(e)(2).
187 31 U.S.C. § 3717(g)(1).
188 See United States v. Spann, 797 F. Supp. 980 (S.D. Fla. 1992).
189 31 U.S.C. § 3717(g)(2).
190 28 U.S.C. § 3011.
191 United States v. Singer, 943 F. Supp. 9 (D.D.C. 1996), aff'd in part, rev'd in part, 132 F.3d 1482 (D.C. Cir. 1997) (Department confessed error and the district court's ordering of 10% surcharge to Department as fees was reversed on appeal); United States v. Smith, 862 F. Supp. 257 (D. Haw. 1994) (proceeding did not involve pre- or post-judgment remedies and therefore government not entitled to 10% surcharge); United States v. Mauldin, 805 F. Supp. 35 (N.D. Ala. 1992).

4.5 Deceptive and Abusive Debt Collection Tactics

4.5.1 Factors That Foster Deception and Abuse in Student Loan Collections

The Department has turned over almost all student loans it holds to private collection agencies. According to a 2006 letter, the Department places about 95% of the defaulted FFEL loans it holds with private collection agencies.[192] Almost all guaranty agencies are doing the same. Consequently, one significant form of student loan collection is dunning letters and other contacts from private collection agencies.[193]

Student loan debt collection contacts, both by private collectors and guarantors, involve a remarkable amount of deceptive, unfair, and illegal conduct. There are several reasons for the extent of these abusive collection actions:

- Millions of student loan obligations are being handled on a "wholesale" basis, with little or no attention being paid to the facts of the individual borrower being dunned.
- Remedies available to collect on student loans are often both unique and misunderstood (for example, federal tax refund intercepts, federal benefits offsets, and non-judicial garnishments), and collectors often misrepresent the exact nature of these remedies when they send collection letters. By all reports, much false information is provided.
- The complexity of the student loan programs leads to much confusion about who is collecting on a debt and makes it easy for an independent collector to misrepresent itself as the government.[194]
- Private collection agencies are delegated the responsibility for determining the size of a reasonable and affordable payment plan. In addition, these collection agencies help determine if students have defenses to wage garnishments and tax refund intercepts, even though the collection agencies' financial incentive is

not to offer reasonable and affordable plans or to acknowledge defenses.[195]
- There appears to be minimal government oversight of collection agencies unrelated to amounts recovered.

For example, in a December 2003 audit report, the Department of Education's Office of Inspector General (OIG) found that the Department's Federal Student Aid Division needed to improve its monitoring of private collection agencies.[196] The OIG reviewed five of the Department's private collection agency contracts and found that the Department did not perform effective monitoring in the following five key areas: (1) tracking complaints; (2) performing desk audits; (3) conducting site visits for technical assistance and trainings; (4) reviewing deliverables; and (5) maintaining contract files. As a result, according to the OIG, the Department was not able to determine whether the contractors complied with the federal debt collection practices act and the Department policies, practices, and contract terms.[197]

The Department frequently cites a low volume of complaints to support its claims of effective oversight. This is troubling in light of the OIG's findings that the Department is not doing an effective job of collecting and tracking complaints. Furthermore, the OIG was unable to determine the resolutions for about 98% of the complaints that were actually logged. The Department claims to be addressing these problems.[198]
- It is very difficult for borrowers to persuade collectors to either suspend collection after a dispute or to return the file to the guaranty agency or Department to resolve disputes. This is the case even though the Department advises its collectors that they should immediately suspend collection activity on an account and refer the issue to the Department or the Department's representative within five days after the borrower disputes the amount owed, raises a legal defense against repayment, or requests a written review or hearing in response to offset or garnishment notice.[199]

---

192 U.S. Dep't of Educ., Federal Student Aid, Borrower Services-Collection Group, FY 06 Collection Costs on Defaulted Loans held by Department of Education and Managed by Borrower Services-Collections Group (Jan. 2006). The letter is on file with NCLC.

193 All guidance from the Department to private collection agencies can be found at www.fsacollections.ed.gov/contractors/pca2004/index.html.

194 *See* Peter v. GC Serv., L.P., 310 F.3d 344 (5th Cir. 2002) (debt collector's use of a Department of Education return address on a student loan collection letter violated the Fair Debt Collection Practices Act); Brider v. Nationwide Credit, 1998 WL 729747 (N.D. Ill. June 24, 1998) (denying motion to dismiss of collector whose collection letter had large bold heading "U.S. Department of Education").

---

195 *See, e.g.,* Arroyo v. Solomon & Solomon, 2001 U.S. Dist. LEXIS 21908 (E.D.N.Y. Nov. 16, 2001) (defendant's summary judgment motion denied in case alleging, among other FDCPA violations, that defendants demanded payments in amount more than borrower could reasonably afford).

196 U.S. Dep't of Educ., Office of Inspector Gen., Final Audit Report, Control #ED-OIG/A19-D0002, Dec. 23, 2003.

197 *Id.*

198 *Id.*

199 U.S. Dep't of Educ., *Agency Review Guide: Internal Procedures for Evaluating Private Collection Agencies (PCAs)* 48 (June 15, 2005), *available at* www.fsacollections.ed.gov/contractors/pca2004/virtual_library/2005%20Agency%20Review%20Guide%206-29-05.doc.

4.5.2 Common Student Loan Debt Collection Abuses

4.5.2.1 Violations Unique to Student Loans

The special rules governing student loan collections lead to a number of collection abuses. This section discusses common fair debt collection violations, followed by a discussion of whether the FDCPA and state debt collection laws apply in the student loan context.

Student loan borrowers may receive dunning letters threatening that the Department will garnish their wages without "legal action." These letters imply that the former student will receive no notice before the wage garnishment and that there will be no opportunity either to contest the validity of the student loan or to present defenses. In truth, the statute and regulations require both notice and an opportunity for an administrative hearing before an employer may be ordered to withhold any wages.[200]

Failure to comply with HEA regulations with respect to garnishment hearing, notice, and venue requirements are all possible federal and state fair debt or UDAP violations.[201]

Collectors may misrepresent a student's ability to obtain a closed-school, unpaid-refund, or false-certification discharge. Collection agencies make no commissions from those obtaining the discharge, while they recover a set percentage on any payments made. These collectors thus have an incentive to discourage discharge applications. For this reason, the Department instructs them not to make any kind of determination concerning a student's eligibility but instead to refer queries related to closed-school, false-certification, or unpaid-refund discharges.[202]

There is considerable confusion as well with respect to federal benefits offsets.[203] For example, borrowers have reported numerous instances of collectors threatening to offset benefits even if the borrower receives SSI payments only. In fact, SSI benefits are completely exempt from offset.[204]

In May 2005, in response to complaints about collection agency threats to seize SSI, the Department sent the following e-mail message to collection contract administrators:

> This is to remind you that Supplement Security Income (SSI) benefits are NOT subject to Treasury offset. These are different from the Social Security Disability benefits that may be subject to offset, under certain conditions. If a borrower advises that their only source of income is SSI, you should not be advising them that this may be offset.
>
> It has been reported that PCA collectors have been misinforming borrowers that their SSI benefits will be offset. This is causing anxiety and distress for these borrowers and has also resulted in complaints due to this misinformation. Please remind your staff immediately concerning this issue.

Borrowers have also reported that the Department routinely continues collection even after borrowers have submitted disability discharge applications. This practice also clearly violates Department regulations.[205]

In addition, collection agencies frequently mislead borrowers with respect to repayment options. In particular, agencies are often very aggressive in steering borrowers into loan consolidation or loan rehabilitation programs. These repayment strategies, as described in detail in Chapter 8, *infra*, benefit many, but not all, borrowers.

At least some industry commentators advise student loan collection companies against pushing consolidation. They point out that consolidation is not actually "collecting" but rather "shuffling dollars from one side of the government's

---

200 Cliff v. Payco Gen. Am. Credits, Inc., 363 F.3d 1113 (11th Cir. 2004) (student loan borrowers allowed to bring claims under state and federal fair debt laws that, among other violations, collection agency falsely represented the claim, amount, or status of the debt; falsely represented or implied that non-payment would result in garnishment; and failed to provide pre-garnishment hearing). The district court granted summary judgment to the collection agency on plaintiff's claim that the agency's notice contained misinformation about the HEA unemployment exemption. The court found that the agency was insulated from liability under the FDCPA's bona fide error defense. The Seventh Circuit agreed. Kort v. Diversified Collection Servs., Inc., 270 F. Supp. 2d 1017 (N.D. Ill. 2003), *aff'd*, 394 F.3d 530 (7th Cir. 2005). *See* Sanders v. OSI Educ. Servs., Inc., 2001 WL 883608 (N.D. Ill. Aug. 3, 2001) (granting class certification based on borrowers' allegations that student loan debt collector violated the Fair Debt Collection Practices Act). *See also* Kort v. Diversified Collection Servs., 2001 WL 88149 (N.D. Ill. Aug. 2, 2001), *class cert. granted in part*, 2001 WL 1617213 (N.D. Ill. Dec. 17, 2001) (denying class certification on plaintiffs' FDCPA claim regarding alleged insufficient time to respond to garnishment notice, but granting class certification on claim that defendants violated the FDCPA by falsely representing that borrowers have an affirmative duty to supply "written proof" of employment history to take advantage of garnishment exception). The court granted summary judgment on plaintiff's claim that the collection letter in this case would cause an unsophisticated consumer to believe that a wage garnishment could occur before expiration of the thirty-day-notice period required by the HEA. Kort v. Diversified Collection Serv., Inc., 270 F. Supp. 2d 1017 (N.D. Ill. 2003). Both cases raised FDCPA violations related to defendants' requiring borrowers to affirmatively prove the exception to garnishment for borrowers who have been involuntarily separated from employment. *See* §§ 5.3.2.1, 5.3.3.1, *infra*.

201 *See, e.g.*, Cliff v. Payco Gen. Am. Credits, Inc., 363 F.3d 1113 (11th Cir. 2004).

202 *Guidelines for Contract Collection Agencies Regarding Treatment of Borrowers Who Claim Relief Against Repayment Due to Closed School or False Certification*, Clearinghouse No. 51,942. *See generally* Ch. 6 (student loan discharges), *infra*.

203 *See* § 5.4, *infra*.

204 *See* § 5.4.1, *infra*.

205 34 C.F.R. § 682.402(c)(1)(iii)(C)(2). *See* § 6.6.5, *infra*.

books to the other."[206] There are also reports that guaranty agencies have begun to realize the drawbacks to consolidation and are reducing fees paid to collection agencies.[207] The Department advises its collectors that they must "truthfully and fully counsel borrowers about [consolidation] advantages, disadvantages and ramifications."[208] In an effort to minimize the pressure many collection agencies were placing on borrowers to consolidate, Congress in 2005 set new standards to ensure that consolidation loans are not an excessive proportion of a guaranty agency's recoveries on defaulted loans.[209]

As discussed in Chapter 8, *infra*, borrowers are also entitled to renew eligibility for financial assistance by making six consecutive reasonable and affordable payments. Here, too, borrowers report frequent misrepresentations. Most commonly, collection agencies will insist, in violation of the federal statute and regulations, that borrowers are required to make minimum monthly payments.[210]

Collectors that charge excessive collection fees may also violate the FDCPA.[211] Collectors that use the Department of Education's name and/or address on the envelope or otherwise deceive borrowers into thinking they are receiving communications from the Department have also been found to be in violation of the FDCPA.[212]

False representation of the amount of any debt should also be grounds for state and/or federal fair debt collection practices violations. These claims may arise in a number of ways, including improper calculation of collection fees and improper crediting of payments. In one case, borrowers successfully argued that the collector's crediting of payments to debtors' accounts on dates after the date of receipt of payment or after the date judgment was entered violated

the fair debt laws.[213] Borrowers argued that, among other violations, the collector's notices contained false statements because the amount listed as due contained improper interest charges attributable to improper crediting practices.[214]

Widespread complaints about student loan collection activity are leading to more litigation. For example, one debt collector was required to pay the maximum $1000 Fair Debt Collection Practices Act (FDCPA) statutory damages and, under state law claims, another $1153 in actual damages and $60,000 in punitive damages for contacting the borrower even after the borrower and the borrower's attorney had advised the collector that the debt had been discharged in bankruptcy.[215] In addition, a number of class actions have been brought in this area.[216]

Private FDCPA actions are in many cases the only way borrowers can get relief when collectors violate Department

---

206 *See* Todd Wolfe, *Student Loan Collection Professionals Face Special Challenges* (Dec. 5, 2002), *at* www.CollectionIndustry.com.

207 *Id. See* § 4.4, *supra*.

208 U.S. Dep't of Educ., *Agency Review Guide: Internal Procedures for Evaluating Private Collection Agencies (PCAs)* 57 (June 15, 2005), *available at* www.fsacollections.ed.gov/contractors/pca2004/virtual_library/2005%20Agency%20Review%20Guide%206-29-05.doc.

209 Pub. L. No. 109-171, 120 Stat. 4 (Feb. 8, 2006), *amending* 20 U.S.C. § 1078. *See* § 4.4.2, *supra*.

210 Misrepresentations about reasonable and affordable payment plans may violate the FDCPA. *See* Arroyo v. Solomon &Solomon, 2001 U.S. Dist. LEXIS 21908 (E.D.N.Y. Nov. 16, 2001) (defendant's summary judgment motion denied in case alleging, among other FDCPA violations, that defendants demanded payments in amounts more than borrower could reasonably afford). *See* § 8.3, *infra*.

211 *See, e.g.*, Padilla v. Payco Gen. Am. Credits, Inc., 161 F. Supp. 2d 264 (S.D.N.Y. 2001) (plaintiff's summary judgment motion granted on claim that collection agency charged fees above the 18.5% allowable limit).

212 *See* Peter v. GC Serv., L.P., 310 F.3d 344 (5th Cir. 2002) (debt collector's use of a Department of Education return address on a student loan collection letter violated the Fair Debt Collection Practices Act).

213 Asch v. Teller, Levit & Silvertrust, P.C., 2003 WL 22232801 (N.D. Ill. Sept. 26, 2003) (borrowers granted summary judgment under federal and state fair debt collection practices laws). In a later ruling, the court granted plaintiff's request for an injunction to prohibit defendants from collecting on accounts affected by defendants' failure to credit payments. Asch v. Teller, Levit & Silvertrust, P.C., 2004 WL 2967441 (N.D. Ill. Nov. 24, 2004) (granting in part and denying in part plaintiff's motion for further summary judgment).

214 *Id.*

215 Miele v. Sid Bailey, Inc., 192 B.R. 611 (S.D.N.Y. 1996). *See also* Padilla v. Payco Gen. Am. Credits, Inc., 161 F. Supp. 2d 264 (S.D.N.Y. 2001) (numerous FDCPA violations raised including charging of excessive collection fees and illegal contacts with the borrower).

216 *See, e.g.*, Kort v. Diversified Collection Servs., Inc., 2001 WL 88149 (N.D. Ill. Aug. 2, 2001), *class cert. granted in part*, 2001 WL 1617213 (N.D. Ill. Dec. 17, 2001) (collector allegedly violated FDCPA by giving borrowers insufficient time to respond to wage garnishment notices and by requiring affirmative proof of unemployment exception to garnishment). The court granted summary judgment on plaintiff's claim that the collection letter in this case would cause an unsophisticated consumer to believe that a wage garnishment could occur before expiration of the thirty-day notice period required by the HEA. Kort v. Diversified Collection Serv., Inc., 270 F. Supp. 2d 1017 (N.D. Ill. 2003). The district court granted summary judgment to the collection agency on plaintiff's claim that the agency's notice contained misinformation about the HEA unemployment exemption. The court found that the agency was insulated from liability under the FDCPA's bona fide error defense. The Seventh Circuit agreed. Kort v. Diversified Collection Servs., Inc., 270 F. Supp. 2d 1017 (N.D. Ill. 2003), *aff'd*, 394 F.3d 530 (7th Cir. 2005); Sanders v. OSI, 2001 WL 883608 (N.D. Ill. Aug. 3, 2001) (similar FDCPA violations alleged as those in *Kort*); Cliff v. Payco Gen. Am. Credits, Inc., Clearinghouse No. 52,132 (M.D. Fla. 1998) (class action complaint) (suit alleges violation of due process rights in collection agencies' administration of wage garnishment procedures); Mitchell v. Educational Credit Mgmt. Corp., Clearinghouse No. 52,038 (N.D. Ill. Oct. 14, 1997) (complaint-class action); Sibley v. Diversified Collection Servs., Clearinghouse No. 51,930 (N.D. Tex. Apr. 26, 1996) (first amended complaint—class action). Sample pleadings in cases challenging private collection agency conduct can be found at Appendix E, *infra*.

of Education collection regulations. Borrowers generally do not have a private right of action under the HEA.[217] However, a collector's failure to follow the law or a collector's misrepresentation of applicable law may violate the FDCPA.

There are limits to using fair debt claims to resolve student loan disputes. The FDCPA is an indirect way of obtaining relief. It is intended to address collection abuses. A collection agency's failure to offer a particular repayment plan or otherwise comply with the HEA is a violation. However, the available remedies are monetary damages. These can be extremely useful, but they do not help borrowers get the repayment plans or discharges to which they are entitled. Advocates that bring these cases should try to directly assist borrowers using the other strategies discussed in this manual or refer borrowers for assistance.

4.5.2.2 Illegal Debt Collection Activity Not Unique to Student Loans

The previous subsection outlined some special forms of illegal debt collection conduct relating solely to student loans. In addition, collectors may engage in a number of other basic forms of illegal debt collection practices that apply to collection of any type of consumer debt.

This subsection briefly lists a number of practices that are prohibited under the federal Fair Debt Collection Practices Act and can lead to actions for actual damages, up to $1000 in statutory damages, plus attorney fees.[218]

The following are examples of fair debt collection standards:

- The collection agency must stop contacting the student if the student so requests in writing.[219]
- The collection agency, in its initial communication or within five days of that communication, must send the student a written notice identifying the debt and the creditor and giving the student the right to dispute the debt or to request the name and address of the original creditor, if different from the current one. If the student raises a dispute, the collector must suspend collection efforts on the disputed portion of the debt until the

collector responds to the request.[220]

The following collection agency conduct also violates the FDCPA:

- Communicating with third parties, such as relatives, employers, friends, or neighbors, about a debt unless the student or a court has given the collector permission to do so. Several narrow exceptions to this prohibition apply. Collectors may contact creditors, attorneys, credit reporting agencies, co-signers, spouses, and parents if the student is a minor. Third-party contacts are also permitted if the contacts are solely for the purpose of locating the student and do not reveal in any way the contact's underlying purpose.[221]
- Communicating with the student at unusual or inconvenient times or places. The times 8:00 a.m. to 9:00 p.m. are generally considered convenient, but daytime contacts with a consumer known to work a night shift may be inconvenient.[222]
- Contacting a student at work if the collector should know that the employer prohibits personal calls, or contacting the student at other inconvenient places, such as a friend's house or the hospital.[223]
- Contacting a student represented by a lawyer, unless the lawyer gives permission for the communication or fails to respond to the collector's communications.[224]
- Using obscene, profane, or abusive language.[225]
- Telephoning repeatedly and frequently with intent to annoy, abuse, or harass the student or other persons at the called number.[226]
- Telephoning without disclosing the collector's identity.[227]
- Making false, misleading or deceptive representations in collecting debts, such as pretending that letters carry legal authority or are from the government.[228]
- Falsely representing the character, amount, or legal status of a debt or of services rendered or compensation owed.[229]
- Falsely stating or implying a lawyer's involvement,

---

217 *See* § 9.3.3.1, *infra.*

218 For more detail, the best resource is National Consumer Law Center's *Fair Credit Reporting* (5th ed. 2002 and Supp.), which details what general collection practices are prohibited and available consumer remedies for such violations.

219 15 U.S.C. § 1692c(c). This provision, in particular, has been cited by collection agencies lobbying Congress to exempt student loan collectors from FDCPA coverage. They point out the conflict between federal student assistance due diligence provisions that require minimum contacts and the FDCPA prohibition against contacting borrowers in certain circumstances. Consumer advocates have responded with alternatives, including exempting collectors from the due diligence contact requirements in these cases, in lieu of wholesale exemption from the FDCPA. This issue is likely to arise again in future legislative sessions.

220 15 U.S.C. § 1692g. *See* Avila v. Rubin, 84 F.3d 222 (7th Cir. 1996) (student loan collector liable when other language overshadowed validation notice).

221 15 U.S.C. §§ 1692b, 1692c(b).

222 15 U.S.C. § 1692c(a)(1).

223 15 U.S.C. § 1692c(a)(3).

224 15 U.S.C. § 1692c(a)(2). *See* Alger v. Ganick, O'Brien & Sarin, 35 F. Supp. 2d 148 (D. Mass. 1999) (contact with represented student loan debtor would be FDCPA violation).

225 15 U.S.C. § 1692d(2).

226 15 U.S.C. § 1692d(5).

227 15 U.S.C. § 1692d(6).

228 15 U.S.C. § 1692e(1), (4), (9), (10), (13). *See* Brider v. Nationwide Credit, 1998 U.S. Dist. LEXIS 22535 (N.D. Ill. June 24, 1998) (denying motion to dismiss of collector whose collection letter had large bold heading "U.S. Department of Education").

229 15 U.S.C. § 1692e(2)(A), (10).

such as form letters written on an attorney's letterhead and bearing an attorney's signature that in fact came from a collection agency and were not reviewed by a lawyer.[230]

- Stating that nonpayment will result in arrest, garnishment, or seizure of property or wages, unless such actions are lawful, and unless the loan holder fully intends to take such action.[231]
- Using any false representation or other deception to collect or attempt to collect any debt or to obtain information about the student.[232]
- Failing to disclose in communications that the collector is attempting to collect a debt.[233]
- Using unfair or unconscionable means to collect debts.[234]
- Collecting fees or charges unless expressly authorized by the agreement creating the debt or permitted by law.[235]

4.5.3 Applicability of the FDCPA to Student Loan Collection Activity

4.5.3.1 General

The federal Fair Debt Collection Practices Act (FDCPA) is the main statute offering students protection from debt collection harassment.[236] The statute specifies numerous prohibited collection techniques, provides debtors with certain rights, and provides students with statutory and actual damages and attorney fees for violations.[237]

The key FDCPA issue for students is whether the Act applies to student loan collection activities. If it does, a student's attorney will often be able to pinpoint FDCPA violations leading to significant recoveries.

The FDCPA applies to collection of "debts" by "debt collectors." "Debt" is defined as "any obligation or alleged obligation of a consumer to pay money arising out of a transaction in which the money, property, insurance, or services that are the subject of the transaction are primarily for personal, family, or household purposes, whether or not such obligation has been reduced to judgment."[238] There is no question that student loan debts fall within this definition.[239]

More controversial, however, is the question of whether an entity seeking to collect a student loan debt meets the FDCPA definition of "debt collector." The basic definition of "debt collector" is "any person who uses any instrumentality of interstate commerce or the mails in any business the principal purpose of which is the collection of any debts, or who regularly collects or attempts to collect, directly or indirectly, debts owed or due or asserted to be owed or due another."[240] There are many qualifications and exceptions to this definition. The analysis varies significantly depending on whether the entity is a private collector or attorney, a nonprofit guarantor, a state agency, or the Department.

If any of these entities are considered "debt collectors," the FDCPA should apply. As one court noted, there is no reason to assume that, given the congressional interest in student loan collection (in this case through wage garnishment), Congress would want to see collection efforts proceeding in an abusive and unfair manner that would otherwise run afoul of the FDCPA.[241]

Another key issue is whether an entity may evade liability by arguing that a violation occurred due to a bona fide error.[242] Debt collectors are not liable under the FDCPA if they can show by a preponderance of evidence that the violation was not intentional and resulted from a bona fide error notwithstanding the maintenance of procedures reasonably adapted to avoid any such error.[243]

---

230 15 U.S.C. § 1692e(3), (10). *See* Avila v. Rubin, 84 F.3d 222 (2d Cir. 1996) (collection letters on attorney's letterhead to student loan debtor misrepresented attorney's involvement).

231 *Id.*

232 15 U.S.C. § 1692e(10). *See* Alger v. Ganick, O'Brien & Sarin, 35 F. Supp. 2d 148 (D. Mass. 1999) (false statements to court that student loan debtor had not been making payments).

233 15 U.S.C. § 1692e(11).

234 15 U.S.C. § 1692f. *See* Alger v. Ganick, O'Brien & Sarin, 35 F. Supp. 2d 148 (D. Mass. 1999) (falsely telling process server that student loan debt was unpaid and instructing him to notify debtor to appear in court would be violation).

235 15 U.S.C. § 1692f(1). *See* Padilla v. Payco Gen. Am. Credits, Inc., 161 F. Supp. 2d 264 (S.D.N.Y. 2001) (plaintiff's summary judgment motion granted on claim that collection agency charged fees above the 18.5% allowable limit); Alger v. Ganick, O'Brien & Sarin, 35 F. Supp. 2d 148 (D. Mass. 1999) (instructing process server to demand inflated amount on student loan debt would be violation).

236 15 U.S.C. § 1692–1692o.

237 The Act is examined in great detail in another NCLC manual, *Fair Debt Collection* (4th ed. 2000 and Supp.).

238 15 U.S.C. § 1692a(5).

239 Brannan v. United Student Aid Funds, Inc., 94 F.3d 1260 (9th Cir. 1996), *cert. denied*, 521 U.S. 1111 (1997); Juras v. Aman Collection Serv., Inc., 829 F.2d 739 (9th Cir. 1987), *cert. denied*, 488 U.S. 875 (1988); McComas v. Financial Collection Agencies, 1997 U.S. Dist. LEXIS 2725 (S.D. W. Va. Mar. 7, 1997); Beaulieu v. American Nat'l Educ. Corp., CV 79-L-271, Clearinghouse No. 30,892 (D. Neb. 1981); Carrigan v. Central Adjustment Bureau, Inc., 494 F. Supp. 824 (N.D. Ga. 1980); FTC Official Staff Commentary on the FDCPA § 803(5), 53 Fed. Reg. 50097, 50102 (Dec. 13, 1988) [reprinted in National Consumer Law Center, Fair Debt Collection Appx. C (5th ed. 2004 and Supp.)].

240 15 U.S.C. § 1692a(6).

241 Kort v. Diversified Collection Serv., Inc., 270 F. Supp. 2d 1017 (N.D. Ill. 2003).

242 Kort v. Diversified Collection Servs., Inc., 394 F.3d 530 (7th Cir. 2005).

243 15 U.S.C. § 1692k(c). *See* National Consumer Law Center, Fair Debt Collection § 7.5 (5th ed. 2004 and Supp.).

4.5.3.2 Independent Collection Agencies and Attorneys

Independent collection agencies present the clearest example of coverage. There should be little question that an independent collection agency is covered by the FDCPA.[244] The FDCPA also applies to attorneys hired to sue or collect on student loans.[245] The FDCPA exception for "any officer or employee of the United States or any State"[246] does not apply to these collectors, since they are not governmental employees but private parties who have governmental contracts.[247]

Although they may acknowledge that they are generally covered by the FDCPA, private collectors may also claim that they are not subject to the FDCPA in cases in which the FDCPA prohibits behavior that is required pursuant to HEA

due diligence collection rules.[248] At least one court concluded that it may be appropriate for specific provisions of the HEA to qualify specific provisions of the FDCPA. However, where the HEA is silent, the court gave full effect to the FDCPA.[249] However, the court also found that the collection agency was not liable for one of the FDCPA violations because it was a bona fide error.[250] The key issue is whether a collector can comply with both the HEA and debt collection laws simultaneously. If so, there should be no conflict with the FDCPA and no preemption of state laws.[251] In cases in which conflicts may arise, the courts are likely to find that the HEA requirements take precedence.[252]

4.5.3.3 Department of Education Employees

The FDCPA specifically excludes any officer or employee of the United States or any state to the extent that their activities are in the performance of their official duties.[253] A court may also find that the Department is not a debt collector within the FDCPA definition because the collection of debts is not a principal purpose of its business and the Department is arguably collecting its own debts and not the debts of another.[254]

244　31 U.S.C. § 3718(a)(2); Cliff v. Payco Gen. Am. Credits, Inc., 363 F.3d 1113 (11th Cir. 2004) (the Secretary of Education has expressed the belief that third-party debt collectors acting on behalf of guaranty agencies to collect federal student loans come within the FDCPA); Kort v. Diversified Collection Serv., 270 F. Supp. 2d 1017 (N.D. Ill. 2003). The district court granted summary judgment to the collection agency on plaintiff's claim that the agency's notice contained misinformation about the HEA unemployment exemption. The court found that the agency was insulated from liability under the FDCPA's bona fide error defense. The Seventh Circuit agreed. Kort v. Diversified Collection Servs., Inc., 270 F. Supp. 2d 1017 (N.D. Ill. 2003), aff'd, 394 F.3d 530 (7th Cir. 2005); Richardson v. Baker, 663 F. Supp. 651 (S.D.N.Y. 1987) (FDCPA applies to collector servicing a tax intercept for the Department of Education); Marritz, FTC Informal Staff Letter (Nov. 6, 1978), *available at* National Consumer Law Center, Fair Debt Collection Appx. B (5th ed. 2004 and Supp) and on the companion CD-Rom to manual. For a good discussion on using the FDCPA in student loan cases, see *Arroyo v. Solomon & Solomon*, 2001 U.S. Dist. LEXIS 21908 (E.D.N.Y. Nov. 16, 2001).

245　Asch v. Teller, Levit & Silvertrust, P.C., 2003 WL 22232801 (N.D. Ill. Sept. 26, 2003) (borrowers granted summary judgment under federal and state fair debt collection practices laws). Defendant law firm collectors were collaterally estopped from contesting liability in a later lawsuit brought under the federal False Claims Act. Alger v. Ganick, O'Brien & Sarin, 35 F. Supp. 2d 148 (D. Mass. 1999); Knight v. Schulman, 102 F. Supp. 2d 867 (S.D. Ohio 1999). *See* United States v. Teller, Levit & Silvertrust, P.C., Case No. 00 C 3290 (N.D. Ill., memorandum opinion and order May 7, 2004). In a later ruling, the court granted plaintiff's request for an injunction to prohibit defendants from collecting on accounts affected by defendants' failure to credit payments. Asch v. Teller, Levit & Silvertrust, P.C., 2004 WL 2967441 (N.D. Ill. Nov. 24, 2004) (granting in part and denying in part plaintiff's motion for further summary judgment). *See also* 31 U.S.C. § 3718. *See generally* Heintz v. Jenkins, 514 U.S. 291, 115 S. Ct. 1489, 131 L. Ed. 2d 395 (1995).

246　15 U.S.C. § 1692a(6)(C).

247　Knight v. Schulman, 102 F. Supp. 2d 867 (S.D. Ohio 1999). *See also* Richardson v. Baker, 663 F. Supp. 651 (S.D.N.Y. 1987) (fact that collector sent letters at behest of Department of Education does not exempt it from FDCPA).

248　Kort v. Diversified Collection Serv., 270 F. Supp. 2d 1017 (N.D. Ill. 2003).

249　*Id.* (defendant collection agency pointed to the following alleged conflicts between the FDCPA and HEA: HEA regulations require a collection agency to send the borrower several written notices while the FDCPA requires debt collectors to terminate communications at the borrower's request; the HEA requires an agency to make diligent attempts to trace a borrower while the FDCPA limits contacts that debt collectors may make with third parties; the HEA requires a contractor performing garnishment services to contact a debtor's employer, an impermissible third-party contact under the FDCPA).

250　Kort v. Diversified Collection Servs., Inc., 394 F.3d 530 (7th Cir. 2005). Debt collectors are not liable under the FDCPA if they can show by a preponderance of evidence that the violation was not intentional and resulted from a bona fide error notwithstanding the maintenance of procedures reasonably adapted to avoid any such error. 15 U.S.C. § 1692k(c).

251　*See* Cliff v. Payco Gen. Am. Credits, Inc., 363 F.3d 1113 (11th Cir. 2004) (claims brought under both federal and state laws); Kort v. Diversified Collection Servs., Inc., 270 F. Supp. 2d 1017 (N.D. Ill. 2003) (claims brought under FDCPA only).

252　*Id. See* § 4.5.4, *infra*.

253　*See, e.g.,* Chatmon v. United States Dep't of Educ., 2003 WL 21501919 (N.D. Tex. June 24, 2003) (Department of Education official does not fall within the FDCPA definition of debt collector because the Department was collecting debt owed to it and because official was acting within the scope of her employment).

254　*See* Chatmon v. United States Dep't of Educ., 2003 WL 21501919 (N.D. Tex. June 24, 2003) (Department had already reimbursed guaranty agencies when the loans were assigned to it and thus Department was attempting to collect for itself). The FDCPA does not apply to creditors collecting their own debts. 15 U.S.C. § 1692a(6)(A). *See generally* National Consumer Law Center, Fair Debt Collection § 4.2 (5th ed. 2004 and Supp.).

Although the law should be clear that the Department's own actions are not covered, while actions by private collectors are, the problem in many cases is determining who in fact engaged in the deceptive conduct—the private collector or the Department. While the Department has turned over almost all its defaulted loans to private collectors, the Department continues to assist those collectors.

Even if the Department is partially responsible for deceptive collection practices, the debt collection agency doing the actual collection may still be liable under the FDCPA. For example, even if the Department actually sent deceptive dunning notices that instruct borrowers to make payments to a private debt collector, the letter may be viewed as an "indirect" attempt by the collection agency to collect a debt, which is within the scope of the FDCPA.[255] In some cases, private collectors use the Department of Education's name and/or address on the envelope or otherwise deceive borrowers into thinking they are receiving communications from the Department. These actions should be violations of the (FDCPA).[256]

4.5.3.4 Secondary Market Lenders and Servicing Agencies

The FDCPA does not apply to creditors collecting their own debts but only to collection agencies and collection attorneys.[257] If a lender has not yet turned an FFEL over to the guarantor or a school is collecting on a Perkins Loan, and if the lender or school is doing the collection activity through its own in-house staff, the FDCPA does not apply. Furthermore, the FDCPA only applies if the third-party collector obtained the debt after it had gone into default.[258] On the other hand, if the lender or school turns a defaulted loan over to a third party for collection, that third party is liable under the FDCPA.

Often an FFEL originating lender will sell the loan *before* default to Sallie Mae or some other secondary market lender. In other situations, an FFEL lender will hire a servicing company *before* default to service the loan payments for the lender. In these situations, the secondary market lender and servicer are not covered by the FDCPA, because they are not assigned the loan post-default and are not taking the loan to collect on a default.[259]

Some advocates have argued that collection agencies should be covered by the FDCPA if they acquired the debt after it became "delinquent" as defined by the student loan regulations, even if it was not yet in "default" as defined by those regulations.[260] The ambiguity arises because the FDCPA does not provide a definition of "default."[261]

The default period in the student loan regulations (previously 180 days, now 270)[262] is unusually long. Borrower advocates argue that allowing such a long period without FDCPA coverage is inconsistent with the purposes of the FDCPA. According to this argument, the definition of "default" in the FDCPA should be the same as "delinquent" in the student loan regulations. The FTC's Official Staff Commentary on the FDCPA lends support to this argument, as it states that the exemption "applies to parties such as mortgage service companies whose business is servicing *current* accounts."[263] Courts have, however, rejected these arguments and interpreted the definition of "default" for FDCPA coverage to be the same as the definition of "default" in student loan regulations.[264]

255 *See* 15 U.S.C. § 1692a(6) (" 'debt collector' means any person who . . . attempts to collect . . . indirectly, debts owed . . . another.") (emphasis added).

256 *See* Peter v. GC Serv., L.P., 310 F.3d 344 (5th Cir. 2002) (debt collector's use of a Department of Education return address on a student loan collection letter violated the Fair Debt Collection Practices Act).

257 15 U.S.C. § 1692a(6)(A). *Cf.* Fischer v. Unipac Serv. Corp., 519 N.W.2d 793 (Iowa 1994) (FDCPA does not apply to loan servicer hired before default). *See generally* Pelfrey v. Educational Credit Mgmt. Corp., 71 F. Supp. 2d 1161 (N.D. Ala. 1999), *aff'd*, 208 F.3d 945 (11th Cir. 2000).

258 15 U.S.C. § 1692a(6)(F)(iii); Gibbs v. SLM Corp., 336 F. Supp. 2d 1 (D. Mass. 2004) (FDCPA does not apply when loan was obtained before the borrower was in default).

259 15 U.S.C. § 1692a(6)(F)(iii); Johnson v. Sallie Mae Servicing Corp., 102 Fed. Appx. 484, 2004 WL 1178200 (7th Cir. May 26, 2004) (servicing corporation was not a "debt collector" subject to FDCPA liability because debtor's student loans clearly were not in default when servicing corporation acquired them); Brumberger v. Sallie Mae Servicing Corp., 2003 WL 1733548 (E.D. La. Mar. 28, 2003), *aff'd*, 84 Fed. Appx. 458, 2004 WL 48901 (5th Cir. Jan. 7, 2004) (FDCPA did not apply to loan servicer because borrower was not in default at the time the servicer began servicing the loan); Fischer v. Unipac Serv. Corp., 519 N.W.2d 793 (Iowa 1994) (FDCPA does not apply to loan servicer hired before default). *See* National Consumer Law Center, Fair Debt Collection § 4.3.10 (5th ed. 2004 and Supp.). *See also* Coppola v. Connecticut Student Loan Found., 1989 U.S. Dist. LEXIS 3415 (D. Conn. Mar. 21, 1989).

260 15 U.S.C. § 1692a(6)(F)(iii).

261 The lack of a definition for the term "default" in the FDCPA has led courts to come up with inconsistent interpretations. At least one court, however, concluded that all the decisions agree that default does not occur until well after a debt becomes outstanding. *See* Alibrandi v. Financial Outsourcing Serv., Inc., 333 F.3d 82, 87 (2d Cir. 2003) (rejecting debtor's argument that default occurs immediately after a debt becomes due; in interpreting "default," court looked to the underlying purpose of the FDCPA. The court concluded that the FDCPA's "pro-debtor" purposes would not be served if it adopted plaintiff's argument that default occurs immediately after payment becomes due. This argument, according to the court, would have the paradoxical effect of immediately exposing debtors to the sort of adverse collection measures from which the FDCPA intended to protect them.).

262 34 C.F.R. §§ 682.200(b) (FFEL), 685.102(b) (Direct Loans). *See generally* § 4.1, *supra*.

263 FTC Official Staff Commentary on the FDCPA § 803-4(f), 53 Fed. Reg. 50097, 50103 (Dec. 13, 1988) (emphasis added).

264 *See* Brannan v. United Student Aid Funds, 94 F.3d 1260, 1262 n.3 (9th Cir. 1996), *cert. denied*, 521 U.S. 1106, 1111 (1997)

4.5.3.5 FDCPA Applicability to Guaranty Agencies

Most collection on FFELs is conducted by guaranty agencies or collection agencies hired by the guarantor. If a guaranty agency hires a private collector, that collector is covered by the FDCPA just as a collector hired by the Department is covered.

Nevertheless, a significant amount of collection activity is still engaged in by the guarantor itself. State-created guaranty agencies may be exempt under the FDCPA's exclusion of state employees, depending upon the structure and authority given the agency by the state legislature.[265]

Private guaranty agencies should clearly fall into the general definition of "collector" under the FDCPA.[266] The governmental exemption does not apply to them, and the guaranty agency meets the other criteria for a debt collector under the FDCPA.[267] To be a debt collector, the guaranty agency's principal purpose must be the collection of debts or it must regularly collect debts owed another,[268] interpreted to mean *originally* owed another.[269]

Guaranty agencies devote most of their resources to collecting on defaulted loans, and their other functions are relatively minor, so there is a strong argument that collection of debts is their principal purpose.[270] Even if this argument is unsuccessful, it is clear that guaranty agencies regularly collect debts owed another and are therefore covered by the FDCPA.[271]

Consequently, the key initial issue in bringing an FDCPA action against a guarantor is determining whether the guarantor is a state or a private entity. Private agencies should clearly fall within the FDCPA's definition of "collector." State agencies, on the other hand, will likely be exempted under the FDCPA's exclusion of state employees.[272]

Advocates should not rely on the name or an agency's prior status as an indication that it is a state agency but should verify this independently. A number of guarantors recently have switched from state to private entities or

---

(holding limited to guaranty agency not fitting within government actor exception and debt in this case obtained after default); Seals v. National Student Loan Program, 2004 WL 3314948 (N.D. W. Va. Aug. 16, 2004), *aff'd*, 124 Fed. Appx. 182 (4th Cir. 2005) (per curiam); Brumberger v. Sallie Mae Servicing Corp., 2003 WL 1733548 (E.D. La. Mar. 28, 2003), *aff'd*, 84 Fed. Appx. 458, 2004 WL 48901 (5th Cir. Jan 7, 2004) (citing Skerry v. Massachusetts Higher Education Assistance Corp. with approval) (court found no viable federal claims under FDCPA, Fair Credit Reporting Act, or Consumer Credit Protection Act); Skerry v. Massachusetts Higher Education Assistance Corp., 73 F. Supp. 2d 47 (D. Mass. 1999); Jones v. Intuition, Inc., 12 F. Supp. 2d 775 (W.D. Tenn. 1998). *See also* Pelfrey v. Educational Credit Mgmt. Corp., 71 F. Supp. 2d 1161 (N.D. Ala. 1999), *aff'd*, 208 F.3d 945 (11th Cir. 2000) (discussing issue, but finding collector exempt for other reasons), *aff'd*, 208 F.3d 945 (11th Cir. 2000); Games v. Cavazos, 737 F. Supp. 1368 (D. Del. 1990) (decision based on government actor exception); Coppola v. Connecticut Student Loan Found., 1989 U.S. Dist. LEXIS 3415 (D. Conn. Mar. 21, 1989) (servicing agency not covered because note not in default when transferred to secondary lender for whom agency serviced loan; facts suggest that plaintiff was current on payments at the time so loan was neither "delinquent" nor in "default").

265 15 U.S.C. § 1692a(6)(C). State guaranty agencies will likely argue that FDCPA claims against them are barred by 11th Amendment sovereign immunity. *See, e.g.,* Sorrell v. Illinois Student Assistance Comm'n, 314 F. Supp. 2d 813 (C.D. Ill. 2004) (plaintiff's FDCPA claims in student loan case barred by 11th Amendment). *See also* Codar, Inc. v. State of Ariz., 168 F.3d 498 (9th Cir. 1999) (in non-student loan case, plaintiff's FDCPA claims were barred by the 11th Amendment). See § 7.3.3, *infra*, for discussion of sovereign immunity in bankruptcy context.

266 Brannan v. United Student Aid Funds, Inc., 94 F.3d 1260 (9th Cir. 1996), *cert. denied*, 521 U.S. 1106, 1111 (1997); Sibley v. Diversified Collection Servs., Inc., 1997 U.S. Dist. LEXIS 23583 (N.D. Tex. June 10, 1997) (ruling on defendants' motion to dismiss). See Appendix G, *infra*, for a complete list of state guaranty agencies and contact information.

267 Brannan v. United Student Aid Funds, Inc., 94 F.3d 1260 (9th Cir. 1996), *cert. denied*, 521 U.S. 1106, 1111 (1997); Student Loan Fund, Inc. v. Duerner, 951 P.2d 1272 (Idaho 1997), *cert.*

denied, 525 U.S. 816 (1998) (court held that guaranty agency was a collector within meaning of FDCPA; guaranty agency "did not become a governmental employee by virtue of its contract with a government agency"). *See also* Spears v. Bowman, 875 F.2d 867 (6th Cir. 1989) (unpublished, full text available at 1989 U.S. App. LEXIS 6208) (reversing ruling that collection agency was exempt as de facto state employee; remanding for factual determination of legal relationship between it and state). *But see* Games v. Cavazos, 737 F. Supp. 1368 (D. Del. 1990) (USA Funds was performing essentially a governmental function in assisting the U.S. in the tax intercept process and, because other state guaranty agencies were in fact state entities, it made no sense to the court to distinguish between guaranty agencies that were private entities and those that were state agencies).

268 15 U.S.C. § 1692a(6). The guaranty agency is not a creditor because it is assigned the debt for the purposes of collecting the debt. *Id.* § 1692a(4).

269 *See* Games v. Cavazos, 737 F. Supp. 1368 (D. Del. 1990); Student Loan Fund, Inc. v. Duerner, 951 P.2d 1272 (Idaho 1997), *cert. denied*, 525 U.S. 816 (1998). *But see* Trubek, FTC Informal Staff Letter (Sept. 12, 1988) (Great Lakes Higher Education Corp. not covered because it is a servicing company and is also a creditor because it owns the loans it guarantees). *See generally* Kimber v. Federal Fin. Corp., 668 F. Supp. 1480 (M.D. Ala. 1987).

270 *See* Games v. Cavazos, 737 F. Supp. 1368 (D. Del. 1990); Student Loan Fund, Inc. v. Duerner, 951 P.2d 1272 (Idaho 1997), *cert. denied*, 525 U.S. 816 (1998) (guaranty agency argued unsuccessfully that it should be excluded from FDCPA coverage because it was collecting a debt that it originated; court held that the bank, not the agency, was the originator of the loans). *But see* Trubek, FTC Informal Staff Letter (Sept. 12, 1988) (Great Lakes Higher Education Corp. not covered because it is a servicing company and is also a creditor because it owns the loans it guarantees).

271 Games v. Cavazos, 737 F. Supp. 1368 (D. Del. 1990); Student Loan Fund, Inc. v. Duerner, 951 P.2d 1272 (Idaho 1997), *cert. denied*, 525 U.S. 816 (1998).

272 15 U.S.C. § 1692a(6)(C).

formed separate subsidiaries.[273] Agencies that appear to be public at first glance may in fact be private and therefore covered by the FDCPA.

A private guaranty agency may try to avoid coverage by arguing that it obtained the debt at the time the agency became the guarantor of the debt (at the initiation of the loan, when the loan was not in default) and that it is therefore exempt.[274] Courts have rejected this specious argument, holding that merely acting as guarantor does not amount to "obtaining" a debt.[275]

To avoid FDCPA coverage, state and private guaranty agencies may also argue that the numerous relationships and connections between the United States government and guaranty agencies place agencies in the position of fiduciaries for the government and, thus, the agencies fall within the exemption for bona fide fiduciaries. This provision of the FDCPA excludes from the definition of "debt collector" any person or agency attempting to collect a debt to the extent such activity is incidental to a bona fide fiduciary obligation or a bona fide escrow arrangement.[276] At least a few courts have exempted nonprofit and private guaranty agencies on this basis.[277]

4.5.4 Applicability of State Debt Collection Law to Student Loans

While the FDCPA exempts creditors and government agencies from its scope, state law often does not. Thus, it is important to explore whether state debt collection laws apply to student loan collection.[278] In addition, state law may specifically prohibit certain collection activity not explicitly restricted by the FDCPA.

State laws that may apply include state debt collection statutes, state UDAP statutes, and common law tort theories. These legal challenges are described in detail in other NCLC manuals.[279]

In any state law challenge to student loan collection practices, advocates should expect a defense that the Higher Education Act's scheme of student loan collection preempts the state debt collection law. There can be no question that state law that directly conflicts with federal law is preempted. However, collectors even argue further that the federal scheme preempts *any* state regulation of student loan collectors.

There is a split in the circuit courts with respect to whether all state regulation is preempted or whether only those state provisions that conflict with the federal scheme are preempted.

In the earlier case, *Brannan v. United Student Aid Funds*, the Ninth Circuit concluded that the federal scheme "totally occupies the field" and thus all state regulation is preempted.[280] The Ninth Circuit held that state law was preempted in any circumstances under which state law regulates pre-litigation collection activity.[281]

The dissent, however, puts forth the better argument that the whole Oregon statute should not be preempted but only those prohibitions that specifically preempt a federal requirement.[282]

In a well-reasoned opinion, *McComas v. Financial Collection Agencies*,[283] a federal court in West Virginia refused to follow the majority opinion in *Brannan* and held that the HEA preempts only those state debt collection provisions that specifically conflict with the federal scheme.[284] The *McComas* court found that

- the federal requirement that student loan collectors telephone debtors does not preempt state law prohibi-

---

273 For example, in 1997 the California Student Aid Commission (CSAC) set up EDFUND as a separate nonprofit corporation. For a complete list of state guaranty agencies, see Appendix G, *infra*. This information is also available on the Department of Education's website at www.ed.gov.

274 See the exemption at 15 U.S.C. § 1692a(6)(F)(iii). *See generally* § 4.5.3.3, *infra*.

275 Sibley v. Diversified Collection Servs., Inc., 1997 U.S. Dist. LEXIS 23583 (N.D. Tex. June 10, 1997). *See also* Games v. Cavazos, 737 F. Supp. 1368 (D. Del. 1990) (fact that guaranty agency once held the debt does not exempt it when it had transferred debt to Department of Education at time of collection activities).

276 15 U.S.C. § 1692a(6)(F)(i).

277 Seals v. National Student Loan Program, 2004 WL 3314948 (N.D. W. Va. Aug. 16, 2004), *aff'd*, 124 Fed. Appx. 182 (4th Cir. 2005) (per curiam). *See* Pelfrey v. Educational Credit Mgmt. Corp., 71 F. Supp. 2d 1161 (N.D. Ala. 1999), *aff'd*, 208 F.3d 945 (11th Cir. 2000); Davis v. United Student Aid Funds, Inc., 45 F. Supp. 2d 1104 (D. Kan. 1998) (in granting motion to dismiss, court found that a nonprofit student loan guaranty agency was a fiduciary and therefore not a debt collector). The *Pelfrey* court repeatedly cited a declaration filed with the court by Larry Oxendine, Director of Guarantor and Lender Oversight Service with the Department of Education. This declaration is a useful summary of the various arguments guaranty agencies will use to support their position that they are exempt from the FDCPA. For a copy of the Oxendine declaration from another case, see Declaration of Larry Oxendine, Mitchell v. Educational Credit Mgmt. Corp., Clearinghouse No. 52492 (N.D. Ill. 1997).

278 Patzka v. Viterbo College, 917 F. Supp. 654 (W.D. Wis. 1996) (school barred from collecting interest when student not informed of interest rate; FDCPA and Wisconsin UDAP violations claimed); Sibley v. Firstcollect, Inc., 913 F. Supp. 469 (M.D. La. 1995).

279 National Consumer Law Center, Fair Debt Collection Chs. 8, 10, 11 (5th ed. 2004 and Supp.); National Consumer Law Center, Unfair and Deceptive Acts and Practices §§ 2.2.2, 5.1.1 (6th ed. 2004 and Supp.).

280 94 F.3d 1260 (9th Cir. 1996), *cert. denied*, 521 U.S. 1106, 1111 (1997).

281 *Id.* at 1263. *See also* Pirouzian v. SLM Corp., 396 F. Supp. 2d 1124 (S.D. Ca. 2005) (*Brannan* holding applies to lenders as well as private collection agencies).

282 *Id.* at 1266 (opinion of J. Fletcher, concurring and dissenting). *See also* Seals v. National Student Loan Program, 2004 WL 3314948 (N.D. W. Va. Aug. 16, 2004), *aff'd*, 124 Fed. Appx. 182 (4th Cir. 2005) (per curiam).

283 1997 U.S. Dist. LEXIS 2725 (S.D. W. Va. Mar. 7, 1997).

284 *Id.*

tions on abusive and deceptive telephone collection techniques;

- the federal requirement that guarantors sue debtors under certain conditions does not preempt a state law prohibition of a collector deceptively threatening legal action it does not intend to take;
- the federal requirement that a guarantor garnish wages in certain circumstances does not preempt a state law prohibition against threatening 33% wage garnishments without first informing the debtor that a court order must first be obtained; and
- the federal scheme does not preempt state laws prohibiting false statements that a collector is affiliated with the government.[285]

A second district court opinion agreed with *McComas*.[286] In March 2004, the Eleventh Circuit took the same position.[287]

There are a number of reasons why the Eleventh Circuit and the district courts are correct. Federal law specifically requires that, when the Department contracts with debt collectors to recover indebtedness, the contract shall provide that the collector is subject to "the laws and regulations of the United States Government and State governments related to debt collection practices."[288] That is, private debt collectors agree in their own contracts to be subject to state debt collection laws.

In addition, the Department's own regulation preempts only state laws "that would conflict with or hinder satisfaction of the requirements of or frustrate the purposes of this section."[289] A subsequent Notice of Interpretation states that the Secretary "intended these provisions ... to preempt contrary or inconsistent State law to the extent necessary to permit compliance with the Federal regulations."[290] *Brannan* found other portions of this Notice of Interpretation to support its conclusion that the federal scheme occupies the field.[291] But the courts rejecting *Brannan* explain how *Brannan* took a particular passage out of context and that the Notice of Interpretation relied on by *Brannan* actually says the exact opposite—that state law is preempted only to the extent it conflicts with the federal scheme.[292]

In *Cliff v. Payco*, the plaintiffs claimed that the collection agency violated state and federal fair debt laws, mainly with respect to its administration of the wage garnishment program.[293] The plaintiffs argued that the "notwithstanding any provision of state law" language in the wage garnishment section of the HEA explicitly preempts only those state laws that regulate garnishment. The court agreed.

In finding that the state debt collection law was not preempted by the HEA, the court disagreed with the defendant's argument that the state law actually conflicted with the HEA. The court found that the agency could comply with the HEA and the state debt collection law simultaneously.[294] However, the court cautioned that this might not always be the case. For example, the court cited the HEA regulation that requires lenders to complete due diligence requirements when attempting to collect a student loan. State laws, the court noted, might be construed to prohibit one or more of these required contacts. In that case, in the view of other courts that have confronted this issue, a claim brought under state law would be preempted.[295]

The *Cliff* court explained in a footnote why it came to a different conclusion than the Ninth Circuit in *Brannan*.[296] This discussion provides a guide for practitioners seeking to raise state law claims against student loan collectors. First, the court pointed out that the *Brannan* majority failed to analyze conflict preemption on a provision-by-provision basis. More importantly, the court also distinguished the two cases. In *Brannan*, the plaintiff alleged that a guaranty agency threatened to cause her to lose her job, communicated with third parties about her debt, and refused to communicate with her about her debt through her attorney. Although it is not entirely clear, according to the *Cliff* court, the HEA regulations might have required the guaranty agency to engage in some or all of these actions. In contrast, *Cliff*'s allegations are based upon a provision of state law that does not hinder the completion of the sequence of contacts.[297]

It is important to note that the plaintiffs in *Cliff* did not argue that the HEA gave them a private right of action,

285 *Id.*

286 Sibley v. Diversified Collection Servs., Inc., 1997 U.S. Dist. LEXIS 23583 (N.D. Tex. June 10, 1997) (ruling on defendants' motion to dismiss) (court declined to follow majority in *Brannan* to the extent it holds that any state statute regulating debt collection practices is per se inconsistent with the collection requirements placed on guarantors by federal regulations).

287 Cliff v. Payco Gen. Am. Credits, Inc., 363 F.3d 1113 (11th Cir. 2004).

288 31 U.S.C. § 3718(a)(2)(B).

289 34 C.F.R. § 682.411(o).

290 55 Fed. Reg. 40120, 40121 (1990).

291 Brannan v. United Student Aid Funds, Inc., 94 F.3d 1260 (9th Cir. 1996), *cert. denied*, 521 U.S. 1106, 1111 (1997). *But see* Cliff v. Payco Gen. Am. Credits, Inc., 363 F.3d 1113 (11th Cir. 2004).

292 *See, e.g.*, McComas v. Financial Collection Agencies, 1997 U.S.

Dist. LEXIS 2725 (S.D. W. Va. Mar. 7, 1997). The *Cliff* court also found the language in the notice of interpretation unpersuasive and allowed plaintiffs to proceed with state claims. Cliff v. Payco Gen. Am. Credits, Inc., 363 F.3d 1113 (11th Cir. 2004).

293 Cliff v. Payco Gen. Am. Credits, Inc., 363 F.3d 1113 (11th Cir. 2004). The issue of HEA preemption was raised as part of the plaintiff's interlocutory appeal of the district court's denial of class certification.

294 *Id.*

295 *Id.* (citing Fischer v. UNIPAC Serv. Corp., 519 N.W.2d 793, 798–99 (Iowa 1994) (concluding that a state law claim brought under Iowa's Consumer Credit Code, which requires a debt collector to communicate with a debtor through the debtor's attorney, was preempted by 34 C.F.R. § 682.411, which requires a particular sequence of written and oral contacts directly with the debtor)).

296 *Id.* at n.12.

297 *Id.*

conceding that this issue had previously been decided against them.[298] Furthermore, the plaintiffs argued that enforcing state debt collection law against the collector is not tantamount to giving borrowers a private right of action. If that were the case, according to the plaintiffs, then the HEA should have preclusive effect on claims under the FDCPA, but courts have consistently held otherwise.[299]

The *Cliff* court also dismissed the defendant's arguments that allowing plaintiffs to proceed under state law would undermine the HEA's enforcement scheme. Finally, the court rejected the defendant's argument that the four-year statute of limitation under state law would discourage lenders from participating in federal loan programs. The court noted that collection agencies are already subject to the one-year statute under the FDCPA and that there is no evidence to suggest that the four-year statute discourage lenders in any way.[300]

4.5.5 Other Remedies for Government Agency Debt Collection Abuse

4.5.5.1 Other Federal Claims

In addition to the FDCPA and state debt collection law, borrowers may have other remedies for debt collection abuse. When the United States is the collector, potential claims include the Federal Tort Claims Act,[301] the Privacy Act, the Administrative Procedure Act, and the Civil Rights Act.[302]

A good example of a constitutional challenge to government student loan collection practices is *Williams v. Illinois State Scholarship Commission*,[303] in which the Illinois Supreme Court ruled that an Illinois statute[304] requiring guaranty agencies to sue only in Cook County violated the Due Process Clause. *Williams* also found violative of due process the guaranty agency's practice, even prior to the passage of the Illinois *special* venue statute, of bringing all its collection actions in Cook County.[305] However, in these cases, the plaintiffs will have to prove that the guaranty agency is a state actor in order to invoke constitutional due process protections.[306]

The guaranty agency in the Illinois case argued that it could bring its collection actions in Cook County because the state's *general* venue statute allows suit in any county with sufficient contacts with the transaction. The guaranty agency claimed it approved student loans from its Cook County offices. The court analyzed the loan process and found there to be insufficient contacts with Cook County.[307] Finally, the Illinois Supreme Court in *Williams* ruled that a venue waiver or forum selection clause found in the actual student loan agreement was against public policy and void.[308]

Similarly, if the Department is responsible for sending dunning letters that mislead students concerning the legal garnishment process (failing to disclose the right to a hearing and failing to disclose various limits to that garnishment right), an argument could be made that those who are misled into making a payment to avoid the garnishment are deprived of that property without notice of their right to a hearing, as required by the HEA and by the Due Process Clause of the Fifth Amendment. Such an argument could form the basis of a civil rights claim against the Department.

If a private collector is involved, advocates should also consider raising claims other than federal and state debt collection laws to challenge abusive collection behavior. There are numerous federal, state, and tort remedies that may apply.[309]

4.5.5.2 Complaining to the Department

Another response to debt collection abuse is to complain to the entity that hired the collection agency. This may not provide any relief to the borrower, but it may help others. If a collector is employed by the Department, borrowers should contact the Department Collection Services divisions or the student loan ombudsman to register complaints.[310]

If a guaranty agency holds a loan, the first place to complain about collection agency misconduct is the state

298 *See* Reply Brief for Appellant, Cliff v. OSI Collection Servs., Inc., f/k/a Payco Gen. Am. Credits, Inc., Case No. 02-12462, October 24, 2002. Plaintiffs noted that the 11th Circuit had recently held that there is no private right of action under the HEA in *McCulloch v. PNC Bank, Inc.*, 298 F.3d 1217 (11th Cir. 2002). This brief, as well as other pleadings, in this case are included on the companion CD-Rom to this manual. For a discussion of actions under the HEA, see § *9.3.5, infra*.

299 *Id. See* § *4.3.3, supra*.

300 Cliff v. Payco Gen. Am. Credits, Inc., 363 F.3d 1113 (11th Cir. 2004).

301 *See, e.g.*, Burgess v. United States Dep't of Educ., 2006 WL 1047064 (D. Vt. Apr. 17, 2006) (FTCA claim for conversion of tax return through tax offset dismissed because of plaintiff's failure to comply with FTCA notice requirements).

302 National Consumer Law Center, Fair Debt Collection § 13.2 (5th ed. 2004 and Supp.).

303 139 Ill. 2d 24, 563 N.E.2d 465 (1990).

304 Ill. Rev. Stat. 1988 Supp. 1, Par. 12.

305 Williams v. Illinois State Scholarship Comm'n, 139 Ill. 2d 24, 563 N.E.2d 465 (1990). *But see* United States v. Frisk, 675 F.2d 1079 (9th Cir. 1982).

306 *See, e.g.*, George W. v. United States Dep't of Ed., 149 F. Supp. 2d 1195 (E.D. Cal. 2000) (in case raising constitutional violations for alleged unreasonable charging of collection fees, court found guaranty agency was not a state actor required to afford borrower due process).

307 Williams v. Illinois State Scholarship Comm'n, 139 Ill. 2d 24, 563 N.E.2d 465 (1990).

308 *Id.*

309 *See generally* National Consumer Law Center, National Consumer Law Center, Fair Debt Collection (5th ed. 2004 and Supp.).

310 *See* § *4.3.2, supra*.

guaranty agency. If the collection misconduct is by an employee of the guaranty agency, it is best to contact an official at a higher level of the agency. If a guaranty agency appears to be systematically failing to follow federal policy, advocates should send the Department or ombudsman the particulars of the complaint. Many guaranty agencies have their own ombudsman offices. They claim to welcome complaints about the agencies that work for them.

The Department claims that it takes complaints about collection agencies very seriously and will handle them as expeditiously as possible. Collection agencies are supposed to suspend collection activity after receiving notice from the Department that a complaint has been received.[311]

Borrowers should also consider complaining to state authorities. For example, the Minnesota Department of Commerce issued a civil penalty in 2005 against a collection agency owned by Sallie Mae.[312] The investigation alleged that the collection agency engaged in more than fifteen violations of Minnesota law, including the following:

- Withdrawing money electronically from a debtor's checking account without authorization
- Contacting debtors at employment after receiving notification to stop
- Disclosing debtor's information to third parties

---

311 U.S. Dep't of Educ., *Agency Review Guide: Internal Procedures for Evaluating Private Collection Agencies* 49 (PCAs) (June 15, 2005), *available at* www.fsacollections.ed.gov/contractors/pca2004/virtual_library/2005%20Agency%20Review%20Guide%206-29-05.doc (last accessed on October 3, 2006).

312 *See* Press Release, Minnesota Department of Commerce, Commerce Commissioner Takes Action Against Collection Agency (Nov. 28, 2005), *available at* www.lawpoint.com/files/nr.arrow.financial.pdf#search=%22Minnesota%20Department%20of%20Commerce%20and%20Arrow%20Financial%20Services%22 (last accessed on October 3, 2006).

Chapter 5 Property and Asset Seizures

5.1 Introduction

In fiscal year 2002, according to the GAO, the Department of Education collected $4.87 billion in defaulted student loans compared to the $2.7 billion that went into default.[1] The default recovery rate was 7.6% without consolidation and 16.8% with consolidations.[2]

Collection information from fiscal year 2003 (through December 31, 2003) indicates that loan rehabilitation accounted for nearly half of the student loan funds recovered that year through methods other than consolidation. Wage garnishment comprised about 16% of these non-consolidation recoveries and Treasury offset about 4%. Signaling the Department's reluctance to litigate these cases, less than 2% of non-consolidation funds collected during this time period came from litigation.[3]

These collection methods often break the budgets of low-income households. Those living on or near the poverty line simply cannot afford to lose a tax refund or hard-earned wages. It is therefore critical for advocates to explore possible ways to cancel, defer, or forebear clients' loans.[4] There may also be affordable repayment options available.[5]

It is also important for advocates to understand the strategies available to challenge property seizures themselves. This chapter focuses on these strategies, highlighting tax refund intercepts, administrative wage garnishments, and federal benefits offsets.

5.2 Tax Refund Interceptions

5.2.1 How Tax Refund Interceptions Work

The tax refund intercept program involves a blanket seizure of almost all tax refunds due to debtors who are in default on their student loans. There is no statute of limitations for such an offset.[6] In addition, a number of states have state laws that authorize state guaranty agencies to intercept state income tax refunds. This subsection, however, focuses exclusively on the federal tax refund interception program.

The federal statute requires an intercept when a debt is owed to a federal agency, including a debt administered by a third party acting as an agent for the federal government.[7] The Department uses this authority to delegate to guaranty agencies the authority to initiate intercepts for loans still held by the guaranty agency.[8] This is significant because, prior to the legislative change allowing interception of debts owed to agents of the federal government, authorization to intercept loans held by guaranty agencies was accomplished by the guarantors assigning the loans to the United States prior to interception. This posed practical problems for obligations that guarantors had already reduced to judgments, particularly since the interception program was not used to collect loans post-judgment. The interception program is now utilized to recover on debts pre- and post-judgment.

Whether the debt is owed to the Department or to the guarantor, the decision of which refunds to intercept is not done on an individual basis. Computer records of *all* borrowers in default meeting certain general criteria are sent to

---

1 *See* U.S. Gen. Accounting Office, Federal Student Aid: Timely Performance Plans and Reports Would Help Guide and Assess Achievement of Default Management Goals, GAO-03-348 (Feb. 2003).

2 *Id.*

3 U.S. Dep't of Educ., Borrower Serv./Collections Group, *Fiscal Year to Date Defaulted Student Loan Recoveries: As of December 31, 2003.*

4 *See* Ch. 3 (deferments and forbearances), *supra*; Ch. 6 (cancellations), *infra.*

5 *See* Ch. 8, *infra.*

6 20 U.S.C. § 1091a(a). Prior to the elimination of the statute of limitations for student loan collections, debts that had been delinquent for more than ten years were not subject to offset. How to count the delinquency was once an issue of some concern (compare Grider v. Cavazos, 911 F.2d 1158 (5th Cir. 1990) *and* Thomas v. Bennett, 856 F.2d 1165, 1169, n.4 (8th Cir. 1988) *with* Jones v. Cavazos, 889 F.2d 1043 (11th Cir. 1989); Roberts v. Bennett, 709 F. Supp. 222 (N.D. Ga. 1989)), but is now irrelevant. *See generally* § 4.2.1, *supra.*

7 31 U.S.C. § 3720A(a). These rules should also apply to Perkins loans that have been assigned to the Department. However, if a school is collecting a Perkins loan, the regulations provide only that the school must attempt to recover the loan through litigation, assign the loan to the United States, or write off the loan. *See* 34 C.F.R. § 674.45(d).

8 *But see* McAfee v. Unger & Assocs. Inc., 730 So. 2d 623 (Ala. Civ. App. 1998), *cert. denied*, 730 So. 2d 626 (Ala. 1999) (federal regulations provide that attachment of an income tax refund can be carried out only by federal government agencies; borrower's attempt to sue collection agency employed by Department of Education failed because agency could not have been involved in the tax intercept process).

the IRS and anyone on that list owed a refund will have that refund intercepted.

5.2.2 How to Challenge Tax Refund Intercepts

5.2.2.1 The Pre-Intercept Notice

The Secretary can refer a debt for offset only after complying with certain procedures.[9] The guarantor (or a computer services contractor for Department-held loans) mails to the borrower a written notice of the Secretary's intent to seek the tax intercept, using the borrower's current address, as determined from the guarantor's Department records.[10] The notice informs the borrower of the intent to refer a past-due debt to the Secretary of the Treasury for offset and provides the borrower with the opportunity to inspect and copy the records on the borrower's debt, obtain a review of the existence, amount, enforceability, or past-due status of the debt, or enter into a written repayment agreement.[11] Courts have held that actual notice is not required, so long as reasonable means are used to provide notice.[12]

5.2.2.2 Inspection of the File and Requesting a Hearing

The borrower must make a written request to inspect a loan file within twenty days of the notice of offset.[13] To obtain a review, the borrower must file a request for review at the address specified in the notice by the *later* of sixty-five days after the date of the notice or fifteen days after the borrower's loan file is provided, if requested.[14] A borrower can request a later hearing, but only a timely hearing request will stop the intercept pending the hearing.

Most loans are held by guarantors, and for these loans the hearing is initially with the guarantor. Only Department-held loans are initially heard by a Department official. If the review is not by the Department, the borrower can request a subsequent review by the Department after receiving the guaranty agency decision. This request for further review must be made within seven days after the agency's initial determination.[15]

The timely request for a hearing stops the intercept until the hearing and any further requests for review have been exhausted. The statute specifies that no intercept can occur until there is a determination that a debt is owed.[16]

When requesting review, the borrower must file identifying information about himself or herself and information about the particular debt, including the borrower's social security number and the name of the loan program. Borrowers must also explain their reasons for contesting debts and file any documents they wish to submit.[17] If the borrower wants an oral hearing, the borrower must also submit the reasons why the review cannot be limited to a review of the documentary evidence and also submit a list of the witnesses the borrower wishes to call, the issues they will testify about, and the reasons why the testimony is necessary.[18] The Secretary has established detailed standards in the regulation about when an oral hearing will be granted and the rules to follow in that hearing.[19]

It is important for borrowers to send the guarantor or the Department of Education all relevant documentation. Even though the Department's file may not contain much useful information, it is still a good practice for borrowers to also request the Department or guaranty agency file.

5.2.2.3 Grounds to Contest a Tax Intercept

While many borrowers report frustration in raising even the most meritorious defenses to a tax intercept, the Department's stated policy is to consider the following types of defenses:[20]

- The borrower has repaid the loan or the Social Security Number is incorrect and the borrower does not owe the loan.
- The borrower has entered into a repayment agreement

---

9   34 C.F.R. § 30.33(a).

10 34 C.F.R. § 30.22(a). *See also* Glover v. Brady, 1994 U.S. Dist. LEXIS 13211 (S.D.N.Y. 1994) (no due process violation found when letter was mailed twice to last known address); Setlech v. United States, 816 F. Supp. 161 (E.D.N.Y. 1993), *aff'd*, 17 F.3d 390, *cert. denied*, 511 U.S. 1085 (1994) (notice need not be received; reasonable efforts must be made in sending the notice; if reasonable efforts are not made, the court would require Department to provide the borrower with a hearing as to whether the debt was due).

11 34 C.F.R. § 30.33(b).

12 *See, e.g.*, Savage v. Scales, 310 F. Supp. 2d 122 (D.D.C. 2004); Shabtai v. United States Dep't of Educ., 2003 WL 21983025 (S.D.N.Y. Aug. 20, 2003); Nelson v. Diversified Collection Servs., Inc., 961 F. Supp. 863 (D. Md. 1997); Setlech v. United States, 816 F. Supp. 161, 167 (E.D.N.Y. 1992) (using an address most recently in the agency's database or an address obtained from plaintiff's most recent tax return has been held to be "reasonably calculated to notify the vast majority of debtors of the intended referral and proposed offset"), *aff'd*, 17 F.3d 390 (2d Cir. 1993) (table). *See also* § 5.3.4, *infra*.

13 34 C.F.R. § 30.33(c)(1).

14 34 C.F.R. § 30.33(d).

15 34 C.F.R. § 30.33(d)(3).

16 31 U.S.C. § 3720A(b)(3).

17 34 C.F.R. § 30.24(b)(1), (2).

18 34 C.F.R. § 30.25.

19 34 C.F.R. § 30.26.

20 U.S. Dep't of Educ., Amendment to Agreement Pursuant to Section 428(b) of the Higher Education Act of 1965, as Amended, with a State or Private Non-profit Institution or Organization for Coverage of Its Student Loan Insurance Program under the Interest Benefits Provision of Section 428(a) of the Act, Clearinghouse No. 51, 926 (July 11, 1994).

with the guaranty agency or the Department and the borrower is making payments as required.

- The borrower has filed for bankruptcy and the case is still open or the loan was discharged in bankruptcy.[21]
- The school failed to pay the borrower an owed refund.
- The borrower is dead or totally and permanently disabled.[22]
- The loan is not enforceable. The Department will apparently recognize forgery or alteration of the loan documents as a defense. It should also recognize school-related defenses on Perkins, Direct, and many FFEL Loans issued after January 1, 1994.[23] It is less clear whether the Department will consider school-related defenses (other than the failure to pay an owed refund) for FFELs issued before that date.[24]
- The borrower is eligible for a closed-school discharge.[25]
- The borrower is eligible for a false-certification discharge.[26]

If the borrower checks the closed school or false certification box, the servicer should mail the borrower the applicable discharge form. The borrower must return the form within sixty days. The tax intercept servicer should not certify the loan for offset until and unless it determines that the borrower fails to qualify for the discharge.[27]

In response to a 2003 FOIA request, the Department reported that, in 2002, it received 1186 requests for review in the Treasury Offset Program in which borrowers claimed a false-certification defense. The number of requests in previous years was higher. For example, the Department received 2266 such requests in 2000 and 1957 in 2001. In 2002, only 397 requests for review claimed a closed-school defense. Again, the numbers were higher in previous years with 816 in 2000 and 732 in 2001. The numbers for unpaid-refund defenses to offset were even lower: 532 in 2000, 471 in 2001, and 275 in 2002.

In addition, although not explicitly recognized by the Department as a defense, the enabling statute for tax intercepts explicitly states that an intercept cannot take place unless the Department has certified that reasonable efforts have been made by the agency to obtain payment of the debt.[28]

The failure to consider evidence should also be grounds to undo a tax intercept. The enabling statute for tax intercepts explicitly states that no intercept can take place until the Department "considers any evidence presented by such person and determines that an amount of such debt is past due and legally enforceable."[29]

5.2.2.4 Due Process Challenges

Unfortunately, there are widespread allegations that guarantors, or contractors hired by the Department, ignore borrower requests for hearings, deny requests on inadequate grounds, ignore valid defenses, or simply fail to respond in any way to student requests concerning pending intercepts. At a minimum, borrowers should be prepared for delays and should be sure to send all correspondence return receipt requested. A file should be created with copies of all correspondence.

When hearings are offered, they often fail to meet even minimum due process standards. In-person hearings are arranged for the convenience of the guarantor or Department and consequently can be thousands of miles from the borrower's residence. The Department has responded to this problem by offering telephone hearings in lieu of in-person hearings.[30] The due process implications of preventing borrowers from presenting their cases in person have not been challenged to date.

There have, however, been challenges to some of the other features of the tax refund intercept program (TRIP). In *Jones v. Cavazos*,[31] the Eleventh Circuit threw out a due process challenge to the intercept procedure because the plaintiff lacked standing, concluding that the plaintiff had no meritorious defense to the tax refund intercept. The clear

---

21 *See* Ch. 7, *infra.*

22 *See* § 6.6, *infra.*

23 *See* § 9.6.2, *infra.*

24 The directions the Department provides guarantors concerning tax intercepts states that school-related defenses will not be accepted except for: (1) the failure to make a refund discussed above; (2) when a state statute specifically provides such lender liability for a seller's conduct; (3) the school made the loan (for example, a Perkins Loan); or (4) the lender and school are so closely related that under applicable law the lender is liable for the school's misconduct. U.S. Dep't of Educ., Amendment to Agreement Pursuant to Section 428(b) of the Higher Education Act of 1965, as Amended, with a State or Private Non-profit Institution or Organization for Coverage of Its Student Loan Insurance Program under the Interest Benefits Provision of Section 428(a) of the Act, Appendix I § 2.4.10, Clearinghouse No. 51,926 (July 11, 1994).

25 *See* § 6.2, *infra.*

26 *See* § 6.3, *infra.*

27 U.S. Dep't of Educ., Amendment to Agreement Pursuant to Section 428(b) of the Higher Education Act of 1965, as Amended, with a State or Private Non-profit Institution or Organization for Coverage of Its Student Loan Insurance Program under the Interest Benefits Provision of Section 428(a) of the Act, Appendix I §§ 2.4.6, 2.4.11, Clearinghouse No. 51,926 (July 11, 1994).

28 31 U.S.C. § 3720A(b)(5).

29 *Id.*

30 U.S. Dep't of Educ., Amendment to Agreement Pursuant to Section 428(b) of the Higher Education Act of 1965, as Amended, with a State or Private Non-profit Institution or Organization for Coverage of Its Student Loan Insurance Program under the Interest Benefits Provision of Section 428(a) of the Act, Appendix I § 2.3.1, Clearinghouse No. 51,926 (July 11, 1994).

31 889 F.2d 1043 (11th Cir. 1989).

lesson is not to raise a constitutional challenge to a hearing procedure on behalf of an individual who has no claims to raise in the hearing.

Richardson v. Baker[32] was a more successful due process challenge to the notice and hearing procedures afforded debtors prior to the tax refund interception. The parties reached a settlement whereby the government modified TRIP procedures for student loan defaulters. The settlement only applies to New York students, but the case is instructive concerning the type of settlement attorneys are likely to reach in other states.

The settlement contains model documents that must be sent in advance of any potential offset of tax refunds, informing recipients in detail about their rights and possible defenses and the nature of their loan obligation. The Department of Education must also send out a form that simplifies and expedites students' requests for a pre-offset hearing. The hearings will be by telephone or in person in New York City. With certain exceptions, the same procedures will be followed for loans held by state guaranty agencies, although hearings will be by telephone or in the office of the guaranty agency. The settlement provides no protections for the residents of the other forty-nine states.

A third case upheld the notice even though it did not list potential defenses, did not disclose the right to an attorney, and was arguably confusing.[33] The same court also found no due process violation when a pre-intercept hearing was offered but never afforded because of a private contractor's negligence, not because of government policy.[34] An unreported district court case also upheld the pre-intercept procedures.[35]

5.2.2.5 Post-Intercept Challenges

The IRS takes the position that there is no right to an administrative review of the intercept within the IRS and courts do not have jurisdiction to hear challenges against the IRS based on the intercept.[36] In denying a borrower's attempt to appeal an offset, one court stated that, although the plaintiff could not seek review of his tax offset against the Department of Treasury, he is "free to pursue any and all

remedies he may have against 'the Federal agency . . . to which the amount of such [income tax refund] reduction was paid.' 26 U.S.C. § 6402(f). 'He may not, however, point the guns of this lawsuit against the Treasury.' "[37] However, in another district court case, the court dismissed a case against the Department of Education when a borrower's wife alleged that her tax refund was improperly seized.[38]

The Department has not set out a formal administrative procedure to review intercepts after they have occurred but has indicated that it will follow the pre-intercept hearing procedure even for hearings requested post-intercept. The only difference is that the intercept is not stayed pending the review.

Whether in fact guarantors or the Department will actually review such post-intercept requests is an open question. Such an administrative appeal may be prudent before filing suit to forestall the Department's argument that the student must first exhaust administrative remedies.[39]

If this request is ignored, the remaining approach, when the student loan is not owed, is to sue the Department of Education for return of the intercepted refund.[40] Such a challenge is generally advisable only if the borrower has a complete defense, because the Department can counterclaim on the student loan note.

5.2.2.6 Repayment Plan in Lieu of Intercept

Borrowers can request written agreements to repay debts if they do so within twenty days of receiving the notice of intent to offset.[41] The Secretary or guarantor provides a repayment schedule, and, to avoid the intercept, the borrower must make the first payment within the later of sixty-five days of receipt of the original notice or seven days after the Secretary's decision if a review of a guaranty agency's decision is requested.[42]

The regulations provide that the repayment agreement must be on terms acceptable to the Secretary.[43] It does not specifically require that the Secretary offer a reasonable and affordable payment plan.[44] However, borrowers may be able to argue that a reasonable and affordable plan should be available in these circumstances. At a minimum, borrowers

---

32 Clearinghouse No. 40,719 (S.D.N.Y. Feb. 9, 1990) (order of settlement).

33 Games v. Cavazos, 737 F. Supp. 1368 (D. Del. 1990).

34 *Id.*

35 Downs v. McPherson, Clearinghouse No. 51,940 (D. Md. July 17, 1989).

36 26 C.F.R. § 301.6402-6(l). *See* Johnson v. Internal Revenue Serv., 2001 WL 1175151 (E.D. Pa. Aug. 21, 2001); Setlech v. United States, 816 F. Supp. 161 (E.D.N.Y. 1993), *aff'd*, 17 F.3d 390 (2d Cir.), *cert. denied*, 511 U.S. 1085 (1994); Richardson v. Baker, 663 F. Supp. 651 (S.D.N.Y. 1987); Sartorious v. United States Dep't of Treasury, 671 F. Supp. 592 (E.D. Wis. 1987); *In re* Blake, 235 B.R. 568 (Bankr. Md. 1998) (although action against Department of Treasury prohibited, borrower could bring suit against the Department of Education; Department ordered to return refund).

37 Albert v. OSI Educ. Serv., Inc., 2004 WL 483166 (D. Minn. Mar. 11, 2004).

38 Burgess v. United States Dep't of Educ., 2006 WL 1047064 (D. Vt. Apr. 17, 2006) ("It is the Treasury Department that performs the tax refund offset, and only at that stage would a government agency become aware of the existence of a joint filer"; Department of Education also had no obligation to provide a non-debtor spouse with notice).

39 *Cf.* Bolden v. Equifax Accounts Receivable Servs., 838 F. Supp. 507 (D. Kan. 1993) (suggesting, over the Department's objection, that administrative remedies need not first be exhausted).

40 *See, e.g., In re* Blake, 235 B.R. 568 (Bankr. Md. 1998).

41 34 C.F.R. § 30.27(a)(1).

42 34 C.F.R. § 30.33(f).

43 34 C.F.R. § 30.27(a).

44 *See* § 8.3 (reasonable and affordable payment plans), *infra.*

should be able to make payments under plans agreed to by the Secretary and then later request reasonable and affordable plans.[45]

5.2.2.7 Can a State Law Exemption Prevent a Tax Refund Intercept?

The Eleventh Circuit overturned a federal district court determination that Alabama's $3000 personal exemption applies to tax refund intercepts.[46] The borrower had argued that the Federal Debt Collection Procedures Act allows debtors to raise state exemptions to federal collection actions.[47] The Eleventh Circuit assumed without any discussion that no exemptions applied under the federal tax intercept statutes[48] and then determined that the tax intercept statutes, and not the Federal Debt Collection Procedures Act, applied.[49]

The court pointed out that the Federal Debt Collection Procedures Act indicates it does not "supersede or modify the operation of . . . statutory rights to set-off. . . ."[50] The court ruled that the intercept was such a set-off. In addition, state law cannot shape the federal tax intercept program. The court held that, when federal law conflicts with state exemption laws, the federal law prevails.[51]

The borrower in this case also argued that he was entitled to a "fairness" exception to the federal income tax offset statutes. The fairness argument was based on the fact that his refund consisted primarily of an earned income tax credit, a benefit available only to low-income families with dependent children.[52] The court rejected this argument as well.[53]

5.2.3 Preventing Intercepts

The only sure-fire method of avoiding a tax refund intercept for a borrower currently in default is to lower federal income tax withholding from earnings and any estimated tax payments. Then, at the end of the year, the taxpayer is not owed a refund and there can be no interception.

This approach is partially available even for those receiving Earned Income Tax Credits (EITC).[54] Employees who are eligible for the EITC *and* who have a qualifying child are entitled to receive EITC payments in their pay during the year if they provide their employer with a completed IRS Form W-5, Earned Income Credit Advance Payment Certificate. The employee, though, can only have a portion of the EITC paid during the year.[55] A riskier strategy is to delay filing a refund. However, clients should be counseled on possible penalties associated with this option.

While most borrowers want to avoid interception of their tax refunds, borrowers who want to immediately pay off their loans may actually be better off having their tax refunds intercepted. Funds from tax intercepts should be applied to principal and interest, not to collection fees.[56] Thus, the balance will decrease more rapidly through tax intercepts than through low monthly payment plans. Borrowers choosing this strategy should wait until the funds taken from the tax intercepts leave them with a small balance left on their loans. Once the borrower has paid down to a small balance, exclusive of collection fees, the Department will frequently agree at this point to compromise the remaining balance and accept a lump sum payment.[57] The Department will usually waive the collection fees when the principal and interest is paid in full. This strategy saves borrowers from paying the huge collection fees that accrue once an account is turned over to a collection agency.[58]

---

45 *Id.*

46 Bosarge v. United States Dep't of Educ., 5 F.3d 1414 (11th Cir. 1993), *cert. denied*, 512 U.S. 1226 (1994).

47 28 U.S.C. §§ 3001–3308 (Debt Collection Procedures Act).

48 26 U.S.C. § 6402(d)(1); 31 U.S.C. § 3720A.

49 Bosarge v. United States Dep't of Educ., 5 F.3d 1414 (11th Cir. 1993), *cert. denied*, 512 U.S. 1226 (1994).

50 28 U.S.C. § 3003(c)(6).

51 Bosarge v. United States Dep't of Educ., 5 F.3d 1414 (11th Cir. 1993), *cert. denied*, 512 U.S. 1226 (1994).

52 *Id.* at 1420.

53 *Id.* (court cannot hold that the earned income tax credit embodies a more valuable social policy than recovery of defaulted student loans). However, some bankruptcy courts have found the earned income tax credit to be a "public benefit" under state statutes and therefore exempt from the bankruptcy estate. *See* § 5.2.4, *infra.*

54 Courts have found that offsets may include the amount of an EITC owed. *See* Sorenson v. Sec. of Treasury, 475 U.S. 851 (1986) (U.S. has authority to seize earned income tax refund); Bosarge v. United States Dep't of Educ., 5 F.3d 1414 (11th Cir. 1993), *cert. denied*, 512 U.S. 1226 (1994).

55 More information about the EITC is available on the IRS website, www.irs.treas.gov, and from the Center on Budget and Policy Priorities, www.cbpp.org, 1-202-408-1080.

56 The Department of Treasury regulations on tax intercepts specify only that offsets can be allocated for past-due debts, less fees charged under 31 C.F.R. § 285.2(i). This section allows fees charged by the Financial Management Service (FMS) of the Department of Treasury and the IRS to be deducted from the amount collected. To the extent allowed by law, federal agencies may add these fees to the debt. Still, the fees deducted, if any, should be less than those charged by collection agencies. *See* § 4.4, *supra.*

57 *See* §§ 4.4.1, 4.4.2, *supra. See also* U.S. Dep't of Educ., Amendment to Agreement Pursuant to Section 428(b) of the Higher Education Act of 1965, as Amended, with a State and Private Non-profit Institution or Organization for Coverage of Its Student Loan Insurance Program under the Interest Benefits Provision of Section 428(a) of the Act, Appendix I § 5.1, Clearinghouse No. 51,926 (July 11, 1994) (if borrower agrees to pay principal within thirty days, agency may enter into a repayment agreement that includes the compromise of interest owed).

58 *See* §§ 4.4.1, 4.4.2, *supra.*

5.2.4 *Using Bankruptcy Filing to Stave Off Intercept*

Filing a personal bankruptcy petition *before* the intercept activates the United States Bankruptcy Code automatic stay provision.[59] The stay prohibits virtually all actions against the debtor's property, including intercepts of owed tax refunds based on a student loan default.[60] The Department claims it will always readily and promptly return any amount taken by an offset during a pending bankruptcy.

It may also be possible to file bankruptcy to protect an impending return and claim any Earned Income Tax Credit (EITC) due as exempt. The majority of courts have found tax credits to be part of the bankruptcy estate under federal law, available for distribution to creditors, but there is some precedent for distinguishing the right to an EITC.[61] The EITC might also be exempt under various state exemption schemes, particularly if a state exemption for "public benefits" is interpreted to include Earned Income Tax Credits.[62]

If the intercept has already occurred, borrowers can still recover that amount if they act quickly. If the borrower files a chapter 7 or 13 bankruptcy within ninety days of the intercept, the borrower can recover the refund as a setoff under 11 U.S.C. § 553.[63]

5.2.5 *Rights of Non-Obligated Spouses*

When the United States intercepts a tax refund due on a joint return, the non-obligated spouse can recover *part* of the seized refund by filing an "injured spouse" claim with the Internal Revenue Service (IRS).[64] IRS regulations require that the United States notify any person who has filed a joint return with the obligated borrower concerning the steps that a non-obligated person can take to secure a proper partial refund.[65] If the non-obligated spouse files a separate return, the United States will seize no portion of a refund due on that return.

5.3 Wage Garnishment

5.3.1 *Federal Statutes Authorize Limited, Non-Judicial Wage Garnishment*

The Higher Education Act authorizes the Secretary and guaranty agencies to garnish borrowers' wages without first obtaining a court order.[66] Prior to 1996, the Department of Education was the only federal agency with this authority. However, the Debt Collection Improvement Act of 1996 (DCIA) extended the "privilege" to other federal agencies collecting debts owed to those agencies.[67]

For a time, there was some question as to whether the Department would continue operating under the authority of the HEA or whether it would try to conform to other agencies and operate under the authority of the DCIA. The mystery was cleared up when the Department published rules to operate garnishment procedures under the authority of the DCIA.[68] As discussed in detail below, these rules

---

59   11 U.S.C. § 362. *See generally* National Consumer Law Center, Consumer Bankruptcy Law and Practice § 2.5.3, Ch. 9, §§ 10.4.2.6.4 (bankruptcy preferences), 10.4.2.6.6 (post-petition transfers), 10.4.2.6.7 (set-off provisions) (7th ed. 2004 and Supp.).

60   An exception to the stay permits the IRS or another taxing authority to set off a pre-petition tax refund against a pre-petition tax debt. 11 U.S.C. § 362(b)(26).

61   *See generally* National Consumer Law Center, Consumer Bankruptcy Law and Practice § 2.5.3 (7th ed. 2004 and Supp.).

62   *See, e.g., In re* Jackson, 2001 Bankr. LEXIS 1125 (Bankr. M.D. Ga. 2001); *In re* Brasher, 253 B.R. 484 (Bankr. M.D. Ala. 2000) (earned-income credit exempt under state "public assistance benefit" exemption); *In re* Longstreet, 246 B.R. 611 (Bankr. S.D. Iowa 2000) (Iowa exemption for any "public assistance benefit" is broad enough to include the federal earned-income credit); *In re* Brockhouse, 220 B.R. 623 (Bankr. C.D. Ill. 1998); *In re* Brown, 186 B.R. 224 (Bankr. W.D. Ky. 1995). *But see In re* Collins, 170 F.3d 512, 513 (5th Cir. 1999) (rejecting earned-income-credit exemption because the Louisiana statute specifically defined exempted assistance to mean "money payments under this title"); *In re* Trudeau, 237 B.R. 803, 807 (B.A.P. 10th Cir. 1999) (Wyoming statute expressly exempts only public assistance and social services provided by the article); *In re* Rutter, 204 B.R. 57 (Bankr. D. Or. 1997). *See generally* National Consumer Law Center, Consumer Bankruptcy Law and Practice § 2.5.3 (7th ed. 2004 and Supp.).

63   *See, e.g., In re* Blake, 235 B.R. 568 (Bankr. Md. 1998) (Department of Education violated the automatic stay by causing improper IRS tax refund intercept; court ordered the Department to refund set-off amount).

64   IRS forms are available on-line at www.irs.treas.gov. The injured spouse form is Form 8379.

65   26 C.F.R. § 301.6402-6(i). *See* Burgess v. United States Dep't of Educ., 2006 WL 1047064 (D. Vt. Apr. 17, 2006) ("It is the Treasury Department that performs the tax refund offset, and only at that stage would a government agency become aware of the existence of a joint filer"; Department of Education also had no obligation to provide a non-debtor spouse with notice).

66   20 U.S.C. § 1095a.

67   Pub. L. No. 104-134, § 31001(o)(1) (Apr. 26, 1996) (codified at 31 U.S.C. § 3720D).

68   The final rules were published in February 2003 and became effective on March 21, 2003. 68 Fed. Reg. 8142 (Feb. 19, 2003) (adding 34 C.F.R. § 34.1–34.30). The switch to the DCIA occurred, among other reasons, because of criticism of the Department in a 2002 General Accounting Office (GAO) report. The GAO criticized the Department of Education and other federal agencies for failing to implement a wage garnishment program under the DCIA. In a letter to the GAO, the Department of Education complained that the report was misleading as it left the impression that no agency was conducting administrative wage garnishment. In fact, the Department of Education began garnishing wages under the authority of the HEA since 1993. *See* U.S. Gen. Accounting Office, Debt Collection Im-

should apply only when the Department initiates garnishment. The previous rules authorized by the Higher Education Act should continue to apply to guaranty agency garnishment actions.

The switch from the HEA-authorized garnishment program to a DCIA-authorized program was more significant prior to July 1, 2006, because there was a difference in the maximum garnishment limits. The DCIA allowed garnishment up to 15% of disposable income and the HEA only up to 10%. As of July 1, 2006, these limits will be the same, set at the higher 15% limit.[69]

5.3.2 HEA Wage Garnishment Program

5.3.2.1 General

The HEA garnishment authority should apply only when guaranty agencies are garnishing.[70] In 2003, the Department confirmed that it would garnish wages under the authority of the Debt Collection Improvement Act (DCIA) while guaranty agencies would continue to operate under HEA statutory authority.[71]

Guaranty agencies are under a general mandate to garnish wages of all eligible borrowers.[72] The only exception to this requirement arises if the agency determines that litigation would be more effective in collecting the debt.[73] The regulations clarify that agencies have the discretion to file lawsuits instead of wage garnishment only if the borrower has no wages that can be garnished or the agency determines that the borrower has sufficient attachable assets or income that is not subject to administrative wage garnishment.[74] The regulations therefore reflect the Department's preference toward using extra-judicial collection methods rather than filing suit.

There are a few substantive and procedural limits to this broad garnishment power in both the statute and the regulations. At least thirty days before beginning garnishment proceedings, agencies must mail borrowers a notice listing the nature and amount of the debt, the intention of the agency to collect the debt through deductions from pay, and an explanation of the borrower's rights.[75] Failure to follow

these notice requirements as well as misrepresentations about the process may violate the FDCPA.[76]

In addition, the guarantor is required to offer the borrower an opportunity to enter into a repayment agreement, in lieu of the garnishment, on terms agreeable to the guarantor.[77] As with tax intercepts, there is no requirement that the payment plan be "reasonable and affordable." However, at a minimum, a borrower should be able to request a reasonable and affordable plan after making a few payments under the plan agreed to by the Secretary.

Garnishment is also prohibited if the borrower has been involuntarily separated from employment until the borrower has been re-employed continuously for twelve months.

Many states place even greater restrictions on wage garnishment or prohibit the practice outright. These state law limitations on garnishment do not apply to garnishments to satisfy student loan obligations.[78] State procedural requirements prior to garnishment are not likely to apply either.[79] On the other hand, certain tribal law restrictions on garnishment should apply.[80]

At least one court has held that the federal wage garnishment provisions do not apply to a state's garnishment efforts.[81] Thus, a state agency was not required to comply with a federal student loan garnishment order against a state

---

provement Act of 1996: Status of Selected Agencies' Implementation of Administrative wage Garnishment, GAO-02-313 (Feb. 2002).

69 Pub. L. No. 109-171 (Higher Education Reconciliation Act).

70 20 U.S.C. § 1095a. The HEA expressly grants authority to guaranty agencies to garnish. The Debt Collection Improvement Ac, in contrast, applies only to "heads" of executive, judicial or legislative agencies. 31 U.S.C. § 3720D(a). See § 5.3.3.1.

71 68 Fed. Reg. 8142, 8148 (Feb. 19, 2003).

72 34 C.F.R. § 682.410(b)(6)(iii).

73 34 C.F.R. § 682.410(b)(6)(iv).

74 *Id.*

75 34 C.F.R. § 682.410(b)(9)(i)(B).

76 *See, e.g.*, Kort v. Diversified Collection Servs., Inc., 2001 WL 88149 (N.D. Ill. Aug. 2, 2001), *class cert. granted in part*, 2001 WL 1617213 (N.D. Ill. Dec. 17, 2001) (alleging that collector violated FDCPA by giving borrowers insufficient time to respond to garnishment notices and by requiring affirmative proof of unemployment exception); Sanders v. OSI Educ. Servs., Inc., 2001 WL 883608 (N.D. Ill. Aug. 3, 2001), *plaintiff's motion for summary judgment granted in part, denied in part*, 2003 WL 21542552 (N.D. Ill. July 8, 2003) (if a deadline for establishing a repayment plan or other response to garnishment is gratuitously established, it must not be misleading to the unsophisticated consumer; FDCPA violation found on this count). The district court granted summary judgment for the collection agency on plaintiff's claim that the agency's notice contained misinformation about the HEA unemployment exemption. The court found that the agency was insulated from liability under the FDCPA's bona fide error defense. The Seventh Circuit agreed. Kort v. Diversified Collection Serv., Inc., 270 F. Supp. 2d 1017 (N.D. Ill. 2003), *aff'd*, 394 F.3d 530 (7th Cir. 2005). *See also* § 4.5, *supra*.

77 20 U.S.C. § 1095a(a)(4); 34 C.F.R. § 682.410(b)(9)(i)(D).

78 20 U.S.C. § 1095a(a) (garnishment requirements are allowed notwithstanding any provisions of state law); Educational Credit Mgmt. Corp. v. Wilson, 2005 WL 1263027 (E.D. Tenn. May 27, 2005) (guaranty agency seeking to garnish pursuant to the HEA need not comply with state laws governing garnishment orders). *See, e.g.*, Clear v. Missouri Coordinating Bd. for Higher Educ., 23 S.W.3d 896 (Mo. App. 2000); Nelson v. Diversified Collection Servs. Inc., 961 F. Supp. 863 (D. Md. 1997).

79 *See* Nelson v. Diversified Collection Servs., Inc., 961 F. Supp. 863 (D. Md. 1997).

80 *See* 59 Fed. Reg. 22,473, Comment 63 (Apr. 29, 1994).

81 United Student Aid Funds, Inc. v. South Carolina Dep't of Health & Envtl. Control, 561 S.E.2d 650 (App. S.C. 2002), *aff'd*, 588 S.E.2d 599 (S.C. 2003).

employee. The court interpreted the federal wage garnishment statute so as not to interfere with the state's sovereign immunity.[82]

5.3.2.2 The Maximum Amount That May Be Garnished

Prior to Congressional changes in 2005, the Higher Education Act administrative wage garnishment statute and regulations allowed garnishment of up to 10% of "disposable pay." As of July 1, 2006, the limit was increased to 15%.[83]

If a guaranty agency decides to increase the withholding rate for a borrower already being garnished at the lesser rate, the agency must notify the borrower that the borrower can obtain a hearing upon request if he or she objects to the increased amount based on hardship. A borrower with new information not presented at the initial garnishment hearing may also request a reconsideration of the existence or the amount of the debt.[84]

Disposable pay is defined as pay remaining after deduction of any amounts required by law to be withheld.[85] The statute provides only that the amount deducted may not exceed 15%.[86] The Department's regulations specify that the amount that can be garnished is the *lesser* of 15% of disposable income and thirty times the prevailing minimum wage (the amount permitted by 15 U.S.C. § 1673).[87] 15 U.S.C. § 1673 also limits total garnishments to 25% of disposable income, so a student loan garnishment and other garnishments should not exceed 25% of income. Both the statute and regulations allow higher garnishments if the borrower gives written consent.[88]

At least one court has concluded that the maximum deduction applies to holders of student loan notes individually rather than collectively.[89] The court allowed each holder of a defaulted loan to garnish up to the maximum 10% of the borrower's wages as long as the total garnishments by all note holders did not exceed 25%.[90] Other courts have disagreed with this interpretation.[91] At least with respect to

garnishment authority under the DCIA, the Department has agreed that the aggregate amount to be withheld cannot exceed the 15% limit.[92]

5.3.2.3 Hearing Rights and Borrower Defenses

The Secretary or guaranty agency must notify the borrower before the garnishment.[93] The borrower must be given the opportunity for a hearing to contest the existence or amount of the debt and the terms of the repayment schedule.[94]

Instead of a hearing, the borrower can request that the holder review the borrower's written statement as to why the garnishment should not go forward. The borrower may (and is even encouraged by the Department's form letter to) request copies of all documentation held by the loan holder on the student loan before requesting the hearing or presenting a statement as to the basis of the student's objection to the garnishment.

The Department suggests (for Department-held loans) that the borrower call the relevant collection agency to obtain copies of the file and also contact the collection agency if the student wants to work out a repayment agreement in lieu of the garnishment. Hearings are reserved for claims that the borrower does not owe the debt in part or in whole.

If the borrower's written request for a hearing is received within fifteen days of the borrower's receipt of the garnishment notice (receipt is presumed within five days of mailing of the notice), no garnishment can issue until the hearing is provided.[95] The Department regulations require guaranty agencies to issue the hearing decision within sixty days.[96]

Possible grounds for contesting the loan obligation include that the loan has already been repaid; the social security numbers are wrong and the individual does not owe the loan; the borrower is making repayments pursuant to a repayment agreement; a bankruptcy proceeding is still pending or the loan was discharged in bankruptcy; the borrower is totally and permanently disabled the school closed while the student was still enrolled; the school falsely certified the student as eligible; the school failed to refund money owed

---

82   *Id.* (interpreting 20 U.S.C. § 1095a).

83   20 U.S.C. § 1095a(a)(1); 34 C.F.R. § 682.410(b)(9)(i)(A).

84   71 Fed. Reg. 45666, 45681–45682 (Aug. 9, 2006) (Interim final regulations).

85   20 U.S.C. § 1095a(e); 34 C.F.R. § 682.410(b)(9)(i)(A).

86   20 U.S.C. § 1095a(a)(1).

87   34 C.F.R. § 682.410(b)(9)(i)(A). The minimum wage can be found at 29 U.S.C. § 206(a)(1). The current minimum wage, as of October 1, 1997, is $5.15/hour. Therefore, $154.50 is protected per week (30 x $5.15 = $154.50).

88   20 U.S.C. § 1095a(a)(1); 34 C.F.R. § 682.410(b)(9)(i)(A). Garnishments may be greater than 25% to garnish for child support.

89   Halperin v. Regional Adjustment Bureau, Inc., 206 F.3d 1063 (11th Cir. 2000).

90   *Id.*

91   *See* United States v. George, 144 F. Supp. 2d 161 (E.D.N.Y. 2001) (because the plaintiff had only one loan, the case was

distinguishable from *Halperin*. However, court criticized the reasoning in *Halperin* as "somewhat forced"; court stated in a footnote that a fair reading of the legislative history "even as recounted in *Halperin*, supports an inference that any limitations on garnishment in the HEA . . . were intended to protect potential garnishees, who were often likely to be poor, from 'severe hardships.' "); Green v. Kentucky Higher Educ. Ass'n, 78 F. Supp. 2d 1259 (S.D. Ala. 1999) (interpreting 20 U.S.C. § 1095a to prevent multiple note holders from collectively garnishing more than 10%).

92   68 Fed. Reg. 8142, 8152 (Feb. 19, 2003).

93   *See* 34 C.F.R. § 682.410(b)(9)(i)(B).

94   34 C.F.R. § 682.410(b)(9)(i)(E).

95   34 C.F.R. § 682.410(b)(9)(i)(K).

96   34 C.F.R. § 682.410(b)(9)(i)(N).

the student; the loan is not enforceable; or the garnishment would result in extreme financial hardship.[97] The borrower, not the employer that receives a garnishment order, must assert any defenses to garnishment.[98]

The extreme financial hardship defense was added in 1998.[99] The Department clarified in a separate letter that it was not creating a new defense but rather making explicit a defense that the statute already allowed.[100] Guaranty agencies have the option of sending the financial disclosure forms needed to prove hardship with all notices or only to those students who raise hardship as a defense. Borrowers should provide as much documentation as possible to support hardship claims. Examples include copies of monthly bills for all expenses, copies of income tax returns, and any recent leave and/or earnings statements for the borrower, borrowers' spouse, and any employed dependents. Borrowers listing credit card payments should provide details about the types of expenses paid with the cards. The agencies may decide to withhold a lesser percentage of the borrower's wages or to completely stop withholding. The Department may reinstate garnishment if the borrower's financial circumstances improve.

Borrowers must inform loan holders that they qualify for the unemployment exception either by checking the appropriate box on the hearing form or by providing other written notice. The regulations depart from the statute in authorizing garnishment unless the guarantor has *knowledge* that this exception applies to a particular borrower.[101] This places the burden on the borrower to notify the guarantor of the lack of continuous employment. The regulations also do not provide notice to the employer in the withholding order of the twelve-months-continuous-employment requirement.[102]

There is some question as to whether borrowers have to provide documentation or other proof that they qualify for the unemployment exception. If documentation is not required, collection letters requiring borrowers to submit affirmative proof of eligibility may violate the FDCPA.[103]

The hearing request form issued by the Department requires that borrowers attach proof of unemployment. Guaranty agencies may also use this form. In a 2005 Seventh Circuit case, the court granted summary judgment for the defendant collection agency on plaintiff's claim that the agency's use of this form violated the FDCPA.[104] The court found that the Department's interpretation of the law as presented on the hearing form might be wrong but that the collection agency was not liable for using the Department's prescribed form.[105] Although the court did not approve the Department's use of the forms, it did observe that the Department's handling of the unemployment exemption in the form was reasonable and proper.[106] According to the court, the HEA is silent on the question of whether a debtor must come forward with documentation to substantiate eligibility. Since Congress gave the Department authority to "fill in gaps in the HEA," the court found the Department's interpretation of the law to be reasonable and noted that it encourages a speedy and amicable resolution of disputes. Furthermore, the court stated that it is an efficient and common-sense approach to require the debtor, who is in a better position to know whether he or she is eligible for the exemption, to share that knowledge and substantiate the claim.[107]

In a training manual for private collection agencies, the Department set out more specifically the type of information borrowers should submit to support the various defenses. For the discharge-related defenses, borrowers should submit the required discharge forms and relevant supporting information. For borrowers claiming that they were entitled to a full or partial refund of their loans, the Department requests that borrowers answer the following questions and provide documentation to support these answers:

---

97 In 1998, the Department issued "Notice prior to Wage Withholding" and "Request for Hearing" notices listing these defenses. These notices are attached to the Department's letter to Guaranty Agency Directors, March 17, 1998, Clearinghouse No. 52, 042. The Department has also developed a form authorized by the Debt Collection Improvement Act for the wage garnishment process. *See* § 5.3.3.2, *infra*.

98 Educational Credit Mgmt. Corp. v. Wilson, 2005 WL 1263027 (E.D. Tenn. May 27, 2005) (employer prohibited from asserting that the borrower did not owe the loan).

99 See U.S. Department of Education's March 17, 1998, "Dear Guaranty Agency Director" letter, Clearinghouse No. 52, 042.

100 Letter from Patricia Newcombe, U.S. Dep't of Educ., to Carol N. Lindsey, Assistant V.P., Texas Guaranteed Student Loan Corp. (Jan. 20, 1998). This letter is included on the companion CD-Rom to this manual.

101 20 U.S.C. § 1095a(a)(d)(7); 34 C.F.R. § 682.410(b)(9)(i)(G).

102 *See* 59 Fed. Reg. 22,474, Comments 72, 73 (Apr. 29, 1994); 34 C.F.R. § 682.410(b)(10)(i)(I) (notice to employer must contain only the information necessary for the employer to comply with the withholding order).

103 However, at least one court found that a collection agency was not liable under the FDCPA even if the information in the notice about the unemployment exception was incorrect. The court agreed with the collection agency's argument that the error was inadvertent because it used the notice form required by the Department of Education and any errors in the form were the responsibility of the Department. Kort v. Diversified Collection Servs., Inc., 2001 WL 881449 (N.D. Ill. Aug. 2, 2001), *class cert. granted in part*, 2001 WL 1617213 (N.D. Ill. Dec. 17, 2001) (alleging that collector violated FDCPA by giving borrowers insufficient time to respond to garnishment notices and by requiring affirmative proof of unemployment exception), *plaintiff's motion for summary judgment granted in part, denied in part*, 270 F. Supp. 2d. 1017 (N.D. Ill. 2003), *aff'd*, 394 F.3d 530 (7th Cir. 2005); Sanders v. OSI Educ. Serv., Inc., 2001 WL 883608 (N.D. Ill. Aug. 3, 2001).

104 Kort v. Diversified Collection Serv., Inc., 394 F.3d 530 (7th Cir. 2005).

105 *Id.*

106 *Id.*

107 *Id.*

- What procedures did you follow to enroll in the school?
- How long after you enrolled did you first attend the school?
- What course did you enroll in?
- What was the cost of the course?
- What did the school charge for tuition, board, and fees?
- Did you receive any other loans or grants to pay for this training?
- What was the refund policy of the school?
- Did the school give you any money from loan(s), or were all loan proceeds used for tuition, board, and fee charges?
- Did you receive any mail-order lessons?
- If so, how many of these lessons did you complete?
- How many days did you attend the school?
- Why did you leave the school?
- What procedures did you follow when you withdrew from the school?
- What was your last day of attendance?
- What steps if any did you take to see if the school issued a refund to the lender?
- Did you notify your lender that you had withdrawn from the school? If so, how did you notify them?[108]

Borrowers may also raise as a defense that the debt is not enforceable. Any viable state, federal, and common law claims should be available.[109]

The borrower is entitled to a hearing with an independent official within the agency. "Independent official" is defined as someone not under the supervision or control of the head of the agency.[110]

The regulations allow the agency to establish the time and location of the hearing or to hold the hearing by telephone conference.[111] A location agreeable to the agency may be very inconvenient for the borrower, possibly thousands of

miles away in another state. There is no requirement that the guarantor tape the hearing, although the agency may do so if it wishes.[112]

The Department's AWG Hearing Guidelines handbook elaborates on the procedures that hearing officers should follow when a borrower raises one of the discharges as a defense to garnishment. According to the handbook, the case law is unanimous that borrowers cannot seek these kinds of discharge relief directly from a court but must present their claim to, and obtain a determination from, the Secretary or the guarantor, who is initially responsible for determining whether the student loan should be discharged.[113]

According to the handbook, when the borrower raises a discharge defense, the Hearing Official must first determine whether the claim has been presented to the guarantor in the manner required by Federal regulations and then whether the guarantor has made a decision on the claim. If these prerequisites have not been met, the Hearing Official may want to adjourn the hearing to accommodate the discharge determination. The Department notes further that the federal regulations generally require the guarantor to suspend collection action on a loan when the guarantor receives reliable information indicating that the borrower may be eligible for discharge relief.[114]

In response to a 2003 FOIA request, the Department reported that, since 1998, it has received 823 requests for review raising false certification of ability to benefit as a defense. Of these, 172 borrowers (about 21%) received discharges. With respect to closed-school defenses, the Department reported receiving 790 requests since 1998 and discharging 277 (about 35%) of these claims. Although the numbers were lower for unpaid-refund discharges, the percentage approved was higher. The Department reported receiving 232 cases of unpaid-refund claims in response to garnishment and discharging 94 (about 40%) of these.

At the hearing, the agency must provide evidence establishing the existence and amount of the debt and the agency's right to administratively garnish the borrower's wages. The case should not be allowed to proceed if, for example, the agency does not have a copy of the loan application and/or promissory note. After the agency has presented this information, the burden shifts to the borrower to provide the facts necessary to support the objection raised. In a 2004 handbook for guaranty agencies, *2004 AWG Handbook*, the Department states that the HEA does not specifically address the issue of burdens of proof. According to the De-

---

108 U.S. Dep't of Educ., Student Financial Assistance, Administrative Wage Garnishment, Hearings Support Manual, Private Collection Agencies (Jan. 2005), *available at* www.fsacollections.ed.gov/contractors/pca2004/awg/PCA%20Training%20Manual%20-%20Revised%2001-%2018-1-05.pdf. These questions and requirements should apply to the DCIA-authorized garnishment process as well. *See* § 5.3.3.2, *infra*.

109 *See generally* § 9.5.3, *infra*.

110 34 C.F.R. § 682.410(b)(9)(i)(M).

111 34 C.F.R. § 682.410(b)(9)(i)(J). The telephone charges are the responsibility of the guaranty agency. In at least one case, a borrower challenged a collection agency's scheduling of a garnishment hearing in another state as a violation of the Fair Debt Collection Practices Act (FDCPA). *See* Lawson v. Management Adjustment Bureau, 1997 U.S. Dist. LEXIS 7275 (N.D. Ill. May 15, 1997) (plaintiff claimed that the scheduling of the hearing in another state violated 15 U.S.C. § 1692i(a)(2), the provision of the FDCPA that requires a collector to bring legal actions on a debt only in the judicial district in which the consumer signed the contract or where the consumer resides; court granted defendant's motion to dismiss this claim, finding that an administrative wage garnishment hearing is not a "legal action" for purposes of the FDCPA venue requirement).

112 *See* 59 Fed. Reg. 22,474, 22,475, Comment 75 (Apr. 29, 1994).

113 Dep't of Educ., AWG Hearing Guidelines (rev. Mar. 1, 2004) (citing *In re* Scholl, 259 B.R. 345 (Bankr. N.D. Iowa 2001) (closed-school claim)); United States v. Wright, 87 F. Supp. 2d 464 (D. Md. 2000); United States v. Bertucci, 2000 WL 1234560 (E.D. La. Aug. 29, 2000); *In re* Bega, 180 B.R. 642 (Bankr. D. Kan. 1995). *See* § 9.5.3.2, *infra*.

114 Dep't of Educ., AWG Hearing Guidelines (rev. Mar. 1, 2004).

partment, however, under the DCIA, the facts necessary to establish objection(s) to the existence of the debt amount, to establish that the proposed garnishment rate would cause financial hardship, or to establish that applicable law bars the Department from collecting the debt by garnishment must be proven by the borrower by a preponderance of the credible evidence.[115] According to the handbook, a similar standard applies to financial hardship claims.[116]

The Department also states that a favorable decision by the guaranty agency on a discharge claim generally moots the garnishment action.[117] If the agency denied the discharge claim, the Hearing Official then must consider the guarantor's determination by applying the same standards a court applies in reviewing other informal administrative agency determinations.[118] Under this standard, the Hearing Official should uphold the denial if he concludes that the decision is "rationally based" and "founded upon a consideration of relevant factors and does not exhibit clear error of judgment."[119] If the Hearing Official finds that the decision does not meet this test, the case should be remanded to the guarantor for further consideration.[120]

In some cases, agencies will be unprepared to offer borrowers proper hearings. As a result, in some cases, when borrowers have pushed for hearings, agencies have simply agreed to withdraw the garnishment order. Advocates should not rely on this possibility. However, borrowers are entitled to at least the procedural rights required in the regulations and should be prepared to aggressively advocate for these rights.[121]

If the borrower does not request a hearing, or if the borrower's objection is denied, the employer is notified to deduct the garnishment amount from the borrower's paycheck. If the borrower is late in requesting a hearing on the garnishment, the garnishment order will proceed, but the borrower should still receive a hearing and a decision within sixty days.[122] If the borrower prevails, the garnishment should be ordered to cease, and, if appropriate, amounts garnished should be returned. In addition, the guaranty agency has discretion to postpone a garnishment pending a hearing, even if the borrower's request for a hearing is late, if the borrower's delay was caused by factors over which the borrower had no control or if the agency receives information that the agency believes justifies a delay.[123]

Guaranty agencies have the authority to adjudicate disputes and make binding decisions.[124] However, unlike federal agency hearings, borrowers have no explicit right to judicial review of guaranty agency actions. This lack of review has been challenged, unsuccessfully to date, on constitutional due process grounds.[125] In 2003 court pleadings, the Department of Education acknowledged the problem and supported implying a private right of action under the HEA for judicial review of guaranty agency administrative wage garnishment hearing decisions.[126] Borrowers should clearly be able to appeal denials when the Department is garnishing.[127]

5.3.3 DCIA Wage Garnishment Program

5.3.3.1 Differences Between Garnishment Under the Debt Collection Improvement Act (DCIA) and the Higher Education Act (HEA)

As discussed earlier, the DCIA authority should apply only when the Department is initiating garnishment and the HEA should apply when guaranty agencies are attempting to garnish. This is because the DCIA, unlike the HEA, applies only to garnishment by the "heads" of executive, judicial, or legislative agencies.[128] It does not specifically apply to agents of the federal departments.

Previously, the most significant difference between the two statutes was that the DCIA authorized garnishment up to 15% and the HEA only up to 10%. However, as of July 1, 2006, both programs allow garnishment of disposable income up to 15%.[129]

The 25% federal limit and special rules regarding child support and minimum wages apply in the DCIA-authorized garnishment process as well.[130] There are other, less significant, differences as well. These are summarized below.

---

115 *Id.* (citing 34 C.F.R. § 34.14(b)–(d)).

116 *Id.*

117 *Id.*

118 *Id.*

119 *Id.* (citing Lee v. Riley, No. 3:96CV-719-H (D.D.C. Feb. 29, 1998)).

120 *Id.* (citing Most v. United States Dep't of Educ., No. 98CV2910 (D.D.C. Dec. 21, 1999)).

121 Whether these procedures comport with due process is discussed in § 5.3.4, *infra*.

122 34 C.F.R. § 684.410(b)(9)(i)(L).

123 *Id.*

124 20 U.S.C. § 1095a.

125 *See* § 5.3.4, *infra*.

126 *See* Hutchins v. United States Dep't of Educ., CV-F-02-6256-OWW-DLB (E.D. Cal. filed Apr. 25, 2003) (U.S. Department of Education Memorandum of Points and Authorities Supporting Motion to Dismiss). The document is included on the companion CD-Rom to this manual.

127 *See, e.g.,* Gorka v. United States Dep't of Educ., 2004 WL 2658071 (N.D. Ill. Oct. 13, 2004) (allowing borrower's claim for improper garnishment but finding that the Department's administrative denial was reasonable). *See* § 6.10, *infra*.

128 31 U.S.C. § 3720D(a). The HEA, in contrast, specifically applies to guaranty agencies as well as the Secretary of Education. 20 U.S.C. § 1095a(a). *See* § 5.3.2.1, *supra*. There may be challenges to the Department's authority to garnish under the DCIA without expressly repealing the HEA. The Department responded to many of these arguments when it published final rules for implementation of DCIA garnishment authority. 68 Fed. Reg. 8142 (Feb. 19, 2003).

129 Pub. L. No. 109-171, 120 Stat. 4 (Feb. 8, 2006).

130 *See* § 5.3.2.2, *supra*.

The DCIA, like the HEA, prohibits garnishment if the borrower has been involuntarily separated from employment until the borrower has been re-employed continuously for twelve months.[131] As discussed above, the Department's garnishment regulations governing guaranty agencies departed from the statute in authorizing garnishment unless the guarantor has *knowledge* that this exception applies.[132] The Department's garnishment regulations implementing the DCIA garnishment authority, in contrast, require that the borrower present credible evidence of involuntary separation from employment.[133] There is not much practical difference between these provisions. Under either garnishment scheme, borrowers have some burden to notify the loan holder of their unemployment status and to prove that they qualify for the unemployment exception.

There is a difference in the definition of "disposable pay." The HEA defines disposable pay as excluding only those amounts required by law to be withheld.[134] The DCIA has a similar definition.[135] However, the Department's regulations follow the Department of Treasury's implementing regulations in defining "disposable pay" as amounts deducted from gross pay for health insurance premiums as well as amounts required by law to be withheld.[136]

In addition, the regulations explicitly grant the Department authority to issue multiple garnishment orders even though there is no provision in the DCIA allowing this practice.[137] Although it can issue multiple garnishment orders, the total amount that may be withheld by a single agency cannot exceed the DCIA garnishment limit of 15%.[138] The total amount may not exceed the smaller of the amount in the orders, the federal limits, or 15%.

5.3.3.2 Hearing Rights and Borrower Defenses

Like the HEA, the DCIA requires notice to the borrower before garnishment.[139] The notice provisions are similar.[140] Notice must be sent by mail to the last known address a minimum of thirty days before the initiation of garnishment procedures.[141] The notice must inform the borrower of the nature and amount of the debt, the agency's intention to initiate garnishment, and an explanation of the borrower's rights.[142]

The regulations specify the borrower rights that must be revealed in the notice. These are (1) right to inspect and copy records; (2) right to enter into a repayment agreement; and (3) right to request a hearing about the existence, amount, or current enforceability of the debt, the rate of withholding, and whether the borrower has been continuously employed less than twelve months after an involuntary separation from employment.[143]

Borrowers must inform loan holders that they qualify for the unemployment exception either by checking the appropriate box on the hearing form or by providing other written notice. There is some question as to whether borrowers should also have to provide documentation or other proof that they qualify for the exception. If documentation is not required, collection letters requiring borrowers to submit affirmative proof of eligibility may violate the FDCPA.[144]

The hearing request form issued by the Department requires that borrowers attach proof of unemployment. Guaranty agencies may also use this form. In a 2005 Seventh Circuit case, the court granted summary judgment for the defendant collection agency on plaintiff's claim that the agency's use of this form violated the FDCPA.[145] The court found that the Department's interpretation of the law as presented on the hearing form might be wrong but that the collection agency was not liable for using the Department's prescribed form.[146] Although the court did not approve the Department's use of the forms, it did observe that the Department's handling of the unemployment exemption in the form was reasonable and proper.[147] According to the court, the HEA is silent on the question of whether a debtor must come forward with documentation to substantiate eligibility. Since Congress gave the Department authority to "fill in gaps in the HEA," the court found the Department's interpretation of the law to be reasonable and noted that it encourages a speedy and amicable resolution of disputes. Furthermore, the court stated that it is an efficient and

---

131 31 U.S.C. § 3720D(b)(6).

132 34 C.F.R. § 682.410(b)(9)(i)(G). *See* § 5.3.2.1, *supra.*

133 34 C.F.R. § 34.23.

134 20 U.S.C. § 1095a(e).

135 31 U.S.C. § 3720D(g).

136 34 C.F.R. § 34.3(a).

137 34 C.F.R. § 34.20 (c). For more on case decisions regarding multiple garnishments, see § 5.3.2.2, *supra.*

138 34 C.F.R. § 34.20(c)(2).

139 31 U.S.C. § 3720D(b)(2).

140 *See* § 5.3.2.3, *supra.*

141 31 U.S.C. § 3720D(b)(2).

142 *Id.*

143 34 C.F.R. §§ 34.6(c).

144 However, at least one court found that a collection agency was not liable under the FDCPA even if the information in the notice about the unemployment exception was incorrect. The court agreed with the collection agency's argument that the error was inadvert because it used the notice form required by the Department of Education and any errors in the form were the responsibility of the Department. Kort v. Diversified Collection Servs., Inc., 2001 WL 881449 (N.D. Ill. Aug. 2, 2001), *class cert. granted in part*, 2001 WL 1617213 (N.D. Ill. Dec. 17, 2001) (alleging that collector violated FDCPA by giving borrowers insufficient time to respond to garnishment notices and by requiring affirmative proof of unemployment exception), *plaintiff's motion for summary judgment granted in part, denied in part*, 270 F. Supp. 2d. 1017 (N.D. Ill. 2003), *aff'd*, 394 F.3d 530 (7th Cir. 2005); Sanders v. OSI Educ. Serv., Inc., 2001 WL 883608 (N.D. Ill. Aug. 3, 2001).

145 Kort v. Diversified Collection Serv., Inc., 394 F.3d 530 (7th Cir. 2005).

146 *Id.*

147 *Id.*

common-sense approach to require the debtor, who is in a better position to know whether he or she is eligible for the exemption, to share that knowledge and substantiate the claim.[148]

Although the grounds for objection are limited to the unemployment defense and defenses regarding the existence, amount, or enforceability of the debt, the Department has issued a "Request for Hearing" form similar to the form for guaranty agencies that includes a list of specific defenses. These defenses including the various discharge programs, including disability, death, closed school, false certification, and unpaid refund. The completed form must be sent to the address listed on the form. As of 2006, this was U.S. Department of Education, P.O. Box 617763, Chicago, IL 60661-7763.[149]

The form also includes a hardship defenses. The information about this defense is printed in bold immediately after the identifying information. There is a separate form, "Financial Disclosure Statement" that the Department requires borrowers seeking a hardship defense to fill out.[150]

In final rules implementing the DCIA hearing requirements, the Department provided a detailed explanation of the hardship exception/defense. The final rules clarify that borrowers may object to a previous garnishment amount within six months after issuance of a garnishment order if the borrower shows, in a request for review, that his or her financial circumstances have substantially worsened.[151]

The Department acknowledged that the garnishment test is less than that required in bankruptcy. In determining a hardship waiver, the Department will compare the debtors' expenses to the average amounts incurred by families of similar size and income. Borrowers bear the burden of proving the necessity of any amounts spent in excess of the national averages. It will use standards adopted by the I.R.S. ("National Standards") to make the comparisons.[152] For example, the borrower may contend that above-average expenses are needed for housing costs, retirement savings, tuition for private schools, charitable contributions, vehicles, utilities, and telephone costs.[153] In contrast, the FFEL regulations for guaranty agencies do not contain any provision that expressly allocates the burden of proof for financial hardship. The HEA regulations also do not require agencies to use national standards to compare borrower expenses.

However, the Department encouraged guaranty agency decision makers to use these same standards.[154]

The Department rejected a proposal to include a separate form for debtors to use to claim hardship.[155] The Department explained that it currently sends financial statement forms to those borrowers who state on their request for hearing that they intend to object on hardship grounds. According to the Department, the overwhelming majority of objections to proposed garnishment are based on hardship. The Department agreed that a "self-explanatory" form would be useful to encourage debtors to present their financial circumstances in a way that makes analysis easier but did not make any commitment to developing this form.[156]

The regulations addressing the format of the hearings are similar to the HEA, with a few notable exceptions. As with the HEA, if the borrower requests a hearing on or before the fifteenth day following notice of garnishment, the garnishment should not proceed until after the hearing.[157] Borrowers can still request hearings after that date, but garnishment may proceed pending a hearing decision.[158]

The regulations provide detail on the hearing process. First, borrowers who want an oral hearing must request one and also must show good reason why the issues cannot be resolved on paper.[159] The oral hearing may be in person or by telephone.[160]

In its final rules, the Department responded to the concern that requiring debtors to state reasons why a written review is insufficient places an unfair burden on debtors.[161] The Department explained that it has limited resources available to conduct oral hearings, citing statistics showing that it received approximately 9000 requests for hearings in its

---

148 *Id.*

149 A copy of the form is included at Appendix D.4.1, *infra*, and on the companion CD-Rom to this manual. It is also available on-line at www.ed.gov/offices/OSFAP/DCS/forms/Request. For.Hearing.pdf.

150 A copy of this form is reprinted at Appendix D. It is also available on-line at www.ed.gov/offices/OSFAP/DCS/forms/fs.pdf. See § 5.3.2.3, *supra*, for a discussion of supporting documentation to submit.

151 68 Fed. Reg. 8142, 8151 (Feb. 19, 2003).

152 67 Fed. Reg. 18072, 18073 (Apr. 12, 2002).

153 68 Fed. Reg. 8142, 8151 (Feb. 19, 2003).

154 *Id.* at 8152.

155 *Id.* at 8151.

156 *Id.*

157 31 U.S.C. § 3720D(c)(1).

158 31 U.S.C. § 3720D(c)(2). It is unclear whether borrowers requesting hearings after the fifteen days may also request in-person hearings. This issue was raised in comments submitted by the National Consumer Law Center, Community Legal Services, and Legal Aid Foundation of Los Angeles. See *Comments to the Department of Education on proposed Administrative Wage Garnishment Regulations* (hereafter *NCLC Wage Garnishment Comments*), which was submitted on June 11, 2002, and is available on the companion CD-Rom to this manual. The final rules did not directly address this issue. However, the Department reaffirmed that it provides hearings even if the request for hearing is untimely, regardless of the type of hearing sought. 68 Fed. Reg. 8142, 8149 (Feb. 19, 2003). The "Request for Hearing" form allows a borrower to choose between a written record, in-person hearing, or telephone hearing. It does not state that only borrowers requesting hearings within fifteen days are entitled to in-person hearings. The form does, however, state that borrowers requesting in-person hearings are required to pay their own expenses. The form is reprinted at Appendix D.4.1, *infra*, and on the companion CD-Rom to this manual.

159 34 C.F.R. § 34.9.

160 34 C.F.R. § 34.9.

161 *Id.* at 8149.

HEA garnishment actions in fiscal year 2000.[162] Although limitations on resources do not warrant curtailing debtor rights, according to the Department, they do militate in favor of the Department avoiding unnecessary hearings.[163] The Department claims that it is simply requiring debtors who seek an oral hearing to show a good reason why the disputed issues cannot be resolved through written review. The Department characterizes this requirement as a "common-sense standard that we have generously applied for years in Federal offset proceedings."[164] Borrowers will be allowed an opportunity to submit evidence and argument after a request for an oral hearing is denied. This is meant to allow borrowers who intended to present evidence and objections at an oral hearing the opportunity to submit this evidence in writing.[165]

The HEA regulations entitle borrowers to a hearing with an independent official from within the Department.[166] In contrast, the DCIA regulations allow the hearing officer to be any "qualified employee" of the Department.[167] Unfortunately for borrowers, the Department does not provide any definition of "qualified employee" and does not explicitly state that the hearing officer must be independent or neutral. The National Consumer Law Center and other advocacy groups have argued that, at minimum, employees of the collections division should not serve as hearing officers.[168]

In its final rules, the Department clarified the role of Department contractors in the hearing process.[169] Department contractors cannot conduct hearings or rule on objections to garnishment because those are inherently governmental functions. The Department itself must provide a hearing and decide debtor objections. This does not, according to the Department, preclude use of contractors to analyze debtor objections and propose resolutions on objections.[170] The Department specifically acknowledged that contractors used to prepare recommendations should be trained to properly analyze debtor objections. The Department also addressed consumer advocates' requests that it adopt guidelines and training procedures for any Department staff designated to conduct hearings. In rejecting these suggestions, the Department merely affirmed that its decisions are

subject to judicial review under the Administrative Procedure Act.[171]

The hearing officer is required to maintain a summary record and issue a written opinion.[172] The hearing decision must rest on evidence in the hearing record and must include a description of the evidence considered in making that decision.[173] The hearing official will consider evidence that was not included in records made available for inspection before the hearing only after the Department has notified the borrower, made the evidence available to the borrower, and provided a reasonable period for rebuttal evidence and argument by the borrower.[174]

Borrowers may submit evidence after sending in a request for hearing. The regulations require that the borrower make a specific request that the record be held open for consideration of such evidence, describe the evidence, and explain why it is relevant. There is a provision for a brief extension of time, upon request, for the borrower to then submit any evidence not previously presented.[175]

Borrowers who object to the decision have the right to request reconsideration.[176] The hearing decision must include a statement not only that the borrower may appeal the ruling in federal court but also explaining the reconsideration rights available.[177] Garnishment will continue pending a decision on reconsideration.[178]

The regulations state that the Department will consider a request for reconsideration only if it determines that:

- the borrower's request is based on grounds of financial hardship and the borrower's financial circumstances, as shown by evidence submitted with the request, have materially changed since issuance of the decision so that the amount to be garnished should be reduced[179] or
- the borrower submitted evidence that was not previously submitted and this evidence demonstrates that the Department should reconsider an objection to the existence, amount, or enforceability of the debt.[180]

The Department may offer a hearing for reconsideration.[181]

162　*Id.* (citing U.S. Gen. Accounting Office, Debt Collection Improvement Act of 1996: Status of Selected Agencies' Implementation of Administrative Wage Garnishment 16, GAO-02-313 (2002)).

163　68 Fed. Reg. 8142, 8149 (Feb. 19, 2003).

164　*Id.*

165　34 C.F.R. § 34.13(d)(4)(iv).

166　34 C.F.R. § 682.410(b)(9)(i)(M). *See* § 5.3.2.3, *supra.*

167　34 C.F.R. § 34.13(a)(2).

168　See *NCLC Administrative Wage Garnishment Comments*, objecting to the lack of any clear standards for hearing officers.

169　68 Fed. Reg. 8142, 8149 (Feb. 19, 2003).

170　*Id.* at 8149–50. The Department also explained that it intended no inference that guaranty agencies could not use contractors as hearing officials.

171　*Id.* at 8150. APA appeal rights, however, may not be available if the guaranty agency makes the decision. *See* § 5.3.4, *infra.*

172　34 C.F.R. § 34.13(b)(3); 34 C.F.R. § 34.16. *See also NCLC Wage Garnishment Comments* (noting that regulations should require hearing officers to provide specific reasons for their decisions).

173　34 C.F.R. § 34.17(a).

174　34 C.F.R. § 34.13(c).

175　34 C.F.R. § 34.13(d)(4)(iii).

176　34 C.F.R. § 34.12.

177　34 C.F.R. § 34.17(a)(4).

178　34 C.F.R. § 34.12(b).

179　34 C.F.R. § 34.12(c)(1).

180　34 C.F.R. § 34.12(c)(2).

181　34 C.F.R. § 34.12(d)(2)(ii).

5.3.4 Due Process Challenges to Garnishment

Serious due process questions are raised regardless of whether garnishment is authorized by the DCIA or HEA. This is particularly true when one considers these procedures in conjunction with the extraordinary statutory authorization for a state or even a private guaranty agency to conduct its own hearing and seize wages without judicial review.

One set of due process issues relates to the notices of hearing. Prior to the Department's issuance of standard notices for garnishment, borrowers challenged a number of misleading and confusing aspects of the withholding and request-for-hearing notices.[182] These challenges have been unsuccessful to date. For example, one court found that the failure to notify plaintiffs of several possible defenses to garnishment in the pre-hearing notice was not a violation of constitutional due process.[183] Even so, the Department later issued new notices that define more clearly the defenses available to borrowers.[184]

Courts have rejected borrowers' due process claims in cases in which actual notice was allegedly not received, but the courts found that the Department had made reasonable efforts to notify the borrowers of offset or other collection processes.[185] Despite the fact that the hearing is likely to be inadequate or even unfair, borrowers seeking to raise due process claims should first request hearings in order to avoid a ruling that the borrower has "slept" on his or her constitutional claims.[186]

There are also many possible challenges to other aspects of the process, including the failure to provide in-person hearings and questions about whether an official provided by the agency is truly an independent arbiter, among other possible violations. It is also very troubling that the Department does not regulate the quality of hearing officers by, for example, publishing minimum qualifications.

In one case, the plaintiffs' due process challenges to the administrative hearing process based on absence of judicial review, inadequacy of hearing procedures, and failure to ensure impartiality of hearing officers were ruled not ripe and dismissed.[187] The court found the claims not ripe because hearings were not actually held for either plaintiff. The court did consider plaintiffs' other due process claims, finding that the failure to offer borrowers the opportunity to appear in-person at the hearing did not violate constitutional due process standards.[188]

The Department has addressed the judicial review problem, suggesting that it supports implying a private right of action under the HEA to allow borrowers to seek review of guaranty agency garnishment decisions.[189] Borrowers should clearly be able to appeal denials when the Department is garnishing.[190]

5.3.5 Participation of Private Collection Agencies in Garnishment

Under the HEA program, the Department has issued guidance to guaranty agencies on the extent to which col-

182 *See, e.g.*, Nelson v. Diversified Collection Servs., Inc., 961 F. Supp. 863 (D. Md. 1997) (USA funds was the guarantor; court found the notice adequate and the existence of pre- and post-intercept hearings before a "neutral" officer sufficient to meet procedural due process concerns; court upheld the notice and hearing procedures without addressing the issue that administrative hearing procedure was entrusted to a non-governmental guaranty agency with direct financial interest in the hearing's outcome); Lawson v. Management Adjustment Bureau, 1997 U.S. Dist. LEXIS 7275 (N.D. Ill. May 15, 1997) (collection agency notice not only stated valid defenses to garnishment but also invalid defenses; court found borrower stated a claim for relief under the Fair Debt Collection Practices Act (FDCPA) and denied defendant's motion for summary judgment); Sibley v. Diversified Collection Servs., Inc., 1997 U.S. Dist. LEXIS 23583 (N.D. Tex. June 10, 1997) (ruling on defendants' motion to dismiss). Class certification was denied on the remaining claims in the *Sibley* case. *See* Sibley v. Diversified Collection Servs., 1998 U.S. Dist. LEXIS 9969 (N.D. Tex. June 30, 1998).
183 Sibley v. Diversified Collection Servs., Inc., 1997 U.S. Dist. LEXIS 23583 (N.D. Tex. June 10, 1997) (ruling on defendant's motion to dismiss). Class certification was denied on the remaining claims. *See* Sibley v. Diversified Collection Servs., 1998 U.S. Dist. LEXIS 9969 (N.D. Tex. June 30, 1998).
184 *See* § 5.3.3.2, *supra*.
185 *See, e.g.*, Savage v. Scales, 310 F. Supp. 2d 122 (D.D.C. 2004); Shabtai v. United States Dep't of Educ., 2003 WL 21983025 (S.D.N.Y. Aug. 20, 2003); Setlech v. United States, 816 F. Sup. 161, 167 (E.D.N.Y. 1992) (using an address most recently in the agency's database or an address obtained from the IRS from plaintiff's most recent tax return has been held to be "reasonably calculated to notify the vast majority of debtors of the intended referral and proposed offset"), *aff'd*, 17 F.3d 390 (2d Cir. 1993)

(table); Nelson v. Diversified Collection Servs., Inc., 961 F. Supp. 863 (D. Md. 1997).
186 Nelson v. Diversified Collection Servs., Inc., 961 F. Supp. 863 (D. Md. 1997)
187 Sibley v. Diversified Collection Servs., Inc., 1997 U.S. Dist. LEXIS 23583 (N.D. Tex. June 10, 1997) (ruling on defendants' motion to dismiss). Class certification was denied on the remaining claims in the Sibley case. *See* Sibley v. Diversified Collection Servs., 1998 U.S. Dist. LEXIS 9969 (N.D. Tex. June 30, 1998).
188 Sibley v. Diversified Collection Servs., Inc., 1997 U.S. Dist. LEXIS 23583 (N.D. Tex. June 10, 1997) (ruling on defendants' motion to dismiss). For a more recent complaint challenging a collection agency's administration of the wage garnishment process, see *Cliff v. Payco Gen. Am. Credits, Inc.*, Clearinghouse No. 52,132 (M.D. Fla. 1998) (class action complaint).
189 *See* Hutchins v. United States Dep't of Educ., CV-F-02-6256-OWW-DLB (E.D. Cal. filed Apr. 25, 2003) (U.S. Department of Education Memorandum of Points and Authorities Supporting Motion to Dismiss). The document is available on the companion CD-Rom to this manual.
190 *See, e.g.*, Gorka v. United States Dep't of Educ., 2004 WL 2658071 (N.D. Ill. Oct. 13, 2004) (allowing borrower's claim for improper garnishment but finding that the Department's administrative denial was reasonable). *See* § 6.10, *infra*.

lection agencies can participate in the garnishment process.[191] The Department prohibits collection personnel from conducting hearings and requires that hearing officers must be independent not only of the guarantor but also of the collector. The collector cannot issue withholding orders to employers and the order cannot appear to come from the collector.

Perhaps even more instructive is the type of collector conduct that the Department allows. This is a good indicator of what types of functions guarantors will turn over to collectors on a systematic basis. Just because the Department allows such involvement by collectors does not mean that the involvement complies with due process requirements.[192]

The Department authorizes collectors to send out the notice of garnishment, respond to debtor inquiries, negotiate repayment arrangements (consumers have a statutory right to avoid garnishment by entering into a repayment arrangement), and receive payments from employers. The contractor may assist in finding independent hearing officers, recommend that garnishment orders be issued, prepare the orders for review, and mail out the orders executed by the guarantor.[193]

In final rules implementing the DCIA authority, the Department clarified its role in the hearing process.[194] Department contractors cannot conduct hearings or rule on objections to garnishment because those are inherently governmental functions. The Department itself must provide a hearing and decide debtor objections. This does not, according to the Department, preclude use of contractors to analyze debtor objections and propose resolutions on objections.[195] The Department specifically acknowledged that contractors used to prepare recommendations should be trained to properly analyze debtor objections. The Department also explained that it did not object to guaranty agencies using contractors as hearing officials.[196]

5.3.6 *Garnishment of Student Loan Funds Generally Prohibited*

Student assistance funds, including loans, grants, and work assistance may be garnished to collect debts owed to the Department of Education.[197] However, these funds (or property traceable to them) cannot be garnished by other collectors.[198] For example, a private collection agency pursuing a student for credit card debt cannot garnish or attach that student's federal student loan funds to collect the debt.

5.4 Seizure of Federal Benefits

5.4.1 *General*

In 1996, Congress further strengthened the debt collection powers of federal agencies.[199] Federal government agencies were given the authority to offset formerly exempt federal benefits to collect debts, such as student loans, owed to the government.[200]

The DCIA and other federal laws prohibit offset against numerous benefits, including Department of Education payments under Title IV of the Higher Education Act,[201] veterans benefits, benefits under Part C of the Black Lung Act, and "tier 2" Railroad Retirement benefits. The Secretary of Treasury also has general authority to exempt any means-tested payments from offset, when so requested by the agency administering the program, and may also exempt other benefits if offset would substantially interfere with or defeat the purposes of the program.[202]

Offset is explicitly allowed against Social Security benefits, benefits under Part B of the Black Lung Act, and some Railroad Retirement benefits.[203] Subsequent regulations

---

191 Letter from Pamela Moran, Chief of the Loans Branch, to Guaranty Agency Directors, Clearinghouse No. 50,424 (Nov. 1, 1994).

192 See *Sibley v. Diversified Collection Servs.*, Clearinghouse No. 51,930 (N.D. Tex. Apr. 26, 1996) (first amended complaint—class action) for an example of a challenge to collection agency participation in the garnishment process. Some aspects of the participation appear to exceed Department guidelines and some aspects appear to be consistent with Department guidelines.

193 Letter from Pamela Moran, Chief of the Loans Branch, to Guaranty Agency Directors, Clearinghouse No. 50,424 (Nov. 1, 1994).

194 68 Fed. Reg. 8142, 8149 (Feb. 19, 2003).

195 *Id.* at 8149–50.

196 *Id.*

---

197 20 U.S.C. § 1095a(d).

198 *Id.*

199 Debt Collection Improvement Act of 1996, Pub. L. No. 104-134 (1996) (Ch. 10).

200 31 U.S.C. § 3716.

201 31 U.S.C. § 3716(c)(1)(C). A list of benefits exempted by all federal laws can be found at www.fms.treas.gov/debt/dmexmpt.pdf.

202 31 U.S.C. § 3716(c)(3)(B). A list of exempted benefits can be found on-line at www.fms.treas.gov/debt/dmexmpt.pdf. For example, as of 2006, the list of benefits exempted by action of the Department of Treasury (as opposed to explicitly exempted by federal laws) included SSI, food stamp benefits and most other Department of Agriculture nutrition programs, a number of FEMA programs including the individual and family grant program, disaster housing, and community disaster loans, Department of Justice payments to eligible claimants of the September 11th Victims Compensation Fund, and numerous HUD programs, including section 8 low-income housing assistance, Indian homeownership grants, and Direct Loans for the Elderly or Handicapped under Section 202.

203 31 U.S.C. § 3716(c)(3)(A)(ii).

specifically exempted SSI payments.[204] The legislation also exempted an annual amount of $9000.[205]

Only regularly recurring monthly benefits should be subject to offset.[206] The regulations specify that only monthly covered payments may be offset, defined as "a covered benefit payment payable to a payee on a recurring basis at monthly intervals that is not expressly limited in duration, at the time the first payment is made, to a period of less than 12 months."[207]

The Department of Treasury and Social Security Administration began implementing the offset process for Social Security payments in 2001.[208] Elders receiving Social Security retirement benefits have been among the most affected by the offset program. These older consumers may have student loan debt, often from many years ago. Some may have incurred loans on behalf of children.

Although this manual focuses on Department of Education's use of this authority to collect student loan debt, federal benefits recipients may also face offsets for collection of debts owed to other federal agencies. For example, the Department of Housing and Urban Development (HUD) has begun using the program to collect debts.[209] In addition, the Social Security Administration is using this power to collect Social Security overpayments. Other agencies have already begun, or are planning to develop, similar programs to collect debts owed to them.

5.4.2 Amount of Offset

The amount of the offset will be the lesser of:

- the amount of the debt;
- an amount equal to 15% of the monthly benefit payment; or
- the amount, if any, by which the monthly benefit exceeds $750.[210]

The maximum amount that will be offset under any circumstances is 15% of the recipient's income. The Financial Management Service (FMS) of the Department of the Treasury provided the following examples:

Example 1: A debtor receives a monthly benefit payment of $850. The amount that is offset is the lesser of $127.50 (15% of 850) or $100 (the amount by which $850 exceeds $750). In this example, $100 would be offset.[211]

Example 2: A debtor receives a monthly benefit of $1250. The amount that is offset is the lesser of $187.50 (15% of 1250) or $500 (the amount by which 1250 exceeds 750). In this example, the offset amount is $187.50 (assuming the debt is $187.50 or more).[212]

If the recipient receives $750 or less, nothing will be offset.[213]

---

204 31 C.F.R. § 285.4(b). In May 2005, in response to complaints about collection agency threats to seize SSI, the Department sent the following e-mail message to collection contract administrators:

> This is to remind you that Supplement Security Income (SSI) benefits are NOT subject to Treasury offset. These are different from the Social Security Disability benefits that may be subject to offset, under certain conditions. If a borrower advises that their only source of income is SSI, you should not be advising them that this may be offset. It has been reported that PCA collectors have been misinforming borrowers that their SSI benefits will be offset. This is causing anxiety and distress for these borrowers and has also resulted in complaints due to this misinformation. Please remind your staff immediately concerning this issue.

See § 4.5.2.1, *supra.*

205 31 U.S.C. § 3716(c)(3)(A)(ii).
206 31 C.F.R. § 285.4.
207 31 C.F.R. § 285.4(a). The statute, however, states only that all payments due to an individual may be offset. 31 U.S.C. § 3716(c)(3).
208 Information about the benefit payment offset program is available on the Department of Treasury website at www.fms.treas.gov/news/factsheets/benefitoffset.html. The Department's Financial Management Service published a notice of proposed rulemaking and an interim rule concerning offsets on August 21, 1998, 63 Fed. Reg. 44991, 44986 (amending 31 C.F.R. Part 285 by adding § 285.4). The interim rule was adopted as final on December 16, 1998, becoming effective on January 22, 1999, 63 Fed. Reg. 71203 (Dec. 23, 1998). Federal agencies must either adopt regulations issued by the Departments of Treasury or Justice or adopt their own regulations consistent with those issued by Treasury or Justice. 31 U.S.C. § 3716(b). The Department of Education adopted regulations for administrative offset prior to the 1996 DCIA amendments. *See* 34 C.F.R. § 30.20 *et seq.* To date, the Department has not issued separate regulations addressing the new powers, including Social Security offsets, authorized by the 1996 amendments. The DOE appears to be following the Treasury regulations at least with respect to general issues regarding offset, such as whether a ten-year limit applies. The Treasury regulations can be found at 31 C.F.R. § 285.4 and 31 C.F.R. § 901.3, *reprinted at* Appx. B, *infra.*

---

209 Note, however, that these agencies should clearly be bound by the ten-year statute of limitations for federal benefits offsets. 31 U.S.C. § 3716(e)(1). This is not the case when the Department of Education is offsetting to collect student loan debt. *See* § 5.4.3.3.
210 31 C.F.R. § 285.4(e).
211 31 C.F.R. § 285.4(e)(3)(i).
212 31 C.F.R. § 285.4(e)(3)(ii).
213 31 C.F.R. § 285.4(e)(3)(iii). In December 2002, the Treasury Department issued interim rules governing the treasury offset process. Among other provisions, the rules describe the order in which deductions will be applied when more than one delinquent debt is submitted to Treasury for the same payee. 67 Fed. Reg. 78936 (Dec. 26, 2002).

5.4.3 *Challenges to Offset*

5.4.3.1 Notice and Hearing Rights

The offset process is managed by the Financial Management Service (FMS) of the Department of Treasury. Before referring a debt to FMS for collection, the federal agency is required to provide the debtor with a notice of intent to offset and an opportunity to review the basis for the debt.[214]

Since the 1996 amendments to the DCIA, the Department of Education has not issued new regulations addressing the additional powers authorized in the amendments. It is therefore unclear which regulations to follow to determine specific borrower rights. The Department of Education appears to be following its existing administrative offset regulations, at least with respect to notice and hearing rights.[215]

The Department of Education regulations require borrowers to request a review within twenty days of receiving a notice of offset.[216] The borrower has the opportunity to first request the opportunity to review and copy relevant documents.[217] Borrowers have the right to request an oral hearing in lieu of a written review but must submit an explanation of why a written review is insufficient.[218] As with other offsets, borrowers should have the right to set up a repayment plan acceptable to the Secretary prior to offset.[219] Borrowers also have a right to request a temporary hardship waiver, as discussed in the next subsection.

FMS has stated that, once DOE (and other federal agencies) refer debts to them, they will subsequently notify the debtor twice, at sixty-day and thirty-day intervals, in writing of the anticipated offset.[220] However, according to the Treasury regulations, the offset remains legal even if the debtor does not receive the notices.[221]

Borrowers are likely to be confused regarding which agency to contact if they wish to challenge offsets or just have questions about them. The Department of Treasury explicitly requires borrowers to contact the "originating" agency (the Department of Education in student loan cases). The FMS notices for student loan administrative offsets list a number at the Department of Education for borrowers to call. Borrowers can contact the FMS at 1-800-304-3107 but

only to find out which agency to contact, particularly if they find that their benefits are being offset but they never received notice.

5.4.3.2 Hardship Reductions

The Department's policy is to allow borrowers to request full or partial reductions of offset based on financial hardship. The Department of Education makes the determinations regarding financial hardship for student loan administrative offsets. However, the availability of this "program" is not specified on the hearing request form.

The Department requires borrowers to submit the following documents before they will review a claim of hardship:

- The notification of offset.
- The notification letter showing the amount of benefit.
- Proof of yearly income.
- A completed financial statement returned to DOE within ten days.[222] If the situation is an emergency, a borrower may submit equivalent information such as an eviction notice or a court order of foreclosure in writing with the completed financial statement.
- A letter explaining the exceptional circumstances that caused the financial hardship along with any other supporting documents.[223]

The Department is currently setting up a review unit in the Chicago Service Center. This unit will examine the documents to determine whether the offset should be reduced partially or fully. Refunds may be granted as well. Documents should be sent to:

United States Department of Education
Attn: Federal Offset Review Unit
P.O. Box 618064
Chicago, IL 60601-8064

In extreme circumstances, the borrower may fax the form to:
1-312-886-5488.

The Department claims that it will notify borrowers of decisions within ten days and that it will send disability discharge applications to borrowers who appear to be eligible.[224]

---

214 31 U.S.C. § 3716(a).

215 34 C.F.R. § 30.20 *et seq.* However, DOE is also referring to the more recent Treasury administrative offset regulations for guidance on issues such as whether a ten-year limit applies in the student loan context. *See* § 5.4.3.3, *infra.*

216 34 C.F.R. § 30.24(a)(1).

217 34 C.F.R. § 30.22(a)(3).

218 34 C.F.R. § 30.25(b)(1). The rules for oral hearings are set out at 34 C.F.R. § 30.26.

219 34 C.F.R. § 30.22(b)(3)(iii). Due process challenges to these review procedures are discussed at §§ 5.2.2.4 (tax refund intercepts) and 5.3.4 (garnishment), *supra.*

220 See the Department of Treasury website at www.fms.treas.gov/news/factsheets/benefitoffset.html.

221 31 C.F.R. § 285.4(f)(3).

---

222 A copy of this form is included at Appendix D, *infra,* and on the companion CD-Rom to this manual. The Department requests, but does not require, that the form be returned within ten days.

223 A sample letter requesting a hardship reduction is included at Appendix E.

224 The procedures are still in flux. In other documents, the DOE has stated that borrowers should send information to the TOP Hardship Review Unit at P.O. Box 4220, Iowa City, Iowa 52244-4220. It is probably best at this point to submit applications to both addresses and, as always, to keep copies. Requests should be sent return receipt requested. The Department reported in 2004 that the Chicago address is the correct address. The Iowa City address was used prior to shifting the processing to the Chicago office.

The unit will determine whether the borrower is entitled to a waiver and, if so, whether the offset amount should be partially or fully reduced. If the Department denies the waiver, they will notify the borrower of the denial and continue offsetting. If the waiver is granted, the borrower may be entitled to a limited refund. The refund will only be for amounts offset above the newly determined offset amount and only for periods during which financial hardship can be shown.

Unfortunately for borrowers, the right to a hardship reduction is not listed in the notices sent by either DOE or FMS. Instead, borrowers may find out about the availability of the hardship reduction when they call the Department of Education number indicated on the notice of federal offset. If borrowers call that number, they will enter into a telephone menu requesting first that they provide identifying information such as name and social security number. After entering this information, borrowers are asked to press a number if they are disputing an offset or administrative wage garnishment. Once a borrower presses this option, they will at some point be asked if the offset is causing severe financial hardship. If the borrower is able to get this far in the process, the borrower will receive information about how to submit an appeal of the offset in writing.

It is unclear how flexible the Department will be in granting these reductions or waivers, particularly with respect to the fifth "exceptional circumstances" category. Exceptional circumstances should clearly include pending evictions or foreclosures but might also include disability status or other "non-temporary" exceptional circumstances. The precise standards to prove financial hardship are also unclear at this point.

In response to an inquiry from NCLC about hardship waiver/reduction policies, the Department replied:

> We use the cost of living standards published annually by the Internal Revenue Service to determine baseline allowable expenses for housing, transportation *etc.* (These standards can be found at the IRS.gov website.) We also consider the borrower's circumstances and may make reasonable modifications to the baseline standards accordingly. Borrowers can request hardship consideration at any point in the collection process, with the following provisos:
>
> — Except in the case of social security benefits, we will not prevent offset of any federal payment based on any hardship claim; once we know the amount of the offset (that is, after it has occurred) we will consider a hardship request for refund.
> — In the case of social security benefits, we will consider either a reduction or suspension of the offset due to hardship even before the offset begins.
> — We will not protect an account from assignment to a collection agency based on total

hardship; only entering a reasonable and affordable payment plan will prevent assignment.

5.4.3.3 The DCIA Statute of Limitations Does Not Apply to Collection of Defaulted Student Loans

The Debt Collection Improvement Act prohibits offset for claims that have been "outstanding" for more than ten years.[225] The issue of whether the ten-year statute of limitations in the DCIA applies to offsets for collection of student loans was litigated beginning in 2001. The U.S. Supreme Court ultimately decided the issue in the government's favor in late 2005.[226] This decision affirmed the Ninth Circuit but overruled contrary decisions (favorable for borrowers) by a 2002 Michigan district court and by the Eighth Circuit in 2004.[227]

Plaintiffs in this line of cases had acknowledged that there is generally no statute of limitations that applies to student loan collections.[228] However, they claimed that this broad authority did not apply in the Social Security context because of the explicit protections of the Social Security anti-attachment statute, 42 U.S.C. § 407. This statute can be abrogated only by statutes that expressly refer to it. The Debt Collection Improvement Act has an explicit reference to § 407 and therefore meets this test.[229] The Higher Education Act (HEA) does not.

The timing of these various laws was critical. Congress eliminated the statute of limitations for student loan collection in 1991 through Higher Education Act Technical Amendments.[230] Among other claims, the plaintiff in the Supreme Court case argued that Congress could not have intended at that time to repeal the Debt Collection Act's statute of limitations as to offsets against Social Security benefits because this method of collection was not authorized until 1996. The Court disagreed.

The Justices' views about express reference provisions appeared to range from impatience to outright hostility. However, the majority opinion did not make any general rulings about the validity of these types of provisions. The Court wrote that it did not have to reach this issue: "Because the Debt Collection Improvement Act clearly makes Social Security benefits subject to offset, it provides exactly the sort of express reference that the Social Security Act says is

---

225 31 U.S.C. § 3716(e)(1).

226 Lockhart v. United States, 126 S. Ct. 699 (2005).

227 *See* Lee v. Paige, 376 F.3d 1179 (8th Cir. 2004); Guillermety v. Secretary of Educ., 241 F. Supp. 2d 727 (E.D. Mich. 2002).

228 The statute of limitations was retroactively eliminated in 1991. *See* § 4.2.1, *supra.*

229 31 U.S.C. § 3716(c)(3)(A)(i).

230 Pub. L. No. 102-26 eliminated the statute of limitations set out in 20 U.S.C. § 1091a(a)(1).

necessary to supersede the anti-attachment provision."[231] However, Justice Scalia in his concurring opinion went further, arguing that § 407's express reference provision was not binding on subsequent Congresses.[232]

It is now clear that the government will not be bound by any time limits when attempting to collect student loans through Social Security offset. This makes it more important than ever for borrowers to assert their rights and for advocates to track the Department's record in enforcing those rights. For example, Department of Education policy allows borrowers to request hardship reductions.[233]

5.4.3.4 Due Process Case Challenges to Offsets

Borrowers' attempts to challenge the offset procedures on constitutional grounds have been unsuccessful to date. In one case, the court concluded that there was no constitutional due process violation when the Department of Education sent written notice to the borrower's last known address and provided him the opportunity for a hearing.[234] A district court also found the offset notices and procedures to be constitutionally adequate.[235]

5.5 Professional License Suspensions and Revocations

At least nine states' laws[236] allow professional and vocational boards to refuse to certify, certify with restrictions, suspend or revoke a member's professional or vocational license, and, in some cases, impose a fine[237] when a member defaults on state[238] and/or federally[239] guaranteed student loans.

While some states' provisions apply to particular professions or vocations—attorneys,[240] health care professionals,[241] teachers,[242] insurance professionals,[243] state officers,[244] and commercial fishermen[245]—others apply more generally to any one whose profession or vocation requires its members to be licensed.[246] Louisiana's catch-all provision is typical. It provides that "default on the repayment of *any* loan guaranteed by the Louisiana Student Financial Assistance Commission . . . shall be grounds for denying an application for, or an application for the renewal of, any license, permit, or certificate required by the state of Louisiana."[247]

Laws that suspend or revoke professional licenses because of student loan defaults typically afford affected individuals notice of the impending action and an opportunity for a hearing. Some states' laws also allow for license reissuance once a licensee in default enters into a loan repayment plan. With the exception of at least one state,[248] all of these laws mandate that the applicable board or department responsible for issuing the license take action, in some cases provisional action, once it receives notice of a member's default.

---

231 Lockhart v. United States, 126 S. Ct. 699 at 702 (2005).

232 *Id.* at 703.

233 *See* § 5.4.3.2.

234 Omgebu v. United States Dep't of Treasury, 2004 WL 3049825 (7th Cir. Dec. 16, 2004) (unpublished order).

235 Stover v. Illinois Student Assistance Comm'n, 2005 WL 3597743 (C.D. Ill. Apr. 21, 2005).

236 Fla. Stat. §§ 456.072, 456.074 (Health Professions and Occupations); Haw. Rev. Stat. § 436C-2 (General); Haw. Rev. Stat. § 189-2(f) (Commercial Marine Licenses); Haw. Rev. Stat. § 302A-807(e) (School Personnel); Haw. Rev. Stat. § 321-15 (Department of Health); Haw. Rev. Stat. § 431:9-235 (Insurance Adjusters and Bill Reviewers); Haw. Rev. Stat. § 431:9A-112 (Insurance Producers); Haw. Rev. Stat. § 457-9 (Nurses); Haw. Rev. Stat. § 466J-8 (Radiological Technology); 2005 Iowa Court Order 05-03: Rule 35.13 (Attorneys); La. Rev. Stat. Ann. § 37:2951 (General); Mass. Gen. Laws Ann. ch. 30A § 13 (State Officers); Mass. Gen. Laws Ann. ch. 112 § 61 (Department of Public Health); N.J. Stat. Ann. § 2A:13-12 (Attorneys); N.J.

Rule of Court 1:20-11B (same); N.J. Stat. Ann. § 18A:71C-19 (General); N.J. Stat. Ann. § 45:1-21.2 (same); N.D. Cent. Code § 28-25-11 (General—Judgment Debtors); Okla. Stat. Ann. tit. 70 § 623.1 (General); Okla. Admin. Code § 595: 10-1-80 (Commercial Drivers); Tenn. Code. Ann. § 56-1-312 (General); Tenn. Code. Ann. § 63-1-141 (Healing Arts Professionals); Tenn. Code. Ann. § 23-3-111 (authorizing Supreme Court to establish guidelines for attorneys); Tenn. Code. Ann. § 49-5-108 (authorizing State Board of Education to establish guidelines for teachers).

237 Fla. Stat. §§ 456.072, 456.074.

238 Florida, Hawaii, Iowa, Louisiana, Massachusetts, New Jersey, North Dakota, and Tennessee.

239 Florida, Hawaii, New Jersey, North Dakota, Oklahoma, and Tennessee.

240 Hawaii, New Jersey, and Tennessee.

241 Florida, Hawaii, Massachusetts, and Tennessee.

242 Hawaii and Tennessee.

243 Hawaii and Tennessee.

244 Massachusetts.

245 Hawaii.

246 Iowa, Louisiana, New Jersey, North Dakota, and Oklahoma.

247 La. Rev. Stat. Ann. § 37:2951 (emphasis added).

248 *See, e.g.,* N.D. Cent. Code § 28-5-11 (2) (providing the court with discretion to suspend a judgment debtor's certificate, license, or permit based on principles of fairness).

Chapter 6   Statutory Discharges of Student Loan Obligations

6.1 Introduction

Statutory discharges (or cancellations) provide the most powerful remedies for student loan borrowers. They offer complete relief as opposed to simply delaying the repayment obligation. After a cancellation, the borrower no longer owes anything on the loan and becomes eligible for new student loans and grants. In some cases, borrowers are also entitled to refunds of past loan payments, deletion of all negative references on their credit records, and renewed eligibility for federal financial aid.

Because these are such powerful remedies, advocates should always consider the various discharges first when evaluating a student loan case, regardless of whether a client is in default. Victims of trade-school fraud, in particular, are likely to be eligible for at least one of these discharges.

The Higher Education Act (HEA) offers seven main ways to discharge or cancel a student loan obligation:

- the school's closure while the student was still enrolled;
- the school's false certification of the student's eligibility (including false certification due to forgery or identity theft);
- the school's failure to pay a refund owed to a student;
- the borrower's permanent and total disability;
- the borrower's death;
- the borrower's profession, such as teaching or military service in limited circumstances; and
- the borrower's bankruptcy.

This chapter considers all of these statutory bases for discharges with the exception of bankruptcy, which is discussed in Chapter 7, *infra*. Common law grounds for raising defenses in student loan collection actions, including claims to cancel student loan obligations, are covered in Chapter 9.

6.2 The Closed-School Discharge

6.2.1 The Closed-School Discharge Applies to Specified Types of Loans

The closed-school discharge applies to FFELs, federal Direct Loans, and Perkins Loans (including NDSLs) re-

ceived at least in part on or after January 1, 1986.[1] The 1986 cut-off means that at least part of the loan must have been disbursed in 1986.[2]

If a borrower consolidates multiple loans, only the portion of the consolidation attributable to the discharge-eligible loan(s) will be discharged. If a borrower consolidates a loan eligible for discharge, the borrower will receive a credit in the amount of the loan(s) relating to the closed school.[3] According to the Department, in the case of a borrower with a consolidated loan who obtains a loan cancellation or discharge of one or more of the underlying loans, the consolidating guarantor (or current guarantor of record) is responsible for refunding any monies due to the borrower.

6.2.2 Determining If a Student Qualifies for a Closed-School Discharge

6.2.2.1 Timing of School Closure

The HEA requires the Secretary to discharge a specified loan if the borrower was unable to complete the program due to the school's closure.[4] The regulations provide this dis-

---

1 20 U.S.C. § 1087(c)(1); 34 C.F.R. §§ 682.402(d)(1)(i) (FFEL), 685.214 (Direct Loans), 674.33(g). As the rules on the six main discharges are substantially the same for the different programs, citations hereafter refer mainly to FFEL rules. In particular, unless otherwise specified, Direct Loans have the same terms and conditions as FFELs. 20 U.S.C. § 1087e(a)(10). For a general description of the different loan programs, see § 1.4, *supra*.

2 34 C.F.R. § 682.402(d)(3)(ii)(A) (FFEL). Borrowers with loans reduced to judgment should also qualify for the closed-school and other federal discharges. This issue came up during spring 2002 negotiated rulemaking sessions with the Department of Education. Among other changes coming out of these sessions, the negotiators agreed to eliminate the rehabilitation right for borrowers with loans reduced to judgment. The Department stated in its explanation in the Federal Register that this change would not affect other rights for borrowers with judgments, including discharge rights. 67 Fed. Reg. 51036, 51038 (Aug. 6, 2002). *See also* § 8.4 (rehabilitation), *infra*.

3 U.S. Dep't of Educ., Dear Colleague Letter 94-G-256, Clearinghouse No. 50,422 (Sept. 1994). The letter is included at Appendix C, *infra*. *See* 34 C.F.R. § 685.220(k)(3) (Direct Consolidation Loans).

4 20 U.S.C. § 1087(c)(1).

charge if the branch of the school at which the student attended closed.[5] For example, if the student goes to branch "A," there is no right to a discharge if only the main campus or branch "B" closed. On the other hand, if branch "A" closes, the student has a right to a discharge even if all other branches stay open. The closed-school discharge applies to any school at which the student obtained a qualified loan, whether or not the school or branch was in fact an eligible institution under the program.[6]

The regulations provide a discharge if the student was still enrolled at the time of the school's closure or if the student withdrew from the school within ninety days before the school's closure.[7] The ninety-day period may be extended if the Secretary determines that exceptional circumstances related to the school's closing would justify an extension.[8] It also may be extended in some circumstances for students who attended correspondence schools.[9]

A student on an approved leave of absence is treated as still enrolled.[10] Until July 2003, with only a few exceptions, each student was only allowed one leave of absence annually. Since that date, schools are allowed to grant multiple leaves of absence at their discretion, as long as the total number of days for all leave does not exceed 180 within a twelve-month period.[11] Students must provide a written, signed, and dated request for a leave that includes the reason for the request.[12] If unforeseen circumstances prevent a student from providing a written request, the school may grant the request as long as it documents the decision and collects the written request at a later date.[13] If the student does not return to school after a leave of absence, the withdrawal date will be the date that the school determines the student began the leave of absence.[14] For purposes of a closed-school discharge, a borrower on an approved leave of absence who tried but could not return to the school because it was closed should still be eligible for the closed-school discharge.

A school's closure date is the date at which it ceases offering *all* programs at a particular branch, not when it stops offering the particular program in which the student is enrolled.[15] Nevertheless, when a particular program at a location ceases four or five months before the branch closes, this would seem to be an appropriate situation for the Secretary to extend the ninety-day period because of the exceptional circumstances related to the school's closing.

Borrowers can obtain closed-school discharges if the school closed before they completed a program, even if the school issued the borrower a diploma or other certificate.[16] On the other hand, if a student completes a program, there is no discharge even if the borrower never received a diploma or certificate.[17]

6.2.2.2 The Official School Closure Date

The Secretary determines the closure date, and, for most situations, the borrower should rely on the Secretary's Cumulative List of Closed Schools to find out the official closure date. The Department periodically updates this list. The easiest way to access the list is through the Department of Education's website. The site allows advocates to search for a specific school's closure date. The general Department website is www.ed.gov. The specific site for the list is http://wdcrobcolp01.ed.gov/CFAPPS/FSA/closedschool/searchpage.cfm.

Initially, numerous errors were reported concerning this list. This is less common now, but errors still appear. For this reason, advocates should not necessarily give up if their client has evidence of a different closing date that would affect eligibility.

Possible sources of evidence of a school's earlier closing date include dated newspaper articles or other media reports about the school's closure and declarations from other students, state regulators, or former school employees regarding the closure date. Advocates may submit to the Department of Education's Closed School Section a request to change a school closing date.[18] A change in a school closing date must be determined by the Department regardless of who holds the loan.

---

5 *See* 34 C.F.R. §§ 682.402(d)(1)(ii)(C) (FFEL), 685.214(a)(2)(ii) (Direct Loans).

6 *See* 34 C.F.R. § 682.402(d)(1)(ii)(C) (FFEL).

7 34 C.F.R. §§ 682.402(d)(1)(i) (FFEL), 685.214(c)(1)(ii) (Direct Loans), 674.33(g)(4)(i)(B) (Perkins). The "90 day rule" is not in the statute, only the regulations. The statute provides for discharges in certain circumstances if the borrower is unable to complete the program due to the closure of the institution. 20 U.S.C. § 1087(c). At least one court found that the plain language of the statute allowed for a closed-school discharge even if the borrower was not enrolled at the time of closure or had not withdrawn within ninety days. *See* Sandler v. U.S. Dep't of Education, 2001 WL 884552 (E.D. Pa. July 19, 2001) (school announced impending closure about a year ahead of time; plaintiff still had over two years of coursework left to complete her program and could not transfer credits to a new location; court found plaintiff's situation fit squarely within the plain language of the statute and therefore court did not consider whether the regulations setting the limit at ninety days were arbitrary and capricious). Advocates should consider continuing to challenge this regulation in court.

8 34 C.F.R. §§ 682.402(d)(1)(i) (FFEL), 685.214(c)(1)(ii) (Direct Loans).

9 *See* § 6.2.2.3, *infra*.

10 34 C.F.R. § 682.402(d)(3)(ii)(B). The definition of an approved leave of absence is found at 34 C.F.R. § 668.22(d).

11 34 C.F.R. § 668.22(d)(vi).

12 34 C.F.R. § 668.22(d)(3)(iii).

13 *Id.*

14 34 C.F.R. § 668.22(d)(2).

15 *See* 34 C.F.R. §§ 682.402(d)(1)(ii)(A) (FFEL), 685.214(a)(2)(i) (Direct Loans).

16 *See* U.S. Dep't of Educ., Dear Colleague Letter GEN-94-256, Clearinghouse No. 50,422 (Sept. 1994), *reprinted at* Appx. C, *infra*.

17 *Id.*

18 United States Department of Education, SFAP/Closed School

Official closure dates have been challenged both informally and in court.[19] In at least one case, the Department entered into a settlement agreeing to change the closure date, discharge the named plaintiff's loans, and provide notice of the new date to borrowers enrolled within 150 days of the new closure date.[20]

6.2.2.3 Correspondence Schools

There are often special problems when a student attended a correspondence school or a correspondence school with a final residential portion to the program. Such schools may stop corresponding with their students well before the school's official closure date. Even though the student's failure to submit lessons was caused by the school, the school's records may indicate, or the Department or guaranty agency might determine, that the student had withdrawn from the school. Similarly, the school's failure to offer the student the residential portion of the program may be misinterpreted as the student dropping out.

In an attempt to address some of the problems associated with correspondence schools, the Department in July 1997 released a "Dear Colleague" letter extending the ninety-day period for students who attended and withdrew from specified correspondence schools.[21] These extended periods apply only to the ten closed correspondence schools listed below:

1. American Career Training Travel/Hart Secretarial School (ACT) (Pompano Beach, Florida, main location). Borrowers who enrolled in ACT and took out a loan with a loan period that began on or after March 1, 1988, may be eligible for the closed-school discharge if they meet all other requirements.

For the other nine schools listed below, borrowers who took out loans with loan periods that began within twelve months of the closure date may be eligible for the closed-school discharge.

2. AMS College, Home Study Division (Alpine, California).
3. Columbia School of Broadcasting (Las Vegas, Nevada).

4. County Schools (Bridgeport, Connecticut).
5. Global Academy (Atlanta, Georgia).
6. National Training Systems (Laurel, Maryland).
7. Northwest Schools (Portland, Oregon).
8. Superior Training Services (Phoenix, Arizona).
9. United Schools (Clearwater, Florida).
10. USA Training Academy Home Study (Newark, Delaware).[22]

The "Dear Colleague" Letter provides that guaranty agencies and lenders must review records to identify borrowers with loan periods that would qualify them for discharges under these extended periods. Agencies must re-evaluate previously denied applications for borrowers identified in this process and mail out applications to all others. Previously denied applicants who meet all the other closed-school-discharge requirements should be granted discharges without the submission of new applications.

6.2.2.4 Teach-Outs

Students are barred from receiving a discharge if they completed the program through a "teach-out" at another school or through transfer of credits or hours earned at the closed school to another school.[23] In a February 1998 decision in the *McComas* case, the United States District Court for the Southern District of West Virginia rejected the argument that the "teach out" bar to discharge contravened the meaning and purpose of the governing statute, 20 U.S.C. § 1087(c)(1). The court granted the Department's summary judgment motion.[24]

The statute states that, in order to qualify for a closed-school discharge, borrowers must be unable to complete the program in which they enrolled. The inability to complete the program must be due to school closure. The ambiguity, challenged in *McComas*, is whether "program" means only the program at the closed school or a general course of study that may be pursued at another school. In *McComas*, the plaintiff was able to transfer credits earned at the closed school to another school. The court agreed that the governing statute was susceptible to two different meanings but did not find clear congressional intent to prohibit the Department's use of the "teach-out/transfer of credits" limitation.

Unit, P.O. Box 23800, L'Enfant Plaza Station, Washington, D.C. 20026; 1-800-4FED-AID. A list of regional closed school unit contacts is available at http://studentaid.ed.gov/PORTALS WebApp/students/english/closedinfo.jsp?tab=attending (last accessed in August 2006).

19 *See* Moorer v. Secretary of Educ., Clearinghouse No. 51,931 (D.D.C. June 7, 1996) (complaint for declaratory and injunctive relief).

20 Settlement Agreement and Stipulation of Dismissal, Tello v. Secretary of Educ., Clearinghouse No. 52,120B (D. Md. Aug. 1998); Class Action Complaint, Tello v. Secretary of Educ., Clearinghouse No. 52,120A (D. Md. 1997).

21 U.S. Dep't of Educ., Dear Colleague Letter 97-G-300, Clearinghouse No. 52,043 (July 1997).

22 All locations listed here are the main locations. Closure dates are not listed because many of these schools had numerous locations, and closure dates vary by location. Closure dates are listed in the Dear Colleague Letter, 97-G-300, Clearinghouse No. 52,043 (July 1997) and The Secretary's Cumulative List of Closed Schools. *See* § 6.2.2.2, *infra*.

23 34 C.F.R. § 682.402(d)(3)(ii)(c).

24 McComas v. Riley, Clearinghouse No. 52,039 (S.D. W. Va. Feb. 27, 1998) (opinion and order granting defendants' renewed motion for summary judgment).

6.2.3　Relief Available for Those Obtaining a Closed-School Discharge

When a borrower receives a closed-school discharge, the borrower (and any other obligor on the note) is no longer obligated to repay the loan or any charges or costs associated with the loan.[25] That is, the loan principal, interest charges, collection costs, and all other charges are forgiven.

In addition, the borrower is reimbursed all amounts paid to date on the loan, whether those payments were voluntary or involuntary, such as through tax intercepts or garnishments.[26] The borrower is no longer regarded in default and is immediately eligible for new loans and grants.[27] The discharge of an FFEL loan must also be reported to all credit reporting agencies to which the holder previously reported the loan's status "so as to delete all adverse credit history assigned to the loan."[28]

The regulations for most of the discharges explicitly provide that both past and current loan obligations may be cancelled.[29] Thus, a borrower should be allowed to seek a discharge even if the borrower's loans are already paid off, possibly through involuntary payments such as tax offsets. Although the current obligation is already extinguished, the borrower should still be able to get a refund and other appropriate relief such as elimination of negative notations on credit reports. However, at least with respect to disability discharges, the Department has indicated that it will not grant discharges for paid-in-full loans.[30]

Revocation of a closed-school discharge is contemplated in the regulations only if the borrower provides testimony, sworn statements, or documentation that does not support the material representations made to obtain the discharge.[31] It is unclear how the Department interprets this provision.

6.2.4　How to Obtain a Closed-School Discharge

6.2.4.1　General

It is rare for the Department and guaranty agencies to provide automatic discharges to those who appear eligible.

Borrowers must apply for the discharge. Guarantors are required to inform those appearing eligible of their right to apply, with an application form, and the guarantors must forbear collecting from these individuals.[32] Presumably, the Department does the same on the loans it is collecting.

If a guaranty agency is holding a loan, borrowers should deal with the guaranty agency in obtaining a discharge. Only if the Department is holding the loan should the student apply directly to the Department. Department-held loans will almost invariably be handled by a private collection agency.

In cases in which the borrower is initially dealing with a collection agency, the Department's policy is that, once the borrower requests a closed-school discharge, the file must be turned over immediately to Department staff. Thus it will be the Department staff, and not the collection agency, that processes the closed-school discharge.

Nevertheless, advocates and borrowers must be prepared for collection agencies (working on a commission basis) to fail to turn accounts over to the Department and to discourage borrowers from seeking the discharge. There have been incidents of collection agencies advising consumers that they are obligated to repay a loan even if the school closed when they were enrolled. When a collection agency misrepresents a borrower's discharge rights, it violates the federal Fair Debt Collection Practices Act (FDCPA).[33]

6.2.4.2　Written Application for Discharge

With a few exceptions discussed below, a written application is required. To apply for a discharge, borrowers will typically fill out forms created by the loan holder and submit the application to the loan holder. For example, if the Department holds the loan, the borrower should use the Department's closed-school-discharge application form and submit the form to the Department.[34] If a guaranty agency holds the loan, that guaranty agency's form should be used.

The borrower only needs to provide the minimum information required by the regulations, including

- whether the borrower has made a claim relating to the loan with a third party such as a state tuition recovery program or surety for the school, and, if so, the amount of any recovery;
- that the borrower received the loan proceeds after January 1, 1986;
- that the borrower did not complete the program because

25　*See* 34 C.F.R. §§ 682.402(d)(2)(i) (FFEL), 685.214(b)(1) (Direct Loans), 674.33(g)(2)(i) (Perkins).

26　*See* 34 C.F.R. §§ 682.402(d)(2)(ii) (FFEL), 685.214(b)(2) (Direct Loans), 674.33(g)(2)(ii) (Perkins).

27　*See* 34 C.F.R. §§ 682.402(d)(2)(iii) (FFEL), 685.214(b)(3) (Direct Loans), 674.33(g)(2)(iii) (Perkins).

28　*See* 34 C.F.R. § 682.402(d)(2)(iv) (FFEL). The language in 34 C.F.R. § 685.214(b)(4) (Direct Loans) is not so extensive, solely requiring the Secretary to report the loan discharge to all credit bureaus to which the Secretary previously reported the status of the loan.

29　34 C.F.R. § 682.402(d)(2)(i) (closed-school discharge); 34 C.F.R. § 682.402(e)(2)(i) (false-certification discharge).

30　*See* § 6.6.3, *infra.*

31　34 C.F.R. § 682.402(d)(4)(ii).

32　34 C.F.R. § 682.402(d)(6).

33　*See generally* Ch. 4, *supra.*

34　*See* Appx. D, *infra.* The form is also available on the Department of Education website at www.ed.gov. If the address to which the borrower is requested to send payments is the National Payment Center in Greenville, TX, borrowers should submit completed forms to U.S. Dept. of Ed., P.O. Box 4222, Iowa City, IA 52244-4222.

of the school's closing while the borrower was enrolled, the borrower was on an approved leave of absence, or the borrower withdrew within ninety days of the school's closure;

- that the borrower did not complete the program through a teach-out at another school or by transferring credits to another school (presumably this would only apply if the borrower received a credit toward tuition at the new school because of attendance at the closed school);
- that the borrower agrees to provide, if requested, other related documentation reasonably available to the borrower;
- that the borrower agrees to cooperate with the Secretary in any action to recover money relating to the loan from third parties, such as the school owners and the school's affiliates.[35]

The regulations contain no requirement that borrowers, in applying for a discharge, reaffirm their debt or waive other rights. If guaranty agencies provide discharge application forms with these extraneous provisions, borrowers should cross these provisions out, with their initials evidencing their intent to delete these items. The Department has also instructed guaranty agencies to process all requests for a closed-school discharge, even if the request is not on the agency's standard form.[36] In practice, however, it is generally most efficient to use the official agency form whenever possible.

6.2.4.3 Oral Applications

The Department and guaranty agencies may grant closed-school discharges without a written application in limited circumstances.[37] Specifically, a discharge may be granted without an application if (1) the borrower received a discharge of a different type of loan for the same program of study or (2) the Department or guaranty agency determines that the borrower qualifies for a discharge based on information in the Secretary or guaranty agency's possession. This may facilitate advocacy that a group of students be given a closed-school discharge in settlement of an action, instead of requiring each student to submit an application.

6.2.4.4 Time Limits and Appeal Rights

There is no time limit on a borrower's eligibility for a discharge.[38] The Department expects guaranty agencies to respond to discharge requests within ninety days, although the Department has not set any time limits for its own response to discharge requests.

Decisions may take years to process. For this reason, advocates should be prepared to request administrative forbearances for borrowers so that collection activities will cease until the discharge has been granted or denied.[39] Guaranty agencies collecting FFEL loans should affirmatively suspend collection if the agency has information about a school not previously known to the Secretary.[40]

The regulations do not set out a review right for denial of a closed-school discharge application. For a discussion on how to appeal an adverse decision, see § 6.10, *infra*.

6.2.5 Effect of School Closure on FISLs and Older FFELs

The closed-school discharge applies only to loans disbursed after January 1, 1986. As a consequence, students whose loans were disbursed *in full* before that date will have to pursue other avenues.

Many loans from the 1970s and early 1980s were Federally Insured Student Loans (FISLs). There was no guaranty agency involvement with these loans. Instead, the lender or even a school acting as lender made the loan, and the loan was directly insured by the United States. Department FISL regulations through 1986 stated that the school's closure while the student was enrolled provided a defense to repayment on the loan.[41]

The Stafford regulations never had such an explicit provision. Nevertheless, the Department had stated a policy, before the closed-school-discharge provision was enacted by Congress, encouraging guaranty agencies to excuse a portion or all of a student's Stafford Loan when the school closed while the student was still enrolled.[42]

Borrowers are excused from paying the percentage of the debt that equals the percentage of the loan period during which the borrower was prevented from attending school because of the school closing. However, the borrower must agree to pay the remainder of the loan and assign to the guaranty agency any right to receive a refund from the school. In addition, the policy does not apply when a borrower has a "teach-out" available from another school.

Apparently, the Department agrees that this policy still applies to pre-1986 loans, although it is unlikely that collection agencies or most personnel hired by the Department or guarantors will be aware of it. Advocates may have to educate these personnel or find a knowledgeable person in the General Counsel's office or elsewhere in the Department such as the Ombudsman office.

Another avenue for pre-1986 Staffords is to raise the school's closure as a school-related claim that the student

---

35 34 C.F.R. § 682.402(d)(3).

36 U.S. Dep't of Educ., Dear Colleague Letter 94-G-256, Clearinghouse No. 50,422 (Sept. 1994), *reprinted at* Appx. C, *infra*.

37 34 C.F.R. §§ 682.402(d)(8) (FFEL), 674.33(g)(3) (Perkins).

38 34 C.F.R. § 682.402(d)(6)(I).

39 34 C.F.R. § 682.211(f)(7). *See also* § 3.3.2, *supra*.

40 34 C.F.R. § 682.402(d)(6)(D).

41 34 C.F.R. § 518 (since rescinded). *See also* United States v. Griffin, 707 F.2d 1477 (D.C. Cir. 1983).

42 Letter, U.S. Dep't of Educ., Compromise and Write-off Procedures 89-G-159, Clearinghouse No. 44,338 (May 1989).

asserts as a defense to the loan.[43] A loan made directly by the school, such as a Perkins loan, is subject to a straightforward breach-of-contract defense if the school closed before the educational services were provided.[44]

6.3 False-Certification Discharge

6.3.1 General

Students are entitled to a loan discharge if they received at least part of an FFEL or Direct loan after January 1, 1986,[45] and if their eligibility to borrow was falsely certified by the school.[46] The discharge does not apply to Perkins loans, but students should be able to raise the school's misconduct as a defense to loan repayment because the school is the original lender.[47]

The Department recognizes four bases for a false-certification discharge:

- the school falsifies a non-high-school graduate's ability to benefit from the program;[48]
- the school enrolls a student unable to meet minimum state employment requirements for the job for which the student is being trained;[49]
- the school forges or alters the student loan note or check endorsements;[50] or
- the borrower is a victim of identity theft.[51]

6.3.2 Discharge Based on Ability-to-Benefit (ATB) Falsification

6.3.2.1 ATB Falsification Defined

Department regulations authorize a false-certification discharge if the student was admitted to a school and the school falsified the student's ability to benefit from the program.[52]

The school is required to test a student's ability to benefit only if the student did not have a high school diploma or its recognized equivalent prior to enrollment.[53] Therefore, borrowers who had high school diplomas or equivalencies at the time they enrolled will not be eligible for this type of false-certification discharge. For enrollments between July 1, 1987, and June 30, 1991, only, both borrowers who had general education diplomas (GEDs) at the time of enrolling *and* those who received the diplomas before completing the program are deemed to have the ability to benefit from the program.[54]

The rules for schools to admit "Ability to Benefit" students changed in 1987, 1991, and 1996. For a school *not* to have falsified the ability of a student enrolled between July 1, 1987, and June 30, 1996,[55] to benefit from the school, the student must have done at least one of the following:

- passed an ability-to-benefit test, the test being approved by the accrediting agency[56] (or, for enrollments after July 1, 1991, by the Secretary) and administered substantially in accordance with the test publisher's or accreditor's requirements for use of the test[57] or
- successfully completed a program of developmental or remedial education provided by the school.[58]

For periods of enrollment after July 1, 1996, and before June 30, 2000, the student must have done at least one of the following:

- obtained a passing score on an independently administered test[59] or

---

43 *See* § 9.6.3.1, *infra*.

44 *See* § 9.6.2.1, *infra*.

45 A loan is dischargeable even if part of it was disbursed in 1985, as long as part was disbursed in 1986. 20 U.S.C. § 1087(c); 34 C.F.R. § 682.402(e)(3)(ii)(A).

46 20 U.S.C. § 1087(c)(1).

47 *See* § 9.6.2.1, *infra*.

48 *See* § 6.3.2, *infra*.

49 *See* § 6.3.3, *infra*.

50 *See* § 6.3.4, *infra*.

51 *See* § 6.3.5, *infra*.

52 34 C.F.R. §§ 682.402(e)(1)(i)(A), 685.215 (Direct Loans). A previous regulatory requirement that borrowers certify that they did not find employment after attending school was struck down in 1999. *See* Jordan v. Secretary of Educ., 194 F.3d 169 (D.C. Cir. 1999), *rev'g* 26 F. Supp. 2d 173 (D.D.C. 1998). The Department agreed to extend the benefits of the ruling to borrowers nationwide. *See* U.S. Dep't of Educ., Dear Colleague Letter #G-00-327 (July 2000), *reprinted at* Appx. C, *infra*.

53 34 C.F.R. § 682.402(e)(1), (e)(13)(iv) (citing student eligibility regulations in 34 C.F.R. § 668.32(e)(1) and ATB test requirements at 34 C.F.R. § 668.141(a)).

54 34 C.F.R. § 682.402(e)(13)(i).

55 For students enrolled before that date, the school had to have developed and consistently applied criteria for determining whether students had the ability to benefit, and the school had to have been able to demonstrate that to the Secretary. *See* 34 C.F.R. § 682.402(e)(13)(ii)(A).

56 For an example of accrediting agency testing standards, see letter from the president of ACCET to ACCET-accredited schools regarding clarification of ATB requirements for all institutions utilizing a test to admit ability-to-benefit students, Clearinghouse No. 51,927 (Feb. 12, 1990). It should be noted that accreditors did not generally grant schools an explicit approval of their ATB tests. Instead, accreditors have guidelines that ATB tests must meet. While some schools were reviewed by accreditors and found to have violated accrediting agency ATB testing rules, the absence of an adverse finding by an accreditor is not tantamount to approval of a school's ATB test or test process.

57 34 C.F.R. § 682.402(e)(13)(ii)(B)(1), (2).

58 34 C.F.R. § 682.402(e)(13)(ii)(C).

59 34 C.F.R. §§ 682.402(e)(13)(ii)(D)(1), 668.32(e)(2). The institution must obtain the results of an approved ATB test directly from either the test publisher or the assessment center that administered the test. There are a number of requirements for

- enrolled in an eligible institution that participates in an alternative admissions process.[60] Alternative processes can be implemented by the states for some or all schools in that state. These processes must be approved by the Secretary of Education. In order to gain approval, the state must present certain information, including proof of a minimum success rate.[61]

For periods of enrollment beginning on or after July 1, 2000, the student must meet one of the two conditions discussed above for July 1, 1996, through June 30, 2000, or meet the requirements for valid home schooling.[62]

A school not administering a valid test when one is required is a clear example of ATB fraud. The Department also considers the following testing errors, even if unintentional, proof of ATB falsification:[63]

- A test requiring an independent test administrator was not so administered.
- The school allowed a student to retake the test earlier than the minimum prescribed waiting period or more frequently than allowed.
- The school allowed more time than permitted to take the test, did not use all required portions of the test, supplied answers to students, allowed students to discuss the answers among themselves, or passed a student whose score did not meet minimum standards.
- Starting after July 1, 1991, the test was not approved by the Department of Education.

Even if an approved ATB test is used, a false-certification discharge may still be granted if the student was not given the appropriate portion of the approved test.[64] In *Pellot v. Riley*, a nursing assistant student who was given only the clerical portion of an approved test was found eligible on appeal for a false-certification discharge. The accreditor guidelines and test publisher instructions made clear that a school should test aptitudes related to the course. In the case of a nursing assistant, this would include verbal and math ability, not just clerical matching skills.

Audit reports and other investigative reports by the Office of the Inspector General (OIG) demonstrate the range of possible ATB fraud. For example, in one case, the OIG uncovered numerous instances of altered ATB test results. School officials in this case admitted changing some test answers.[65]

Another common abuse occurs when schools improperly enroll students who are unable to benefit from the coursework because of limited English language skills. The regulations allow schools to give admission tests in non-English languages only in specific situations. If a student is not a native English speaker and is not fluent in English, the school may give a test in that person's language only if the coursework is conducted entirely in that language. The test must be linguistically accurate and culturally sensitive.[66] If the coursework is in English with an English as a Second Language (ESL) component, and the student is enrolled in both the coursework and the ESL component, students may be given an approved ESL test or an approved test in their native language.[67] If the course is in English without an ESL component or if the student is not enrolled in the ESL component, he or she must be given an approved test in English.[68] There are also specific testing requirements for students with disabilities.[69]

These rules are routinely violated by unscrupulous vocational schools. In particular, many students are given tests in

---

independently administered tests, including that the test be given at an assessment center by a test administrator who has no financial or ownership interest in the school. The regulations for independently administered tests are set out at 34 C.F.R. § 668, Subpart J. 34 C.F.R. § 668.151 relates to the administration of tests. In addition, the test is not independently administered if the school pays a test administrator a bonus or other incentive. 34 C.F.R. § 668.151(c).

60 34 C.F.R. § 682.402(e)(13)(D)(2) (citing regulations for approved state processes at 34 C.F.R. § 668.156).

61 34 C.F.R. § 668.156(b).

62 34 C.F.R. § 682.402(e)(13)(ii)(E)(1), (2). The home schooling regulations can be found at 34 C.F.R. § 668.32(e)(4).

63 U.S. Dep't of Educ., Dear Colleague Letter Gen-95-42, at 5, 6, Clearinghouse No. 51,675 (Sept. 1995) (from Elizabeth M. Hicks, Deputy Assistant Secretary for Student Financial Assistance), *reprinted at* Appx. C, *infra*.

64 Order, Pellot v. Riley, Clearinghouse No. 52,116A (E.D. Pa. 1998); Memorandum of Law in Support of Plaintiff's Motion for Summary Judgment, Pellot v. Riley, Clearinghouse No. 52,116B (E.D. Pa. 1998). The Secretary provides a list of approved "Ability-to-Benefit" (ATB) tests and passing scores. *See, e.g.*, 71 Fed. Reg. 29135 (May 19, 2006).

65 Office of Inspector Gen., *In re* Maurice Charles Academy of Hair Styling, Docket #91-18-ST (1991). *See also* Office of Inspector Gen., Advanced Career Training Institute's Administration of the Title IV Higher Education Act Programs, Final Audit Report # ED-OIG/A04-B0019 (Sept. 2003) (finding that the school had disbursed aid to students who did not pass ability-to-benefit tests); Office of Inspector Gen., Audit of Lincoln Technical Institute, Final Audit Report #ED-OIG/A03-BC0013 (May 2002) (finding that the school compromised the security of ability-to-benefit tests); U.S. Dept. of Educ. Office of Hearings & Appeals, In the Matter of Roswell Beauty College of Cosmetology Arts & Sciences, Docket No. 03-16-SP (Sept. 15, 2003) (finding, among other problems, failure to meet ability-to-benefit testing requirements); U.S. Dept. of Educ., Office of Hearings and Appeals, In the Matter of Nationwide Beauty Sch., Docket No. 02-63-SP (Jan. 15, 2003) (findings included routine practice of falsifying or fabricating documents used to support proof of eligibility for federal student financial assistance); U.S. Dept. of Educ., Office of Hearings and Appeals, In the Matter of Hamilton Prof'l Sch., Docket No. 02-49-SP (June 11, 2003) (finding that the school falsified ability-to-benefit tests to obtain federal assistance funds for ineligible students).

66 34 C.F.R. § 668.153(a)(1).

67 34 C.F.R. § 668.153(a)(2).

68 34 C.F.R. § 668.153(a)(3).

69 34 C.F.R. § 668.153(b).

their native languages in order to make them feel more comfortable and to ease them through the process. However, in many cases, these students are enrolled in courses offered in English only without an ESL component. This is a violation of the ATB testing rules and should be grounds for a false-certification discharge.

It may also be possible to argue that even an approved test did not adequately measure a student's ability to benefit. Support for this argument can be found in OIG audits showing that the Department failed to properly monitor ATB test publishers.[70] The Federal Student Aid Office (FSA) has acknowledged many of these problems. It is important for advocates to monitor whether FSA has addressed them. Regardless of any future progress, the audit reports should be useful as evidence that the Department did not exercise proper oversight in the past.

6.3.2.2 Using Independent Evidence to Prove ATB Falsification

6.3.2.2.1 Challenging Department denials based on lack of corroborating evidence

Often, the borrower's own statement on the discharge application form is the only available evidence of ATB falsification (for example, the student certifying that no test was given or that the school helped the student pass the test). The Department is skeptical of such applications and requires the presentation of additional independent evidence of ATB falsification, such as a finding by an entity that had oversight responsibility, statements by school officials, or statements by other students, including statements made in other claims for discharge relief.[71] This is a huge obstacle for borrowers seeking false-certification discharges.

The Department's practices in this area are ripe for legal challenge. One key issue is the level of review required once the Department receives a borrower's discharge application. The regulations provide that, when a borrower applies for a false-certification discharge, the guaranty agency shall "review the borrower's request and supporting sworn statement in light of information available from the records of the agency and from other sources, including other guaranty agencies, state authorities, and cognizant accrediting associations."[72] However, in a 1995 "Dear Colleague" Letter, the Department directed guaranty agencies that an absence of findings of improper ATB practices by authorities with

oversight powers "raises an inference that no improper practices were reported because none were taking place."[73] The Department's reasoning in the "Dear Colleague" letter is that responsible authorities should have discovered ATB fraud, and the fact that these agencies did not issue such a report implies that no ATB fraud occurred. This is truly incredible. In fact, Congress in 1992 provided for the false-certification discharge and overhauled the student loan system because such supervising authorities (including the Department) had failed to do their job.[74]

The Department's practices have been challenged in court in at least two separate cases.[75] There were two main issues raised in these cases. First, plaintiffs challenged the Department's assertion that the regulations require them only to look for *findings* from oversight agencies. The Department, at least in some cases, has stated that this means they do not need to examine other materials, such as student complaints.[76]

A second issue relates to Department practices after investigating a complaint. Even if the Department looks beyond investigative "findings," they will often not find evidence to support the borrower's statements. In these cases, the Department will deny the discharge and generally allow the borrower to respond by submitting any corroborating evidence. A typical Department denial under these circumstances states:

> This office has reviewed information from entities responsible for overseeing the school's compliance with ability-to-benefit regulations, and has concluded that either no evidence of ability-benefit-violations exist[s] or the evidence does not support the issues raised in your discharge request. If you wish to contest this decision, it is your responsibility to present corroborating evidence that the school improperly determined your ability-to-benefit.[77]

---

70 *See, e.g.*, ED-OIG/A03-B0001 (Aug. 22, 2002); ED-OIG/A03-B0024 (May 13, 2002) (audit of American College Testing); and ED-OIG/A03-B0022 (Feb. 5, 2002) (audit of Wonderlic).

71 U.S. Dep't of Educ., Dear Colleague Letter Gen-95-42, Clearinghouse No. 51,675 (Sept. 1995) (from Elizabeth M. Hicks, Deputy Assistant Secretary for Student Financial Assistance), *reprinted at* Appx. C, *infra*.

72 34 C.F.R. § 682.402(e)(6)(iv).

73 U.S. Dep't of Educ., Dear Colleague Letter GEN-95-42 (Sept. 1995), *reprinted at* Appx. C, *infra*.

74 *See, e.g.*, *Abuses in Federal Student Grant Programs: Hearings before the Permanent Subcommittee on Investigations of the Committee on Governmental Affairs*, 103d Cong. S. Hearing 103-491 (Oct. 1993). *See generally* Ch. 9 (challenging vocational school fraud), *infra*.

75 Two of these complaints, *Cofan v. Paige*, Civil Action No. 01-4239 (E.D. Pa. 2001), and *Gill v. Riley*, CV-00-5453 (E.D.N.Y. 2000), are reprinted at Appendix E, *infra*. The complaints and other documents from these cases are also available on the companion CD-Rom to this manual. The *Cofan* case settled and the *Gill* case was still pending at the time this manual was printed.

76 *Gill v. Riley*, CV-00-5453 (E.D.N.Y. 2000), *reprinted at* Appx. E, *infra*.

77 This was the notice received by the plaintiff in the *Cofan* case. *Cofan v. Paige*, Civil Action No. 01-4239 (E.D. Pa. complaint filed 2001). This notice is available on the companion CD-Rom to this manual.

In at least one case, the plaintiffs argued that, if the Department does not find evidence to contradict the borrower's statement, the Department must grant the discharge.[78] The first district court to consider these issues rejected most of the borrowers' arguments.[79] The court found that requiring additional evidence beyond a borrower's sworn statement was not in conflict with the false-certification statute.[80] The court also rejected the borrowers' argument that the Department's policy conflicted with the regulations.[81] The borrowers' procedural arguments, based on the Department's announcing the policy in a "Dear Colleague" letter rather than formal regulations, were also rejected.[82] According to the court, the notice and comment requirements do not apply to interpretive rules, general statements of policy, or rules of agency organizations, procedure, or practice.

There was one issue left outstanding in the case. The plaintiffs requested additional discovery to develop the record regarding their claim that the adoption of the "Dear Colleague" letter was arbitrary and capricious. The plaintiffs alleged that the Department should have known that agencies it relied upon to make ATB findings provided inadequate oversight.[83] The court agreed that the facts were not sufficiently developed to determine whether the Secretary considered and rejected or entirely failed to consider the performance of accrediting agencies at policing proprietary schools. Summary judgment for the Department was denied on this issue only.[84]

6.3.2.2.2 Obtaining investigatory files through Freedom of Information Act requests

Lack of documentation has been the primary obstacle to the granting of false-certification discharges. There is no magic solution to gathering evidence, but there are a number of sources to try.

One good source of information is state or federal regulators' investigatory files. The Department of Education's files on a school may be obtained through a Freedom of Information Act request. Important documents include the school's application for eligibility with accompanying documents, any program reviews, or reviews shared with the Department by guaranty agencies, state agencies, or accreditors.[85] It is also important to request any "Emergency Action" memos issued by the Department in relation to the school.

A separate request should be made to the Department's Inspector General for audit and investigations concerning the school. State licensing agencies may also have files on schools, including investigation reports, which may be available under state sunshine laws.[86] Private accrediting agencies will not usually share files on schools without a subpoena.

The Freedom of Information Act contains standards for waiver of fees for search and duplication under the statute.[87] There is also a provision that the agency should not charge for the first 100 pages of copying.[88] The following language should be included in requests to obtain a waiver of fees:

> These records are not requested for any commercial purpose but to gather information on [how the agency has carried out its obligations in the area covered by the records]. Accordingly, I request that any fees be waived as disclosure of this information is in the public interest because it is likely to contribute significantly to public understanding of the operations or activities of the government. 5 U.S.C. § 552(a)(4)(A)(iii). If there are any proposed charges which are not waived and they exceed [Fill in amount], please notify me before they are incurred.

For advocates seeking records to expose misconduct of a school operating under the loan program, it is important to emphasize the public benefit of disclosure concerning what the Department knew abut the school's operations and whether it acted effectively in enforcing HEA standards.

In addition, both the Department of Education's Office of Hearings and Appeals (OHA) and Office of Inspector General (OIG) have investigative and audit reports on-line.[89]

6.3.2.2.3 School files

Advocates should try to obtain copies of all the school's files on the student. This information is generally difficult to obtain directly from the school if it has already closed. In that case, students can often obtain the schools' student records from the state agency responsible for regulating the schools. Typically, a student has an academic file and a financial aid file. The academic file will be the more important. Information about state licensing agencies is available on the Department of Education website.[90]

---

78 Gill v. Riley, CV-00-5453 (E.D.N.Y. 2000), *reprinted at* Appx. E, *infra*.

79 Gill v. Paige, 226 F. Supp. 2d 366 (E.D.N.Y. 2002).

80 *Id.* at 372.

81 *Id.* at 373.

82 *Id.* at 374.

83 *Id.* at 375.

84 *Id.* at 376.

85 Sample FOIA requests can be found at Appendix F, *infra*.

86 State licensing agency contact information can be found on the Department's website at www.studentaid.ed.gov/students/attachments/siteresources/StateLicensingAgency TelephoneNumbers_1.doc.

87 5 U.S.C. § 552(a)(4)(A)(iii).

88 *Id.*

89 The Office of Inspector General website is at www.ed.gov/about/offices/list/oig/index.html?src=mr (last accessed on October 5, 2006). The Office of Hearings and Appeals website is at www.ed-oha.org (last accessed on October 5, 2006).

90 *See* www.ed.gov/offices/OSFAP/Students/closedschool/statelicensing.html.

Advocates should look for a copy of an admission test in the file or a description of the type of test used. The absence of a test or any reference to a test is evidence that the test was never given. In fact, for independent testing done after 1991, the Department regulations state that the school is liable to the Department for all funds disbursed if the school is unable to *document* that the student received a passing score on an approved test.[91]

6.3.2.2.4 Testing company information

If the file (or the school or state licensing agency) can identify the company giving the test, consider contacting the testing agency. The Wonderlic Company tests were widely used by trade schools for ATB testing. Wonderlic can provide appropriate information on whether a particular social security number matches one of its registered test results.[92] If the student was to have received the Wonderlic test, but the test score is not registered, this may provide evidence that a proper test was not given. Wonderlic may also provide additional information about the validity of test scores at a particular school that administered the Wonderlic test for ATB purposes.

6.3.2.2.5 Information on specific schools

The National Consumer Law Center has compiled information on a few schools (unfortunately just a small fraction of those involved in ATB falsification). Advocates should contact the Center if they need more information on any of the following schools:

- Academy of Court Reporting (Cleveland, Ohio)—2006 report obtained in a FOIA request for investigations, inquiries, and other actions from 1985–2006.
- American Business Institute (Chicago, Illinois; closed in 1990)—1989 Illinois State Board of Education findings.
- Austin School of Beauty Culture (Chicago, Illinois; closed on July 3, 1990—1988 Department of Education review.
- Chicago Institute of Technology, Inc. (closed in 1990)—Higher Education Assistance Foundation, Accrediting Bureau of Health Education Schools reviews.
- County Schools—information about ATB testing.
- Debbie's School of Beauty Culture (Chicago, four lo-

cations; closed between 1989 and 1993)—Higher Education Assistance Foundation and Department of Education review.
- Hausman Computer School (New York)—copy of federal court decision finding the school guilty of criminal conduct, including ATB fraud, and imprisoning the owners. United States v. Grundhofer, 916 F.2d 788 (2d Cir. 1990).
- IADE American Schools (various locations in southern California; all schools closed by 1995)—Student Financial Assistance proceeding finding that, from July 1989 through June 1991, IADE disbursed student assistance funds to students who had failed the ATB test; copy of 1997 news release with information about the indictment of IADE's owner and financial aid director.
- Illinois School of Commerce (Chicago, Illinois; closed in 1988)—Department of Education reports and copies of complaints against former president and owner.
- Marion Adult Education and Career Training Center, (Chicago, Illinois; closed in 1990)—1990 Department of Education audit report.
- Metropolitan Business College (Evergreen Park, Illinois; closed in 1992)—1987 and 1990 Department of Education audits.
- Molder Hairstyling College (Chicago, IL).
- National Business Academy (California, accredited by ACCET)—State attorney general office submitted compilation of materials to California guaranty agency showing ATB fraud.
- National Technical College (accredited by ABHES and ACCT)—Evidence shows, among other violations, that NTC routinely falsely certified students as having the ability to benefit from the training.
- Phillips Junior College (Augusta and Columbus, Georgia; Spokane, Washington; Campbell, California; Georgia locations closed in 1993, Washington location in 1995, and Campbell in 1996)—Department of Education audit reports.
- PTC Career Institute (Philadelphia, Atlanta, Chicago, Baltimore, Newark, Cleveland, District of Columbia; accredited by ACCSCT/CCATTS (NATTS))—Department's Office of Inspector General audit report finds ATB problems, as does an affidavit from Wonderlic Personnel Test, Inc., and an affidavit used to support application by Community Legal Services in Philadelphia for false-certification discharges. The Department has authorized false-certification discharges to PTC Philadelphia students during the audit period.
- Rome Academy of Cosmetology (Chicago, Illinois; closed in 1992)—1993 Department of Education program review.
- SCS Business and Technical Institute (Jamaica, New York)
- Tarkio College (Tarkio, Missouri)—Information obtained from Missouri Department of Higher Education,

---

91   34 C.F.R. § 668.154(c).

92   Call Wonderlic at 1-800-323-3742 and ask to talk to the ATB Department; mail a request to Wonderlic Personnel Test, Inc., 1795 N. Butterfield Rd., Libertyville, IL 60048; or visit www.wonderlic.com. *See also Tests in Print 6: An Index to Tests, Test Reviews, and the Literature on Specific Tests* (Barbara Plake et al eds., July 2002) (providing a description of most tests and their appropriate uses, along with the addresses of the publishers).

including numerous newspaper articles about the school.

- Trainco Business School (Chicago, Illinois; two locations; closed in 1990)—Illinois Attorney General complaint.
- United Business Institute (New York, Florida, Georgia, and New Jersey; accredited by SACCOE)—New York State Education Department found ATB fraud.
- United Education and Software (UES) Schools (California; includes National Technical Schools—Home Study, Pacific Coast Technical Institutes, and Pacific Coast Colleges; all accredited by CCATTS (NATTS))—Court found systematic ATB fraud, as did two Department Office of Inspector General audits.
- Wilfred Academy of Hair and Beauty (Illinois; two locations; closed in 1991 and 1992)—Audited Financial Statements 1985–1987.

In addition, advocates should check the Department of Education's Office of Hearings and Appeals website and the Office of Inspector General website.[93] Many schools have also faced state and federal investigations and lawsuits. The lawsuits are mainly a combination of whistleblower, wrongful-termination, and shareholder suits.[94]

6.3.2.2.6 Other evidence of ATB fraud

Additional information can be provided by obtaining affidavits of other students who attended the same school as the client and who can testify that they were not tested or were improperly tested. In cases in which the client did not speak English at the time of enrollment or had a low reading aptitude, advocates should consider getting an official evaluation of the client's reading level.

For example, a monolingual Spanish-speaking client who dropped out of school in the fifth or sixth grade in the client's home country should submit an affidavit regarding his or her inability to speak English at the time of enrollment, that he or she dropped out of school, and that he or she was never tested or was improperly tested. This testimony, along with an official assessment of the client's reading level, should be strong evidence for an ATB discharge, even in the absence of official investigatory records.[95]

6.3.2.3 Group Discharges

The Department will provide false-certification discharges upon proper application *without* independent evidence for a particular cohort of students (such as non-high-school graduates who were admitted at a particular branch

of a school during a certain time period) if *the Department* determines that a school committed pervasive and serious violations of ATB regulations.[96]

A partial list of group discharges provided by the Department in 1998 included the following schools:

1. 10/31/96, Draughon College (Oklahoma City)—Approval of ATB borrowers enrolled from 7/1/87–6/30/91.[97]

2. 12/20/96, National Technical Schools Home Study Division—Approval of ATB borrowers enrolled from 8/18/87–11/15/88.

3. 12/20/96, six branches of UES/Pacific Coast College—Approval of ATB borrowers enrolled from 2/1/87–5/31/89.[98]

4. 5/20/97, Andover Tractor Trailer School—Approval of ATB borrowers enrolled from 6/1/86–4/30/89. This limited time period was successfully challenged in subsequent litigation. The group discharge should apply to any Andover borrower during any time period who did not have a high school diploma or GED at the time of enrollment and who otherwise meets the criteria for a false-certification discharge.[99]

Another cohort of students includes all those with loans currently or subsequently held by the Department related to enrollments at any PTC Career Institute[100] or USA Training Academy. The Department has also granted a group discharge for Cambridge Technical School students.[101] The

---

93 *See* § 6.3.2.2.2, *supra.*

94 *See* § 9.1.2, *infra.*

95 See § 6.3.2.1, *supra,* for a discussion of ATB testing of non-English speaking students.

96 Requests to have schools treated in this way should be sent, with accompanying evidence, to Chief, General Provisions Branch, Policy, Training, and Analysis Service, Policy Development Division, U.S. Department of Education, 600 Independence Ave. SW, Washington D.C. 20202-5346; (202) 708-7888. *See* U.S. Dep't of Educ., Dear Colleague Letter GEN-95-42, Clearinghouse No. 51,675 (Sept. 1995), *reprinted at* Appx. C, *infra.*

97 *See* Letter from Carney M. McCollough to Glendon Forgey, Oklahoma Guaranteed Student Loan Program (July 31, 1996) (on file with the U.S. Department of Education). The letter is included on the companion CD-Rom to this manual.

98 *See* Letter from Carney M. McCollough to Susan Donald, California Student Aid Comm'n (Dec. 20, 1996) (on file with the U.S. Department of Education). The letter is included on the companion CD-Rom to this manual.

99 U.S. Dep't of Educ., Letter from Carney M. McCollough to Irv Ackelsberg, Community Legal Services, Clearinghouse No. 52,135 (May 20, 1997). The deadline and other issues were challenged in *White v. Riley*, Clearinghouse No. 52,121 (E.D. Pa. 1998) (class action complaint). The letter to Irv Ackelsberg is included on the companion CD-Rom to this manual.

100 PTC had schools in Philadelphia, Atlanta, Chicago, Baltimore, Newark, Cleveland, and the District of Columbia. The group discharge applies to students whose first day of attendance occurred from July 1, 1987, through June 30, 1990. *See* Letter from Pamela A. Moran to Irv Ackelsberg, Community Legal Services (June 30, 1995) (on file with the U.S. Department of Education). The letter is included on the companion CD-Rom to this manual.

101 U.S. Dep't of Educ., Letter from Carney M. McCollough to Stephen Olden, Legal Aid Society of Cincinnati, Clearinghouse No. 52,491 (Apr. 30, 1999). The letter is included on the companion CD-Rom to this manual.

Department also granted a group ATB discharge for certain former students who enrolled in Programming Systems Incorporated (PSI). The group discharge covers ATB students who attended any PSI school from January 1, 1986, until the school's closing. It applies to every campus of PSI, including those in New York, Baltimore, Silver Spring (Maryland), Columbus, Cleveland, Southfield (Michigan), Indianapolis, Philadelphia, Miami, Charlotte, and Flint. Loans are held by at least sixteen different guaranty agencies in addition to the Department. The Department was supposed to notify all these agencies of the group discharge.[102]

This list is not exhaustive because to date the Department has not made a list of approved false-certification group discharges widely available. There may be other schools for which group discharges have been granted by the Department.

Another way to prove ATB falsification without evidence from an independent entity is to aggregate a number of students with ATB claims against the same school and then send those applications in as a group with a cover letter. An alternative approach is to send in only one application but refer to other previously filed applications in a cover letter. Each application should then serve as independent evidence for each of the other applications.

6.3.3 Discharge Based on Student's Inability to Meet Minimum State Job Requirements

Even students with a high school diploma can receive a false-certification discharge if, *at the time of the student's enrollment*, "the student would not meet the requirements for employment (in the student's state of residence) in the occupation for which the training program supported by the loan was intended because of physical or mental condition, or age, or criminal record or other reason accepted by the Secretary."[103] According to the Department, "[t]hose provisions apply to all categories of students at all schools, including students for whom the school was not required to make ability-to-benefit determinations or for whom the school made such determinations properly."[104]

For example, students with less than a tenth-grade education should receive a false-certification discharge if they attended a cosmetology school in one of a number of states (such as Pennsylvania and California) that requires licensed cosmetologists to have at least a tenth-grade education.[105] Other examples include those with felony records being trained as security guards or one-armed students being trained as truck-drivers when state law disqualifies those individuals from those occupations.

Monolingual Spanish students taught exclusively in Spanish are another example if the state licensing test is given only in English. Even absent a licensing exam requirement, it may be that a Spanish-speaking student would not "meet the requirements for employment" if the employment required the employee to be English speaking. The fact that the course was allegedly in English would not affect the fact that the student could only speak Spanish "at the time of the student's enrollment." The equities of this argument are even stronger when the school failed to provide promised English-as-a-second-language training. However, according to anecdotal reports from advocates, the Department has generally, but not always, rejected this argument. To date, these denials have not been appealed.

The discharge should also apply when the school's program, instead of the student, does not meet minimum state requirements. For example, a discharge should be available when a program was not certified by the state and graduation from a certified program is a precondition under state law for employment.

Borrowers should submit detailed documentation of the status or condition that prevents them from working in the particular field. In addition, the Department will generally require a copy of the state statute or regulation showing the requirements for employment in the particular field and that the condition or status would prevent the student from meeting those requirements.

6.3.4 Forgery

A third important basis for a false-certification discharge is if the student's signature was forged on the loan application, promissory note, loan check endorsement, or authorization for an electronic funds transfer.[106] Advocates may find more forged checks than loan applications because students may have changed their enrollment decision after they signed the application, but before a first or subsequent check was cut, and thus not have been available or willing to endorse the check to the school.

---

102 A copy of the application for group discharge submitted by Legal Aid Society of Cleveland is included on the companion CD-Rom to this volume. Community Legal Services in Philadelphia also submitted a group discharge application on behalf of former PSI students. The Department's letter approving the group discharge is reproduced on the companion CD-Rom to this manual.

103 34 C.F.R. § 682.402(e)(13)(iii)(B).

104 U.S. Dep't of Educ., Dear Colleague Letter Gen-95-42, at 9, Clearinghouse No. 51,675 (Sept. 1995) (from Elizabeth M. Hicks, Deputy Assistant Secretary for Student Financial Assistance), *reprinted at* Appx. C, *infra*. The letter does state that a defense to the discharge would be evidence that the school

asked the student about such a disqualifying condition and the student did not divulge it.

105 Apparently guaranty agencies are quite erratic in whether they require more than just the student's statement that the student did not complete the tenth grade. Guaranty agencies requiring additional proof the interesting problem of proof for students to show the negative—that the student never completed the tenth grade at any school.

106 34 C.F.R. § 682.402(e)(1)(i)(B), (e)(1)(ii).

It is essential to obtain copies not only of the loan application and promissory note but of all canceled checks evidencing the indebtedness. If the borrower's signature appears forged, the student must submit five specimens of the student's own signature, two of which had to have been within one year of the forgery.[107]

A false-certification discharge for a forged check is only available if the proceeds of the forged check went toward tuition payments that the student was not obligated to pay, such as that portion of tuition not owed under the applicable refund formula after the student had dropped out.[108] The regulations and a "Dear Colleague" letter appear to place the burden not on the student but on the guaranty agency to determine whether the forged check proceeds went toward a legitimate student obligation or not.[109] The Department will not grant a discharge based on forgery if the borrower benefited from the loan.[110]

6.3.5 Identity Theft

The Higher Education Reconciliation Act of 2005 provides for discharges of FFEL or Direct loans if the borrower's eligibility to borrow was falsely certified due to identity theft.[111] This basis for a discharge became effective on July 1, 2006.

The regulations published in August 2006 require a borrower seeking this discharge to

- certify that the borrower did not sign the promissory note or that any other means of identification used to obtain the loan was used without the borrower's authorization;
- certify that the borrower did not receive or benefit from the proceeds of the loan with knowledge that the loan had been made without the borrower's authorization; and
- provide a copy of a local, state, or federal court verdict or judgment that conclusively determines that the borrower was a victim of the crime of identity theft and that the loan in question was made as a result of that theft.[112]

If the judicial determination of the crime does not expressly state that the loan was obtained as a result of the crime, the borrower must provide authentic samples of his or her signature or other means of identification and a statement of facts that demonstrate that the borrower's eligibility for the loan in question was falsely certified as a result of identity theft.

The Department clarifies in the interim regulations that it is not suggesting in any way that borrowers are liable for loans they did not execute or authorize when there is no crime of identity theft.[113] Borrowers may also be eligible for false-certification discharges due to forgery.[114] In addition, they may have common law contract defenses or other defenses derived from HEA regulations. For example, FFEL program regulations provide that benefits are payable to loan holders only when the lender obtained a legally enforceable promissory note to evidence the loan.[115] Lender rights are also subject to the obligation of the lender to exercise due diligence in making the loan.[116]

6.3.6 Relief Available for Those Obtaining a False-Certification Discharge

The relief available is identical to that for a closed-school discharge, as detailed in § 6.2.3, *supra*. Revocation of a false-certification discharge is contemplated in the regulations only if the borrower provides testimony, sworn statements, or documentation that does not support the material representations made to obtain the discharge.[117] It is unclear how the Department interprets this provision.

6.3.7 How to Apply for a False-Certification Discharge

There is no time limit on a student's eligibility for a false-certification discharge.[118] Whether a student seeks a discharge based on a disqualifying condition, ATB falsification, or a forged check, the application should be directed to the entity holding the loan. For a defaulted loan, the holder is almost always either a guaranty agency or the Department of Education. Guaranty agencies have their own forms, and the Department has three different false-certification-discharge forms for loans it is holding, one relating to claims of a disqualifying condition, one for ATB fraud, and one for forgery claims.[119]

While it is important to fill out the forms in their entirety, it is useful to know what the regulations say is required of

---

107 34 C.F.R. § 682.402(e)(3)(iii), (iv).

108 34 C.F.R. § 682.402(e)(1)(ii).

109 U.S. Dep't of Educ., Dear Colleague Letter 94-G-256 item 11 Clearinghouse No. 51,670 (Sept. 1994) (from Leo Kornfeld, Deputy Assistant Secretary for Student Financial Assistance Programs).

110 34 C.F.R. § 682.402(e)(1)(ii).

111 Pub. L. No. 109-171, 120 Stat. 4 (Feb. 8, 2006).

112 34 C.F.R. § 682.402(e)(3)(v) (interim final rule). *See* 71 Fed. Reg. 45666 (Aug. 9, 2006).

113 71 Fed. Reg. 45666 (Aug. 9, 2006).

114 *See* § 6.3.4, *supra*.

115 71 Fed. Reg. 45666 (Aug. 9, 2006) (citing 34 C.F.R. § 682.402(e)(1)(i)(B), 682.406(a)(1)). *See* § 9.5.3, *infra*.

116 *Id.* (citing 34 C.F.R. § 682.206(a)(2)).

117 34 C.F.R. § 682.402(e)(4)(ii).

118 34 C.F.R. § 682.402(e)(6)(v).

119 The Department of Education forms are reprinted at Appendix D, *infra*. They are also available on the Department's website at www.ed.gov. The Department should also be making available a form for the identity theft discharge.

an application. According to the regulations, the student must submit a written request for a discharge and a sworn statement (not notarized, but sworn under the penalty of perjury) attesting

(1) whether the student has made a claim against another party on the loan (such as from a state tuition recovery fund);

(2) that at least part of the loan was disbursed after January 1, 1986;

(3) that the student agrees to provide, at the Secretary's request, additional information concerning the student's eligibility for a discharge; and

(4) that the student will cooperate with the Secretary in enumerated enforcement actions and to assign to the Secretary certain rights the student has to recover from third parties.[120]

For ATB falsification applications, students must also state that they had not graduated from high school before being admitted and that they did not have the ability to benefit from the course.

For false-certification discharges based on the school's forging of the student's signature on the loan application, the promissory note, a check endorsement, or electronic funds transfer authorization, the student must also state that a signature on one of these documents is not the student's and provide five signature specimens (two of which are within one year of the disputed signature).[121] When the forgery is on a check endorsement or transfer authorization, the student must state that the student never received the loan proceeds and those proceeds were never credited to amounts owed to the school for that portion of the program that the student completed.[122]

The regulations contain no requirement that students, in applying for a discharge, reaffirm their debt or waive other rights. If guaranty agencies provide discharge application forms with these extraneous provisions, students should cross these provisions out, with their initials evidencing their intent to delete these items. The Department has also instructed guaranty agencies to process all requests for a discharge, even if the request is not on the agency's standard form.[123] In practice, however, it is generally expeditious to use the official agency form whenever possible. In addition, the loan may be discharged without a written application if the guaranty agency, with the Secretary's permission, determines that the borrower qualifies for a discharge based on information in its possession.[124]

In general, borrowers will find it difficult to obtain a false-certification discharge. It will often be necessary to continue following up on applications and to dispute denials. Since discharge applications often take many years to process, advocates should be prepared to request administrative forbearances for students so that collection activities will cease until the discharge has been granted or denied.[125] The regulations do not specifically grant borrowers an automatic collection stay after applying for a discharge. Stays are granted only if the holder of the loan receives information it believes to be reliable indicating that a borrower is eligible for a discharge.[126] The borrower must respond within sixty days of receiving this notice in order to suspend collection.[127]

In response to a 2003 FOIA request, the Department reported the following statistics for the false-certification discharge program:

• In fiscal year 1998, the Department received 4753 applications but claimed it did not have information about approval rates.

• In fiscal year 1999, the Department received 6571 applications but claimed it did not have information about approval rates.

• In fiscal year 2000, the Department received 9576 applications but claimed it did not have information about approval rates.

• In fiscal year 2001, the Department received 4713 applications and reported 1211 approvals after December 18, 2000. This is an approximately 25% approval rate. The Department reported that this represented $7,766,156.57 in discharged funds.

• In fiscal year 2002, the Department received 5272 applications and reported approving 44% or 2317. The total amount discharged was $11,928,735.98.

In fiscal year 2003 through June 30, the Department had received 6145 applications and reported approving 3757 or 61%.

The Department expects guaranty agencies to respond to discharge requests within ninety days, although the Department has not set any time limits for its own response to discharge requests. The Department's delays in making decisions on false-certification discharges were among the issues raised in a 1998 class action complaint. The complaint alleged that the Secretary had not assigned adequate staff to administer the program, resulting in a backlog of over 10,000 undecided applications, some of which had been pending for years.[128]

---

120 34 C.F.R. § 682.402 (e)(3), (e)(4). There is questionable statutory authority for this requirement since the statute provides for assignment of rights only against the school and its affiliates and principals.

121 34 C.F.R. § 682.402(e)(3)(iii), (iv).

122 34 C.F.R. § 682.402(e)(3)(iv).

123 U.S. Dep't of Educ., Dear Colleague Letter 94-G-256, Clearinghouse No. 50,422 (Sept. 1994), *reprinted at* Appx. C, *infra*.

124 34 C.F.R. § 682.402(e)(14).

125 34 C.F.R. § 682.211(f)(7). *See also* § 3.3.2, *supra*.

126 34 C.F.R. § 682.402(e)(6)(ii).

127 34 C.F.R. § 682.402(e)(6)(iv).

128 White v. Riley, Clearinghouse No. 52,121 (E.D. Pa. 1998) (class action complaint). A copy of a letter from the Department in a successful false-certification discharge case is reprinted at Appendix D.

The student has a right to seek review by the Secretary of a guaranty agency denial of a false-certification discharge application.[129]

6.4 Discharge for Unpaid Refunds

6.4.1 General

Failure to provide refunds was one of the most common complaints during the heyday of trade school fraud in the 1980s and early 1990s. Many borrowers signed up for schools, never attended classes, but were still charged the full amount of the loan. The unpaid-refund discharge fills in some of the gaps left by the closed-school and false-certification discharges, which provide relief for many, but not all, victims of trade school abuses. It provides for discharge based on the school's failure to make an owed refund to the student.[130]

6.4.2 Criteria for Unpaid-Refund Discharge

The discharge applies to the following types of loans entered into after January 1, 1986: Guaranteed Student (Stafford) Loans, Unsubsidized Stafford Loans, Supplemental Loans for Students (SLSs), PLUS (parent borrower) loans, and Federal Direct Loans. Students already can raise an unpaid refund as a defense to the Perkins Loan collection action.[131] The unpaid-refund discharge became effective as of July 1, 2000.[132]

The unpaid-refund discharge applies to students who signed up for a school but never attended, who withdrew, or who terminated within a time frame that entitled them to a refund but never received the refund from the school. Students who completed 60% or more of the loan period are not entitled to refunds and therefore not entitled to the discharge.[133] A student should not have to show written proof or other formal proof of withdrawal or termination in order to qualify.

Students who never received the owed refund are eligible to reduce their current obligations by the amount that should have been refunded plus interest and related charges. Based on previous experience with the closed-school and false-certification discharges, thousands of students who attended scam vocational schools will likely be eligible for this discharge. Implementation problems will arise in figuring out the amount of discharges due, pressuring the Department

to grant the discharges in a timely manner, tracking down eligible borrowers, and educating them on this new right.

6.4.3 Determining Amount of Discharge

The amount of the unpaid refund will be determined based on information the holder of the loan has or the borrower can provide or by applying the appropriate refund formula to information that the borrower provides or that is otherwise available to the agency. If the actual school refund formula is not available, the regulations set out a substitute formula to determine the amount eligible for discharge.[134]

In these circumstances, the guaranty agency is required to use the following formula to determine the amount eligible for discharge:

- In the case of a student who fails to attend or whose withdrawal or termination date is before October 7, 2000, and who completes less than 60% of the loan period, the guaranty agency discharges the lesser of the institutional charges unearned or the loan amount.[135] The guaranty agency determines the amount of the institutional charges unearned by (A) calculating the ratio of the amount of time in the loan period after the student's last day of attendance to the actual length of the loan period and (B) multiplying the resulting factor by the institutional charges assessed the student for the loan period.[136]
- In the case of a student who fails to attend or whose withdrawal or termination date is on or after October 7, 2000, and who completes less than 60% of the loan period, the guaranty agency discharges the loan amount unearned. This is determined by (A) calculating the ratio of the amount of time remaining in the loan period after the student's last day of attendance to the actual length of the loan period and (B) multiplying the resulting factor by the total amount of title IV grants and loans received by the student or, if unknown, the loan amount.[137]

The borrower needs three pieces of information to calculate a refund: the tuition, the school's refund formula, and the percentage of the course or term the borrower completed. The school catalog or the written enrollment agreement will have the tuition, refund policy, and number of weeks per term. State licensing agencies sometimes have school catalogs and/or enrollment contract forms in their files for closed schools. The student must supply the enrollment date and last date of attendance to figure the percentage of the course completed. A refund is calculated based on the

---

129 *See* 34 C.F.R. § 682.402(e)(11). *See* § 6.10 (appeals), *infra*.

130 20 U.S.C. § 1087(c); 34 C.F.R. § 682.402(l) (FFEL), 685.216 (Direct Loans).

131 *See* § 9.6.2.1, *infra*.

132 64 Fed. Reg. 58,937–58,970 (Nov. 1, 1999).

133 34 C.F.R. § 682.402(o)(2)(iii).

134 34 C.F.R. § 682.402(o)(2).

135 34 C.F.R. § 682.402(o)(2)(i).

136 *Id.*

137 34 C.F.R. § 682.402(o)(2)(ii).

student's last date of attendance (LDA), regardless of whether the student notified the school of his or her withdrawal.

Federal rules have generally required that schools apply refunds of unearned tuition to loans first, and then to grants. This rule benefits the borrower because even a partial tuition refund may eliminate the loan balance in full. For example, if the student was entitled to a 50% refund of a $5000 tuition and had a $2500 loan and $2500 in grants, the entire loan should have been refunded by the school. The unpaid refund should be for 100% of the loan amount.

Students who completed 60% or more of the loan period are not entitled to refunds and therefore not entitled to the discharge.[138] On the other hand, most students who never attended classes at all were entitled to a full refund of their loan amount and therefore should get a full discharge of their loans.

6.4.4 *Applying for the Discharge*

The procedures and timing for a loan discharge are slightly different depending on whether the school is currently open or closed. If the school is still open, to qualify for the discharge, the borrower and guarantor must document that they attempted to resolve the problem within 120 days from the date that the borrower submitted a completed application for discharge.[139] This requirement does not apply if the school is closed.

Except when the guaranty agency (with the Department's approval) determines, based on information in its possession, that the borrower qualifies for a discharge, borrowers must submit written discharge applications.[140] Applications should be sent to the holder or guaranty agency. In most cases the holder will be the guaranty agency.[141]

The Department has developed a uniform application form.[142] In addition, the regulations require agencies to send discharge applications to potentially eligible borrowers.[143] Once they do so, they must cease collection until the application is resolved.[144] If the borrower does not return the application within sixty days, collection actions can resume.[145]

There is no time limit for the agency to make a decision. However, once an application is granted, the holder must suspend collection within thirty days, discharge the appropriate amount, and inform the borrower of the determination.[146]

If the application is denied, the holder must notify the borrower in writing of the reason for the determination and of the borrower's right to request review within thirty days of the borrower's submission of additional documentation. Collection must be suspended during the review period.[147]

In response to a 2003 FOIA request, the Department reported the following statistics for the unpaid-refund discharge program:

- In fiscal year 2001, after 12/18/00, the Department received 1345 applications and approved 1005 or about 75%. The amount discharged was $3,530,970.52.
- In fiscal year 2002, the Department received 5979 applications and approved 4031 or about 67%. The amount discharged was $16,271,331.35.
- Through June 30, 2003, of fiscal year 2003, the Department received 3600 applications and approved 1839 or about 51%. Not all claims had been processed at the time this information was provided and the Department had not yet calculated the amount discharged.
- To date, the approval rates for unpaid-refund discharges are considerably higher than in the other discharge programs.

6.4.5 *Relief Available for Those Obtaining a Discharge*

Eligible borrowers will be granted a discharge in the amount of the unpaid refund, including any accrued interest and any collection of other charges relating to the amount of the unpaid refund.[148] If the borrower has already paid off part of the loan, and the amount still owing on the loan is less than the unpaid refund, part of the unpaid refund will be used to fully discharge the loan. The rest of the unpaid refund will be paid the borrower in cash to the extent the borrower has made payments of that amount on the loan. The holder of the loan is also required to report the discharge to all credit reporting agencies to which the holder previously reported the status of the loan.[149]

6.5 Relationship Between Closed-School, False-Certification, and Unpaid-Refund Discharges

Many victims of trade school fraud will be eligible for multiple discharges. The same borrower can apply for more than one discharge but cannot obtain duplicate relief.

---

138 34 C.F.R. § 682.402(o)(2)(iii).

139 34 C.F.R. § 682.402(l)(2)(ii).

140 34 C.F.R. § 682.402(l)(5)(iv).

141 The regulations are slightly different if the lender holds the loan. In these circumstances, lenders are required to provide the guaranty agency with documentation related to the borrower's qualification for discharge. 34 C.F.R. § 682.402(m).

142 *See* U.S. Dep't of Educ., Dear Guaranty Agency Director Letter Gen-01-15 (Nov. 2001). The form is included at Appendix C, *infra*, and available on the Department's website at www.ed.gov.

143 34 C.F.R. § 682.402(l)(5).

144 34 C.F.R. § 682.402(l)(5)(ii).

145 34 C.F.R. § 682.402(l)(5)(iii).

146 34 C.F.R. § 682.402(l)(5)(vi).

147 34 C.F.R. § 682.402(l)(5)(vii). *See* § 6.10 (administrative appeals), *infra*.

148 34 C.F.R. § 682.402(l)(3)(i).

149 34 C.F.R. § 682.402(l)(3)(ii).

Many clients who were truly victims of trade school fraud will not meet the criteria for one or more of the discharges. For this reason, it is always critical to consider all three. For example, many borrowers attended schools that closed, but the borrowers may not have been in attendance (or they cannot show they were in attendance) at the time the school closed or within ninety days of the closure. If a particular borrower is also a high school graduate, he or she may not be eligible for either a closed-school or false-certification-of-ability-to-benefit discharge even if the schooling was worthless. The borrower may, however, be eligible to get at least partial relief from an unpaid-refund discharge. Similarly, a borrower who withdrew from a school within a short period of enrolling, or who never attended classes, may have both a false-certification-by-forgery and an unpaid-refund claim.

Another avenue to consider, discussed in § 6.6, *infra*, is a disability discharge. In addition, some states have tuition recovery funds that may reimburse all or part of a student's obligation.[150] Bankruptcy, discussed in detail in Chapter 7, *infra*, may also be a viable option, particularly for borrowers with bleak long-term financial prospects.

6.6 Disability Discharge

6.6.1 General

The borrower's permanent and total disability is grounds for a student loan discharge.[151] Prior to 1999, a disabled borrower simply had a licensed physician certify that the borrower was permanently disabled, with an onset date after the date of the loan. This had to be done on the proper form and the discharge was generally granted.

In 1999, the Department's Inspector General (IG) conducted a study that led to a Department crackdown on alleged fraud. The IG found that 23% of borrowers who received disability discharges in a specified time period worked and earned money after the disability determination was made or the loan was discharged.[152]

In response to these findings, the Department in November 1999 sent out a "Dear Colleague" letter detailing a more aggressive approach to the existing regulation.[153] It then made the disability discharge a focus of the 2000 round of negotiated rulemaking. Some of the new regulations that

resulted from rulemaking went into effect on July 1, 2001, although the most significant changes became effective on July 1, 2002.

Most importantly, the Department established a conditional discharge system. Under this program, borrowers who apply for a discharge must first get preliminary approval from their loan holder. If approved, borrowers are placed in a three-year "waiting period." The period begins from the date that the borrower became totally and permanently disabled. There are numerous complications related to the conditional system, described in detail below.

6.6.2 Definition of Total and Permanent Disability

A borrower's FFEL, Direct Loan, and Perkins loan may be discharged if the borrower is found to be totally and permanently disabled.[154] Borrowers must provide certification from a physician that they are unable to work and earn money because of an illness or injury that is expected to continue indefinitely or result in death.[155]

This is a very restrictive standard, generally higher than the standards in most other disability programs, such as Social Security. At least one court has recognized the difficulty of meeting this definition.[156] The court affirmed that the physician's statements in this case were sufficient to show that the borrower was totally and permanently disabled even though, in the court's word, the doctor could not say flatly and unequivocally as a matter of medical certainty, "I can't salvage him."

Due to advances in modern medicine, it is rare for a physician to be able to state with absolute certainty that a debilitating condition will continue indefinitely or result in death. Practically, this means that many doctors will be reluctant to sign the discharge form even if they have given a dire diagnosis. However, regulations that allow borrowers to regain eligibility for federal student aid implicitly acknowledge that a physician's honest evaluation at a particular point in time may change.[157] In fact, the Department has explicitly stated that advances in medical treatment may

---

150 *See* § 9.8, *infra*.

151 20 U.S.C. § 1087(a); 34 C.F.R. §§ 674.61 (Perkins), 682.402(c) (FFEL), 685.213 (Direct Loan).

152 U.S. Dep't of Education, Office of the Inspector Gen., Improving the Process for Forgiving Student Loans, (June 7, 1999) (ACN A06-80001). The report is cited in Dear Colleague Letter No. GEN-99-36, Clearinghouse No. 52, 492 (Nov. 1999), *reprinted at* Appx. C, *infra*.

153 Dear Colleague Letter No. GEN-99-36, Clearinghouse No. 52, 492 (Nov. 1999), *reprinted at* Appx. C, *infra*.

154 20 U.S.C. § 1087(a); 34 C.F.R. §§ 674.61 (Perkins), 682.402(c) (FFEL), 685.213 (Direct Loans). The definition of total and permanent disability can be found at 34 C.F.R. §§ 674.51(s) (Perkins), 682.200 (FFEL), 685.102 (Direct Loans).

155 The requirement that borrowers also not be able to attend school was removed in 2001. *See* 65 Fed. Reg. 65,680–65,695 (Nov. 1, 2000) (amending 34 C.F.R. §§ 674.51(s) (Perkins), 682.200 (FFEL), 685.102 (Direct Loans)). Initially, there was some indication that the Department continued to use the old definition and required borrowers to show they could not attend school. *See, e.g.,* U.S. v. Norton, 2002 WL 1774238 (N.D. Iowa Feb. 5, 2002).

156 United States v. Norton, 2002 WL 1774238 (N.D. Iowa Feb. 5, 2002).

157 *See* § 6.6.4, *infra*.

result in an improvement in the borrower's condition that could not be predicted at the time of the physician's certification.[158]

To address these concerns, advocates have pushed the Department to tie its definition of disability to the standard used in other government programs. The Department considered but ultimately dropped this proposal in the 2002 final rules, finding that there was no documentation currently issued by Social Security Administration that would effectively establish disability under the Department's standards.[159] Various Congressional bills introduced since then include language tying disability discharge determinations to Social Security and U.S. Department of Veterans Affairs standards.[160]

6.6.3 Eligible Loans

Borrowers with FFEL or Direct Stafford loans and Perkins loans are eligible for the disability discharge. Parents with PLUS loans may apply for discharges based on their own disabilities, not those of their children. For a PLUS loan, the disability of only one of two obligated parents does not discharge the debt.[161] For consolidated loans, borrowers are considered disabled if they would meet the definition for all of the loans included in the consolidation loan.[162]

Partial discharges are explicitly allowed for borrowers with joint consolidation loans and if one borrower becomes disabled, but the other borrower does not qualify for a discharge.[163] The amount discharged is equal to the portion of the outstanding balance of the consolidation loan attributable to the eligible borrower's loans. However, partial discharge of a joint consolidation loan under any of the discharge programs other than the death discharge does not eliminate joint and several liability for the remaining balance of the loan.[164]

For example: Borrower A and Borrower B have a joint consolidation loan. The joint loan is made up of Borrower A's loans totaling $10,000 and Borrower B's loans totaling $10,000. Borrower A receives a disability discharge with an effective date of June 1, 2000. Borrower A's loan from before that date ($10,000) should be discharged. There is still an outstanding balance of $10,000, which includes all of Borrower B's outstanding loans. Both Borrower A and Borrower B are jointly and severally liable for the $10,000 balance.

This issue will be less relevant because of 2005 legislation that eliminated joint consolidation loans effective July 1, 2006.[165]

To complicate the issue, the Department has stated that the right to obtain a partial discharge of a consolidation loan, other than a joint consolidation loan, applies only to borrowers who qualify for false-certification, closed-school, or unpaid-refund discharges, not for disability.[166] The Department's argument is that the only way that some, but not all, of a borrower's consolidated loans could be eligible for a discharge would be if the ineligible loans were made after the date the borrower became totally and permanently disabled, and this would mean that the borrower was not eligible for a discharge.[167] Yet the Department has also stated that a borrower can in some circumstances get new loans after receiving a final disability discharge.[168]

There are also separate regulations allowing disability discharges for Health Education Assistance Loan Program (HEAL) loan borrowers. The Secretary of Health and Human Services (HHS) has the authority to discharge HEAL loans based on a finding of total and permanent disability.[169] Borrowers must provide HHS with medical evidence no more than four months old to substantiate disability claims.[170] The definition of total and permanent disability for HEAL loans is similar, but not precisely the same, as the definition for most other federal loans. HEAL loans may be discharged if the borrower is "unable to engage in any substantial gainful activity because of a medically determinable impairment, which the Secretary expects to continue for a long and indefinite period of time or to result in death."[171]

There is some question as to whether loans paid in full are eligible to be discharged. The Department apparently has a policy that a loan that has already been paid in full may not be discharged based on the borrower's total and permanent disability.[172] The reasons cited for this policy are first that the regulations do not specifically provide for discharge of paid-in-full loans. Second, according to the Department, a paid-in-full loan no longer exists and borrowers cannot claim benefits related to a "non-existent" debt. In addition, the Department argues that a borrower who is able to repay

---

158   *See* 65 Fed. Reg. 65687, 65681 (Nov. 1, 2000).

159   65 Fed. Reg. 65,678, 65,684 (Nov. 1, 2000).

160   *See* The College Access and Opportunity Act of 2004, H.R. 4283, 108th Cong. § 428(j) (May 5, 2004); The College Access and Opportunity Act of 2005, H.R. 609, 109th Cong. § 428(j) (Feb. 8, 2005); The Borrower Bill of Rights, S. 3255, 109th Cong. (introduced, May 26, 2006).

161   34 C.F.R. § 682.402(a)(3).

162   34 C.F.R. § 682.402(c)(1)(iv).

163   34 C.F.R. §§ 682.402(a)(2), 685.220(l)(3)(ii).

164   67 Fed. Reg. 67048, 67068 (Nov. 1, 2002).

165   Pub. L. No. 109-171, 120 Stat. 4 (Feb. 8, 2006).

166   Expanding the partial discharge for disability was considered and rejected during spring 2002 negotiated rulemaking sessions. *See* 67 Fed. Reg. 51036, 51041 (Aug. 6, 2002). In fact, it is possible for a borrower to obtain a final disability discharge and later take out new loans. *See* § 6.6.7, *infra*.

167   *See* 67 Fed. Reg. 51036, 51041 (Aug. 6, 2002).

168   *See* §§ 6.6.6, 6.6.7.

169   42 C.F.R. § 60.39(b)(1). *See, e.g.*, Student Loan Mktg. Ass'n v. Herdman, 2005 WL 648143 (Cal. App. Mar. 22, 2005) (not officially published).

170   42 C.F.R. § 60.39(b)(2).

171   42 C.F.R. § 60.39(b)(1).

172   This policy is described in copies of e-mail messages obtained in an FOIA request by NCLC.

the loan after the date he or she is determined to be totally and permanently discharged is presumably not truly disabled.

There are a number of holes in the Department's logic and this may be an issue that could be successfully challenged. The last rationale is particularly problematic. There are many ways that a borrower can pay off a loan other than through the borrower's own work earnings. For example, a borrower may not have voluntarily paid off his or her loan. Instead, the loan could have been repaid through offsets and other involuntary collection methods.[173] It is also possible that someone else, such as the borrower's parents, may have paid off the loan. The Department appears to take the position that the borrower is solely responsible for learning that the disability discharge is available and is out of luck if the borrower learns of the discharge after the loan is paid off. In contrast, most of the other discharges explicitly allow discharge of both past and current loan obligations.[174]

6.6.4 Onset Date of Disability and Timing Issues

6.6.4.1 General

There are a number of key timing issues, including

1. how a borrowers can get discharges if they experience substantial deterioration of a condition that existed when they took out the loan;
2. figuring out the extent to which work earnings prior to the disability determination or during the conditional discharge period disqualify a borrower; and
3. understanding how the Department handles cases in which the borrower applies for a discharge after the conditional period (based on the disability onset date) has expired.[175]

6.6.4.2 Substantial Deterioration

A borrower is not considered disabled based on a condition that existed at the time the borrower applied for the loan unless the condition substantially deteriorated after the loan was made.[176] The key distinction here is between the terms "condition" and "disability." The Department interprets this provision to allow borrowers with medical "conditions" to later apply for discharges if those conditions, due to deterioration, later rise to the level of permanent and total

disabilities. However, according to the Department, if the borrower is already permanently and totally disabled when the borrower incurred the loan, later deterioration is irrelevant and those loans could not be discharged. According to the Department:

> "If the date of the loan in question was made between the date the borrower's condition began and the date the borrower became unable to work and earn money in any capacity, no additional information explaining that the condition deteriorated is needed. The loan is eligible for cancellation if otherwise eligible. . . . If the date of the loan in question was made after the date the borrower became unable to work and earn money in any capacity, the loan is not eligible for a disability cancellation. A statement from the physician indicating that the borrower's condition has substantially deteriorated has no impact. The loan cannot be cancelled for disability.[177]

Advocates should be very careful to discuss the difference between "condition" and "disability" with the physician. It is possible to submit a second application if the first is denied on this basis, but this will likely raise suspicions that the borrower is trying to "game" the system. On the other hand, physicians do make errors, and it is often difficult to pinpoint the precise moment when a condition became permanently disabling.

6.6.4.3 When Work Is Allowed

The question of whether a "disabled" borrower can work and, if so, when, is particularly confusing. There are numerous contradictions in Department regulations and policy in this area.

With respect to the definition of disability, the Department takes the position that the borrower cannot be working at the time a physician pronounces the borrower to be totally and permanently disabled. This is because the definition, discussed above, requires that the borrower must be unable to work and earn money because of an illness or injury that is expected to continue indefinitely or result in death. According to the Department, a physician may not certify that a borrower has a total and permanent disability if, at the time of the physician's certification, the borrower is currently able or is expected to be able to work and earn money.

However, the regulations are contradictory in at least two fundamental ways. First, as discussed in § 6.6.6, *infra*, the borrower is allowed to have minimal earnings during the conditional discharge period. Second, the borrower may get new loans, go back to school, and presumably earn money

---

173 In an e-mail from the Department obtained in an FOIA request, a Department employee states that there may be rare exceptions to the policy against discharges for paid-in-full loans when a final offset that pays a loan in full could not be stopped in time before a disability application was processed.

174 *See, e.g.,* 34 C.F.R. § 682.402(d)(2)(i) (closed school).

175 *See* § 6.6.6, *infra.*

176 34 C.F.R. § 682.402(c)(1)(iii).

177 U.S. Dep't of Educ., Notes to Contract Administrators, *Disabilities and "Pre-Existing Conditions"* (May 13, 2005), *available at* www.fsacollections.ed.gov/contractors/pca2004/cotr/051305.htm.

after the conditional discharge period is over and after he or she has received a final discharge. There are certain requirements that the borrower must meet to get a new loan in these circumstances.[178]

The Department has acknowledged that advances in medical treatment may result in an improvement in the borrower's condition that could not be predicted at the time of the physician's certification.[179] In addition, changes in employment conditions may allow a borrower to return to work despite his or her condition. The Department has stated that it does not wish to discourage disabled individuals from attempting employment. Accordingly, the regulations do not disqualify borrowers who have minimal earnings during the conditional discharge period. However, at least at the time the physician makes the determination, the borrower should not be working, even just minimally.

6.6.5 *Application and Evaluation Process*

The Department initially set out a more restrictive approach to evaluating disability discharges in a November 1999 "Dear Colleague" letter.[180] A subsequent May 2002 "Dear Colleague" letter reiterated these standards and clarified the disability process under the new disability discharge regulations.[181]

An area that is ripe for legal challenge is the way in which the Department has developed the new disability discharge program. Although the switch to a conditional process came out of negotiated rulemaking sessions, there has been no corresponding revision in the HEA statute. In addition, the Department has issued much of its guidance on this issue through informal "Dear Colleague" letters instead of regulatory or statutory amendments.[182]

The disability procedures under the conditional program are as follows:

The borrower applies to the loan holder for a discharge. If a borrower has different loan holders, the borrower should submit a separate application to each. There is a standardized form, reprinted at Appendix D, *infra*, and on the companion CD-Rom to this manual, that should be used.

Unfortunately, borrowers will often find that a discharge is denied even after they have submitted a properly completed physician's certification of total and permanent disability. Such denials may be appealed under the judicial review provision of the Administrative Procedures Act.[183]

The loan holder makes a preliminary determination as to whether the borrower meets the criteria for a disability discharge. For Perkins loans, the school makes this determination. In the FFEL program, the current holder makes the determination. For Direct loans, the Department's direct loan staff makes the decision.[184]

The Department intends for this preliminary determination to be a rigorous process. The Department's expectations were initially set out in the November 1999 "Dear Colleague" letter and affirmed in the May 2002 letter.

The Department requires guaranty agencies and others making preliminary disability determinations at a minimum to do the following:

- Require additional information to support the borrower's application when the information provided is not definitive, is illegible, or incomplete.
- Reaffirm the physician's certification if the diagnosis and prognosis do not appear to reach the standard of total and permanent disability. (The Department emphasized that guaranty agencies should ensure that physicians understand that the FFEL definition of total and permanent disability is generally a higher standard than that used by other federal or state agencies for disability.)
- Assist borrowers to obtain deferments or forbearances in cases when it does not appear that the borrower is totally and permanently disabled.[185]

The Department also suggests that agencies may want to seek the assistance of a qualified physician to evaluate discharge requests.[186]

Lenders are required to provide guaranty agencies with disability claims within sixty days of the date on which they determine that a borrower is totally and permanently disabled.[187]

For FFEL loans, the loan is assigned to the Disability Discharge Unit if both the loan holder and the guaranty agency, if different, decide that the borrower is eligible for discharge.[188] The loan holder is required to notify the borrower that the loan will be sent to the Department for further review. The Department suggests that the notice also explain

---

178 *See* § 6.6.7, *infra*.

179 *See* 65 Fed. Reg. 65687, 65681 (Nov. 1, 2000).

180 U.S. Dep't of Educ., Dear Colleague Letter No. GEN-99-36, Clearinghouse No. 52, 492 (Nov. 1999), *reprinted at* Appx. C, *infra*.

181 U.S. Dep't of Educ., Dear Colleague Letter No. GEN-02-03 (May 2002), *reprinted at* Appx. C, *infra*.

182 Sample complaints challenging the Department's process of adopting the new disability discharge program are included at Appendix E, *infra*, and on the companion CD-Rom to this manual.

183 *See* § 6.10, *infra*.

184 *Id.*

185 U.S. Dep't of Educ., Dear Colleague Letter No. GEN-99-36, Clearinghouse No. 52,492 (Nov. 1999), *reprinted at* Appx. C, *infra*; U.S. Dep't of Educ., Dear Colleague Letter No. GEN-02-03 (May 2002), *reprinted at* Appx. C, *infra*.

186 U.S. Dep't of Educ., Dear Colleague Letter GEN-02-03 (May 2002), *reprinted at* Appx. C, *infra*.

187 34 C.F.R. § 682.402(g)(2).

188 U.S. Dep't of Educ., Dear Colleague Letter No. GEN-02-03 (May 2002), *reprinted at* Appx. C, *infra*. *See also* 34 C.F.R. § 682.402(c)(11).

the Department's procedures for reviewing discharges when preliminary approval has been granted and explain that the Department will be requesting information on the borrower's income from earnings during the conditional period.[189] If the application is denied, the loan holder is required to notify the borrower of the denial, including reasons for the decision.[190] In cases in which preliminary approval is granted, Perkins loans holders (schools) are required to assign the loans to the Department's Disability Discharge Unit and notify borrowers of the assignment.[191]

The Department will then review all preliminarily approved loans to affirm that the borrower meets the disability discharge criteria. If the Department agrees with the preliminary determination, the borrower is placed in a conditional-discharge status for three years *beginning on the date the borrower became totally and permanently disabled.*[192]

If a lender or its agent is the loan holder, the borrower should submit the application and supporting documentation to that entity. The lender may continue collection until it receives the certification of disability.[193] After receiving the certification, the lender must cease collection efforts.[194] The Department interprets the regulations to apply only to lenders. According to the Department, a guaranty agency or the Department may continue at least certain collection efforts even after receipt of a disability discharge application. However, the Department claims that, if it is the loan holder, action on a completed application should occur within a few days.

Thus, it is critical that borrowers submit completed applications. Common problems include failure to fill in the onset of disability date, failure to sign the application, illegible applications, and failure to provide sufficient supporting documentation. It is critical for the borrower to provide information from the physician that explains the borrower's condition and why this condition is disabling.

In some cases, the borrower may be dealing with a collection agency throughout this process. A sample of a letter from an agency requesting additional information for a discharge is reprinted at Appendix D, *infra.*

Guaranty agencies, according to the Department, should also make timely decisions on completed applications.[195] If the guaranty agency makes a preliminary determination of eligibility, the agency should stop all collection efforts at that point. Even though it may take three or four months for the agency to assign the account to the Department, the borrower should not be facing collection efforts during this time. The Department has stated that the delay in processing occurs because the guarantor must request reinsurance (which occurs once a month); wait for reinsurance payment (which takes approximately a month); update the student loan database to reflect that reinsurance was paid (which occurs once a month); wait ten days to confirm reporting to the student loan database; and assign the loan.

The Department describes the review process post-assignment as a three-step process. Before getting to this point, both the lender and guaranty agency (or solely the guaranty agency if the lender had assigned the loan to the agency before the borrower applied for discharge) must have made a preliminary determination of disability. The loan is then assigned to the Department. At this point, the Department will review the previous determinations. This review will generally include further contact with the borrower's physician.

A 2005 report by the Department's Inspector General contains different estimates of the percentage of physicians contacted after disability applications are received. A nurse in the Conditional Disability Discharge Unit reported that physicians are contacted for approximately half of the disability discharge applications the Unit receives. The Department responded that its contractor follows up with physicians for approximately 70% of cancellation applications received.[196]

The Department's process can be time-consuming. However, during this review period, all collection activity should cease and interest should not be accruing on the borrower's loans.[197]

If there is a delay after submission of a completed application, the borrower may request an administrative forbearance to stop collection during the review period. Loan holders may grant discretionary forbearances to disabled borrowers. The regulations are slightly different for FFEL and Direct loans. For Direct loans, forbearances may be granted for a period after the Secretary receives reliable information indicating that the borrower has become totally and permanently disabled until the Secretary receives docu-

---

189 U.S. Dep't of Educ., Dear Colleague Letter No. GEN-02-03 (May 2002), *reprinted at* Appx. C, *infra.*

190 U.S. Dep't of Educ., Dear Colleague Letter No. GEN-02-03 (May 2002), *reprinted at* Appx. C, *infra. See also* 34 C.F.R. § 682.402(c)(7).

191 34 C.F.R. § 674.61(b)(3).

192 34 C.F.R. §§ 674.61(b) (Perkins), 682.402(c)(1) (FFEL), 685.213(a) (Direct Loans).

193 34 C.F.R. § 682.402(c)(3).

194 *Id.*

195 The regulations require guaranty agencies to review discharge claims promptly and pay the lender on approved claims not later than forty-five days after the claim was filed by the lender for death and bankruptcy claims and not later than ninety days after the claim was filed by the lender for disability, closed-school, or

false-certification claims. 34 C.F.R. § 682.402(h)(1).

196 U.S. Dep't of Educ., Office of Inspector Gen., Final Audit Report: Death and Total and Permanent Disability Discharges of FFEL and Direct Loan Program Loans, Control Number ED-OIG/A04E006 at 15 (Nov. 14, 2005).

197 Department staff confirmed in a July 2003 conversation with NCLC that it would not continue to collect while still reviewing loans. They did not cite regulatory authority, but the Department should be bound by 34 C.F.R. § 682.402(c)(1)(iv)(C)(3), which requires that lenders cease collection activity after receiving the disability certification.

mentation of total and permanent disability.[198] There may be conflicting interpretations of this provision within the Department. Although the Department acknowledges that it will sometimes cease collection upon receipt of a disability discharge request, staff may be reluctant to call this cessation a "forbearance." However, the regulation cited above clearly gives the Department discretion to grant a forbearance in these circumstances. A similar provision applies to FFEL loans.[199]

The Department recommends that borrowers contact the loan holders to which they submitted the application if they have questions. If the loan holder makes a favorable preliminary determination, it will notify the borrower that his or her loan will be assigned to the Department and will provide the borrower with a detailed explanation of the conditional discharge process. The Department has set up a Disability Discharge Loan Servicing Center. The Center can be contacted by phone at 1-888-869-4169, by e-mail at disability_discharge@acs-inc.com, or by regular mail at U.S. Department of Education Conditional Total and Permanent Disability Assignments, P.O. Box 7200, Utica, NY 13504. Hearing-impaired individuals with access to a TDD can call 1-888-636-6401.

The Department provided NCLC with the following explanation of the procedures for disability discharges for borrowers who are already facing collection. According to the Department,

> [i]f certain collection activities are in place when a borrower applies for a total and permanent disability discharge, it would be administratively burdensome and costly to require the loan holder to cease those collection activities only to restart them if the borrower does not qualify for the discharge. Therefore, in cases in which a judgment against the borrower has already been obtained, the loan holder is not required to suspend enforcement of the judgment or vacate the judgment during the review period. If the loan holder approves the discharge claim, the judgment should be transferred to the Department when the loan is assigned. Similarly, if an AWG [administrative wage garnishment] wage withholding order was already in place when the borrower submitted the application for disability discharge, the loan holder is not required to withdraw the wage withholding order during the review period. If Federal or State Offset has already been initiated by the Federal or State government, the loan holder is not required to halt the Offset during the

review process. After a loan holder makes a preliminary determination that the borrower meets the criteria for a total and permanent disability discharge, the loan holder must withdraw the wage withholding order, halt State Offset, or send a record on its next Weekly Update tape to inactivate the account from the Treasury Offset Program. If a loan holder makes a preliminary determination that the borrower does not meet the criteria for a total and permanent disability discharge, the loan holder should resume routine collection activity. Borrowers that receive a favorable preliminary determination are assigned to the Department for further review. If the Department finds such a borrower ineligible at any point in the conditional discharge process, the Department will reinstate that borrower to servicing and collection activity will resume.

If the borrower satisfies the criteria for a total and permanent disability discharge during and at the end of the conditional discharge period, the balance of the loan is discharged and any payments received after the date the borrower became totally and permanently disabled should be returned.[200]

6.6.6 *The Conditional Discharge Period*

The conditional period begins on the date the borrower is certified as permanently and totally disabled. This means that, for many borrowers, the conditional period will have expired by the time they apply for a discharge. In these cases, an initial determination of eligibility will also be the final determination of eligibility. The borrower will not have to wait three years to get a discharge.[201]

For example, Borrower A applies for a disability discharge in 2006. Her doctor certifies that the onset date of her disability was 2000. Since this is more than three years before the application date, if the Department agrees with the doctor's evaluation, Borrower A can immediately get a loan discharge. If the onset date was 2005 and she applied in 2006, she would have to wait two additional years (the conditional period) for a final discharge.

It is important to understand the factors that the Department will consider during the conditional period to assess continued eligibility. The two main factors are whether the borrower has earnings beyond a minimally acceptable amount and whether the borrower has incurred new federal student loans. There is no requirement that the borrower obtain a medical review of his or her condition.

With respect to earnings, borrowers will satisfy the criteria for a discharge after the three years if their annual earnings from employment during that time do not exceed 100% of the poverty line for a family of two and they did not

---

198 34 C.F.R. § 685.205(b)(5).

199 34 C.F.R. § 682.211(f)(5). The Department may argue that these regulations apply only after the discharge application is submitted to the conditional disability discharge unit. Borrowers should challenge this restrictive reading of the regulation. However, borrowers may get the same result by requesting an agreement to cease collection rather than a forbearance.

200 34 C.F.R. § 682.402(c)(1)(i). *See* § 6.6.7, *infra.*

201 U.S. Dep't of Educ., Dear Colleague Letter No. GEN-02-03 (May 2002), *reprinted at* Appx. C, *infra.*

receive a student loan during that time, except for an FFEL or Direct Consolidation loan that does not include any loans that have a conditional-discharge status.[202]

As discussed above, the earnings limit during the conditional period recognizes that advances in medical treatment may result in an improvement in the borrower's condition that could not be predicted at the time of the physician's certification.[203] In addition, changes in employment conditions may allow a borrower to return to work despite his or her condition. The Department has stated that it does not wish to discourage disabled individuals from attempting employment. Accordingly, the regulations do not disqualify borrowers who have minimal earnings during the conditional discharge period.

The earnings limit is relatively straightforward if the borrower applies for a discharge before the conditional period has expired. It is more complicated when the period is already expired. The question in these cases is whether the Department will examine earnings only during the conditional period (when minimal earnings are allowed) or whether they will also look at earnings records from before or after this period. This is significant because, according to a 2005 Inspector General report, about 54% of the applications for borrowers who received discharges in their study were received more than three years after the disability date.[204]

According to the Inspector General report and informal information from the Department, the Department will examine earnings records during the conditional period only. However, the Department has cautioned that. if they receive documentation which indicates that the borrower is currently working and earning money, even if the conditional period has expired, that information might call into question the validity of the physician's determination. This policy is questionable since the physician's determination was made on information available to the physician at that time and the Department has acknowledged that an individual's medical condition could improve over time.

In one e-mail message, the Department acknowledged that allowing the three-year period to be entirely retroactive has "created a lot of issues we didn't anticipate."[205] However, they state that it was presumably not their intent to grant discharges to individuals who would have met the definition if they had applied for the discharge several years ago, but who no longer meet that definition by the time they actually submit a discharge application.

The Inspector General in a 2005 report criticizes the Department for reviewing earnings during the conditional period only. They have called for revised regulations to ensure that current income and loan information is considered when determining disability. Specifically, they have suggested that the three-year period begin on the date the borrower submits the applications rather than from the disability onset date.[206]

Advocates should look for cases in which the Department or a guaranty agency appears to automatically deny a discharge for a borrower who has worked after the physician's determination of total and permanent disability. The underlying rationale of allowing minimal earnings during the conditional period should also apply if the borrower made attempts to work after that period or before the physician's determination.

The second requirement is that borrowers may not incur new federal student loans during the conditional period. The regulations only prohibit borrowers from receiving new loans under the Perkins, FFEL, or Direct Loan programs.[207] These borrowers should be able to go to school without jeopardizing eligibility for a discharge and they can even take out non-federal loans or grants.

The only exception to the federal loan prohibition is that the borrower is permitted to receive an FFEL or Direct Consolidation loan during the conditional period as long as it does not include any loans that have a conditional-discharge status.[208] This means that the borrower could have received loans prior to the disability that the borrower later chose to consolidate.

Another complicating factor is whether a borrower is disqualified if the borrower did not incur a new loan prior to the conditional period but rather signed up for a loan prior to the period that was disbursed during the conditional period. The Department's policy is that a subsequent disbursement is to be considered the same as a new loan for disability discharge purposes. Thus, a borrower who accepts a disbursement that was made after the disability date is not eligible for a discharge. According to information from the Department, as of 2005, there was nothing in writing to support this policy. In fact, the Department acknowledges that, in other situations, they do not consider a subsequent disbursement to be a new loan.

During the conditional period, borrowers are not required to make any payments on the loan. The loan is not considered past due or in default. Borrowers are required to notify the Department if their annual earnings exceed the poverty line limit.[209] If at any time during the three-year period, the

---

202   34 C.F.R. § 682.402(c)(1)(ii)(A), (B).

203   *See* 65 Fed. Reg. 65687, 65681 (Nov. 1, 2000).

204   U.S. Dept' of Educ., Office of Inspector Gen., Final Audit Report: Death and Total and Permanent Disability Discharges of FFEL and Direct Loan Program Loans, Control Number ED-OIG/A04E006 (Nov. 14, 2005).

205   This policy is described in copies of e-mail messages obtained in an FOIA request by NCLC.

206   U.S. Dep't of Educ., Office of Inspector Gen., Final Audit Report: Death and Total and Permanent Disability Discharges of FFEL and Direct Loan Program Loans, Control Number ED-OIG/A04E006 (Nov. 14, 2005).

207   34 C.F.R. § 682.402(c)(1)(ii)(B).

208   34 C.F.R. § 682.402(c)(1)(ii)(B).

209   34 C.F.R. § 682.402(c)(14).

Department finds that the borrower does not meet the eligibility requirements, the Department will resume collection. The borrower is not required to pay any interest that accrued on the loan from the date of the initial determination through the end of the conditional discharge.[210] Presumably if the Department finds evidence that the borrower is no longer disabled midway through the conditional period, interest will begin to accrue at the point that the conditional discharge is officially terminated.

6.6.7 *Effect of Final Discharge*

If the borrower satisfies the criteria for a disability discharge during and at the end of the conditional discharge period, the balance of the loan will be discharged.[211] Any payments received after the date the borrower became disabled are to be returned.[212] The borrower is responsible for providing information requested by the Department to prove that the borrower did not have excess earnings or otherwise failed to meet the requirements for final discharge. The Department has stated that borrowers often fail to respond to these requests. Although the Department will wait up to 100 days or longer for a response, it will ultimately resume collection if the borrower does not respond.

There are no specific provisions in the regulation allowing the Department to revoke a disability discharge if it discovers potentially disqualifying evidence after the conditional period has expired. Yet there are reports that the Department has attempted to revoke discharges particularly if a borrower who received a final discharge later attempts to take out a new student loan.

Borrowers who have received final discharges but wish to take out a new loan must obtain certification from a physician that they are able to engage in substantial gainful activity and sign a statement acknowledging that the loan they receive cannot be discharged in the future on the basis of any impairment present when the new loan is made, unless that impairment substantially deteriorates.[213] A third requirement applies only to borrowers who received final discharges on or after July 1, 2001, and before July 1, 2002. These borrowers must meet the two other conditions discussed above. In addition, if they apply for another loan within three years from the disability onset date, they must reaffirm the previously discharged loan before receiving the

new loan.[214] This provision mirrors the requirements in the conditional discharge program that became effective in July 2002.

Borrowers who have received only a conditional discharge must obtain certification from a physician that they are able to engage in substantial gainful activity and sign a statement acknowledging that the loan they receive cannot be discharged in the future on the basis of any impairment present when they applied for a total and permanent disability discharge or when the new loan is made unless the impairment substantially deteriorates. In addition, these borrowers must sign a statement acknowledging that the loan that has been conditionally discharged cannot be discharged in the future on the basis of any impairment present when the borrower applied for a total and permanent disability discharge or when the new loan is made unless the impairment substantially deteriorates and acknowledges that collection activity will resume on any loans in a conditional discharge period.[215] This is confusing because the regulations refer to loans that have been placed in a conditional discharge period prior to a final determination of total and permanent disability. In fact, the borrower is required to obtain a determination of total and permanent disability before the borrower can get a conditional discharge. Perhaps the Department is referring to borrowers who have obtained conditional discharges but have not yet served their time to get a final discharge.

6.7 Discharge Based on Death

The borrower's death is a defense to collection actions on Stafford, SLS, Perkins, and Federal Direct loans.[216] The death of both parents (assuming both parents are obligated) or the death of the student discharges PLUS loans.[217] The death of only one of the two obligated parents does not discharge a PLUS loan.[218] This is only the case if the parents were co-borrowers.

Partial discharges are explicitly allowed for borrowers with joint consolidation loans if one borrower dies but the other is still alive.[219] The amount discharged is equal to the portion of the outstanding balance of the consolidation loan attributable to the eligible borrower's loans.

Even the death discharge has become controversial. In the same IG report that found alleged disability discharge abuse, the Department of Education concluded that some borrowers were continuing to live and work after receiving death

---

210 34 C.F.R. § 682.402(c)(16). The OIG criticized subsidizing of interest during the conditional period. U.S. Dep't of Educ., Office of Inspector Gen., Final Audit Report: Death and Total and Permanent Disability Discharges of FFEL and Direct Loan Program Loans, Control Number ED-OIG/A04E006 (Nov. 14, 2005).

211 34 C.F.R. § 682.402(c)(15).

212 34 C.F.R. § 682.402(c)(1)(i), (r)(2), (3).

213 34 C.F.R. § 682.201(a)(6)(i), (ii).

214 34 C.F.R. § 682.201(a)(6)(iii).

215 34 C.F.R. § 682.201(a)(7).

216 20 U.S.C. § 1087; 34 C.F.R. §§ 674.61(a), 682.402(b), 685.212(a).

217 34 C.F.R. § 682.402(b)(1).

218 20 U.S.C. § 1087(a); 34 C.F.R. § 682.402(a)(3).

219 34 C.F.R. §§ 682.402(a)(2), 685.220(l)(3)(ii).

discharges.[220] The Department has expressed concern that documentation used to support death discharges may be easily forged or may not provide definitive proof of death. To address this issue, the Department requires an original or certified copy of a death certificate in most circumstances.[221]

6.8 Other Loan Cancellations

Perkins loans may be completely canceled in certain circumstances, including the debtor's service in Head Start or in the military service in an area "of hostilities."[222]

The Perkins program was also the first to provide for cancellations of loans for teachers in low-income school districts and for other service, including military and volunteer service.[223]

Despite the language in the statute and regulations, there is still some ambiguity regarding eligibility for some of the Perkins loan cancellations. For example, a class of public interest attorneys sued the Department after the Department terminated them from the Perkins "Children's and Family Service" cancellation program.[224] The district court held that the Perkins Loan public service employment cancellation did not apply to public service attorneys working for New York City's Administration for Children's Services.[225] The Second Circuit reversed.[226] The Second Circuit refused to defer to the Department's informal interpretations of qualifications for the Perkins "Full-time Employment in a Public or Private Nonprofit Child or Family Service Agency" cancellation. In reaching this decision, the court found that, based on the criteria listed in the statute, the plaintiffs qualified for cancellation of their Perkins loans.

The Second Circuit noted that the Department's regulations setting out the qualifications for this cancellation simply repeat the statutory language verbatim.[227] Furthermore, the Department's restrictive interpretation of the eligibility criteria was derived not from the regulations but from the Federal Student Aid Office's *Financial Aid Handbook* and informal e-mail messages from Department of Education staff. The Second Circuit found that the *Chevron* deference to the Department in this case was clearly inapplicable.[228]

Perkins cancellations are available even for borrowers in default under certain circumstances.[229] In general, to qualify for a Perkins discharge, borrowers must perform uninterrupted service as a teacher or perform other qualifying service for a specific length of time. The Department has waived this requirement of uninterrupted and/or consecutive service for borrowers who are members of the military reserves called or ordered to active duty for a period of more than thirty days or who are regular active duty members of the Armed Forces reassigned to a different duty station for more than thirty days as a result of a military mobilization.[230]

"Affected individuals" includes borrowers serving on active duty during a war or other military operation or national emergency; performing qualifying National Guard duty during a war or other military operation or national emergency; residing or employed in an area that is declared a disaster area by any federal, state, or local official in connection with a national emergency; or suffering direct economic hardship as a direct result of a war or other military operation or national emergency, as determined by the Secretary.[231] The reason for the interruption in service must be related to the borrower's status as an "affected individual."[232]

The FFEL and Direct Loan programs also have loan-forgiveness programs for teachers.[233] The teacher forgiveness or cancellation under FFEL and Direct loans will repay up to a maximum of $5000 for individuals who are full-time teachers over five consecutive years in certain schools that serve low-income families.[234] The limit is $17,500 for borrowers who teach five consecutive years as highly qualified math or science teachers in eligible secondary schools or as special education teachers in eligible elementary or secondary schools.[235]

The FFEL and Direct Loan programs apply only to borrowers with no outstanding loan balances as of October

---

220 See U.S. Dep't of Educ., Dear Colleague Letter GEN-99-36 (Nov. 1999), which is reprinted at Appx. C, *infra*, citing an Office of Inspector General study that found that 2% of borrowers who received death discharges were working and earning money after the loan was discharged. In a 2005 report, the Inspector General concluded that the new controls over the death-discharge process were adequate. U.S. Dep't of Educ., Office of Inspector Gen., Final Audit Report: Death and Total and Permanent Disability Discharges of FFEL and Direct Loan Program Loans, Control Number ED-OIG/A04E0006 (Nov. 14, 2005).

221 34 C.F.R. §§ 682.402(b)(2) (FFEL), 685.212(a)(3) (Direct Loans).

222 34 C.F.R. §§ 674.58 (Head Start cancellation), 674.59 (military cancellations).

223 34 C.F.R. §§ 674.55 (teacher cancellations), 674.56 (employment in certain professions such as nursing or medical technicians), 674.57 (law enforcement), 674.59 (military service), 674.60 (volunteer service including Peace Corps).

224 De La Mota v. United States Dep't of Educ., 412 F.3d 71 (2d Cir. 2005).

225 De La Mota v. United States Dep't of Educ., 2003 WL 22038741 (S.D.N.Y. Aug. 29, 2003).

226 De La Mota v. United States Dep't of Educ., 412 F.3d 71 (2d Cir. 2005).

227 *Id.* (citing 34 C.F.R. § 674.56(b)(1); 20 U.S.C. § 1087ee(a) (2)(I)).

228 De La Mota v. United States Dep't of Educ., 412 F.3d 71 (2d Cir. 2005) (citing Chevron U.S.A., Inc. v. NRDC, 467 U.S. 837 (1984)).

229 34 C.F.R. § 674.52(c).

230 68 Fed. Reg. 25821 (May 14, 2003).

231 68 Fed. Reg. 69312 (Dec. 12, 2003).

232 *Id.*

233 34 C.F.R. §§ 682.215 (FFEL), 685.217 (Direct Loans).

234 *Id.*

235 34 C.F.R. § 682.215(a) (FFEL).

1, 1998, or later. Unlike the Perkins programs, FFEL and Direct loan borrowers are not eligible for teacher-loan forgiveness for defaulted loans unless they first make satisfactory repayment arrangements and reestablish loan eligibility.[236] Proposed rules issued in August 2002 for the Direct Loan program include new language stating that a joint Direct Consolidation loan may be partially discharged if one of the borrowers qualifies for teacher-loan forgiveness.[237]

In addition, the Department administers a loan-forgiveness-demonstration program for certain child care providers with FFEL or Direct loans.[238] This program is contingent upon annual appropriations. Under this program, borrowers who have received an associate's or bachelor's degree in early childhood education or child care and who are providing full-time child care services in child care facilities that serve certain low-income communities are eligible for forgiveness of up to 100% of their total eligible loans. Only loans made after October 7, 1998, qualify. This program is available on a first-come, first-served basis. The Secretary has not yet issued regulations to implement this program. In January 2004, the Department published the application for this cancellation program.[239]

Congress routinely considers various proposals to grant loan forgiveness to borrowers in other professions such as nursing and to employees of nonprofit organizations. Other proposals have been introduced to cancel loans for spouses, surviving joint debtors, and parents of individuals who died or who became permanently disabled due to the September 11 attacks.[240]

Despite the numerous proposals to expand loan-forgiveness programs, there has been very little assessment of the effectiveness of these programs. A 2004 report funded by the Lumina Foundation examined state and federal loan-forgiveness programs.[241] The scope of the report was limited, as the researchers gathered data on only 100 of the approximately 161 programs. About 75% of these programs were loan-forgiveness programs and the others were loan-

repayment programs that repay existing education debt in exchange for specified work. Teaching, nursing, and medicine were the three fields most likely to be covered by such programs.

Only 48 of the 122 loan-forgiveness programs were able to provide any data about how many students had fulfilled their work commitments. Those programs reported that, on average, 63% of participants had completed at least some job service.[242]

This report provides a starting point for measuring the effectiveness of these programs with respect to the numbers of borrowers who drop out of the programs, the extent to which the programs help address labor shortages, and whether the programs attract students who otherwise might not have entered the targeted occupations.

The need for relief for borrowers who work in low-paying professions is clear. These programs are intended to address the concern that, if the cost of education continues to grow at its current pace, lower- and middle-income students will simply be unable to work as teachers, social workers, or doctors or lawyers serving under-privileged communities. This is a very serious issue. However, many of these borrowers are receiving some income and are able to make some payments. The problem is that their monthly payments are often too high and the total amount to be repaid is unaffordable. The State PIRGs found, for example, that 23% of public college and 38% of private college graduates would have unmanageable debt as starting teachers. The percentages are even higher for social workers, with 37% of public college and 55% of private college graduates facing unmanageable debt.[243]

6.9 Income Tax Issues

There should not be tax consequences when a borrower's loan is cancelled. The I.R.S. has stated that it may issue guidance on this issue in the future but, in the meantime, lenders and guaranty agencies are not subject to penalties for failure to report amounts forgiven pursuant to the terms of a debt obligation. This specifically includes forgiveness upon a stated event such as death, disability, or service as a teacher.[244] In addition, the Internal Revenue Code specifically allows tax-free treatment for loans that are cancelled through programs tied to work for certain amounts of time in certain professions, such as teaching.[245] There are, however, potential tax consequences when a borrower's loan is

---

236   34 C.F.R. §§ 682.215 (c)(8), 685.217 (c)(8).

237   67 Fed. Reg. 51036 (Aug. 6, 2002) (amending 34 C.F.R. § 685.220(l)). According to the Department, similar changes were not made to FFEL consolidation regulations because the construction of those regulations already provides for a partial discharge under these circumstances.

238   *See* 67 Fed. Reg. 55385 (Aug. 29, 2002).

239   U.S. Dep't of Educ., Dear Colleague Letter #GEN-04-01 (Jan. 2004). The form is available on the Department of Education's website at www.ed.gov.

240   *See, e.g.,* H.R. 12, H.R. 438, and H.R. 3180. These proposals had not passed at the time this manual was written.

241   Rita J. Kirshstein, Andrea R. Berger, Elana Benatar, & David Rhodes, American Inst. for Research, *Workforce Contingent Financial Aid: How States Link Financial Aid to Employment* (Feb. 2004). The report is available on-line at www.luminafoundation.org/research/Workforce.pdf (July 2004). *See also* Peter Schmidt, *Programs That Pay Tuition in Exchange for Work Are Unproved, Report Says,* The Chron. of Higher Educ., Feb. 27, 2004, at A20.

242   *Id.*

243   The State PIRGS' Higher Education Project, *Paying Back, Not Giving Back: Student Debt's Negative Impact on Public Service Career Opportunities* (April 2006), *available at* http://pirg.org/highered/payingback.pdf.

244   69 Fed. Reg. 62181 (Oct. 25, 2004).

245   *See* Internal Revenue Serv., Publication 970, *Tax Benefits for Education* (2004); 26 U.S.C. 108(f).

written off after paying for twenty-five years using an income-contingent repayment plan.[246]

6.10 Appealing Adverse Discharge Decisions

Before seeking judicial review of a discharge denial, student loan borrowers should be certain that they have presented a complete and fully documented application. If a discharge was denied for want of evidence that is now available or on the basis of erroneous facts, the borrower should resubmit an accurate and complete application rather than seeking judicial review. The Department will generally reconsider a prior discharge denial, particularly if circumstances have changed.

In addition, for false-certification and unpaid-refund discharges only, FFEL borrowers should first seek administrative review from the Department.[247] The closed-school and disability discharge regulations do not provide for this type of "internal" review.

The Administrative Procedure Act (APA) is available only after borrowers have exhausted administrative remedies. Borrowers cannot initiate the discharge process in court.[248] A district court in North Carolina summarized the problem for borrowers.[249] In a case pending before that court, the borrower sought to enjoin the government from collecting on loans that the borrower alleged were paid for instruction he never received. The court noted that the plaintiff's claims appealed to the equities found in the law.[250] The court also noted that Congress had addressed the problem by passing the various administrative discharges.[251] However, these claims must be presented through the administrative process and not as defensive claims in civil litigation.

The Administrative Procedure Act governs judicial review of any informal agency adjudication, including denial of a student loan discharge by the Department of Education. The pertinent section provides that the court shall hold unlawful and set aside agency action, findings, and conclusions found to be "arbitrary, capricious, an abuse of discre-

tion, or otherwise not in accordance with law. . . ."[252] Section 706 "require[s] the reviewing court to engage in a substantial inquiry."[253] In determining whether an agency's action was unlawful under § 706(2)(A), the court must "consider whether the decision was based on a consideration of the relevant factors and whether there has been a clear error in judgment."[254] If the court determines that the agency relied on factors Congress did not intend for it to consider, or has failed to consider an important aspect of the problem, the action should be set aside as arbitrary and capricious.[255]

An agency is bound by its own regulations.[256] If an agency's action does not comport with its regulations, the action is contrary to law and should be reversed by a reviewing court.[257]

In many cases, the Department may not even be relying on regulations to set policy. The Department frequently sets standards for student loan discharges and other programs through informal "Dear Colleague" letters or other informal methods such as staff interpretations or communications. Courts should be persuaded that these types of informal decisions are not due the same type of deference as regulations that have been issued through the public notice and comment process.[258]

Because the Department of Education's decision to deny a student loan discharge is an informal adjudication, there is no formal record. The district court will consider all material that was presented to the Department by the borrower and should also consider any other information or documents the Department relied on. The government will typically prepare and submit what it considers to be the administrative record. The borrower, however, is free to present to the court any additional evidence that had a bearing on the agency's decision. The guaranty agencies act as agents for the Department in reviewing discharge requests. Material submitted to the guaranty agencies should also be submitted as part of the agency record.[259]

---

246 *See* § 8.2.2.6, *infra*.

247 34 C.F.R. §§ 682.402(e)(11)(ii) (false-certification administrative appeals), 682.402(l)(5)(vii) (unpaid-refund administrative appeals).

248 Courts have consistently found that only the Department of Education has the discretion to discharge the loans based on the various discharge programs. *See, e.g.*, United States v. Levreau, 2001 WL 1690059 (D. Minn. Dec. 14, 2001) (discharge claims must be pursued administratively and may not be asserted as a defense in a collection action); United States v. Bertucci, 2000 WL 1234560 (E.D. La. 2000); United States v. Wright, 87 F. Supp. 2d 464 (D. Md. 2000); *In re* Bega, 180 B.R. 642 (Bankr. D. Kan. 1995).

249 Green v. United States, 163 F. Supp. 2d 593 (W.D.N.C. 2000).

250 *Id.* at 597.

251 *Id.* at 597–598.

252 5 U.S.C. § 706(2)(A). *See also* Jordan v. Secretary of Educ. of the U.S., 194 F.3d 169 (D.C. Cir. 1999).

253 Citizens to Preserve Overton Park, Inc. v. Volpe, 401 U.S. 402, 415 (1971); C.K. v. New Jersey Dep't of Health & Human Servs., 92 F.3d 171, 182 (3d Cir. 1996).

254 Citizens to Preserve Overton Park, Inc. v. Volpe, 401 U.S. 416 (1971) (citations omitted); C.K. v. New Jersey Dep't of Health & Human Servs., 92 F.3d 182 (3d Cir. 1996).

255 Frisby v. United States Dep't of Housing & Urban Dev., 755 F.2d 1052, 1055 (3d Cir. 1985) (citing Motor Vehicle Mfrs. Ass'n v. State Farm Mut. Auto. Ins. Co., 463 U.S. 29, 43 (1983)).

256 *See* United States v. Nixon, 418 U.S. 683, 696 (1974).

257 *See* Frisby v. United States Dep't of Housing & Urban Dev., 755 F.2d 1055–56 (3d Cir. 1985); Kelly v. Railroad Ret. Bd., 625 F.2d 486, 491–92 (3d Cir. 1980).

258 *See, e.g.*, De La Mota v. United States Dep't of Educ., 412 F.3d 71 (2d Cir. 2005).

259 A sample APA appeal can be found at Appendix E, *infra*. See § 5.3.2.3, *supra*, for a discussion of APA claims when a guaranty agency, rather than the Department, makes the underlying decision.

An action for APA review is filed in federal district court. There is no time limit in the APA for seeking judicial review. Most courts have looked to 28 U.S.C. § 2401(a) as the relevant statute of limitations for appeals of agency decisions.[260] This section requires that civil actions against the United States be filed within six years after the right of action first accrued.

The APA provides for relief pending review.[261] When an agency finds that justice so requires, it may postpone the effective date of action taken by it, pending judicial review. The test is generally similar to that required for preliminary injunctions.

There are limits to APA relief. Monetary damages are not available under the APA.[262] However, plaintiffs may argue that the government has waived sovereign immunity on claims for monetary relief in certain circumstances.[263] The APA does create a potential cause of action for declaratory relief.[264] Regardless of the relief sought, review under the APA is available only when there is no other adequate remedy in a court.[265] However, the Supreme Court has held that this limitation should not be construed to defeat the central purpose of providing a broad spectrum of judicial review of agency action. The restriction is designed primarily to ensure that federal courts do not duplicate the previously established statutory procedures relating to specific agencies.[266] The agency action challenged must also be final.[267]

---

260 *See, e.g.,* Southwest Williamson County Cmty. Ass'n, Inc. v. Slater, 173 F.3d 1033, 1036 (6th Cir. 1999); Chemical Weapons Work Group v. Department of Army, 111 F.3d 1485 (10th Cir. 1997); Village of Elk Grove Vill. v. Evans, 997 F.2d 328, 331 (7th Cir. 1993); Impro Prods., Inc. v. Block, 722 F.2d 845 (D.C. Cir. 1983); Lewis v. Glickman, 104 F. Supp. 2d 1311 (D. Kan. 2000), *aff'd sub nom.* Jones v. Glickman, 2002 WL 1435904, 42 Fed. Appx. 292 (10th Cir. 2002).

261 5 U.S.C. § 705.

262 5 U.S.C. § 702 ("An action in a court of the United States seeking relief other than money damages and stating a claim that an agency or an officer or employee thereof acted or failed to act in an official capacity or under color of legal authority shall not be dismissed nor relief therein be denied on the ground that it is against the United States or that the United States is an indispensable party. The United States may be named as a defendant in any such action, and a judgment or decree may be entered against the United States.").

263 *See, e.g.,* De La Mota v. United States Dep't of Educ., 2003 WL 21919774 (S.D.N.Y. Aug. 12, 2003) (discussing and rejecting various theories to waive sovereign immunity on claims for monetary relief).

264 *See id.* (HEA anti-injunction provision waives the Secretary's immunity from suit seeking declaratory relief). *See also* § 9.4.1.1, *infra.*

265 5 U.S.C. § 704. *See* Marlow v. United States Dep't of Educ., 820 F.2d 581, 583 n.3 (2d Cir. 1987); Infante v. Drug Enforcement Admin., 938 F. Supp. 1149 (E.D.N.Y. 1996).

266 *See* Bowen v. Massachusetts, 487 U.S. 879, 108 S. Ct. 2722, 101 L. Ed. 2d 749 (1988). *See also* De La Mota v. United States Dep't of Educ., 2003 WL 21919774 (S.D.N.Y. Aug. 12, 2003) (court allowed APA action to proceed in case in which alternative remedy of breach-of-contact action against the plaintiffs' law schools was not an adequate remedy), *rev'd on other grounds,* 412 F.3d 71 (2d Cir. 2005).

267 5 U.S.C. § 704.

Discharging Student Loans in Bankruptcy

7.1 About the Bankruptcy Option

Discharging student loans in bankruptcy is an important strategy for low-income consumers, either through a chapter 7 ("straight") or a chapter 13 ("wage earner plan") bankruptcy filing.[1] Though a series of amendments to the Bankruptcy Code have made it more difficult to discharge student loans, it is still an option consumers struggling with debt may consider.[2] In addition, even when a student loan cannot be discharged in bankruptcy, a chapter 13 bankruptcy filing offers other important options for the student loan borrower.

Deciding whether to file for bankruptcy to deal with a student loan requires at least two decisions. The first decision—whether bankruptcy can effectively deal with a student loan—is described later in this chapter. The other issue is whether bankruptcy makes sense for a consumer in light of the consumer's total debt picture. This question is detailed in another NCLC manual[3] and will only be briefly summarized here.

The 2005 Bankruptcy Abuse Prevention and Consumer Protection Act (BAPCPA) amendments to the Bankruptcy Code limit consumers' access to bankruptcy relief in a number of ways. Generally effective for cases filed as of October 17, 2005, the amendments created new paperwork and counseling requirements for consumer debtors. The scope of bankruptcy relief has been restricted in specific areas, and important new limits on repeat filings are now in effect.[4] However, the recent amendments did not change the general standards and procedures applicable to student loan discharge determinations.[5] The extensive pre-BAPCPA case law construing the "undue hardship" dischargeability standards under § 523(a)(8) of the Code will remain pertinent under the new regime.

In a chapter 7 bankruptcy, virtually all of a consumer's debts are eliminated (discharged) with no obligation to make payments, and the consumer will be able to keep exempt property. Non-exempt property, however, may be liquidated. It is therefore critical for a consumer's attorney to carefully study the consumer's exemption, redemption, and other rights if the consumer wishes to retain a home, car, or other significant asset. Nevertheless, exemption statutes will permit many low-income persons to retain all their assets in a chapter 7 proceeding.

If a consumer is concerned about his or her ability to retain a home, car, or other asset, a chapter 13 filing will often be a successful approach. In a chapter 13 bankruptcy, a debtor pays some portion (even if only 5% or 10%) of his or her unsecured debts in accordance with a court-approved ("confirmed") plan, usually over a three- to five-year period.[6] At the conclusion of the plan, the remaining obligations on any unsecured debts are discharged.[7] The opportunity to cure defaults on or to restructure secured debt is also available.[8]

Another consideration is that filing a chapter 7 or chapter 13 bankruptcy instantly protects the student from most collection actions on claims arising before the bankruptcy. For example, the "automatic stay" would prevent a student loan creditor from continuing with an administrative wage garnishment.[9]

Currently, the fee is $299 for filing a chapter 7 and $274 for filing a chapter 13 bankruptcy.[10] Debtors in chapter 7 may now seek wavier of the filing fee through the *in forma*

---

1 For a general introduction to bankruptcy law, see National Consumer Law Center, Consumer Bankruptcy Law and Practice Chs. 1–6 (8th ed. 2006).

2 In 1998, student loan debtors suffered a major setback to their ability to discharge student loans. For all bankruptcy cases filed on or after October 7, 1998, the discharge of student loans that first became due more than seven years prior to the bankruptcy filing is no longer allowed. Pub. L. No. 105-244 § 971 (Oct. 7, 1998) (Higher Education Programs Authorization Extension Act).

3 National Consumer Law Center, Consumer Bankruptcy Law and Practice (8th ed. 2006).

4 *Id.*

5 The primary area related to student loans in bankruptcy affected by the BACPA amendments is the expanded definition of entities covered by the exception from discharge for educational

loans. These changes are discussed at § 7.2.2, *infra*.

6 National Consumer Law Center, Consumer Bankruptcy Law and Practice Ch. 4 (8th ed. 2006).

7 11 U.S.C. § 1328(c).

8 *See* National Consumer Law Center, Consumer Bankruptcy Law and Practice Ch. 11 (8th ed. 2006).

9 *See* 11 U.S.C. § 362. The automatic stay remains in effect while the bankruptcy case is pending or until such time as it is lifted by the court upon request by a creditor based on grounds specified in § 362 of the Bankruptcy Code. See § 5.2.4, *supra*, for a discussion of the automatic stay in relation to tax intercepts.

10 Fees effective April 9, 2006.

pauperis provisions enacted with BAPCPA.[11] The filing fees generally cannot be waived in chapter 13 but may be paid in installments in both chapter 13 and chapter 7.[12]

7.2 When Can a Student Loan Be Discharged in Bankruptcy?

7.2.1 Special Restriction on Dischargeability Applies to Most Student Loans

A chapter 7 or 13 discharge eliminates all of a debtor's unsecured debts, with certain statutory exceptions. While student loans are technically unsecured debts subject to discharge, the Bankruptcy Code limits their dischargeability. Educational loans can only be discharged if the consumer can show that payment of the debt "will impose an undue hardship on the debtor and the debtor's dependents."[13]

This special restriction on dischargeability applies to educational loans "made, insured or guaranteed by any governmental unit, or made under any program funded in whole or in part by a government unit or a nonprofit institution."[14] Consequently, the dischargeability of Stafford, SLS, Federal Direct, and Perkins loans are all restricted. Most courts find these limitations apply not only to student borrowers but also to parents who co-sign a student loan or take out a PLUS or other loan for their child's education.[15]

The exception to discharge applies to loans by state agencies and nonprofit organizations.[16] Under pre-BAPCPA law, loans made by for-profit institutions were dischargeable.[17] The 2005 amendments expanded the scope of the discharge exception to encompass most for-profit lenders as well.[18] The restriction on dischargeability also applies to educational benefit overpayments (such as Pell grant overpayments) and obligations to repay funds received as educational benefits, scholarships, or stipends.[19] Occasionally an employer pays off the costs associated with an employee's education and training as part of a hiring agreement. The courts have found these payments to be dischargeable debts because the employer made the payments for business purposes, as a hiring incentive, and not as education loans.[20]

---

11 28 U.S.C. § 1930(f)(1).

12 Part of each fee is a mandatory noticing fee rather than a filing fee. That part of the fee is waivable in most jurisdictions. For more information about bankruptcy court fee waivers, see National Consumer Law Center, Consumer Bankruptcy Law and Practice §§ 7.2, 13.6 (8th ed. 2006).

13 11 U.S.C. § 523(a)(8).

14 11 U.S.C. §§ 523(a)(8)(A)(i), 1328(a)(2); *In re* O'Brien, 419 F.3d 104 (2d Cir. 2005) (the term "funded," as used in bankruptcy statute excepting student loans from discharge "made under any program funded in whole or in part by a governmental unit or non-profit institution," modified the word "program" rather than the word "loan" and did not require nonprofit institution that guaranteed debtor's student loans to actually supply any portion of funding for the loans in order for discharge exception to apply). In general, it is the purpose for which the loan was made that controls rather than the use of the loan proceeds. *In re* Murphy, 282 F.3d 868 (5th Cir. 2002) (student loans nondischargeable even if portion used by debtor to purchase car, housing, food, and other living expenses). See also National Consumer Law Center, Consumer Bankruptcy Law and Practice § 14.4.2 (8th ed. 2006), for a discussion on the dischargeability of student loans.

15 *See In re* Pelkowski, 990 F.2d 737 (3d Cir. 1993); *In re* Varma, 149 B.R. 817 (N.D. Tex. 1992); *In re* Wilcon, 143 B.R. 4 (D. Mass. 1992); Uterhark v. Great Lakes Higher Educ. Corp. (*In re* Uterhark), 185 B.R. 39 (Bankr. N.D. Ohio 1995); Owens v. Nebraska Higher Educ. Loan Program, Inc. (Matter of Owens), 161 B.R. 829 (Bankr. D. Neb. 1993). *But see In re* Kirkish, 144 B.R. 367 (Bankr. W.D. Mich. 1992); *In re* Behr, 80 B.R. 124

(Bankr. N.D. Iowa 1987). Courts have been less willing to find that the exception to discharge applies to co-signers who are not the student's parents. *See, e.g., In re* Pryor, 234 B.R. 716 (Bankr. W.D. Tenn. 1999) (exception not applicable to non-student co-signer); *In re* Meier, 85 B.R. 805 (Bankr. W.D. Wis. 1986) (exception not applicable to accommodation party).

16 *See* TI Federal Credit Union v. DelBonis, 72 F.3d 921 (1st Cir. 1995) (federally chartered credit union is a governmental unit for purposes of exception to discharge); *In re* Merchant, 958 F.2d 738 (6th Cir. 1992) (loan guaranteed by nonprofit institution was nondischargeable); *In re* Roberts, 149 B.R. 547 (C.D. Ill. 1993) (loan from nonprofit credit union nondischargeable). *Cf. In re* Reis, 274 B.R.46 (Bankr. D. Mass. 2002) (private student loan made by grandparents not excepted from discharge because not made pursuant to student loan program of governmental unit or by nonprofit entity).

17 *In re* Scott, 287 B.R. 470 (Bankr. E.D. Mo. 2002) (loan made by for-profit truck driving school dischargeable); *In re* Jones, 242 B.R. 441 (Bankr. W.D. Tenn. 1999) (debt to for-profit trade school was not within scope of § 523(a)(8)); *In re* Shorts, 209 B.R. 818 (Bankr. D.R.I. 1997) (same); *In re* Simmons, 175 B.R. 624 (Bankr. E.D. Va. 1994) (credit union was not a nonprofit institution and loan was not made pursuant to a program within meaning of § 523(a)(8)); *In re* Sinclair-Ganos, 133 B.R. 382 (Bankr. W.D. Mich. 1991) (credit union not a nonprofit institution within meaning of § 523(a)(8)). *But see In re* Pilcher, 149 B.R. 595 (B.A.P. 9th Cir. 1993) (private loan received from for-profit lender as part of Law Access program involving two nonprofit institutions was covered by exception to discharge); *In re* O'Brien, 299 B.R. 725 (Bankr. S.D.N.Y. 2003) (same), *aff'd,* 419 F.3d 104 (2d Cir. 2005); *In re* Bolen, 287 B.R. 127 (Bankr. D. Vt. 2002) (same).

18 *See* § 7.2.2, *infra.*

19 11 U.S.C. § 523(a)(8); *In re* Burks, 244 F.3d 1245 (11th Cir. 2001) (obligation to repay stipend due to failure to fulfill stipend agreement to teach in "other race" institution after receiving degree was nondischargeable); U.S. Dep't of Health & Human Servs. v. Smith, 807 F.2d 122 (8th Cir. 1986) (scholarship grants received to finance medical training in exchange for agreement to practice in designated physician shortage area nondischargeable). *See also In re* Coole, 202 B.R. 518 (Bankr. D.N.M. 1996) (an "educational benefit overpayment" involves a program like the "GI Bill," wherein students receive payments based on their attendance at school and overpayment occurs when student continues to receive payments after leaving school).

20 *See In re* Segal, 57 F.3d 342 (3d Cir. 1995) (when nonprofit hospital paid off debtor's student loans, replacing it with new loans, those new loans were dischargeable because they were

However, obligations to fulfill military service duties in return for education subsidies give rise to nondischargeable debts if the military service is not completed.[21]

The restriction on dischargeability should also apply in the same way to consolidation loans.[22] However, it does not apply to a student's nonpayment of tuition or room and board when the charges are not incurred as an extension of credit or under an appropriate program.[23] In addition, the restriction may not apply to non-students who sign as co-obligors to finance a third party's education.[24]

7.2.2 New Bankruptcy Law and Student Loans

The 2005 bankruptcy law, the Bankruptcy Abuse Prevention, Consumer Protection Act, effective October 17, 2005, includes some significant revisions to the student loan dischargeability standards in § 523(a)(8).[25] The general principle that student loans are nondischargeable unless the borrower can prove undue hardship remains the same. However, the new law restructures the student loan section such that some student loans that are currently dischargeable will fall into the nondischargeable category.

There are two major structural changes to the section. First, new section A(i) provides that an educational benefit overpayment or loan made, insured, or guaranteed by a government unit—or made under any program funded in whole or in part by a government unit or nonprofit institution—is nondischargeable. Section A(ii) provides separately that an obligation to repay funds received as an education benefit, scholarship, or stipend is nondischargeable.

The new law also adds section (B), a kind of catch-all category. In addition to the student loans in section (A), section (B) provides that any other education loan that is a qualified educational loan, as defined in § 221(d)(1) of the Internal Revenue Code, is nondischargeable. This is especially significant because it means most private loans, which were dischargeable unless the lender proved that the loan was made or funded by a government unit or nonprofit institution, will be nondischargeable unless the debtor can prove hardship.

There are a few limits to new section (B). These limits are derived from the Internal Revenue Code definition of a "qualified education loan," which is explicitly referenced in

---

not made under a "program" of giving educational loans); *In re* Hawkins, 317 B.R. 104 (B.A.P. 9th Cir. 2004) (tuition subsidy related to continued medical practice in Ohio was not an educational loan subject to § 523(a)(8)); *In re* Rezendez, 324 B.R. 689 (N.D. Ind. 2004) (cost of plumbers' union apprentice program was dischargeable because not an educational loan and not subject to agreement to pay any fixed amount); *In re* Nies, 324 B.R. 495 (Bankr. D. Mass. 2005) (hospital recruitment program that paid doctor's student loans as a hiring incentive was not an educational loan).

21 *In re* Udell, 454 F.3d 180 (3d Cir. 2006) (dismissed cadet's obligation to repay costs of Air Force Academy attendance must be treated as education loan subject to § 523(a)(8) after the initial five-year period of absolute nondischargeability under 19 U.S.C. § 2005(d) has passed); *In re* Dunn, 325 B.R. 807 (Bankr. N.D. Iowa 2005) (same rule applies to obligations to repay private college subsidy under ROTC program).

22 *See In re* Flint, 238 B.R. 676 (E.D. Mich. 1999), *rev'g* 231 B.R. 611 (Bankr. E.D. Mich. 1999); *In re* Shaffer, 237 B.R. 617 (Bankr. N.D. Tex. 1999); *In re* Cobb, 196 B.R. 34 (Bankr. E.D. Va. 1996).

23 *In re* Chambers, 348 F.3d 650 (7th Cir. 2003) (tuition debt and related charges held dischargeable as no evidence parties entered into loan arrangement prior to services being provided); *In re* Mehta, 310 F.3d 308 (3d Cir. 2002) (student's unilateral decision not to pay tuition does not create a loan); Cazenovia College v. Renshaw, 222 F.3d 82 (2d Cir. 2000) (tuition debt not a loan); *In re* Nelson, 188 B.R. 32 (D.S.D. 1995) (debt for tuition, room, and board to university was not a loan); *In re* Navarro, 284 B.R. 727 (Bankr. C.D. Cal. 2002) (agreement that student would be responsible for tuition and fees was not a promissory note for sum certain and therefore was dischargeable); *In re* Ray, 262 B.R. 544 (Bankr. D. Okla. 2001) (tuition debt was neither "loan" nor "obligation to repay funds received as an educational benefit"); *In re* Pelzman, 233 B.R. 575 (Bankr. D.D.C. 1999) (room and board for first semester nondischargeable because pursuant to program but not for remaining semesters when extension of credit violated school policy); *In re* Gordon, 231 B.R. 459 (Bankr. D. Conn. 1999) (residency program assistance not student loan); *In re* Feyes, 228 B.R. 887 (Bankr. N.D. Ohio 1998) (credit extension was dischargeable when school allowed student to attend classes on a credit basis and pay for them when he could and no promissory note was signed); *In re* Johnson, 222 B.R. 783 (Bankr. E.D. Va. 1998) (debt for tuition was not obligation for funds received on a loan and there was no "program"); *In re* Meinhart, 211 B.R. 750 (Bankr. D. Colo. 1997) (debt to school was not an obligation to repay "funds received" as required by statute); *In re* Coole, 202 B.R. 518 (Bankr. D.N.M. 1996) (debt to school for services rendered was not a loan); *In re* Alibatya, 178 B.R. 335 (Bankr. E.D.N.Y. 1995) (no loan when debtor failed to pay student housing rent under lease with university). *See also In re* Parker, 334 B.R. 529 (Bankr. D. Mass. 2005) (university violated automatic stay and discharge injunction by refusing to allow student to register for class unless she paid past tuition bill

discharged in bankruptcy). *Cf. In re* DePasquale, 225 B.R. 830 (B.A.P. 1st Cir. 1998) (payment agreement for overdue tuition constituted "loan"); *In re* Johnson, 218 B.R. 449 (B.A.P. 8th Cir. 1998) (debtor who signed promissory note to college for unpaid tuition had student loan). For a more extensive summary of cases on the subject of distinguishing student loans from student tuition account debts, see Matthew C. Welnicki, *Dischargeability of Student Financial Obligations: Student Loans Versus Student Tuition Account Debts*, 31 J.C. & U.L. 665 (2005).

24 *See In re* Pryor, 234 B.R. 716 (W.D. Tenn. 1999) (exception not applicable to non-student co-debtor); Kirkish v. Meritor Sav. Bank, 144 B.R. 367 (Bankr. W.D. Mich. 1992). *But see In re* Pelkowski, 990 F.2d 737 (3d Cir. 1993) (language of statute does not limit exception to discharge to exclude parent co-signers); *In re* Varma, 149 B.R. 817 (N.D. Tex. 1992); *In re* Wilcon, 143 B.R. 5. (D. Mass. 1992); *In re* Salter, 207 B.R. 272 (Bankr. M.D. Fla. 1997) (exception applies to co-maker as focus should be type of debt involved rather than who signed).

25 Pub. L. No. 109-8, § 220.

the bankruptcy law.[26] Only "qualified education loans" will be nondischargeable under this new category.

The Internal Revenue Code defines qualified education loans as any indebtedness incurred by the taxpayer *solely* to pay qualified higher education expenses.[27] This may allow borrowers who incur debt for education that is commingled with other types of debt to argue that the education debt was not incurred *solely* to pay higher education expenses and is thus dischargeable.

In order to be considered a qualified education loan, the loan must also be taken out to pay expenses for education furnished during a period in which the recipient was an eligible student.[28] There are circumstances under which a student may take out a loan to attend school but may not necessarily be an eligible student. For example, aggressive proprietary schools in some cases enroll non-high-school graduates without properly administering the required "ability to benefit test."[29] Students improperly enrolled in this way are eligible to administratively cancel their loans and should also be categorized as "ineligible" students.

There may also be some wiggle room in the definition of qualified higher education expenses. There are two parts to this definition. First, the expenses must fit within the federal Higher Education Act (HEA) category of items and services considered to be "the cost of attendance." Second, the expenses must be for attendance at an "eligible education institution."[30]

The HEA definition of "cost of attendance" is quite broad, including tuition and fees and costs for rental or purchase of equipment, materials, and supplies.[31] It also includes room and board. Most education-related expenses will likely be covered.

The requirement that expenses must be for attendance at an "eligible education institution" may be more helpful for borrowers. Eligible institutions are defined as institutions that are eligible to participate in a Title IV program.[32] Title IV refers to the title of the HEA that governs federal financial assistance programs. Most, but not all, schools are eligible to participate in these programs. For example, numerous unaccredited schools have gone in and out of business in recent years. These unaccredited schools are not eligible to participate in the Title IV programs. Other scam programs such as "diploma mills" are also not eligible to participate in Title IV programs. Borrowers with student

loans from these schools should be able to discharge the loans without having to prove hardship.

7.2.3 Discharging Student Loans over Seven Years Old No Longer Allowed for Cases Filed After October 7, 1998

In 1998, student loan debtors suffered a major setback to their ability to discharge student loans. For all bankruptcy cases filed after October 7, 1998, the discharge of student loans that first became due more than seven years prior to the bankruptcy filing will no longer be allowed.[33] Cases filed before October 7, 1998, are not affected by the change in the law. The following discussion of discharges under the seven-year rule is still relevant for consumers who filed before the change in law and there remains a question as to whether a student loan was discharged.

For cases filed before October 7, 1998, if the first student loan installment became due more than seven years prior to the bankruptcy filing, then the entire loan and not just the first installment is discharged.[34] The most important issue in counting the seven-year period is that the seven years are "exclusive of any applicable suspension of the repayment period."[35] This means that a deferment or forbearance may lengthen the seven-year period if repayments were suspended during that period.[36] On the other hand, the seven-year period should not be lengthened just because the consumer was allowed to make reduced payments or entered into a reasonable and affordable repayment agreement, because payments were not suspended.[37] Consolidating one or more student loans, though, will likely start the seven-year

---

26 26 U.S.C. § 221(d).

27 26 U.S.C. § 221(d)(1). Note that the expenses must be incurred on behalf of the taxpayer, the taxpayer's spouse, or any dependent of the taxpayer, and must be paid or incurred within a reasonable period of time before or after the indebtedness is incurred and attributable to education furnished during a period in which the recipient was an eligible student.

28 26 U.S.C. § (d)(1)(C).

29 *See* § 6.3.2, *supra.*

30 26 U.S.C. § 221(d)(2).

31 20 U.S.C. § 1087*ll.*

32 26 U.S.C. § 221(d)(2) (referring to 26 U.S.C. § 25A(f)(2)(B)).

33 Pub. L. No. 105-244 § 971 (Oct. 7, 1998) (Higher Education Programs Authorization Extension Act).

34 *See, e.g., In re* Nunn, 788 F.2d 617 (9th Cir. 1986).

35 11 U.S.C. § 523(a)(8)(A); U.S. Dep't of Ed. v. Scott (*In re* Scott), 147 F.3d 788 (8th Cir. 1998) (loan first became due after six-month grace period expired, not when student left school). *See also* National Consumer Law Center, Consumer Bankruptcy Law and Practice § 14.4.3.8 (8th ed. 2006).

36 *In re* Huber, 169 B.R. 82 (Bankr. W.D.N.Y. 1994) (deferment period counts even when debtor eventually found not eligible for deferment when repayment requirement was suspended); *In re* Barciz, 123 B.R. 771 (Bankr. N.D. Ohio 1990) (forbearance tolls running of period). *But see In re* Flynn, 190 B.R. 139 (Bankr. D.N.H. 1995) (a reference to a period of forbearance did not refer to a suspension of payment).

37 *In re* Salter, 207 B.R. 272 (Bankr. M.D. Fla. 1997) (stipulation changing amount of payments did not constitute a new obligation that would restart the seven-year time period); *In re* Marlewski, 168 B.R. 378 (Bankr. E.D. Wis. 1994) (repayment agreement does not toll period when agreement did not call for suspension of payments or lengthening of repayment period). *See also In re* Manriquez, 207 B.R. 890 (B.A.P. 9th Cir. 1996) (retroactive forbearance agreement signed after seven years had already run did not render loan nondischargeable).

period running all over again as of the date of the consolidated loan.[38]

7.2.4 Undue Hardship As Basis for Discharging Student Loan

7.2.4.1 General

A student loan may be discharged if payment of the debt "will impose an undue hardship on the debtor and the debtor's dependents."[39] There is no statutory definition of "undue hardship." Generally, it means the consumer's present income is inadequate to pay the loan and this situation is not likely to change even after considering the consumer's future earning potential.

Many bankruptcy courts have adopted the three-prong test for determining undue hardship set forth in the Second Circuit decision in *Brunner v. New York State Higher Educ. Servs. Corp.*[40] The *Brunner* test requires a showing that (1) the debtor cannot maintain, based on current income and expenses, a "minimal" standard of living for the debtor and the debtor's dependents if forced to repay the student loans; (2) additional circumstances exist indicating that this state of affairs is likely to persist for a significant portion of the repayment period of the student loans; and (3) the debtor has made good faith efforts to repay the loans.[41]

While the *Brunner* test is widely followed, some courts have chosen to apply other tests or to consider other criteria.[42] Another commonly used test that preceded *Brunner*

and is similar in some ways is the *Johnson* test.[43] Like *Brunner*, the *Johnson* test has three parts:

(1) The Mechanical Test: Courts will ask whether the debtor's future financial resources will be sufficient to support the debtor and dependents (similar to steps one and two of *Brunner*).

(2) The Good Faith Test: Here the courts ask whether the debtor was negligent or irresponsible in his or her efforts to maximize income and minimize expenses and, if so, whether the absence of such negligence would have altered the answer to the mechanical test (similar to step three in *Brunner*).

(3) The Policy Test: The courts ask whether the circumstances, particularly the amount and percentage of total indebtedness of the student loan, indicate that the dominant purpose of the bankruptcy petition was to discharge the student debt. Courts will favor debtors who have truly fallen on hard times after incurring student loan debt and are unlikely to derive future benefits from the education financed with the loan.[44]

This third step, unlike the *Brunner* test, takes into account whether the debtor benefited or is likely to benefit financially from the education. Though this prong of the *Johnson* test can be restrictive, it should be more favorably applied to low-income students who have attended scam vocational schools and never benefited from the education.

Other courts have rejected the rigid tests set out in both *Brunner* and *Johnson*, choosing instead to use a more

---

38 See, e.g., Hiatt v. Indiana State Student Assistance Comm'n, 36 F.3d 21 (7th Cir. 1994), *cert. denied*, 513 U.S. 1154 (1995); United States v. McGrath, 143 B.R. 820 (D. Md. 1992), *aff'd without opinion*, 8 F.3d 821 (4th Cir. 1993); In re Burns, 334 B.R. 521 (Bankr. D. Mass. 2005) (debtor had initially filed for chapter 7 relief in 1988; five-year limit not met because loans were consolidated in 1984); In re Cobb, 196 B.R. 34 (Bankr. E.D. Va. 1996); In re Hasselgrave, 177 B.R. 681 (Bankr. D. Or. 1995); In re Menendez, 151 B.R. 972 (Bankr. M.D. Fla. 1993); In re Martin, 137 B.R. 770 (Bankr. W.D. Mo. 1992). One court has held that a consolidation loan obtained by duress was void, permitting the debtor to obtain a discharge under the former seven-year rule. In re Mason, 300 B.R. 160 (Bankr. D. Conn. 2003).

39 11 U.S.C. § 523(a)(8)(B).

40 831 F.2d 395 (2d Cir. 1987).

41 The Second Circuit's *Brunner* test has been adopted by the Third, Fourth, Fifth, Sixth, Seventh, Ninth, Tenth, and Eleventh Circuits. See In re Frushour, 433 F.3d 393 (4th Cir. 2005); In re Oyler, 397 F.3d 382 (6th Cir. 2005); Educational Credit Mgmt. Corp. v. Polleys, 356 F.3d 1302 (10th Cir. 2004); In re Gerhardt, 348 F.3d 89 (5th Cir. 2003); In re Cox, 338 F.3d 1238 (11th Cir. 2003); Goulet v. Educational Credit Mgmt. Corp., 284 F.3d 773 (7th Cir. 2002); In re Brightful, 267 F.3d 324 (3d Cir. 2001); In re Rifino, 245 F.3d 1083 (9th Cir. 2001), *cert. denied sub nom.* Nowland v. United States, 534 U.S. 927 (2001).

42 Since the *Brunner* decision, courts have tended to "mix and match" both restrictive and less restrictive elements from vari-

ous cases. See United Student Aid Funds v. Pena (In re Pena), 155 F.3d 1108 (9th Cir. 1998) (adopting *Brunner* test); In re Faish, 72 F.3d 298 (3d Cir. 1995), *cert. denied*, 116 S. Ct. 2532 (1996); In re Cheesman, 25 F.3d 356 (6th Cir. 1994) (no specific test adopted but *Brunner* analysis followed), *cert. denied*, 513 U.S. 1081 (1995); In re Roberson, 999 F.2d 1132 (7th Cir. 1993) ("dischargeability of student loan should be based on certainty of hopelessness, not simply a present inability to fulfill financial commitment"); In re Mayer, 210 B.R. 677 (E.D. Pa. 1997), *aff'g* 198 B.R. 116 (Bankr. E.D. Pa. 1996), *aff'd without opinion*, 156 F.3d 1225 (3d Cir. 1998). Still other courts have cited the more restrictive language in *Roberson* to deny discharges. See, e.g., In re Coveney, 192 B.R. 140 (Bankr. W.D. Tex. 1996); In re Walcott, 185 B.R. 721 (Bankr. E.D.N.C. 1995); In re Hawkins, 187 B.R. 294 (Bankr. N.D. Iowa 1995). See generally Andrew M. Campbell, *Bankruptcy Discharge of Student Loan on Ground of Undue Hardship Under § 523(a)(8)(B) of Bankruptcy Code of 1978 (11 U.S.C.S. § 523(a)(8)(B) Discharge of Student Loans)*, 144 A.L.R. Fed. 1 (1998).

43 In re Johnson, 1979 U.S. Dist. LEXIS 11428, 5 B.C.D. 532 (Bankr. E.D. Pa. 1979). See also In re Roe, 226 B.R. 258 (Bankr. N.D. Ala. 1998); In re Taylor, 198 B.R. 700 (Bankr. N.D. Ohio 1996). For decisions comparing the *Brunner* and *Johnson* tests, see In re Kopf, 245 B.R. 731 (Bankr. D. Me. 2000); In re Lehman, 226 B.R. 805 (Bankr. D. Vt. 1998) (court chooses *Brunner* test and denies discharge); In re Holtorf, 204 B.R. 567 (Bankr. S.D. Cal. 1997); In re Hawkins, 187 B.R. 294 (Bankr. N.D. Iowa 1995) (*Brunner* test applied after discussing both *Brunner* and *Johnson* tests).

44 In re Johnson, 1979 U.S. Dist. LEXIS 11428, 5 B.C.D. 532 (Bankr. E.D. Pa. 1979).

flexible test and consider the "totality of the debtor's circumstances."[45] This test does not necessarily conflict with *Brunner* and *Johnson* but expands the scope of factors a court may consider, taking into consideration more fully the student's personal circumstances.[46]

In still other cases, courts have not necessarily rejected the *Brunner* or *Johnson* tests but rather refined or expanded some of the prongs in making their decisions.[47] And at least

one court has introduced a "poverty test" in which a debtor's loans were presumptively considered nondischargeable if the debtor's income exceeded the federal poverty guidelines, unless the debtor could show extreme circumstances.[48]

Regardless of the test used, courts must ultimately engage in the discretionary determination of when "hardship" becomes "undue." Courts are generally in agreement that "ordinary" or "garden variety" hardship, however defined, is simply not sufficient. On the other extreme are courts that require extraordinary circumstances such as the total physical incapacity of the debtor.[49] One court recently criticized these latter decisions, finding the requisite hardship to be more "mundane":

> To conclude that the debtor must demonstrate something approaching a "certainty of hopelessness" or "total incapacity" would be to sacrifice the notion of "fresh start" at the altar of "undue hardship."[50]

---

45 Long v. Educational Credit Mgmt. Corp., 322 F.3d 549 (8th Cir. 2003) (totality-of-circumstances test adopted, which considers (1) debtor's past, current, and reasonably reliable future financial resources; (2) debtor and debtor's dependents' reasonable necessary living expenses; and (3) any other relevant facts and circumstances applicable to bankruptcy case). On remand, the court applied the totality-of-circumstances test and concluded that the student loans should not be discharged. *In re* Long, 292 B.R. 635 (B.A.P. 8th Cir. 2003). *See also In re* Reynolds, 425 F.3d 526 (8th Cir. 2005) (in granting discharge of law school loan debts under "totality of circumstances" test, court gives significant weight to evidence of long-term debt's detrimental effect upon the emotional state of debtor who suffers from depression, anxiety, and personality disorder); *In re* Cumberworth, 347 B.R. 652 (B.A.P. 8th Cir. 2006) (rejecting DOE's efforts to apply "certainty of financial hopelessness" and "indefinite and extraordinary hardship" tests, panel upholds finding of undue hardship when student loan debtor and her husband received long-term disability benefits under Social Security and VA programs); *In re* Lee, 345 B.R. 911 (Bankr. W.D. Ark. 2006) (granting discharge for student loan debtor who has no health impairments but who is sole support of two minor children and works at low-paying clerical job); *In re* Dufresne, 341 B.R. 391 (Bankr. D. Mass. 2006) (court has discretion to "consider all the relevant facts and circumstances" without adhering to any particular test and holds that debtor who failed bar exam nine times may discharge her law school student loans); *In re* Kopf, 245 B.R. 731 (Bankr. D. Me. 2000); *In re* Phelps, 237 B.R. 527 (Bankr. D.R.I. 1999); *In re* Clark, 240 B.R. 758 (Bankr. W.D. Mo. 1999) (applying the *Andrews* test); *In re* Law, 159 B.R. 287 (Bankr. D.S.D. 1993) (described as a "case-by-case approach that is fact sensitive").

46 The Court of Appeals for the First Circuit allows the bankruptcy courts to develop their own standards for "undue hardship" without doctrinal adherence to either the *Brunner* or "totality of the circumstances" standards. *In re* Nash, 446 F.3d 188 (1st Cir. 2006) (First Circuit has not adopted either the *Brunner* test or the Eighth Circuit "totality of circumstances" standard, and court declines to mandate either one); *In re* Lorenz, 337 B.R. 423 (B.A.P. 1st Cir. 2006) (debtor's household income did not establish undue hardship under either major standard); *In re* Kelley, 312 B.R. 200 (B.A.P. 1st Cir. 2004) (bankruptcy court was free to choose its own approach and use of the totality-of-the-circumstances test in granting partial discharge); *In re* Paul, 337 B.R. 730 (Bankr. D. Mass. 2006) (courts in First Circuit are free to choose their own approach in determining undue hardship, noting most courts within the First Circuit have adopted the "totality of the circumstances" test); *In re* Hicks, 331 B.R. 18 (Bankr. D. Mass. 2005) (after thoroughly analyzing *Brunner* and "totality of circumstances" standards, court develops its own test: "Can the debtor now, and in the foreseeable future, maintain a reasonable, minimal standard of living for the debtor and the debtor's dependents and still afford to make payments on the debtors' student loans?").

47 *See, e.g.*, Educational Credit Mgmt. Corp. v. Polleys, 356 F.3d

1302 (10th Cir. 2004) (good faith prong of *Brunner* test should consider debtor's reasons for seeking discharge and whether debtor is intentionally creating hardship); *In re* Faish, 72 F.3d 298 (3d Cir. 1995), *cert. denied*, 116 S. Ct. 2532 (1996); *In re* Roberson, 999 F.2d 1132 (7th Cir. 1993).

48 *In re* Bryant, 72 B.R. 913, 916–17 (Bankr. E.D. Pa. 1987). The *Bryant* test was rejected by the Third Circuit in *In re* Faish, 72 F.3d 298 (3d Cir. 1995), *cert. denied*, 518 U.S. 1009 (1996). The substantial amount of student loan debt many consumers now confront, in some cases exceeding $100,000, has caused several courts to find undue hardship even for debtors with incomes well above the poverty level. *E.g.*, *In re* Nys, 308 B.R. 436 (B.A.P. 9th Cir. 2004), *aff'd*, 446 F.3d 938 (9th Cir. 2005).

49 *E.g.*, *In re* Frushour, 433 F.3d 393, 401 (4th Cir. 2005) (only "rare" circumstances will satisfy "additional circumstances" test of *Brunner*); *In re* Oyler, 397 F.3d 382, 386 (6th Cir. 2005) (facts indicating a "certainty of hopelessness" "may include illness, disability, a lack of usable job skills, or the existence of a large number of dependents"); *In re* Gerhardt, 348 F.3d 89 (5th Cir. 2003) (exceptional circumstances necessary to satisfy second prong of *Brunner* test).

50 *In re* Kopf, 245 B.R. 731, 744 (Bankr. D. Me. 2000). Other courts have rejected the onerous requirement that a debtor show extraordinary circumstances beyond the likelihood of continuing financial hardship. *Accord In re* Woody, 345 B.R. 246, 253 (B.A.P. 10th 2006); *In re* Hicks, 331 B.R. 18, 27 n.12 (Bankr. D. Mass. 2005) (the focus of many courts on the "certainty of hopelessness" language makes it appear that "any room for optimism will result in a finding of nondischargeability"). *See* Educational Credit Mgmt. Corp. v. Polleys, 356 F.3d 1302 (10th Cir. 2004) (courts need not require a "certainty of hopelessness"). A useful study of the development of the "undue hardship" standard under § 523(a)(8) can be found in Rafael I Pardo & Michelle R. Lacey, *Undue Hardship in the Bankruptcy Courts: An Empirical Assessment of the Discharge of Educational Debt*, 74 U. Cin. L. Rev. 405 (Winter 2005). From an evaluation of hundreds of published undue-hardship decisions applying the *Brunner* standard, the authors conclude that the rule has become useless as a predictable and reliable legal standard. Debtors similarly situated by demographics and financial circumstances are typically not treated the same when

In reaching a similar conclusion, the Court of Appeals for the Tenth Circuit noted that bankruptcy judges must have discretion to consider all relevant matters and that the *Brunner* "test must be applied such that debtors who truly cannot afford to repay their loans may have their loans discharged."[51]

In a decision following *Educational Credit Management v. Polleys*, the Bankruptcy Appellate Panel for the Tenth Circuit again emphasized the need for more flexibility in applying *Brunner*.[52] The panel affirmed the discharge of a 58-year old debtor's Department of Education and HEAL loans. The debtor was employed as an IRS staffer at a modest income of approximately $38,000 annually. He had incurred the loans to attend a chiropractic program, which he never completed. His expenses approximately equaled his income. The court noted that it was unlikely that this debtor's income would increase materially through promotion or other means until his planned retirement at age 65. The panel affirmed the bankruptcy court's conclusion that payment of the loans currently and for the foreseeable future would deprive the debtor of "the ability to afford life's basic necessities, such as health care, transportation, food, housing, utilities, or even the ability to care for oneself upon impending retirement."[53]

In another recent decision, the Ninth Circuit rejected an overly restrictive construction of the second prong of the *Brunner* test.[54] This is the requirement that the debtor show "additional circumstances" indicating that the current inability to afford loan payments is likely to persist for a significant portion of loan repayment period. Lenders, and many courts, have taken this standard to mean that the

debtor must show "exceptional circumstances" beyond the current and foreseeable inability to pay. According to this view, the "exceptional" circumstances must be something beyond the likely persistence of the debtor's financial problems, such as proof of serious illness, psychiatric problems, or disability of a dependent. The court in *In re Nys* rejected this narrow focus and instead developed a non-exclusive list of twelve "additional circumstances" that courts may consider in reviewing the second prong of the *Brunner* test.[55] Significantly, these factors include the "maximized income potential in the chosen educational field, and no other more lucrative job skills"; "limited number of years remaining in the debtor's work life to allow payment of the loan"; and "age or other factors that prevent retraining or relocation as a means for payment of the loan."[56] There is nothing particularly "exceptional" about these circumstances. These characteristics apply to many debtors who made reasonable decisions regarding a course of study, made reasonable career decisions after completing school and, despite being in good health and working hard, do not earn enough to pay for basic necessities for their family and still pay on a student loan. The Ninth Circuit decision goes some distance in recognizing the hardship that these debtors face and suggests a more flexible standard for evaluating their loan discharge claims.

The approaches taken by the courts in the recent decisions from the Ninth and Tenth Circuits offer a counterweight to those rulings that, in effect, force debtors to prove a negative with respect to their future prospects.[57] Under the second prong of *Brunner,* the debtor cannot fairly be called upon to prove to a "certainty" that every chance of improvement is impossible. Instead, the debtor should first show that he or she is unable to afford life's basic necessities: healthcare, transportation, food, housing, utilities, and care for oneself upon retirement. Then the debtor must show that it is more likely than not that these financial difficulties will continue for a substantial part of the loan repayment period.

7.2.4.2 Applying the Hardship Tests

The Sixth Circuit decision in *In re Cheesman* provides an example of the application of the undue hardship standard.[58] Though the Sixth Circuit did not adopt any specific test in *Cheesman*, it examined the three factors found in the *Brunner* test.

The court concluded first that the debtors could not maintain a minimal standard of living if they were required to repay their loans.[59] The debtors, though college-educated,

---

different courts apply the standard. The authors conclude that "those debtors granted a discharge and those denied a discharge predominantly resemble one another and that there are few statistically significant differences in the factual circumstances of the two groups." *Id.* at 412. Furthermore, the authors find that the extensive body of judicial interpretation built upon the "good faith" and "additional circumstances" prongs of *Brunner* have no concrete support in the legislative history of the "undue hardship" exception in § 523(a)(8). In practice, the *Brunner* "good faith" test has allowed courts to apply personal value judgments to conduct that is irrelevant to the "undue hardship" concept referenced in the statute. *Id.* at 514–19. Similarly, future ability to pay meant something quite different when *Brunner* was decided in 1987. At that time, all student loan debts that had been due for five years were dischargeable without reference to hardship. Thus, predicting the duration of future financial hardship was a more reasonable undertaking under the Code as it existed in 1987. Since then, with changes to the statute that ended fixed-time-period discharges and with the advent of ICRPs extending loan payments for up to twenty-five years, the requirement to predict the debtor's financial future has become an open field for the exercise of unlimited judicial discretion. *Id.* at 512–13, n.415.

51 Educational Credit Mgmt. Corp. v. Polleys, 356 F.3d 1302, 1309 (10th Cir. 2004).

52 *In re* Woody, 345 B.R. 246 (B.A.P. 10th Cir. 2006).

53 *Id.* at 259.

54 *In re* Nys, 446 F.3d 938 (9th Cir. 2006).

55 *Id.* at 947.

56 *Id.*

57 *See* note 49, *supra*, note 72, *infra*.

58 25 F.3d 356 (6th Cir. 1994). More recently, the Sixth Circuit has adopted the *Brunner* test. *See In re* Oyler, 397 F.3d 382 (6th Cir. 2005).

59 In proving that the debtor is maintaining a minimal standard of living

were barely above poverty level; even a frugal budget would require $400 a month more in expenses than their anticipated income.[60]

Second, the court concluded that it was not likely there would be significant improvement in their financial circumstances in the near future.[61] The court evaluated only realistic expectations rather than speculation concerning future prospects,[62] noting that the debtors "chose to work in

---

living, it may be helpful in some cases to present evidence that the debtor's actual living expenses are below certain national standards for allowable living expenses. *See* Internal Revenue Serv., U.S. Dep't of the Treasury, *National Standards for Allowable Living Expenses*, *at* www.irs.gov/individuals/article/0,id=96543,00.html. On the other hand, debtors should be able to show reasonable and necessary expenses that may exceed those used for IRS collection purposes. *See In re* Howe, 319 B.R. 886 (B.A.P. 9th Cir. 2005) (reversing bankruptcy court for adhering to IRS guidelines when debtor had reasonable medical expenses over the guideline amounts); *In re* Albee, 338 B.R. 407 (Bankr. W.D. Mo. 2006) (lender cannot rely on IRS guidelines only to show certain expenses over guidelines and ignore those below the guidelines). For information about food budgets, also visit the U.S. Department of Agriculture, Center for Nutrition Policy and Promotion, website at www.usda.gov/cnpp/using3.html.

60   *See also In re* Pena, 155 F.3d 1108 (9th Cir. 1998) (debtors' monthly deficit of $41 after deducting average expenses from net income cannot support minimal standard of living); *In re* Hornsby, 144 F.3d 433 (6th Cir. 1998) (debtors did not need to be at poverty level to show undue hardship); *In re* Murphy, 305 B.R. 780 (Bankr. E.D. Va. 2004); *In re* Alston, 297 B.R. 410 (Bankr. E.D. Pa. 2003) (debtor's use of Earned Income Tax Credit refunds of approximately $3000 to $5000 for necessary home repairs and furniture, expenses that are normally part of a monthly budget, did not establish debtor was living beyond a minimal standard of living); *In re* McGinnis, 289 B.R. 257 (Bankr. M.D. Ga. 2003) (debtor's income can exceed poverty level and still satisfy *Brunner* test); *In re* Ivory, 269 B.R. 890 (Bankr. N.D. Ala. 2001) (applying both a subjective and objective evaluation of debtor's income and expenses and citing studies showing that income far higher than poverty level needed for minimal standard of living). Courts have generally refused to find ordinary household expenses, if not excessive, to be inconsistent with a minimal standard of living. *In re* Frushour, 433 F.3d 393 (4th Cir. 2005) ($95.00 monthly expense for cable and internet not unreasonable, but debt found nondischargeable on other grounds); *In re* Allen, 329 B.R. 544 (Bankr. W.D. Pa. 2005) ($111.67 monthly payment to retirement account is a reasonable expense); *In re* Fullbright, 319 B.R. 650 (Bankr. D. Mont. 2005) ($430 monthly church tithing expense is excessive); *In re* Innes, 284 B.R. 496 (D. Kan. 2002) (modest holiday gifts for the debtors' children, a "single frugal" summer vacation, and the debtors' use of a tax refund to make home repairs not incompatible with a minimal standard of living); *In re* Cheney, 280 B.R. 648 (N.D. Iowa 2002) ("lifestyle choices" should not be questioned if expenses are not excessive); *In re* Durrani, 311 B.R. 496 (Bankr. N.D. Ill. 2004), *aff'd*, 320 B.R. 357 (N.D. Ill. 2005) ($52.00-per-month cable bill not inappropriate); *In re* Myers, 280 B.R. 416 (Bankr. S.D. Ohio 2002) (expenses for cell phone, satellite T.V., and three vehicles were within minimum standards of living for family with nine children); *In re* Lewis, 276 B.R. 912 (Bankr. C.D. Ill. 2002) (debtor not required to purchase less expensive auto). In considering a student's ability to repay a student loan in cases in which the student does not file bankruptcy with his or her spouse, courts frequently consider the non-filing spouse's income and contributions to household expenses. *See, e.g., In re* Bray, 332 B.R. 186, 192–93 (Bankr. W.D. Mo. 2005) ("Overwhelming authority requires that a court consider the spouse's income."); *In re* Dolan, 256 B.R. 230 (Bankr. D. Mass. 2000); *In re* Greco, 251

B.R. 670 (Bankr. E.D. Pa. 2000); *In re* Koch, 144 B.R. 959 (Bankr. W.D. Pa. 1992); *In re* Albert, 25 B.R. 98 (Bankr. N.D. Ohio 1982). A bankruptcy appellate panel has recently ruled that the bankruptcy court must consider the income of the debtor's long-term domestic partner. *In re* Lorenz, 337 B.R. 423 (B.A.P. 1st Cir. 2006). Expenses for a child in college have been considered reasonable household expenditures, *In re* Reed, 2005 WL 1398479 (Bankr D. Vt. 2005), while necessary medical expenses for an emancipated twenty-four year old child have been excluded. *In re* Gill, 326 B.R. 611 (Bankr. E.D. Va. 2005). One court found it appropriate to consider the debtor's expenditures for care of her mother. *In re* Doe, 325 B.R. 69 (Bankr. S.D.N.Y. 2005) (applying IRS definition of dependent).

61   *See also In re* Cline, 248 B.R. 347 (B.A.P. 8th Cir. 2000) (single woman unable to increase income would need decades to repay $53,000 in loans); Queen v. Pennsylvania H.E.A.A., 210 B.R. 677 (E.D. Pa. 1997), *aff'd without opinion sub nom. In re* Mayer, 156 F.3d 1225 (3d Cir. 1998) (discharge granted to single-parent manual laborer with uncompleted masters degree; any salary increase from full-time work would be offset by day-care costs); *In re* Thomson, 234 B.R. 506 (Bankr. D. Mont. 1999) (discharge granted to veteran with permanent and total disability); *In re* Kasey, 227 B.R. 473 (Bankr. W.D. Va. 1998) (discharge granted for single mother suffering from depression with three young children, unlikely to finish education, who had attempted payments), *aff'd in unpublished opinion*, 187 F.3d 630 (4th Cir. 1999); *In re* Bessette, 226 B.R. 103 (Bankr. D. Idaho 1998) (chapter 7 debtor had two minor dependents, limited job skills, and limited potential for increasing income); *In re* Young, 225 B.R. 312 (Bankr. E.D. Pa. 1998) (discharge granted when court also considered race and age as factors in determining whether hardship conditions were likely to persist); *In re* Lebovits, 223 B.R. 265 (Bankr. E.D.N.Y. 1998) (discharge granted to parent with M.S.W. with seven children when religious convictions required parochial schooling); *In re* Doherty, 219 B.R. 665 (Bankr. W.D.N.Y. 1998) (chapter 7 debtor satisfied her burden of proving that her present inability to repay the debt was likely to continue, presenting undisputed evidence of an incurable mental illness that was the cause of present inability to earn a sufficient wage); *In re* Shankwiler, 208 B.R. 701 (Bankr. C.D. Cal. 1997); *In re* Dotson-Cannon, 206 B.R. 530 (Bankr. W.D. Mo. 1997) (student loans discharged when single 51-year-old woman with B.S. in public administration was only able to obtain $7/hour clerical work); *In re* Coats, 214 B.R. 397 (Bankr. N.D. Okla. 1997); *In re* Windland, 201 B.R. 178 (Bankr. N.D. Ohio 1996); *In re* Derby, 199 B.R. 328 (Bankr. W.D. Pa. 1996); Hoyle v. Pennsylvania Higher Educ. Assistance Agency, 199 B.R. 518 (Bankr. E.D. Pa. 1996); *In re* Fuertes, 198 B.R. 379 (Bankr. S.D. Fla. 1996). *But see In re* Garybush, 265 B.R. 587 (Bankr. S.D. Ohio 2001) (no discharge when family income should improve because debtor can resume part-time employment when youngest child enters school); *In re* Vinci, 232 B.R. 644 (Bankr. E.D. Pa. 1999); *In re* Pantelis, 229 B.R. 716 (Bankr. N.D. Ohio 1999) (no discharge when no documentation of physical disability and no showing of effective job search); *In re* Elmore, 230 B.R. 22 (Bankr. D. Conn. 1999); *In re* McLeod, 197 B.R. 624 (Bankr. N.D. Ohio 1996).

62   *See also In re* Doherty, 219 B.R. 665 (Bankr. W.D.N.Y. 1998)

worthwhile albeit low-paying professions."[63] And, finally, the court concluded that the consumers had acted in good faith, after limiting that inquiry to a finding that they had attempted to make minimal payments on the loan over a period of several years[64] and that they had no prospect of embarking on lucrative careers in the private sector.

However, in a more troubling aspect of the decision, the court concluded that a bankruptcy court has the discretion to defer making a final determination about the dischargeability of a student loan for as long as eighteen months after the case is heard in order to determine if the debtor's situation has improved. This conclusion is hard to accept as proper. A finding of undue hardship always calls for a prediction by a court. A deferral process shirks the courts' responsibility to make the necessary forecast of the debtors' ability to pay during the remaining repayment period and delays the debtors' fresh start.[65] Although, as the dissent points out, in

some circumstances a delay may result in an improved opportunity to establish undue hardship, more often the delay will create an unnecessary uncertainty about the debtor's ongoing responsibilities.[66]

7.2.4.3 Other Hardship Factors

The student's undue hardship argument may be stronger when the student loan arose from a private vocational school that closed down or defrauded the student. Absent a meaningful educational experience, the student has no job skills and, because of the default, is ineligible for future government educational loans. If a discharge is not granted, the student will not be able to go back to school and will not be able to obtain a decent paying job, making repayment now or in the future an undue hardship.

In addition, the nature of the schooling will be relevant to whether the education enabled or would enable the debtor to obtain substantially higher income.[67] Another bankruptcy court has put it this way:

(court took judicial notice of prognosis for debtor suffering from bipolar disorder).

63 *In re* Cheesman, 25 F.3d 360 (6th Cir. June 2, 1994). *See also In re* Gerhardt, 348 F.3d 89 (5th Cir. 2003) (debtor failed second prong of *Brunner* test by choosing to work only as a cellist in the low-paying field in which he was trained); *In re* Oyler, 300 B.R. 255 (B.A.P. 6th Cir. 2003) (debtor's choice to work in low-paying field as minister not by itself evidence of bad faith and should not be used against debtor under undue hardship test), *rev'd*, 397 F.3d 382 (6th Cir. 2005) (pastor failed to meet *Brunner* test because his decision not to maximize his earnings, though commendable, was voluntarily made).

64 *See also* Educational Credit Mgmt. Corp. v. Polleys, 356 F.3d 1302 (10th Cir. 2004) (failure to make any payments, by itself, does not establish lack of good faith); *In re* Alston, 297 B.R. 410 (Bankr. E.D. Pa. 2003); *In re* McGinnis, 289 B.R. 257 (Bankr. M.D. Ga. 2003) (actual payments not required to show good faith, and requests for forbearances not evidence of bad faith). *Cf. In re* Innes, 284 B.R. 496 (D. Kan. 2002) (finding of good faith effort not precluded by debtor's failure to make payments, as debtor lacked sufficient income to make minimum monthly payments); *In re* Nary, 253 B.R. 752 (N.D. Tex. 2000). The test requiring a good faith effort to pay the loan does not require that repayment actually occurred, although it may require some effort to deal with the loan prior to bankruptcy. *In re* Ivory, 269 B.R. 890 (Bankr. N.D. Ala. 2001) (no bad faith when debtor never had ability to repay loan); *In re* Coats, 214 B.R. 397 (Bankr. N.D. Okla. 1997); *In re* Maulin, 190 B.R. 153 (Bankr. W.D.N.Y. 1995). *But cf.* Tennessee Student Assistance Corp. v. Hornsby (*In re* Hornsby), 144 F.3d 433 (6th Cir. 1998) (debtors had not made any payments; court holds that loan is nondischargeable because they had not done everything possible to minimize expenses and maximize income). Courts should consider any good faith efforts made to pay prior student loans that are subsequently consolidated and not simply consider the debtor's repayment efforts on the consolidation loan. *See In re* Lewis, 276 B.R. 912 (Bankr. C.D. Ill. 2002) (court rejected application of court decisions construing effect of loan consolidation on counting of seven-year period under former § 523(a)(8)).

65 The pertinent time frame for the court's prediction of future prospects under the second prong of the *Brunner* test is the remaining period for repayment under the loan obligations. One court has held that a consolidation loan that effectively restruc-

tured a student loan with the same lender at the end of the original ten-year term did not "restart the clock" on a new fifteen-year repayment period for purposes of considering future inability to repay. *See In re* Ordaz, 287 B.R. 912 (Bankr. C.D. Ill. 2002). *See also In re* Coatney, 345 B.R. 905 (Bankr. C.D. Ill. 2006) (court defers ruling on dischargeability because debtor did not present evidence of original loan term; time frame under ICRP not relevant to second prong of *Brunner* test).

66 *See In re* Shirzadi, 269 B.R. 664 (Bankr. S.D. Ind. 2001) (since hardship discharge denied under *Brunner* test because debtor failed to maximize income by pursuing child support, determination of whether debtor should be granted partial discharge deferred for nine months to get update on her efforts to collect support); *In re* Jones v. Catholic Univ. of Am., 1997 Bankr. LEXIS 92, 1997 WL 52188 (Bankr. D.D.C. Feb. 4, 1997) (debts discharged for eighteen months, after which the debtor would become re-obligated; debtor could amend the judgment as the eighteen months approached with proof that present financial situation would persist). *See also* § 7.2.4.5, *infra*.

67 United Student Aid Funds v. Pena (*In re* Pena), 155 F.3d 1108 (9th Cir. 1998) (value of education relevant to future ability to pay student loans); *In re* Carter, 295 B.R. 555 (Bankr. W.D. Pa. 2003) (debtor never completed program for position as medical assistant); *In re* Lewis, 276 B.R. 912 (Bankr. C.D. Ill. 2002) (lack of benefit from uncompleted junior college program considered under second prong of *Brunner* test); *In re* Evans, 131 B.R. 372 (Bankr. S.D. Ohio 1991) (trade school education in word-processing did not improve debtor's ability to repay her student loans); Price v. Bureau of Student Fin. Assistance (*In re* Price), 25 B.R. 256, 258 (Bankr. W.D. Mo. 1982). *See also* Correll v. Union Nat'l Bank of Pittsburgh, 105 B.R. 302 (Bankr. W.D. Pa. 1989); Carter v. Kent State Univ. (*In re* Carter), 29 B.R. 228 (Bankr. N.D. Ohio 1983); Love v. Department of Health, Education & Welfare (*In re* Love), 28 B.R. 475 (Bankr. S.D. Ind. 1983); Ford v. New York State Higher Educ. Servs. Corp. (*In re* Ford), 22 B.R. 442 (Bankr. W.D.N.Y. 1982); Littell v. State of Oregon (*In re* Littell), 6 B.R. 85 (Bankr. D. Or. 1980); *In re* Johnson, 5 B.C.D. 532 (Bankr. E.D. Pa. 1979). *But see In re* Chapman, 238 B.R. 450 (Bankr. W.D. Mo. 1999) (court rejected debtor's argument that his loans were not really student loans because he did not receive any educational benefit; in

There is thus great pressure and temptation on the part of college authorities to encourage students to apply for loans and grant them when in effect it is not a sound economic thing to do. This should be a substantial factor in determining whether a student loan should be dischargeable. Was the student inveigled into obtaining the loan and taking particular courses in college when the college authorities should have known that upon graduation from college the student had little chance of obtaining employment in that field?[68]

Yet another bankruptcy court has used an investment analysis. Education is an investment with the hope that the student will obtain a higher-paying job in the future. For example, it would be inequitable for a doctor to discharge his medical school debts just before embarking on a well-paid career made possible because of his educational loans. But this exception should not apply when a student attends a cosmetology school and the schooling did not increase the student's job skills in any significant amount.[69]

The fact that the student was swindled by the school may also be relevant to the consumer's good faith in seeking to discharge the loan. The student may not have felt that the obligation was owed in circumstances under which the school referred the consumer to the lender and the school had defrauded the student.

Courts have also considered whether there should be a different hardship test applied in chapter 13 cases. Sometimes creditors argue against a chapter 13 undue hardship discharge for a student loan on the basis that a debtor can only propose a chapter 13 plan if the debtor has disposable income. If the debtor has disposable income, can it be an undue hardship to repay the student loan? Courts generally reject this argument and apply the same undue hardship standards for chapter 13 and 7 bankruptcies.[70]

Finally, debtors seeking a hardship discharge before a sympathetic bankruptcy court that is inclined to grant a discharge must still be vigilant in proving all the elements of the appropriate hardship test.[71] Appellate courts in several recent cases have reversed judgments in favor of the debtors on the basis that the record evidence failed to support findings that the debtors' financial circumstances were likely to persist.[72]

Evidence of the debtor's future financial prospects can be based on the debtor's own testimony. For example, courts have not required the introduction of expert testimony to prove that a debtor's financial outlook and earning capacity have been impaired by the debtor's psychological, emotional, or substance dependency problems.[73] But when the

---

applying *Brunner* and totality-of-circumstances tests, court failed to find undue hardship); *In re* O'Flaherty, 204 B.R. 793 (Bankr. N.D. Ala. 1997) (in applying *Brunner* test, court considered debtor's current income and expenses rather than his ability to utilize education he acquired through loan; debtor was unable to fulfill goal of ordination as Catholic priest).

68 Littell v. State of Oregon (*In re* Littell), 6 B.R. 85 (Bankr. D. Or. 1980). *See also* Correll v. Union Nat'l Bank of Pittsburgh, 105 B.R. 302 (Bankr. W.D. Pa. 1989).

69 Powelson v. Stewart School of Hairstyling, Inc., 25 B.R. 274 (Bankr. D. Neb. 1982). *See also In re* Law, 159 B.R. 287 (Bankr. D.S.D. 1993) (debtor obtained no benefit from $20,000 student loan for two-and-a-half weeks of flight training).

70 *In re* Strauss, 216 B.R. 638 (Bankr. N.D. Cal. 1998); *In re* Oswalt, 215 B.R. 337 (Bankr. W.D.N.Y. 1997) (chapter 13 debtor entitled to undue hardship discharge); *In re* Goranson, 183 B.R. 52 (Bankr. W.D.N.Y. 1995); *In re* Evans, 131 B.R. 372 (Bankr. S.D. Ohio 1991). *See also In re* Elebrashy, 189 B.R. 922 (Bankr. N.D. Ohio 1995).

71 The debtor has the burden of proof on all elements of the hardship test. Goulet v. Educational Credit Management Corp., 284 F.3d 773 (7th Cir. 2002); *In re* Rifino, 245 F.3d 1083 (9th Cir. 2001); *In re* Faish, 72 F.3d 298 (3d Cir. 1995), *cert. denied sub nom.* Nowland v. United States, 534 U.S. 927 (2001). *See In re* Nys, 446 F.3d 938 (9th Cir. 2005) (in assessing debtor's future prospects, court will not presume that the present inability to make payments will continue; rather, debtor has burden to provide additional evidence to show that the inability to pay is likely to persist)

72 *In re* Frushour, 433 F.3d 393 (4th Cir. 2005) (reversing lower courts, the court of appeals opines that childcare costs and the need to replace old car, among other barriers, will not deter debtor, a single mother, from finding a better-paying job; dissent strongly criticizes reversal of lower courts' fact findings); *In re* Tirch, 409 F.3d 677 (6th Cir. 2005) (debtor presented insufficient evidence of extent and duration of claimed impairments); *In re* Oyler, 397 F.3d 382 (6th Cir. 2005) (debtor fails second *Brunner* prong because he chose to work as a low-paid pastor when he should have chosen work that pays more); *In re* O'Hearn, 339 F.3d 559 (7th Cir. 2003) (vacating bankruptcy court decision based on factual inferences not supported by record); Goulet v. Educational Credit Mgmt. Corp., 284 F.3d 773 (7th Cir. 2002) (record devoid of evidence that debtor's problems with alcoholism and a felony conviction, which predated several of his student loan obligations, were "insurmountable," or that they prevented debtor from being gainfully employed); *In re* Rifino, 245 F.3d 1083 (9th Cir. 2001) (debtor failed to prove that her financial circumstances were likely to persist by rebutting creditor's testimony concerning the debtors' earning potential as a social worker), *cert. denied sub nom.* Nowland v. United States, 534 U.S. 927 (2001); *In re* Brightful, 267 F.3d 324 (3d Cir. 2001) (debtor failed to introduce evidence that her mental and emotional condition prevented her from using her skills as a legal secretary to secure full-time employment). Student debtors should also carefully evaluate whether to file a cross-appeal in cases in which they have been granted less than a full discharge and the student loan creditor has filed an appeal. *See In re* Alderete, 308 B.R. 495 (B.A.P. 10th Cir. 2004) (BAP found that entire debt should have been discharged but was compelled to affirm bankruptcy court decision not to discharge loan principal because debtor had not filed cross-appeal), *rev'd in part on other grounds*, 412 F.3d 1200 (10th Cir. 2005) (bankruptcy court cannot order partial discharge absent a finding of undue hardship).

73 *In re* Brightful, 267 F.3d 324 (3d Cir. 2001) (bankruptcy judge may make reasonable conclusions concerning debtor's emotional state without expert testimony); *In re* Pena, 155 F.3d 1108 (9th Cir. 1998) (debtor's testimony about mental impairment, combined with evidence of her Social Security disability award related to condition, are sufficient evidence to establish medical

debtor can present corroborating testimony that his or her condition is not likely to improve, either from friends, family members or treating professionals, this certainly will improve the likelihood of obtaining a hardship discharge and having it survive on appeal.[74]

7.2.4.4 Relevance of Older Loans (Seven Years or More) in Making Undue Hardship Claims

The elimination of the seven-year discharge rule means that more debtors will seek discharge based on undue hardship. There have been few hardship cases involving loans more than seven years old since, previously. These debtors were able to get discharges without a showing of hardship. However, the fact that a loan remains unpaid after seven years should influence evaluation of the standards in several ways.

Previous inability to pay over seven years is solid evidence of the second factor discussed in *Brunner*, that financial problems are likely to persist into the future.[75] To the

extent the court is being asked to make a prediction, there could be little evidence that is more relevant than past experience.

A debtor's history over seven years would also be important to the analysis of good faith (the *Brunner* third factor).[76] Presumably most debtors with older student loans will have made payment during some part of the seven-year period. Every effort should be made to explain why the debtor was able to make payments at one time but is no longer able to do so now. The goal should be to establish that the debtor "tried but failed" to make payments for a valid reason.

Finally, judges may be more willing to discharge older student loans. Judges should be reminded that, since there is no statute of limitations for collection of most student loans, failure to make an undue hardship discharge may mean that debtors take their student loans to their graves.

7.2.4.5 Partial Discharge or Modification of Student Loan

In cases involving large student loan debts owed by middle-class debtors, courts have been exploring the possibility of offering a partial hardship discharge. The court may find that the student has future earnings potential but that the amount of debt is still excessive. In this situation, several courts have discharged only part of the debt and require the balance to be paid out over time.[77] The recent trend is for

---

condition); *In re* Barrett, 337 B.R. 896 (B.A.P. 6th Cir. 2006) (court takes judicial notice of National Institute of Health literature on debtor's medical condition); *In re* Hertzel, 329 B.R. 221 (B.A.P. 6th Cir. 2005) (court takes judicial notice of well known medical facts about debtor's condition of multiple sclerosis); *In re* Cline, 248 B.R. 347 (B.A.P. 8th Cir. 2000) (court's findings were not unreliable simply because no expert testimony was presented that debtor was clinically disabled); *In re* Cheney, 280 B.R. 648 (N.D. Iowa 2002) (debtor not required to submit expert evidence of clinical diagnoses of depression or mental disability, particularly when debtor's testimony about her condition was not rebutted); Mosko v. American Educ. Servs., 2006 WL 995854 (Bankr. M.D.N.C. 2006), *aff'd*, 2006 WL 2668437 (M.D.N.C. Sept. 15, 2006) (corroborating medical expert not required); *In re* Mosley, 330 B.R. 832 (Bankr. N.D. Ga. 2005) (after review of cases on medical corroboration in student loan discharge cases, court find that homeless veteran, appearing *pro se*, met *Brunner* standards through his own testimony regarding his physical and emotional ailments). *But see In re* Nash, 446 F.3d 188 (1st Cir. 2006) (to prevail in discharge action, debtor must present opinion of qualified expert concerning the expected duration of her psychological disorders); *In re* Burton, 339 B.R. 856 (Bankr. E.D. Va. 2006) (collecting cases on use of medical evidence in dischargeability cases, declining to give corroborating weight to social security disability determination); *In re* Burkhead, 304 B.R. 560 (Bankr. D. Mass. 2004) (although debtor documented through medical records that her medical condition was serious, she failed to testify or provide expert testimony that her condition would persist).

74 *See In re* Reynolds, 425 F.3d 526 (8th Cir. 2005) (extensive testimony of debtor corroborated by testimony of psychiatric expert witness as to her medical and psychological condition and by attorney expert as to debtor's inability to gain admission to the Minnesota bar); *In re* Kelsey, 287 B.R. 132 (Bankr. D. Vt. 2001) (treating psychiatrist testified at length and established that it was more likely than not that the debtor's debilitating condition would persist for a significant portion of the repayment period).

75 *In re* Lewis, 276 B.R. 912 (Bankr. C.D. Ill. 2002) (based on "temporal element" found in *Brunner's* second prong, older

student loans more likely to be discharged).

76 At least one court has commented that the "good faith" and "policy" factors are less relevant following the elimination of the seven-year discharge rule, as courts previously were concerned that debtors who sought a discharge before the seven-year period had passed "might not yet have given repayment efforts a chance." *In re* Kopf, 245 B.R. 731, 741 (Bankr. D. Me. 2000).

77 *See In re* Hornsby, 144 F.3d 433 (6th Cir. 1998) (partial discharge is permitted under court's equitable powers); *In re* Saxman, 325 F.3d 1168 (9th Cir. 2003) (bankruptcy court may exercise equitable power to partially discharge student loan if debtor satisfies undue hardship test as to portion of debt to be discharged); *In re* Blair, 291 B.R. 514 (B.A.P. 9th Cir. 2003); *In re* Nary, 253 B.R. 752 (N.D. Tex. 2000); *In re* Kapinos, 243 B.R. 271 (W.D. Va. 2000); *In re* Brown, 239 B.R. 204 (S.D. Cal. 1999); *In re* Muto, 216 B.R. 325 (Bankr. N.D.N.Y. 1996); *In re* Ammirati, 187 B.R. 902 (D.S.C. 1995), *aff'd with unpublished opinion*, 85 F.3d 615 (4th Cir. 1996); *In re* Siegel, 282 B.R. 629 (Bankr. N.D. Ohio 2002) (based on debtor's $400 per month in disposable income, discharge allowed for $13,500 out of $30,000 debt, with $16,500 balance to be paid with no interest over twelve years); *In re* Barron, 264 B.R. 833 (Bankr. E.D. Tex. 2001) (bankruptcy court may use equitable power under § 105(a) of Bankruptcy Code to grant partial discharge and restructure student loan debt); *In re* Lohr, 252 B.R. 84 (Bankr. E.D. Va. 2000) (discharge allowed for $30,500 out of $35,000 in student loans; recommendation that $4500 balance be paid at 7% interest amortized over ten years); *In re* Rivers, 213 B.R. 616 (Bankr. S.D. Ga. 1997) ($40,000 out of $55,000 consolidated student loans held nondischargeable); *In re* Wetzel, 213 B.R. 220 (Bankr. N.D.N.Y. 1996); *In re* Raimondo, 183 B.R.

courts that allow partial discharges to require consumer to show undue hardship for the portion of the loans to be discharged.[78] Another approach is for the court to discharge some, but not all, of a debtor's individual student loans. This approach rejects a pro rata reduction but still offers the debtor some relief by applying the hardship test on a loan-by-loan basis.[79]

Other courts have used the dischargeability proceeding to restructure the loan, reducing the amount owed and establishing a modified repayment schedule. For example, courts have discharged collection fees and accrued interest and delayed for several years the obligation to make payments, during which time no further interest would accrue.[80]

Despite recent interest in partial discharges, the view most consistent with the statutory language is that courts should determine simply whether the debt is or is not dischargeable.[81] Courts that have created the middle ground approach of a partial discharge should not apply it to low-income debtors with limited future earnings potential. The partial discharge should be relevant only to debtors with significant future earnings potential but with extremely large student loan debt loads, such as $50,000 to $100,000.[82] If repayment of a relatively small student loan will likely be a hardship for the foreseeable future, the debt should be completely discharged to allow the debtor a fresh start.

7.2.4.6 Effect of Income-Contingent Repayment Plans

In recent cases, student loan authorities and the Department of Education have argued that courts need not find that repayment will impose an undue hardship on students because the Department's regulations provide for payment relief in the form of income-contingent repayment plans (ICRP).[83] Several courts of appeals have ruled that, while participation in an ICRP is not required to satisfy the *Brunner* "good faith" test, the debtor's response to the availability of an ICRP may be treated as an important factor

---

677 (Bankr. W.D.N.Y. 1995); *In re* Fox, 189 B.R. 115 (Bankr. N.D. Ohio 1995); *In re* Gammoh 174 B.R. 707 (Bankr. N.D. Ohio 1994). *See also* Graves v. Myrvang, 232 F.3d 1116 (9th Cir. 2000) (Ninth Circuit applies *Hornsby* analysis to dischargeability provision relating to child support).

78 *See, e.g., In re* Alderete, 412 F.3d 1200 (10th Cir. 2005); *In re* Miller, 377 F.3d 616 (6th Cir. 2004); *In re* Cox, 338 F.3d 1238 (11th Cir. 2003); *In re* Saxman, 325 F.3d 1168 (9th Cir. 2003).

79 Educational Credit Mgmt. Corp. v. Kelly, 312 B.R. 200 (B.A.P. 1st Cir. 2004) (based on "such debt" language in § 523(a)(8), court adopted "hybrid approach," which provides that undue hardship test should be applied independently as to each loan, absent evidence that loans were consolidated); *In re* Andresen, 232 B.R. 127 (B.A.P. 8th Cir. 1999) (affirms bankruptcy court's discharge of two of three loans); *In re* Allen, 329 B.R. 544 (Bankr. W.D. Pa. 2005) (the larger of two loans discharged when debtor could divert her $130 monthly church tithing contribution to pay the smaller loan); *In re* Myers, 280 B.R. 416 (Bankr. S.D. Ohio 2002) (three loans totaling $59,438 discharged and three smaller loans totaling $5472 found nondischargeable); *In re* Morris, 277 B.R. 910 (Bankr. W.D. Ark. 2002) (largest student loan in amount of $65,912 discharged but not smaller loans totaling $41,741); *In re* Grigas, 252 B.R. 866 (Bankr. D.N.H. 2000) (based on court's finding that debtor could pay $224 per month for fifteen years, debtor's fifteen student loans should be analyzed in chronological order so that only those that can first be fully repaid within fifteen years will be excepted from discharge); *In re* Shankwiler, 208 B.R. 701 (Bankr. C.D. Cal. 1997) (holding that each loan should be treated separately); *In re* Hinkle, 200 B.R. 690 (Bankr. W.D. Wash. 1996) (discharging three out of six student loans).

80 *See In re* Fields, 326 B.R. 676 (B.A.P. 6th Cir. 2005) (for debtor with $129,801 in student loans, court reduces current monthly payments to amount being garnished and abates accrual and capitalization of interest for six years, with twenty-five-year payment term remaining in effect); *In re* Davis, 336 B.R. 604 (Bankr. W.D.N.Y. 2006) (student loan debt reduced to an amount based on calculation of what creditor could obtain from debtor by garnishment and attachment under state law for twenty years; the indebtedness in excess of this amount is discharged); *In re* Grove, 323 B.R. 216 (Bankr. N.D. Ohio 2005) (any student loan debt still owing at end of twenty-five-year ICRP is discharged in order to avoid potential tax assessment); *In re* Shirzadi, 269 B.R. 664 (Bankr. S.D. Ind. 2001) (court reduced monthly payment amount and suspended accrual of interest and late fees for nine months pending rehearing on whether debtor entitled to partial discharge); *In re* Garybush, 265 B.R. 587 (Bankr. S.D. Ohio 2001) (court discharged all interest, costs, and fees, granted four-year deferment on pay-

ments, and set monthly amount to be paid on principal after deferment); *In re* Kapinos, 253 B.R. 709 (Bankr. W.D. Va. 2000) (discharging accrued interest and future interest for period of five years, at which time debtor may reopen case to seek further discharge relief); *In re* Griffin, 197 B.R. 144 (Bankr. E.D. Okla. 1996) (discharging accrued interest and attorney fees on loans but not principal); *In re* Heckathorn, 199 B.R. 188 (Bankr. N.D. Okla. 1996) (court found debt nondischargeable but deferred repayment for five years and suspended accrual of interest for three years); *In re* O'Donnell, 198 B.R. 1 (Bankr. D.N.H. 1996); *In re* Mayes, 183 B.R. 261 (Bankr. E.D. Okla. 1995).

81 Courts rejecting partial discharges have done so largely based on a strict construction of § 523(a)(8)—that the statutory language does not use the phrase "to the extent" as found in other sections providing for partial discharge. Educational Credit Mgmt. Corp. v. Carter, 279 B.R. 872 (M.D. Ga. 2002) (bankruptcy court lacks authority under § 523(a)(8) and § 105(a) to grant partial discharge). *See also In re* Cox, 338 B.R. 1238 (11th Cir. 2003) (bankruptcy court's equitable powers under § 105 cannot override plain language of § 523(a)(8)); *In re* Pincus, 280 B.R. 303 (Bankr. S.D.N.Y. 2002) (no language in § 523(a)(8) permits granting of partial discharge); *In re* Brown, 249 B.R. 525 (Bankr. W.D. Mo. 2000) (court grants full discharge after determining that Bankruptcy Code precludes partial discharge); *In re* Young, 225 B.R. 312 (Bankr. E.D. Pa. 1998); *In re* Skaggs, 196 B.R. 865 (Bankr. W.D. Okla. 1996); *In re* Hawkins, 187 B.R. 294 (Bankr. N.D. Iowa 1995); *In re* Barrows, 182 B.R. 640 (Bankr. D.N.H. 1994). *Cf. In re* Richardson, 334 B.R. 316 (Bankr. D. Mass. 2005) (while court would allow discharge of separate individual loans, a single consolidated loan cannot be subject to partial discharge—so court discharges entire loan for debtor who meets undue hardship test).

82 *Cf. In re* Heckathorn, 199 B.R. 188 (Bankr. N.D. Okla. 1996).

83 *See* 20 U.S.C. §§ 1078(m), 1087a; 34 C.F.R. § 685.209(a)(2)(i); Ch. 8, *infra*.

in the evaluation.[84] In granting only a partial discharge, one court found that the debtor had an ability to repay some of her student loans because she could enter into an ICRP providing for $56-per-month payments for twenty-five years.[85] Courts applying "totality of the circumstances" test recognize the option to participate in an ICRP as a factor in determining undue hardship, but not a determining one.[86]

While some courts may embrace arguments relating to the availability of these payment plans, the Bankruptcy Code undeniably provides an opportunity for a debtor to obtain an absolute and immediate discharge of student loans if the statutory conditions are met,[87] and no comparable discharge is available under the Department's regulations and administrative collection programs.[88] At least one court has concluded that such payment plans should not present an opportunity for courts to abdicate their obligation to apply the bankruptcy law as written.[89]

---

84 *In re* Nys, 446 F.3d 938, 947 (9th Cir. 2005) (debtor's consideration of ICRP option is an important indicator of good faith); *In re* Frushour, 433 F.3d 393,402 (4th Cir. 2005) (important component of good faith inquiry); *In re* Alderete, 412 F.3d 1200,1206 (10th Cir. 2005) (carries "significant weight" in evaluating good faith); *In re* Tirch, 409 F.3d 677, 682 (6th Cir. 2005) (decision not to take advantage of ICRP probative of debtor's intent to repay). The Fourth Circuit has held that the availability of an ICRP should be considered under the "unconscionability" standard for HEAL loans. U.S. Dep't of Health & Human Servs. v. Smitley, 347 F.3d 109 (4th Cir. 2003). *See also In re* Hollins, 286 B.R. 310 (Bankr. N.D. Tex. 2002) (debtor's eligibility for ICRP precluded her from satisfying second prong of *Brunner* test); *In re* Douglass, 237 B.R. 652 (Bankr. N.D. Ohio 1999) (debtor who failed to make any payments on student loans or negotiate an ICRP denied discharge based on lack of good faith effort to repay under *Brunner* test). *But see* Educational Credit Mgmt. Corp. v. Porrazzo, 307 B.R. 345 (Bankr. D. Conn. 2004) (no lack of good faith as debtor's decision to reject ICRP was appropriate given that regular status reviews over twenty-five-year period would exacerbate his anxiety disorder).

85 *In re* DeRose, 316 B.R. 606 (Bankr. W.D.N.Y. 2004) (debtor did not prove undue hardship because she could repay through an ICRP); *In re* Chambers, 239 B.R. 767 (Bankr. N.D. Ohio 1999). *Cf. In re* Durrani, 311 B.R. 496 (Bankr. N.D. Ill. 2004), *aff'd*, 320 B.R. 357 (N.D. Ill. 2005) (first prong of *Brunner* test looks at whether debtor can maintain minimal standard of living and "repay this loan," not whether the debtor has some surplus income available to pay accruing interest or some portion of the loan).

86 *In re* Cumberworth, 347 B.R. 652 (B.A.P. 8th Cir. 2006) (recognizing the standards for eligibility for an ICRP and the test for "undue hardship" under § 523(a)(8) as two separate and distinct determinations); *In re* Standfuss, 245 B.R. 356 (Bankr. E.D. Mo. 2000) ("flexibility" of ICRP plan considered in determining debtors' ability to repay student loan). *See also In re* Ford, 269 B.R. 673 (B.A.P. 8th Cir. 2001) (availability of ICRP is merely one factor considered in totality-of-circumstances test and not determinative in case in which ICRP would result in 62-year-old woman with arthritic condition carrying large and increasing debt that would not be forgiven until she is 87 years old).

87 *See In re* Barrett, 337 B.R. 896 (B.A.P. 6th Cir. 2006) (no evidence of Congressional intent that ICRP program eliminates discharge option, particularly when there is no reasonable likelihood that the debtor will ever be able to repay the loan); *In re* Dufresne, 341 B.R. 391 (Bankr. D. Mass. 2006) (unlike discharge, the ICRP "simply condemns a debtor whose honesty and efforts are not otherwise in question to privation beyond

reasonable limits—to an ever-present and ever-growing mountain of debt which, given her reasonably foreseeable financial prospects (derived from her actual past and present circumstances), will not likely ever be repaid."); *In re* Alston, 297 B.R. 410 (Bankr. E.D. Pa. 2003) (requiring debtor to wait twenty-five years to obtain discharge under ICRP is contrary to the "fresh start" purpose of the Bankruptcy Code). *But see In re* Kehler, 326 B.R. 142 (Bankr. N.D. Ind. 2005) (discharge denied, court finding that 62 year-old debtor can make monthly $87.97 ICRP payments on a $62,000 educational loan over next twenty-five years).

88 If Congress had intended for the ICRP and other payment programs to meet all hardship situations, it would have repealed the hardship provisions in the Bankruptcy Code. In fact, Congress has not eliminated the bankruptcy hardship discharge despite having made amendments to § 523(a)(8) since the student loan payment programs were enacted. *See also In re* Nanton-Marie, 303 B.R. 228 (Bankr. S.D. Fla. 2003) (nothing in Bankruptcy Code requires consideration of ICRP as condition precedent to undue hardship discharge); *In re* Johnson, 299 B.R. 676, 682 (Bankr. M.D. Ga. 2003) ("If Congress had intended the question of dischargeability of student loans to be delegated to a non-judicial entity, no matter how fair its formulas or intentions, it could have provided for such."); *In re* Korhonen, 296 B.R. 492, 496 (Bankr. D. Minn. 2003) ("[ICRP] cannot trump the Congressionally mandated individualized determination of undue hardship"). For a thorough discussion of the relationship between § 523(a)(8)'s discharge provision and the ICRP option, see Terrence L. Michael & Janie M. Phelps, *Judges?!—We Don't Need No Stinking Judges!!!": The Discharge of Student Loans in Bankruptcy Cases and The Income Contingent Repayment Plan* 38 Tex. Tech. L. Rev. 73 (Fall 2005) (one of the authors is a bankruptcy judge).

89 *In re* Kopf, 245 B.R. 731 (Bankr. D. Me. 2000) (no matter how flexible or "humanely executed" such programs may be, they simply are not the equivalent of a discharge). The *Kopf* court noted that, even when a debtor's monthly payment obligation is reduced to zero under an ICRP, this will only "postpone repayment indefinitely and, unless interest is abated, permit additional interest accruals." *Id.* at 735. *See also In re* Durrani, 311 B.R. 496 (Bankr. N.D. Ill. 2004) ("Courts must not turn to the ICRP as a substitute for the thoughtful and considered exercise of . . . discretion" required under the *Brunner* test). An ICRP actually allows the loan balance to increase, with capitalization of some interest, and does not prevent the discharge of a remaining balance after twenty-five years from being deemed taxable income to the debtor. *See also In re* Durrani, 311 B.R. 496 (Bankr. N.D. Ill. 2004), *aff'd*, 320 B.R. 357 (N.D. Ill. 2005) (unlike discharge in bankruptcy, ICRP discharge may result in substantial nondischargeable tax liability for debtor because unpaid amount and accrued interest over twenty-five-year period treated as income); *In re* Korhonen, 296 B.R. 492, 496 (Bankr. D. Minn. 2003); *In re* Thomsen, 234 B.R. 506, 514 (Bankr. D. Mont. 1999) (debtors will simply replace nondischargeable student loans with another nondischargeable debt in form of income taxes). See generally § 8.2.2.6, *infra*, for a discussion of the long-term consequences for borrowers making small payments under an ICRP.

In addition, by considering a debtor's ability to pay under an ICRP for a period of up to twenty-five years, courts following the *Brunner* test may misapply its second prong, which looks to whether the debtor's inability to repay will persist for a significant portion of the remaining repayment period under the original loan obligations.[90] It should not be overlooked that *Brunner* was decided in 1987. At that time, *any* student loan could be discharged after it had been due for five years. As a practical matter, the loan repayment periods within the court's contemplation in 1987 were always subject to this potential for discharge. It is therefore questionable that *Brunner* should be relied upon to support arguments that a twenty-five year loan repayment period should be imposed upon a debtor in lieu of discharging the debt.[91] Similarly, courts should not require that students apply for an ICRP as an exhaustion of administrative remedies before seeking a hardship discharge in bankruptcy.[92]

In addition, students should present evidence of any obstacles they have faced in attempting to negotiate an affordable plan. An agency's claim of flexible payment arrangements will be undercut by testimony that the agency failed to cooperate with the student and ultimately demanded payments in excess of the student's ability to pay, or when the student was told that affordable payment plans simply do not exist.[93] Even when the debtor intends to argue

that an ICRP should not be a substitute for a bankruptcy discharge, the debtor should review available payment options before the discharge hearing[94] and be prepared to present evidence when an ICRP is not feasible, particularly when the accrual of interest will effectively prevent any meaningful repayment of the loan.[95] Since payments must be made under an ICRP if the debtor's income is even slightly above poverty level, the debtor should present evidence that making these payments will prevent the debtor from maintaining a minimal standard of living.[96]

Many bankruptcy courts that focus on the ICRP operate on the mistaken assumption that this option is nearly universally available. This is not the case. In fact, there are a number of restrictions on these plans. It is essential for consumers and their attorneys to present evidence with respect to whether the consumer is eligible for an ICRP. Even eligible consumers should be prepared to present evidence that the plan is not affordable without causing hardship or that their current lenders have told them that the plans are not eligible.

The first restriction is that the ICRP is available through the Direct Loan program only. Students may borrow through the Direct Loan program if the school they are attending

---

90   *See, e.g., In re* Ordaz, 287 B.R. 912 (Bankr. C.D. Ill. 2002) (consolidation loan that effectively restructured student loan with same lender at the end of original ten-year term did not "restart the clock" on new fifteen-year repayment period for purposes of considering future inability to repay). However, applying a totality-of-circumstances test, the Eighth Circuit Bankruptcy Appellate Panel has concluded that a twenty-five-year repayment period under an ICRP would not impose an undue hardship on a debtor under the circumstances of that case. *See* Long v. Educational Credit Mgmt. Corp., 292 B.R. 635 (B.A.P. 8th Cir. 2003). *See also In re* Coatney, 345 B.R. 905 (Bankr. C.D. Ill. 2006) (declining to rule on dischargeability when only evidence before court was duration of ICRP and no facts presented regarding the original loan repayment period).

91   *See* Rafael I. Pardo & Michelle R. Lacey, *Undue Hardship in the Bankruptcy Courts: An Empirical Assessment of the Discharge of Educational Debt*, 74 U. Cin. L. Rev. 405 n.415 (Winter 2005).

92   However, in a case that did not involve an ICRP, one court denied a hardship discharge adversary complaint without prejudice because the student had failed to exhaust administrative remedies by first seeking an unpaid-refund discharge. *See In re* Scholl, 259 B.R. 345 (Bankr. N.D. Iowa 2001).

93   *In re* Cheney, 280 B.R. 648 (N.D. Iowa 2002) (student loan creditor failed to prove that it had properly advised debtor of availability of ICRP and other programs or to assist the debtor in pursuing them); *In re* Lee, 345 B.R. 911, 918 (Bankr. W.D. Ark. 2006) (court will not fault debtor who was never advised of various options such as ICRP); *In re* Thomsen, 234 B.R. 506, 514 (Bankr. D. Mont. 1999) (debtor made three separate requests for affordable payment plans but DOE never sent application and instead demanded excessive payments contrary to rule for "satisfactory payment arrangements"). Some courts have rejected generalized statements made by student loan creditors about the availability of ICRPs and other payment

programs without proof that the debtor would in fact be eligible for such programs. Educational Credit Mgmt. Corp. v. Porrazzo, 307 B.R. 345 (Bankr. D. Conn. 2004) (student loan creditor failed to prove that debtor was eligible for Ford Program); *In re* Strand, 298 B.R. 367 (Bankr. D. Minn. 2003).

94   *See In re* Chambers, 239 B.R. 767 (Bankr. N.D. Ohio 1999) (debtor admitted on cross-examination that she was unaware of availability of ICRP before filing bankruptcy and that she would have participated in the payment program had she known). *See also In re* Schilling, 333 B.R. 716 (Bankr. W.D. Pa. 2005) (debtor fails *Brunner* "good faith" test when she did not articulate any reason for deciding not to pursue an ICRP).

95   *In re* Barrett, 337 B.R. 896 (B.A.P. 6th Cir. 2006) (lender's emphasis on ICRP "fails to take account of the additional worry and anxiety that the Debtor is likely to suffer if he is compelled to watch his debt steadily increase knowing that he does not have the ability to repay it for reasons beyond his control"); *In re* Dufresne, 341 B.R. 391 (Bankr. D. Mass. 2006) (rejecting ICRP alternative and noting that the lender's calculus ignored "the indefinite and perhaps decades-long duration of the forbearance, the ongoing accruals of interest added to current debt, the public credit reporting of a large and growing debt in a perpetual default status, the tax consequences of a debt forgiven many years hence"); *In re* Strand, 298 B.R. 367 (Bankr. D. Minn. 2003) (interest accruing over twenty-five-year period under ICRP will leave debtor "hamstrung into poverty for the rest of his life" and prevent him from obtaining credit or approval of rental applications).

96   *In re* Greenwood, __ B.R. __, 2006 WL 2556396 (Bankr. D. Ariz. Sept. 5, 2006) (no lack of good faith when debtor rejects ICRP requiring $260 monthly payments that he cannot afford); *In re* Bray, 332 B.R. 186, 198 (Bankr. W.D. Mo. 2005) (ICRP with monthly payments of $200 "not a viable option" for debtor who meets undue hardship test); *In re* Carter, 295 B.R. 555 (Bankr. W.D. Pa. 2003) (loan consolidation and repayment plan not viable alternative for debtor unable to provide for basic necessities).

participates in the program and the student chooses to take out a Direct Loan to pay for his or her education-related expenses. Alternatively, the borrower may obtain a Direct *consolidation* loan while he or she is still in school or afterwards. Since Direct Loans comprise only about 25% of the total student loan market, most students will initially borrow through other loan programs and will access the Direct Loan program only if attempting to get a consolidation loan.[97]

However, not all borrowers will be eligible to consolidate their loans through the Direct Loan program. The first requirement is that borrowers have at least one FFEL or Direct loan in order to consolidate through Direct Loans.[98] for example, a borrower with only Perkins loans cannot consolidate with Direct Loans and obtain an ICRP. This issue takes on added importance under the new bankruptcy law that went into effect in October 2005. The new law extends the nondischargeability presumption to many private student loans as well. Unlike Perkins loans, private loans cannot be consolidated even if the borrower has an FFEL or Direct loan that he or she is also consolidating.[99]

Another obstacle is that the Department will not re-consolidate a consolidation loan if the underlying loans in the defaulted consolidation loan had been in default. In practice, this means that borrowers can consolidate defaulted loans with the Direct Loan program only once.

There are additional limitations passed as part of the Higher Education Reconciliation Act in 2005, effective July 1, 2006. First, defaulted Direct consolidation loans may no longer be consolidated.[100] Under the post-July 1, 2006, rules, a borrower who already has a consolidation loan with either FFEL or Direct will not be able to "reconsolidate" with either program, except in limited circumstances. These following are such circumstances:

- if the borrower receives eligible student loans after the date of receipt of the consolidation loan;
- when loans received prior to the date of the consolidation loan are added during the 180-day period following the making of the consolidation loan;
- when loans received following the making of the consolidation loan are added during the 180-day period following the making of the consolidation loan;

- when loans received prior to the date of the first consolidation are added to a subsequent consolidation loans; and
- when FFEL consolidation borrowers obtain a Direct consolidation loan only for the purposes of obtaining an ICRP and only if the loan has been submitted to the guaranty agency for default aversion.[101]

As of July 1, 2006, there are additional, important limits affecting which loans may be consolidated with Direct Loans. Prior to this date, the rules for Direct Loan consolidation were significantly more flexible for borrowers than FFEL consolidation. Most, but not all, of this flexibility was eliminated.

For example, prior to July 1, 2006, the Department, at its discretion, could consolidate loans that were reduced to judgment, loans of borrowers facing wage garnishment, and defaulted consolidation loans. Similar to the FFEL program, loans that have been reduced to judgment may now be consolidated with Direct only if the judgment has been vacated.[102] If the borrower is facing wage garnishment, he or she may consolidate with Direct only if the garnishment order is lifted.[103]

Furthermore, many borrowers who are eligible for the ICRP will be told erroneously by the private lenders holding their loans that they cannot consolidate with Direct Loans. In fact, borrowers with only FFEL loans can consolidate with Direct Loans if they are unable to obtain an FFEL consolidation loan or are eligible for the ICRP and unable to obtain an FFEL consolidation loan with acceptable income-sensitive repayment terms.[104]

It is also misleading for courts to claim that borrowers can get complete relief after twenty-five years. While the Department of Education is supposed to forgive the loan balance after twenty-five consecutive years of ICRP repayments, the borrower may face significant tax liabilities at that time on the amount forgiven.[105]

---

97 *See* Stephen Burd, *Direct Lending in Distress*, Chron. of Higher Educ., July 8, 2005 (Direct Loans comprise only about 25% of the total student loan market). *See generally* Ch. 8, *infra* (loan consolidation).

98 34 C.F.R. § 685.220(d). *See* § 8.2.2.2, *infra*.

99 *See* § 7.2.2, *supra*.

100 This may not be much different from current practice. In general, even prior to July 1, 2006, the Department had the discretion to consolidate in these circumstances but had a policy against "re-consolidating" a consolidation loan if the underlying loans in the defaulted consolidation loan had been in default. *See* § 8.2.2.2, *infra*.

101 20 U.S.C. §§ 1078-3(a)(3)(B)(FFEL), 1087e(g) (Direct). The regulations that limit "re-consolidation" to FFEL borrowers with defaulted loans may go beyond the provisions of the Higher Education Reconciliation Act.

102 34 C.F.R. § 685.220(d)(ii)(E).

103 34 C.F.R. § 685.220(d)(ii)(F).

104 34 C.F.R. § 685.220(d)(1)(i). *See* § 8.2.2.3, *infra*.

105 Some courts have begun to address the important tax implications of loan forgiveness under an ICRP, albeit their remedies for the problem have been less than satisfactory. *See In re* Coatney, 345 B.R. 905 (Bankr. C.D. Ill. 2006). The court in *Coatney* noted that the debtor's participation in an ICRP would be extremely problematic. With a current loan balance of $120,000, the indebtedness could grow to hundreds of thousands of dollars by the end of the eighteen-year ICRP term. This could leave the debtor with tens of thousands of dollars in nondischargeable income taxes due. *Id.* at 911. However, rather than finding the underlying debt dischargeable, the court granted the debtor a four-year deferment, after which he could seek another dischargeability determination based on a more com-

Some of the courts that have addressed this issue have acknowledged that not all borrowers are eligible for ICRPs. These courts note that borrowers must then present evidence that they inquired about the program and found out they were not eligible. The court would then treat this as evidence establishing good faith for the *Brunner* test.[106]

7.2.4.7 Special Rule for HEAL Loans

The limits on dischargeability of Health Education Assistance Loans (HEALs) are more severe than for other student loans. They can be discharged only if the court finds denial of discharge would be "unconscionable," and the student cannot seek a discharge during the first seven years of the loan repayment period.[107] A Bankruptcy Appellate Panel for the Tenth Circuit affirmed the discharge of a HEAL loan when the bankruptcy court had concluded that depriving the debtor of the ability to afford life's basic necessities, such a health care, transportation, food, housing, utilities, and the ability to care for himself upon his impending retirement would be "unconscionable."[108] The Sixth Circuit has concluded that the unconscionability standard for HEAL loans is "significantly more stringent" than the undue hardship standard[109] and, therefore, only debtors presenting the most compelling facts will be granted a discharge.[110] This standard can be particularly harsh on

students who never benefited from the HEAL loans.[111] However, under a plain language reading of 11 U.S.C. § 523(b), HEALs may be more easily dischargeable if the debtor receives a second bankruptcy discharge.[112]

Some students may have both HEAL and non-HEAL student loans. The Fourth Circuit has held that a bankruptcy court should first consider the dischargeability of the non-HEAL loans, since the discharge of the non-HEAL loans could affect the repayment analysis under the more stringent unconscionability standard for the remaining HEAL loans.[113]

7.3 The Dischargeability Determination

7.3.1 Procedure for Determining Dischargeability of Student Loan

Whether a student loan is discharged based on hardship is not automatically determined in the bankruptcy proceeding. The debtor must affirmatively seek such a determination. If the debtor fails to do so, and a loan holder subsequently attempts to collect on the loan, the loan's dischargeability can be resolved at that later date either by the bankruptcy court or by a state court in a proceeding relating to the note's collection. In general, it is best to resolve the loan's dischargeability in the bankruptcy court while the case is pending.

If there is no dispute about a student loan being dischargeable, it should be relatively easy to resolve this at the time of the bankruptcy. For example, if the loan was clearly over seven years old for cases filed before October 7, 1998, even accounting for all deferments, forbearances, consolidations, and the like, the guaranty agency or the Department will usually admit the loan's dischargeability.[114] A written stipulation of this sort may even make it unnecessary for the bankruptcy court to rule on the issue.

Requests for stipulations are usually fruitless when the student seeks a hardship discharge or when the seven-year period is in doubt. Guaranty agencies are strongly urged by the Department of Education to contest dischargeability.[115]

plete record. In another decision, the court focused upon the "undue hardship" that would arise from assessment of taxes at the time of loan forgiveness at the end of a twenty-five year ICRP. *In re* Grove, 323 B.R. 216, 230 (Bankr. N.D. Ohio 2005). Here, rather than discharging the debt, the court granted a partial discharge to the extent of any indebtedness remaining at the end of the ICRP term, thus precluding assessment of taxes against the forgiven indebtedness. While addressing one problem, the *Grove* decision unfortunately left the debtor, at age 57, with the full burden of growing indebtedness for the future twenty-five-year term of the ICRP.

106 *See, e.g., In re* Alderete, 412 F.3d 1200 (10th Cir. 2005).

107 42 U.S.C. § 294f(g). As under § 523(a)(8), the debtor must affirmatively seek a determination that the grounds for discharge of a HEAL debt have been satisfied. *See* United States v. Rushing, 287 B.R. 343 (D.N.J. 2002).

108 *In re* Woody, 345 B.R. 246, 259 (B.A.P. 10th Cir. 2006) (debtor was 58, in poor health, and had no prospect of increasing his income as IRS employee).

109 *In re* Rice, 78 F.3d 1144, 1149 (6th Cir. 1996) (denial not unconscionable; nondischarge of the loan must be "shockingly unfair, harsh, or unjust"). *See also* U.S. Dep't of Health & Human Servs. v. Smitley, 347 F.3d 109 (4th Cir. 2003); *In re* Malloy, 155 B.R. 940 (E.D. Va. 1993), *aff'd without opinion*, 23 F.3d 402 (4th Cir. 1994).

110 *See In re* Buracker, 2004 WL 950771 (Bankr. C.D. Ill. May 3, 2004) (sixty-one-year-old chiropractor whose circumstances were not likely to improve granted discharge of $123,000 in HEAL loans); *In re* Ascue, 268 B.R. 739 (Bankr. W.D. Va. 2001), *aff'd with unpublished opinion*, 2002 WL 192561 (W.D. Va., Feb. 7, 2002) (partial discharge eliminating $300,000 in interest on National Health Service Corps loan for debtor whose earnings were limited).

111 *In re* Rogers, 250 B.R. 883 (Bankr. S.D. Ohio 2000) (debtor never received health education degree and employed as shipping clerk).

112 *In re* Tanski, 195 B.R. 408 (Bankr. E.D. Wis. 1996).

113 U.S. Dep't of Health & Human Servs. v. Smitley, 347 F.3d 109 (4th Cir. 2003).

114 However, some prodding may be required. One or more letters requesting a stipulation that the loan is dischargeable can be followed up with a request for the court to determine the issue if no agreement is forthcoming. In any event, it is important to create a paper trail establishing the dischargeability in order to prevent later disputes.

115 34 C.F.R. § 682.402(f), (g), (h), (i).

Schools making Perkins loans are instructed to oppose dischargeability if they determine that legal costs are not expected to exceed one-third of the amount owed.[116]

Even when the student loan creditor intends to contest the loan's dischargeability, it is usually the best approach to resolve the loan's dischargeability at the time of the bankruptcy filing. The student may do this by bringing an adversary proceeding in the bankruptcy court seeking a declaratory judgment that a particular debt is dischargeable.[117] An "adversary proceeding" is a lawsuit within the bankruptcy case initiated by the filing of an adversary complaint. It is subject to rules almost identical to the Federal Rules of Civil Procedure, including those relating to discovery procedure.[118] For a more detailed discussion of adversary proceedings, see National Consumer Law Center, Consumer Bankruptcy Law and Practice (8th ed. 2006). In addition, sample adversary complaints and related pleadings in student loan cases are provided at Appendix E, *infra*, and on the companion CD-Rom to this manual.[119]

An adversary proceeding to determine dischargeability of a student loan may be brought at any time, and a bankruptcy case that has been closed may be reopened without payment of an additional filing fee in order to obtain a dischargeability determination.[120] Likewise, courts have held that, since the denial of a hardship discharge is generally made without prejudice, a student may renew a request for discharge relief when there has been a change in circumstances.[121] In some instances the courts have expressly invited debtors to reopen and seek discharge upon the occurrence of certain future events.[122]

Since there are no time limitations on when the action can be filed, a student may consider reopening a bankruptcy case to seek a hardship discharge when the student's situation has taken a turn for the worse after the bankruptcy case is closed.[123] In some situations, a student may also defer filing the adversary proceeding until some time after the bankruptcy is closed when the student's ability to prove the elements of the hardship test may improve with time.[124] Particularly when the student needs to file bankruptcy for other reasons, but may not be in a position to prove all of the elements of the applicable hardship test, the student should attempt to avoid a premature filing of the hardship adversary proceeding.[125] However, the right to reopen a bankruptcy case is not limitless. The court will reopen a case only for cause.[126] A court may refuse to reopen a case if the debtor does not provide sufficient facts to show cause.[127] However,

---

116 34 C.F.R. § 674.49(c)(4).

117 *In re* Doane, 2004 WL 1433436, 102 Fed. Appx. 312 (4th Cir. June 28, 2004) (debtor must file an adversary proceeding even if bankruptcy court issued a discharge order that purported to discharge student loans, since discharge was not sought nor authorized). *See* Fed. R. Bankr. P. 7001. The student has the burden to prove entitlement to a hardship discharge, though the student loan creditor generally has the initial burden to establish the existence of the debt. *In re* Kopf, 245 B.R. 731 (Bankr. D. Me. 2000); *In re* Green, 238 B.R. 727 (Bankr. N.D. Ohio 1999).

118 *See* Fed. R. Bankr. P. 7001–7087. Under the present fee schedule adopted by the Administrative Office of the federal courts, there is no filing fee for an adversary complaint brought by a debtor in a bankruptcy case.

119 For reasons discussed in § 7.3.3, *infra*, concerning sovereign immunity, in preparing the adversary complaint it is generally advisable to name the director of the student loan agency as a defendant in order to invoke the *Ex parte Young* doctrine.

120 *See* Fed. R. Bankr. P. 4007(b) and 11 U.S.C. § 350(b). If the student is eligible for a discharge under the Higher Education Act as discussed in Chapter 6, *supra*, it is advisable that the student apply for an administrative discharge before filing a bankruptcy adversary complaint. *See In re* Scholl, 259 B.R. 345 (Bankr. N.D. Iowa 2001) (hardship discharge adversary complaint denied without prejudice when student failed to exhaust administrative remedies by first seeking an unpaid-refund discharge). Borrowers may also be eligible for disability discharges through the Department of Education. Most borrowers found to be eligible for this discharge are given a three-year conditional discharge period. *See* § 6.6, *supra*. At least one court has held that it is not fitting to adjudicate an undue hardship case during this conditional discharge period since the borrower may potentially receive complete relief outside of bankruptcy. *See In re* Furrow, 2005 WL 1397156 (Bankr. W.D. Mo. May 24, 2005).

121 *In re* Andrews, 661 F.2d 702 (8th Cir. 1981) (recommending that the denial of a hardship discharge by bankruptcy courts should be made without prejudice to permit the debtor to seek relief under Rule 4007 when there has been a change in circumstances); *In re* Sobh, 61 B.R. 576 (E.D. Mich. 1986) (res judicata does not bar a debtor from filing a new complaint seeking a hardship discharge based on new facts). *But see In re* Bugos, 288 B.R. 435 (Bankr. E.D. Va. 2003) (absent circumstances that are foreseeable or that relate current situation to the time petition was filed, bankruptcy case should not be reopened to determine undue hardship); *In re* Kapsin, 265 B.R. 778 (Bankr. N.D. Ohio 2001) (change in circumstances one-and-one-half years later did not constitute "cause" for reopening bankruptcy). The Bankruptcy Code also provides that a student loan that was excepted from discharge in a prior bankruptcy may be discharged in a subsequent bankruptcy case if the debtor can satisfy the undue hardship test. *See* 11 U.S.C. § 523(b).

122 *In re* Nash, 446 F.3d 188, 194 (1st Cir. 2006) (debtor may reopen case to bring new dischargeability action if she obtains more supportive medical evidence); *In re* Coatney, 345 B.R. 905, 911 (Bankr. C.D. Ill. 2006) (debtor may reopen and raise claims again at end of four-year deferment granted by court); *In re* Grove, 323 B.R. 216 (Bankr. N.D. Ohio 2005) (debtor may reopen case if he is turned down for ICRP).

123 *In re* Fisher, 223 B.R. 377 (Bankr. M.D. Fla. 1998) (debtor may reopen bankruptcy two years later when debtor's medical condition did not manifest until after case closed).

124 *See In re* Doherty, 219 B.R. 665 (Bankr. W.D.N.Y. 1998) (good faith shown when debtor tried to make payments for year-and-a-half before reopening her case to bring discharge proceeding).

125 *In re* Kraft, 161 B.R. 82 (Bankr. W.D.N.Y. 1993) (hardship complaint filed too early as debtor could not prove good faith under *Brunner* test). However, a consolidation loan entered into after the bankruptcy case has been closed may cut off the student's right to seek a hardship discharge of the original loans. *In re* Clarke, 266 B.R. 301 (Bankr. E.D. Pa. 2001) (consolidation loan extinguishes original student loans).

126 11 U.S.C. § 350(b).

127 Courts have found that the party seeking to reopen the case has the burden of demonstrating cause. *See, e.g., In re* Cloninger, 209 B.R. 125 (Bankr. E.D. Ark. 1997).

even if the court denies a motion to reopen, the debtor should still be able to file a new bankruptcy case and initiate an adversary proceeding to prove undue hardship based on his or her current circumstances.[128]

If the student does not obtain a stipulation or court determination of a student loan's dischargeability at the time of the bankruptcy, then the loan's dischargeability is left in limbo—the lack of prosecution of the issue prejudices neither the debtor nor creditor's position. If the loan's dischargeability is not determined, the guaranty agency or Department can be expected to try to collect on the loan through tax intercepts, garnishments, and collection contacts. The student would then have to argue before a collection agency or in an administrative hearing that the debt is not owed because the loan was discharged by the bankruptcy. Such arguments may not go far in such proceedings even when the student can prove the application of the seven-year rule but certainly will be of no avail when hardship is the basis for discharge.

The better approach is to apply to the bankruptcy court (even after the bankruptcy case has been closed) for a determination that the loan is discharged by the bankruptcy. Then the court determination can be presented to the collector or guarantor.

If the Department or other party is pressing a collection action on the note in state court, the student has two choices. The student can ask the state court judge to rule on the dischargeability of the debt. Alternatively, the student can seek to remove the action to the bankruptcy court for such a determination[129] (or request that the state action be stayed pending the reopening of the bankruptcy case).

7.3.2 Undue Hardship Determination in Chapter 13

Chapter 13 debtors may also file an adversary proceeding to determine the dischargeability of student loan obligations. The issue may be raised at any time during the three- to five-year period of the plan,[130] and similar timing consid-

erations apply as discussed previously.[131] However, some courts have required that the student wait until the end of the chapter 13 plan before seeking a hardship discharge.[132] Another way to obtain a student loan hardship determination is through the chapter 13 plan confirmation process. However, courts have become increasingly hostile to this strategy.[133] A shrinking minority of courts are willing to give res judicata effect to provisions in a confirmed chapter 13 plan allowing discharge based on undue hardship.[134] For courts that enforce such provisions against student loan creditors, the key factor is whether an objection to the provision is made prior to or after plan confirmation. If an objection is made before confirmation, courts will generally deny the plan provision on the ground that dischargeability determinations should be made in an adversary proceeding.[135]

---

131 *See* § 7.3.1, *supra.*

132 *In re* Bender, 368 F.3d 846 (8th Cir. 2004) (student loan discharge determination in chapter 13 case not ripe for adjudication until conclusion of plan at time of discharge); *In re* Pair, 269 B.R. 719 (Bankr. N.D. Ala. 2001). *See, e.g., In re* Raisor, 180 B.R. 163 (Bankr. E.D. Tex. 1995).

133 For example, two courts have warned that the insertion of an undue hardship finding in a plan or confirmation order is never appropriate and may be grounds for setting such finding aside and/or sanctions. *See In re* Mersmann, 318 B.R. 537 (B.A.P. 10th Cir. 2004); *In re* Whelton, 312 B.R. 508, 517 (D. Vt. 2004), *aff'd*, 432 F.3d 150 (2d Cir. 2005) (plan provision purporting to effect undue hardship determination through plan confirmation order will not be given res judicata effect; debtor must comply with adversary action procedures, including service of summons and complaint upon creditor). *See also In re* Hanson, 397 F.3d 482 (7th Cir. 2005) (same); *In re* Ruehle, 412 F.3d 679 (6th Cir. 2005) (same); Poland v. Educational Credit Mgmt. Corp., 382 F.3d 1185 (10th Cir. 2004) (questioning *Anderson* decision and limiting holding); Banks v. Sallie Mae Servicing Corp. (*In re* Banks), 299 F.3d 296 (4th Cir. 2002) (confirmed plan providing for discharge of post-petition interest violated student loan creditor's due process rights when creditor not served with adversary complaint and summons and therefore plan not given preclusive effect); *In re* Ransom, 336 B.R. 790 (B.A.P. 9th Cir. 2005) (plan provision purporting to discharge post-petition interest accruing on student loan has no res judicata effect); *In re* Repp, 307 B.R. 144, 149 (B.A.P. 9th Cir. 2004) (joining "emerging consensus" that undue hardship discharge by plan provision violates creditor's due process rights); *In re* Key, 128 B.R. 742 (Bankr. S.D. Ohio 1991) (plan provision cannot render claim dischargeable).

134 Great Lakes Higher Educ. Corp. v. Pardee (*In re* Pardee), 193 F.3d 1083 (9th Cir. 1999) (confirmation of chapter 13 plan providing that post-petition interest on student loan would be discharged bound the creditor); *In re* Andersen, 179 F.3d 1253 (10th Cir. 1999) (court found that confirmation of chapter 13 plan including a provision of undue hardship bound the creditor); Educational Credit Mgmt. Corp. v. Boyer, 305 B.R. 42 (Bankr. D. Kan. 2004), *rev'd in part by In re* Nelson, 318 B.R. 532 (B.A.P. 10th Cir. 2004), *aff'd in part by In re* Mersmann 318 B.R. 537 (B.A.P. 10th Cir. 2004).

135 Kielisch v. Educational Credit Management Corp. (*In re* Kielisch), 258 F.3d 315 (4th Cir. 2001) (plan provision providing for non-accrual of post-petition interest not effective when debtor has not brought adversary proceeding to obtain hardship discharge); *In re* Webber, 251 B.R. 554 (Bankr. D. Ariz. 2000);

---

128 *See, e.g., In re* Root, 318 B.R. 851 (Bankr. W.D. Mont. 2004) (court denied debtor's motion to reopen case thirteen years after case was closed).

129 28 U.S.C. § 1452; Fed. R. Bankr. P. 9027.

130 *In re* Ekenasi, 325 F.3d 541 (4th Cir. 2003) (although debtor need not wait until end of chapter 13 plan to bring dischargeability proceeding, debtor must demonstrate that *Brunner* factors can be predicted with sufficient certainty if seeking discharge earlier in case); *In re* Coleman, 345 B.R. 203 (N.D. Cal. 2006) (debtor may bring undue hardship dischargeability action before completion of plan); *In re* Strahm, 327 B.R. 319 (Bankr. S.D. Ohio 2005) (same). *See also* Educational Credit Mgmt. Corp. v. Repp, 307 B.R. 144 (B.A.P. 9th Cir. 2004) (notice of plan containing student loan discharge provision must be provided in manner substantially similar to that used for service of adversary proceeding).

If no objection is raised and the plan is confirmed, the existence of the plan provision will constitute an additional ground to establish that the debt is dischargeable. If the court rules otherwise, an adversary proceeding can be filed at that time. In addition, a plan provision seeking to discharge post-petition interest, if it is not objected to and is given preclusive effect,[136] can be an effective way to ensure that a student who has paid a student loan claim in a chapter 13 plan does not emerge from the bankruptcy owing post-petition interest.

Plan provisions should be drafted with care in order to preclude an argument that the plan did not give the creditor adequate notice of dischargeability.[137] Once the plan is filed, it should be served on the affected creditor to avoid the lack-of-notice argument.[138]

The strategy of discharging student loans through chapter 13 plan provisions became popular after the Tenth Circuit ruling in *In re Anderson*.[139] Since that decision, the Tenth Circuit revisited this issue and limited the *Anderson* holding to the facts of the case.[140] In this later case, the court focused on one "all important difference" from *Anderson*: the confirmed plan in the later case made no mention of undue hardship and stated only the fact, the amount, and the disputed nature of the student loan debt and that, if no proof of claim was filed by the creditor, the claim shall be discharged.[141] According to the later decision, the *Anderson* ruling rested on the fact that confirmation of the plan, to which there was no objection, amounted to a binding adjudication of undue hardship, thereby turning a nondischargeable debt into a dischargeable debt. In the later decision, the court emphasized that the proper way to discharge a student loan debt is through an adversary proceeding in which the debtor established undue hardship.[142] In a footnote, the court stated that *Anderson* was wrongly decided and should be reconsidered. The unfortunate result of *Anderson*, the court noted, is that attorneys now insert student loan discharge language into chapter 13 plans hoping to achieve preclusive effect.[143] Since courts have increasingly looked disfavorably on such practice, the better route is to file an adversary proceeding.

7.3.3 Discharge of Student Loans Owed to State Agencies

Following the Supreme Court decision in *Seminole Tribe v. Florida*, state agencies collecting student loan debts aggressively asserted Eleventh Amendment immunity (sovereign immunity) as a way of barring debtors from discharging student loans in bankruptcy.[144] The issue of sovereign immunity arises because debtors must affirmatively seek student loan discharges through an adversary proceeding. State agencies had argued that this proceeding, which they characterized as a private suit in federal court against the state, was barred by the Eleventh Amendment.[145]

Fortunately for student loan debtors, the sovereign immunity issue in undue hardship cases has now been resolved favorably by the Supreme Court. In *Tennessee Student Assistance Corp. v. Hood*,[146] the Court relied upon an exception previously carved out for admiralty proceedings and held that a bankruptcy dischargeability suit brought against the state does not implicate a state's Eleventh Amendment immunity from suit.

Drawing on a distinction between *in rem* and *in personam* proceedings, the Court in *Hood* noted that a bankruptcy court's jurisdiction is "premised on the debtor and his estate, and not on the creditors," and therefore the discharge of a

In re Mammel, 221 B.R. 238 (Bankr. N.D. Iowa 1998).

136 *In re* Pardee, 193 F.3d 1083 (9th Cir. 1999); *In re* York, 250 B.R. 842 (Bankr. D. Del. 2000) (res judicata prevents student loan creditor from objecting to plan provision providing for discharge of post-petition interest).

137 See *In re* Andersen, 215 B.R. 792 (B.A.P. 10th Cir. 1998), *aff'd*, 179 F.3d 1253 (10th Cir. 1999), for a good model plan provision. *Cf. In re* Loving, 269 B.R. 655 (Bankr. S.D. Ind. 2001) (no preclusive effect given when debtor's plan did not explicitly provide for discharge of student loans upon completion of plan payments).

138 Advocates may take note that the Fourth Circuit has held that, although the mailing of a proposed plan, confirmation order, and hearing notice satisfies the notice requirements of Bankruptcy Rule 2002, it is not sufficient to protect a student loan creditor's due process rights; a plan seeking discharge of interest requires the filing of an adversary complaint and service of process under Bankruptcy Rule 7004. Banks v. Sallie Mae Servicing Corp. (*In re* Banks), 299 F.3d 296 (4th Cir. 2002).

139 *In re* Anderson, 179 F.3d 1253 (10th Cir. 1999).

140 *In re* Poland, 382 F.3d 1185 (10th Cir. 2004). *See also In re* Hanson, 397 F.3d 482 (7th Cir. 2005) (embracing *Banks* and *Poland*); *In re* Kaufman, 122 Fed. Appx. 815 (6th Cir. 2004) (distinguishing facts from *Anderson* in holding that res judicata doctrine could not be invoked to find that student loan was dischargeable).

141 *In re* Poland, 382 F.3d 1185 (10th Cir. 2004).

142 *Id.*

143 *Id.* at n.2.

144 Seminole Tribe v. Florida, 517 U.S. 44 (1996). *See generally* Patricia L. Barsalou & Scott A. Stengel, *Ex Parte Young: Relativity in Practice*, 72 Am. Bankr. L.J. 455 (1998); National Consumer Law Center, Consumer Bankruptcy Law and Practice § 13.3.2.2 (8th ed. 2005).

145 The doctrine of sovereign immunity acts as a jurisdictional bar to suits filed by private individuals against non-consenting states. For a good summary of the doctrine in student loan cases, see *In re* Greenwood, 237 B.R. 128 (N.D. Tex. 1999) (upholding state agency's sovereign immunity claim). For other cases in which sovereign immunity was affirmed, see, for example, *Murphy v. Michigan Guar. Agency (In re Murphy)*, 271 F.3d 629 (5th Cir. 2001) (adversary proceeding seeking student loan discharge was "suit" against the state barred by Eleventh Amendment); *In re* Kahl, 240 B.R. 524 (Bankr. E.D. Pa. 1999); *In re* Stout, 231 B.R. 313 (Bankr. W.D. Mo. 1999); and *In re* Schmitt, 220 B.R. 68 (Bankr. W.D. Mo. 1998).

146 541 U.S. 440 (2004).

debt by a bankruptcy court is an *in rem* proceeding.[147] This permitted the Court to rely upon its earlier decision holding that the Eleventh Amendment does not bar federal jurisdiction over certain *in rem* admiralty proceedings.[148] Since the bankruptcy court's jurisdiction is "premised on the *res*," a state is bound by a discharge determination even if it elects not to participate in the bankruptcy proceeding.[149] The Eleventh Circuit in 2004 applied the Supreme Court's ruling to a debtor's dischargeability claim, finding that the Eleventh Amendment was not implicated on that claim and denying the guaranty agency's motion to dismiss.[150] However, the debtor also sought damages from the state agencies for their attempts to collect the student loans after receiving notice of the bankruptcy filing. This claim, according to the court, was premised on the persona of the state, not on the *res* of the debtor's property, and so was not obviated by the Supreme Court decision.[151] The court held that Congress had not abrogated the state's sovereign immunity with respect to *in persona* bankruptcy cases and that the district court should have granted the state agency's motion to dismiss as to the damages claim.[152]

The *Hood* opinion makes clear that debtors may now directly bring an adversary proceeding against the state to obtain student loan dischargeability determinations. If the debtor seeks additional relief against a state agency, such as an order to enforce the automatic stay or discharge injunction or to enjoin the agency from discriminating against the debtor based on a student loan discharge,[153] there can be little doubt after *Hood* that the bankruptcy court's *in personam* jurisdiction against the agency will be invoked and that an Eleventh Amendment immunity defense will be asserted. In this situation, the debtor may rely upon the following three exceptions to sovereign immunity:

1. Pursuant to the *Ex Parte Young* doctrine, suits against state officials in their individual capacities seeking prospective declaratory or injunctive relief for ongoing violations of federal law are not barred.[154] A number of bankruptcy courts prior to *Hood* had dismissed discharge actions against state agencies on sovereign immunity grounds subject to the debtor's possible use of the *Young* doctrine in bringing an action against a state official.[155]

2. The second exception to sovereign immunity is that Congress may abrogate it by unequivocally expressing an intent to do so and acting pursuant to a valid exercise of power.[156] While courts are in general agreement that Congress clearly intended to abrogate immunity through § 106(a) of the Bankruptcy Code, they are divided on whether this provision is valid.[157]

---

147 *Id.* at 447. *See also* Central Va. Comm. College v. Katz, 126 S. Ct. 990 (2006) (holding that trustee's proceeding to set aside debtor's preferential transfers to state agencies not barred by sovereign immunity).

148 California v. Deep Sea Research, Inc., 523 U.S. 491 (1998).

149 The Court in *Hood* also addressed the guaranty agency's concern that it had been served with a summons and complaint in an adversary proceeding, since the Court had previously ruled that the primary purpose of the Eleventh Amendment is to prevent the "indignity" of subjecting a state to court process. *See* Alden v. Maine, 527 U.S. 706 (1999). It concluded that the Bankruptcy Rule requirement that an adversary proceeding be filed to obtain a discharge under § 523(a)(8) did not transform the substantive nature of the matter from an *in rem* to an *in personam* proceeding. The Court sensibly observed that, "[t]o conclude that the issuance of a summons, which is required only by the Rules, precludes Hood from exercising her statutory right to an undue hardship determination would give the Rules an impermissible effect." *Tennessee Student Assistance Corp. v. Hood*, 541 U.S. 454.

150 *In re* Crow, 394 F.3d 918 (11th Cir. 2004).

151 *Id.*

152 *Id.*

153 *See* § 7.5, *infra*.

154 *Ex Parte* Young, 209 U.S. 123 (1908) (allowing federal court suit against state official acting *ultra vires* to proceed). *See also* Idaho v. Coeur d'Alene Tribe of Idaho, 521 U.S. 261 (1997). To invoke the *Young* doctrine, the party seeking enforcement of federal law must establish the following two elements. First, the party must allege that a state official is acting in violation of federal law. *See* Pennhurst State Sch. & Hosp. v. Halderman, 465 U.S. 89, 106 (1984). Second, the relief sought must be prospective in that the party must seek to enjoin future violations of federal law rather than obtain monetary compensation or other retrospective relief for past violations. Green v. Mansour, 474 U.S. 64, 68 (1985); Quern v. Jordan, 440 U.S. 332, 346–49 (1979).

155 *In re* Kahl, 240 B.R. 524 (Bankr. E.D. Pa. 1999) (case dismissed without prejudice to afford debtor opportunity to invoke the *Young* doctrine if relevant); *In re* Schmitt, 220 B.R. 68 (Bankr. W.D. Mo. 1998); *In re* Morrell, 218 B.R. 87 (Bankr. C.D. Cal. 1997) (granting debtors leave to amend in state franchise tax case to invoke *Young* doctrine). *But see In re* Stout, 231 B.R. 313 (Bankr. W.D. Mo. 1999) (*Young* doctrine does not give blanket authorization for suits against state officials to obtain injunctive relief).

156 For a good discussion of this exception, see *Hood v. Tennessee Student Assistance Corp.*, 319 F.3d 755 (6th Cir. 2003), *aff'd on other grounds*, 541 U.S. 440 (2004).

157 *See* Nelson v. La Crosse County Dist. Att'y (State of Wis.), 301 F.3d 820 (7th Cir. 2002) (Constitution's Bankruptcy Clause not valid authority for abrogating states' sovereign immunity); *In re* Sacred Heart Hosp. of Norristown, 133 F.3d 237 (3d Cir. 1997) (section 106 not valid abrogation); *In re* Estate of Fernandez, 123 F.3d 241 (5th Cir. 1997) (section 106(a) violates the Eleventh Amendment and therefore unconstitutional); *In re* Creative Goldsmiths, 119 F.3d 1140 (4th Cir. 1997), *cert. denied*, 523 U.S. 1075 (1998). *Cf.* Wilson v. S.C. State Educ. Assistance Auth., 258 B.R. 303 (Bankr. S.D. Ga. 2001) (section 108 valid abrogation as enacted pursuant to privileges and immunities clause of the Fourteenth Amendment); Lees v. Tennessee Student Assistance Corp., 252 B.R. 441 (Bankr. W.D. Tenn. 2000), *aff'd on other grounds*, 264 B.R. 884 (W.D. Tenn. 2001). A few courts have held that the issue of whether immunity had been waived or abrogated need not be considered in regard to dischargeability proceedings because the states, in ratifying the Constitution, ceded their sovereignty over discharge matters to Congress. Hood v. Tennessee Student Assistance Corp., 319 F.3d 755 (6th Cir. 2003) (Congress validly abrogated states'

And though this was the question on which the Supreme Court granted certiorari in *Hood*, it ultimately declined to rule on whether the abrogation in § 106(a) was valid based on authority found in the Bankruptcy Clause of the Constitution (Article I, § 8, clause 4).

3. The third exception is that states may waive Eleventh Amendment immunity and therefore consent to suit in federal courts. For example, participation in the federal loan program may act as a waiver of the state's Eleventh Amendment immunity in bankruptcy or other federal proceedings.[158] Mere participation, however, is generally insufficient to waive sovereign immunity without some indication of affirmative assent to suit.[159]

For example, the filing of a proof of claim by a college or guaranty agency can itself be a waiver of sovereign immunity.[160]

Another issue that may arise in these cases is the threshold question of whether the state actor collecting the loan is truly an "arm of the state."[161] If not, the state actor should not be entitled to assert sovereign immunity.

Most circuit courts have established a multi-prong test to determine whether an agency is an "arm of the state."[162] The foremost factor under these tests is whether the state will be financially burdened by the action in question.[163] This should be a strong argument in the student loan context, within which states are usually not responsible for guaranty agencies' financial obligations,[164] because such entities typically have a legal existence distinct from the state.[165] Moreover, based on their contractual arrangement with the Department of Education, guaranty agencies are reimbursed by the federal government for most of the indebtedness on discharged loans.[166] One court has applied the various factors of the "arm of the state" test to a student loan authority and found that it was not entitled to claim sovereign immunity.[167]

---

sovereign immunity under Constitution's Bankruptcy Clause and Fourteenth Amendment), *aff'd on other grounds*, 541 U.S. 440 (2004); *In re* Bleimeister, 251 B.R. 383 (Bankr. D. Ariz. 2000), *aff'd on other grounds*, 296 F.3d 858 (9th Cir. 2002).

158   *See In re* Innes, 184 F.3d 1275 (10th Cir. 1999), *cert. denied*, 529 U.S. 1037 (2000); *In re* Rose, 187 F.3d 926 (8th Cir. 1999); *In re* Huffine, 246 B.R. 405 (Bankr. E.D. Wash. 2000) (waiver found based on a review of Perkins Loan program as a whole, including the statute, the participation contract, and the governing regulations). *But see In re* Janc, 251 B.R. 525 (Bankr. W.D. Mo. 2000) (state guaranty agency did not waive sovereign immunity by participating in student loan program).

159   *See generally* College Sav. Bank v. Florida Prepaid Postsecondary Educ. Expense Bd., 527 U.S. 666 (1999) (rejecting doctrine of "constructive waiver"); Atascadero v. Scanlon, 473 U.S. 234 (1985). *See also In re* Innes, 184 F.3d 1275 (10th Cir. 1999), *cert. denied*, 529 U.S. 1037 (2000); *In re* Rose, 187 F.3d 926 (8th Cir. 1999); *In re* Phelps, 237 B.R. 527 (Bankr. D.R.I. 1999) (waiver found when, among other actions, creditor acknowledged it was a party to discharge proceeding and only raised immunity issue after unfavorable decision on hardship). While sovereign immunity may be raised for the first time on appeal, it is not an ordinary limitation on subject matter jurisdiction and therefore federal courts are not required to *sua sponte* consider a possible immunity defense. Wisconsin Dep't of Corrections v. Schacht, 524 U.S. 381, 389–391 (1998); Toll v. Moreno, 458 U.S. 1, 17–19 (1982). *See also* Parella v. Ret. Bd. of Rhode Island Employee Ret. Sys., 173 F.3d 46 (1st Cir. 1999).

160   *See* Gardner v. New Jersey, 329 U.S. 565 (1947); Rose v. U.S. Dep't of Educ., 187 F.3d 926 (8th Cir. 1999); *In re* Straight, 143 F.3d 1387 (10th Cir. 1998), *cert. denied*, 525 U.S. 982 (1998); State of Georgia Dep't of Revenue v. Burke, 146 F.3d 1313 (11th Cir. 1998), *cert. denied*, 119 S. Ct. 2410 (1999); *In re* Stanley, 273 B.R. 907 (Bankr. N.D. Fla. 2002) (state guaranty agency that waived sovereign immunity by filing proof of claim could not reinstate immunity defense by later withdrawing claim).

161   *See* Lake County Estates, Inc. v. Tahoe Reg'l Planning Agency, 440 U.S. 391 (1979).

162   *See, e.g.*, Duke v. Grady Muni. Schs., 127 F.3d 972 (10th Cir. 1997); Mancuso v. New York State Thruway Auth., 86 F.3d 289 (2d Cir. 1996), *cert. denied*, 519 U.S. 992 (1996); Hadley v. North Arkansas Cmty. Technical Coll., 76 F.3d 1437 (8th Cir. 1996), *cert. denied*, 519 U.S. 1148 (1997); Harter v. C.D. Vernon, 101 F.3d 334 (4th Cir. 1996), *cert. denied*, 521 U.S. 1120 (1997); Christy v. Pennsylvania Turnpike Comm'n, 54 F.3d 1140 (3d Cir. 1995), *cert. denied*, 516 U.S. 932 (1995); Metcalf & Eddy v. Puerto Rico Aqueduct & Sewer Auth., 991 F.2d 935 (1st. Cir. 1993). For a more detailed discussion of this topic, see NCLC REPORTS, *Bankruptcy and Foreclosures Ed.* (Nov./Dec. 2000).

163   *See* Metcalf & Eddy v. Puerto Rico Aqueduct & Sewer Auth., 991 F.2d 935 (1st Cir. 1993).

164   The enabling statutes of guaranty agencies often provide that their bonds and loan guaranties are not an obligation of the state. *See, e.g.*, Iowa Code § 261.38; Mich. Comp. Laws § 390.1154; N.J. Stat. Ann. § 18A:71A-18 (same for New Jersey Higher Education Student Assistance Authority); N.C. Gen. Stat. § 116-202; 24 Pa. Cons. Stat. § 5105.1(b) (bonds and notes of Pennsylvania Higher Education Assistance Authority not debt of Pennsylvania); R.I. Gen. Laws § 16-57-12.

165   *See In re* Muir, 239 B.R. 213 (Bankr. D. Mont. 1999) (student loan guaranty agency failed to satisfy burden of demonstrating that it was an arm of the state and entitled to Eleventh Amendment immunity). *But see In re* Kahl, 240 B.R. 524 (Bankr. E.D. Pa. 1999) (finding Texas agency to be an arm of the state, but no waiver of sovereign immunity). *See generally* Duke v. Grady Muni. Schs., 127 F.3d 972 (10th Cir. 1997) (court must focus on legal liability for a judgment rather than practical or indirect impact a judgment would have on a state's treasury); Metcalf & Eddy v. Puerto Rico Aqueduct & Sewer Auth., 991 F.2d 935 (1st Cir. 1993) (rejecting among other arguments the state agency's claim that it could claim immunity solely on the basis that judgments against it might absorb unrestricted funds donated by the state and in that way lead indirectly to the depletion of the state's treasury).

166   *See* 10 U.S.C. § 1087(b).

167   Lees v. Tennessee Student Assistance Corp., 264 B.R. 884 (W.D. Tenn. 2001).

7.3.4 Use of Older Dischargeability Standards Today When Student's Pre-1998 Bankruptcy Did Not Determine Student Loan's Dischargeability

Unless the student or another party seeks a determination in the bankruptcy proceeding concerning a student loan's dischargeability, the loan's dischargeability will *not* be determined in a bankruptcy proceeding—the loan is neither ruled discharged nor enforceable. Instead, whether the loan has been discharged by the bankruptcy will not be determined until a later date, perhaps many years later, when a guarantor or the Department seeks to collect on that debt in court or when the student seeks a judicial determination of the loan's enforceability.

When a student loan's dischargeability is determined after the bankruptcy proceeding, the test will be whether the loan was dischargeable based on the Bankruptcy Code in effect at the time of the bankruptcy case, not at the time the loan's dischargeability is determined. This distinction may have a significant impact on whether the debt is dischargeable.

For example, the dischargeability exception for bankruptcies filed before November 1990 was that student loans more than *five* years old were dischargeable in chapter 7 bankruptcies (compared to the subsequent seven-year standard).[168] Also, a chapter 13 discharge operated to discharge a student loan obligation, even one less than five years old (compared to the present, wherein dischargeability is treated the same for chapter 13 and 7 cases).[169]

Thus, when a loan was first due in 1983, and the loan's dischargeability was not determined in a chapter 7 bankruptcy filed in 1989, a court today should determine that the loan was discharged by that bankruptcy.[170] While the loan is not dischargeable under the present Code, it is dischargeable under the five-year test in place at that time. Likewise, a loan

that first became due in 1990 was discharged in a bankruptcy filed in 1998 (before October 7, 1998) under the seven-year rule.

7.4 Advantages of a Chapter 13 Bankruptcy When Student Loan Cannot Be Discharged

7.4.1 Separate Classification

If a student loan cannot be discharged based on undue hardship in a chapter 7 or 13 bankruptcy filing, there are still strategic advantages to filing a chapter 13 bankruptcy.[171] One advantage is that the student's chapter 13 plan, not the loan holder, determines the size of a student's loan payments. For the three- to five-year life of the chapter 13 plan, the plan will determine how much the student pays each unsecured creditor, including student loan creditors.

For many plans, this would mean that only 5% or 10% of the outstanding loan would be paid off over those three to five years. At the end of the plan, the student could seek a determination that repayment of the balance would cause an undue hardship. During the three- to five-year pendency of the plan, no collection action, garnishment, or tax intercepts can be taken against the student, though interest on the debt will continue to accrue.[172]

Nevertheless, if the remainder of the debt is not dischargeable after the plan has terminated, the student is then obligated to pay the remainder. When that is the case, it is in the student's interest to pay off as much of the student loan in the chapter 13 plan as possible, at the expense of other unsecured creditors—creditors whose remaining balance *will* be dischargeable after the plan is completed.

One way to pay more on the student loan than on other unsecured debts is to classify separately the student loan for

---

168 Section 523(a)(8) was amended by Pub. L. No. 101-647, 104 Stat 4964, § 3621 (Nov. 29, 1990).

169 Section 1328(a)(2) of the Bankruptcy Code was amended by Pub. L. No. 101-508, § 3007 (Nov. 5, 1990).

170 Similarly, between November 6, 1978, and August 14, 1979, there was no statutory restriction in place on the dischargeability of student loans. Thus students can argue today that any student loan listed as a debt in a bankruptcy during that period is discharged, no matter how recently the debt was first due before the bankruptcy proceeding. 20 U.S.C. § 1087-3, dealing with the discharge of student loans in bankruptcy, was repealed by the Bankruptcy Reform Act, Pub. L. No. 95-598 § 317 (1978). It was replaced as to cases filed on and after August 14, 1979, by the United States Bankruptcy Code. *See* S. Rep. No. 230, 96th Cong., 1st Sess. (1979) *reprinted in* 1979 U.S.C.C.A.N. 936, 938. *But see* Adamo v. New York State Higher Educ. Servs. Corp. (*In re* Adamo), 619 F.2d 216 (2d Cir. 1980), *cert. denied*, 449 U.S. 843 (1980).

171 For more details, see National Consumer Law Center, Consumer Bankruptcy Law and Practice § 14.4.3.8.5 (8th ed. 2006).

172 If the student loan debt is nondischargeable, post-petition interest will not be discharged. *See* Kielisch v. Educational Credit Mgmt. Corp. (*In re* Kielisch), 258 F.3d 315 (4th Cir. 2001); *In re* Pardee, 218 B.R. 916 (B.A.P. 9th Cir. 1998), *aff'd*, 187 F.3d 648 (9th Cir. 1999); *In re* Jordan, 146 B.R. 31 (D. Colo. 1992). In addition, § 502(b)(2) of the Code provides that general unsecured creditors such as student loan creditors may not include unmatured, post-petition interest in their bankruptcy claims. Leeper v. Pennsylvania Higher Educ. Assistance Agency, 49 F.3d 98 (3d Cir. 1995) (interest accruing during pendency of plan not discharged, even though debtor paid pre-petition debt in full through chapter 13 plan). One court has held that, while unmatured, post-petition interest may not be included in the student loan creditor's claim, § 502(b) does not prevent the creditor from applying chapter 13 plan payments to accrued interest, including post-petition interest, on the nondischargeable debt. Kielisch v. Educational Credit Mgmt. Corp. (*In re* Kielisch), 258 F.3d 315 (4th Cir. 2001).

payments at a higher percentage than other unsecured debts pursuant to 11 U.S.C. § 1322(b)(1). Recent cases have been divided, both in the means of analysis and the result, as to whether students can separately classify student loans, some allowing separate classification[173] and some not.[174] Some courts have even issued opinions providing guidance as to the amount of discrimination that will be allowed.[175]

A useful alternative to separate classification, in those jurisdictions where separate classification has not been approved, is to cure a default on the student loan pursuant to 11 U.S.C. § 1322(b)(5).[176] This allows the debtor to cure an arrearage on the student loan over time while maintaining the post-petition payments during the life of the plan. A number of courts have already permitted debtors to make ongoing student loan payments from income on this basis outside the plan.[177] An added benefit of this approach is that the ongoing payments will include post-petition interest that would not otherwise be paid as part of a claim under the plan.[178] By failing to give effect to § 1322(b)(5) as a distinct plan provision, some courts have required debtors proposing to pay student loans outside the plan to satisfy the unfair discrimination test under § 1322(b)(1).[179]

A final approach might be to establish a five-year plan, not separately classify the student loan for the first three years of the plan, but then to classify it for greater payment during the plan's final two years.[180] The basis for this approach is the Bankruptcy Code provision that requires disposable income only to be paid out over three years.[181] Any amount that creditors receive in the final two years would be a bonus in any event. Courts have split on whether they will allow this separate classification of student loans in years four and five of a chapter 13 plan.[182]

7.4.2 Co-Debtor Stay

Another advantage of chapter 13 is that there is an additional type of "automatic stay" that goes into effect when the case is filed. This stay prohibits any act or legal action to collect a debtor's consumer debt from a co-debtor

---

173 *In re* Cox, 186 B.R. 744 (Bankr. N.D. Fla. 1995); *In re* Tucker, 159 B.R. 325 (Bankr. D. Mont. 1993); Matter of Foreman, 136 B.R. 532 (Bankr. S.D. Iowa 1992); *In re* Boggan, 125 B.R. 533 (Bankr. N.D. Ill. 1991); *In re* Freshley, 69 B.R. 96 (Bankr. N.D. Ga. 1987). *See also In re* Sullivan, 195 B.R. 649 (Bankr. W.D. Tex. 1996); *In re* Dodds, 140 B.R. 542 (Bankr. D. Mont. 1992).

On the analogous question of whether nondischargeable child support debts may be separately classified, many courts have concluded in the affirmative. *E.g., In re* Leser, 939 F.2d 669 (8th Cir. 1991); *In re* Husted, 142 B.R. 72 (Bankr. W.D.N.Y. 1992); *In re* Whittaker, 113 B.R. 531 (Bankr. D. Minn. 1990) (allowing a fresh start is sufficient to justify discriminatory classification in favor of nondischargeable support debt).

174 *In re* Groves, 39 F.3d 212 (8th Cir. 1994) (plan could not discriminate in favor of student loans solely due to their nondischargeability); *In re* Bentley, 266 B.R. 229 (B.A.P. 1st Cir. 2001) (chapter 13 plan that favored student loan creditor failed unfair discrimination test by altering the "allocation of benefits and burdens" to detriment of other unsecured creditors); *In re* Sperna, 173 B.R. 654 (B.A.P. 9th Cir. 1994) (plan could not discriminate in favor of student loans solely due to their nondischargeability); McCullough v. Brown, 162 B.R. 506 (N.D. Ill. 1993); *In re* Thibodeau, 248 B.R. 699 (Bankr. D. Mass. 2000) (plan was not proposed in nondiscriminatory manner based on debtor's sizeable income and lack of good faith); *In re* Burns, 216 B.R. 945 (Bankr. S.D. Cal. 1998); *In re* Gonzalez, 206 B.R. 239 (Bankr. S.D. Fla. 1997); *In re* Coonce, 213 B.R. 344 (Bankr. S.D. Ill. 1997); *In re* Willis, 189 B.R. 203 (Bankr. N.D. Okla. 1995), *rev'd and remanded*, 197 B.R. 912 (N.D. Okla. 1996); *In re* Colfer, 159 B.R. 602 (Bankr. D. Me. 1993) (refusing to allow separate classification); *In re* Smalberger, 157 B.R. 472 (Bankr. D. Or. 1993), *aff'd*, 170 B.R. 707 (D. Or. 1994); *In re* Chapman, 146 B.R. 411 (Bankr. N.D. Ill. 1992); *In re* Scheiber, 129 B.R. 604 (Bankr. D. Minn. 1991); *In re* Furlow, 70 B.R. 973 (Bankr. E.D. Pa. 1987) (separate classification of student loan debt not allowed without further explanation of reasons).

175 *In re* Simmons, 288 B.R. 737 (Bankr. N.D. Tex. 2003) (plan providing for 100% repayment of student loan and 0% to general unsecured creditors may be confirmed when all of debtor's disposable income paid into plan for first thirty-six months and student loan creditor paid in months forty-one through forty-eight of plan); *In re* Williams, 253 B.R. 220 (Bankr. W.D. Tenn. 2000) (plan that provides for 100% repayment of student loan will be confirmed only if other unsecured creditors are paid at least 70%; debtors may show "unique circumstances" to justify confirmation of plans with more than 30% difference in repayment percentage).

176 Section 1322(b)(5) permits the curing of defaults under the plan and maintenance of ongoing payments, typically made outside the plan, on any secured or unsecured claims when the last payment on the debt is due after the final payment under the plan.

177 *See In re* Williams, 253 B.R. 220 (Bankr. W.D. Tenn. 2000); *In re* Chandler, 210 B.R. 898 (Bankr. D.N.H. 1997); *In re* Sullivan, 195 B.R. 649 (Bankr. W.D. Tex. 1996); *In re* Cox, 186 B.R. 744 (Bankr. N.D. Ill. 1995); *In re* Christophe, 151 B.R. 475 (Bankr. N.D. Ill. 1993) (plan can propose cure of student loan default pursuant to § 1322(b)(5)); *In re* Benner, 156 B.R. 631 (Bankr. D. Minn. 1993); *In re* Saulter, 133 B.R. 148 (Bankr. W.D. Mo. 1991).

178 *See* note 172, *supra*; *In re* Williams, 253 B.R. 220 (Bankr. W.D. Tenn. 2000) (maintenance of ongoing payments on student loans under § 1322(b)(5) includes the payment of post-petition interest).

179 *In re* Labib-Kiyarash, 271 B.R. 189 (B.A.P. 9th Cir. 2001) (use of § 1322(b)(5) subject to debtor showing that classification is fair under § 1322(b)(1)); *In re* Simmons, 288 B.R. 737 (Bankr. N.D. Tex. 2003); *In re* Edwards, 263 B.R. 690 (Bankr. R.I. 2001); *In re* Thibodeau, 248 B.R. 699 (Bankr. D. Mass. 2000).

180 *In re* Strickland, 181 B.R. 598 (Bankr. N.D. Ala. 1995) (court held nondischargeable student loan debt could not be treated more favorably than other unsecured claims for first thirty-six months of chapter 13 plan, but remaining twenty-four months could be devoted solely to payment of student loan).

181 11 U.S.C. § 1325(b)(1)(B).

182 *Compare In re* Stickland, 181 B.R. 598 (Bankr. N.D. Ala. 1995) (allowing separate treatment in years four and five); *In re* Rudy, 1993 WL 365370 (Bankr. S.D. Ohio 1993) (same) *with In re* Sullivan, 195 B.R. 649 (Bankr. W.D. Tex. 1996) (not allowing separate classification).

or co-obligor.[183] Students who file under chapter 13 can thus protect from collection parents or other family members who may have co-signed a student loan as long as the student's plan provides for payment of the student loan.[184] In addition, the need to retain the co-debtor stay may provide an additional justification for the separate classification of a student loan in a chapter 13 plan.[185]

7.4.3 Raising Defenses in Response to Creditor Claims

The chapter 13 claim allowance process may also present an opportunity for consumers to raise defenses to a student loan obligation. In addition to the various grounds for objections to creditors' claims that may be raised under the Bankruptcy Code,[186] no claim may be allowed to the extent that it is unenforceable against the debtor.[187] This means that the student may assert as objections any defenses, counterclaims, or setoffs the debtor may have, including for instance defenses relating to the school's misconduct.[188] The objection will generally be treated by the bankruptcy court as a "contested matter."[189]

For students who are confronted with unlawful or excessive interest and collection fees or the miscrediting of payments by loan servicers, this process also provides an opportunity for the student to challenge the amount owed on the student loan. A student loan creditor is bound by a determination disallowing collection costs as part of its claim in bankruptcy regardless of whether the student loan debt is nondischargeable. Student loan creditors may be denied collection costs and fees as part of their claims when no entitlement exists under the relevant regulations or contract provisions.[190] Unfortunately, the courts have rejected

several recent challenges to guarantee agency's fixed-percentage collection fees.[191]

7.5 Student's Rights After Bankruptcy Discharge

If there has been a judicial determination that a student loan is discharged in bankruptcy, the debtor is no longer liable for the obligation and is protected from any attempt to collect the debt.[192] The lender should not accept any further payments on the loan, such as payments the lender may receive through a tax intercept program or even those voluntarily made by the debtor. Department of Education regulations provide that, if a guaranty agency receives payments on a discharged loan on which the Department previously paid a claim to the agency, the agency must return the payments to the sender and notify the borrower that there is no obligation to pay the loan.[193]

Similarly, a school cannot withhold a former student's transcripts just because the debt has been discharged in bankruptcy.[194] The 1994 amendments to the Bankruptcy Code clarified this principle, prohibiting discrimination with respect to student loans or grants based upon discharge of a prior debt. Prior to this time, courts had split on whether schools could deny transcripts after discharge and also on whether schools could deny transcripts to students who filed for bankruptcy but had not yet received a discharge.[195] Some courts have continued to allow denial of transcripts in the

---

183 *See* 11 U.S.C. § 1301. For a more detailed discussion of the co-debtor stay in chapter 13, see National Consumer Law Center, Consumer Bankruptcy Law and Practice § 9.4.4 (8th ed. 2006).

184 The Department of Education regulations acknowledge the chapter 13 co-debtor stay by noting that guaranty agencies must suspend all collection efforts against a "co-maker or endorser" if the student borrower has filed under chapter 13. *See* 34 C.F.R. § 682.402(f)(2).

185 11 U.S.C. 1322(b)(1). *See* § 7.4.1, *supra*.

186 For a detailed discussion of objections to claims, see National Consumer Law Center, Consumer Bankruptcy Law and Practice § 13.4.3 (7th ed. 2004 and Supp.).

187 11 U.S.C. § 502(b)(1).

188 *See also In re* Mason, 300 B.R. 160 (Bankr. D. Conn. 2003) (consolidation loan obtained by duress held void and unenforceable). *See generally* Ch. 9, *infra*.

189 Such proceedings are governed by Fed. R. Bankr. P. 9014.

190 *In re* Schlehr, 290 B.R. 387 (Bankr. D. Mont. 2003) (objection to collection fees included in student loan creditor's proofs of claim denied as chapter 13 trustee failed to rebut prima facie validity of claims); *In re* McAlpin, 254 B.R. 449 (Bankr. D. Minn. 2000), *rev'd on other grounds*, 263 B.R. 881 (B.A.P. 8th Cir. 2001), *aff'd*, 278 F.3d 866 (8th Cir. 2002) (collection costs

and fees disallowed, based on 34 C.F.R. § 674.45(e) *et seq.*, when creditor failed to prove they were reasonable, and limited to actual or average cost incurred).

191 Black v. Educational Credit Management Corp., 459 F.3d 796 (7th Cir. 2006), *aff'g*, Educational Credit Management Corp. v. Barnes, 318 B.R. 482 (S.D. Ind. 2004) (DOE regulation that authorizes collection charges based on annual aggregate agency costs, up to 25% of outstanding principal and interest for the individual loan, is a valid exercise of statutory authority); *In re* Belton, 337 B.R. 471 (Bankr. W.D. N.Y. 2006) (same); *In re* Evans, 322 B.R. 429 (Bankr. W.D. Wash. 2005) (25% fees based on agency's purported aggregate costs are authorized by federal regulation and notes). *See also* United States v. Vilus, 419 F. Supp. 2d 293 (E.D.N.Y. 2005) (percentage fees upheld in student loan debt collection cases, rejecting debtors' arguments that fees should be based on hourly rates for work actually performed).

192 11 U.S.C. § 524(a)(2). Damages and attorney fees are available if improper collection activities occur. *See* National Consumer Law Center, Consumer Bankruptcy Law and Practice § 14.5.5.6 (8th ed. 2006).

193 34 C.F.R. § 682.402(r)(1).

194 *Id. See also* National Consumer Law Center, Consumer Bankruptcy Law and Practice § 14.5.5.2 (7th ed. 2004 and Supp.).

195 *In re* Merchant, 958 F.2d 738 (6th Cir. 1992); Juras v. Aman Collection, 829 F.2d 739 (9th Cir. 1987), *cert. denied*, 488 U.S. 875, 977 (1988) (institutions cannot withhold transcripts from students who have had their loans discharged, who are making payments under chapter 13 plan, or who have filed for bankruptcy but not yet received a discharge); *In re* Gustafson, 111 B.R. 282 (B.A.P. 9th Cir. 1990), *rev'd on other grounds*, 934

latter situation (in which a debtor filed bankruptcy but has not yet been granted a discharge). The debtor's response in this situation should be that, as soon as a bankruptcy is filed, acts such as withholding of transcripts are prohibited by the automatic stay.[196]

While the Department of Education in the early 1990s stated that students who discharged student loans in bankruptcy would not be eligible for new student loans,[197] the question of a student's eligibility for new loans and grants after discharging a student loan in bankruptcy has now been resolved by Congressional action. The Bankruptcy Reform Act of 1994 specifies that those discharging student loans in bankruptcy remain eligible for new loans and grants. The United States, guarantors, and lenders cannot discriminate

against those who have not paid their student loans when those loans were discharged in bankruptcy.[198]

The Act's legislative history states that the "section clarifies the anti-discrimination provisions of the Bankruptcy Code to ensure that applicants for student loans or grants are not denied those benefits due to a prior bankruptcy. The section overrules *In re Goldrich.* . . ."[199]

The Department responded by changing its regulations so that students no longer have to reaffirm student loans discharged in bankruptcy to be eligible for new loans or grants. The Department states that such a reaffirmation requirement is no longer permissible because the Bankruptcy Reform Act prohibits denial of a loan or loan guarantee based on a bankruptcy discharge.[200] Consequently, the offending language has been deleted from the regulations.[201]

Nevertheless, the Department will look to a prior bankruptcy in considering an applicant's future creditworthiness in applying for PLUS loans. A PLUS loan is a specialized type of loan taken out by parents of the student, during the application for which, by statute, the Department is required to consider the parent(s)' creditworthiness. Thus applicants for PLUS loans will be required to explain the bankruptcy or secure a credit-worthy endorser.

F.2d 216 (9th Cir. 1991); *In re* Carson, 150 B.R. 228 (Bankr. E.D. Mo. 1993) (protections of the automatic stay override creditor's ability to collect student loan debt until such time as debt is determined to be nondischargeable; therefore no withholding of transcripts until debt is found to be nondischargeable). *But see In re* Joyner, 171 B.R. 759 (Bankr. E.D. Pa. 1994); *In re* Najafi, 154 B.R. 185 (Bankr. E.D. Pa. 1993) (rejecting *Gustafson*, reasoning that it is unfair to the creditor if students can get transcripts up until the moment the debt is found to be nondischargeable; court found college had right comparable to a "security interest" in the transcript). Both the *Najafi* and *Joyner* courts ordered the colleges to release transcripts upon payment of $300 in each case by the students to the colleges. Both cases involved private colleges and, in both cases, the student debts were found nondischargeable. *See generally* Ana Kellia Ramares, *Annotation: Validity, Constructions, and Application of Statutes, Regulations, or Policies Allowing Denial of Student Loans, Student Loan Guarantees, or Educational Services to Debtors Who Have Had Student Loans Scheduled in Bankruptcy*, 107 A.L.R. Fed. 192 (1998).

196 Loyola v. McClarty, 234 B.R. 386 (E.D. La. 1999).

197 Its position was that the Bankruptcy Code's prohibition of governmental discrimination at 11 U.S.C. § 525(a) did not apply to the granting of credit, such as a student loan. *See, e.g., In re* Goldrich, 771 F.2d 28 (2d Cir. 1985) (student loan not within scope of § 525(a)). Of course, the Code discrimination prohibition will clearly apply to Pell and other student *grants*.

198 11 U.S.C. § 525(c). *See* Pub. L. No. 103-394 § 313 (amending 11 U.S.C. § 525 (Oct. 22, 1994)). *See also* 140 Cong. Rec. H10, 7771 (daily ed. Oct. 4, 1994). While the Act applies to bankruptcies filed after October 22, 1994, unless otherwise noted, the language of § 313 makes clear a Congressional intent to apply that section to any student loan discharged in bankruptcy, even to student loans discharged under the Bankruptcy Act, that is, discharged before 1979.

199 H.R. Rep. No. 103-835 (Judiciary Comm.) at 58 (1994), *reprinted in* 1994 U.S.C.C.A.N. 3340, 3367.

200 59 Fed. Reg. 61212 (Nov. 29, 1994) (FFEL loans). *See also* 59 Fed. Reg. 61667 (Dec. 1, 1994) (FDSL loans).

201 59 Fed. Reg. 61215 (Nov. 29, 1994) (amending 34 C.F.R. § 682.201(4)(i)).

Chapter 8   Repayment Strategies for Getting Out of Default

8.1 Introduction

Many low-income student loan defaulters have been placed in an impossible situation. Their inability to repay their student loans makes them ineligible for new student loans and grants that might help them pull themselves out of poverty. It also damages their credit ratings, leads to interception of Earned Income Tax Credits, wage garnishment, aggressive collection efforts, and assessment of high collection fees.

The primary goal for most of these borrowers is to get out of default. Some hope to go back to school. Others simply want to stop the government collection onslaught. Whatever their reasons, there are numerous possibilities for low-income borrowers to get out of default by making payments on their loans. In many cases, the payments will be very low and affordable.

This chapter reviews the primary repayment options for clients in default. These include loan consolidation, renewal of eligibility through reasonable and affordable payment plans, and loan rehabilitation. Some clients may have the ability to pay a lump sum to settle the loan. The Department's discretionary authority to compromise or even write off all or part of the loan is also discussed in this chapter. Pre-default repayment options are covered in Chapter 2, *supra*.

Discharges and bankruptcy will also renew eligibility. These options should be considered before attempting to set up payment plans. Discharge rights are discussed in Chapter 6, *supra*. Low-income victims of vocational school fraud will often qualify for discharges. Bankruptcy, as discussed in Chapter 7, *supra*, is a more remote possibility due to restrictions on when student loans can be discharged in bankruptcy. State tuition recovery funds, discussed in Chapter 9, *infra*, should also be considered when available.

Many borrowers, however, will not qualify for any of the federal or state discharges discussed in Chapters 6 and 9 and/or will be unable to discharge their loans in bankruptcy as discussed in Chapter 7. Even if they do qualify for discharges, borrowers may still want to set up repayment plans pending resolution of their discharge applications. This may be preferable in some cases to the administrative forbearance options discussed in Chapter 3, *supra*.

8.2 Consolidation Loans

8.2.1 General

Consolidation can be an effective solution to get out of default. Low-income borrowers can consolidate their defaulted student loans into a new Direct consolidation loan with an income-contingent repayment plan (ICRP). An alternative is to obtain a Federal Family Education Consolidation Loan (FFEL) with an income-sensitive repayment plan (ISRP).[1]

After obtaining a consolidation loan, the borrower gets a fresh start, becoming eligible for new loans, grants, and even deferments. Borrowers will no longer be listed as currently in default on their credit records, and no longer subject to tax intercepts, garnishments, or other collection efforts.

Consolidation is an option for borrowers outside of default as well. The FFEL consolidation program in particular has grown at a staggering pace since the late 1990s. This growth is attributable to a number of factors, including unprecedented low interest rates that spurred many borrowers to refinance their higher-rate loans into fixed rate, lower-interest consolidation loans. Loan brokers and consolidation companies aggressively selling consolidation loans also emerged.

The costs have been as staggering as the growth. For example, subsidy costs for FFEL consolidation grew from $0.651 billion for loans made in fiscal year 2002 to $2.135 billion for loans made in fiscal year 2003.[2]

The increased profile of consolidation lending has generated considerable controversy and debate in Congress. Many advocates and policymakers sought to curb the growth, arguing that consolidation loans were never intended to be tools to secure low interest rates. Proponents countered that borrowers desperately needed the ability to refinance. They acknowledged the costs but suggested that savings could be better realized without penalizing borrowers, such as by cutting subsidies to lenders.

---

1 Direct Consolidation Loans are discussed beginning at § 8.2.2, *infra*; FFEL Consolidation loans at § 8.2.3, *infra*.

2 U.S. Gen. Accounting Office, Student Loan Programs: Lower Interest Rates and Higher Loan Volume Have Increased Federal Consolidation Loan Costs, GAO-04-568T (Mar. 17, 2004).

Large consolidation lenders such as Sallie Mae protested against the opening up of the consolidation market. They argued that the third-party marketers and other consolidation lenders luring student loan borrowers into consolidating their loans undermined the student loan originating industry. In their view, student loan originators would simply leave the loan program if they believed that their loan portfolios will be later "stolen" by other companies offering to consolidate loans at favorable terms.[3]

Lower-income borrowers were affected by the massive competition in the consolidation sector. Consolidation is currently the one way a borrower with defaulted loans or with exclusively FFEL loans can obtain the Direct Consolidation Loans income-contingent repayment plan. However, aggressive marketing by FFEL lenders and the refusal of many FFEL lenders to allow borrowers to consolidate with the Federal Direct Loan program unfairly shut the door to an ICRP for many needy borrowers.

One measure of FFEL lenders' success in steering borrowers away from the Direct consolidation program is the substantial growth in the FFEL consolidation program. From fiscal year 1998 to fiscal year 2002, the share of underlying FFEL and Direct loan volume consolidated into FFEL increased significantly.[4] In fiscal year 2002 alone, 84% of FFEL loan volume that was consolidated was consolidated through the FFEL program. With respect to Direct loans, 58% were consolidated with FFEL.[5] Defaulted loans, however, from either the FFEL or Direct Loan program were much more likely to be consolidated into the Direct Loan program.[6]

After many years of debate, Congress made significant changes to the consolidation programs in 2005 and 2006. For the most part, these changes will likely make consolidation less attractive for refinancing purposes. The two consolidation programs, FFEL and Direct, will also look much more alike. Other changes should reduce the incentives for collectors to pressure borrowers into consolidation. These changes became effective on July 1, 2006. Despite the significant revisions, the borrower's right to consolidate defaulted loans into a Direct consolidation loan and obtain an ICRP survived largely intact.

8.2.2 Direct Consolidation Loans

8.2.2.1 How to Obtain a Direct Consolidation Loans Application

Prior to July 1, 2006, there were three categories of Direct consolidation loans: (1) Direct Subsidized Consolidation Loans,[7] (2) Direct Unsubsidized Consolidation Loans,[8] and (3) Direct PLUS Consolidation Loans.[9] For loans for which applications are received after July 1, 2006, there will be only a single Direct consolidation loan, but it may include up to three separate components representing subsidized, unsubsidized, and PLUS loans.

There is no charge to obtain a Direct consolidation loan. The first step is to request an application by calling the current toll-free number, 1-800-557-7392 or, for TDD, 1-800-557-7395. Borrowers can also apply for Direct consolidation loans using the Internet. The website is www.ed.gov/DirectLoan.[10] The Direct Loan website has information about interest rates and payment plans for consolidation loans. It also provides a number of calculators to help borrowers estimate their monthly repayments under the various plans.

8.2.2.2 Which Loans Can Be Consolidated Under the Direct Loan Program

Under the Direct Consolidation Loan program, borrowers can consolidate subsidized and unsubsidized Stafford loans, supplemental loans for students (SLSs), federally insured

---

3   Tensions between third-party marketers and traditional consolidation lenders led to a 2002 lawsuit filed by the College Loan Corporation (CLC) against SLM Corporation (*Sallie Mae College Loan Corp. v. SLM Corp.*, Civil No. 02-1377-A (E.D. Va.). Pleadings and decisions in this case are available on the website of the National Council of Higher Education Loan Programs (NCHELP) at www.nchelp.org (e-library) (2006). CLC and SLM were parties to a contract that provided that CLC would send consolidation loans to SLM for servicing and processing. CLC alleged that SLM, motivated by a desire to increase their own profitability, began mishandling loans sent to them by CLC. CLC alleged that SLM contacted the borrowers whose applications were mishandled in an attempt to get them to have their loans funded through SLM rather than CLC. In June 2003, a jury found in favor of the defendant SLM and affiliates on the remaining claims in the case, including CLC's allegations of breach of contract, breach of fiduciary duty, and interference with prospective economic advantage. CLC appealed and the parties settled the case in May 2005. SLM paid $14 million, net of insurance, but did not admit liability. *See also* College Loan Corp. v. SLM Corp., 396 F.3d 588 (4th Cir. 2005) (College Loan Corporation's state law claims not preempted).

4   U.S. Gov't Accountability Office, Student Consolidation Loans: Future Analysis Could Lead to Enhanced Default Assumptions for Budgetary Cost Estimates, GAO-04-843 (Aug. 2004).

5   *Id.*

6   *Id.*

---

7   Interest is not charged to the borrower during in-school grace and deferment periods. 34 C.F.R. § 685.102(b). *See generally* § 1.4.2, *supra.*

8   Borrowers are responsible for the interest that accrues during any period on these loans.

9   The PLUS loan category includes the traditional Parent Loans and the new (as of 2006) PLUS loans for graduate and professional students. In general, the conditions and terms for the PLUS parent loans will apply to the graduate/professional PLUS loans, including credit requirements. *See* § 1.4.2.1, *supra.*

10 A copy of the most recent Direct Consolidation application form is reprinted at Appendix D, *infra.*

student loans (FISLs), PLUS Loans, Direct loans, Perkins loans, Health Education Assistance loans (HEALs), and just about any other type of federal student loan.[11] Loans that are not eligible for consolidation include state or private loans that are not federally guaranteed; law, medical, and graduate access loans; and graduate extension loans.

Although all of these different loans may be consolidated, the borrower must have at least one outstanding FFEL or Direct loan to obtain a Direct consolidation loan.[12] This means, for example, that a Perkins loan on its own cannot be consolidated into a Direct loan.

If the "qualifying" loan is an FFEL loan, the borrower must also certify that he or she was unable to obtain FFEL consolidation or is unable to obtain an FFEL consolidation loan with acceptable income-sensitive repayment terms and is eligible for the income-contingent repayment plan.[13]

Prior to July 1, 2006, borrowers could even obtain a Direct consolidation loan when they were still in school. In-school consolidation was eliminated by the Higher Education Reconciliation Act.[14] This change applies to applications for loans received on or after July 1, 2006.

Borrowers have the option to consolidate all, just some, or even just one of their existing student loans. There is no minimum or maximum size for a Direct consolidation loan.

Prior to July 1, 2006, married borrowers could choose to consolidate loans from both spouses or jointly consolidate the loans of either spouse. Both borrowers had to agree to be jointly and severally liable for repayment. In addition, the borrowers had to agree to repay the joint loan regardless of any change in marital status. Perhaps because of the dubious advantages of this program, Congress eliminated it as of July 1, 2006.[15]

Borrowers can consolidate if they are out of school but in repayment or, most importantly for many low-income borrowers, if they are already in default.[16] To obtain a Direct consolidation loan, borrowers in default *either* have to make three consecutive reasonable and affordable payments based on their total financial circumstances (sometimes set as low as $5 a month) *or* agree to accept an income-contingent repayment plan (ICRP) and consent to the IRS disclosing to the Department certain tax return information for the purposes of calculating a monthly repayment amount.[17]

The three payments need not be consecutive if the borrower is an "affected individual," defined to include those who are serving on active duty during a war or other military operation or national emergency, are performing qualifying National Guard duty during a war or other military operation or national emergency, reside or are employed in an area that is declared a disaster area by any federal, state, or local official in connection with a national emergency, or suffered economic hardship as a direct result of a war or other military operation or national emergency, as determined by the Secretary.[18]

However, due to changes passed by Congress in 2005 and 2006, defaulted Direct consolidation loans may no longer be consolidated.[19] Under the rules after July 1, 2006, a borrower who already has a consolidation loan with either FFEL or Direct will not be able to "reconsolidate" with either program, except in the following limited circumstances:

- if the borrower receives eligible student loans after the date of receipt of the consolidation loan;
- if loans received prior to the date of the consolidation loan are added during the 180-day period following the making of the consolidation loan;
- if loans received following the making of the consolidation loan are added during the 180-day period following the making of the consolidation loan;
- if loans received prior to the date of the first consolidation are added to a subsequent consolidation loans; and
- if FFEL consolidation borrowers obtain a Direct consolidation loan only for the purposes of obtaining an ICRP and only if the loan has been submitted to the guaranty agency for default aversion.[20]

Congress imposed these limits to address problems with so-called "two step" consolidation. Prior to these changes, there were no limits on FFEL consolidation borrowers' ability to consolidate with Direct. The FFEL lenders often encouraged borrowers who had already consolidated with FFEL to first consolidate with Direct. The borrowers were then able to turn around and consolidate the new Direct consolidation loan with an FFEL consolidation lender. This was basically a way for FFEL lenders and borrowers to get around the rule that prevented FFEL consolidation borrowers from "re-consolidating" their loans with FFEL.

As of July 1, 2006, there are additional, important limits affecting which loans may be consolidated with Direct loans. Prior to this date, the rules for Direct loan consoli-

---

11   34 C.F.R. § 685.220(b).

12   34 C.F.R. § 685.220(d).

13   34 C.F.R. § 685.220(d)(1)(i)(B). *See* § 8.2.2.3.

14   Pub. L. No. 109-171, 120 Stat. 4 (Feb. 8, 2006). *See also* 71 Fed. Reg. 45666 (Aug. 9, 2006) (Interim Final Regulations, effective September 8, 2006).

15   Pub. L. No. 109-171, 120 Stat. 4 (Feb. 8, 2006).

16   34 C.F.R. § 685.220(d)(1)(ii)(C), (D).

17   34 C.F.R. § 685.220(d)(1)(ii)(C), (D).

18   68 Fed. Reg. 69312 (Dec. 12, 2003).

19   This may not be much different from current practice. In general, even prior to July 1, 2006, the Department had the discretion to consolidation in these circumstances but had a policy against "re-consolidating" a consolidation loan if the underlying loans in the defaulted consolidation loan had been in default.

20   20 U.S.C. § 1078-3(a)(3)(B)(FFEL), 20 U.S.C. § 1087e(g) (Direct). The regulations that limit "re-consolidation" to FFEL borrowers with defaulted loans may go beyond the provisions of the Higher Education Reconciliation Act.

dation were significantly more flexible for borrowers than FFEL consolidation. Most, but not all, of this flexibility was eliminated.

For example, prior to July 1, 2006, the Department, at its discretion, could consolidate loans that were reduced to judgment, loans of borrowers facing wage garnishment, and borrowers with defaulted consolidation loans. Similar to the FFEL program, loans that have been reduced to judgment may now be consolidated with Direct only if the judgment has been vacated.[21] If the borrower is facing wage garnishment, he or she may consolidate with Direct only if the garnishment order is lifted.[22]

8.2.2.3 Borrower Certification That FFEL Consolidation Loan Is Not Satisfactory

Borrowers with outstanding balances on Direct loans are eligible for Direct loan consolidation. However, many borrowers, particularly low-income trade school students, will not meet this requirement. This is primarily because the number of schools participating in the Direct Loan program is limited.[23] Many borrowers will have initially borrowed with FFEL.

Fortunately, borrowers with FFEL loans are also eligible for Direct consolidation loans. However, these borrowers must meet one of the following two conditions: (1) the borrower must be unable to obtain an FFEL consolidation loan, *or* (2) the borrower must be unable to obtain an FFEL consolidation loan with income-sensitive repayment terms acceptable to the borrower. To meet this second condition, the borrower must also be eligible for the Income Contingent Repayment Plan (ICRP) program under the Direct Consolidation Loan program.[24] Low-income borrowers generally will have no difficulty meeting the second alternative category. They do not also have to certify that they have first been turned down or even applied for an FFEL consolidation (the first category).[25]

To meet the second category, the borrower must certify that he or she is unable to obtain an FFEL consolidation loan with acceptable income-sensitive repayment terms. This is a subjective assessment based on information about available FFEL income-sensitive repayment plans compared to available Direct Loan income-contingent repayment plans. The borrower determines what is acceptable, and, for nearly all low-income borrowers, FFEL Income Sensitive Repayment Plan program terms will not be as good as Direct Loan ICRP terms. FFELs at a minimum require payments that equal *all* interest as it accrues while Direct loans can have even zero

payment amounts.[26] The borrower is not required to present any special evidence or justification why the Direct loan is more acceptable. To meet the second condition, the borrower must also certify that he or she is eligible for a Direct Consolidation Loan ICRP. Again, most low-income borrowers will have no problems meeting this standard.[27]

Even though borrowers who can meet the second category are not required to show that they attempted to obtain an FFEL consolidation loan, many FFEL lenders will nevertheless claim that borrowers will be perjuring themselves if they do not apply for an FFEL consolidation loan prior to applying for a Direct consolidation loan. This is clearly not the case. Not only is actually applying for an FFEL consolidation loan *not* a precondition for applying for a Direct consolidation loan, but the application may delay or even prevent the borrower from obtaining a Direct consolidation loan. Direct consolidation loan applicants must certify that no other application to consolidate their loans is pending with any other lender.[28]

Congress eliminated this "self-certification" process in the Higher Education Reconciliation Act of 2005 but then restored it in the 2006 Appropriations Act.[29] The process was restored for borrowers with FFEL non-consolidation loans only.[30]

8.2.2.4 Filling Out the Direct Loan Consolidation Application

Within a week or two after the borrower calls the current toll-free number (1-800-557-7392), the Department will send an informational package with a projected payment schedule, application, and various other forms to be completed. The borrower must return the filled-out application to the Department. It is important for Direct Consolidation Loan applicants to include accurate information about all loans to be consolidated. Borrowers may also apply online.[31]

For Department-held loans other than Direct loans, one way for borrowers to obtain information about their loans is to call the Federal Student Aid Center at 1-800-4-FED-AID.

---

21 34 C.F.R. § 685.220(d)(ii)(E).

22 34 C.F.R. § 685.220(d)(ii)(F).

23 *See* § 1.4.2.1.2, *supra*.

24 34 C.F.R. § 685.220(d)(1)(i), (B).

25 *Id.*

26 34 C.F.R. § 682.209(a)(7)(iv) (FFEL). Those borrowers under an ISRP that cannot afford to pay all accrued interest can apply each year for forbearance or a deferment, but this is not an automatic part of the ISRP, and the deferments or forbearance are usually limited to three years. *See generally* Ch. 3 (forbearances and deferments), *supra*.

27 *See* § 8.2.2.5 (income contingent repayment plans), *infra*.

28 34 C.F.R. § 685.220(d)(1)(iii).

29 Pub. L. No. 109-171, 120 Stat. 4 (Feb. 8, 2006) (Higher Education Reconciliation Act); Pub. L. No. 109-234, 120 Stat. 418 (June 15, 2006) (Appropriations Act). *See* U.S. Dep't of Educ., Dear Colleague Letter GEN-06-12, Consolidation Loans Made Under the Federal Family Education Loan (FFEL) and William D. Ford Federal Direct Programs (June 23, 2006).

30 *See* § 8.2.2.2, *supra*.

31 The current website at which to apply is www.ed.gov/DirectLoan/consolid2.html.

For guaranty-agency-held loans, the borrower will generally have to obtain the loan information from the guaranty agency.

Another excellent resource is the Department's National Student Loan Data System (NSLDS). The system can be accessed on-line at www.nslds.ed.gov or by calling the federal student aid information center at 1-800-4-FED-AID or, for TDD, at 1-800-730-8913. The database includes information about all federal loans, regardless of who holds the loans, and Pell grants. Borrowers can find out about loan and/or grant amounts, outstanding balances, loan status, and disbursements. In order to use the data base, borrowers need to provide their social security number, first two digits of last name, date of birth, and a personal identification number (PIN).[32]

If the loan balances on the borrower's application are incorrect, the Department notifies the borrower of the correct amount. The Department sends out a promissory note with the correct loan amount only after the consolidation has been approved. The borrower is then required to sign and return this promissory note to the Department.

Once the information about the borrower's loans is compiled, the next step is to complete the application. Among other information, the application calls for two references. These individuals will not be financially obligated on the loan and do not have to possess good credit records. The references are used only if the Department cannot locate the borrower.

Virtually all low-income student loan defaulters will want an income-contingent repayment plan (ICRP). In fact, they must make this selection if they have not, prior to consolidation, made at least three consecutive reasonable and affordable payments.[33] Borrowers requesting ICRPs must complete the "Repayment Plan Selection" and "Income Contingent Repayment Plan Consent to Disclosure of Tax Information" forms that accompany the application and promissory note.[34]

In some cases, borrowers will be required to fill out an "Alternative Documentation of Income" form.[35] This is required if the borrower is repaying Direct loans under the ICRP and

- is in his or her first year of repayment;
- is in his or her second year of repayment and has been notified that alternative documentation of income is required; or
- has been notified that the I.R.S. is unable to provide the

Department with adjusted gross income (AGI) information for the borrower or the borrower's spouse.

A borrower may also, at the borrower's discretion, choose to use the alternative documentation form if the borrower's AGI or borrower's spouse's AGI, as reported on the most recently filed federal tax return, does not reasonably reflect current income and/or ability to repay in circumstances such as loss or change of employment.

Within about two months (sometimes less) of the borrower sending in all the application papers, the Direct consolidation loan should be in effect. The holders of the prior loans also notify the borrower that the loans have been paid in full.

In recent years, borrowers with FFEL loans have often run into FFEL lenders who would not "release" borrowers into the Direct program. At least some of these lenders reportedly cited the FFEL "single holder rule" as a justification for not allowing borrowers to switch to the Direct Loan program.[36] This was an incorrect interpretation of that rule. The "single holder rule" simply restricted borrowers who had only one FFEL loan holder from shopping around and consolidating with a different FFEL consolidation lender. It did not bar borrowers with multiple loan holders from seeking loan consolidation with another lender.[37] In addition, the rule explicitly did not apply to borrowers who had been unable to receive a loan from their holder with income-sensitive repayment terms.[38]

The Department issued a series of confusing (and often contradictory) letters on this topic, followed by an Inspector General report that found that many FFEL lenders were either intentionally or unintentionally preventing borrowers from consolidating with Direct or unduly delaying the process.[39] This issue should now be resolved, as Congress eliminated the "single holder rule" in 2006.[40]

8.2.2.5 Calculating the Monthly Payment Under ICRP

The ICRP payment for a Direct Consolidation Loan can go up or down over time as the borrower's income changes. The monthly payment is based on annual income and the loan amount. The payments should be zero for families living at the poverty line or below.[41] The payments are

---

32 Borrowers can obtain their own PINs on-line through the National Student Loan Data System website at www.nslds.ed.gov. PINs will be sent by mail. *See generally* § 1.6 (National Student Loan Data System), *supra*.

33 34 C.F.R. § 685.220(h)(2).

34 These forms are included on the companion CD-Rom to this manual.

35 A copy of this form is reprinted at Appendix D.1.3, *infra*, and included on the companion CD-Rom to this manual.

36 34 C.F.R. § 682.201(c)(3)(iv) ("single holder rule").

37 34 C.F.R. § 682.201(c)(3)(iv)(B)(1).

38 34 C.F.R. § 682.201(c)(3)(iv)(B)(2).

39 U.S. Dep't of Educ., Office of the Inspector Gen., Final Audit Report ED-OIG/A07-D0027 (Feb. 10, 2005). A number of the key Dear Colleague letters on this topic are reprinted at Appendix C and included on the companion CD Rom to this manual.

40 Pub. L. No. 109-234 § 7015, 120 Stat. 418 (June 15, 2006) (Appropriations Act).

41 The HHS poverty guidelines are published every year. The 2006 guidelines can be found at 71 Fed. Reg. 3848 (Jan. 24, 2006). The 2006 poverty guideline is $13,200 for a family of two living

minimal for those earning several thousand dollars more than that amount. The exact formulae for determining the ICRP are set out in Department regulations.[42]

In general, the annual amount payable under an ICRP is the lesser of:

(1) the amount the borrower would repay annually over twelve years using standard amortization multiplied by an income percentage factor that corresponds to the borrower's adjusted gross income (AGI) as shown in the income percentage factor table in a notice published annually by the Secretary in the Federal Register;[43] or

(2) 20% of discretionary income. Discretionary income is defined as a borrower's AGI minus the amounts in the poverty guidelines. If a borrower provides acceptable documentation that he or she has more than one person in her family, the Secretary should apply the poverty guidelines for the borrower's family size.[44]

The Department provides information to help borrowers calculate the monthly payments. The following example was published in the 2006 *Federal Register*:[45]

> Example: This example assumes you are a single borrower with $15,000 in Direct Loans, the interest rate being charged is 6.80 percent, and you have an adjusted gross income (AGI) of $35,260.
>
> Step 1: Determine your annual payments based on what you would pay over 12 years using standard amortization. To do this, multiply your loan balance by the constant multiplier for 6.80 percent interest (0.122130).[46]
>
> $0.122130 \times \$15,000 = \$1,831.95$.
>
> Step 2: Multiply the result of Step 1 by the income percentage factor shown in the income percentage factor table that corresponds to your income and divide that result by 100.[47]
>
> 88.77 (the income percentage factor) × $1,831.95/100 = \$1,626.22$.
>
> Step 3: Determine 20 percent of your discretion-

ary income. Because you are a single borrower, subtract the poverty level for a family of one, as published in the *Federal Register*, from your income and multiply the result by 20%.

> $\$35,260 - \$9800 = \$25,460$.
>
> $\$25,460 \times 0.20 = \$5,092.00$.
>
> Step 4: Compare the amount from Step 2 with the amount from Step 3. The lower of the two will be your annual payment amount. In this example, you will be paying the amount calculated under Step 2. To determine your monthly payment amount, divide the annual amount by 12.
>
> $\$1,626.2/12 = \$135.52$.

A married borrower who wants to make payments under the ICRP and who has filed a separate income tax return must provide his or her spouse's written consent to disclosure of tax information.[48] This requirement does not apply if the borrower and the borrower's spouse are separated. The adjustable gross income for both spouses is used to calculate the monthly payment.[49] If both have loans, married borrowers may also choose to repay jointly.[50]

The following example for married borrowers is from the 2006 *Federal Register*:[51]

> Example: This example assumes you are married. You and your spouse have a combined adjusted gross income (AGI) of $66,631 and are repaying your loans jointly under the Income Contingent Repayment Plan. You have no children. You have a Direct Loan balance of $10,000, and your spouse has a Direct Loan balance of $15,000. Your interest rate is 6.80%.
>
> Step 1: Add your loan balances and your spouse's Direct Loan balances together to determine your aggregate loan balance:
>
> $\$10,000 + \$15,000 = \$25,000$
>
> Step 2: Determine the annual payment based on what you would pay over 12 years using standard amortization. To do this, multiply your aggregate loan balance by the constant multiplier for 6.80% interest (0.122130).
>
> $0.122130 \times \$25,000 = \$3,053.25$
>
> Step 3: Multiply the result of Step 2 by the income percentage factor shown in the income percentage factors table that corresponds to your and your spouse's income and then divide the result by 100.
>
> $109.40 \times \$3,053.25/100 = \$3,340.26$
>
> Step 4: Determine 20 percent of your discretion-

---

42 in the contiguous states and the District of Columbia.

42 Each year the Department publishes, in an annual notice to the Federal Register, the income percentage factors, case examples of calculations, a constant multiplier chart, and sample first-year monthly repayment tables for various income and debt levels. *See* 71 Fed. Reg. 36758 (June 28, 2006).

43 34 C.F.R. § 685.209(a)(2). *See* 71 Fed. Reg. 36758 (June 28, 2006).

44 34 C.F.R. § 685.209(a)(3). See examples of single and married borrowers discussed later in this subsection.

45 71 Fed. Reg. 36758 (June 29, 2006).

46 The multipliers for various interest rates are included in a table in the annual Federal Register notice updating the ICRP formula. For 2006 updates, see 71 Fed. Reg. 36758 (June 28, 2006).

47 The income percentage factors are also included in the annual Federal Register update. For 2006 updates, see 71 Fed. Reg. 36758 (June 28, 2006).

---

48 34 C.F.R. § 685.209(b)(1).

49 *Id.*

50 34 C.F.R. § 685.209(b)(2).

51 71 Fed. Reg. 36758 (June 28, 2006).

ary income. To do this, subtract the poverty level for a family of two from your aggregate income and multiply the result by 20 percent:

$66,631 − $13,200 = $53,431.00

$53,431.00 × 0.20 = $10,686.20.

Step 5: Compare the amount from Step 3 with the amount from Step 4. The lower of the two will be your annual payment amount. You and your spouse will pay the amount calculated under Step 3. To determine your monthly repayment amount, divide the annual amount by 12.

$3,340.26/12 = $278.36.

The Department website offers an excellent resource to help borrowers figure out their monthly payment amounts under an ICRP. Budget, monthly repayment, and Direct Consolidation Loans calculators are available on-line at www.ed.gov/DirectLoan/calc.html.[52]

A Direct consolidation loan with an ICRP can be a lifesaver for many low-income borrowers. However, it is important that only borrowers who can afford even very low monthly payments choose this option. If a borrower in default gets a consolidation loan, the borrower will not be able to later "re-consolidate" if he or she goes into default.[53] Unfortunately, the default rate among consolidation borrowers with previously defaulted loans is quite high. According to a 2000 General Accounting Office study, over 20,000 borrowers repaying consolidation loans under the income-contingent option had already defaulted on one or more of their underlying loans. This group of previous defaulters had default rates on their consolidation loans over 40%.[54]

8.2.2.6 What Happens to the Loan Obligation While Borrower Makes Only Minimal Payments

Unlike an FFEL income-sensitive repayment plan (ISRP), a Direct Loan income-sensitive repayment plan (ICRP) can create negative amortization. Even though the borrower makes all required payments, the minimal amount of the payment does not cover accrued interest, and the amount owed is increased to include this unpaid interest. Interest is then charged on the accrued interest ("capitalization"), resulting in the loan balance increasing beyond the original amount due.

Three features of the Direct Consolidation Loans program mitigate the consequences of negative amortization. First,

borrowers can seek loan deferments, during which period the United States pays for accrued interest.[55] Borrowers in school can obtain deferments for as long as they are in school. Borrowers may also be eligible for unemployment, economic, and other deferments for periods as long as three years.[56] Many low-income borrowers, even those in default on older loans, will qualify for these deferments as soon as they obtain Direct consolidation loans.

A second feature limiting negative amortization is the ICRP's limitation of interest capitalization to 10% of the loan amount.[57] Unpaid interest is capitalized until the outstanding principal amount is 10% greater than the original principal amount. After that point, interest continues to accrue but is not capitalized.

The third limit on negative amortization is that, after twenty-five years of ICRP payments (even if the payment amount was zero over the whole twenty-five-year period), the remainder of the loan is cancelled.[58] Deferment or forbearance periods are excluded from the twenty-five-year ICRP period.

There may be negative consequences for borrowers if the loan is written off after twenty-five years. Most importantly, when the balance of the loan is forgiven, under current tax law the amount forgiven will be taxable income for the borrower. This may not be particularly worrisome for many borrowers since they will not have to worry about the tax liability for twenty-five years.

However, the "25 year issue" is a legitimate concern for many advocates and their clients. At a minimum, clients should be counseled about the potential problems that may arise in the future. In addition, borrowers should be counseled that they may be able to avoid future tax consequences. In particular, they will not have to report the cancelled debt as income to the extent they are insolvent at the time the debt is written off.[59] To establish insolvency, a borrower must send the IRS a statement concerning the

---

52 For a more sophisticated calculator program, see www.finaid.org/calculators/icr.phtml (last accessed in August 2006). This calculator uniquely computes present value so that the cost of a loan paid under various methods can more accurately be compared to the cost of income-contingent repayment.

53 *See* § 8.2.2.2, *supra.*

54 *See* U.S. Gen. Accounting Office, Direct Loan Default Rates, GAO-01-68 (Oct. 2000), *available at* www.gao.gov.

55 This is the case for that portion of the consolidation loan whose underlying loans were GSLs, Staffords, FISLs, Perkins, Direct Loans, or other subsidized loans. Interest continues to accrue during a deferment period for that portion of the consolidation loan that derives from an unsubsidized loan, such as an SLS or unsubsidized Stafford. See Chapter 2, *supra*, for more information on deferments.

56 34 C.F.R. § 682.210. *See generally* Ch. 3, *supra* (deferments).

57 34 C.F.R. § 685.209(c)(5). Advocates should keep in mind that the original consolidation balance will often be much greater than the original loan amount.

58 34 C.F.R. § 685.209(c)(4)(iv). For a discussion of a proposal to reduce the number of years required before a loan is written off, see Philip G. Schrag, *The Federal Income Contingent Repayment Option for Law Student Loans*, 29 Hofstra L. Rev. 733 (Spring 2001). This proposal has been included in various Congressional bills. For example, see S. 371, 109th Congress (as introduced on February 14, 2005), which would allow loan forgiveness for borrowers employed in the public sector who have made ten years of payments through ICRP plans.

59 26 U.S.C. § 108.

discharged debt along with a list that shows that, at the time of forgiveness, the borrower had more debts (including the forgiven debt) than assets.[60]

For example, after twenty-five years, Borrower A receives a loan cancellation worth $10,000. Immediately before the cancellation, her liabilities totaled $20,000 and the fair market value of her assets was $15,000. The amount of the insolvency in this case is $20,000 − $15,000 = $5000. She can exclude up to $5000 of the $10,000 debt cancellation from taxable income because that is the amount by which she was insolvent. The remaining $5000 must be included in income. If her liabilities totaled $30,000, her insolvency would be $15,000 ($30,000 − $15,000) and she would be able to exclude all of the $10,000 cancellation from income.

Even borrowers who are not insolvent may be able to escape the post-twenty-five-year negative tax consequences. In particular, some borrowers may have only temporary financial difficulties that require them to repay loans using an ICRP. As their financial circumstances improve, they will be able to move to a different repayment plan that allows them to pay off their loans more quickly. These borrowers will not qualify for the twenty-five-year loan write-off because they will not meet the condition that borrowers must be in repayment under an ICRP for twenty-five consecutive years.[61] A strict reading of this regulation leads to the conclusion that a borrower could choose another repayment plan at any point along the way, even after twenty-four years, and avoid having the debt forgiven.

In addition, in most transactions, only principal amounts canceled are considered taxable income. Cancelled interest and fees are generally not counted as income. Such amounts were never available as income to the consumer. Advocates should consult a tax professional if advising borrowers on these issues.

Although it is possible that the tax code will be amended before many clients reach the twenty-five-year mark, it is still important to counsel clients on the drawbacks of ICRPs. In general, negative amortization or other low payment plans should be viewed, if possible, as temporary solutions. In practice, some clients will never be able to break out of the cycle of low monthly payments. It is still critical to consider other options for these clients. For example, if their financial hardship seems likely to continue into the future, they may be able to discharge their loans in bankruptcy.[62] As always, the cancellation options discussed in Chapter 6, *supra*, should also be considered.[63]

Borrowers should also be counseled that the low monthly payments may not last forever. ICRP payment amounts are reviewed annually.[64] If a borrower's financial situation improves, the borrower will be required to make higher payments.

8.2.2.7 Terms of Direct Consolidation Loans

Prior to July 1, 2006, consolidation interest rates were fixed while rates for most other federal student loan programs were variable. The variable rate era ended, at least for now, on July 1, 2006. As of July 1, 2006, and for loans for which disbursement is made on or after July 1, 2006, Stafford loans will have a fixed 6.8% interest rate. PLUS loans incurred after July 1, 2006, will also have fixed interest rates.

Interest rates for consolidation loans will remain fixed. The fixed rate is based on the weighted average of the interest rates on the loans at the time of consolidation, rounded up to the nearest one-eighth of a percentage point. The interest rate must not exceed 8.25%.[65]

The repayment period for a Direct consolidation loan begins on the day the loan is disbursed.[66] With the exception of borrowers choosing FFEL income-sensitive or Direct income-contingent plans, the repayment plan options for borrowers entering repayment for consolidation loans after July 1, 2006, are the same for both FFEL and Direct.[67] Direct consolidation loan borrowers may choose between standard, extended, graduated, and income-contingent plans.[68] The Department may also provide alternative repayment plans for borrowers who demonstrate that the terms and conditions of the other repayment plans are not adequate to accommodate the borrower's exceptional circumstances.[69]

Repayment periods are also specified by regulation. For example, the repayment period for standard and graduated repayment plans is as follows:

If the sum of the amount of the consolidation loan and the unpaid balance on other student loans to the applicant:

- is less than $7500, the borrower must repay the consolidation loan in not more than ten years;
- is equal to or greater than $7,500 but less than $10,000, the borrower must repay the consolidation loan in not more than twelve years;
- is equal to or greater than $10,000 but less than $20,000, the borrower must repay the consolidation

---

60 More information about reporting cancelled debts is available on the IRS website at www.irs.gov. In particular, see *Publication 908: Bankruptcy Tax Guide*, available at www.irs.gov/pub/irs-pdf/p908.pdf (last accessed in October 2006).

61 34 C.F.R. § 685.209(c)(4)(iv).

62 *See* Ch. 7, *supra*.

63 There should not be tax consequences when a borrower's loan is cancelled. *See* § 6.9, *supra*.

64 34 C.F.R. § 685.209(a)(5).

65 The formulae may be slightly different for consolidation loans incurred prior to 1999. *See* 20 U.S.C. § 1087e(b); 34 C.F.R. § 685.202(a)(3)(i)(E) (Direct).

66 34 C.F.R. § 685.220(i)(1).

67 For repayment plan options for borrowers entering repayment before July 1, 2006, see 34 C.F.R. § 685.208.

68 34 C.F.R. § 685.208(a)(iii). *See* 2.7.3, *supra*.

69 34 C.F.R. § 685.220(l).

loan in not more than fifteen years;

- is equal to or greater than $20,000 but less than $40,000, the borrower must repay the consolidation loan in not more than twenty years;
- is equal to or greater than $40,000 but less than $60,000, the borrower must repay the consolidation loan in not more than twenty-five years; or
- is equal to or greater than $60,000, the borrower must repay the consolidation loan in not more than thirty years.[70]

When originating a consolidation loan consisting of underlying loans in default, collection costs may be charged in an amount not to exceed 18.5% of the outstanding principal and interest.[71]

In an effort to minimize the pressure many collection agencies were placing on borrowers to consolidate, Congress in 2005 set new standards to ensure that consolidation loans are not an excessive proportion of a guaranty agency's recoveries on defaulted loans.[72]

Under the new rules, if a borrower repays a defaulted loan through an FFEL consolidation loan on or after October 1, 2006, collection fees are still capped at 18.5%. However, when returning proceeds to the Department after consolidation, a guaranty agency that charged the borrower collection costs after October 1, 2006, must remit an amount that equals the lesser of the actual collection costs charged or 8.5% of the outstanding principal and interest.[73] By Oct. 1, 2009, guaranty agencies will have to remit the entire collection cost charged when returning proceeds from the consolidation of a defaulted loan that is paid off with excess consolidation proceeds. Excess proceeds means the amount of proceeds from the consolidation of defaulted loans under FFEL that exceed 45% of the agency's total collections on defaulted loans in that fiscal year.[74]

8.2.3 FFEL Consolidation Loans

8.2.3.1 Growth (and Decline?) of FFEL Consolidation

In 1998, Congress moved to foster competition among lenders and give borrowers more repayment options. Before 1998, borrowers trying to get an FFEL Consolidation loan had to use one of the lenders who held their loans. Congress amended the law to allow borrowers with loans from dif-

ferent lenders to consolidate their loans with any eligible consolidation lender. Only borrowers with loans all from a single lender had to first try to consolidate with that lender. This so-called "single holder rule," eliminated in 2006, contributed to growth in the FFEL consolidation program.

This change stimulated competition and led to the growth of many new companies seeking to lure borrowers away from Sallie Mae (the largest FFEL consolidator) and the Direct Loan program. Many of these companies are "third party marketers" that work as contractors for banks hoping to attract student loan borrowers. These third-party marketers often use aggressive marketing techniques.

Low interest rates also increased competition among loan consolidators.[75] Students were bombarded with loan consolidation offers, often while they were still enrolled in school. More and more of these students chose to consolidate. For example, in 2001–2, borrowers consolidated more than $17 billion in loans, twice as much as the year before.[76] The pressure to consolidate also came from collection agencies that stood to benefit financially even if consolidation is not in the borrower's best interest.[77]

Growth in the consolidation loan programs has been staggering. Direct and FFEL consolidation loans combined accounted for about 48% of the $87.4 billion in total new student loan dollars that originated during fiscal year 2003.[78] FFEL loans comprised about 84% of the total consolidation loan volume, while Direct consolidation loans accounted for the remaining 16%. This growth is due mainly to an unprecedented period of low interest rates and aggressive marketing of consolidation loans.

The growth in consolidation lending is very expensive. A major cost, associated with FFEL consolidation only, is attributable to government subsidies to lenders. These are special allowances paid by the government to lenders to provide them a guaranteed rate of return on the student loans they make.[79] For example, subsidy costs for FFEL consolidation grew from $0.651 billion for loans made in fiscal year 2002 to $2.135 billion for loans made in fiscal year 2003.[80] Low interest rates increase these costs because FFEL consolidation loans carry a government-guaranteed rate of return to lenders that is higher than the fixed interest rate paid by consolidation loan borrowers. When the interest rate paid by borrowers does not provide the full guarantee rate to lenders, the federal government pays the difference to the lenders. Direct loans, in contrast, are made by the govern-

---

70 34 C.F.R. § 685.208(j).

71 34 C.F.R. § 685.220(f)(iii) (authorizes collection costs to be charged in the same way as in the FFEL program). *See* 34 C.F.R. § 682.401(b)(27) (FFEL).

72 Pub. L. Rev. 109-171, 120 Stat. 4 (Feb. 8, 2006) (amending 20 U.S.C. § 1078).

73 34 C.F.R. § 682.401(b)(27).

74 *Id.*

75 *See* § 8.2.1, *supra.*

76 Will Potter, *Interest Rates on Student Loans Are Expected to Hit All-Time Low*, The Chron. of Higher Educ. May 23, 2003, at A23.

77 *See* § 4.5.2.1, *supra.*

78 U.S. Gen. Accounting Office, Student Loan Programs: Lower Interest Rates and Higher Loan Volume Have Increased Federal Consolidation Loan Costs, GAO-04-568T (Mar. 17, 2004).

79 *Id.*

80 *Id.*

ment and thus carry no interest rate guarantee to lenders.[81] In both fiscal years 2002 and 2003, there was no net subsidy cost to the government for Direct loan consolidation because the interest rate paid by borrowers who consolidated their loans was greater than the interest rate the Department paid to the Treasury to finance its lending. However, the government's net gain from Direct consolidation loan borrowers has declined.[82]

Although not tracked as closely, administrative costs have likely risen in both programs. According to the GAO, costs in fiscal year 2002 associated with Direct loan consolidation totaled roughly $52.3 million. The estimate for fiscal year 2003 was slightly higher.[83] Administrative costs for FFEL consolidation loans were likely to be smaller, according to the GAO.[84] In a 2005 report, the GAO concluded that providing consolidations loans exclusively through the Direct Loan program could save the government over $3 billion.[85]

The landscape after July 1, 2006, should be significantly different in many ways. First, Congress made changes to stop "two step consolidation." This means that FFEL lenders should not be able to encourage borrowers who wish to reconsolidate to consolidate first with Direct and then return to FFEL.[86] In addition, the switch to fixed interest rates for Stafford and PLUS loans means that consolidation loan rates will become more standardized over time. This is because the underlying loans to be consolidated will eventually have the same or similar rates. Since the consolidation loan interest rate is based on an average of the underlying loans, the consolidation rate will eventually be close to the fixed rates of the underlying loans. Presumably, consolidation will become less popular as the interest rate advantages decline. However, this will not occur overnight. Many borrowers will consolidate loans incurred before July 1, 2006, which still have variable interest rates that will rise and fall with Treasury bill rates.[87]

8.2.3.2 Which Loans Can Be Consolidated

FFEL Consolidation lenders do not have to include non-FFEL loans in the new consolidation loan. They may do so at their discretion.[88] In March 2004, the Department clarified that non-FFEL loans cannot be consolidated into an

FFEL consolidation loan without an FFEL loan being included in the consolidation.[89]

As is now also the case with Direct consolidation loans, loans that have been reduced to judgment may not be consolidated with FFEL unless the judgment has been vacated.[90] If the borrower is facing wage garnishment, the borrower may consolidate with FFEL only if the garnishment order is lifted.[91]

A borrower in default applying for an FFEL consolidation loan must first make three consecutive reasonable and affordable monthly payments or arrange to pay under an ISRP.[92] The difference between the Direct Loan ICRP and the FFEL ISRP is that the ISRP will require low-income borrowers to make higher monthly payments than the Direct Loan program's ICRP.[93]

The three payments need not be consecutive if the borrower is an "affected individual," defined to include those who are serving on active duty during a war or other military operation or national emergency; are performing qualifying National Guard duty during a war or other military operation or national emergency; reside or are employed in an area that is declared a disaster area by any federal, state, or local official in connection with a national emergency; or suffered economic hardship as a direct result of a war or other military operation or national emergency, as determined by the Secretary.[94]

As with Direct loans, with only a few exceptions, borrowers with defaulted FFEL consolidation loans will not be able to re-consolidate with FFEL or Direct.[95]

Borrowers have many choices with respect to loan consolidation lenders and brokers. The maximum interest rates are set by federal law, although lenders are free to offer lower rates.[96] The differences between programs can be seen mainly in discounts the lenders can offer. Many lenders offer discounts to borrowers who enroll in the lender's automatic bill payment program. Another discount is often given as a reward for making a series of on-time payments, usually after a few years. Sallie Mae, for example, has offered a 0.25% immediate interest-rate reduction to borrowers who enroll in automatic payment and an additional 1% reduction to those who make regular, on-time payments for three years

---

81 *Id.*

82 *Id.*

83 *Id.*

84 *Id.*

85 U.S. Gov't Accountability Office, Student Consolidation Loans: Potential Effects of Making Fiscal Year 2006 Consolidations Loans Exclusively Through the Direct Loan Program, GAO-06-195 (Dec. 2005).

86 *See* § 8.2.2.2, *supra.* There may, however, be ways in which FFEL lenders and borrowers will get around the rules. This remains to be seen.

87 *See* § 2.1, *supra.*

88 34 C.F.R. § 682.201(d).

89 Dept. of Educ., Dear Colleague Letter #FP-04-05 (Apr. 29, 2004). The Department was responding to a question from the National Council of Higher Education Loan Programs inquiring into whether a borrower who has both FFEL and non-FFEL loans could obtain an FFEL consolidation loan that would consolidate only the borrower's non-FFEL loans.

90 20 U.S.C. § 1078-3(a)(3)(A)(i); 34 C.F.R. § 682.201(d)(1)(B).

91 20 U.S.C. § 1078-3(a)(3)(A)(i); 34 C.F.R. § 682.201(d)(1)(C).

92 *See* 34 C.F.R. § 682.200 (satisfactory repayment arrangement); 20 U.S.C. § 1078-3(a)(3)(A)(III); 34 C.F.R. § 682.201(d)(1)(i)(3).

93 *See* §§ 2.7.3.2, 8.2.2.3, *supra.*

94 68 Fed. Reg. 69312 (Dec. 12, 2003).

95 *See* § 8.2.2.2, *supra.*

96 *See* §§ 2.1, 8.2.2.7, *supra.*

on loan balances of more than $10,000. Some lenders will provide cash rebates to borrowers who make regular on-time payments rather than lowering interest rates.

To obtain an FFEL consolidation loan, the best approach is to contact the party holding the note. That party will generally be eager to process the FFEL consolidation loan. In fact, there are instances in which debt collectors hired by the Department have steered consumers to FFEL consolidations when they would have been better off with a Direct loan consolidation from the Department. The Department has approved common loan forms for FFEL consolidation loans.[97]

The available repayment plans are now the same for both FFEL and Direct consolidation loans, except that an ICRP is only available through the Direct program.[98]

8.2.4 Pros and Cons of Consolidation

There are some disadvantages to consolidation regardless of which program the borrower chooses. When a borrower in default consolidates a loan through either program, presently 18.5% is added to the amount due for collection fees.[99] This may be preferable to existing collection fees that may be as high as 43%.[100] Lenders automatically add the 18.5% fee to the consolidation. It is theoretically possible to request a waiver of collection fees before consolidation, but a waiver is very unlikely to occur in practice. After the consolidation, the fees become part of the amount due on the new loan.

Consolidation may not be a wise strategy for borrowers who owe a lot of interest on their loans. Consolidating will end up converting much of that interest into principal.

In general, depending on how much a borrower owes and the length of the consolidated loan, a borrower who chooses to consolidate could end up spending more in interest over the longer time period. The Department of Education warns that, in some situations, consolidation can double a borrower's total interest expense. Consolidation can also add additional fees to the borrower's balance, including collection fees, as noted above. In addition, the interest rate advantages of consolidation are likely to diminish now that interest rates on non-consolidation loans are fixed.[101]

Another problem to consider is that many borrowers who consolidate a defaulted student loan will default again within twelve months. This is particularly true among borrowers who consolidate defaulted loans. According to a 2000 General Accounting Office study, over 20,000 borrowers repaying consolidation loans under the income-contingent option (ICRP) had already defaulted on one or more of their underlying loans. This group of previous defaulters had default rates on their consolidation loans over 40%.[102]

Both FFEL and Direct loan borrowers who had defaulted prior to consolidation are more likely to default on their consolidation loans than those who did not default prior to consolidation. According to the GAO, the Department now has the data available to link consolidation loans to borrowers' underlying loans and determine whether re-default rates vary by type of school.[103] In the meantime, the GAO did its own analysis and found that FFEL consolidation borrowers were less likely than Direct consolidation loan borrowers to have attended a proprietary school prior to consolidation. The overall default rate for consolidation loan borrowers with an underlying defaulted loan was higher for borrowers who had attended a two-year or proprietary school than for those who had attended a four-year school. For FFEL loans, the rate of default was 45.5% for borrowers who had attended proprietary schools compared with 29.6% for borrowers who had attended a four-year school. The Direct Loan consolidation program had similar relative default rates.[104]

Another disadvantage to consolidation relates to credit reporting. Consolidation results in a notation on a borrower's credit report that the defaulted loan was paid in full. In contrast, rehabilitation removes the default notation completely.[105] This may be of concern to some clients. However, rehabilitation is not always an attractive option for low-income borrowers due to potentially higher monthly payments.[106]

In addition, borrowers may have more opportunity to compromise the amount owed on an old loan than on a consolidation loan. However, this will usually require a lump sum payment of a significant portion of the loan, something that is rarely possible for most low-income consumers.[107]

Generally, borrowers should always first consider loan cancellation options.[108] Low-income borrowers with bleak financial prospects should also seriously consider filing bankruptcy to discharge student loan debt. Many of these borrowers will be able to meet the undue hardship test required to discharge student loans in bankruptcy.[109]

---

97 *See* U.S. Dep't of Educ., Dear Guaranty Agency Director Letter GEN-00-16, Approved Federal Consolidation Loan Application Forms for Use Within the Federal Family Education Loan Program (FFELP) (Oct. 2000). The forms are included on the companion CD-Rom to this manual.

98 *See* § 8.2.2.7, *supra*.

99 34 C.F.R. § 685.220(f)(iii) (Direct), using amount in 34 C.F.R. § 682.401(b)(27) (FFEL).

100 *See generally* § 4.4, *supra*.

101 *See generally* §§ 8.2.3.1, 8.2.2.7, *supra*.

102 *See* U.S. Gen. Accounting Office, Direct Loan Default Rates, GAO-01-68 (Oct. 2000), *available at* www.gao.gov.

103 U.S. Gov't Accountability Office, Student Consolidation Loans: Further Analysis Could Lead to Enhanced Default Assumptions for Budgetary Cost Estimates, GAO-04-843 (Aug. 2004).

104 *Id.*

105 *See generally* § 8.4 (rehabilitation), *infra*.

106 *See* § 8.4 (rehabilitation), *infra*.

107 *See* § 8.5, *infra*.

108 *See* Ch. 6, *supra*.

109 *See* Ch. 7, *supra*.

The main advantages of consolidation are that it generally leads to lower monthly payments and allows borrowers to submit only one payment each month instead of making two or more payments with different due dates. For low-income borrowers, a key advantage is that it is the only way for borrowers who initially borrowed FFEL loans to obtain a Direct Loan ICRP.[110]

However, by consolidating a loan through either the FFEL or Direct Consolidation Loan programs, the borrower's ability to raise school-related defenses may be muddled. Borrowers can still obtain a closed-school discharge for that portion of the consolidation loan which relates to an original loan that would be eligible for the closed-school discharge, and the same guidelines apply for false-certification and unpaid-refund discharges.[111] For consolidated loans, borrowers are considered disabled if they would meet the definition for all of the loans included in the consolidation loan.[112]

The situation for other school-related claims is less clear. It is possible that a court would find that borrowers consolidating their loans waive their right to bring claims and defenses concerning the original loan.[113] The difference between FFEL and Direct loan consolidations is that FFEL loans after January 1, 1994, contain the FTC Holder Notice making the note holder liable for school-related defenses when the school is for-profit and related to the lender. The Direct Consolidation Loan note does not include this notice. The issue of raising school-related defenses is discussed at Chapter 9, *infra*.

8.3 Renewing Eligibility Through Reasonable and Affordable Payment Plans

8.3.1 Basic Requirements

Another option for FFEL and Direct Loan borrowers in default is to reschedule their payments through reasonable and affordable payment plans based on their total financial circumstances. The defaulted borrower has a statutory right

to such a plan, and payments can be as low as $5 a month or less.[114] Whether the Department or a guaranty agency holds the loan, the borrower, to renew eligibility, must enter a satisfactory repayment arrangement, defined as six consecutive on-time monthly payments.[115]

A reasonable and affordable payment plan to renew eligibility must be sharply distinguished from a normal repayment plan in which the student may be asked to pay hundreds of dollars a month. Payments under reasonable and affordable plans can be much lower, often not even covering interest payments.

If a borrower wants eventually to pay off a loan, monthly payments that at least equal accrued monthly interest will avoid negative amortization. Borrowers who cannot afford payments that high may still want to set up reasonable and affordable payment plans. They may not be particularly concerned about the total amount of interest that will accrue on the loan over time. It is for these borrowers that payments as low as $5 a month or less may provide the needed avenue back to school.

While the borrower will still technically be in default while making reasonable and affordable payments, the borrower will not be subject to tax intercepts, wage garnishments, collection contacts, or collection lawsuits. The borrower's credit record will most likely still show a default unless he or she rehabilitates the loan. Rehabilitation is discussed in § 8.4, *infra*.

8.3.2 Eligible Borrowers

Borrowers who previously set up reasonable and affordable payment plans and became delinquent on their payments cannot renew eligibility through a new reasonable and affordable plan. Therefore, a borrower has only one chance to renew eligibility with a reasonable and affordable repayment agreement.[116]

Borrowers have only one chance to renew eligibility but more than one chance to *try* to renew eligibility. For example, if the borrower successfully makes six consecutive

---

110　NCLC and other advocacy groups have recommended revisions in the law to allow qualified borrowers in all of the main federal loan programs to access the ICR directly rather than through the consolidation program. This option should be available before and after default. *See generally* Deanne Loonin, National Consumer Law Center, *No Way Out: Student Loans, Financial Distress and the Need for Policy Reform* (June 2006), *available at* www.nclc.org/news/content/nowayout.pdf and on the companion CD-Rom to this manual.

111　Dear Colleague Letter 94-G-256, Clearinghouse No. 50,422 (Sept. 1994), *reprinted at* Appx. C, *infra*; 34 C.F.R. § 685.216(l)(3).

112　34 C.F.R. § 682.402(c)(1)(iv); § 6.6.3, *supra*.

113　*But see* Crawford v. The American Inst. of Prof'l Careers, Inc., Clearinghouse No. 51,258 (D. Ariz. Feb. 8, 1996).

114　20 U.S.C. § 1078-6(b). The Conference Report for this provision states that it is intended to provide a second chance at educational loans and grants for low-income students previously defrauded by trade schools. *See* H.R. Conf. Rep. No. 630, at 467 (1992) (Conf. Rep.). Although the statute refers to guaranty agencies, the Conference Report makes clear that the Secretary must offer the same opportunity to renew eligibility when the Department of Education is holding the loan.

115　The regulation that provides for reinstatement of borrower eligibility, 34 C.F.R. § 682.401(a)(4) (FFEL), requires the borrower to make satisfactory repayment arrangements as defined in § 682.200. Section 682.200 provides that the borrower must make six timely payments and that the amount must be reasonable and affordable. *See also* 34 C.F.R. §§ 685.200(d), 685.102 (definition of satisfactory repayment arrangement for purposes of regaining eligibility).

116　34 C.F.R. §§ 682.200 (FFEL) (definition of "satisfactory repayment arrangement"), 685.102 (Direct Loans).

on-time payments, renews eligibility and then defaults, the borrower is not eligible under the regulations for another chance at a reasonable and affordable payment plan. However, if the borrower makes five payments and then stops paying, the borrower never actually renewed eligibility and should thus be able to try again in the future to renew eligibility through reasonable and affordable payments.[117]

Borrowers with loans subject to a judgment for failure to repay may also be eligible to renew eligibility as long as the borrower repays the debt in full or makes repayment arrangements that are satisfactory to the holder.[118] The "one-time" requirement applies here as well.[119]

The Department has stated that a judgment holder may require more stringent repayment arrangements that it considers appropriate. The benefits that the judgment holder may offer the borrower include the return of eligibility and removal of a borrower's negative credit history.[120] Alternatively, the holder may offer to vacate the judgment and allow the borrower to sign a new promissory note after the borrower complies with the conditions of the agreement.[121]

Borrowers who stay current on the reasonable and affordable plan can apparently keep on the plan indefinitely at that level of payment. The level will change if the borrower's financial circumstances change.

The problem with staying on a reasonable and affordable payment plan indefinitely is that borrowers will not be able to get out of default. To get out of default, they must rehabilitate or consolidate their loans.[122]

8.3.3 Determining a Reasonable and Affordable Payment Amount

A satisfactory repayment arrangement involves an amount that is determined to be reasonable and affordable based on the borrower's total financial circumstances.[123] To come up with that amount, the guaranty agency (and the Department on loans which it holds) must consider the borrower's and his or her spouse's disposable income. Disposable income is defined as income from any source that remains after the deduction of any amounts required by law to be withheld (for example, taxes and wage garnishments) or any child support or alimony payments under court order or legally enforceable agreement.[124]

The note holder must also consider the borrower's and his or her spouse's necessary expenses, including but not lim-

ited to housing, utilities, food, medical costs, dependent-care costs, work-related expenses, and other student loan repayments.[125]

No formula is specified, but the note holder *cannot* establish a minimum payment amount—for example, $50 per month—for all borrowers. That is, if it is determined that $30 is reasonable and affordable based on the borrower's total financial circumstances, then this lesser amount prevails.[126] However, in this example, the guarantor must maintain documentation in the student's file if the amount is less than $50.[127]

An important document relating to the minimum repayment amount is a February 1, 1993, letter to the Secretary of Education from United States Representative Bruce F. Vento, who had originally introduced the renewed eligibility provisions in Congress.[128] The Congressman objected to the $50-minimum standard being use by certain guarantors and indicated that Congress' intent was to require only "nominal payments well below $50 per month for those with very low incomes."

The regulations do not provide a specific formula for determining how to compute a reasonable and affordable repayment amount. When a borrower's necessary expenses exceed income, advocates should argue that the reasonable and affordable amount is either nothing or a nominal amount, since the regulations require consideration of these necessary expenses.

On the other hand, some collectors and guarantors have demanded payment plans based on the size of the outstanding loan. Department officials have made it clear that this is wrong. The payment amount must be based on the borrower's ability to pay and not on the size of the outstanding loan. Confusion arises because guarantors or collectors are allowed to base "normal" payment plans on the amount outstanding. Borrowers should clearly state to the collector or guarantor that they are not seeking a normal repayment agreement but a special agreement to renew eligibility that is reasonable and affordable based on their total financial circumstances.

The guarantor, for its part, must provide the borrower with a written statement of the monthly payment amount and provide the borrower with an opportunity to object to its terms.[129]

---

117 The regulations at 34 C.F.R. § 682.200 ("satisfactory repayment arrangement") state that a borrower may only obtain the benefit of a reasonable and affordable payment plan *"with respect to renewed eligibility once."* [emphasis added]

118 34 C.F.R. § 668.35(b).

119 34 C.F.R. § 668.35(c).

120 67 Fed. Reg. 67048, 67061 (Nov. 1, 2002).

121 *Id.*

122 *See* §§ 8.2 (consolidation), *supra*, 8.4 (rehabilitation), *infra*.

123 34 C.F.R. § 682.200 ("satisfactory repayment arrangement").

124 34 C.F.R. § 682.200 (disposable income).

125 34 C.F.R. § 682.401(b)(4)(i)(A).

126 34 C.F.R. § 682.401(b)(4)(i)(B).

127 *Id.*

128 Letter from Representative Bruce F. Vento to the Honorable Rich Riley, Secretary of Education, Clearinghouse No. 47,962 (Feb. 1, 1993).

129 34 C.F.R. § 682.401(b)(4)(iii).

8.3.4 *How to Obtain a Reasonable and Affordable Payment Plan*

As a practical matter, the first step in seeking a reasonable and affordable repayment agreement is to determine who is servicing the loan. Since this right only applies to loans already in default, the entity is almost always a state guaranty agency or a collection agency hired by the Department of Education for Department-held loans. Most trade school loans that are ten years old or older are held by the Department and serviced by a collection agency. On the other hand, most loans taken out within the last six years are still held by a state guaranty agency.[130]

The next step is to contact the party servicing the loan to request a reasonable and affordable payment plan. It is typical for the loan servicer to tell a student that a repayment plan is not available or that the plan will require a down payment and minimum monthly payments. This is because the borrower has not specifically requested "a reasonable and affordable payment plan to renew eligibility" or words to that effect. However, the borrower should not have to use any "magic words" in order to get a reasonable and affordable payment plan.[131]

There have been widespread reports of guarantors and collectors still refusing to acknowledge the existence of the option for reasonable and affordable plans even after the borrower specifically requests one. This is a very serious matter. Collectors hired by the Department have been given lengthy training about this option and all guarantors have established such an option.

The refusal of a staffer to acknowledge the existence of such a plan or to misrepresent the requirements implies either deliberate deception by that individual or grossly deficient supervision and training of that individual. This conduct should rise to the level of a federal Fair Debt Collection Practices Act violation for collectors and private guarantors and perhaps a due process or other violation for state employees.[132] More on actions against this type of misconduct is detailed in Chapter 4, *supra*.

The Department's regulations specify the type of documentation the borrower should provide in seeking a reasonable and affordable repayment agreement. The borrower should provide to the guarantor, or to the Department's collector handling the debt, documentation of income, expenses, and the amount owed on all student loans. Evidence of current income might include proof of receipt of public assistance or the borrower's two most recent pay stubs. Expenses might be proved by filling in a form provided by the guaranty agency showing the borrower's monthly household budget.[133]

In theory, there is no reason for a borrower in default to accept another type of payment plan. However, in practice, it is often difficult for advocates and borrowers to convince loan holders that they must offer these plans. In many situations, consolidation will be an easier option.[134] In either case, borrowers should be advised to think seriously about whether they can make even minimal payments. If not, repaying student loan debt may not be possible until the borrower's financial circumstances improve, and it might not be worth jeopardizing the one-time only option of a reasonable and affordable payment plan.

8.4 Loan Rehabilitation

8.4.1 *General*

A student can renew eligibility for new loans and grants and cure the loan default by "rehabilitating" the defaulted loan. Loan rehabilitation for FFELs and Direct loans may be requested after the borrower has made nine payments within twenty days of the due date during a period of ten consecutive months.[135] Prior to July 1, 2006, twelve consecutive payments were required. The longer requirement still applies to Perkins loan rehabilitations.[136]

For a rehabilitation agreement that began prior to July 1, a guaranty agency may consider the borrower to have met the new rehabilitation standard if at least one of the borrower's payments is due to be made after July 1, even if that payment is received prior to July 1, but within twenty days of the required due date in July. The agency must treat all borrowers in this situation equally. In this situation, the Department will consider the borrower to have met the new standards if the borrower makes payments as required under the existing agreement and at least one of the nine payments made by the borrower was due on or after July 1, 2006, even if that specific payment was received prior to July 1, but within twenty days of the July due date.[137]

To assist borrowers serving in the military, the Department has waived the consecutive payment requirement for "affected individuals," defined to include those who are

130 For a list of state guaranty agencies, see Appendix G, *infra*. See also § 8.2.2.4, *supra*, for information on finding loan holders.

131 *See, e.g.*, Arroyo v. Solomon & Solomon, P.C., 2001 U.S. Dist. LEXIS 21908 (E.D.N.Y. 2001) (borrower's claim that collection agency violated the Fair Debt Collection Practices Act by misrepresenting the requirements for a reasonable and affordable payment plan survived summary judgment). *See* §§ 4.5.2, 4.5.3, *supra*.

132 *See* Arroyo v. Solomon & Solomon, P.C., 2001 U.S. Dist. LEXIS 21908 (E.D.N.Y. 2001) (borrower's claim that collection agency violated the Fair Debt Collection Practices Act by misrepresenting the requirements for a reasonable and affordable payment plan survived summary judgment). *See* §§ 4.5.2, 4.5.3, *supra*.

133 34 C.F.R. § 682.401(b)(4)(i)(C).

134 *See* § 8.2, *supra*.

135 *See* 34 C.F.R. § 682.405(a)(2)(FFEL); 34 C.F.R. § 685.211(f) (Direct).

136 *See* § 8.4.3, *infra*.

137 71 Fed. Reg. 45666 (Aug. 9, 2006).

serving on active duty during a war or other military operation or national emergency; are performing qualifying National Guard duty during a war or other military operation or national emergency; reside or are employed in an area that is declared a disaster area by any federal, state, or local official in connection with a national emergency; or suffered economic hardship as a direct result of a war or other military operation or national emergency, as determined by the Secretary.[138] Loan holders should not treat any payment missed during the time that a borrower is an affected individual, or a payment missed during the three-month transition period, as an interruption in the number of consecutive monthly on-time payments required for loan rehabilitation.[139]

The payment amount is determined by the guaranty agency (or the United States if it is holding the loan) in the same way as a reasonable and affordable payment plan to renew eligibility, described in the prior subsection.[140]

Some borrowers are incorrectly told by their loan holders that they must make payments beyond what they can afford. Even those borrowers who obtain reasonable and affordable plans are often kicked into the standard ten-year plan after the loan is rehabilitated. This often results in a monthly payment amount after rehabilitation that exceeds what is affordable for low-income borrowers. The main problem is that there is no standard formula to determine the affordable monthly amount, and the Department has stated that borrowers are not eligible for an ICRP while their loans are in rehabilitation.

Department staff told NCLC in 2004 that resolving this problem was likely as straightforward as fixing the Department's computers so that borrowers have the option of choosing which plan to continue with after the official rehabilitation period is over. Yet reports persist of borrowers not being given this choice and not even understanding that they have this choice. As a result, too many borrowers just recently lifted out of default fall right back in during the transition period when the rehabilitated loan is sold.

Another problem is that collection does not necessarily cease during the rehabilitation period. The Department has explained in response to questions from NCLC and other advocates that collection will stop only if the rehabilitation agreement specifically provides for a cessation. Otherwise, borrowers will continue to face the usual range of collection tactics, including tax offset, even though they have made a repayment commitment and are in the process of rehabilitating their loans. This seems particularly counterproductive since borrowers are likely to quickly get discouraged from making payments if they continue to face collection efforts.

The payments made under the rehabilitation agreement must be "voluntary." Voluntary payments are those made directly by the borrower and do not include payments obtained by federal offset, garnishment, income or asset execution, or after a judgment has been entered on a loan.[141]

For FFEL loans, after the borrower makes the required timely monthly payments under the new plan and requests rehabilitation, the guarantor or the United States must attempt to secure a lender to purchase the loan.[142] If the loan is sold—it may not be if no lender agrees to purchase the loan—the loan is removed from default status and the borrower is eligible for new loans and grants.[143] According to the Department, it is an industry practice not to repurchase FFEL program loans with a balance of less than $1500. If an FFEL loan cannot be resold, it will not be rehabilitated.[144] In addition, collection fees of up to 18.5% of the unpaid principal and accrued interest at the time of sale are added to the new loan.[145]

An eligible lender purchasing a rehabilitated loan must establish a repayment schedule which meets the same requirements that are applicable to other FFEL program loans made under the same loan type and which provides for the borrower to make monthly payments at least as great as the average of the monthly payments received by the guaranty agency.[146]

Loans that have been reduced to judgment may not be rehabilitated. However, borrowers in this situation may be able to renew eligibility in certain circumstances.[147]

8.4.2 Advantages and Disadvantages of Loan Rehabilitation

Rehabilitation can be preferable to consolidation because successful rehabilitation wipes out the borrower's past history of default on credit reports and the borrower is not at risk of losing rights through consolidation.[148] However, because rehabilitation is a business proposition—requiring that a lender purchase the rehabilitated loan—the program is not always an accessible or useful tool for the lowest-income borrowers who can pay only relatively small monthly amounts.

Loan rehabilitation has certain benefits. Rehabilitation removes the default notation from the borrower's credit report. For FFEL loans, guaranty agencies must report within ninety days to all national credit bureaus that the loan

---

138 68 Fed. Reg. 69312 (Dec. 12, 2003).

139 *Id.*

140 20 U.S.C. § 1078-6(a)(1); 34 C.F.R. § 682.405(b)(1))(i)(B) (no minimum requirement for reasonable and affordable payment plan).

141 34 C.F.R. § 682.405(b)(2).

142 34 C.F.R. § 682.405(b)(1).

143 20 U.S.C. § 1078-6(a)(3); 34 C.F.R. § 682.405(a)(3).

144 U.S. Dep't of Educ., Direct Consolidation Loan Guide for Schools 11 (2000), *available at* http://eric.ed.gov/ERICDocs/data/ericdocs2/content_storage_01/0000000b/80/21/f9/94.pdf.

145 34 C.F.R. § 682.405(b)(1)(iv).

146 34 C.F.R. § 682.405(b)(3).

147 *See* § 8.3.2, *supra.*

148 § 8.2.4, *supra.*

is no longer in a default status and that the default is to be removed from the borrower's credit history.[149]

Collection fees are reduced to 18.5% of the unpaid principal and accrued interest at the time of the sale.[150] All ill effects of having a defaulted loan are removed, and the borrower becomes eligible for all benefits afforded other borrowers, such as deferrals and forbearance.[151]

8.4.3 Perkins Rehabilitation

Perkins loan borrowers may also rehabilitate defaulted loans.[152] Borrowers must make twelve consecutive on-time payments as determined by the institution.[153] The Perkins regulations do not explicitly state that the payments must be reasonable and affordable but rather that they must be determined by the school.[154] Loans reduced to judgment may not be consolidated.[155]

A difference between Perkins and the other loan rehabilitation programs is that Perkins regulations specify that defaulted loans may be rehabilitated only once.[156] A borrower may rehabilitate only once, but there should not be a limit to the number of times a borrower is permitted to attempt rehabilitation. Collection costs related to Perkins Loan rehabilitations cannot exceed 24%.[157]

Under the Perkins program, schools have thirty days after receiving a borrower's last on-time monthly payment to instruct any credit bureau to which the default was reported to remove the default from the borrower's credit history.[158]

8.5 Compromise and Write-Off Authority

8.5.1 Compromise

The Department has authority to compromise FFEL or Perkins loans of any amount or to suspend or terminate collection of these loans.[159] The regulations state that the Department will use the standard set out by the Department of Treasury for compromise of federal claims.[160]

---

149 34 C.F.R. § 682.405(b)(2).
150 34 C.F.R. § 682.405(b)(1)(iv).
151 20 U.S.C. § 1078-6(a)(4); 34 C.F.R. § 682.405(a)(3), (b)(2) (removal of default from credit report).
152 34 C.F.R. § 674.39.
153 34 C.F.R. § 674.39(a)(2).
154 34 C.F.R. § 674.39(a)(2).
155 34 C.F.R. § 674.39(a).
156 34 C.F.R. § 674.39(e).
157 34 C.F.R. § 674.39(c)(1).
158 34 C.F.R. § 674.39(b)(3).
159 34 C.F.R. § 30.70(h). Compromises for other types of debts are set out in 34 C.F.R. § 30.70(a)–(f).
160 34 C.F.R. § 30.70(a) (referring to 4 C.F.R. § 103; regulations now found at 31 C.F.R. § 902).

The Treasury regulations give federal agencies discretion to compromise debts if they cannot collect the full amount because

(1) the debtor is unable to pay the full amount in a reasonable time, as verified through credit reports or other financial information;[161]

(2) the government is unable to collect the debt in full within a reasonable time by enforced collection proceedings;

(3) the cost of collecting the debt does not justify the enforced collection of the full amount;[162] or

(4) there is significant doubt concerning the government's ability to prove its case in court.[163]

Agencies are discouraged from accepting compromises payable in installments.[164] However, this is allowed as long as the agency obtains a legally enforceable written agreement providing that, in the event of default, the full original principal balance of the debt prior to compromise, less sums paid, is reinstated.[165] Agencies are also encouraged to obtain security for repayment.

The Department has also approved Standardized Compromise and Write-Off Procedures, described below, for use by all guaranty agencies for FFELs.[166] The compromise standards relate to a negotiated agreement between the student loan borrower and the guaranty agency to accept less than full payment as full liquidation of the entire debt.

This compromise is often, but not always, binding on the United States. It is important for borrowers to secure written verification of this point to ensure that the United States will not demand the student's balance at a later date.

1. *Collection costs* can be waived to obtain payment of all principal and interest in full. Guaranty agencies can make this determination through the supervisor directly charged with collections. In practice, many guaranty agencies will quickly agree to waive collection fees.

2. *30% of principal and interest owing* also can be

---

161 Debtors are required to submit a current financial statement executed under penalty of perjury showing assets, liabilities, income, and expenses. 31 C.F.R. § 902.2(g).
162 In these circumstances, agencies may impose an appropriate discount on the amount accepted in compromise for the administrative and litigative costs of collection, with consideration given to the time it will take to effect collection. The regulations state that collection costs may be a substantial factor in the settlement of small debts. 31 C.F.R. § 902.2(e).
163 31 C.F.R. § 902.2(a).
164 31 C.F.R. § 902.2(f).
165 *Id.*
166 *See* Letter from Jean Frohlicher, President of the National Council of Higher Education Loan Programs, Inc., regarding Compromise and Write-Off Procedures (Nov. 7, 1993), with attached approval by Robert W. Evans, Director, Division of Policy Development (Nov. 24, 1993), and attached Standardized Compromise and Write-Off Procedures, all found at Clearinghouse No. 49,168. The letter is reprinted in Appendix D, *infra*, and is included on the companion CD-Rom to this manual.

waived to recover the remaining 70%. If the amount waived only involves interest, the determination can be made by the supervisor directly charged with collections. If principal is to be waived, then the next level of management must make the determination. Guaranty agencies are less likely to agree to compromise interest and principal because the amounts compromised apparently will be taken out of the 30% guaranty agencies make on a loan collection. On the other hand, guaranty agencies still have an incentive to compromise up to 30%. If the guaranty agencies do not collect anything, they will eventually turn the loan over to the United States and keep none of the 30%.

3. *Compromises involving more than 30%* of outstanding principal and interest will bind only the guaranty agency, *not* the United States. Such compromises cannot waive the Secretary's right to collect the remaining balance due. The guaranty agency can compromise this larger amount as long as it can document the reasons for the action, the guaranty agency director approves the compromise, and the compromise does not bind the United States.

The write-off procedures for FFEL loans are intended only to stop guaranty agency collection activity. In general, write-off does not relieve the debtor of the debt. This is in contrast to Perkins write-offs, through which the borrower can be relieved of all repayment obligations.[167] The rules for Perkins write-offs differ depending on whether the school or the Department holds the loan. The Department may take a restrictive interpretation of the regulations if the school is holding the loan. In those cases, the Department may find that the school cannot write off a loan unless the borrower has a very low balance.[168] In contrast, if the school has assigned the loan to the Department, borrowers should be entitled to request a write-off and the Department has discretion to grant one regardless of the loan amount.[169] Once a guaranty agency has written off an FFEL loan, it must permanently assign the loan to the Department of Educa-

tion.[170] The exception to this policy is that guaranty agencies have the authority to write off loans with principal balances of less than $100 and a total balance of less than $1000, and any loans in which the remaining balance represents only interest, attorney fees, court costs, or collection costs without requiring the permanent assignment of the loan to the Department.[171]

The Department sets out guidelines for guaranty agencies to consider in deciding whether to write off loans and cease collection activity. Agencies are required to consider the debtor's and, if applicable, an endorser's current inability to repay the debt. Examples of borrowers who might qualify include borrowers who are repeatedly unemployed and have no prospects for future employment; borrowers who repeatedly are public assistance recipients; borrowers who are chronically ill, partially disabled, or of an age that results in their inability to work; borrowers whose potential for future earnings is limited or non-existent; and borrowers who have no other funds available to them from other sources, such as inheritance. Borrowers who receive a compromise or write-off must reaffirm the amount compromised or written off if they later want to receive an FFEL loan.[172] Perkins lenders have discretion to write off a loan balance less than $25 or less than $50 if, for a period of at least two years, the borrower has been billed (and has not paid) the balance.[173] When a school writes off an account, the borrower is relieved of all repayment obligations.[174]

The Department has told NCLC that it offers compromises only when they conclude that it is in the best federal fiscal interest to do so. They might also offer a compromise if there are mitigating circumstances in favor of a settlement. They acknowledged that they do not publicize compromise standards "externally," since doing so could prejudice negotiations and make it more difficult for the government to obtain the amount that is deemed reasonable for any particular borrower.

---

167 34 C.F.R. § 674.47(h)(3).

168 34 C.F.R. § 674.47(h) (schools may write off accounts with balances less than $25 or $50 if a borrower has been billed, but has not paid, the balance for a period of at least two years).

169 34 C.F.R. § 30.70(h).

170 *See* Letter from Jean Frolicher re: Compromise and Write-off Procedures (Nov. 7, 1993), Clearinghouse No. 49,168. The letter is reprinted in Appendix D and is included on the companion CD-Rom to this manual.

171 *Id.*

172 *Id.*

173 67 Fed. Reg. 67048 (amending 34 C.F.R. § 674.47(h), effective July 1, 2003). The write-off amount was increased from $5.

174 *Id.* (amending 34 C.F.R. § 674.47(h)(3)).

Chapter 9 — Defending Student Loan Collection Actions and Challenging Trade School Abuses

9.1 Trade School Abuses

9.1.1 Brief History

Unfair and deceptive vocational and correspondence school practices are a tremendous source of frustration, financial loss, and loss of opportunity for consumers, particularly low-income consumers hoping to break out of poverty. Attracted by the financing provided by government student loan and grant programs, many vocational school scams and ill-conceived schools have exploited federally funded student assistance programs.

Abuses were particularly widespread during the 1980s and early 1990s when student financial assistance became more widely available for non-high-school graduates and for vocational training.[1] The abuses were fueled by a federal student loan system that created a con artist's perfect dream. Schools were able to pressure vulnerable and low-income consumers into signing documents obligating them to thousands of dollars. Many schools promised that students would not have to repay loans until they found high-paying jobs. The schools then literally took the money and ran, leaving loan collection to third parties and the government.

This problem, for the most part, grew out of good intentions. In 1979, Congress amended the Higher Education Act (HEA) to encourage lenders to market loans to for-profit vocational school students.[2] Congress hoped to open up the student financial assistance market, particularly to non-high-school graduates and others wishing to pursue vocational training. Unfortunately, these changes not only opened the door to eager students but also to unscrupulous for-profit school operators and lenders.

The tragedy of trade school fraud is that it robs vulnerable people of their dreams. According to testimony given by a former truck-driver-training-school owner, "In the proprietary school business what you sell is dreams and so ninety-nine percent of the sales were made in poor, black areas [at] welfare offices and unemployment lines, and in housing projects. My approach was that if [a prospect] could breathe, scribble his name, had a driver's license, and was over 18 years of age, he was qualified for North American's program."[3]

Although the situation has improved significantly, the abuses of the past are still relevant. Many clients need help dealing with older student loan debt that may be preventing them from going back to school, from getting good credit, or even from buying a house. There are also new concerns and new abuses in the trade school industry, discussed below. Unless addressed through loan cancellation, repayment, or other remedies, these problems can literally last forever because of the elimination of a statute of limitations for most student loan collection.[4]

9.1.2 Recent Growth in Proprietary Higher Education and Current Concerns

Trade school fraud is by no means only a legacy of the past. New abuses have emerged. A number of problems are tied to the aggressive push for growth in the sector. The booming for-profit educational market is increasingly dominated by regional and even national franchises, many with stock shares traded on Wall Street. There are already many

---

1 For a good history of student financial assistance for vocational schools, see C. Mansfield, *The Federal Trade Commission Holder Rules and Its Applicability to Student Loans—Re-Allocating the Risk of Proprietary School Failure*, 26 Wake Forest L. Rev. 635 (1991). In addition, although the issue was not briefed by the parties in the litigation, the *Armstrong* court on its own initiative summarized some of the changes that made federal student aid more widely available over time. *See* Armstrong v. Accrediting Council for Continuing Education & Training, 168 F. Rep. 3d 1362, 1364 (D.C. Cir. 1999).

2 Higher Education Technical Amendments of 1979, Pub. L. No. 96-49, 93 Stat. 351 (1979). The 1979 amendments removed a ceiling on the federal interest subsidy paid to participating guaranteed student loan program lenders. Later amendments removed other limitations on student borrowers attending for-profit schools. *See* Education Amendments of 1980, Pub. L. No. 96-374, 94 Stat. 1367 (1980); Higher Education Amendments of 1986, Pub. L. No. 99-498, §§ 425, 1075(a), 100 Stat. 1268, 1359 (1986).

3 S. Rep. No. 102-58 at 12–13 (1991) (testimony), *quoted in* Patrick F. Linehan, *Dreams Protected: A New Approach to Policing Proprietary Schools' Misrepresentations*, 89 Geo. L.J. 753 (Mar. 2001).

4 *See* § 4.2.1, *supra*.

complaints about some of these "mega-schools."[5] Many of these companies are expanding internationally as well.[6]

Even the Department of Education's Inspector General concedes that reducing risk in the student aid programs is still a management challenge for the Department and that it continues to find fraud and abuse by program participants as well as weaknesses in program administration.[7]

Although this manual generally refers to the issue as "trade school fraud," the problem is much broader. Issues arise with respect to proprietary schools generally. Proprietary education has evolved from mostly small, local, vocation-oriented schools into much larger corporate institutions that provide two-year and longer programs.[8] Over the years, there has been a decline in the number of schools offering shorter programs.

The for-profit higher education sector flourished even during the Wall Street bear market of the early 2000s. Apollo, Career Education, and Corinthian were three of the hottest public offerings in the past decade.[9] However, government investigations and private lawsuits in the sector have led to greater market volatility.[10]

For example, beginning in around 2004, state agencies in six states—California, Florida, Kentucky, New Jersey, Oregon, and Pennsylvania—conducted regulatory reviews or investigations into the activities of various for-profit colleges. In 2006, the New York State Board of Regents endorsed a package of proposals designed to provide greater oversight of new for-profit colleges and those undergoing a change of ownership. The board also called for increasing scrutiny of the admissions practices of all such colleges operating in the state.[11]

The emphasis on growth in the proprietary school sector, particularly among the publicly traded companies, has increased competition and led schools to unleash aggressive marketing campaigns. A market orientation can theoretically lead to innovation and flexibility. However, unless constrained by reasonable protections for consumers and taxpayers, it can also induce schools to engage in practices that harm students and taxpayers. Unfortunately, the system creates incentives for schools to inflate or otherwise misrepresent performance data such as completion and job placement rates in order to maintain and grow profits.[12]

A 2003 Department of Education program review of University of Phoenix (UOP) provides a detailed look at an aggressive marketing structure and the problems this creates. The report describes extensive use of incentive compensation based on enrollments for those involved in recruiting or admission activities, in violation of the HEA requirements.[13] According to a 2006 news article, a former recruiter at a Career Education Colleges campus said that there is pressure to enroll students "by any means necessary."[14]

A case against another school, based mainly on allegations of race discrimination, describes a system that requires admissions employees to meet enrollment targets that are set by management.[15] A Fair Labor Standards Act case against another proprietary school provides additional insight into an aggressive marketing strategy. In order to avoid paying

---

5   The Chronicle of Higher Education keeps an index of for-profit education, noting changes in stock prices, profits, and acquisitions. The index was developed by the Center for Research in Security Prices at the University of Chicago's Graduate School of Business.

6   The trend toward greater consolidation in the for-profit higher education market is continuing as well. For example, Education Management Corporation announced in June 2003 that it was purchasing a system of eighteen junior colleges with locations in eight states. This was the company's third purchase of smaller competitors since April 2003. Corinthian Colleges, Inc., also made three acquisitions in June 2003, including schools in Canada. Several other for-profit companies, including DeVry, Inc., and Career Education Corporation also made major purchases in 2003. *See* Goldie Blumenstyk & Elizabeth F. Farrell, In For-Profit Higher Education, Buying Binge Heats Up, The Chron. of Higher Educ., July 11, 2003, at A25.

7   Office of Inspector Gen., Semiannual Report to Congress: No. 48, Oct. 1, 2003–Mar. 31, 2004; Office of Inspector Gen., Semiannual Report to Congress: No. 47, Apr. 1, 2003–Sept. 30, 2003. Reports are available on the OIG website at www.ed.gov/about/offices/list/oig. Inspector General John P. Higgins testified in May 2005 that the student financial assistance program is a high-risk area that remains vulnerable. *Hearing Before the U.S. House Committee on Government Reform*, 109th Cong. (May 26, 2005) (statement of John P. Higgins, Jr., Inspector General, Department of Education).

8   *See* NEA Higher Educ. Research Ctr., *Proprietary Education: Threat, or Not?*, 10 Update, No. 4 (Sept. 2004), *available at* www2.nea.org/he/heupdate/images/vol10no4.pdf (last accessed in October 2006).

9   *See* Stephen Schurr, *Market Insight: What Short-Sellers Can Teach Us, at* www.FT.com (last visited in June 2004). Publicly traded postsecondary education stocks rose 460% over the period of 2000–2003, compared to a 24% loss for the Standard & Poor's 500-stock index. Eryn Brown, *Can For-Profit Schools Pass an Ethics Test*, N.Y. Times, Dec. 12, 2004.

10 *See generally* National Consumer Law Center, *Making the Numbers Count: Why Proprietary School Performance Data*

Doesn't Add Up and What Can Be Done About It (June 2005), *available at* www.nclc.org and on the companion CD Rom to this manual. For an in-depth investigative article about one of Career Education Corporation's campuses, see Stephen Burd, *Promises and Profits*, The Chron. of Higher Educ., Jan. 13, 2006, at A21.

11 *See* Xiao-Bo Yuan, *Disputes Over Regulating For-Profit Colleges Come to a Head in California*, The Chron. of Higher Educ., Aug. 11, 2006.

12 *See* § 9.2.4, *infra.*

13 U.S. Dep't of Educ., Student Financial Assistance Program Review Report, PCRN 200340922254, Univ. of Phoenix, Site Visit of 8/18/03 to 8/22/03 (on file with NCLC). A false claims lawsuit against UOP makes similar allegations. U.S. *ex rel.* Hendow and Albertson v. Univ. of Phoenix, Case # Civ. 5-03-0457 (E.D. Ca. complaint filed Mar. 7, 2003). *See* § 9.2.6.

14 Stephen Burd, *Promises and Profits*, The Chron. of Higher Educ., Jan. 13, 2006, at A21.

15 Legrand v. New York Restaurant Sch., 2004 WL 1555102 (S.D.N.Y. July 12, 2004).

overtime, the school argued that field representatives who engaged in a range of activities—including high school visits and calls to prospective students—were actually salespeople.[16] The court noted that college recruiters are ordinarily not engaged in selling services. In contrast, the employees in this case not only identified prospective students but also were paid based on inducing them to enroll. As discussed in the decision, the employee's potential for salary enhancements and eligibility for recognition and rewards was based primarily on the number of tuition-paying "student starts" the employee collected.[17]

Yet another problem area is the for-profit education sector's growing use of mandatory arbitration clauses in school enrollment agreements.[18]

9.1.3 Scholarship Scams

Companies that take advance payment from consumers to find them scholarships and grants is another growing form of abuse. These companies may send high school and college students postcards advertising that, for an advance fee, the service can find "unclaimed" scholarship and grant funds from private companies. They promise to refund the fee if the student does not receive a minimum amount. Nevertheless, these companies all too often provide neither the promised financial aid nor the promised refunds.[19] Other

times, they claim a refund is not owing because the small print places onerous conditions on receiving a refund.[20] When they cannot get the student to send money up front, the companies may find out the student's checking account number and take money out of the account with an unauthorized demand draft or telecheck.[21]

Sometimes these companies merely provide consumers with lists of financial aid sources to which the consumers must apply on their own.[22] One company agreed to stop its practice of selling employment and financial aid directories which it misrepresented as programs guaranteeing students jobs with free room, board, and transportation or free financial aid.[23]

In 2000, Congress passed legislation specifically addressing this issue. The College Scholarship Fraud Prevention Act of 2000 required the United States Sentencing Commission to provide enhanced penalties for financial aid fraud.[24] The Act also requires the Departments of Education, Justice and Federal Trade Commission to coordinate enforcement and outreach activities in this area.[25]

Another problem is the rise of so-called "diploma mills." "Diploma mills" and other unaccredited schools resemble the distance education programs that have managed to secure legitimate accreditation. Although there is no formal definition of a "diploma mill," it is generally an on-line operation that offers degrees for money alone or, in some cases, for money and a little work.[26]

---

16   Nielsen v. Devry Inc., 302 F. Supp. 2d 747 (W.D. Mich. 2003).

17   *Id.*

18   According to one San Diego-based lawyer who represents large post-secondary education clients, "[i]f you're a proprietary school and you don't have [an arbitration provision], you're insane." Elizabeth F. Farrell, *Signer Beware*, The Chron. of Higher Educ., Apr. 18, 2003, at A33 (quoting Keith Zakarin). The Chronicle of Higher Education reports that many large for-profit college systems, including ITT Educational Services, Corinthian, Education Management Corporation, Kaplan, and Whitman Education Group (soon to be acquired by Career Education Corporation), include arbitration provisions in their enrollment contracts. For a detailed discussion of problems with mandatory arbitration clauses and how advocates can challenge these clauses, see National Consumer Law Center, Consumer Arbitration Agreements (4th ed. 2004). *See, e.g.*, Cross v. Maric College, 2006 WL 1769779 (Cal. App. June 29, 2006) (school failed to carry initial burden of proof to show a valid arbitration agreement existed); Thornton v. Career Training Ctr., 128 Cal. App. 4th 116, 26 Cal. Rptr. 3d 723 (Cal. App. 2005) (arbitration clauses in promissory notes executed by students to obtain student loans did not apply to student action against vocational training school alleging state UDAP claims), *rev. granted*, 31 Cal. Rptr. 3d 457, 115 P.3d 1121 (Cal. 2005).

19   FTC v. National Scholarship Found., Inc., 5 Trade Reg. Rep. (CCH) ¶ 24,512 (S.D. Fla. 1998) (order for permanent injunction); FTC v. Deco Consulting Servs., Inc., 5 Trade Reg. Rep. (CCH) ¶ 24,363 (S.D. Fla. 1998) (consent decree); FTC v. National Grant Found., Inc., 5 Trade Reg. Rep. (CCH) ¶ 24,427 (S.D. Fla. 1998) (proposed consent decree); FTC v. College Assistance Servs., Inc., 5 Trade Reg. Rep. (CCH) ¶ 24,357 (S.D. Fla. 1998) (proposed consent decree); FTC v. Career Assistance Planning, Inc., 5 Trade Reg. Rep. (CCH) ¶ 24,218 (N.D. Ga.

1997) (consent decree); FTC v. Nwaigwe, 5 Trade Reg. Rep. (CCH) ¶ 24,253 (D. Md. 1997) (proposed consent decree).

20   FTC v. Student Aid Inc., 5 Trade Reg. Rep. (CCH) ¶ 24,312 (S.D.N.Y. 1997) (proposed consent decree).

21   *Id. See* National Consumer Law Center, Unfair and Deceptive Acts and Practices §§ 5.1.10.1–5.1.10.3 (6th ed. 2004 and Supp.), for a discussion of demand drafts or telechecks.

22   FTC v. National Grant Found., Inc., 5 Trade Reg. Rep. (CCH) ¶ 24,427 (S.D. Fla. 1998) (proposed consent decree).

23   FTC v. Progressive Media, Inc., 5 Trade Reg. Rep. (CCH) ¶ 24,304 (W.D. Wash. 1997) (proposed consent decree). More information can be found on the Department of Education's website at www.ed.gov.

24   Scholarship Fraud Prevention Act, Pub. L. No. 106-420, 114 Stat. 1867 (Nov. 1, 2000). *See* 20 U.S.C. § 1092d.

25   Project Scholarscam is the FTC's ongoing project to prevent and prosecute scholarship fraud. For more information, see www.ftc.gov/bcp/conline/edcams/scholarship/index.html. The Department of Education also has consumer education information to help borrowers avoid scholarship scams, available at www.ed.gov/studentaid or by calling 1-800-4FED-AID (1-800-433-3243). *See also* U.S. Dep't of Justice, U.S. Dep't of Educ., Federal Trade Comm'n, Scholarship Fraud Prevention Act of 2000: First Annual Report to Congress (May 2002).

26   *See, e.g.*, U.S. Gen. Accounting Office, Diploma Mills: Federal Employees Have Obtained Degrees from Diploma Mills and Other Unaccredited Schools, Some at Government Expense, GAO-04-77IT (May 2004); Thomas Bartlett & Scott Smallwood, *Inside the Multimillion-Dollar World of Diploma Mills*, The Chron. of Higher Educ., June 25, 2004, at A8. *See* § 9.2.3 (distance education), *supra.*

9.2 Regulation of Trade Schools

9.2.1 General

The Department of Education (DOE) does not review the educational quality of schools before certifying their eligibility to participate in the federal student aid programs. Instead, the DOE requires the schools to be licensed by a state agency, and the Department recognizes various private accrediting agencies and associations whose job it is to review the educational standards of the school.[27]

The current regulatory structure for schools participating in federal financial assistance programs is often referred to as the "triad." The three "arms" of the triad consist of the federal Department of Education, state agencies, and accrediting agencies. The Department of Education relies heavily on the other two arms to determine program standards.[28] The federal Department mainly plays a gate-keeping role, verifying institutions' eligibility, certifying their financial and administrative capacities, and granting recognition to accrediting agencies.

The state-based regulatory approach varies widely. Some states have developed standards that set, for example, minimum qualifications for trade school teachers.[29] Others have created state tuition recovery funds.[30] Overall, nearly every state agency is understaffed and under-funded.

The role of the accrediting agencies has been particularly controversial.[31] During Senate hearings in the early 1990s, the Senate noted the inherent conflict of interest in accreditation: once an agency approves a school for accreditation, the agency thereafter assumes the role of the school's advocate.[32] Despite these conflicts, the basic model persists, allowing for a buffer between trade schools and direct federal oversight.

Accreditation agencies are supposed to demonstrate that they have rigorous standards. The regulations set out factors that accreditation agencies must address in evaluating the quality of an institution, including success with respect to student achievement and, as appropriate, consideration of course completion, state licensing examination, and job placement rates.[33] Inspector General audit reports have concluded, however, that many accreditation agencies have not followed through on these responsibilities.[34] These findings are especially disturbing given that the Government Accountability Office recommended in 1996 that accreditation agencies develop and make public uniform performance-based consumer protection standards, including information on completion and placement rates.[35]

Over the years, Congress has enacted various laws to bolster enforcement of the laws regulating proprietary schools. Some of these provisions apply only to proprietary schools. Others apply more broadly but tend to disproportionately impact the proprietary sector. Key laws and regulations are discussed in this chapter. Congress has also passed certain cancellation rights for victims of proprietary school fraud, discussed in Chapter 6, *supra*.

For the most part, the requirements discussed below are proxies for quality. It is difficult to directly measure and monitor a school's performance. However, there are warning signs of problems that are measurable, including high default rates and over-reliance on federal funds. These are the types of standards Congress has developed over the years to help curb fraud.

Nearly all of the laws passed to protect borrowers from proprietary school abuses are under attack. Despite the real potential for abuse, the strong trade school lobby argues that the bad schools from the past are gone and that the industry now deserves relief from strict regulation. The lobby has succeeded and some restrictions, such as limits on federal aid for distance education, have been eliminated.[36]

9.2.2 Restrictions on Percentage of Federal Financial Aid Funds

The reliance of many for-profit trade schools on federal student assistance funds has been an issue of concern throughout the history of trade school regulation and fraud. The main problem, according to a GAO study, is that proprietary schools that rely more heavily on student assistance tend to have poorer student outcomes, including lower completion and placement rates and higher default rates.[37] These schools are also more likely to push students into taking out loans that they will not be able to repay.

In March 2005, Department of Education Chief Operating Officer Theresa Shaw reported in a presentation to the career college trade association that federal student assis-

---

27 For more information on accreditors, see § 9.4.1.2, *infra*.

28 *See generally* U.S. Gen. Accounting Office, Higher Education: Ensuring Quality Education From Proprietary Institutions, GAO/T-HEHS-96-158 (June 1996).

29 *See* § 9.3.2.2, *infra*.

30 *See* § 9.7, *infra*.

31 *See, e.g.*, S. Rep. No. 102-58 at 20 (1991). For a summary of newspaper articles exposing these issues as well as government investigations, see Patrick F. Linehan, *Dreams Protected: A New Approach to Policing Proprietary Schools' Misrepresentations*, 89 Geo. L.J. 753 (Mar. 2001).

32 S. Rep. No. 102-58 (1991).

33 20 U.S.C. § 1099b; 34 C.F.R. § 602.16.

---

34 *Enforcement of Federal Anti-Fraud Laws in For-Profit Education: Hearings Before the U.S. House Committee on Education and the Workforce*, 109th Cong. (Mar. 1, 2005) (reports cited in statement of Thomas A. Carter, Deputy Inspector General).

35 U.S. Gen. Accounting Office, Department of Education: Status of Actions to Improve the Management of Student Financial Aid, GAO/HEHS-96-143 (July 1996).

36 *See* § 9.2.3, *infra*.

37 U.S. Gen. Accounting Office, Proprietary Schools: Poorer Student Outcomes at Schools That Rely More on Federal Student Aid, GAO/HEHS-97-103 (June 1997).

tance funding for proprietary schools increased by 54% between 2001 and 2002 and between 2003 and 2004, with a 70% increase for publicly held schools.[38]

In annual reports and other information to investors, the companies repeatedly discuss their reliance on federal student aid to stay in business and to grow. *Forbes Magazine* noted this trend, describing Career Education Corporation (CEC) as a "company built to swallow Title IV [federal student assistance] funds in the way a whale gathers up plankton."[39]

Congress passed the 85/15 (now 90/10) rule to address this problem. Enacted as part of the 1992 Higher Education Act reauthorization, the rule requires each school to limit the percentage of revenues it receives from federal financial assistance.[40] Schools are required to calculate the federal student assistance dollars its students receive as the numerator, and total revenues from educational programs as the denominator. The maximum result (equaling the school's federal student assistance dollars as a percentage of total revenues) was initially set at 85% and then increased to 90%.[41]

A 1997 GAO report affirmed the importance of this rule. Interestingly, the GAO suggested that decreasing the percentage from 85% would be more likely to reduce defaults. However, the agency noted that this might lead to fewer low-income students enrolling in trade schools.[42] Instead, Congress went the other way, increasing the percentage to 90% (now known as the 90/10 rule).[43] This issue is very likely to come up again in the future. A number of bills have been introduced in Congress to eliminate the 90/10 rule.[44]

Unfortunately, the actual requirements of the rule are often obscured by political rhetoric. The rule requires that schools receive no more than 90% of their revenues from federal aid funds. Some students at these schools may still receive full financial aid, however, as long as at least 10% of the school's revenues used to pay for the education and training of students is derived from other funds. These other funds may include students' private funds, private loans, scholarships, or other funds.

9.2.3 Restrictions on Distance Education, Correspondence, and Telecommunications

Another area of concern is the growing field of distance education. While technological innovation may in some cases provide benefits for students, there are also dangers that diminished classroom (or seat time) will lead to abuses by unscrupulous school operators.

Prior to 2006, schools that offered primarily distance education courses had their participation in federal assistance programs limited in a number of ways. These limits were tied to restrictions on correspondence courses. Schools offering bogus correspondence courses were guilty of some of the most abusive practices during the 1980s and early 1990s. As a result, Congress barred federal funding for most correspondence courses that are not part of programs leading to bachelors, associates, or graduate degrees.[45]

The prohibitions on federal aid for correspondence courses are still in place. Degree-granting schools that offer more than 50% of their courses by correspondence are not eligible to participate in the federal financial assistance programs.[46] These schools, even if otherwise eligible, are also considered ineligible if the school enrolls 50% or more of its regular students in correspondence courses.[47]

However, due to changes passed in the Higher Education Reconciliation Act, the 50% limit no longer applies to "telecommunications" courses.[48] The main difference between correspondence and telecommunications courses is that correspondence courses are "home study courses" in which schools provide instructional materials and examinations. When students complete a portion of the instructional materials, the students take the examinations that relate to that portion of the materials and return the examinations to the institution for grading.[49] Correspondence courses may include courses offered by videocassette and discs if the school does not offer comparable instruction to students physically attending classes.[50] If a course is part correspondence and part residential training, the Secretary considers the course to be a correspondence course.

In contrast, telecommunications courses are defined as courses offered principally through the use of television, audio, or computer transmission.[51] The courses "deliver instruction to students who are separated from the instructor and . . . support regular and substantive interaction between these students and the instructor, either synchronously or asynchronously. The term does not include a course that is

---

38 Theresa S. Shaw, U.S. Dep't of Educ., *Federal Student Aid Update* (Mar. 16, 2005) (presentation to Career College Association), *available at* www.career.org/Template.cfm?Section=News_You_Can_Use&CONTENTID=2967&TEMPLATE=/ContentManagement/ContentDisplay.cfm#15 (last accessed in October 2005).

39 Daniel Kruger, *Blackboard Jungle*, Forbes Magazine, Dec. 13, 2004.

40 34 C.F.R. § 600.5(a)(8). *See* U.S. Dep't of Educ., Dear Colleague Letter Gen-99-33 (Oct. 1999).

41 34 C.F.R. § 600.5(a)(8), 600.5(d).

42 U.S. Gen. Accounting Office, Proprietary Schools: Poorer Student Outcomes at Schools That Rely More on Federal Student Aid, GAO/HEHS-97-103 (June 1997).

43 34 C.F.R. § 600.5(a)(8).

44 As of summer 2006, Congress had not yet acted to eliminate the 90/10 rule.

45 20 U.S.C. § 1091(k).

46 34 C.F.R. § 600.7(a)(1)(i).

47 34 C.F.R. § 600.7(a)(1)(ii).

48 20 U.S.C. § 1002(a)(3).

49 34 C.F.R. § 600.2.

50 34 C.F.R. § 600.2.

51 20 U.S.C. § 1091(l)(4); 34 C.F.R. § 600.2.

delivered using video cassettes or disc recordings unless that course is delivered to students physically attending classes at the institution providing the course during the same award year. If the course does not qualify as a telecommunications course, it is considered to be a correspondence course."[52]

An otherwise eligible program that is offered in whole or in part through telecommunications is now eligible for federal financial aid if the program is offered by an institution, other than a foreign institution, that has been evaluated and is accredited for its effective delivery of distance education programs by an accrediting agency or association that is recognized by the Secretary and has accreditation of distance education within the scope of its recognition.[53]

The Department has expressed concern that schools may try to disguise "correspondence" courses by making minimal, cosmetic changes and calling them "telecommunications" courses. The Department addressed this issue in its amended regulations. The Department emphasized that the definition of telecommunications does not focus exclusively on technology.[54] According to the Department, basing the definition solely on whether the course has a technological component might lead to an erroneous interpretation that an institution could qualify for full participation in federal aid programs upon introduction of minor e-mail contact between students and a grader. The amended definition, the Department states, acknowledges the importance of interactivity between instructors and students and clearly distinguishes telecommunications from correspondence.[55]

The limits on telecommunications courses had little effect until recently as more schools began to offer "distance education" courses. The percentage of higher education institutions offering courses through distance education grew by one-third from 1995 to 1997–98 and continues to grow.[56] According to a 2003 report, all types of schools expect to see growth in on-line learning enrollments, with for-profit schools likely to see the largest percentage increases.[57]

The limits on federal aid for distance education were increasingly seen as barriers to integrating distance education into trade school course offerings. However, the GAO found in a February 2004 report that only fourteen schools were either adversely affected by the restrictions on financial aid for distance education or likely to be affected in the future. Eight of these schools had already been granted waivers from the restrictions.[58] Waivers were granted through a Distance Education Demonstration Project passed as part of the 1998 Higher Education Act (HEA) Amendments.[59]

Congress passed the legislation eliminating the restrictions on telecommunications courses despite a GAO study showing that eliminating the restrictions with no additional monitoring would trigger a medium- to high-risk of fraud and abuse and could lead to substantial cost increases.[60] The GAO also found significant variation in accrediting agencies' oversight of distance education programs. This is particularly troubling since the accrediting agencies are given substantial flexibility by the DOE to determine standards and monitor schools.

9.2.4 *Job Placement and Completion Statistics*

Proprietary schools have an explicit directive to prepare students for employment in recognized occupations. While this is an important goal for all higher education institutions, only proprietary schools are required by law to fulfill this mission. Specifically, programs at a proprietary institution of higher education may be eligible for federal financial assistance only if the school provides an eligible program of training to prepare students for gainful employment in a recognized occupation and is accredited by a nationally recognized accrediting agency.[61]

There are a number of additional regulatory requirements that at a minimum mandate that schools collect and retain data on completions and job placement and in some cases

---

52   34 C.F.R. § 600.2.

53   34 C.F.R. § 668.8(m).

54   71 Fed. Reg. 45666, 45667–68 (Aug. 9, 2006).

55   *Id.*

56   National Ctr. for Educ. Statistics, Distance Education at Post-secondary Education Institutions: 1997–1998, at 5 (Dec. 1999), *cited in* U.S. Dep't of Educ., Office of Postsecondary Education, Policy, Planning and Innovation, Report to Congress on the Distance Education Demonstration Programs, Washington, D.C. (Jan. 2001); U.S. Dep't of Educ., Office of Postsecondary Educ., Policy, Planning and Innovation, Second Report to Congress on the Distance Education Program (July 2003); I. Elaine Allen & Jeff Seaman, The Sloan Consortium, Sizing the Opportunity: The Quality and Extent of Online Education in the United States, 2002 and 2003 (Sept. 2003). In September 2004, the Department's Inspector General (IG) issued a report finding that the Department's Second Report to Congress contained statements that were not supported by information in the report or in other documents provided to the IG. *See* Dep't of Educ., Office of Inspector Gen., Final Audit Report: U.S. Department of Education's Administration of the Distance Education Demonstration Program, Ed-OIG/A09-D0010 (Sept. 2004). *See also* U.S. Dep't of Educ., Office of Postsecondary Educ., Third

Report to Congress on the Distance Education Demonstration Program (Apr. 2005).

57   I. Elaine Allen & Jeff Seaman, The Sloan Consortium, Sizing the Opportunity: The Quality and Extent of Online Education in the United States, 2002 and 2003 (Sept. 2003).

58   U.S. Gen. Accounting Office, Distance Education: Improved Data on Program Costs and Guidelines on Quality Assessments Needed to Inform Federal Policy, GAO-04-279 (Feb. 2004).

59   20 U.S.C. § 1093.

60   *See* U.S. Gen. Accounting Office, Distance Education: Improved Data on Program Costs and Guidelines on Quality Assessments Needed to Inform Federal Policy, GAO-04-279 (Feb. 2004).

61   20 U.S.C. § 1002(b).

require that this information be disclosed to prospective students. Key requirements are summarized below.

1. *Minimum Placement and Completion Standards*: Proprietary schools offering educational programs of at least 300 clock hours of instruction, but less than 600 hours, offered during a minimum of 10 weeks, are not eligible to participate in the FFEL and Direct Loan programs unless they have a verified completion rate for those programs of at least 70% and a verified job placement rate of at least 70%.[62]

Placement rates are calculated by first determining the number of students who, during the award year, received the degree, certificate, or other recognized educational credential awarded for successfully completing the program. Of this total, the school must determine the number of students who, within 180 days of the day they received their degree, certificate, or other recognized educational credential, obtained gainful employment in the recognized occupation for which they were trained or in a related comparable recognized occupation and, on the date of this calculation, are employed or have been employed for at least 13 weeks following receipt of the credential.[63] The rate is the number of students placed divided by the total.

Schools are also required to collect documentation to support the numbers of students categorized as "placed" in jobs. Examples of satisfactory documentation of a student's gainful employment include, but are not limited to

(i)   a written statement from the student's employer;

(ii) signed copies of State or Federal income tax forms; and

(iii) written evidence of payments of Social Security taxes.[64]

2. *Accreditation Agency Standards*. The regulations set out factors that accreditation agencies must address in evaluating the quality of an institution, including success with respect to student achievement, which includes, as appropriate, consideration of course completion, state licensing examination, and job placement rates.[65]

3. *Disclosure Requirements for Completion and Placement*. Institutions must sign participation agreements with the Secretary of Education in order to participate in federal student assistance programs. Institutions that advertise job placement rates as a means of attracting students to enroll must make available to prospective students, at or before the time that those students apply for enrollment, the most recent available data concerning employment statistics, graduation statistics, and any other information necessary to substantiate the truthfulness of the advertisements.[66]

4. *Completion Disclosure Requirements*. An institution must make available to any enrolled student or prospective student, on request and through appropriate publications, mailings, or electronic media, information concerning financial assistance and the institution's completion or graduation rate and, if applicable, its transfer-out rate. In the case of a prospective student, the information must be made available prior to the student's enrolling or entering into any financial obligation with the institution.[67]

5. *Annual Reporting of Completion Rates*. Institutions must make completion or graduation rates available annually.[68]

Many recent cases against proprietary schools and government investigations have focused on misrepresentations about job placement rates. This is a serious problem because it is almost impossible to determine the "real" rates. Although there are serious flaws with the completion data itself and the reporting of completion data, it is at least collected in some consistent way. This is not the case with job placement data. The Department does not collect job placement rates for any type of institution.

Because there is little or no oversight, there is tremendous room for the schools to manipulate the placement rates.[69] A 2005 *60 Minutes* story about Career Education Corporation (CEC) described ways in which school officials pump up placement rates by including students placed in any job, not necessarily jobs they were trained for.[70]

The lack of enforcement occurs not only with respect to reporting of data but also with respect to investigating whether the school is substantiating data. As noted above, the schools are supposed to document placement information by, for example, retaining written statements from a student's employer or signed copies of state or federal income tax forms. Although not a panacea, this type of documentation at least provides one way of evaluating the types of employment reported.

Another problem is that even legitimate trade schools may offer courses in areas with bleak job prospects. A 1997 General Accounting Office (GAO) study found that a large percentage of the federal assistance money that goes to trade school students is used to train students for these low-demand jobs.[71] In some cases, the data was dramatic, with students being trained for occupations in which local supply exceeded demand by ratios of 10 to 1 or more. Common

---

62   20 U.S.C. § 1088(b)(2)(A).

63   34 C.F.R. § 668.8(g).

64   *Id.*

65   34 C.F.R. § 602.16.

66   34 C.F.R. § 668.14.

67   34 C.F.R. § 668.41.

68   34 C.F.R. § 668.45.

69   *See, e.g.*, Brent Hunsberger, *Degrees of Risk*, The Oregonian, Sept. 10, 2006.

70   *60 Minutes: An Expensive Lesson; Career Education Corporation Schools* (CBS News Transcripts Jan. 30, 2005).

71   *See* U.S. Gen. Accounting Office, Proprietary Schools: Millions Spent to Train Students for Oversupplied Occupations, GAO/HEHS-97-104 (June 1997). In contrast, several major federal job training programs restrict training to fields with favorable job projections. Most welfare-to-work programs also require welfare agencies to work with private industry councils and ensure that programs provided training for jobs likely to become available in the area. *See id.*

trade school courses, such as barbering/cosmetology and appliance/equipment repair were oversupplied for all states in the study.[72]

9.2.5 Cohort Default Rate Sanctions

9.2.5.1 General

Throughout the late 1980s and early 1990s, vocational school abuses led to tremendous increases in student loan default rates. The government worked to curb growing default rates by expanding collection powers, as discussed throughout this manual, and by initiating a program to punish schools with high default rates. Under this sanctions program, the Department has the authority to terminate high-default schools from the federal student aid programs.[73]

Since the inception of the program in 1991, according to the Department, more than 1100 schools have lost student loan program eligibility.[74] The number of schools subject to sanctions has dropped dramatically since the peak of 642 in 1994. Department of Education records show that no schools were sanctioned in 2001 and only one was sanctioned in 2002.

The default-rate programs apply to all institutions. However, due to higher default rates in the proprietary sector, these schools have historically been more likely to face sanctions or the threat of sanctions.

The Department calculates default rates for institutions and may initiate proceedings against any institution with an FFEL, Direct Loan, or weighted average rate that is more than 40% for any fiscal year.[75] The rates are gathered for specific groups of borrowers during specific time periods. Each group is called a "cohort." Schools with cohort default rates of 25% or more for three consecutive years face loss of eligibility in the loan and Federal Pell Grant programs.[76]

9.2.5.2 How School Default Rates Are Calculated

For schools with thirty borrowers or more, the cohort default rate is the percentage of a school's borrowers who enter repayment on most FFEL and/or Direct loans during a fiscal year and default before the end of the following fiscal year.[77] FFEL and Direct PLUS, FISL, and Perkins loans are not included in the calculation. Perkins loans have separate cohort default-rate calculations.[78]

The cohort rate is a misleading indicator for several reasons. It tracks borrowers for just the first two years after they go into repayment. For schools with twenty-nine or fewer borrowers entering repayment during a fiscal year, the cohort rate data includes borrowers entering repayment over a three-year period.[79] This is a mere snapshot in time that does not give a full picture of default trends.

Both the GAO and Department of Education Inspector General have released reports describing the ways in which these default rates are understated.[80] The Inspector General Report, for example, cited a number of problems, including that the rates reflect defaults during the two-year cohort period and not the life of the loan, that PLUS loans and certain consolidation loans are excluded, and that the rates are calculated based on the number of borrowers in a cohort and not on the number of loans or the loan amount.[81]

An additional problem is that the Department counts borrowers with deferments and forbearances among those who are successfully repaying their loans.[82] This means that the number of borrowers in default is divided by a number larger than the total number of borrowers who are actually repaying their loans. As a result, the default rate is understated.[83] Further distorting the statistics, these borrowers are not placed in subsequent cohorts and are thus never included in calculations of a school's default rate even if they default on their loans after the deferment or forbearance period is over.

Both the GAO and the Department of Education's Inspector General found that excluding these borrowers from the denominator of the calculation rate would significantly increase the cohort default rates in all school sectors. Both agencies concluded that these borrowers should be excluded from the cohort default rate calculation. They concluded further that the borrowers should be added to subsequent

---

72 U.S. Gen. Accounting Office, Proprietary Schools: Millions Spent to Train Students for Oversupplied Occupations, GAO/HEHS-97-104 (June 1997).

73 20 U.S.C. § 1085.

74 Press Release, U.S. Dep't of Educ., Accountability for Results Works: College Loan Default Rates Continue to Decline (Sept. 19, 2001).

75 34 C.F.R. § 668.187(a)(1).

76 34 C.F.R. § 668.187(a)(2). Historically black colleges or universities and tribally controlled community colleges or Navajo community colleges are not subject to loss of eligibly as long as they meet certain requirements such as submission of a default management plan. 20 U.S.C. § 1085(a)(5); 34 C.F.R. § 668.198.

77 34 C.F.R. § 668.183(d).

78 34 C.F.R. § 674.5.

79 34 C.F.R. § 668.183(a)(1).

80 U.S. Dep't of Educ., Office of the Inspector Gen., Audit to Determine If Cohort Default Rates Provide Sufficient Information on Defaults in the Title IV Loan Programs, ED-OIG/A03-C0017 (Dec. 2003); U.S. Gen. Accounting Office, Federal Student Aid: Timely Performance Plans and Reports Would Help Guide and Assess Achievement of Default Management Goals, GAO-03-348 (Feb. 2003); U.S. Gen. Accounting Office, Student Loans: Default Rates Need to be Computed More Appropriately, GAO/HEHS-99-135 (July 1999).

81 U.S. Dep't of Educ., Office of the Inspector Gen., Audit to Determine If Cohort Default Rates Provide Sufficient Information on Defaults in the Title IV Loan Programs, ED-OIG/A03-C0017 (Dec. 2003).

82 *Id.*

83 *Id.*

default cohorts in the year in which their deferments or forbearances end and they have begun repaying their loans.[84]

9.2.5.3 School Appeals Process

Schools have the right to appeal disciplinary action. Over the years, Congress has steadily expanded the grounds for appeal. In particular, provisions in the 1998 HEA allowed schools to appeal based on mitigating circumstances.[85] The "mitigating circumstance" most relevant for low-income clients is the exemption from sanctions for schools serving primarily low-income students. This is known as the "economically disadvantaged appeal."[86]

There are two types of economically disadvantaged appeals. The first applies to non-degree-granting schools and is based on the percentage of low-income students at the school ("low income rate") and employment placement rate.[87] These schools must show that the low-income rate and the school's placement rate (generally, the percentage of students who became employed in the occupation for which the school trained them) is 44% or more.[88]

The second, applying to degree-granting schools, is based on low-income rate and program completion rate.[89] Degree-granting schools must show that the school's low-income rate is two-thirds or more and the school's completion rate (generally, the percentage of students who completed their program) is 70% or more.[90]

The low-income rate is defined as the percentage of students who are eligible to receive a federal Pell grant of at least one-half the maximum award or have an adjusted gross income that, if added to the student's parents' income (unless the student is an independent student) or added to the spouse's income if the student is a married independent student, is less than the poverty level for the student's family size.[91] Schools can also appeal based on errors or inaccuracies in the calculation of the default rate.[92]

It is important for advocates representing low-income clients to understand the cohort default appeals process. Vocational schools, particularly those in low-income communities, rely almost exclusively on federal assistance to stay in business.[93] They are very aware of the need to stay

below the cohort default triggers. As a result, they may push borrowers into certain repayment options (such as consolidation) that may not make sense for a particular borrower. They also may try to mischaracterize certain types of employment as related to the student's program of study at the school. At a minimum, understanding these incentives is likely to give advocates additional leverage when negotiating with schools on behalf of low-income clients. It is also a good idea to check on a current school's default rate for a client who is complaining of problems with a particular school. A high default rate is usually a tip-off that there are serious problems with the school.

9.2.6 Limits on Incentive Compensation and Commissions

All institutions that wish to receive federal financial aid must enter into program participation agreements with the Department of Education. Among the requirements in these agreements are bans on paying recruiters on a per-student basis.[94] This provision is meant to curb the risk that recruiters will sign up poorly qualified students who will derive little benefit from the subsidy and may be unable or unwilling to repay federally guaranteed loans.[95]

The limits on incentive compensation have been significantly diluted in recent years. The previous regulations generally followed the statutory language in prohibiting commissions, bonuses, and other incentive payments by school recruiters when those payments were tied directly or indirectly to success in securing enrollments or financial aid.[96] Legislation pending in Congress in 2002 would have taken much of the bite out of this law.[97] However, the Department of Education bypassed the legislative process by enacting new regulations that contained many of the provisions in the Congressional bill.[98]

The regulations added a number of safe harbors for schools. For example, the following are exempted from the definition of "incentive compensation":

- the payment of fixed compensation, such as a fixed annual salary or a fixed hourly wage, as long as that compensation is not adjusted up or down more than twice during any twelve-month period and any adjustment is not based solely on the number of students recruited, admitted, enrolled, or awarded financial aid. For this purpose, an increase in fixed compensation resulting from a cost-of-living increase that is paid to all

---

84 *Id.*
85 20 U.S.C. § 1085(a)(4)–(6).
86 34 C.F.R. § 668.194.
87 34 C.F.R. § 668.194(b), (d).
88 *Id.* The regulation explicitly states that a former student is not considered to have been employed based on any employment by the institution. 34 C.F.R. § 668.194(d)(2).
89 34 C.F.R. § 668.194(b), (c).
90 *Id.*
91 34 C.F.R. § 668.194(b).
92 34 C.F.R. § 668.192 (erroneous data appeals).
93 The main barrier keeping schools from relying exclusively on student assistance revenue is the 90/10 (previously 85/15) rule. 34 C.F.R. § 600.5. *See* § 9.2.2, *supra.*

94 20 U.S.C. § 1094(a)(20).
95 *See* U.S., ex rel. Hendow v. University of Phoenix, __ F. 3d __, 2006 WL 2530394 (9th Cir. Sept. 5, 2006).
96 20 U.S.C. § 1094(a)(20); 34 C.F.R. § 668.24.
97 Internet Equity and Education Act of 2001, S. 1445, 107th Cong. (2001).
98 67 Fed. Reg. 67048 (Nov. 1, 2002) (amending 34 C.F.R. § 668.14(b)(22)).

or substantially all full-time employees is not considered an adjustment;[99]

- compensation to recruiters based upon their recruitment of students who enroll only in programs that are not eligible for title IV, HEA program funds;[100]

- compensation paid to employees who perform clerical "pre-enrollment" activities, such as answering telephone calls, referring inquiries, or distributing institutional materials;[101]

- compensation to managerial or supervisory employees who do not directly manage or supervise employees who are directly involved in recruiting or admissions activities or the awarding of title IV, HEA program funds;[102] and

- compensation paid for Internet-based recruitment and admission activities that provide information about the institution to prospective students, refer prospective students to the institution, or permit prospective students to apply for admission on-line.[103]

9.3 Key Legal Claims in Student Loan Cases

9.3.1 Introduction

In most cases, clients will seek legal help for student loans long after they have left or graduated from school. As noted above, the complete elimination of a statute of limitations for most student loans means that collection efforts can go on indefinitely.[104] Some clients may seek legal assistance for loans from ten, twenty, or even thirty years ago.

Although the majority of student loan cases will be defensive, affirmative suits may still be viable in some cases. For victims of proprietary school abuses, particularly those with pre-1994 FFELS, affirmative claims may be the only available relief. This is because some courts refuse to allow borrowers to raise school-related claims defensively.[105]

The subsections below discuss claims to consider in student loan cases. The analysis focuses on claims relevant to school-related problems or abuses. However, many of these claims will also apply when a borrower attends a "legitimate" school but runs into problems with his or her student loan, such as a school or guaranty agency's failure to grant a reasonable and affordable repayment plan.

---

99 34 C.F.R. § 668.14(b)(22)(ii)(A).
100 34 C.F.R. § 668.14(b)(22)(ii)(B).
101 34 C.F.R. § 668.14(b)(22)(ii)(F).
102 34 C.F.R. § 668.14(b)(22)(ii)(G).
103 34 C.F.R. § 668.14(b)(22)(ii)(J).
104 *See* § 4.2.1, *supra*.
105 § 9.6, *infra*.

9.3.2 State Claims

9.3.2.1 UDAP Theories

9.3.2.1.1 General and preemption

Unfair and Deceptive Acts and Practices (UDAP) claims are generally well-suited to challenge trade school abuses. Oral and print misrepresentations can be deceptive; the failure to disclose can be deceptive; and enrolling students unable to benefit from a program can be unfair or unconscionable.[106] The student's proof burden is simplified with a UDAP claim because the student normally need not prove intent, scienter, or other components of a common law fraud claim.[107] Some states do, however, require proof of reliance on the deceptive statement or conduct.[108] UDAP remedies often offer multiple or punitive damages and attorney fees.[109]

Despite the existence of federal regulation of the student loan program, the Higher Education Act should generally not preempt all UDAP claims against a school. Specifically, only state claims that conflict with the purposes or provisions of the HEA should be preempted.[110] Conflict preemption may arise under two circumstances: from a direct conflict between state and federal law, such that compliance with both is impossible (called "direct conflict"), or because a state law "stands as an obstacle to the accomplishment and execution of the full purposes and objectives of Congress"

---

106 *See generally* National Consumer Law Center, Unfair and Deceptive Acts and Practices §§ 4.3, 4.4 (6th ed. 2004 and Supp.).
107 *See id.* § 4.2.
108 *See id.* §§ 7.5.2, 10.5.2. *See, e.g.,* Finstad v. Washburn Univ. of Topeka, 845 P.2d 685 (Kan. 1993) (in UDAP case, court found students failed to demonstrate causation between school's false statement regarding accreditation and students' injuries; students did not claim they were induced to enroll by the false statement).
109 *See* National Consumer Law Center, Unfair and Deceptive Acts and Practices Ch. 8 (6th ed. 2004 and Supp.).
110 Courts have consistently concluded that the HEA does not occupy the field of higher education loans, so "field preemption" is not appropriate in these cases. *See, e.g.,* College Loan Corp. v. SLM Corp., 396 F.3d 588 (4th Cir. 2005). *See* Cliff v. Payco Gen. Am. Credits, 363 F.3d 1113 (11th Cir. 2004) (HEA does not occupy the field of student loan debt collection, and state fair debt collection claims not preempted); Morgan v. Markerdowne Corp., 976 F. Supp. 301 (D.N.J. 1997) (HEA preempts only those state laws which are in conflict with it), *class cert. denied*, 201 F.R.D. 341 (D.N.J. 2001) (court found no typical and predominant questions whether the plaintiffs relied on school's misrepresentations in deciding to enroll); Williams v. National Sch. of Health Tech., Inc., 836 F. Supp. 273 (E.D. Pa. 1993), *aff'd*, 37 F.3d 1491 (3d Cir. 1994).

(called "obstacle preemption").[111] Courts have found conflicts in numerous cases and preempted state claims.[112]

A few sections of the HEA expressly preempt certain state law claims. These include state usury laws,[113] state statutes of limitations,[114] state infancy defenses,[115] and state disclosure requirements.[116] The fact that certain provisions are expressly preempted bolsters the argument that Congress did not intend the HEA to so "occupy the field" that it would automatically preempt all state laws.[117]

The Fourth Circuit addressed these issues in a 2005 case, overturning the district court's ruling that the plaintiff's state claims were preempted based on "obstacle preemption."[118] According to the court, the existence of extensive regulations pursuant to the HEA does not automatically mean that non-conflicting state law is preempted.[119] Furthermore, the fact that there is no private right of action to enforce the HEA does not lead to the conclusion that the plaintiff's pursuit of state law claims would obstruct the federal scheme.[120] To the contrary, the court emphasized that the Supreme Court has recognized that the availability of a state law claim is even more important in an area where no federal private right of action exists.[121] In this case, the plaintiff sought redress under state law for the defendant's alleged violation of the HEA provision requiring lenders who receive loan verification certificates to complete and return these certificates within ten days.[122]

9.3.2.1.2 FTC guides and rule

The FTC has issued guides concerning unfair and deceptive private vocational school practices.[123] The guides specify that schools cannot misrepresent, through their name or otherwise, that they are connected with government agencies or civil service commissions or that they are an employment agency or employer.[124]

Among other provisions, the FTC Guides require that schools disclose if the course is offered through correspondence.[125] It is deceptive for a school to misrepresent the nature of its approval or accreditation or the extent to which former students, employers, or counselors recommend a course.[126]

The FTC updated its vocational school guides in 1998, renaming them "Guides for Private Vocational and Distance Education Schools."[127] The most significant change was a provision addressing misrepresentations about a school's placement success following training. The guides now specifically state that it is deceptive for a school, in promoting a course of training, to misrepresent the availability of employment after graduation from a course, the success that

---

111 See the discussion in *College Loan Corp. v. SLM Corp.*, 396 F.3d 588 (4th Cir. 2005).

112 *See, e.g.*, Armstrong v. Accrediting Council for Continuing Educ. and Training, Inc., 168 F. 3d 1362 (D.C. Cir. 1999) (federal student loan policy preempted student loan recipient's state law mistake and illegality claims as well as assertion of vocational school misconduct as a defense to collection); Washkoviak v. Student Loan Mktg. Ass'n, 849 A. 2d 37 (D.C. Ct. App. 2004) (UDAP claims based on lenders failure to disclose information about late fees and for improper charging of late fees preempted by HEA), *on subsequent appeal* 900 A. 2d 168 (D.C. Ct. App. 2006). For a detailed discussion of whether the HEA preempts state debt collection claims, see § 4.5.4, *supra.*

113 20 U.S.C. § 1078(d). *See* § 2.1.2, *supra.*

114 20 U.S.C. § 1091a(a).

115 20 U.S.C. § 1091a(b)(2).

116 20 U.S.C. § 1099. *See* § 2.4, *supra.*

117 *See, e.g.*, College Loan Corp. v. SLM Corp., 396 F.3d 588 (4th Cir. 2005).

118 *Id.*

119 *Id.* (citing Abbott by Abbott v. American Cyanamid Co., 844 F.2d at 1108 (4th Cir. 1988)). See § 4.5.4, *supra*, for a discussion of possible conflicts with the FDCPA.

120 College Loan Corp. v. SLM Corp., 396 F.3d 588 (4th Cir. 2005). *See also* § 9.6.3.3, *infra.*

121 College Loan Corp. v. SLM Corp., 396 F.3d 588 (4th Cir. 2005) (citing Silkwood v. Kerr-McGee Corp., 464 U.S. 238, 104 S. Ct. 615 (1984), *cited in* Worm v. American Cyanamid Co., 970 F.2d 1301 (4th Cir. 1992)), *on appeal after remand*, 5 F.3d 744 (4th Cir. 1993). The *College Loan Corp.* court noted in its opinion that defendant Salle Mae's argument boils down to a contention that "it was free to enter into a contract that invoked a federal standard as the indicator of compliance, then to proceed to breach its duties thereunder and to shield its breach by pleading preemption. In this case at least, federal supremacy does not mandate such a result."

122 34 C.F.R. § 682.209(j). *See* § 8.2.2.3, *supra.*

123 Guides for Private Vocational and Distance Education Schools, 16 C.F.R. §§ 254.0–254.10. In 1978, the FTC also promulgated a rule related to private trade school activities. Trade Regulation Rule Concerning Proprietary Vocational and Home-Study Schools, 43 Fed. Reg. 60,795 (Dec. 18, 1978). The Commission withdrew the Vocational School Rule's effective date pending further Commission action and, in 1988, finally terminated the Rule. 53 Fed. Reg. 29,482 (Aug. 5, 1988). Nevertheless, the Rule's Statement of Basis and Purpose, 43 Fed. Reg. 60,791 (Dec. 18, 1978), and the FTC staff report recommending the rule still provide a useful factual and legal background to vocational school issues. Bureau of Consumer Protection, Proprietary Vocational and Home-Study Schools, Final Report and Proposed Trade Regulation Rule, Clearinghouse No. 31,041 (1976).

124 16 C.F.R. § 254.2. *See also* FTC v. Couture Sch. of Modeling, 5 Trade Reg. Rep. (CCH) ¶ 22,815 (D. Md. 1990) (injunction); United States v. Eyler, 5 Trade Reg. Rep. (CCH) ¶ 22,891 (M.D. Fla. 1990) (consent decree); People v. Wilshire Computer College, Clearinghouse No. 46,309B (Cal. Super. Ct. 1991) (preliminary injunction pursuant to stipulation).

125 16 C.F.R. § 254.2(c).

126 16 C.F.R. § 254.3. *See also* Malone v. Academy of Court Reporting, 64 Ohio App. 3d 588, 582 N.E.2d 54 (1990) (concealment of fact that school was not certified or accredited to issue promised associate degree violates UDAP); Cavaliere v. Duff's Bus. Inst., 605 A.2d 397 (Pa. Super. Ct. 1992); Webster College v. Speier, 605 S.W.2d 712 (Tex. App. 1980). *But see* Lidecker v. Kendall Coll., 550 N.E.2d 1121 (Ill. App. Ct. 1990) (failure to inform prospective students of nursing school's lack of accreditation not a UDAP violation when school did not intend that students rely on the omission, and the lack of accreditation did not cause the student harm).

127 63 Fed. Reg. 42,570 (Aug. 10, 1998) (amending 16 C.F.R. part 254); 63 Fed. Reg. 72,350 (Dec. 31, 1998) (corrections).

the member's graduates have realized in obtaining such employment, or the salary that the member's graduates will receive in such employment.[128] The guides also state that it is deceptive for a school to misrepresent that the lack of a high school education or prior training is not an impediment to successful completion of a course or obtaining employment.[129]

9.3.2.1.3 Other precedent

Courts have identified a number of other trade school practices not enumerated in the FTC Guides as unfair or deceptive. State UDAP precedent and FTC case law provide important additional principles concerning job and earnings claims, student loans, and refund policies.

Schools may not deceive students with respect to the nature, terms, or conditions of contractual obligations, veterans' educational benefits, and federally insured student loans.[130] A school may not misrepresent its refund policy or deceive students into attending additional classes before dropping out with the result that their contractual obligation is significantly increased under the refund formula.[131] Schools must also pay all owed refunds.[132]

It is deceptive to misrepresent the amount of personalized instruction available in a correspondence course or the difficulty of the correspondence courses themselves.[133] Schools cannot misrepresent students' ability to benefit from

a course. Schools cannot fail to meet state entrance standards,[134] nor can schools encourage students to falsify their identity or immigration status.[135]

Also deceptive are misrepresentations concerning the nature of school placement services.[136] For example, in one UDAP case, consumer recovery was based on the school's "admissions officers" (who worked on commission and made as much as $56,000 a year) promising 90% to 95% job placement when in fact the school was reporting to its accrediting agency job placement rates averaging only 47%. The school's higher 90%–95% figure was derived only from students who kept in touch with the school's placement office, not the total number of the school's graduates.[137]

9.3.2.2 State Education Laws

Another source of precedent on unfair or deceptive trade school practices may be found in a state's education statutes, such as California's Maxine Waters Student Protection Act.[138] In some cases, these statutes will provide for a private right of action. If not, a violation of these standards may be actionable under a state UDAP statute.

A few states set minimum standards for schools, in some cases only for vocational or "career" schools.[139] Others

128 16 C.F.R. § 254.4(d).

129 16 C.F.R. § 254.5.

130 Bell & Howell Co., 95 F.T.C. 761 (1980) (consent order); People v. Wilshire Computer Coll., Clearinghouse No. 46,309B (Cal. Super. Ct. 1991) (preliminary injunction pursuant to stipulation); Manley v. Wichita Bus. Coll., 237 Kan. 427, 701 P.2d 893 (1985). *But see* Finstad v. Washburn Univ. of Topeka, 845 P.2d 685 (Kan. 1993) (overruling the holding in *Manley* that actual damages are not required in Kansas UDAP cases); Gamble v. University Sys. of N.H., 610 A.2d 357 (N.H. 1992) (university's imposition of mid-semester tuition increase due to fiscal crisis not a UDAP violation when it notified almost all affected students of possible increase in letter accompanying initial billing for semester).

131 People v. Wilshire Computer Coll., Clearinghouse No. 46,309B (Cal. Super. Ct. 1991) (preliminary injunction pursuant to stipulation); Manley v. Wichita Business Coll., 237 Kan. 427, 701 P.2d 893 (1985); Reynolds v. Sterling Coll., Inc., 750 A.2d 1020 (Vt. 2000) (summary judgment awarded to student on contractual claim; consumer fraud claim remanded; change in refund policy after substantial tuition payments had been made found to be a unilateral modification of specific contractual term for which no consideration had been received). *But see* Finstad v. Washburn Univ. of Topeka, 845 P.2d 685 (Kan. 1993) (overruling the holding in *Manley* that actual damages are not required in Kansas UDAP cases).

132 United States v. Eyler, 5 Trade Reg. Rep. (CCH) ¶ 22,891 (M.D. Fla. 1990) (consent decree); People v. Wilshire Computer Coll., Clearinghouse No. 46,309B (Cal. Super. Ct. 1991) (preliminary injunction pursuant to stipulation). In addition, there is now a federal discharge program to reimburse students for unpaid refunds. *See* § 6.4, *supra*.

133 Bell & Howell Co., 95 F.T.C. 761 (1980) (consent order).

134 People v. Wilshire Computer Coll., Clearinghouse No. 46,309B (Cal. Super. Ct. 1991) (preliminary injunction pursuant to stipulation).

135 *Id.*

136 Control Data Corp., 97 F.T.C. 84 (1981) (consent order); Bell & Howell Co., 95 F.T.C. 761 (1980) (consent order); Universal Training Serv. Inc., 94 F.T.C. 167 (1979) (consent order); Art Instruction Schs. Inc., 93 F.T.C. 32 (1979) (consent order); Driver Training Inst. Inc., 92 F.T.C. 235 (1978) (consent order); Commercial Programming Unlimited Inc., 88 F.T.C. 913 (1976) (consent order); Lafayette United Corp., 88 F.T.C. 683 (1976) (consent order); Lear Siegler Inc., 86 F.T.C. 860 (1975) (consent order); Weaver Airline Personnel Sch., 85 F.T.C. 237 (1975) (consent order); Eastern Detective Academy Inc., 78 F.T.C. 1428 (1971); Missouri Coll. of Automation, 67 F.T.C. 258 (1965) (consent order); People *ex rel.* Abrams v. New York Vocational Sch., Inc., Clearinghouse No. 43,088 (N.Y. Sup. Ct. 1987); Fla. Admin. Code Ann. r. 2-18.002 (Contracts for Future Consumer Services).

137 Beckett v. Computer Career Inst., Inc. (Or. Cir. Ct. July 2, 1990), *aff'd in part and rev'd in part*, 120 Or. App. 143, 852 P.2d 840 (1993).

138 Cal. Educ. Code § 94850 (formerly § 94316). Most of the provisions in the California Student Protection Act apply only to violations that occurred after January 1, 1990. For some provisions, the effective date is January 1, 1991. There are some more limited protections in the California Code for pre-1990 violations.

139 *See, e.g.,* Alaska Stat. § 14.48.060 (postsecondary educational institutions); Colo. Rev. Stat. Ann. § 12-59-106 (private occupational school standards); Ga. Code Ann. § 20-3-250.6 (nonpublic postsecondary educational institutions); Mo. Rev. Stat. § 173.604 (proprietary schools).

prohibit false statements or misrepresentations or require schools to provide certain disclosures.[140]

9.3.2.3 Other State Claims

In some states, a state RICO claim may provide superior remedies than a UDAP claim, or the two together may provide more relief than just a UDAP claim. For example, in Oregon, one UDAP and state RICO case against a school resulted in a jury verdict of $320,000 in multiple and punitive damages for nine former computer school students.[141] On appeal, the state RICO recovery was reversed on technical grounds, but all the UDAP actual and punitive damages were affirmed, as was the award of attorney fees to the consumers.[142]

9.3.3 Federal Claims

9.3.3.1 Higher Education Act and RICO

In general, the consumer should have a good reason to seek federal instead of state court jurisdiction, because there are serious drawbacks with RICO and particularly with HEA claims.

A RICO claim requires consumers to prove various technical elements, which will significantly complicate a case.[143] Nevertheless, RICO claims have proved successful in a number of vocational school cases.[144] The RICO claim has the benefit of treble damages and attorney fees, and its structure is well-suited to bringing in as defendants the school, school personnel, lenders, accrediting associations, and other parties.

The HEA claim may be dismissed outright, because most courts find there is no implied private right of action under the statute.[145] The HEA also explicitly states that failure to comply with its loan disclosure requirements does *not* provide a basis for a claim for civil damages.[146]

---

140 *See, e.g.,* Fla. Stat. Ann. § 1005.04 (nonpublic postsecondary education); 105 Ill. Comp. Stat. Ann. § 425/26 (Private Business and Vocational School Act includes private right of action); Mass. Gen. Laws Ann. ch. 93 § 21 (private trade schools, includes private enforcement right); Minn. Stat. Ann. § 141.28 (private career schools); N.D. Cent. Code § 15-20.4-09 (postsecondary educational institutions, private enforcement right); Tex. Educ. Code § 132.151 (career schools or colleges); Wash. Rev. Code Ann. § 28C.10.110 (unfair practices of private vocational schools).

141 Beckett v. Computer Career Inst., Inc. (Or. Cir. Ct. July 2, 1990), *aff'd in part and rev'd in part*, 120 Or. App. 143, 852 P.2d 840 (1993).

142 Beckett v. Computer Career Inst., Inc., 120 Or. App. 143, 852 P.2d 840 (1993).

143 18 U.S.C. §§ 1961–1968. *See* National Consumer Law Center, Unfair and Deceptive Acts and Practices § 9.2 (6th ed. 2004 and Supp.).

144 *See* Rosario v. Livaditis, 963 F.2d 1013 (7th Cir. 1992), *cert. denied*, 506 U.S. 1051 (1993) (Illinois law); Rodriguez v. McKinney, 878 F. Supp. 744 (E.D. Pa. 1995); Moy v. Adelphi Inst., Inc., 866 F. Supp. 696 (E.D.N.Y. 1994), *ex rel.* Moy v. Terranova, 1999 WL 118773 (E.D.N.Y. Mar. 2, 1999); Gonzalez v. North Am. Coll., 700 F. Supp. 362 (S.D. Tex. 1988) (students sufficiently alleged RICO claim). *But see* Johnson v. Midland Career Inst., 1996 U.S. Dist. LEXIS 1308 (N.D. Ill. 1996).

145 20 U.S.C. §§ 1001–1010. *See* Thomas M. Cooley Law School v. The American Bar Ass'n, 2006 WL 2355598 (6th Cir. Aug. 16, 2006); Christopher v. United States, 64 Fed. Appx. 132, 2003 WL 1904785 (10th Cir. Apr. 21, 2003); McCulloch v. PNC Bank, Inc., 298 F.3d 1217 (11th Cir. 2002) (in enacting the HEA, Congress expressly provided a detailed regulatory scheme which confers on the Secretary of Education the exclusive authority to monitor and enforce the provisions of the HEA); Labickas v. Arkansas State Univ., 78 F.3d 333 (8th Cir. 1996), *cert. denied*, 117 S. Ct. 395 (1997); Gibbs v. SLM Corp., 336 F. Supp. 2d 1 (D. Mass. 2004); White v. The Apollo Group, 241 F. Supp. 2d 710 (W.D. Tex. 2003); Robinett v. Delgado Cmty. Coll., 2000 WL 798407 (E.D. La. June 19, 2000); Waugh v. Conn. Student Loan Found., 966 F. Supp. 141 (D. Conn. 1997); Morgan v. Markerdowne Corp., 976 F. Supp. 301 (D.N.J. 1997); Bartels v. Alabama Commercial Coll., 918 F. Supp. 1565 (S.D. Ga. 1995), *aff'd without published opinion*, 189 F.3d 483 (11th Cir. 1999), *cert. denied*, 528 U.S. 1074 (2000); Moy v. Adelphi Inst., Inc., 866 F. Supp. 696 (E.D.N.Y. 1994); Spinner v. Chesapeake Bus. Inst. of Va., Clearinghouse No. 49,131A (E.D. Va. Feb. 5, 1993) Jackson v. Culinary Sch. of Wash., 811 F. Supp. 714 (D.D.C. 1993) (claim dismissed based on summary judgment motion that students had not presented evidence of origination relationship), *aff'd on other grounds*, 27 F.3d 573 (D.C. Cir. 1994) (origination theory not enforceable against the Secretary), *vacated on other grounds*, 115 S. Ct. 2573 (1995) (appellate court used de novo instead of abuse of discretion standard to review district court's decision to decide state law issues in declaratory judgment action), *remanded to district court on state law claims, aff'g own ruling on origination*, 59 F.3d 254 (D.C. Cir. 1995) (to determine on what basis federal court decided to rule on state law issues), *motion dismissed*, 1995 U.S. App. LEXIS 22304 (D.C. Cir. 1995); Keams v. Tempe Tech. Inst., 807 F. Supp. 569 (D. Ariz. 1992); Shorter v. Alexander, Clearinghouse No. 47,950 (N.D. Ga. Dec. 8, 1992); Graham v. Security Sav. & Loan, 125 F.R.D. 687 (N.D. Ind. 1989), *aff'd sub nom.* Veal v. First Am. Sav. Bank, 914 F.2d 909 (7th Cir. 1990). *But see* Gibbs v. SLM Corp., 336 F. Supp. 2d 1 (D. Mass 2004) (duress claim dismissed because plaintiff failed to show that (1) one side involuntarily accepted the terms of another, (2) circumstances permitted no other alternative, and (3) said circumstances were the result of coercive acts of the opposing party); Tipton v. Northeastern Bus. Coll., Clearinghouse No. 44,339 (S.D. W. Va. Jan. 8, 1988) (private right of action); Chavez v. LTV Aerospace Corp., 412 F. Supp. 4 (N.D. Tex. 1976) (private cause of action when school allegedly imposed illegal charges on students). In 2003 court pleadings, the Department of Education suggested that it supports implying a private right of action under the HEA in very limited circumstances. Specifically, the Department supported a private right for borrowers to seek judicial review of guaranty agency administrative wage garnishment hearing decisions. Borrowers already have this right in cases in which the Department conducts the hearing. *See* Memorandum of Points and Authorities in Support of Motion to Dismiss, Hutchins et al. v. USA et al., Case No. 02-CV-6256 (E.D. Ca. memorandum filed Apr. 25, 2003).

146 Federal student loan lenders are also not subject to Truth in Lending requirements. 20 U.S.C. § 1083(c).

Federal court jurisdiction is the only benefit of an HEA claim. No multiple or statutory damages or attorney fees will be available. In addition, anything that violates the HEA should also be a UDAP, contract, or tort violation. This may be the only way most borrowers can privately enforce the HEA. HEA violations may also form the basis of federal Fair Debt Collection Practices Act claims.[147]

9.3.3.2 False Claims Act

The federal False Claims Act may be used against schools that violate federal regulations. The Act is intended to reach all types of fraud that might result in financial loss to the government. It makes liable anyone who "knowingly makes, uses or causes to be made or used, a false record or statement to get a false or fraudulent claim paid or approved by the Government."[148] The Act authorizes the United States to institute a civil action against an alleged false claimant as well as grants individuals the right to act as private attorneys general to bring a civil action in the United State's name as a realtor.[149]

False Claims Act cases against various schools have survived motions to dismiss. In one case, former enrollment counselors sued the University of Phoenix alleging that the university knowingly made false promises to comply with the incentive compensation ban.[150] The Ninth Circuit agreed with the realtors that a claim could be made based either on the theory of false certification or promissory fraud.

The former theory is that a defendant may falsely certify compliance with a state or regulation. In order to state a claim under the False Claims Act, the statement must be false when made and must be material to the government's decision to pay money. Furthermore, there must be an actual claim on the government's fisc. The "promissory fraud" theory holds defendants liable for each claim submitted to the government under a contract, when the contract or extension of government benefit was originally obtained through false statements or fraudulent conduct.

9.3.3.3 Other Federal Claims

Another potential claim in the typical vocational school/student loan case is that the Department of Education failed to adequately supervise the school and improperly recognized the accrediting agency. The Federal Tort Claims Act[151] sharply limits a party's ability to recover *damages* from a federal agency, but the Act does not prevent the student from receiving reimbursement of amounts improperly paid or otherwise receiving money to be made whole.[152] Before initiating an action, the borrower must first exhaust administrative remedies.[153]

The Secretary is likely to argue that the Department has no responsibility to review the educational quality of the school. The counter-argument is that the Secretary has an obligation under the Higher Education Act to evaluate the fiscal responsibility of the school.[154]

At least one federal court decision found that students could proceed on this theory.[155] The court allowed the students to proceed to trial to try to prove any of the following: (1) that the Secretary acted arbitrarily and capriciously in certifying branch campuses to participate in the loan program; (2) that certain campuses were not affiliated with any other eligible school and thus never approved for participation in the program; or (3) that the courses did not provide education for a recognized occupation or "useful employment." The court also allowed the students to proceed in their mandamus action against the Secretary to force the school to repay program funds when the program failed to satisfy federal standards.[156]

There are other federal claims to consider as well. The federal Fair Debt Collections Practices Act (FDCPA) is

---

147 *See, e.g.,* Cliff v. Payco Gen. Am. Credits, 363 F.3d 1113 (11th Cir. 2004) (HEA does not occupy the field of student loan debt collection, and state fair debt collection claims not preempted). *See* § 4.5, *supra*.

148 31 U.S.C. § 3729(a)(2).

149 31 U.S.C. § 3 730(b)(1).

150 United States *ex rel.* Hendow v. University of Phoenix, ___ F. 3d ___, 2006 WL 2530394 (9th Cir. Sept. 5, 2006) (False Claims Act cases survived motion to dismiss). *See also* United States *ex rel.* Main v. Oakland City Univ., 426 F. 3d 914 (7th Cir. 2005), *cert. denied*, 126 S. Ct. 1786, 164 L. Ed. 2d 519 (U.S. 2006) (former university recruiter brought False Claims Act case, contending that the university falsely represented that it would not pay recruiters fees for enrolling students); United States v. Chapman Univ., 2006 WL 1562231 (C.D. Cal. May 23, 2006) (False Claims Act claim survived motion to dismiss except for claims based on student applications for state licensing). *See* § 9.2.6 (incentive compensation).

151 28 U.S.C. § 1346(b).

152 Florence County Sch. Dist. Four v. Carter, 510 U.S. 7 (1993); Burlington Sch. Comm. v. Massachusetts Dep't of Educ., 471 U.S. 359 (1985); Army & Air Force Exch. Serv. v. Sheehan, 456 U.S. 728, 739 n.11 (1982); United States v. Testan, 424 U.S. 392, 401–02 (1976); Porter v. Warner Holding Co., 328 U.S. 395 (1946); Muller v. Comm'n on Special Educ. of E. Islip Sch. Dist., 145 F.3d 95 (2d Cir. 1998); Gadsby by Gadsby v. Grasmick, 109 F.3d 940 (4th Cir. 1997); Whayne v. United States Dep't of Educ., 915 F. Supp. 1143 (D. Kan. 1996) (Federal Tort Claims cause of action dismissed due to plaintiff's failure to exhaust administrative remedies).

153 *See, e.g.,* Shabtai v. United States Dep't of Educ., 2003 WL 21983025 (S.D.N.Y. Aug. 20, 2003) (borrower's federal tort claim alleging that the Department had failed to grant loan cancellation and other issues dismissed due to failure to exhaust administrative remedies).

154 *See* 34 C.F.R. §§ 668.14, 668.15.

155 Hernandez v. Alexander, Clearinghouse No. 46,792 (D. Nev. May 18, 1992). *But see* Armand v. Secretary of Educ., Clearinghouse No. 51,298 (S.D. Fla. July 19, 1995).

156 For a discussion of declaratory relief and injunctive actions against the Department, see § 9.4.1.1, *infra*. In general, the HEA states that no injunction shall be issued against the Secretary. 20 U.S.C. § 1082(a)(2). Strategies to address this prohibition are discussed in § 9.4.1.1, *infra*.

essential in challenging abusive student loan collection practices. Private FDCPA actions are in many cases the only way borrowers can get relief when collectors violate Department of Education collection regulations.[157]

There are limits, however, to using fair debt claims to resolve student loan disputes. The FDCPA is an indirect way of obtaining relief. It is intended to address collection abuses. A collection agency's failure to offer a particular repayment plan or otherwise comply with the HEA is a violation. However, the available remedies are monetary damages. These can be extremely useful, but they do not help borrowers get the repayment plans or discharges to which they are entitled.

The federal Fair Credit Reporting Act (FCRA) may also be used to challenge problems related to the reporting of student loans on credit reports.[158] Federal student loan lenders are not subject to Truth in Lending Act (TILA) disclosure requirements.[159] However, as long as the credit extended is less than $25,000, TILA should apply to private student loans.[160]

9.3.4 Common Law Claims

9.3.4.1 General

State UDAP claims are key to school cases, but other theories should also be considered. Common law fraud, in particular, should not be overlooked because of the possibility of punitive damages.[161]

However, fraud and negligence claims may be difficult to bring in trade school cases. To prove fraudulent misrepresentation, for example, plaintiffs must show that (1) the defendant made a false representation; (2) the defendant acted with an intent to deceive; (3) the defendant made a representation directed at a particular person; (4) the plaintiff relied on the representation; and (5) the plaintiff was damaged as a result.

The first element may be particularly difficult as many trade school employees make representations that are clearly misleading but often difficult to prove as false. For example, representations about job placement made before a student enrolls may be different when the student graduates due to many factors, including the student's academic performance and unexpected changes in the labor market.[162] Proving causation can also be a problem if the plaintiff is trying to prove that his or her failure to learn marketable skills is the schools' fault.[163]

Similarly, a common problem with negligence claims is showing that the school had a duty of care to the plaintiff student. The main barrier to these claims is the judicial academic abstention doctrine.[164] This doctrine developed from judicial concern that decisions about educational quality are often subjective. In addition, courts are hesitant to appear to be creating educational policy, preferring to leave this to educational experts.[165]

Courts have also, on a variety of legal theories, rescinded enrollment agreements and directed schools to reimburse students for their tuition payments or student loan debts.[166]

9.3.4.2 Contract Claims

The threshold question in contract claims against schools is whether there is an enforceable contractual promise. Courts are reluctant to enforce a school's representations

---

157 *See* § 4.5, *supra.*

158 *See* § 4.3.4.2.3, *supra.*

159 20 U.S.C. § 1083(c).

160 15 U.S.C. § 1603(3); Reg. Z § 226.3(b). *See, e.g.,* Blanco v. Keybank USA, 2005 WL 4135013 (N.D. Ohio Sept. 30, 2005) (denying creditor's motion to dismiss private student loan borrower's TILA claim). *See* National Consumer Law Center, Truth in Lending § 2.4 (5th ed. 2003 and Supp.). *See also* § 2.4, *supra.*

161 *See* Harman v. Sullivan Univ. Sys., Inc., 2005 WL 1353752 (W.D. Ky. June 6, 2005) (sufficient evidence for plaintiff to proceed on fraudulent misrepresentation claim); Moy v. Adelphi Inst., Inc., 866 F. Supp. 696 (E.D.N.Y. 1994) (misrepresentation and fraud claims survived motion to dismiss, but not claim for negligent misrepresentation or breach of fiduciary duty), *ex rel.* Moy v. Terranova, 1999 WL 118773 (E.D.N.Y. Mar. 2 1999); Phillips Coll. of Ala., Inc. v. Lester, 622 So. 2d 308 (Ala. 1993) (a valid fraud claim asserted against school that had promised in written materials but failed to provide a specific number of hours of practical training); Craig v. Forest Inst. of Prof'l Psychology, 713 So. 2d 967 (Ala. Civ. App. 1997). *But see* Spafford v. Cuyahoga Cmty. College, 2005 WL 797936 (Ohio. App. Apr. 7, 2005) (upholding trial court's directed verdict for defendant on fraud, breach of contract, and UDAP claims).

162 *See generally* Patrick F. Linehan, *Dreams Protected: A New Approach to Policing Proprietary Schools' Misrepresentations,* 89 Geo. L. J. 753 (Mar. 2001).

163 *See, e.g.,* Idrees v. American Univ. of the Caribbean, 546 F. Supp. 1342 (S.D.N.Y. 1982).

164 *See, e.g.,* Alsides v. Brown Inst., Ltd., 592 N.W.2d 468 (Minn. App. 1999) (rejecting claims against educational institutions outside of a contractual relationship). *See generally* Patrick F. Linehan, *Dreams Protected: A New Approach to Policing Proprietary Schools' Misrepresentations,* 89 Geo. L. J. 753 (Mar. 2001). *See also* § 9.3.4.2 (educational malpractice claims), *supra.*

165 *Id.*

166 André v. Pace Univ., 170 Misc. 2d 893, 655 N.Y.S.2d 777 (1996), *rev'g* 161 Misc. 2d 613, 618 N.Y.S.2d 975 (1994) (school's complete failure to provide course at promised level allows damages and rescission); Brown v. Hambric, 638 N.Y.S.2d 873, 168 Misc. 2d 502 (1995) (travel agents school found to be a deceptive pyramid scheme; rescission of contract warranted and failure to deliver the promised support and training was unconscionable and deceptive business practice); James v. SCS Bus. & Technical Inst., 595 N.Y.S.2d 885 (Civ. Ct. County of N.Y. 1992) (unconscionability and lack of consideration); Cavaliere v. Duff's Bus. Inst., 605 A.2d 397 (Pa. Super. Ct. 1992) (general claim of lack of quality education not actionable, but misrepresentation or breach of contract would be).

that it will provide a "quality education" or other assertions about the value of the school's diploma because of the subjective inquiry involved.

In general, courts are more likely to find a breach of a contractual obligation if the student's claim is based, at least in part, on objective promises or guarantees, particularly if they are set forth in written materials, such as catalogs or advertisements.[167] School catalogs, bulletins, and regulations should be considered part of the contract between the school and its students.[168]

The general rule is that courts will not allow a claim for educational malpractice but may allow a contract claim based on failure to provide any instruction or a specific service.[169] This view is based on the belief that there is no clear standard of care in education.

For example, the court in one case, in reviewing student claims of breach of contract based on alleged unsuitable computer courses, held that an inquiry into whether the courses were appropriate was "best left to the educational community. A different situation might be presented if defendants were to provide 'no educational services' or failed to meet its contractual obligation to provide certain specified services, such as a designated number of hours of instruction. . . ."[170]

The difference between educational malpractice and a contract claim is not always clear. In general, the more limited the claim (for example, a school's failure to offer a particular promised course) and the more the claim is tied to written promises, the stronger the case.[171]

Courts have found a lack of consideration in some education cases. For example, failure of consideration was found when the school accepted the student's tuition and failed to provide the promised educational services.[172] In another case, the court awarded summary judgment to a student, agreeing that a change in the school's refund policy after substantial tuition payments had been made was a unilateral modification of a specific contractual term for

---

167 Another good source to establish a contractual relationship is a student handbook. *See generally* Idrees v. American Univ. of the Caribbean, 546 F. Supp. 1342 (S.D.N.Y. 1982) (inaccurate and misleading statements in a university brochure about facilities, equipment, and faculty constituted fraudulent misrepresentation); Ralph D. Mawdsley, *Litigation Involving Higher Education Employee and Student Handbooks*, 109 Ed. Law. Rep. 1031 (1996); Claudia G. Catalano, *Liability of Private School or Educational Institution for Breach of Contract Arising from Provision of Deficient Educational Instruction*, 46 A.L.R.5th 581 (1997).

168 Ross v. Creighton Univ., 957 F.2d 410 (7th Cir. 1992) (basic legal relationship between student and school is contractual in nature); Harman v. Sullivan Univ. Sys., Inc., 2005 WL 1353752 (W.D. Ky. June 6, 2005) (sufficient evidence for plaintiff to proceed on breach-of-contract claim when school's handbook falsely claimed that program met certain accreditation standards and that graduates would be eligible to take the national certifying exam in radiology). *See also* Gally v. Columbia Univ., 22 F. Supp. 2d 199 (S.D.N.Y. 1998) (implied contract between students and school required university to act in good faith and students to satisfy academic requirements and comply with school procedures); Zumbrun v. University of S. Cal., 25 Cal. App. 3d 1, 101 Cal. Rptr. 499 (1972); Wickstrom v. North Idaho Coll., 725 P.2d 155 (Idaho 1986).

169 Ambrose v. New England Ass'n of Schs. and Colls., Inc., 2000 WL 1195363 (D. Me. Aug. 7, 2000), *aff'd*, 252 F.3d 488 (1st Cir. 2001); Whayne v. United States Dep't of Educ., 915 F. Supp. 1143 (D. Kan. 1996) (allegation that education simply was not good enough insufficient to state a claim for breach of contract; educational malpractice claim rejected as a matter of state law); Cencor Inc. v. Tolman, 868 P.2d 396 (Colo. 1994) (although no claim for educational malpractice, plaintiff may have a claim for failure to provide a specific service); Page v. Klein Tools, Inc., 610 N.W.2d 900 (Mich. 2000) (explains policy considerations underlying various courts' rejection of educational malpractice claims); Alsides v. Brown Inst., 592 N.W.2d 468 (Minn. Ct. App. 1999) (courts may consider contract, fraud, and misrepresentation claims only if they do not require inquiry into the nuances of educational processes and theories); Andre v. Pace Univ., 170 Misc. 2d 893, 655 N.Y.S.2d 777 (1996), *rev'g* 161 Misc. 2d 613, 618 N.Y.S.2d 975 (1994); Cavaliere v. Duff's Bus. Inst., 413 Pa. Super. 357, 605 A.2d 397 (1992) (if the contract with the school were to provide for certain specified services such as, for example, a designated number of hours of instruction and the school failed to meet its

obligation, then a contract action with appropriate consequential damages might be viable).

170 Andre v. Pace Univ., 170 Misc. 2d 893, 655 N.Y.S.2d 777 (1996), *rev'g* 161 Misc. 2d 613, 618 N.Y.S.2d 975 (1994).

171 Dillon v. Ultrasound Diagnostic Schs., 1997 U.S. Dist. LEXIS 20795 (E.D. Pa. 1997) (plaintiff's complaints identified specific alleged benefits and services which defendants promised and failed to provide so as to state a claim for breach of educational contract); Gundlach v. Reinstein, 924 F. Supp. 684 (E.D. Pa. 1996) (no written contract between law school and student; student failed to identify specific manner in which school breached contract), *aff'd*, 114 F.3d 1172 (3rd Cir. 1997); Cencor Inc. v. Tolman, 868 P.2d 396 (Colo. 1994) (court agreed that enrollment agreement and school catalog constituted the express terms of the contract and that students showed specific services which had not been provided; also found failure to provide qualified teacher); Wickstrom v. North Idaho Coll., 725 P.2d 155 (Idaho 1986); Collins v. Minnesota Sch. of Bus., Inc., 655 N.W.2d 320 (Minn. 2003); Alsides v. Brown Inst., 592 N.W.2d 468 (Minn. Ct. App. 1999) (allowing students to proceed with claims involving a computer school's promises to provide instruction on a particular software program and particular types of computers; frequent absences or tardiness of instructors; insufficient operable computers; outdated hardware and software; and failure to deliver the number of hours of instruction promised); Squires v. Sierra Nevada Educ. Found., 823 P.2d 256 (Nev. 1991); Brown v. Hambric, 638 N.Y.S.2d 873, 168 Misc. 2d 502 (1995); Ryan v. University of N.C. Hosps., 494 S.E.2d 789 (N.C. App. 1998) (court upheld claim for breach of contract); Britt v. Chestnut Hill Coll., 429 Pa. Super. 263, 632 A.2d 557 (Pa. Super. 1993); Thomas v. French, 30 Wash. App. 811, 638 P.2d 613 (1981), *rev'd on other grounds*, 99 Wash. 2d 95, 659 P.2d 1097 (1983) (viable contract claim when private cosmetology school's contract expressly required the school to prepare the students to take a state cosmetology exam).

172 595 N.Y.S.2d 885 (N.Y. Civ. Ct. 1992) (withdrawn from publication).

which no consideration had been received.[173] It is also possible to raise contract defenses such as duress when appropriate.[174]

9.4 Additional Issues to Consider When Bringing Affirmative Litigation Against Vocational Schools

9.4.1 Potential Defendants

9.4.1.1 Suing the Department

The HEA contains an explicit grant of federal jurisdiction for suits against the Secretary of Education.[175] In general, courts will not allow injunctive relief against the Secretary except when the Secretary exercises powers that are clearly outside his or her statutory authority.[176] This is a high standard. For example, according to one court, the anti-injunction provision may not be overcome merely because the Secretary exercised poor judgment or even if the Secretary violated the specific mandates of another statutory scheme.[177] An anti-injunction provision may also be over-ruled if the court finds that the plaintiff has no alternative legal remedy.[178] Courts have generally rejected this argument in the student loan context, finding that plaintiff schools or borrowers bringing actions against the Secretary have an available alternative in the Administrative Procedures Act (APA).[179]

Although injunction actions are subject to these restrictions, actions for declaratory relief should not be similarly barred.[180] Thus, even courts that have accepted the view that an agency or officer is immune from injunction have held that declaratory relief is available.[181] The key difference, according to one court, is that an injunction is a coercive order by a court directing a party to do or refrain from doing something and applies to future actions. A declaratory judgment states the existing legal rights in a controversy but does not, in itself, coerce any party or enjoin any future action.[182] A declaratory judgment is a milder remedy that is frequently available in situations in which an injunction is unavailable

---

173 Reynolds v. Sterling Coll., Inc., 750 A.2d 1020 (Vt. 2000).

174 *See, e.g., In re* Mason, 300 B.R. 160 (Bankr. D. Conn. 2003) (consolidation loan was obtained through duress and was therefore null and void under state law). *But see* Gibbs v. SLM Corp., 336 F. Supp. 2d 1 (D. Mass 2004) (duress claim dismissed because plaintiff failed to show that (1) one side involuntarily accepted the terms of another, (2) circumstances permitted no other alternative, and (3) said circumstances were the result of coercive acts of the opposing party). *See* § 9.5.3.1, *infra.*

175 20 U.S.C. § 1082(a).

176 *See, e.g.,* Shabtai v. United States Dep't of Educ., 2003 WL 21983025 (S.D.N.Y. Aug. 20, 2003); De La Mota v. United States Dep't of Educ., 2003 WL 21919774 (S.D.N.Y. Aug. 12, 2003) (plaintiffs did not point to a specific provision of the HEA that overrides the explicit and express prohibition against injunctive relief), *rev'd on other grounds,* 412 F.3d 71 (2d Cir. 2005); Kitchen v. United States Dep't of Educ., 1998 WL 167325 (S.D.N.Y. Apr. 9, 1998) (collection of student loans within Secretary's statutory authority, and borrower's motion for preliminary injunctive relief denied); Advanced Career Training v. Riley, 1997 WL 214863 (E.D. Pa. Apr. 25, 1997) (plaintiff schools failed to show that the Secretary acted clearly outside of his statutory authority); Coalition of N.Y. State Private Career Sch. Inc. v. Riley, 1996 WL 678453 (N.D.N.Y. Nov. 15, 1996); Calise Beauty Sch., Inc. v. Riley, 941 F. Supp. 425 (S.D.N.Y. Sept. 30, 1996) (injunctive relief denied to vocational schools that were removed from federal loan programs; secretary did not exceed his HEA authority by allegedly violating non-discretionary duties in calculating and publishing cohort default rates and ruling on appeals; even if Secretary did violate these duties, such violations would at most constitute wrongful exercise of proper administrative functions).

177 Advanced Career Training v. Riley, 1997 WL 214863 (E.D. Pa. Apr. 25, 1997).

178 South Carolina v. Regan, 465 U.S. 367, 104 S. Ct. 1107, 79 L. Ed. 2d 372 (1984) (in tax case, Court held that Anti-Injunction Act was not intended to bar action when Congress has not provided plaintiff with alternative legal way to challenge validity of the tax).

179 *See, e.g.,* Advanced Career Training v. Riley, 1997 WL 214863 (E.D. Pa. April 25, 1997) (APA claim allows a plaintiff to obtain either declaratory relief or a remand to the Department for further evaluation).

180 Section 1082(a)(2) does not by its terms exclude declaratory relief from the forms of relief as to which the Secretary may "sue and be sued." A number of such class actions seeking declaratory relief have been certified. *See* Keams v. Tempe Technical Inst., 39 F.3d 222 (9th Cir. 1994), *appeal after remand,* 103 F.3d 138 (9th Cir. 1996), *redesignated as opinion,* 110 F.3d 44 (9th Cir. 1997), *claims against all defendants dismissed,* 16 F. Supp. 2d 1119 (D. Ariz. 1998); Shorter v. Riley, Clearinghouse No. 47,950B (N.D. Ga. Nov. 18, 1993); Genzale v. Zenzi's Beauty Coll., Clearinghouse No. 49,931 (Cal. Super. Ct. Apr. 19, 1993) (order certifying the class).

181 In higher education cases, see for example *Thomas v. Bennett,* 856 F.2d 1165, 1168 (8th Cir. 1988) (affirming denial of Secretary's motion to dismiss plaintiff's declaratory relief complaint in which individual taxpayer challenged a student-loan-related tax offset, notwithstanding the anti-injunction provision); *De La Mota v. U.S. Dep't of Educ.,* 2003 WL 21919774 (S.D.N.Y. Aug. 12, 2003), *summary judgment granted,* 2003 WL 22038741 (S.D.N.Y. Aug. 29, 2003), *rev'd on other grounds,* 412 F.3d 71 (2d Cir. 2005); *Bank of America NT & SA v. Riley,* 940 F. Supp. 348, 350–51 (D.D.C. 1996), *aff'd,* 132 F.3d 1480 (D.C. Cir. 1997); *Student Loan Mktg. Ass'n v. Riley,* 907 F. Supp. 464 (D.D.C. 1995) (refusing to dismiss, for lack of jurisdiction, Salle Mae's declaratory relief action challenging Secretary's announced intention to apply a statutory offset fee to certain assets), *aff'd,* 104 F.3d 397 (D.C. Cir.), *cert. denied,* 522 U.S. 913, 118 S. Ct. 295, 139 L. Ed. 2d 227 (1997); and *Pro Schs., Inc. v. Riley,* 824 F. Supp. 1314–16 (E.D. Wis. 1993) (allowing cosmetology schools operator to challenge Secretary's termination of its FFEL eligibility in an action for declaratory relief).

182 Ulstein Maritime, Ltd. v. United States, 833 F.2d 1052 (1st Cir. 1987).

or inappropriate.[183] However, a court may find declaratory relief to be barred as well if such relief would produce the same effect as an injunction.[184]

The limit on injunctive actions is not always fatal. In some collection cases, the guaranty agency will be the loan holder and an injunction can generally be crafted to fully protect students without naming the Secretary. In other cases, additional agencies, such as the Department of Treasury, will be involved in collection efforts. These agencies should be named in cases seeking injunction relief.[185]

In bringing affirmative actions against the Department, borrowers should also be prepared that the Department or other loan holder might file a suit to collect on the loan.

Borrowers might also use the Administrative Procedures Act claims to challenge Department decisions in garnishment or offset hearings or other matters. Appellate review is discussed in Chapter 5, *supra*.

9.4.1.2 Claims Against Private Accrediting Agencies

Attorneys representing defrauded students may want to consider adding as a party to the lawsuit the private accrediting agency that accredited the defendant school. Although usually nonprofit organizations, these agencies may be an important alternative source of assets particularly when schools are bankrupt or insolvent.

The United States Department of Education does not review the educational quality of private vocational schools before certifying their eligibility to participate in the GSL program. Instead the Department of Education recognizes various private accrediting agencies and associations whose job it is to review the educational standards of the schools.

A private accrediting association is responsible for monitoring the school's educational program, admissions procedures, advertising, and sales techniques. The school's accreditation makes a school eligible for government assistance programs, and the failure to adequately examine a school may be directly connected to the student's injury.

As outlined by the Department of the Education, the functions of accreditation include

- certifying that an institution or program has met established standards;
- assisting students in identifying acceptable institutions;
- assisting institutions in determining the acceptability of transfer credits;
- creating goals for self-improvement of weaker programs and stimulating a general raising of standards among educational institutions;
- establishing criteria for professional certification and licensure; and
- identifying institutions and programs for the investment of public and private funds.[186]

Accreditation agencies are required to demonstrate that they have rigorous standards. The regulations set out factors that accreditation agencies must address in evaluating the quality of an institution, including success with respect to student achievement and, as appropriate, consideration of course completion, state licensing examination, and job placement rates.[187]

In general, the agency must have the administrative and fiscal capacity to carry out accrediting activities.[188] The agency is required to demonstrate that it has standards for accreditation that are sufficiently rigorous to ensure that the agency is a reliable authority on the quality of education or training in institutions it accredits.[189]

Inspector General audit reports have concluded, however, that many accreditation agencies have not followed through on these responsibilities.[190] These findings are especially disturbing given that the Government Accountability Office recommended in 1996 that accreditation agencies develop and make public uniform performance-based consumer protection standards, including information on completion and placement rates.[191]

The Secretary of Education recognizes approximately 100 major national accrediting agencies, including

- Accrediting Bureau for Health Education Schools (ABHES);
- Accrediting Council for Continuing Education and Training (ACCET);
- Accrediting Council for Independent Colleges and Schools;

---

183 *Id.*

184 Am. Ass'n of Cosmetology Schs. v. Riley, 170 F.3d 1250 (9th Cir. 1999) (the anti-injunction bar cannot be skirted by the simple expedient of labeling an action that really seeks injunctive relief as an action for "declaratory relief"). Courts have on occasion refused to grant declaratory relief in cases in which the effect would be identical to a legally impermissible injunction. Great Lakes Co. v. Huffman, 319 U.S. 293, 63 S. Ct. 1070, 87 L. Ed. 1407 (1943); Samuels v. Mackell, 401 U.S. 66, 91 S. Ct. 764, 27 L. Ed. 2d 688 (1971), *cited in* Ulstein Maritime, Ltd. v. United States, 833 F.2d 1052 (1st Cir. 1987).

185 This issue was raised in litigation challenging the government's right to offset Social Security benefits for old student loans. *See* § 5.4.3.3, *supra*. Pleadings and discovery requests can be found at Appendices E and F, *infra*, and on the companion CD-Rom to this manual.

186 U.S. Gen. Accounting Office, Higher Education: Ensuring Quality Education From Proprietary Institutions, GAO/T-HEHS-96-158 (June 1996).

187 34 C.F.R. § 602.16.

188 34 C.F.R. § 602.15.

189 34 C.F.R. § 602.16.

190 *Enforcement of Federal Anti-Fraud Laws in For-Profit Education: Hearings Before the U.S. House Committee on Education and the Workforce*, 109th Cong. (Mar. 1, 2005) (reports cited in statement of Thomas A. Carter, Deputy Inspector Gen.).

191 U.S. Gen. Accounting Office, Department of Education: Status of Actions to Improve the Management of Student Financial Aid, GAO/HEHS-96-143 (July 1996).

- National Accrediting Commission of Cosmetology Arts and Sciences (NACCAS);
- Accrediting Bureau of Health Education Schools; and
- Southern Association of Colleges and Schools, the Commission on Colleges.[192]

The process by which the Department of Education recognizes accrediting agencies has been severely criticized. The staff of the United States Senate Permanent Subcommittee on Investigations issued a report finding that owners "can get an unaccredited school accredited simply by buying an already accredited school and developing some connection, however tenuous, between the two."[193] Similarly, a small accredited school can suddenly sprout dozens of branch schools all over the country, and the accrediting association will grant the branches automatic accreditation. Similar conclusions were reached by the Department of Education's own Inspector General.[194] Unfortunately, the Department rarely invokes its power to suspend or terminate an agency's recognition.[195]

Advocates have met with mixed success in their attempts to hold agencies liable for the bad acts of schools they accredit. Most courts have found that accrediting agencies are not responsible for students damaged by inferior schools accredited by these agencies. For example, the Ninth Circuit found that accrediting agencies owed no tort law duty under state law to students who attended the schools accredited by those agencies.[196]

Students in another federal court action in the District of Columbia presented UDAP and common law claims against an accrediting agency. The court found that the District of Columbia UDAP statute did not apply to accrediting agencies but did allow the students to pursue common law claims for misrepresentation and fraud against the accrediting agency.[197]

Both sides sought summary judgment in the case. The students claimed that the accreditor fraudulently provided accreditation even though the accreditor had no knowledge of whether the school met the accreditor's standards. The court found that the students could go forward with their case to trial, having met all the prima facie elements of fraud.[198]

A settlement was reached with the accreditor in this case.[199] Without admitting any liability or fault, the accreditor agreed to make payments to members of the class. The amount paid to each class member varies depending on the total number of claims received.

A claim of negligence against an accrediting agency is even more difficult. The borrower has to show a duty of the accreditor to the student, reliance on the accreditor's certification, negligence in the accreditation process, in causing proximate injury to the consumer. The little case law in this area generally relates to personal injury relating to products that received independent certification.[200] At least a few courts have considered the issue in the student loan context and found that an accrediting agency did not owe a duty to the students upon which a negligence action could be brought.[201]

9.4.1.3 Claims Against State Licensing Agencies

Claims may be available against state licensing agencies that have even greater responsibility than the Department of Education to review a school's operation. For example, a New York appellate court allowed a claim to proceed when the students sought declaratory and injunctive relief that the state education department fulfill its statutory obligation in supervising private vocational schools.[202]

---

192 The Department of Education publishes the lists of agencies applying for initial or renewed recognition as accreditors. *See, e.g.*, 67 Fed. Reg. 48450 (July 24, 2002). For the most recent list, see 71 Fed. Reg. 6059 (Feb. 6, 2006).

193 Staff of S. Permanent Subcomm. on Investigations of the Comm. on Gov't Affairs, 102d Cong., Abuses in Federal Student Aid Programs, Part 2: Licensing, Accreditation, Certification and Eligibility, Clearinghouse No. 45,922 (Sept. 12, 1990).

194 *See* S. Permanent Subcomm. on Investigation of the Comm. on Gov't Affairs., Clearinghouse No. 45,923 (Sept. 12, 1990) (statement of James Thomas, Jr., U.S. Department of Education Inspector General).

195 The regulatory authority for revocation can be found at 34 C.F.R. §§ 602.40–.43.

196 Keams v. Tempe Technical Inst., 39 F.3d 222 (9th Cir. 1994), *appeal after remand*, 103 F.3d 138 (9th Cir. 1996), *redesignated as opinion*, 110 F.3d 44 (9th Cir. 1997) (students failed to identify a single decision in which any court has held that accrediting agencies owe a tort law duty to students), *claims against all defendants dismissed*, 16 F. Supp. 2d 1119 (D. Ariz. 1998).

197 Armstrong v. Accrediting Council for Continuing Educ. & Training, Inc., 832 F. Supp. 419 (D.D.C. 1993).

198 Armstrong v. Accrediting Council for Continuing Educ. & Training, Inc., 961 F. Supp. 305 (D.D.C. 1997).

199 Armstrong v. Accrediting Council for Continuing Educ. & Training, Inc., Clearinghouse No. 52,040 (D.D.C. Mar. 30, 1998) (settlement agreement and order approving settlement).

200 *See* Jerald A. Jacobs & Jefferson Caffery Glassie, Am. Soc'y of Ass'n Execs., Certification and Accreditation Law Handbook Ch. 3 (1992).

201 Keams v. Tempe Technical Inst., 39 F.3d 222 (9th Cir. 1994), *appeal after remand*, 103 F.3d 138 (9th Cir. 1996), *redesignated as opinion*, 110 F.3d 44 (9th Cir. 1997), *claims against all defendants dismissed*, 16 F. Supp. 2d 1119 (D. Ariz. 1998); Ambrose v. New England Ass'n of Schs. & Colls., 2000 WL 1195363 (D. Me. Aug. 7, 2000) (analogizing negligent accreditation claims to educational malpractice; court found it improper for courts to make these subjective determinations; summary judgment granted to defendant accrediting organization), *aff'd*, 252 F.3d 488 (1st Cir. 2001).

202 Figueroa v. Market Training Inst., Inc., 167 A.D.2d 503, 562 N.Y.S.2d 175 (App. Div. 1990).

9.4.1.4 Suing the School and Individual Owners and Operators

A major obstacle to affirmative litigation against schools is that, in many cases, the school will already be closed by the time the client seeks assistance. It is also very common for schools to close during the course of litigation. As a result, relying on a recovery from the school can be frustrating. In these circumstances, the borrower will be forced to raise the school-related claim, by way of recoupment, to an action to collect on the debt or as a declaratory action that the debt is not owed.[203] However, affirmative claims against schools should still be considered, especially in cases in which the school is still open.

If the school is already in bankruptcy, advocates should consider recovering a judgment in bankruptcy. Students may have a consumer priority, giving them first crack at any school assets ahead of unsecured creditors.[204] Another benefit arises if the student's attorney serves on a creditor's committee. In these cases, the attorney fees for that service will be paid out of the school's assets.[205]

Another possible approach to recover from a bankrupt school is to jump ahead of other creditors by means of a criminal restitution order. *United States v. Grundhoefer*[206] affirms an order of almost $1 million in criminal restitution to students victimized by a private vocational school. Brooklyn and Bronx Legal Services suggested to two different federal judges sentencing several principals of the school that all the criminal restitution go to defrauded students and not to the school's other creditors. The judges agreed, instructing the government and the legal services attorneys to work out a restitution plan. The school's bankruptcy trustee, representing the school's other creditors, appealed. The Second Circuit found no abuse of discretion in the restitution plan and no standing by the other creditors to object to the courts' orders.[207]

When dealing with an insolvent school, advocates should also explore the following potential alternative defendants:

- *A bonding company or state tuition recovery fund*, since schools are licensed by many states, and a bond or contribution to a state tuition recovery fund is usually a pre-condition to licensure.[208]
- *The parent company or franchisor* is often a deep pocket and may aid or abet the school's misrepresentations.
- *Owners, officers,*[209] *and employees are responsible* for their own actions, even if they are acting as a corporate agent. Individuals dealing directly with a student, and those supervising those individuals, are potential defendants, as is a school's owner to the extent the owner supervises the school or to the extent the corporate veil can be pierced.
- *Advertising agencies, accountants, lawyers, or others aiding and abetting a fraudulent scheme* are individually liable for their own misconduct.[210]

9.4.2 Deciding Between Class and Individual Actions

An individual action is one way to pursue a trade school case. A second, and often more efficient, approach is to join a number of individual students as plaintiffs.[211] Sometimes it is easier to obtain punitive damages on behalf of a limited number of students than on behalf of a class. The case can easily be brought before a jury, where sympathetic facts on each individual plaintiff can be presented directly to the jury.[212] A class action, in contrast, might not allow as effective a presentation of each student's case and might not result in a punitive damages award.

A class action against a trade school may also lead to successful results. For example, in one case, a class action against a cosmetology school recovered $640,000 UDAP actual damages and $271,000 in UDAP attorney fees.[213]

---

203 *See* § 9.6, *infra*.

204 *See, e.g., In re* Longo, 144 B.R. 305 (Bankr. Md. 1992) (Maryland Higher Education Commission brought tuition recovery claims on behalf of student borrowers; court granted consumer deposit priority pursuant to 11 U.S.C. § 507(a)(6); school president argued unsuccessfully that school's services were business and not consumer in nature).

205 A more detailed analysis of a consumer creditor's rights when a company has filed for bankruptcy can be found in National Consumer Law Center's *Unfair and Deceptive Acts and Practices* § 6.9 (6th ed. 2004 and Supp.) and *Consumer Bankruptcy Law and Practice* Ch. 17 (7th ed. 2004 and Supp.).

206 916 F.2d 788 (2d Cir. 1990).

207 *Id.*

208 *See* § 9.8, *infra* (student tuition recovery funds).

209 *See* Goldsmith v. Rodano, Clearinghouse No. 50,943C (Cal. Super. Ct. Aug. 21, 1995) (former president agrees to pay $100,000 to seventy-five students and $30,000 to student's attorney).

210 *See* National Consumer Law Center, Unfair and Deceptive Acts and Practices § 6.5 (6th ed. 2004 and Supp.).

211 *See, e.g.*, Cross v. Acad. of Court Reporting, Inc., Clearinghouse No. 46,794 (Ohio Summit Cty. 1991) (thirty-four individual students brought an action against a trade school; all the students recovered actual damages, ranging from $2600 to $12,200, and punitive damages of either $2500 or $3000 each; total recovery exceeded $400,000), *aff'd in part and remanded in part sub nom.* Matulin v. Acad. of Court Reporting, 1992 WL 74210 (Ohio Ct. App. Apr. 8, 1992) (upholding virtually all counts but remanding the case for redetermination of the attorney fee award of $116,000, which it found to be inadequate); Beckett v. Computer Career Inst., Inc. (Or. Cir. Ct. July 2, 1990), *aff'd in part and rev'd in part*, 120 Or. App. 143, 852 P.2d 840 (1993) (significant recovery for nine students).

212 *See* Beckett v. Computer Career Inst., Inc. (Or. Cir. Ct. July 2, 1990), *aff'd in part and rev'd in part*, 120 Or. App. 143, 852 P.2d 840 (1993) (significant recovery for nine students).

213 Rosario v. Livaditis, Clearinghouse No. 47,927B (N.D. Ill. 1989), *aff'd*, 963 F.2d 1013 (7th Cir. 1992) (Illinois law). *See*

Because each student may be subjected to a different oral sales presentation, the Rule 23(b)(2) commonality requirement may be a problem in vocational school class action litigation. However, courts may find that each of these individual presentations is sufficiently close to the school's standard sales script to present common issues of fact, and the core issue in question may be whether the school operated pursuant to an ongoing scheme to defraud and deceive students.[214]

For example, one federal court certified a class of about 400 Native Americans recruited to attend the TTI trade school by one particular salesperson over a fifteen-month period.[215] Although the bulk of the evidence related to oral sales presentations, the court found enough commonality in the salesman's presentations to justify the class action.

When seeking a declaration that the student does not owe on a Federal Family Education Loan (FFEL) because of school-related defenses, it usually makes sense to do so on behalf of a class of students who were victimized by the same program and who took out FFELs to attend. To proceed as a class, it will be necessary to convince the court that the class action requirements have been met.

In theory, if an action meets that test, then issues of lender liability should be sufficiently common to the class that the class should be certified. In fact, the standards may even be easier for a declaratory judgment action than in a damage action against a school. At least one court has ruled that an action seeking to declare loans unenforceable is not a damage action and that only the requirements of Rule 23(b)(2), not (b)(3), need be met.[216] Class actions seeking damages or restitution actions are often problematic in the trade school context.[217]

9.4.3 Developing a Case

One of the best ways to develop evidence of school malfeasance is to find disgruntled former employees—both commissioned sales representatives and faculty. The names, addresses, and dates of employment of present and past school employees can be obtained through discovery. The names of disgruntled sales representatives may also be obtained from court records, since many of them must sue the school for their back commissions. Not only can these people provide crucial evidence, but the "educational" institution's use of commissioned enrollment officers probably will have an impact on the jury or judge. Clients may also remember instructors' names and/or be able to provide a school catalog with this information.

Advocates should also be sure to obtain the school's sales manuals, marketing memos, and sales training materials. It is critical to find out how the student was enrolled, for example, outside a welfare office or in a high-pressure door-to-door sale.

Other information can be found on file with private accrediting associations, state licensing agencies, and the Department of Education. Advocates may want to focus on drop-out and job placement rates.[218] Although data on completion and job placement can be very useful in developing a case, it is also very difficult to find reliable data. In many cases, schools are required to keep this information and in some cases meet minimum standards for completion and job placement.[219]

Some of this data is available through the National Center for Education Statistics (NCES), which administers the Integrated Postsecondary Education Data System (IPEDS). This is an on-line data collection program that compiles information on all postsecondary institutions in the U.S. It contains institutional data such as tuition and salaries of instructional staff as well as student data, which include enrollment numbers and the race and gender of students.[220] The most recent cohort enrollments and completion data can be found here as well. However, NCES does not collect job placement rates for any type of institution.

FOIA requests sent to federal and state agencies are also useful in collecting information, particularly with respect to possible investigations against schools.[221]

---

generally National Consumer Law Center, Unfair and Deceptive Acts and Practices § 8.5 (6th ed. 2004 and Supp.).

214 *See* Shorter v. Riley, Clearinghouse No. 47,950B (N.D. Ga. Nov. 18, 1993).

215 Keams v. Tempe Technical Inst., 807 F. Supp. 569 (D. Ariz. 1992), *rev'd*, 39 F.3d 222 (9th Cir. 1994), *appeal after remand*, 103 F.3d 138 (9th Cir. 1996), *redesignated as opinion*, 110 F.3d 44 (9th Cir. 1997), *claims against all defendants dismissed*, 16 F. Supp. 2d 1119 (D. Ariz. 1998).

216 Shorter v. Riley, Clearinghouse No. 47,950B (N.D. Ga. Nov. 18, 1993). *See generally* National Consumer Law Center, Unfair and Deceptive Acts and Practices § 8.5 (6th ed. 2004 and Supp.); National Consumer Law Center, Consumer Class Actions (6th ed. 2006).

217 *See, e.g.*, Morgan v. Markerdowne Corp., 201 F.R.D. 341 (D.N.J. 2001).

218 For information on gathering evidence from state licensing agencies, including Freedom of Information Act requests, see § 6.3.2.2, *supra*.

219 *See* § 9.2.4, *supra*.

220 *See* Integrated Postsecondary Educ. Data Sys., *About IPEDS*, at http://nces.ed.gov/AboutIPEDS.asp. Additional data can be found on the "College Opportunities Online" (COOL) database at http://nces.ed.gov/ipeds/cool.

221 *See* § 6.3.2.2.2, *supra*. Sample FOIA requests are included in Appendix F. Advocates should be prepared to respond if agencies deny fee waivers for FOIA requests. *See* Students for Sensible Drug Policy, Harmful Drug Law Hits Home (Apr. 17, 2006) (describing battle with the federal Department of Education regarding FOIA requests and fee waivers; the group and Public Citizen filed a lawsuit against the Department in January 2006 and the Department settled the case and provided the data free of charge), *available at* http://www.ssdp.org/states/ssdp-state-report.pdf (last accessed in October 2006).

9.4.4 *Proving Actual Damages*

Student plaintiffs may have suffered a variety of actual damages as a result of vocational school fraud. In one case, the plaintiffs successfully argued that they would never have attended had they known of the school's actual placement rate, which was lower than represented. The students' actual damages were found to be their *total* tuition (even though most had graduated from the school) plus the students' lost wages incurred when they left their jobs to attend the school.[222]

Other damage claims to consider in these cases include child care and transportation expenses incurred while students attended school. In addition, many students were encouraged or required by schools to purchase equipment or materials. For example, many schools purporting to teach automobile mechanic skills required students to purchase their own tools. These costs can also be claimed as damages.

9.5 Additional Issues to Consider in Defending Student Loan Collection Actions

9.5.1 *Standing and Other Procedural Issues*

There are different issues to consider depending on which entity is suing to collect the loan. If the loan is a Perkins loan, the school may be bringing the action. Alternatively, the loan may have been assigned to the Department.

In some cases, a collection agency may be the party suing to collect. In these cases, advocates will want to explore whether the collection agency is in fact the owner of the loan. Borrowers can seek through discovery the original instrument and the originals of all evidence of assignment or transfer. There may also be questions about unauthorized practice of law. States have taken very different positions as to what activities of a collection agency constitute unauthorized practice of law.[223] Some states, for example, prohibit a contingent-fee collector from filing suit in its own name.

A consumer sued on a loan by a guaranty agency or the United States should consider not just raising school-related defenses to the collection action but also impleading the school if it is still solvent. Joining the school will also aid discovery and paint a clearer picture for the judge.

When the United States (as opposed to a state guaranty agency) is bringing the lawsuit, there should be little ques-

tion of the student's right to implead the school or other parties against whom the student has student-loan-related claims. The Federal Debt Collection Procedures Act authorizes debtors sued by the United States to join, as a defendant in the same lawsuit, any party owing the debtor money related to the same transaction that forms the basis of the government's suit against the debtor.[224]

The Act not only permits students to implead the school[225] but also authorizes the United States to do so as well. When the student has neither the legal resources to implead the school nor the financial resources to satisfy a judgment, the United States' best course would be to implead the school and seek payment from that party.

When no collection action has been brought against the student, but when tax refund intercepts and other collection contacts are threatened and the school is insolvent, another approach is to bring an affirmative action for declaratory relief that the loan amount is not owed to the guarantors or the Department because of school-related claims.[226]

Clients may already have judgments entered against them. In these cases, advocates should consider attempting to vacate the judgments. This is especially critical because borrowers have fewer rights if judgments have already been entered against them. For example, they may not consolidate loans in these circumstances.[227] Advocates may negotiate with creditors to vacate judgments or file motions in court.[228]

There also may be a question about which party has the burden of proof, particularly in cases in which the borrower is claiming that he or she repaid the loan.[229]

9.5.2 *Statute of Limitations Not a Defense to Federal Student Loan Collection*

The Higher Education Technical Amendments of 1991 (HEA) eliminated all statutes of limitations for any collection action by a school, guaranty agency, or the United States under a federal loan program.[230] These amendments

---

222   Beckett v. Computer Career Inst., Inc. (Or. Cir. Ct. July 2, 1990), *aff'd in part and rev'd in part*, 120 Or. App. 143, 852 P.2d 840 (1993).

223   *See generally* National Consumer Law Center, Fair Debt Collection § 11.5.2 (5th ed. 2004 and Supp.).

224   28 U.S.C. § 3012.

225   *See* H.R. Rep. No. 736, 101st Cong., 2d Sess. 30 (Sept. 21, 1990), *reprinted in* 1991 U.S.C.C.A.N. 6638.

226   *See* § 9.4.1.1, *supra*.

227   *See* § 8.2.2.2, *supra*.

228   *See, e.g.,* United States v. Cagle, 2006 WL 1409100 (E.D. Mich. Apr. 17, 2006) (default judgment vacated; default was grossly unfair and inequitable because it was entered only three weeks after borrower was served and borrower alleged a meritorious defense that the debt had been paid and account closed).

229   *See, e.g.,* Proctor v. United States Dep't of Educ., 2006 WL 2430485 (6th Cir. Aug. 21, 2006) (the Department satisfied its initial burden by showing that the borrower signed promissory notes, received loans and defaulted; borrower then had to present evidence supporting his repayment defense).

230   Pub. L. No. 102-26 eliminated the statute of limitations set out in 20 U.S.C. § 1091a(a). While the elimination of the limitations period was to have sunset on November 15, 1992, the Higher

also eliminated all limitation periods for tax intercepts, wage garnishments, and other collection efforts.[231]

The elimination of the statute of limitations applies to collection by government agencies and their agents. The statute specifically applies to institutions collecting federal grant or work assistance refunds; guaranty agencies that have agreements with the Department and are collecting federal loans; institutions that have agreements with the Department and are collecting government loans; and the Secretary of Education, Attorney General, or administrative head of another federal agency to collect government grants and loans.[232] Collection of private student loans is not covered.

9.5.3 Forgery, Mistake, Infancy, and Other Defenses to Loan Enforceability

9.5.3.1 General

A student's obligation to pay a student loan is conditioned upon the loan agreement being enforceable under basic contract principles—such as forgery, mistake, and fraud— that affect a borrower's obligation on any note. The only common law contract defense not available to student loan borrowers is infancy, that is, that the student was under age when signing the loan document. The HEA specifies that the United States and guaranty agencies, irrespective of state law on the issue, shall *not* be subject to a claim of infancy.[233]

The HEA does not limit other contract defenses. These defenses should therefore apply to student loans just as they do to any other type of loan. Borrowers have, for example, successfully raised duress as a defense.[234]

The Department on numerous occasions has stated that the student does not owe on a loan, and guaranty agencies should not seek payment, to the extent to which the loan obligation is not enforceable under state law.[235]

If a student did not sign a student loan note, and the student's signature was forged or altered, the student should have no liability under that note. It should make no difference whether the forger is the school or lender.

Similarly, when checks are presented to pay school tuition, the federal statute requires that the student's endorsement be included before the check is cashed.[236] Forgery of that endorsement or failure to obtain that endorsement should also void the student's liability for that check.

A 1993 letter from the Department of Education spells out student rights when a check lacks the student's endorsement or the endorsement is forged.[237] A student is not liable for the amount of a check when the student did not endorse the check, unless under state law the holder can show that the borrower is legally obligated for the amount disbursed. Holders cannot presume that a borrower who remained enrolled at a school after a check was cashed thereby received its proceeds or condoned the school's action in cashing the check.

According to the Department letter, if a student is not obligated on the amount involving the check without proper endorsement, the guarantor should correct the student's credit record to reflect that fact, must make sure that the failure to pay that amount is not causing the student to be ineligible for future loans and grants, and must return any amount collected concerning that check, including any tax intercept.

In 2006 regulations related to false certifications due to identity theft, the Department affirmed that a person is ordinarily not liable on an instrument, such as a promissory note or check, unless that person signed that instrument or authorized another to sign on his or her behalf.[238] The Department cited FFEL regulations that provided that FFEL program benefits are payable to the holder of the loan only when the lender obtained a legally enforceable promissory note to evidence the loan and also regulations providing that reinsurance may be received only with respect to a claim on a legally enforceable loan.[239]

When a promissory note or check endorsement is forged, the student may have two different approaches to discharging the loan. One is to apply for a false-certification discharge based on the forgery.[240] The other is to claim that the obligation is unenforceable under common law principles.

Education Amendments of 1992 § 1551, codified at 20 U.S.C. § 1091a, extended indefinitely the abolition of the statute of limitations for student loan collections. *See* § 4.2.1, *supra*.

231 *Id.* A lingering argument to apply a time limit for Social Security offsets was finally put to rest, unfortunately for borrowers, by the U.S. Supreme Court in 2005. *See* Lockhart v. United States, 126 S. Ct. 699 (2005). *See* § 5.4.3.3, *supra*.

232 20 U.S.C. § 1091a(a).

233 20 U.S.C. § 1091a(b)(2). This provision only applies explicitly to FFELs and not Perkins loans. While the provision does not mention Direct loans, it will apply to Direct loans because, unless otherwise specified, Direct loans "shall have the same terms, conditions, and benefits" as FFELs. 20 U.S.C. § 1087e(a)(1).

234 *See, e.g., In re* Mason, 300 B.R. 160 (Bankr. D. Conn. 2003) (consolidation loan was obtained through duress and was therefore null and void under state law). *But see* Gibbs v. SLM Corp., 336 F. Supp. 2d 1 (D. Mass. 2004) (duress claim dismissed because plaintiff failed to show that (1) one side involuntarily accepted the terms of another, (2) circumstances permitted no other alternative, and (3) said circumstances were the result of coercive acts of the opposing party).

235 A good enunciation of this policy is found in a letter from Acting Assistant Secretary Whitehead to Congressman Stephen Solarz, Clearinghouse No. 44,343 (May 19, 1988). *See also* 71 Fed. Reg. 45666, 45676–77 (Aug. 9, 2006).

236 20 U.S.C. § 1078(b)(1)(O).

237 Letter of William Morant, Acting Deputy Assistant Secretary for Student Financial Assistance, Nos. 93-L-156, 93-G-236, Clearinghouse No. 49,163 (July 1993).

238 71 Fed. Reg. 45666, 45676–77 (Aug. 9, 2006).

239 *Id.* (citing 34 C.F.R. § 682.402(e)(1)(i)(B), 682.406(a)(1)).

240 *See* § 6.3.4, *supra*.

In the appropriate case, both of these strategies should work, and the student can choose which way to proceed first. Department regulations state that the false-certification discharge based on forgery applies only if the *school* signed the borrower's name without authorization.[241] If the forgery was done by someone else, relief is available under the common law or state law defense of forgery.

Fraud in obtaining the consumer's signature should also be a defense. For example, there are many reported cases of consumers signing promissory notes unaware that they were obligating themselves on a loan. The consumers typically thought they were just applying to a school or applying for a grant. The student never went to the school or realized the existence of the debt until much later when a lender tried to collect on the loan. While such facts should provide a valid defense on the note, advocates should be prepared for the Department and guaranty agencies to give little credibility to such claims.

9.5.3.2 Connection Between Contract Defenses and Statutory Discharges

Any student entitled to a school-related discharge might also consider raising school-related claims as a defense on a loan, since, by definition, the student has serious claims against the school. In part because of Department regulations, students should demonstrate some care concerning the interrelationship of school-based discharges and raising school-related defenses.

Borrowers cannot initiate the discharge process in court.[242] A discharge-related issue may be resolved in court, but only after a borrower has exhausted the administrative process and is seeking judicial review.[243] A district court in North Carolina summarized the problem for borrowers.[244] In a case pending before that court, the borrower sought to enjoin the government from collecting for loans that the borrower alleged were paid for instruction he never received. The court noted that plaintiff's claims appealed to the equities found in the law.[245] The court also noted that Congress had addressed the problem by passing the various administrative discharges.[246] However, these claims must be

presented through the administrative process and not as defensive claims in civil litigation.

The safest course is always to raise the discharge claim first and then raise school-related defenses later. If borrowers are sued for collection, they should file an answer to the collection suit asserting the right to a discharge as a defense. The court should be asked not to enter judgment until the discharge application has been ruled on. If the Department of Education is suing, the United States Attorney will usually agree to stay the litigation until the Department rules on the discharge request.

9.5.4 Defenses for Servicemembers

9.5.4.1 Servicemember Civil Relief Act Protections

The Servicemember Civil Relief Act (SCRA) limits collection tactics and enforcement of claims against active duty military personnel.[247] In general, everyone on active duty is entitled to the benefit of the Act, whether or not they are stationed in a war zone and whether they enlisted or were called up. Active duty includes full-time training duty, annual training duty, and attendance at a military school while in active military service.[248]

The interest rate protections under the Act do not apply to government student loans.[249] They should, however, apply to private student loans. The Act requires that creditors reduce the interest rate to 6% on any obligation incurred by a servicemember before active duty.[250] The reduction lasts as long as the sevicemember is on active duty.

The protections in civil judicial and administrative proceedings should apply to student loan collection proceedings. These are relatively new protections arising under 2003 amendments to the Act that extended coverage to administrative as well as judicial proceedings.[251] The Act also restricts execution upon assets of the servicemember.

The protections in judicial and administrative procedures are divided into two main categories: cases in which the servicemember has not been notified of the proceeding and cases in which the servicemember has been notified. In cases in which the servicemember has not been notified, courts are prohibited from entering default judgments in cases in

---

241 34 C.F.R. § 682.402(e)(1)(i)(B). *See* § 6.3.4, *supra.*

242 Courts have consistently found that only the Department of Education has the discretion to discharge the loans based on the various discharge programs. *See, e.g.*, United States v. Levreau, 2001 WL 1690059 (D. Minn. Dec. 14, 2001) (discharge claims must be pursued administratively and may not be asserted as a defense in a collection action), United States v. Bertucci, 2000 WL 1234560 (E.D. La. 2000); United States v. Wright, 87 F. Supp. 2d 464 (D. Md. 2000); *In re* Bega, 180 B.R. 642 (Bankr. D. Kan. 1995).

243 *See* § 6.10, *supra* (APA appeals).

244 Green v. United States, 163 F. Supp. 2d 593 (W.D.N.C. 2000).

245 *Id.* at 597.

246 *Id.* at 597–598.

---

247 50 U.S.C. app. §§ 501–596. *See generally* National Consumer Law Center, Fair Debt Collection § 9.12 (5th ed. 2004 and Supp.).

248 For a discussion of servicemembers protected by the Act, see National Consumer Law Center, Fair Debt Collection § 9.12.2 (5th ed. 2004 and Supp.).

249 20 U.S.C. § 1078(d).

250 § 207 (50 U.S.C. app. § 527).

251 § 101(5) (defining "court" to include state and federal administrative agencies); § 2(2) (referring to administrative proceedings in purpose clause); § 102(b) (Act applies to any judicial or administrative proceeding commenced in any court or agency).

which the defendant has not appeared, unless the plaintiff files an affidavit stating whether or not the defendant is in military service and showing facts in support of the statement. If it appears that the defendant is in military service, the court may not enter a judgment until it appoints an attorney to represent the defendant, and there are special provisions for stays.[252] The Act also gives a servicemember who has been notified of an action or proceeding other than an eviction the right to an automatic, non-discretionary ninety-day stay upon request.[253] The servicemember may seek an additional stay, but this extension is not automatic. In addition, the Act allows the court to stay execution of any judgment against a servicemember and to vacate or stay any pre- or post-judgment attachment or garnishment of property.[254] There are also provisions tolling statutes of limitations during the period of active duty.[255]

9.5.4.2 Other Protections for Servicemembers

Federal law provides unique deferment, forbearance, and other rights for active duty servicemembers.[256] There may be state claims as well to protect service members attending school. For example, Ohio requires that institutions of higher education grant active duty military students a leave of absence without academic penalty while the student is serving on active duty. There are also provisions for refunds or credits of tuition.[257]

These issues are increasingly important as military members are increasingly seeking education, often online, while serving. The University of Phoenix online, for example, has a separate division that handles military students.[258] In addition, many schools, including large proprietary schools, target those leaving the service.

9.6 Raising School-Related Defenses

9.6.1 General

Defrauded students may have no other practical recourse than to raise school-related defenses on their student loans. While it is almost always preferable to obtain a discharge than to raise school-related defenses, many defrauded stu-

dents will not receive such discharges.[259] Similarly, most defrauded students will not want to file for bankruptcy or may not be able to obtain a bankruptcy discharge of their student loans.[260] Affirmative suits against the school raise many practical problems, not the least of which is that the school may now be insolvent or insolvent by the time a judgment is entered against the school.[261]

Consequently, for millions of students defrauded by trade schools, raising school-related defenses on their student loans is critical. This same right to raise seller-related claims on loans has proven essential for other defrauded consumers as well, such as those victimized by home improvement contractors or used-car dealers. In most cases, when the seller refers the consumer to the lender or when the seller and lender have a business arrangement, these other consumers can successfully raise as a defense to their loans all claims and defenses they have against the seller.[262]

Unfortunately, it is not as clear whether defrauded students can raise school-related defenses to their loans. The analysis depends at least initially on the type of student loan involved. Students can raise school-related defenses for Perkins loans, Direct loans, and usually on federally insured student loans (FISLs). They can also raise these defenses on FFELs extended on or after January 1, 1994, when a for-profit school has a referral or other business relationship with the lender.

The situation for earlier FFELs, on the other hand, is far from clear. In addition, special issues arise when an FFEL has lost its guaranteed status or when a student loan is consolidated into a new student loan.

This section sets out existing standards for raising school-related defenses for all of these types of loans. Advocates must properly match their client's type of loan with the appropriate discussion below.[263] The types of claims to raise defensively are similar to those that can be raised in affirmative cases. These issues are discussed above.

9.6.2 The Clearer Picture: Loans for Which School-Related Defenses Should Be Available

9.6.2.1 Perkins Loans

Schools are the lender for Perkins loans. In these cases, the lender (that is, the school) should be subject to school-related defenses. In addition, the lender may *assign* the note

---

252 *See* National Consumer Law Center, Fair Debt Collection § 9.12.3.2 (5th ed. 2004 and Supp.).
253 *Id.* § 9.12.3.3.
254 50 U.S.C. App. § 524.
255 50 U.S.C. App. § 526(a).
256 *See* §§ 3.2.4.4 (deferments), 3.3 (forbearance).
257 Ohio Rev. Code § 1713.60 (includes private right of enforcement); Ohio Rev. Code § 3332.20 (leave of absence and other requirements apply to career colleges and schools).
258 *See* Dan Carnevale, *Be All You Can Be-Online*, The Chron. of Higher Educ., July 7, 2006, at A31.

259 *See generally* Ch. 6, *supra* (discharges).
260 *See* Ch. 7, *supra.*
261 *See* § 9.4.1.4, *supra.*
262 *See generally* National Consumer Law Center, National Consumer Law Center, Unfair and Deceptive Acts and Practices § 6.6 (6th ed. 2004 and Supp.).
263 For information on how to find out what type of loan a client has, see § 1.6, *supra.*

to the United States for collection.[264] The United States, as assignee, should be subject to all defenses that could be raised against the assignor.[265] While this legal theory is straightforward and unassailable, few if any students have raised school-related defenses on Perkins loans.

9.6.2.2 Direct Loans

The HEA specifies that, notwithstanding any other provision of state or federal law, the Secretary shall, for Direct loans, specify in regulations when school misconduct may be asserted as a defense to loan repayment, but the student's recovery pursuant to such a defense cannot exceed the amount the student has repaid on the loan.[266]

The regulations state that, in any proceeding to collect on a Direct loan, the borrower may assert as a defense against repayment any act or omission of the school that would give rise to a cause of action against the school under applicable state law.[267] In addition, the Secretary may determine that all or part of amounts already paid on the loan should be refunded to the student and may also correct negative credit reports.[268] These defenses can be raised not only in litigation but also in tax offset, wage garnishment, and other salary offset proceedings.[269]

9.6.2.3 FISLs

Federally insured student loans (FISLs) usually date back to the 1970s or early 1980s. Loans from a bank or even from a school were insured directly by the United States. Students can raise many school-related defenses to FISLs because, until 1986 (when it was dropped without comment), an FISL regulation explicitly stated that the United States would not collect an FISL to the extent that a school had closed or students had certain school-related defenses.[270] This regulation should apply at least to FISLs entered into before 1986. Moreover, when the school was the originating lender, students should also be able to raise all defenses against the assignee (the United States) based on the same rationale as with Perkins loans.[271]

---

264 *See* 34 C.F.R. §§ 674.8(d), 674.50 (assignment of defaulted loans).

265 The note is not a negotiable instrument so that the United States cannot be a holder in due course. *See generally* National Consumer Law Center, Unfair and Deceptive Acts and Practices § 6.6 (6th ed. 2004 and Supp.).

266 20 U.S.C. § 1087e(h).

267 34 C.F.R. § 685.206(c)(1).

268 34 C.F.R. § 685.206(c)(2).

269 34 C.F.R. § 685.206(c)(1).

270 34 C.F.R. § 518 (1985) (since rescinded). *See also* United States v. Griffin, 707 F.2d 1477 (D.C. Cir. 1983).

271 *See* § 9.6.2.1, *supra. Cf.* United States v. Griffin, 707 F.2d 1477 (D.C. Cir. 1983) (not ruling on whether the United States was an assignee or surety because Department regulations authorized students to raise defenses).

9.6.2.4 FFELs Extended After January 1, 1994

Starting on January 1, 1994, all FFELs use a common promissory note that is drafted by the United States Department of Education. The note includes an adaptation of the FTC Holder Notice:

> If this loan is made by the school, or if the proceeds of this loan are used to pay tuition and charges of a for-profit school that refers loan applicants to the lender, or that is affiliated with the lender by common control, contract or business arrangement, any holder of this Note is subject to all claims and defenses which I could assert against the school. My recovery under this provision shall not exceed the amount I paid on this loan.[272]

Students whose notes include this loan provision will be in a strong position to raise school-related claims. Nevertheless, this loan provision, by its very terms, only allows consumers to raise school-related defenses to an FFEL *if* the school is for-profit and *if* the school refers students to the lender or is affiliated with the lender by common control, contract, or business arrangement. In raising school-related defenses, the student should thus allege that the school is for-profit and that it refers students or has a business arrangement with the lender.

The Department has issued a letter giving its interpretations as to when a referral relationship exists.[273] Such a relationship does not exist if the only relationship between school and lender is based on certain specific duties required of the school and lender by the Higher Education Act or regulations. Moreover, simply giving students a list of available lenders does not create a referral relationship.

On the other hand, if a school seeks out a lender to add to its list of lenders, such a relationship is more likely to exist. The relationship does not exist if the list of lenders is obtained from a third source, such as a guaranty agency or trade association.

There is a referral relationship when the school recommends a particular lender, but only when the lender knows about the recommendation. If a lender sends the school promotional material about its lending activity, the lender should expect that students seeking loans have been recommended by the school. On the other hand, credible assurances to a lender that the school will do no more than include its name on a list of willing lenders is not knowledge of the recommendation.

The Department statement concludes that FTC interpretations will ordinarily be dispositive as to whether a referral

---

272 *See* Common Application Material and Promissory Note, Clearinghouse No. 47,974 (Apr. 16, 1993).

273 Div. of Policy Dev., Office of the Assistant Sec'y for Postsecondary Educ., Overview of the Federal Trade Commission Holder Rule, Clearinghouse No. 49,162 (July 2, 1993).

relationship exists. Interested parties should consider statements from the FTC staff on the Holder Rule's application.[274]

Advocates should also check to see if the lender waives origination fees the school must pay or otherwise provides special privileges to the school. This is excellent evidence of a business arrangement.

9.6.3 Less Clarity As to Raising School-Related Defenses for FFELs Extended Before 1994

9.6.3.1 Introduction

It is quite frustrating to students that lenders, guaranty agencies, and the Department still, in large part, refuse to recognize legitimate school-related defenses for FFELs entered into before 1994. For these loans, the only undisputed right to relief is through a closed-school, unpaid-refund, or false-certification discharge.[275]

The key question in determining whether students can raise school-related defenses to FFELs extended before 1994 is whether the originating lender (usually a bank) is subject to the student's claims against the school. If the bank is subject to the claims, then so are its assignees—a secondary market lender, a guaranty agency, and the United States.[276]

Unlike a Perkins loan, the school is not the originating lender. While the school may assist the lender and refer the student to the lender, the loan goes directly from the bank or other lender to the student. Lenders argue that they have nothing to do with the school—they are not assignees of the school, do not guaranty school quality, and are not subject to any school-related defenses.

Nevertheless, in other analogous consumer transactions, a direct lender is liable for the misconduct of a related seller, such as when a finance company arranges for a homeowner's payment to a home improvement contractor.[277] Well-established legal principles and statutes protect consumers in these situations. When a seller refers the consumer to the lender or otherwise has an arrangement or course of dealing with that lender, the lender is generally subject to all the consumer's claims and defenses against the seller.[278]

An important avenue for relief for students would be if these general principles of lender liability for other consumer transactions and for other student loans (including FFELs after January 1, 1994) also applied to FFELs prior to 1994. Since the lender would be liable for the school's misconduct, the same would be true for the guaranty agency and the Department, who are merely assignees of the lender.[279] Legal theories allowing the student to raise

---

274 The Department statement particularly references 40 Fed. Reg. 53,506 (Nov. 18, 1975); 41 Fed. Reg. 43,594 (Aug. 16, 1976); 57 Fed. Reg. 28,814 (June 29, 1992).

275 *See* Ch. 6, *supra* (discharges).

276 There may be additional issues that arise in trying to hold secondary market purchasers liable for a school's fraud or negligence. *See* Crawford v. The American Inst. of Prof'l Careers, Inc., 934 F. Supp. 335 (D. Ariz. 1996) (state law claims against secondary purchasers deemed preempted by the HEA; court agreed that purchasers could not comply with state law and the anti-discrimination provisions of the HEA, which require purchasers to purchase certain loans without any independent oversight or control over school programs; no separate fraud or wrongdoing alleged against purchaser in this case).

277 Williams v. ITT Fin. Servs., 1997 Ohio App. LEXIS 2721 (Ohio App. June 25, 1997) (state appellate court upheld $1.5 million punitive damages award against finance company for failing to warn borrower that a home improvement contractor was fraudulent; liability upheld even though home improvement contractor was not an agent of finance company and did not receive payment from company). The *Williams* court approach should apply in the student loan context both to argue for punitive damages against a lender in excess of the FTC Holder Rule cap on liability and to create a claim against a direct lender when the FTC Holder Rule is not contained in the loan documents.

278 *See* National Consumer Law Center, Unfair and Deceptive Acts and Practices § 6.6 (6th ed. 2004 and Supp.). There is a Congressional intent that this general rule of lender liability apply to at least certain GSLs. The House version of the Higher Education Amendments of 1992 provided lenders with extensive immunity from students' school-related defenses, but the House acceded to the Senate version that provided no such immunity, indicating a Congressional intent that banks be liable in at least certain situations, as to be determined by the courts:

> The conferees are reluctant to legislate in this area while the issue is pending in the courts. The conferees have instead chosen to leave to the courts the complex determination as to when a student should and should not be able to raise the school's fraud or other misconduct as a defense to the student's loans. Courts will have to consider many factors, including the exact nature of the lender's relationship and dealings with the school. In deciding to leave this matter to the courts, the conferees weighed several important, but in some cases conflicting, considerations. Allowing victimized students to raise defenses on their loans may also have the salutary effect of causing increased scrutiny of schools, thereby effectively policing sham schools. At the same time, the ability of schools to refer students to lenders willing to make loans to them, the participation of national lenders and servicers, and cooperative efforts to improve service to students and reduce defaults are important to improve service to students and reduce defaults are important to achieving nationwide loan access.

H.R. Rep No. 630, at 508 (1992) (Conf. Rep.).

279 Guaranty agencies at one time argued (but appear to have given up arguing) that, even if the lenders are liable for school-related claims, the guaranty agency enforcing that loan obligation is not. More common is for the guaranty agency to argue that it is not liable even if the lender is liable because the guaranty agency is not an assignee of the lender but the students'

school-related claims and defenses against the lender, the guaranty agency, and the United States are set out below.

In some cases, the student may not be facing a collection lawsuit but other collection methods such as tax intercepts and/or wage garnishments. It is difficult to raise school-related defenses in response to a threatened tax intercept, garnishment, or collection contact.[280]

One way to address this problem is for students to bring an affirmative action in state or federal court for declaratory relief that the student does not owe the loan. The student can then use the declaration as a defense in any tax intercept or other administrative collection action. An action for declaratory relief should not violate the HEA's anti-injunction provision.[281]

9.6.3.2 Agency and Other Common Law Theories

One ground for lender liability for school-related claims is that the lender has appointed the school its agent for certain functions and that, under *respondeat superior*, the principal is liable for the acts of its agent within the actual or apparent scope of the agent's authority. Typically, in many vocational school enrollments, the school acts as the lender's agent in giving the loan papers to the student, filling out the lender's portion of the loan paperwork, helping the student fill out the student portion, and forwarding that paperwork to the lender.[282]

The key question is whether the federal regulatory scheme preempts application of the state or federal common law of *respondeat superior*. Unfortunately for borrowers, the current judicial trend favors federal preemption in these circumstances.[283]

Even if the claim survives preemption, a weakness of the agency approach is that the principal will only be liable for acts within the actual or apparent authority of the agent. This will usually relate to the student's enrollment in the school and not to the school's quality of teaching, equipment, or placement services.

However, the principal should also be responsible for misrepresentations made by the agency. The strength of the agency approach therefore lies in misrepresentation, rather than contract, claims against the school. If the school makes misrepresentations to induce the student to enroll and sign the forms, those misrepresentations can be raised against the lender if the school had actual or apparent authority to make such representations.

Another agency argument is that the school was acting as the Department of Education's agent in administering the HEA and that the Department should thus be estopped from collecting on a loan involving misconduct by its agent.[284] Other common law theories that may be applicable in some states include close connectedness and joint enterprise,[285] and that the enrollment contract and loan papers were integrated contracts, making the breach of the enrollment contract a defense as to enforcement of the loan.[286]

"guarantor." At common law, a guarantor seeking reimbursement from the primary obligor is not subject to that primary obligor's defenses against the lender unless the guarantor had notice of those defenses before it paid off the lender.

There are three principal reasons why the common law rule protecting "guarantors" is not available in the student loan context: (1) At common law, the entities that are labeled "guarantors" would have been considered insurers under the HEA, not guarantors. Insurers were not covered by the rule that foreclosed borrower defenses if the loan was repaid without prior notice of the defense. (2) Even under common law, the rule concerning prior notice was only available when the guarantor was acting to accommodate the borrower because of a relationship with the borrower. That relationship does not exist in the HEA when the guarantor becomes involved because of its contractual relationship with the lender. (3) Guarantors often have actual or constructive notice of the school-related claims before they pay off the insurance claims by the lenders.

280   *See* §§ 5.2.2.3 (tax offset), 5.3.3.2 (garnishment), *supra*.

281   Bank of America, NT & SA v. Riley, 940 F. Supp. 348 (D.D.C. 1996) (HEA's anti-injunctive provision does not apply to a declaratory judgment action against the Secretary), *aff'd*, 132 F.3d 1480 (D.C. Cir. 1997). *See also* Thomas v. Bennett, 856 F.2d 1165 (8th Cir. 1988); Student Loan Marketing Ass'n v. Riley, 907 F. Supp. 464 (D.D.C. 1995), *aff'd and remanded*, 104 F.3d 397 (D.C. 1997); Pro Schools, Inc. v. Riley, 824 F. Supp. 1314 (E.D. Wis. 1993). A number of briefs filed on behalf of students have also persuasively countered the argument that the anti-injunctive provision applies to actions for declaratory relief. *See* § 9.4.1.1, *supra*.

282   *See* Shorter v. Riley, Clearinghouse No. 47,950B (N.D. Ga. Nov. 18, 1993); Hicks v. Riley, Clearinghouse No. 49,133 (N.D. Ga.

May 27, 1993) (plaintiff's motion to approve settlement and brief in support thereof); Tillis v. Bank of America, Clearinghouse No. 49,932 (Cal. Super. Ct. Nov. 17, 1993).

283   *See, e.g.*, Keams v. Tempe Technical Inst., 39 F.3d 222 (9th Cir. 1994), *appeal after remand*, 103 F.3d 138 (9th Cir. 1996), *redesignated as opinion*, 110 F.3d 44 (9th Cir. 1997), *claims against all defendants dismissed*, 16 F. Supp. 2d 1119 (D. Ariz. 1998); Morgan v. Markerdowne Corp., 976 F. Supp. 301 (D.N.J. 1997) (New Jersey's law of agency and close connectedness preempted to the extent they would hold the lenders and guarantors liable for alleged misrepresentations by the school); Crawford v. American Inst. of Prof'l Careers, 934 F. Supp. 335 (D. Ariz. 1996); Bartels v. Alabama Commercial Coll., Inc., 918 F. Supp. 1565 (N.D. Ga. 1995), *aff'd without published opinion*, 189 F.3d 483 (11th Cir. Ga. 1999), *cert. denied*, 528 U.S. 1074 (2000) (only relationship between guarantors or secondary market holders and school were functions required by the HEA; liability based on such functions would conflict with the HEA; court never considered whether there were special functions delegated by the originating lender to the school); Bogart v. Nebraska Student Loan Program, 313 Ark. 656, 858 S.W.2d 78 (1993) (court finds that federal law preempts state law claim based on agency, the students apparently not bringing to court's attention various federal court rulings limiting preemption).

284   Spinner v. Chesapeake Bus. Inst. of Va., Clearinghouse No. 49,131A (E.D. Va. Feb. 5, 1993).

285   Tillis v. Bank of America, Clearinghouse No. 49,932 (Cal. Super. Ct. Nov. 17, 1993).

286   *But see* Bartels v. Alabama Commercial College, Inc., 918 F. Supp. 1565 (S.D. Ga. 1995), *aff'd without published opinion*, 189 F.3d 483 (11th Cir. 1999), *cert. denied*, 528 U.S. 1074

9.6.3.3 State Lender Liability Statutes

A number of states have enacted statutes specifically requiring that lenders be liable for the acts of their related sellers, specifying in some detail the type of relationship between the seller and lender that is sufficient to allow the consumer to raise seller-related defenses on the loan.[287] While these statutes in some states are vague,[288] they still may provide a basis for a student raising school-related defenses to an FFEL.[289]

The major obstacle yet again is federal preemption of the state statutes. In theory, the HEA should not preempt state laws because the Department of Education now requires that student loans provide for the same protection specified in these state laws.[290] Specifically, in post-1994 student loans containing the FTC Holder Notice, lenders should be liable for school-related claims.

Courts have generally agreed that the HEA does not expressly preempt state lender liability statutes and that it does not implicitly preempt the field of lender liability.[291]

Therefore, these state statutes should be preempted only if they are in actual conflict with federal requirements or objectives.[292]

The problem for students is that courts have generally found that some federal requirements or objectives conflict with the state statutory provisions. For example, state statutes finding lenders liable when the loan is conditioned on the proceeds going to a particular purpose or when the lender provides forms to the seller have been considered preempted.[293] These judicial interpretations have far-reaching consequences since the HEA requires all lenders to condition the loan on the student using the money to go to school and all lenders must supply forms to schools.

Even more troubling for student litigants, though, is a judicial trend toward courts finding certain state statutory provisions to conflict with federal "objectives" that are not embodied in any statute or regulation. The 1999 *Armstrong* decision is illustrative of this trend. The loan at issue in that case was made in 1988. The *Armstrong* court refused to

---

(2000); Shorter v. Alexander, Clearinghouse No. 47,950 (N.D. Ga. Dec. 8, 1992).

287 *See generally* National Consumer Law Center, Unfair and Deceptive Acts and Practices § 6.6.4.6 (6th ed. 2004 and Supp.).

288 Armstrong v. Accrediting Council for Continuing Educ. & Training, Inc., 84 F.3d 1452 (D.C. Cir. 1996), *on remand*, 950 F. Supp. 1 (D.D.C. 1996) (court maintained jurisdiction of pendent claims and found case to be appropriate for declaratory relief), *on further remand*, 980 F. Supp. 53 (D.D.C. 1997), *aff'd*, 168 F.3d 1362 (D.C. Cir. 1999) (state law claims preempted by pre-1992 federal policy to protect lenders; in essence, all state law claims prior to 1993 preempted unless there is an origination relationship), *cert. denied*, 528 U.S. 1073 (2000); Jackson v. Culinary Sch. of Washington, Ltd., 811 F. Supp. 714 (D.D.C. 1993) (summary judgment) (state statute required that lender act at express request of seller and seller receive compensation from lender; court found insufficient facts to establish such compensation), *aff'd on other grounds*, 27 F.3d 573 (D.C. Cir. 1994) (court declines to consider complex state law issues in declaratory judgment action), *affirmance vacated*, 115 S. Ct. 2573 (1995) (appellate court used de novo instead of abuse of discretion standard to review district court's decision to decide state law issues in declaratory judgment action), *remanded to district court on state law claims*, 59 F.3d 254 (D.C. Cir. 1995) (to determine on what basis federal court decided to rule on state law issues), *motion dismissed*, 1995 U.S. App. LEXIS 22304 (D.C. Cir. 1995); Williams v. National Sch. of Health Tech., Inc., 836 F. Supp. 273 (E.D. Pa. 1993) (state retail installment sales act applies to loans directly from a seller, not to loans directly from a lender; student loan directly from lender was not structured to avoid this Pennsylvania law but was structured pursuant to federal scheme; consequently, installment sales act does not apply by its very terms and there is no reason to extend statute to third-party student loans).

289 *See* Tipton v. Secretary of Educ., 768 F. Supp. 540 (S.D. W. Va. 1991).

290 *See* § 9.6.2.4, *supra*.

291 *See, e.g.*, Armstrong v. Accrediting Council for Continuing Educ. & Training, Inc., 84 F.3d 1452 (D.C. Cir. 1996), *on remand*, 950 F. Supp. 1 (D.D.C. 1996) (court maintained juris-

diction of pendent claims and found case to be appropriate for declaratory relief), *on further remand*, 980 F. Supp. 53 (D.D.C. 1997), *aff'd*, 168 F.3d 1362 (D.C. Cir. 1999) (state law claims preempted by pre-1992 federal policy to protect lenders; in essence, all state law claims prior to 1993 preempted unless there is an origination relationship), *cert. denied*, 528 U.S. 1073 (2000); Keams v. Tempe Technical Inst., 39 F.3d 222 (9th Cir. 1994), *appeal after remand*, 103 F.3d 138 (9th Cir. 1996), *redesignated as opinion*, 110 F.3d 44 (9th Cir. 1997), *claims against all defendants dismissed*, 16 F. Supp. 2d 1119 (D. Ariz. 1998); Jackson v. Culinary Sch. of Washington, Ltd., 27 F.3d 573 (D.C. Cir. 1994), *vacated on other grounds*, 115 S. Ct. 2573 (1995) (appellate court used de novo instead of abuse of discretion standard to review district court's decision to decide state law issues in declaratory judgment action), *remanded to district court on state law claims*, 59 F.3d 254 (D.C. Cir. 1995) (to determine on what basis federal court decided to rule on state law issues), *motion dismissed*, 1995 U.S. App. LEXIS 22304 (D.C. Cir. 1995); Spinner v. Chesapeake Bus. Inst. of Va., Clearinghouse No. 49,131A (E.D. Va. Feb. 5, 1993); Jackson v. Culinary Sch. of Washington, Ltd., 811 F. Supp. 714 (D.D.C. 1993) (claim dismissed based on summary judgment motion that students had not presented evidence of origination relationship), *aff'd on other grounds*, 27 F.3d 573 (D.C. Cir. 1994) (origination theory not enforceable against the Secretary), *vacated on other grounds*, 115 S. Ct. 2573 (1995) (appellate court used de novo instead of abuse of discretion standard to review district court's decision to decide state law issues in declaratory judgment action), *remanded to district court on state law claims, aff'g own ruling on origination*, 59 F.3d 254 (D.C. Cir. 1995) (to determine on what basis federal court decided to rule on state law issues), *motion dismissed*, 1995 U.S. App. LEXIS 22304 (D.C. Cir. 1995); Hernandez v. Alexander, Clearinghouse No. 46,792 (D. Nev. May 18, 1992); Tipton v. Secretary of Educ., Clearinghouse No. 45,765D (S.D. W. Va. Mar. 31, 1992) (denial of permission for an interlocutory appeal); Tipton v. Secretary of Educ., 768 F. Supp. 540 (S.D. W. Va. 1991); Wilson v. Manufacturers Hanover Trust Co., Clearinghouse No. 45,921 (4th Cir. Sept. 25, 1990). *See* § 9.3.2.1.1, *supra*.

292 *See* § 9.3.2.1.1, *supra*.

293 Tipton v. Secretary of Educ., 768 F. Supp. 540 (S.D. W. Va. 1991).

imply the FTC Holder Rule terms and concluded that state law claims were preempted.[294] The court found that state laws that would allow school-related defenses to be raised against lenders were preempted during the period that the FTC had decided not to enforce the Holder Rule with respect to student loans.[295]

In a blow to student advocates, the court stuck to this position even while acknowledging that the FTC and the Secretary of Education have since concluded that the Holder Rule does apply and that it did apply during this period of non-enforcement.[296] The *Armstrong* court seemed uneasy about the result, acknowledging that students with these older loans are left "holding the bag," but claimed they had no authority to protect the students.[297]

9.6.3.4 Private Remedy for Failure to Include FTC Holder Notice

As described above, all student loans extended on or after January 1, 1994, include a provision based on the FTC Holder Rule allowing students to raise school-related defenses when certain conditions are met.[298] Unfortunately for students, virtually no student loans before that date contained such a provision.

Federal law is clear that many of those pre-1994 FFELs should have included the FTC Holder Notice. The FTC Holder Rule specifies that, when a for-profit seller (such as a proprietary trade school) refers the consumer to a particular lender, then the FTC Holder Notice must be included in the promissory note.

The FTC staff in charge of enforcing the Holder Rule has unambiguously stated that the Holder Rule applies to FFELs.[299]

The Secretary of Education[300] and a 1993 Congressional Conference Report[301] reach the same conclusion. These 1991, 1992, and 1993 interpretations supersede a few earlier courts that ruled otherwise.[302] Subsequent court rulings are in line with the FTC, Department, and Congressional interpretation that the Holder Rule does apply to FFELs.[303]

The problem for students is that, while courts may assume that the FTC Holder Notice should have been included in the GSL note, courts are leery of providing consumers with a *remedy* for the lenders' failure to include that notice. There is no direct private right of action for violation of an FTC Rule.[304] As a result, consumers must use state law theories to claim violations of the FTC Rule. To date, such state law claims have met with limited success.

---

294 Armstrong v. Accrediting Counsel for Continuing Educ. & Training, Inc., 168 F.3d 1362 (D.C. Cir. 1999), *cert. denied*, 528 U.S. 1073 (2000).

295 This period was from 1982 to 1993, or possibly from 1982 to 1991, depending on a court's historical interpretation. The court noted that a common promissory note with the FTC Holder Rule was instituted in 1993, although the FTC began enforcing the Rule again in 1991. Armstrong v. Accrediting Counsel for Continuing Educ. & Training, Inc., 168 F.3d 1362, 1365 (D.C. Cir. 1999), *cert. denied*, 528 U.S. 1073 (2000).

296 Armstrong v. Accrediting Council for Continuing Educ. & Training, Inc., 168 F.3d 1362, 1368 (D.C. Cir. 1999), *cert. denied*, 528 U.S. 1073 (2000).

297 *Id.* at 1370. As discussed below in § 9.6.3.5, the *Armstrong* court indicated that state law claims were not preempted, even during the period of FTC non-enforcement, when the school and lender had an "origination relationship" under federal law.

298 *See* § 9.6.2.4, *supra*. The Federal Trade Commission Trade Regulation Rule Concerning the Preservation of Consumers' Claims and Defenses, 16 C.F.R. § 433, is discussed in detail at National Consumer Law Center, Unfair and Deceptive Acts and Practices § 6.6 (6th ed. 2004 and Supp.).

299 *See* F.T.C. Staff Letter from David Medine, Associate Director for Credit Practices, Clearinghouse No. 47,975 (Feb. 11, 1993); F.T.C. Staff Opinion Letter to Jonathan Sheldon, National Consumer Law Center, Clearinghouse No. 46,752 (July 24, 1991).

These letters reverse a prior letter on the subject, F.T.C. Informal Staff Letter (Esposito), Clearinghouse No. 44,341 (Jan. 9, 1989). The full Federal Trade Commission, while not formally adopting the 1991 staff opinion, did refer to that opinion with apparent approval in 1992. In a Commission decision not to amend the Holder Rule, the Commission stated that "the Commission staff has provided NCLC with an opinion letter stating that such educational loans are not exempt from the Rule." 57 Fed. Reg. 28815, n.11 (June 29, 1992). *But see* Armstrong v. Accrediting Council for Continuing Educ. & Training, Inc., 168 F.3d 1362 (D.C. Cir. 1999), *cert. denied*, 528 U.S. 1073 (2000).

300 The introductory material to the Department's common promissory note, at page 7, states: "The Secretary of Education has determined that the Governing Law and Notices section of the common promissory note must include the Federal Trade Commission (FTC) consumer defense clause as required by the FTC regulations, 16 CFR Section 433.2." *See* Common Application Material and Promissory Note, Clearinghouse No. 47,974 (Apr. 16, 1993).

301 "The Holder Rule applies to student loan borrowers attending for-profit institutions, and the new Federal Family Education Loan promissory note includes the required notice." Omnibus Budget Reconciliation Act of 1993, H.R. 2264 (Conf. Rep.), H.R. Rep. No. 213, 455, 103d Cong. (1st Sess. Aug. 4, 1993). In addition, Congress, in the Higher Education Amendments of 1992, had an opportunity, by adopting the House version, to limit significantly the FTC Holder Rule's applicability to GSLs. Instead, Congress decided to adopt the Senate version that would not limit the Holder Rule's applicability.

302 Veal v. First Am. Savs. Bank, 914 F.2d 909 (7th Cir. 1990). *See also* McVey v. U.S. Training Acad., Clearinghouse No. 44,344 (Bankr. E.D. Ky. Aug. 25, 1988); Molina v. Crown Bus. Inst., Clearinghouse No. 45,920 (N.Y. Sup. Ct. 1990).

303 *See, e.g.,* Morgan v. Markerdowne Corp., 976 F. Supp. 301 (D.N.J. 1997); Jackson v. Culinary Sch. of Washington, Ltd., 788 F. Supp. 1233 (D.D.C. 1992) (see note 145, *supra*, for subsequent history). *See also* Spinner v. Chesapeake Bus. Inst. of Va., Clearinghouse No. 49,131A (E.D. Va. Feb. 5, 1993); C. Mansfield, *The Federal Trade Commission Holder Rule and its Applicability to Student Loans—Re-Allocating the Risk of Proprietary School Failure*, 26 Wake Forest L. Rev. 635 (1991). *But cf.* Hernandez v. Alexander, Clearinghouse No. 46,792 (D. Nev. May 18, 1992).

304 *See* National Consumer Law Center, Unfair and Deceptive Acts and Practices § 6.6.2 (6th ed. 2004 and Supp.).

In other contexts, courts have had little difficulty finding a violation of an FTC Rule to be a state UDAP violation.[305] Yet in the student loan context, courts have usually found ways to avoid UDAP liability for FFELs violating the FTC Holder Rule.[306]

Despite this judicial reluctance, in many states a consumer should be able to challenge a lender's systematic failure to comply with the FTC Holder Rule as a state UDAP violation.[307] This is particularly the case for loans entered into after April 16, 1993, when the Department of Education announced to lenders and guarantors that the FTC Holder Rule applies to student loans.[308] Lenders after that date had no excuse not to include the Holder Notice in their promissory notes, when applicable.

Another approach is to seek to enforce the Holder language as an implied term in the note even though the notice is not present.[309] This approach has not been successful in the student loan context.[310] Also not successful to date has been the argument that the lender should be estopped from taking advantage of the illegality in the note or that an illegal note cannot be enforced.[311]

It may also be possible to argue that the note without the FTC Holder Rule is unconscionable and thus unenforceable or that the Department, guaranty agency, or the lender had a fiduciary duty to the borrower or were engaged in constructive fraud. At least one federal court rejected the fiduciary duty argument but let go to trial both the arguments that the note involved constructive fraud and was unconscionable.[312] A RICO claim is another possibility.[313] Failure to include the FTC holder notice is a growing problem among private student lenders.[314]

9.6.3.5 Origination Theory

The Secretary of Education recognizes that students can raise school-related defenses to FFEL collection actions

---

305 *See generally* National Consumer Law Center, Unfair and Deceptive Acts and Practices § 6.6.4.4 (6th ed. 2004 and Supp.).

306 *See, e.g.,* Armstrong v. Accrediting Council for Continuing Educ. & Training, Inc., 84 F.3d 1452 (D.C. Cir. 1996), *on remand,* 950 F. Supp. 1 (D.D.C. 1996) (court maintained jurisdiction of pendent claims and found case to be appropriate for declaratory relief), *on further remand,* 980 F. Supp. 53 (D.D.C. 1997) (court determined that California law controls and invited plaintiff to amend complaint to assert claims and defenses under California consumer protection laws), *aff'd,* 168 F.3d 1362 (D.C. Cir. 1999) (affirming district court's dismissal of claims), *cert. denied,* 528 U.S. 1073 (2000); Keams v. Tempe Technical Inst., Inc., 993 F. Supp. 714 (D. Ariz. 1997) (since student loan contracts did not include terms of Holder Rule, former vocational school students were not able to assert claims and defenses arising from school's behavior against assignee), *claims against all defendants dismissed,* 16 F. Supp. 2d 1119 (D. Ariz. 1998); Morgan v. Markerdowne Corp., 976 F. Supp. 301 (D.N.J. 1997); United States v. Ornecipe, Clearinghouse No. 51,941 (S.D. Fla. 1995) (Florida UDAP statute does not apply to banks); Jackson v. Culinary Sch. of Washington, Ltd., 811 F. Supp. 714 (D.D.C. 1993) (summary judgment) (court found insufficient facts to find UDAP liability), *aff'd on other grounds,* 27 F.3d 573 (D.C. Cir. 1994) (court declined to consider complex state law issue in declaratory judgment action), *vacated,* 115 S. Ct. 2573 (1995) (appellate court used de novo instead of abuse of discretion standard to review district court's decision to decide state law issues in declaratory judgment action), *remanded to district court on state law claims,* 59 F.3d 254 (D.C. Cir. 1995) (to determine on what basis federal court decided to rule on state law issues), *motion dismissed,* 1995 U.S. App. LEXIS 22304 (D.C. Cir. 1995); Williams v. National Sch. of Health Tech., Inc., 836 F. Supp. 273 (E.D. Pa. 1993) (United States committed no wrongdoing, so no UDAP violation; court failed to consider that lender did engage in wrongdoing and that the United States is an assignee of the lender); Spinner v. Chesapeake Bus. Inst. of Va., Clearinghouse No. 49,131A (E.D. Va. Feb. 5, 1993) (UDAP statute exempted practices authorized by federal laws or regulations and the court determined that the student loan contracts were authorized); Hernandez v. Alexander, Clearinghouse No. 46,792 (D. Nev. May 18, 1992). *But see* Keams v. Tempe Technical Inst., Inc., Clearinghouse No. 41,793J (D. Ariz. Oct. 19, 1995).

307 *See* Keams v. Tempe Technical Inst., 39 F.3d 222 (9th Cir. 1994), *appeal after remand,* 103 F.3d 138 (9th Cir. 1996), *redesignated as opinion,* 110 F.3d 44 (9th Cir. 1997), *claims against all defendants dismissed,* 16 F. Supp. 2d 1119 (D. Ariz. 1998); Jackson v. Culinary Sch. of Washington, Ltd., 788 F. Supp. 1233 (D.D.C. 1992) (see note 145, *supra,* for the subsequent history in this case); Shorter v. Alexander, Clearinghouse No. 47,950 (N.D. Ga. Dec. 8, 1992). *But see* Armand v. Secretary of Educ., Clearinghouse No. 51,298 (S.D. Fla. July 19, 1995) (Florida UDAP statute does not apply to banks).

308 Common Application Material and Promissory Note, Clearinghouse No. 47,974 (Apr. 16, 1993).

309 *See* Anderson v. Central States Waterproofing, Clearinghouse No. 40,627 (Minn. Dist. Ct. Hennepin Cty. 1982). *See also* White, *Coping with Violations of the Federal Trade Commission's Holder In Due Course Rule,* 66 Temple L. Rev. 661 (1993).

310 Armstrong v. Accrediting Council for Continuing Educ. & Training, Inc., 84 F.3d 1452 (D.C. Cir. 1996), *on remand,* 950 F. Supp. 1 (D.D.C. 1996), *on further remand,* 980 F. Supp. 53 (D.D.C. 1997), *aff'd,* 168 F.3d 1362 (D.C. Cir. 1999), *cert. denied,* 528 U.S. 1073 (2000); Lee v. Riley, Clearinghouse No. 52,041 (W.D. Ky. Feb. 27, 1998) (memorandum opinion); Bartels v. Alabama Commercial Coll., Inc., 918 F. Supp. 1565 (S.D. Ga. 1995), *rev'd on other grounds,* 54 F.3d 702 (11th Cir. 1995); Spinner v. Chesapeake Bus. Inst. of Va., Clearinghouse No. 49,131A (E.D. Va. Feb. 5, 1993); Jackson v. Culinary Sch. of Washington, Ltd., 788 F. Supp. 1233 (D.D.C. 1992) (see note 145, *supra,* for subsequent history in this case); Hernandez v. Alexander, Clearinghouse No. 46,792 (D. Nev. May 18, 1992); Shorter v. Alexander, Clearinghouse No. 47,950 (N.D. Ga. Dec. 8, 1992).

311 Armstrong v. Accrediting Council for Continuing Educ. & Training, Inc., 84 F.3d 1452 (D.C. Cir. 1996), *on remand,* 950 F. Supp. 1 (D.D.C. 1996), *on further remand,* 980 F. Supp. 53 (D.D.C. 1997), *aff'd,* 168 F.3d 1362 (D.C. Cir. 1999), *cert. denied,* 528 U.S. 1073 (2000); Spinner v. Chesapeake Bus. Inst. of Va., Clearinghouse No. 49,131A (E.D. Va. Feb. 5, 1993).

312 Spinner v. Chesapeake Bus. Inst. of Va., Clearinghouse No. 49,131A (E.D. Va. Feb. 5, 1993).

313 *See* §§ 9.3.2.3, 9.3.3.1 (federal RICO claims), 9.3.4.1 (state RICO claims), *supra.*

314 *See* § 1.5.1, *supra.*

when the school is in an "origination relationship" with the lender.[315] Therefore, if an origination relationship can be proven, even loans from the period prior to the inclusion of the FTC Holder Notice should be subject to school-related defenses. The *Armstrong* court affirmed this concept, citing the origination relationship as a major exception to lenders' protection from student suits prior to re-enforcement of the FTC Holder Rule.[316]

Unfortunately for students, the District of Columbia Circuit has ruled that the Secretary has not sufficiently communicated an intention to be bound by the origination policy so as to create a legally enforceable right grounded in federal law.[317] The *Armstrong* decision, however, indicates that, if there was an origination relationship, a state law theory of lender liability would not be preempted even during the period of FTC non-enforcement.[318]

Some courts have found the origination theory binding on the Department and guarantors,[319] based on the Department's statements that it expects guaranty agencies not to collect unenforceable loans when an origination relationship exists.[320] Other courts find that, even if the Department's statements are binding on the Department, the statements have never been promulgated as a rule and are not binding on guarantors.[321]

If a court allows a consumer to raise defenses when there is an origination relationship, the next step is to present sufficient proof of the relationship. Department regulations define origination as a special relationship in which the lender delegates to the school substantial functions normally performed by lenders.[322] The regulations also, until 1994, gave three examples in which the Secretary determined that an origination relationship exists:

- the school determines who receives a loan and the amount of the loan;
- the lender has the school verify the identity of the borrower; *or*
- the lender has the school complete forms normally completed by the lender.[323]

The burden of proving this relationship is on the student.[324]

---

315 A good enunciation of this policy is found in a letter from Acting Assistant Secretary Whitehead to Congressman Stephen Solarz, Clearinghouse No. 44,343 (May 19, 1988). In addition, a recent Department of Education regulation requires schools to warn students that students cannot raise school-related defenses against lenders "other than a loan made or originated by the school." 34 C.F.R. § 682.604(f)(2)(iii). Also see 41 Fed. Reg. 4,496 (Jan. 29, 1976) for an explanation of the origins of this policy.

One early case dismissed the origination theory as applied to GSL because the plaintiffs had mistakenly relied on FISL regulations. *See* Veal v. First American Savs. Bank, 914 F.2d 909 (7th Cir. 1990). The Department itself has stated that, while the FISL regulations do not regulate GSLs, the origination theory is independently applicable to GSLs. Letter from Fred J. Marinucci, U.S. Department of Education Office of General Counsel, to the Honorable John T. Copenhaver, Jr., federal district court judge, Clearinghouse No. 45,919 (Nov. 9, 1990).

316 Armstrong v. Accrediting Council for Continuing Educ. & Training, 168 F.3d 1362, 1365 (D.C. Cir. 1999) (as long as lenders avoided school origination relationships, they could make and sell loans without fear that students could assert school misconduct as a defense against repaying their loans), *cert. denied*, 528 U.S. 1073 (2000); Morgan v. Markerdowne Corp., 976 F. Supp. 301 (D.N.J. 1997) (origination relationship between lender and school subjects lenders and guarantors to school-related defenses).

317 Jackson v. Culinary Sch. of Washington, Ltd., 27 F.3d 573 (D.C. Cir. 1994), *vacated on other grounds*, 115 S. Ct. 2573 (1995) (appellate court used de novo instead of abuse of discretion standard to review district court's decision to decide state law issues in declaratory judgment action), *remanded to district court on state law claims, aff'g ruling on origination*, 59 F.3d 254 (D.C. Cir. 1995) (to determine on what basis federal court decided to rule on state law issues), *motion dismissed*, 1995 U.S. App. LEXIS 22304 (D.C. Cir. 1995); Williams v. National Sch. of Health Tech., Inc. 836 F. Supp. 273 (E.D. Pa. 1993), *aff'd without opinion*, 37 F.3d 1491 (3d Cir. 1994). *See also* Bartels v. Alabama Commercial Coll., Inc., 918 F. Supp. 1565 (S.D. Ga. 1995), *aff'd without published opinion*, 189 F.3d 483 (11th Cir. Ga. 1999), *cert. denied*, 528 U.S. 1074 (2000).

318 *See* § 9.6.3.3, *supra*. Armstrong v. Accrediting Council for Continuing Educ. & Training, Inc., 168 F.3d 1362 (D.C. Cir. 1999), *cert. denied*, 528 U.S. 1073 (2000).

319 Morgan v. Markerdowne Corp., 976 F. Supp. 301 (D.N.J. 1997); Tipton v. Secretary of Educ., 768 F. Supp. 540 (S.D. W. Va. 1991). *See also* Hernandez v. Alexander, Clearinghouse No. 46,792 (D. Nev. May 18, 1992); Alberto v. School of Bus. Machs., Clearinghouse No. 46,755 (N.J. Super. Ct. July 26, 1991). *Cf.* Plaintiff's Opposition to Motions to Dismiss of Defendants Bank of America, California Student Loan Finance Corp., the Higher Education Assistance Foundation, and the Secretary of Education, Armstrong v. Accrediting Council for Continuing Educ. & Training, Inc., Clearinghouse No. 46,789 (D.D.C. filed Apr. 1, 1992).

320 *See, e.g.*, Letter from Acting Assistant Secretary Whitehead to Congressman Stephen Solarz, Clearinghouse No. 44,343 (May 19, 1988).

321 Armstrong v. Accrediting Council for Continuing Educ. & Training, Inc., 84 F.3d 1452 (D.C. Cir. 1996), *on remand*, 950 F. Supp. 1 (D.D.C. 1996), *on further remand*, 980 F. Supp. 53 (D.D.C. 1997), *aff'd*, 168 F.3d 1362 (D.C. Cir. 1999) (affirming district court's dismissal of claims), *cert. denied*, 528 U.S. 1073 (2000); Bartels v. Alabama Commercial Coll., Inc., 918 F. Supp. 1565 (S.D. Ga. 1995), *aff'd without published opinion*, 189 F.3d 483 (11th Cir. 1999), *cert. denied*, 528 U.S. 1074 (2000); Williams v. National Sch. of Health Tech., Inc., 836 F. Supp. 273 (E.D. Pa. 1993); Spinner v. Chesapeake Bus. Inst. of Va., Clearinghouse No. 49,131A (E.D. Va. Feb. 5, 1993); Shorter v. Alexander, Clearinghouse No. 47,950 (N.D. Ga. Dec. 8, 1992).

322 34 C.F.R. § 682.200(b) ("Origination").

323 *Id.* Morgan v. Markerdowne Corp., 976 F. Supp. 301 (D.N.J. 1997) (origination relationship existed when school chose the banks from which borrowers would obtain financing, obtained all of the necessary financial papers, either completed the papers or assisted borrowers in completing the papers, verified borrowers' information, and had borrowers sign the documents).

324 Jackson v. Culinary Sch. of Washington, Ltd., 811 F. Supp. 714 (D.D.C. 1993) (claim dismissed based on summary judgment

9.6.3.6 Ineligible School

When a guaranty agency or the Department is seeking collection on a guaranteed loan, a possible defense is that the loan never should have been guaranteed and that the guarantor or the Department should not be collecting on the loan.[325]

In certain cases, the school was not an eligible institution when the loan was extended, so under federal law the loan was not eligible for a federal guarantee. More common is the situation in which the Department recognized a school as eligible when the school should not in fact have been found to be eligible. No court has yet found this as a basis to refuse to enforce an FFEL.[326] In addition, there are an increasing number of cases in which schools that are ineligible to participate in the federal student assistance programs stay in business by steering students to private loan products.[327]

9.6.4 Raising School-Related Defenses when FFELs Have Lost Their Guaranteed Status

An FFEL may lose its guaranteed status if a lender does not exercise due diligence, if the school was not an eligible institution, or for some other reason. While the promissory note between the lender and student will not be automatically cancelled, the guaranty agency and the United States no longer back up the loan. Typically the lender will sell the loan to some private entity, and that entity (not a guaranty agency) will try to collect from the student on the loan.

When this private entity collects on what is now a private loan, state laws should apply as to the loan's enforceability. The state's applicable statute of limitations should apply. State common law and statutory theories of lender liability should also apply. There can no longer be any issue of preemption of state law because of a conflict with the HEA, since the loan is no longer part of the federal program.

The FTC Holder Rule should be inserted in the loan as well, and there is no excuse that the guaranty agency or the United States approved of a loan without such notice, since this is no longer a guaranteed loan. Thus state remedies for failure to comply with the Holder Notice should apply as well.

If the FFEL lost its guaranteed status because the school was never an eligible program, this should be raised as a defense on any collection of the now non-guaranteed loan. The school was almost certainly the original lender's agent in signing the student up for the school. The school's fraud in signing the student up for an ineligible loan should be imputed to its principal and thus to all subsequent assignees of the loan.[328]

Moreover, if the loan lost its guaranteed status because of the lender's lack of due diligence, it may be possible to argue that this lack of due diligence also acts as a defense to the student's obligation to pay the loan.[329] Such loans may also be dischargeable in bankruptcy even though the loan does not meet the substantial hardship test because the loan is not insured by a government unit.[330] Even though a loan has lost its guaranteed status, the Department has stated that the student is still eligible for a closed-school or false-certification discharge.[331]

9.6.5 Raising School-Related Defenses After Loan Has Been Consolidated

A loan consolidation has significant benefits for most student loan borrowers in default.[332] However, one problem is that consolidating a student loan may make it more

---

motion that students had not presented evidence of origination relationship), *aff'd on other grounds*, 27 F.3d 573 (D.C. Cir. 1994) (origination theory not enforceable against the Secretary), *vacated on other grounds*, 115 S. Ct. 2573 (1995) (appellate court used de novo instead of abuse of discretion standard to review district court's decision to decide state law issues in declaratory judgment action), *remanded to district court on state law claims, aff'g own ruling on origination*, 59 F.3d 254 (D.C. Cir. 1995) (to determine on what basis federal court decided to rule on state law issues), *motion dismissed*, 1995 U.S. App. LEXIS 22304 (D.C. Cir. 1995); Hernandez v. Alexander, 845 F. Supp. 1417 (D. Nev. 1993) (not sufficient to allege that school determined amount of loan requested but not of loan actually lent, verified identity of borrower—there being no requirement that lender verify borrower's identity—and filled in portions of note normally filled in by student and school but not by lender). *See also* Armand v. Secretary of Educ., Clearinghouse No. 51,298 (S.D. Fla. July 19, 1995). *But cf.* Shorter v. Riley, Clearinghouse No. 47,950B (N.D. Ga. Nov. 18, 1993) (question of whether there is an origination relationship must be decided at trial and not based on either sides' summary judgment motions).

325 See § 9.6.4, *infra*, for a discussion of loans that have lost their guaranteed status.

326 *But see* Hernandez v. Alexander, Clearinghouse No. 46,792 (D. Nev. May 18, 1992) (court appears to accept argument that loan could be unenforceable because school was improperly certified as eligible).

327 *See* § 1.5, *supra*.

328 *See* § 9.6.3.2, *supra*.

329 *See* United States v. Rhodes, 788 F. Supp. 339 (E.D. Mich. 1992). *But see* United States v. Gould, 2006 WL 1522071 (E.D. Mich. May 30, 2006); United States v. Lewis 2001 WL 789224 (D. Kan. June 29, 2001) (borrower may not invoke the lender's due diligence obligations against the United States on her own behalf); Vanderbilt Univ. v. Henderson, 2001 WL 1216980 (Tenn. Ct. App. Oct. 12, 2001) (borrowers cannot use the statutes and regulations governing the administration of the NDSL program to defend against University's collection efforts). Also see the discussion in 71 Fed. Reg. 45777, 45677 (Aug. 9, 2006).

330 *Id.*

331 Dear Colleague Letter 94-G-256, Clearinghouse No. 50,422 (Sept. 1994).

332 *See* § 8.2, *supra*.

difficult to raise school-related defenses on that loan. The lender may argue that the new consolidated loan is a novation and that defenses to the old loan do not apply to the new loan. Even though the post-1994 FFEL loans contain the FTC Holder Notice, the Direct consolidation loan does not.

At least one federal court has rejected this argument, holding instead that a student does not waive his or her defenses to an original student loan by exchanging that loan for a federal consolidation loan.[333] The court found insufficient policy grounds to rule as a matter of law that the consolidation was a new loan extinguishing defenses to the old loan. The court also found unpersuasive the language in the loan consolidation that explicitly stated that the borrower was waiving all defenses on the original loan. The court found the waiver language not sufficiently conspicuous and not based on a knowing and voluntary agreement. The court found that there was no novation because there was no mutual agreement that the student was waiving defenses.

Another argument why a consolidation loan does not waive student defenses is that the Department of Education has stated that the student can continue, despite the consolidation, to apply for a closed-school, unpaid-refund, or false-certification discharge.[334] The policy grounds for the ability to continue raising school-related defenses should apply with equal force.

9.7 Issues Unique to Private Student Loans

Schools that are not eligible to participate in federal loan programs or do not wish to follow the federal rules may decide instead to work with private student lenders. This strategy raises a number of concerns. First, many students may be steered to private loan products even though they may qualify for more affordable federal loans. Second, private loan borrowers who attend "scam" schools will not have the same remedies as federal loan borrowers if problems arise.

A 2003 survey of twenty-three members of the National Association of State Administrators and Supervisors of Private Schools showed that, in 2002, over one hundred computer schools closed in their states.[335] Of those schools, only twenty-five gave any advance notice of the closing.[336] This study is extremely limited because it does not include states such as California, Virginia, North Carolina, and Florida that have suffered extensive closings. For example,

in 2003, officials with the North Carolina Community College System identified approximately 300 unlicensed trade schools operating in that state.[337]

Banks and other financial institutions make private student loans without any direct financial backing from the federal government. They are not subsidized, meaning that interest starts to accrue at the time the loans are obtained. There are many different types of private loans, each program with specific rules and requirements. Private loans are also known as private-label or alternative loans.

The private student loan business has experienced tremendous growth in recent years. Despite the boom in private lending, the vast majority of students still borrow primarily federal loan products. However, private loan products are coming on strong. Private borrowing by students rose to about $5 billion in 2001–2002, up from about $1 billion in 1995–1996.[338] The total volume of private loans has surpassed the amounts awarded annually under the Federal Student Education Opportunity Grant, Work-Study, and Perkins Loan programs combined.[339]

A 2003 report found that private loans comprise about 10% of total student loan volume. The percentage is much higher among professional students, 16% of whom borrowed private loans during 1999–2000.[340] Overall, the number of private loan products grew from 79 in March 1997 to 272 in March 2003, an increase of 244%.[341]

Recent cases against Sallie Mae illustrate some of the claims that have arisen in private student loan cases.[342] SLM Corporation, commonly known as Sallie Mae, is one of the largest private lenders, selling products for all types of student borrowers (www.salliemae.com).[343] The plaintiffs

---

333 Crawford v. The American Inst. of Prof'l Careers, Inc., 934 F. Supp. 335 (D. Ariz. 1996).

334 *See, e.g.,* § 6.2.1, *supra.*

335 Nat'l Ass'n of State Adm'rs and Supervisors of Private Schs., *2003 Survey of Members of the National Association of State Administrators and Supervisors of Private Schools: Computer Schools,* at www.nasasps.com/Computer-Survey-NASASPS-4-22-03.pdf (last accessed in October 2006).

336 *Id.*

337 Tom Domonoske, Nat'l Assoc. of Consumer Advocates, *The Finance Industry Fuels Revival of Trade School Scams,* Consumer Advocate, No. 4 (Oct./Nov./Dec. 2003).

338 Kate Rube, State PIRGS' Higher Educ. Project, Private Loans Who's Borrowing and Why (Apr. 2003). The study also found that private borrowing at for-profit institutions was higher than at public institutions. At less-than-two-year institutions, the average private loan was $6095.

339 Inst. for Higher Educ. Policy, Private Loans and Choice in Financing in Higher Education (2003), *available at* www.ihep.com. Pubs/PDF/PvtLoans.pdf and on the companion CD-Rom to this manual.

340 *Id.* at 33.

341 *Id.* at 14.

342 The complaint in one class action, *Barnes v. SLM Financial Corporation,* is included in Appendix E.7.1, *infra,* and is also included, along with another complaint against SLM, on the companion CD-Rom to this manual.

343 Sallie Mae was founded in 1972 as a government-sponsored enterprise and was initially a secondary market resource for student loans. In 1997, the company began a privatization process and started expanding into new areas. SLM Financial Corporation was established as a wholly owned subsidiary of Sallie Mae in 1999 to sell non-federal loans. According to Sallie Mae, the government-sponsored enterprise model will be fully phased out by 2006 and the company will be fully privatized at that point. Sallie Mae owns and manages federal loans and also

allege that SLM has arrangements with certain schools that allow them to market its private loan products. In some cases, these schools are not properly licensed or certified. The plaintiffs further allege that SLM uses the schools to solicit loans and then place the loans with banks. Sallie Mae immediately purchases the loans back and engages in collection efforts on the loans.

The plaintiffs raise a number of federal and state causes of action, including violations of the federal Truth in Lending Act for improper loan disclosures, violations of the Equal Credit Opportunity Act, as well as RICO and UDAP violations. Because the loans are private, the Truth in Lending Act's exemption for government-backed loans does not apply.[344]

The plaintiffs also allege that SLM intentionally denies borrowers the benefits of the Federal Trade Commission Holder Rule. Although the Holder notice is included in at least some contracts, these loan contracts contradict the notice by stating that, if the student is dissatisfied with the school or fails to complete the course, the student still must repay the note in full. Thus, SLM denies all responsibility for school-related claims. Among other school-related claims, the plaintiffs allege that schools have operated without proper licensing, falsely and illegally guaranteed jobs, and failed to provide proper equipment or materials. Other allegations include deceptive representations that the loan contracts were final when, in fact, the terms and amount were subject to SLM approval and could be altered later in the process.

By structuring the loans such that the Sallie Mae subsidiary arranges but does not initially fund the loan, Sallie Mae may also be subjecting itself to a number of state credit repair statutes that apply to those who assist consumers in obtaining loans for a fee.[345] These statutes tend to have very strong private remedies and detailed substantive requirements.[346]

If a court views SLM not as a loan arranger but as the actual lender—such that the credit repair statute does not apply—then the court should find that state laws regulating lenders apply. It is also possible that a sham relationship with an out-of-state bank and the alleged misrepresentation that the original loan was with Sallie Mae may be seen as an unfair or deceptive attempt to confuse students with regard to the identity of the lender or even as a means to evade state usury laws. According to one of the lawyers involved in cases against SLM, Sallie Mae has reported that it no longer provides loans to unlicensed schools or the full amount of the tuition up-front for a sequence of courses.[347]

Keybank has also been sued for similar practices. In the Sallie Mae cases, borrowers have challenged the lender's practice of including the FTC Holder Rule in promissory notes but then contradicting the notice in supplementary documents. In contrast, in the Keybank cases, the plaintiffs challenge the bank's refusal to even include the notice in the first place. Keybank's legal justification is that the FTC does not regulate banks and the bank bears no responsibility for the schools' violation of the Holder Rule.[348] At least one court, in *Abel v. Keybank U.S.A.*, has agreed with the bank's justification.[349] In this case, the plaintiff sued the bank under a state law provision that grants consumers the right to assert the protections of the Holder notice regardless of whether the notice is included in the note or contract. The court found that the National Bank Act and corresponding federal regulations preempted the state law provision.[350] The court found that this type of state-imposed liability significantly interferes with a national bank's ability to negotiate promissory notes and lend money.[351]

However, another district court disagreed with this result. The court noted that the *Abel* decision cites cases involving state laws that were either significantly more burdensome or more directly controlling than in the present case in which the state retail installment act does not directly control the federal bank activity.[352] The court noted that the plaintiffs

---

sells private loans. The company has expanded into these areas, often by acquiring other entities. For example, in 1999, Sallie Mae acquired Nellie Mae in order to begin originating student loans. It merged with USA Group in 2000 and acquired Student Loan Funding, increasing the company's loan portfolio by about 20%. A merger with a higher education consulting firm led to a greater presence in guarantee servicing and debt management. The company also acquired two collection agencies, General Revenue Corporation and Pioneer Credit Recovery, to help in its growing student loan collection business. For more information, see www.salliemae.com. SLM is a major player in the loan consolidation market as well. *See* Ch. 8, *infra*. In August 2004, Sallie Mae announced that it had offered to buy, for cash, $4.3 billion of its Student Loan Marketing Association subsidiary's debt in a major step toward privatizing the company. According to Salle Mae officials, the company is on track to fully convert to a private-sector company in early 2005. *See* Bureau of Nat'l Affairs, *Salle Mae Offers to Buy for Cash Subsidiary's Debt, Privatizing Company*, 83 Banking Report, No. 5 (Aug. 2, 2004). *See also* Albert B. Crenshaw, *Student Loans Are Private Affairs: Sallie Mae Cleaned Up When It Cut Public Ties*, Wash. Post, Nov. 22, 2004.

344 15 U.S.C. § 1603; Reg. Z § 226.3(f). *See* National Consumer Law Center, Truth in Lending § 2.4.5.2 (5th ed. 2003 and Supp.).

345 *See* National Consumer Law Center, Fair Credit Reporting Appx. B (5th ed. 2002 and Supp.).

346 *Id.* at Ch. 15.

347 Tom Domonoske, Nat'l Assoc. of Consumer Advocates, *The Finance Industry Fuels Revival of Trade School Scams*, 9 Consumer Advocate, No. 4 (Oct./Nov./Dec. 2003).

348 For more information about enforcing the FTC Holder Rule, see National Consumer Law Center, Unfair and Deceptive Acts and Practices § 6.6 (6th ed. 2004 and Supp.).

349 Abel v. Keybank U.S.A., 313 F. Supp. 2d 720 (N.D. Ohio Mar. 3, 2004).

350 *Id.*

351 For a detailed discussion of preemption and national banks, see National Consumer Law Center, The Cost of Credit: Regulation, Preemption, and Industry Abuses § 3.4.6 (3d ed. 2005 and Supp.).

352 Blanco v. Keybank USA, 2005 WL 4135013 (N.D. Ohio Sept.

are not suggesting that the retail installment act prohibits banks from negotiating promissory notes. Rather, "it would have the incidental effect of encouraging all lenders—national or otherwise—to engage in a closer risk analysis in purchasing consumer promissory notes."[353] The court also agreed with the plaintiff's argument that the Federal Trade Commission "holder rule" should be used to interpret the preemptive scope of the National Bank Act narrowly.

9.8 Student Claims Against Tuition Recovery Funds

9.8.1 General

State tuition recovery funds (STRFs) can be a valuable source of relief for defrauded students when a school is insolvent and when the student cannot obtain a closed-school or false-certification discharge. STRFs contain deposits of money collected from schools approved to operate in the state. The funds are disbursed to victimized students under specified conditions.

Many states have either an STRF or a bond program to reimburse defrauded students. States with STRFs tend to have two different funds—one for degree-granting institutions and one for schools that offer non-degree-granting vocational programs.[354]

The STRF is an important student remedy because it will provide relief in situations in which defrauded students cannot obtain a closed-school, unpaid-refund, or false-certification discharge. The California STRF, for example, will pay claims when a student ceased attending a school because of a breach or anticipatory breach of the agreement for the course of instruction.[355] The California STRF also pro-

---

353   *Id.*

354   The following is a fairly current list of states that have STRFs, including contact information:

Arizona: Student Tuition Recovery Fund, Arizona State Board for Private Postsecondary Education, 1401 W. Washington, Room 260, Phoenix, AZ 85007; 602-542-5709.

Arkansas: State Board of Higher Education, 114 E. Capital, Little Rock, Ark. 72201; 501-371-2000.

California: Bureau for Private Postsecondary and Vocational Education, California Department of Consumer Affairs, Student Tuition Recovery Fund, 1625 North Market Blvd., Suite S202, Sacramento, CA 95834; 916-574-7720.

Connecticut: Department of Higher Education, P.O. Box 2219, Hartford, CT 06145.

Delaware: Department of Education, 401 Federal St., P.O. Box 1402, Dover, DE 19903-1402; 302-739-4601.

Florida: Florida Student Protection Fund, Florida Department of Education, Commission for Independent Education, 944 Turlington Bldg., 325 W. Gaines St., Tallahassee, FL 32399.

Georgia: Tuition Guaranteed Trust Fund, 2189 N. Lake Pkwy, Bldg. 10, Suite 100, Tucker, GA 30084; 770-414-3300.
Non-Public Post Secondary Commission, 2100 E. Exchange Pl. #203, Tucker, GA 30303; 770-414-3302.

Idaho: Student Tuition Recovery Account, Board of Education, P.O. Box 83720, Boise, ID 83720; 208-334-2270.

Kentucky: Student Protection Fund, State Board for Proprietary Education, P.O. Box 1360, Frankfort, KY 40602; 502-564-3296, x227.

Louisiana: Student Protection Fund, P.O. Box 94064, Baton Rouge, LA 70804-4064.

Maryland: Guaranty Student Tuition Fund, Maryland Higher Education Commission, 839 Bestgate Rd., Suite 400, Annapolis, MD 21401; 410-260-4500.

Massachusetts: Board of Cosmetology, 239 Causeway Street, Boston, MA 02114; 617-727-3067.
Board of Higher Education, One Ashburton Pl, Suite 1401, Boston, MA 02108; 617-727-7785.
Private Postsecondary Schools, 350 Main St., Malden, MA 02148.

Nebraska: Department of Education, 310 Centennial Mall South, Lincoln, NE 68509; 402-471-2295.

Nevada: Student Indemnification Account, Nevada Commission on Postsecondary Education, 1820 East Sahara Ave., Suite 111, Las Vegas, NV 89104; 702-486-7330.

New Mexico: Post-Secondary Educational Institution Fund, Higher Education Department, 1068 Cerrillos Rd., Santa Fe, NM 87505; 505-476-6500.

New York: Tuition Reimbursement Account, 116 W. 32d St., 14th Floor, New York, NY 10001; 212-643-4760.

Ohio: Student Tuition Recovery Fund, Student Tuition Recovery Authority, c/o State Board of Career Colleges and Schools, 35 East Gay St., Suite 403, Columbus, OH 43215; 614-446-2752.

Oklahoma: Board of Private Vocational Schools, 2200 North Classen Blvd., Oklahoma City, OK 73106; 405-521-2225.

Oregon: Tuition Protection Fund, Education Department, 255 Capital Street, NE, Salem, OR 97310-0203; 503-378-3600; www.ode.state.or.us.

Tennessee: Tuition Guarantee Fund, 404 James Robertson Parkway, Suite 1900, Nashville, TN 37243; 615-741-5293.

Texas: Tuition Trust Account, Texas Workforce Commission, Career Schools and Colleges, 101 East 15th St., Austin, TX 78778; 512-936-3100.

Vermont: Career and Lifelong Learning Department, 120 State St., Montpelier, VT 05620; 802-828-5139.
Vermont State Board of Cosmetology, 109 State St., Montpelier, VT 05609; 802-828-2373.

Virginia: Student Tuition Recovery Fund, P.O. Box 2120, Richmond, VA 23218; 804-225-2848.

Washington: Tuition Recovery Trust Fund, Workforce Training and Education Coordinating Board, 128 10th Ave., S.W., P.O. Box 43105, Olympia, WA 98504-3105; 360-753-5662.

355   Cal. Educ. Code § 94944(a)(1)(A)(iv). The Act is scheduled to be repealed as of January 1, 2008. *See* Cal. Educ. Code § 94999.

30, 2005) (National Banking Act does not preempt the state RISA).

vides relief for students who have obtained judgments against schools for violations of the state student protection act provisions but are unable to collect the judgment after diligent efforts.[356] The operation of STRFs varies significantly by state. Advocates will need to contact their own state regulatory agency concerning detailed information on their STRF.

9.8.2 Relationship of STRF to Closed-School and False-Certification Discharges

Quite often students entitled to relief under an STRF are also entitled under federal law to a school-related discharge.[357] For example, the California STRF pays claims to students who suffered losses as a result of the closure of an institution.[358]

Students entitled to recovery under the STRF and a federal discharge provision can expect to be placed in the middle of a tug-a-war between the state agency and the Department, as each agency tries to have the other pay for the student's loss. For example, the Department's closed-school regulations require students to specify whether they have applied to an STRF and what payment they received from the STRF.[359] The applicant for a closed-school discharge also assigns to the government, upon discharge, all the student's rights a loan received, including STRF funds received from a private party.[360]

State agencies often respond by delaying processing on an STRF application until the closed-school or false-certification application is resolved. As a result, STRF applications are often held in limbo for long periods of time. Despite these delays, it is important for students to apply to the STRF in any case and keep records of application dates as the state STRF, unlike the federal discharge programs, may limit the time period for applications.[361] Students who do not apply to the STRF pending decisions on their federal discharge applications risk losing the tuition fund remedy. Students should also contact the STRF periodically to check on the status of their recovery fund applications.

---

356 Cal. Educ. Code § 94944(a)(2).
357 *See* Ch. 6 (loan cancellations), *supra*.
358 Cal. Educ. Code § 94944(a)(1)(i).

359 34 C.F.R. § 682.402(d)(3)(i).
360 34 C.F.R. § 682.402(d)(5)(i).
361 For example, see Cal. Educ. Code §§ 94944(d)(1)(F), 94944(d)(2).

Federal Student Loan Statutes

Most of the statutory authority for federal student assistance can be found at 20 U.S.C. § 1070 *et seq.* Section 1070a (not reprinted here) relates to Pell grants. The Federal Family Education Loan Program (FFEL) statutory authority begins at § 1071. This appendix includes most of the relevant authority from these sections. It also includes selected authority for the Federal Direct Loan Program (§ 1087a *et seq.*) and the Perkins Loan Program (§ 1087aa *et seq.*). These and additional statutory sections for all these programs can be found on the companion CD-Rom to this manual.

A.1 Federal Statutes

A.1.1 FFEL

20 U.S.C. sec.

1078-3. Federal consolidation loans.
1087. Repayment by Secretary of loans of bankrupt, deceased, or disabled borrowers; treatment of borrowers attending closed schools or falsely certified as eligible to borrow

§ 1078-3. Federal consolidation loans

(a) Agreements with eligible lenders
(1) Agreement required for insurance coverage
For the purpose of providing loans to eligible borrowers for consolidation of their obligations with respect to eligible student loans, the Secretary or a guaranty agency shall enter into agreements in accordance with subsection (b) of this section with the following eligible lenders:
(A) the Student Loan Marketing Association or the Holding Company of the Student Loan Marketing Association, including any subsidiary of the Holding Company, created pursuant to section 1087-3 of this title;
(B) State agencies described in subparagraphs (D) and (F) of section 1085(d)(1) of this title; and
(C) other eligible lenders described in subparagraphs (A), (B), (C), (E), and (J) of such section.
(2) Insurance coverage of consolidation loans
Except as provided in section 1079(e) of this title, no contract of insurance under this part shall apply to a consolidation loan unless such loan is made under an agreement pursuant to this section and is covered by a certificate issued in accordance with subsection (b)(2) of this section. Loans covered by such a certificate that is issued by a guaranty agency shall be considered to be insured loans for the purposes of reimbursements under section 1078(c) of this title, but no payment shall be made with respect to such loans under section 1078(f) of this title to any such agency.

(3) Definition of eligible borrower
(A) For the purpose of this section, the term "eligible borrower" means a borrower who—
    (i) is not subject to a judgment secured through litigation with respect to a loan under this subchapter and part C of subchapter I of chapter 34 of Title 42 or to an order for wage garnishment under section 1095a of this title; and
    (ii) at the time of application for a consolidation loan—
        (I) is in repayment status as determined under section 1078(b)(7)(A);
        (II) is in a grace period preceding repayment; or
        (III) is a defaulted borrower who has made arrangements to repay the obligation on the defaulted loans satisfactory to the holders of the defaulted loans.
(B)(i)[1] An individual's status as an eligible borrower under this section or under section 1087e(g) terminates under both sections upon receipt of a consolidation loan under this section or under section 1087e(g), except that—
        (I) an individual who receives eligible student loans after the date of receipt of the consolidation loan may receive a subsequent consolidation loan;
        (II) loans received prior to the date of the consolidation loan may be added during the 180-day period following the making of the consolidation loan;
        (III) loans received following the making of the consolidation loan may be added during the 180-day period following the making of the consolidation loan;
        (IV) loans received prior to the date of the first consolidation loan may be added to a subsequent consolidation loan; and
        (V) an individual may obtain a subsequent consolidation loan under section 1087e(g) only for the purposes of obtaining an income contingent repayment plan, and only if the loan has been submitted to the guaranty agency for default aversion."
(4) "Eligible student loans" defined
For the purpose of paragraph (1), the term "eligible student loans" means loans—
(A) made, insured, or guaranteed under this part, including loans on which the borrower has defaulted (but has made arrangements to repay the obligation on the defaulted loans

---

1 So in original. No cl. (ii) has been enacted.

satisfactory to the Secretary or guaranty agency, whichever insured the loans);

(B) made under part D of this subchapter;

(C) made under part C of this subchapter;

(D) made under subpart II of part A of title VII of the Public Health Service Act (42 U.S.C. § 292 *et seq.*); or

(E) made under subpart II of part B of title VIII of the Public Health Service Act (42 U.S.C. § 297a *et seq.*).

(b) Contents of agreements, certificates of insurance, and loan notes

(1) Agreements with lenders

Any lender described in subparagraph (A), (B), or (C) of subsection (a)(1) of this section who wishes to make consolidation loans under this section shall enter into an agreement with the Secretary or a guaranty agency which provides—

(A) that, in the case of all lenders described in subsection (a)(1), the lender will make a consolidation loan to an eligible borrower (on request of that borrower) only if the borrower certifies that the borrower has no other application pending for a loan under this section;

(B) that each consolidation loan made by the lender will bear interest, and be subject to repayment, in accordance with subsection (c) of this section;

(C) that each consolidation loan will be made, notwithstanding any other provision of this part limiting the annual or aggregate principal amount for all insured loans made to a borrower, in an amount (i) which is not less than the minimum amount required for eligibility of the borrower under subsection (a)(3) of this section, and (ii) which is equal to the sum of the unpaid principal and accrued unpaid interest and late charges of all eligible student loans received by the eligible borrower which are selected by the borrower for consolidation;

(D) that the proceeds of each consolidation loan will be paid by the lender to the holder or holders of the loans so selected to discharge the liability on such loans;

(E) that the lender shall offer an income-sensitive repayment schedule, established by the lender in accordance with the regulations promulgated by the Secretary, to the borrower of any consolidation loan made by the lender on or after July 1, 1994; and

(F) such other terms and conditions as the Secretary or the guaranty agency may specifically require of the lender to carry out this section.

(2) Issuance of certificate of comprehensive insurance coverage

The Secretary shall issue a certificate of comprehensive insurance coverage under section 1079(b) of this title to a lender which has entered into an agreement with the Secretary under paragraph (1) of this subsection. The guaranty agency may issue a certificate of comprehensive insurance coverage to a lender with which it has an agreement under such paragraph. The Secretary shall not issue a certificate to a lender described in subparagraph (B) or (C) of subsection (a)(1) of this section unless the Secretary determines that such lender has first applied to, and has been denied a certificate of insurance by, the guaranty agency which insures the preponderance of its loans (by value).

(3) Contents of certificate

A certificate issued under paragraph (2) shall, at a minimum, provide—

(A) that all consolidation loans made by such lender in confor-

mity with the requirements of this section will be insured by the Secretary or the guaranty agency (whichever is applicable) against loss of principal and interest;

(B) that a consolidation loan will not be insured unless the lender has determined to its satisfaction, in accordance with reasonable and prudent business practices, for each loan being consolidated—

(i) that the loan is a legal, valid, and binding obligation of the borrower;

(ii) that each such loan was made and serviced in compliance with applicable laws and regulations; and

(iii) in the case of loans under this part, that the insurance on such loan is in full force and effect;

(C) the effective date and expiration date of the certificate;

(D) the aggregate amount to which the certificate applies;

(E) the reporting requirements of the Secretary on the lender and an identification of the office of the Department of Education or of the guaranty agency which will process claims and perform other related administrative functions;

(F) the alternative repayment terms which will be offered to borrowers by the lender;

(G) that, if the lender prior to the expiration of the certificate no longer proposes to make consolidation loans, the lender will so notify the issuer of the certificate in order that the certificate may be terminated (without affecting the insurance on any consolidation loan made prior to such termination); and

(H) the terms upon which the issuer of the certificate may limit, suspend, or terminate the lender's authority to make consolidation loans under the certificate (without affecting the insurance on any consolidation loan made prior to such limitation, suspension, or termination).

(4) Terms and conditions of loans

A consolidation loan made pursuant to this section shall be insurable by the Secretary or a guaranty agency pursuant to paragraph (2) only if the loan is made to an eligible borrower who has agreed to notify the holder of the loan promptly concerning any change of address and the loan is evidenced by a note or other written agreement which—

(A) is made without security and without endorsement, except that if the borrower is a minor and such note or other written agreement executed by him or her would not, under applicable law, create a binding obligation, endorsement may be required;

(B) provides for the payment of interest and the repayment of principal in accordance with subsection (c) of this section;

(C)(i) provides that periodic installments of principal need not be paid, but interest shall accrue and be paid in accordance with clause (ii), during any period for which the borrower would be eligible for a deferral under section 1078(b)(1)(M) of this title, and that any such period shall not be included in determining the repayment schedule pursuant to subsection (c)(2) of this section; and

(ii) provides that interest shall accrue and be paid during any such period—

(I) by the Secretary, in the case of a consolidation loan for which the application is received by an eligible lender before November 13, 1997, that consolidated only Federal Stafford Loans for which the student borrower received an interest subsidy under section 1078 of this title;

 (II) by the Secretary, in the case of a consolidation loan for which the application is received by an eligible lender on or after November 13, 1997 except that the Secretary shall pay such interest only on that portion of the loan that repays Federal Stafford Loans for which the student borrower received an interest subsidy under section 1078 of this title or Federal Direct Stafford Loans for which the borrower received an interest subsidy under section 1087e of this title; or

 (III) by the borrower, or capitalized, in the case of a consolidation loan other than a loan described in subclause (I) or (II);

(D) entitles the borrower to accelerate without penalty repayment of the whole or any part of the loan; and

(E)(i) contains a notice of the system of disclosure concerning such loan to credit bureau organizations under section 1080a of this title, and (ii) provides that the lender on request of the borrower will provide information on the repayment status of the note to such organizations.

(5) Direct loans

In the event that a borrower is unable to obtain a consolidation loan from a lender with an agreement under subsection (a)(1), or is unable to obtain a consolidation loan with income-sensitive repayment terms acceptable to the borrower from such a lender, the Secretary shall offer any such borrower who applies for it, a Federal Direct Consolidation loan. Such direct consolidation loan shall, as requested by the borrower, be repaid either pursuant to income contingent repayment under part C of this subchapter or pursuant to any other repayment provision under this section. The Secretary shall not offer such loans if, in the Secretary's judgment, the Department of Education does not have the necessary origination and servicing arrangements in place for such loans.

(6) Nondiscrimination in loan consolidation

An eligible lender that makes consolidation loans under this section shall not discriminate against any borrower seeking such a loan—

(A) based on the number or type of eligible student loans the borrower seeks to consolidate, except that a lender is not required to consolidate loans described in subparagraph (D) or (E) of subsection (a)(4) of this section or subsection (d)(1)(C)(ii) of this section;

(B) based on the type or category of institution of higher education that the borrower attended;

(C) based on the interest rate to be charged to the borrower with respect to the consolidation loan; or

(D) with respect to the types of repayment schedules offered to such borrower.

(c) Payment of principal and interest

(1) Interest rate

(A) Notwithstanding subparagraphs (B) and (C), with respect to any loan made under this section for which the application is received by an eligible lender—

 (i) on or after October 1, 1998, and before July 1, 2006, the applicable interest rate shall be determined under section 427A(k)(4); or

 (ii) on or after July 1, 2006, the applicable interest rate shall be determined under section 427A(l)(3).

(B) A consolidation loan made before July 1, 1994, shall bear interest at an annual rate on the unpaid principal balance of the loan that is equal to the greater of—

 (i) the weighted average of the interest rates on the loans consolidated, rounded to the nearest whole percent; or

 (ii) 9 percent.

(C) A consolidation loan made on or after July 1, 1994, shall bear interest at an annual rate on the unpaid principal balance of the loan that is equal to the weighted average of the interest rates on the loans consolidated, rounded upward to the nearest whole percent.

(D) A consolidation loan for which the application is received by an eligible lender on or after November 13, 1997, and before October 1, 1998, shall bear interest at an annual rate on the unpaid principal balance of the loan that is equal to the rate specified in section 1077a(f) of this title, except that the eligible lender may continue to calculate interest on such a loan at the rate previously in effect and defer, until not later than April 1, 1998, the recalculation of the interest on such a loan at the rate required by this subparagraph if the recalculation is applied retroactively to the date on which the loan is made.

(2) Repayment schedules

(A) Notwithstanding any other provision of this part, to the extent authorized by its certificate of insurance under subsection (b)(2)(F) of this section and approved by the issuer of such certificate, the lender of a consolidation loan shall establish repayment terms as will promote the objectives of this section, which shall include the establishment of graduated or income-sensitive repayment schedules, established by the lender in accordance with the regulations of the Secretary. Except as required by such income-sensitive repayment schedules, or by the terms of repayment pursuant to income contingent repayment offered by the Secretary under subsection (b)(5) of this section, such repayment terms shall require that if the sum of the consolidation loan and the amount outstanding on other student loans to the individual—

 (i) is less than $7,500, then such consolidation loan shall be repaid in not more than 10 years;

 (ii) is equal to or greater than $7,500 but less than $10,000, then such consolidation loan shall be repaid in not more than 12 years;

 (iii) is equal to or greater than $10,000 but less than $20,000, then such consolidation loan shall be repaid in not more than 15 years;

 (iv) is equal to or greater than $20,000 but less than $40,000, then such consolidation loan shall be repaid in not more than 20 years;

 (v) is equal to or greater than $40,000 but less than $60,000, then such consolidation loan shall be repaid in not more than 25 years; or

 (vi) is equal to or greater than $60,000, then such consolidation loan shall be repaid in not more than 30 years.

(B) The amount outstanding on other student loans which may be counted for the purpose of subparagraph (A) may not exceed the amount of the consolidation loan.

(3) Additional repayment requirements

Notwithstanding paragraph (2)—

(A) a repayment schedule established with respect to a consolidation loan shall require that the minimum installment payment be an amount equal to not less than the accrued unpaid interest; and

(B) except as required by the terms of repayment pursuant to income contingent repayment offered by the Secretary under subsection (b)(5) of this section, the lender of a consolidation loan may, with respect to repayment on the loan, when the amount of a monthly or other similar payment on the loan is not a multiple of $5, round the payment to the next highest whole dollar amount that is a multiple of $5.

(4) Commencement of repayment

Repayment of a consolidation loan shall commence within 60 days after all holders have, pursuant to subsection (b)(1)(D) of this section, discharged the liability of the borrower on the loans selected for consolidation.

(5) Insurance premiums prohibited

No insurance premium shall be charged to the borrower on any consolidation loan, and no insurance premium shall be payable by the lender to the Secretary with respect to any such loan, but a fee may be payable by the lender to the guaranty agency to cover the costs of increased or extended liability with respect to such loan.

(d) Special program authorized

(1) General rule and definition of eligible student loan

(A) In general

Subject to the provisions of this subsection, the Secretary or a guaranty agency shall enter into agreements with eligible lenders described in subparagraphs (A), (B), and (C) of subsection (a)(1) of this section for the consolidation of eligible student loans.

(B) Applicability rule

Unless otherwise provided in this subsection, the agreements entered into under subparagraph (A) and the loans made under such agreements for the consolidation of eligible student loans under this subsection shall have the same terms, conditions, and benefits as all other agreements and loans made under this section.

(C) Definition

For the purpose of this subsection, the term "eligible student loans" means loans—

    (i)   of the type described in subparagraphs (A), (B), and (C) of subsection (a)(4) of this section; and

    (ii) made under subpart I of part A of title VII of the Public Health Service Act (42 U.S.C. 292 *et seq.*).

(2) Interest rate rule

(A) In general

The portion of each consolidated loan that is attributable to an eligible student loan described in paragraph (1)(C)(ii) shall bear interest at a rate not to exceed the rate determined under subparagraph (B).

(B) Determination of the maximum interest rate

For the 12-month period beginning after July 1, 1992, and for each 12-month period thereafter, beginning on July 1 and ending on June 30, the interest rate applicable under subparagraph (A) shall be equal to the average of the bond equivalent rates of the 91-day Treasury bills auctioned for the quarter prior to July 1, for each 12-month period for which the determination is made, plus 3 percent.

(C) Publication of maximum interest rate

The Secretary shall determine the applicable rate of interest under subparagraph (B) after consultation with the Secretary of the Treasury and shall publish such rate in the Federal Register as soon as practicable after the date of such determination.

(3) Special rules

(A) No special allowance rule

No special allowance under section 1087-1 of this title shall be paid with respect to the portion of any consolidated loan under this subsection that is attributable to any loan described in paragraph (1)(C)(ii).

(B) No interest subsidy rule

No interest subsidy under section 1078(a) of this title shall be paid on behalf of any eligible borrower for any portion of a consolidated loan under this subsection that is attributable to any loan described in paragraph (1)(C)(ii).

(C) Additional reserve rule

Notwithstanding any other provision of this chapter, additional reserves shall not be required for any guaranty agency with respect to a loan made under this subsection.

(D) Insurance rule

Any insurance premium paid by the borrower under subpart I of part A of title VII of the Public Health Service Act (42 U.S.C. 292 *et seq.*) with respect to a loan made under that subpart and consolidated under this subsection shall be retained by the student loan insurance fund established under section 710 of the Public Health Service Act (42 U.S.C. 292i).

(4) Regulations

The Secretary is authorized to promulgate such regulations as may be necessary to facilitate carrying out the provisions of this subsection.

(e) Termination of authority

The authority to make loans under this section expires at the close of September 30, 2012. Nothing in this section shall be construed to authorize the Secretary to promulgate rules or regulations governing the terms or conditions of the agreements and certificates under subsection (b) of this section. Loans made under this section which are insured by the Secretary shall be considered to be new loans made to students for the purpose of section 1074(a) of this title.

(f) Interest payment rebate fee

(1) In general

For any month beginning on or after October 1, 1993, each holder of a consolidation loan under this section for which the first disbursement was made on or after October 1, 1993, shall pay to the Secretary, on a monthly basis and in such manner as the Secretary shall prescribe, a rebate fee calculated on an annual basis equal to 1.05 percent of the principal plus accrued unpaid interest on such loan.

(2) Special rule

For consolidation loans based on applications received during the period from October 1, 1998 through January 31, 1999, inclusive, the rebate described in paragraph (1) shall be equal to 0.62 percent of the principal plus accrued unpaid interest on such loan.

(3) Deposit

The Secretary shall deposit all fees collected pursuant to subsection (a) of this section into the insurance fund established in section 1081 of this title.

[Pub. L. 89-329, title IV, Sec. 428C, as added Pub. L. 99-498, title IV, Sec. 402(a), Oct. 17, 1986, 100 Stat. 1388; amended Pub. L.

100-50, Sec. 10(s), June 3, 1987, 101 Stat. 345; Pub. L. 102-325, title IV, Sec. 419, July 23, 1992, 106 Stat. 532; Pub. L. 102-408, title III, Sec. 306(a), (b), Oct. 13, 1992, 106 Stat. 2084, 2086; Pub. L. 103-66, title IV, Sec. 4046(a), (b)(2), 4106(a), Aug. 10, 1993, 107 Stat. 360, 363, 368; Pub. L. 103-208, Sec. 2(c)(33)-(37), Dec. 20, 1993, 107 Stat. 2466; Pub. L. 103-382, title III, Sec. 356, Oct. 20, 1994, 108 Stat. 3967; Pub. L. 104-208, div. A, title I, Sec. 101(e) (title VI, Sec. 602(b)(1)(A)(ii)), Sept. 30, 1996, 110 Stat. 3009-233, 3009-283; Pub. L. 105-33, title VI, Sec. 6104(3), Aug. 5, 1997, 111 Stat. 652; Pub. L. 105-78, title VI, Sec. 609(b)-(e), Nov. 13, 1997, 111 Stat. 1522, 1523; Pub. L. 105-244, title IV, Sec. 416(b)(2), 420, Oct. 7, 1998, 112 Stat. 1682, 1695; Pub. L. 107-139, Feb. 8, 2002, 116 Stat. 8; Pub. L. 109-171, Feb. 8, 2006, 120 Stat. 4; Pub. L. 109-234, June 15, 2006, 120 Stat. 418]

§ 1087. Repayment by Secretary of loans of bankrupt, deceased, or disabled borrowers; treatment of borrowers attending schools that fail to provide a refund, attending closed schools, or falsely certified as eligible to borrow

(a) Repayment in full for death and disability

If a student borrower who has received a loan described in subparagraph (A) or (B) of section 1078(a)(1) of this title dies or becomes permanently and totally disabled (as determined in accordance with regulations of the Secretary), then the Secretary shall discharge the borrower's liability on the loan by repaying the amount owed on the loan.

(b) Payment of claims on loans in bankruptcy

The Secretary shall pay to the holder of a loan described in section 1078(a)(1)(A) or (B), 1078-1, 1078-2, 1078-3, or 1078-8 of this title, the amount of the unpaid balance of principal and interest owed on such loan—

(1) when the borrower files for relief under chapter 12 or 13 of title 11 [11 U.S.C.A. § 1201 *et seq.* or 1301 *et seq.*];

(2) when the borrower who has filed for relief under chapter 7 or 11 of such title [11 U.S.C.A. § 701 *et seq.* or 1101 *et seq.*] commences an action for a determination of dischargeability under section 523(a)(8)(B) of such title; or

(3) for loans described in section 523(a)(8)(A) of such title, when the borrower files for relief under chapter 7 or 11 of such title [11 U.S.C.A. § 701 *et seq.* or 1101 *et seq.*].

(c) Discharge

(1) In general

If a borrower who received, on or after January 1, 1986, a loan made, insured, or guaranteed under this part and the student borrower, or the student on whose behalf a parent borrowed, is unable to complete the program in which such student is enrolled due to the closure of the institution or if such student's eligibility to borrow under this part [20 U.S.C.A. § 1071 *et seq.*] was falsely certified by the eligible institution or was falsely certified as a result of a crime of identity theft, or if the institution failed to make a refund of loan proceeds which the institution owed to such student's lender, then the Secretary shall discharge the borrower's liability on the loan (including interest and collection fees) by repaying the amount owed on the loan and shall subsequently pursue any claim available to such borrower against the institution and its affiliates and principals or settle the loan obligation pursuant to the financial responsibility authority under subpart 3 of part G [20 U.S.C.A. § 1099 *et seq.*]. In the case of a discharge based upon a failure to refund, the amount of the discharge shall not exceed that portion of the loan which should have been refunded. The

Secretary shall report to the Committee on Education and the Workforce of the House of Representatives and the Committee on Labor and Human Resources of the Senate annually as to the dollar amount of loan discharges attributable to failures to make refunds.

(2) Assignment

A borrower whose loan has been discharged pursuant to this subsection shall be deemed to have assigned to the United States the right to a loan refund up to the amount discharged against the institution and its affiliates and principals.

(3) Eligibility for additional assistance

The period of a student's attendance at an institution at which the student was unable to complete a course of study due to the closing of the institution shall not be considered for purposes of calculating the student's period of eligibility for additional assistance under this subchapter and part C of subchapter I of chapter 34 of title 42.

(4) Special rule

A borrower whose loan has been discharged pursuant to this subsection shall not be precluded from receiving additional grants, loans, or work assistance under this subchapter and part C of subchapter I of chapter 34 of Title 42 for which the borrower would be otherwise eligible (but for the default on such discharged loan). The amount discharged under this subsection shall be treated the same as loans under section 1087ee(a)(5) of this title.

(5) Reporting

The Secretary shall report to credit bureaus with respect to loans which have been discharged pursuant to this subsection.

(d) Repayment of loans to parents

If a student on whose behalf a parent has received a loan described in section 1078-2 of this title dies, then the Secretary shall discharge the borrower's liability on the loan by repaying the amount owed on the loan.

[Pub. L. 89-329, title IV, Sec. 437, as added Pub. L. 99-498, title IV, Sec. 402(a), Oct. 17, 1986, 100 Stat. 1414; amended Pub. L. 102-325, title IV, Sec. 428, July 23, 1992, 106 Stat. 551; Pub. L. 103-208, Sec. 2(c)(63)–(65), Dec. 20, 1993, 107 Stat. 2469; Pub. L. 105-244, title IV, Sec. 431, Oct. 7, 1998, 112 Stat. 1709.]

A.1.2 Direct Loans

20 U.S.C. sec.

1087e. Terms and conditions of loans

§ 1087e. Terms and conditions of loans

(a) In general

(1) Parallel terms, conditions, benefits, and amounts

Unless otherwise specified in this part [20 U.S.C.A. § 1087a *et seq.*], loans made to borrowers under this part shall have the same terms, conditions, and benefits, and be available in the same amounts, as loans made to borrowers under sections 1078, 1078-2, 1078-3 and 1078-8 of this title.

(2) Designation of loans

Loans made to borrowers under this part that, except as otherwise specified in this part, have the same terms, conditions, and benefits as loans made to borrowers under—

(A) section 1078 of this title shall be known as "Federal Direct Stafford Loans";

(B) section 1078-2 of this title shall be known as "Federal Direct PLUS Loans";

(C) section 1078-3 shall be known as "Federal Direct Consolidation Loans"; and

(D) section 1078-8 of this title shall be known as "Federal Direct Unsubsidized Stafford Loans."

(b) Interest rate

(1) Rates for FDSL and FDUSL

For Federal Direct Stafford Loans and Federal Direct Unsubsidized Stafford Loans for which the first disbursement is made on or after July 1, 1994, the applicable rate of interest shall, during any 12-month period beginning on July 1 and ending on June 30, be determined on the preceding June 1 and be equal to—

(A) the bond equivalent rate of 91-day Treasury bills auctioned at the final auction held prior to such June 1; plus

(B) 3.1 percent, except that such rate shall not exceed 8.25 percent.

(2) In school and grace period rules

(A) Notwithstanding the provisions of paragraph (1), but subject to paragraph (3), with respect to any Federal Direct Stafford Loan or Federal Direct Unsubsidized Stafford Loan for which the first disbursement is made on or after July 1, 1995, the applicable rate of interest for interest which accrues—

(i) prior to the beginning of the repayment period of the loan; or

(ii) during the period in which principal need not be paid (whether or not such principal is in fact paid) by reason of a provision described in section 1078(b)(1)(M) or 1077(a)(2)(C) of this title, shall not exceed the rate determined under subparagraph (B).

(B) For the purpose of subparagraph (A), the rate determined under this subparagraph shall, during any 12-month period beginning on July 1 and ending on June 30, be determined on the preceding June 1 and be equal to—

(i) the bond equivalent rate of 91-day Treasury bills auctioned at the final auction prior to such June 1; plus

(ii) 2.5 percent, except that such rate shall not exceed 8.25 percent.

(3) Out-year rule

Notwithstanding paragraphs (1) and (2), for Federal Direct Stafford Loans and Federal Direct Unsubsidized Stafford Loans made on or after July 1, 1998, the applicable rate of interest shall, during any 12-month period beginning on July 1 and ending on June 30, be determined on the preceding June 1 and be equal to—

(A) the bond equivalent rate of the security with a comparable maturity as established by the Secretary; plus

(B) 1.0 percent, except that such rate shall not exceed 8.25 percent.

(4) Rates for FDPLUS

(A) For Federal Direct PLUS Loans for which the first disbursement is made on or after July 1, 1994, the applicable rate of interest shall, during any 12-month period beginning on July 1 and ending on June 30, be determined on the preceding June 1 and be equal to—

(i) the bond equivalent rate of 52-week Treasury bills auctioned at final auction held prior to such June 1; plus

(ii) 3.1 percent, except that such rate shall not exceed 9 percent.

(B) For Federal Direct PLUS loans made on or after July 1, 1998, the applicable rate of interest shall, during any 12-month period beginning on July 1 and ending on June 30, be determined on the preceding June 1 and be equal to—

(i) the bond equivalent rate of the security with a comparable maturity as established by the Secretary; plus

(ii) 2.1 percent, except that such rate shall not exceed 9 percent.

(5) Temporary interest rate provision

(A) Rates for FDSL and FDUSL

Notwithstanding the preceding paragraphs of this subsection, for Federal Direct Stafford Loans and Federal Direct Unsubsidized Stafford Loans for which the first disbursement is made on or after July 1, 1998, and before October 1, 1998, the applicable rate of interest shall, during any 12-month period beginning on July 1 and ending on June 30, be determined on the preceding June 1 and be equal to—

(i) the bond equivalent rate of 91-day Treasury bills auctioned at the final auction held prior to such June 1; plus

(ii) 2.3 percent, except that such rate shall not exceed 8.25 percent.

(B) In school and grace period rules

Notwithstanding the preceding paragraphs of this subsection, with respect to any Federal Direct Stafford Loan or Federal Direct Unsubsidized Stafford Loan for which the first disbursement is made on or after July 1, 1998, and before October 1, 1998, the applicable rate of interest for interest which accrues—

(i) prior to the beginning of the repayment period of the loan; or

(ii) during the period in which principal need not be paid (whether or not such principal is in fact paid) by reason of a provision described in section 1078(b)(1)(M) or 1077(a)(2)(C) of this title, shall be determined under subparagraph (A) by substituting "1.7 percent" for "2.3 percent."

(C) PLUS loans

Notwithstanding the preceding paragraphs of this subsection, with respect to Federal Direct PLUS Loan for which the first disbursement is made on or after July 1, 1998, and before October 1, 1998, the applicable rate of interest shall be determined under subparagraph (A)—

(i) by substituting "3.1 percent" for "2.3 percent"; and

(ii) by substituting "9.0 percent" for "8.25 percent."

(6) Interest rate provision for new loans on or after October 1, 1998, and before July 1, 2006

(A) Rates for FDSL and FDUSL

Notwithstanding the preceding paragraphs of this subsection, for Federal Direct Stafford Loans and Federal Direct Unsubsidized Stafford Loans for which the first disbursement is made on or after October 1, 1998, and before July 1, 2006, the applicable rate of interest shall, during any 12-month period beginning on July 1 and ending on June 30, be determined on the preceding June 1 and be equal to—

(i) the bond equivalent rate of 91-day Treasury bills auctioned at the final auction held prior to such June 1; plus

(ii) 2.3 percent, except that such rate shall not exceed 8.25 percent.

(B) In school and grace period rules

Notwithstanding the preceding paragraphs of this subsection, with respect to any Federal Direct Stafford Loan or Federal Direct Unsubsidized Stafford Loan for which the first disbursement is made on or after October 1, 1998, and before July 1, 2006, the applicable rate of interest for interest which accrues—

(i) prior to the beginning of the repayment period of the loan; or

(ii) during the period in which principal need not be paid (whether or not such principal is in fact paid) by reason of a provision described in section 1078(b)(1)(M) or 1077(a)(2)(C) of this title, shall be determined under subparagraph (A) by substituting "1.7 percent" for "2.3 percent."

(C) PLUS loans

Notwithstanding the preceding paragraphs of this subsection, with respect to Federal Direct PLUS Loan for which the first disbursement is made on or after October 1, 1998, and before July 1, 2003, the applicable rate of interest shall be determined under subparagraph (A)—

(i) by substituting "3.1 percent" for "2.3 percent"; and

(ii) by substituting "9.0 percent" for "8.25 percent."

(D) Consolidation loans

Notwithstanding the preceding paragraphs of this subsection, any Federal Direct Consolidation loan for which the application is received on or after February 1, 1999, and before July 1, 2003, shall bear interest at an annual rate on the unpaid principal balance of the loan that is equal to the lesser of—

(i) the weighted average of the interest rates on the loans consolidated, rounded to the nearest higher one-eighth of one percent; or

(ii) 8.25 percent.

(E) Temporary rules for consolidation loans

Notwithstanding the preceding paragraphs of this subsection, any Federal Direct Consolidation loan for which the application is received on or after October 1, 1998, and before February 1, 1999, shall bear interest at an annual rate on the unpaid principal balance of the loan that is equal to—

(i) the bond equivalent rate of 91-day Treasury bills auctioned at the final auction held prior to such June 1; plus

(ii) 2.3 percent, except that such rate shall not exceed 8.25 percent.

(7) Interest rate provision for new loans on or after July 1, 2006

(A) Rates for FDSL and FDUSL

Notwithstanding the preceding paragraphs of this subsection, for Federal Direct Stafford Loans and Federal Direct Unsubsidized Stafford Loans for which the first disbursement is made on or after July 1, 2006, the applicable rate of interest shall be 6.8 percent on the unpaid principal balance of the loan.

(B) PLUS loans

Notwithstanding the preceding paragraphs of this subsection, with respect to any Federal Direct PLUS loan for which the first disbursement is made on or after July 1, 2006, the applicable rate of interest shall be 7.9 percent on the unpaid principal balance of the loan.

(C) Consolidation loans

Notwithstanding the preceding paragraphs of this subsection, any Federal Direct Consolidation loan for which the application is received on or after July 1, 2006, shall bear interest at an annual rate on the unpaid principal balance of the loan that is equal to the lesser of—

(i) the weighted average of the interest rates on the loans consolidated, rounded to the nearest higher one-eighth of one percent; or

(ii) 8.25 percent.

(8) Repayment incentives

(A) In general

Notwithstanding any other provision of this part [20 U.S.C.A. § 1087a *et seq.*], the Secretary is authorized to prescribe by regulation such reductions in the interest rate or origination fee paid by a borrower of a loan made under this part as the Secretary determines appropriate to encourage on-time repayment of the loan. Such reductions may be offered only if the Secretary determines the reductions are cost neutral and in the best financial interest of the Federal Government. Any increase in subsidy costs resulting from such reductions shall be completely offset by corresponding savings in funds available for the William D. Ford Federal Direct Loan Program in that fiscal year from section 1087h of this title and other administrative accounts.

(B) Accountability

Prior to publishing regulations proposing repayment incentives, the Secretary shall ensure the cost neutrality of such reductions. The Secretary shall not prescribe such regulations in final form unless an official report from the Director of the Office of Management and Budget to the Secretary and a comparable report from the Director of the Congressional Budget Office to the Congress each certify that any such reductions will be completely cost neutral. Such reports shall be transmitted to the Committee on Labor and Human Resources of the Senate and the Committee on Education and the Workforce of the House of Representatives not less than 60 days prior to the publication of regulations proposing such reductions.

(9) Publication

The Secretary shall determine the applicable rates of interest under this subsection after consultation with the Secretary of the Treasury and shall publish such rate in the Federal Register as soon as practicable after the date of determination.

(c) Loan fee—

(1) In general—

The Secretary shall charge the borrower of a loan made under this part [20 U.S.C.A. § 1087a *et seq.*] an origination fee of 4.0 percent of the principal amount of loan.

(2) Subsequent reduction.—Paragraph (1) shall be applied to loans made under this part, other than Federal Direct Consolidation loans and Federal Direct PLUS loans—

(A) by substituting "3.0 percent" for "4.0 percent" with respect to loans for which the first disbursement of principal is made on or after the date of enactment of the Higher Education Reconciliation Act of 2005, and before July 1, 2007;

(B) by substituting "2.5 percent" for "4.0 percent" with respect to loans for which the first disbursement of principal is made on or after July 1, 2007, and before July 1, 2008;

(C) by substituting "2.0 percent" for "4.0 percent" with respect to loans for which the first disbursement of principal is made on or after July 1, 2008, and before July 1, 2009;

(D) by substituting "1.5 percent" for "4.0 percent" with respect to loans for which the first disbursement of principal is made on or after July 1, 2009, and before July 1, 2010; and

(E) by substituting "1.0 percent" for "4.0 percent" with respect to loans for which the first disbursement of principal is made on or after July 1, 2010.

(d) Repayment plans

(1) Design and selection

Consistent with criteria established by the Secretary, the Secretary shall offer a borrower of a loan made under this part [20 U.S.C.A. § 1087a *et seq.*] a variety of plans for repayment of such loan, including principal and interest on the loan. The borrower shall be entitled to accelerate, without penalty, repayment on the borrower's loans under this part. The borrower may choose—

(A) a standard repayment plan, consistent with subsection (a)(1) of this section and with section 1078(b)(9)(A)(i);

(B) a graduated repayment plan, consistent with section 1078(b)(9)(A)(ii);

(C) an extended repayment plan, consistent with section 1078(b)(9)(A)(v), except that the borrower shall annually repay a minimum amount determined by the Secretary in accordance with section 1078(b)(1)(L); and

(D) an income contingent repayment plan, with varying annual repayment amounts based on the income of the borrower, paid over an extended period of time prescribed by the Secretary, not to exceed 25 years, except that the plan described in this subparagraph shall not be available to the borrower of a Federal Direct PLUS loan.

(2) Selection by Secretary

If a borrower of a loan made under this part [20 U.S.C.A. § 1087a *et seq.*] does not select a repayment plan described in paragraph (1), the Secretary may provide the borrower with a repayment plan described in subparagraph (A), (B), or (C) of paragraph (1).

(3) Changes in selections

The borrower of a loan made under this part may change the borrower's selection of a repayment plan under paragraph (1), or the Secretary's selection of a plan for the borrower under paragraph (2), as the case may be, under such terms and conditions as may be established by the Secretary.

(4) Alternative repayment plans

The Secretary may provide, on a case by case basis, an alternative repayment plan to a borrower of a loan made under this part [20 U.S.C.A. § 1087a *et seq.*] who demonstrates to the satisfaction of the Secretary that the terms and conditions of the repayment plans available under paragraph (1) are not adequate to accommodate the borrower's exceptional circumstances. In designing such alternative repayment plans, the Secretary shall ensure that such plans do not exceed the cost to the Federal Government, as determined on the basis of the present value of future payments by such borrowers, of loans made using the plans available under paragraph (1).

(5) Repayment after default

The Secretary may require any borrower who has defaulted on a loan made under this part [20 U.S.C.A. § 1087a *et seq.*] to—

(A) pay all reasonable collection costs associated with such loan; and

(B) repay the loan pursuant to an income contingent repayment plan.

(e) Income contingent repayment

(1) Information and procedures

The Secretary may obtain such information as is reasonably necessary regarding the income of a borrower (and the borrower's spouse, if applicable) of a loan made under this part that is, or may be, repaid pursuant to income contingent repayment, for the purpose of determining the annual repayment obligation of the borrower. Returns and return information (as defined in section 6103 of Title 26) may be obtained under the preceding sentence only to the extent authorized by section 6103(*l*)(13) of Title 26. The Secretary shall establish procedures for determining the borrower's repayment obligation on that loan for such year, and such other procedures as are necessary to implement effectively income contingent repayment.

(2) Repayment based on adjusted gross income

A repayment schedule for a loan made under this part [20 U.S.C.A. § 1087a *et seq.*] and repaid pursuant to income contingent repayment shall be based on the adjusted gross income (as defined in section 62 of Title 26 [26 U.S.C.A. § 62]) of the borrower or, if the borrower is married and files a Federal income tax return jointly with the borrower's spouse, on the adjusted gross income of the borrower and the borrower's spouse.

(3) Additional documents

A borrower who chooses, or is required, to repay a loan made under this part [20 U.S.C.A. § 1087a *et seq.*] pursuant to income contingent repayment, and for whom adjusted gross income is unavailable or does not reasonably reflect the borrower's current income, shall provide to the Secretary other documentation of income satisfactory to the Secretary, which documentation the Secretary may use to determine an appropriate repayment schedule.

(4) Repayment schedules

Income contingent repayment schedules shall be established by regulations promulgated by the Secretary and shall require payments that vary in relation to the appropriate portion of the annual income of the borrower (and the borrower's spouse, if applicable) as determined by the Secretary.

(5) Calculation of balance due

The balance due on a loan made under this part [20 U.S.C.A. § 1087a *et seq.*] that is repaid pursuant to income contingent repayment shall equal the unpaid principal amount of the loan, any accrued interest, and any fees, such as late charges, assessed on such loan. The Secretary may promulgate regulations limiting the amount of interest that may be capitalized on such loan, and the timing of any such capitalization.

(6) Notification to borrowers

The Secretary shall establish procedures under which a borrower of a loan made under this part [20 U.S.C.A. 1087a *et seq.*] who chooses or is required to repay such loan pursuant to income contingent repayment is notified of the terms and conditions of such plan, including notification of such borrower—

(A) that the Internal Revenue Service will disclose to the Secretary tax return information as authorized under section 6103(l)(13) of Title 26 [20 U.S.C.A. § 6103(*l*)(13)]; and

(B) that if a borrower considers that special circumstances, such as a loss of employment by the borrower or the borrower's spouse, warrant an adjustment in the borrower's loan repayment as determined using the information described in subparagraph (A), or the alternative documentation described in paragraph (3), the borrower may contact the Secretary, who shall determine whether such adjustment is appropriate, in accordance with criteria established by the Secretary.

(f) Deferment

(1) Effect on principal and interest

A borrower of a loan made under this part [20 U.S.C.A. § 1087a *et seq*.] who meets the requirements described in paragraph (2) shall be eligible for a deferment, during which periodic installments of principal need not be paid, and interest—

(A) shall not accrue, in the case of a—

   (i) Federal Direct Stafford Loan; or

   (ii) a Federal Direct Consolidation Loan that consolidated only Federal Direct Stafford Loans, or a combination of such loans and Federal Stafford Loans for which the student borrower received an interest subsidy under section 1078 of this title; or

(B) shall accrue and be capitalized or paid by the borrower, in the case of a Federal Direct PLUS Loan, a Federal Direct Unsubsidized Stafford Loan, or a Federal Direct Consolidation Loan not described in subparagraph (A)(ii).

(2) Eligibility

A borrower of a loan made under this part shall be eligible for a deferment during any period—

(A) during which the borrower—

   (i) is carrying at least one-half the normal full-time work load for the course of study that the borrower is pursuing, as determined by the eligible institution (as such term is defined in section 1085(a) of this title) the borrower is attending; or

   (ii) is pursuing a course of study pursuant to a graduate fellowship program approved by the Secretary, or pursuant to a rehabilitation training program for individuals with disabilities approved by the Secretary, except that no borrower shall be eligible for a deferment under this subparagraph, or a loan made under this part [20 U.S.C.A. § 1087a *et seq*.] (other than a Federal Direct PLUS Loan or a Federal Direct Consolidation Loan), while serving in a medical internship or residency program;

(B) not in excess of 3 years during which the borrower is seeking and unable to find full-time employment;

(C) not in excess of 3 years during which the borrower—

   (i) is serving on active duty during a war or other military operation or national emergency; or

   (ii) is performing qualifying National Guard duty during a war or other military operation or national emergency; or

(D) not in excess of 3 years during which the Secretary determines, in accordance with regulations prescribed under section 1085(*o*) of this title, that the borrower has experienced or will experience an economic hardship.

(3) Definition of borrower

For the purpose of this subsection, the term "borrower" means an individual who is a new borrower on the date such individual applies for a loan under this part for which the first disbursement is made on or after July 1, 1993.

(4) Deferments for previous part B loan borrowers

A borrower of a loan made under this part [20 U.S.C.A. § 1087a *et seq*.], who at the time such individual applies for such loan, has an outstanding balance of principal or interest owing on any loan made, insured, or guaranteed under part B of this subchapter [20 U.S.C.A. § 1071 *et seq*.] prior to July 1, 1993, shall be eligible for a deferment under section 1077(a)(2)(C) of this title or section 1078(b)(1)(M) of this title as such sections were in effect on July 22, 1992.

(g) Federal Direct Consolidation Loans

A borrower of a loan made under this part may consolidate such loan with the loans described in section 1078-3(a)(4) of this title. To be eligible for a consolidation loan under this part, a borrower shall meet the eligibility criteria set forth in section 1078-3(a)(3) of this title. The Secretary, upon application for such a loan, shall comply with the requirements applicable to a lender under section 1078-3(b)(1)(F) of this title.

(h) Borrower defenses

Notwithstanding any other provision of State or Federal law, the Secretary shall specify in regulations (except as authorized under section 1087g(a)(1) of this title) which acts or omissions of an institution of higher education a borrower may assert as a defense to repayment of a loan made under this part [20 U.S.C.A. § 1087a *et seq*.], except that in no event may a borrower recover from the Secretary, in any action arising from or relating to a loan made under this part, an amount in excess of the amount such borrower has repaid on such loan.

(*i*) Loan application and promissory note

The common financial reporting form required in section 1090(a)(1) of this title shall constitute the application for loans made under this part [20 U.S.C.A. § 1087a *et seq*.] (other than a Federal Direct PLUS loan). The Secretary shall develop, print, and distribute to participating institutions a standard promissory note and loan disclosure form.

(j) Loan disbursement

(1) In general

Proceeds of loans to students under this part [20 U.S.C.A. § 1087a *et seq*.] shall be applied to the student's account for tuition and fees, and, in the case of institutionally owned housing, to room and board. Loan proceeds that remain after the application of the previous sentence shall be delivered to the borrower by check or other means that is payable to and requires the endorsement or other certification by such borrower.

(2) Payment periods

The Secretary shall establish periods for the payments described in paragraph (1) in a manner consistent with payment of Federal Pell Grants under subpart 1 of part A of this subchapter [20 U.S.C.A. § 1070a *et seq*.].

(k) Fiscal control and fund accountability

(1) In general

(A) An institution shall maintain financial records in a manner consistent with records maintained for other programs under this subchapter [20 U.S.C.A. § 1070 *et seq*.].

(B) Except as otherwise required by regulations of the Secretary, or in a notice under section 1087g(a)(1) of this title, an institution may maintain loan funds under this part in the same account as other Federal student financial assistance.

(2) Payments and refunds

Payments and refunds shall be reconciled in a manner consistent with the manner set forth for the submission of a payment summary report required of institutions participating in the program under subpart 1 of part A of this subchapter [20 U.S.C.A. § 1070a *et seq.*], except that nothing in this paragraph shall prevent such reconciliations on a monthly basis.

(3) Transaction histories

All transaction histories under this part shall be maintained using the same system designated by the Secretary for the provision of Federal Pell Grants under subpart 1 of part A of this subchapter [20 U.S.C.A. § 1070a *et seq.*].

(*l*) Armed forces student loan interest payment program

(1) Authority

Using funds received by transfer to the Secretary under section 2174 of Title 10 for the payment of interest on a loan made under this part to a member of the Armed Forces, the Secretary shall pay the interest on the loan as due for a period not in excess of 36 consecutive months. The Secretary may not pay interest on such a loan out of any funds other than funds that have been so transferred.

(2) Forbearance

During the period in which the Secretary is making payments on a loan under paragraph (1), the Secretary shall grant the borrower forbearance, in the form of a temporary cessation of all payments on the loan other than the payments of interest on the loan that are made under that paragraph.

[Pub. L. 89-329, title IV, Sec. 455, as added Pub. L. 99-498, title IV, Sec. 404, Oct. 17, 1986, 100 Stat. 1439; amended Pub. L. 102-325, title IV, Sec. 451, July 23, 1992, 106 Stat. 572; Pub. L. 103-66, title IV, Sec. 4021, Aug. 10, 1993, 107 Stat. 346; Pub. L. 103-382, title III, Sec. 359, Oct. 20, 1994, 108 Stat. 3968; Pub. L. 105-178, title VIII, Sec. 8301(c), June 9, 1998, 112 Stat. 498; Pub. L. 105-244, title IV, Sec. 401(g)(6), 452(a)(1), (b), (c), Oct. 7, 1998, 112 Stat. 1652, 1715–1717; Pub. L. 106-554, § 1(a)(1), Dec. 21, 2000, 114 Stat. 2763, 2763A-49; Pub. L. 107-139, § 1(b), (c), Feb. 8, 2002, 116 Stat. 9; Pub. L. 107-314, § 651(c), Dec. 2, 2002, 116 Stat. 2458; Pub. L. 109-171, Feb. 8, 2006, 120 Stat. 4]

A.1.3 Perkins Loans

20 U.S.C. sec.

1087bb. Allocation of funds.
1087cc. Agreements with institutions of higher education.
1087dd. Terms of loans.

§ 1087bb. Allocation of funds

(a) Allocation based on previous allocation

(1) From the amount appropriated pursuant to section 1087aa(b) of this title for each fiscal year, the Secretary shall first allocate to each eligible institution an amount equal to—

(A) 100 percent of the amount received under subsections (a) and (b) of this section for fiscal year 1999 (as such subsections were in effect with respect to allocations for such fiscal year), multiplied by

(B) the institution's default penalty, as determined under subsection (e) of this section, except that if the institution has a cohort default rate in excess of the applicable maximum cohort default rate under subsection (f) of this section, the

institution may not receive an allocation under this paragraph.

(2)(A) From the amount so appropriated, the Secretary shall next allocate to each eligible institution that began participation in the program under this part after fiscal year 1999 but is not a first or second time participant, an amount equal to the greater of-

(i) $5,000; or

(ii) 100 percent of the amount received and expended under this part for the first year it participated in the program.

(B) From the amount so appropriated, the Secretary shall next allocate to each eligible institution that began participation in the program under this part after fiscal year 1999 and is a first or second time participant, an amount equal to the greatest of—

(i) $5,000;

(ii) an amount equal to (I) 90 percent of the amount received and used under this part in the second preceding fiscal year by eligible institutions offering comparable programs of instruction, divided by (II) the number of students enrolled at such comparable institutions in such fiscal year, multiplied by (III) the number of students enrolled at the applicant institution in such fiscal year; or

(iii) 90 percent of the institution's allocation under this part for the preceding fiscal year.

(C) Notwithstanding subparagraphs (A) and (B) of this paragraph, the Secretary shall allocate to each eligible institution which—

(i) was a first-time participant in the program in fiscal year 2000 or any subsequent fiscal year, and

(ii) received a larger amount under this subsection in the second year of participation,

an amount equal to 90 percent of the amount it received under this subsection in its second year of participation.

(D) For any fiscal year after a fiscal year in which an institution receives an allocation under subparagraph (A), (B), or (C), the Secretary shall allocate to such institution an amount equal to the product of—

(i) the amount determined under subparagraph (A), (B), or (C), multiplied by

(ii) the institution's default penalty, as determined under subsection (e) of this section, except that if the institution has a cohort default rate in excess of the applicable maximum cohort default rate under subsection (f) of this section, the institution may not receive an allocation under this paragraph.

(3)(A) If the amount appropriated for any fiscal year is less than the amount required to be allocated to all institutions under paragraph (1) of this subsection, then the amount of the allocation to each such institution shall be ratably reduced.

(B) If the amount appropriated for any fiscal year is more than the amount required to be allocated to all institutions under paragraph (1) but less than the amount required to be allocated to all institutions under paragraph (2), then—

(i) the Secretary shall allot the amount required to be allocated to all institutions under paragraph (1), and

(ii) the amount of the allocation to each institution under

paragraph (2) shall be ratably reduced.

(C) If additional amounts are appropriated for any such fiscal year, such reduced amounts shall be increased on the same basis as they were reduced (until the amount allocated equals the amount required to be allocated under paragraphs (1) and (2) of this subsection).

(b) Allocation of excess based on share of excess eligible amounts

(1) From the remainder of the amount appropriated pursuant to section 1087aa(b) of this title after making the allocations required by subsection (a) of this section, the Secretary shall allocate to each eligible institution which has an excess eligible amount an amount which bears the same ratio to such remainder as such excess eligible amount bears to the sum of the excess eligible amounts of all such eligible institutions (having such excess eligible amounts).

(2) For any eligible institution, the excess eligible amount is the amount, if any, by which—

(A)(i) that institution's eligible amount (as determined under paragraph (3)), divided by

(ii) the sum of the eligible amounts of all institutions (as so determined), multiplied by

(iii) the amount appropriated pursuant to section 1087aa(b) of this title for the fiscal year; exceeds

(B) the amount required to be allocated to that institution under subsection (a) of this section, except that an eligible institution which has a cohort default rate in excess of the applicable maximum cohort default rate under subsection (f) of this section may not receive an allocation under this paragraph.

(3) For any eligible institution, the eligible amount of that institution is equal to—

(A) the amount of the institution's self-help need, as determined under subsection (c) of this section; minus

(B) the institution's anticipated collections; multiplied by

(C) the institution's default penalty, as determined under subsection (e) of this section;

except that, if the institution has a cohort default rate in excess of the applicable maximum cohort default rate under subsection (f) of this section, the eligible amount of that institution is zero.

(c) Determination of institution's self-help need

(1) The amount of an institution's self-help need is equal to the sum of the self-help need of the institution's eligible undergraduate students and the self-help need of the institution's eligible graduate and professional students.

(2) To determine the self-help need of an institution's eligible undergraduate students, the Secretary shall—

(A) establish various income categories for dependent and independent undergraduate students;

(B) establish an expected family contribution for each income category of dependent and independent undergraduate students, determined on the basis of the average expected family contribution (computed in accordance with part E of this subchapter) of a representative sample within each income category for the second preceding fiscal year;

(C) compute 25 percent of the average cost of attendance for all undergraduate students;

(D) multiply the number of eligible dependent students in each income category by the lesser of—

　(i)　25 percent of the average cost of attendance for all

undergraduate students determined under subparagraph (C); or

　(ii)　the average cost of attendance for all undergraduate students minus the expected family contribution determined under subparagraph (B) for that income category, except that the amount computed by such subtraction shall not be less than zero;

(E) add the amounts determined under subparagraph (D) for each income category of dependent students;

(F) multiply the number of eligible independent students in each income category by the lesser of—

　(i)　25 percent of the average cost of attendance for all undergraduate students determined under subparagraph (C); or

　(ii)　the average cost of attendance for all undergraduate students minus the expected family contribution determined under subparagraph (B) for that income category, except that the amount computed by such subtraction for any income category shall not be less than zero;

(G) add the amounts determined under subparagraph (F) for each income category of independent students; and

(H) add the amounts determined under subparagraphs (E) and (G).

(3) To determine the self-help need of an institution's eligible graduate and professional students, the Secretary shall—

(A) establish various income categories for graduate and professional students;

(B) establish an expected family contribution for each income category of graduate and professional students, determined on the basis of the average expected family contribution (computed in accordance with part E of this subchapter) of a representative sample within each income category for the second preceding fiscal year;

(C) determine the average cost of attendance for all graduate and professional students;

(D) subtract from the average cost of attendance for all graduate and professional students (determined under subparagraph (C)), the expected family contribution (determined under subparagraph (B)) for each income category, except that the amount computed by such subtraction for any income category shall not be less than zero;

(E) multiply the amounts determined under subparagraph (D) by the number of eligible students in each category;

(F) add the amounts determined under subparagraph (E) for each income category.

(4)(A) For purposes of paragraphs (2) and (3), the term "average cost of attendance" means the average of the attendance costs for undergraduate students and for graduate and professional students, which shall include (i) tuition and fees determined in accordance with subparagraph (B), (ii) standard living expenses determined in accordance with subparagraph (C), and (iii) books and supplies determined in accordance with subparagraph (D).

(B) The average undergraduate and graduate and professional tuition and fees described in subparagraph (A)(i) shall be computed on the basis of information reported by the institution to the Secretary, which shall include (i) total revenue received by the institution from undergraduate and graduate tuition and fees for the second year preceding the year for which it is applying for an allocation, and (ii) the institution's enrollment for such second preceding year.

(C) The standard living expense described in subparagraph (A)(ii) is equal to 150 percent of the difference between the income protection allowance for a family of five with one in college and the income protection allowance for a family of six with one in college for a single independent student.

(D) The allowance for books and supplies described in subparagraph (A)(iii) is equal to $450.

(d) Anticipated collections

(1) An institution's anticipated collections are equal to the amount which was collected during the second year preceding the beginning of the award period, multiplied by 1.21.

(2) The Secretary shall establish an appeals process by which the anticipated collections required in paragraph (1) may be waived for institutions with low cohort default rates in the program assisted under this part.

(e) Default penalties

(1) Years preceding fiscal year 2000

For any fiscal year preceding fiscal year 2000, any institution with a cohort default rate that—

(A) equals or exceeds 15 percent, shall establish a default reduction plan pursuant to regulations prescribed by the Secretary, except that such plan shall not be required with respect to an institution that has a default rate of less than 20 percent and that has less than 100 students who have loans under this part in such academic year;

(B) equals or exceeds 20 percent, but is less than 25 percent, shall have a default penalty of 0.9;

(C) equals or exceeds 25 percent, but is less than 30 percent, shall have a default penalty of 0.7; and

(D) equals or exceeds 30 percent shall have a default penalty of zero.

(2) Years following fiscal year 2000

For fiscal year 2000 and any succeeding fiscal year, any institution with a cohort default rate (as defined under subsection (g) of this section) that equals or exceeds 25 percent shall have a default penalty of zero.

(3) Ineligibility

(A) In general

For fiscal year 2000 and any succeeding fiscal year, any institution with a cohort default rate (as defined in subsection (g) of this section) that equals or exceeds 50 percent for each of the 3 most recent years for which data are available shall not be eligible to participate in a program under this part for the fiscal year for which the determination is made and the 2 succeeding fiscal years, unless, within 30 days of receiving notification from the Secretary of the loss of eligibility under this paragraph, the institution appeals the loss of eligibility to the Secretary. The Secretary shall issue a decision on any such appeal within 45 days after the submission of the appeal. Such decision may permit the institution to continue to participate in a program under this part if—

(i) the institution demonstrates to the satisfaction of the Secretary that the calculation of the institution's cohort default rate is not accurate, and that recalculation would reduce the institution's cohort default rate for any of the 3 fiscal years below 50 percent; or

(ii) there are, in the judgment of the Secretary, such a small number of borrowers entering repayment that the application of this subparagraph would be inequitable.

(B) Continued participation

During an appeal under subparagraph (A), the Secretary may permit the institution to continue to participate in a program under this part.

(C) Return of funds

Within 90 days after the date of any termination pursuant to subparagraph (A), or the conclusion of any appeal pursuant to subparagraph (B), whichever is later, the balance of the student loan fund established under this part by the institution that is the subject of the termination shall be distributed as follows:

(i) The Secretary shall first be paid an amount which bears the same ratio to such balance (as of the date of such distribution) as the total amount of Federal capital contributions to such fund by the Secretary under this part bears to the sum of such Federal capital contributions and the capital contributions to such fund made by the institution.

(ii) The remainder of such student loan fund shall be paid to the institution.

(D) Use of returned funds

Any funds returned to the Secretary under this paragraph shall be reallocated to institutions of higher education pursuant to subsection (i) of this section.

(E) Definition

For the purposes of subparagraph (A), the term "loss of eligibility" shall be defined as the mandatory liquidation of an institution's student loan fund, and assignment of the institution's outstanding loan portfolio to the Secretary.

(f) Applicable maximum cohort default rate

(1) Award years prior to 2000

For award years prior to award year 2000, the applicable maximum cohort default rate is 30 percent.

(2) Award year 2000 and succeeding award years

For award year 2000 and subsequent years, the applicable maximum cohort default rate is 25 percent.

(g) "Cohort default rate" defined

(1)(A) The term "cohort default rate" means, for any award year in which 30 or more current and former students at the institution enter repayment on loans under this part (received for attendance at the institution), the percentage of those current and former students who enter repayment on such loans (received for attendance at that institution) in that award year who default before the end of the following award year.

(B) For any award year in which less than 30 of the institution's current and former students enter repayment, the term "cohort default rate" means the percentage of such current and former students who entered repayment on such loans in any of the three most recent award years and who default before the end of the award year immediately following the year in which they entered repayment.

(C) A loan on which a payment is made by the institution of higher education, its owner, agency, contractor, employee, or any other entity or individual affiliated with such institution, in order to avoid default by the borrower, is considered as in default for the purposes of this subsection.

(D) In the case of a student who has attended and borrowed at more than one school, the student (and his or her subsequent repayment or default) is attributed to the school for attendance at which the student received the loan that entered repayment in the award year.

(E) In determining the number of students who default before the end of such award year, the institution, in calculating the cohort default rate, shall exclude—

  (i) any loan on which the borrower has, after the time periods specified in paragraph (2)—

    (I) voluntarily made 6 consecutive payments;

    (II) voluntarily made all payments currently due;

    (III) repaid in full the amount due on the loan; or

    (IV) received a deferment or forbearance, based on a condition that began prior to such time periods;

  (ii) any loan which has, after the time periods specified in paragraph (2), been rehabilitated or canceled; and

  (iii) any other loan that the Secretary determines should be excluded from such determination.

(F) The Secretary shall prescribe regulations designed to prevent an institution from evading the application to that institution of a cohort default rate determination under this subsection through the use of such measures as branching, consolidation, change of ownership or control or other means as determined by the Secretary.

(2) For purposes of calculating the cohort default rate under this subsection, a loan shall be considered to be in default—

(A) 240 days (in the case of a loan repayable monthly), or

(B) 270 days (in the case of a loan repayable quarterly), after the borrower fails to make an installment payment when due or to comply with other terms of the promissory note.

(h) Filing deadlines

The Secretary shall, from time to time, set dates before which institutions must file applications for allocations under this part.

(*i*) Reallocation of excess allocations

(1) In general

(A) If an institution of higher education returns to the Secretary any portion of the sums allocated to such institution under this section for any fiscal year, the Secretary shall reallocate 80 percent of such returned portions to participating institutions in an amount not to exceed such participating institution's excess eligible amounts as determined under paragraph (2).

(B) For the purpose of this subsection, the term "participating institution" means an institution of higher education that—

  (i) was a participant in the program assisted under this part in fiscal year 1999; and

  (ii) did not receive an allocation under subsection (a) of this section in the fiscal year for which the reallocation determination is made.

(2) Excess eligible amount

For any participating institution, the excess eligible amount is the amount, if any, by which—

(A)(i) that institution's eligible amount (as determined under subsection (b)(3) of this section), divided by

  (ii) the sum of the eligible amounts of all participating institutions (as determined under paragraph (3)), multiplied by

  (iii) the amount of funds available for reallocation under this subsection; exceeds

(B) the amount required to be allocated to that institution under subsection (b) of this section.

(3) Remainder

The Secretary shall reallocate the remainder of such returned portions in accordance with regulations of the Secretary.

(4) Allocation reductions

If under paragraph (1) of this subsection an institution returns more than 10 percent of its allocation, the institution's allocation for the next fiscal year shall be reduced by the amount returned. The Secretary may waive this paragraph for a specific institution if the Secretary finds that enforcing it is contrary to the interest of the program.

[Pub. L. 89-329, title IV, Sec. 462, as added Pub. L. 99-498, title IV, Sec. 405(a), Oct. 17, 1986, 100 Stat. 1440; amended Pub. L. 100-50, Sec. 13(a)-(d), June 3, 1987, 101 Stat. 348; Pub. L. 102-325, title IV, Sec. 462, July 23, 1992, 106 Stat. 576; Pub. L. 103-208, Sec. 2(f)(1)-(4), Dec. 20, 1993, 107 Stat. 2470, 2471; Pub. L. 105-244, title IV, Sec. 462(a)(1), (2), (b)-(e), Oct. 7, 1998, 112 Stat. 1720–1723.)

§ 1087cc. Agreements with institutions of higher education

(a) Contents of agreements

An agreement with any institution of higher education for the payment of Federal capital contributions under this part shall—

(1) provide for the establishment and maintenance of a student loan fund for the purpose of this part;

(2) provide for the deposit in such fund of—

(A) Federal capital contributions from funds appropriated under section 1087aa of this title;

(B) a capital contribution by an institution in an amount equal to one-third of the Federal capital contributions described in subparagraph (A);

(C) collections of principal and interest on student loans made from deposited funds;

(D) charges collected pursuant to regulations under section 1087dd(c)(1)(H) of this title; and

(E) any other earnings of the funds;

(3) provide that such student loan fund shall be used only for—

(A) loans to students, in accordance with the provisions of this part;

(B) administrative expenses, as provided in subsection (b) of this section;

(C) capital distributions, as provided in section 1087ff of this title; and

(D) costs of litigation, and other collection costs agreed to by the Secretary in connection with the collection of a loan from the fund (and interest thereon) or a charge assessed pursuant to regulations under section 1087dd(c)(1)(H) of this title;

(4) provide that where a note or written agreement evidencing a loan has been in default despite due diligence on the part of the institution in attempting collection thereon—

(A) if the institution has knowingly failed to maintain an acceptable collection record with respect to such loan, as determined by the Secretary in accordance with criteria established by regulation, the Secretary may—

  (i) require the institution to assign such note or agreement to the Secretary, without recompense; and

  (ii) apportion any sums collected on such a loan, less an amount not to exceed 30 percent of any sums collected to cover the Secretary's collection costs, among other institutions in accordance with section 1087bb of this title; or

(B) if the institution is not one described in subparagraph (A), the Secretary may—

    (i)   allow such institution to transfer its interest in such loan to the Secretary, for collection, and the Secretary may use any collections thereon (less an amount not to exceed 30 percent of any such sums collected to cover the Secretary's collection costs) to make allocations to institutions of additional capital contributions in accordance with section 1087bb of this title; or

    (ii) allow such institution to refer such note or agreement to the Secretary, without recompense, except that any sums collected on such a loan (less an amount not to exceed 30 percent of any such sums collected to cover the Secretary's collection costs) shall be repaid to such institution no later than 180 days after collection by the Secretary and treated as an additional capital contribution;

(5) provide that, if an institution of higher education determines not to service and collect student loans made available from funds under this part, the institution will assign, at the beginning of the repayment period, notes or evidence of obligations of student loans made from such funds to the Secretary and the Secretary shall apportion any sums collected on such notes or obligations (less an amount not to exceed 30 percent of any such sums collected to cover that Secretary's collection costs) among other institutions in accordance with section 1087bb of this title;

(6) provide that, notwithstanding any other provision of law, the Secretary will provide to the institution any information with respect to the names and addresses of borrowers or other relevant information which is available to the Secretary, from whatever source such information may be derived;

(7) provide assurances that the institution will comply with the provisions of section 1087cc-1 of this title;

(8) provide that the institution of higher education will make loans first to students with exceptional need; and

(9) include such other reasonable provisions as may be necessary to protect the United States from unreasonable risk of loss and as are agreed to by the Secretary and the institution.

(b) Administrative expenses

An institution which has entered into an agreement under subsection (a) of this section shall be entitled, for each fiscal year during which it makes student loans from a student loan fund established under such agreement, to a payment in lieu of reimbursement for its expenses in administering its student loan program under this part during such year. Such payment shall be made in accordance with section 1096 of this title.

(c) Cooperative agreements with credit bureau organizations

(1) For the purpose of promoting responsible repayment of loans made pursuant to this part, the Secretary and each institution of higher education participating in the program under this part shall enter into cooperative agreements with credit bureau organizations to provide for the exchange of information concerning student borrowers concerning whom the Secretary has received a referral pursuant to section 1087gg of this title and regarding loans held by the Secretary or an institution.

(2) Each cooperative agreement made pursuant to paragraph (1) shall be made in accordance with the requirements of section 1080a

of this title except that such agreement shall provide for the disclosure by the Secretary or an institution, as the case may be, to such organizations, with respect to any loan held by the Secretary or the institution, respectively, of—

(A) the date of disbursement and the amount of such loans made to any borrower under this part at the time of disbursement of the loan;

(B) information concerning the repayment and collection of any such loan, including information concerning the status of such loan; and

(C) the date of cancellation of the note upon completion of repayment by the borrower of any such loan, or upon cancellation or discharge of the borrower's obligation on the loan for any reason.

(3) Notwithstanding paragraphs (4) and (6)[2] of subsection (a) of section 1681c of title 15, a consumer reporting agency may make a report containing information received from the Secretary or an institution regarding the status of a borrower's account on a loan made under this part until the loan is paid in full.

(4)(A) Except as provided in subparagraph (B), an institution of higher education, after consultation with the Secretary and pursuant to the agreements entered into under paragraph (1), shall disclose at least annually to any credit bureau organization with which the Secretary has such an agreement the information set forth in paragraph (2), and shall disclose promptly to such credit bureau organization any changes to the information previously disclosed.

(B) The Secretary may promulgate regulations establishing criteria under which an institution of higher education may cease reporting the information described in paragraph (2) before a loan is paid in full.

(5) Each institution of higher education shall notify the appropriate credit bureau organizations whenever a borrower of a loan that is made and held by the institution and that is in default makes 6 consecutive monthly payments on such loan, for the purpose of encouraging such organizations to update the status of information maintained with respect to that borrower.

(d) Limitation on use of interest bearing accounts

In carrying out the provisions of subsection (a)(9) of this section, the Secretary may not require that any collection agency, collection attorney, or loan servicer collecting loans made under this part deposit amounts collected on such loans in interest bearing accounts, unless such agency, attorney, or servicer holds such amounts for more than 45 days.

(e) Special due diligence rule

In carrying out the provisions of subsection (a)(5)[3] of this section relating to due diligence, the Secretary shall make every

---

2 Paragraph (6) of subsection (a) of section 1681c of title 15, referred to in subsec. (c)(3), was redesignated paragraph (5) of subsection (a) of section 1681c of title 15 by Pub. L. 105-347, Sec. 5(4), Nov. 2, 1998, 112 Stat. 3211.

    Subsection (a)(5) of this section relating to due diligence, referred to in subsec. (e), was redesignated subsec. (a)(4), by Pub. L. 105-244, title IV, Sec. 463(a)(3), Oct. 7, 1998, 112 Stat. 1724.

3 Paragraph (6) of subsection (a) of section 1681c of title 15, referred to in subsec. (c)(3), was redesignated paragraph (5) of subsection (a) of section 1681c of title 15 by Pub. L. 105-347, Sec. 5(4), Nov. 2, 1998, 112 Stat. 3211.

effort to ensure that institutions of higher education may use Internal Revenue Service skip-tracing collection procedures on loans made under this part.

[Pub. L. 89-329, title IV, Sec. 463, as added Pub. L. 99-498, title IV, Sec. 405(a), Oct. 17, 1986, 100 Stat. 1444; amended Pub. L. 100-50, Sec. 13(e), (f), June 3, 1987, 101 Stat. 349; Pub. L. 102-325, title IV, Sec. 463(a), (b), July 23, 1992, 106 Stat. 579; Pub. L. 103-208, Sec. 2(f)(5)-(7), Dec. 20, 1993, 107 Stat. 2471; Pub. L. 105-244, title IV, Sec. 463, Oct. 7, 1998, 112 Stat. 1724]

§ 1087dd. Terms of loans

(a) Terms and conditions

(1) Loans from any student loan fund established pursuant to an agreement under section 1087cc of this title to any student by any institution shall, subject to such conditions, limitations, and requirements as the Secretary shall prescribe by regulation, be made on such terms and conditions as the institution may determine.

(2)(A) Except as provided in paragraph (4), the total of loans made to a student in any academic year or its equivalent by an institution of higher education from a loan fund established pursuant to an agreement under this part shall not exceed—

   (i) $4,000, in the case of a student who has not successfully completed a program of undergraduate education; or

   (ii) $6,000, in the case of a graduate or professional student (as defined in regulations issued by the Secretary).

(B) Except as provided in paragraph (4), the aggregate unpaid principal amount for all loans made to a student by institutions of higher education from loan funds established pursuant to agreements under this part may not exceed—

   (i) $40,000, in the case of any graduate or professional student (as defined by regulations issued by the Secretary, and including any loans from such funds made to such person before such person became a graduate or professional student);

   (ii) $20,000, in the case of a student who has successfully completed 2 years of a program of education leading to a bachelor's degree but who has not completed the work necessary for such a degree (determined under regulations issued by the Secretary), and including any loans from such funds made to such person before such person became such a student; and

   (iii) $8,000, in the case of any other student.

(3) Regulations of the Secretary under paragraph (1) shall be designed to prevent the impairment of the capital student loan funds to the maximum extent practicable and with a view toward the objective of enabling the student to complete his course of study.

(4) In the case of a program of study abroad that is approved for credit by the home institution at which a student is enrolled and that has reasonable costs in excess of the home institution's budget, the annual and aggregate loan limits for the student may exceed the amounts described in paragraphs (2)(A) and (2)(B) by 20 percent.

Subsection (a)(5) of this section relating to due diligence, referred to in subsec. (e), was redesignated subsec. (a)(4), by Pub. L. 105-244, title IV, Sec. 463(a)(3), Oct. 7, 1998, 112 Stat. 1724.

(b) Demonstration of need and eligibility required

(1) A loan from a student loan fund assisted under this part may be made only to a student who demonstrates financial need in accordance with part E of this subchapter, who meets the requirements of section 1091 of this title, and who provides the institution with the student's drivers license number, if any, at the time of application for the loan. A student who is in default on a loan under this part shall not be eligible for an additional loan under this part unless such loan meets one of the conditions for exclusion under section 1087bb(g)(1)(E) of this title.

(2) If the institution's capital contribution under section 1087bb of this title is directly or indirectly based in part on the financial need demonstrated by students who are (A) attending the institution less than full time, or (B) independent students, then a reasonable portion of the loans made from the institution's student loan fund containing the contribution shall be made available to such students.

(c) Contents of loan agreement

(1) Any agreement between an institution and a student for a loan from a student loan fund assisted under this part—

(A) shall be evidenced by note or other written instrument which, except as provided in paragraph (2), provides for repayment of the principal amount of the loan, together with interest thereon, in equal installments (or, if the borrower so requests, in graduated periodic installments determined in accordance with such schedules as may be approved by the Secretary) payable quarterly, bimonthly, or monthly, at the option of the institution, over a period beginning nine months after the date on which the student ceases to carry, at an institution of higher education or a comparable institution outside the United States approved for this purpose by the Secretary, at least one-half the normal full-time academic workload, and ending 10 years and 9 months after such date except that such period may begin earlier than 9 months after such date upon the request of the borrower;

(B) shall include provision for acceleration of repayment of the whole, or any part, of such loan, at the option of the borrower;

(C)(i) may provide, at the option of the institution, in accordance with regulations of the Secretary, that during the repayment period of the loan, payments of principal and interest by the borrower with respect to all outstanding loans made to the student from a student loan fund assisted under this part shall be at a rate equal to not less than $40 per month, except that the institution may, subject to such regulations, permit a borrower to pay less than $40 per month for a period of not more than one year where necessary to avoid hardship to the borrower, but without extending the 10-year maximum repayment period provided for in subparagraph (A) of this paragraph; and

   (ii) may provide that the total payments by a borrower for a monthly or similar payment period with respect to the aggregate of all loans held by the institution may, when the amount of a monthly or other similar payment is not a multiple of $5, be rounded to the next highest whole dollar amount that is a multiple of $5;

(D) shall provide that the loan shall bear interest, on the unpaid balance of the loan, at the rate of 5 percent per year in the case of any loan made on or after October 1, 1981, except that no interest shall accrue (I) prior to the beginning date of repayment determined under paragraph (2)(A)(i), or (II) during any period in which repayment is suspended by reason of paragraph (2);

(E) shall provide that the loan shall be made without security and without endorsement;

(F) shall provide that the liability to repay the loan shall be canceled upon the death of the borrower, or if he becomes permanently and totally disabled as determined in accordance with regulations of the Secretary;

(G) shall provide that no note or evidence of obligation may be assigned by the lender, except upon the transfer of the borrower to another institution participating under this part (or, if not so participating, is eligible to do so and is approved by the Secretary for such purpose), to such institution, and except as necessary to carry out section 1087cc(a)(6)[4] of this title;

(H) pursuant to regulations of the Secretary, shall provide for an assessment of a charge with respect to the loan for failure of the borrower to pay all or part of an installment when due, which shall include the expenses reasonably incurred in attempting collection of the loan, to the extent permitted by the Secretary, except that no charge imposed under this subparagraph shall exceed 20 percent of the amount of the monthly payment of the borrower; and

(*I*) shall contain a notice of the system of disclosure of information concerning default on such loan to credit bureau organizations under section 1087cc(c) of this title.

(2)(A) No repayment of principal of, or interest on, any loan from a student loan fund assisted under this part shall be required during any period—

    (i) during which the borrower—

        (I) is pursuing at least a half-time course of study as determined by an eligible institution; or

        (II) is pursuing a course of study pursuant to a graduate fellowship program approved by the Secretary, or pursuant to a rehabilitation training program for disabled individuals approved by the Secretary, except that no borrower shall be eligible for a deferment under this clause, or loan made under this part while serving in a medical internship or residency program;

    (ii) not in excess of 3 years during which the borrower is seeking and unable to find full-time employment;

    (iii) not in excess of 3 years during which the borrower—

        (I) is serving on active duty during a war or other military operation or national emergency; or

        (II) is performing qualifying National Guard duty during a war or other military operation or national emergency;

    (iv) not in excess of 3 years for any reason which the lender determines, in accordance with regulations prescribed by the Secretary under section 1085(o) of this title, has caused or will cause the borrower to

have an economic hardship; or

    (v) during which the borrower is engaged in service described in section 1087ee(a)(2) of this title; and

provides that any such period shall not be included in determining the 10-year period described in subparagraph (A) of paragraph (1).

(B) No repayment of principal of, or interest on, any loan for any period described in subparagraph (A) shall begin until 6 months after the completion of such period.

(C) An individual with an outstanding loan balance who meets the eligibility criteria for a deferment described in subparagraph (A) as in effect on October 7, 1998, shall be eligible for deferment under this paragraph notwithstanding any contrary provision of the promissory note under which the loan or loans were made, and notwithstanding any amendment (or effective date provision relating to any amendment) to this section made prior to the date of such deferment.

(3)(A) The Secretary is authorized, when good cause is shown, to extend, in accordance with regulations, the 10-year maximum repayment period provided for in subparagraph (A) of paragraph (1) with respect to individual loans.

(B) Pursuant to uniform criteria established by the Secretary, the repayment period for any student borrower who during the repayment period is a low-income individual may be extended for a period not to exceed 10 years and the repayment schedule may be adjusted to reflect the income of that individual.

(4) The repayment period for a loan made under this part shall begin on the day immediately following the expiration of the period, specified in paragraph (1)(A), after the student ceases to carry the required academic workload, unless the borrower requests and is granted a repayment schedule that provides for repayment to commence at an earlier point in time, and shall exclude any period of authorized deferment, forbearance, or cancellation.

(5) The institution may elect—

(A) to add the amount of any charge imposed under paragraph (1)(H) to the principal amount of the loan as of the first day after the day on which the installment was due and to notify the borrower of the assessment of the charge; or

(B) to make the amount of the charge payable to the institution not later than the due date of the next installment.

(6) Requests for deferment of repayment of loans under this part by students engaged in graduate or post-graduate fellowship-supported study (such as pursuant to a Fulbright grant) outside the United States shall be approved until completion of the period of the fellowship.

(7) There shall be excluded from the 9-month period that begins on the date on which a student ceases to carry at least one-half the normal full-time academic workload (as described in paragraph (1)(A)) any period not to exceed 3 years during which a borrower who is a member of a reserve component of the Armed Forces named in section 10101 of title 10 is called or ordered to active duty for a period of more than 30 days (as defined in section 101(d)(2) of such title). Such period of exclusion shall include the period necessary to resume enrollment at the borrower's next available regular enrollment period.

(d) Availability of loan fund to all eligible students

---

4 Section 1087cc(a) of this title, referred to in subsec. (c)(1)(G), was amended by Pub. L. 105-244, title IV, Sec. 463(a)(3), Oct. 7, 1998, 112 Stat. 1724, which redesignated pars. (6) and (7) as (5) and (6), respectively.

An agreement under this part for payment of Federal capital contributions shall include provisions designed to make loans from the student loan fund established pursuant to such agreement reasonably available (to the extent of the available funds in such fund) to all eligible students in such institutions in need thereof.

(e) Forbearance

The Secretary shall ensure that, upon written request, an institution of higher education shall grant a borrower forbearance of principal and interest or principal only, renewable at 12-month intervals for a period not to exceed 3 years, on such terms as are otherwise consistent with the regulations issued by the Secretary and agreed upon in writing by the parties to the loan, if—

(1) the borrower's debt burden equals or exceeds 20 percent of such borrower's gross income;

(2) the institution determines that the borrower should qualify for forbearance for other reasons; or

(3) the borrower is eligible for interest payments to be made on such loan for service in the Armed Forces under section 2174 of Title 10 and, pursuant to that eligibility, the interest on such loan is being paid under subsection (j) of this section, except that the form of a forbearance under this paragraph shall be a temporary cessation of all payments on the loan other than payments of interest on the loan that are made under subsection (j) of this section.

(f) Special repayment rule authority

(1) Subject to such restrictions as the Secretary may prescribe to protect the interest of the United States, in order to encourage repayment of loans made under this part which are in default, the Secretary may, in the agreement entered into under this part, authorize an institution of higher education to compromise on the repayment of such defaulted loans in accordance with paragraph (2). The Federal share of the compromise repayment shall bear the same relation to the institution's share of such compromise repayment as the Federal capital contribution to the institution's loan fund under this part bears to the institution's capital contribution to such fund.

(2) No compromise repayment of a defaulted loan as authorized by paragraph (1) may be made unless the student borrower pays—

(A) 90 percent of the loan under this part;

(B) the interest due on such loan; and

(C) any collection fees due on such loan;

in a lump sum payment.

(g) Discharge

(1) In general

If a student borrower who received a loan made under this part on or after January 1, 1986, is unable to complete the program in which such student is enrolled due to the closure of the institution, then the Secretary shall discharge the borrower's liability on the loan (including the interest and collection fees) and shall subsequently pursue any claim available to such borrower against the institution and the institution's affiliates and principals, or settle the loan obligation pursuant to the financial responsibility standards described in section 1099c(c) of this title.

(2) Assignment

A borrower whose loan has been discharged pursuant to this subsection shall be deemed to have assigned to the United States the right to a loan refund in an amount that does not exceed the amount discharged against the institution and the institution's affiliates and principals.

(3) Eligibility for additional assistance

The period during which a student was unable to complete a course of study due to the closing of the institution shall not be considered for purposes of calculating the student's period of eligibility for additional assistance under this subchapter and part C of subchapter I of chapter 34 of title 42.

(4) Special rule

A borrower whose loan has been discharged pursuant to this subsection shall not be precluded, because of that discharge, from receiving additional grant, loan, or work assistance under this subchapter and part C of subchapter I of chapter 34 of title 42 for which the borrower would be otherwise eligible (but for the default on the discharged loan). The amount discharged under this subsection shall be treated as an amount canceled under section 1087ee(a) of this title.

(5) Reporting

The Secretary or institution, as the case may be, shall report to credit bureaus with respect to loans that have been discharged pursuant to this subsection.

(h) Rehabilitation of loans

(1) Rehabilitation

(A) In general

If the borrower of a loan made under this part who has defaulted on the loan makes 12 ontime, consecutive, monthly payments of amounts owed on the loan, as determined by the institution, or by the Secretary in the case of a loan held by the Secretary, the loan shall be considered rehabilitated, and the institution that made that loan (or the Secretary, in the case of a loan held by the Secretary) shall request that any credit bureau organization or credit reporting agency to which the default was reported remove the default from the borrower's credit history.

(B) Comparable conditions

As long as the borrower continues to make scheduled repayments on a loan rehabilitated under this paragraph, the rehabilitated loan shall be subject to the same terms and conditions, and qualify for the same benefits and privileges, as other loans made under this part.

(C) Additional assistance

The borrower of a rehabilitated loan shall not be precluded by section 1091 of this title from receiving additional grant, loan, or work assistance under this subchapter and part C of subchapter I of chapter 34 of title 42 (for which the borrower is otherwise eligible) on the basis of defaulting on the loan prior to such rehabilitation.

(D) Limitations

A borrower only once may obtain the benefit of this paragraph with respect to rehabilitating a loan under this part.

(2) Restoration of eligibility

If the borrower of a loan made under this part who has defaulted on that loan makes 6 ontime, consecutive, monthly payments of amounts owed on such loan, the borrower's eligibility for grant, loan, or work assistance under this subchapter and part C of subchapter I of chapter 34 of title 42 shall be restored to the extent that the borrower is otherwise eligible. A borrower only once may obtain the benefit of this paragraph with respect to restored eligibility.

(*i*) Incentive repayment program

(1) In general

Each institution of higher education may establish, with the approval of the Secretary, an incentive repayment program designed to reduce default and to replenish student loan funds established under this part. Each such incentive repayment program may—

    (A) offer a reduction of the interest rate on a loan on which the borrower has made 48 consecutive, monthly repayments, but in no event may the rate be reduced by more than 1 percent;

    (B) provide for a discount on the balance owed on a loan on which the borrower pays the principal and interest in full prior to the end of the applicable repayment period, but in no event may the discount exceed 5 percent of the unpaid principal balance due on the loan at the time the early repayment is made; and

    (C) include such other incentive repayment options as the institution determines will carry out the objectives of this subsection.

  (2) Limitation

No incentive repayment option under an incentive repayment program authorized by this subsection may be paid for with Federal funds, including any Federal funds from the student loan fund, or with institutional funds from the student loan fund.

  (j) Armed Forces student loan interest payment program

  (1) Authority

Using funds received by transfer to the Secretary under section 2174 of Title 10 for the payment of interest on a loan made under this part to a member of the Armed Forces, the Secretary shall pay the interest on the loan as due for a period not in excess of 36 consecutive months. The Secretary may not pay interest on such a loan out of any funds other than funds that have been so transferred.

  (2) Forbearance

During the period in which the Secretary is making payments on a loan under paragraph (1), the institution of higher education shall grant the borrower forbearance in accordance with subsection (e)(3) of this section.

[Pub. L. 89-329, title IV, Sec. 462, as added Pub. L. 99-498, title IV, Sec. 405(a), Oct. 17, 1986, 100 Stat. 1440; amended Pub. L. 100-50, Sec. 13(a)-(d), June 3, 1987, 101 Stat. 348; Pub. L. 102-325, title IV, Sec. 462, July 23, 1992, 106 Stat. 576; Pub. L. 103-208, Sec. 2(f)(1)–(4), Dec. 20, 1993, 107 Stat. 2470, 2471; Pub. L. 105-244, title IV, Sec. 462(a)(1), (2), (b)–(e), Oct. 7, 1998, 112 Stat. 1720–1723; Pub. L. 107-314, Div. A, title VI, § 651(c), Dec. 2, 2002, 116 Stat. 2458; Pub. L. 109-171, Feb. 8, 2006, 120 Stat. 4)

A.1.4 General Provisions

20 U.S.C. sec.

1091. Student eligibility.
1091a. Statute of limitations, and State court judgments.
1091b. Institutional refunds.
1095a. Wage garnishment requirements.

§ 1091. Student eligibility

  (a) In general

In order to receive any grant, loan, or work assistance under this subchapter and part C of subchapter I of chapter 34 of Title 42, a student must—

  (1) be enrolled or accepted for enrollment in a degree, certifi-

cate, or other program (including a program of study abroad approved for credit by the eligible institution at which such student is enrolled) leading to a recognized educational credential at an institution of higher education that is an eligible institution in accordance with the provisions of section 1094 of this title, except as provided in subsections (b)(3) and (b)(4) of this section, and not be enrolled in an elementary or secondary school;

  (2) if the student is presently enrolled at an institution, be maintaining satisfactory progress in the course of study the student is pursuing in accordance with the provisions of subsection (c) of this section;

  (3) not owe a refund on grants previously received at any institution under this subchapter and part C of subchapter I of chapter 34 of Title 42, or be in default on any loan from a student loan fund at any institution provided for in part D of this subchapter, or a loan made, insured, or guaranteed by the Secretary under this subchapter and part C of subchapter I of chapter 34 of Title 42 for attendance at any institution;

  (4) file with the Secretary, as part of the original financial aid application process, a certification,,[5] which need not be notarized, but which shall include—

    (A) a statement of educational purpose stating that the money attributable to such grant, loan, or loan guarantee will be used solely for expenses related to attendance or continued attendance at such institution; and

    (B) such student's social security number, except that the provisions of this subparagraph shall not apply to a student from the Republic of the Marshall Islands, the Federated States of Micronesia, or the Republic of Palau;[6]

  (5) be a citizen or national of the United States, a permanent resident of the United States, able to provide evidence from the Immigration and Naturalization Service that he or she is in the United States for other than a temporary purpose with the intention of becoming a citizen or permanent resident,[7] a citizen of any one of the Freely Associated States; and

  (6) if the student has been convicted of, or has pled nolo contendere or guilty to, a crime involving fraud in obtaining funds under this title, have completed the repayment of such funds to the Secretary, or to the holder in the case of a loan under this title obtained by fraud.

  (b) Eligibility for student loans

  (1) In order to be eligible to receive any loan under this subchapter and part C of subchapter I of chapter 34 of Title 42 (other than a loan under section 1078-2 or 1078-3 of this title) for any period of enrollment, a student who is not a graduate or professional student (as defined in regulations of the Secretary), and who is enrolled in a program at an institution which has a participation agreement with the Secretary to make awards under subpart 1 of part A of this subchapter, shall—

    (A) (i) have received a determination of eligibility or ineligibility for a Pell Grant under such subpart 1 for such period of enrollment; and

      (ii) if determined to be eligible, have filed an application for a Pell Grant for such enrollment period; or (B) have (A) filed an application with the Pell Grant processor for such institution for such enrollment

---

5 So in original.
6 So in original. Probably should be followed by "and".
7 So in original. Probably should be followed by "or".

period, and (B) received from the financial aid administrator of the institution a preliminary determination of the student's eligibility or ineligibility for a grant under such subpart 1.

(2) In order to be eligible to receive any loan under section 1078-1[8] of this title for any period of enrollment, a student shall—

(A) have received a determination of need for a loan under section 1078(a)(2)(B) of this title;

(B) if determined to have need for a loan under section 1078 of this title, have applied for such a loan; and

(C) has applied for a loan under section 1078-8 of this title, if such student is eligible to apply for such a loan.

(3) A student who—

(A) is carrying at least one-half the normal full-time work load for the course of study that the student is pursuing, as determined by an eligible institution, and

(B) is enrolled in a course of study necessary for enrollment in a program leading to a degree or certificate,

shall be, notwithstanding paragraph (1) of subsection (a) of this section, eligible to apply for loans under part B or C of this subchapter. The eligibility described in this paragraph shall be restricted to one 12-month period.

(4) A student who—

(A) is carrying at least one-half the normal full-time work load for the course of study the student is pursuing, as determined by the institution, and

(B) is enrolled or accepted for enrollment in a program at an eligible institution necessary for a professional credential or certification from a State that is required for employment as a teacher in an elementary or secondary school in that State,

shall be, notwithstanding paragraph (1) of subsection (a) of this section, eligible to apply for loans under part B, C, or D of this subchapter or work- study assistance under part C of subchapter I of chapter 34 of Title 42.

(5) Notwithstanding any other provision of this subsection, no incarcerated student is eligible to receive a loan under this subchapter and part C of subchapter I of chapter 34 of Title 42.

(c) Satisfactory progress

---

8 Section 1078-1 of this title, referred to in subsec. (b)(2), was repealed by Pub. L. 103-66, title IV, Sec. 4047(b)-(d), Aug. 10, 1993, 107 Stat. 364, eff. July 1, 1994, except with respect to loans provided under that section as it existed prior to Aug. 10, 1993. Subsequently, a new section 1078-1, relating to voluntary flexible agreements with guaranty agencies, was enacted by Pub. L. 105-244, title IV, Sec. 418, Oct. 7, 1998, 112 Stat. 1691.

Subsection (h) of this section, referred to in subsecs. (h)(2), (3) and (i), was redesignated subsec. (g) of this section by Pub. L. 103-208, Sec. 2(h)(25), Dec. 20, 1993, 107 Stat. 2477.

Section 2471 of this title, referred to in subsec. (l)(1)(B)(i), was omitted in the general amendment of chapter 44 (Sec. 2301 *et seq.*) of this title by Pub. L. 105-332, Sec. 1(b), Oct. 31, 1998, 112 Stat. 3076.

Section 1113 of Public Law 97-252, referred to in subsec. (n), amended section 462 of Title 50, Appendix, War and National Defense, and enacted provisions set out as a note under section 462 of Title 50, Appendix.

This chapter, referred to in subsec. (o), was in the original "this Act", meaning Pub. L. 89-329, as amended, known as the Higher Education Act of 1965. For complete classification of this Act to the Code, see Short Title note set out under section 1001 of this title and Tables.

(1) For the purpose of subsection (a)(2) of this section, a student is maintaining satisfactory progress if—

(A) the institution at which the student is in attendance, reviews the progress of the student at the end of each academic year, or its equivalent, as determined by the institution, and

(B) the student has a cumulative C average, or its equivalent or academic standing consistent with the requirements for graduation, as determined by the institution, at the end of the second such academic year.

(2) Whenever a student fails to meet the eligibility requirements of subsection (a)(2) of this section as a result of the application of this subsection and subsequent to that failure the student has academic standing consistent with the requirements for graduation, as determined by the institution, for any grading period, the student may, subject to this subsection, again be eligible under subsection (a)(2) of this section for a grant, loan, or work assistance under this subchapter and part C of subchapter I of chapter 34 of Title 42.

(3) Any institution of higher education at which the student is in attendance may waive the provisions of paragraph (1) or paragraph (2) of this subsection for undue hardship based on—

(A) the death of a relative of the student,

(B) the personal injury or illness of the student, or

(C) special circumstances as determined by the institution.

(d) Students who are not high school graduates

In order for a student who does not have a certificate of graduation from a school providing secondary education, or the recognized equivalent of such certificate, to be eligible for any assistance under subparts 1, 3, and 4 of part A and parts B, C, and D of this subchapter and part C of subchapter I of chapter 34 of Title 42, the student shall meet one of the following standards:

(1) The student shall take an independently administered examination and shall achieve a score, specified by the Secretary, demonstrating that such student can benefit from the education or training being offered. Such examination shall be approved by the Secretary on the basis of compliance with such standards for development, administration, and scoring as the Secretary may prescribe in regulations.

(2) The student shall be determined as having the ability to benefit from the education or training in accordance with such process as the State shall prescribe. Any such process described or approved by a State for the purposes of this section shall be effective 6 months after the date of submission to the Secretary unless the Secretary disapproves such process. In determining whether to approve or disapprove such process, the Secretary shall take into account the effectiveness of such process in enabling students without high school diplomas or the equivalent thereof to benefit from the instruction offered by institutions utilizing such process, and shall also take into account the cultural diversity, economic circumstances, and educational preparation of the populations served by the institutions.

(3) The student has completed a secondary school education in a home school setting that is treated as a home school or private school under State law.

(e) Certification for GSL eligibility

Each eligible institution may certify student eligibility for a loan by an eligible lender under part B of this subchapter prior to completing the review for accuracy of the information submitted by the applicant required by regulations issued under this subchapter and part C of subchapter I of chapter 34 of Title 42, if—

(1) checks for the loans are mailed to the eligible institution prior to disbursements;

(2) the disbursement is not made until the review is complete; and

(3) the eligible institution has no evidence or documentation on which the institution may base a determination that the information submitted by the applicant is incorrect.

(f) Loss of eligibility for violation of loan limits

(1) No student shall be eligible to receive any grant, loan, or work assistance under this subchapter and part C of subchapter I of chapter 34 of Title 42 if the eligible institution determines that the student fraudulently borrowed in violation of the annual loan limits under part B, part C, or part D of this subchapter in the same academic year, or if the student fraudulently borrowed in excess of the aggregate maximum loan limits under such part B, part C, or part D.

(2) If the institution determines that the student inadvertently borrowed amounts in excess of such annual or aggregate maximum loan limits, such institution shall allow the student to repay any amount borrowed in excess of such limits prior to certifying the student's eligibility for further assistance under this subchapter and part C of subchapter I of chapter 34 of Title 42.

(g) Verification of immigration status

(1) In general

The Secretary shall implement a system under which the statements and supporting documentation, if required, of an individual declaring that such individual is in compliance with the requirements of subsection (a)(5) of this section shall be verified prior to the individual's receipt of a grant, loan, or work assistance under this subchapter and part C of subchapter I of chapter 34 of Title 42.

(2) Special rule

The documents collected and maintained by an eligible institution in the admission of a student to the institution may be used by the student in lieu of the documents used to establish both employment authorization and identity under section 1324a(b)(1)(B) of Title 8 to verify eligibility to participate in work-study programs under part C of subchapter I of chapter 34 of Title 42.

(3) Verification mechanisms

The Secretary is authorized to verify such statements and supporting documentation through a data match, using an automated or other system, with other Federal agencies that may be in possession of information relevant to such statements and supporting documentation.

(4) Review

In the case of such an individual who is not a citizen or national of the United States, if the statement described in paragraph (1) is submitted but the documentation required under paragraph (2) is not presented or if the documentation required under paragraph (2)(A) is presented but such documentation is not verified under paragraph (3)—

(A) the institution—

   (i)   shall provide a reasonable opportunity to submit to the institution evidence indicating a satisfactory immigration status, and

   (ii)   may not delay, deny, reduce, or terminate the individual's eligibility for the grant, loan, or work assistance on the basis of the individual's immigration status until such a reasonable opportunity has been provided; and

(B) if there are submitted documents which the institution determines constitute reasonable evidence indicating such status—

   (i)   the State shall transmit to the Immigration and Naturalization Service either photostatic or other similar copies of such documents, or information from such documents, as specified by the Immigration and Naturalization Service, for official verification,

   (ii)   pending such verification, the institution may not delay, deny, reduce, or terminate the individual's eligibility for the grant, loan, or work assistance on the basis of the individual's immigration status, and

   (iii)   the institution shall not be liable for the consequences of any action, delay, or failure of the Service to conduct such verification.

(h) Limitations of enforcement actions against institutions

The Secretary shall not take any compliance, disallowance, penalty, or other regulatory action against an institution of higher education with respect to any error in the institution's determination to make a student eligible for a grant, loan, or work assistance based on citizenship or immigration status—

(1) if the institution has provided such eligibility based on a verification of satisfactory immigration status by the Immigration and Naturalization Service,

(2) because the institution, under subsection (h)(4)(A)(i)[9] of this section, was required to provide a reasonable opportunity to submit documentation, or

(3) because the institution, under subsection (h)(4)(B)(i)[10] of this section, was required to wait for the response of the Immigration and Naturalization Service to the institution's request for official verification of the immigration status of the student.

---

9   Section 1078-1 of this title, referred to in subsec. (b)(2), was repealed by Pub. L. 103-66, title IV, Sec. 4047(b)-(d), Aug. 10, 1993, 107 Stat. 364, eff. July 1, 1994, except with respect to loans provided under that section as it existed prior to Aug. 10, 1993. Subsequently, a new section 1078-1, relating to voluntary flexible agreements with guaranty agencies, was enacted by Pub. L. 105-244, title IV, Sec. 418, Oct. 7, 1998, 112 Stat. 1691. .

Subsection (h) of this section, referred to in subsecs. (h)(2), (3) and (i), was redesignated subsec. (g) of this section by Pub. L. 103-208, Sec. 2(h)(25), Dec. 20, 1993, 107 Stat. 2477.

Section 2471 of this title, referred to in subsec. (l)(1)(B)(i), was omitted in the general amendment of chapter 44 (Sec. 2301 *et seq.*) of this title by Pub. L. 105-332, Sec. 1(b), Oct. 31, 1998, 112 Stat. 3076.

Section 1113 of Public Law 97-252, referred to in subsec. (n), amended section 462 of Title 50, Appendix, War and National Defense, and enacted provisions set out as a note under section 462 of Title 50, Appendix.

This chapter, referred to in subsec. (o), was in the original "this Act", meaning Pub. L. 89-329, as amended, known as the Higher Education Act of 1965. For complete classification of this Act to the Code, see Short Title note set out under section 1001 of this title and Tables.

10   Section 1078-1 of this title, referred to in subsec. (b)(2), was repealed by Pub. L. 103-66, title IV, Sec. 4047(b)-(d), Aug. 10, 1993, 107 Stat. 364, eff. July 1, 1994, except with respect to loans provided under that section as it existed prior to Aug. 10, 1993. Subsequently, a new section 1078-1, relating to voluntary flexible agreements with guaranty agencies, was enacted by Pub. L. 105-244, title IV, Sec. 418, Oct. 7, 1998, 112 Stat. 1691.

Subsection (h) of this section, referred to in subsecs. (h)(2), (3) and (i), was redesignated subsec. (g) of this section by Pub. L. 103-208, Sec. 2(h)(25), Dec. 20, 1993, 107 Stat. 2477.

(*i*) Validity of loan guarantees for loan payments made before immigration status verification completed

Notwithstanding subsection (h)[11] of this section, if—

(1) a guaranty is made under this subchapter and part C of subchapter I of chapter 34 of Title 42 for a loan made with respect to an individual,

(2) at the time the guaranty is entered into, the provisions of subsection (h) of this section had been complied with,

(3) amounts are paid under the loan subject to such guaranty, and

(4) there is a subsequent determination that, because of an unsatisfactory immigration status, the individual is not eligible for the loan,

the official of the institution making the determination shall notify and instruct the entity making the loan to cease further payments under the loan, but such guaranty shall not be voided or otherwise nullified with respect to such payments made before the date the entity receives the notice.

(j) Assistance under subparts 1 and 3 of part A, and part C

Notwithstanding any other provision of law, a student shall be eligible until September 30, 2004, for assistance under subparts 1 and 3 of part A of this subchapter, and part C of subchapter 1 of chapter 34 of Title 42, if the student is otherwise qualified and—

(1) is a citizen of any one of the Freely Associated States and attends an institution of higher education in a State or a public or nonprofit private institution of higher education in the Freely Associated States; or

---

Section 2471 of this title, referred to in subsec. (l)(1)(B)(i), was omitted in the general amendment of chapter 44 (Sec. 2301 *et seq.*) of this title by Pub. L. 105-332, Sec. 1(b), Oct. 31, 1998, 112 Stat. 3076.

Section 1113 of Public Law 97-252, referred to in subsec. (n), amended section 462 of Title 50, Appendix, War and National Defense, and enacted provisions set out as a note under section 462 of Title 50, Appendix.

This chapter, referred to in subsec. (o), was in the original "this Act", meaning Pub. L. 89-329, as amended, known as the Higher Education Act of 1965. For complete classification of this Act to the Code, see Short Title note set out under section 1001 of this title and Tables.

11 Section 1078-1 of this title, referred to in subsec. (b)(2), was repealed by Pub. L. 103-66, title IV, Sec. 4047(b)–(d), Aug. 10, 1993, 107 Stat. 364, eff. July 1, 1994, except with respect to loans provided under that section as it existed prior to Aug. 10, 1993. Subsequently, a new section 1078-1, relating to voluntary flexible agreements with guaranty agencies, was enacted by Pub. L. 105-244, title IV, Sec. 418, Oct. 7, 1998, 112 Stat. 1691.

Subsection (h) of this section, referred to in subsecs. (h)(2), (3) and (i), was redesignated subsec. (g) of this section by Pub. L. 103-208, Sec. 2(h)(25), Dec. 20, 1993, 107 Stat. 2477.

Section 2471 of this title, referred to in subsec. (l)(1)(B)(i), was omitted in the general amendment of chapter 44 (Sec. 2301 *et seq.*) of this title by Pub. L. 105-332, Sec. 1(b), Oct. 31, 1998, 112 Stat. 3076.

Section 1113 of Public Law 97-252, referred to in subsec. (n), amended section 462 of Title 50, Appendix, War and National Defense, and enacted provisions set out as a note under section 462 of Title 50, Appendix.

This chapter, referred to in subsec. (o), was in the original "this Act", meaning Pub. L. 89-329, as amended, known as the Higher Education Act of 1965. For complete classification of this Act to the Code, see Short Title note set out under section 1001 of this title and Tables.

(2) meets the requirements of subsection (a)(5) of this section and attends a public or nonprofit private institution of higher education in any one of the Freely Associated States.

(k) Special rule for correspondence courses

A student shall not be eligible to receive grant, loan, or work assistance under this subchapter and part C of subchapter I of chapter 34 of Title 42 for a correspondence course unless such course is part of a program leading to an associate, bachelor or graduate degree.

(*l*) Courses offered through telecommunications

(1) Relation to correspondence courses

(A) In general

A student enrolled in a course of instruction at an institution of higher education that is offered in whole or in part through telecommunications and leads to a recognized certificate, or a recognized associate, baccalaureate, or graduate degree, conferred by such institution, shall not be considered to be enrolled in correspondence courses.

(B) Exception

Subparagraph (A) shall not apply to an institution or school described in section 3(3)(C) of the Carl D. Perkins Vocational and Technical Education Act of 1998.

(2) Restriction or reductions of financial aid

A student's eligibility to receive grants, loans, or work assistance under this subchapter and part C of subchapter I of chapter 34 of Title 42 shall be reduced if a financial aid officer determines under the discretionary authority provided in section 1087tt of this title that telecommunications instruction results in a substantially reduced cost of attendance to such student.

(3) Special rule

For award years prior to July 23, 1992, the Secretary shall not take any compliance, disallowance, penalty, or other action against a student or an eligible institution when such action arises out of such institution's prior award of student assistance under this subchapter and part C of subchapter I of chapter 34 of Title 42 if the institution demonstrates to the satisfaction of the Secretary that its course of instruction would have been in conformance with the requirements of this subsection.

(4) "Telecommunications, defined

For the purposes of this subsection, the term "telecommunications" means the use of television, audio, or computer transmission, including open broadcast, closed circuit, cable, microwave, or satellite, audio conferencing, computer conferencing, or video cassettes or discs, except that such term does not include a course that is delivered using video cassette or disc recordings at such institution and that is not delivered in person to other students of that institution.

(m) Students with a first baccalaureate or professional degree

A student shall not be ineligible for assistance under parts B, C, and D of this subchapter and part C of subchapter I of chapter 34 of Title 42 because such student has previously received a baccalaureate or professional degree.

(n) Data base matching

To enforce the Selective Service registration provisions of section 1113 of Public Law 97-252, the Secretary shall conduct data base matches with the Selective Service, using common demographic data elements. Appropriate confirmation, through an application output document or through other means, of any person's registration shall fulfill the requirement to file a separate statement of compliance. In the absence of a confirmation from such data matches, an institution may also use data or documents that support either the student's registration, or the absence of a registration requirement for the student, to fulfill the requirement to file a separate statement of compliance. The mechanism for reporting the resolution of nonconfirmed matches shall be prescribed by the Secretary in regulations.

(o) Study abroad

Nothing in this chapter shall be construed to limit or otherwise prohibit access to study abroad programs approved by the home institution at which a student is enrolled. An otherwise eligible student who is engaged in a program of study abroad approved for academic credit by the home institution at which the student is enrolled shall be eligible to receive grant, loan, or work assistance under this subchapter and part C of subchapter I of chapter 34 of Title 42, without regard to whether such study abroad program is required as part of the student's degree program.

(p) Verification of social security number

The Secretary of Education, in cooperation with the Commissioner of the Social Security Administration, shall verify any social security number provided by a student to an eligible institution under subsection (a)(4) of this section and shall enforce the following conditions:

(1) Except as provided in paragraphs (2) and (3), an institution shall not deny, reduce, delay, or terminate a student's eligibility for assistance under this part because social security number verification is pending.

(2) If there is a determination by the Secretary that the social security number provided to an eligible institution by a student is incorrect, the institution shall deny or terminate the student's eligibility for any grant, loan, or work assistance under this subchapter and part C of subchapter I of chapter 34 of Title 42 until such time as the student provides documented evidence of a social security number that is determined by the institution to be correct.

(3) If there is a determination by the Secretary that the social security number provided to an eligible institution by a student is incorrect, and a correct social security number cannot be provided by such student, and a loan has been guaranteed for such student under part B of this subchapter, the institution shall notify and instruct the lender and guaranty agency making and guaranteeing the loan, respectively, to cease further disbursements of the loan, but such guaranty shall not be voided or otherwise nullified with respect to such disbursements made before the date that the lender and the guaranty agency receives such notice.

(4) Nothing in this subsection shall permit the Secretary to take any compliance, disallowance, penalty, or other regulatory action against—

(A) any institution of higher education with respect to any error in a social security number, unless such error was a result of fraud on the part of the institution; or

(B) any student with respect to any error in a social security number, unless such error was a result of fraud on the part of the student.

(q) Verification of income data

(1) Confirmation with IRS

The Secretary of Education, in cooperation with the Secretary of the Treasury, is authorized to confirm with the Internal Revenue Service the information specified in section 6103(l)(13) of the Internal Revenue Code of 1986 reported by applicants (including parents) under this title on their Federal income tax returns for the purpose of verifying the information reported by applicants on student financial aid applications.

(2) Notification

The Secretary shall establish procedures under which an applicant is notified that the Internal Revenue Service will disclose to the Secretary tax return information as authorized under section 6103(l)(13) of Title 26.

(r) Suspension of eligibility for drug-related offenses

(1) In general

A student who is convicted of any offense under any Federal or State law involving the possession or sale of a controlled substance for conduct that occurred during a period of enrollment for which the student was receiving any grant, loan, or work assistance under this title shall not be eligible to receive any grant, loan, or work assistance under this title from the date of that conviction for the period of time specified in the following table:

If convicted of an offense involving:

The possession of a controlled substance:	Ineligibility period is:
First offense	1 year
Second offense	2 years
Third offense	Indefinite.
The sale of a controlled substance:	Ineligibility period is:
First offense	2 years
Second offense	Indefinite.

(2) Rehabilitation

A student whose eligibility has been suspended under paragraph (1) may resume eligibility before the end of the ineligibility period determined under such paragraph if—

(A) the student satisfactorily completes a drug rehabilitation program that—

(i) complies with such criteria as the Secretary shall prescribe in regulations for purposes of this paragraph; and

(ii) includes two unannounced drug tests; or

(B) the conviction is reversed, set aside, or otherwise rendered nugatory.

(3) Definitions

In this subsection, the term "controlled substance" has the meaning given the term in section 802(6) of Title 21.

[Pub. L. 89-329, Title IV, § 484, as added Pub. L. 99-498, Title IV, § 407(a), Oct. 17, 1986, 100 Stat. 1479, and amended Pub. L. 99-603, Title I, § 121(a)(3), Nov. 6, 1986, 100 Stat. 3388; Pub. L. 100-50, § 15(7) to (9), June 3, 1987, 101 Stat. 356, 357; Pub. L. 100-369, §§ 1, 2, 6, July 18, 1988, 102 Stat. 835, 836; Pub. L. 100-525, § 2(g), Oct. 24, 1988, 102 Stat. 2611; Pub. L. 101-508, Title III, § 3005(a), Nov. 5, 1990, 104 Stat. 1388-27; Pub. L. 102-26, § 2(b), (c)(2), (d)(2)(A), Apr. 9, 1991, 105 Stat. 123, 124; Pub. L. 102-73, Title VIII, § 801(a), July 25, 1991, 105 Stat. 359; Pub. L. 102-325, Title IV, § 484(a), (b)(1), (c) to (h), July 23, 1992, 106 Stat. 615 to 619; Pub. L. 103-208, § 2(h)(13) to (25), Dec. 20, 1993, 107 Stat. 2476, 2477; Pub. L. 103-382, Title III, § 360A, Oct. 20, 1994, 108 Stat. 3969; Pub. L. 104-208, Div. C, Title V, § 507(b), Sept. 30, 1996, 110 Stat. 3009-673; Pub. L. 105-244, Title IV, § 483(a) to (f)(1), Oct. 7, 1998, 112 Stat. 1735, 1736; Pub. L. 109-171, Feb. 8, 2006, 120 Stat. 4]

§ 1091a. Statute of limitations, and State court judgments

(a) In general

(1) It is the purpose of this subsection to ensure that obligations to repay loans and grant overpayments are enforced without regard to any Federal or State statutory, regulatory, or administrative limitation on the period within which debts may be enforced.

(2) Notwithstanding any other provision of statute, regulation, or administrative limitation, no limitation shall terminate the period within which suit may be filed, a judgment may be enforced, or an offset, garnishment, or other action initiated or taken by—

(A) an institution that receives funds under this subchapter and part C of subchapter I of chapter 34 of Title 42 that is seeking to collect a refund due from a student on a grant made, or work assistance awarded, under this subchapter and part C of subchapter I of chapter 34 of Title 42;

(B) a guaranty agency that has an agreement with the Secretary under section 1078(c) of this title that is seeking the repayment of the amount due from a borrower on a loan made under part B of this subchapter after such guaranty agency reimburses the previous holder of the loan for its loss on account of the default of the borrower;

(C) an institution that has an agreement with the Secretary pursuant to section 1087c or 1087cc(a) of this title that is seeking the repayment of the amount due from a borrower on a loan made under part C or D of this subchapter after the default of the borrower on such loan; or

(D) the Secretary, the Attorney General, or the administrative head of another Federal agency, as the case may be, for payment of a refund due from a student on a grant made under this subchapter and part C of subchapter I of chapter 34 of Title 42, or for the repayment of the amount due from a borrower on a loan made under this subchapter and part C of subchapter I of chapter 34 of Title 42 that has been assigned to the Secretary under this subchapter and part C of subchapter I of chapter 34 of Title 42.

(b) Assessment of costs and other charges

Notwithstanding any provision of State law to the contrary—

(1) a borrower who has defaulted on a loan made under this subchapter and part C of subchapter I of chapter 34 of title 42 shall be required to pay, in addition to other charges specified in this subchapter and part C of subchapter I of chapter 34 of title 42 reasonable collection costs; and

(2) in collecting any obligation arising from a loan made under part B of this subchapter, a guaranty agency or the Secretary shall not be subject to a defense raised by any borrower based on a claim of infancy.

(c) State court judgments

A judgment of a State court for the recovery of money provided as grant, loan, or work assistance under this subchapter that has been assigned or transferred to the Secretary under this subchapter may be registered in any district court of the United States by filing a certified copy of the judgment and a copy of the assignment or transfer. A judgment so registered shall have the same force and effect, and may be enforced in the same manner, as a judgment of the district court of the district in which the judgment is registered.

[Pub. L. 89-329, title IV, Sec. 484A, as added Pub. L. 99-498, title IV, Sec. 407(a), Oct. 17, 1986, 100 Stat. 1482; amended Pub. L. 102-26, Sec. 3(a), Apr. 9, 1991, 105 Stat. 124; Pub. L. 105-244, title IV, Sec. 484, Oct. 7, 1998, 112 Stat. 1737.)

§ 1091b. Institutional refunds

(a) Return of title IV funds

(1) In general

If a recipient of assistance under this subchapter and part C of subchapter I of chapter 34 of Title 42 [42 U.S.C.A. § 2751 *et seq.*] withdraws from an institution during a payment period or period of enrollment in which the recipient began attendance, the amount of grant or loan assistance (other than assistance received under part C of subchapter I of chapter 34 of Title 42 [12 U.S.C.A. § 2751 *et seq.*]) to be returned to the title IV programs is calculated according to paragraph (3) and returned in accordance with subsection (b) of this section.

(2) Leave of absence

(A) Leave not treated as withdrawal

In the case of a student who takes 1 or more leaves of absence from an institution for not more than a total of 180 days in any 12-month period, the institution may consider the student as not having withdrawn from the institution during the leave of absence, and not calculate the amount of grant and loan assistance provided under this subchapter [20 U.S.C.A. § 1070 *et seq.*] and part C of subchapter I of chapter 34 of Title 42 [42 U.S.C.A. § 2751 *et seq.*] that is to be returned in accordance with this section if—

(i) the institution has a formal policy regarding leaves of absence;

(ii) the student followed the institution's policy in requesting a leave of absence; and

(iii) the institution approved the student's request in accordance with the institution's policy.

(B) Consequences of failure to return

If a student does not return to the institution at the expiration of an approved leave of absence that meets the requirements of subparagraph (A), the institution shall calculate the amount of grant and loan assistance provided under this subchapter [20 U.S.C.A. § 1070 *et seq.*] and part C of subchapter I of chapter 34 of Title 42 [42 U.S.C.A. § 2751 *et seq.*] that is to be returned in accordance with this section based on the day the student withdrew (as determined under subsection (c) of this section.

(3) Calculation of amount of title IV assistance earned

(A) In general

The amount of grant or loan assistance under this subchapter [20 U.S.C.A. § 1070 *et seq.*] and part C of subchapter I of chapter 34 of Title 42 [42 U.S.C.A. § 2751 *et seq.*] that is earned by the recipient for purposes of this section is calculated by—

(i) determining the percentage of grant and loan assistance under this subchapter [20 U.S.C.A. § 1070 *et seq.*] and part C of subchapter I of chapter 34 of Title 42 [42 U.S.C.A. 2751 *et seq.*] that has been earned by the student, as described in subparagraph (B); and

(ii) applying such percentage to the total amount of such grant and loan assistance that was disbursed (and that could have been disbursed) to the student, or on the student's behalf, for the payment period or period of enrollment for which the assistance was awarded, as of the day the student withdrew.

(B) Percentage earned

For purposes of subparagraph (A)(i), the percentage of grant or loan assistance under this subchapter [20 U.S.C.A.

§ 1070 *et seq.*] and part C of subchapter I of chapter 34 of Title 42 [42 U.S.C.A. § 2751 *et seq.*] that has been earned by the student is—

    (i) equal to the percentage of the payment period or period of enrollment for which assistance was awarded that was completed (as determined in accordance with subsection (d)) as of the day the student withdrew, provided that such date occurs on or before the completion of 60 percent of the payment period or period of enrollment; or

    (ii) 100 percent, if the day the student withdrew occurs after the student has completed (as determined in accordance with subsection (d)) 60 percent of the payment period or period of enrollment.

(C) Percentage and amount not earned

For purposes of subsection (b), the amount of grant and loan assistance awarded under this subchapter [20 U.S.C.A. § 1070 *et seq.*] and part C of subchapter I of chapter 34 of Title 42 [42 U.S.C.A. § 2751 *et seq.*] that has not been earned by the student shall be calculated by—

    (i) determining the complement of the percentage of grant assistance under subparts 1 and 3 of part A, or loan assistance under parts B, D, and E, and part C of subchapter I of chapter 34 of Title 42 that has been earned by the student described in subparagraph (B); and

    (ii) applying the percentage determined under clause (i) to the total amount of such grant and loan assistance that was disbursed (and that could have been disbursed) to the student, or on the student's behalf, for the payment period or period of enrollment, as of the day the student withdrew.

(4) Differences between amounts earned and amounts received

(A) In general

After determining the eligibility of the student for a late disbursement or post-withdrawal disbursement (as required in regulations prescribed by the Secretary), the institution of higher education shall contact the borrower and obtain confirmation that the loan funds are still required by the borrower. In making such contact, the institution shall explain to the borrower the borrower's obligation to repay the funds following any such disbursement. The institution shall document in the borrower's file the result of such contact and the final determination made concerning such disbursement.

(B) Return

If the student has received more grant or loan assistance than the amount earned as calculated under paragraph (3)(A), the unearned funds shall be returned by the institution or the student, or both, as may be required under paragraphs (1) and (2) of subsection [20 U.S.C.A. § 1070 *et seq.*] (b), to the programs under this subchapter and part C of subchapter I of chapter 34 of title 42 [42 U.S.C.A. § 2751 *et seq.*] in the order specified in subsection (b)(3).

(b) Return of title IV program funds

(1) Responsibility of the institution

The institution shall return not later than 45 days from the determination of withdrawal, in the order specified in paragraph (3), the lesser of—

(A) the amount of grant and loan assistance awarded under this subchapter [20 U.S.C.A. § 1070 *et seq.*] and part C of subchapter I of chapter 34 of Title 42 [42 U.S.C.A. § 2751]

that has not been earned by the student, as calculated under subsection (a)(3)(C); or

(B) an amount equal to—

    (i) the total institutional charges incurred by the student for the payment period or period of enrollment for which such assistance was awarded; multiplied by

    (ii) the percentage of grant and loan assistance awarded under this subchapter and part C of subchapter I of chapter 34 of title 42 that has not been earned by the student, as described in subsection (a)(3)(C)(i)

(2) Responsibility of the student

(A) In general

The student shall return assistance that has not been earned by the student as described in subsection (a)(3)(C)(ii) in the order specified in paragraph (3) minus the amount the institution is required to return under paragraph (1).

(B) Special rule

The student (or parent in the case of funds due to a loan borrowed by a parent under part B or C of this subchapter [20 U.S.C.A. § 1071 *et seq.*]) shall return or repay, as appropriate, the amount determined under subparagraph (A) to—

    (i) a loan program under this subchapter [20 U.S.C.A. § 1070] and part C of subchapter I of chapter 34 of Title 42 [42 U.S.C.A. § 2751 *et seq.*] in accordance with the terms of the loan; and

    (ii) a grant program under this subchapter and part C of subchapter I of chapter 34 of title 42, as an overpayment of such grant and shall be subject to—

        (I) repayment arrangements satisfactory to the institution; or

        (II) overpayment collection procedures prescribed by the Secretary.

(C) Grant Overpayment Requirements

    (i) In general.—Notwithstanding subparagraphs (A) and (B), a student shall only be required to return grant assistance in the amount (if any) by which—

        (I) the amount to be returned by the student (as determined under subparagraphs (A) and (B)), exceeds

        (II) 50 percent of the total grant assistance received by the student under this title for the payment period or period of enrollment.

    (ii) Minimum.—A student shall not be required to return amounts of $50 or less.

(D) Waivers of Federal Pell Grant repayment by students affected by disasters.—The Secretary may waive the amounts that students are required to return under this section with respect to Federal Pell Grants if the withdrawals on which the returns are based are withdrawals by students—

    (i) who were residing in, employed in, or attending an institution of higher education that is located in an area in which the President has declared that a major disaster exists, in accordance with section 401 of the Robert T. Stafford Disaster Relief and Emergency Assistance Act (42 U.S.C. 5170);

    (ii) whose attendance was interrupted because of the impact of the disaster on the student or the institution; and

    (iii) whose withdrawal ended within the academic year during which the designation occurred or during the next succeeding academic year.

(E) Waivers of grant assistance repayment by students affected by disasters.—In addition to the waivers authorized by subparagraph (D), the Secretary may waive the amounts that students are required to return under this section with respect to any other grant assistance under this title if the withdrawals on which the returns are based are withdrawals by students—

   (i) who were residing in, employed in, or attending an institution of higher education that is located in an area in which the President has declared that a major disaster exists, in accordance with section 401 of the Robert T. Stafford Disaster Relief and Emergency Assistance Act (42 U.S.C. 5170);

   (ii) whose attendance was interrupted because of the impact of the disaster on the student or the institution; and

   (iii) whose withdrawal ended within the academic year during which the designation occurred or during the next succeeding academic year.

(3) Order of return of title IV funds

(A) In general

Excess funds returned by the institution or the student, as appropriate, in accordance with paragraph (1) or (2), respectively, shall be credited to outstanding balances on loans made under this subchapter and part C of subchapter I of chapter 34 of title 42 to the student or on behalf of the student for the payment period or period of enrollment for which a return of funds is required. Such excess funds shall be credited in the following order:

   (i) To outstanding balances on loans made under section 1078-8 of this title for the payment period or period of enrollment for which a return of funds is required.

   (ii) To outstanding balances on loans made under section 1078 of this title for the payment period or period of enrollment for which a return of funds is required.

   (iii) To outstanding balances on unsubsidized loans (other than parent loans) made under part C of this subchapter [20 U.S.C.A. 1087a *et seq.*] for the payment period or period of enrollment for which a return of funds is required.

   (iv) To outstanding balances on subsidized loans made under part C of this subchapter for the payment period or period of enrollment for which a return of funds is required.

   (v) To outstanding balances on loans made under part D of this subchapter [20 U.S.C.A. § 1087a *et seq.*] for the payment period or period of enrollment for which a return of funds is required.

   (vi) To outstanding balances on loans made under section 1078-2 of this title for the payment period or period of enrollment for which a return of funds is required.

   (vii) To outstanding balances on parent loans made under part C of this subchapter for the payment period or period of enrollment for which a return of funds is required.

(B) Remaining excesses

If excess funds remain after repaying all outstanding loan amounts, the remaining excess shall be credited in the following order:

   (i) To awards under subpart 1 of part A of this subchap-

ter for the payment period or period of enrollment for which a return of funds is required.

   (ii) To awards under subpart 3 of part A of this subchapter for the payment period or period of enrollment for which a return of funds is required.

   (iii) To other assistance awarded under this subchapter and part C of subchapter I of chapter 34 of title 42 for which a return of funds is required.

(c) Withdrawal date

(1) In general

In this section, the term "day the student withdrew"—

(A) is the date that the institution determines—

   (i) the student began the withdrawal process prescribed by the institution;

   (ii) the student otherwise provided official notification to the institution of the intent to withdraw; or

   (iii) in the case of a student who does not begin the withdrawal process or otherwise notify the institution of the intent to withdraw, the date that is the midpoint of the payment period for which assistance under this subchapter [20 U.S.C.A. § 1070 *et seq.*] and part C of subchapter I of chapter 34 of Title 42 [42 U.S.C.A. § 2751 *et seq.*] was disbursed or a later date documented by the institution; or

(B) for institutions required to take attendance, is determined by the institution from such attendance records.

(2) Special rule

Notwithstanding paragraph (1), if the institution determines that a student did not begin the withdrawal process, or otherwise notify the institution of the intent to withdraw, due to illness, accident, grievous personal loss, or other such circumstances beyond the student's control, the institution may determine the appropriate withdrawal date.

(d) Percentage of the payment period or period of enrollment completed

For purposes of subsection (a)(3)(B), the percentage of the payment period or period of enrollment for which assistance was awarded that was completed, is determined—

(1) in the case of a program that is measured in credit hours, by dividing the total number of calendar days comprising the payment period or period of enrollment for which assistance is awarded into the number of calendar days completed in that period as of the day the student withdrew; and

(2) in the case of a program that is measured in clock hours scheduled to be completed by the student in that period as of the day the student withdrew.

(e) Effective date

The provisions of this section shall take effect 2 years after October 7, 1998. An institution of higher education may choose to implement such provisions prior to that date.

[Pub. L. 89-329, title IV, Sec. 484B, as added Pub. L. 102-325, title IV, Sec. 485(a), July 23, 1992, 106 Stat. 619; amended Pub. L. 103-208, Sec. 2(h)(26), (27), Dec. 20, 1993, 107 Stat. 2477; Pub. L. 105-244, title IV, Sec. 485, Oct. 7, 1998, 112 Stat. 1737; Pub. L. 109-66, Sept. 21 2005, 119 Stat. 1999; Pub. L. 109-67, Sept. 21, 2005, 119 Stat. 2001; Pub. L. 109-171, Feb. 8, 2006, 120 Stat. 4]

§ 1095a. Wage garnishment requirement

(a) Garnishment requirements

Notwithstanding any provision of State law, a guaranty agency, or the Secretary in the case of loans made, insured or guaranteed under this subchapter [20 U.S.C.A. 1070 *et seq.*] and part C of subchapter I of chapter 34 of title 42 [42 U.S.C.A. § 2751 *et seq.*] that are held by the Secretary, may garnish the disposable pay of an individual to collect the amount owed by the individual, if he or she is not currently making required repayment under a repayment agreement with the Secretary, or, in the case of a loan guaranteed under part B of this subchapter on which the guaranty agency received reimbursement from the Secretary under section 1078(c) of this title, with the guaranty agency holding the loan, as appropriate, provided that—

(1) the amount deducted for any pay period may not exceed 15 percent of disposable pay, except that a greater percentage may be deducted with the written consent of the individual involved;

(2) the individual shall be provided written notice, sent by mail to the individual's last known address, a minimum of 30 days prior to the initiation of proceedings, from the guaranty agency or the Secretary, as appropriate, informing such individual of the nature and amount of the loan obligation to be collected, the intention of the guaranty agency or the Secretary, as appropriate, to initiate proceedings to collect the debt through deductions from pay, and an explanation of the rights of the individual under this section;

(3) the individual shall be provided an opportunity to inspect and copy records relating to the debt;

(4) the individual shall be provided an opportunity to enter into a written agreement with the guaranty agency or the Secretary, under terms agreeable to the Secretary, or the head of the guaranty agency or his designee, as appropriate, to establish a schedule for the repayment of the debt;

(5) the individual shall be provided an opportunity for a hearing in accordance with subsection (b) of this section on the determination of the Secretary or the guaranty agency, as appropriate, concerning the existence or the amount of the debt, and, in the case of an individual whose repayment schedule is established other than by a written agreement pursuant to paragraph (4), concerning the terms of the repayment schedule;

(6) the employer shall pay to the Secretary or the guaranty agency as directed in the withholding order issued in this action, and shall be liable for, and the Secretary or the guaranty agency, as appropriate, may sue the employer in a State or Federal court of competent jurisdiction to recover, any amount that such employer fails to withhold from wages due an employee following receipt of such employer of notice of the withholding order, plus attorneys' fees, costs, and, in the court's discretion, punitive damages, but such employer shall not be required to vary the normal pay and disbursement cycles in order to comply with this paragraph;

(7) if an individual has been reemployed within 12 months after having been involuntarily separated from employment, no amount may be deducted from the disposable pay of such individual until such individual has been reemployed continuously for at least 12 months; and

(8) an employer may not discharge from employment, refuse to employ, or take disciplinary action against an individual subject to wage withholding in accordance with this section by reason of the fact that the individual's wages have been subject to garnishment under this section, and such individual may sue in a State or Federal court of competent jurisdiction any employer who takes such action. The court shall award attorneys' fees to a prevailing employee and, in its discretion, may order reinstatement of the individual, award punitive damages and back pay to the employee, or order such other remedy as may be reasonably necessary.

(b) Hearing requirements

A hearing described in subsection (a)(5) of this section shall be provided prior to issuance of a garnishment order if the individual, on or before the 15th day following the mailing of the notice described in subsection (a)(2) of this section, and in accordance with such procedures as the Secretary or the head of the guaranty agency, as appropriate, may prescribe, files a petition requesting such a hearing. If the individual does not file a petition requesting a hearing prior to such date, the Secretary or the guaranty agency, as appropriate, shall provide the individual a hearing under subsection (a)(5) of this section upon request, but such hearing need not be provided prior to issuance of a garnishment order. A hearing under subsection (a)(5) of this section may not be conducted by an individual under the supervision or control of the head of the guaranty agency, except that nothing in this sentence shall be construed to prohibit the appointment of an administrative law judge. The hearing official shall issue a final decision at the earliest practicable date, but not later than 60 days after the filing of the petition requesting the hearing.

(c) Notice requirements

The notice to the employer of the withholding order shall contain only such information as may be necessary for the employer to comply with the withholding order.

(d) No attachment of student assistance

Except as authorized in this section, notwithstanding any other provision of Federal or State law, no grant, loan, or work assistance awarded under this subchapter [20 U.S.C.A. 1070 *et seq.*] and part C of subchapter I of chapter 34 of Title 42 [42 U.S.C.A. § 2751 *et seq.*], or property traceable to such assistance, shall be subject to garnishment or attachment in order to satisfy any debt owed by the student awarded such assistance, other than a debt owed to the Secretary and arising under this subchapter and part C of subchapter I of chapter 34 of title 42.

(e) "Disposable pay" defined

For the purpose of this section, the term "disposable pay" means that part of the compensation of any individual from an employer remaining after the deduction of any amounts required by law to be withheld.

[Pub. L. 89-329, title IV, Sec. 488A, as added Pub. L. 102-164, title VI, Sec. 605(a), Nov. 15, 1991, 105 Stat. 1066; amended Pub. L. 105-244, title IV, Sec. 490A, Oct. 7, 1998, 112 Stat. 1753.]

A.1.5 *Selected Debt Collection Statutes*

The following is selected statutory authority from the federal Debt Collection Act. These provisions apply to all federal agencies including the Department of Education.

31 U.S.C. sec.

3716. Administrative offset.
3720A. Reduction of tax refund by amount of debt.
3720D. Garnishment.

§ 3716. Administrative offset

(a) After trying to collect a claim from a person under section 3711(a) of this title, the head of an executive, judicial, or legislative agency may collect the claim by administrative offset. The head of the agency may collect by administrative offset only after giving the debtor—

(1) written notice of the type and amount of the claim, the intention of the head of the agency to collect the claim by administrative offset, and an explanation of the rights of the debtor under this section;

(2) an opportunity to inspect and copy the records of the agency related to the claim;

(3) an opportunity for a review within the agency of the decision of the agency related to the claim; and

(4) an opportunity to make a written agreement with the head of the agency to repay the amount of the claim.

(b) Before collecting a claim by administrative offset, the head of an executive, judicial, or legislative agency must either—

(1) adopt, without change, regulations on collecting by administrative offset promulgated by the Department of Justice, the General Accounting Office, or the Department of the Treasury; or

(2) prescribe regulations on collecting by administrative offset consistent with the regulations referred to in paragraph (1).

(c)(1)(A) Except as otherwise provided in this subsection, a disbursing official of the Department of the Treasury, the Department of Defense, the United States Postal Service, or any other government corporation, or any disbursing official of the United States designated by the Secretary of the Treasury, shall offset at least annually the amount of a payment which a payment certifying agency has certified to the disbursing official for disbursement, by an amount equal to the amount of a claim which a creditor agency has certified to the Secretary of the Treasury pursuant to this subsection.

(B) An agency that designates disbursing officials pursuant to section 3321(c) of this title is not required to certify claims arising out of its operations to the Secretary of the Treasury before such agency's disbursing officials offset such claims.

(C) Payments certified by the Department of Education under a program administered by the Secretary of Education under title IV of the Higher Education Act of 1965 shall not be subject to administrative offset under this subsection.

(2) Neither the disbursing official nor the payment certifying agency shall be liable—

(A) for the amount of the administrative offset on the basis that the underlying obligation, represented by the payment before the administrative offset was taken, was not satisfied; or

(B) for failure to provide timely notice under paragraph (8).

(3)(A)(i) Notwithstanding any other provision of law (including sections 207 and 1631(d)(1) of the Social Security Act (42 U.S.C. 407 and 1383(d)(1)), section 413(b) of Public Law 91-173 (30 U.S.C. 923(b)), and section 14 of the Act of August 29, 1935 (45 U.S.C. 231m)), except as provided in clause (ii), all payments due to an individual under—

    (I)   the Social Security Act,

    (II) part B of the Black Lung Benefits Act, or

    (III) any law administered by the Railroad Retirement Board (other than payments that such Board determines to be tier 2 benefits),

shall be subject to offset under this section.

(ii) An amount of $9,000 which a debtor may receive under Federal benefit programs cited under clause (i) within a 12-month period shall be exempt from offset under this subsection. In applying the $9,000 exemption, the disbursing official shall—

    (I)   reduce the $9,000 exemption amount for the 12-month period by the amount of all Federal benefit payments made during such 12-month period which are not subject to offset under this subsection; and

    (II) apply a prorated amount of the exemption to each periodic benefit payment to be made to the debtor during the applicable 12-month period.

For purposes of the preceding sentence, the amount of a periodic benefit payment shall be the amount after any reduction or deduction required under the laws authorizing the program under which such payment is authorized to be made (including any reduction or deduction to recover any overpayment under such program).

(B) The Secretary of the Treasury shall exempt from administrative offset under this subsection payments under means-tested programs when requested by the head of the respective agency. The Secretary may exempt other payments from administrative offset under this subsection upon the written request of the head of a payment certifying agency. A written request for exemption of other payments must provide justification for the exemption under standards prescribed by the Secretary. Such standards shall give due consideration to whether administrative offset would tend to interfere substantially with or defeat the purposes of the payment certifying agency's program. The Secretary shall report to the Congress annually on exemptions granted under this section.

(C) The provisions of sections 205(b)(1), 809(a)(1), and 1631(c)(1) of the Social Security Act shall not apply to any administrative offset executed pursuant to this section against benefits authorized by title II, VIII, or title XVI of the Social Security Act, respectively.

(4) The Secretary of the Treasury may charge a fee sufficient to cover the full cost of implementing this subsection. The fee may be collected either by the retention of a portion of amounts collected pursuant to this subsection, or by billing the agency referring or transferring a claim for those amounts. Fees charged to the agencies shall be based on actual administrative offsets completed. Amounts received by the United States as fees under this subsection shall be deposited into the account of the Department of the Treasury under section 3711(g)(7) of this title, and shall be collected and accounted for in accordance with the provisions of that section.

(5) The Secretary of the Treasury in consultation with the Commissioner of Social Security and the Director of the Office of Management and Budget, may prescribe such rules, regulations, and procedures as the Secretary of the Treasury considers necessary to carry out this subsection. The Secretary shall consult with the heads of affected agencies in the development of such rules, regulations, and procedures.

(6) Any Federal agency that is owed by a person a past due, legally enforceable nontax debt that is over 180 days delinquent, including nontax debt administered by a third party acting as an agent for the Federal Government, shall notify the Secretary of the

Treasury of all such nontax debts for purposes of administrative offset under this subsection.

(7)(A) The disbursing official conducting an administrative offset with respect to a payment to a payee shall notify the payee in writing of—

(i) the occurrence of the administrative offset to satisfy a past due legally enforceable debt, including a description of the type and amount of the payment otherwise payable to the payee against which the offset was executed;

(ii) the identity of the creditor agency requesting the offset; and

(iii) a contact point within the creditor agency that will handle concerns regarding the offset.

(B) If the payment to be offset is a periodic benefit payment, the disbursing official shall take reasonable steps, as determined by the Secretary of the Treasury, to provide the notice to the payee not later than the date on which the payee is otherwise scheduled to receive the payment, or as soon as practical thereafter, but no later than the date of the administrative offset. Notwithstanding the preceding sentence, the failure of the debtor to receive such notice shall not impair the legality of such administrative offset.

(8) A levy pursuant to the Internal Revenue Code of 1986 shall take precedence over requests for administrative offset pursuant to other laws.

(d) Nothing in this section is intended to prohibit the use of any other administrative offset authority existing under statute or common law.

(e) This section does not apply—

(1) to a claim under this subchapter that has been outstanding for more than 10 years; or

(2) when a statute explicitly prohibits using administrative offset or setoff to collect the claim or type of claim involved.

(f) The Secretary may waive the requirements of sections 552a(o) and (p) of title 5 for administrative offset or claims collection upon written certification by the head of a State or an executive, judicial, or legislative agency seeking to collect the claim that the requirements of subsection (a) of this section have been met.

(g) The Data Integrity Board of the Department of the Treasury established under 552a(u) of title 5 shall review and include in reports under paragraph (3)(D) of that section a description of any matching activities conducted under this section. If the Secretary has granted a waiver under subsection (f) of this section, no other Data Integrity Board is required to take any action under section 552a(u) of title 5.

(h)(1) The Secretary may, in the discretion of the Secretary, apply subsection (a) with respect to any past-due, legally-enforceable debt owed to a State if—

(A) the appropriate State disbursing official requests that an offset be performed; and

(B) a reciprocal agreement with the State is in effect which contains, at a minimum—

(i) requirements substantially equivalent to subsection (b) of this section; and

(ii) any other requirements which the Secretary considers appropriate to facilitate the offset and prevent duplicative efforts.

(2) This subsection does not apply to—

(A) the collection of a debt or claim on which the administrative costs associated with the collection of the debt or claim exceed the amount of the debt or claim;

(B) any collection of any other type, class, or amount of claim, as the Secretary considers necessary to protect the interest of the United States; or

(C) the disbursement of any class or type of payment exempted by the Secretary of the Treasury at the request of a Federal agency.

(3) In applying this section with respect to any debt owed to a State, subsection (c)(3)(A) shall not apply.

[Added Pub. L. 97-452, § 1(16)(A), Jan. 12, 1983, 96 Stat. 2471; amended Pub. L. 104-134, Title III, § 31001(c)(1), (d)(2), (e), (f), Apr. 26, 1996, 110 Stat. 1321-359, 1321-362; Pub. L. 106-169, Title II, § 251(b)(10), Dec. 14, 1999, 113 Stat. 1856.]

§ 3720A. Reduction of tax refund by amount of debt

(a) Any Federal agency that is owed by a person a past-due, legally enforceable debt (including debt administered by a third party acting as an agent for the Federal Government) shall, and any agency subject to section 9 of the Act of May 18, 1933 (16 U.S.C. 831h), owed such a debt may, in accordance with regulations issued pursuant to subsections (b) and (d), notify the Secretary of the Treasury at least once each year of the amount of such debt.

(b) No Federal agency may take action pursuant to subsection (a) with respect to any debt until such agency—

(1) notifies the person incurring such debt that such agency proposes to take action pursuant to such paragraph with respect to such debt;

(2) gives such person at least 60 days to present evidence that all or part of such debt is not past-due or not legally enforceable;

(3) considers any evidence presented by such person and determines that an amount of such debt is past due and legally enforceable;

(4) satisfies such other conditions as the Secretary may prescribe to ensure that the determination made under paragraph (3) with respect to such debt is valid and that the agency has made reasonable efforts (determined on a government-wide basis) to obtain payment of such debt; and

(5) certifies that reasonable efforts have been made by the agency (pursuant to regulations) to obtain payment of such debt.

(c) Upon receiving notice from any Federal agency that a named person owes to such agency a past-due legally enforceable debt, the Secretary of the Treasury shall determine whether any amounts, as refunds of Federal taxes paid, are payable to such person. If the Secretary of the Treasury finds that any such amount is payable, he shall reduce such refunds by an amount equal to the amount of such debt, pay the amount of such reduction to such agency, and notify such agency of the individual's home address.

(d) The Secretary of the Treasury shall issue regulations prescribing the time or times at which agencies must submit notices of past-due legally enforceable debts, the manner in which such notices must be submitted, and the necessary information that must be contained in or accompany the notices. The regulations shall specify the minimum amount of debt to which the reduction procedure established by subsection (c) may be applied and the fee that an agency must pay to reimburse the Secretary of the Treasury for the full cost of applying such procedure. Any fee paid to the Secretary pursuant to the preceding sentence may be used to reimburse appropriations which bore all or part of the cost of applying such procedure.

(e) Any Federal agency receiving notice from the Secretary of the Treasury that an erroneous payment has been made to such agency under subsection (c) shall pay promptly to the Secretary, in accordance with such regulations as the Secretary may prescribe, an amount equal to the amount of such erroneous payment (without regard to whether any other amounts payable to such agency under such subsection have been paid to such agency).

(f)(1) Subsection (a) shall apply with respect to an OASDI overpayment made to any individual only if such individual is not currently entitled to monthly insurance benefits under title II of the Social Security Act.

(2)(A) The requirements of subsection (b) shall not be treated as met in the case of the recovery of an OASDI overpayment from any individual under this section unless the notification under subsection (b)(1) describes the conditions under which the Commissioner of Social Security is required to waive recovery of an overpayment, as provided under section 204(b) of the Social Security Act.

(B) In any case in which an individual files for a waiver under section 204(b) of the Social Security Act within the 60-day period referred to in subsection (b)(2), the Commissioner of Social Security shall not certify to the Secretary of the Treasury that the debt is valid under subsection (b)(4) before rendering a decision on the waiver request under such section 204(b). In lieu of payment, pursuant to subsection (c), to the Commissioner of Social Security of the amount of any reduction under this subsection based on an OASDI overpayment, the Secretary of the Treasury shall deposit such amount in the Federal Old-Age and Survivors Insurance Trust Fund or the Federal Disability Insurance Trust Fund, whichever is certified to the Secretary of the Treasury as appropriate by the Commissioner of Social Security.

(g) In the case of refunds of business associations, this section shall apply only to refunds payable on or after January 1, 1995. In the case of refunds of individuals who owe debts to Federal agencies that have not participated in the Federal tax refund offset program prior to the date of enactment of this subsection, this section shall apply only to refunds payable on or after January 1, 1994.

(h)(1)[12] The disbursing official of the Department of the Treasury—

(1) shall notify a taxpayer in writing of—

(A) the occurrence of an offset to satisfy a past-due legally enforceable nontax debt;

(B) the identity of the creditor agency requesting the offset; and

(C) a contact point within the creditor agency that will handle concerns regarding the offset;

(2) shall notify the Internal Revenue Service on a weekly basis of—

(A) the occurrence of an offset to satisfy a past-due legally enforceable non-tax[13] debt;

(B) the amount of such offset; and

(C) any other information required by regulations; and

(3) shall match payment records with requests for offset by using a name control, taxpayer identifying number (as that term is used in section 6109 of the Internal Revenue Code of 1986), and any other necessary identifiers.

(h)(2)[14] The term "disbursing official" of the Department of the Treasury means the Secretary or his designee.

(i) An agency subject to section 9 of the Act of May 18, 1933 (16 U.S.C. 831h), may implement this section at its discretion.

[Added Pub. L. 98-369, Title VI, § 2653(a)(1), July 18, 1984, 98 Stat. 1153, and amended Pub. L. 101-508, Title V, § 5129(b), Nov. 5, 1990, 104 Stat. 1388-287; Pub. L. 102-589, § 3, Nov. 10, 1992, 106 Stat. 5133; Pub. L. 103-296, Title I, § 108(j)(2), Aug. 15, 1994, 108 Stat. 1488; Pub. L. 104-134, Title III, § 31001(u)(1), (v)(1), (w), Apr. 26, 1996, 110 Stat. 1321-375.]

§ 3720D. Garnishment

(a) Notwithstanding any provision of State law, the head of an executive, judicial, or legislative agency that administers a program that gives rise to a delinquent nontax debt owed to the United States by an individual may in accordance with this section garnish the disposable pay of the individual to collect the amount owed, if the individual is not currently making required repayment in accordance with any agreement between the agency head and the individual.

(b) In carrying out any garnishment of disposable pay of an individual under subsection (a), the head of an executive, judicial, or legislative agency shall comply with the following requirements:

(1) The amount deducted under this section for any pay period may not exceed 15 percent of disposable pay, except that a greater percentage may be deducted with the written consent of the individual.

(2) The individual shall be provided written notice, sent by mail to the individual's last known address, a minimum of 30 days prior to the initiation of proceedings, from the head of the executive, judicial, or legislative agency, informing the individual of—

(A) the nature and amount of the debt to be collected;

(B) the intention of the agency to initiate proceedings to collect the debt through deductions from pay; and

(C) an explanation of the rights of the individual under this section.

(3) The individual shall be provided an opportunity to inspect and copy records relating to the debt.

(4) The individual shall be provided an opportunity to enter into a written agreement with the executive, judicial, or legislative agency, under terms agreeable to the head of the agency, to establish a schedule for repayment of the debt.

(5) The individual shall be provided an opportunity for a hearing in accordance with subsection (c) on the determination of the head of the executive, judicial, or legislative agency concerning—

(A) the existence or the amount of the debt, and

(B) in the case of an individual whose repayment schedule is established other than by a written agreement pursuant to paragraph (4), the terms of the repayment schedule.

---

12 So in original. Subsec. (h) contains two pars. designated (1) and (2).

13 So in original. Probably should not be hyphenated.

14 So in original. Subsec. (h) contains two pars. designated (1) and (2).

(6) If the individual has been reemployed within 12 months after having been involuntarily separated from employment, no amount may be deducted from the disposable pay of the individual until the individual has been reemployed continuously for at least 12 months.

(c)(1) A hearing under subsection (b)(5) shall be provided prior to issuance of a garnishment order if the individual, on or before the 15th day following the mailing of the notice described in subsection (b)(2), and in accordance with such procedures as the head of the executive, judicial, or legislative agency may prescribe, files a petition requesting such a hearing.

(2) If the individual does not file a petition requesting a hearing prior to such date, the head of the agency shall provide the individual a hearing under subsection (a)(5) [FN1] upon request, but such hearing need not be provided prior to issuance of a garnishment order.

(3) The hearing official shall issue a final decision at the earliest practicable date, but not later than 60 days after the filing of the petition requesting the hearing.

(d) The notice to the employer of the withholding order shall contain only such information as may be necessary for the employer to comply with the withholding order.

(e)(1) An employer may not discharge from employment, refuse to employ, or take disciplinary action against an individual subject to wage withholding in accordance with this section by reason of the fact that the individual's wages have been subject to garnishment under this section, and such individual may sue in a State or Federal court of competent jurisdiction any employer who takes such action.

(2) The court shall award attorneys' fees to a prevailing employee and, in its discretion, may order reinstatement of the individual, award punitive damages and back pay to the employee, or order such other remedy as may be reasonably necessary.

(f)(1) The employer of an individual—

(A) shall pay to the head of an executive, judicial, or legislative agency as directed in a withholding order issued in an action under this section with respect to the individual, and

(B) shall be liable for any amount that the employer fails to withhold from wages due an employee following receipt by such employer of notice of the withholding order, plus attorneys' fees, costs, and, in the court's discretion, punitive damages.

(2)(A) The head of an executive, judicial, or legislative agency may sue an employer in a State or Federal court of competent jurisdiction to recover amounts for which the employer is liable under paragraph (1)(B).

(B) A suit under this paragraph may not be filed before the termination of the collection action, unless earlier filing is necessary to avoid expiration of any applicable statute of limitations period.

(3) Notwithstanding paragraphs (1) and (2), an employer shall not be required to vary its normal pay and disbursement cycles in order to comply with this subsection.

(g) For the purpose of this section, the term "disposable pay" means that part of the compensation of any individual from an employer remaining after the deduction of any amounts required by any other law to be withheld.

(h) The Secretary of the Treasury shall issue regulations to implement this section.

[Added Pub. L. 104-134, Title III, § 31001(o)(1), Apr. 26, 1996, 110 Stat. 1321–369]

Appendix B   Federal Regulations

Reprinted below are selected regulations for the FFEL, Direct Loan and Perkins Loan programs, as well as general debt collection regulations. Additional regulations can be found on the companion CD-Rom to this manual. Key proposed regulations are also available on the companion CD-Rom.

B.1 Selected Debt Collection Procedures

B.1.1 Administrative Offset

34 C.F.R. sec.

30.20 To what do Secs. 30.20–30.31 apply?

30.21 When may the Secretary offset a debt?

30.22 What notice does the debtor receive before the commencement of offset?

30.23 How must a debtor request an opportunity to inspect and copy records relating to a debt?

30.24 What opportunity does the debtor receive to obtain a review of the existence or amount of a debt?

30.25 How may a debtor obtain an oral hearing?

30.26 What special rules apply to an oral hearing?

30.27 When does the Secretary enter into a repayment agreement rather than offset?

30.28 When may the Secretary offset before completing the procedures under §§ 30.22–30.27?

30.29 What procedures apply when the Secretary offsets to collect a debt owed another agency?

30.30 What procedures apply when the Secretary requests another agency to offset a debt owed under a program or activity of the Department?

30.31 How does the Secretary apply funds recovered by offset if multiple debts are involved?

Source: 51 Fed. Reg. 24099, July 1, 1986; 53 Fed. Reg. 33425, Aug. 30, 1988, unless otherwise noted.

§ 30.20 To what do §§ 30.20–30.31 apply?

(a)(1)(i) Sections 30.20–30.31 establish the general procedures used by the Secretary to collect debts by administrative offset.

(ii) The Secretary uses the procedures established under other regulations, including § 30.33, What procedures does the Secretary follow for IRS tax refund offsets?, 34 CFR part 31, Salary Offset for Federal Employees Who Are Indebted to the United States Under Programs Administered by the Secretary of Education, and 34 CFR part 32, Salary Offset to Recover Overpayments of Pay or Allowances from Department of Education Employees, if the conditions requiring application of those special procedures exists.

(2) The word "offset" is used in this subpart to refer to the collection of a debt by administrative offset.

(b) The Secretary does not rely on 31 U.S.C. 3716 as authority for offset if:

(1) The debt is owed by a State or local government;

(2) The debt, or the payment against which offset would be taken, arises under the Social Security Act;

(3) The debt is owed under:

(i)   The Internal Revenue Code of 1954; or

(ii) The tariff laws of the United States; or

(4) The right to collect the debt first accrued more than ten years before initiation of the offset.

(c)(1) The Secretary may rely on 31 U.S.C. 3716 as authority for offset of a debt to which paragraph (b)(4) of this section would otherwise apply if facts material to the Government's right to collect the debt were not known and could not reasonably have been known by the official or officials of the Government who are charged with the responsibility to discover and collect the debt.

(2) If paragraph (c)(1) of this section applies, the Secretary may rely on 31 U.S.C. 3716 as authority for offset up to 10 years after the date that the official or officials described in that paragraph first knew or reasonably should have known of the right of the United States to collect the debt.

(d) The Secretary determines when the right to collect a debt first accrued under the existing law regarding accrual of debts such as 28 U.S.C. 2415.

(Authority: 20 U.S.C. 1221e-3(a)(1) and 1226a-1, 31 U.S.C. 3716(b))

[51 Fed. Reg. 24099, July 1, 1986, as amended at 51 Fed. Reg. 35646, Oct. 7, 1986; 53 Fed. Reg. 33425, Aug. 30, 1988; 54 Fed. Reg. 43583, Oct. 26, 1989]

§ 30.21 When may the Secretary offset a debt?

(a) The Secretary may offset a debt if:

(1) The debt is liquidated or certain in amount; and

(2) Offset is feasible and not otherwise prohibited.

(b)(1) Whether offset is feasible is determined by the Secretary in the exercise of sound discretion on a case-by-case basis, either:

(i)   For each individual debt or offset; or

(ii) For each class of similar debts or offsets.

(2) The Secretary considers the following factors in making this determination:

(i)   Whether offset can be practically and legally accomplished.

(ii)   Whether offset will further and protect the interests of the United States.

(c) The Secretary may switch advance funded grantees to a reimbursement payment system before initiating an offset.

(Authority: 20 U.S.C. 1221e-3(a)(1) and 1226a-1, 31 U.S.C. 3716(b))

§ 30.22 What notice does the debtor receive before the commencement of offset?

(a)(1) Except as provided in §§ 30.28 and 30.29, the Secretary provides a debtor with written notice of the Secretary's intent to offset before initiating the offset.

(2) The Secretary mails the notice to the debtor at the current address of the debtor, as determined by the Secretary from information regarding the debt maintained by the Department.

(b) The written notice informs the debtor regarding:

(1) The nature and amount of the debt;

(2) The Secretary's intent to collect the debt by offset;

(3) The debtor's opportunity to:

(i)   Inspect and copy Department records pertaining to the debt;

(ii) Obtain a review within the Department of the existence or amount of the debt; and

(iii) Enter into a written agreement with the Secretary to repay the debt;

(4) The date by which the debtor must request an opportunity set forth under paragraph (b)(3) of this section; and

(5) The Secretary's decision, in appropriate cases, to switch the debtor from advance funding to a reimbursement payment system.

(c)(1) In determining whether a debtor has requested an opportunity set forth under paragraph (b)(3) of this section in a timely manner, the Secretary relies on:

(i)   A legibly dated U.S. Postal Service postmark for the debtor's request; or

(ii) A legibly stamped U.S. Postal service mail receipt for debtor's request.

(2) The Secretary does not rely on either of the following as proof of mailing;

(i)   A private metered postmark.

(ii) A mail receipt that is not dated by the U.S. Postal Service.

NOTE: The U.S. Postal Service does not uniformly provide a dated postmark. Before relying on this method for proof of mailing, a debtor should check with its local post office.

(d) If a debtor previously has been notified of the Secretary's intent to offset or offered an opportunity to take any of the actions set forth in paragraph (b)(3) of this section in connection with the same debt, the Secretary may offset without providing the debtor with an additional notice of intent or opportunity to take any of those actions under these offset procedures.

(Authority: 20 U.S.C. 1221e-3(a)(1) and 1226a-1, 31 U.S.C. 3716(b))

§ 30.23 How must a debtor request an opportunity to inspect and copy records relating to a debt?

(a) If a debtor wants to inspect and copy Department documents relating to the debt, the debtor must:

(1) File a written request to inspect and copy the documents within 20 days after the date of the notice provided under § 30.22; and

(2) File the request at the address specified in that notice.

(b) A request filed under paragraph (a) of this section must contain:

(1) All information provided to the debtor in the notice under § 30.22 or § 30.33(b) that identifies the debtor and the debt, including the debtor's Social Security number and the program under which the debt arose, together with any corrections of that identifying information; and

(2) A reasonably specific identification of the records the debtor wishes to have available for inspection and copying.

(c) The Secretary may decline to provide an opportunity to inspect and copy records if the debtor fails to request inspection and copying in accordance with this section.

(Approved by the Office of Management and Budget under control number 1880-0515)

(Authority: 20 U.S.C. 1221e-3(a)(1) and 1226a-1, 31 U.S.C. 3716(b))

[51 Fed. Reg. 24099, July 1, 1986, as amended at 51 Fed. Reg. 35646, Oct. 7, 1986]

§ 30.24 What opportunity does the debtor receive to obtain a review of the existence or amount of a debt?

(a) If a debtor wants a review within the Department of the issues identified in the notice under § 30.22(b)(3)(ii) or § 30.33(b)(3)(ii), the debtor must:

(1) File a request for review within 20 days after the date of the notice provided under § 30.22; and

(2) File a request at the address specified in that notice.

(b) A request filed under paragraph (a) of this section must contain:

(1) All information provided to the debtor in the notice under § 30.22 or § 30.33(b) that identifies the debtor and the particular debt, including the debtor's Social Security number and the program under which the debt arose, together with any corrections of that identifying information; and

(2) An explanation of the reasons the debtor believes that the notice the debtor received under § 30.22 or § 30.33(b) inaccurately states any facts or conclusions relating to the debt.

(c) The Secretary may decline to provide an opportunity for review of a debt if the debtor fails to request the review in accordance with this section.

(d)(1) The debtor shall:

(i)   File copies of any documents relating to the issues identified in the notice under § 30.22(b)(3)(ii) or § 30.33(b)(3)(ii) that the debtor wishes the Secretary to consider in the review;

(ii) File the documents at the address specified in that notice, and

(iii) File the documents no later than:

(A) 20 days after the date of the notice provided under § 30.22; or

(B) If the debtor has requested an opportunity to inspect and copy records under § 30.23 within the time period specified in that section, 15 days after the date on which the Secretary makes available to the debtor the relevant, requested records.

(2) The Secretary may decline to consider any reasons or documents that the debtor fails to provide in accordance with

paragraphs (b) and (d) of this section.

(e) If the Secretary bases the review on only the documentary evidence, the Secretary:

(1) Reviews the documents submitted by the debtor and other relevant evidence; and

(2) Notifies the debtor in writing of the Secretary's decision regarding the issues identified in the notice under § 30.22(b)(3)(ii) or § 30.33(b)(3)(ii) and, if appropriate, the question of waiver of the debt.

(Approved by the Office of Management and Budget under control number 1880-0515)

(Authority: 20 U.S.C. 1221e-3(a)(1) and 1226a-1, 31 U.S.C. 3716(b))

[51 Fed. Reg. 24099, July 1, 1986, as amended at 51 Fed. Reg. 35646, Oct. 7, 1986]

§ 30.25 How may a debtor obtain an oral hearing?

(a) If a debtor wants the Secretary to conduct the review requested under § 30.24 as an oral hearing, the debtor must file a written request for an oral hearing together with the request for review filed under § 30.24(a).

(b) A request filed under paragraph (a) of this section must contain the following in addition to the information filed under § 30.24(b):

(1) An explanation of reason(s) why the debtor believes the Secretary cannot resolve the issues identified in the notice under § 30.22(b)(3)(ii) or § 30.33(b)(3)(ii) through a review of the documentary evidence.

(2) An identification of:

(i)   The individuals that the debtor wishes to have testify at the oral hearing;

(ii) The specific issues identified in the notice regarding which each individual is prepared to testify; and

(iii) The reasons why each individual's testimony is necessary to resolve the issue.

(c) The Secretary grants a debtor's request for an oral hearing regarding the issues identified in the notice under § 30.22(b)(3)(ii) or § 30.33(b)(3)(ii) only if:

(1)(i) A statute authorizes or requires the Secretary to consider waiver of the indebtedness involved;

(ii) The debtor files a request for waiver of the indebtedness with the request for review filed under paragraph (a)(1) of this section; and

(iii) The question of waiver of the indebtedness turns on an issue of credibility or veracity; or

(2) The Secretary determines that the issues identified in the notice under § 30.22(b)(3)(ii) or § 30.33(b)(3)(ii) cannot be resolved by review of only the documentary evidence.

(d) Notwithstanding paragraph (b) of this section, the Secretary may deny oral hearings for a class of similar debts if:

(1) The issues identified in the notice under § 30.22(b)(3)(ii) or 30.33(b)(3)(ii) for which an oral hearing was requested, or the issue of waiver, rarely involve issues of credibility or veracity; and

(2) The Secretary determines that review of the documentary evidence is ordinarily an adequate means to correct mistakes.

(e) The Secretary may decline to consider any reasons that the debtor fails to provide in accordance with paragraph (b)(1) of this section.

(Approved by the Office of Management and Budget under control number 1880-0515)

(Authority: 20 U.S.C. 1221e-3(a)(1) and 1226a-1, 31 U.S.C. 3716(b))

[51 Fed. Reg. 24099, July 1, 1986, as amended at 51 Fed. Reg. 35647, Oct. 7, 1986]

§ 30.26 What special rules apply to an oral hearing?

(a) The oral hearing under § 30.25 is not a formal evidentiary hearing subject to 5 U.S.C. 554, unless required by law.

(b) If the Secretary grants an oral hearing, the Secretary notifies the debtor in writing of:

(1) The time and place for the hearing;

(2) The debtor's right to representation; and

(3) The debtor's right to present and cross examine witnesses.

(c) If the Secretary grants an oral hearing, the Secretary designates an official to:

(1) Govern the conduct of the hearing;

(2) Take all necessary action to avoid unreasonable delay in the proceedings;

(3) Review the evidence presented at the hearing, the documents submitted by the debtor, and other relevant evidence; and

(4) After considering the evidence, notify the debtor in writing of the official's decision regarding the issues identified in the notice under § 30.22(b)(3)(ii) or § 30.33(b)(3)(ii) and, if appropriate, the question of waiver of the debt.

(d) The official designated under paragraph (c) of this section may decline to hear any witnesses or testimony not identified by the debtor in accordance with § 30.25(b)(2).

(e) The decision of the designated official under paragraph (c) of this section constitutes the final decision of the Secretary.

(Authority: 20 U.S.C. 1221-3(a)(1) and 1226a-1, 31 U.S.C. 3716(b))

§ 30.27 When does the Secretary enter into a repayment agreement rather than offset?

(a) If a debtor wants an opportunity to enter into a written agreement to repay a debt on terms acceptable to the Secretary, the debtor must:

(1) File a request to enter into such agreement within 20 days after the date of the notice provided under § 30.22; and

(2) File the request at the address specified in the notice.

(b) A request filed under paragraph (a) of this section must contain all information provided to the debtor in the notice under § 30.22 or § 30.33(b) that identifies the debtor and the debt, including the debtor's Social Security number and the program under which the debt arose, together with any corrections of that identifying information.

(c) If the Secretary receives a request filed in accordance with this section, the Secretary may enter into a written agreement requiring repayment in accordance with 4 CFR 102.11, instead of offsetting the debt.

(d) In deciding whether to enter into the agreement, the Secretary may consider:

(1) The Government's interest in collecting the debt; and

(2) Fairness to the debtor.

(e)(1) A debtor that enters into a repayment agreement with the Secretary under this section waives any right to further review by the Secretary of the issues relating to the original debt identified in the notice under § 30.22(b)(3)(ii) or § 30.33(b)(3)(ii).

(2) If a debtor breaches a repayment agreement, the Secretary may offset, or, under § 30.30, refer to another agency for offset:

(i)   The amount owing under the agreement; or

(ii) The entire original debt, to the extent not repaid.

(Authority: 20 U.S.C. 1221-3(a)(1) and 1226a-1, 31 U.S.C. 3716(b))

[51 Fed. Reg. 24099, July 1, 1986, as amended at 51 Fed. Reg. 35647, Oct. 7, 1986]

§ 30.28 When may the Secretary offset before completing the procedures under §§ 30.22–30.27?

(a) The Secretary may offset before completing the procedures otherwise required by §§ 30.22–30.27 if:

(1) Failure to offset would substantially prejudice the Government's ability to collect the debt; and

(2) The amount of time remaining before the payment by the United States which is subject to offset does not reasonably permit completion of the procedures under §§ 30.22–30.27.

(b) If the Secretary offsets under paragraph (a) of this section, the Secretary:

(1) Promptly completes the procedures under §§ 30.22–30.27 after initiating the offset; and

(2) Refunds any amounts recovered under the offset that are later found not to be owed to the United States.

(Authority: 20 U.S.C. 1221e-3(a)(1) and 1226a-1, 31 U.S.C. 3716(b))

§ 30.29 What procedures apply when the Secretary offsets to collect a debt owed another agency?

The Secretary may initiate offset to collect a debt owed another Federal agency if:

(a) An official of that agency certifies in writing:

(1) That the debtor owes a debt to the United States;

(2) The amount of the debt; and

(3) That the agency has complied with 4 CFR 102.3; and

(b) For offsets under 31 U.S.C. 3716, the Secretary makes an independent determination that the offset meets the standards under § 30.21(a)(2).

(Authority: 20 U.S.C. 1221e-3(a)(1) and 1226a-1, 31 U.S.C. 3716(b))

§ 30.30 What procedures apply when the Secretary requests another agency to offset a debt owed under a program or activity of the Department?

(a) The Secretary may request another Federal agency to offset a debt owed under a program or activity of the Department if the Secretary certifies in writing to the other Federal agency:

(1) That the debtor owes a debt to the United States;

(2) The amount of the debt; and

(3) That the Secretary has complied with 4 CFR 102.3.

(b) Before providing the certification required under paragraph (a) of this section, the Secretary complies with the procedures in §§ 30.20–30.27.

(Authority: 20 U.S.C. 1221e-3(a)(1) and 1226a-1, 31 U.S.C. 3716(b))

§ 30.31 How does the Secretary apply funds recovered by offset if multiple debts are involved?

If the Secretary collects more than one debt of a debtor by administrative offset, the Secretary applies the recovered funds to satisfy those debts based on the Secretary's determination of the best interests of the United States, determined by the facts and circumstances of the particular case.

(Authority: 20 U.S.C. 1221e-3(a)(1) and 1226a-1, 31 U.S.C. 3716(b))

B.1.2 Tax Refund Offset

34 C.F.R. sec.

§ 30.33 What procedures does the Secretary follow for IRS tax refund offsets?

(a) If a named person owes a debt under a program or activity of the Department, the Secretary may refer the debt for offset to the Secretary of the Treasury after complying with the procedures in §§ 30.20–30.28, as modified by this section.

(b) Notwithstanding § 30.22(b), the notice sent to a debtor under § 30.22 informs the debtor that:

(1) The debt is past due;

(2) The Secretary intends to refer the debt for offset to the Secretary of Treasury;

(3) The debtor has an opportunity to:

(i)   Inspect and copy Department records regarding the existence, amount, enforceability, or past-due status of the debt;

(ii) Obtain a review within the Department of the existence, amount, enforceability, or past-due status of the debt;

(iii) Enter into a written agreement with the Secretary to repay the debt; and

(4) The debtor must take an action set forth under paragraph (b)(3) by a date specified in the notice.

(c) Notwithstanding § 30.23(a), if a debtor wants to inspect and copy Department records regarding the existence, amount, enforceability, or past-due status of the debt, the debtor must:

(1) File a written request to inspect and copy the records within 20 days after the date of the notice provided under § 30.22; and

(2) File the request at the address specified in that notice.

(d) Notwithstanding the time frame under § 30.24(a), if a debtor wants a review under that paragraph, the debtor must file a request for review at the address specified in the notice by the later of:

(1) Sixty-five days after the date of the notice provided under § 30.22;

(2) If the debtor has requested an opportunity to inspect and copy records within the time period specified in paragraph (c) of this section, 15 days after the date on which the Secretary makes available to the debtor the relevant, requested records; or

(3) If the debtor has requested a review within the appropriate time frame under paragraph (d) (1) or (2) of this section and the Secretary has provided an initial review by a guarantee agency, seven days after the date of the initial determination by the guarantee agency.

(e) Notwithstanding the time frames under § 30.24(d), a debtor shall file the documents specified under that paragraph with the request for review.

(f) Notwithstanding the time frame under § 30.27(a), a debtor must agree to repay the debt under terms acceptable to the Secretary and make the first payment due under the agreement by the latest of:

(1) The seventh day after the date of decision of the Secretary if the debtor requested a review under § 30.24;

(2) The sixty-fifth day after the date of the notice under § 30.22(b), if the debtor did not request a review under § 30.24, or an opportunity to inspect and copy records of the Department under § 30.23; or

(3) The fifteenth day after the date on which the Secretary made available relevant records regarding the debt, if the debtor filed a timely request under § 30.23(a).

(Authority: 20 U.S.C. 1221e-3(a)(1) and 1226a-1, 31 U.S.C. 3720A)

* * *

B.1.3 *Administrative Wage Garnishment*

34 C.F.R. sec.

34.1 Purpose of this part.
34.2 Scope of this part.
34.3 Definitions.
34.4 Notice of proposed garnishment.
34.5 Contents of a notice of proposed garnishment.
34.6 Rights in connection with garnishment.
34.7 Consideration of objection to the rate or amount of withholding.
34.8 Providing a hearing.
34.9 Conditions for an oral hearing.
34.10 Conditions for a paper hearing.
34.11 Timely request for a hearing.
34.12 Request for reconsideration.
34.13 Conduct of a hearing.
34.14 Burden of proof.
34.15 Consequences of failure to appear for an oral hearing.
34.16 Issuance of the hearing decision.
34.17 Content of decision.
34.18 Issuance of the wage garnishment order.
34.19 Amounts to be withheld under a garnishment order.
34.20 Amount to be withheld under multiple garnishment orders.
34.21 Employer certification.
34.22 Employer responsibilities.
34.23 Exclusions from garnishment.
34.24 Claim of financial hardship by debtor subject to garnishment.
34.25 Determination of financial hardship.
34.26 Ending garnishment.
34.27 Actions by employer prohibited by law.
34.28 Refunds of amounts collected in error.
34.29 Enforcement action against employer for noncompliance with garnishment order.
34.30 Application of payments and accrual of interest.

Source: 68FR 8142, Feb. 19, 2003, unless otherwise noted.

Authority: 31 U.S.C. 3720D, unless otherwise noted.

§ 34.1 **Purpose of this part.**

This part establishes procedures the Department of Education uses to collect money from a debtor's disposable pay by means of administrative wage garnishment to satisfy delinquent debt owed to the United States.

(Authority: 31 U.S.C. 3720D)

§ 34.2 **Scope of this part.**

(a) This part applies to collection of any financial obligation owed to the United States that arises under a program we administer.

(b) This part applies notwithstanding any provision of State law.

(c) We may compromise or suspend collection by garnishment of a debt in accordance with applicable law.

(d) We may use other debt collection remedies separately or in conjunction with administrative wage garnishment to collect a debt.

(e) To collect by offset from the salary of a Federal employee, we use the procedures in 34 CFR part 31, not those in this part.

(Authority: 31 U.S.C. 3720D)

§ 34.3 **Definitions.**

As used in this part, the following definitions apply:

Administrative debt means a debt that does not arise from an individual's obligation to repay a loan or an overpayment of a grant received under a student financial assistance program authorized under Title IV of the Higher Education Act.

Business day means a day Monday through Friday, unless that day is a Federal holiday.

Certificate of service means a certificate signed by an authorized official of the U.S. Department of Education (the Department) that indicates the nature of the document to which it pertains, the date we mail the document, and to whom we are sending the document.

Day means calendar day. For purposes of computation, the last day of a period will be included unless that day is a Saturday, a Sunday, or a Federal legal holiday; in that case, the last day of the period is the next business day after the end of the period.

Debt or *claim* means any amount of money, funds, or property that an appropriate official of the Department has determined an individual owes to the United States under a program we administer.

Debtor means an individual who owes a delinquent nontax debt to the United States under a program we administer.

Disposable pay. This term—

(a)(1) Means that part of a debtor's compensation for personal services, whether or not denominated as wages, from an employer that remains after the deduction of health insurance premiums and any amounts required by law to be withheld.

(2) For purposes of this part, "amounts required by law to be withheld include amounts for deductions such as social security taxes and withholding taxes, but do not include any amount withheld" under a court order; and

(b) Includes, but is not limited to, salary, bonuses, commissions, or vacation pay.

Employer. This term—

(a) Means a person or entity that employs the services of another and that pays the latter's wages or salary;

(b) Includes, but is not limited to, State and local governments; and

(c) Does not include an agency of the Federal Government.

Financial hardship means an inability to meet basic living expenses for goods and services necessary for the survival of the debtor and his or her spouse and dependents.

Garnishment means the process of withholding amounts from an employee's disposable pay and paying those amounts to a creditor in satisfaction of a withholding order.

We means the United States Department of Education.

Withholding order. (a) This term means any order for withholding or garnishment of pay issued by this Department, another Federal agency, a State or private non-profit guaranty agency, or a judicial or administrative body.

(b) For purposes of this part, the terms "wage garnishment order" and "garnishment order" have the same meaning as "withholding order."

You means the debtor.

(Authority: 31 U.S.C. 3720D)

§ 34.4 Notice of proposed garnishment.

(a) We may start proceedings to garnish your wages whenever we determine that you are delinquent in paying a debt owed to the United States under a program we administer.

(b) We start garnishment proceedings by sending you a written notice of the proposed garnishment.

(c) At least 30 days before we start garnishment proceedings, we mail the notice by first class mail to your last known address.

(d)(1) We keep a copy of a certificate of service indicating the date of mailing of the notice.

(2) We may retain this certificate of service in electronic form.

(Authority: 31 U.S.C. 3720D)

§ 34.5 Contents of a notice of proposed garnishment.

In a notice of proposed garnishment, we inform you of—

(a) The nature and amount of the debt;

(b) Our intention to collect the debt through deductions from pay until the debt and all accumulated interest, penalties, and collection costs are paid in full; and

(c) An explanation of your rights, including those in § 34.6, and the time frame within which you may exercise your rights.

(Authority: 31 U.S.C. 3720D)

§ 34.6 Rights in connection with garnishment.

Before starting garnishment, we provide you the opportunity—

(a) To inspect and copy our records related to the debt;

(b) To enter into a written repayment agreement with us to repay the debt under terms we consider acceptable;

(c) For a hearing in accordance with § 34.8 concerning—

(1) The existence, amount, or current enforceability of the debt;

(2) The rate at which the garnishment order will require your employer to withhold pay; and

(3) Whether you have been continuously employed less than 12 months after you were involuntarily separated from employment.

(Authority: 31 U.S.C. 3720D)

§ 34.7 Consideration of objection to the rate or amount of withholding.

(a) We consider objections to the rate or amount of withholding only if the objection rests on a claim that withholding at the proposed rate or amount would cause financial hardship to you and your dependents.

(b) We do not provide a hearing on an objection to the rate or amount of withholding if the rate or amount we propose to be withheld does not exceed the rate or amount agreed to under a repayment agreement reached within the preceding six months after a previous notice of proposed garnishment.

(c) We do not consider an objection to the rate or amount of withholding based on a claim that by virtue of 15 U.S.C. 1673, no amount of wages are available for withholding by the employer.

(Authority: 31 U.S.C. 3720D)

§ 34.8 Providing a hearing.

(a) We provide a hearing if you submit a written request for a hearing concerning the existence, amount, or enforceability of the debt or the rate of wage withholding.

(b) At our option the hearing may be an oral hearing under § 34.9 or a paper hearing under § 34.10.

(Authority: 31 U.S.C. 3720D)

§ 34.9 Conditions for an oral hearing.

(a) We provide an oral hearing if you—

(1) Request an oral hearing; and

(2) Show in the request a good reason to believe that we cannot resolve the issues in dispute by review of the documentary evidence, by demonstrating that the validity of the claim turns on the credibility or veracity of witness testimony.

(b) If we determine that an oral hearing is appropriate, we notify you how to receive the oral hearing.

(c)(1) At your option, an oral hearing may be conducted either in person or by telephone conference.

(2) We provide an in-person oral hearing with regard to administrative debts only in Washington D.C.

(3) We provide an in-person oral hearing with regard to debts based on student loan or grant obligations only at our regional service centers in Atlanta, Chicago, or San Francisco.

(4) You must bear all travel expenses you incur in connection with an in person hearing.

(5) We bear the cost of any telephone calls we place in order to conduct an oral hearing by telephone.

(d)(1) To arrange the time and location of the oral hearing, we ordinarily attempt to contact you first by telephone call to the number you provided to us.

(2) If we are unable to contact you by telephone, we leave a message directing you to contact us within 5 business days to arrange the time and place of the hearing.

(3) If we can neither contact you directly nor leave a message with you by telephone—

(i)   We notify you in writing to contact us to arrange the time and place of the hearing; or

(ii) We select a time and place for the hearing, and notify you in writing of the time and place set for the hearing.

(e) We consider you to have withdrawn the request for an oral hearing if—

(1) Within 15 days of the date of a written notice to contact us, we receive no response to that notice; or

(2) Within five business days of the date of a telephone message to contact us, we receive no response to that message.

(Authority: 31 U.S.C. 3720D)

§ 34.10 Conditions for a paper hearing.

We provide a paper hearing—

(a) If you request a paper hearing;

(b) If you requested an oral hearing, but we determine under § 34.9(e) that you have withdrawn that request;

(c) If you fail to appear for a scheduled oral hearing, as provided in § 34.15; or

(d) If we deny a request for an oral hearing because we conclude that, by a review of the written record, we can resolve the issues raised by your objections.

(Authority: 31 U.S.C. 3720D)

§ 34.11 Timely request for a hearing.

(a) A hearing request is timely if—

(1) You mail the request to the office designated in the garnishment notice and the request is postmarked not later than the 30th day following the date of the notice; or

(2) The designated office receives the request not later than the 30th day following the date of the garnishment notice.

(b) If we receive a timely written request from you for a hearing, we will not issue a garnishment order before we—

(1) Provide the requested hearing; and

(2) Issue a written decision on the objections you raised.

(c) If your written request for a hearing is not timely—

(1) We provide you a hearing; and

(2) We do not delay issuance of a garnishment order unless—

(i) We determine from credible representations in the request that the delay in filing the request for hearing was caused by factors over which you had no control; or

(ii) We have other good reason to delay issuing a garnishment order.

(d) If we do not complete a hearing within 60 days of an untimely request, we suspend any garnishment order until we have issued a decision.

(Authority: 31 U.S.C. 3720D)

§ 34.12 Request for reconsideration.

(a) If you have received a decision on an objection to garnishment you may file a request for reconsideration of that decision.

(b) We do not suspend garnishment merely because you have filed a request for reconsideration.

(c) We consider your request for reconsideration if we determine that—

(1) You base your request on grounds of financial hardship, and your financial circumstances, as shown by evidence submitted with the request, have materially changed since we issued the decision so that we should reduce the amount to be garnished under the order; or

(2)(i) You submitted with the request evidence that you did not previously submit; and

(ii) This evidence demonstrates that we should reconsider your objection to the existence, amount, or enforceability of the debt.

(d)(1) If we agree to reconsider the decision, we notify you.

(2)(i) We may reconsider based on the request and supporting evidence you have presented with the request; or

(ii) We may offer you an opportunity for a hearing to present evidence.

(Authority: 31 U.S.C. 3720D)

§ 34.13 Conduct of a hearing.

(a)(1) A hearing official conducts any hearing under this part.

(2) The hearing official may be any qualified employee of the Department whom the Department designates to conduct the hearing.

(b)(1) The hearing official conducts any hearing as an informal proceeding.

(2) A witness in an oral hearing must testify under oath or affirmation.

(3) The hearing official maintains a summary record of any hearing.

(c) Before the hearing official considers evidence we obtain that was not included in the debt records available for inspection when we sent notice of proposed garnishment, we notify you that additional evidence has become available, may be considered by the hearing official, and is available for inspection or copying.

(d) The hearing official considers any objection you raise and evidence you submit—

(1) In or with the request for a hearing;

(2) During an oral hearing;

(3) By the date that we consider, under §34.9(e), that a request for an oral hearing has been withdrawn; or

(4) Within a period we set, ordinarily not to exceed seven business days, after—

(i) We provide you access to our records regarding the debt, if you requested access to records within 20 days after the date of the notice under § 34.4;

(ii) We notify you that we have obtained and intend to consider additional evidence;

(iii) You request an extension of time in order to submit specific relevant evidence that you identify to us in the request; or

(iv) We notify you that we deny your request for an oral hearing.

(Authority: 31 U.S.C. 3720D)

§ 34.14 Burden of proof.

(a)(1) We have the burden of proving the existence and amount of a debt.

(2) We meet this burden by including in the record and making available to the debtor on request records that show that—

(i) The debt exists in the amount stated in the garnishment notice; and

(ii) The debt is currently delinquent.

(b) If you dispute the existence or amount of the debt, you must prove by a preponderance of the credible evidence that—

(1) No debt exists;

(2) The amount we claim to be owed on the debt is incorrect, or

(3) You are not delinquent with respect to the debt.

(c)(1) If you object that the proposed garnishment rate would cause financial hardship, you bear the burden of proving by a preponderance of the credible evidence that withholding the amount of wages proposed in the notice would leave you unable to meet the basic living expenses of you and your dependents.

(2) The standards for proving financial hardship are those in § 34.24.

(d)(1) If you object on the ground that applicable law bars us from collecting the debt by garnishment at this time, you bear the burden of proving the facts that would establish that claim.

(2) Examples of applicable law that may prevent collection by garnishment include the automatic stay in bankruptcy (11 U.S.C. 362(a)), and the preclusion of garnishment action against a debtor who was involuntarily separated from employment and has been reemployed for less than a continuous period of 12 months (31 U.S.C. 3720D(b)(6)).

(e) The fact that applicable law may limit the amount that an employer may withhold from your pay to less than the amount or rate we state in the garnishment order does not bar us from issuing the order.

(Authority: 31 U.S.C. 3720D)

§ 34.15 Consequences of failure to appear for an oral hearing.

(a) If you do not appear for an in-person hearing you requested, or you do not answer a telephone call convening a telephone hearing, at the time set for the hearing, we consider you to have withdrawn your request for an oral hearing.

(b) If you do not appear for an oral hearing but you demonstrate that there was good cause for not appearing, we may reschedule the oral hearing.

(c) If you do not appear for an oral hearing you requested and we do not reschedule the hearing, we provide a paper hearing to review your objections, based on the evidence in your file and any evidence you have already provided.

(Authority: 31 U.S.C. 3720D)

§ 34.16 Issuance of the hearing decision.

(a) Date of decision. The hearing official issues a written opinion stating his or her decision, as soon as practicable, but not later than 60 days after the date on which we received the request for hearing.

(b) If we do not provide you with a hearing and render a decision within 60 days after we receive your request for a hearing—

(1) We do not issue a garnishment order until the hearing is held and a decision rendered; or

(2) If we have already issued a garnishment order to your employer, we suspend the garnishment order beginning on the 61st day after we receive the hearing request until we provide a hearing and issue a decision.

(Authority: 31 U.S.C. 3720D)

§ 34.17 Content of decision.

(a) The written decision is based on the evidence contained in the hearing record. The decision includes—

(1) A description of the evidence considered by the hearing official;

(2) The hearing official's findings, analysis, and conclusions regarding objections raised to the existence or amount of the debt;

(3) The rate of wage withholding under the order, if you objected that withholding the amount proposed in the garnishment notice would cause an extreme financial hardship; and

(4) An explanation of your rights under this part for reconsideration of the decision.

(b) The hearing official's decision is the final action of the Secretary for the purposes of judicial review under the Administrative Procedure Act (5 U.S.C. 701 *et seq.*).

(Authority: 31 U.S.C. 3720D)

§ 34.18 Issuance of the wage garnishment order.

(a)(1) If you fail to make a timely request for a hearing, we issue a garnishment order to your employer within 30 days after the deadline for timely requesting a hearing.

(2) If you make a timely request for a hearing, we issue a withholding order within 30 days after the hearing official issues a decision to proceed with garnishment.

(b)(1) The garnishment order we issue to your employer is signed by an official of the Department designated by the Secretary.

(2) The designated official's signature may be a computer-generated facsimile.

(c)(1) The garnishment order contains only the information we consider necessary for your employer to comply with the order and for us to ensure proper credit for payments received from your employer.

(2) The order includes your name, address, and social security number, as well as instructions for withholding and information as to where your employer must send the payments.

(d)(1) We keep a copy of a certificate of service indicating the date of mailing of the order.

(2) We may create and maintain the certificate of service as an electronic record.

(Authority: 31 U.S.C. 3720D)

§ 34.19 Amounts to be withheld under a garnishment order.

(a)(1) After an employer receives a garnishment order we issue, the employer must deduct from all disposable pay of the debtor during each pay period the amount directed in the garnishment order unless this section or § 34.20 requires a smaller amount to be withheld.

(2) The amount specified in the garnishment order does not apply if other law, including this section, requires the employer to withhold a smaller amount.

(b) The employer must comply with our garnishment order by withholding the lesser of—

(1) The amount directed in the garnishment order; or—

(2) The amount specified in 15 U.S.C. 1673(a)(2) (Restriction on Garnishment); that is, the amount by which a debtor's disposable pay exceeds an amount equal to 30 times the minimum wage. (See 29 CFR 870.10.)

(Authority: 31 U.S.C. 3720D)

§ 34.20 Amount to be withheld under multiple garnishment orders.

If a debtor's pay is subject to several garnishment orders, the employer must comply with our garnishment order as follows:

(a) Unless other Federal law requires a different priority, the employer must pay us the amount calculated under § 34.19(b) before the employer complies with any later garnishment orders, except a family support withholding order.

(b) If an employer is withholding from a debtor's pay based on a garnishment order served on the employer before our order, or if a withholding order for family support is served on an employer at any time, the employer must comply with our garnishment order by withholding an amount that is the smaller of—

(1) The amount calculated under § 34.19(b); or

(2) An amount equal to 25 percent of the debtor's disposable pay less the amount or amounts withheld under the garnishment order or orders with priority over our order.

(c)(1) If a debtor owes more than one debt arising from a program we administer, we may issue multiple garnishment orders.

(2) The total amount withheld from the debtor's pay for orders we issue under paragraph (c)(1) of this section does not exceed the amounts specified in the orders, the amount specified in § 34.19(b)(2), or 15 percent of the debtor's disposable pay, whichever is smallest.

(d) An employer may withhold and pay an amount greater than that amount in paragraphs (b) and (c) of this section if the debtor gives the employer written consent.

(Authority: 31 U.S.C. 3720D)

§ 34.21 Employer certification.

(a) Along with a garnishment order, we send to an employer a certification in a form prescribed by the Secretary of the Treasury.

(b) The employer must complete and return the certification to us within the time stated in the instructions for the form.

(c) The employer must include in the certification information about the debtor's employment status, payment frequency, and disposable pay available for withholding.

(Authority: 31 U.S.C. 3720D)

§ 34.22 Employer responsibilities.

(a)(1) Our garnishment order indicates a reasonable period of time within which an employer must start withholding under the order.

(2) The employer must promptly pay to the Department all amounts the employer withholds according to the order.

(b) The employer may follow its normal pay and disbursement cycles in complying with the garnishment order.

(c) The employer must withhold the appropriate amount from the debtor's wages for each pay period until the employer receives our notification to discontinue wage garnishment.

(d) The employer must disregard any assignment or allotment by an employee that would interfere with or prohibit the employer from complying with our garnishment order, unless that assignment or allotment was made for a family support judgment or order.

(Authority: 31 U.S.C. 3720D)

§ 34.23 Exclusions from garnishment.

(a) We do not garnish your wages if we have credible evidence that you—

(1) Were involuntarily separated from employment; and

(2) Have not yet been reemployed continuously for at least 12 months.

(b) You have the burden of informing us of the circumstances surrounding an involuntary separation from employment.

(Authority: 31 U.S.C. 3720D)

§ 34.24 Claim of financial hardship by debtor subject to garnishment.

(a) You may object to a proposed garnishment on the ground that

withholding the amount or at the rate stated in the notice of garnishment would cause financial hardship to you and your dependents. (See § 34.7)

(b) You may, at any time, object that the amount or the rate of withholding which our order specifies your employer must withhold causes financial hardship.

(c)(1) We consider an objection to an outstanding garnishment order and provide you an opportunity for a hearing on your objection only after the order has been outstanding for at least six months.

(2) We may provide a hearing in extraordinary circumstances earlier than six months if you show in your request for review that your financial circumstances have substantially changed after the notice of proposed garnishment because of an event such as injury, divorce, or catastrophic illness.

(d)(1) You bear the burden of proving a claim of financial hardship by a preponderance of the credible evidence.

(2) You must prove by credible documentation—

(i) The amount of the costs incurred by you, your spouse, and any dependents, for basic living expenses; and

(ii) The income available from any source to meet those expenses.

(e)(1) We consider your claim of financial hardship by comparing—

(i) The amounts that you prove are being incurred for basic living expenses; against

(ii) The amounts spent for basic living expenses by families of the same size and similar income to yours.

(2) We regard the standards published by the Internal Revenue Service under 26 U.S.C. 7122(c)(2) (the "National Standards") as establishing the average amounts spent for basic living expenses for families of the same size as, and with family incomes comparable to, your family.

(3) We accept as reasonable the amount that you prove you incur for a type of basic living expense to the extent that the amount does not exceed the amount spent for that expense by families of the same size and similar income according to the National Standards.

(4) If you claim for any basic living expense an amount that exceeds the amount in the National Standards, you must prove that the amount you claim is reasonable and necessary.

(Authority: 31 U.S.C. 3720D)

§ 34.25 Determination of financial hardship.

(a)(1) If we conclude that garnishment at the amount or rate proposed in a notice would cause you financial hardship, we reduce the amount of the proposed garnishment to an amount that we determine will allow you to meet proven basic living expenses.

(2) If a garnishment order is already in effect, we notify your employer of any change in the amount the employer must withhold or the rate of withholding under the order.

(b) If we determine that financial hardship would result from garnishment based on a finding by a hearing official or under a repayment agreement we reached with you, this determination is effective for a period not longer than six months after the date of the finding or agreement.

(c)(1) After the effective period referred to in paragraph (b) of this section, we may require you to submit current information regarding your family income and living expenses.

(2) If we conclude from a review of that evidence that we should

increase the rate of withholding or payment, we—

(i)   Notify you; and

(ii) Provide you with an opportunity to contest the determination and obtain a hearing on the objection under the procedures in § 34.24.

(Authority: 31 U.S.C. 3720D)

§ 34.26 Ending garnishment.

(a)(1) A garnishment order we issue is effective until we rescind the order.

(2) If an employer is unable to honor a garnishment order because the amount available for garnishment is insufficient to pay any portion of the amount stated in the order, the employer must—

(i)   Notify us; and

(ii) Comply with the order when sufficient disposable pay is available.

(b) After we have fully recovered the amounts owed by the debtor, including interest, penalties, and collection costs, we send the debtor's employer notification to stop wage withholding.

(Authority: 31 U.S.C. 3720D)

§ 34.27 Actions by employer prohibited by law.

An employer may not discharge, refuse to employ, or take disciplinary action against a debtor due to the issuance of a garnishment order under this part.

(Authority: 31 U.S.C. 3720D)

§ 34.28 Refunds of amounts collected in error.

(a) If a hearing official determines under §§ 34.16 and 34.17 that a person does not owe the debt described in our notice or that an administrative wage garnishment under this part was barred by law at the time of the collection action, we promptly refund any amount collected by means of this garnishment.

(b) Unless required by Federal law or contract, we do not pay interest on a refund.

(Authority: 31 U.S.C. 3720D)

§ 34.29 Enforcement action against employer for noncompliance with garnishment order.

(a) If an employer fails to comply with § 34.22 to withhold an appropriate amount from wages owed and payable to an employee, we may sue the employer for that amount.

(b)(1) We do not file suit under paragraph (a) of this section before we terminate action to enforce the debt as a personal liability of the debtor.

(2) However, the provision of paragraph (b)(1) of this section may not apply if earlier filing of a suit is necessary to avoid expiration of any applicable statute of limitations.

(c)(1) For purposes of this section, termination of an action to enforce a debt occurs when we terminate collection action in accordance with the FCCS, other applicable standards, or paragraph (c)(2) of this section.

(2) We regard termination of the collection action to have occurred if we have not received for one year any payments to satisfy the debt, in whole or in part, from the particular debtor whose wages were subject to garnishment.

(Authority: 31 U.S.C. 3720D)

§ 34.30 Application of payments and accrual of interest.

We apply payments received through a garnishment in the following order—

(a) To costs incurred to collect the debt;

(b) To interest accrued on the debt at the rate established by—

(1) The terms of the obligation under which it arises; or

(2) Applicable law; and

(c) To outstanding principal of the debt.

(Authority: 31 U.S.C. 3720D)

B.1.4 Collection Costs and Penalties

34 C.F.R. sec.

§ 30.60 What costs does the Secretary impose on delinquent debtors?

Source: 51 Fed. Reg. 24099, July 1, 1986; 53 Fed. Reg. 33425, Aug. 30, 1988, unless otherwise noted.

§ 30.60 What costs does the Secretary impose on delinquent debtors?

(a) The Secretary may charge a debtor for the costs associated with the collection of a particular debt. These costs include, but are not limited to—

(1) Salaries of employees performing Federal loan servicing and debt collection activities;

(2) Telephone and mailing costs;

(3) Costs for reporting debts to credit bureaus;

(4) Costs for purchase of credit bureau reports;

(5) Costs associated with computer operations and other costs associated with the maintenance of records;

(6) Bank charges;

(7) Collection agency costs;

(8) Court costs and attorney fees; and

(9) Costs charged by other Governmental agencies.

(b) Notwithstanding any provision of State law, if the Secretary uses a collection agency to collect a debt on a contingent fee basis, the Secretary charges the debtor, and collects through the agency, an amount sufficient to recover—

(1) The entire amount of the debt; and

(2) The amount that the Secretary is required to pay the agency for its collection services.

(c)(1) The amount recovered under paragraph (b) of this section is the entire amount of the debt, multiplied by the following fraction:

[*Graphic Omitted*]

(2) In paragraph (c)(1) of this section, cr equals the commission rate the Department pays to the collection agency.

(d) If the Secretary uses more than one collection agency to collect similar debts, the commission rate (cr) described in paragraph (c)(2) of this section is calculated as a weighted average of the commission rates charged by all collection agencies collecting similar debts, computed for each fiscal year based on the formula

[*Graphic Omitted*]

where—

(1) Xi equals the dollar amount of similar debts placed by the Department with an individual collection agency as of the end of the preceding fiscal year;

(2) Yi equals the commission rate the Department pays to that collection agency for the collection of the similar debts;

(3) Z equals the dollar amount of similar debts placed by the Department with all collection agencies as of the end of the preceding fiscal year; and

(4) N equals the number of collection agencies with which the Secretary has placed similar debts as of the end of the preceding fiscal year.

(e) If a debtor has agreed under a repayment or settlement agreement with the Secretary to pay costs associated with the collection of a debt at a specified amount or rate, the Secretary collects those costs in accordance with the agreement.

(f) The Secretary does not impose collection costs against State or local governments under paragraphs (a) through (d) of this section.

(Authority: 20 U.S.C. 1221e-3(a)(1) and 1226a-1, 31 U.S.C. 3711(e), 3717(e)(1), 3718)

§ 30.61 What penalties does the Secretary impose on delinquent debtors?

(a) If a debtor does not make a payment on a debt, or portion of a debt, within 90 days after the date specified in the first demand for payment sent to the debtor, the Secretary imposes a penalty on the debtor.

(b)(1) The amount of the penalty imposed under paragraph (a) of this section is 6 percent per year of the amount of the delinquent debt.

(2) The penalty imposed under this section runs from the date specified in the first demand for payment to the date the debt (including the penalty) is paid.

(c) If a debtor has agreed under a repayment or settlement agreement with the Secretary to pay a penalty for failure to pay a debt when due, or has such an agreement under a grant or contract under which the debt arose, the Secretary collects the penalty in accordance with the agreement, grant, or contract.

(d) The Secretary does not impose a penalty against State or local governments under paragraphs (a) and (b) of this section.

(Authority: 20 U.S.C. 1221e-3(a)(1) and 1226a-1, 31 U.S.C. 3711(e))

B.1.5 Compromise of Debts

34 C.F.R. sec.

30.70 How does the Secretary exercise discretion to compromise a debt or to suspend or terminate collection of a debt?

§ 30.70 How does the Secretary exercise discretion to compromise a debt or to suspend or terminate collection of a debt?

(a) The Secretary uses the standards in the FCCS, 4 CFR part 103, to determine whether compromise of a debt is appropriate if—

(1) The debt must be referred to the Department of Justice under this section; or

(2) The amount of the debt is less than or equal to $20,000 and

the Secretary does not follow the procedures in paragraph (e) of this section.

(b) The Secretary refers a debt to the Department of Justice to decide whether to compromise a debt if—

(1) The debt was incurred under a program or activity subject to section 452(f) of the General Education Provisions Act and the initial determination of the debt was more than $50,000; or

(2) The debt was incurred under a program or activity not subject to section 452(f) of the General Education Provisions Act and the amount of the debt is more than $20,000.

(c) The Secretary may compromise the debt under the procedures in paragraph (e) of this section if—

(1) The debt was incurred under a program or activity subject to section 452(f) of the General Education Provisions Act; and

(2) The initial determination of the debt was less than or equal to $50,000.

(d) The Secretary may compromise a debt without following the procedure in paragraph (e) of this section if the amount of the debt is less than or equal to $20,000.

(e) The Secretary may compromise the debt pursuant to paragraph (c) of this section if—

(1) The Secretary determines that—

(i) Collection of any or all of the debt would not be practical or in the public interest; and

(ii) The practice that resulted in the debt has been corrected and will not recur;

(2) At least 45 days before compromising the debt, the Secretary publishes a notice in the Federal Register stating—

(i) The Secretary's intent to compromise the debt; and

(ii) That interested persons may comment on the proposed compromise; and

(3) The Secretary considers any comments received in response to the Federal Register notice before finally compromising the debt.

(f)(1) The Secretary uses the standards in the FCCS, 4 CFR part 104, to determine whether suspension or termination of collection action is appropriate.

(2) The Secretary—

(i) Refers the debt to the Department of Justice to decide whether to suspend or terminate collection action if the amount of the debt at the time of the referral is more than $20,000; or

(ii) May decide to suspend or terminate collection action if the amount of the debt at the time of the Secretary's decision is less than or equal to $20,000.

(g) In determining the amount of a debt under paragraphs (a) through (f) of this section, the Secretary excludes interest, penalties, and administrative costs.

(h) Notwithstanding paragraphs (b) through (f) of this section, the Secretary may compromise a debt, or suspend or terminate collection of a debt, in any amount if the debt arises under the Guaranteed Student Loan Program authorized under title IV, part B, of the Higher Education Act of 1965, as amended, or the Perkins Loan Program authorized under title IV, part E, of the Higher Education Act of 1965, as amended.

(*i*) The Secretary refers a debt to the General Accounting Office (GAO) for review and approval before referring the debt to the Department of Justice for litigation if—

(1) The debt arose from an audit exception taken by GAO to a payment made by the Department; and

(2) The GAO has not granted an exception from the GAO referral requirement.

(j) Nothing in this section precludes—

(1) A contracting officer from exercising his authority under applicable statutes, regulations, or common law to settle disputed claims relating to a contract; or

(2) The Secretary from redetermining a claim.

(Authority: 20 U.S.C. 1082(a) (5) and (6), 1087hh, 1221e-3(a)(1), 1226a-1, and 1234a(f), 31 U.S.C. 3711(e))

[51 Fed. Reg. 24099, July 1, 1986; 53 Fed. Reg. 33425, Aug. 30, 1988; 53 Fed. Reg. 33426, Aug. 30, 1988]

B.1.6 Department of Treasury Debt Collection Regulations

31 C.F.R. sec.

§ 285.4 Offset of Federal benefit payments to collect past-due legally enforceable nontax debt.

* * *

§ 901.3 Collection by administrative offset.

Source: 65 Fed. Reg. 70395, Nov. 22, 2000, unless otherwise noted.

§ 285.4 Offset of Federal benefit payments to collect past-due, legally enforceable nontax debt.

(a) *Scope.*

(1) This section sets forth special rules applicable to the offset of Federal benefit payments payable to an individual under the Social Security Act (other than Supplemental Security Income (SSI) payments), part B of the Black Lung Benefits Act, or any law administered by the Railroad Retirement Board (other than payments that such Board determines to be tier 2 benefits) to collect delinquent nontax debt owed to the United States.

(2) As used in this section, benefit payments "due to" an individual, "payable to" an individual, and/or benefit payments "received by" an individual, refer to those benefit payments expected to be paid to an individual before any amounts are offset to satisfy the payee's delinquent debt owed to the United States. Nothing in these phrases, similar phrases, or this section is intended to imply or confer any new or additional rights or benefits on an individual with respect to his or her entitlement to benefit payments. The Financial Management Service (FMS), the Social Security Administration, the Railroad Retirement Board, and other payment agencies are not liable for the amount offset from an individual's benefit payment on the basis that the underlying obligation, represented by the payment before the offset was taken, was not satisfied. See 31 U.S.C. 3716(c)(2)(A).

(b) *Definitions.* As used in this section:

Administrative offset or *offset* means withholding funds payable by the United States (including funds payable by the United States on behalf of a State government) to, or held by the United States for, a person to satisfy a debt.

Agency or *Federal agency* means a department, agency, court, court administrative office, or instrumentality in the executive, judicial, or legislative branch of the Federal Government, including government corporations.

Covered benefit payment means a Federal benefit payment payable to an individual under the Social Security Act (other than SSI payments), part B of the Black Lung Benefits Act, or any law administered by the Railroad Retirement Board (other than payments that such Board determines to be tier 2 benefits). The amount of the covered benefit payment payable to a debtor for purposes of this section will be the amount after reduction or deduction required under the laws authorizing the program. Reductions to recover benefit overpayments are excluded from the covered benefit payment when calculating amounts available for offset.

Creditor agency means a Federal agency owed a debt that seeks to collect that debt through administrative offset.

Debt or *claim* means an amount of money, funds, or property which has been determined by an agency official to be due the United States from any person, organization, or entity except another Federal agency. Debt or claim does not include a debt or claim arising under the Internal Revenue Code of 1986 or the tariff laws of the United States.

Debtor means a person who owes a debt. The term "person" includes any individual, organization or entity, except another Federal agency.

Disbursing official means an official who has authority to disburse public money pursuant to 31 U.S.C. 3321 or another law, including an official of the Department of the Treasury, the Department of Defense, the United States Postal Service, or any other government corporation, or any official of the United States designated by the Secretary of the Treasury to disburse public money.

FMS means the Financial Management Service, a bureau of the Department of the Treasury.

Monthly covered benefit payment means a covered benefit payment payable to a payee on a recurring basis at monthly intervals that is not expressly limited in duration, at the time the first payment is made, to a period of less than 12 months.

Payee means a person who is due a payment from a disbursing official. For purposes of this section, a "payee" is a person who is entitled to the benefit of all or part of a payment from a disbursing official.

Taxpayer identifying number means the identifying number described under section 6109 of the Internal Revenue Code of 1986 (26 U.S.C. 6109). For an individual, the taxpayer identifying number generally is the individual's social security number.

(c) *Administrative offset, generally.* Disbursing officials shall offset payments to satisfy, in whole or in part, debts owed by the payee. Disbursing officials shall compare payment records with records of debts submitted to FMS for collection by administrative offset. A match will occur when the taxpayer identifying number and name of the payee (as defined in paragraph (b) of this section) on a payment record are the same as the taxpayer identifying number and name of the debtor on a debt record. When a match occurs and all other requirements for offset have been met, the disbursing official shall offset the payment to satisfy, in whole or in part, the debt. Any amounts not offset shall be paid to the payee. Covered benefit payments, i.e., payments made to individuals under the Social Security Act (other than Supplemental Security Income (SSI) payments), part B of the Black Lung Benefits Act, or any law administered by the Railroad Retirement Board (RRB) (other than tier 2 benefit payments) are among the types of payments which may be offset to collect debts owed to the United States. Offset of covered benefit payments are subject to the limitations contained in this section. Offsets of covered benefit payments will occur only if the name and taxpayer identifying number of the person who is entitled to the benefit of all or a part of the payment matches the name and taxpayer identifying number of the debtor.

(d) *Submission of debts to FMS for collection by administrative offset.* Creditor agencies must notify FMS of all past-due, legally enforceable debt delinquent for more than 180 days for purposes of collection by administrative offset. Creditor agencies may notify FMS of all debt delinquent for less than 180 days for purposes of collection by administrative offset. Prior to such notification, creditor agencies must certify to FMS that the debt is past-due, legally enforceable, and that the creditor agency has provided the debtor with notice and an opportunity for a review in accordance with the provisions of 31 U.S.C. 3716(a) and other applicable law.

(e) *Offset amount.*

(1) The amount offset from a monthly covered benefit payment shall be the lesser of:

(i) The amount of the debt, including any interest, penalties and administrative costs;

(ii) An amount equal to 15% of the monthly covered benefit payment; or

(iii) The amount, if any, by which the monthly covered benefit payment exceeds $750.

(2) A debtor shall not receive a refund of any amounts offset if the debtor's monthly covered benefit payments are reduced, suspended, terminated, or otherwise not received for a period of 12 months.

(3) *Examples.*

(i) A debtor receives monthly Social Security benefits of $850. The amount offset is the lesser of $127.50 (15% of $850) or $100 (the amount by which $850 exceeds $750). In this example, the amount offset is $100 (assuming the debt is $100 or more).

(ii) A debtor receives monthly Social Security benefits of $1250. The amount offset is the lesser of $187.50 (15% of $1250) or $500 (the amount by which $1250 exceeds $750). In this example, the amount offset is $187.50 (assuming the debt is $187.50 or more).

(iii) A debtor receives monthly Social Security payments of $650. No amount will be offset because $650 is less than $750.

(f) *Notification of offset.*

(1) Before offsetting a covered benefit payment, the disbursing official will notify the payee in writing of the date offset will commence. The notice shall inform the payee of the type of payment that will be offset; the identity of the creditor agency which requested the offset; and a contact point within the creditor agency that will handle concerns regarding the offset.

(2) The disbursing official conducting the offset will notify the payee in writing of the occurrence of the offset to satisfy, in whole or in part, a delinquent debt owed to the United States. The notice shall inform the payee of the type and amount of the payment that was offset; the identity of the creditor agency which requested the offset; and a contact point within the creditor agency that will handle concerns regarding the offset.

(3) Non-receipt by the debtor of the notices described in paragraphs (f)(1) and (f)(2) of this section shall not impair the legality of the administrative offset.

(g) *Fees.* A fee which FMS has determined to be sufficient to cover the full cost of the offset procedure, shall be deducted from each offset amount. Creditor agencies may add this fee to the debt

if not otherwise prohibited by law.

(h) *Disposition of amounts collected.* The disbursing official conducting the offset will transmit amounts collected for debts, less fees charged under paragraph (g) of this section, to the appropriate creditor agency. If an erroneous offset payment is made to a creditor agency, the disbursing official will notify the creditor agency that an erroneous offset payment has been made. The disbursing official may deduct the amount of the erroneous offset payment from future amounts payable to the creditor agency. Alternatively, upon the disbursing official's request, the creditor agency shall return promptly to the disbursing official or the affected payee an amount equal to the amount of the erroneous payment. The disbursing official and the creditor agency shall adjust the debtor records appropriately.

[63 Fed. Reg. 44988, Aug. 21, 1998; 63 Fed. Reg. 71204, Dec. 23, 1998]

* * *

§ 901.3 Collection by administrative offset.

(a) *Scope.*

(1) The term "administrative offset" has the meaning provided in 31 U.S.C. 3701(a)(1).

(2) This section does not apply to:

(i) Debts arising under the Social Security Act, except as provided in 42 U.S.C. 404;

(ii) Payments made under the Social Security Act, except as provided for in 31 U.S.C. 3716(c) (*see* 31 CFR 285.4, Federal Benefit Offset);

(iii) Debts arising under, or payments made under, the Internal Revenue Code (*see* 31 CFR 285.2, Tax Refund Offset) or the tariff laws of the United States;

(iv) Offsets against Federal salaries to the extent these standards are inconsistent with regulations published to implement such offsets under 5 U.S.C. 5514 and 31 U.S.C. 3716 (*see* 5 CFR part 550, subpart K, and 31 CFR 285.7, Federal Salary Offset);

(v) Offsets under 31 U.S.C. 3728 against a judgment obtained by a debtor against the United States;

(vi) Offsets or recoupments under common law, State law, or Federal statutes specifically prohibiting offsets or recoupments of particular types of debts; or

(vii) Offsets in the course of judicial proceedings, including bankruptcy.

(3) Unless otherwise provided for by contract or law, debts or payments that are not subject to administrative offset under 31 U.S.C. 3716 may be collected by administrative offset under the common law or other applicable statutory authority.

(4) Unless otherwise provided by law, administrative offset of payments under the authority of 31 U.S.C. 3716 to collect a debt may not be conducted more than 10 years after the Government's right to collect the debt first accrued, unless facts material to the Government's right to collect the debt were not known and could not reasonably have been known by the official or officials of the Government who were charged with the responsibility to discover and collect such debts. This limitation does not apply to debts reduced to a judgment.

(5) In bankruptcy cases, agencies should seek legal advice from their agency counsel concerning the impact of the Bankruptcy

Code, particularly 11 U.S.C. 106, 362, and 553, on pending or contemplated collections by offset.

(b) *Mandatory centralized administrative offset.*

(1) Creditor agencies are required to refer past due, legally enforceable nontax debts which are over 180 days delinquent to the Secretary for collection by centralized administrative offset. Debts which are less than 180 days delinquent also may be referred to the Secretary for this purpose. *See* § 901.3(b)(5) for debt certification requirements.

(2) The names and taxpayer identifying numbers (TINs) of debtors who owe debts referred to the Secretary as described in paragraph (b)(1) of this section shall be compared to the names and TINs on payments to be made by Federal disbursing officials. Federal disbursing officials include disbursing officials of Treasury, the Department of Defense, the United States Postal Service, other Government corporations, and disbursing officials of the United States designated by the Secretary. When the name and TIN of a debtor match the name and TIN of a payee and all other requirements for offset have been met, the payment will be offset to satisfy the debt.

(3) Federal disbursing officials will notify the debtor/payee in writing that an offset has occurred to satisfy, in part or in full, a past due, legally enforceable delinquent debt. The notice shall include a description of the type and amount of the payment from which the offset was taken, the amount of offset that was taken, the identity of the creditor agency requesting the offset, and a contact point within the creditor agency who will respond to questions regarding the offset.

(4)(i) Before referring a delinquent debt to the Secretary for administrative offset, agencies must have prescribed administrative offset regulations consistent with this section or have adopted this section without change by cross-reference.

(ii) Such regulations shall provide that offsets may be initiated only after the debtor:

(A) Has been sent written notice of the type and amount of the debt, the intention of the agency to use administrative offset to collect the debt, and an explanation of the debtor's rights under 31 U.S.C. 3716; and

(B) The debtor has been given:

(1) The opportunity to inspect and copy agency records related to the debt;

(2) The opportunity for a review within the agency of the determination of indebtedness; and

(3) The opportunity to make a written agreement to repay the debt.

(iii) Agency regulations may provide for the omission of the procedures set forth in paragraph (a)(4)(ii) of this section when:

(A) The offset is in the nature of a recoupment;

(B) The debt arises under a contract as set forth in *Cecile Industries, Inc. v. Cheney*, 995 F.2d 1052 (Fed. Cir. 1993) (notice and other procedural protections set forth in 31 U.S.C. 3716(a) do not supplant or restrict established procedures for contractual offsets accommodated by the Contracts Disputes Act); or

(C) In the case of non-centralized administrative offsets conducted under paragraph (c) of this section, the agency first learns of the existence of the amount owed by the debtor when there is insufficient time before payment would be made to the debtor/payee to allow for prior notice and an opportunity for review. When prior notice and an opportunity for review are omitted, the agency shall give the debtor such notice and an opportunity for review as soon as practicable and shall promptly refund any money ultimately found not to have been owed to the Government.

(iv) When an agency previously has given a debtor any of the required notice and review opportunities with respect to a particular debt (*see, e.g.*, § 901.2), the agency need not duplicate such notice and review opportunities before administrative offset may be initiated.

(5) Agencies referring delinquent debts to the Secretary must certify, in a form acceptable to the Secretary, that:

(i) The debt(s) is (are) past due and legally enforceable; and

(ii) The agency has complied with all due process requirements under 31 U.S.C. 3716(a) and the agency's regulations.

(6) Payments that are prohibited by law from being offset are exempt from centralized administrative offset. The Secretary shall exempt payments under means-tested programs from centralized administrative offset when requested in writing by the head of the payment certifying or authorizing agency. Also, the Secretary may exempt other classes of payments from centralized offset upon the written request of the head of the payment certifying or authorizing agency.

(7) Benefit payments made under the Social Security Act (42 U.S.C. 301 *et seq.*), part B of the Black Lung Benefits Act (30 U.S.C. 921 *et seq.*), and any law administered by the Railroad Retirement Board (other than tier 2 benefits), may be offset only in accordance with Treasury regulations, issued in consultation with the Social Security Administration, the Railroad Retirement Board, and the Office of Management and Budget. See 31 CFR 285.4.

(8) In accordance with 31 U.S.C. 3716(f), the Secretary may waive the provisions of the Computer Matching and Privacy Protection Act of 1988 concerning matching agreements and post-match notification and verification (5 U.S.C. 552a(*o*) and (p)) for centralized administrative offset upon receipt of a certification from a creditor agency that the due process requirements enumerated in 31 U.S.C. 3716(a) have been met. The certification of a debt in accordance with paragraph (b)(5) of this section will satisfy this requirement. If such a waiver is granted, only the Data Integrity Board of the Department of the Treasury is required to oversee any matching activities, in accordance with 31 U.S.C. 3716(g). This waiver authority does not apply to offsets conducted under paragraphs (c) and (d) of this section.

(c) *Non-centralized administrative offset.*

(1) Generally, non-centralized administrative offsets are ad hoc case-by-case offsets that an agency conducts, at the agency's discretion, internally or in cooperation with the agency certifying or authorizing payments to the debtor. Unless otherwise prohibited by law, when centralized administrative offset is not available or appropriate, past due, legally enforceable nontax delinquent debts may be collected through non-centralized administrative offset. In these cases, a creditor agency may make a request directly to a payment authorizing agency to offset a payment due a debtor to collect a delinquent debt. For example, it may be appropriate for a creditor agency to request that the Office of Personnel Management (OPM) offset a Federal employee's lump sum payment upon leaving Government service to satisfy an unpaid advance.

(2) Before requesting a payment authorizing agency to conduct

a non-centralized administrative offset, agencies must adopt regulations providing that such offsets may occur only after:

(i) The debtor has been provided due process as set forth in paragraph (b)(4) of this section; and

(ii) The payment authorizing agency has received written certification from the creditor agency that the debtor owes the past due, legally enforceable delinquent debt in the amount stated, and that the creditor agency has fully complied with its regulations concerning administrative offset.

(3) Payment authorizing agencies shall comply with offset requests by creditor agencies to collect debts owed to the United States, unless the offset would not be in the best interests of the United States with respect to the program of the payment authorizing agency, or would otherwise be contrary to law. Appropriate use should be made of the cooperative efforts of other agencies in effecting collection by administrative offset.

(4) When collecting multiple debts by non-centralized administrative offset, agencies should apply the recovered amounts to those debts in accordance with the best interests of the United States, as determined by the facts and circumstances of the particular case, particularly the applicable statute of limitations.

(d) *Requests to OPM to offset a debtor's anticipated or future benefit payments under the Civil Service Retirement and Disability Fund.* Upon providing OPM written certification that a debtor has been afforded the procedures provided in paragraph (b)(4) of this section, creditor agencies may request OPM to offset a debtor's anticipated or future benefit payments under the Civil Service Retirement and Disability Fund (Fund) in accordance with regulations codified at 5 CFR 831.1801–831.1808. Upon receipt of such a request, OPM will identify and "flag" a debtor's account in anticipation of the time when the debtor requests, or becomes eligible to receive, payments from the Fund. This will satisfy any requirement that offset be initiated prior to the expiration of the time limitations referenced in paragraph (a)(4) of this section.

(e) *Review requirements.*

(1) For purposes of this section, whenever an agency is required to afford a debtor a review within the agency, the agency shall provide the debtor with a reasonable opportunity for an oral hearing when the debtor requests reconsideration of the debt and the agency determines that the question of the indebtedness cannot be resolved by review of the documentary evidence, for example, when the validity of the debt turns on an issue of credibility or veracity.

(2) Unless otherwise required by law, an oral hearing under this section is not required to be a formal evidentiary hearing, although the agency should carefully document all significant matters discussed at the hearing.

(3) This section does not require an oral hearing with respect to debt collection systems in which a determination of indebtedness rarely involves issues of credibility or veracity and the agency has determined that review of the written record is ordinarily an adequate means to correct prior mistakes.

(4) In those cases when an oral hearing is not required by this section, an agency shall accord the debtor a "paper hearing," that is, a determination of the request for reconsideration based upon a review of the written record.

B.2 FFEL Regulations

34 C.F.R. sec.

682.200 Definitions.
682.201 Eligible borrowers.
682.202 Permissible charges by lenders to borrowers.

* * *

682.209 Repayment of a loan.
682.210 Deferment.
682.211 Forbearance.

* * *

682.402 Death, disability, closed school, false certification, unpaid refunds, and bankruptcy payments.

* * *

682.405 Loan rehabilitation agreement.

* * *

682.410 Fiscal, administrative, and enforcement requirements.
682.411 Lender due diligence in collecting guaranty agency loans.

Source: 57 Fed. Reg. 60323, Dec. 18, 1992; 58 Fed. Reg. 36870, July 9, 1993, unless otherwise noted.

§ 682.200 Definitions.

(a)(1) The definitions of the following terms used in this part are set forth in subpart A of the Student Assistance General Provisions, 34 CFR part 668:

Academic year
Campus-based programs
Dependent student
Eligible program
Eligible student
Enrolled
Expected family contribution
Federal Consolidation Loan Program
Federal Pell Grant Program
Federal Perkins Loan Program
Federal PLUS Program
Federal Work-Study (FWS) Program
Full-time student
Independent student
Leveraging Educational Assistance Partnership (LEAP) Program
National of the United States (Referred to as U.S. Citizen or National in 34 CFR 668.2)
Payment period
Supplemental Educational Opportunity Grant (SEOG) Program
Supplemental Loans for Students (SLS) Program

(2) The following definitions are set forth in the regulations for Institutional Eligibility under the Higher Education Act of 1965, as amended, 34 CFR part 600:

Accredited
Clock hour
Correspondence course
Educational program
Federal Family Education Loan Program (formerly known as the Guaranteed Student Loan (GSL) Program)
Institution of higher education (§ 600.4)

Nationally recognized accrediting agency
Postsecondary Vocational Institution
Preaccredited
Secretary
State

(3) The definition for cost of attendance is set forth in section 472 of the Act, as amended.

(b) The following definitions also apply to this part:

Act. The Higher Education Act of 1965, as amended, 20 U.S.C. 1071 *et seq.*

Actual interest rate. The annual interest rate a lender charges on a loan, which may be equal to or less than the applicable interest rate on that loan.

Applicable interest rate. The maximum annual interest rate that a lender may charge under the Act on a loan.

Authority. Any private non-profit or public entity that may issue tax-exempt obligations to obtain funds to be used for the making or purchasing of FFEL loans. The term "Authority" also includes any agency, including a State postsecondary institution or any other instrumentality of a State or local governmental unit, regardless of the designation or primary purpose of that agency, that may issue tax-exempt obligations, any party authorized to issue those obligations on behalf of a governmental agency, and any non-profit organization authorized by law to issue tax-exempt obligations.

Borrower. An individual to whom a FFEL Program loan is made.

Co-Maker. One of two married individuals who jointly borrow a Consolidation loan, each of whom are eligible and who are jointly and severally liable for repayment of the loan. The term co-maker also includes one of two parents who are joint borrowers as previously authorized in the PLUS Program.

Default. The failure of a borrower and endorser, if any, or joint borrowers on a PLUS or Consolidation loan, to make an installment payment when due, or to meet other terms of the promissory note, the Act, or regulations as applicable, if the Secretary or guaranty agency finds it reasonable to conclude that the borrower and endorser, if any, no longer intend to honor the obligation to repay, provided that this failure persists for—

(1) 270 days for a loan repayable in monthly installments; or

(2) 330 days for a loan repayable in less frequent installments.

Disbursement. The transfer of loan proceeds by a lender to a holder, in the case of a Consolidation loan, or to a borrower, a school, or an escrow agent by issuance of an individual check, a master check or by electronic funds transfer that may represent loan amounts for borrowers.

Disposable income. That part of an individual's compensation from an employer and other income from any source, including spousal income, that remains after the deduction of any amounts required by law to be withheld, or any child support or alimony payments that are made under a court order or legally enforceable written agreement. Amounts required by law to be withheld include, but are not limited to, Federal, State, and local taxes, Social Security contributions, and wage garnishment payments.

Endorser. An individual who signs a promissory note and agrees to repay the loan in the event that the borrower does not.

Escrow agent. Any guaranty agency or other eligible lender that receives the proceeds of a FFEL program loan as an agent of an eligible lender for the purpose of transmitting those proceeds to the borrower or the borrower's school.

Estimated financial assistance.

(1) The estimated amount of assistance for a period of enrollment that a student (or a parent on behalf of a student) will receive from Federal, State, institutional, or other sources, such as, scholarships, grants, the net earnings from need-based employment, or loans, including but not limited to—

(i) Except as provided in paragraph (2)(iii) of this definition, national service education awards or post-service benefits under title I of the National and Community Service Act of 1990 (AmeriCorps) and veterans' educational benefits paid under chapters 30 (Montgomery GI Bill—Active Duty), 31 (Vocational Rehabilitation and Employment Program), 32 (Veterans' Educational Assistance Program, and 35 (Dependents' Educational Assistance Program) of title 38 of the United States Code;

(ii) Educational benefits paid under Chapters 31 (National Call to Service), 1606 (Montgomery GI Bill-Selected Reserve), and 1607 (Reserve Educational Assistance Program) of Title 10 of the United States Code;

(iii) Reserve Officer Training Corps (ROTC) scholarships and subsistence allowances awarded under Chapter 2 of Title 10 and Chapter 2 of Title 37 of the United States Code;

(iv) Benefits paid under Pub. L. 96-342, section 903: Educational Assistance Pilot Program;

(v) Any educational benefits paid because of enrollment in a postsecondary education institution, or to cover postsecondary education expenses;

(vi) Fellowships or assistantships, except non-need-based employment portions of such awards;

(vii) Insurance programs for the student's education; and

(viii) The estimated amount of other Federal student financial aid, including but not limited to a Federal Pell Grant, Academic Competitiveness Grant, National SMART Grant, campus-based aid, and the gross amount (including fees) of subsidized and unsubsidized Federal Stafford Loans or subsidized and unsubsidized Federal Direct Stafford/Ford Loans, and Federal PLUS or Federal Direct PLUS Loans.

(2) Estimated financial assistance does not include—

(i) Those amounts used to replace the expected family contribution, including the amounts of any unsubsidized Federal Stafford or Federal Direct Stafford/Ford Loans, Federal PLUS or Federal Direct PLUS Loans, and non-federal non-need-based loans, including private, state-sponsored, and institutional loans. However, if the sum of the loan amounts received that are being used to replace the student's EFC exceed the EFC, the excess amount is treated as estimated financial assistance;

(ii) Federal Perkins loan and Federal Work-Study funds that the student has declined;

(iii) For the purpose of determining eligibility for a subsidized Stafford loan, veterans' educational benefits paid under chapter 30 of title 38 of the United States Code (Montgomery GI Bill—Active Duty) and national service education awards or post-service benefits under title I of the National and Community Service Act of 1990 (AmeriCorps);

(iv) Any portion of the estimated financial assistance described in paragraph (1) of this definition that is included in the calculation of the student's expected family contribution (EFC);

(v) Non-need-based employment earnings; and

(vi) Assistance not received under this title, if that assistance is designated to offset all or a portion of a specific amount of the cost of attendance and that component is excluded from the cost of attendance as well. If that assistance is excluded from either estimated financial assistance or cost of attendance, it must be excluded from both.

Federal GSL programs. The Federal Insured Student Loan Program, the Federal Supplemental Loans for Students Program, the Federal PLUS Program, and the Federal Consolidation Loan Program.

Federal Insured Student Loan Program. The loan program authorized by title IV-B of the Act under which the Secretary directly insures lenders against losses.

Foreign school. A school not located in a State.

Grace period. The period that begins on the day after a Stafford loan borrower ceases to be enrolled as at least a half-time student at an institution of higher education and ends on the day before the repayment period begins. See also "Post-deferment grace period." For an SLS borrower who also has a Federal Stafford loan on which the borrower has not yet entered repayment, the grace period is an equivalent period after the borrower ceases to be enrolled as at least a half-time student at an institution of higher education.

Graduate or professional student. A student who, for a period of enrollment—

(1) Is enrolled in a program above the baccalaureate level at an institution of higher education or is enrolled in a program leading to a first professional degree;

(2) Has completed the equivalent of at least three academic years of full-time study at an institution of higher education, either before entrance into the program or as part of the program itself; and

(3) Is not receiving aid under title IV of the Act as an undergraduate student for the same period of enrollment. Guaranty agency. A State or private nonprofit organization that has an agreement with the Secretary under which it will administer a loan guarantee program under the Act.

Half-time student. A student who is enrolled in an institution of higher education, and is carrying an academic workload that amounts to at least one-half the workload of a full-time student, as determined by the school, and is not a full-time student as defined in 34 CFR 668.2. A student enrolled solely in an eligible correspondence course as defined in 34 CFR 668.8 is considered a half-time student.

Holder. An eligible lender owning an FFEL Program loan including a Federal or State agency or an organization or corporation acting on behalf of such an agency and acting as a conservator, liquidator, or receiver of an eligible lender.

Legal guardian. An individual appointed by a court to be a "guardian" of a person and specifically required by the court to use his or her financial resources for the support of that person.

Lender.

(1) The term "eligible lender" is defined in section 435(d) of the Act, and in paragraphs (2)–(5) of this definition.

(2) With respect to a National or State chartered bank, a mutual savings bank, a savings and loan association, a stock savings bank, or a credit union—

(i) The phrase "subject to examination and supervision" in

section 435(d) of the Act means "subject to examination and supervision in its capacity as a lender";

(ii) The phrase "does not have as its primary consumer credit function the making or holding of loans made to students under this part" in section 435(d) of the Act means that the lender does not, or in the case of a bank holding company, the company's wholly-owned subsidiaries as a group do not at any time, hold FFEL Program loans that total more than one-half of the lender's or subsidiaries' combined consumer credit loan portfolio, including home mortgages held by the lender or its subsidiaries. For purposes of this paragraph, loans held in trust by a trustee lender are not considered part of the trustee lender's consumer credit function.

(3) A bank that is subject to examination and supervision by an agency of the United States, making student loans as a trustee, may be an eligible lender if it makes loans under an express trust, operated as a lender in the FFEL programs prior to January 1, 1975, and met the requirements of this paragraph prior to July 23, 1992.

(4) The corporate parent or other owner of a school that qualifies as an eligible lender under section 435(d) of the Act is not an eligible lender unless the corporate parent or owner itself qualifies as an eligible lender under section 435(d) of the Act.

(5) The term "eligible lender" does not include any lender that the Secretary determines, after notice and opportunity for a hearing before a designated Department official, has—

(i) Offered, directly or indirectly, points, premiums, payments, or other inducements, to any school or other party to secure applicants for FFEL loans, except that a lender is not prohibited from providing assistance to schools comparable to the kinds of assistance provided by the Secretary to schools under, or in furtherance of, the Federal Direct Loan Program.

(ii) Conducted unsolicited mailings to a student or a student's parents of FFEL loan application forms, except to a student who previously has received a FFEL loan from the lender or to a student's parent who previously has received a FFEL loan from the lender;

(iii) Offered, directly or indirectly, a FFEL loan to a prospective borrower to induce the purchase of a policy of insurance or other product or service by the borrower or other person; or

(iv) Engaged in fraudulent or misleading advertising with respect to its FFEL program loan activities.

(6) The term eligible lender does not include any lender that—

(i) Is debarred or suspended, or any of whose principals or affiliates (as those terms are defined in 34 CFR part 85) is debarred or suspended under Executive Order (E.O.) 12549 (3 CFR, 1986 Comp., p. 189) or the Federal Acquisition Regulation (FAR), 48 CFR part 9, subpart 9.4;

(ii) Is an affiliate, as defined in 34 CFR part 85, of any person who is debarred or suspended under E.O. 12549 (3 CFR 1986 Comp., p. 189) or the FAR, 48 CFR part 9, subpart 9.4; or

(iii) Employs a person who is debarred or suspended under E.O. 12549 (3 CFR, 1986 Comp., p. 189) or the FAR, 48 CFR part 9, subpart 9.4, in a capacity that involves the administration or receipt of FFEL program funds.

Master Promissory Note (MPN). A promissory note under which the borrower may receive loans for a single period of enrollment or multiple periods of enrollment.

National credit bureau. A credit bureau with a service area that encompasses more than a single region of the country. Nonsubsidized Stafford loan. A Stafford loan made prior to October 1, 1992 that does not qualify for interest benefits under § 682.301(b) or special allowance payments under § 682.302.

Origination relationship. A special business relationship between a school and a lender in which the lender delegates to the school, or to an entity or individual affiliated with the school, substantial functions or responsibilities normally performed by lenders before making FFEL program loans. In this situation, the school is considered to have "originated" a loan made by the lender.

Origination fee. A fee that the lender is required to pay the Secretary to help defray the Secretary's costs of subsidizing the loan. The lender may pass this fee on to the Stafford loan borrower. The lender must pass this fee on to the SLS or PLUS borrower.

Participating school. A school that has in effect a current agreement with the Secretary under § 682.600. Period of enrollment. The period for which a Stafford, SLS, or PLUS loan is intended. The period of enrollment must coincide with a bona fide academic term established by the school for which institutional charges are generally assessed (e.g., semester, trimester, quarter, length of the student's program or academic year). The period of enrollment is also referred to as the loan period.

Post-deferment grace period. For a loan made prior to October 1, 1981, a single period of six consecutive months beginning on the day following the last day of an authorized deferment period.

Repayment period.

(1) For a Stafford loan, the period beginning on the date following the expiration of the grace period and ending no later than 10 years, or 25 years under an extended repayment schedule, from the date the first payment of principal is due from the borrower, exclusive of any period of deferment or forbearance.

(2) For unsubsidized Stafford loans, the period that begins on the day after the expiration of the applicable grace period that follows after the student ceases to be enrolled on at least a half-time basis and ending no later than 10 years or 25 years under an extended repayment schedule, from that date, exclusive of any period of deferment or forbearance. However, payments of interest are the responsibility of the borrower during the in-school and grace period, but may be capitalized by the lender.

(3) For SLS loans, the period that begins on the date the loan is disbursed, or if the loan is disbursed in more than one installment, on the date the last disbursement is made and ending no later than 10 years from that date, exclusive of any period of deferment or forbearance. The first payment of principal is due within 60 days after the loan is fully disbursed unless a borrower who is also a Stafford loan borrower but who, has not yet entered repayment on the Stafford loan requests that commencement of repayment on the SLS loan be delayed until the borrower's grace period on the Stafford loan expires. Interest on the loan accrues and is due and payable from the date of the first disbursement of the loan. The borrower is responsible for paying interest on the loan during the grace period and periods of deferment, but the interest may be capitalized by the lender.

(4) For Federal PLUS loans, the period that begins on the date the loan is disbursed, or if the loan is disbursed in more than one installment, on the date the last disbursement is made and ending no later than 10 years, or 25 years under an extended repayment schedule from that date, exclusive of any period of deferment or

forbearance. Interest on the loan accrues and is due and payable from the date of the first disbursement of the loan.

(5) For Federal Consolidation loans, the period that begins on the date the loan is disbursed and ends no later than 10, 12, 15, 20, 25, or 30 years from that date depending upon the sum of the amount of the Consolidation loan, and the unpaid balance on other student loans, exclusive of any period of deferment or forbearance.

Satisfactory repayment arrangement.

(1) For purposes of regaining eligibility under § 682.401(b)(4), the making of six (6) consecutive, on-time, voluntary full monthly payments on a defaulted loan. A borrower may only obtain the benefit of this paragraph with respect to renewed eligibility once.

(2) For purposes of consolidating a defaulted loan under 34 CFR 682.201(c)(1)(iii)(C), the making of three (3) consecutive, on-time, voluntary full monthly payments on a defaulted loan.

(3) The required full monthly payment amount may not be more than is reasonable and affordable based on the borrower's total financial circumstances. Voluntary payments are those payments made directly by the borrower, and do not include payments obtained by income tax off-set, garnishment, or income or asset execution. On-time means a payment received by the Secretary or a guaranty agency or its agent within 15 days of the scheduled due date.

School.

(1) An "institution of higher education" as that term is defined in 34 CFR 600.4.

(2) For purposes of an in-school deferment, the term includes an institution of higher education, whether or not it participates in any Title IV program or has lost its eligibility to participate in the FFEL program because of a high default rate.

School lender. A school, other than a correspondence school, that has entered into a contract of guarantee under this part with the Secretary or, a similar agreement with a guaranty agency.

Stafford Loan Program. The loan program authorized by Title IV-B of the Act which encourages the making of subsidized and unsubsidized loans to undergraduate, graduate, and professional students and is one of the Federal Family Education Loan programs.

State lender. In any State, a single State agency or private nonprofit agency designated by the State that has entered into a contract of guarantee under this part with the Secretary, or a similar agreement with a guaranty agency.

Subsidized Stafford Loan: A Stafford loan that qualifies for interest benefits under § 682.301(b) and special allowance under § 682.302.

Temporarily totally disabled. The condition of an individual who, though not totally and permanently disabled, is unable to work and earn money or attend school, during a period of at least 60 days needed to recover from injury or illness. With regard to a disabled dependent of a borrower, this term means a spouse or other dependent who, during a period of injury or illness, requires continuous nursing or similar services for a period of at least 90 days.

Third-party servicer. Any State or private, profit or nonprofit organization or any individual that enters into a contract with a lender or guaranty agency to administer, through either manual or automated processing, any aspect of the lender's or guaranty agency's FFEL programs required by any statutory provision of or applicable to Title IV of the HEA, any regulatory provision prescribed under that statutory authority, or any applicable special arrangement, agreement, or limitation entered into under the authority of statutes applicable to Title IV of the HEA that governs the FFEL programs, including, any applicable function described in the definition of third-party servicer in 34 CFR part 668; originating, guaranteeing, monitoring, processing, servicing, or collecting loans; claims submission; or billing for interest benefits and special allowance.

Totally and permanently disabled. The condition of an individual who is unable to work and earn money because of an injury or illness that is expected to continue indefinitely or result in death.

Undergraduate student. A student who is enrolled at a school in a program of study, at or below the baccalaureate level, that usually does not exceed four academic years, or is up to five academic years in length, and is designed to lead to a degree or certificate at or below the baccalaureate level.

Unsubsidized Stafford loan. A loan made after October 1, 1992, authorized under section 428H of the Act for borrowers who do not qualify for interest benefits under § 682.301(b) but do qualify for special allowance under § 682.302.

Write-off. Cessation of collection activity on a defaulted FFEL loan due to a determination in accordance with applicable standards that no further collection activity is warranted.

(Approved by the Office of Management and Budget under control number 1845-0020)

(Authority: 8 U.S.C. 1101; 20 U.S.C. 1070 to 1087-2, 1088–1098, 1141; E.O. 12549 (3 CFR, 1986 Comp., p. 189), E.O. 12689 (3 CFR, 1989 Comp., p. 235))

[59 Fed. Reg. 22454, April 29, 1994; 59 Fed. Reg. 25744, May 17, 1994; 59 Fed. Reg. 32656, June 24, 1994; 59 Fed. Reg. 33348, June 28, 1994; 59 Fed. Reg. 61215, Nov. 29, 1994; 60 Fed. Reg. 32912, June 26, 1995; 60 Fed. Reg. 61756, Dec. 1, 1995; 61 Fed. Reg. 60608, Nov. 29, 1996; 64 Fed. Reg. 18975, April 16, 1999; 64 Fed. Reg. 58952, Nov. 1, 1999; 65 Fed. Reg. 38729, June 22, 2000; 65 Fed. Reg. 65691, Nov. 1, 2000; 67 Fed. Reg. 67078, Nov. 1, 2002; 69 Fed. Reg. 12274, Mar. 16, 2004; 71 Fed. Reg. 45666, Sept. 8, 2006]

§ 682.201 Eligible borrowers.

(a) Student Stafford borrower. Except for a refinanced SLS/PLUS loan made under § 682.209(e) or (f), a student is eligible to receive a Stafford loan, and an independent undergraduate student, a graduate or professional student, or, subject to paragraph (a)(3) of this section, a dependent undergraduate student, is eligible to receive an unsubsidized Stafford loan, if the student who is enrolled or accepted for enrollment on at least a half-time basis at a participating school meets the requirements for an eligible student under 34 CFR part 668, and—

(1) In the case of an undergraduate student who seeks a Stafford loan or unsubsidized Stafford loan for the cost of attendance at a school that participates in the Pell Grant Program, has received a final determination, or, in the case of a student who has filed an application with the school for a Pell Grant, a preliminary determination, from the school of the student's eligibility or ineligibility for a Pell Grant and, if eligible, has applied for the period of enrollment for which the loan is sought;

(2) In the case of any student who seeks an unsubsidized Stafford loan for the cost of attendance at a school that participates in the Stafford Loan Program, the student must—

(i) Receive a determination of need for a subsidized Stafford loan; and

(ii) If the determination of need is in excess of $200, have made a request to a lender for a subsidized Stafford loan;

(3) For purposes of a dependent undergraduate student's eligibility for an additional unsubsidized Stafford loan amount, as described at § 682.204(d), is a dependent undergraduate student for whom the financial aid administrator determines and documents in the school's file, after review of the family financial information provided by the student and consideration of the student's debt burden, that the student's parents likely will be precluded by exceptional circumstances (e.g., denial of a PLUS loan to a parent based on adverse credit, the student's parent receives only public assistance or disability benefits, is incarcerated, or his or her whereabouts are unknown) from borrowing under the PLUS Program and the student's family is otherwise unable to provide the student's expected family contribution. A parent's refusal to borrow a PLUS loan does not constitute an exceptional circumstance;

(4)(i) Reaffirms any FFEL loan amount on which there has been a total cessation of collection activity, including all principal interest, collection costs, legal costs, and late charges that have accrued on that amount up to the date of reaffirmation.

(ii) For purposes of this section, reaffirmation means the acknowledgment of the loan by the borrower in a legally binding manner. The acknowledgment may include, but is not limited to, the borrower—

(A) Signing a new promissory note that includes the same terms and conditions as the original note signed by the borrower or repayment schedule; or

(B) Making a payment on the loan.

(5) The suspension of collection activity has been lifted from any loan on which collection activity had been suspended based on a conditional determination that the borrower was totally and permanently disabled under § 682.402(c).

(6) In the case of a borrower whose prior loan under title IV of the Act was discharged after a final determination of total and permanent disability, the student must—

(i) Obtain certification from a physician that the borrower is able to engage in substantial gainful activity;

(ii) Sign a statement acknowledging that the FFEL loan the borrower receives cannot be discharged in the future on the basis of any impairment present when the new loan is made, unless that impairment substantially deteriorates; and

(iii) In the case of a borrower whose previous loan under title IV of the Act was discharged due to a total and permanent disability on or after July 1, 2001 and before July 1, 2002, meets the requirements of paragraphs (a)(6)(i) and (a)(6)(ii) of this section. If the borrower applies for another loan within three years from the date that the borrower became totally and permanently disabled, as certified by the physician, the borrower must reaffirm the previously discharged loan before receiving the new loan.

(7) In the case of a borrower whose prior loan under title IV of the HEA was conditionally discharged based on an initial determination that the borrower was totally and permanently disabled, the borrower must—

(i) Comply with the requirements of paragraphs (a)(6)(i) and (a)(6)(ii) of this section; and

(ii) Sign a statement acknowledging that—

    (A) The loan that has been conditionally discharged prior to a final determination of total and permanent disability cannot be discharged in the future on the basis of any impairment present when the borrower applied for a total and permanent disability discharge or when the new loan is made unless that impairment substantially deteriorates; and

    (B) Collection activity will resume on any loans in a conditional discharge period, as described in paragraph 682.402(c)(16).

(8) In the case of any student who seeks a loan but does not have a certificate of graduation from a school providing secondary education or the recognized equivalent of such a certificate, the student meets the requirements under 34 CFR Part 668.32(e).

(9) Is not serving in a medical internship or residency program, except for an internship in dentistry.

(b) *Student PLUS borrower.* A graduate or professional student who is enrolled or accepted for enrollment on at least a half-time basis at a participating school is eligible to receive a PLUS Loan on or after July 1, 2006, if the student—

(1) Meets the requirements for an eligible student under 34 CFR 668;

(2) Meets the requirements of paragraphs (a)(4), (a)(5), (a)(6), (a)(7), (a)(8), and (a)(9) of this section, if applicable;

(3) Has received a determination of his or her annual loan maximum eligibility under the Federal Subsidized and Unsubsidized Stafford Loan Program; and

(4) Does not have an adverse credit history in accordance with paragraphs (c)(2)(i) through (c)(2)(v) of this section, or obtains an endorser who has been determined not to have an adverse credit history, as provided for in paragraph (c)(1)(vii) of this section.

(c)(1) *Parent PLUS borrower.* A parent borrower, is eligible to receive a PLUS Program loan, other than a loan made under § 682.209(e), if the parent—

    (i) Is borrowing to pay for the educational costs of a dependent undergraduate student who meets the requirements for an eligible student set forth in 34 CFR Part 668;

    (ii) Provides his or her and the student's social security number;

    (iii) Meets the requirements pertaining to citizenship and residency that apply to the student in 34 CFR 668.33;

    (iv) Meets the requirements concerning defaults and overpayments that apply to the student in 34 CFR 668.35 and meets the requirements of judgment liens that apply to the student under 34 CFR 668.32(g)(3);

    (v) Except for the completion of a Statement of Selective Service Registration Status, complies with the requirements for submission of a Statement of Educational Purpose that apply to the student in 34 CFR part 668;

    (vi) Meets the requirement of paragraphs (a)(4) and (a)(6), as applicable of this section;

    (vi) Meets the requirements of paragraphs (a)(4), (a)(5), (a)(6), and (a)(7) of this section, as applicable; and

    (vii) In the case of a Federal PLUS loan made on or after July 1, 1993, does not have an adverse credit history or obtains an endorser who has been determined not to have an adverse credit history as provided in paragraph (b)(2)(ii) of this section.

(viii) Has completed repayment of any title IV, HEA program assistance obtained by fraud, if the parent has been convicted of, or has pled nolo contendere or guilty to, a crime involving fraud in obtaining title IV, HEA program assistance.

(2)(i) For purposes of this section, the lender must obtain a credit report on each applicant from at least one national credit bureau. The credit report must be secured within a timeframe that would ensure the most accurate, current representation of the borrower's credit history before the first day of the period of enrollment for which the loan is intended.

(ii) Unless the lender determines that extenuating circumstances existed, the lender must consider each applicant to have an adverse credit history based on the credit report if—

    (A) The applicant is considered 90 or more days delinquent on the repayment of a debt; or

    (B) The applicant has been the subject of a default determination, bankruptcy discharge, foreclosure, repossession, tax lien, wage garnishment, or write-off of a Title IV debt, during the five years preceding the date of the credit report.

(iii) Nothing in this paragraph precludes the lender from establishing more restrictive credit standards to determine whether the applicant has an adverse credit history.

(iv) The absence of any credit history is not an indication that the applicant has an adverse credit history and is not to be used as a reason to deny a PLUS loan to that applicant.

(v) The lender must retain a record of its basis for determining that extenuating circumstances existed. This record may include, but is not limited to, an updated credit report, a statement from the creditor that the borrower has made satisfactory arrangements to repay the debt, or a satisfactory statement from the borrower explaining any delinquencies with outstanding balances of less than $500.

(3) For purposes of paragraph (b)(1) of this section, a "parent" includes the individuals described in the definition of "parent" in 34 CFR 668.2 and the spouse of a parent who remarried, if that spouse's income and assets would have been taken into account when calculating a dependent student's expected family contribution.

(d) *Consolidation program borrower.*

(1) An individual is eligible to receive a Consolidation loan if the individual—

    (i) On the loans being consolidated—

        (A) Is, at the time of application for a Consolidation loan—

            (1) In a grace period preceding repayment;

            (2) In repayment status;

            (3) In a default status and has either made satisfactory repayment arrangements as defined in applicable program regulations or has agreed to repay the consolidation loan under the income-sensitive repayment plan described in § 682.209(a)(7)(viii);

        (B) Not subject to a judgment secured through litigation, unless the judgment has been vacated;

        (C) Not subject to an order for wage garnishment under section 488A of the Act, unless the order has been lifted;

        (D) Not in default status resulting from a claim filed under § 682.412.

    (ii) Certifies that no other application for a Consolidation loan is pending; and

(iii) Agrees to notify the holder of any changes in address.

(2) A borrower may not consolidate a loan under this section for which the borrower is wholly or partially responsible.

(e) A borrower's eligibility to receive a Consolidation loan terminates upon receipt of a Consolidation loan except that—

(1) Eligible loans received prior to the date a Consolidation loan was made and loans received during the 180-day period following the date a Consolidation loan was made, may be added to the Consolidation loan based on the borrower's request received by the lender during the 180-day period after the date the Consolidation loan was made;

(2) A borrower who receives an eligible loan before or after the date a Consolidation loan is made may receive a subsequent Consolidation loan;

(3) A Consolidation loan borrower may consolidate an existing Consolidation loan if the borrower has at least one other eligible loan made before or after the existing Consolidation loan that will be consolidated; and

(4) If the consolidation loan has been submitted to the guaranty agency for default aversion, the borrower may obtain a subsequent consolidation loan under the Federal Direct Consolidation Loan Program for purposes of obtaining an income contingent repayment plan.

(Authority: 20 U.S.C. 1077, 1078, 1078-1, 1078-2, 1078-3, 1082, and 1091)

[59 Fed. Reg. 25745, May 17, 1994; 59 Fed. Reg. 33349, June 28, 1994; 59 Fed. Reg. 61215, Nov. 29, 1994; 60 Fed. Reg. 32912, June 26, 1995; 60 Fed. Reg. 61756, 61815, Dec. 1, 1995; 62 Fed. Reg. 63433, Nov. 28, 1997; 64 Fed. Reg. 18975, 18976, April 16, 1999; 64 Fed. Reg. 58952, Nov. 1, 1999; 65 Fed. Reg. 65619, 65691, Nov. 1, 2000; 66 Fed. Reg. 44007, Aug. 21, 2001; 68 Fed. Reg. 75427, Dec. 31, 2003; 71 Fed. Reg. 45666, Sept. 8, 2006]

§ 682.202 Permissible charges by lenders to borrowers.

The charges that lenders may impose on borrowers, either directly or indirectly, are limited to the following:

(a) *Interest.* The applicable interest rates for FFEL Program loans are given in paragraphs (a)(1) through (a)(4) of this section.

(1) *Stafford Loan Program.*

(i) For loans made prior to July 1, 1994, if, the borrower, on the date the promissory note evidencing the loan is signed, has an outstanding balance of principal or interest on a previous Stafford loan, the interest rate is the applicable interest rate on that previous Stafford loan.

(ii) If the borrower, on the date the promissory note evidencing the loan is signed, has no outstanding balance on any FFEL Program loan, and the first disbursement is made—

(A) Prior to October 1, 1992, for a loan covering a period of instruction beginning on or after July 1, 1988, the interest rate is 8 percent until 48 months elapse after the repayment period begins, and 10 percent thereafter; or

(B) On or after October 1, 1992 and prior to July 1, 1994, the interest rate is a variable rate, applicable to each July 1–June 30 period, that equals the lesser of—

  (1) The bond equivalent rate of the 91-day Treasury bills auctioned at the final auction prior to the June 1 immediately preceding the July 1–June 30 period, plus 3.10 percent; or

  (2) 9 percent.

(iii) For a Stafford loan for which the first disbursement is made before October 1, 1992—

(A) If the borrower, on the date the promissory note is signed, has no outstanding balance on a Stafford loan but has an outstanding balance of principal or interest on a PLUS or SLS loan made for a period of enrollment beginning before July 1, 1988, or on a Consolidation loan that repaid a loan made for a period of enrollment beginning before July 1, 1988, the interest rate is 8 percent; or

(B) If the borrower, on the date the promissory note evidencing the loan is signed, has an outstanding balance of principal or interest on a PLUS or SLS loan made for a period of enrollment beginning on or after July 1, 1988, or on a Consolidation loan that repaid a loan made for a period of enrollment beginning on or after July 1, 1988, the interest rate is 8 percent until 48 months elapse after the repayment period begins, and 10 percent thereafter.

(iv) For a Stafford loan for which the first disbursement is made on or after October 1, 1992 but before December 20, 1993, if the borrower, on the date the promissory note evidencing the loan is signed, has no outstanding balance on a Stafford loan but has an outstanding balance of principal or interest on a PLUS, SLS, or Consolidation loan, the interest rate is 8 percent.

(v) For a Stafford loan for which the first disbursement is made on or after December 20, 1993 and prior to July 1, 1994, if the borrower, on the date the promissory note is signed, has no outstanding balance on a Stafford loan but has an outstanding balance of principal or interest on a PLUS, SLS, or Consolidation loan, the interest rate is the rate provided in paragraph (a)(1)(ii)(B) of this section.

(vi) For a Stafford loan for which the first disbursement is made on or after July 1, 1994 and prior to July 1, 1995, for a period of enrollment that includes or begins on or after July 1, 1994, the interest rate is a variable rate, applicable to each July 1–June 30 period, that equals the lesser of—

(A) The bond equivalent rate of the 91-day Treasury bills auctioned at the final auction prior to the June 1 immediately preceding the July 1–June 30 period, plus 3.10; or

(B) 8.25 percent.

(vii) For a Stafford loan for which the first disbursement is made on or after July 1, 1995 and prior to July 1, 1998 the interest rate is a variable rate applicable to each July 1–June 30 period, that equals the lesser of—

(A) The bond equivalent rate of the 91-day Treasury bills auctioned at the final auction prior to the June 1 immediately preceding the July 1–June 30 period, plus 2.5 percent during the in-school, grace and deferment period and 3.10 percent during repayment; or

(B) 8.25 percent.

(viii) For a Stafford loan for which the first disbursement is made on or after July 1, 1998, and prior to July 1, 2006, the interest rate is a variable rate, applicable to each July 1–June 30 period, that equals the lesser of—

(A) The bond equivalent rate of the 91-day Treasury bills auctioned at the final auction prior to the June 1 immediately preceding the July 1–June 30 period plus 1.7 percent during the in-school, grace and deferment periods and 2.3 percent during repayment; or

    (B) 8.25 percent.

(ix) For a Stafford loan for which the first disbursement is made on or after July 1, 2006, the interest rate is 6.8 percent.

(2) *PLUS Program.*

(i) For a combined repayment schedule under § 682.209d), the interest rate i the weighted average of the rates of all loans included under that schedule.

(ii) For a loan disbursed on or after July 1, 1987 but prior to October 1, 1992, and for any loan made under § 682.209 (e) or (f), the interest rate is a variable rate, applicable to each July 1–June 30 period, that equals the lesser of—

    (A) The bond equivalent rate of the 52-week Treasury bills auctioned at the final auction prior to the June 1 immediately preceding the July 1–June 30 period, plus 3.25 percent; or

    (B) 12 percent.

(iii) For a loan disbursed on or after October 1, 1992 and prior to July 1, 1994, the interest rate is a variable rate, applicable to each July 1–June 30 period, that equals the lesser of—

    (A) The bond equivalent rate of the 52-week Treasury bills auctioned at the final auction prior to the June 1 immediately preceding the July 1–June 30 period, plus 3.10 percent; or

    (B) 10 percent.

(iv) For a loan for which the first disbursement is made on or after July 1, 1994 and prior to July 1, 1998, the interest rate is a variable rate applicable to each July 1–June 30 period, that equals the lesser of—

    (A) The bond equivalent rate of the 52-week Treasury bills auctioned at the final auction prior to the June 1 immediately preceding the July 1–June 30 period, plus 3.10 percent; or

    (B) 9 percent.

(v) For a loan for which the first disbursement is made on or after July 1, 1998, the interest rate is a variable rate, applicable to each July 1–June 30 period, that equals the lesser of—

    (A) The bond equivalent rate of the 91-day Treasury bills auctioned at the final auction prior to the June 1 immediately preceding the July 1–June 30 period, plus 3.10 percent; or

    (B) 9 percent.

(vi)(A) Beginning on July 1, 2001, and prior to July 1, 2006, the interest rate on the loans described in paragraphs (a)(2)(ii) through (iv) of this section is a variable rate applicable to each July 1–June 30, as determined on the preceding June 26, and is equal to the weekly average 1-year constant maturity Treasury yield, as published by the Board of Governors of the Federal Reserve System, for the last calendar week ending on or before such June 26; plus—

    (1) 3.25 percent for loans described in paragraph (a)(2)(ii) of this section; or

    (2) 3.1 percent for loans described in paragraphs (a)(2)(iii) and (iv) of this section.

    (B) The interest rates calculated under paragraph (a)(2)(vi)(A) of this section shall not exceed the limits specified in paragraphs (a)(2)(ii)(B), (a)(2)(iii)(B), and

(a)(2)(iv)(B) of this section, as applicable.

(vii) For a PLUS loan first disbursed on or after July 1, 2006, the interest rate is 8.5 percent.

(3) *SLS Program.*

(i) For a combined repayment schedule under § 682.209(d), the interest rate is the weighted average of the rates of all loans included under that schedule.

(ii) For a loan disbursed on or after July 1, 1987 but prior to October 1, 1992, and for any loan made under § 682.209 (e) or (f), the interest rate is a variable rate, applicable to each July 1–June 30 period, that equals the lesser of—

    (A) The bond equivalent rate of the 52-week Treasury bills auctioned at the final auction prior to the June 1 immediately preceding the July 1–June 30 period, plus 3.25 percent; or

    (B) 12 percent.

(iii) For a loan disbursed on or after October 1, 1992, the interest rate is a variable rate, applicable to each July 1–June 30 period, that equals the lesser of—

    (A) The bond equivalent rate of the 52-week Treasury bills auctioned at the final auction prior to the June 1 immediately preceding the July 1–June 30 period, plus 3.10 percent; or

    (B) 11 percent.

(iv)(A) Beginning on July 1, 2001, the interest rate on the loans described in paragraphs (a)(3)(ii) and (iii) of this section is a variable rate applicable to each July 1–June 30, as determined on the preceding June 26, and is equal to the weekly average 1-year constant maturity Treasury yield, as published by the Board of Governors of the Federal Reserve System, for the last calendar week ending on or before such June 26; plus—

    (1) 3.25 percent for loans described in paragraph (a)(3)(ii) of this section; or

    (2) 3.1 percent for loans described in paragraph (a)(3)(iii) of this section.

    (B) The interest rates calculated under paragraph (a)(3)(iv)(A) of this section shall not exceed the limits specified in paragraphs (a)(3)(ii)(B) and (a)(3)(iii)(B) of this section, as applicable.

(4) *Consolidation Program.*

(i) A Consolidation Program loan made before July 1, 1994 bears interest at the rate that. is the greater of—

    (A) The weighted average of interest rates on the loans consolidated, rounded to the nearest whole percent; or

    (B) 9 percent.

(ii) A Consolidation loan made on or after July 1, 1994, for which the loan application was received by the lender before November 13, 1997, bears interest at the rate that is equal to the weighted average of interest rates on the loans consolidated, rounded upward to the nearest whole percent.

(iii) For a Consolidation loan for which the loan application was received by the lender on or after November 13, 1997 and before October 1, 1998, the interest rate for the portion of the loan that consolidated loans other than HEAL loans is a variable rate, applicable to each July 1–June 30 period, that equals the lesser of—

    (A) The bond equivalent rate of the 91-day Treasury bills auctioned at the final auction held prior to June 1 of each year plus 3.10 percent; or

(B) 8.25 percent.

(iv) For a Consolidation loan for which the application was received by the lender on or after October 1, 1998, the interest rate for the portion of the loan that consolidated loans other than HEAL loans is a fixed rate that is the lesser of—

  (A) The weighted average of interest rates on the loans consolidated, rounded to the nearest higher one-eighth of one percent; or

  (B) 8.25 percent.

(v) For a Consolidation loan for which the application was received by the lender on or after November 13, 1997, the annual interest rate applicable to the portion of each consolidation loan that repaid HEAL loans is a variable rate adjusted annually on July 1 and must be equal to the average of the bond equivalent rates of the 91-day Treasury bills auctioned for the quarter ending June 30, plus 3 percent. There is no maximum rate on this portion of the loan.

(5) *Actual interest rates under the Stafford loan, SLS, PLUS, and Consolidation Programs.* A lender may charge a borrower an actual rate of interest that is less than the applicable interest rate specified in paragraphs (a)(1)–(4) of this section.

(6) *Refund of excess interest paid on Stafford loans.*

(i) For a loan with an applicable interest rate of 10 percent made prior to July 23, 1992, and for a loan with an applicable interest rate of 10 percent made from July 23, 1992 through September 30, 1992, to a borrower with no outstanding FFEL Program loans—

  (A) If during any calendar quarter, the sum of the average of the bond equivalent rates of the 91-day Treasury bills auctioned for that quarter, plus 3.25 percent, is less than 10 percent, the lender shall calculate an adjustment and credit the adjustment as specified under paragraph (a)(6)(i)(B) of this section if the borrower's account is not more than 30 days delinquent on December 31. The amount of the adjustment for a calendar quarter is equal to—

    (1) 10 percent minus the sum of the average of the bond equivalent rates of the 91-day Treasury bills auctioned for the applicable quarter plus 3.25 percent;

    (2) Multiplied by the average daily principal balance of the loan (not including unearned interest added to principal); and

    (3) Divided by 4;

  (B) No later than 30 calendar days after the end of the calendar year, the holder of the loan shall credit any amounts computed under paragraph (a)(6)(i)(A) of this section to—

    (1) The Secretary, for amounts paid during any period in which the borrower is eligible for interest benefits;

    (2) The borrower's account to reduce the outstanding principal balance as of the date the holder adjusts the borrower's account, provided that the borrower's account was not more than 30 days delinquent on that December 31; or

    (3) The Secretary, for a borrower who on the last day of the calendar year is delinquent for more than 30 days.

(ii) For a fixed interest rate loan made on or after July 23, 1992

to a borrower with an outstanding FFEL Program loan—

  (A) If during any calendar quarter, the sum of the average of the bond equivalent rates of the 91-day Treasury bills auctioned for that quarter, plus 3.10 percent, is less than the applicable interest rate, the lender shall calculate an adjustment and credit the adjustment to reduce the outstanding principal balance of the loan as specified under paragraph (a)(6)(ii)(C) of this section if the borrower's account is not more than 30 days delinquent on December 31. The amount of an adjustment for a calendar quarter is equal to—

    (1) The applicable interest rate minus the sum of the average of the bond equivalent rates of the 91-day Treasury bills auctioned for the applicable quarter plus 3.10 percent;

    (2) Multiplied by the average daily principal balance of the loan (not including unearned interest added to principal); and

    (3) Divided by 4;

  (B) For any quarter or portion thereof that the Secretary was obligated to pay interest subsidy on behalf of the borrower, the holder of the loan shall refund to the Secretary, no later than the end of the following quarter, any excess interest calculated in accordance with paragraph (a)(6)(ii)(A) of this section;

  (C) For any other quarter, the holder of the loan shall, within 30 days of the end of the calendar year, reduce the borrower's outstanding principal by the amount of excess interest calculated under paragraph (a)(6)(ii)(A) of this section, provided that the borrower's account was not more than 30 days delinquent as of December 31;

  (D) For a borrower who on the last day of the calendar year is delinquent for more than 30 days, any excess interest calculated shall be refunded to the Secretary; and

  (E) Notwithstanding paragraphs (a)(6)(ii)(B), (C) and (D) of this section, if the loan was disbursed during a quarter, the amount of any adjustment refunded to the Secretary or credited to the borrower for that quarter shall be prorated accordingly.

(7) *Conversion to Variable Rate.*

(i) A lender or holder shall convert the interest rate on a loan under paragraphs (a)(6)(i) or (ii) of this section to a variable rate.

(ii) The applicable interest rate for each 12-month period beginning on July 1 and ending on June 30 preceding each 12-month period is equal to the sum of—

  (A) The bond equivalent rate of the 91-day Treasury bills auctioned at the final auction prior to June 1; and

  (B) 3.25 percent in the case of a loan described in paragraph (a)(6)(i) of this section or 3.10 percent in the case of a loan described in paragraph (a)(6)(ii) of this section.

(iii)(A) In connection with the conversion specified in paragraph (a)(6)(ii) of this section for any period prior to the conversion for which a rebate has not been provided under paragraph (a)(6) of this section, a lender or holder shall convert the interest rate to a variable rate.

  (B) The interest rate for each period shall be reset quarterly and the applicable interest rate for the quarter or portion shall equal the sum of—

    (1) The average of the bond equivalent rates of 91-day Treasury

bills auctioned for the preceding 3-month period; and

(2) 3.25 percent in the case of loans as specified under paragraph (a)(6)(i) of this section or 3.10 percent in the case of loans as specified under paragraph (a)(6)(ii) of this section.

(iv)(A) The holder of a loan being converted under paragraph (a)(7)(iii)(A) of this section shall complete such conversion on or before January 1, 1995.

(B) The holder shall, not later than 30 days prior to the conversion, provide the borrower with—

(1) A notice informing the borrower that the loan is being converted to a variable interest rate;

(2) A description of the rate to the borrower;

(3) The current interest rate; and

(4) An explanation that the variable rate will provide a substantially equivalent benefit as the adjustment otherwise provided under paragraph (a)(6) of this section.

(v) The notice may be provided as part of the disclosure requirement as specified under § 682.205.

(vi) The interest rate as calculated under this paragraph may not exceed the maximum interest rate applicable to the loan prior to the conversion.

(b) *Capitalization.*

(1) A lender may add accrued interest and unpaid insurance premiums to the borrower's unpaid principal balance in accordance with this section. This increase in the principal balance of a loan is called "capitalization."

(2) Except as provided in paragraph (b)(4) of this section, a lender may capitalize interest payable by the borrower that has accrued—

(i) For the period from the date the first disbursement was made to the beginning date of the in-school period;

(ii) For the in-school or grace periods, or for a period needed to align repayment of an SLS with a Stafford loan, if capitalization is expressly authorized by the promissory note (or with the written consent of the borrower);

(iii) For a period of authorized deferment;

(iv) For a period of authorized forbearance; or

(v) For the period from the date the first installment payment was due until it was made.

(3) A lender may capitalize accrued interest under paragraphs (b)(2)(ii) through (iv) of this section no more frequently than quarterly. Capitalization is again permitted when repayment is required to begin or resume. A lender may capitalize accrued interest under paragraph (b)(2)(i) and (v) of this section only on the date repayment of principal is scheduled to begin.

(4)(i) For unsubsidized Stafford loans disbursed on or after October 7, 1998 and prior to July 1, 2000, the lender may capitalize the unpaid interest that accrues on the loan according to the requirements of section 428H(e)(2) of the Act.

(ii) For Stafford loans first disbursed on or after July 1, 2000, the lender may capitalize the unpaid interest—

(A) When the loan enters repayment;

(B) At the expiration of a period of authorized deferment;

(C) At the expiration of a period of authorized forbearance; and

(D) When the borrower defaults.

(5) For any borrower in an in-school or grace period or the period needed to align repayment, deferment, or forbearance status, during which the Secretary does not pay interest benefits and for which the borrower has agreed to make payments of interest, the lender may capitalize past due interest provided that the lender has notified the borrower that the borrower's failure to resolve any delinquency constitutes the borrower's consent to capitalization of delinquent interest and all interest that will accrue through the remainder of that period.

(c) *Fees for FFEL Program loans.*

(1)(i) For Stafford loans first disbursed prior to July 1, 2006, a lender may charge a borrower an origination fee not to exceed 3 percent of the principal amount of the loan.

(ii) For Stafford loans first disbursed on or after July 1, 2006, but before July 1, 2007, a lender may charge a borrower an origination fee not to exceed 2 percent of the principal amount of the loan.

(iii) For Stafford loans first disbursed on or after July 1, 2007, but before July 1, 2008, a lender may charge a borrower an origination fee not to exceed 1.5 percent of the principal amount of the loan.

(iv) For Stafford loans first disbursed on or after July 1, 2008, but before July 1, 2009, a lender may charge a borrower an origination fee not to exceed 1 percent of the principal amount of the loan.

(v) For Stafford loans first disbursed on or after July 1, 2009, but before July 1, 2010, a lender may charge a borrower an origination fee not to exceed. 5 percent of the principal amount of the loan.

(vi) For Stafford loans first disbursed on or after July 1, 2010, a lender may not charge a borrower an origination fee.

(vii) Except as provided in paragraph (c)(2) of this section, a lender must charge all borrowers the same origination fee.

(2)(i) A lender may charge a lower origination fee than the amount specified in paragraph (c)(1) of this section to a borrower whose expected family contribution (EFC), used to determine eligibility for the loan, is equal to or less than the maximum qualifying EFC for a Federal Pell Grant at the time the loan is certified or to a borrower who qualifies for a subsidized Stafford loan. A lender must charge all such borrowers the same origination fee.

(ii) With the approval of the Secretary, a lender may use a standard comparable to that defined in paragraph (c)(2)(i) of this section.

(3) If a lender charges a lower origination fee on unsubsidized loans under paragraph (c)(1) or (c)(2) of this section, the lender must charge the same fee on subsidized loans.

(4)(i) For purposes of this paragraph (c), a lender is defined as:

(A) All entities under common ownership, including ownership by a common holding company, that make loans to borrowers in a particular state; and

(B) Any beneficial owner of loans that provides funds to an eligible lender trustee to make loans on the beneficial owner's behalf in a particular state.

(ii) If a lender as defined in paragraph(c)(4)(i) charges a lower origination fee to any borrower in a particular state under paragraphs (c)(1) or (c)(2) of this section, the lender must charge all such borrowers who reside in that state or attend school in that state the same origination fee.

(5) Shall charge a borrower an origination fee on a PLUS loan of 3 percent of the principal amount of the loan;

(6) Shall deduct a pro rata portion of the fee (if charged) from each disbursement; and

(7) Shall refund by a credit against the borrower's loan balance the portion of the origination fee previously deducted from the loan that is attributable to any portion of the loan—

(i) That is returned by a school to a lender in order to comply with the Act or with applicable regulations;

(ii) That is repaid or returned within 120 days of disbursement, unless—

(A) The borrower has no FFEL Program loans in repayment status and has requested, in writing, that the repaid or returned funds be used for a different purpose; or

(B) The borrower has a FFEL Program loan in repayment status, in which case the payment is applied in accordance with § 682.209(b) unless the borrower has requested, in writing, that the repaid or returned funds be applied as a cancellation of all or part of the loan;

(iii) For which a loan check has not been negotiated within 120 days of disbursement; or

(iv) For which loan proceeds disbursed by electronic funds transfer or master check in accordance with § 682.207(b)(1)(ii)(B) and (C) have not been released from the restricted account maintained by the school within 120 days of disbursement.

(d) *Insurance premium and Federal default fee.*

(1) For loans guaranteed prior to July 1, 2006, a lender may charge the borrower the amount of the insurance premium paid by the lender to the guarantor (up to 1 percent of the principal amount of the loan) if that charge is provided for in the promissory note.

(2) For loans guaranteed on or after July 1, 2006, other than an SLS or PLUS loan refinanced under § 682.209(e) or (f), a lender may charge the borrower the amount of the Federal default fee paid by the lender to the guarantor (up to 1 percent of the principal amount of the loan) if that charge is provided for in the promissory note.

(3) If the borrower is charged the insurance premium or the Federal default fee, the amount charged must be deducted proportionately from each disbursement of the borrower's loan proceeds, if the loan is disbursed in more than one installment.

(4) The lender shall refund the insurance premium or Federal default fee paid by the borrower in accordance with the circumstances and procedures applicable to the return of origination fees, as described in paragraph (c)(7) of this section.

(e) *Administrative charge for a refinanced PLUS or SLS Loan.* A lender may charge a borrower up to $100 to cover the administrative costs of making a loan to a borrower under § 682.209(e) for the purpose of refinancing a PLUS or SLS loan to secure a variable interest rate.

(f) *Late charge.*

(1) If authorized by the borrower's promissory note, the lender may require the borrower to pay a late charge under the circumstances described in paragraph (f)(2) of this section. This charge may not exceed six cents for each dollar of each late installment.

(2) The lender may require the borrower to pay a late charge if the borrower fails to pay all or a portion of a required installment payment within 15 days after it is due.

(g) *Collection charges.*

(1) If provided for in the borrower's promissory note, and notwithstanding any provisions of State law, the lender may require that the borrower or any endorser pay costs incurred by the lender or its agents in collecting installments not paid when due, including, but not limited to—

(i) Attorney's fees;

(ii) Court costs; and

(iii) Telegrams.

(2) The costs referred to in paragraph (g)(1) of this section may not include routine collection costs associated with preparing letters or notices or with making personal contacts with the borrower (e.g., local and long-distance telephone calls).

(h) *Special allowance.* Pursuant to § 682.412(c), a lender may charge a borrower the amount of special allowance paid by the Secretary on behalf of the borrower.

(Authority: 20 U.S.C. 1077, 1078, 1078-1, 1078-2, 1078-3, 1079, 1082, 1087-1, 1091a)

[59 Fed. Reg. 22475, April 29, 1994; 59 Fed. Reg. 25745, May 17, 1994; 59 Fed. Reg. 29543, June 8, 1994; 59 Fed. Reg. 35625, July 13, 1994; 59 Fed. Reg. 61427, Nov. 30, 1994; 60 Fed. Reg. 32912, June 26, 1995; 61 Fed. Reg. 60486, Nov. 27, 1996; 62 Fed. Reg. 63434, Nov. 28, 1997; 64 Fed. Reg. 18976, April 16, 1999; 64 Fed. Reg. 58953, Nov. 1, 1999; 66 Fed. Reg. 34762, June 29, 2001; 71 Fed. Reg. 45666, Sept. 8, 2006]

§ 682.209 Repayment of a loan.

(a) *Conversion of a loan to repayment status.*

(1) For a Consolidation loan, the repayment period begins on the date the loan is disbursed. The first payment is due within 60 days after the date the loan is disbursed.

(2)(i) For a PLUS loan, the repayment period begins on the date of the last disbursement made on the loan. Interest accrues and is due and payable from the date of the first disbursement of the loan. The first payment is due within 60 days after the date the loan is fully disbursed.

(ii) For an SLS loan, the repayment period begins on the date the loan is disbursed, or, if the loan is disbursed in multiple installments, on the date of the last disbursement of the loan. Interest accrues and is due and payable from the date of the first disbursement of the loan. Except as provided in paragraph (a)(2)(iii), (a)(2)(iv), and (a)(2)(v) of this section the first payment is due within 60 days after the date the loan is fully disbursed.

(iii) For an SLS borrower who has not yet entered repayment on a Stafford loan, the borrower who has not yet entered repayment on a Stafford loan, the borrower may postpone payment, consistent with the grace period on the borrower's Stafford loan.

(iv) If the lender first learns after the fact that an SLS borrower has entered the repayment period, the repayment begins no later than 75 days after the date the lender learns that the borrower has entered the repayment period.

(v) The lender may establish a first payment due date that is no more than an additional 30 days beyond the period specified in paragraphs (a)(2)(ii)–(a)(2)(vi) of this section in order for the lender to comply with the required deadline contained in § 682.205(c)(1).

(3)(i) Except as provided in paragraph (a)(4) of this section, for a Stafford loan the repayment period begins—

(A) For a borrower with a loan for which the applicable interest rate is 7 percent per year, not less than 9 nor more than 12 months following the date on which the borrower is no longer enrolled on at least a half-time basis at an eligible school. The length of this grace period is determined by the lender for loans made under the FISL Program, and by the guaranty agency for loans guaranteed by the agency;

(B) For a borrower with a loan for which the initial applicable interest rate is 8 or 9 percent per year, the day after 6 months following the date on which the borrower is no longer enrolled on at least a half-time basis at an institution of higher education and

(C) For a borrower with a loan with a variable interest rate, the day after 6 months following the date on which the borrower is no longer enrolled on at least a half-time basis at an institution of higher education.

(ii) The first payment on a Stafford loan is due on a date established by the lender that is no more than—

  (A) 60 days following the first day that the repayment period begins;

  (B) 60 days from the expiration of a deferment or forbearance period;

  (C) 60 days following the end of the post deferment grace period;

  (D) If the lender first learns after the fact that the borrower has entered the repayment period, no later than 75 days after the date the lender learns that the borrower has entered the repayment period; or

  (E) An additional 30 days beyond the period specified in paragraphs (a)(3)(ii)(A)–(a)(3)(ii)(D) of this section in order for the lender to comply with the required deadlines contained in § 682.205(c)(1).

(iii) When determining the date that the student was no longer enrolled on at least a half-time basis, the lender must use a new date it receives from a school, unless the lender has already disclosed repayment terms to the borrower and the new date is within the same month and year as the most recent date reported to the lender.

(4) For a borrower of a Stafford loan who is a correspondence student, the grace period specified in paragraph (a)(3)(i) of this section begins on the earliest of—

(i) The day after the borrower completes the program;

(ii) The day after withdrawal as determined pursuant to 34 CFR 668.22; or

(iii) 60 days following the last day for completing the program as established by the school.

(5) For purposes of establishing the beginning of the repayment period for Stafford and SLS loans, the grace periods referenced in paragraphs (a)(2)(iii) and (a)(3)(i) of this section exclude any period during which a borrower who is a member of a reserve component of the Armed Forces named in section 10101 of title 10, United States Code is called or ordered to active duty for a period of more than 30 days. Any single excluded period may not exceed three years and includes the time necessary for the borrower to resume enrollment at the next available regular enrollment period. Any Stafford or SLS borrower who is in a grace period when called or ordered to active duty as specified in this paragraph is entitled to a full grace period upon completion of the excluded period.

(6)(i) The repayment schedule may provide for substantially equal installment payments or for installment payments that increase or decrease in amount during the repayment period. If the loan has a variable interest rate that changes annually, the lender may establish a repayment schedule that—

(A) Provides for adjustments of the amount of the installment payment to reflect annual changes in the variable interest rate; or

(B) Contains no provision for an adjustment of the amount of the installment payment to reflect annual changes in the variable interest rate, but requires the lender to grant a forbearance to the borrower (or endorser, if applicable) for a period of up to 3 years of payments in accordance with § 682.211(i)(5) in cases where the effect of a variable interest rate on a standard or graduated repayment schedule would result in a loan not being repaid within the maximum repayment term.

(ii) If a graduated or income-sensitive repayment schedule is established, it may not provide for any single installment that is more than three times greater than any other installment. An agreement as specified in paragraph (c)(1)(ii) of this section is not required if the schedule provides for less than the minimum annual payment amount specified in paragraph (c)(1)(i) of this section.

(iii) Not more than six months prior to the date that the borrower's first payment is due, the lender must offer the borrower a choice of a standard, income-sensitive, graduated, or, if applicable, an extended repayment schedule.

(iv) The repayment schedule must require that each payment equal at least the interest that accrues during the interval between scheduled payments.

(v) The lender shall require the borrower to repay the loan under a standard repayment schedule described in paragraph (a)(6)(vi) of this section if the borrower—

  (A) Does not select an income-sensitive, a graduated, or if applicable, an extended repayment schedule within 45 days after being notified by the lender to choose a repayment schedule; or

  (B) Chooses an income-sensitive repayment schedule, but does not provide the documentation requested by the lender under paragraph (a)(7)(viii)(C) of this section within the time period specified by the lender.

(vi) Under a standard repayment schedule, the borrower is scheduled to pay either—

  (A) The same amount for each installment payment made during the repayment period, except that the borrower's final payment may be slightly more or less than the other payments; or

  (B) An installment amount that will be adjusted to reflect annual changes in the loan's variable interest rate.

(vii) Under a graduated repayment schedule—

  (A)(1) The amount of the borrower's installment payment is scheduled to change (usually by increasing) during the course of the repayment period; or

    (2) If the loan has a variable interest rate that changes annually, the lender may establish a repayment schedule that may have adjustments in the payment amount as provided under paragraph (a)(6)(i) of this section; and

  (B) An agreement as specified in paragraph (c)(1)(ii) of this section is not required if the schedule provides for less than the minimum annual payment amount specified in paragraph (c)(1)(i) of this section.

(viii) Under an income-sensitive repayment schedule—

  (A)(1) The amount of the borrower's installment payment is

adjusted annually, based on the borrower's expected total monthly gross income received by the borrower from employment and from other sources during the course of the repayment period; or

(2) If the loan has a variable interest rate that changes annually, the lender may establish a repayment schedule that may have adjustments in the payment amount as provided under paragraph (a)(6)(i) of this section; and

(B) In general, the lender shall request the borrower to inform the lender of his or her income no earlier than 90 days prior to the due date of the borrower's initial installment payment and subsequent annual payment adjustment under an income-sensitive repayment schedule. The income information must be sufficient for the lender to make a reasonable determination of what the borrower's payment amount should be. If the lender receives late notification that the borrower has dropped below half-time enrollment status at a school, the lender may request that income information earlier than 90 days prior to the due date of the borrower's initial installment payment;

(C) If the borrower reports income to the lender that the lender considers to be insufficient for establishing monthly installment payments that would repay the loan within the applicable maximum repayment period, the lender shall require the borrower to submit evidence showing the amount of the most recent total monthly gross income received by the borrower from employment and from other sources including, if applicable, pay statements from employers and documentation of any income received by the borrower from other parties;

(D) The lender shall grant a forbearance to the borrower (or endorser, if applicable) for a period of up to 5 years of payments in accordance with § 682.211(i)(5) in cases where the effect of decreased installment amounts paid under an income-sensitive repayment schedule would result in a loan not being repaid within the maximum repayment term; and

(E) The lender shall inform the borrower that the loan must be repaid within the time limits specified under paragraph (a)(7) of this section.

(ix) Under an extended repayment schedule, a new borrower whose total outstanding principal and interest in FFEL loans exceed $30,000 may repay the loan on a fixed annual repayment amount or a graduated repayment amount for a period that may not exceed 25 years. For purposes of this section, a "new borrower" is an individual who has no outstanding principal or interest balance on an FFEL Program loan as of October 7, 1998, or on the date he or she obtains an FFEL Program loan after October 7, 1998.

(x) A borrower may request a change in the repayment schedule on a loan. The lender must permit the borrower to change the repayment schedule no less frequently than annually.

(xi) For purposes of this section, a lender shall, to the extent practicable require that all FFEL loans owed by a borrower to the lender be combined into one account and repaid under one repayment schedule. In that event, the word "loan" in this section shall mean all of the borrower's loans that were combined by the lender into that account.

(7)(i) Subject to paragraphs (a)(7)(ii) through (iv) of this section, and except as provided in paragraph (a)(6)(ix) a lender shall allow a borrower at least 5 years, but not more than 10 years, or 25 years under an extended repayment plan to repay a Stafford, SLS, or Plus loan, calculated from the beginning of the repayment period. Except in the case of a FISL loan for a period of enrollment beginning on or after July 1, 1986, the lender shall require a borrower to fully repay a FISL loan within 15 years after it is made.

(ii) If the borrower receives an authorized deferment or is granted forbearance, as described in § 682.210 or § 682.211 respectively, the periods of deferment or forbearance are excluded from determinations of the 5-, 10-, 15- and 25-year periods, and from the 10-, 12-, 15-, 20-, 25-, and 30-year periods for repayment of a Consolidation loan pursuant to § 682.209(h).

(iii) If the minimum annual repayment required in paragraph (c) of this section would result in complete repayment of the loan in less than 5 years, the borrower is not entitled to the full 5-year period.

(iv) The borrower may, prior to the beginning of the repayment period, request and be granted by the lender a repayment period of less than 5 years. Subject to paragraph (a)(8)(iii) of this section, a borrower who makes such a request may notify the lender at any time to extend the repayment period to a minimum of 5 years.

(8) If, with respect to the aggregate of all loans held by a lender, the total payment made by a borrower for a monthly or similar payment period would not otherwise be a multiple of five dollars, the lender may round that periodic payment to the next highest whole dollar amount that is a multiple of five dollars.

(b) *Payment application and prepayment.*

(1) The lender may credit the entire payment amount first to any late charges accrued or collection costs and then to any outstanding interest and then to outstanding principal.

(2)(i) The borrower may prepay the whole or any part of a loan at any time without penalty.

(ii) If the prepayment amount equals or exceeds the monthly payment amount under the repayment schedule established for the loan, the lender shall apply the prepayment to future installments by advancing the next payment due date, unless the borrower requests otherwise. The lender must either inform the borrower in advance using a prominent statement in the borrower coupon book or billing statement that any additional full payment amounts submitted without instructions to the lender as to their handling will be applied to future scheduled payments with the borrower's next scheduled payment due date advanced consistent with the number of additional payments received, or provide a notification to the borrower after the payments are received informing the borrower that the payments have been so applied and the date of the borrower's next scheduled payment due date. Information related to next scheduled payment due date need not be provided to borrower's making such prepayments while in an in-school, grace, deferment, or forbearance period when payments are not due.

(c) *Minimum annual payment.*

(1)(i) Subject to paragraph (c)(1)(ii) of this section and except as otherwise provided by a graduated, income-sensitive, or extended repayment plan selected by the borrower, during each year of the repayment period, a borrower's total payments to all holders of the borrower's FFEL Program loans must total at least $600 or the unpaid balance of all loans, including interest, whichever amount is less.

(ii) If the borrower and the lender agree, the amount paid may be less.

(2) The provisions of paragraphs (c)(1)(i) and (ii) of this section may not result in an extension of the maximum repayment period unless forbearance as described in § 682.211, or deferment described in § 682.210, has been approved.

(d) *Combined repayment of a borrower's student PLUS and SLS loans held by a lender.*

(1) A lender may, at the request of a student borrower, combine the borrower's student PLUS and SLS loans held by it into a single repayment schedule.

(2) The repayment period on the loans included in the combined repayment schedule must be calculated based on the beginning of repayment of the most recent included loan.

(3) The interest rate on the loans included in the new combined repayment schedule must be the weighted average of the rates of all included loans.

(e) *Refinancing a fixed-rate PLUS or SLS Program loan to secure a variable interest rate.*

(1) Subject to paragraph (g) of this section, a lender may, at the request of a borrower, refinance a PLUS or SLS loan with a fixed interest rate in order to permit the borrower to obtain a variable interest rate.

(2) A loan made under paragraph (e)(1) of this section—

(i) Must bear interest at the variable rate described in § 682.202(a)(2)(ii) and (3)(ii) as appropriate; and

(ii) May not extend the repayment period provided for in paragraph (a)(7)(i) of this section.

(3) The lender may not charge an additional insurance premium or Federal default fee on the loan, but may charge the borrower an administrative fee pursuant to § 682.202(e).

(f) *Refinancing of a fixed-rate PLUS or SLS Program loan to secure a variable interest rate by a discharge of previous loan.*

(1) Subject to paragraph (g) of this section, a borrower who has applied for, but been denied, a refinanced loan authorized under paragraph (e) of this section by the holder of the borrower's fixed rate PLUS or SLS loan, may obtain a loan from another lender for the purpose of discharging the fixed-rate loan and obtaining a variable interest rate.

(2) A loan made under paragraph (f)(1) of this section—

(i) Must bear interest at the variable interest rate described in § 682.202(a)(2)(ii) and (3)(ii), as appropriate;

(ii) May not operate to extend the repayment period provided for in paragraph (a)(7)(i) of this section; and

(iii) Must be disbursed to the holder of the fixed-rate loan to discharge the borrower's obligation thereon.

(3) Upon receipt of the proceeds of a loan made under paragraph (f)(1) of this section, the holder of the fixed-rate loan shall, within five business days, apply the proceeds to discharge the borrower's obligation on the fixed-rate loan, and provide the refinancing lender with either a copy of the borrower's original promissory note evidencing the fixed-rate loan or the holder's written certification that the borrower's obligation on the fixed-rate loan has been fully discharged.

(4) The refinancing lender may charge the borrower an insurance premium on a loan made under paragraph (f)(1) of this section, but may not charge a fee to cover administrative costs.

(5) For purposes of deferments under § 682.210, the refinancing loan—

(i) Is considered a PLUS loan if any of the included loans is a PLUS loan made to a parent;

(ii) Is considered an SLS loan if the combined loan does not include a PLUS loan made to a parent; or

(iii) Is considered a loan to a "new borrower" as defined in § 682.210(b)(7), if all the loans that were refinanced were made on or after July 1, 1987, for a period of enrollment beginning on or after that date.

(g) *Conditions for refinancing certain loans.*

(1) A lender may not refinance a loan under paragraphs (e) or (f) of this section if that loan is in default, involves a violation of a condition of reinsurance described in § 682.406, or, in the case of a Federal SLS or Federal PLUS loan, is uninsured by the Secretary.

(2)(i) Prior to refinancing a fixed-rate under paragraph (f) of this section, the lender shall obtain a written statement from the holder of the loan certifying that—

(A) The holder has refused to refinance the fixed-rate loan under paragraph (e) of this section; and

(B) The fixed-rate loan is eligible for insurance or reinsurance under paragraph (g)(1) of this section.

(ii) The holder of a fixed-rate loan shall, within 10 business days of receiving a lender's written request to provide a certification under paragraph (g)(1)(i) of this section, provide the lender with that certification, or provide the lender and the guarantor on the loan with a written explanation of the reasons for its inability to provide the certification to the requesting lender.

(iii) The refinancing lender may rely in good faith on the certification provided by the holder of the fixed-rate loan under paragraph (g)(2)(ii) of this section.

(h) *Consolidation loans.*

(1) For a Consolidation loan, the repayment period begins on the day of disbursement, with the first payment due within 60 days after the date of disbursement.

(2) If the sum of the amount of the Consolidation loan and the unpaid balance on other student loans to the applicant—

(i) Is less than $7,500, the borrower shall repay the Consolidation loan in not more than 10 years;

(ii) Is equal to or greater than $7,500 but less than $10,000, the borrower shall repay the Consolidation loan in not more than 12 years;

(iii) Is equal to or greater than $10,000 but less than 20,000, the borrower shall repay the Consolidation loan in not more than 15 years;

(iv) Is equal to or greater than $20,000 but less than $40,000, the borrower shall repay the Consolidation loan in not more than 20 years;

(v) Is equal to or greater than $40,000 but less than $60,000, the borrower shall repay the Consolidation loan in not more than 25 years; or

(vi) Is equal to or greater than $60,000, the borrower shall repay the Consolidation loan in not more than 30 years.

(3) For the purpose of paragraph (h)(2) of this section, the

unpaid balance on other student loans—

(i) May not exceed the amount of the Consolidation loan; and

(ii) With the exception of the defaulted title IV loans on which the borrower has made satisfactory repayment arrangements with the holder of the loan, does not include the unpaid balance on any defaulted loans.

(4) A repayment schedule for a Consolidation loan—

(i) Must be established by the lender;

(ii) Must require that each payment equal at least the interest that accrues during the interval between scheduled payments.

(5) Upon receipt of the proceeds of a loan made under paragraph (h)(2) of this section, the holder of the underlying loan shall promptly apply the proceeds to discharge fully the borrower's obligation on the underlying loan, and provide the consolidating lender with the holder's written certification that the borrower's obligation on the underlying loan has been fully discharged.

(i) *Treatment by a lender of borrowers' title IV, HEA program funds received from schools if the borrower withdraws.*

(1) A lender shall treat a refund or a return of title IV, HEA program funds under § 668.22 when a student withdraws received by the lender from a school as a credit against the principal amount owed by the borrower on the borrower's loan.

(2)(i) If a lender receives a refund or a return of title IV, HEA program funds under § 668.22 when a student withdraws from a school on a loan that is no longer held by that lender, or that has been discharged by another lender by refinancing under § 682.209(f) or by a Consolidation loan, the lender must transmit the amount of the payment, within 30 days of its receipt, to the lender to whom it assigned the loan, or to the lender that discharged the prior loan, with an explanation of the source of the payment.

(ii) Upon receipt of a refund or a return of title IV, HEA program funds transmitted under paragraph (i)(2)(i) of this section, the holder of the loan promptly must provide written notice to the borrower that the holder has received the return of title IV, HEA program funds.

(j) *Certification on loans to be repaid through consolidation.*

Within 10 business days after receiving a written request for a certification from a lender under § 682.206(f), a holder shall either provide the requesting lender the certification or, if it is unable to certify to the matters described in that paragraph, provide the requesting lender and the guarantor on the loan at issue with a written explanation of the reasons for its inability to provide the certification.

(Approved by the Office of Management and Budget under control number 1845-0020)

(Authority: 20 U.S.C. 1077, 1078, 1078-1, 1078-2, 1078-3, 1079, 1082, 1085)

[59 Fed. Reg. 33352, June 28, 1994; 59 Fed. Reg. 33593, June 29, 1994; 60 Fed. Reg. 30788, June 12, 1995; 60 Fed. Reg. 32912, June 26, 1995; 60 Fed. Reg. 61756, Dec. 1, 1995; 61 Fed. Reg. 16718, April 17, 1996; 62 Fed. Reg. 63434, Nov. 28, 1997; 64 Fed. Reg. 18977, April 16, 1999; 64 Fed. Reg. 58957, 59043, Nov. 1, 1999; 66 Fed. Reg. 34763, June 29, 2001; 67 Fed. Reg. 67078, Nov. 1, 2002; 68 Fed. Reg. 75427, Dec. 31, 2003; 71 Fed. Reg. 45666, Sept. 8, 2006]

§ 682.210 Deferment.

(a) *General.*

(1)(i) A borrower is entitled to have periodic installment payments of principal deferred during authorized periods after the beginning of the repayment period, pursuant to paragraph (b) of this section.

(ii) With the exception of a deferment authorized under paragraph (*o*) of this section, a borrower may continue to receive a specific type of deferment that is limited to a maximum period of time only if the total amount of time that the borrower has received the deferment does not exceed the maximum time period allowed for the deferment.

(2)(i) For a loan made before October 1, 1981, the borrower is also entitled to have periodic installments of principal deferred during the six-month period (post-deferment grace period) that begins after the completion of each deferment period or combination of those periods, except as provided in paragraph (a)(2)(ii) of this section.

(ii) Once a borrower receives a post-deferment grace period following an unemployment deferment, as described in paragraph (b)(1)(v) of this section, the borrower does not qualify for additional post-deferment grace periods following subsequent unemployment deferments.

(3) Interest accrues and is paid by the borrower during the deferment period and the post-deferment grace period, if applicable, unless interest accrues and is paid by the Secretary for a Stafford loan and for all or a portion of a qualifying Consolidation loan that meets the requirements under § 682.301.

(4) As a condition for receiving a deferment, except for purposes of paragraphs (c)(1)(ii) and (iii) of this section, the borrower must request the deferment, and provide the lender with all information and documents required to establish eligibility for a specific type of deferment.

(5) An authorized deferment period begins on the date that the holder determines is the date that the condition entitling the borrower to the deferment first existed, except that an initial unemployment deferment as described in paragraph (h)(2) of this section cannot begin more than 6 months before the date the holder receives a request and documentation required for the deferment.

(6) An authorized deferment period ends on the earlier of—

(i) The date when the condition establishing the borrower's eligibility for the deferment ends;

(ii) Except as provided in paragraph (a)(6)(iv) of this section, the date on which, as certified by an authorized official, the borrower's eligibility for the deferment is expected to end;

(iii) Except as provided in paragraph (a)(6)(iv) of this section, the expiration date of the period covered by any certification required by this section to be obtained for the deferment;

(iv) In the case of an in-school deferment, the student's anticipated graduation date as certified by an authorized official of the school; or

(v) The date when the condition providing the basis for the borrower's eligibility for the deferment has continued to exist for the maximum amount of time allowed for that type of deferment.

(7) A lender may not deny a borrower a deferment to which the borrower is entitled, even though the borrower may be delinquent, but not in default, in making required installment payments. The

270- or 330-day period required to establish default does not run during the deferment and post-deferment grace periods. Unless the lender has granted the borrower forbearance under § 682.211, when the deferment and, if applicable, the post-deferment grace period expire, a borrower resumes any delinquency status that existed when the deferment period began.

(8) A borrower whose loan is in default is not eligible for a deferment on that loan, unless the borrower has made payment arrangements acceptable to the lender prior to the payment of a default claim by a guaranty agency.

(9) The borrower promptly must inform the lender when the condition entitling the borrower to a deferment no longer exists.

(10) Authorized deferments are described in paragraph (b) of this section. Specific requirements for each deferment are set forth in paragraphs (c) through (s) of this section.

(11) If two individuals are jointly liable for repayment of a PLUS loan or a Consolidation loan, the lender shall grant a request for deferment if both individuals simultaneously meet the requirements of this section for receiving the same, or different deferments.

(b) *Authorized deferments.*

(1) Deferment is authorized for a FFEL borrower during any period when the borrower is—

(i) Except as provided in paragraph (c)(5) of this section, engaged in full-time study at a school, or at a school that is operated by the Federal Government (e.g., the service academies), unless the borrower is not a national of the United States and is pursuing a course of study at a school not located in a State;

(ii) Engaged in a course of study under an eligible graduate fellowship program;

(iii) Engaged in a rehabilitation training program for disabled individuals;

(iv) Temporarily totally disabled, or unable to secure employment because the borrower is caring for a spouse or other dependent who is disabled and requires continuous nursing or similar services for up to three years; or

(v) Conscientiously seeking, but unable to find, full-time employment in the United States, for up to two years.

(2) For a borrower of a Stafford or SLS loan, and for a parent borrower of a PLUS loan made before August 15, 1983, deferment is authorized during any period when the borrower is—

(i) On active duty status in the United States Armed Forces, or an officer in the Commissioned Corps of the United States Public Health Service, for up to three years (including any period during which the borrower received a deferment authorized under paragraph (b)(5)(i) of this section);

(ii) A full-time volunteer under the Peace Corps Act, for up to three years;

(iii) A full-time volunteer under Title I of the Domestic Volunteer Service Act of 1973 (ACTION programs), for up to three years;

(iv) A full-time volunteer for a tax-exempt organization, for up to three years; or

(v) Engaged in an internship of residency program, for up to two years (including any period during which the borrower received a deferment authorized under paragraph (b)(5)(iii) of this section).

(3) For a borrower of a Stafford or SLS loan who has been enrolled on at least a half-time basis at an institution of higher education during the six months preceding the beginning of this deferment, deferment is authorized during a period of up to six months during which the borrower is—

(i)(A) Pregnant;

(B) Caring for his or her newborn child; or

(C) Caring for a child immediately following the placement of the child with the borrower before or immediately following adoption; and

(ii) Not attending a school or gainfully employed.

(4) For a "new borrower," as defined in paragraph (b)(7) of this section, deferment is authorized during periods when the borrower is engaged in at least half-time study at a school, unless the borrower is not a national of the United States and is pursuing a course of study at a school not located in a State.

(5) For a new borrower, as defined in paragraph (b)(7) of this section, of a Stafford or SLS loan, deferment is authorized during any period when the borrower is—

(i) On active duty status in the National Oceanic and Atmospheric Administration Corps, for up to three years (including any period during which the borrower received a deferment authorized under paragraph (b)(2)(i) of this section);

(ii) Up to three years of service as a full-time teacher in a public or non-profit private elementary or secondary school in a teacher shortage area designated by the Secretary under paragraph (q) of this section.

(iii) Engaged in an internship or residency program, for up to two years (including any period during which the borrower received a deferment authorized under paragraph (c)(2)(v) of this section); or

(iv) A mother who has preschool-age children (i.e., children who have not enrolled in first grade) and who is earning not more than $1 per hour above the Federal minimum wage, for up to 12 months of employment, and who began that full-time employment within one year of entering or re-entering the work force. Full-time employment involves at least 30 hours of work a week and it expected to last at least 3 months.

(6) For a parent borrower of a PLUS loan, deferment is authorized during any period when a student on whose behalf the parent borrower received the loan—

(i) Is not independent as defined in section 480(d) of the Act; and

(ii) Meets the conditions and provides the required documentation, for any of the deferments described in paragraphs (b)(1)(i)–(iii) and (b)(4) of this section.

(7) For purposes of paragraph (b)(5) of this section, a "new borrower" with respect to a loan is a borrower who, on the date he or she signs and promissory note, has no outstanding balance on—

(i) A Stafford, SLS, or PLUS loan made prior to July 1, 1987 for a period of enrollment beginning prior to July 1, 1987; or

(ii) A Consolidation loan that repaid a loan made prior to July 1, 1987 and or a period of enrollment beginning prior to July 1, 1987.

(c) *In-school deferment.*

(1) Except as provided in paragraph (c)(5) of this section, the lender processes a deferment for full-time study or half-time study at a school, when—

(i) The borrower submits a request and supporting documentation for a deferment;

(ii) The lender receives information from the borrower's school about the borrower's eligibility in connection with a new loan; or

(iii) The lender receives student status information from the borrower's school, either directly or indirectly, indicating that the borrower's enrollment status supports eligibility for a deferment.

(2) The lender must notify the borrower that a deferment has been granted based on paragraph (c)(1)(ii) or (iii) of this section and that the borrower has the option to pay interest that accrues on an unsubsidized FFEL Program loan or to cancel the deferment and continue paying on the loan. The lender must include in the notice an explanation of the consequences of these options.

(3) The lender must consider a deferment granted on the basis of a certified loan application or other information certified by the school to cover the period lasting until the anticipated graduation date appearing on the application, and as updated by notice or SSCR update to the lender from the school or guaranty agency, unless and until it receives notice that the borrower has ceased the level of study (i.e., full-time or half-time) required for the deferment.

(4) In the case of a FFEL borrower, the lender shall treat a certified loan application or other form certified by the school or for multiple holders of a borrower's loans, shared data from the Student Status Confirmation Report, as sufficient documentation for an in-school deferment for any outstanding FFEL loan previously made to the borrower that is held by the lender.

(5) A borrower serving in a medical internship or residency program, except for an internship in dentistry, is prohibited from receiving or continuing a deferment on a Stafford, or a PLUS (unless based on the dependent's status) SLS, or Consolidation loan under paragraph (c) of this section.

(d) *Graduate fellowship deferment.*

(1) To qualify for a deferment for study in a graduate fellowship program, a borrower shall provide the lender with a statement from an authorized official of the borrower's fellowship program certifying—

(i) That the borrower holds at least a baccalaureate degree conferred by an institution of higher education;

(ii) That the borrower has been accepted or recommended by an institution of higher education for acceptance on a full-time basis into an eligible graduate fellowship program; and

(iii) The borrower's anticipated completion date in the program.

(2) For purposes of paragraph (d)(1) of this section, an eligible graduate fellowship program is a fellowship program that—

(i) Provides sufficient financial support to graduate fellows to allow for full-time study for at least six months;

(ii) Requires a written statement from each applicant explaining the applicant's objectives before the award of that financial support;

(iii) Requires a graduate fellow to submit periodic reports, projects, or evidence of the fellow's progress; and

(iv) In the case of a course of study at a foreign university, accepts the course of study for completion of the fellowship program.

(e) *Rehabilitation training program deferment.*

(1) To qualify for a rehabilitation training program deferment, a borrower shall provide the lender with a statement from an authorized official of the borrower's rehabilitation training program certifying that the borrower is either receiving, or is scheduled to receive, services under an eligible rehabilitation training program for disabled individuals.

(2) For purposes of paragraph (e)(1) of this section, an eligible rehabilitation training program for disabled individuals is a program that—

(i) Is licensed, approved, certified, or otherwise recognized as providing rehabilitation training to disabled individuals by—

(A) A State agency with responsibility for vocational rehabilitation programs;

(B) A State agency with responsibility for drug abuse treatment programs;

(C) A State agency with responsibility for mental health services program;

(D) a State agency with responsibility for alcohol abuse treatment programs; or

(E) The Department of Veterans Affairs; and

(ii) Provides or will provide the borrower with rehabilitation services under a written plan that—

(A) Is individualized to meet the borrower's needs;

(B) Specifies the date on which the services to the borrower are expected to end; and

(C) Is structured in a way that requires a substantial commitment by the borrower to his or her rehabilitation. The Secretary considers a substantial commitment by the borrower to be a commitment of time and effort that normally would prevent an additional from engaging in full-time employment, either because of the number of hours that must be devoted to rehabilitation or because of the nature of the rehabilitation. For the purpose of this paragraph, full-time employment involves at least 30 hours of work per week and is expected to last at least three months.

(f) *Temporary total disability deferment.*

(1) To qualify for a temporary total disability deferment, a borrower shall provide the lender with a statement from a physician, who is a doctor of medicine or osteopathy and is legally authorized to practice, certifying that the borrower is temporarily totally disabled as defined in § 682.200(b).

(2) A borrower is not considered temporarily totally disabled on the basis of a condition that existed before he or she applied for the loan, unless the condition has substantially deteriorated so as to render the borrower temporarily totally disabled, as substantiated by the statement required under paragraph (f)(1) of this section, after the borrower submitted the loan application.

(3) A lender may not grant a deferment based on a single certification under paragraph (f)(1) of this section beyond the date that is six months after the date of certification.

(g) *Dependent's disability deferment.*

(1) To qualify for a deferment given to a borrower whose spouse or other dependent requires continuous nursing or similar services for a period of at least 90 days, the borrower shall provide the lender with a statement—

(i) From a physician, who is a doctor of medicine or osteopathy and is legally authorized to practice, certifying that the borrower's spouse or dependent requires continuous nursing or similar services for a period of at least 90 days; and

(ii) From the borrower, certifying that the borrower is unable to secure full-time employment because he or she is providing continuous nursing or similar services to the borrower's spouse or other dependent. For the purpose of this paragraph, full-time employment involves at least 30 hours of work per week and is expected to last at least three months.

(2) A lender may not grant a deferment based on a single certification under paragraph (g)(1) of this section beyond the date that is six months after the date of the certification.

(h) *Unemployment deferment.*

(1) A borrower qualifies for an unemployment deferment by providing evidence of eligibility for unemployment benefits to the lender.

(2) A borrower also qualifies for an unemployment deferment by providing to the lender a written certification, or an equivalent as approved by the Secretary, that—

(i) The borrower has registered with a public or private employment agency, if one is available to the borrower within a 50-mile radius of the borrower's current address; and

(ii) For all requests beyond the initial request, the borrower has made at least six diligent attempts during the preceding 6-month period to secure full-time employment.

(3) For purposes of obtaining an unemployment deferment under paragraph (h)(2) of this section, the following rules apply:

(i) A borrower may qualify for an unemployment deferment whether or not the borrower has been previously employed.

(ii) An unemployment deferment is not justified if the borrower refuses to seek or accept employment in kinds of positions or at salary and responsibility levels for which the borrower feels over qualified by virtue of education or previous experience.

(iii) Full-time employment involves at least 30 hours of work a week and is expected to last at least three months.

(iv) The initial period of unemployment deferment may be granted for a period of unemployment beginning up to 6 months before the date the lender receives the borrower's request, and may be granted for up to 6 months after that date.

(4) A lender may not grant an unemployment deferment beyond the date that is 6 months after the date the borrower provides evidence of the borrower's eligibility for unemployment insurance benefits under paragraph (h)(1) of this section or the date the borrower provides the written certification, or an approved equivalent, under paragraph (h)(2) of this section.

(i) *Military deferment.*

(1) To qualify for a military deferment, a borrower shall provide the lender with—

(i) A written statement from the borrower's commanding or personnel officer certifying—

(A) That the borrower is on active duty in the Armed Forces of the United States;

(B) The date on which the borrower's service began; and

(C) The date on which the borrower's service is expected to end; or

(ii)(A) A copy of the borrower's official military orders; and

(B) A copy of the borrower's military identification.

(2) For the purpose of this section, the Armed Forces means the Army, Navy, Air Force, Marine Corps, and the Coast Guard.

(3) A borrower enlisted in a reserve component of the Armed Forces may qualify for a military deferment only for service on a full-time basis that is expected to last for a period of at least one year in length, as evidenced by official military orders, unless an order for national mobilization of reservists is issued.

(4) A borrower enlisted in the National Guard qualifies for a military deferment only while the borrower is on active duty status as a member of the U.S. Army or Air Force Reserves, and meets the requirements of paragraph (i)(3) of this section.

(j) *Public Health Service deferment.* To qualify for a Public Health Service deferment, the borrower shall provide the lender with a statement from an authorized official of the United States Public Health Service (USPHS) certifying—

(1) That the borrower is engaged in full-time service as an officer in the Commissioned Corps of the USPHS;

(2) The date on which the borrower's service began; and

(3) The date on which the borrower's service is expected to end.

(k) *Peace Corps deferment.*

(1) To qualify for a deferment for service under the Peace Corps Act, the borrower shall provide the lender with a statement from an authorized official of the Peace Corps certifying—

(i) That the borrower has agreed to serve for a term of at least one year;

(ii) The date on which the borrower's service began; and

(iii) The date on which the borrower's service is expected to end.

(2) The lender must grant a deferment for the borrower's full term of service in the Peace Corps, not to exceed three years.

(*l*) *Full-time volunteer service in the ACTION programs.* To qualify for a deferment as a full-time paid volunteer in an ACTION program, the borrower shall provide the lender with a statement from an authorized official of the program certifying—

(1) That the borrower has agreed to serve for a term of at least one year;

(2) The date on which the borrower's service began; and

(3) The date on which the borrower's service is expected to end.

(m) *Deferment for full-time volunteer service for a tax-exempt organization.* To qualify for a deferment as a full-time paid volunteer for a tax-exempt organization, a borrower shall provide the lender with a statement from an authorized official of the volunteer program certifying—

(1) That the borrower—

(i) Serves in an organization that has obtained an exemption from taxation under section 501(c)(3) of the Internal Revenue Code of 1986;

(ii) Provides service to low-income persons and their communities to assist them in eliminating poverty and poverty-related human, social, and environmental conditions;

(iii) Does not receive compensation that exceeds the rate prescribed under section 6 of the Fair Labor Standards Act of 1938 (the Federal minimum wage), except that the tax-exempt organization may provide health, retirement, and other fringe benefits to the volunteer that are substantially equivalent to the benefits offered to other employees of the organization;

(iv) Does not, as part of his or her duties, give religious instruction, conduct worship services, engage in religious proselytizing, or engage in fund-raising to support religious activities; and

(v) Has agreed to serve on a full-time basis for a term of at least one year;

(2) The date on which the borrower's service began; and

(3) The date on which the borrower's service is expected to end.

(n) *Internship or residency deferment.*

(1) To qualify for an internship or residency deferment under paragraphs (b)(2)(v) or (b)(5)(iii) of this section, the borrower shall provide the lender with a statement from an authorized official of the organization with which the borrower is undertaking the internship or residency program certifying—

(i) That the internship or residency program is a supervised training program that requires the borrower to hold at least a baccalaureate degree prior to acceptance into the program;

(ii) That, except for a borrower that provides the statement from a State official described in paragraph (n)(2) of this section, the internship or residency program leads to a degree or certificate awarded by an institution of higher education, a hospital, or a health care facility that offers postgraduate training;

(iii) That the borrower has been accepted into the internship or residency program; and

(iv) The anticipated dates on which the borrower will begin and complete the internship or residency program, or, in the case of a borrower providing the statement described in paragraph (n)(2) of this section, the anticipated date on which the borrower will begin and complete the minimum period of participation in the internship program that the State requires be completed before an individual may be certified for professional practice or service.

(2) For a borrower who does not provide a statement certifying to the matters set forth in paragraph (n)(1)(ii) of this section to qualify for an internship deferment under paragraph (b)(2)(v) of this section, the borrower shall provide the lender with a statement from an official of the appropriate State licensing agency certifying that the internship or residency program, or a portion thereof, is required to be completed before the borrower may be certified for professional practice or service.

(*o*) *Parental-leave deferment.*

(1) To qualify for the parental-leave deferment described in paragraph (b)(3) of this section, the borrower shall provide the lender with—

(i) A statement from an authorized official of a participating school certifying that the borrower was enrolled on at least a half-time basis during the six months preceding the beginning of the deferment period;

(ii) A statement from the borrower certifying that the borrower—

(A) Is pregnant, caring for his or her newborn child, or caring for a child immediately following the placement of the child with the borrower in connection with an adoption;

(B) Is not, and will not be, attending school during the deferment period; and

(C) Is not, and will not be, engaged in full-time employment during the deferment period; and

(iii) A physician's statement demonstrating the existence of the pregnancy, a birth certificate, or a statement from the adoption agency official evidencing a pre-adoption placement.

(2) For purposes of paragraph (*o*)(1)(ii)(C) of this section, full-time employment involves at least 30 hours of work per week and is expected to last at least three months.

(p) *NOAA deferment.* To qualify for a National Oceanic and Atmospheric Administration (NOAA) deferment, the borrower shall provide the lender with a statement from an authorized official of the NOAA corps, certifying—

(1) That the borrower is on active duty service in the NOAA corps;

(2) The date on which the borrower's service began; and

(3) The date on which the borrower's service is expected to end.

(q) *Targeted teacher deferment.*

(1) To qualify for a targeted teacher deferment under paragraph (b)(5)(ii) of this section, the borrower, for each school year of service for which a deferment is requested, must provide to the lender—

(i) A statement by the chief administrative officer of the public or nonprofit private elementary or secondary school in which the borrower is teaching, certifying that the borrower is employed as a full-time teacher; and

(ii) A certification that he or she is teaching in a teacher shortage area designated by the Secretary as provided in paragraphs (q)(5) through (7) of this section, as described in paragraph (q)(2) of this section.

(2) In order to satisfy the requirement for certification that a borrower is teaching in a teacher shortage area designated by the Secretary, a borrower must do one of the following:

(i) If the borrower is teaching in a State in which the Chief State School Officer has complied with paragraph (q)(3) of this section and provides an annual listing of designated teacher shortage areas to the State's chief administrative officers whose schools are affected by the Secretary's designations, the borrower may obtain a certification that he or she is teaching in a teacher shortage area from his or her school's chief administrative officer.

(ii) If a borrower is teaching in a State in which the Chief State School Officer has not complied with paragraph (q)(3) of this section or does not provide an annual listing of designated teacher shortage areas to the State's chief administrative officers whose schools are affected by the Secretary's designations, the borrower must obtain certification that he or she is teaching in a teacher shortage area from the Chief State School Officer for the State in which the borrower is teaching.

(3) In the case of a State in which borrowers wish to obtain certifications as provided for in paragraph (q)(2)(i) of this section, the State's Chief State School Officer must first have notified the Secretary, by means of a one-time written assurance, that he or she provides annually to the State's chief administrative officers whose schools are affected by the Secretary's designations and the guaranty agency for that State, a listing of the teacher shortage areas designated by the Secretary as provided for in paragraph (q)(5) through (7) of this section.

(4) If a borrower who receives a deferment continues to teach in the same teacher shortage areas as that in which he or she was teaching when the deferment was originally granted, the borrower shall, at the borrower's request, continue to receive the deferment for those subsequent years, up to the three-year maximum deferment period, even if his or her position does not continue to be within an area designated by the Secretary as a teacher shortage area in those subsequent years. To continue to receive the deferment in a subsequent year under this paragraph, the borrower shall provide the lender with a statement by the chief administrative officer of the public or nonprofit private elementary or secondary

school that employs the borrower, certifying that the borrower continues to be employed as a full-time teacher in the same teacher shortage area for which the deferment was received for the previous year.

(5) For purposes on this section a teacher shortage area is—

(i)(A) A geographic region of the State in which there is a shortage of elementary or secondary school teachers; or

(B) A specific grade level or academic, instructional, subject-matter, or discipline classification in which there is a statewide shortage of elementary or secondary school teachers; and

(ii) Designated by the Secretary under paragraphs (q)(6) or (q)(7) of this section.

(6)(i) In order for the Secretary to designate on or more teacher shortage areas in a State for a school year, the Chief State School Officer shall by January 1 of the calendar year in which the school year begins, and in accordance with objective written standards, propose teacher shortage areas to the Secretary for designation. With respect to private nonprofit schools included in the recommendation, the Chief State School Officer shall consult with appropriate officials of the private nonprofit schools in the State prior to submitting the recommendation.

(ii) In identifying teacher shortage areas to propose for designation under paragraph (q)(6)(i) of this section, the Chief State School Officer shall consider data from the school year in which the recommendation is to be made, unless the data is not yet available, in which case he or she may use data from the immediately preceding school year, with respect to—

(A) Teaching positions that are unfilled;

(B) Teaching positions that are filled by teachers who are certified by irregular, provisional, temporary, or emergency certification; and

(C) Teaching positions that are filled by teachers who are certified, but who are teaching in academic subject areas other than their area of preparation.

(iii) If the total number of unduplicated full-time equivalent (FTE) elementary or secondary teaching positions identified under paragraph (q)(6)(ii) of this section in the shortage areas proposed by the State for designation does not exceed 5 percent of the total number of FTE elementary and secondary teaching positions in the State, the Secretary designates those areas as teacher shortage areas.

(iv) If the total number of unduplicated FTE elementary and secondary teaching positions identified under paragraph (q)(6)(ii) of this section in the shortage areas proposed by the State for designation exceeds 5 percent of the total number of elementary and secondary FTE teaching positions in the State, the Chief State School Officer shall submit, with the list of proposes areas, supporting documentation showing the methods used for identifying shortage areas, and an explanation of the reasons why the Secretary should nevertheless designate all of the proposed areas as teacher shortage areas. The explanation must include a ranking of the proposed shortage areas according to priority, to assist the Secretary in determining which areas should be designated. The Secretary, after considering the explanation, determines which shortage areas to designate as teacher shortage areas.

(7) A Chief State School Officer may submit to the Secretary for approval an alternative written procedure to the one described in paragraph (q)(6) of this section, for the Chief State School Officer to use to select the teacher shortage areas recommended to the Secretary for designation, and for the Secretary to use to choose the areas to be designated. If the Secretary approves the proposed alternative procedure, in writing, that procedure, once approved, may be used instead of the procedure described in paragraph (q)(6) of this section for designation of teacher shortage areas in that State.

(8) For purposes of paragraphs (q)(1) through (7) of this section—

(i) The definition of the term *school* in § 682.200(b) does not apply;

(ii) *Elementary school* means a day or residential school that provides elementary education, as determined under State law;

(iii) *Secondary school* means a day or residential school that provides secondary education, as determined under State law. In the absence of applicable State law, the Secretary may determine, with respect to that State, whether the term "secondary school" includes education beyond the twelfth grade;

(iv) *Teacher* means a professional who provides direct and personal services to students for their educational development through classroom teaching;

(v) *Chief State School Officer* means the highest ranking educational official for elementary and secondary education for the State;

(vi) *School year* means the period from July 1 of a calendar year through June 30 of the following calendar year;

(vii) *Teacher shortage area* means an area of specific grade, subject matter, or discipline classification, or a geographic area in which the Secretary determines that there is an inadequate supply of elementary or secondary school teachers; and

(viii) *Full-time equivalent* means the standard used by a State in defining full-time employment, but not less than 30 hours per week. For purposes of counting full-time equivalent teacher positions, a teacher working part of his or her total hours in a position that is designated as a teacher shortage area is counted on a pro rata basis corresponding to the percentage of his or her working hours spent in such a position.

(r) *Working-mother deferment.*

(1) To qualify for the working-mother deferment described in paragraph (b)(5)(iv) of this section, the borrower shall provide the lender with a statement certifying that she—

(i) Is the mother of a preschool-age child;

(ii) Entered or reentered the workforce not more than one year before the beginning date of the period for which the deferment is being sought;

(iii) Is currently engaged in full-time employment; and

(iv) Does not receive compensation that exceeds $1 per hour above the rate prescribed under section 6 of the Fair Labor Standards Act of 1938 (the Federal minimum wage).

(2) In addition to the certification required under paragraph (r)(1) of this section, the borrower shall provide to the lender documents demonstrating the age of her child (e.g., a birth certifi-

cate) and the rate of her compensation (e.g., a pay stub showing her hourly rate of pay).

(3) For purposes of this paragraph—

(i)   A preschool-age child is one who has not yet enrolled in first grade or a higher grade in elementary school; and

(ii) Full-time employment involves at least 30 hours of work a week and is expected to last at least 3 months.

(s) *Deferments for new borrowers on or after July 1, 1993—*

(1) *General.* A new borrower who receives an FFEL Program loan first disbursed on or after July 1, 1993 is entitled to receive deferments under paragraphs (s)(2) through (s)(6) of this section. For purposes of paragraphs (s)(2) through (s)(6) of this section, a "new borrower" is an individual who has no outstanding principal or interest balance on an FFEL Program loan as of July 1, 1993 or on the date he or she obtains a loan on or after July 1, 1993. This term also includes a borrower who obtains a Federal Consolidation Loan on or after July 1, 1993 if the borrower has no other outstanding FFEL Program loan when the Consolidation Loan was made.

(2) *In-school deferment.* An eligible borrower is entitled to a deferment based on the borrower's at least half-time study in accordance with the rules prescribed in § 682.210(c), except that the borrower is not required to obtain a Stafford or SLS loan for the period of enrollment covered by the deferment.

(3) *Graduate fellowship deferment.* An eligible borrower is entitled to a graduate fellowship deferment in accordance with the rules prescribed in § 682.210(d).

(4) *Rehabilitation training program deferment.* An eligible borrower is entitled to a rehabilitation training program deferment in accordance with the rules prescribed in § 682.210(e).

(5) *Unemployment deferment.* An eligible borrower is entitled to an unemployment deferment in accordance with the rules prescribed in § 682.210(h) for periods that, collectively, do not exceed 3 years.

(6) *Economic hardship deferment.* An eligible borrower is entitled to an economic hardship deferment for periods of up to one year at a time that, collectively, do not exceed 3 years (except that a borrower who receives a deferment under paragraph (s)(6)(vi) of this section is entitled to an economic hardship deferment for the lesser of the borrower's full term of service in the Peace Corps or the borrower's remaining period of economic hardship deferment eligibility under the 3-year maximum), if the borrower provides documentation satisfactory to the lender showing that the borrower is within any of the categories described in paragraphs (s)(6)(I) through (s)(6)(vi) of this section.

(i)   Has been granted an economic hardship deferment under either the Direct Loan or Federal Perkins Loan Programs for the period of time for which the borrower has requested an economic hardship deferment for his or her FFEL loan.

(ii) Is receiving payment under a Federal or State public assistance program, such as Aid to Families with Dependent Children, Supplemental Security Income, Food Stamps, or State general public assistance.

(iii) Is working full-time and has a monthly income that does not exceed the greater of (as calculated on a monthly basis)—

(A) The minimum wage rate described in section 6 of the Fair Labor Standards Act of 1938; or

(B) An amount equal to 100 percent of the poverty line for a family of two, as determined in accordance with

section 673(2) of the Community Services Block Grant Act.

(iv) Is working full-time and has a Federal education debt burden that equals or exceeds 20 percent of the borrower's monthly income, and that income, minus the borrower's Federal education debt burden, is less than 220 percent of the amount described in paragraph (s)(6)(iii) of this section.

(v)   Is not working full-time and has a monthly income that—

(A) Does not exceed twice the amount described in paragraph (s)(6)(iii) of this section; and

(B) After deducting an amount equal to the borrower's Federal education debt burden, the remaining amount of the borrower's income does not exceed the amount described in paragraph (s)(6)(iii) of this section.

(vi) Is serving as a volunteer in the Peace Corps.

(vii) In determining a borrower's Federal education debt burden for purposes of an economic hardship deferment under paragraphs (s)(6)(iv) and (v) of this section, the lender shall—

(A) If the Federal postsecondary education loan is scheduled to be repaid in 10 years or less, use the actual monthly payment amount (or a proportional share if the payments are due less frequently than monthly);

(B) If the Federal postsecondary education loan is scheduled to be repaid in more than 10 years, use a monthly payment amount (or a proportional share if the payments are due less frequently than monthly) that would have been due on the loan if the loan had been scheduled to be repaid in 10 years; and

(C) Require the borrower to provide evidence that would enable the lender to determine the amount of the monthly payments that would have been owed by the borrower during the deferment period.

(viii) For an initial period of deferment granted under paragraphs (s)(6)(iii) through (v) of this section, the lender must require the borrower to submit evidence showing the amount of the borrower's monthly income.

(ix) To qualify for a subsequent period of deferment that begins less than one year after the end of a period of deferment under paragraphs (s)(6)(iii) through (v) of this section, the lender must require the borrower to submit evidence showing the amount of the borrower's monthly income or a copy of the borrower's most recently filed Federal income tax return.

(x)   For purposes of paragraph (s)(6) of this section, a borrower's monthly income is the gross amount of income received by the borrower from employment and from other sources, or one-twelfth of the borrower's adjusted gross income, as recorded on the borrower's most recently filed Federal income tax return.

(xi) For purposes of paragraph (s)(6) of this section, a borrower is considered to be working full-time if the borrower is expected to be employed for at least three consecutive months at 30 hours per week.

(t) Military service deferments for loans for which the first disbursement is made on or after July, 1, 2001—

(1) A borrower who receives an FFEL Program loan first disbursed on or after July 1, 2001, may receive a military service

deferment for such loans for any period not to exceed 3 years during which the borrower is—

(i)   Serving on active duty during a war or other military operation or national emergency; or

(ii) Performing qualifying National Guard duty during a war or other military operation or national emergency.

(2) Serving on active duty during a war or other military operation or national emergency means service by an individual who is—

(i)   A Reserve of an Armed Force ordered to active duty under 10 U.S.C. 12301(a), 12301(g), 12302, 12304 or 12306;

(ii) A retired member of an Armed Force ordered to active duty under 10 U.S.C. 688 for service in connection with a war or other military operation or national emergency, regardless of the location at which such active duty service is performed; or

(iii) Any other member of an Armed Force on active duty in connection with such emergency or subsequent actions or conditions who has been assigned to a duty station at a location other than the location at which member is normally assigned.

(3) Qualifying National Guard duty during a war or other operation or national emergency means service as a member of the National Guard on full-time National Guard duty, as defined in 10 U.S.C. 101(d)(5), under a call to active service authorized by the President or the Secretary of Defense for a period of more than 30 consecutive days under 32 U.S.C. 502(f) in connection with a war, other military operation, or national emergency declared by the President and supported by Federal funds.

(4) Payments made by or on behalf of a borrower during a period for which the borrower qualified for a military service deferment are not refunded.

(5) A borrower is eligible for a military service deferment on a Federal Consolidation Loan only if the borrower meets the conditions described in this section and all of the title IV loans included in the Consolidation Loan were first disbursed on or after July 1, 2001.

(6) As used in this section—

(i)   Active duty means active duty as defined in 10 U.S.C. 101(d)(1) except that it does not include active duty for training or attendance at a service school;

(ii) Military operation means a contingency operation as defined in 10 U.S.C. 101(a)(13); and

(iii) National emergency means the national emergency by reason of certain terrorist attacks declared by the President on September 14, 2001, or subsequent national emergencies declared by the President by reason of terrorist attacks.

(Approved by the Office of Management and Budget under control number 1845-0020)

(Authority: 20 U.S.C. 1077, 1078, 1078-1, 1078-2, 1078-3, 1082, 1085)

[58 Fed. Reg. 9120, Feb. 19, 1993; 59 Fed. Reg. 25746, May 17, 1994; 59 Fed. Reg. 33594, June 29, 1994; 59 Fed. Reg. 61215, Nov. 29, 1994; 60 Fed. Reg. 30788, June 12, 1995; 60 Fed. Reg. 32912, June 26, 1995; 60 Fed. Reg. 61756, Dec. 1, 1995; 61 Fed. Reg. 16718, April 17, 1996; 64 Fed. Reg. 18977, April 16, 1999; 64 Fed. Reg. 57531, Oct. 25, 1999; 64 Fed. Reg. 58626, Oct. 29, 1999; 64 Fed. Reg. 58958, Nov. 1, 1999; 65 Fed. Reg. 65619, Nov.

1, 2000; 66 Fed. Reg. 34763, June 29, 2001; 67 Fed. Reg. 67078, Nov. 1, 2002; 68 Fed. Reg. 75427, Dec. 31, 2003; 71 Fed. Reg. 45666, Sept. 8, 2006]

§ 682.211 Forbearance.

(a)(1) The Secretary encourages a lender to grant forbearance for the benefit of a borrower or endorser in order to prevent the borrower or endorser from defaulting on the borrower's or endorser's repayment obligation, or to permit the borrower or endorser to resume honoring that obligation after default. *Forbearance* means permitting the temporary cessation of payments, allowing an extension of time for making payments, or temporarily accepting smaller payments than previously were scheduled.

(2) Subject to paragraph (g) of this section, a lender may grant forbearance to payments of principal and interest under paragraphs (b), (c), and (d) of this section only if—

(i)   The lender reasonably believes, and documents in the borrower's file, that the borrower or endorser intends to repay the loan but, due to poor health or other acceptable reasons, is currently unable to make scheduled payments; or

(ii) The borrower's payments of principal are deferred under § 682.210 and the Secretary does not pay interest benefits on behalf of the borrower under § 682.301.

(3) If two individuals are jointly liable for repayment of a PLUS loan or a Consolidation loan, the lender may grant forbearance on repayment of the loan only if the ability of both individuals to make scheduled payments has been impaired based on the same or differing conditions.

(4) Except as provided in paragraph (f)(10) of this section, if payments of interest are forborne, they may be capitalized as provided in § 682.202(b).

(b) A lender may grant forbearance if—

(1) The lender and the borrower or endorser agree to the terms of the forbearance and, unless the agreement was in writing, the lender sends, within 30 days, a notice to the borrower or endorser confirming the terms of the forbearance and records the terms of the forbearance in the borrower's file; or

(2) In the case of forbearance of interest during a period of deferment, if the lender informs the borrower at the time the deferment is granted that interest payments are to be forborne.

(c) A lender may grant forbearance for a period of up to one year at a time if both the borrower or endorser and an authorized official of the lender agree to the terms of the forbearance. If the lender and the borrower or endorser agree to the terms orally, the lender must notify the borrower or endorser of the terms within 30 days of that agreement.

(d) A guaranty agency may authorize a lender to grant forbearance to permit a borrower or endorser to resume honoring the agreement to repay the debt after default but prior to claim payment. The terms of the forbearance agreement in this situation must include a new signed agreement to repay the debt.

(e) Except in the case of forbearance of interest payments during a deferment period, if a forbearance involves the postponement of all payments, the lender must contact the borrower or endorser at least once every six months during the period of forbearance to inform the borrower or endorser of—

(1) The outstanding obligation to repay;

(2) The amount of the unpaid principal balance and any unpaid interest that has accrued on the loan;

(3) The fact that interest will accrue on the loan for the full term of the forbearance; and

(4) The borrower's or endorser's option to discontinue the forbearance at any time.

(f) A lender may grant forbearance, upon notice to the borrower or if applicable, the endorser, with respect to payments of interest and principal that are overdue or would be due—

(1) For a properly granted period of deferment for which the lender leans the borrower did not qualify;

(2) Upon the beginning of an authorized deferment period under § 682.210, or an administrative forbearance period as specified under paragraph (f)(11) or (i)(2) of this section;

(3) For the period beginning when the borrower entered repayment without the lender's knowledge until the first payment due date was established;

(4) For the period prior to the borrower's filing of a bankruptcy petition as provided in § 682.402(f);

(5) For the periods described in § 682.402(c) in regard to the borrower's total and permanent disability;

(6) For a period not to exceed an additional 60 days after the lender has suspended collection activity for the initial 60-day period required pursuant to § 682.211(i)(6) and § 682.402(b)(3), when the lender receives reliable information that the borrower (or student in the case of a parent PLUS loan) has died;

(7) For periods necessary for the Secretary or guaranty agency to determine the borrower's eligibility for discharge of the loan because of an unpaid refund, attendance at a closed school or false certification of loan eligibility, pursuant to § 682.402(d) or (e), or the borrower's or, if applicable, endorser's bankruptcy, pursuant to § 682.402(f);

(8) For a period of delinquency at the time a loan is sold or transferred, if the borrower or endorser is less than 60 days delinquent on the loan at the time of sale or transfer;

(9) For a period of delinquency that may remain after a borrower ends a period of deferment or mandatory forbearance until the next due date, which can be no later than 60 days after the period ends;

(10) For a period not to exceed 60 days necessary for the lender to collect and process documentation supporting the borrower's request for a deferment, forbearance, change in repayment plan, or consolidation loan. Interest that accrues during this period is not capitalized; or

(11) For a period not to exceed 3 months when the lender determines that a borrower's ability to make payments has been adversely affected by a natural disaster, a local or national emergency as declared by the appropriate government agency, or a military mobilization.

(g) In granting a forbearance under this section, except for a forbearance under paragraph (i)(5) of this section, a lender shall grant a temporary cessation of payments, unless the borrower chooses another form of forbearance subject to paragraph (a)(1) of this section.

(h) *Mandatory forbearance.*

(1) Medical or dental interns or residents. Upon receipt of a request and sufficient supporting documentation, as described in § 682.210(n), from a borrower serving in a medical or dental internship or residency program, a lender shall grant increments (or a lesser period equal to the actual period during which the borrower is eligible) if the borrower has exhausted his or her eligibility for a deferment under § 682.210(n), or the borrower's promissory note does not provide for such a deferment—

(i) For the length of time remaining in the borrower's medical or dental internship or residency that must be successfully completed before the borrower may begin professional practice or service; or

(ii) For the length of time that the borrower is serving in a medical or dental internship or residency program leading to a degree or certificate awarded by an institution of higher education, a hospital, or a health care facility that offers postgraduate training.

(2) Borrowers who are not medical or dental interns or residents, and endorsers. Upon receipt of a request and sufficient supporting documentation from an endorser (if applicable), or from a borrower (other than a borrower who is serving in a medical or dental internship or residency described in paragraph (h)(1) of this section), a lender shall grant forbearance—

(i) In increments up to one year, for periods that collectively do not exceed three years, if—

(A) The borrower or endorser is currently obligated to make payments on Title IV loans; and

(B) The amount of those payments each month (or a proportional share if the payments are due less frequently than monthly) is collectively equal to or greater than 20 percent of the borrower's or endorser's total monthly income;

(ii) In yearly increments (or a lesser period equal to the actual period during which the borrower is eligible) for as long as a borrower—

(A) Is serving in a national service position for which the borrower receives a national service educational award under the National and Community Service Trust Act of 1993;

(B) Is performing the type of service that would qualify the borrower for a partial repayment of his or her loan under the Student Loan Repayment Programs administered by the Department of Defense under 10 U.S.C. 2171; or

(C) Is performing the type of service that would qualify the borrower for loan forgiveness and associated forbearance under the requirements of the teacher loan forgiveness program in § 682.215.

(3) Written agreement. The terms of the forbearance must be agreed to in writing—

(i) By the lender and the borrower for a forbearance under paragraphs (h)(1) or (h)(2)(ii)(A) of this section; or

(ii) By the lender and the borrower or endorser for a forbearance under paragraph (h)(2)(i) of this section.

(4) Documentation.

(i) Before granting a forbearance to a borrower or endorser under paragraph (h)(2)(i) of this section, the lender shall require the borrower or endorser to submit at least the following documentation:

(A) Evidence showing the amount of the most recent total monthly gross income received by the borrower or endorser from employment and from other sources; and

(B) Evidence showing the amount of the monthly payments owed by the borrower or endorser to other entities for the most recent month for the borrower's or endorser's Title IV loans.

(ii) Before granting a forbearance to a borrower or endorser under paragraph (h)(2)(ii)(B) of this section, the lender shall require the borrower or endorser to submit documentation showing the beginning and ending dates that the Department of Defense considers the borrower to be eligible for a partial repayment of his or her loan under the Student Loan Repayment Programs.

(iii) Before granting a forbearance to a borrower under paragraph (h)(2)(ii)(C) of this section, the lender must require the borrower to—

(A) Submit documentation for the period of the annual forbearance request showing the beginning and anticipated ending dates that the borrower is expected to perform, for that year, the type of service described in § 682.215(c); and

(B) Certify the borrower's intent to satisfy the requirements of § 682.215(c).

(Approved by the Office of Management and Budget under control number 1845-0020)

(i) Mandatory administrative forbearance.

(1) The lender shall grant a mandatory administrative forbearance for the periods specified in paragraph (i)(2) of this section until the lender is notified by the Secretary or a guaranty agency that the forbearance period no longer applies. The lender may not require a borrower who is eligible for a forbearance under paragraph (i)(2)(ii) of this section to submit a request or supporting documentation, but shall require a borrower (or endorser, if applicable) who requests forbearance because of a military mobilization to provide documentation showing that he or she is subject to a military mobilization as described in paragraph (i)(4) of this section.

(2) The lender is not required to notify the borrower (or endorser, if applicable) at the time the forbearance is granted, but shall grant a forbearance to a borrower or endorser during a period, and the 30 days following the period, when the lender is notified by the Secretary that—

(i) Exceptional circumstances exist, such as a local or national emergency or military mobilization; or

(ii) The geographical area in which the borrower or endorser resides has been designated a disaster area by the president of the United States or Mexico, the prime minister of Canada, or by a governor of a state.

(3) As soon as feasible, or by the date specified by the Secretary, the lender shall notify the borrower (or endorser, if applicable) that the lender has granted a forbearance and the date that payments should resume. The lender's notification shall state that the borrower or endorser—

(i) May decline the forbearance and continue to be obligated to make scheduled payments; or

(ii) Consents to making payments in accordance with the lender's notification if the forbearance is not declined.

(4) For purposes of paragraph (i)(2)(i) of this section, the term "military mobilization" shall mean a situation in which the Department of Defense orders members of the National Guard or Reserves to active duty under sections 688, 12301(a), 12301(g), 12302, 12304, and 12306 of title 10, United States Code. This term also includes the assignment of other members of the Armed Forces to duty stations at locations other than the locations at which they were normally assigned, only if the military mobilization involved the activation of the National Guard or Reserves.

(5) The lender shall grant a mandatory administrative forbearance to a borrower (or endorser, if applicable) during a period when the borrower (or endorser, if applicable) is making payments for a period of—

(i) Up to 3 years of payments in cases where the effect of a variable interest rate on a standard or graduated repayment schedule would result in a loan not being repaid within the maximum repayment term; or

(ii) Up to 5 years of payments in cases where the effect of decreased installment amounts paid under an income-sensitive repayment schedule would result in the loan not being repaid within the maximum repayment term.

(6) The lender shall grant a mandatory administrative forbearance to a borrower for a period not to exceed 60 days after the lender receives reliable information indicating that the borrower (or student in the case of a PLUS loan) has died, until the lender receives documentation of death pursuant to § 682.402(b)(3).

(Approved by the Office of Management and Budget under control number 1845-0020)

(Authority: 20 U.S.C. 1077, 1078, 1078-1, 1078-2, 1078-3, 1080, 1082)

[58 Fed. Reg. 9120, Feb. 19, 1993; 59 Fed. Reg. 25746, May 17, 1994; 59 Fed. Reg. 33595, June 29, 1994; 60 Fed. Reg. 30788, June 12, 1995; 60 Fed. Reg. 32912, June 26, 1995; 60 Fed. Reg. 61756, Dec. 1, 1995; 61 Fed. Reg. 16718, April 17, 1996; 64 Fed. Reg. 18977, April 16, 1999; 64 Fed. Reg. 58626, Oct. 29, 1999; 64 Fed. Reg. 58959, Nov. 1, 1999; 65 Fed. Reg. 65627, Nov. 1, 2000; 66 Fed. Reg. 34763, June 29, 2001; 66 Fed. Reg. 44007, Aug. 21, 2001; 67 Fed. Reg. 67079, Nov. 1, 2002; 68 Fed. Reg. 75429, Dec. 31, 2003; 71 Fed. Reg. 45666, Sept. 8, 2006; 71 Fed. Reg. 45666, Sept. 8, 2006]

§ 682.402 Death, disability, closed school, false certification, unpaid refunds, and bankruptcy payments.

(a) *General.*

(1) Rules governing the payment of claims based on filing for relief in bankruptcy, and discharge of loans due to death, total and permanent disability, attendance at a school that closes, false certification by a school of a borrower's eligibility for a loan, and unpaid refunds by a school are set forth in this section.

(2) If a Consolidation loan was obtained jointly by a married couple, the amount of the Consolidation loan that is discharged if one of the borrowers dies or becomes totally and permanently disabled is equal to the portion of the outstanding balance of the Consolidation loan, as of the date the borrower died or became totally and permanently disabled, attributable to any of that borrower's loans that would have been eligible for discharge.

(3) If a PLUS loan was obtained by two parents as co-makers, and only one of the borrowers dies, becomes totally and permanently disabled, has collection of his or her loan obligation stayed by a bankruptcy filing, or has that obligation discharged in bankruptcy, the other borrower remains obligated to repay the loan unless that borrower would qualify for discharge of the loan under these regulations.

(4) Except for a borrower's loan obligation discharged by the Secretary under the false certification discharge provision of paragraphs paragraph (e)(1)(ii) or (iii) of this section, a loan qualifies for payment under this section and as provided in paragraph (h)(1)(iv) of this section, only to the extent that the loan is legally enforceable under applicable law by the holder of the loan.

(5) For purposes of this section—

(i) The legal enforceability of a loan is conclusively determined on the basis of a ruling by a court or administrative tribunal of competent jurisdiction with respect to that loan, or a ruling with respect to another loan in a judgment that collaterally estops the holder from contesting the enforceability of the loan;

(ii) A loan is conclusively determined to be legally unenforceable to the extent that the guarantor determines, pursuant to an objection presented in a proceeding conducted in connection with credit bureau reporting, tax refund offset, wage garnishment, or in any other administrative proceeding, that the loan is not legally enforceable; and

(iii) If an objection has been raised by the borrower or another party about the legal enforceability of the loan and no determination has been made under paragraph (a)(5)(i) or (ii) of this section, the Secretary may authorize the payment of a claim under this section under conditions the Secretary considers appropriate. If the Secretary determines in that or any other case that a claim was paid under this section with respect to a loan that was not a legally enforceable obligation of the borrower, the recipient of that payment must refund that amount of the payment to the Secretary.

(b) *Death.*

(1) If an individual borrower dies, or the student for whom a parent received a PLUS loan dies, the obligation of the borrower and any endorser to make any further payments on the loan is discharged.

(2) A discharge of a loan based on the death of the borrower (or student in the case of a PLUS loan) must be based on an original or certified copy of the death certificate. Under exceptional circumstances and on a case-by-case basis, the chief executive officer of the guaranty agency may approve a discharge based upon other reliable documentation supporting the discharge request.

(3) After receiving reliable information indicating that the borrower (or student) has died, the lender must suspend any collection activity against the borrower and any endorser for up to 60 days and promptly request the documentation described in paragraph (b)(2) of this section. If additional time is required to obtain the documentation, the period of suspension of collection activity may be extended up to an additional 60 days. If the lender is not able to obtain an original or certified copy of the death certificate or other documentation acceptable to the guaranty agency, under the provisions of paragraph (b)(2) of this section, during the period of suspension, the lender must resume collection activity from the point that it had been discontinued. The lender is deemed to have exercised forbearance as to repayment of the loan during the period when collection activity was suspended.

(4) Once the lender has determined under paragraph (b)(2) of this section that the borrower (or student) has died, the lender may not attempt to collect on the loan from the borrower's estate or from any endorser.

(5) The lender shall return to the sender any payments received from the estate or paid on behalf of the borrower after the date of the borrower's (or student's) death.

(6) In the case of a Federal Consolidation Loan that includes a Federal PLUS or Direct PLUS loan borrowed for a dependent who has died, the obligation of the borrower or any endorser to make any further payments on the portion of the outstanding balance of the Consolidation Loan attributable to the Federal PLUS or Direct

PLUS loan is discharged as of the date of the dependent's death.

(c) *Total and permanent disability.*

(1)(i) If the Secretary has made an initial determination that the borrower is totally and permanently disabled, as defined in § 682.200(b), the loan is conditionally discharged for up to three years from the date that the borrower became totally and permanently disabled, as certified by a physician. The Secretary suspends collection activity on the loan from the date of the initial determination of total and permanent disability until the end of the conditional period. If the borrower satisfies the criteria for a total and permanent disability discharge during and at the end of the conditional discharge period, the balance of the loan is discharged at the end of the conditional discharge period and any payments received after the date the borrower became totally and permanently disabled as certified under § 682.402(c)(2), are returned to the sender.

(ii) A borrower satisfies the criteria for a discharge of a loan based on a total and permanent disability if, during and at the end of the three-year period described in paragraph (c)(1)(i) of this section—

(A) The borrower's annual earnings from employment do not exceed 100 percent of the poverty line for a family of two, as determined in accordance with the Community Service Block Grant Act; and

(B) The borrower does not receive a new loan under the Perkins, FFEL, or Direct Loan programs, except for a FFEL or Direct Consolidation loan that does not include any loans that are in a conditional discharge status.

(iii) Except as provided in paragraph (c)(1)(iv)(A) of this section, a borrower is not considered totally and permanently disabled based on a condition that existed at the time the loan was made unless the borrower's condition substantially deteriorated.

(iv)(A) For a Consolidation Loan, a borrower is considered totally and permanently disabled if he or she would be considered totally and permanently disabled under paragraphs (c)(1)(i) through (iii) of this section for all of the loans that were included in the Consolidation Loan if those loans had not been consolidated.

(B) For the purposes of discharging a loan under paragraph (c)(1)(iv)(A) of this section, provisions in paragraphs (c)(1)(i) through (iii) of this section apply to each loan included in the Consolidation Loan, even if the loan is not a FFEL Program loan.

(C) If requested, a borrower seeking to discharge a loan obligation under paragraph (c)(1)(iv)(A) of this section must provide the lender with the disbursement dates of the underlying loans if the lender does not possess that information.

(2) After being notified by the borrower or the borrower's representative that the borrower claims to be totally and permanently disabled, the lender promptly requests that the borrower or the borrower's representative submit, on a form approved by the Secretary, a certification by a physician, who is a doctor of medicine or osteopathy and legally authorized to practice in a State, that the borrower is totally and permanently disabled as defined in § 682.200(b).

(3) The lender must continue collection activities until it receives either the certification of total and permanent disability from

a physician or a letter from a physician stating that the certification has been requested and that additional time is needed to determine if the borrower is totally and permanently disabled. Except as provided in paragraph (c)(5) or (c)(7) of this section, after receiving the physician's certification or letter the lender may not attempt to collect from the borrower or any endorser.

(4) The lender must submit a disability claim to the guaranty agency if the borrower submits a certification by a physician and the lender makes a determination that the certification supports the conclusion that the borrower meets the criteria for a total and permanent disability discharge, as defined in § 682.200(b).

(5) If the lender determines that a borrower who claims to be totally and permanently disabled is not totally and permanently disabled, or if the lender does not receive the physician's certification of total and permanent disability within 60 days of the receipt of the physician's letter requesting additional time, as described in paragraph (c)(3) of this section, the lender must resume collection and is deemed to have exercised forbearance of payment of both principal and interest from the date collection activity was suspended. The lender may capitalize, in accordance with § 682.202(b), any interest accrued and not paid during that period.

(6) The guaranty agency must pay a claim submitted by the lender if the guaranty agency has reviewed the application and determined that it is complete and that it supports the conclusion that the borrower meets the criteria for a total and permanent disability discharge, as defined in § 682.200(b).

(7) If the guaranty agency does not pay the disability claim, the guaranty agency must return the claim to the lender with an explanation of the basis for the agency's denial of the claim. Upon receipt of the returned claim, the lender must notify the borrower that the application for a disability discharge has been denied, provide the basis for the denial, and inform the borrower that the lender will resume collection on the loan. The lender is deemed to have exercised forbearance of both principal and interest from the date collection activity was suspended until the first payment due date. The lender may capitalize, in accordance with § 682.202(b), any interest accrued and not paid during that period.

(8) If the guaranty agency pays the disability claim, the lender must notify the borrower that the loan will be assigned to the Secretary for determination of eligibility for a total and permanent disability discharge.

(9) After receiving a claim payment from the guaranty agency, the lender must forward to the guaranty agency any payments subsequently received from or on behalf of the borrower.

(10) The Secretary reimburses the guaranty agency for a disability claim paid to the lender after the agency pays the claim to the lender.

(11) The guaranty agency must assign the loan to the Secretary after the guaranty agency pays the disability claim.

(12) If the Secretary determines that the certification and information provided by the borrower do not support the conclusion that the borrower meets the criteria for a total and permanent disability discharge, the Secretary notifies the borrower that the application for a disability discharge has been denied, and that the loan is due and payable under the terms of the promissory note.

(13) If the Secretary makes an initial determination that the borrower is totally and permanently disabled, the Secretary notifies the borrower that the loan is conditionally discharged and that the conditional discharge period will last for up to three years after the date the borrower became totally and permanently disabled as certified under § 682.402(c)(2). The notification identifies the conditions of the conditional discharge period specified in paragraphs (c)(13) through (c)(16) of this section and specifies that all or part of the three-year period may predate the Secretary's initial determination.

(14) During the conditional discharge period, the borrower—

(i)   Is not required to make any payments on the loan;

(ii) Is not considered delinquent or in default on the loan, unless the borrower was delinquent or in default at the time the conditional discharge was granted;

(iii) Must promptly notify the Secretary of any changes in address or phone number;

(iv) Must promptly notify the Secretary if the borrower's annual earnings from employment exceed the amount specified in paragraph (c)(1)(ii)(A) of this section; and

(v)   Must provide the Secretary, upon request, with additional documentation or information related to the borrower's eligibility for discharge under this section.

(15) If, during and at the end of the conditional discharge period, the borrower continues to satisfy the eligibility criteria for a total and permanent disability discharge, as described in § 682.402(c)(1)(ii), the balance of the loan is discharged.

(16) If, at any time during the three-year conditional discharge period, the borrower does not continue to meet the eligibility requirements for a total and permanent disability discharge, the Secretary resumes collection activity on the loan. The Secretary does not require the borrower to pay any interest that accrued on the loan from the date of the initial determination described in paragraph (c)(13) of this section through the end of the conditional discharge period.

(d) *Closed school.*

(1) *General.*

(i)   The Secretary reimburses the holder of a loan received by a borrower on or after January 1, 1986, and discharges the borrower's obligation with respect to the loan in accordance with the provisions of paragraph (d) of this section, if the borrower (or the student for whom a parent received a PLUS loan) could not complete the program of study for which the loan was intended because the school at which the borrower (or student) was enrolled, closed, or the borrower (or student) withdrew from the school not more than 90 days prior to the date the school closed. This 90-day period may be extended if the Secretary determines that exceptional circumstances related to a school's closing would justify an extension.

(ii) For purposes of the closed school discharge authorized by this section—

(A) A school's closure date is the date that the school ceases to provide educational instruction in all programs, as determined by the Secretary;

(B) The term "borrower" includes all endorsers on a loan; and

(C) A "school" means a school's main campus or any location or branch of the main campus, regardless of whether the school or its location or branch is considered eligible.

(2) *Relief available pursuant to discharge.*

(i)   Discharge under paragraph (d) of this section relieves the borrower of an existing or past obligation to repay the loan and any charges imposed or costs incurred by the holder with respect to the loan that the borrower is, or was otherwise obligated to pay.

(ii) A discharge of a loan under paragraph (d) of this section qualifies the borrower for reimbursement of amounts paid voluntarily or through enforced collection on a loan obligation discharged under paragraph (d) of this section.

(iii) A borrower who has defaulted on a loan discharged under paragraph (d) of this section is not regarded as in default on the loan after discharge, and is eligible to receive assistance under the Title IV, HEA programs.

(iv) A discharge of a loan under paragraph (d) of this section must be reported by the loan holder to all credit reporting agencies to which the holder previously reported the status of the loan, so as to delete all adverse credit history assigned to the loan.

(3) *Borrower qualification for discharge.* Except as provided in paragraph (d)(8) of this section, in order to qualify for a discharge of a loan under paragraph (d) of this section, a borrower must submit a written request and sworn statement to the holder of the loan. The statement need not be notarized, but must be made by the borrower under the penalty of perjury, and, in the statement, the borrower must state—

(i) Whether the student has made a claim with respect to the school's closing with any third party, such as the holder of a performance bond or a tuition recovery program, and if so, the amount of any payment received by the borrower (or student) or credited to the borrower's loan obligation;

(ii) That the borrower (or the student for whom a parent received a PLUS loan)—

(A) Received, on or after January 1, 1986, the proceeds of any disbursement of a loan disbursed, in whole or in part, on or after January 1, 1986 to attend a school;

(B) Did not complete the educational program at that school because the school closed while the student was enrolled or on an approved leave of absence in accordance with § 682.605(c), or the student withdrew from the school not more than 90 days before the school closed; and

(C) Did not complete the program of study through a teach-out at another school or by transferring academic credits or hours earned at the closed school to another school;

(iii) That the borrower agrees to provide, upon request by the Secretary or the Secretary's designee, other documentation reasonably available to the borrower that demonstrates, to the satisfaction of the Secretary or the Secretary's designee, that the student meets the qualifications in paragraph (d) of this section; and

(iv) That the borrower agrees to cooperate with the Secretary or the Secretary's designee in enforcement actions in accordance with paragraph (d)(4) of this section, and to transfer any right to recovery against a third party in accordance with paragraph (d)(5) of this section.

(4) *Cooperation by borrower in enforcement actions.*

(i) In any judicial or administrative proceeding brought by the Secretary or the Secretary's designee to recover for amounts discharged under paragraph (d) of this section or to take other enforcement action with respect to the conduct on which those claims were based, a borrower who requests or receives a discharge under paragraph (d) of this section must cooperate with the Secretary of the Secretary's

designee. At the request of the Secretary or the Secretary's designee, and upon the Secretary's or the Secretary's designee's tendering to the borrower the fees and costs as are customarily provided in litigation to reimburse witnesses, the borrower shall—

(A) Provide testimony regarding any representation made by the borrower to support a request for discharge; and

(B) Produce any documentation reasonably available to the borrower with respect to those representations and any sworn statement required by the Secretary with respect to those representations and documents.

(ii) The Secretary revokes the discharge, or denies the request for discharge, of a borrower who—

(A) Fails to provide testimony, sworn statements, or documentation to support material representations made by the borrower to obtain the discharge; or

(B) Provides testimony, a sworn statement, or documentation that does not support the material representations made by the borrower to obtain the discharge.

(5) *Transfer to the Secretary of borrower's right of recovery against third parties.*

(i) Upon discharge under paragraph (d) of this section, the borrower is deemed to have assigned to and relinquished in favor of the Secretary any right to a loan refund (up to the amount discharged) that the borrower (or student) may have by contract or applicable law with respect to the loan or the enrollment agreement for the program for which the loan was received, against the school, its principals, affiliates and their successors, its sureties, and any private fund, including the portion of a public fund that represents funds received from a private party.

(ii) The provisions of paragraph (d) of this section apply notwithstanding any provision of State law that would otherwise restrict transfer of such rights by the borrower (or student), limit or prevent a transferee from exercising those rights, or establish procedures or a scheme of distribution that would prejudice the Secretary's ability to recover on those rights.

(iii) Nothing in this section shall be construed as limiting or foreclosing the borrower's (or student's) right to pursue legal and equitable relief regarding disputes arising from matters otherwise unrelated to the loan discharged.

(6) *Guaranty agency responsibilities—*

(i) *Procedures applicable if a school closed on or after January 1, 1986, but prior to June 13, 1994.*

(A) If a borrower received a loan for attendance at a school with a closure date on or after January 1, 1986, but prior to June 13, 1994, the loan may be discharged in accordance with the procedures specified in paragraph (d)(6)(i) of this section.

(B) If a loan subject to paragraph (d) of this section was discharged in part in accordance with the Secretary's "Closed School Policy" as authorized by section IV of Bulletin 89-G-159, the guaranty agency shall initiate the discharge of the remaining balance of the loan not later than August 13, 1994.

(C) A guaranty agency shall review its records and identify all schools that appear to have closed on or after January 1, 1986 and prior to June 13, 1994, and shall identify the loans made to any borrower (or student) who appears to have been enrolled at the school on the school closure date or who withdrew not more than 90 days prior to the closure date.

(D) A guaranty agency shall notify the Secretary immediately if it determines that a school not previously known to have closed appears to have closed, and, within 30 days of making that determination, notify all lenders participating in its program to suspend collection efforts against individuals with respect to loans made for attendance at the closed school, if the student to whom (or on whose behalf) a loan was made, appears to have been enrolled at the school on the closing date, or withdrew not more than 90 days prior to the date the school appears to have closed. Within 30 days after receiving confirmation of the date of a school's closure from the Secretary, the agency shall—

(1) Notify all lenders participating in its program to mail a discharge application explaining the procedures and eligibility criteria for obtaining a discharge and an explanation of the information that must be included in the sworn statement (which may be combined) to all borrowers who may be eligible for a closed school discharge; and

(2) Review the records of loans that it holds, identify the loans made to any borrower (or student) who appears to have been enrolled at the school on the school closure date or who withdrew not more than 90 days prior to the closure date, and mail a discharge application and an explanation of the information that must be included in the sworn statement (which may be combined) to the borrower. The application shall inform the borrower of the procedures and eligibility criteria for obtaining a discharge.

(E) If a loan identified under paragraph (d)(6)(i)(D)(2) of this section is held by the guaranty agency as a defaulted loan and the borrower's current address is known, the guaranty agency shall immediately suspend any efforts to collect from the borrower on any loan received for the program of study for which the loan was made (but may continue to receive borrower payments), and notify the borrower that the agency will provide additional information about the procedures for requesting a discharge after the agency has received confirmation from the Secretary that the school had closed.

(F) If a loan identified under paragraph (d)(6)(i)(D)(2) of this section is held by the guaranty agency as a defaulted loan and the borrower's current address is unknown, the agency shall, by June 13, 1995, further refine the list of borrowers whose loans are potentially subject to discharge under paragraph (d) of this section by consulting with representatives of the closed school, the school's licensing agency, accrediting agency, and other appropriate parties. Upon learning the new address of a borrower who would still be considered potentially eligible for a discharge, the guaranty agency shall, within 30 days after learning the borrower's new address, mail to the borrower a discharge application that meets the requirements of paragraph (d)(6)(i)(E) of this section.

(G) If the guaranty agency determines that a borrower identified in paragraph (d)(6)(i)(E) or (F) of this section has satisfied all of the conditions required for a discharge, the agency shall notify the borrower in writing of that determination within 30 days after making that determination.

(H) If the guaranty agency determines that a borrower identified in paragraph (d)(6)(i)(E) or (F) of this section does not qualify for a discharge, the agency shall notify the borrower in writing of that determination and the reasons for it within 30 days after the date the agency—

(1) Made that determination based on information available to the guaranty agency;

(2) Was notified by the Secretary that the school had not closed;

(3) Was notified by the Secretary that the school had closed on a date that was more than 90 days after the borrower (or student) withdrew from the school;

(4) Was notified by the Secretary that the borrower (or student) was ineligible for a closed school discharge for other reasons; or

(5) Received the borrower's completed application and sworn statement.

(I) If a borrower described in paragraph (d)(6)(i)(E) or (F) of this section fails to submit the written request and sworn statement described in paragraph (d)(3) of this section within 60 days of being notified of that option, the guaranty agency shall resume collection and shall be deemed to have exercised forbearance of payment of principal and interest from the date it suspended collection activity. The agency may capitalize, in accordance with § 682.202(b), any interest accrued and not paid during that period.

(J) A borrower's request for discharge may not be denied solely on the basis of failing to meet any time limits set by the lender, guaranty agency, or the Secretary.

(ii) *Procedures applicable if a school closed on or after June 13, 1994.*

(A) A guaranty agency shall notify the Secretary immediately whenever it becomes aware of reliable information indicating a school may have closed. The designated guaranty agency in the state in which the school is located shall promptly investigate whether the school has closed and, within 30 days after receiving information indicating that the school may have closed, report the results of its investigation to the Secretary concerning the date of the school's closure and whether a teach-out of the closed school's program was made available to students.

(B) If a guaranty agency determines that a school appears to have closed, it shall, within 30 days of making that determination, notify all lenders participating in its program to suspend collection efforts against individuals with respect to loans made for attendance at the closed school, if the student to whom (or on whose behalf) a loan was made, appears to have been enrolled at the school on the closing date, or withdrew not more than 90 days prior to the date the school appears to have closed. Within 30 days after receiving confirmation of the date of a school's closure from the Secretary, the agency shall—

(1) Notify all lenders participating in its program to mail

a discharge application explaining the procedures and eligibility criteria for obtaining a discharge and an explanation of the information that must be included in the sworn statement (which may be combined) to all borrowers who may be eligible for a closed school discharge; and

(2) Review the records of loans that it holds, identify the loans made to any borrower (or student) who appears to have been enrolled at the school on the school closure date or who withdrew not more than 90 days prior to the closure date, and mail a discharge application and an explanation of the information that must be included in the sworn statement (which may be combined) to the borrower. The application shall inform the borrower of the procedures and eligibility criteria for obtaining a discharge.

(C) If a loan identified under paragraph (d)(6)(ii)(B)(2) of this section is held by the guaranty agency as a defaulted loan and the borrower's current address is known, the guaranty agency shall immediately suspend any efforts to collect from the borrower on any loan received for the program of study for which the loan was made (but may continue to receive borrower payments), and notify the borrower that the agency will provide additional information about the procedures for requesting a discharge after the agency has received confirmation from the Secretary that the school had closed.

(D) If a loan identified under paragraph (d)(6)(ii)(B)(2) of this section is held by the guaranty agency as a defaulted loan and the borrower's current address is unknown, the agency shall, within one year after identifying the borrower, attempt to locate the borrower and further determine the borrower's potential eligibility for a discharge under paragraph (d) of this section by consulting with representatives of the closed school, the school's licensing agency, accrediting agency, and other appropriate parties. Upon learning the new address of a borrower who would still be considered potentially eligible for a discharge, the guaranty agency shall, within 30 days after learning the borrower's new address, mail to the borrower a discharge application that meets the requirements of paragraph (d)(6)(ii)(B) of this section.

(E) If the guaranty agency determines that a borrower identified in paragraph (d)(6)(ii)(C) or (D) of this section has satisfied all of the conditions required for a discharge, the agency shall notify the borrower in writing of that determination within 30 days after making that determination.

(F) If the guaranty agency determines that a borrower identified in paragraph (d)(6)(ii)(C) or (D) of this section does not qualify for a discharge, the agency shall notify the borrower in writing of that determination and the reasons for it within 30 days after the date the agency—

(1) Made that determination based on information available to the guaranty agency;

(2) Was notified by the Secretary that the school had not closed;

(3) Was notified by the Secretary that the school had closed on a date that was more than 90 days after the borrower (or student) withdrew from the school;

(4) Was notified by the Secretary that the borrower (or student) was ineligible for a closed school discharge for other reasons; or

(5) Received the borrower's completed application and sworn statement.

(G) Upon receipt of a closed school discharge claim filed by a lender, the agency shall review the borrower's request and supporting sworn statement in light of information available from the records of the agency and from other sources, including other guaranty agencies, state authorities, and cognizant accrediting associations, and shall take the following actions—

(1) If the agency determines that the borrower satisfies the requirements for discharge under paragraph (d) of this section, it shall pay the claim in accordance with § 682.402(h) not later than 90 days after the agency received the claim; or

(2) If the agency determines that the borrower does not qualify for a discharge, the agency shall, not later than 90 days after the agency received the claim, return the claim to the lender with an explanation of the reasons for its determination.

(H) If a borrower fails to submit the written request and sworn statement described in paragraph (d)(3) of this section within 60 days of being notified of that option, the lender or guaranty agency shall resume collection and shall be deemed to have exercised forbearance of payment of principal and interest from the date it suspended collection activity. The lender or guaranty agency may capitalize, in accordance with § 682.202(b), any interest accrued and not paid during that period.

(I) A borrower's request for discharge may not be denied solely on the basis of failing to meet any time limits set by the lender, guaranty agency, or the Secretary.

(7) *Lender responsibilities.*

(i) A lender shall comply with the requirements prescribed in paragraph (d) of this section. In the absence of specific instructions from a guaranty agency or the Secretary, if a lender receives information from a source it believes to be reliable indicating that an existing or former borrower may be eligible for a loan discharge under paragraph (d) of this section, the lender shall immediately notify the guaranty agency, and suspend any efforts to collect from the borrower on any loan received for the program of study for which the loan was made (but may continue to receive borrower payments).

(ii) If the borrower fails to submit the written request and sworn statement described in paragraph (d)(3) of this section within 60 days after being notified of that option, the lender shall resume collection and shall be deemed to have exercised forbearance of payment of principal and interest from the date the lender suspended collection activity. The lender may capitalize, in accordance with § 682.202(b), any interest accrued and not paid during that period.

(iii) The lender shall file a closed school claim with the guaranty agency in accordance with § 682.402(g) no later than 60 days after the lender receives the borrower's written request and sworn statement described in paragraph (d)(3) of this section. If a lender receives a payment made by or on behalf of the borrower on the loan after the lender files a claim on the loan with the guaranty agency, the lender shall forward the payment to the guaranty agency within 30 days of its receipt. The lender shall assist the guaranty agency and the borrower in determining whether the borrower is eligible for discharge of the loan.

(iv) Within 30 days after receiving reimbursement from the guaranty agency for a closed school claim, the lender shall notify the borrower that the loan obligation has been discharged, and request that all credit bureaus to which it previously reported the status of the loan delete all adverse credit history assigned to the loan.

(v) Within 30 days after being notified by the guaranty agency that the borrower's request for a closed school discharge has been denied, the lender shall resume collection and notify the borrower of the reasons for the denial. The lender shall be deemed to have exercised forbearance of payment of principal and interest from the date the lender suspended collection activity, and may capitalize, in accordance with § 682.202(b), any interest accrued and not paid during that period.

(8) *Discharge without an application.* A borrower's obligation to repay an FFEL Program loan may be discharged without an application from the borrower if the—

(i) Borrower received a discharge on a loan pursuant to 34 CFR 674.33(g) under the Federal Perkins Loan Program, or 34 CFR 685.213 under the William D. Ford Federal Direct Loan Program; or

(ii) The Secretary or the guaranty agency, with the Secretary's permission, determines that the borrower qualifies for a discharge based on information in the Secretary or guaranty agency's possession.

(e) *False certification by a school of a student's eligibility to borrow and unauthorized disbursements*—

(1) *General.*

(i) The Secretary reimburses the holder of a loan received by a borrower on or after January 1, 1986, and discharges a current or former borrower's obligation with respect to the loan in accordance with the provisions of paragraph (e) of this section, if the borrower's (or the student for whom a parent received a PLUS loan) eligibility to receive the loan was falsely certified by an eligible school. On or after July 1, 2006, the Secretary reimburses the holder of a loan, and discharges a borrower's obligation with respect to the loan in accordance with the provisions of paragraph (e) of this section, if the borrower's eligibility to receive the loan was falsely certified as a result of a crime of identity theft. For purposes of a false certification discharge, the term "borrower" includes all endorsers on a loan. A student's or other individual's eligibility to borrow shall be considered to have been falsely certified by the school if the school—

(A) Certified the student's eligibility for a FFEL Program loan on the basis of ability to benefit from its training and the student did not meet the applicable requirements described in 34 CFR Part 668 and section 484(d) of the Act, as applicable and as described in paragraph (e)(13) of this section; or

(B) Signed the borrower's name without authorization by the borrower on the loan application or promissory note.

(C) Certified the eligibility of an individual for an FFEL

Program loan as a result of the crime of identity theft committed against the individual, as that crime is defined in § 682.402(e)(14).

(ii) The Secretary discharges the obligation of a borrower with respect to a loan disbursement for which the school, without the borrower's authorization, endorsed the borrower's loan check or authorization for electronic funds transfer, unless the student for whom the loan was made received the proceeds of the loan either by actual delivery of the loan funds or by a credit in the amount of the contested disbursement applied to charges owed to the school for that portion of the educational program completed by the student. However, the Secretary does not reimburse the lender with respect to any amount disbursed by means of a check bearing an unauthorized endorsement unless the school also executed the application or promissory note for that loan for the named borrower without that individual's consent.

(iii) If a loan was made as a result of the crime of identity theft that was committed by an employee or agent of the lender, or if at the time the loan was made, an employee or agent of the lender knew of the identity theft of the individual named as the borrower—

(A) The Secretary does pay reinsurance, and does not reimburse the holder, for any amount disbursed on the loan; and

(B) Any amounts received by a holder as interest benefits and special allowance payments with respect to the loan must be refunded to the Secretary, as provided in paragraphs (e)(8)(ii)(B)(4) and (e)(10)(ii)(D) of this section.

(2) *Relief available pursuant to discharge.*

(i) Discharge under paragraph (e)(1)(i) of this section relieves the borrower of an existing or past obligation to repay the loan certified by the school, and any charges imposed or costs incurred by the holder with respect to the loan that the borrower is, or was, otherwise obligated to pay.

(ii) A discharge of a loan under paragraph (e) of this section qualifies the borrower for reimbursement of amounts paid voluntarily or through enforced collection on a loan obligation discharged under paragraph (e) of this section.

(iii) A borrower who has defaulted on a loan discharged under paragraph (e) of this section is not regarded as in default on the loan after discharge, and is eligible to receive assistance under the Title IV, HEA programs.

(iv) A discharge of a loan under paragraph (e) of this section is reported by the loan holder to all credit reporting agencies to which the holder previously reported the status of the loan, so as to delete all adverse credit history assigned to the loan.

(v) Discharge under paragraph (e)(1)(ii) of this section qualifies the borrower for relief only with respect to the amount of the disbursement discharged.

(3) *Borrower qualification for discharge.* Except as provided in paragraph (e)(14) of this section, to qualify for a discharge of a loan under paragraph (e) of this section, the borrower must submit to the holder of the loan a written request and a sworn statement. The statement need not be notarized, but must be made by the borrower under penalty of perjury, and, in the statement, the borrower must—

(i) State whether the student has made a claim with respect to the school's false certification with any third party, such as the holder of a performance bond or a tuition recovery program, and if so, the amount of any payment received by the borrower (or student) or credited to the borrower's loan obligation;

(ii) In the case of a borrower requesting a discharge based on defective testing of the student's ability to benefit, state that the borrower (or the student for whom a parent received a PLUS loan)—

  (A) Received, on or after January 1, 1986, the proceeds of any disbursement of a loan disbursed, in whole or in part, on or after January 1, 1986 to attend a school; and

  (B) Was admitted to that school on the basis of ability to benefit from its training and did not meet the applicable requirements for admission on the basis of ability to benefit as described in paragraph (e)(13) of this section;

(iii) In the case of a borrower requesting a discharge because the school signed the borrower's name on the loan application or promissory note—

  (A) State that the signature on either of those documents was not the signature of the borrower; and

  (B) Provide five different specimens of his or her signature, two of which must be not earlier or later than one year before or after the date of the contested signature;

(iv) In the case of a borrower requesting a discharge because the school, without authorization of the borrower, endorsed the borrower's name on the loan check or signed the authorization for electronic funds transfer or master check, the borrower shall—

  (A) Certify that he or she did not endorse the loan check or sign the authorization for electronic funds transfer or master check, or authorize the school to do so;

  (B) Provide five different specimens of his or her signature, two of which must be not earlier or later than one year before or after the date of the contested signature; and

  (C) State that the proceeds of the contested disbursement were not received either through actual delivery of the loan funds or by a credit in the amount of the contested disbursement applied to charges owed to the school for that portion of the educational program completed by the student;

(v) In the case of an individual who is requesting a discharge of a loan because the individual's eligibility was falsely certified as a result of a crime of identity theft committed against the individual—

  (A) Certify that the individual did not sign the promissory note, or that any other means of identification used to obtain the loan was used without the authorization of the individual claiming relief;

  (B) Certify that the individual did not receive or benefit from the proceeds of the loan with knowledge that the loan had been made without the authorization of the individual;

  (C) Provide a copy of a local, State, or Federal court verdict or judgment that conclusively determines that the individual who is named as the borrower of the loan was the victim of a crime of identify theft;

  (D) If the judicial determination of the crime does not expressly state that the loan was obtained as a result of the crime, provide—

    (1) Authentic specimens of the signature of the individual, as provided in paragraph (e)(3)(iii)(B), or other means of identification of the individual, as applicable, corresponding to the means of identification falsely used to obtain the loan; and

    (2) A statement of facts that demonstrate, to the satisfaction of the Secretary, that eligibility for the loan in question was falsely certified as a result of the crime of identity theft committed against that individual.

(vi) That the borrower agrees to provide upon request by the Secretary or the Secretary's designee, other documentation reasonably available to the borrower, that demonstrates, to the satisfaction of the Secretary or the Secretary's designee, that the student meets the qualifications in paragraph (e) of this section; and

(vii) That the borrower agrees to cooperate with the Secretary or the Secretary's designee in enforcement actions in accordance with paragraph (e)(4) of this section, and to transfer any right to recovery against a third party in accordance with paragraph (e)(5) of this section.

(4) *Cooperation by borrower in enforcement actions.*

(i) In any judicial or administrative proceeding brought by the Secretary or the Secretary's designee to recover for amounts discharged under paragraph (e) of this section or to take other enforcement action with respect to the conduct on which those claims were based, a borrower who requests or receives a discharge under paragraph (e) of this section must cooperate with the Secretary or the Secretary's designee. At the request of the Secretary or the Secretary's designee, and upon the Secretary's or the Secretary's designee's tendering to the borrower the fees and costs as are customarily provided in litigation to reimburse witnesses, the borrower shall—

  (A) Provide testimony regarding any representation made by the borrower to support a request for discharge; and

  (B) Produce any documentation reasonably available to the borrower with respect to those representations and any sworn statement required by the Secretary with respect to those representations and documents.

(ii) The Secretary revokes the discharge, or denies the request for discharge, of a borrower who—

  (A) Fails to provide testimony, sworn statements, or documentation to support material representations made by the borrower to obtain the discharge; or

  (B) Provides testimony, a sworn statement, or documentation that does not support the material representations made by the borrower to obtain the discharge.

(5) *Transfer to the Secretary of borrower's right of recovery against third parties.*

(i) Upon discharge under paragraph (e) of this section, the borrower is deemed to have assigned to and relinquished in favor of the Secretary any right to a loan refund (up to the amount discharged) that the borrower (or student) may have by contract or applicable law with respect to the loan or the enrollment agreement for the program for which the loan was received, against the school, its principals, affiliates and their successors, its sureties, and any private fund, including the portion of a public fund that represents funds received from a private party.

(ii) The provisions of paragraph (e) of this section apply notwithstanding any provision of state law that would otherwise restrict transfer of such rights by the borrower (or student), limit or prevent a transferee from exercising those rights, or establish procedures or a scheme of distribution that would prejudice the Secretary's ability to recover on those rights.

(iii) Nothing in this section shall be construed as limiting or foreclosing the borrower's (or student's) right to pursue legal and equitable relief regarding disputes arising from matters otherwise unrelated to the loan discharged.

(6) *Guaranty agency responsibilities—general.*

(i) A guaranty agency shall notify the Secretary immediately whenever it becomes aware of reliable information indicating that a school may have falsely certified a student's eligibility or caused an unauthorized disbursement of loan proceeds, as described in paragraph (e)(3) of this section. The designated guaranty agency in the state in which the school is located shall promptly investigate whether the school has falsely certified a student's eligibility and, within 30 days after receiving information indicating that the school may have done so, report the results of its preliminary investigation to the Secretary.

(ii) If the guaranty agency receives information it believes to be reliable indicating that a borrower whose loan is held by the agency may be eligible for a discharge under paragraph (e) of this section, the agency shall immediately suspend any efforts to collect from the borrower on any loan received for the program of study for which the loan was made (but may continue to receive borrower payments), and inform the borrower of the procedures for requesting a discharge.

(iii) If the borrower fails to submit the written request and sworn statement described in paragraph (e)(3) of this section within 60 days of being notified of that option, the guaranty agency shall resume collection and shall be deemed to have exercised forbearance of payment of principal and interest from the date it suspended collection activity. The agency may capitalize, in accordance with § 682.202(b), any interest accrued and not paid during that period.

(iv) Upon receipt of a discharge claim filed by a lender or a request submitted by a borrower with respect to a loan held by the guaranty agency, the agency shall have up to 90 days to determine whether the discharge should be granted. The agency shall review the borrower's request and supporting sworn statement in light of information available from the records of the agency and from other sources, including other guaranty agencies, state authorities, and cognizant accrediting associations.

(v) A borrower's request for discharge and sworn statement may not be denied solely on the basis of failing to meet any time limits set by the lender, the Secretary or the guaranty agency.

(7) *Guaranty agency responsibilities with respect to a claim filed by a lender based on the borrower's assertion that he or she did not sign the loan application or the promissory note that he or she was a victim of the crime of identity theft, or that the school failed to test, or improperly tested, the student's ability to benefit.*

(i) The agency shall evaluate the borrower's request and consider relevant information it possesses and information available from other sources, and follow the procedures described in paragraph (e)(7) of this section.

(ii) If the agency determines that the borrower satisfies the requirements for discharge under paragraph (e) of this section, it shall, not later than 30 days after the agency makes that determination, pay the claim in accordance with § 682.402(h) and—

(A) Notify the borrower that his or her liability with respect to the amount of the loan has been discharged, and that the lender has been informed of the actions required under paragraph (e)(7)(ii)(C) of this section;

(B) Refund to the borrower all amounts paid by the borrower to the lender or the agency with respect to the discharged loan amount, including any late fees or collection charges imposed by the lender or agency related to the discharged loan amount; and

(C) Notify the lender that the borrower's liability with respect to the amount of the loan has been discharged, and that the lender must—

(1) Immediately terminate any collection efforts against the borrower with respect to the discharged loan amount and any charges imposed or costs incurred by the lender related to the discharged loan amount that the borrower is, or was, otherwise obligated to pay; and

(2) Within 30 days, report to all credit reporting agencies to which the lender previously reported the status of the loan, so as to delete all adverse credit history assigned to the loan; and

(D) Within 30 days, demand payment in full from the perpetrator of the identity theft committed against the individual, and if payment is not received, pursue collection action thereafter against the perpetrator.

(iii) If the agency determines that the borrower does not qualify for a discharge, it shall, within 30 days after making that determination—

(A) Notify the lender that the borrower's liability on the loan is not discharged and that, depending on the borrower's decision under paragraph (e)(7)(iii)(B) of this section, the loan shall either be returned to the lender or paid as a default claim; and

(B) Notify the borrower that the borrower does not qualify for discharge, and state the reasons for that conclusion. The agency shall advise the borrower that he or she remains obligated to repay the loan and warn the borrower of the consequences of default, and explain that the borrower will be considered to be in default on the loan unless the borrower submits a written statement to the agency within 30 days stating that the borrower—

(1) Acknowledges the debt and, if payments are due, will begin or resume making those payments to the lender; or

(2) Requests the Secretary to review the agency's decision.

(iv) Within 30 days after receiving the borrower's written statement described in paragraph (e)(7)(iii)(B)(1) of this section, the agency shall return the claim file to the lender and notify the lender to resume collection efforts if payments are due.

(v) Within 30 days after receiving the borrower's request for review by the Secretary, the agency shall forward the claim file to the Secretary for his review and take the actions required under paragraph (e)(11) of this section.

(vi) The agency shall pay a default claim to the lender within 30 days after the borrower fails to return either of the written statements described in paragraph (e)(7)(iii)(B) of this section.

(8) *Guaranty agency responsibilities with respect to a claim filed by a lender based only on the borrower's assertion that he or she did not sign the loan check or the authorization for the release of loan funds via electronic funds transfer or master check.*

(i) The agency shall evaluate the borrower's request and consider relevant information it possesses and information available from other sources, and follow the procedures described in paragraph (e)(8) of this section.

(ii) If the agency determines that a borrower who asserts that he or she did not endorse the loan check satisfies the requirements for discharge under paragraph (e)(3)(iv) of this section, it shall, within 30 days after making that determination—

(A) Notify the borrower that his or her liability with respect to the amount of the contested disbursement of the loan has been discharged, and that the lender has been informed of the actions required under paragraph (e)(8)(ii)(B) of this section;

(B) Notify the lender that the borrower's liability with respect to the amount of the contested disbursement of the loan has been discharged, and that the lender must—

(1) Immediately terminate any collection efforts against the borrower with respect to the discharged loan amount and any charges imposed or costs incurred by the lender related to the discharged loan amount that the borrower is, or was, otherwise obligated to pay;

(2) Within 30 days, report to all credit reporting agencies to which the lender previously reported the status of the loan, so as to delete all adverse credit history assigned to the loan;

(3) Refund to the borrower, within 30 days, all amounts paid by the borrower with respect to the loan disbursement that was discharged, including any charges imposed or costs incurred by the lender related to the discharged loan amount; and

(4) Refund to the Secretary, within 30 days, all interest benefits and special allowance payments received from the Secretary with respect to the loan disbursement that was discharged; and

(C) Transfer to the lender the borrower's written assignment of any rights the borrower may have against third parties with respect to a loan disbursement that was discharged because the borrower did not sign the loan check.

(iii) If the agency determines that a borrower who asserts that he or she did not sign the electronic funds transfer or master check authorization satisfies the requirements for discharge under paragraph (e)(3)(iv) of this section, it shall, within 30 days after making that determination, pay the claim in accordance with § 682.402(h) and—

(A) Notify the borrower that his or her liability with respect to the amount of the contested disbursement of the loan has been discharged, and that the lender has been in-

formed of the actions required under paragraph (e)(8)(iii)(C) of this section;

(B) Refund to the borrower all amounts paid by the borrower to the lender or the agency with respect to the discharged loan amount, including any late fees or collection charges imposed by the lender or agency related to the discharged loan amount; and

(C) Notify the lender that the borrower's liability with respect to the contested disbursement of the loan has been discharged, and that the lender must—

(1) Immediately terminate any collection efforts against the borrower with respect to the discharged loan amount and any charges imposed or costs incurred by the lender related to the discharged loan amount that the borrower is, or was, otherwise obligated to pay; and

(2) Within 30 days, report to all credit reporting agencies to which the lender previously reported the status of the loan, so as to delete all adverse credit history assigned to the loan.

(iv) If the agency determines that the borrower does not qualify for a discharge, it shall, within 30 days after making that determination—

(A) Notify the lender that the borrower's liability on the loan is not discharged and that, depending on the borrower's decision under paragraph (e)(8)(iv)(B) of this section, the loan shall either be returned to the lender or paid as a default claim; and

(B) Notify the borrower that the borrower does not qualify for discharge, and state the reasons for that conclusion. The agency shall advise the borrower that he or she remains obligated to repay the loan and warn the borrower of the consequences of default, and explain that the borrower will be considered to be in default on the loan unless the borrower submits a written statement to the agency within 30 days stating that the borrower—

(1) Acknowledges the debt and, if payments are due, will begin or resume making those payments to the lender; or

(2) Requests the Secretary to review the agency's decision.

(v) Within 30 days after receiving the borrower's written statement described in paragraph (e)(8)(iv)(B)(1) of this section, the agency shall return the claim file to the lender and notify the lender to resume collection efforts if payments are due.

(vi) Within 30 days after receiving the borrower's request for review by the Secretary, the agency shall forward the claim file to the Secretary for his review and take the actions required under paragraph (e)(11) of this section.

(vii) The agency shall pay a default claim to the lender within 30 days after the borrower fails to return either of the written statements described in paragraph (e)(8)(iv)(B) of this section.

(9) *Guaranty agency responsibilities in the case of a loan held by the agency for which a discharge request is submitted by a borrower based on the borrower's assertion that he or she did not sign the loan application or the promissory note that he or she was a victim of the crime of identity theft, or that the school failed to test, or improperly tested, the student's ability to benefit.*

(i) The agency shall evaluate the borrower's request and consider relevant information it possesses and information available from other sources, and follow the procedures described in paragraph (e)(9) of this section.

(ii) If the agency determines that the borrower satisfies the requirements for discharge under paragraph (e)(3) of this section, it shall immediately terminate any collection efforts against the borrower with respect to the discharged loan amount and any charges imposed or costs incurred by the agency related to the discharged loan amount that the borrower is, or was otherwise obligated to pay and, not later than 30 days after the agency makes the determination that the borrower satisfies the requirements for discharge—

(A) Notify the borrower that his or her liability with respect to the amount of the loan has been discharged;

(B) Report to all credit reporting agencies to which the agency previously reported the status of the loan, so as to delete all adverse credit history assigned to the loan;

(C) Refund to the borrower all amounts paid by the borrower to the lender or the agency with respect to the discharged loan amount, including any late fees or collection charges imposed by the lender or agency related to the discharged loan amount; and

(D) Within 30 days, demand payment in full from the perpetrator of the identity theft committed against the individual, and if payment is not received, pursue collection action thereafter against the perpetrator.

(iii) If the agency determines that the borrower does not qualify for a discharge, it shall, within 30 days after making that determination, notify the borrower that the borrower's liability with respect to the amount of the loan is not discharged, state the reasons for that conclusion, and if the borrower is not then making payments in accordance with a repayment arrangement with the agency on the loan, advise the borrower of the consequences of continued failure to reach such an arrangement, and that collection action will resume on the loan unless within 30 days the borrower—

(A) Acknowledges the debt and, if payments are due, reaches a satisfactory arrangement to repay the loan or resumes making payments under such an arrangement to the agency; or

(B) Requests the Secretary to review the agency's decision.

(iv) Within 30 days after receiving the borrower's request for review by the Secretary, the agency shall forward the borrower's discharge request and all relevant documentation to the Secretary for his review and take the actions required under paragraph (e)(11) of this section.

(v) The agency shall resume collection action if within 30 days of giving notice of its determination the borrower fails to seek review by the Secretary or agree to repay the loan.

(10) *Guaranty agency responsibilities in the case of a loan held by the agency for which a discharge request is submitted by a borrower based only on the borrower's assertion that he or she did not sign the loan check or the authorization for the release of loan proceeds via electronic funds transfer or master check.*

(i) The agency shall evaluate the borrower's request and consider relevant information it possesses and information available from other sources, and follow the procedures described in paragraph (e)(10) of this section.

(ii) If the agency determines that a borrower who asserts that he or she did not endorse the loan check satisfies the requirements for discharge under paragraph (e)(3)(iv) of this section, it shall refund to the Secretary the amount of reinsurance payment received with respect to the amount discharged on that loan less any repayments made by the lender under paragraph (e)(10)(ii)(D)(2) of this section, and within 30 days after making that determination—

(A) Notify the borrower that his or her liability with respect to the amount of the contested disbursement of the loan has been discharged;

(B) Report to all credit reporting agencies to which the agency previously reported the status of the loan, so as to delete all adverse credit history assigned to the loan;

(C) Refund to the borrower all amounts paid by the borrower to the lender or the agency with respect to the discharged loan amount, including any late fees or collection charges imposed by the lender or agency related to the discharged loan amount;

(D) Notify the lender to whom a claim payment was made that the lender must refund to the Secretary, within 30 days—

(1) All interest benefits and special allowance payments received from the Secretary with respect to the loan disbursement that was discharged; and

(2) The amount of the borrower's payments that were refunded to the borrower by the guaranty agency under paragraph (e)(10)(ii)(C) of this section that represent borrower payments previously paid to the lender with respect to the loan disbursement that was discharged;

(E) Notify the lender to whom a claim payment was made that the lender must, within 30 days, reimburse the agency for the amount of the loan that was discharged, minus the amount of borrower payments made to the lender that were refunded to the borrower by the guaranty agency under paragraph (e)(10)(ii)(C) of this section; and

(F) Transfer to the lender the borrower's written assignment of any rights the borrower may have against third parties with respect to the loan disbursement that was discharged.

(iii) In the case of a borrower who requests a discharge because he or she did not sign the electronic funds transfer or master check authorization, if the agency determines that the borrower meets the conditions for discharge, it shall immediately terminate any collection efforts against the borrower with respect to the discharged loan amount and any charges imposed or costs incurred by the agency related to the discharged loan amount that the borrower is, or was, otherwise obligated to pay, and within 30 days after making that determination—

(iv) The agency shall take the actions required under paragraphs (e)(9)(iii) through (v) if the agency determines that the borrower does not qualify for a discharge.

(11) *Guaranty agency responsibilities if a borrower requests a review by the Secretary.*

(i) Within 30 days after receiving the borrower's request for review under paragraph (e)(7)(iii)(B)(2), (e)(8)(iv)(B)(2), (e)(9)(iii)(B), or (e)(10)(iv) of this section, the agency shall forward the borrower's discharge request and all relevant documentation to the Secretary for his review.

(ii) The Secretary notifies the agency and the borrower of a determination on review. If the Secretary determines that the borrower is not eligible for a discharge under paragraph (e) of this section, within 30 days after being so informed, the agency shall take the actions described in paragraphs (e)(8)(iv) through (vii) or (e)(9)(iii) through (v) of this section, as applicable.

(iii) If the Secretary determines that the borrower meets the requirements for a discharge under paragraph (e) of this section, the agency shall, within 30 days after being so informed, take the actions required under paragraph (e)(7)(ii), (e)(8)(ii), (e)(8)(iii), (e)(9)(ii), (e)(10)(ii), or (e)(10)(iii) of this section, as applicable.

(12) *Lender Responsibilities.*

(i) If the lender is notified by a guaranty agency or the Secretary, or receives information it believes to be reliable from another source indicating that a current or former borrower may be eligible for a discharge under paragraph (e) of this section, the lender shall immediately suspend any efforts to collect from the borrower on any loan received for the program of study for which the loan was made (but may continue to receive borrower payments) and, within 30 days of receiving the information or notification, inform the borrower of the procedures for requesting a discharge.

(ii) If the borrower fails to submit the written request and sworn statement described in paragraph (e)(3) of this section within 60 days of being notified of that option, the lender shall resume collection and shall be deemed to have exercised forbearance of payment of principal and interest from the date the lender suspended collection activity. The lender may capitalize, in accordance with § 682.202(b), any interest accrued and not paid during that period.

(iii) The lender shall file a claim with the guaranty agency in accordance with § 682.402(g) no later than 60 days after the lender receives the borrower's written request and sworn statement described in paragraph (e)(3) of this section. If a lender receives a payment made by or on behalf of the borrower on the loan after the lender files a claim on the loan with the guaranty agency, the lender shall forward the payment to the guaranty agency within 30 days of its receipt. The lender shall assist the guaranty agency and the borrower in determining whether the borrower is eligible for discharge of the loan.

(iv) The lender shall comply with all instructions received from the Secretary or a guaranty agency with respect to loan discharges under paragraph (e) of this section.

(v) The lender shall review a claim that the borrower did not endorse and did not receive the proceeds of a loan check. The lender shall take the actions required under paragraphs (e)(8)(ii)(A) and (B) of this section if it determines that the borrower did not endorse the loan check, unless the lender secures persuasive evidence that the proceeds of the loan were received by the borrower or the student for whom the loan was made, as provided in paragraph (e)(1)(ii). If the lender determines that the loan check was properly endorsed or the proceeds were received by the borrower or student, the lender may consider the borrower's objection to repayment as a statement of intention not to repay the loan, and may file a claim with the guaranty agency for reimbursement on that ground, but shall not report the loan to credit bureaus as in default until the guaranty agency, or, as applicable, the Secretary, reviews the claim for relief. By filing such a claim, the lender shall be deemed to have agreed to the following—

(A) If the guarantor or the Secretary determines that the borrower endorsed the loan check or the proceeds of the loan were received by the borrower or the student, any failure to satisfy due diligence requirements by the lender prior to the filing of the claim that would have resulted in the loss of reinsurance on the loan in the event of default will be waived by the Secretary; and

(B) If the guarantor or the Secretary determines that the borrower did not endorse the loan check and that the proceeds of the loan were not received by the borrower or the student, the lender will comply with the requirements specified in paragraph (e)(8)(ii)(B) of this section.

(vi) Within 30 days after being notified by the guaranty agency that the borrower's request for a discharge has been denied, the lender shall notify the borrower of the reasons for the denial and, if payments are due, resume collection against the borrower. The lender shall be deemed to have exercised forbearance of payment of principal and interest from the date the lender suspended collection activity, and may capitalize, in accordance with § 682.202(b), any interest accrued and not paid during that period.

(13) *Requirements for certifying a borrower's eligibility for a loan.*

(i) For periods of enrollment beginning between July 1, 1987 and June 30, 1991, a student who had a general education diploma or received one before the scheduled completion of the program of instruction is deemed to have the ability to benefit from the training offered by the school.

(ii) A student not described in paragraph (e)(13)(i) of this section is considered to have the ability to benefit from training offered by the school if the student—

(A) For periods of enrollment beginning prior to July 1, 1987, was determined to have the ability to benefit from the school's training in accordance with the requirements of 34 CFR 668.6, as in existence at the time the determination was made;

(B) For periods of enrollment beginning between July 1, 1987 and June 30, 1996, achieved a passing grade on a test—

(1) Approved by the Secretary, for periods of enrollment beginning on or after July 1, 1991, or by the accrediting agency, for other periods; and

(2) Administered substantially in accordance with the requirements for use of the test;

(C) Successfully completed a program of developmental or remedial education provided by the school; or

(D) For periods of enrollment beginning on or after July 1, 1996 through June 30, 2000—

(1) Obtained, within 12 months before the date the student initially receives title IV, HEA program assistance, a passing score specified by the Secretary on an independently administered test in accordance with subpart J of 34 CFR part 668; or

(2) Enrolled in an eligible institution that participates in a State process approved by the Secretary under subpart J of 34 CFR part 668.

(E) For periods of enrollment beginning on or after July 1, 2000—

　(1) Met either of the conditions described in paragraph (e)(13)(ii)(D) of this section; or

　(2) Was home schooled and met the requirements of 34 CFR 668.32(e)(4).

(iii) Notwithstanding paragraphs (e)(13)(i) and (ii) of this section, a student did not have the ability to benefit from training offered by the school if—

(A) The school certified the eligibility of the student for a FFEL Program loan; and

(B) At the time of certification, the student would not meet the requirements for employment (in the student's State of residence) in the occupation for which the training program supported by the loan was intended because of a physical or mental condition, age, or criminal record or other reason accepted by the Secretary.

(iv) Notwithstanding paragraphs (e)(13)(i) and (ii) of this section, a student has the ability to benefit from the training offered by the school if the student received a high school diploma or its recognized equivalent prior to enrollment at the school.

(14) *Identity theft.*

(i) The unauthorized use of the identifying information of another individual that is punishable under 18 U.S.C. 1028, 1029, or 1030, or substantially comparable State or local law.

(ii) Identifying information includes, but is not limited to—

(A) Name, Social Security number, date of birth, official State or government issued driver's license or identification number, alien registration number, government passport number, and employer or taxpayer identification number;

(B) Unique biometric data, such as fingerprints, voiceprint, retina or iris image, or unique physical representation;

(C) Unique electronic identification number, address, or routing code; or

(D) Telecommunication identifying information or access device (as defined in 18 U.S.C. 1029(e)).

(15) Discharge without an application. A borrower's obligation to repay all or a portion of an FFEL Program loan may be discharged without an application from the borrower if the Secretary, or the guaranty agency with the Secretary's permission, determines that the borrower qualifies for a discharge based on information in the Secretary or guaranty agency's possession.

(f) *Bankruptcy*—

(1) *General.* If a borrower files a petition for relief under the Bankruptcy Code, the Secretary reimburses the holder of the loan for unpaid principal and interest on the loan in accordance with paragraphs (h) through (k) of this section.

(2) *Suspension of collection activity.*

(i) If the lender is notified that a borrower has filed a petition for relief in bankruptcy, the lender must immediately suspend any collection efforts outside the bankruptcy proceeding against the borrower and—

(A) Must suspend any collection efforts against any co-maker or endorser if the borrower has filed for relief under Chapters 12 or 13 of the Bankruptcy Code; or

(B) May suspend any collection efforts against any co-maker or endorser if the borrower has filed for relief under Chapters 7 or 11 of the Bankruptcy Code.

(ii) If the lender is notified that a co-maker or endorser has filed a petition for relief in bankruptcy, the lender must immediately suspend any collection efforts outside the bankruptcy proceeding against the co-maker or endorser and—

(A) Must suspend collection efforts against the borrower and any other parties to the note if the co-maker or endorser has filed for relief under Chapters 12 or 13 of the Bankruptcy Code; or

(B) May suspend any collection efforts against the borrower and any other parties to the note if the co-maker or endorser has filed for relief under Chapters 7 or 11 of the Bankruptcy Code.

(3) *Determination of filing.* The lender must determine that a borrower has filed a petition for relief in bankruptcy on the basis of receiving a notice of the first meeting of creditors or other proof of filing provided by the debtor's attorney or the bankruptcy court.

(4) *Proof of claim.*

(i) Except as provided in paragraph (f)(4)(ii) of this section, the holder of the loan shall file a proof of claim with the bankruptcy court within—

(A) 30 days after the holder receives a notice of first meeting of creditors unless, in the case of a proceeding under chapter 7, the notice states that the borrower has no assets; or

(B) 30 days after the holder receives a notice from the court stating that a chapter 7 no-asset case has been converted to an asset case.

(ii) A guaranty agency that is a state guaranty agency, and on that basis may assert immunity from suit in bankruptcy court, and that does not assign any loans affected by a bankruptcy filing to another guaranty agency—

(A) Is not required to file a proof of claim on a loan already held by the guaranty agency; and

(B) May direct lenders not to file proofs of claim on loans guaranteed by that agency.

(5) *Filing of bankruptcy claim with the guaranty agency.*

(i) The lender shall file a bankruptcy claim on the loan with the guaranty agency in accordance with paragraph (g) of this section, if—

(A) The borrower has filed a petition for relief under Chapters 12 or 13 of the Bankruptcy Code; or

(B) The borrower has filed a petition for relief under Chapters 7 or 11 of the Bankruptcy Code before October 8, 1998 and the loan has been in repayment for more than seven years (exclusive of any applicable suspension of the repayment period) from the due date of the first payment until the date of the filing of the petition for relief; or

(C) The borrower has begun an action to have the loan obligation determined to be dischargeable on grounds of undue hardship.

(ii) In cases not described in paragraph (f)(5)(i) of this section, the lender shall continue to hold the loan notwithstanding the bankruptcy proceeding. Once the bankruptcy proceeding is completed or dismissed, the lender shall treat the loan as if the lender had exercised forbearance as to repayment of principal and interest accrued from the date of the borrower's filing of the bankruptcy petition until the date the lender is notified that the bankruptcy proceeding is completed or dismissed.

(g) *Claim procedures for a loan held by a lender—*

(1) *Documentation.* A lender shall provide the guaranty agency with the following documentation when filing a death, disability, closed school, false certification, or bankruptcy claim:

(i) The original or a true and exact copy of the promissory note.

(ii) The loan application, if a separate loan application was provided to the lender.

(iii) In the case of a death claim, an original or certified death certificate, or other documentation supporting the discharge request that formed the basis for the determination of death.

(iv) In the case of a disability claim, a copy of the certification of disability described in paragraph (c)(2) of this section.

(v) In the case of a bankruptcy claim—

(A) Evidence that a bankruptcy petition has been filed, all pertinent documents sent to or received from the bankruptcy court by the lender, and an assignment to the guaranty agency of any proof of claim filed by the lender regarding the loan; and

(B) A statement of any facts of which the lender is aware that may form the basis for an objection or exception to the discharge of the borrower's loan obligation in bankruptcy and all documents supporting those facts.

(vi) In the case of a closed school claim, the documentation described in paragraph (d)(3) of this section, or any other documentation as the Secretary may require;

(vii) In the case of a false certification claim, the documentation described in paragraph (e)(3) of this section.

(2) *Filing deadlines.* A lender shall file a death, disability, closed school, false certification, or bankruptcy claim within the following periods:

(i) Within 60 days of the date on which the lender determines that a borrower (or the student on whose behalf a parent obtained a PLUS loan) has died, or the lender determines that the borrower is totally and permanently disabled.

(ii) In the case of a closed school claim, the lender shall file a claim with the guaranty agency no later than 60 days after the borrower submits to the lender the written request and sworn statement described in paragraph (d)(3) of this section or after the lender is notified by the Secretary or the Secretary's designee or by the guaranty agency to do so.

(iii) In the case of a false certification claim, the lender shall file a claim with the guaranty agency no later than 60 days after the borrower submits to the lender the written request and sworn statement described in paragraph (e)(3) of this section or after the lender is notified by the Secretary or the Secretary's designee or by the guaranty agency to do so.

(iv) A lender shall file a bankruptcy claim with the guaranty agency by the earlier of—

(A) 30 days after the date on which the lender receives notice of the first meeting of creditors or other information described in paragraph (f)(3) of this section; or

(B) 15 days after the lender is served with a complaint or motion to have the loan determined to be dischargeable on grounds of undue hardship, or, if the lender secures an extension of time within which an answer may be filed, 25 days before the expiration of that extended period, whichever is later.

(h) *Payment of death, disability, closed school, false certification, and bankruptcy claims by the guaranty agency.*

(1) *General.*

(i) The guaranty agency shall review a death, disability, bankruptcy, closed school, or false certification claim promptly and shall pay the lender on an approved claim the amount of loss in accordance with paragraphs (h)(2) and (h)(3) of this section—

(A) Not later than 45 days after the claim was filed by the lender for death and bankruptcy claims; and

(B) Not later than 90 days after the claim was filed by the lender for disability, closed school, or false certification claims.

(ii) In the case of a bankruptcy claim, the guaranty agency shall, upon receipt of the claim from the lender, immediately take those actions required under paragraph (i) of this section to oppose the discharge of the loan by the bankruptcy court.

(iii) In the case of a closed school claim or a false certification claim based on the determination that the borrower did not sign the loan application, the promissory note, or the authorization for the electronic transfer of loan funds, or that the school failed to test, or improperly tested, the student's ability to benefit, the guaranty agency shall document its determination that the borrower is eligible for discharge under paragraphs (d) or (e) of this section and pay the borrower or the holder the amount determined under paragraph (h)(2) of this section.

(iv) In reviewing a claim under this section, the issue of confirmation of subsequent loans under an MPN will not be reviewed and a claim will not be denied based on the absence of any evidence relating to confirmation in a particular loan file. However, if a court rules that a loan is unenforceable solely because of the lack of evidence of the confirmation process or processes, insurance benefits must be repaid.

(2)(i) The amount of loss payable—

(A) On a death or disability claim is equal to the sum of the remaining principal balance and interest accrued on the loan, collection costs incurred by the lender and applied to the borrower's account within 30 days of the date those costs were actually incurred, and unpaid interest up to the date the lender should have filed the claim.

(B) On a bankruptcy claim is equal to the unpaid balance of principal and interest determined in accordance with paragraph (h)(3) of this section.

(ii) The amount of loss payable to a lender on a closed school claim or on a false certification claim is equal to the sum of the remaining principal balance and interest accrued on the loan, collection costs incurred by the lender and applied to the borrower's account within 30 days of the date those costs were actually incurred, and unpaid interest determined in accordance with paragraph (h)(3) of this section.

(iii) In the case of a closed school or false certification claim filed by a lender on an outstanding loan owed by the borrower, on the same date that the agency pays a claim to the lender, the agency shall pay the borrower an amount equal to the amount paid on the loan by or on behalf of the borrower, less any school tuition refunds or payments received by the holder or the borrower from a tuition recovery fund, performance bond, or other third-party source.

(iv) In the case of a claim filed by a lender based on a request received from a borrower whose loan had been repaid in full by, or on behalf of the borrower to the lender, on the same date that the agency notifies the lender that the borrower is eligible for a closed school or false certification discharge, the agency shall pay the borrower an amount equal to the amount paid on the loan by or on behalf of the borrower, less any school tuition refunds or payments received by the holder or the borrower from a tuition recovery fund, performance bond, or other third-party source.

(v) In the case of a loan that has been included in a Consolidation Loan, the agency shall pay to the holder of the borrower's Consolidation Loan, an amount equal to—

(A) The amount paid on the loan by or on behalf of the borrower at the time the loan was paid through consolidation;

(B) The amount paid by the consolidating lender to the holder of the loan when it was repaid through consolidation; minus

(C) Any school tuition refunds or payments received by the holder or the borrower from a tuition recovery fund, performance bond, or other third-party source if those refunds or payments were—

(1) Received by the borrower or received by the holder and applied to the borrower's loan balance before the date the loan was repaid through consolidation; or

(2) Received by the borrower or received by the Consolidation Loan holder on or after the date the consolidating lender made a payment to the former holder to discharge the borrower's obligation to that former holder.

(3) *Payment of interest.* If the guarantee covers unpaid interest, the amount payable on an approved claim includes the unpaid interest that accrues during the following periods:

(i) During the period before the claim is filed, not to exceed the period provided for in paragraph (g)(2) of this section for filing the claim.

(ii) During a period not to exceed 30 days following the receipt date by the lender of a claim returned by the guaranty agency for additional documentation necessary for the claim to be approved by the guaranty agency.

(iii) During the period required by the guaranty agency to approve the claim and to authorize payment or to return the claim to the lender for additional documentation not to exceed—

(A) 45 days for death or bankruptcy claims; or

(B) 90 days for disability, closed school, or false certification claims.

(i) *Guaranty agency participation in bankruptcy proceedings—*

(1) *Undue hardship claims.*

(i) In response to a petition filed prior to October 8, 1998 with regard to any bankruptcy proceeding by the borrower for discharge under 11 U.S.C. 523(a)(8) on the grounds of undue hardship, the guaranty agency must, on the basis of reasonably available information, determine whether the first payment on the loan was due more than 7 years (exclusive of any applicable suspension of the repayment period) before the filing of that petition and, if so, process the claim.

(ii) In all other cases, the guaranty agency must determine whether repayment under either the current repayment schedule or any adjusted schedule authorized under this part would impose an undue hardship on the borrower and his or her dependents.

(iii) If the guaranty agency determines that repayment would not constitute an undue hardship, the guaranty agency must then determine whether the expected costs of opposing the discharge petition would exceed one-third of the total amount owed on the loan, including principal, interest, late charges, and collection costs. If the guaranty agency has determined that the expected costs of opposing the discharge petition will exceed one-third of the total amount of the loan, it may, but is not required to, engage in the activities described in paragraph (i)(1)(iv) of this section.

(iv) The guaranty agency must use diligence and may assert any defense consistent with its status under applicable law to avoid discharge of the loan. Unless discharge would be more effectively opposed by not taking the following actions, the agency must—

(A) Oppose the borrower's petition for a determination of dischargeability; and

(B) If the borrower is in default on the loan, seek a judgment for the amount owed on the loan.

(v) In opposing a petition for a determination of dischargeability on the grounds of undue hardship, a guaranty agency may agree to discharge of a portion of the amount owed on a loan if it reasonably determines that the agreement is necessary in order to obtain a judgment on the remainder of the loan.

(2) *Response by a guaranty agency to plans proposed under Chapters 11, 12, and 13.* The guaranty agency shall take the following actions when a petition for relief in bankruptcy under Chapters 11, 12, or 13 is filed:

(i) The agency is not required to respond to a proposed plan that—

(A) Provides for repayment of the full outstanding balance of the loan;

(B) Makes no provision with regard to the loan or to general unsecured claims.

(ii) In any other case, the agency shall determine, based on a review of its own records and documents filed by the debtor in the bankruptcy proceeding—

(A) What part of the loan obligation will be discharged under the plan as proposed;

(B) Whether the plan itself or the classification of the loan under the plan meets the requirements of 11 U.S.C. 1129, 1225, or 1325, as applicable; and

(C) Whether grounds exist under 11 U.S.C. 1112, 1208, or 1307, as applicable, to move for conversion or dismissal of the case.

(iii) If the agency determines that grounds exist to challenge the proposed plan, the agency shall, as appropriate, object to the plan or move to dismiss the case, if—

(A) The costs of litigation of these actions are not reasonably expected to exceed one-third of the amount of the loan to be discharged under the plan; and

(B) With respect to an objection under 11 U.S.C. 1325, the additional amount that may be recovered under the plan if an objection is successful can reasonably be expected to equal or exceed the cost of litigating the objection.

(iv) The agency shall monitor the debtor's performance under a confirmed plan. If the debtor fails to make payments required under the plan or seeks but does not demonstrate entitlement to discharge under 11 U.S.C. 1328(b), the agency shall oppose any requested discharge or move to dismiss the case if the costs of litigation together with the costs incurred for objections to the plan are not reasonably expected to exceed one-third of the amount of the loan to be discharged under the plan.

(j) *Mandatory purchase by a lender of a loan subject to a bankruptcy claim.*

(1) The lender shall repurchase from the guaranty agency a loan held by the agency pursuant to a bankruptcy claim paid to that lender, unless the guaranty agency sells the loan to another lender, promptly after the earliest of the following events:

(i) The entry of an order denying or revoking discharge or dismissing a proceeding under any chapter.

(ii) A ruling in a proceeding under chapter 7 or 11 that the loan is not dischargeable under 11 U.S.C. 523(a)(8) or other applicable law.

(iii) The entry of an order granting discharge under chapter 12 or 13, or confirming a plan of arrangement under chapter 11, unless the court determined that the loan is dischargeable under 11 U.S.C. 523(a)(8) on grounds of undue hardship.

(2) The lender may capitalize all outstanding interest accrued on a loan purchased under paragraph (j) of this section to cover any periods of delinquency prior to the bankruptcy action through the date the lender purchases the loan and receives the supporting loan documentation from the guaranty agency.

(k) *Claims for reimbursement from the Secretary on loans held by guarantee agencies.*

(1)(i) The Secretary reimburses the guaranty agency for its losses on bankruptcy claims paid to lenders after—

(A) A determination by the court that the loan is dischargeable under 11 U.S.C. 523(a)(8) with respect to a proceeding initiated under chapter 7 or chapter 11; or

(B) With respect to any other loan, after the agency pays the claim to the lender.

(ii) The guaranty agency shall refund to the Secretary the full amount of reimbursement received from the Secretary on a loan that a lender repurchases under this section.

(2) The Secretary pays a death, disability, bankruptcy, closed school, or false certification claim in an amount determined under § 682.402(k)(5) on a loan held by a guaranty agency after the agency has paid a default claim to the lender thereon and received payment under its reinsurance agreement. The Secretary reimburses the guaranty agency only if—

(i) The guaranty agency determines that the borrower (or the student for whom a parent obtained a PLUS loan or each of the co-makers of a PLUS loan) has died, or the borrower (or each of the co-makers of a PLUS loan) has become totally and permanently disabled since applying for the loan, or has filed for relief in bankruptcy, in accordance with the procedures in paragraphs (b), (c), or (f) of this section, or the student was unable to complete an educational program because the school closed, or the borrower's eligibility to borrow (or the student's eligibility in the case of a PLUS loan) was falsely certified by an eligible school. For purposes of this paragraph, references to the "lender" and "guaranty agency" in paragraphs (b) through (f) of this section mean the guaranty agency and the Secretary respectively;

(ii) In the case of a Stafford, SLS, or PLUS loan, the guaranty agency determines that the borrower (or the student for whom a parent obtained a PLUS loan, or each of the co-makers of a PLUS loan) has died, or the borrower (or each of the co-makers of a PLUS loan) has become totally and permanently disabled since applying for the loan, or has filed the petition for relief in bankruptcy within 10 years of the date the borrower entered repayment, exclusive of periods of deferment or periods of forbearance granted by the lender that extended the 10-year maximum repayment period, or the borrower (or the student for whom a parent received a PLUS loan) was unable to complete an educational program because the school closed, or the borrower's eligibility to borrow (or the student's eligibility in the case of a PLUS loan) was falsely certified by an eligible school;

(iii) In the case of a Consolidation loan, the borrower (or one of the co-makers) has died, is determined to be totally and permanently disabled under Sec. 682.402(c), or has filed the petition for relief in bankruptcy within the maximum repayment period described in Sec. 682.209(h)(2), exclusive of periods of deferment or periods of forbearance granted by the lender that extended the maximum repayment period;

(iv) The guaranty agency has not written off the loan in accordance with the procedures established by the agency under § 682.410(b)(6)(x), except for closed school and false certification discharges; and

(v) The guaranty agency has exercised due diligence in the collection of the loan in accordance with the procedures established by the agency under § 682.410(b)(6)(x), until the borrower (or the student for whom a parent obtained a PLUS loan, or each of the co-makers of a PLUS loan) has died, or the borrower (or each of the co-makers of a PLUS loan) has become totally and permanently disabled or filed a Chapter 12 or Chapter 13 petition, or had the loan discharged in bankruptcy, or for closed school and false certification claims, the guaranty agency receives a request for discharge from the borrower or another party.

(3) [*Reserved*]

(4) Within 30 days of receiving reimbursement for a closed school or false certification claim, the guaranty agency shall pay—

(i) The borrower an amount equal to the amount paid on the loan by or on behalf of the borrower, less any school tuition refunds or payments received by the holder, guaranty agency, or the borrower from a tuition recovery fund, performance bond, or other third-party source; or

(ii) The amount determined under paragraph (h)(2)(iv) of this section to the holder of the borrower's Consolidation Loan.

(5) The Secretary pays the guaranty agency a percentage of the outstanding principal and interest that is equal to the complement of the reinsurance percentage paid on the loan. This interest

includes interest that accrues during—

(i) For death or bankruptcy claims, the shorter of 60 days or the period from the date the guaranty agency determines that the borrower (or the student for whom a parent obtained a PLUS loan, or each of the co-makers of a PLUS loan) died, or filed a petition for relief in bankruptcy until the Secretary authorizes payment;

(ii) For disability claims, the shorter of 60 days or the period from the date the guaranty agency makes a preliminary determination that the borrower became totally and permanently disabled until the Secretary authorizes payment; or

(iii) For closed school or false certification claims, the period from the date on which the guaranty agency received payment from the Secretary on a default claim to the date on which the Secretary authorizes payment of the closed school or false certification claim.

(l) *Unpaid refund discharge.*

(1) *Unpaid refunds in closed school situations.* In the case of a school that has closed, the Secretary reimburses the guarantor of a loan and discharges a former or current borrower's (and any endorser's) obligation to repay that portion of an FFEL Program loan (disbursed, in whole or in part, on or after January 1, 1986) equal to the refund that should have been made by the school under applicable Federal law and regulations, including this section. Any accrued interest and other charges (late charges, collection costs, origination fees, and insurance premiums) associated with the unpaid refund are also discharged.

(2) *Unpaid refunds in open school situations.* In the case of a school that is open, the guarantor discharges a former or current borrower's (and any endorser's) obligation to repay that portion of an FFEL loan (disbursed, in whole or in part, on or after January 1, 1986) equal to the amount of the refund that should have been made by the school under applicable Federal law and regulations, including this section, if—

(i) The borrower (or the student on whose behalf a parent borrowed) is not attending the school that owes the refund; and

(ii) The guarantor receives documentation regarding the refund and the borrower and guarantor have been unable to resolve the unpaid refund within 120 days from the date the guarantor receives a complete application in accordance with paragraph (l)(4) of this section. Any accrued interest and other charges (late charges, collection costs, origination fees, and insurance premiums) associated with the amount of the unpaid refund amount are also discharged.

(3) *Relief to borrower (and any endorser) following discharge.*

(i) If a borrower receives a discharge of a portion of a loan under this section, the borrower is reimbursed for any amounts paid in excess of the remaining balance of the loan (including accrued interest, late charges, collection costs, origination fees, and insurance premiums) owed by the borrower at the time of discharge.

(ii) The holder of the loan reports the discharge of a portion of a loan under this section to all credit reporting agencies to which the holder of the loan previously reported the status of the loan.

(4) *Borrower qualification for discharge.* To receive a discharge of a portion of a loan under this section, a borrower must submit a written application to the holder or guaranty agency except as provided in paragraph (l)(5)(iv) of this section. The application

requests the information required to calculate the amount of the discharge and requires the borrower to sign a statement swearing to the accuracy of the information in the application. The statement need not be notarized but must be made by the borrower under penalty of perjury. In the statement, the borrower must—

(i) State that the borrower (or the student on whose behalf a parent borrowed)—

(A) Received the proceeds of a loan, in whole or in part, on or after January 1, 1986 to attend a school;

(B) Did not attend, withdrew, or was terminated from the school within a timeframe that entitled the borrower to a refund; and

(C) Did not receive the benefit of a refund to which the borrower was entitled either from the school or from a third party, such as a holder of a performance bond or a tuition recovery program.

(ii) State whether the borrower has any other application for discharge pending for this loan; and

(iii) State that the borrower—

(A) Agrees to provide upon request by the Secretary or the Secretary's designee other documentation reasonably available to the borrower that demonstrates that the borrower meets the qualifications for an unpaid refund discharge under this section; and

(B) Agrees to cooperate with the Secretary or the Secretary's designee in enforcement actions in accordance with paragraph (e) of this section and to transfer any right to recovery against a third party to the Secretary in accordance with paragraph (d) of this section.

(5) *Unpaid refund discharge procedures.*

(i) Except for the requirements of paragraph (l)(5)(iv) of this section related to an open school, if the holder or guaranty agency learns that a school did not pay a refund of loan proceeds owed under applicable law and regulations, the holder or the guaranty agency sends the borrower a discharge application and an explanation of the qualifications and procedures for obtaining a discharge. The holder of the loan also promptly suspends any efforts to collect from the borrower on any affected loan.

(ii) If the borrower returns the application, specified in paragraph (l)(4) of this section, the holder or the guaranty agency must review the application to determine whether the application appears to be complete. In the case of a loan held by a lender, once the lender determines that the application appears complete, it must provide the application and all pertinent information to the guaranty agency including, if available, the borrower's last date of attendance. If the borrower returns the application within 60 days, the lender must extend the period during which efforts to collect on the affected loan are suspended to the date the lender receives either a denial of the request or the unpaid refund amount from the guaranty agency. At the conclusion of the period during which the collection activity was suspended, the lender may capitalize any interest accrued and not paid during that period in accordance with § 682.202(b).

(iii) If the borrower fails to return the application within 60 days, the holder of the loan resumes collection efforts and grants forbearance of principal and interest for the period during which the collection activity was suspended. The holder may capitalize any interest accrued and not paid during that period in accordance with § 682.202(b).

(iv) The guaranty agency may, with the approval of the Secretary, discharge a portion of a loan under this section without an application if the guaranty agency determines, based on information in the guaranty agency's possession, that the borrower qualifies for a discharge.

(v) If the holder of the loan or the guaranty agency determines that the information contained in its files conflicts with the information provided by the borrower, the guaranty agency must use the most reliable information available to it to determine eligibility for and the appropriate payment of the refund amount.

(vi) If the holder of the loan is the guaranty agency and the agency determines that the borrower qualifies for a discharge of an unpaid refund, the guaranty agency must suspend any efforts to collect on the affected loan and, within 30 days of its determination, discharge the appropriate amount and inform the borrower of its determination. Absent documentation of the exact amount of refund due the borrower, the guaranty agency must calculate the amount of the unpaid refund using the unpaid refund calculation defined in paragraph (*o*) of this section.

(vii) If the guaranty agency determines that a borrower does not qualify for an unpaid refund discharge, (or, if the holder is the lender and is informed by the guarantor that the borrower does not qualify for a discharge)—

(A) Within 30 days of the guarantor's determination, the agency must notify the borrower in writing of the reason for the determination and of the borrower's right to request a review of the agency's determination. The guaranty agency must make a determination within 30 days of the borrower's submission of additional documentation supporting the borrower's eligibility that was not considered in any prior determination. During the review period, collection activities must be suspended; and

(B) The holder must resume collection if the determination remains unchanged and grant forbearance of principal and interest for any period during which collection activity was suspended under this section. The holder may capitalize any interest accrued and not paid during these periods in accordance with § 682.202(b).

(viii) If the guaranty agency determines that a current or former borrower at an open school may be eligible for a discharge under this section, the guaranty agency must notify the lender and the school of the unpaid refund allegation. The notice to the school must include all pertinent facts available to the guaranty agency regarding the alleged unpaid refund. The school must, no later than 60 days after receiving the notice, provide the guaranty agency with documentation demonstrating, to the satisfaction of the guarantor, that the alleged unpaid refund was either paid or not required to be paid.

(ix) In the case of a school that does not make a refund or provide sufficient documentation demonstrating the refund was either paid or was not required, within 60 days of its receipt of the allegation notice from the guaranty agency, relief is provided to the borrower (and any endorser) if the guaranty agency determines the relief is appropriate. The agency must forward documentation of the school's failure to pay the unpaid refund to the Secretary.

(m) *Unpaid refund discharge procedures for a loan held by a lender.* In the case of an unpaid refund discharge request, the lender must provide the guaranty agency with documentation related to the borrower's qualification for discharge as specified in paragraph (l)(4) of this section.

(n) *Payment of an unpaid refund discharge request by a guaranty agency.*

(1) *General.* The guaranty agency must review an unpaid refund discharge request promptly and must pay the lender the amount of loss as defined in paragraphs (l)(1) and (l)(2) of this section, related to the unpaid refund not later than 45 days after a properly filed request is made.

(2) *Determination of the unpaid refund discharge amount to the lender.* The amount of loss payable to a lender on an unpaid refund includes that portion of an FFEL Program loan equal to the amount of the refund required under applicable Federal law and regulations, including this section, and including any accrued interest and other charges (late charges, collection costs, origination fees, and insurance premiums) associated with the unpaid refund.

(*o*)(1) *Determination of amount eligible for discharge.* The guaranty agency determines the amount eligible for discharge based on information showing the refund amount or by applying the appropriate refund formula to information that the borrower provides or that is otherwise available to the guaranty agency. For purposes of this section, all unpaid refunds are considered to be attributed to loan proceeds.

(2) If the information in paragraph (*o*)(1) of this section is not available, the guaranty agency uses the following formulas to determine the amount eligible for discharge:

(i) In the case of a student who fails to attend or whose withdrawal or termination date is before October 7, 2000 and who completes less than 60 percent of the loan period, the guaranty agency discharges the lesser of the institutional charges unearned or the loan amount. The guaranty agency determines the amount of the institutional charges unearned by—

(A) Calculating the ratio of the amount of time in the loan period after the student's last day of attendance to the actual length of the loan period; and

(B) Multiplying the resulting factor by the institutional charges assessed the student for the loan period.

(ii) In the case of a student who fails to attend or whose withdrawal or termination date is on or after October 7, 2000 and who completes less than 60 percent of the loan period, the guaranty agency discharges the loan amount unearned. The guaranty agency determines the loan amount unearned by—

(A) Calculating the ratio of the amount of time remaining in the loan period after the student's last day of attendance to the actual length of the loan period; and

(B) Multiplying the resulting factor by the total amount of title IV grants and loans received by the student, or if unknown, the loan amount.

(iii) In the case of a student who completes 60 percent or more of the loan period, the guaranty agency does not discharge any amount because a student who completes 60 percent or more of the loan period is not entitled to a refund.

(p) *Requests for reimbursement from the Secretary on loans held by guaranty agencies.* The Secretary reimburses the guaranty agency for its losses on unpaid refund request payments to lenders or borrowers in an amount that is equal to the amount specified in paragraph (n)(2) of this section.

(q) *Payments received after the guaranty agency's payment of an unpaid refund request.*

(1) The holder must promptly return to the sender any payment on a fully discharged loan, received after the guaranty agency pays an unpaid refund request unless the sender is required to pay (as in the case of a tuition recovery fund) in which case, the payment amount must be forwarded to the Secretary. At the same time that the holder returns the payment, it must notify the borrower that there is no obligation to repay a loan fully discharged.

(2) If the holder has returned a payment to the borrower, or the borrower's representative, with the notice described in paragraph (q)(1) of this section, and the borrower (or representative) continues to send payments to the holder, the holder must remit all of those payments to the Secretary.

(3) If the loan has not been fully discharged, payments must be applied to the remaining debt.

(r)(1) If the guaranty agency receives any payments from or on behalf of the borrower on or attributable to a loan that has been discharged in bankruptcy on which the Secretary previously paid a bankruptcy claim, the guaranty agency must return 100 percent of these payments to the sender. The guaranty agency must promptly return, to the sender, any payment on a cancelled or discharged loan made by the sender and received after the Secretary pays a closed school or false certification claim. At the same time that the agency returns the payment, it must notify the borrower that there is no obligation to repay a loan discharged on the basis of death, bankruptcy, false certification, or closing of the school.

(2) If the guaranty agency receives any payments from or on behalf of the borrower on or attributable to a loan that has been assigned to the Secretary for determination of eligibility for a total and permanent disability discharge, the guaranty agency must forward those payments to the Secretary for crediting to the borrower's account. At the same time that the agency forwards the payments, it must notify the borrower that there is no obligation to make payments on the loan while it is conditionally discharged prior to a final determination of eligibility for a total and permanent disability discharge, unless the Secretary directs the borrower otherwise.

(3) When the Secretary makes a final determination to discharge the loan, the Secretary returns to the sender any payments received on the loan after the date the borrower became totally and permanently disabled.

(4) The guaranty agency shall remit to the Secretary all payments received from a tuition recovery fund, performance bond, or other third party with respect to a loan on which the Secretary previously paid a closed school or false certification claim.

(5) If the guaranty agency has returned a payment to the borrower, or the borrower's representative, with the notice described in paragraphs (r)(1) or (r)(2) of this section, and the borrower (or representative) continues to send payments to the guaranty agency, the agency must remit all of those payments to the Secretary.

(s) *Applicable suspension of the repayment period.* For purposes of this section and 11 U.S.C. 523(a)(8)(A) with respect to loans guaranteed under the FFEL Program, an applicable suspension of the repayment period—

(1) Includes any period during which the lender does not require the borrower to make a payment on the loan.

(2) Begins on the date on which the borrower qualifies for the requested deferment as provided in § 682.210(a)(5) or the lender grants the requested forbearance;

(3) Closes on the later of the date on which—

(i) The condition for which the requested deferment or forbearance was received ends; or

(ii) The lender receives notice of the end of the condition for which the requested deferment or forbearance was received, if the condition ended earlier than represented by the borrower at the time of the request and the borrower did not notify timely the lender of the date on which the condition actually ended

(4) Includes the period between the end of the borrower's grace period and the first payment due date established by the lender in the case of a borrower who entered repayment without the knowledge of the lender;

(5) Includes the period between the filing of the petition for relief and the date on which the proceeding is completed or dismissed, unless payments have been made during that period in amounts sufficient to meet the amount owed under the repayment schedule in effect when the petition was filed.

(Approved by the Office of Management and Budget under control number 1845-0020)

(Authority: 20 U.S.C. 1078, 1078-1, 1078-2, 1078-3, 1082, 1087)

[58 Fed. Reg. 9120, Feb. 19, 1993; 59 Fed. Reg. 22476, April 29, 1994; 59 Fed. Reg. 25746, May 17, 1994; 59 Fed. Reg. 29543, June 8, 1994; 59 Fed. Reg. 35625, July 13, 1994; 59 Fed. Reg. 46175, Sept. 7, 1994; 59 Fed. Reg. 61216, Nov. 29, 1994; 59 Fed. Reg. 61428, Nov. 30, 1994; 60 Fed. Reg. 32912, June 26, 1995; 60 Fed. Reg. 61757, Dec. 1, 1995; 62 Fed. Reg. 63434, Nov. 28, 1997; 64 Fed. Reg. 18979, April 16, 1999; 64 Fed. Reg. 58628, Oct. 29, 1999; 64 Fed. Reg. 58960, Nov. 1, 1999; 65 Fed. Reg. 65620, 65691, Nov. 1, 2000; 66 Fed. Reg. 34763, June 29, 2001; 67 Fed. Reg. 67080, Nov. 1, 2002; 68 Fed. Reg. 75429, Dec. 31, 2003; 71 Fed. Reg. 45666, Sept. 8, 2006]

§ 682.405 Loan rehabilitation agreement.

(a) *General.*

(1) A guaranty agency that has a basic program agreement must enter into a loan rehabilitation agreement with the Secretary. The guaranty agency must establish a loan rehabilitation program for all borrowers with an enforceable promissory note for the purpose of rehabilitating defaulted loans, except for loans for which a judgment has been obtained, loans on which a default claim was filed under § 682.412, and loans on which the borrower has been convicted of, or has pled nolo contendere or guilty to, a crime involving fraud in obtaining title IV, HEA program assistance, so that the loan may be purchased, if practicable, by an eligible lender and removed from default status.

(2) A loan is considered to be rehabilitated only after—

(i) The borrower has made and the guaranty agency has received nine of the ten payments required under a monthly repayment agreement.

(A) Each of which payments is—

(1) Made voluntarily;

(2) In the full amount required; and

(3) Received within 20 days of the due date for the payment, and

(B) All nine payments are received within a 10-month period that begins with the month in which the first required due date falls and ends with the ninth consecutive calendar month following that month, and

(ii) The loan has been sold to an eligible lender.

(3) After the loan has been rehabilitated, the borrower regains all benefits of the program, including any remaining deferment eligibility under section 428(b)(1)(M) of the Act, from the date of the rehabilitation.

(b) *Terms of agreement.* In the loan rehabilitation agreement, the guaranty agency agrees to ensure that its loan rehabilitation program meets the following requirements at all times:

(1) A borrower may request rehabilitation of the borrower's defaulted loan held by the guaranty agency. In order to be eligible for rehabilitation of the loan, the borrower must voluntarily make at least nine of the ten payments required under a monthly repayment agreement.

(i) Each of which payment is—

(A) Made voluntarily,

(B) In the full amount required, and

(C) Received within 20 days of the due date for the payment, and

(ii) All nine payments are received within a ten-month period that begins with the month in which the first required due date falls and ends with the ninth consecutive calendar month following that month.

(2) For the purposes of this section, payment in the full amount required means payment of an amount that is reasonable and affordable, based on the borrower's total financial circumstances, as agreed to by the borrower and the agency. Voluntary payments are those made directly by the borrower and do not include payments obtained by Federal offset, garnishment, income or asset execution, or after a judgment has been entered on a loan. A guaranty agency must attempt to secure a lender to purchase the loan at the end of the 9- or 10-month payment period as applicable.

(3) The guaranty agency must report to all national credit bureaus within 90 days of the date the loan was rehabilitated that the loan is no longer in a default status and that the default is to be removed from the borrower's credit history.

(4) An eligible lender purchasing a rehabilitated loan must establish a repayment schedule that meets the same requirements that are applicable to other FFEL Program loans made under the same loan type and provides for the borrower to make monthly payments at least as great as the average of the 9 monthly payments received by the guaranty agency. For the purposes of the maximum loan repayment period, the lender must treat the first payment made under the 9 payments as the first payment under the applicable maximum repayment term, as defined under sections 682.209(a) or (h).

(Approved by the Office of Management and Budget under control number 1845-0020)

(Authority: 20 U.S.C. 1078-6)

[59 Fed. Reg. 33355, June 28, 1994; 60 Fed. Reg. 30788, June 12, 1995; 64 Fed. Reg. 18980, April 16, 1999; 64 Fed. Reg. 58965,

Nov. 1, 1999; 66 Fed. Reg. 34764, June 29, 2001; 67 Fed. Reg. 67090, Nov. 1, 2002; 68 Fed. Reg. 75429, Dec. 31, 2003; 71 Fed. Reg. 45666, Sept. 8, 2006]

§ 682.410 Fiscal, administrative, and enforcement requirements.

(a) *Fiscal requirements—*

(1) *Reserve fund assets.* A guaranty agency shall establish and maintain a reserve fund to be used solely for its activities as a guaranty agency under the FFEL Program ("guaranty activities"). The guaranty agency shall credit to the reserve fund—

(i) The total amount of insurance premiums and federal deferment fees collected;

(ii) Funds received from a State for the agency's guaranty activities, including matching funds under section 422(a) of the Act;

(iii) Federal advances obtained under sections 422(a) and (c) of the Act;

(iv) Federal payments for default, bankruptcy, death, disability, closed schools, and false certification claims;

(v) Supplemental preclaims assistance payments;

(vi) Transitional support payments received under section 458(a) of the Act;

(vii) Funds collected by the guaranty agency on FFEL Program loans on which a claim has been paid;

(viii) Investment earnings on the reserve fund; and

(ix) Other funds received by the guaranty agency from any source for the agency's guaranty activities.

(2) *Uses of reserve fund assets.* A guaranty agency may not use the assets of the reserve fund established under paragraph (a)(1) of this section to pay costs prohibited under § 682.418, but shall use the assets of the reserve fund to pay only—

(i) Insurance claims;

(ii) Costs that are reasonable, as defined under § 682.410(a)(11)(iii), and that are ordinary and necessary for the agency to fulfill its responsibilities under the HEA, including costs of collecting loans, providing preclaims assistance, monitoring enrollment and repayment status, and carrying out any other guaranty activities. Those costs must be—

(A) Allocable to the FFEL Program;

(B) Not higher than the agency would incur under established policies, regulations, and procedures that apply to any comparable non-Federal activities of the guaranty agency;

(C) Not included as a cost or used to meet cost sharing or matching requirements of any other federally supported activity, except as specifically provided by Federal law;

(D) Net of all applicable credits; and

(E) Documented in accordance with applicable legal and accounting standards;

(iii) The Secretary's equitable share of collections;

(iv) Federal advances and other funds owed to the Secretary;

(v) Reinsurance fees;

(vi) Insurance premiums and Federal default fees related to cancelled loans;

(vii) Borrower refunds, including those arising out of student or other borrower claims and defenses;

(vii)(A) The repayment, on or after December 29, 1993, of amounts credited under paragraphs (a)(1)(ii) or (a)(1)(ix) of this section, if the agency provides the Secretary

30 days prior notice of the repayment and demonstrates that—

(1) These amounts were originally received by the agency under appropriate contemporaneous documentation specifying that receipt was on a temporary basis only;

(2) The objective for which these amounts were originally received by the agency has been fully achieved; and

(3) Repayment of these amounts would not cause the agency to fail to comply with the minimum reserve levels provided by paragraph (a)(10) of this section, except that the Secretary may, for good cause, provide written permission for a payment that meets the other requirements of this paragraph (a)(2)(ix)(A).

(B) The repayment, prior to December 29, 1993, of amounts credited under paragraphs (a)(1)(ii) or (a)(1)(ix) of this section, if the agency demonstrates that—

(1) These amounts were originally received by the agency under appropriate contemporaneous documentation that receipt was on a temporary basis only; and

(2) The objective for which these amounts were originally received by the agency has been fully achieved.

(ix) Any other costs or payments ordinary and necessary to perform functions directly related to the agency's responsibilities under the HEA and for their proper and efficient administration;

(x) Notwithstanding any other provision of this section, any other payment that was allowed by law or regulation at the time it was made, if the agency acted in good faith when it made the payment or the agency would otherwise be unfairly prejudiced by the nonallowability of the payment at a later time; and

(xi) Any other amounts authorized or directed by the Secretary.

(3) *Accounting basis.* Except as approved by the Secretary, a guaranty agency shall credit the items listed in paragraph (a)(1) of this section to its reserve fund upon their receipt, without any deferral for accounting purposes, and shall deduct the items listed in paragraph (a)(2) of this section from its reserve fund upon their payment, without any accrual for accounting purposes.

(4) *Accounting records.*

(i) The accounting records of a guaranty agency must reflect the correct amount of sources and uses of funds under paragraph (a) of this section.

(ii) A guaranty agency may reverse prior credits to its reserve fund if—

(A) The agency gives the Secretary prior notice setting forth a detailed justification for the action;

(B) The Secretary determines that such credits were made erroneously and in good faith; and

(C) The Secretary determines that the action would not unfairly prejudice other parties.

(iii) A guaranty agency shall correct any other errors in its accounting or reporting as soon as practicable after the errors become known to the agency.

(iv) If a general reconstruction of a guaranty agency's historical accounting records is necessary to make a change under paragraphs (a)(4)(ii) and (a)(4)(iii) of this section or any other retroactive change to its accounting records, the agency may make this reconstruction only upon prior approval by the Secretary and without any deduction from its reserve fund for the cost of the reconstruction.

(5) *Investments.* The guaranty agency shall exercise the level of care required of a fiduciary charged with the duty of investing the money of others when it invests the assets of the reserve fund described in paragraph (a)(1) of this section. It may invest these assets only in low-risk securities, such as obligations issued or guaranteed by the United States or a State.

(6) *Development of assets.*

(i) If the guaranty agency uses in a substantial way for purposes other than the agency's guaranty activities any funds required to be credited to the reserve fund under paragraph (a)(1) of this section or any assets derived from the reserve fund to develop an asset of any kind and does not in good faith allocate a portion of the cost of developing and maintaining the developed asset to funds other than the reserve fund, the Secretary may require the agency to—

(A) Correct this allocation under paragraph (a)(4)(iii) of this section; or

(B) Correct the recorded ownership of the asset under paragraph (a)(4)(iii) of this section so that—

(1) If, in a transaction with an unrelated third party, the agency sells or otherwise derives revenue from uses of the asset that are unrelated to the agency's guaranty activities, the agency promptly shall deposit into the reserve fund described in paragraph (a)(1) of this section a percentage of the sale proceeds or revenue equal to the fair percentage of the total development cost of the asset paid with the reserve fund monies or provided by assets derived from the reserve fund; or

(2) If the agency otherwise converts the asset, in whole or in part, to a use unrelated to its guaranty activities, the agency promptly shall deposit into the reserve fund described in paragraph (a)(1) of this section a fair percentage of the fair market value or, in the case of a temporary conversion, the rental value of the portion of the asset employed for the unrelated use.

(ii) If the agency uses funds or assets described in paragraph (a)(6)(i) of this section in the manner described in that paragraph and makes a cost and maintenance allocation erroneously and in good faith, it shall correct the allocation under paragraph (a)(4)(iii) of this section.

(7) *Third-party claims.* If the guaranty agency has any claim against any other party to recover funds or other assets for the reserve fund, the claim is the property of the United States.

(8) *Related-party transactions.* All transactions between a guaranty agency and a related organization or other person that involve funds required to be credited to the agency's reserve fund under paragraph (a)(1) of this section or assets derived from the reserve fund must be on terms that are not less advantageous to the reserve fund than would have been negotiated on an arm's-length basis by unrelated parties.

(9) *Scope of definition.* The provisions of this § 682.410(a) define reserve funds and assets for purposes of sections 422 and 428 of the Act. These provisions do not, however, affect the Secretary's authority to use all funds and assets of the agency pursuant to section 428(c)(9)(F)(vi) of the Act.

(10) *Minimum reserve fund level.* The guaranty agency must maintain a current minimum reserve level of not less than—

(i) .5 percent of the amount of loans outstanding, for the fiscal year of the agency that begins in calendar year 1993;

(ii) .7 percent of the amount of loans outstanding, for the fiscal year of the agency that begins in calendar year 1994;

(iii) .9 percent of the amount of loans outstanding, for the fiscal year of the agency that begins in calendar year 1995; and

(iv) 1.1 percent of the amount of loans outstanding, for each fiscal year of the agency that begins on or after January 1, 1996.

(11) *Definitions.* For purposes of this section—

(i) *Reserve fund level* means—

(A) The total of reserve fund assets as defined in paragraph (a)(1) of this section;

(B) Minus the total amount of the reserve fund assets used in accordance with paragraphs (a)(2) and (a)(3) of this section; and

(ii) *Amount of loans outstanding* means—

(A) The sum of—

(1) The original principal amount of all loans guaranteed by the agency; and

(2) The original principal amount of any loans on which the guarantee was transferred to the agency from another guarantor, excluding loan guarantees transferred to another agency pursuant to a plan of the Secretary in response to the insolvency of the agency;

(B) Minus the original principal amount of all loans on which—

(1) The loan guarantee was cancelled;

(2) The loan guarantee was transferred to another agency;

(3) Payment in full has been made by the borrower;

(4) Reinsurance coverage has been lost and cannot be regained; and

(5) The agency paid claims.

(iii) *Reasonable cost* means a cost that, in its nature and amount, does not exceed that which would be incurred by a prudent person under the circumstances prevailing at the time the decision was made to incur the cost. The burden of proof is upon the guaranty agency, as a fiduciary under its agreements with the Secretary, to establish that costs are reasonable. In determining reasonableness of a given cost, consideration must be given to—

(A) Whether the cost is of a type generally recognized as ordinary and necessary for the proper and efficient performance and administration of the guaranty agency's responsibilities under the HEA;

(B) The restraints or requirements imposed by factors such as sound business practices, arms-length bargaining, Federal, State, and other laws and regulations, and the terms and conditions of the guaranty agency's agreements with the Secretary; and

(C) Market prices of comparable goods or services.

(b) *Administrative requirements*—

(1) *Independent audits.* The guaranty agency shall arrange for an independent financial and compliance audit of the agency's FFEL program as follows:

(i) With regard to a guaranty agency that is an agency of a State government, an audit must be conducted in accordance with 31 U.S.C. 7502 and 34 CFR part 80, appendix G.

(ii) With regard to a guaranty agency that is a nonprofit organization, an audit must be conducted in accordance with OMB Circular A-133, Audits of Institutions of Higher Education and Other Nonprofit Organizations and 34 CFR 74.61(h)(3). If a nonprofit guaranty agency meets the criteria in Circular A-133 to have a program specific audit, and chooses that option, the program specific audit must meet the following requirements:

(A) The audit must examine the agency's compliance with the Act, applicable regulations, and agreements entered into under this part.

(B) The audit must examine the agency's financial management of its FFEL program activities.

(C) The audit must be conducted in accordance with the standards for audits issued by the United States General Accounting Office's (GAO) Government Auditing Standards. Procedures for audits are contained in an audit guide developed by, and available from, the Office of the Inspector General of the Department.

(D) The audit must be conducted annually and must be submitted to the Secretary within six months of the end of the audit period. The first audit must cover the agency's activities for a period that includes July 23, 1992, unless the agency is currently submitting audits on a biennial basis, and the second year of its biennial cycle starts on or before July 23, 1992. Under these circumstances, the agency shall submit a biennial audit that includes July 23, 1992 and submit its next audit as an annual audit.

(2) *Collection charges.* Whether or not provided for in the borrower's promissory note and subject to any limitation on the amount of those costs in that note, the guaranty agency shall charge a borrower an amount equal to reasonable costs incurred by the agency in collecting a loan on which the agency has paid a default or bankruptcy claim. These costs may include, but are not limited to, all attorney's fees, collection agency charges, and court costs. Except as provided in §§ 682.401(b)(27) and 682.405(b)(1)(iv), the amount charged a borrower must equal the lesser of—

(i) The amount the same borrower would be charged for the cost of collection under the formula in 34 CFR 30.60; or

(ii) The amount the same borrower would be charged for the cost of collection if the loan was held by the U.S. Department of Education.

(3) *Interest charged by guaranty agencies.* The guaranty agency shall charge the borrower interest on the amount owed by the borrower after the capitalization required under paragraph (b)(4) of this section has occurred at a rate that is the greater of—

(i) The rate established by the terms of the borrower's original promissory note;

(ii) In the case of a loan for which a judgment has been obtained, the rate provided for by State law.

(4) *Capitalization of unpaid interest.* The guaranty agency shall capitalize any unpaid interest due the lender from the borrower at the time the agency pays a default claim to the lender.

(5) *Credit bureau reports.*

(i) After the completion of the procedures in paragraph (b)(5)(ii) of this section, the guaranty agency shall, after it has paid a default claim, report promptly, but not less than sixty days after completion of the procedures in paragraph (b)(6)(v) of this section, and on a regular basis, to all national credit bureaus—

(A) The total amount of loans made to the borrower and the remaining balance of those loans;

(B) The date of default;

(C) Information concerning collection of the loan, including the repayment status of the loan;

(D) Any changes or corrections in the information reported by the agency that result from information received after the initial report; and

(E) The date the loan is fully repaid by or on behalf of the borrower or discharged by reason of the borrower's death, bankruptcy, total and permanent disability, or closed school or false certification.

(ii) The guaranty agency, after it pays a default claim on a loan but before it reports the default to a credit bureau or assesses collection costs against a borrower, shall, within the time-frame specified in paragraph (b)(6)(v) of this section, provide the borrower with—

(A) Written notice that meets the requirements of paragraph (b)(5)(vi) of this section regarding the proposed actions;

(B) An opportunity to inspect and copy agency records pertaining to the loan obligation;

(C) An opportunity for an administrative review of the legal enforceability or past-due status of the loan obligation; and

(D) An opportunity to enter into a repayment agreement on terms satisfactory to the agency.

(iii) The procedures set forth in 34 CFR 30.20–30.33 (administrative offset) satisfy the requirements of paragraph (b)(5)(ii) of this section.

(iv)(A) In response to a request submitted by a borrower, after the deadlines established under agency rules, for access to records, an administrative review, or for an opportunity to enter into a repayment agreement, the agency shall provide the requested relief but may continue reporting the debt to credit bureaus until it determines that the borrower has demonstrated that the loan obligation is not legally enforceable or that alternative repayment arrangements satisfactory to the agency have been made with the borrower.

(B) The deadline established by the agency for requesting administrative review under paragraph (b)(5)(ii)(C) of this section must allow the borrower at least 60 days from the date the notice described in paragraph (b)(5)(ii)(A) of this section is sent to request that review.

(v) An agency may not permit an employee, official, or agent to conduct the administrative review required under this paragraph if that individual is—

(A) Employed in an organizational component of the agency or its agent that is charged with collection of loan obligations; or

(B) Compensated on the basis of collections on loan obligations.

(vi) The notice sent by the agency under paragraph (b)(5)(ii)(A) of this section must—

(A) Advise the borrower that the agency has paid a default claim filed by the lender and has taken assignment of the loan;

(B) Identify the lender that made the loan and the school for attendance at which the loan was made;

(C) State the outstanding principal, accrued interest, and any other charges then owing on the loan;

(D) Demand that the borrower immediately begin repayment of the loan;

(E) Explain the rate of interest that will accrue on the loan, that all costs incurred to collect the loan will be charged to the borrower, the authority for assessing these costs, and the manner in which the agency will calculate the amount of these costs;

(F) Notify the borrower that the agency will report the default to all national credit bureaus to the detriment of the borrower's credit rating;

(G) Explain the opportunities available to the borrower under agency rules to request access to the agency's records on the loan, to request an administrative review of the legal enforceability or past-due status of the loan, and to reach an agreement on repayment terms satisfactory to the agency to prevent the agency from reporting the loan as defaulted to credit bureaus and provide deadlines and method for requesting this relief;

(H) Unless the agency uses a separate notice to advise the borrower regarding other proposed enforcement actions, describe specifically any other enforcement action, such as offset against federal or state income tax refunds or wage garnishment that the agency intends to use to collect the debt, and explain the procedures available to the borrower prior to those other enforcement actions for access to records, for an administrative review, or for agreement to alternative repayment terms;

(I) Describe the grounds on which the borrower may object that the loan obligation as stated in the notice is not a legally enforceable debt owed by the borrower;

(J) Describe any appeal rights available to the borrower from an adverse decision on administrative review of the loan obligation;

(K) Describe any right to judicial review of an adverse decision by the agency regarding the legal enforceability or past-due status of the loan obligation; and

(L) Describe the collection actions that the agency may take in the future if those presently proposed do not result in repayment of the loan obligation, including the filing of a lawsuit against the borrower by the agency and assignment of the loan to the Secretary for the filing of a lawsuit against the borrower by the Federal Government.

(vii) As part of the guaranty agency's response to a borrower who appeals an adverse decision resulting from the agency's administrative review of the loan obligation, the agency must provide the borrower with information on the availability of the Student Loan Ombudsman's office.

(6) *Collection efforts on defaulted loans.*

(i) A guaranty agency must engage in reasonable and documented collection activities on a loan on which it pays a default claim filed by a lender. For a non-paying borrower, the agency must perform at least one activity every 180 days to collect the debt, locate the borrower (if necessary), or determine if the borrower has the means to repay the debt.

(ii) A guaranty agency must attempt an annual Federal offset against all eligible borrowers. If an agency initiates proceedings to offset a borrower's State or Federal income tax refunds and other payments made by the Federal Government to the borrower, it may not initiate those proceedings sooner than 60 days after sending the notice described in paragraph (b)(5)(ii)(A) of this section.

(iii) A guaranty agency must initiate administrative wage garnishment proceedings against all eligible borrowers, except as provided in paragraph (b)(6)(iv) of this section, by following the procedures described in paragraph (b)(9) of this section.

(iv) A guaranty agency may file a civil suit against a borrower to compel repayment only if the borrower has no wages that can be garnished under paragraph (b)(9) of this section, or the agency determines that the borrower has sufficient attachable assets or income that is not subject to administrative wage garnishment that can be used to repay the debt, and the use of litigation would be more effective in collection of the debt.

(v) Within 45 days after paying a lender's default claim, the agency must send a notice to the borrower that contains the information described in paragraph (b)(5)(ii) of this section. During this time period, the agency also must notify the borrower, either in the notice containing the information described in paragraph (b)(5)(ii) of this section, or in a separate notice, that if he or she does not make repayment arrangements acceptable to the agency, the agency will promptly initiate procedures to collect the debt. The agency's notification to the borrower must state that the agency may administratively garnish the borrower's wages, file a civil suit to compel repayment, offset the borrower's State and Federal income tax refunds and other payments made by the Federal Government to the borrower, assign the loan to the Secretary in accordance with § 682.409, and take other lawful collection means to collect the debt, at the discretion of the agency. The agency's notification must include a statement that borrowers may have certain legal rights in the collection of debts, and that borrowers may wish to contact counselors or lawyers regarding those rights.

(vi) Within a reasonable time after all of the information described in paragraph (b)(6)(v) of this section has been sent, the agency must send at least one notice informing the borrower that the default has been reported to all national credit bureaus (if that is the case) and that the borrower's credit rating may thereby have been damaged.

(7) *Special conditions for agency payment of a claim.*

(i) A guaranty agency may adopt a policy under which it pays a claim to a lender on a loan under the conditions described in § 682.509(a)(1).

(ii) Upon the payment of a claim under a policy described in paragraph (b)(7)(i) of this section, the guaranty agency shall—

(A) Perform the loan servicing functions required of a lender under § 682.208, except that the agency is not required to follow the credit bureau reporting requirements of that section;

(B) Perform the functions of the lender during the repayment period of the loan, as required under § 682.209;

(C) If the borrower is delinquent in repaying the loan at the time the agency pays a claim thereon to the lender or becomes delinquent while the agency holds the loan, exercise due diligence in accordance with § 682.411 in attempting to collect the loan from the borrower and any endorser or co-maker; and

(D) After the date of default on the loan, if any, comply with

paragraph (b)(6) of this section with respect to collection activities on the loan, with the date of default treated as the claim payment date for purposes of those paragraphs.

(8) *Preemption of State law.* The provisions of paragraphs (b)(2), (5), and (6) of this section preempt any State law, including State statutes, regulations, or rules, that would conflict with or hinder satisfaction of the requirements of these provisions.

(9) *Administrative Garnishment.*

(i) If a guaranty agency decides to garnish the disposable pay of a borrower who is not making payments on a loan held by the agency, on which the Secretary has paid a reinsurance claim, it shall do so in accordance with the following procedures:

(A) The employer shall deduct and pay to the agency from a borrower's wages an amount that does not exceed the lesser of 15 percent of the borrower's disposable pay for each pay period or the amount permitted by 15 U.S.C. 1673, unless the borrower provides the agency with written consent to deduct a greater amount. For this purpose, the term "disposable pay" means that part of the borrower's compensation from an employer remaining after the deduction of any amounts required by law to be withheld.

(B) At least 30 days before the initiation of garnishment proceedings, the guaranty agency shall mail to the borrower's last known address, a written notice of the nature and amount of the debt, the intention of the agency to initiate proceedings to collect the debt through deductions from pay, and an explanation of the borrower's rights.

(C) The guaranty agency shall offer the borrower an opportunity to inspect and copy agency records related to the debt.

(D) The guaranty agency shall offer the borrower an opportunity to enter into a written repayment agreement with the agency under terms agreeable to the agency.

(E) The guaranty agency shall offer the borrower an opportunity for a hearing in accordance with paragraph (b)(9)(i)(J) of this section concerning the existence or the amount of the debt and, in the case of a borrower whose proposed repayment schedule under the garnishment order is established other than by a written agreement under paragraph (b)(9)(i)(D) of this section, the terms of the repayment schedule.

(F) The guaranty agency shall sue any employer for any amount that the employer, after receipt of the garnishment notice provided by the agency under paragraph (b)(9)(i)(H) of this section, fails to withhold from wages owed and payable to an employee under the employer's normal pay and disbursement cycle.

(G) The guaranty agency may not garnish the wages of a borrower whom it knows has been involuntarily separated from employment until the borrower has been reemployed continuously for at least 12 months.

(H) Unless the guaranty agency receives information that the agency believes justifies a delay or cancellation of the withholding order, it shall send a withholding order to the employer within 20 days after the borrower fails to make a timely request for a hearing, or, if a timely request for a hearing is made by the borrower, within 20 days after a final decision is made by the agency to proceed with garnishment.

(I) The notice given to the employer under paragraph (b)(9)(i)(H) of this section must contain only the information as may be necessary for the employer to comply with the withholding order.

(J) The guaranty agency shall provide a hearing, which, at the borrower's option, may be oral or written, if the borrower submits a written request for a hearing on the existence or amount of the debt or the terms of the repayment schedule. The time and location of the hearing shall be established by the agency. An oral hearing may, at the borrower's option, be conducted either in-person or by telephone conference. All telephonic charges must be the responsibility of the guaranty agency.

(K) If the borrower's written request is received by the guaranty agency on or before the 15th day following the borrower's receipt of the notice described in paragraph (b)(9)(i)(B) of this section, the guaranty agency may not issue a withholding order until the borrower has been provided the requested hearing. For purposes of this paragraph, in the absence of evidence to the contrary, a borrower shall be considered to have received the notice described in paragraph (b)(9)(i)(B) of this section 5 days after it was mailed by the agency. The guaranty agency shall provide a hearing to the borrower in sufficient time to permit a decision, in accordance with the procedures that the agency may prescribe, to be rendered within 60 days.

(L) If the borrower's written request is received by the guaranty agency after the 15th day following the borrower's receipt of the notice described in paragraph (b)(9)(i)(B) of this section, the guaranty agency shall provide a hearing to the borrower in sufficient time that a decision, in accordance with the procedures that the agency may prescribe, may be rendered within 60 days, but may not delay issuance of a withholding order unless the agency determines that the delay in filing the request was caused by factors over which the borrower had no control, or the agency receives information that the agency believes justifies a delay or cancellation of the withholding order. For purposes of this paragraph, in the absence of evidence to the contrary, a borrower shall be considered to have received the notice described in paragraph (b)(9)(i)(B) of this section 5 days after it was mailed by the agency.

(M) The hearing official appointed by the agency to conduct the hearing may be any qualified individual, including an administrative law judge, not under the supervision or control of the head of the guaranty agency.

(N) The hearing official shall issue a final written decision at the earliest practicable date, but not later than 60 days after the guaranty agency's receipt of the borrower's hearing request.

(O) As specified in section 488A(a)(8) of the HEA, the borrower may seek judicial relief, including punitive damages, if the employer discharges, refuses to employ, or takes disciplinary action against the borrower due to the issuance of a withholding order.

(ii) References to "the borrower" in this paragraph include all endorsers on a loan.

(10) *Conflicts of interest.*

(i) A guaranty agency shall maintain and enforce written standards of conduct governing the performance of its employees, officers, directors, trustees, and agents engaged in the selection, award, and administration of contracts or agreements. The standards of conduct must, at a minimum, require disclosure of financial or other interests and must mandate disinterested decision-making. The standards must provide for appropriate disciplinary actions to be applied for violations of the standards by employees, officers, directors, trustees, or agents of the guaranty agency, and must include provisions to—

(A) Prohibit any employee, officer, director, trustee, or agent from participating in the selection, award, or decision-making related to the administration of a contract or agreement supported by the reserve fund described in paragraph (a) of this section, if that participation would create a conflict of interest. Such a conflict would arise if the employee, officer, director, trustee, or agent, or any member of his or her immediate family, his or her partner, or an organization that employs or is about to employ any of those parties has a financial or ownership interest in the organization selected for an award or would benefit from the decision made in the administration of the contract or agreement. The prohibitions described in this paragraph do not apply to employees of a State agency covered by codes of conduct established under State law;

(B) Ensure sufficient separation of responsibility and authority between its lender claims processing as a guaranty agency and its lending or loan servicing activities, or both, within the guaranty agency or between that agency and one or more affiliates, including independence in direct reporting requirements and such management and systems controls as may be necessary to demonstrate, in the independent audit required under § 682.410(b)(1), that claims filed by another arm of the guaranty agency or by an affiliate of that agency receive no more favorable treatment than that accorded the claims filed by a lender or servicer that is not an affiliate or part of the guaranty agency; and

(C) Prohibit the employees, officers, directors, trustees, and agents of the guaranty agency, his or her partner, or any member of his or her immediate family, from soliciting or accepting gratuities, favors, or anything of monetary value from contractors or parties to agreements, except that nominal and unsolicited gratuities, favors, or items may be accepted.

(ii) *Guaranty agency restructuring.* If the Secretary determines that action is necessary to protect the Federal fiscal interest because of an agency's failure to meet the requirements of § 682.410(b)(10)(i), the Secretary may require the agency to comply with any additional measures that the Secretary believes are appropriate, including the total divestiture of the agency's non-FFEL functions and the agency's interests in any affiliated organization.

(c) *Enforcement requirements.* A guaranty agency shall take such measures and establish such controls as are necessary to ensure its vigorous enforcement of all Federal, State, and guaranty agency requirements, including agreements, applicable to its loan guarantee program, including, at a minimum, the following:

(1) Conducting comprehensive biennial on-site program reviews, using statistically valid techniques to calculate liabilities to the Secretary that each review indicates may exist, of at least—

(i)(A) Each participating lender whose dollar volume of FFEL loans made or held by the lender and guaranteed by the agency in the preceding year—

(1) Equaled or exceeded two percent of the total of all loans guaranteed in that year by the agency;

(2) Was one of the ten largest lenders whose loans were guaranteed in that year by the agency; or

(3) Equaled or exceeded $10 million in the most recent fiscal year;

(B) Each lender described in section 435(d)(1)(D) or (J) of the Act that is located in any State in which the agency is the principal guarantor and, at the option of each guaranty agency, the Student Loan Marketing Association; and

(C) Each participating school, located in a State for which the guaranty agency is the principal guaranty agency, that has a cohort default rate, as described in subpart M of 34 CFR part 668, for either of the 2 immediately preceding fiscal years, as defined in 34 CFR 668.182, that exceeds 20 percent, unless the school is under a mandate from the Secretary under subpart M of 34 CFR part 668 to take specific default reduction measures or if the total dollar amount of loans entering repayment in each fiscal year on which the cohort default rate over 20 percent is based does not exceed $100,000; or

(ii) The schools and lenders selected by the agency as an alternative to the reviews required by paragraphs (c)(1)(A)–(C) of this section if the Secretary approves the agency's proposed alternative selection methodology.

(2) Demanding prompt repayment by the responsible parties to lenders, borrowers, the agency, or the Secretary, as appropriate, of all funds found in those reviews to be owed by the participants with regard to loans guaranteed by the agency, whether or not the agency holds the loans, and monitoring the implementation by participants of corrective actions, including these repayments, required by the agency as a result of those reviews.

(3) Referring to the Secretary for further enforcement action any case in which repayment of funds to the Secretary is not made in full within 60 days of the date of the agency's written demand to the school, lender, or other party for payment, together with all supporting documentation, any correspondence, and any other documentation submitted by that party regarding the repayment.

(4) Adopting procedures for identifying fraudulent loan applications.

(5) Undertaking or arranging with State or local law enforcement agencies for the prompt and thorough investigation of all allegations and indications of criminal or other programmatic misconduct by its program participants, including violations of Federal law or regulations.

(6) Promptly referring to appropriate State and local regulatory agencies and to nationally recognized accrediting agencies and associations for investigation information received by the guaranty agency that may affect the retention or renewal of the license or accreditation of a program participant.

(7) Promptly reporting all of the allegations and indications of misconduct having a substantial basis in fact, and the scope, progress, and results of the agency's investigations thereof to the Secretary.

(8) Referring appropriate cases to State or local authorities for criminal prosecution or civil litigation.

(9) Promptly notifying the Secretary of—

(i) Any action it takes affecting the FFEL program eligibility of a participating lender or school;

(ii) Information it receives regarding an action affecting the FFEL program eligibility of a participating lender or school taken by a nationally recognized accrediting agency, association, or a State licensing agency;

(iii) Any judicial or administrative proceeding relating to the enforceability of FFEL loans guaranteed by the agency or in which tuition obligations of a school's students are directly at issue, other than a proceeding relating to a single borrower or student; and

(iv) Any petition for relief in bankruptcy, application for receivership, or corporate dissolution proceeding brought by or against a school or lender participating in its loan guarantee program.

(10) Cooperating with all program reviews, investigations, and audits conducted by the Secretary relating to the agency's loan guarantee program.

(11) Taking prompt action to protect the rights of borrowers and the Federal fiscal interest respecting loans that the agency has guaranteed when the agency learns that a participating school or holder of loans is experiencing problems that threaten the solvency of the school or holder, including—

(i) Conducting on-site program reviews;

(ii) Providing training and technical assistance, if appropriate;

(iii) Filing a proof of claim with a bankruptcy court for recovery of any funds due the agency and any refunds due to borrowers on FFEL loans that it has guaranteed when the agency learns that a school has filed a bankruptcy petition;

(iv) Promptly notifying the Secretary that the agency has determined that a school or holder of loans is experiencing potential solvency problems; and

(v) Promptly notifying the Secretary of the results of any actions taken by the agency to protect Federal funds involving such a school or holder.

(Approved by the Office of Management and Budget under control number 1845-0020)

(Authority: 20 U.S.C. 1078, 1078-1, 1078-2, 1078-3, 1080a, 1082, 1087, 1091a, and 1099)

[58 Fed. Reg. 9119, Feb. 19, 1993; 59 Fed. Reg. 22487, April 29, 1994; 59 Fed. Reg. 25747, May 17, 1994; 59 Fed. Reg. 33357, June 28, 1994; 59 Fed. Reg. 35625, July 13, 1994; 59 Fed. Reg. 46175, Sept. 7, 1994; 59 Fed. Reg. 60691, Nov. 25, 1994; 60 Fed. Reg. 32912, June 26, 1995; 61 Fed. Reg. 60436, 60486, Nov. 27, 1996; 64 Fed. Reg. 18980, April 16, 1999; 64 Fed. Reg. 58630, Oct. 29, 1999; 64 Fed. Reg. 58965, Nov. 1, 1999; 65 Fed. Reg. 65621, Nov. 1, 2000; 65 Fed. Reg. 65650, Nov. 1, 2000; 66 Fed. Reg. 34764, June 29, 2001; 68 Fed. Reg. 75427, Dec. 31, 2003; 71 Fed. Reg. 45666, Sept. 8, 2006]

§ 682.411 Lender due diligence in collecting guaranty agency loans.

(a) *General.* In the event of delinquency on an FFEL Program loan, the lender must engage in at least the collection efforts described in paragraphs (c) through (n) of this section, except that in the case of a loan made to a borrower who is incarcerated, residing outside a State, Mexico, or Canada, or whose telephone number is unknown, the lender may send a forceful collection letter instead of each telephone effort required by this section.

(b) *Delinquency.*

(1) For purposes of this section, delinquency on a loan begins on the first day after the due date of the first missed payment that is not later made. The due date of the first payment is established by the lender but must occur by the deadlines specified in § 682.209(a) or, if the lender first learns after the fact that the borrower has entered the repayment period, no later than 75 days after the day the lender so learns, except as provided in § 682.209(a)(2)(v) and (a)(3)(ii)(E). If a payment is made late, the first day of delinquency is the day after the due date of the next missed payment that is not later made. A payment that is within five dollars of the amount normally required to advance the due date may nevertheless advance the due date if the lender's procedures allow for that advancement.

(2) At no point during the periods specified in paragraphs (c), (d), and (e) of this section may the lender permit the occurrence of a gap in collection activity, as defined in paragraph (j) of this section, of more than 45 days (60 days in the case of a transfer).

(3) As part of one of the collection activities provided for in this section, the lender must provide the borrower with information on the availability of the Student Loan Ombudsman's office.

(c) *1–15 days delinquent.* Except in the case in which a loan is brought into this period by a payment on the loan, expiration of an authorized deferment or forbearance period, or the lender's receipt from the drawee of a dishonored check submitted as a payment on the loan, the lender during this period must send at least one written notice or collection letter to the borrower informing the borrower of the delinquency and urging the borrower to make payments sufficient to eliminate the delinquency. The notice or collection letter sent during this period must include, at a minimum, a lender or servicer contact, a telephone number, and a prominent statement informing the borrower that assistance may be available if he or she is experiencing difficulty in making a scheduled repayment.

(d) *16–180 days delinquent (16–240 days delinquent for a loan repayable in installments less frequently than monthly).*

(1) Unless exempted under paragraph (d)(4) of this section, during this period the lender must engage in at least four diligent efforts to contact the borrower by telephone and send at least four collection letters urging the borrower to make the required payments on the loan. At least one of the diligent efforts to contact the borrower by telephone must occur on or before, and another one must occur after, the 90th day of delinquency. Collection letters sent during this period must include, at a minimum, information for the borrower regarding deferment, forbearance, income-sensitive repayment and loan consolidation, and other available options to avoid default.

(2) At least two of the collection letters required under paragraph (d)(1) of this section must warn the borrower that, if the loan is not paid, the lender will assign the loan to the guaranty agency that, in turn, will report the default to all national credit bureaus,

and that the agency may institute proceedings to offset the borrower's State and Federal income tax refunds and other payments made by the Federal Government to the borrower or to garnish the borrower's wages, or to assign the loan to the Federal Government for litigation against the borrower.

(3) Following the lender's receipt of a payment on the loan or a correct address for the borrower, the lender's receipt from the drawee of a dishonored check received as a payment on the loan, the lender's receipt of a correct telephone number for the borrower, or the expiration of an authorized deferment or forbearance period, the lender is required to engage in only—

   (i) Two diligent efforts to contact the borrower by telephone during this period, if the loan is less than 91 days delinquent (121 days delinquent for a loan repayable in installments less frequently than monthly) upon receipt of the payment, correct address, correct telephone number, or returned check, or expiration of the deferment or forbearance; or

   (ii) One diligent effort to contact the borrower by telephone during this period if the loan is 91–120 days delinquent (121–180 days delinquent for a loan repayable in installments less frequently than monthly) upon receipt of the payment, correct address, correct telephone number, or returned check, or expiration of the deferment or forbearance.

(4) A lender need not attempt to contact by telephone any borrower who is more than 120 days delinquent (180 days delinquent for a loan repayable in installments less frequent than monthly) following the lender's receipt of—

   (i) A payment on the loan;

   (ii) A correct address or correct telephone number for the borrower;

   (iii) A dishonored check received from the drawee as a payment on the loan; or

   (iv) The expiration of an authorized deferment or forbearance.

(e) *181–270 days delinquent (241–330 days delinquent for a loan repayable in installments less frequently than monthly).* During this period the lender must engage in efforts to urge the borrower to make the required payments on the loan. These efforts must, at a minimum, provide information to the borrower regarding options to avoid default and the consequences of defaulting on the loan.

(f) *Final demand.* On or after the 241st day of delinquency (the 301st day for loans payable in less frequent installments than monthly) the lender must send a final demand letter to the borrower requiring repayment of the loan in full and notifying the borrower that a default will be reported to a national credit bureau. The lender must allow the borrower at least 30 days after the date the letter is mailed to respond to the final demand letter and to bring the loan out of default before filing a default claim on the loan.

(g) *Collection procedures when borrower's telephone number is not available.* Upon completion of a diligent but unsuccessful effort to ascertain the correct telephone number of a borrower as required by paragraph (m) of this section, the lender is excused from any further efforts to contact the borrower by telephone, unless the borrower's number is obtained before the 211th day of delinquency (the 271st day for loans repayable in installments less frequently than monthly).

(h) *Skip-tracing.*

(1) Unless the letter specified under paragraph (f) of this section

has already been sent, within 10 days of its receipt of information indicating that it does not know the borrower's current address, the lender must begin to diligently attempt to locate the borrower through the use of effective commercial skip-tracing techniques. These efforts must include, but are not limited to, sending a letter to or making a diligent effort to contact each endorser, relative, reference, individual, and entity, identified in the borrower's loan file, including the schools the student attended. For this purpose, a lender's contact with a school official who might reasonably be expected to know the borrower's address may be with someone other than the financial aid administrator, and may be in writing or by phone calls. These efforts must be completed by the date of default with no gap of more than 45 days between attempts to contact those individuals or entities.

(2) Upon receipt of information indicating that it does not know the borrower's current address, the lender must discontinue the collection efforts described in paragraphs (c) through (f) of this section.

(3) If the lender is unable to ascertain the borrower's current address despite its performance of the activities described in paragraph (h)(1) of this section, the lender is excused thereafter from performance of the collection activities described in paragraphs (c) through (f) and (l)(1) through (l)(3) and (l)(5) of this section unless it receives communication indicating the borrower's address before the 241st day of delinquency (the 301st day for loans payable in less frequent installments than monthly).

(4) The activities specified by paragraph (m)(1)(i) or (ii) of this section (with references to the "borrower" understood to mean endorser, reference, relative, individual, or entity as appropriate) meet the requirement that the lender make a diligent effort to contact each individual identified in the borrower's loan file.

(*i*) *Default aversion assistance.* Not earlier than the 60th day and no later than the 120th day of delinquency, a lender must request default aversion assistance from the guaranty agency that guarantees the loan.

(*j*) *Gap in collection activity.* For purposes of this section, the term *gap in collection activity* means, with respect to a loan, any period—

(1) Beginning on the date that is the day after—

(i)   The due date of a payment unless the lender does not know the borrower's address on that date;

(ii) The day on which the lender receives a payment on a loan that remains delinquent notwithstanding the payment;

(iii) The day on which the lender receives the correct address for a delinquent borrower;

(iv) The day on which the lender completes a collection activity;

(v)   The day on which the lender receives a dishonored check submitted as a payment on the loan;

(vi) The expiration of an authorized deferment or forbearance period on a delinquent loan; or

(vii) The day the lender receives information indicating it does not know the borrower's current address; and

(2) Ending on the date of the earliest of—

(i)   The day on which the lender receives the first subsequent payment or completed deferment request or forbearance agreement;

(ii) The day on which the lender begins the first subsequent collection activity;

(iii) The day on which the lender receives written communication from the borrower relating to his or her account; or

(iv) Default.

(*k*) *Transfer.* For purposes of this section, the term transfer with respect to a loan means any action, including, but not limited to, the sale of the loan, that results in a change in the system used to monitor or conduct collection activity on a loan from one system to another.

(*l*) *Collection activity.* For purposes of this section, the term collection activity with respect to a loan means—

(1) Mailing or otherwise transmitting to the borrower at an address that the lender reasonably believes to be the borrower's current address a collection letter or final demand letter that satisfies the timing and content requirements of paragraph (c), (d), (e), or (f) of this section;

(2) Making an attempt to contact the borrower by telephone to urge the borrower to begin or resume repayment;

(3) Conducting skip-tracing efforts, in accordance with paragraph (h)(1) or (m)(1)(iii) of this section, to locate a borrower whose correct address or telephone number is unknown to the lender;

(4) Mailing or otherwise transmitting to the guaranty agency a request for default aversion assistance available from the agency on the loan at the time the request is transmitted; or

(5) Any telephone discussion or personal contact with the borrower so long as the borrower is apprised of the account's past-due status.

(*m*) *Diligent effort for telephone contact.*

(1) For purposes of this section, the term *diligent effort with respect to telephone contact* means—

(i)   A successful effort to contact the borrower by telephone;

(ii) At least two unsuccessful attempts to contact the borrower by telephone at a number that the lender reasonably believes to be the borrower's correct telephone number; or

(iii) An unsuccessful effort to ascertain the correct telephone number of a borrower, including, but not limited to, a directory assistance inquiry as to the borrower's telephone number, and sending a letter to or making a diligent effort to contact each reference, relative, and individual identified in the most recent loan application or most recent school certification for that borrower held by the lender. The lender may contact a school official other than the financial aid administrator who reasonably may be expected to know the borrower's address or telephone number.

(2) If the lender is unable to ascertain the borrower's correct telephone number despite its performance of the activities described in paragraph (m)(1)(iii) of this section, the lender is excused thereafter from attempting to contact the borrower by telephone unless it receives a communication indicating the borrower's current telephone number before the 211th day of delinquency (the 271st day for loans repayable in installments less frequently than monthly).

(3) The activities specified by paragraph (m)(1)(i) or (ii) of this section (with references to "the borrower" understood to mean endorser, reference, relative, or individual as appropriate), meet the requirement that the lender make a diligent effort to contact each endorser or each reference, relative, or individual identified on the borrower's most recent loan application or most recent school certification.

(n) *Due diligence for endorsers.*

(1) Before filing a default claim on a loan with an endorser, the lender must—

(i) Make a diligent effort to contact the endorser by telephone; and

(ii) Send the endorser on the loan two letters advising the endorser of the delinquent status of the loan and urging the endorser to make the required payments on the loan with at least one letter containing the information described in paragraph (d)(2) of this section (with references to "the borrower" understood to mean the endorser).

(2) On or after the 241st day of delinquency (the 301st day for loans payable in less frequent installments than monthly) the lender must send a final demand letter to the endorser requiring repayment of the loan in full and notifying the endorser that a default will be reported to a national credit bureau. The lender must allow the endorser at least 30 days after the date the letter is mailed to respond to the final demand letter and to bring the loan out of default before filing a default claim on the loan.

(3) Unless the letter specified under paragraph (n)(2) of this section has already been sent, upon receipt of information indicating that it does not know the endorser's current address or telephone number, the lender must diligently attempt to locate the endorser through the use of effective commercial skip-tracing techniques. This effort must include an inquiry to directory assistance.

(*o*) *Preemption of State law.* The provisions of this section preempt any State law, including State statutes, regulations, or rules, that would conflict with or hinder satisfaction of the requirements or frustrate the purposes of this section.

(Approved by the Office of Management and Budget under control number 1845-0020)

(Authority: 20 U.S.C. 1078, 1078-1, 1078-2, 1078-3, 1080a, 1082, 1087)

[58 Fed. Reg. 9119, Feb. 19, 1993; 59 Fed. Reg. 22489, April 29, 1994; 59 Fed. Reg. 25747, May 17, 1994; 59 Fed. Reg. 46175, Sept. 7, 1994; 60 Fed. Reg. 32912, June 26, 1995; 61 Fed. Reg. 60486, Nov. 27, 1996; 62 Fed. Reg. 13539, March 21, 1997; 64 Fed. Reg. 18981, April 16, 1999; 64 Fed. Reg. 58630, Oct. 29, 1999; 64 Fed. Reg. 58965, Nov. 1, 1999]

B.3 Direct Loan Regulations

34 C.F.R. sec

685.102 Definitions.

* * *

685.200 Borrower eligibility.

* * *

685.204 Deferment.
685.205 Forbearance.
685.206 Borrower responsibilities and defenses.
685.207 Obligation to repay.
685.208 Repayment plans.
685.209 Income contingent repayment plan.
685.210 Choice of repayment plan.
685.211 Miscellaneous repayment provisions.

685.212 Discharge of a loan obligation.
685.213 Total and permanent disability discharge.
685.214 Closed school discharge.
685.215 Discharge for false certification of student eligibility or unauthorized payment.
685.216 Unpaid refund discharge.

Authority: 20 U.S.C. 1087a *et seq.*, unless otherwise noted.

§ 685.102 Definitions.

(a)(1) The definitions of the following terms used in this part are set forth in subpart A of the Student Assistance General Provisions, 34 CFR part 668:

Academic year
Campus-based programs
Dependent student
Disburse
Eligible program
Eligible student
Enrolled
Expected family contribution
Federal Consolidation Loan Program
Federal Direct Student Loan Program (Direct Loan Program)
Federal Pell Grant Program
Federal Perkins Loan Program
Federal PLUS Program
Federal Supplemental Educational Opportunity Grant Program
Federal Work-Study Program
Independent student
Leveraging Educational Assistance Partnership Program
One-third of an academic year
Parent
Payment period
State
Two-thirds of an academic year
U.S. citizen or national

(2) The following definitions are set forth in the regulations for Institutional Eligibility under the Higher Education Act of 1965, as amended, 34 CFR Part 600:

Accredited
Clock hour
Educational program
Eligible institution
Federal Family Education Loan (FFEL) Program
Institution of higher education
Nationally recognized accrediting agency or association
Preaccredited
Program of study by correspondence
Secretary

(3) The following definitions are set forth in the regulations for the Federal Family Education Loan (FFEL) Program, 34 CFR Part 682:

Act
Endorser
Federal Insured Student Loan (FISL) Program
Federal Stafford Loan Program
Foreign school
Full-time student

Graduate or professional student
Guaranty agency
Holder
Legal guardian
Lender
Totally and permanently disabled
Undergraduate student

(b) The following definitions also apply to this part:

Alternative originator: An entity under contract with the Secretary that originates Direct Loans to students and parents of students who attend a Direct Loan Program school that does not originate loans.

Consortium: For purposes of this part, a consortium is a group of two or more schools that interacts with the Secretary in the same manner as other schools, except that the electronic communication between the Secretary and the schools is channeled through a single point. Each school in a consortium shall sign a Direct Loan Program participation agreement with the Secretary and be responsible for the information it supplies through the consortium.

Default: The failure of a borrower and endorser, if any, to make an installment payment when due, or to meet other terms of the promissory note, if the Secretary finds it reasonable to conclude that the borrower and endorser, if any, no longer intend to honor the obligation to repay, provided that this failure persists for 270 days.

Estimated financial assistance:

(1) The estimated amount of assistance for a period of enrollment that a student (or a parent on behalf of a student) will receive from Federal, State, institutional, or other sources, such as scholarships, grants, net earnings from need-based employment, or loans, including but not limited to—

(i) Except as provided in paragraph (2)(iv) of this definition, veterans' educational benefits paid under chapters 30 (Montgomery GI Bill—Active Duty), 31 (Vocational Rehabilitation and Employment Program), 32 (Veterans' Educational Assistance Program), and 35 (Dependents' Educational Assistance Program) of title 38 of the United States Code;

(ii) Educational benefits paid under chapters 31 (National Call to Service), 1606 (Montgomery GI Bill—Selected Reserve), and 1607 (Reserve Educational Assistance Program) of title 10 of the United States Code;

(iii) Reserve Officer Training Corps (ROTC) scholarships and subsistence allowances awarded under chapter 2 of title 10 and chapter 2 of title 37 of the United States Code;

(iv) Benefits paid under Public Law 96-342, section 903: Educational Assistance Pilot Program;

(v) Any educational benefits paid because of enrollment in a postsecondary education institution, or to cover postsecondary education expenses;

(vi) Fellowships or assistantships, except non-need-based employment portions of such awards;

(vii) Insurance programs for the student's education;

(viii) The estimated amount of other Federal student financial aid, including but not limited to a Federal Pell Grant, Academic Competitiveness Grant, National SMART Grant, campus-based aid, and the gross amount (including fees) of subsidized and unsubsidized Federal Stafford Loans or subsidized and unsubsidized Direct Stafford Loans and Federal PLUS or Direct PLUS Loans; and

(ix) Except as provided in paragraph (2)(iii) of this definition, national service education awards or post-service benefits under title I of the National and Community Service Act of 1990 (AmeriCorps).

(2) Estimated financial assistance does not include—

(i) Those amounts used to replace the expected family contribution (EFC), including the amounts of any unsubsidized Federal Stafford Loans or Direct Stafford Loans, Federal PLUS or Direct PLUS Loans, and non-federal non-need-based loans, including private, state-sponsored, and institutional loans. However, if the sum of the loan amounts received that are being used to replace the student's EFC exceed the EFC, the excess amount must be treated as estimated financial assistance;

(ii) Federal Perkins loan and Federal Work-Study funds that the student has declined;

(iii) Non-need-based employment earnings;

(iv) For the purpose of determining eligibility for a Direct Subsidized Loan, veterans' educational benefits paid under chapter 30 of title 38 of the United States Code (Montgomery GI Bill—Active Duty) and national service education awards or post-service benefits under title I of the National and Community Service Act of 1990 (AmeriCorps);

(v) Any portion of the estimated financial assistance described in paragraph (1) of this definition that is included in the calculation of the student's EFC; and

(vi) Assistance not received under this part if that assistance is designated to offset all or a portion of a specific amount of the cost of attendance and that component is excluded from the cost of attendance as well. If that assistance is excluded from either estimated financial assistance or cost of attendance, it must be excluded from both.

Federal Direct Consolidation Loan Program:

(1) A loan program authorized by title IV, part D of the Act that provides loans to borrowers who consolidate certain Federal educational loan(s), and one of the components of the Direct Loan Program. Loans made under this program are referred to as Direct Consolidation Loans.

(2) The term "Direct Subsidized Consolidation Loan" refers to the portion of a Direct Consolidation Loan attributable to certain subsidized title IV education loans that were repaid by the consolidation loan. Interest is not charged to the borrower during deferment periods, or, for a borrower whose consolidation application was received before July 1, 2006, during in-school and grace periods.

(3) The term "Direct Unsubsidized Consolidation Loan" refers to the portion of a Direct Consolidation Loan attributable to unsubsidized title IV education loans, certain subsidized title IV education loans, and certain other Federal education loans that were repaid by the consolidation loan. The borrower is responsible for the interest that accrues during any period.

(4) The term "Direct PLUS Consolidation Loan" refers to the portion of a Direct Consolidation Loan attributable to Direct PLUS Loans, Direct PLUS Consolidation Loans, Federal PLUS Loans, and Parent Loans for Undergraduate Students that were repaid by the consolidation loan. The borrower is responsible for the interest that accrues during any period.

Federal Direct PLUS Program: A loan program authorized by title IV, Part D of the Act that is one of the components of the

Federal Direct Loan Program. The Federal Direct PLUS Program provides loans to parents of dependent students attending schools that participate in the Direct Loan Program. The Federal Direct PLUS Program also provides loans to graduate or professional students attending schools that participate in the Direct Loan Program. The borrower is responsible for the interest that accrues during any period. Loans made under this program are referred to as Direct PLUS Loans.

Federal Direct Stafford/Ford Loan Program: A loan program authorized by title IV, part D of the Act that provides loans to undergraduate, graduate, and professional students attending Direct Loan Program schools, and one of the components of the Direct Loan Program. The Secretary subsidizes the interest while the borrower is in an in-school, grace, or deferment period. Loans made under this program are referred to as Direct Subsidized Loans.

Federal Direct Unsubsidized Stafford/Ford Loan Program: A loan program authorized by title IV, part D of the Act that provides loans to undergraduate, graduate, and professional students attending Direct Loan Program schools, and one of the components of the Direct Loan Program. The borrower is responsible for the interest that accrues during any period. Loans made under this program are referred to as Direct Unsubsidized Loans.

Grace period: A six-month period that begins on the day after a Direct Loan Program borrower ceases to be enrolled as at least a half-time student at an eligible institution and ends on the day before the repayment period begins.

Half-time student: A student who is not a full-time student and who is enrolled in an institution of higher education and is carrying an academic workload that is at least one-half the workload of a full-time student, as determined by the school. A student enrolled solely in an eligible program of study by correspondence is considered a half-time student.

Interest rate: The annual interest rate that is charged on a loan, under title IV, part D of the Act.

Loan fee: A fee, payable by the borrower, that is used to help defray the costs of the Direct Loan Program.

Master Promissory Note (MPN):

(1) A promissory note under which the borrower may receive loans for a single academic year or multiple academic years.

(2) For MPNs processed by the Secretary before July 1, 2003, loans may no longer be made under an MPN after the earliest of—

(i)   The date the Secretary or the school receives the borrower's written notice that no further loans may be disbursed;

(ii)   One year after the date of the borrower's first anticipated disbursement if no disbursement is made during that twelve-month period; or

(iii) Ten years after the date of the first anticipated disbursement, except that a remaining portion of a loan may be disbursed after this date.

(3) For MPNs processed by the Secretary on or after July 1, 2003, loans may no longer be made under an MPN after the earliest of—

(i)   The date the Secretary or the school receives the borrower's written notice that no further loans may be made;

(ii)   One year after the date the borrower signed the MPN or the date the Secretary receives the MPN, if no disbursements are made under that MPN; or

(iii) Ten years after the date the borrower signed the MPN or the date the Secretary receives the MPN, except that a remaining portion of a loan may be disbursed after this date.

Period of enrollment: The period for which a Direct Subsidized, Direct Unsubsidized, or Direct PLUS Loan is intended. The period of enrollment must coincide with one or more academic terms established by the school (such as semester, trimester, quarter, academic year, and length of the program of study), for which institutional charges are generally assessed. The period of enrollment is also referred to in this part as the loan period.

Satisfactory repayment arrangement.

(1) For the purpose of regaining eligibility under section 428F(b) of the HEA, the making of six consecutive, voluntary, on-time, full monthly payments on a defaulted loan. A borrower may only obtain the benefit of this paragraph with respect to renewed eligibility once.

(2) For the purpose of consolidating a defaulted loan under 34 CFR 685.220(d)(1)(ii)(C), the making of three consecutive, voluntary, on-time, full monthly payments on a defaulted loan.

(3) The required monthly payment amount may not be more than is reasonable and affordable based on the borrower's total financial circumstances. "On-time" means a payment made within 15 days of the scheduled due date, and voluntary payments are those payments made directly by the borrower and do not include payments obtained by Federal offset, garnishment, or income or asset execution.

School origination option 1: In general, under this option the school performs the following functions: creates a loan origination record, transmits the record to the Servicer, prepares the promissory note, obtains a completed and signed promissory note from a borrower, transmits the promissory note to the Servicer, receives the funds electronically, disburses a loan to a borrower, creates a disbursement record, transmits the disbursement record to the Servicer, and reconciles on a monthly basis. The Servicer initiates the drawdown of funds for schools participating in school origination option 1. The Secretary may modify the functions performed by a particular school.

School origination option 2: In general, under this option the school performs the following functions: creates a loan origination record, transmits the record to the Servicer, prepares the promissory note, obtains a completed and signed promissory note from a borrower, transmits the promissory note to the Servicer, determines funding needs, initiates the drawdown of funds, receives the funds electronically, disburses a loan to a borrower, creates a disbursement record, transmits the disbursement record to the Servicer, and reconciles on a monthly basis. The Secretary may modify the functions performed by a particular school.

Servicer: An entity that has contracted with the Secretary to act as the Secretary's agent in providing services relating to the origination or servicing of Direct Loans.

Standard origination: In general, under this option the school performs the following functions: creates a loan origination record, transmits the record to the Servicer, receives funds electronically, disburses funds, creates a disbursement record, transmits the disbursement record to the Servicer, and reconciles on a monthly basis. The Servicer prepares the promissory note, obtains a completed and signed promissory note from a borrower, and initiates the drawdown of funds for schools participating in standard origination. The Secretary may modify the functions performed by a particular school.

(Authority: 20 U.S.C. 1087a *et seq.*)

[60 Fed. Reg. 61793, Dec. 1, 1995; 61 Fed. Reg. 29899, June 12, 1996; 61 Fed. Reg. 60610, Nov. 29, 1996; 64 Fed. Reg. 58965, Nov. 1, 1999; 65 Fed. Reg. 38729, June 22, 2000; 65 Fed. Reg. 65629, Nov. 1, 2000; 66 Fed. Reg. 34765, June 29, 2001; 67 Fed. Reg. 67081, Nov. 1, 2002; 68 Fed. Reg. 75427, Dec. 31, 2003; 69 Fed. Reg. 12274, Mar. 16, 2004; 71 Fed. Reg. 45666, Sept. 8, 2006]

* * *

§ 685.200 Borrower eligibility.

(a) *Student Direct Subsidized or Direct Unsubsidized borrower.*

(1) A student is eligible to receive a Direct Subsidized Loan, a Direct Unsubsidized Loan, or a combination of these loans, if the student meets the following requirements:

(i) The student is enrolled, or accepted for enrollment, on at least a half-time basis in a school that participates in the Direct Loan Program.

(ii) The student meets the requirements for an eligible student under 34 CFR Part 668.

(iii) In the case of an undergraduate student who seeks a Direct Subsidized Loan or a Direct Unsubsidized Loan at a school that participates in the Federal Pell Grant Program, the student has received a determination of Federal Pell Grant eligibility for the period of enrollment for which the loan is sought.

(iv)(A) In the case of a borrower whose prior loan under title IV of the Act was discharged after a final determination of total and permanent disability, the borrower—

(1) Obtains a certification from a physician that the borrower is able to engage in substantial gainful activity; and

(2) Signs a statement acknowledging that the Direct Loan the borrower receives cannot be discharged in the future on the basis of any impairment present when the new loan is made, unless that impairment substantially deteriorates.

(B) In the case of a borrower whose prior loan under title IV of the Act was discharged on or after July 1, 2001 and before July 1, 2002 after a final determination of total and permanent disability, the borrower—

(1) Complies with the requirements of paragraph (a)(1)(iv)(A) of this section; and

(2) If the borrower applies for another loan within three years from the date that the borrower became totally and permanently disabled, as certified by the physician, reaffirms the previously discharged loan before receiving the new loan. For the purposes of this paragraph, reaffirmation means the acknowledgement of the loan by the borrower in a legally binding manner. The acknowledgement may include, but is not limited to, the borrower signing a new promissory note that includes the same terms and conditions as the original note signed by the borrower, making a payment on the loan, or signing a repayment agreement.

(C) In the case of a borrower whose prior loan under title IV of the Act was conditionally discharged based on an initial determination that the borrower was totally and permanently disabled—

(1) The suspension of collection activity on the prior loan has been lifted;

(2) The borrower complies with the requirements in paragraphs (a)(1)(iv)(A)(1) and (2) of this section;

(3) The borrower signs a statement acknowledging that the loan that has been conditionally discharged prior to a final determination of total and permanent disability cannot be discharged in the future on the basis of any impairment present when the borrower applied for a total and permanent disability discharge or when the new loan is made, unless that impairment substantially deteriorates; and

(4) The borrower signs a statement acknowledging that the suspension of collection activity on the prior loan will be lifted.

(v) In the case of a student who seeks a loan but does not have a certificate of graduation from a school providing secondary education or the recognized equivalent of such a certificate, the student meets the requirements under 34 CFR 668.32(e)(2), (3), or (4).

(2)(i) A Direct Subsidized Loan borrower must demonstrate financial need in accordance with title IV, part F of the Act.

(ii) The Secretary considers a member of a religious order, group, community, society, agency, or other organization who is pursuing a course of study at an institution of higher education to have no financial need if that organization—

(A) Has as its primary objective the promotion of ideals and beliefs regarding a Supreme Being;

(B) Requires its members to forego monetary or other support substantially beyond the support it provides; and

(C)(1) Directs the member to pursue the course of study; or

(2) Provides subsistence support to its members.

(b) *Student PLUS borrower.*

(1) A graduate or professional student is eligible to receive a Direct PLUS Loan originated on or after July 1, 2006, if the student meets the following requirements—

(i) The student is enrolled, or accepted for enrollment, on at least a half-time basis in a school that participates in the Direct Loan Program.

(ii) The student meets the requirements for an eligible student under 34 CFR part 668.

(iii) The student meets the requirements of paragraphs (a)(1)(iv) and (a)(1)(v) of this section, if applicable.

(iv) The student has received a determination of his or her annual loan maximum eligibility under the Federal Direct Stafford/Ford Loan Program and the Federal Direct Unsubsidized and Stafford/Ford Loan Program; and

(v) The student does not have an adverse credit history in accordance with paragraph (c)(1)(vii) of this section.

(c)(1) *Parent PLUS borrower.* A parent is eligible to receive a Direct PLUS Loan if the parent meets the following requirements:

(i) The parent is borrowing to pay for the educational costs of a dependent undergraduate student who meets the requirements for an eligible student under 34 CFR Part 668.

(ii) The parent provides his or her and the student's social security number.

(iii) The parent meets the requirements pertaining to citizenship and residency that apply to the student under 34 CFR 668.33.

(iv)   The parent meets the requirements concerning defaults and overpayments that apply to the student in 34 CFR 668.32(g).

(v)   The parent complies with the requirements for submission of a Statement of Educational Purpose that apply to the student under 34 CFR Part 668, except for the completion of a Statement of Selective Service Registration Status.

(vi)   The parent meets the requirements that apply to a student under paragraph (a)(1)(iv) of this section.

(vii)(A)   The parent—

(1)   Does not have an adverse credit history;

(2)   Has an adverse credit history but has obtained an endorser who does not have an adverse credit history; or

(3)   Has an adverse credit history but documents to the satisfaction of the Secretary that extenuating circumstances exist.

(B)   For purposes of paragraph (c)(1)(vii)(A) of this section, an adverse credit history means that as of the date of the credit report, the applicant—

(1)   Is 90 or more days delinquent on any debt; or

(2)   Has been the subject of a default determination, bankruptcy discharge, foreclosure, repossession, tax lien, wage garnishment, or write-off of a debt under title IV of the Act during the five years preceding the date of the credit report.

(C)   For the purposes of (c)(1)(vii)(A) of this section, the Secretary does not consider the absence of a credit history as an adverse credit history and does not deny a Direct PLUS loan on that basis.

(2)   For purposes of paragraph (c)(1) of this section, a "parent" includes the individuals described in the definition of "parent" in 34 CFR 668.2 and the spouse of a parent who remarried, if that spouse's income and assets would have been taken into account when calculating a dependent student's expected family contribution.

(3)   Has completed repayment of any title IV, HEA program assistance obtained by fraud, if the parent has been convicted of, or has pled nolo contendere or guilty to, a crime involving fraud in obtaining title IV, HEA program assistance.

(d)   *Defaulted FFEL Program and Direct Loan borrowers.* Except as noted in 685.220(d)(1)(ii)(D), in the case of a student or parent borrower who is currently in default on an FFEL Program or a Direct Loan Program Loan, the borrower shall make satisfactory repayment arrangements, as described in paragraph (2) of the definition of that term under § 685.102(b), on the defaulted loan.

(e)   *Use of loan proceeds to replace expected family contribution.* The amount of a Direct Unsubsidized Loan, a Direct PLUS loan, or a non-federal non-need based loan, including a private, state-sponsored, or institution loan, obtained for a loan period may be used to replace the expected family contribution for that loan period.

(Authority: 20 U.S.C. 1087a *et seq.*)

[60 Fed. Reg. 61816, Dec. 1, 1995; 61 Fed. Reg. 29900, June 12, 1996; 65 Fed. Reg. 65629, 65693, Nov. 1, 2000; 66 Fed. Reg. 34765, June 29, 2001; 66 Fed. Reg. 44007, Aug. 21, 2001; 68 Fed.

Reg. 75427, Dec. 31, 2003; 71 Fed. Reg. 45666, Sept. 8, 2006]

* * *

§ 685.204 Deferment.

(a)(1)   A Direct Loan borrower whose loan is eligible for interest subsidies and who meets the requirements described in paragraphs (b) and (e) of this section is eligible for a deferment during which periodic installments of principal and interest need not be paid.

(2)   A Direct Loan borrower whose loan is not eligible for interest subsidies and who meets the requirements described in paragraphs (b) and (e) of this section is eligible for a deferment during which periodic installments of principal need not be paid but interest does accrue and is capitalized or paid by the borrower.

(b)   Except as provided in paragraph (d) and (f) of this section, a Direct Loan borrower is eligible for a deferment during any period during which the borrower meets any of the following requirements:

(1)(i)   The borrower—

(A)   Is carrying at least one-half the normal full-time work load for the course of study that the borrower is pursuing, as determined by the eligible school the borrower is attending;

(B)   Is pursuing a course of study pursuant to a graduate fellowship program approved by the Secretary; or

(C)   Is pursuing a rehabilitation training program, approved by the Secretary, for individuals with disabilities; and

(ii)   The borrower is not serving in a medical internship or residency program, except for a residency program in dentistry.

(iii)(A)   For the purpose of paragraph (b)(1)(i) of this section, the Secretary processes a deferment when—

(1)   The borrower submits a request to the Secretary along with documentation verifying the borrower's eligibility;

(2)   The Secretary receives information from the borrower's school indicating that the borrower is eligible to receive a new loan; or

(3)   The Secretary receives student status information from the borrower's school, either directly or indirectly, indicating that the borrower is enrolled on at least a half-time basis.

(B)(1)   Upon notification by the Secretary that a deferment has been granted based on paragraph (b)(1)(iii)(A)(2) or (3) of this section, the borrower has the option to continue paying on the loan.

(2)   If the borrower elects to cancel the deferment and continue paying on the loan, the borrower has the option to make the principal and interest payments that were deferred. If the borrower does not make the payments, the Secretary applies a deferment for the period in which payments were not made and capitalizes the interest.

(2)(i)   The borrower is seeking and unable to find full-time employment.

(ii)   For purposes of paragraph (b)(2)(i) of this section, the Secretary determines whether a borrower is eligible for a deferment due to the inability to find full-time employment using the standards and procedures set forth in 34 CFR 682.210(h) with references to the lender understood to mean the Secretary.

(3)(i) The borrower has experienced or will experience an economic hardship.

(ii) For purposes of paragraph (b)(3)(i) of this section, the Secretary determines whether a borrower is eligible for a deferment due to an economic hardship using the standards and procedures set forth in 34 CFR 682.210(s)(6) with references to the lender understood to mean the Secretary.

(c) No deferment under paragraphs (b)(2) or (3) of this section may exceed three years.

(d) If, at the time of application for a borrower's first Direct Loan, a borrower has an outstanding balance of principal or interest owing on any FFEL Program loan that was made, insured, or guaranteed prior to July 1, 1993, the borrower is eligible for a deferment during—

(1) the periods described in paragraph (b) and (e) of this section; and

(2) the periods described in 34 CFR 682.210(b), including those periods that apply to a "new borrower" as that term is defined in 34 CFR 682.210(b)(7).

(e)(1) A borrower who receives a Direct Loan Program loan first disbursed on or after July 1, 2001, may receive a military service deferment for such loan for any period not to exceed 3 years during which the borrower is—

(i) Serving on active duty during a war or other military operation or national emergency; or

(ii) Performing qualifying National Guard duty during a war or other military operation or national emergency.

(2) Serving on active duty during a war or other military operation or national emergency means service by an individual who is—

(i) A Reserve of an Armed Force ordered to active duty under 10 U.S.C. 12301(a), 12301(g), 12302, 12304, or 12306;

(ii) A retired member of an Armed Force ordered to active duty under 10 U.S.C. 688 for service in connection with a war or other military operation or national emergency, regardless of the location at which such active duty service is performed; or

(iii) Any other member of an Armed Force on active duty in connection with such emergency or subsequent actions or conditions who has been assigned to a duty station at a location other than the location at which the member is normally assigned.

(3) Qualifying National Guard duty during a war or other operation or national emergency means service as a member of the National Guard on full-time National Guard duty, as defined in 10 U.S.C. 101(d)(5) under a call to active service authorized by the President or the Secretary of Defense for a period of more than 30 consecutive days under 32 U.S.C. 502(f) in connection with a war, other military operation, or national emergency declared by the President and supported by Federal funds.

(4) These provisions do not authorize the refunding of any payments made by or on behalf of a borrower during a period for which the borrower qualified for a military service deferment.

(5) A borrower is eligible for a military service deferment on a Direct Consolidation Loan only if the borrower meets the conditions described in this section and all of the title IV loans included in the Consolidation Loan were first disbursed on or after July 1, 2001.

(6) As used in this section—

(i) Active duty means active duty as defined in 10 U.S.C.

101(d)(1) except that it does not include active duty for training or attendance at a service school;

(ii) Military operation means a contingency operation as defined in 10 U.S.C. 101(a)(13); and

(iii) National emergency means the national emergency by reason of certain terrorist attacks declared by the President on September 14, 2001, or subsequent national emergencies declared by the President by reason of terrorist attacks.

(f) A borrower whose loan is in default is not eligible for a deferment, unless the borrower has made payment arrangements satisfactory to the Secretary.

(Approved by the Office of Management and Budget under control number 1845-0021)

(Authority: 20 U.S.C. 1087a *et seq.*)

[60 Fed. Reg. 33345, June 28, 1995; 61 Fed. Reg. 29900, June 12, 1996; 64 Fed. Reg. 58968, Nov. 1, 1999; 71 Fed. Reg. 45666, Sept. 8, 2006]

§ 685.205 Forbearance.

(a) *General.* "Forbearance" means permitting the temporary cessation of payments, allowing an extension of time for making payments, or temporarily accepting smaller payments than previously scheduled. The borrower has the option to choose the form of forbearance. Except as provided in paragraph (b)(9) of this section, if payments of interest are forborne, they are capitalized. The Secretary grants forbearance if the borrower or endorser intends to repay the loan but requests forbearance and provides sufficient documentation to support this request, and—

(1) The Secretary determines that, due to poor health or other acceptable reasons, the borrower or endorser is currently unable to make scheduled payments;

(2) The borrower's payments of principal are deferred under § 685.204 and the Secretary does not subsidize the interest benefits on behalf of the borrower;

(3) The borrower is in a medical or dental internship or residency that must be successfully completed before the borrower may begin professional practice or service, or the borrower is serving in a medical or dental internship or residency program leading to a degree or certificate awarded by an institution of higher education, a hospital, or a health care facility that offers postgraduate training;

(4) The borrower is serving in a national service position for which the borrower is receiving a national service education award under title I of the National and Community Service Act of 1990; or

(5) The borrower—

(i) Is performing the type of service that would qualify the borrower for loan forgiveness under the requirements of the teacher loan forgiveness program in § 685.217; and

(ii) Is required, by the Secretary, before a forbearance is granted under § 685.205(a)(5)(i) to—

(A) Submit documentation for the period of the annual forbearance request showing the beginning and ending dates that the borrower is expected to perform, for that year, the type of service described in § 685.217(c); and

(B) Certify the borrower's intent to satisfy the requirements of § 685.217(c).

(6) For not more than three years during which the borrower or endorser—

(i) Is currently obligated to make payments on loans under title IV of the Act; and

(ii) The sum of these payments each month (or a proportional share if the payments are due less frequently than monthly) is equal to or greater than 20 percent of the borrower's or endorser's total monthly gross income.

(b) *Administrative forbearance.* In certain circumstances, the Secretary grants forbearance without requiring documentation from the borrower. These circumstances include but are not limited to—

(1) A properly granted period of deferment for which the Secretary learns the borrower did not qualify;

(2) The period for which payments are overdue at the beginning of an authorized deferment period;

(3) The period beginning when the borrower entered repayment without the secretary's knowledge until the first payment due date was established;

(4) The period prior to a borrower's filing of a bankruptcy petition;

(5) A period after the Secretary receives reliable information indicating that the borrower (or the student in the case of a Direct PLUS Loan obtained by a parent borrower) has died, or the borrower has become totally and permanently disabled, until the Secretary receives documentation of death or total and permanent disability;

(6) Periods necessary for the Secretary to determine the borrower's eligibility for discharge—

(i) Under § 685.214;

(ii) Under § 685.215;

(iii) Under § 685.216; or

(iv) Under § 685.217; or

(v) Due to the borrower's or endorser's (if applicable) bankruptcy;

(7) A period of up to three years in cases where the effect of a variable interest rate on a fixed-amount or graduated repayment schedule causes the extension of the maximum repayment term;

(8) A period during which the Secretary has authorized forbearance due to a national military mobilization or other local or national emergency; or

(9) A period of up to 60 days necessary for the Secretary to collect and process documentation supporting the borrower's request for a deferment, forbearance, change in repayment plan, or consolidation loan. Interest that accrues during this period is not capitalized.

(c) *Period of forbearance.*

(1) The Secretary grants forbearance for a period of up to one year.

(2) The forbearance is renewable, upon request of the borrower, for the duration of the period in which the borrower meets the condition required for the forbearance.

(Authority: 20 U.S.C. 1087a *et seq.*)

[61 Fed. Reg. 29900, June 12, 1996; 64 Fed. Reg. 58968, Nov. 1, 1999; 65 Fed. Reg. 65629, Nov. 1, 2000; 66 Fed. Reg. 34765, June 29, 2001; 68 Fed. Reg. 75430, Dec. 31, 2003; 71 Fed. Reg. 45666, Sept. 8, 2006]

§ 685.206 Borrower responsibilities and defenses.

(a) The borrower shall give the school the following information as part of the origination process for a Direct Subsidized, Direct Unsubsidized, or Direct PLUS Loan:

(1) A statement, as described in 34 CFR Part 668, that the loan will be used for the cost of the student's attendance.

(2) Information demonstrating that the borrower is eligible for the loan.

(3) Information concerning the outstanding FFEL Program and Direct Loan Program loans of the borrower and, for a parent borrower, of the student, including any Federal Consolidation Loan or Direct Consolidation Loan.

(4) A statement authorizing the school to release to the Secretary information relevant to the student's eligibility to borrow or to have a parent borrow on the student's behalf (e.g., the student's enrollment status, financial assistance, and employment records).

(b)(1) The borrower shall promptly notify the Secretary of any change of name, address, student status to less than half-time, employer, or employer's address; and

(2) The borrower shall promptly notify the school of any change in address during enrollment.

(c) *Borrower defenses.*

(1) In any proceeding to collect on a Direct Loan, the borrower may assert as a defense against repayment, any act or omission of the school attended by the student that would give rise to a cause of action against the school under applicable State law. These proceedings include, but are not limited to, the following:

(i) Tax refund offset proceedings under 34 CFR 30.33.

(ii) Wage garnishment proceedings under section 488A of the Act.

(iii) Salary offset proceedings for Federal employees under 34 CFR Part 31.

(iv) Credit bureau reporting proceedings under 31 U.S.C. 3711(f).

(2) If the borrower's defense against repayment is successful, the Secretary notifies the borrower that the borrower is relieved of the obligation to repay all or part of the loan and associated costs and fees that the borrower would otherwise be obligated to pay. The Secretary affords the borrower such further relief as the Secretary determines is appropriate under the circumstances. Further relief may include, but is not limited to, the following:

(i) Reimbursing the borrower for amounts paid toward the loan voluntarily or through enforced collection.

(ii) Determining that the borrower is not in default on the loan and is eligible to receive assistance under title IV of the Act.

(iii) Updating reports to credit bureaus to which the Secretary previously made adverse credit reports with regard to the borrower's Direct Loan.

(3) The Secretary may initiate an appropriate proceeding to require the school whose act or omission resulted in the borrower's successful defense against repayment of a Direct Loan to pay to the Secretary the amount of the loan to which the defense applies. However, the Secretary does not initiate such a proceeding after the period for the retention of records described in § 685.309(c) unless the school received actual notice of the claim during that period.

(Approved by the Office of Management and Budget under control number 1845-0021)

(Authority: 20 U.S.C. 1087a *et seq.*)

[60 Fed. Reg. 33345, June 28, 1995; 64 Fed. Reg. 58972, Nov. 1, 1999]

§ 685.207 Obligation to repay.

(a) *Obligation of repayment in general.*

(1) A borrower is obligated to repay the full amount of a Direct Loan, including the principal balance, fees, any collection costs charged under § 685.202(e), and any interest not subsidized by the Secretary, unless the borrower is relieved of the obligation to repay as provided in this part.

(2) The borrower's repayment of a Direct Loan may also be subject to the deferment provisions in § 685.204, the forbearance provisions in § 685.205, and the discharge provisions in § 685.212.

(b) *Direct Subsidized Loan repayment.*

(1) During the period in which a borrower is enrolled at an eligible school on at least a half-time basis, the borrower is in an "in-school" period and is not required to make payments on a Direct Subsidized Loan unless—

  (i) The loan entered repayment before the in-school period began; and

  (ii) The borrower has not been granted a deferment under § 685.204.

(2)(i) When a borrower ceases to be enrolled at an eligible school on at least a half-time basis, a six-month grace period begins, unless the grace period has been previously exhausted.

  (ii)(A) Any borrower who is a member of a reserve component of the Armed Forces named in section 10101 of title 10, United States Code and is called or ordered to active duty for a period of more than 30 days is entitled to have the active duty period excluded from the six-month grace period. The excluded period includes the time necessary for the borrower to resume enrollment at the next available regular enrollment period. Any single excluded period may not exceed 3 years.

  (B) Any borrower who is in a grace period when called or ordered to active duty as specified in paragraph (b)(2)(ii)(A) of this section is entitled to a full six-month grace period upon completion of the excluded period.

  (iii) During a grace period, the borrower is not required to make any principal payments on a Direct Subsidized Loan.

(3) A borrower is not obligated to pay interest on a Direct Subsidized Loan for in-school or grace periods unless the borrower is required to make payments on the loan during those periods under paragraph (b)(1) of this section.

(4) The repayment period for a Direct Subsidized Loan begins the day after the grace period ends. A borrower is obligated to repay the loan under paragraph (a) of this section during the repayment period.

(c) *Direct Unsubsidized Loan repayment.*

(1) During the period in which a borrower is enrolled at an eligible school on at least a half-time basis, the borrower is in an "in-school" period and is not required to make payments of principal on a Direct Unsubsidized Loan unless—

  (i) The loan entered repayment before the in-school period began; and

  (ii) The borrower has not been granted a deferment under § 685.204.

(2)(i) When a borrower ceases to be enrolled at an eligible school on at least a half-time basis, a six-month grace period begins, unless the grace period has been previously exhausted.

  (ii)(A) Any borrower who is a member of a reserve component of the Armed Forces named in section 10101 of title 10, United States Code and is called or ordered to active duty for a period of more than 30 days is entitled to have the active duty period excluded from the six-month grace period. The excluded period includes the time necessary for the borrower to resume enrollment at the next available regular enrollment period. Any single excluded period may not exceed 3 years.

  (B) Any borrower who is in a grace period when called or ordered to active duty as specified in paragraph (c)(2)(ii)(A) of this section is entitled to a full six-month grace period upon completion of the excluded period.

  (iii) During a grace period, the borrower is not required to make any principal payments on a Direct Unsubsidized Loan.

(3) A borrower is responsible for the interest that accrues on a Direct Unsubsidized Loan during in-school and grace periods. Interest begins to accrue on the day the first installment is disbursed. Interest that accrues may be capitalized or paid by the borrower.

(4) The repayment period for a Direct Unsubsidized Loan begins the day after the grace period ends. A borrower is obligated to repay the loan under paragraph (a) of this section during the repayment period.

(d) *Direct PLUS Loan repayment.* The repayment period for a Direct PLUS Loan begins on the day the loan is fully disbursed. Interest begins to accrue on the day the first installment is disbursed. A borrower is obligated to repay the loan under paragraph (a) of this section during the repayment period.

(e) *Direct Consolidation Loan repayment.*

(1) Except as provided in paragraphs (e)(2) and (e)(3) of this section, the repayment period for a Direct Consolidation Loan begins and interest begins to accrue on the day the loan is made. The borrower is obligated to repay the loan under paragraph (a) of this section during the repayment period.

(2) In the case of a borrower whose consolidation application was received before July 1, 2006, a borrower who obtains a Direct Subsidized Consolidation Loan during an in-school period will be subject to the repayment provisions in paragraph (b) of this section.

(3) In the case of a borrower whose consolidation application was received before July 1, 2006, a borrower who obtains a Direct Unsubsidized Consolidation Loan during an in-school period will be subject to the repayment provisions in paragraph (c) of this section.

(f) *Determining the date on which the grace period begins for a borrower in a correspondence program.* For a borrower of a Direct Subsidized or Direct Unsubsidized Loan who is a correspondence student, the grace period specified in paragraphs (b)(2) and (c)(2) of this section begins on the earliest of—

(1) The day after the borrower completes the program;

(2) The day after withdrawal as determined pursuant to 34 CFR 668.22; or

(3) 60 days following the last day for completing the program as established by the school.

(Authority: 20 U.S.C. 1087a *et seq.*)

[64 Fed. Reg. 58968, Nov. 1, 1999; 68 Fed. Reg. 75430, Dec. 31, 2003; 71 Fed. Reg. 45666, Sept. 8, 2006]

§ 685.208 Repayment plans.

(a) *General.*

(1) *Borrowers who entered repayment before July 1, 2006.*

(i) A borrower may repay a Direct Subsidized Loan, a Direct Unsubsidized Loan, a Direct Subsidized Consolidation Loan, or a Direct Unsubsidized Consolidation Loan under the standard repayment plan, the extended repayment plan, the graduated repayment plan, or the income contingent repayment plan, in accordance with paragraphs (b), (d), (f), and (k) of this section, respectively.

(ii) A borrower may repay a Direct PLUS Loan or a Direct PLUS Consolidation Loan under the standard repayment plan, the extended repayment plan, or the graduated repayment plan, in accordance with paragraphs (b), (d), and (f) of this section, respectively.

(2) *Borrowers entering repayment on or after July 1, 2006.*

(i) A borrower may repay a Direct Subsidized Loan or a Direct Unsubsidized Loan under the standard repayment plan, the extended repayment plan, the graduated repayment plan, or the income contingent repayment plan, in accordance with paragraphs (b), (e), (g), and (k) of this section, respectively.

(ii) A borrower may repay a Direct PLUS Loan under the standard repayment plan, the extended repayment plan, or the graduated repayment plan, in accordance with paragraphs (b), (e), and (g) of this section, respectively.

(iii) A borrower may repay a Direct Consolidation Loan under the standard repayment plan, the extended repayment plan, the graduated repayment plan, or the income contingent repayment plan, in accordance with paragraphs (c), (e), (h), and (k) of this section, respectively.

(3) The Secretary may provide an alternative repayment plan in accordance with paragraph (l) of this section.

(4) All Direct Loans obtained by one borrower must be repaid together under the same repayment plan, except that—

(i) A borrower of a Direct PLUS Loan may repay the Direct PLUS Loan separately from other Direct Loans obtained by the borrower; and

(ii) A borrower of a Direct PLUS Consolidation Loan that entered repayment before July 1, 2006 may repay the Direct PLUS Consolidation Loan separately from other Direct Loans obtained by that borrower.

(5) The repayment period for any of the repayment plans described in this section does not include periods of authorized deferment or forbearance.

(b) *Standard repayment plan for all Direct Subsidized Loan, Direct Unsubsidized Loan, and Direct PLUS Loan borrowers, regardless of when they entered repayment, and for Direct Consolidation Loan borrowers who entered repayment before July 1, 2006.*

(1) Under this repayment plan, a borrower must repay a loan in full within ten years from the date the loan entered repayment by making fixed monthly payments.

(2) A borrower's payments under this repayment plan are at least $50 per month, except that a borrower's final payment may be less than $50.

(3) The number of payments or the fixed monthly repayment amount may be adjusted to reflect changes in the variable interest rate identified in § 685.202(a).

(c) *Standard repayment plan for Direct Consolidation Loan borrowers entering repayment on or after July 1, 2006.*

(1) Under this repayment plan, a borrower must repay a loan in full by making fixed monthly payments over a repayment period that varies with the total amount of the borrower's student loans, as described in paragraph (j) of this section.

(2) A borrower's payments under this repayment plan are at least $50 per month, except that a borrower's final payment may be less than $50.

(d) *Extended repayment plan for all Direct Loan borrowers who entered repayment before July 1, 2006.*

(1) Under this repayment plan, a borrower must repay a loan in full by making fixed monthly payments within an extended period of time that varies with the total amount of the borrower's loans, as described in paragraph (i) of this section.

(2) A borrower makes fixed monthly payments of at least $50, except that a borrower's final payment may be less than $50.

(3) The number of payments or the fixed monthly repayment amount may be adjusted to reflect changes in the variable interest rate identified in § 685.202(a).

(e) *Extended repayment plan for all Direct Loan borrowers entering repayment on or after July 1, 2006.*

(1) Under this repayment plan, a new borrower with more than $30,000 in outstanding Direct Loans accumulated on or after October 7, 1998 must repay either a fixed annual or graduated repayment amount over a period not to exceed 25 years from the date the loan entered repayment. For this repayment plan, a new borrower is defined as an individual who has no outstanding principal or interest balance on a Direct Loan as of October 7, 1998, or on the date the borrower obtains a Direct Loan on or after October 7, 1998.

(2) A borrower's payments under this plan are at least $50 per month, and will be more if necessary to repay the loan within the required time period.

(3) The number of payments or the monthly repayment amount may be adjusted to reflect changes in the variable interest rate identified in § 685.202(a).

(f) *Graduated repayment plan for all Direct Loan borrowers who entered repayment before July 1, 2006.*

(1) Under this repayment plan, a borrower must repay a loan in full by making payments at two or more levels within a period of time that varies with the total amount of the borrower's loans, as described in paragraph (i) of this section.

(2) The number of payments or the monthly repayment amount may be adjusted to reflect changes in the variable interest rate identified in § 685.202(a).

(3) No scheduled payment under this repayment plan may be less than the amount of interest accrued on the loan between monthly payments, less than 50 percent of the payment amount that would be required under the standard repayment plan described in paragraph (b) of this section, or more than 150 percent of the payment amount that would be required under the standard repayment plan described in paragraph (b) of this section.

(g) *Graduated repayment plan for Direct Subsidized Loan, Direct Unsubsidized Loan, and Direct PLUS Loan borrowers entering repayment on or after July 1, 2006.*

(1) Under this repayment plan, a borrower must repay a loan in full by making payments at two or more levels over a period of

time not to exceed ten years from the date the loan entered repayment.

(2) The number of payments or the monthly repayment amount may be adjusted to reflect changes in the variable interest rate identified in § 685.202(a).

(3) A borrower's payments under this repayment plan are at least $50 per month, except that a borrower's final payment may be less than $50. No single payment under this plan will be more than three times greater than any other payment.

(h) *Graduated repayment plan for Direct Consolidation Loan borrowers entering repayment on or after July 1, 2006.*

(1) Under this repayment plan, a borrower must repay a loan in full by making monthly payments that gradually increase in stages over the course of a repayment period that varies with the total amount of the borrower's student loans, as described in paragraph (j) of this section.

(2) A borrower's payments under this repayment plan are at least $50 per month, except that a borrower's final payment may be less than $50.

(i) *Repayment period for the extended and graduated plans described in paragraphs (d) and (f) of this section, respectively.* Under these repayment plans, if the total amount of the borrower's Direct Loans is—

    (1) Less than $10,000, the borrower must repay the loans within 12 years of entering repayment;

    (2) Greater than or equal to $10,000 but less than $20,000, the borrower must repay the loans within 15 years of entering repayment;

    (3) Greater than or equal to $20,000 but less than $40,000, the borrower must repay the loans within 20 years of entering repayment;

    (4) Greater than or equal to $40,000 but less than $60,000, the borrower must repay the loans within 25 years of entering repayment; and

    (5) Greater than or equal to $60,000, the borrower must repay the loans within 30 years of entering repayment.

(j) *Repayment period for the standard and graduated repayment plans described in paragraphs (c) and (h) of this section, respectively.* Under these repayment plans, if the total amount of the Direct Consolidation Loan and the borrower's other student loans, as defined in § 685.220(i), is—

(1) Less then $7,500, the borrower must repay the Consolidation Loan within 10 years of entering repayment;

(2) Equal to or greater than $7,500 but less than $10,000, the borrower must repay the Consolidation Loan within 12 years of entering repayment;

(3) Equal to or greater than $10,000 but less than $20,000, the borrower must repay the Consolidation Loan within 15 years of entering repayment;

(4) Equal to or greater than $20,000 but less than $40,000, the borrower must repay the Consolidation Loan within 20 years of entering repayment;

(5) Equal to or greater than $40,000 but less than $60,000, the borrower must repay the Consolidation Loan within 25 years of entering repayment; and

(6) Equal to or greater than $60,000, the borrower must repay the Consolidation Loan within 30 years of entering repayment.

(k) *Income contingent repayment plan.*

(1) Under the income contingent repayment plan, a borrower's monthly repayment amount is generally based on the total amount

of the borrower's Direct Loans, family size, and Adjusted Gross Income (AGI) reported by the borrower for the most recent year for which the Secretary has obtained income information. The borrower's AGI includes the income of the borrower's spouse. A borrower must make payments on a loan until the loan is repaid in full or until the loan has been in repayment through the end of the income contingent repayment period.

(2) The regulations in effect at the time a borrower enters repayment and selects the income contingent repayment plan or changes into the income contingent repayment plan from another plan govern the method for determining the borrower's monthly repayment amount for all of the borrower's Direct Loans, unless—

    (i) The Secretary amends the regulations relating to a borrower's monthly repayment amount under the income contingent repayment plan; and

    (ii) The borrower submits a written request that the amended regulations apply to the repayment of the borrower's Direct Loans.

(3) Provisions governing the income contingent repayment plan are in § 685.209.

(l) *Alternative repayment.*

(1) The Secretary may provide an alternative repayment plan for a borrower who demonstrates to the Secretary's satisfaction that the terms and conditions of the repayment plans specified in paragraphs (b) through (h) of this section are not adequate to accommodate the borrower's exceptional circumstances.

(2) The Secretary may require a borrower to provide evidence of the borrower's exceptional circumstances before permitting the borrower to repay a loan under an alternative repayment plan.

(3) If the Secretary agrees to permit a borrower to repay a loan under an alternative repayment plan, the Secretary notifies the borrower in writing of the terms of the plan. After the borrower receives notification of the terms of the plan, the borrower may accept the plan or choose another repayment plan.

(4) A borrower must repay a loan under an alternative repayment plan within 30 years of the date the loan entered repayment, not including periods of deferment and forbearance.

(5) If the amount of a borrower's monthly payment under an alternative repayment plan is less than the accrued interest on the loan, the unpaid interest is capitalized until the outstanding principal amount is 10 percent greater than the original principal amount. After the outstanding principal amount is 10 percent greater than the original principal amount, interest continues to accrue but is not capitalized. For purposes of this paragraph, the original principal amount is the amount owed by the borrower when the borrower enters repayment.

(Authority: 20 U.S.C. 1087a *et seq.*)

[61 Fed. Reg. 31359, June 19, 1996; 62 Fed. Reg. 25515, May 9, 1997; 66 Fed. Reg. 34765, June 29, 2001; 71 Fed. Reg. 45666, Sept. 8, 2006]

§ 685.209 Income contingent repayment plan.

(a) *Repayment amount calculation.*

(1) The amount the borrower would repay is based upon the borrower's Direct Loan debt when the borrower's first loan enters repayment, and this basis for calculation does not change unless the borrower obtains another Direct Loan or the borrower and the borrower's spouse obtain approval to repay their loans jointly under paragraph (b)(2) of this section. If the borrower obtains

another Direct Loan, the amount the borrower would repay is based on the combined amounts of the loans when the last loan enters repayment. If the borrower and the borrower's spouse repay the loans jointly, the amount the borrowers would repay is based on both borrowers' Direct Loan debts at the time they enter joint repayment.

(2) The annual amount payable under the income contingent repayment plan by a borrower is the lesser of—

   (i)   The amount the borrower would repay annually over 12 years using standard amortization multiplied by an income percentage factor that corresponds to the borrower's adjusted gross income (AGI) as shown in the income percentage factor table in a notice published annually by the Secretary in the Federal Register; or

   (ii) 20 percent of discretionary income.

(3) For purposes of this section, discretionary income is defined as a borrower's AGI minus the amount of the "HHS Poverty Guidelines for all States (except Alaska and Hawaii) and the District of Columbia" as published by the United States Department of Health and Human Services on an annual basis.[1] For residents of Alaska and Hawaii, discretionary income is defined as a borrower's AGI minus the amounts in the "HHS Poverty Guidelines for Alaska" and the "HHS Poverty Guidelines for Hawaii" respectively. If a borrower provides documentation acceptable to the Secretary that the borrower has more than one person in the borrower's family, the Secretary applies the HHS Poverty Guidelines for the borrower's family size.

(4) For exact incomes not shown in the income percentage factor table in the annual notice published by the Secretary, an income percentage factor is calculated, based upon the intervals between the incomes and income percentage factors shown on the table.

(5) Each year, the Secretary recalculates the borrower's annual payment amount based on changes in the borrower's AGI, the variable interest rate, the income percentage factors in the table in the annual notice published by the Secretary, and updated HHS Poverty Guidelines (if applicable).

(6) If a borrower's monthly payment is calculated to be greater than $0 but less than or equal to $5.00, the amount payable by the borrower shall be $5.00.

(7) For purposes of the annual recalculation described in paragraph (a)(5) of this section, after periods in which a borrower makes payments that are less than interest accrued on the loan, the payment amount is recalculated based upon unpaid accrued interest and the highest outstanding principal loan amount (including amount capitalized) calculated for that borrower while paying under the income contingent repayment plan.

(8) For each calendar year after calendar year 1996, the Secretary publishes in the Federal Register a revised income percentage factor table reflecting changes based on inflation. This revised table is developed by changing each of the dollar amounts contained in the table by a percentage equal to the estimated percentage changes in the Consumer Price Index (as determined by the Secretary) between December 1995 and the December next preceding the beginning of such calendar year.

---

   1   The HHS Poverty Guidelines are available from the Office of the Assistant Secretary for Planning and Evaluation, Department of Health and Human Services (HHS), Room 438F, Humphrey Building, 200 Independence Avenue, S.W., Washington, D.C. 20201.

(9) Examples of the calculation of monthly repayment amounts and tables that show monthly repayment amounts for borrowers at various income and debt levels are included in the annual notice published by the Secretary.

(b) *Treatment of married borrowers.*

(1) A married borrower who wishes to repay under the income contingent repayment plan and who has filed an income tax return separately from his or her spouse must provide his or her spouse's written consent to the disclosure of certain tax return information under paragraph (c)(5) of this section (unless the borrower is separated from his or her spouse). The AGI for both spouses is used to calculate the monthly repayment amount.

(2) Married borrowers may repay their loans jointly. The outstanding balances on the loans of each borrower are added together to determine the borrowers' payback rate under (a)(1) of this section.

(3) The amount of the payment applied to each borrower's debt is the proportion of the payments that equals the same proportion as that borrower's debt to the total outstanding balance, except that the payment is credited toward outstanding interest on any loan before any payment is credited toward principal.

(c) *Other features of the income contingent repayment plan.*

(1) *Alternative documentation of income.* If a borrower's AGI is not available or if, in the Secretary's opinion, the borrower's reported AGI does not reasonably reflect the borrower's current income, the Secretary may use other documentation of income provided by the borrower to calculate the borrower's monthly repayment amount.

(2) *First and second year borrowers.* The Secretary requires alternative documentation of income from borrowers in their first and second years of repayment, when in the Secretary's opinion, the borrower's reported AGI does not reasonably reflect the borrower's current income.

(3) *Adjustments to repayment obligations.* The Secretary may determine that special circumstances, such as a loss of employment by the borrower or the borrower's spouse, warrant an adjustment to the borrower's repayment obligations.

(4) *Repayment period.*

   (i)   The maximum repayment period under the income contingent repayment plan is 25 years.

   (ii)(A) The repayment period includes—

(1) Periods in which the borrower makes payments under the standard repayment plan described in § 685.208(b); and

(2) If the repayment period is not more than 12 years, periods in which the borrower makes payments under the extended repayment plans described in § 685.208(d) and (e), or the standard repayment plan described in § 685.208(c).

   (B) The repayment period does not include—

(1) Periods in which the borrower makes payments under the graduated repayment plans described in § 685.208(f), § 685.208(g) and § 685.208(h);

(2) Periods in which the borrower makes payments under an alternative repayment plan;

(3) Periods of authorized deferment or forbearance; or

(4) Periods in which the borrower makes payments under the extended repayment plans described in § 685.208(d) and (e) in which payments are based on a repayment period that is longer than 12 years.

   (iii) If a borrower repays more than one loan under the income contingent repayment plan, a separate repayment period for each loan begins when that loan enters repayment.

(iv) If a borrower has not repaid a loan in full at the end of the 25-year repayment period under the income contingent repayment plan, the Secretary cancels the unpaid portion of the loan.

(v) At the beginning of the repayment period under the income contingent repayment plan, a borrower shall make monthly payments of the amount of interest that accrues on the borrower's Direct Loans until the Secretary calculates the borrower's monthly repayment amount on the basis of the borrower's income.

(5) *Limitation on capitalization of interest.* If the amount of a borrower's monthly payment is less than the accrued interest, the unpaid interest is capitalized until the outstanding principal amount is ten percent greater than the original principal amount. After the outstanding principal amount is ten percent greater than the original amount, interest continues to accrue but is not capitalized. For purposes of this paragraph, the original amount is the amount owed by the borrower when the borrower enters repayment.

(6) *Notification of terms and conditions.* When a borrower elects or is required by the Secretary to repay a loan under the income contingent repayment plan, the Secretary notifies the borrower of the terms and conditions of the plan, including—

(i) That the Internal Revenue Service will disclose certain tax return information to the Secretary or the Secretary's agents; and

(ii) That if the borrower believes that special circumstances warrant an adjustment to the borrower's repayment obligations, as described in § 685.209(c)(3), the borrower may contact the Secretary and obtain the Secretary's determination as to whether an adjustment is appropriate.

(7) *Consent to disclosure of tax return information.*

(i) A borrower shall provide written consent to the disclosure of certain tax return information by the Internal Revenue Service (IRS) to agents of the Secretary for purposes of calculating a monthly repayment amount and servicing and collecting a loan under the income contingent repayment plan. The borrower shall provide consent by signing a consent form, developed consistent with 26 CFR 301.6103(c)-1 and provided to the borrower by the Secretary, and shall return the signed form to the Secretary.

(ii) The borrower shall consent to disclosure of the borrower's taxpayer identity information as defined in 26 U.S.C. 6103(b)(6), tax filing status, and AGI.

(iii) The borrower shall provide consent for a period of five years from the date the borrower signs the consent form. The Secretary provides the borrower a new consent form before that period expires. The IRS does not disclose tax return information after the IRS has processed a borrower's withdrawal of consent.

(iv) The Secretary designates the standard repayment plan for a borrower who selects the income contingent repayment plan but—

(A) Fails to provide the required written consent;

(B) Fails to renew written consent upon the expiration of the five-year period for consent; or

(C) Withdraws consent and does not select another repayment plan.

(v) If a borrower defaults and the Secretary designates the income contingent repayment plan for the borrower but the borrower fails to provide the required written consent, the Secretary mails a notice to the borrower establishing a repayment schedule for the borrower.

(Approved by the Office of Management and Budget under control number 1845-0021)

(Authority: 20 U.S.C. 1087a *et seq.*)

[60 Fed. Reg. 33345, June 28, 1995; 60 Fed. Reg. 61823, Dec. 1, 1995; 61 Fed. Reg. 24447, May 15, 1996; 61 Fed. Reg. 31359, June 19, 1996; 64 Fed. Reg. 29183, May 28, 1999; 64 Fed. Reg. 58972, Nov. 1, 1999; 71 Fed. Reg. 45666, Sept. 8, 2006]

§ 685.210 Choice of repayment plan.

(a) *Initial selection of a repayment plan.*

(1) Before a Direct Loan enters into repayment, the Secretary provides the borrower a description of the available repayment plans and requests the borrower to select one. A borrower may select a repayment plan before the loan enters repayment by notifying the Secretary of the borrower's selection in writing.

(2) If a borrower does not select a repayment plan, the Secretary designates the standard repayment plan described in § 685.208(b) for the borrower.

(b) *Changing repayment plans.*

(1) A borrower may change repayment plans at any time after the loan has entered repayment by notifying the Secretary. However, a borrower who is repaying a defaulted loan under the income contingent repayment plan under § 685.211(d)(3)(ii) may not change to another repayment plan unless—

(i) The borrower was required to and did make a payment under the income contingent repayment plan in each of the prior three (3) months; or

(ii) The borrower was not required to make payments but made three reasonable and affordable payments in each of the prior three months; and

(iii) The borrower makes and the Secretary approves a request to change plans.

(2)(i) A borrower may not change to a repayment plan that has a maximum repayment period of less than the number of years the loan has already been in repayment, except that a borrower may change to the income contingent repayment plan at any time.

(ii) If a borrower changes plans, the repayment period is the period provided under the borrower's new repayment plan, calculated from the date the loan initially entered repayment. However, if a borrower changes to the income contingent repayment plan, the repayment period is calculated as described in § 685.209(c)(4).

(Authority: 20 U.S.C. 1087a *et seq.*)

[65 Fed. Reg. 65629, Nov. 1, 2000; 68 Fed. Reg. 75430, Dec. 31, 2003]

§ 685.211 Miscellaneous repayment provisions.

(a) *Payment application and prepayment.*

(1) The Secretary applies any payment first to any accrued charges and collection costs, then to any outstanding interest, and then to outstanding principal.

(2) A borrower may prepay all or part of a loan at any time without penalty. If a borrower pays any amount in excess of the

amount due, the excess amount is a prepayment.

(3) If a prepayment equals or exceeds the monthly repayment amount under the borrower's repayment plan, the Secretary—

(i) Applies the prepaid amount according to paragraph (a)(1) of this section;

(ii) Advances the due date of the next payment unless the borrower requests otherwise; and

(iii) Notifies the borrower of any revised due date for the next payment.

(4) If a prepayment is less than the monthly repayment amount, the Secretary applies the prepayment according to paragraph (a)(1) of this section.

(b) *Repayment incentives.* To encourage on-time repayment, the Secretary may reduce the interest rate for a borrower who repays a loan under a system or on a schedule that meets requirements specified by the Secretary.

(c) *Refunds and returns of title IV, HEA program funds from schools.* The Secretary applies any refund or return of title IV, HEA program funds that the Secretary receives from a school under § 668.22 against the borrower's outstanding principal and notifies the borrower of the refund or return.

(d) *Default.*

(1) *Acceleration.* If a borrower defaults on a Direct Loan, the entire unpaid balance and accrued interest are immediately due and payable.

(2) *Collection charges.* If a borrower defaults on a Direct Loan, the Secretary assesses collection charges in accordance with § 685.202(e).

(3) *Collection of a defaulted loan.*

(i) The Secretary may take any action authorized by law to collect a defaulted Direct Loan including, but not limited to, filing a lawsuit against the borrower, reporting the default to national credit bureaus, requesting the Internal Revenue Service to offset the borrower's Federal income tax refund, and garnishing the borrower's wages.

(ii) If a borrower defaults on a Direct Subsidized Loan, a Direct Unsubsidized Loan, or a Direct Consolidation Loan, the Secretary may designate the income contingent repayment plan for the borrower.

(e) *Ineligible borrowers.*

(1) The Secretary determines that a borrower is ineligible if, at the time the loan was made and without the school's or the Secretary's knowledge, the borrower (or the student on whose behalf a parent borrowed) provided false or erroneous information, has been convicted of, or has pled nolo contendere or guilty to, a crime involving fraud in obtaining title IV, HEA program funds, or took actions that caused the borrower or student—

(i) To receive a loan for which the borrower is wholly or partially ineligible;

(ii) To receive interest benefits for which the borrower was ineligible; or

(iii) To receive loan proceeds for a period of enrollment for which the borrower was not eligible.

(2) If the Secretary makes the determination described in paragraph (e)(1) of this section, the Secretary sends an ineligible borrower a demand letter that requires the borrower to repay some or all of a loan, as appropriate. The demand letter requires that within 30 days from the date the letter is mailed, the borrower repay any principal amount for which the borrower is ineligible and

any accrued interest, including interest subsidized by the Secretary, through the previous quarter.

(3) If a borrower fails to comply with the demand letter described in paragraph (e)(2) of this section, the borrower is in default on the entire loan.

(4) A borrower may not consolidate a loan under § 685.220 for which the borrower is wholly or partially ineligible.

(f) *Rehabilitation of defaulted loans.*

(1) A defaulted Direct Loan, except for a loan on which a judgment has been obtained, is rehabilitated if the borrower makes nine voluntary, reasonable, and affordable monthly payments within 20 days of the due date during ten consecutive months. The amount of such a payment is determined on the basis of the borrower's total financial circumstances. If a defaulted loan is rehabilitated, the Secretary instructs any credit bureau to which the default was reported to remove the default from the borrower's credit history.

(2) A defaulted Direct Loan on which a judgment has been obtained may not be rehabilitated.

(3) A Direct Loan obtained by fraud for which the borrower has been convicted of, or has pled nolo contendere or guilty to, a crime involving fraud in obtaining title IV, HEA program assistance may not be rehabilitated.

(Authority: 20 U.S.C. 1087a *et seq.*)

[64 Fed. Reg. 57961, Oct. 27, 1999; 64 Fed. Reg. 59043, Nov. 1, 1999; 65 Fed. Reg. 65629, Nov. 1, 2000; 66 Fed. Reg. 34765, June 29, 2001; 67 Fed. Reg. 67081, Nov. 1, 2002; 71 Fed. Reg. 45666, Sept. 8, 2006]

§ 685.212 Discharge of a loan obligation.

(a) *Death.*

(1) If a borrower (or the student on whose behalf a parent borrowed a Direct PLUS Loan) dies, the Secretary discharges the obligation of the borrower and any endorser to make any further payments on the loan based on an original or certified copy of the borrower's (or student's in the case of a Direct PLUS loan obtained by a parent borrower) death certificate.

(2) If an original or certified copy of the death certificate is not available, the Secretary discharges the loan only based on other reliable documentation that establishes, to the Secretary's satisfaction, that the borrower (or student) has died. The Secretary discharges a loan based on documentation other than an original or certified copy of the death certificate only under exceptional circumstances and on a case-by-case basis.

(3) In the case of a Direct PLUS Consolidation Loan that repaid a Direct PLUS Loan or a Federal PLUS Loan obtained on behalf of a student who dies, the Secretary discharges an amount equal to the portion of the outstanding balance of the consolidation loan, as of the date of the student's death, attributable to that Direct PLUS Loan or Federal PLUS Loan.

(b) *Total and permanent disability.* If a borrower meets the requirements in § 685.213(c), the Secretary discharges the obligation of the borrower and any endorser to make any further payments on the loan.

(c) *Bankruptcy.* If a borrower's obligation to repay a loan is discharged in bankruptcy, the Secretary does not require the borrower to make any further payments on the loan.

(d) *Closed schools.* If a borrower meets the requirements in § 685.214, the Secretary discharges the obligation of the borrower and any endorser to make any further payments on the loan. In the case of a Direct Consolidation Loan, the Secretary discharges the portion of the consolidation loan equal to the amount of the discharge applicable to any loan disbursed, in whole or in part, on or after January 1, 1986 that was included in the consolidation loan.

(e) *False certification and unauthorized disbursement.* If a borrower meets the requirements in § 685.215, the Secretary discharges the obligation of the borrower and any endorser to make any further payments on the loan. In the case of a Direct Consolidation Loan, the Secretary discharges the portion of the consolidation loan equal to the amount of the discharge applicable to any loan disbursed, in whole or in part, on or after January 1, 1986 that was included in the consolidation loan.

(f) *Unpaid refunds.* If a borrower meets the requirements in § 685.216, the Secretary discharges the obligation of the borrower and any endorser to make any further payments on the amount of the loan equal to the unpaid refund and any accrued interest and other charges associated with the unpaid refund. In the case of a Direct Consolidation Loan, the Secretary discharges the portion of the consolidation loan equal to the amount of the unpaid refund owed on any loan disbursed, in whole or in part, on or after January 1, 1986 that was included in the consolidation loan.

(g) *Payments received after eligibility for discharge.*

(1) *For the discharge conditions in paragraphs (a), (c), (d), and (e) of this section.* Upon receipt of acceptable documentation and approval of the discharge request, the Secretary returns to the sender, or, for a discharge based on death, the borrower's estate, any payments received after the date that the eligibility requirements for discharge were met.

(2) *For the discharge condition in paragraph (b) of this section.* Upon making a final determination of eligibility for discharge based on total and permanent disability, the Secretary returns to the sender any payments received after the date the borrower became totally and permanently disabled, as certified under § 685.213(b).

(3) *For the discharge condition in paragraph (f) of this section.* Upon receipt of acceptable documentation and approval of the discharge request, the Secretary returns to the sender payments received in excess of the amount owed on the loan after applying the unpaid refund.

(h) *Teacher loan forgiveness program.* If a new borrower meets the requirements in § 685.217, the Secretary repays up to $5,000, or up to $17,500, of the borrower's Direct Subsidized Loans, Direct Unsubsidized Loans, and, in certain cases, Direct Consolidation Loans.

(Approved by the Office of Management and Budget under control number 1845-0021)

(Authority: 20 U.S.C. 1087a *et seq.*)

[61 Fed. Reg. 29900, June 12, 1996; 62 Fed. Reg. 30412, June 3, 1997; 62 Fed. Reg. 63435, Nov. 28, 1997; 63 Fed. Reg. 34816, June 26, 1998; 64 Fed. Reg. 58969, Nov. 1, 1999; 65 Fed. Reg. 65629, 65694, Nov. 1, 2000; 66 Fed. Reg. 34765, June 29, 2001; 67 Fed. Reg. 67081, Nov. 1, 2002; 71 Fed. Reg. 45666, Sept. 8, 2006]

§ 685.213 Total and permanent disability discharge.

(a) *General.*

(1) If the Secretary makes an initial determination that a borrower is totally and permanently disabled, the Secretary—

(i)   Notifies the borrower that the loan will be in a conditional

discharge status for up to three years from the date that the borrower became totally and permanently disabled, as certified under 685.213(b). The Secretary also notifies the borrower of the conditions of the conditional discharge period, and that all or part of the three-year conditional discharge period may predate the Secretary's initial determination.

(ii)   Suspends any efforts to collect on the loan from the date of the initial determination described in paragraph (a)(1) of this section until the end of the conditional discharge period.

(2) If the borrower continues to meet the eligibility requirements for total and permanent disability discharge during and at the end of the three-year conditional discharge period, the Secretary—

(i)   Discharges the obligation of the borrower and any endorser to make any further payments on the loan at the end of that period; and

(ii)   Returns to the borrower any payments received after the date the borrower became totally and permanently disabled, as certified under § 685.213(b).

(3) If the borrower does not continue to meet the eligibility requirements for a total and permanent disability discharge at any time during or at the end of the three-year conditional discharge period, the Secretary resumes collection activity on the loan. The Secretary does not require the borrower to pay any interest that accrued on the loan from the date of the initial determination described in paragraph (a)(1) of this section through the end of the conditional discharge period.

(4) Except as provided in paragraph (e)(1) of this section, a borrower is not considered totally and permanently disabled based on a condition that existed at the time the loan was made, unless the borrower's condition substantially deteriorated after the loan was made so as to render the borrower totally and permanently disabled.

(b) *Initial determination of total and permanent disability.* The Secretary makes an initial determination that a borrower is totally and permanently disabled if the borrower (or the borrower's representative) provides the Secretary with a certification (on a form approved by the Secretary) by a physician who is a doctor of medicine or osteopathy and legally authorized to practice in a State that the borrower is totally and permanently disabled as defined in 34 CFR 682.200(b).

(c) *Eligibility requirements for total and permanent disability discharge.* A borrower meets the eligibility requirements for total and permanent disability discharge if, during and at the end of the three-year conditional discharge period described in paragraph (a)(1) of this section—

(1) The borrower's annual earnings from employment do not exceed 100 percent of the poverty line for a family of two, as determined in accordance with the Community Service Block Grant Act; and

(2) The borrower does not receive a new loan under the Perkins, FFEL, or Direct Loan programs, except for a FFEL or Direct consolidation loan that does not include any loans that are in a conditional discharge status.

(d) *Conditional discharge period.* During the conditional discharge period described in paragraph (a)(1) of this section, the borrower—

(1) Is not required to make any payments of principal or interest on the loan beginning on the date the Secretary makes an initial

determination that the borrower is totally and permanently disabled;

(2) Is not considered to be delinquent or in default on the loan, unless the loan was delinquent or in default at the time the conditional discharge was granted;

(3) Must promptly notify the Secretary of any changes in the borrower's address or telephone number;

(4) Must promptly notify the Secretary if the borrower's annual earnings from employment exceed the amount specified in paragraph (c)(1) of this section; and

(5) Must provide the Secretary, upon request, with additional documentation or information related to the borrower's eligibility for discharge under this section.

(e) *Provisions for discharge of Direct Consolidation Loans.*

(1) For a Direct Consolidation Loan, a borrower is considered totally and permanently disabled if he or she would be considered totally and permanently disabled under the provisions of this section for all of the loans that were included in the Direct Consolidation Loan if those loans had not been consolidated.

(2) For the purposes of discharging a loan under paragraph (e)(1) of this section, the provisions of this section apply to each loan included in the Direct Consolidation Loan, even if the loan is not a Direct Loan Program loan.

(3) If requested, a borrower seeking to discharge a loan obligation under paragraph (e)(1) of this section must provide the Secretary with the disbursement dates of the underlying loans.

(Authority: 20 U.S.C. 1087a *et seq.*)

[65 Fed. Reg. 65629, 65694, Nov. 1, 2000]

§ 685.214 Closed school discharge.

(a) *General.*

(1) The Secretary discharges the borrower's (and any endorser's) obligation to repay a Direct Loan in accordance with the provisions of this section if the borrower (or the student on whose behalf a parent borrowed) did not complete the program of study for which the loan was made because the school at which the borrower (or student) was enrolled closed, as described in paragraph (c) of this section.

(2) For purposes of this section—

(i) A school's closure date is the date that the school ceases to provide educational instruction in all programs, as determined by the Secretary; and

(ii) "School" means a school's main campus or any location or branch of the main campus.

(b) *Relief pursuant to discharge.*

(1) Discharge under this section relieves the borrower of any past or present obligation to repay the loan and any accrued charges or collection costs with respect to the loan.

(2) The discharge of a loan under this section qualifies the borrower for reimbursement of amounts paid voluntarily or through enforced collection on the loan.

(3) The Secretary does not regard a borrower who has defaulted on a loan discharged under this section as in default on the loan after discharge, and such a borrower is eligible to receive assistance under programs authorized by title IV of the Act.

(4) The Secretary reports the discharge of a loan under this section to all credit reporting agencies to which the Secretary previously reported the status of the loan.

(c) *Borrower qualification for discharge.* In order to qualify for

discharge of a loan under this section, a borrower shall submit to the Secretary a written request and sworn statement, and the factual assertions in the statement must be true. The statement need not be notarized but must be made by the borrower under penalty of perjury. In the statement, the borrower shall—

(1) State that the borrower (or the student on whose behalf a parent borrowed)—

(i) Received the proceeds of a loan, in whole or in part, on or after January 1, 1986 to attend a school;

(ii) Did not complete the program of study at that school because the school closed while the student was enrolled, or the student withdrew from the school not more than 90 days before the school closed (or longer in exceptional circumstances); and

(iii) Did not complete the program of study through a teach-out at another school or by transferring academic credits or hours earned at the closed school to another school;

(2) State whether the borrower (or student) has made a claim with respect to the school's closing with any third party, such as the holder of a performance bond or a tuition recovery program, and, if so, the amount of any payment received by the borrower (or student) or credited to the borrower's loan obligation; and

(3) State that the borrower (or student)—

(i) Agrees to provide to the Secretary upon request other documentation reasonably available to the borrower that demonstrates that the borrower meets the qualifications for discharge under this section; and

(ii) Agrees to cooperate with the Secretary in enforcement actions in accordance with paragraph (d) of this section and to transfer any right to recovery against a third party to the Secretary in accordance with paragraph (e) of this section.

(d) *Cooperation by borrower in enforcement actions.*

(1) In order to obtain a discharge under this section, a borrower shall cooperate with the Secretary in any judicial or administrative proceeding brought by the Secretary to recover amounts discharged or to take other enforcement action with respect to the conduct on which the discharge was based. At the request of the Secretary and upon the Secretary's tendering to the borrower the fees and costs that are customarily provided in litigation to reimburse witnesses, the borrower shall—

(i) Provide testimony regarding any representation made by the borrower to support a request for discharge;

(ii) Produce any documents reasonably available to the borrower with respect to those representations; and

(iii) If required by the Secretary, provide a sworn statement regarding those documents and representations.

(2) The Secretary denies the request for a discharge or revokes the discharge of a borrower who—

(i) Fails to provide the testimony, documents, or a sworn statement required under paragraph (d)(1) of this section; or

(ii) Provides testimony, documents, or a sworn statement that does not support the material representations made by the borrower to obtain the discharge.

(e) *Transfer to the Secretary of borrower's right of recovery against third parties.*

(1) Upon discharge under this section, the borrower is deemed to have assigned to and relinquished in favor of the Secretary any right to a loan refund (up to the amount discharged) that the borrower (or student) may have by contract or applicable law with

respect to the loan or the enrollment agreement for the program for which the loan was received, against the school, its principals, its affiliates and their successors, its sureties, and any private fund, including the portion of a public fund that represents funds received from a private party.

(2) The provisions of this section apply notwithstanding any provision of State law that would otherwise restrict transfer of those rights by the borrower (or student), limit or prevent a transferee from exercising those rights, or establish procedures or a scheme of distribution that would prejudice the Secretary's ability to recover on those rights.

(3) Nothing in this section limits or forecloses the borrower's (or student's) right to pursue legal and equitable relief regarding disputes arising from matters unrelated to the discharged Direct Loan.

(f) *Discharge procedures.*

(1) After confirming the date of a school's closure, the Secretary identifies any Direct Loan borrower (or student on whose behalf a parent borrowed) who appears to have been enrolled at the school on the school closure date or to have withdrawn not more than 90 days prior to the closure date.

(2) If the borrower's current address is known, the Secretary mails the borrower a discharge application and an explanation of the qualifications and procedures for obtaining a discharge. The Secretary also promptly suspends any efforts to collect from the borrower on any affected loan. The Secretary may continue to receive borrower payments.

(3) If the borrower's current address is unknown, the Secretary attempts to locate the borrower and determines the borrower's potential eligibility for a discharge under this section by consulting with representatives of the closed school, the school's licensing agency, the school's accrediting agency, and other appropriate parties. If the Secretary learns the new address of a borrower, the Secretary mails to the borrower a discharge application and explanation and suspends collection, as described in paragraph (f)(2) of this section.

(4) If a borrower fails to submit the written request and sworn statement described in paragraph (c) of this section within 60 days of the Secretary's mailing the discharge application, the Secretary resumes collection and grants forbearance of principal and interest for the period in which collection activity was suspended. The Secretary may capitalize any interest accrued and not paid during that period.

(5) If the Secretary determines that a borrower who requests a discharge meets the qualifications for a discharge, the Secretary notifies the borrower in writing of that determination.

(6) If the Secretary determines that a borrower who requests a discharge does not meet the qualifications for a discharge, the Secretary notifies that borrower in writing of that determination and the reasons for the determination.

(Approved by the Office of Management and Budget under control number 1845-0021)

(Authority: 20 U.S.C. 1087a *et seq.*)

[60 Fed. Reg. 33345, June 28, 1995; 64 Fed. Reg. 58972, Nov. 1, 1999; 65 Fed. Reg. 65629, Nov. 1, 2000; 66 Fed. Reg. 34765, June 29, 2001]

§ 685.215 Discharge for false certification of student eligibility or unauthorized payment.

(a) *Basis for discharge.*

(1) *False certification.* The Secretary discharges a borrower's (and any endorser's) obligation to repay a Direct Loan in accordance with the provisions of this section if a school falsely certifies the eligibility of the borrower (or the student on whose behalf a parent borrowed) to receive the loan. The Secretary considers a student's eligibility to borrow to have been falsely certified by the school if the school—

(i) Certified the student's eligibility for a Direct Loan on the basis of ability to benefit from its training and the student did not meet the eligibility requirements described in 34 CFR part 668 and section 484(d) of the Act, as applicable;

(ii) Signed the borrower's name on the loan application or promissory note without the borrower's authorization; or

(iii) Certified the eligibility of a student who, because of a physical or mental condition, age, criminal record, or other reason accepted by the Secretary, would not meet the requirements for employment (in the student's State of residence when the loan was originated) in the occupation for which the training program supported by the loan was intended.

(iv) Certified the individual's eligibility for a Direct Loan as a result of the crime of identity theft committed against the individual, as that crime is defined in § 682.402(e)(14).

(2) *Unauthorized payment.* The Secretary discharges a borrower's (and any endorser's) obligation to repay a Direct Loan if the school, without the borrower's authorization, endorsed the borrower's loan check or signed the borrower's authorization for electronic funds transfer, unless the proceeds of the loan were delivered to the student or applied to charges owed by the student to the school.

(b) *Relief pursuant to discharge.*

(1) Discharge for false certification under paragraph (a)(1) of this section relieves the borrower of any past or present obligation to repay the loan and any accrued charges and collection costs with respect to the loan.

(2) Discharge for unauthorized payment under paragraph (a)(2) of this section relieves the borrower of the obligation to repay the amount of the payment discharged.

(3) The discharge under this section qualifies the borrower for reimbursement of amounts paid voluntarily or through enforced collection on the discharged loan or payment.

(4) The Secretary does not regard a borrower who has defaulted on a loan discharged under this section as in default on the loan after discharge, and such a borrower is eligible to receive assistance under programs authorized by title IV of the Act.

(5) The Secretary reports the discharge under this section to all credit reporting agencies to which the Secretary previously reported the status of the loan.

(c) *Borrower qualification for discharge.* In order to qualify for discharge under this section, the borrower shall submit to the Secretary a written request and a sworn statement, and the factual assertions in the statement must be true. The statement need not be notarized but must be made by the borrower under penalty of perjury. In the statement, the borrower shall meet the requirements in paragraphs (c)(1) through (6) of this section.

(1) *Ability to benefit.* In the case of a borrower requesting a discharge based on defective testing of the student's ability to

benefit, the borrower shall state that the borrower (or the student on whose behalf a parent borrowed)—

    (i) Received a disbursement of a loan, in whole or in part, on or after January 1, 1986 to attend a school; and

    (ii) Received a Direct Loan at that school on the basis of an ability to benefit from the school's training and did not meet the eligibility requirements described in 34 CFR Part 668 and section 484(d) of the Act, as applicable.

(2) *Unauthorized loan.* In the case of a borrower requesting a discharge because the school signed the borrower's name on the loan application or promissory note without the borrower's authorization, the borrower shall—

    (i) State that he or she did not sign the document in question or authorize the school to do so; and

    (ii) Provide five different specimens of his or her signature, two of which must be within one year before or after the date of the contested signature.

(3) *Unauthorized payment.* In the case of a borrower requesting a discharge because the school, without the borrower's authorization, endorsed the borrower's loan check or signed the borrower's authorization for electronic funds transfer, the borrower shall—

    (i) State that he or she did not endorse the loan check or sign the authorization for electronic funds transfer or authorize the school to do so;

    (ii) Provide five different specimens of his or her signature, two of which must be within one year before or after the date of the contested signature;

    (iii) State that the proceeds of the contested disbursement were not delivered to the student or applied to charges owed by the student to the school.

(4) *Identity theft.* In the case of an individual whose eligibility to borrow was falsely certified because he or she was a victim of the crime of identity theft and is requesting a discharge, the individual shall—

    (i) Certify that the individual did not sign the promissory note, or that any other means of identification used to obtain the loan was used without the authorization of the individual claiming relief;

    (ii) Certify that the individual did not receive or benefit from the proceeds of the loan with knowledge that the loan had been made without the authorization of the individual;

    (iii) Provide a copy of a local, State, or Federal court verdict or judgment that conclusively determines that the individual who is named as the borrower of the loan was the victim of a crime of identity theft; and

    (iv) If the judicial determination of the crime does not expressly state that the loan was obtained as a result of the crime of identity theft, provide—

        (A) Authentic specimens of the signature of the individual, as provided in paragraph (c)(2)(ii), or of other means of identification of the individual, as applicable, corresponding to the means of identification falsely used to obtain the loan; and

        (B) A statement of facts that demonstrate, to the satisfaction of the Secretary, that eligibility for the loan in question was falsely certified as a result of the crime of identity theft committed against that individual.

(5) *Claim to third party.* The borrower shall state whether the borrower (or student) has made a claim with respect to the school's false certification or unauthorized payment with any third party,

such as the holder of a performance bond or a tuition recovery program, and, if so, the amount of any payment received by the borrower (or student) or credited to the borrower's loan obligation.

(6) *Cooperation with Secretary.* The borrower shall state that the borrower (or student)—

    (i) Agrees to provide to the Secretary upon request other documentation reasonably available to the borrower that demonstrates that the borrower meets the qualifications for discharge under this section; and

    (ii) Agrees to cooperate with the Secretary in enforcement actions as described in § 685.214(d) and to transfer any right to recovery against a third party to the Secretary as described in § 685.214(e).

(7) *Discharge without an application.* The Secretary may discharge a loan under this section without an application from the borrower if the Secretary determines, based on information in the Secretary's possession, that the borrower qualifies for a discharge.

(d) *Discharge procedures.*

(1) If the Secretary determines that a borrower's Direct Loan may be eligible for a discharge under this section, the Secretary mails the borrower a disclosure application and an explanation of the qualifications and procedures for obtaining a discharge. The Secretary also promptly suspends any efforts to collect from the borrower on any affected loan. The Secretary may continue to receive borrower payments.

(2) If the borrower fails to submit the written request and sworn statement described in paragraph (c) of this section within 60 days of the Secretary's mailing the disclosure application, the Secretary resumes collection and grants forbearance of principal and interest for the period in which collection activity was suspended. The Secretary may capitalize any interest accrued and not paid during that period.

(3) If the borrower submits the written request and sworn statement described in paragraph (c) of the section, the Secretary determines whether to grant a request for discharge under this section by reviewing the request and sworn statement in light of information available from the Secretary's records and from other sources, including guaranty agencies, State authorities, and cognizant accrediting associations.

(4) If the Secretary determines that the borrower meets the applicable requirements for a discharge under paragraph (c) of this section, the Secretary notifies the borrower in writing of that determination.

(5) If the Secretary determines that the borrower does not qualify for a discharge, the Secretary notifies the borrower in writing of that determination and the reasons for the determination.

(Approved by the Office of Management and Budget under control number 1845-0021)

(Authority: 20 U.S.C. 1087a *et seq.*)

[60 Fed. Reg. 33345, June 28, 1995; 61 Fed. Reg. 29900, June 12, 1996; 64 Fed. Reg. 58972, Nov. 1, 1999; 65 Fed. Reg. 65622, 65629, Nov. 1, 2000; 66 Fed. Reg. 34765, June 29, 2001; 71 Fed. Reg. 45666, Sept. 8, 2006]

§ 685.216 Unpaid refund discharge.

  (a)(1) *Unpaid refunds in closed school situations.* In the case of a school that has closed, the Secretary discharges a former or current borrower's (and any endorser's) obligation to repay that portion of a Direct Loan equal to the refund that should have been made by the school under applicable law and regulations, including this section. Any accrued interest and other charges associated with the unpaid refund are also discharged.

(2) *Unpaid refunds in open school situations.*

(i) In the case of a school that is open, the Secretary discharges a former or current borrower's (and any endorser's) obligation to repay that portion of a Direct Loan equal to the refund that should have been made by the school under applicable law and regulations, including this section, if—

(A) The borrower (or the student on whose behalf a parent borrowed) is not attending the school that owes the refund;

(B) The borrower has been unable to resolve the unpaid refund with the school; and

(C) The Secretary is unable to resolve the unpaid refund with the school within 120 days from the date the borrower submits a complete application in accordance with paragraph (c)(1) of this section regarding the unpaid refund. Any accrued interest and other charges associated with the unpaid refund are also discharged.

(ii) For the purpose of paragraph (a)(2)(i)(C) of this section, within 60 days of the date notified by the Secretary, the school must submit to the Secretary documentation demonstrating that the refund was made by the school or that the refund was not required to be made by the school.

(b) *Relief to borrower following discharge.*

(1) If the borrower receives a discharge of a portion of a loan under this section, the borrower is reimbursed for any amounts paid in excess of the remaining balance of the loan (including accrued interest and other charges) owed by the borrower at the time of discharge.

(2) The Secretary reports the discharge of a portion of a loan under this section to all credit reporting agencies to which the Secretary previously reported the status of the loan.

(c) *Borrower qualification for discharge.*

(1) Except as provided in paragraph (c)(2) of this section, to receive a discharge of a portion of a loan under this section, a borrower must submit a written application to the Secretary. The application requests the information required to calculate the amount of the discharge and requires the borrower to sign a statement swearing to the accuracy of the information in the application. The statement need not be notarized but must be made by the borrower under penalty of perjury. In the statement, the borrower must—

(i) State that the borrower (or the student on whose behalf a parent borrowed)—

(A) Received the proceeds of a loan, in whole or in part, on or after January 1, 1986 to attend a school;

(B) Did not attend, withdrew, or was terminated from the school within a timeframe that entitled the borrower to a refund; and

(C) Did not receive the benefit of a refund to which the borrower was entitled either from the school or from a third party, such as the holder of a performance bond or a tuition recovery program;

(ii) State whether the borrower (or student) has any other application for discharge pending for this loan; and

(iii) State that the borrower (or student)—

(A) Agrees to provide to the Secretary upon request other

documentation reasonably available to the borrower that demonstrates that the borrower meets the qualifications for discharge under this section; and

(B) Agrees to cooperate with the Secretary in enforcement actions as described in § 685.214(d) and to transfer any right to recovery against a third party to the Secretary as described in § 685.214(e).

(2) The Secretary may discharge a portion of a loan under this section without an application if the Secretary determines, based on information in the Secretary's possession, that the borrower qualifies for a discharge.

(d) *Determination of amount eligible for discharge.*

(1) The Secretary determines the amount eligible for discharge based on information showing the refund amount or by applying the appropriate refund formula to information that the borrower provides or that is otherwise available to the Secretary. For purposes of this section, all unpaid refunds are considered to be attributed to loan proceeds.

(2) If the information in paragraph (d)(1) of this section is not available, the Secretary uses the following formulas to determine the amount eligible for discharge:

(i) In the case of a student who fails to attend or whose withdrawal or termination date is before October 7, 2000 and who completes less than 60 percent of the loan period, the Secretary discharges the lesser of the institutional charges unearned or the loan amount. The Secretary determines the amount of the institutional charges unearned by—

(A) Calculating the ratio of the amount of time remaining in the loan period after the student's last day of attendance to the actual length of the loan period; and

(B) Multiplying the resulting factor by the institutional charges assessed the student for the loan period.

(ii) In the case of a student who fails to attend or whose withdrawal or termination date is on or after October 7, 2000 and who completes less than 60 percent of the loan period, the Secretary discharges the loan amount unearned. The Secretary determines the loan amount unearned by—

(A) Calculating the ratio of the amount of time remaining in the loan period after the student's last day of attendance to the actual length of the loan period; and

(B) Multiplying the resulting factor by the total amount of title IV grants and loans received by the student, or, if unknown, the loan amount.

(iii) In the case of a student who completes 60 percent or more of the loan period, the Secretary does not discharge any amount because a student who completes 60 percent or more of the loan period is not entitled to a refund.

(e) *Discharge procedures.*

(1) Except as provided in paragraph (c)(2) of this section, if the Secretary learns that a school did not make a refund of loan proceeds owed under applicable law and regulations, the Secretary sends the borrower a discharge application and an explanation of the qualifications and procedures for obtaining a discharge. The Secretary also promptly suspends any efforts to collect from the borrower on any affected loan. The Secretary may continue to receive borrower payments.

(2) If a borrower who is sent a discharge application fails to submit the application within 60 days of the Secretary's sending the discharge application, the Secretary resumes collection and grants forbearance of principal and interest for the period in which

collection activity was suspended. The Secretary may capitalize any interest accrued and not paid during that period.

(3) If a borrower qualifies for a discharge, the Secretary notifies the borrower in writing. The Secretary resumes collection and grants forbearance of principal and interest on the portion of the loan not discharged for the period in which collection activity was suspended. The Secretary may capitalize any interest accrued and not paid during that period.

(4) If a borrower does not qualify for a discharge, the Secretary notifies the borrower in writing of the reasons for the determination. The Secretary resumes collection and grants forbearance of principal and interest for the period in which collection activity was suspended. The Secretary may capitalize any interest accrued and not paid during that period.

(Approved by the Office of Management and Budget under control number 1845-0021)

(Authority: 20 U.S.C. 1087a *et seq.*)

[64 Fed. Reg. 58969, Nov. 1, 1999; 65 Fed. Reg. 65629, Nov. 1, 2000; 66 Fed. Reg. 34765, June 29, 2001]

* * *

§ 685.220 Consolidation.

(a) *Direct Consolidation Loans.* A borrower may consolidate education loans made under certain Federal programs into a Direct Consolidation Loan. Loans consolidated into a Direct Consolidation Loan are discharged when the Direct Consolidation Loan is originated.

(b) *Loans eligible for consolidation.* The following loans may be consolidated into a Direct Consolidation Loan:

(1) Federal Subsidized Stafford Loans.

(2) Guaranteed Student Loans.

(3) Federal Insured Student Loans (FISL).

(4) Direct Subsidized Loans.

(5) Direct Subsidized Consolidation Loans.

(6) Federal Perkins Loans.

(7) National Direct Student Loans (NDSL).

(8) National Defense Student Loans (NDSL).

(9) Federal PLUS Loans.

(10) Parent Loans for Undergraduate Students (PLUS).

(11) Direct PLUS Loans.

(12) Direct PLUS Consolidation Loans.

(13) Federal Unsubsidized Stafford Loans.

(14) Federal Supplemental Loans for Students (SLS).

(15) Federal Consolidation Loans.

(16) Direct Unsubsidized Loans.

(17) Direct Unsubsidized Consolidation Loans.

(18) Auxiliary Loans to Assist Students (ALAS).

(19) Health Professions Student Loans (HPSL) and Loans for Disadvantaged Students (LDS) made under subpart II of part A of title VII of the Public Health Service Act.

(20) Health Education Assistance Loans (HEAL).

(21) Nursing loans made under subpart II of part B of title VIII of the Public Health Service Act.

(c) *Subsidized, unsubsidized, and PLUS components of Direct Consolidation Loans.*

(1) The portion of a Direct Consolidation Loan attributable to the loans identified in paragraphs (b)(1) through (5) of this section, and to Federal Consolidation Loans under paragraph (b)(15) of this section if they are eligible for interest benefits during a deferment

period under Section 428C(b)(4)(C) of the Act, is referred to as a Direct Subsidized Consolidation Loan.

(2) Except as provided in paragraph (c)(1) of this section, the portion of a Direct Consolidation Loan attributable to the loans identified in paragraphs (b)(6) through (8) and (b)(13) through (21) of this section is referred to as a Direct Unsubsidized Consolidation Loan.

(3) The portion of a Direct Consolidation Loan attributable to the loans identified in paragraphs (b)(9) through (12) of this section is referred to as a Direct PLUS Consolidation Loan.

(d) *Eligibility for a Direct Consolidation Loan.*

(1) A borrower may obtain a Direct Consolidation Loan if, at the time the borrower applies for such a loan, the borrower meets the following requirements:

(i) The borrower either—

(A) Has an outstanding balance on a Direct Loan; or

(B) Has an outstanding balance on an FFEL loan and—

(1) The borrower is unable to obtain a FFEL consolidation loan;

(2) The borrower is unable to obtain a FFEL consolidation loan with income-sensitive repayment terms acceptable to the borrower; or

(3) The borrower has an FFEL Consolidation Loan that has been submitted to the guaranty agency by the lender for default aversion, and the borrower wants to consolidate the FFEL Consolidation Loan into the Direct Loan Program for the purpose of obtaining an income contingent repayment plan.

(ii) On the loans being consolidated, the borrower is—

(A) In a six-month grace period;

(B) In a repayment period but not in default;

(C) In default but has made satisfactory repayment arrangements, as defined in applicable program regulations, on the defaulted loan; or

(D) Except as provided in paragraph (d)(4) of this section, in default but agrees to repay the consolidation loan under the income contingent repayment plan described in § 685.208(k) and signs the consent form described in § 685.209(d)(5).

(E) Not subject to a judgment secured through litigation, unless the judgment has been vacated; or

(F) Not subject to an order for wage garnishment under section 488A of the Act, unless the order has been lifted.

(iii) The borrower certifies that no other application to consolidate any of the borrower's loans listed in paragraph (b) of this section is pending with any other lender.

(iv) The borrower agrees to notify the Secretary of any change in address.

(2) A borrower may not consolidate a Direct Consolidation Loan into a new consolidation loan under this section or under § 682.201(c) unless at least one additional eligible loan is included in the consolidation.

(3) Eligible loans received before or after the date a Direct Consolidation Loan is made may be added to a subsequent Direct Consolidation Loan.

(4) A borrower may not consolidate a defaulted Direct Consolidation Loan.

(e) *Application for a Direct Consolidation Loan.* To obtain a Direct Consolidation Loan, a borrower shall submit a completed application to the Secretary.

(f) *Origination of a consolidation loan.*

(1)(i) The holder of a loan that a borrower wishes to consolidate into a Direct Loan shall complete and return the Secretary's request for certification of the amount owed within 10 business days of receipt or, if it is unable to provide the certification, provide to the Secretary a written explanation of the reasons for its inability to provide the certification.

(ii) If the Secretary approves an application for a consolidation loan, the Secretary pays to each holder of a loan selected for consolidation the amount necessary to discharge the loan.

(iii) For a Direct loan or FFEL Program loan that is in default, the Secretary limits collection costs that may be charged to the borrower to no more than those authorized under the FFEL Program.

(2) Upon receipt of the proceeds of a Direct Consolidation Loan, the holder of a consolidated loan shall promptly apply the proceeds to fully discharge the borrower's obligation on the consolidated loan. The holder of a consolidated loan shall notify the borrower that the loan has been paid in full.

(3) The principal balance of a Direct Consolidation Loan is equal to the sum of the amounts paid to the holders of the consolidated loans.

(4) If the amount paid by the Secretary to the holder of a consolidated loan exceeds the amount needed to discharge that loan, the holder of the consolidated loan shall promptly refund the excess amount to the Secretary to be credited against the outstanding balance of the Direct Consolidation Loan.

(5) If the amount paid by the Secretary to the holder of the consolidated loan is insufficient to discharge that loan, the holder shall notify the Secretary in writing of the remaining amount due on the loan. The Secretary promptly pays the remaining amount due.

(g) *Interest rate.* The interest rate on a Direct Subsidized Consolidation Loan or a Direct Unsubsidized Consolidation Loan is the rate established in Sec. 685.202(a)(3)(i). The interest rate on a Direct PLUS Consolidation Loan is the rate established in Sec. 685.202(a)(3)(ii).

(h) *Repayment plans.* A borrower may choose a repayment plan for a Direct Consolidation Loan in accordance with § 685.208, except that a borrower who became eligible to consolidate a defaulted loan under paragraph (d)(1)(ii)(D) of this section must repay the consolidation loan under the income contingent repayment plan unless—

(1) The borrower was required to and did make a payment under the income contingent repayment plan in each of the prior three (3) months; or

(2) The borrower was not required to make payments but made three reasonable and affordable payments in each of the prior three (3) months; and

(3) The borrower makes and the Secretary approves a request to change plans.

(i) *Repayment period.*

(1) Except as noted in paragraph (i)(4) of this section, the repayment period for a Direct Consolidation Loan begins on the day the loan is disbursed.

(2)(i) Borrowers who entered repayment before July 1, 2006. The Secretary determines the repayment period under § 685.208(i) on the basis of the outstanding balances on all of the borrower's loans that are eligible for consolidation

and the balances on other education loans except as provided in paragraphs (i)(3)(i), (ii), and (iii) of this section.

(ii) Borrowers entering repayment on or after July 1, 2006. The Secretary determines the repayment period under § 685.208(j) on the basis of the outstanding balances on all of the borrower's loans that are eligible for consolidation and the balances on other education loans except as provided in paragraphs (i)(3)(i) and (ii) of this section.

(3)(i) The total amount of outstanding balances on the other education loans used to determine the repayment period under §§ 685.208(i) and (j) may not exceed the amount of the Direct Consolidation Loan.

(ii) The borrower may not be in default on the other education loan unless the borrower has made satisfactory repayment arrangements with the holder of the loan.

(iii) The lender of the other educational loan may not be an individual.

(4) Borrowers whose consolidation application was received before July 1, 2006. A Direct Consolidation Loan receives a grace period if it includes a Direct Loan or FFEL Program loan for which the borrower is in an in-school period at the time of consolidation. The repayment period begins the day after the grace period ends.

(j) *Repayment schedule.*

(1) The Secretary provides a borrower of a Direct Consolidation Loan a repayment schedule before the borrower's first payment is due. The repayment schedule identifies the borrower's monthly repayment amount under the repayment plan selected.

(2) If a borrower adds an eligible loan to the consolidation loan under paragraph (e) of this section, the Secretary makes appropriate adjustments to the borrower's monthly repayment amount and repayment period.

(k) *Refunds and returns of title IV, HEA program funds received from schools.* If a lender receives a refund or return of title IV, HEA program funds from a school on a loan that has been consolidated into a Direct Consolidation Loan, the lender shall transmit the refund or return and an explanation of the source of the refund or return to the Secretary within 30 days of receipt.

(*l*) *Special provisions for joint consolidation loans.* The provisions of paragraphs (*l*)(1) through (3) of this section apply to a Direct Consolidation Loan obtained by two married borrowers.

(1) Deferment. To obtain a deferment on a joint Direct Consolidation Loan under Sec. 685.204, both borrowers must meet the requirements of that section.

(2) Forbearance. To obtain forbearance on a joint Direct Consolidation Loan under Sec. 685.205, both borrowers must meet the requirements of that section.

(3) Discharge.

(i) If a borrower dies and the Secretary receives the documentation described in Sec. 685.212(a), the Secretary discharges an amount equal to the portion of the outstanding balance of the consolidation loan, as of the date of the borrower's death, attributable to any of that borrower's loans that were repaid by the consolidation loan.

(ii) If a borrower meets the requirements for total and permanent disability discharge under Sec. 685.212(b), the Secretary discharges an amount equal to the portion of the outstanding balance of the consolidation loan, as of the date the borrower became totally and permanently disabled, attributable to any of that borrower's loans that were repaid by the consolidation loan.

(iii) If a borrower meets the requirements for discharge under Sec. 685.212(d), (e), or (f) on a loan that was consolidated into a joint Direct Consolidation Loan, the Secretary discharges the portion of the consolidation loan equal to the amount of the loan that would be eligible for discharge under the provisions of Sec. 685.212(d), (e), or (f) as applicable, and that was repaid by the consolidation loan.

(iv) If a borrower meets the requirements for loan forgiveness under Sec. 685.212(h) on a loan that was consolidated into a joint Direct Consolidation Loan, the Secretary repays the portion of the outstanding balance of the consolidation loan attributable to the loan that would be eligible for forgiveness under the provisions of Sec. 685.212(h), and that was repaid by the consolidation loan.

(Approved by the Office of Management and Budget under control number 1845-0021)

(Authority: 20 U.S.C. 1078-8, 1087a *et seq.*)

[59 Fed. Reg. 61690, Dec. 1, 1994. Redesignated and amended at 64 Fed. Reg. 58969, 58970, 59044, Nov. 1, 1999; 65 Fed. Reg. 37045, June 13, 2000. Redesignated at 65 Fed. Reg. 65629, Nov. 1, 2000, as amended at 66 Fed. Reg. 34765, June 29, 2001; 67 Fed. Reg. 67082, Nov. 1, 2002; 68 Fed. Reg. 75427, Dec. 31, 2003; 71 Fed. Reg. 45666, Sept. 8, 2006]

B.4 Perkins Regulations

34 C.F.R. sec.

674.33 Repayment.

674.34 Deferment of repayment—Federal Perkins loans, NDSLs and Defense loans.

* * *

674.38 Deferment procedures.

674.39 Loan rehabilitation.

674.50 Assignment of defaulted loans to the United States.

674.51 Special definitions.

674.52 Cancellation procedures.

* * *

674.61 Discharge for death or disability.

Source: 52 Fed. Reg. 45555, Nov. 30, 1987; 52 Fed. Reg. 45747, Dec. 1, 1987; 52 Fed. Reg. 45754, Dec. 1, 1987, unless otherwise noted.

Authority: 20 U.S.C. 1087aa–1087hh and 20 U.S.C. 421–429, unless otherwise noted.

§ 674.33 Repayment.

(a) *Repayment Plan.*

(1) The institution shall establish a repayment plan before the student ceases to be at least a half-time regular student.

(2) If the last scheduled payment would be $25 or less the institution may combine it with the next-to-last repayment.

(3) If the installment payment for all loans made to a borrower by an institution is not a multiple of $5, the institution may round that payment to the next highest dollar amount that is a multiple of $5.

(4) The institution shall apply any payment on a loan in the following order:

(i) Collection costs.

(ii) Late charges.

(iii) Accrued interest.

(iv) Principal.

(b) *Minimum monthly repayment—*

(1) *Minimum monthly repayment option.*

(i) An institution may require a borrower to pay a minimum monthly repayment if—

(A) The promissory note includes a minimum monthly repayment provision specifying the amount of the minimum monthly repayment; and

(B) The monthly repayment of principal and interest for a 10-year repayment period is less than the minimum monthly repayment; or

(ii) An institution may require a borrower to pay a minimum monthly repayment if the borrower has received loans with different interest rates at the same institution and the total monthly repayment would otherwise be less than the minimum monthly repayment.

(2) *Minimum monthly repayment of loans from more than one institution.* If a borrower has received loans from more than one institution and has notified the institution that he or she wants the minimum monthly payment determination to be based on payments due to other institutions, the following rules apply:

(i) If the total of the monthly repayments is equal to at least the minimum monthly repayment, no institution may exercise a minimum monthly repayment option.

(ii) If only one institution exercises the minimum monthly repayment option when the monthly repayment would otherwise be less than the minimum repayment option, that institution receives the difference between the minimum monthly repayment and the repayment owed to the other institution.

(iii) If each institution exercises the minimum repayment option, the minimum monthly repayment must be divided among the institutions in proportion to the amount of principal advanced by each institution.

(3) *Minimum monthly repayment of both Defense and NDSL or Federal Perkins loans from one or more institutions.* If the borrower has notified the institution that he or she wants the minimum monthly payment determination to be based on payments due to other institutions, and if the total monthly repayment is less than $30 and the monthly repayment on a Defense loan is less than $15 a month, the amount attributed to the Defense loan may not exceed $15 a month.

(4) *Minimum monthly repayment of loans with differing grace periods and deferments.* If the borrower has received loans with different grace periods and deferments, the institution shall treat each note separately, and the borrower shall pay the applicable minimum monthly payment for a loan that is not in the grace or deferment period.

(5) *Hardship.* The institution may reduce the borrower's scheduled repayments for a period of not more than one year at a time if—

(i) It determines that the borrower is unable to make the scheduled repayments due to hardship (see § 674.33(c)); and

(ii) The borrower's scheduled repayment is the minimum monthly repayment described in paragraph (b) of this section.

(6) *Minimum monthly repayment rates.* For the purposes of this section, the minimum monthly repayment rate is—

(i) $15 for a Defense loan;

(ii) $30 for an NDSL or for a Federal Perkins loan made before October 1, 1992, or for a Federal Perkins loan made on or after October 1, 1992, to a borrower who, on the date the loan is made, has an outstanding balance of principal or interest owing on any loan made under this part; or

(iii) $40 for a Federal Perkins loan made on or after October 1, 1992, to a borrower who, on the date the loan is made, has no outstanding balance of principal or interest owing on any loan made under this part.

(7) The institution shall determine the minimum repayment amount under paragraph (b) of this section for loans with repayment installment intervals greater than one month by multiplying the amounts in paragraph (b) of this section by the number of months in the installment interval.

(c) *Extension of repayment period*—

(1) *Hardship.* The institution may extend a borrower's repayment period due to prolonged illness or unemployment.

(2) *Low-income individual.*

(i) For Federal Perkins loans and NDSLs made on or after October 1, 1980, the institution may extend the borrower's repayment period up to 10 additional years beyond the 10-year maximum repayment period if the institution determines during the course of the repayment period that the borrower is a "low-income individual." The borrower qualifies for an extension of the repayment period on the basis of low-income status only during the period in which the borrower meets the criteria described in paragraph (c)(2)(i)(A) or (B) of this section. The term *low-income individual* means the following:

(A) For an unmarried borrower without dependents, an individual whose total income for the preceding calendar year did not exceed 45 percent of the Income Protection Allowance for the current award year for a family of four with one in college.

(B) For a borrower with a family that includes the borrower and any spouse or legal dependents, an individual whose total family income for the preceding calendar year did not exceed 125 percent of the Income Protection Allowance for the current award year for a family with one in college and equal in size to that of the borrower's family.

(ii) The institution shall use the Income Protection Allowance published annually in accordance with section 478 of the HEA in making this determination.

(iii) The institution shall review the borrower's status annually to determine whether the borrower continues to qualify for an extended repayment period based on his or her status as a "low-income individual."

(iv) Upon determining that a borrower ceases to qualify for an extended repayment period under this section, the institution shall amend the borrower's repayment schedule. The term of the amended repayment schedule may not exceed the number of months remaining on the original repayment schedule, provided that the institution may not include the time elapsed during any extension of the repayment period granted under this section in determining the number of months remaining on the original repayment schedule.

(3) Interest continues to accrue during any extension of a repayment period.

(d) *Forbearance.*

(1) Forbearance means the temporary cessation of payments, allowing an extension of time for making payments, or temporarily accepting smaller payments than previously were scheduled.

(2) Upon receipt of a written request and supporting documentation, the institution shall grant the borrower forbearance of principal and, unless otherwise indicated by the borrower, interest renewable at intervals of up to 12 months for periods that collectively do not exceed three years.

(3) The terms of forbearance must be agreed upon, in writing, by the borrower and the institution.

(4) In granting a forbearance under this section, an institution shall grant a temporary cessation of payments, unless the borrower chooses another form of forbearance subject to paragraph (d)(1) of this section.

(5) An institution shall grant forbearance if—

(i) The amount of the payments the borrower is obligated to make on title IV loans each month (or a proportional share if the payments are due less frequently than monthly) is collectively equal to or greater than 20 percent of the borrower's total monthly gross income;

(ii) The institution determines that the borrower should qualify for the forbearance due to poor health or for other acceptable reasons; or

(iii) The Secretary authorizes a period of forbearance due to a national military mobilization or other national emergency.

(6) Before granting a forbearance to a borrower under paragraph (d)(5)(i) of this section, the institution shall require the borrower to submit at least the following documentation:

(i) Evidence showing the amount of the most recent total monthly gross income received by the borrower; and

(ii) Evidence showing the amount of the monthly payments owed by the borrower for the most recent month for the borrower's title IV loans.

(7) Interest accrues during any period of forbearance.

(8) The institution may not include the periods of forbearance described in this paragraph in determining the 10-year repayment period.

(e) *Compromise of repayment.*

(1) An institution may compromise on the repayment of a defaulted loan if—

(i) The institution has fully complied with all due diligence requirements specified in subpart C of this part; and

(ii) The student borrower pays in a single lump-sum payment—

(A) 90 percent of the outstanding principal balance on the loan under this part;

(B) The interest due on the loan; and

(C) Any collection fees due on the loan.

(2) The Federal share of the compromise repayment must bear the same relation to the institution's share of the compromise repayment as the Federal capital contribution to the institution's loan Fund under this part bears to the institution's capital contribution to the Fund.

(f)(1) *Incentive repayment program.* An institution may establish the following repayment incentives:

(i) A reduction of no more than one percent of the interest rate on a loan on which the borrower has made 48 consecutive, monthly repayments.

(ii) A discount of no more than five percent on the balance owed on a loan which the borrower pays in full prior to the end of the repayment period.

(iii) With the Secretary's approval, any other incentive the institution determines will reduce defaults and replenish its Fund.

(2) *Limitation on the use of funds.*

(i) The institution must reimburse its Fund, on at least a quarterly basis, for money lost to its Fund that otherwise would have been paid by the borrower as a result of establishing a repayment incentive under paragraphs (f)(1)(i), (ii) and (iii) of this section.

(ii) An institution may not use Federal funds, including Federal funds from the student loan fund, or institutional funds from the student loan fund to pay for any repayment incentive authorized by this section.

(g) *Closed school discharge.*

(1) *General.*

(i) The holder of an NDSL or a Federal Perkins Loan discharges the borrower's (and any endorser's) obligation to repay the loan if the borrower did not complete the program of study for which the loan was made because the school at which the borrower was enrolled closed.

(ii) For the purposes of this section—

(A) A school's closure date is the date that the school ceases to provide educational instruction in all programs, as determined by the Secretary;

(B) "School" means a school's main campus or any location or branch of the main campus; and

(C) The "holder" means the Secretary or the school that holds the loan.

(2) *Relief pursuant to discharge.*

(i) Discharge under this section relieves the borrower of any past or present obligation to repay the loan and any accrued interest or collection costs with respect to the loan.

(ii) The discharge of a loan under this section qualifies the borrower for reimbursement of amounts paid voluntarily or through enforced collection on the loan.

(iii) A borrower who has defaulted on a loan discharged under this section is not considered to have been in default on the loan after discharge, and such a borrower is eligible to receive assistance under programs authorized by title IV of the HEA.

(iv) The Secretary or the school, if the school holds the loan, reports the discharge of a loan under this section to all credit bureaus to which the status of the loan was previously reported.

(3) *Determination of borrower qualification for discharge by the Secretary.* The Secretary may discharge the borrower's obligation to repay an NDSL or Federal Perkins Loan without an application if the Secretary determines that—

(i) The borrower qualified for and received a discharge on a loan pursuant to 34 CFR 682.402(d) (Federal Family Education Loan Program) or 34 CFR 685.213 (Federal Direct Loan Program), and was unable to receive a discharge on an NDSL or Federal Perkins Loan because the Secretary lacked the statutory authority to discharge the loan; or

(ii) Based on information in the Secretary's possession, the borrower qualifies for a discharge.

(4) *Borrower qualification for discharge.* Except as provided in paragraph (g)(3) of this section, in order to qualify for discharge of an NDSL or Federal Perkins Loan, a borrower must submit to the holder of the loan a written request and sworn statement, and the factual assertions in the statement must be true. The statement need not be notarized but must be made by the borrower under penalty of perjury. In the statement the borrower must—

(i) State that the borrower—

(A) Received the proceeds of a loan to attend a school;

(B) Did not complete the program of study at that school because the school closed while the student was enrolled, or the student withdrew from the school not more than 90 days before the school closed (or longer in exceptional circumstances); and

(C) Did not complete and is not in the process of completing the program of study through a teachout at another school as defined in 34 CFR 602.2 and administered in accordance with 34 CFR 602.207(b)(6), by transferring academic credit earned at the closed school to another school, or by any other comparable means;

(ii) State whether the borrower has made a claim with respect to the school's closing with any third party, such as the holder of a performance bond or a tuition recovery program, and, if so, the amount of any payment received by the borrower or credited to the borrower's loan obligation; and

(iii) State that the borrower—

(A) Agrees to provide to the holder of the loan upon request other documentation reasonably available to the borrower that demonstrates that the borrower meets the qualifications for discharge under this section; and

(B) Agrees to cooperate with the Secretary in enforcement actions in accordance with paragraph (g)(6) of this section and to transfer any right to recovery against a third party to the Secretary in accordance with paragraph (g)(7) of this section.

(5) *Fraudulently obtained loans.* A borrower who secured a loan through fraudulent means, as determined by the ruling of a court or an administrative tribunal of competent jurisdiction, is ineligible for a discharge under this section.

(6) *Cooperation by borrower in enforcement actions.*

(i) In order to obtain a discharge under this section, a borrower must cooperate with the Secretary in any judicial or administrative proceeding brought by the Secretary to recover amounts discharged or to take other enforcement action with respect to the conduct on which the discharge was based. At the request of the Secretary and upon the Secretary's tendering to the borrower the fees and costs that are customarily provided in litigation to reimburse witnesses, the borrower must—

(A) Provide testimony regarding any representation made by the borrower to support a request for discharge;

(B) Provide any documents reasonably available to the borrower with respect to those representations; and

(C) If required by the Secretary, provide a sworn statement regarding those documents and representations.

(ii) The holder denies the request for a discharge or revokes the discharge of a borrower who—

(A) Fails to provide the testimony, documents, or a sworn statement required under paragraph (g)(6)(i) of this section; or

(B) Provides testimony, documents, or a sworn statement that does not support the material representations made by the borrower to obtain the discharge.

(7) *Transfer to the Secretary of borrower's right of recovery against third parties.*

(i) In the case of a loan held by the Secretary, upon discharge under this section, the borrower is deemed to have assigned to and relinquished in favor of the Secretary any right to a loan refund (up to the amount discharged) that the borrower may have by contract or applicable law with respect to the loan or the enrollment agreement for the program for which the loan was received, against the school, its principals, its affiliates and their successors, its sureties, and any private fund, including the portion of a public fund that represents funds received from a private party.

(ii) The provisions of this section apply notwithstanding any provision of State law that would otherwise restrict transfer of those rights by the borrower, limit or prevent a transferee from exercising those rights, or establish procedures or a scheme of distribution that would prejudice the Secretary's ability to recover on those rights.

(iii) Nothing in this section limits or forecloses the borrower's right to pursue legal and equitable relief regarding disputes arising from matters unrelated to the discharged NDSL or Federal Perkins Loan.

(8) *Discharge procedures.*

(i) After confirming the date of a school's closure, the holder of the loan identifies any NDSL or Federal Perkins Loan borrower who appears to have been enrolled at the school on the school closure date or to have withdrawn not more than 90 days prior to the closure date.

(ii) If the borrower's current address is known, the holder of the loan mails the borrower a discharge application and an explanation of the qualifications and procedures for obtaining a discharge. The holder of the loan also promptly suspends any efforts to collect from the borrower on any affected loan. The holder of the loan may continue to receive borrower payments.

(iii) In the case of a loan held by the Secretary, if the borrower's current address is unknown, the Secretary attempts to locate the borrower and determine the borrower's potential eligibility for a discharge under this section by consulting with representatives of the closed school or representatives of the closed school's third-party billing and collection servicers, the school's licensing agency, the school accrediting agency, and other appropriate parties. If the Secretary learns the new address of a borrower, the Secretary mails to the borrower a discharge application and explanation and suspends collection, as described in paragraph (g)(8)(ii) of this section.

(iv) In the case of a loan held by a school, if the borrower's current address is unknown, the school attempts to locate the borrower and determine the borrower's potential eligibility for a discharge under this section by taking steps required to locate the borrower under § 674.44.

(v) If the borrower fails to submit the written request and sworn statement described in paragraph (g)(4) of this section within 60 days of the holder of the loan's mailing the discharge application, the holder of the loan resumes collection and grants forbearance of principal and interest

for the period during which collection activity was suspended.

(vi) If the holder of the loan determines that a borrower who requests a discharge meets the qualifications for a discharge, the holder of the loan notifies the borrower in writing of that determination.

(vii) In the case of a loan held by the Secretary, if the Secretary determines that a borrower who requests a discharge does not meet the qualifications for a discharge, the Secretary notifies that borrower, in writing, of that determination and the reasons for the determination.

(viii) In the case of a loan held by a school, if the school determines that a borrower who requests a discharge does not meet the qualifications for discharge, the school submits that determination and all supporting materials to the Secretary for approval. The Secretary reviews the materials, makes an independent determination, and notifies the borrower in writing of the determination and the reasons for the determination.

(ix) In the case of a loan held by a school and discharged by either the school or the Secretary, the school must reimburse its Fund for the entire amount of any outstanding principal and interest on the loan, and any collection costs charged to the Fund as a result of collection efforts on a discharged loan. The school must also reimburse the borrower for any amount of principal, interest, late charges or collection costs the borrower paid on a loan discharged under this section.

(Approved by the Office of Management and Budget under control number 1845-0019)

(Authority: 20 U.S.C. 425 and 1087dd, sec. 137(d) of Pub. L. 92-318)

[57 Fed. Reg. 32345, July 21, 1992; 57 Fed. Reg. 60706, Dec. 21, 1992; 58 Fed. Reg. 36870, 36871, July 9, 1993; 59 Fed. Reg. 61409, Nov. 30, 1994; 60 Fed. Reg. 61814, Dec. 1, 1995; 62 Fed. Reg. 50848, Sept. 26, 1997; 64 Fed. Reg. 58309, Oct. 28, 1999; 65 Fed. Reg. 18002, 18003, April 6, 2000; 65 Fed. Reg. 26136, May 5, 2000; 67 Fed. Reg. 67076, Nov. 1, 2002]

§ 674.34 Deferment of repayment—Federal Perkins loans, NDSLs and Defense loans.

(a) The borrower may defer making a scheduled installment repayment on a Federal Perkins loan, an NDSL, or a Defense loan, regardless of contrary provisions of the borrower's promissory note and regardless of the date the loan was made, during periods described in paragraphs (b), (c), (d), (e), (f), and (g) of this section.

(b)(1) The borrower need not repay principal, and interest does not accrue, during a period after the commencement or resumption of the repayment period on a loan, when the borrower is—

(i) Enrolled and in attendance as a regular student in at least a half-time course of study at an eligible institution;

(ii) Enrolled and in attendance as a regular student in a course of study that is part of a graduate fellowship program approved by the Secretary;

(iii) Engaged in graduate or post-graduate fellowship-supported study (such as a Fulbright grant) outside the United States; or

(iv) Enrolled in a course of study that is part of a rehabilitation training program for disabled individuals approved by the Secretary as described in paragraph (g) of this section.

(2) No borrower is eligible for a deferment under paragraph (b)(1) of this section while serving in a medical internship or residency program, except for a residency program in dentistry.

(3) The institution of higher education at which the borrower is enrolled does not need to be participating in the Federal Perkins Loan program for the borrower to qualify for a deferment.

(4) If a borrower is attending an institution of higher education as at least a half-time regular student for a full academic year and intends to enroll as at least a half-time regular student in the next academic year, the borrower is entitled to a deferment for 12 months.

(5) If an institution no longer qualifies as an institution of higher education, the borrower's deferment ends on the date the institution ceases to qualify.

(c)(1) The borrower of a Federal Perkins loan need not repay principal, and interest does not accrue, for any period during which the borrower is engaged in service described in §§ 674.53, 674.54, 674.56, 674.57, 674.58, 674.59, and 674.60.

(2) The borrower of an NDSL need not repay principal, and interest does not accrue, for any period during which the borrower is engaged in service described in §§ 674.53, 674.54, 674.56, 674.57, 674.58, and 674.59.

(d) The borrower need not repay principal, and interest does not accrue, for any period not to exceed 3 years during which the borrower is seeking and unable to find full-time employment.

(e) The borrower need not repay principal, and interest does not accrue, for periods of up to one year at a time (except that a deferment under paragraph (e)(6) of this section may be granted for the lesser of the borrower's full term of service in the Peace Corps or the borrower's remaining period of economic hardship deferment eligibility) that, collectively, do not exceed 3 years, during which the borrower is suffering an economic hardship, if the borrower provides documentation satisfactory to the institution showing that the borrower is within any of the categories described in paragraphs (e)(1) through (e)(6) of this section.

(1) Has been granted an economic hardship deferment under either the FDSL or FFEL programs for the period of time for which the borrower has requested an economic hardship deferment for his or her Federal Perkins loan.

(2) Is receiving payment under a federal or state public assistance program, such as Aid to Families with Dependent Children, Supplemental Security Income, Food Stamps, or state general public assistance.

(3) Is working full-time and earning a total monthly gross income that does not exceed the greater of—

(i) The monthly earnings of an individual earning the minimum wage described in section 6 of the Fair Labor Standards Act of 1938; or

(ii) An amount equal to 100 percent of the poverty line for a family of two, as determined in accordance with section 673(2) of the Community Service Block Grant Act.

(4) Is not receiving total monthly gross income that exceeds twice the amount specified in paragraph (e)(3) of this section and, after deducting an amount equal to the borrower's monthly payments on federal postsecondary education loans, as determined under paragraph (e)(10) of this section, the remaining amount of that income does not exceed the amount specified in paragraph (e)(3) of this section;

(5) Is working full-time and has a Federal education debt burden as determined under paragraph (e)(10) of this section that equals or exceeds 20 percent of the borrower's total monthly gross income, and the borrower's income minus such burden is less than 220 percent of the amount calculated under paragraph (3) of this section.

(6) Is serving as a volunteer in the Peace Corps.

(7) For a deferment granted under paragraph (e)(4) or (e)(5) of this section, the institution shall require the borrower to submit at least the following documentation to qualify for an initial period of deferment—

(i) Evidence showing the amount of the borrower's most recent total monthly gross income, as defined in section 674.2; and

(ii) Evidence that would enable the institution to determine the amount of the monthly payments that would have been owed by the borrower during the deferment period to other entities for federal postsecondary education loans in accordance with paragraph (e)(9) of this section.

(8) To qualify for a subsequent period of deferment that begins less than one year after the end of a period of deferment under paragraphs (e)(3), (e)(4), or (e)(5) of this section, the institution shall require the borrower to submit a copy of the borrower's federal income tax return if the borrower filed a tax return within eight months prior to the date the deferment is requested.

(9) For purposes of paragraphs (e)(3) and (e)(5) of this section, a borrower is considered to be working full-time if the borrower is expected to be employed for at least three consecutive months at 30 hours per week.

(10) In determining a borrower's Federal education debt burden under paragraphs (e)(4) and (e)(5) of this section, the institution shall—

(i) If the Federal postsecondary education loan is scheduled to be repaid in 10 years or less, use the actual monthly payment amount (or a proportional share if the payments are due less frequently than monthly); or

(ii) If the Federal postsecondary education loan is scheduled to be repaid in more than 10 years, use a monthly payment amount (or a proportional share if the payments are due less frequently than monthly) that would have been due on the loan if the loan had been scheduled to be repaid in 10 years.

(f) To qualify for a deferment for study as part of a graduate fellowship program pursuant to paragraph (b)(1)(ii) of this section, a borrower must provide the institution certification that the borrower has been accepted for or is engaged in full-time study in the institution's graduate fellowship program.

(g) To qualify for a deferment for study in a rehabilitation training program, pursuant to paragraph (b)(1)(iv) of this section, the borrower must be receiving, or be scheduled to receive, services under a program designed to rehabilitate disabled individuals and must provide the institution with the following documentation:

(1) A certification from the rehabilitation agency that the borrower is either receiving or scheduled to receive rehabilitation training services from the agency.

(2) A certification from the rehabilitation agency that the rehabilitation program—

(i) Is licensed, approved, certified, or otherwise recognized by one of the following entities as providing rehabilitation training to disabled individuals—

(A) A State agency with responsibility for vocational rehabilitation programs;

(B) A State agency with responsibility for drug abuse treatment programs;

(C) A State agency with responsibility for mental health services programs;

(D) A State agency with responsibility for alcohol abuse treatment programs; or

(E) The Department of Veterans Affairs; and

(ii) Provides or will provide the borrower with rehabilitation services under a written plan that—

(A) Is individualized to meet the borrower's needs;

(B) Specifies the date on which the services to the borrower are expected to end; and

(C) Is structured in a way that requires a substantial commitment by the borrower to his or her rehabilitation. The Secretary considers a substantial commitment by the borrower to be a commitment of time and effort that would normally prevent an individual from engaging in full-time employment either because of the number of hours that must be devoted to rehabilitation or because of the nature of the rehabilitation.

(h)(1) The borrower need not pay principal and interest does not accrue on a Federal Perkins Loan made on or after July 1, 2001, for any period not to exceed 3 years during which the borrower is—

(i) Serving on active duty during a war or other military operation or national emergency; or

(ii) Performing qualifying National Guard duty during a war or other military operation or national emergency.

(2) Serving on active duty during a war or other military operation or national emergency means service by an individual who is—

(i) A Reserve of an Armed Force ordered to active duty under 10 U.S.C. 12301(a), 12301(g), 12302, 12304, or 12306;

(ii) A retired member of an Armed Force ordered to active duty under 10 U.S.C. 688 for service in connection with a war or other military operation or national emergency, regardless of the location at which such active duty service is performed; or

(iii) Any other member of an Armed Force on active duty in connection with such emergency or subsequent actions or conditions who has been assigned to a duty station at a location other than the location at which the member is normally assigned.

(3) Qualifying National Guard duty during a war or other operation or national emergency means service as a member of the National Guard on full-time National Guard duty, as defined in 10 U.S.C. 101(d)(5), under a call to active service authorized by the President or the Secretary of Defense for a period of more than 30 consecutive days under 32 U.S.C. 502(f) in connection with a war, other military operation, or national emergency declared by the President and supported by Federal funds.

(4) As used in this section—

(i) Active duty means active duty as defined in 10 U.S.C. 101(d)(1) except that it does not include active duty for training or attendance at a service school;

(ii) Military operation means a contingency operation as defined in 10 U.S.C. 101(a)(13); and

(iii) National emergency means the national emergency by reason of certain terrorist attacks declared by the President on September 14, 2001, or subsequent national emergencies declared by the President by reason of terrorist attacks.

(5) These provisions do not authorize the refunding of any payments made by or on behalf of a borrower during a period for which the borrower qualified for a military service deferment.

(i) The institution may not include the deferment periods described in paragraphs (b), (c), (d), (e), (f), (g), and (h) of this section and the period described in paragraph (j) of this section in determining the 10-year repayment period.

(j) The borrower need not pay principal and interest does not accrue until six months after completion of any period during which the borrower is in deferment under paragraphs (b), (c), (d), (e), (f), (g) , and (h) of this section.

(Approved by the Office of Management and Budget under control number 1845-0019)

(Authority: 20 U.S.C. 1087dd)

[59 Fed. Reg. 61410, Nov. 30, 1994; 60 Fed. Reg. 31410, June 15, 1995; 60 Fed. Reg. 61815, Dec. 1, 1995; 62 Fed. Reg. 50848, Sept. 26, 1997; 64 Fed. Reg. 57531, Oct. 25, 1999; 64 Fed. Reg. 58311, Oct. 28, 1999; 65 Fed. Reg. 18003, April 6, 2000; 65 Fed. Reg. 26136, May 5, 2000; 67 Fed. Reg. 67076, Nov. 1, 2002; 71 Fed. Reg. 45666, Sept. 8, 2006]

* * *

§ 674.38 Deferment procedures.

(a)(1) Except as provided in paragraph (a)(2)of this section, a borrower must request the deferment and provide the institution with all information and documents required by the institution by the date that the institution establishes.

(2) In the case of an in school deferment, the institution may grant the deferment based on student enrollment information showing that a borrower is enrolled as a regular student on at least a half-time basis, if the institution notifies the borrower of the deferment and of the borrower's option to cancel the deferment and continue paying on the loan.

(3) If the borrower fails to meet the requirements of paragraph (a)(1) of this section, the institution may declare the loan to be in default, and may accelerate the loan.

(b)(1) The institution may grant a deferment to a borrower after it has declared a loan to be a default.

(2) As a condition for a deferment under this paragraph, the institution—

(i) Shall require the borrower to execute a written repayment agreement on the loan; and

(ii) May require the borrower to pay immediately some or all of the amounts previously scheduled to be repaid before the date on which the institution determined that the borrower had demonstrated that grounds for a deferment existed, plus late charges and collection costs.

(c) If the information supplied by the borrower demonstrates that for some or all of the period for which a deferment is requested, the borrower had retained in-school status or was within the initial grace period on the loan, the institution shall—

(1) Redetermine the date on which the borrower was required to commence repayment on the loan;

(2) Deduct from the loan balance any interest accrued and late charges added before the date on which the repayment period commenced, as determined in paragraph (c)(1) of this section; and

(3) Treat in accordance with paragraph (b) of this section, the

request for deferment for any remaining portion of the period for which deferment was requested.

(d) The institution must determine the continued eligibility of a borrower for a deferment at least annually, except that a borrower engaged in service described in §§ 674.34(e)(6), 674.35(c)(3), 674.36(c)(2), 674.37(c)(2), and § 674.60(a)(1) must be granted a deferment for the lesser of the borrower's full term of service in the Peace Corps, or the borrower's remaining period of eligibility for a deferment under § 674.34(e), not to exceed 3 years.

(Approved by the Office of Management and Budget under control number 1845-0019)

(Authority: 20 U.S.C. 425, 1087dd)

[53 Fed. Reg. 49147, Dec. 6, 1988; 59 Fed. Reg. 61410, 61411, Nov. 30, 1994; 64 Fed. Reg. 57531, Oct. 25, 1999; 64 Fed. Reg. 58315, Oct. 28, 1999]

§ 674.39 Loan rehabilitation.

(a) Each institution must establish a loan rehabilitation program for all borrowers for the purpose of rehabilitating defaulted loans made under this part, except for loans for which a judgment has been secured or loans obtained by fraud for which the borrower has been convicted of, or has pled nolo contendere or guilty to, a crime involving fraud in obtaining title IV, HEA program assistance. The institution's loan rehabilitation program must provide that—

(1) A defaulted borrower is notified of the option and consequences of rehabilitating a loan; and

(2) A loan is rehabilitated if the borrower makes an on-time, monthly payment, as determined by the institution, each month for twelve consecutive months and the borrower requests rehabilitation.

(b) Within 30 days of receiving the borrower's last on-time, consecutive, monthly payment, the institution must—

(1) Return the borrower to regular repayment status;

(2) Treat the first payment made under the 12 consecutive payments as the first payment under the 10-year repayment maximum; and

(3) Instruct any credit bureau to which the default was reported to remove the default from the borrower's credit history.

(c) Collection costs on a rehabilitated loan—

(1) If charged to the borrower, may not exceed 24 percent of the unpaid principal and accrued interest as of the date following application of the twelfth payment;

(2) That exceed the amounts specified in paragraph (c)(1) of this section, may be charged to an institution's Fund until July 1, 2002 in accordance with § 674.47(e)(5); and

(3) Are not restricted to 24 percent in the event the borrower defaults on the rehabilitated loan.

(d) After rehabilitating a defaulted loan and returning to regular repayment status, the borrower regains the balance of the benefits and privileges of the promissory note as applied prior to the borrower's default on the loan. Nothing in this paragraph prohibits an institution from offering the borrower flexible repayment options following the borrower's return to regular repayment status on a rehabilitated loan.

(e) The borrower may rehabilitate a defaulted loan only one time.

(Approved by the Office of Management and Budget under control number 1845-0023)

[53 Fed. Reg. 49147, Dec. 6, 1988; 57 Fed. Reg. 32346, July 21, 1992; 58 Fed. Reg. 36870, July 9, 1993; 59 Fed. Reg. 61410, 61411, Nov. 30, 1994; 64 Fed. Reg. 58311, Oct. 28, 1999; 65 Fed. Reg. 65614, Nov. 1, 2000; 67 Fed. Reg. 67077, Nov. 1, 2002; 71 Fed. Reg. 45666, Sept. 8, 2006]

§ 674.50 Assignment of defaulted loans to the United States.

(a) An institution may submit a defaulted loan note to the Secretary for assignment to the United States if—

(1) The institution has been unable to collect on the loan despite complying with the diligence procedures, including at least a first level collection effort as described in § 674.45(a) and litigation, if required under § 674.46(a), to the extent these actions were required by regulations in effect on the date the loan entered default;

(2) The amount of the borrower's account to be assigned, including outstanding principal, accrued interest, collection costs and late charges is $25.00 or greater; and

(3) The loan has been accelerated.

(b) An institution may submit a defaulted note for assignment only during the submission period established by the Secretary.

(c) The Secretary may require an institution to submit the following documents for any loan it proposes to assign—

(1) An assignment form provided by the Secretary and executed by the institution, which must include a certification by the institution that it has complied with the requirements of this subpart, including at least a first level collection effort as described in § 674.45(a) in attempting collection on the loan.

(2) The original promissory note or a certified copy of the original note.

(3) A copy of the repayment schedule.

(4) A certified copy of any judgment order entered on the loan.

(5) A complete statement of the payment history.

(6) Copies of all approved requests for deferment and cancellation.

(7) A copy of the notice to the borrower of the effective date of acceleration and the total amount due on the loan.

(8) Documentation that the institution has withdrawn the loan from any firm that it employed for address search, billing, collection or litigation services, and has notified that firm to cease collection activity on the loans.

(9) Copies of all pleadings filed or received by the institution on behalf of a borrower who has filed a petition in bankruptcy and whose loan obligation is determined to be nondischargeable.

(10) Documentation that the institution has complied with all of the due diligence requirements described in paragraph (a)(1) of this section if the institution has a cohort default rate that is equal to or greater than 20 percent as of June 30 of the second year preceding the submission period.

(d) Except as provided in paragraph (e) of this section, and subject to paragraph (g) of this section, the Secretary accepts an assignment of a note described in paragraph (a) of this section and submitted in accordance with paragraph (c) of this section.

(e) The Secretary does not accept assignment of a loan if—

(1) The institution has not provided the Social Security number of the borrower;

(2) The borrower has received a discharge in bankruptcy, unless—

(i) The bankruptcy court has determined that the loan obligation is nondischargeable and has entered judgment against the borrower; or

(ii) A court of competent jurisdiction has entered judgment against the borrower on the loan after the entry of the discharge order; or

(3) The institution has initiated litigation against the borrower, unless the judgment has been entered against the borrower and assigned to the United States.

(f)(1) The Secretary provides an institution written notice of the acceptance of the assignment of the note. By accepting assignment, the Secretary acquires all rights, title, and interest of the institution in that loan.

(2) The institution shall endorse and forward to the Secretary any payment received from the borrower after the date on which the Secretary accepted the assignment, as noted in the written notice of acceptance.

(g)(1) The Secretary may determine that a loan assigned to the United States is unenforceable in whole or in part because of the acts or omissions of the institution or its agent. The Secretary may make this determination with or without a judicial determination regarding the enforceability of the loan.

(2) The Secretary may require the institution to reimburse the Fund for that portion of the outstanding balance on a loan assigned to the United States which the Secretary determines to be unenforceable because of an act or omission of that institution or its agent.

(3) Upon reimbursement to the Fund by the institution, the Secretary shall transfer all rights, title and interest of the United States in the loan to the institution for its own account.

(h) An institution shall consider a borrower whose loan has been assigned to the United States for collection to be in default on that loan for the purpose of eligibility for title IV financial assistance, until the borrower provides the institution confirmation from the Secretary that he or she has made satisfactory arrangements to repay the loan.

(Approved by the Office of Management and Budget under control number 1845-0019)

(Authority: 20 U.S.C. 424, 1087cc)

[53 Fed. Reg. 49147, Dec. 6, 1988; 57 Fed. Reg. 32347, July 21, 1992; 57 Fed. Reg. 60706, Dec. 21, 1992; 58 Fed. Reg. 36870, 36871, July 9, 1993; 59 Fed. Reg. 61412, Nov. 30, 1994; 64 Fed. Reg. 58315, Oct. 28, 1999; 65 Fed. Reg. 65614, Nov. 1, 2000; 67 Fed. Reg. 67077, Nov. 1, 2002]

§ 674.51 Special definitions.

The following definitions apply to this Subpart:

(a) *Academic year or its equivalent for elementary and secondary schools and special education*:

(1) One complete school year, or two half years from different school years, excluding summer sessions, that are complete and consecutive and generally fall within a 12-month period.

(2) If such a school has a year-round program of instruction, the Secretary considers a minimum of nine consecutive months to be the equivalent of an academic year.

(b) *Academic year or its equivalent for institutions of higher education*: A period of time in which a full-time student is expected to complete—

(1) The equivalent of 2 semesters, 2 trimesters, or 3 quarters at an institution using credit hours; or

(2) At least 900 clock hours of training for each program at an institution using clock hours.

(c) Title I Children: Children of ages 5 through 17 who are counted under section 1124(c)(1) of the Elementary and Secondary Education Act of 1965, as amended.

(d) *Children and youth with disabilities*: Children and youth from ages 3 through 21, inclusive, who require special education and related services because they have disabilities as defined in section 602(a)(1) of the Individuals with Disabilities Education Act.

(e) *Early intervention services*: Those services defined in section 672(2) of the Individuals with Disabilities Education Act that are provided to infants and toddlers with disabilities.

(f) *Elementary school*: A school that provides elementary education, including education below grade 1, as determined by—

(1) State law; or

(2) The Secretary, if the school is not in a State.

(g) *Handicapped children*: Children of ages 3 through 21 inclusive who require special education and related services because they are—

(1) Mentally retarded;

(2) Hard of hearing;

(3) Deaf;

(4) Speech and language impaired;

(5) Visually handicapped;

(6) Seriously emotionally disturbed;

(7) Orthopedically impaired;

(8) Specific learning disabled; or

(9) Otherwise health impaired.

(h) *High-risk children*: Individuals under the age of 21 who are low-income or at risk of abuse or neglect, have been abused or neglected, have serious emotional, mental, or behavioral disturbances, reside in placements outside their homes, or are involved in the juvenile justice system.

(i) *Infants and toddlers with disabilities*: Infants and toddlers from birth to age 2, inclusive, who need early intervention services for specified reasons, as defined in section 672(1) of the Individuals with Disabilities Education Act.

(j) *Local educational agency*:

(1) A public board of education or other public authority legally constituted within a State to administer, direct, or perform a service function for public elementary or secondary schools in a city, county, township, school district, other political subdivision of a State; or such combination of school districts of counties as are recognized in a State as an administrative agency for its public elementary or secondary schools.

(2) Any other public institution or agency having administrative control and direction of a public elementary or secondary school.

(k) *Low-income communities*: Communities in which there is a high concentration of children eligible to be counted under title I of the Elementary and Secondary Education Act of 1965, as amended.

(l) *Medical technician*: An allied health professional (working in fields such as therapy, dental hygiene, medical technology, or nutrition) who is certified, registered, or licensed by the appropriate State agency in the State in which he or she provides health care services. An allied health professional is someone who assists, facilitates, or complements the work of physicians and other specialists in the health care system.

(m) *Nurse*: A licensed practical nurse, a registered nurse, or other individual who is licensed by the appropriate State agency to provide nursing services.

(n) *Qualified professional provider of early intervention services*: A provider of services as defined in section 672(2) of the Individuals with Disabilities Education Act.

(o) *Secondary school*:

(1) A school that provides secondary education, as determined by—

(i) State law; or

(ii) The Secretary, if the school is not in a State.

(2) However, State laws notwithstanding, secondary education does not include any education beyond grade 12.

(p) *State education agency*:

(1) The State board of education; or

(2) An agency or official designated by the Governor or by State law as being primarily responsible for the State supervision of public elementary and secondary schools.

(q) *Teacher*:

(1) A teacher is a person who provides—

(i) Direct classroom teaching;

(ii) Classroom-type teaching in a non-classroom setting; or

(iii) Educational services to students directly related to classroom teaching such as school librarians or school guidance counselors.

(2) A supervisor, administrator, researcher, or curriculum specialist is not a teacher unless he or she primarily provides direct and personal educational services to students.

(3) An individual who provides one of the following services does not qualify as a teacher unless that individual is licensed, certified, or registered by the appropriate State education agency for that area in which he or she is providing related special educational services, and the services provided by the individual are part of the educational curriculum for handicapped children:

(i) Speech and language pathology and audiology;

(ii) Physical therapy;

(iii) Occupational therapy;

(iv) Psychological and counseling services; or

(v) Recreational therapy.

(r) *Teaching in a field of expertise*: The majority of classes taught are in the borrower's field of expertise.

(s) *Total and permanent disability*: The condition of an individual who is unable to work and earn money because of an injury or illness that is expected to continue indefinitely or result in death.

(Authority: 20 U.S.C. 425, 1087ee, 1141, and 1401(1))

[59 Fed. Reg. 61412, Nov. 30, 1994; 65 Fed. Reg. 65690, Nov. 1, 2000]

§ 674.52 Cancellation procedures.

(a) *Application for cancellation*. To qualify for cancellation of a loan, a borrower shall submit to the institution to which the loan is owed, by the date that the institution establishes, both a written request for cancellation and any documentation required by the institution to demonstrate that the borrower meets the conditions for the cancellation requested.

(b) *Part-time employment*.

(1)(i) An institution may refuse a request for cancellation based on a claim of simultaneously teaching in two or more schools or institutions if it cannot determine easily from the documentation supplied by the borrower that the teaching is full-time. However, it shall grant the cancellation if one school official certifies that a teacher worked full-time for a full academic year.

(ii) An institution may refuse a request for cancellation based on a claim of simultaneous employment as a nurse or medical technician in two or more facilities if it cannot determine easily from the documentation supplied by the borrower that the combined employment is full-time. However, it shall grant the cancellation if one facility official certifies that a nurse or medical technician worked full-time for a full year.

(2) If the borrower is unable due to illness or pregnancy to complete the academic year, the borrower still qualifies for the cancellation if—

(i) The borrower completes the first half of the academic year, and has begun teaching the second half; and

(ii) The borrower's employer considers the borrower to have fulfilled his or her contract for the academic year for purposes of salary increment, tenure, and retirement.

(c) *Cancellation of a defaulted loan*.

(1) Except with regard to cancellation on account of the death or disability of the borrower, a borrower whose defaulted loan has not been accelerated may qualify for a cancellation by complying with the requirements of paragraph (a) of this section.

(2) A borrower whose defaulted loan has been accelerated—

(i) May qualify for a loan cancellation for services performed before the date of acceleration; and

(ii) Cannot qualify for a cancellation for services performed on or after the date of acceleration.

(3) An institution shall grant a request for cancellation on account of the death or disability of the borrower without regard to the repayment status of the loan.

(d) *Concurrent deferment period*. The Secretary considers a Perkins Loan, NDSL or Defense Loan borrower's loan deferment under § 674.34(c) to run concurrently with any period for which cancellation under §§ 674.53, 674.54, 674.55, 674.56, 674.57, 674.58, 674.59, and 674.60 is granted.

(e) *National community service*. No borrower who has received a benefit under subtitle D of title I of the National and Community Service Act of 1990 may receive a cancellation under this subpart.

(Approved by the Office of Management and Budget under control number 1845-0019)

(Authority: 20 U.S.C. 425, 1087ee)

[53 Fed. Reg. 49147, Dec. 6, 1988; 57 Fed. Reg. 32347, July 21, 1992; 58 Fed. Reg. 36870, July 9, 1993; 59 Fed. Reg. 61413, Nov. 30, 1994; 62 Fed. Reg. 50848, Sept. 26, 1997; 64 Fed. Reg. 58313, Oct. 28, 1999; 65 Fed. Reg. 18003, April 6, 2000; 65 Fed. Reg. 26136, May 5, 2000]

* * *

§ 674.61 Discharge for death or disability.

(a) *Death*. An institution must discharge the unpaid balance of a borrower's Defense, NDSL, or Perkins loan, including interest, if the borrower dies. The institution must discharge the loan on the basis of an original or certified copy of the death certificate. Under exceptional circumstances and on a case-by-case basis, the chief financial officer of the institution may approve a discharge based upon other reliable documentation supporting the discharge request.

(b) *Total and permanent disability*.

(1) If the Secretary has made an initial determination that the borrower is totally and permanently disabled, as defined in § 674.51(s), the loan is conditionally discharged for up to three years from the date that the borrower became totally and permanently disabled, as certified by a physician. The Secretary suspends collection activity on the loan from the date of the initial determination of total and permanent disability until the end of the three-year conditional period. If the borrower satisfies the criteria for a total and permanent disability discharge during and at the end of the conditional discharge period, the balance of the loan is discharged at the end of the conditional discharge period and any payments received after the date the borrower became totally and permanently disabled as certified under § 674.61(b)(3) are returned to the sender.

(2) A borrower satisfies the criteria for a discharge of a loan based on a total and permanent disability if, during and at the end of the three-year conditional discharge period described in paragraph (b)(1) of this section—

(i) The borrower's annual earnings from employment do not exceed 100 percent of the poverty line for a family of two, as determined in accordance with the Community Service Block Grant Act; and

(ii) The borrower does not receive a new loan under the Perkins, FFEL or Direct Loan programs, except for a FFEL or Direct Consolidation Loan that does not include any loans that are in a conditional discharge status.

(3) If a borrower becomes totally and permanently disabled after receiving a Defense, NDSL, or Perkins loan, the institution must assign the loan to the Secretary if the borrower submits a certification by a physician and the institution reviewed the application and determined that it is complete and that it supports the conclusion that the borrower has a total and permanent disability as defined in § 674.51(s).

(4) At the time the loan is assigned to the Secretary the institution must notify the borrower that the loan has been assigned to the Secretary for determination of eligibility for a total and permanent disability discharge.

(5) If the Secretary determines that the certification provided by the borrower does not support the conclusion that the borrower meets the criteria for a total and permanent disability discharge, the Secretary notifies the borrower that the application for a disability discharge has been denied, and that the loan is due and payable under the terms of the promissory note.

(6) If the Secretary makes an initial determination that the borrower is totally and permanently disabled, the Secretary notifies the borrower that the loan will be in a conditional discharge status for a period of up to three years after the date the borrower became totally and permanently disabled as certified under § 674.61(b)(3). This notification identifies the conditions of the conditional discharge period specified in paragraphs (b)(6) through (b)(9) of this section and specifies that all or part of the three-year period may predate the Secretary's initial determination.

(7) During the conditional discharge period, the borrower—

(i) Is not required to make any payments on the loan;

(ii) Is not considered past due or in default on the loan, unless the loan was past due or in default at the time the conditional discharge was granted;

(iii) Must promptly notify the Secretary of any changes in address or phone number;

(iv) Must promptly notify the Secretary if the borrower's an-

nual earnings from employment exceed the amount specified in paragraph (b)(2)(i) of this section; and

(v) Must provide the Secretary, upon request, with additional documentation or information related to the borrower's eligibility for discharge under this section.

(8) If, during and at the end of the conditional discharge period, the borrower continues to satisfy the eligibility criteria for a total and permanent disability discharge, as described in paragraph (b)(2) of this section, the balance of the loan is discharged.

(9) If, at any time during or at the end of the three-year conditional discharge period, the borrower does not continue to meet the eligibility requirements for total and permanent disability discharge, the Secretary resumes collection activity on the loan. The Secretary does not require the borrower to pay any interest that accrued on the loan from the date of the initial determination described in paragraph (b)(6) of this section through the end of the conditional discharge period.

(10) If the institution receives any payments from or on behalf of the borrower on or attributable to a loan that has been assigned to the Secretary for determination of eligibility for a total and permanent disability discharge, the institution must forward those payments to the Secretary for crediting to the borrower's account. At the same time that the institution forwards the payment, it must notify the borrower that there is no obligation to make payments on the loan while it is conditionally discharged prior to a final determination of eligibility for a total and permanent disability discharge, unless the Secretary directs the borrower otherwise.

(11) When the Secretary makes a final determination to discharge the loan, the Secretary returns to the sender any payments received on the loan after the date the borrower became totally and permanently disabled.

(c) *No Federal reimbursement.* No Federal reimbursement is made to an institution for cancellation of loans due to death or disability.

(d) *Retroactive.* Cancellation for death or disability applies retroactively to all Defense, NDSL or Perkins loans.

(Approved by the Office of Management and Budget under control number 1845-0019)

(Authority: 20 U.S.C. 425 and 1087dd and sec. 130(g)(2) of the Education Amendments of 1976, Pub. L. 94-482)

[53 Fed. Reg. 49147, Dec. 6, 1988; 59 Fed. Reg. 61413, 61415, Nov. 30, 1994; 64 Fed. Reg. 58315, Oct. 28, 1999; 65 Fed. Reg. 18002, April 6, 2000; 65 Fed. Reg. 26136, May 5, 2000; 65 Fed. Reg. 65690, Nov. 1, 2000; 66 Fed. Reg. 44007, Aug. 21, 2001; 68 Fed. Reg. 75427, Dec. 31, 2003]

B.5 Other Federal Financial Assistance Regulations

B.5.1 Selected Institutional Eligibility Requirements

34 C.F.R. sec.

§ 600.1 Scope.

This part establishes the rules and procedures that the Secretary uses to determine whether an educational institution qualifies in whole or in part as an eligible institution of higher education under the Higher Education Act of 1965, as amended (HEA). An eligible institution of higher education may apply to participate in programs authorized by the HEA (HEA programs).

(Authority: 20 U.S.C. 1088, 1094, 1099b, 1099c, and 1141)

[59 Fed. Reg. 22336, Apr. 29, 1994]

§ 600.2 Definitions.

The following definitions apply to terms used in this part:

Accredited: The status of public recognition that a nationally recognized accrediting agency grants to an institution or educational program that meets the agency's established requirements.

Award year: The period of time from July 1 of one year through June 30 of the following year.

Branch Campus: A location of an institution that is geographically apart and independent of the main campus of the institution. The Secretary considers a location of an institution to be independent of the main campus if the location—

(1) Is permanent in nature;

(2) Offers courses in educational programs leading to a degree, certificate, or other recognized educational credential;

(3) Has its own faculty and administrative or supervisory organization; and

(4) Has its own budgetary and hiring authority.

Clock hour: A period of time consisting of—

(1) A 50- to 60-minute class, lecture, or recitation in a 60-minute period;

(2) A 50- to 60-minute faculty-supervised laboratory, shop training, or internship in a 60-minute period; or

(3) Sixty minutes of preparation in a correspondence course.

Correspondence course:

(1) A "home study" course provided by an institution under which the institution provides instructional materials, including examinations on the materials, to students who are not physically attending classes at the institution. When students complete a portion of the instructional materials, the students take the examinations that relate to that portion of the materials, and return the examinations to the institution for grading.

(2) A home study course that provides instruction in whole or in part through the use of video cassettes or video discs in an award year is a correspondence course unless the institution also delivers the instruction on the cassette or disc to students physically attending classes at the institution during the same award year.

(3) If a course is part correspondence and part residential training, the Secretary considers the course to be a correspondence course.

Direct assessment program: A program as described in 34 CFR 668.10.

Educational program: (1) A legally authorized postsecondary program of organized instruction or study that:

(i) Leads to an academic, professional, or vocational degree, or certificate, or other recognized educational credential; and

(ii) May, in lieu of credit hours or clock hours as a measure of student learning, utilize direct assessment of student learning, or recognize the direct assessment of student learning by others, if such assessment is consistent with the accreditation of the institution or program utilizing the results of the assessment and with the provisions of § 668.10.

(2) The Secretary does not consider that an institution provides an educational program if the institution does not provide instruction itself (including a course of independent study) but merely gives credit for one or more of the following: Instruction provided by other institutions or schools; examinations or direct assessments provided by agencies or organizations; or other accomplishments such as "life experience."

Eligible institution: An institution that—

(1) Qualifies as—

(i) An institution of higher education, as defined in Sec. 600.4;

(ii) A proprietary institution of higher education, as defined in Sec. 600.5; or

(iii) A postsecondary vocational institution, as defined in Sec. 600.6; and

(2) Meets all the other applicable provisions of this part.

Federal Family Education Loan (FFEL) Programs: The loan programs (formerly called the Guaranteed Student Loan (GSL) programs) authorized by title IV-B of the HEA, including the Federal Stafford Loan, Federal PLUS, Federal Supplemental Loans for Students (Federal SLS), and Federal Consolidation Loan programs, in which lenders use their own funds to make loans to enable students or their parents to pay the costs of the students' attendance at eligible institutions. The Federal Stafford Loan, Federal PLUS, Federal SLS, and Federal Consolidation Loan programs are defined in 34 CFR part 668.

Incarcerated student: A student who is serving a criminal sentence in a Federal, State, or local penitentiary, prison, jail, reformatory, work farm, or other similar correctional institution. A student is not considered incarcerated if that student is in a half-way house or home detention or is sentenced to serve only weekends.

Legally authorized: The legal status granted to an institution through a charter, license, or other written document issued by the appropriate agency or official of the State in which the institution is physically located.

Nationally recognized accrediting agency: An agency or association that the Secretary recognizes as a reliable authority to determine the quality of education or training offered by an institution or a program offered by an institution. The Secretary recognizes these agencies and associations under the provisions of 34 CFR part 602 and publishes a list of the recognized agencies in the Federal Register.

Nonprofit institution: An institution that—

(1) Is owned and operated by one or more nonprofit corporations or associations, no part of the net earnings of which benefits any private shareholder or individual;

(2) Is legally authorized to operate as a nonprofit organization by

each State in which it is physically located; and

(3) Is determined by the U.S. Internal Revenue Service to be an organization to which contributions are tax-deductible in accordance with section 501(c)(3) of the Internal Revenue Code (26 U.S.C. 501(c)(3)).

One-academic-year training program: An educational program that is at least one academic year as defined under 34 CFR 668.2.

Preaccredited: A status that a nationally recognized accrediting agency, recognized by the Secretary to grant that status, has accorded an unaccredited public or private nonprofit institution that is progressing toward accreditation within a reasonable period of time.

Recognized equivalent of a high school diploma: The following are the equivalent of a high school diploma—

(1) A General Education Development Certificate (GED);

(2) A State certificate received by a student after the student has passed a State-authorized examination that the State recognizes as the equivalent of a high school diploma;

(3) An academic transcript of a student who has successfully completed at least a two-year program that is acceptable for full credit toward a bachelor's degree; or

(4) For a person who is seeking enrollment in an educational program that leads to at least an associate degree or its equivalent and who has not completed high school but who excelled academically in high school, documentation that the student excelled academically in high school and has met the formalized, written policies of the institution for admitting such students.

Recognized occupation: An occupation that is—

(1) Listed in an "occupational division" of the latest edition of the Dictionary of Occupational Titles, published by the U.S. Department of Labor; or

(2) Determined by the Secretary in consultation with the Secretary of Labor to be a recognized occupation.

Regular student: A person who is enrolled or accepted for enrollment at an institution for the purpose of obtaining a degree, certificate, or other recognized educational credential offered by that institution.

Secretary: The Secretary of the Department of Education or an official or employee of the Department of Education acting for the Secretary under a delegation of authority.

State: A State of the Union, American Samoa, the Commonwealth of Puerto Rico, the District of Columbia, Guam, the Virgin Islands, the Commonwealth of the Northern Mariana Islands, the Republic of the Marshall Islands, the Federated States of Micronesia, and the Republic of Palau. The latter three are also known as the Freely Associated States.

Telecommunications course: A course offered principally through the use of one or a combination of technologies including television, audio, or computer transmission through open broadcast, closed circuit, cable, microwave, or satellite; audio conferencing; computer conferencing; or video cassettes or discs to deliver instruction to students who are separated from the instructor and to support regular and substantive interaction between these students and the instructor, either synchronously or asynchronously. The term does not include a course that is delivered using video cassettes or disc recordings unless that course is delivered to students physically attending classes at the institution providing the course during the same award year. If the course does not qualify as a telecommunications course, it is considered to be a correspondence course.

Title IV, HEA program: Any of the student financial assistance programs listed in 34 CFR 668.1(c).

(Authority: 20 U.S.C. 1071 *et seq.*, 1078-2, 1088, 1099b, 1099c, and 1141 and 26 U.S.C. 501(c).)

[59 Fed. Reg. 22336, Apr. 29, 1994, as amended at 63 Fed. Reg. 40622, July 29, 1998; 64 Fed. Reg. 58615, Oct. 29, 1999; 71 Fed. Reg. 45666, Sept. 8, 2006]

§ 600.3 [Reserved]

§ 600.4 Institution of higher education.

(a) An institution of higher education is a public or private nonprofit educational institution that—

(1) Is in a State, or for purposes of the Federal Pell Grant, Federal Supplemental Educational Opportunity Grant, Federal Work-Study, and Federal TRIO programs may also be located in the Federated States of Micronesia or the Marshall Islands;

(2) Admits as regular students only persons who—

(i)   Have a high school diploma;

(ii) Have the recognized equivalent of a high school diploma; or

(iii) Are beyond the age of compulsory school attendance in the State in which the institution is physically located;

(3) Is legally authorized to provide an educational program beyond secondary education in the State in which the institution is physically located;

(4) Provides an educational program—

(i)   For which it awards an associate, baccalaureate, graduate, or professional degree;

(ii) That is at least a two-academic-year program acceptable for full credit toward a baccalaureate degree; or

(iii) That is at least a one-academic-year training program that leads to a certificate, degree, or other recognized educational credential and prepares students for gainful employment in a recognized occupation; and

(5) Is—

(i)   Accredited or preaccredited; or

(ii) Approved by a State agency listed in the Federal Register in accordance with 34 CFR part 603, if the institution is a public postsecondary vocational educational institution that seeks to participate only in Federal student assistance programs.

(b) An institution is physically located in a State if it has a campus or other instructional site in that State.

(c) The Secretary does not recognize the accreditation or preaccreditation of an institution unless the institution agrees to submit any dispute involving the final denial, withdrawal, or termination of accreditation to initial arbitration before initiating any other legal action.

(Authority: 20 U.S.C. 1094, 1099b, and 1141(a))

[59 Fed. Reg. 22337, Apr. 29, 1994, as amended at 64 Fed. Reg. 58615, Oct. 29, 1999]

§ 600.5 Proprietary institution of higher education.

(a) A proprietary institution of higher education is an educational institution that—

(1) Is not a public or private nonprofit educational institution;

(2) Is in a State;

(3) Admits as regular students only persons who—

(i)   Have a high school diploma;

(ii) Have the recognized equivalent of a high school diploma; or

(iii) Are beyond the age of compulsory school attendance in the State in which the institution is physically located;

(4) Is legally authorized to provide an educational program beyond secondary education in the State in which the institution is physically located;

(5) Provides an eligible program of training, as defined in 34 CFR 668.8, to prepare students for gainful employment in a recognized occupation;

(6) Is accredited;

(7) Has been in existence for at least two years; and

(8) Has no more than 90 percent of its revenues derived from title IV, HEA program funds, as determined under paragraph (d) of this section.

(b)(1) The Secretary considers an institution to have been in existence for two years only if—

(i)   The institution has been legally authorized to provide, and has provided, a continuous educational program to prepare students for gainful employment in a recognized occupation during the 24 months preceding the date of its eligibility application; and

(ii) The educational program that the institution provides on the date of its eligibility application is substantially the same in length and subject matter as the program that the institution provided during the 24 months preceding the date of its eligibility application.

(2)(i) The Secretary considers an institution to have provided a continuous educational program during the 24 months preceding the date of its eligibility application even if the institution did not provide that program during normal vacation periods, or periods when the institution temporarily closed due to a natural disaster that directly affected the institution or the institution's students.

(ii) The Secretary considers an institution to have satisfied the provisions of paragraph (b)(1)(ii) of this section if the institution substantially changed the subject matter of the educational program it provided during that 24-month period because of new technology or the requirements of other Federal agencies.

(3) In determining whether an applicant institution satisfies the requirement contained in paragraph (b)(1) of this section, the Secretary—

(i)   Counts any period during which the applicant institution has been certified as a branch campus; and

(ii) Except as provided in paragraph (b)(3)(i) of this section, does not count any period during which the applicant institution was a part of another eligible proprietary institution of higher education, postsecondary vocational institution, or vocational school.

(c) An institution is physically located in a State if it has a campus or other instructional site in that State.

(d)(1) An institution satisfies the requirement contained in paragraph (a)(8) of this section by examining its revenues under the following formula for its latest complete fiscal year: Title IV, HEA program funds the institution used to satisfy its students' tuition, fees, and other institutional charges to students. The sum of revenues including title IV, HEA program funds generated by the institution from: tuition, fees, and other institutional charges for students enrolled in eligible programs as defined in 34 CFR 668.8; and activities conducted by the institution, to the extent not included in tuition, fees, and other institutional charges, that are necessary for the education or training of its students who are enrolled in those eligible programs.

(2) An institution must use the cash basis of accounting when calculating the amount of title IV, HEA program funds in the numerator and the total amount of revenue generated by the institution in the denominator of the fraction contained in paragraph (d)(1) of this section.

(3) Under the cash basis of accounting—

(i)   In calculating the amount of revenue generated by the institution from institutional loans, the institution must include only the amount of loan repayments received by the institution during the fiscal year; and

(ii) In calculating the amount of revenue generated by the institution from institutional scholarships, the institution must include only the amount of funds it disbursed during the fiscal year from an established restricted account and only to the extent that the funds in that account represent designated funds from an outside source or income earned on those funds.

(e) With regard to the formula contained in paragraph (d)(1) of this section—

(1) The institution may not include as title IV, HEA program funds in the numerator nor as revenue generated by the institution in the denominator—

(i)   The amount of funds it received under the Federal Work-Study (FWS) Program, unless the institution used those funds to pay a student's institutional charges in which case the FWS program funds used to pay those charges would be included in the numerator and denominator.

(ii) The amount of funds it received under the Leveraging Educational Assistance Partnership (LEAP) Program. (The LEAP Program was formerly called the State Student Incentive Grant or SSIG Program.);

(iii) The amount of institutional funds it used to match title IV, HEA program funds;

(iv) The amount of title IV, HEA program funds that must be refunded or returned under Sec. 668.22; or

(v) The amount charged for books, supplies, and equipment unless the institution includes that amount as tuition, fees, or other institutional charges.

(2) In determining the amount of title IV, HEA program funds received by the institution under the cash basis of accounting, except as provided in paragraph (e)(3) of this section, the institution must presume that any title IV, HEA program funds disbursed or delivered to or on behalf of a student will be used to pay the student's tuition, fees, or other institutional charges, regardless of whether the institution credits those funds to the student's account or pays those funds directly to the student, and therefore must include those funds in the numerator and denominator.

(3) In paragraph (e)(2) of this section, the institution may not presume that title IV, HEA program funds were used to pay tuition, fees, and other institutional charges to the extent that those charges were satisfied by—

(i)   Grant funds provided by non-Federal public agencies, or private sources independent of the institution;

(ii) Funds provided under a contractual arrangement described in Sec. 600.7(d), or

(iii) Funds provided by State prepaid tuition plans.

(4) With regard to the denominator, revenue generated by the institution from activities it conducts, that are necessary for its students' education or training, includes only revenue from those activities that—

(i) Are conducted on campus or at a facility under the control of the institution;

(ii) Are performed under the supervision of a member of the institution's faculty; and

(iii) Are required to be performed by all students in a specific educational program at the institution.

(f) An institution must notify the Secretary within 90 days following the end of the fiscal year used in paragraph (d)(1) of this section if it fails to satisfy the requirement contained in paragraph (a)(8) of this section.

(g) If an institution loses its eligibility because it failed to satisfy the requirement contained in paragraph (a)(8) of this section, to regain its eligibility it must demonstrate compliance with all eligibility requirements for at least the fiscal year following the fiscal year used in paragraph (d)(1) of this section.

(h) The Secretary does not recognize the accreditation of an institution unless the institution agrees to submit any dispute involving the final denial, withdrawal, or termination of accreditation to initial arbitration before initiating any other legal action.

(Approved by the Office of Management and Budget under control number 1840-0098)

(Authority: 20 U.S.C. 1088)

[59 Fed. Reg. 22337, Apr. 29, 1994; 59 Fed. Reg. 32082, June 22, 1994, as amended at 59 Fed. Reg. 47801, Sept. 19, 1994; 59 Fed. Reg. 61177, Nov. 29, 1994; 61 Fed. Reg. 29901, June 12, 1996; 61 Fed. Reg. 60569, Nov. 29, 1996; 64 Fed. Reg. 58615, Oct. 29, 1999]

§ 600.6 Postsecondary vocational institution.

(a) A postsecondary vocational institution is a public or private nonprofit educational institution that—

(1) Is in a State;

(2) Admits as regular students only persons who—

(i) Have a high school diploma;

(ii) Have the recognized equivalent of a high school diploma; or

(iii) Are beyond the age of compulsory school attendance in the State in which the institution is physically located;

(3) Is legally authorized to provide an educational program beyond secondary education in the State in which the institution is physically located;

(4) Provides an eligible program of training, as defined in 34 CFR 668.8, to prepare students for gainful employment in a recognized occupation;

(5) Is—

(i) Accredited or preaccredited; or

(ii) Approved by a State agency listed in the Federal Register in accordance with 34 CFR part 603, if the institution is a public postsecondary vocational educational institution that seeks to participate only in Federal assistance programs; and

(6) Has been in existence for at least two years.

(b)(1) The Secretary considers an institution to have been in existence for two years only if—

(i) The institution has been legally authorized to provide, and has provided, a continuous education or training program to prepare students for gainful employment in a recognized occupation during the 24 months preceding the date of its eligibility application; and

(ii) The education or training program it provides on the date of its eligibility application is substantially the same in length and subject matter as the program it provided during the 24 months preceding the date of its eligibility application.

(2)(i) The Secretary considers an institution to have provided a continuous education or training program during the 24 months preceding the date of its eligibility application even if the institution did not provide that program during normal vacation periods, or periods when the institution temporarily closed due to a natural disaster that affected the institution or the institution's students.

(ii) The Secretary considers an institution to have satisfied the provisions of paragraph (b)(1)(ii) of this section if the institution substantially changed the subject matter of the educational program it provided during that 24-month period because of new technology or the requirements of other Federal agencies.

(3) In determining whether an applicant institution satisfies the requirement contained in paragraph (b)(1) of this section, the Secretary—

(i) Counts any period during which the applicant institution qualified as an eligible institution of higher education;

(ii) Counts any period during which the applicant institution was part of another eligible institution of higher education, provided that the applicant institution continues to be part of an eligible institution of higher education;

(iii) Counts any period during which the applicant institution has been certified as a branch campus; and

(iv) Except as provided in paragraph (b)(3)(iii) of this section, does not count any period during which the applicant institution was a part of another eligible proprietary institution of higher education or postsecondary vocational institution.

(c) An institution is physically located in a State or other instructional site if it has a campus or instructional site in that State.

(d) The Secretary does not recognize the accreditation or preaccreditation of an institution unless the institution agrees to submit any dispute involving the final denial, withdrawal, or termination of accreditation to initial arbitration before initiating any other legal action.

(Authority: 20 U.S.C. 1088 and 1094(c)(3))

[59 Fed. Reg. 22339, Apr. 29, 1994, as amended at 64 Fed. Reg. 58616, Oct. 29, 1999]

§ 600.7 Conditions of institutional ineligibility.

(a) *General rule.* For purposes of title IV of the HEA, an educational institution that otherwise satisfies the requirements contained in Secs. 600.4, 600.5, or 600.6 nevertheless does not qualify as an eligible institution under this part if—

(1) For its latest complete award year—

(i)   More than 50 percent of the institution's courses were correspondence courses as calculated under paragraph (b) of this section;

(ii) Fifty percent or more of the institution's regular enrolled students were enrolled in correspondence courses;

(iii) More than twenty-five percent of the institution's regular enrolled students were incarcerated;

(iv) More than fifty percent of its regular enrolled students had neither a high school diploma nor the recognized equivalent of a high school diploma, and the institution does not provide a four-year or two-year educational program for which it awards a bachelor's degree or an associate degree, respectively;

(2) The institution, or an affiliate of the institution that has the power, by contract or ownership interest, to direct or cause the direction of the management of policies of the institution—

(A) Files for relief in bankruptcy, or

(B) Has entered against it an order for relief in bankruptcy; or

(3) The institution, its owner, or its chief executive officer—

(i)   Has pled guilty to, has pled nolo contendere to, or is found guilty of, a crime involving the acquisition, use, or expenditure of title IV, HEA program funds; or

(ii) Has been judicially determined to have committed fraud involving title IV, HEA program funds.

(b) *Special provisions regarding correspondence courses and students*—

(1) Calculating the number of correspondence courses. For purposes of paragraphs (a)(1)(i) and (ii) of this section—

(i)   A correspondence course may be a complete educational program offered by correspondence, or one course provided by correspondence in an on-campus (residential) educational program;

(ii) A course must be considered as being offered once during an award year regardless of the number of times it is offered during that year; and

(iii) A course that is offered both on campus and by correspondence must be considered two courses for the purpose of determining the total number of courses the institution provided during an award year.

(2) Exceptions.

(i)   The provisions contained in paragraphs (a)(1)(i) and (ii) of this section do not apply to an institution that qualifies as a "technical institute or vocational school used exclusively or principally for the provision of vocational education to individuals who have completed or left high school and who are available for study in preparation for entering the labor market" under section 3(3)(C) of the Carl D. Perkins Vocational and Applied Technology Education Act of 1995.

(ii) The Secretary waives the limitation contained in paragraph (a)(1)(ii) of this section for an institution that offers a 2-year associate-degree or a 4-year bachelor's-degree program if the students enrolled in the institution's correspondence courses receive no more than 5 percent of the title IV, HEA program funds received by students at that institution.

(c) *Special provisions regarding incarcerated students*—

(1) Exception. The Secretary may waive the prohibition contained in paragraph (a)(1)(iii) of this section, upon the application of an institution, if the institution is a nonprofit institution that provides four-year or two-year educational programs for which it awards a bachelor's degree, an associate degree, or a postsecondary diploma.

(2) Waiver for entire institution. If the nonprofit institution that applies for a waiver consists solely of four-year or two-year educational programs for which it awards a bachelor's degree, an associate degree, or a postsecondary diploma, the Secretary waives the prohibition contained in paragraph (a)(1)(iii) of this section for the entire institution.

(3) Other waivers. If the nonprofit institution that applies for a waiver does not consist solely of four-year or two-year educational programs for which it awards a bachelor's degree, an associate degree, or a postsecondary diploma, the Secretary waives the prohibition contained in paragraph (a)(1)(iii) of this section—

(i)   For the four-year and two-year programs for which it awards a bachelor's degree, an associate degree or a postsecondary diploma; and

(ii) For the other programs the institution provides, if the incarcerated regular students enrolled in those other programs have a completion rate of 50 percent or greater.

(d) *Special provision for a nonprofit institution if more than 50 percent of its enrollment consists of students who do not have a high school diploma or its equivalent.*

(1) Subject to the provisions contained in paragraphs (d)(2) and (d)(3) of this section, the Secretary waives the limitation contained in paragraph (a)(1)(iv) of this section for a nonprofit institution if that institution demonstrates to the Secretary's satisfaction that it exceeds that limitation because it serves, through contracts with Federal, State, or local government agencies, significant numbers of students who do not have a high school diploma or its recognized equivalent.

(2) Number of critical students. The Secretary grants a waiver under paragraph (d)(1) of this section only if no more than 40 percent of the institution's enrollment of regular students consists of students who—

(i)   Do not have a high school diploma or its equivalent; and

(ii) Are not served through contracts described in paragraph (d)(3) of this section.

(3) Contracts with Federal, State, or local government agencies. For purposes of granting a waiver under paragraph (d)(1) of this section, the contracts referred to must be with Federal, State, or local government agencies for the purpose of providing job training to low-income individuals who are in need of that training. An example of such a contract is a job training contract under the Job Training Partnership Act (JPTA).

(e) *Special provisions.*

(1) For purposes of paragraph (a)(1)of this section, when counting regular students, the institution shall—

(i)   Count each regular student without regard to the full-time or part-time nature of the student's attendance (*i.e.*, "head count" rather than "full-time equivalent");

(ii) Count a regular student once regardless of the number of times the student enrolls during an award year; and

(iii) Determine the number of regular students who enrolled in the institution during the relevant award year by—

(A) Calculating the number of regular students who enrolled during that award year; and

(B) Excluding from the number of students in paragraph (e)(1)(iii)(A) of this section, the number of regular students who enrolled but subsequently withdrew or were expelled from the institution and were entitled to receive a 100 percent refund of their tuition and fees less any administrative fee that the institution is permitted to keep under its fair and equitable refund policy.

(2) For the purpose of calculating a completion rate under paragraph (c)(3)(ii) of this section, the institution shall—

(i) Determine the number of regular incarcerated students who enrolled in the other programs during the last completed award year;

(ii) Exclude from the number of regular incarcerated students determined in paragraph (e)(2)(i) of this section, the number of those students who enrolled but subsequently withdrew or were expelled from the institution and were entitled to receive a 100 percent refund of their tuition and fees, less any administrative fee the institution is permitted to keep under the institution's fair and equitable refund policy;

(iii) Exclude from the total obtained in paragraph (e)(2)(ii) of this section, the number of those regular incarcerated students who remained enrolled in the programs at the end of the applicable award year;

(iv) From the total obtained in paragraph (e)(2)(iii) of this section, determine the number of regular incarcerated students who received a degree, certificate, or other recognized educational credential awarded for successfully completing the program during the applicable award year; and

(v) Divide the total obtained in paragraph (e)(2)(iv) of this section by the total obtained in paragraph (e)(2)(iii) of this section and multiply by 100.

(f)(1) If the Secretary grants a waiver to an institution under this section, the waiver extends indefinitely provided that the institution satisfies the waiver requirements in each award year.

(2) If an institution fails to satisfy the waiver requirements for an award year, the institution becomes ineligible on June 30 of that award year.

(g)(1) For purposes of paragraph (a)(1) of this section, and any applicable waiver or exception under this section, the institution shall substantiate the required calculations by having the certified public accountant who prepares its audited financial statement under 34 CFR 668.15 or its title IV, HEA program compliance audit under 34 CFR 668.23 report on the accuracy of those determinations.

(2) The certified public accountant's report must be based on performing an "attestation engagement" in accordance with the American Institute of Certified Public Accountants (AICPA's) Statement on Standards for Attestation Engagements. The certified public accountant shall include that attestation report with or as part of the audit report referenced in paragraph (g)(1) of this section.

(3) The certified public accountant's attestation report must indicate whether the institution's determinations regarding paragraph (a)(1) of this section and any relevant waiver or exception under paragraphs (b), (c), and (d) of this section are accurate; *i.e.*, fairly presented in all material respects.

(h) *Notice to the Secretary.* An institution shall notify the Secretary—

(1) By July 31 following the end of an award year if it falls within one of the prohibitions contained in paragraph (a)(1) of this section, or fails to continue to satisfy a waiver or exception granted under this section; or

(2) Within 10 days if it falls within one of the prohibitions contained in paragraphs (a)(2) or (a)(3) of this section.

(i) *Regaining eligibility.*

(1) If an institution loses its eligibility because of one of the prohibitions contained in paragraph (a)(1) of this section, to regain its eligibility, it must demonstrate—

(i) Compliance with all eligibility requirements;

(ii) That it did not fall within any of the prohibitions contained in paragraph (a)(1) of this section for at least one award year; and

(iii) That it changed its administrative policies and practices to ensure that it will not fall within any of the prohibitions contained in paragraph (a)(1) of this section.

(2) If an institution loses its eligibility because of one of the prohibitions contained in paragraphs (a)(2) and (a)(3) of this section, this loss is permanent. The institution's eligibility cannot be reinstated.

(Approved by the Office of Management and Budget under control number 1840-0098)

(Authority: 20 U.S.C. 1088)

[59 Fed. Reg. 22339, Apr. 29, 1994; 59 Fed. Reg. 32082, June 22, 1994, as amended at 59 Fed. Reg. 47801, Sept. 19, 1994; 60 Fed. Reg. 34430, June 30, 1995; 64 Fed. Reg. 58616, Oct. 29, 1999; 71 Fed. Reg. 45666, Sept. 8, 2006]

§ 600.8 Treatment of a branch campus.

A branch campus of an eligible proprietary institution of higher education or a postsecondary vocational institution must be in existence for at least two years as a branch campus after the branch is certified as a branch campus before seeking to be designated as a main campus or a free-standing institution.

(Authority: 20 U.S.C. 1099c)

[59 Fed. Reg. 22340, Apr. 29, 1994, as amended at 64 Fed. Reg. 58616, Oct. 29, 1999; 67 Fed. Reg. 67070, Nov. 1, 2002]

§ 600.9 [Reserved]

[59 Fed. Reg. 22340, Apr. 29, 1994, as amended 65 Fed. Reg. 65671, Nov. 1, 2000]

§ 600.10 Date, extent, duration, and consequence of eligibility.

(a) *Date of eligibility.*

(1) If the Secretary determines that an applicant institution satisfies all the statutory and regulatory eligibility requirements, the Secretary considers the institution to be an eligible institution as of the date—

(i) The Secretary signs the institution's program participation agreement described in 34 CFR part 668, subpart B, for purposes of participating in any title IV, HEA program; and

(ii) The Secretary receives all the information necessary to make that determination for purposes other than participating in any title IV, HEA program.

(2) [*Reserved*]

(b) *Extent of eligibility.*

(1) If the Secretary determines that the entire applicant institution, including all its locations and all its educational programs, satisfies the applicable requirements of this part, the Secretary extends eligibility to all educational programs and locations iden-

tified on the institution's application for eligibility.

(2) If the Secretary determines that only certain educational programs or certain locations of an applicant institution satisfy the applicable requirements of this part, the Secretary extends eligibility only to those educational programs and locations that meet those requirements and identifies the eligible educational programs and locations in the eligibility notice sent to the institution under Sec. 600.21.

(3) Eligibility does not extend to any location that an institution establishes after it receives its eligibility designation if the institution provides at least 50 percent of an educational program at that location, unless—

    (i)   The Secretary approves that location under Sec. 600.20(e)(4); or

    (ii)   The location is licensed and accredited, the institution does not have to apply to the Secretary for approval of that location under Sec. 600.20(c), and the institution has reported to the Secretary that location under Sec. 600.21.

(c) *Subsequent additions of educational programs.*

(1) Except as provided in paragraph (c)(2) of this section, if an eligible institution adds an educational program after it has been designated as an eligible institution by the Secretary, the institution must apply to the Secretary to have that additional program designated as an eligible program of that institution.

(2) An eligible institution that adds an educational program after it has been designated as an eligible institution by the Secretary does not have to apply to the Secretary to have that additional program designated as an eligible program of that institution except as provided in 34 CFR 668.10 if the additional program—

    (i)   Leads to an associate, baccalaureate, professional, or graduate degree; or

    (ii)(A)   Prepares students for gainful employment in the same or related recognized occupation as an educational program that has previously been designated as an eligible program at that institution by the Secretary; and

    (B)   Is at least 8 semester hours, 12 quarter hours, or 600 clock hours.

(3) If an institution incorrectly determines under paragraph (c)(2) of this section that an educational program satisfies the applicable statutory and regulatory eligibility provisions without applying to the Secretary for approval, the institution is liable to repay to the Secretary all HEA program funds received by the institution for that educational program, and all the title IV, HEA program funds received by or on behalf of students who were enrolled in that educational program.

(d) *Duration of eligibility.*

(1) If an institution participates in the title IV, HEA programs, the Secretary's designation of the institution as an eligible institution under the title IV, HEA programs expires when the institution's program participation agreement, as described in 34 CFR part 668, subpart B, expires.

(2) If an institution participates in an HEA program other than a title IV, HEA program, the Secretary's designation of the institution as an eligible institution, for purposes of that non-title IV, HEA program, does not expire as long as the institution continues to satisfy the statutory and regulatory requirements governing its eligibility.

(e) *Consequence of eligibility.*

(1) If, as a part of its institutional eligibility application, an institution indicates that it wishes to participate in a title IV, HEA

program and the Secretary determines that the institution satisfies the applicable statutory and regulatory requirements governing institutional eligibility, the Secretary will determine whether the institution satisfies the standards of administrative capability and financial responsibility contained in 34 CFR part 668, subpart B.

(2) If, as part of its institutional eligibility application, an institution indicates that it does not wish to participate in any title IV, HEA program and the Secretary determines that the institution satisfies the applicable statutory and regulatory requirements governing institutional eligibility, the institution is eligible to apply to participate in any HEA program listed by the Secretary in the eligibility notice it receives under Sec. 600.21. However, the institution is not eligible to participate in those programs, or receive funds under those programs, merely by virtue of its designation as an eligible institution under this part.

(Approved by the Office of Management and Budget under control number 1845-0098)

(Authority: 20 U.S.C. 1088 and 1141)

[59 Fed. Reg. 22340, Apr. 29, 1994, as amended at 59 Fed. Reg. 47801, Sept. 19, 1994; 65 Fed. Reg. 65671, Nov. 1, 2000; 71 Fed. Reg. 45666, Sept. 8, 2006]

§ 600.11 Special rules regarding institutional accreditation or preaccreditation.

(a) *Change of accrediting agencies.* For purposes of Secs. 600.4(a)(5)(i), 600.5(a)(6), and 600.6(a)(5)(i), the Secretary does not recognize the accreditation or preaccreditation of an otherwise eligible institution if that institution is in the process of changing its accrediting agency, unless the institution provides to the Secretary—

(1) All materials related to its prior accreditation or preaccreditation; and

(2) Materials demonstrating reasonable cause for changing its accrediting agency.

(b) *Multiple accreditation.* The Secretary does not recognize the accreditation or preaccreditation of an otherwise eligible institution if that institution is accredited or preaccredited as an institution by more than one accrediting agency, unless the institution—

(1) Provides to each such accrediting agency and the Secretary the reasons for that multiple accreditation or preaccreditation;

(2) Demonstrates to the Secretary reasonable cause for that multiple accreditation or preaccreditation; and

(3) Designates to the Secretary which agency's accreditation or preaccreditation the institution uses to establish its eligibility under this part.

(c) *Loss of accreditation or preaccreditation.*

(1) An institution may not be considered eligible for 24 months after it has had its accreditation or preaccreditation withdrawn, revoked, or otherwise terminated for cause, unless the accrediting agency that took that action rescinds that action.

(2) An institution may not be considered eligible for 24 months after it has withdrawn voluntarily from its accreditation or preaccreditation status under a show-cause or suspension order issued by an accrediting agency, unless that agency rescinds its order.

(d) *Religious exception.*

(1) If an otherwise eligible institution loses its accreditation or preaccreditation, the Secretary considers the institution to be accredited or preaccredited for purposes of complying with the

provisions of Secs. 600.4, 600.5, and 600.6 if the Secretary determines that its loss of accreditation or preaccreditation—

　(i)　Is related to the religious mission or affiliation of the institution; and

　(ii)　Is not related to its failure to satisfy the accrediting agency's standards.

(2) If the Secretary considers an unaccredited institution to be accredited or preaccredited under the provisions of paragraph (d)(1) of this section, the Secretary will consider that unaccredited institution to be accredited or preaccredited for a period sufficient to allow the institution to obtain alternative accreditation or preaccreditation, except that period may not exceed 18 months.

[59 Fed. Reg. 22341, Apr. 29, 1994]

(Authority: 20 U.S.C. 1099b)

B.5.2　Selected Student Assistance General Provisions

34 C.F.R. sec.

§ 668.1　Scope.

(a) This part establishes general rules that apply to an institution that participates in any student financial assistance program authorized by Title IV of the Higher Education Act of 1965, as amended (Title IV, HEA program). To the extent that an institution contracts with a third-party servicer to administer any aspect of the institution's participation in any Title IV, HEA program, the applicable rules in this part also apply to that servicer. An institution's use of a third-party servicer does not alter the institution's responsibility for compliance with the rules in this part.

(b) As used in this part, an "institution" includes—

(1) An institution of higher education as defined in 34 CFR 600.4;

(2) A proprietary institution of higher education as defined in 34 CFR 600.5; and

(3) A postsecondary vocational institution as defined in 34 CFR 600.6.

(c) The Title IV, HEA programs include—

(1) The Federal Pell Grant Program (20 U.S.C. 1070a *et seq.*; 34 CFR part 690);

(2) The National Early Intervention Scholarship and Partnership (NEISP) Program (20 U.S.C. 1070a-21 *et seq.*; 34 CFR part 693);

(3) The Federal Supplemental Educational Opportunity Grant (FSEOG) Program (20 U.S.C. 1070b *et seq.*; 34 CFR parts 673 and 676);

(4) The Leveraging Educational Assistance Partnership (LEAP) Program (20 U.S.C. 1070c *et seq.*; 34 CFR part 692);

(5) The Federal Stafford Loan Program (20 U.S.C. 1071 *et seq.*; 34 CFR part 682);

(6) The Federal PLUS Program (20 U.S.C. 1078-2; 34 CFR part 682);

(7) The Federal Consolidation Loan Program (20 U.S.C. 1078-3; 34 CFR part 682);

(8) The Federal Work-Study (FWS) Program (42 U.S.C. 2751 *et seq.*; 34 CFR parts 673 and 675);

(9) The William D. Ford Federal Direct Loan (Direct Loan) Program (20 U.S.C. 1087a *et seq.*; 34 CFR part 685); and

(10) The Federal Perkins Loan Program (20 U.S.C. 1087aa *et seq.*; 34 CFR parts 673 and 674).

(Authority: 20 U.S.C. 1070 *et seq.*)

[52 Fed. Reg. 45724, Dec. 1, 1987, as amended at 56 Fed. Reg. 36696, July 31, 1991; 59 Fed. Reg. 22418, Apr. 29, 1994; 61 Fed. Reg. 60396, Nov. 27, 1996; 63 Fed. Reg. 40623, July 29, 1998; 65 Fed. Reg. 38729, June 22, 2000]

§ 668.2　General definitions.

(a) The following definitions are contained in the regulations for Institutional Eligibility under the Higher Education Act of 1965, as Amended, 34 CFR part 600:

Accredited
Award year
Branch campus
Clock hour
Correspondence course
Educational program
Eligible institution
Federal Family Education Loan (FFEL) programs
Incarcerated student
Institution of higher education
Legally authorized
Nationally recognized accrediting agency
Nonprofit institution
One-year training program
Postsecondary vocational institution
Preaccredited
Proprietary institution of higher education
Recognized equivalent of a high school diploma
Recognized occupation
Regular student
Secretary
State
Telecommunications course

(b) The following definitions apply to all Title IV, HEA programs:

Campus-based programs:

(1) The Federal Perkins Loan Program (34 CFR parts 673 and 674);

(2) The Federal Work-Study (FWS) Program (34 CFR parts 673 and 675); and

(3) The Federal Supplemental Educational Opportunity Grant (FSEOG) Program (34 CFR parts 673 and 676).

Defense loan: A loan made before July 1, 1972, under Title II of the National Defense Education Act of 1958.

(Authority: 20 U.S.C. 421–429)

Dependent student: Any student who does not qualify as an independent student (see Independent student).

Designated department official: An official of the Department of Education to whom the Secretary has delegated responsibilities indicated in this part.

Direct Loan Program loan: A loan made under the William D. Ford Federal Direct Loan Program.

(Authority: 20 U.S.C. 1087a *et seq.*)

Direct PLUS Loan: A loan made under the Federal Direct PLUS Program.

(Authority: 20 U.S.C. 1078-2 and 1087a *et seq.*)

Direct Subsidized Loan: A loan made under the Federal Direct Stafford/Ford Loan Program.

(Authority: 20 U.S.C. 1071 and 1087a *et seq.*)

Direct Unsubsidized Loan: A loan made under the Federal Direct Unsubsidized Stafford/Ford Loan Program.

(Authority: 20 U.S.C. 1087a *et seq.*)

Enrolled: The status of a student who—

(1) Has completed the registration requirements (except for the payment of tuition and fees) at the institution that he or she is attending; or

(2) Has been admitted into an educational program offered predominantly by correspondence and has submitted one lesson, completed by him or her after acceptance for enrollment and without the help of a representative of the institution.

(Authority: 20 U.S.C. 1088)

Expected family contribution (EFC): The amount, as determined under title IV, part F of the HEA, an applicant and his or her spouse and family are expected to contribute toward the applicant's cost of attendance.

Federal Consolidation Loan program: The loan program authorized by Title IV-B, section 428C, of the HEA that encourages the making of loans to borrowers for the purpose of consolidating their repayment obligations, with respect to loans received by those borrowers, under the Federal Insured Student Loan (FISL) Program as defined in 34 CFR part 682, the Federal Stafford Loan, Federal PLUS (as in effect before October 17, 1986), Federal Consolidation Loan, Federal SLS, ALAS (as in effect before October 17, 1986), Federal Direct Student Loan, and Federal Perkins Loan programs, and under the Health Professions Student Loan (HPSL) Program authorized by subpart II of part C of Title VII of the Public Health Service Act, for Federal PLUS borrowers whose loans were made after October 17, 1986, and for Higher Education Assistance Loans (HEAL) authorized by subpart I of part A of Title VII of the Public Health Services Act.

(Authority: 20 U.S.C. 1078-3)

Federal Direct PLUS Program: A loan program authorized by title IV, Part D of the HEA that is one of the components of the Direct Loan Program. The Federal Direct PLUS Program provides loans to parents of dependent students attending schools that participate in the Direct Loan Program. The Federal Direct PLUS Program also provides loans to graduate or professional students attending schools that participate in the Direct Loan Program. The borrower is responsible for the interest that accrues during any period.

(Authority: 20 U.S.C. 10782 and 1087a *et seq.*)

Federal Direct Stafford/Ford Loan Program: A loan program authorized by Title IV, Part D of the HEA that is one of the components of the Direct Loan Program. The Federal Direct Stafford/Ford Loan Program provides loans to undergraduate, graduate, and professional students attending schools that participate in the Direct Loan Program. The Secretary subsidizes the interest while the borrower is in an in-school, grace, or deferment period.

(Authority: 20 U.S.C. 1071 and 1087a *et seq.*)

Federal Direct Unsubsidized Stafford/Ford Loan Program: A loan program authorized by Title IV, Part D of the HEA that is one of the components of the Direct Loan Program. The Federal Direct Unsubsidized Stafford/Ford Loan Program provides loans to undergraduate, graduate, and professional students attending schools that participate in the Direct Loan Program. The borrower is responsible for the interest that accrues during any period.

(Authority: 20 U.S.C. 1087a *et seq.*)

Federal Pell Grant Program: The grant program authorized by Title IV-A-1 of the HEA.

(Authority: 20 U.S.C. 1070a)

Federal Perkins loan: A loan made under Title IV-E of the HEA to cover the cost of attendance for a period of enrollment beginning on or after July 1, 1987, to an individual who on July 1, 1987, had no outstanding balance of principal or interest owing on any loan previously made under Title IV-E of the HEA.

(Authority: 20 U.S.C. 1087aa *et seq.*)

Federal Perkins Loan program: The student loan program authorized by Title IV-E of the HEA after October 16, 1986. Unless otherwise noted, as used in this part, the Federal Perkins Loan Program includes the National Direct Student Loan Program and the National Defense Student Loan Program.

(Authority: 20 U.S.C. 1087aa–1087ii)

Federal PLUS loan: A loan made under the Federal PLUS Program.

(Authority: 20 U.S.C. 1078-2)

Federal PLUS program: The loan program authorized by Title IV-B, section 428B, of the HEA, that encourages the making of loans to parents of undergraduate students. Before October 17, 1986, the PLUS Program also provided for making loans to graduate, professional, and independent undergraduate students. Before July 1, 1993, the PLUS Program also provided for making loans to parents of dependent graduate students. Beginning July 1, 2006, the PLUS Program provides for making loans to graduate and professional students.

(Authority: 20 U.S.C. 1078-2)

Federal SLS loan: A loan made under the Federal SLS Program.

(Authority: 20 U.S.C. 1078-1)

Federal Stafford loan: A loan made under the Federal Stafford Loan Program.

(Authority: 20 U.S.C. 1071 *et seq.*)

Federal Stafford Loan program: The loan program authorized by Title IV-B (exclusive of sections 428A, 428B, and 428C) that encourages the making of subsidized Federal Stafford and unsubsidized Federal Stafford loans as defined in 34 CFR part 682 to undergraduate, graduate, and professional students.

(Authority: 20 U.S.C. 1071 *et seq.*)

Federal Supplemental Educational Opportunity Grant (FSEOG) program: The grant program authorized by Title IV-A-2 of the HEA.

(Authority: 20 U.S.C. 1070b *et seq.*)

Federal Supplemental Loans for Students (Federal SLS) Program: The loan program authorized by Title IV-B, section 428A of the HEA, as in effect for periods of enrollment that began before July 1, 1994. The Federal SLS Program encourages the making of loans to graduate, professional, independent undergraduate, and certain dependent undergraduate students.

(Authority: 20 U.S.C. 1078-1)

Federal Work Study (FWS) program: The part-time employment program for students authorized by Title IV-C of the HEA.

(Authority: 42 U.S.C. 2751–2756b)

FFELP loan: A loan made under the FFEL programs.

(Authority: 20 U.S.C. 1071 *et seq.*)

Full-time student: An enrolled student who is carrying a full-time academic workload (other than by correspondence) as determined by the institution under a standard applicable to all students enrolled in a particular educational program. The student's workload may include any combination of courses, work, research, or special studies that the institution considers sufficient to classify the student as a full-time student. However, for an undergraduate student, an institution's minimum standard must equal or exceed one of the following minimum requirements:

(1) Twelve semester hours or 12 quarter hours per academic term in an educational program using a semester, trimester, or quarter system.

(2) Twenty-four semester hours or 36 quarter hours per academic year for an educational program using credit hours but not using a semester, trimester, or quarter system, or the prorated equivalent for a program of less than one academic year.

(3) Twenty-four clock hours per week for an educational program using clock hours.

(4) In an educational program using both credit and clock hours, any combination of credit and clock hours where the sum of the following fractions is equal to or greater than one:

(i) For a program using a semester, trimester, or quarter system—

Number of credit hours per term

12

+

Number of clock hours per week

24

(ii) For a program not using a semester, trimester, or quarter system—

Number of semester or trimester hours per academic year

24

+

Number of quarter hours per academic year

36

+

Number of clock hours per week

24

(5) A series of courses or seminars that equals 12 semester hours or 12 quarter hours in a maximum of 18 weeks.

(6) The work portion of a cooperative education program in which the amount of work performed is equivalent to the academic workload of a full-time student.

HEA: The Higher Education Act of 1965, as amended.

(Authority: 20 U.S.C. 1070 *et seq.*)

Independent student: A student who qualifies as an independent student under section 480(d) of the HEA.

(Authority: 20 U.S.C. 1087vv)

Initiating official: The designated department official authorized to begin an emergency action under 34 CFR 668.83.

Leveraging Educational Assistance Partnership (LEAP) Program: The grant program authorized by Title IV-A-4 of the HEA.

National Defense Student Loan program: The student loan program authorized by Title II of the National Defense Education Act of 1958.

(Authority: 20 U.S.C. 421–429)

National Direct Student Loan (NDSL) program: The student loan program authorized by Title IV-E of the HEA between July 1, 1972, and October 16, 1986.

(Authority: 20 U.S.C. 1087aa–1087ii)

National Early Intervention Scholarship and Partnership (NEISP) program: The scholarship program authorized by Chapter 2 of subpart 1 of Title IV-A of the HEA.

(Authority: 20 U.S.C. 1070a-21 *et seq.*)

One-third of an academic year: A period that is at least one-third of an academic year as determined by an institution. At a minimum, one-third of an academic year must be a period that begins on the first day of classes and ends on the last day of classes or examinations and is a minimum of 10 weeks of instructional time during which, for an undergraduate educational program, a full-time student is expected to complete at least 8 semester or trimester hours or 12 quarter hours in an educational program whose length is measured in credit hours or 300 clock hours in an educational program whose length is measured in clock hours. For an institution whose academic year has been reduced under § 668.3, one-third of an academic year is the pro-rated equivalent, as measured in weeks and credit or clock hours, of at least one-third of the institution's academic year.

(Authority: 20 U.S.C. 1088)

Output document: The Student Aid Report (SAR), Electronic Student Aid Report (ESAR), or other document or automated data generated by the Department of Education's central processing system or Multiple Data Entry processing system as the result of the processing of data provided in a Free Application for Federal Student Aid (FAFSA).

Parent: A student's biological or adoptive mother or father or the student's stepparent, if the biological parent or adoptive mother or father has remarried at the time of application.

Participating institution: An eligible institution that meets the standards for participation in Title IV, HEA programs in subpart B and has a current program participation agreement with the Secretary.

Show-cause official: The designated department official authorized to conduct a show-cause proceeding for an emergency action under 34 CFR 668.83.

(Authority: 20 U.S.C. 1070c *et seq.*)

Third-party servicer:

(1) An individual or a State, or a private, profit or nonprofit organization that enters into a contract with an eligible institution to administer, through either manual or automated processing, any aspect of the institution's participation in any Title IV, HEA program. The Secretary considers administration of participation in a Title IV, HEA program to—

   (i)   Include performing any function required by any statutory provision of or applicable to Title IV of the HEA, any regulatory provision prescribed under that statutory authority, or any applicable special arrangement, agreement, or limitation entered into under the authority of statutes applicable to Title IV of the HEA, such as, but not restricted to—

     (A) Processing student financial aid applications;

     (B) Performing need analysis;

     (C) Determining student eligibility and related activities;

     (D) Certifying loan applications;

     (E) Processing output documents for payment to students;

     (F) Receiving, disbursing, or delivering Title IV, HEA program funds, excluding lock-box processing of loan payments and normal bank electronic fund transfers;

     (G) Conducting activities required by the provisions governing student consumer information services in subpart D of this part;

     (H) Preparing and certifying requests for advance or reimbursement funding;

     (I) Loan servicing and collection;

     (J) Preparing and submitting notices and applications required under 34 CFR part 600 and subpart B of this part; and

     (K) Preparing a Fiscal Operations Report and Application to Participate (FISAP);

   (ii) Exclude the following functions—

     (A) Publishing ability-to-benefit tests;

     (B) Performing functions as a Multiple Data Entry Processor (MDE);

     (C) Financial and compliance auditing;

     (D) Mailing of documents prepared by the institution;

     (E) Warehousing of records; and

     (F) Providing computer services or software; and

   (iii) Notwithstanding the exclusions referred to in paragraph (1)(ii) of this definition, include any activity comprised of any function described in paragraph (1)(i) of this definition.

(2) For purposes of this definition, an employee of an institution is not a third-party servicer. The Secretary considers an individual to be an employee if the individual—

   (i)   Works on a full-time, part-time, or temporary basis;

   (ii) Performs all duties on site at the institution under the supervision of the institution;

   (iii) Is paid directly by the institution;

   (iv) Is not employed by or associated with a third-party servicer; and

   (v) Is not a third-party servicer for any other institution.

(Authority: 20 U.S.C. 1088)

Two-thirds of an academic year: A period that is at least two-thirds of an academic year as determined by an institution. At a minimum, two-thirds of an academic year must be a period that begins on the first day of classes and ends on the last day of classes or examinations and is a minimum of 20 weeks of instructional time during which, for an undergraduate educational program, a full-time student is expected to complete at least 16 semester or trimester hours or 24 quarter hours in an educational program whose length is measured in credit hours or 600 clock hours in an educational program whose length is measured in clock hours. For an institution whose academic year has been reduced under § 668.3, two-thirds of an academic year is the pro-rated equivalent as measured in weeks and credit or clock hours, of at least two-thirds of the institution's academic year.

(Authority: 20 U.S.C. 1088)

U.S. citizen or national: (1) A citizen of the United States; or (2) A person defined in the Immigration and Nationality Act, 8 U.S.C. 1101(a)(22), who, though not a citizen of the United States, owes permanent allegiance to the United States.

(Authority: 8 U.S.C. 1101)

Valid institutional student information report (valid ISIR): A valid institutional student information report as defined in 34 CFR 690.2 for purposes of the Federal Pell Grant Program.

Valid student aid report (valid SAR): A valid student aid report (valid SAR) as defined in 34 CFR 690.2 for purposes of the Federal Pell Grant Program.

(Authority: 20 U.S.C. 1070 *et seq.*, unless otherwise noted)

William D. Ford Federal Direct Loan (Direct Loan) Program: The loan program authorized by Title IV, Part D of the HEA.

(Authority: 20 U.S.C. 1087a *et seq.*)

[52 Fed. Reg. 45725, Dec. 1, 1987; 56 Fed. Reg. 36696, July 31, 1991; 57 Fed. Reg. 27703, June 22, 1992; 58 Fed. Reg. 13343, March 10, 1993; 58 Fed. Reg. 32200, June 8, 1993; 58 Fed. Reg. 36871, July 9, 1993; 59 Fed. Reg. 12520, March 16, 1994; 59 Fed. Reg. 21866, April 26, 1994; 59 Fed. Reg. 22418, April 29, 1994; 59 Fed. Reg. 32657, June 24, 1994; 59 Fed. Reg. 61178, Nov. 29, 1994; 60 Fed. Reg. 61809, Dec. 1, 1995; 61 Fed. Reg. 60396, Nov. 27, 1996; 63 Fed. Reg. 40623, July 29, 1998; 65 Fed. Reg. 38729, June 22, 2000; 65 Fed. Reg. 65674, Nov. 1, 2000; 67 Fed. Reg. 67071, Nov. 1, 2002; 69 Fed. Reg. 12275, March 16, 2004; 71 Fed. Reg. 45666, Sept. 8, 2006]

§ 668.3 Academic year.

(a) *General.* Except as provided in paragraph (c) of this section, an academic year for a program of study must include—

   (1)(i) For a program offered in credit hours, a minimum of 30 weeks of instructional time; or

(ii) For a program offered in clock hours, a minimum of 26 weeks of instructional time; and

(2) For an undergraduate educational program, an amount of instructional time whereby a full-time student is expected to complete at least—

(i) Twenty-four semester or trimester credit hours or 36 quarter credit hours for a program measured in credit hours; or

(ii) 900 clock hours for a program measured in clock hours.

(b) *Definitions.* For purposes of paragraph (a) of this section—

(1) A week is a consecutive seven-day period;

(2) A week of instructional time is any week in which at least one day of regularly scheduled instruction or examinations occurs or, after the last scheduled day of classes for a term or payment period, at least one day of study for final examinations occurs; and

(3) Instructional time does not include any vacation periods, homework, or periods of orientation or counseling.

(c) *Reduction in the length of an academic year.*

(1) Upon the written request of an institution, the Secretary may approve, for good cause, an academic year of 26 through 29 weeks of instructional time for educational programs offered by the institution if the institution offers a two-year program leading to an associate degree or a four-year program leading to a baccalaureate degree.

(2) An institution's written request must—

(i) Identify each educational program for which the institution requests a reduction, and the requested number of weeks of instructional time for that program;

(ii) Demonstrate good cause for the requested reductions; and

(iii) Include any other information that the Secretary may require to determine whether to grant the request.

(3)(i) The Secretary approves the request of an eligible institution for a reduction in the length of its academic year if the institution has demonstrated good cause for granting the request and the institution's accrediting agency and State licensing agency have approved the request.

(ii) If the Secretary approves the request, the approval terminates when the institution's program participation agreement expires. The institution may request an extension of that approval as part of the recertification process.

(Approved by the Office of Management and Budget under control number 1845-0022)

(Authority: 20 U.S.C. 1088)

[59 Fed. Reg. 22421, Apr. 29, 1994; 59 Fed. Reg. 32657, June 24, 1994; 59 Fed. Reg. 34964, July 7, 1994; 59 Fed. Reg. 61178, Nov. 29, 1994; 60 Fed. Reg. 42408, Aug. 15, 1995; 67 Fed. Reg. 67071, Nov. 1, 2002; 71 Fed. Reg. 45666, Sept. 8, 2006]

§ 668.4 Payment period.

(a) *Payment periods for an eligible program that measures progress in credit hours and has academic terms.* For a student enrolled in an eligible program that measures progress in credit hours and has academic terms, the payment period is the academic term.

(b) *Payment periods for an eligible program that measures progress in credit hours and does not have academic terms.*

(1) For a student enrolled in an eligible program that is one academic year or less in length—

(i) The first payment period is the period of time in which the student completes half the number of credit hours in the program and half the number of weeks in the program; and

(ii) The second payment period is the period of time in which the student completes the program.

(2) For a student enrolled in an eligible program that is more than one academic year in length—

(i) For the first academic year and any subsequent full academic year—

(A) The first payment period is the period of time in which the student completes half the number of credit hours in the academic year and half the number of weeks in the academic year; and

(B) The second payment period is the period of time in which the student completes the academic year.

(ii) For any remaining portion of an eligible program that is more than one-half an academic year but less than a full academic year in length—

(A) The first payment period is the period of time in which the student completes half the number of credit hours in the remaining portion of the program and half the number of weeks remaining in the program; and

(B) The second payment period is the period of time in which the student completes the remainder of the program.

(iii) For any remaining portion of an eligible program that is not more than half an academic year, the payment period is the remainder of the program.

(3) For purposes of paragraphs (b)(1) and (b)(2) of this section, if an institution is unable to determine when a student has completed half of the credit hours in a program, academic year, or remainder of a program; the student is considered to begin the second payment period of the program, academic year, or remainder of a program at the later of—

(i) The date, as determined by the institution, on which the student has completed half of the academic coursework in the program, academic year, or remainder of the program; or

(ii) The calendar midpoint between the first and last scheduled days of class of the program, academic year, or remainder of the program.

(c) *Payment periods for an eligible program that measures progress in clock hours.*

(1) For a student enrolled in an eligible program that is one academic year or less in length—

(i) The first payment period is the period of time in which the student completes half the number of clock hours in the program; and

(ii) The second payment period is the period of time in which the student completes the program.

(2) For a student enrolled in an eligible program that is more than one academic year in length—

(i) For the first academic year and any subsequent full academic year—

(A) The first payment period is the period of time in which the student completes half the number of clock hours in the academic year; and

(B) The second payment period is the period of time in which the student completes the academic year.

(ii) For any remaining portion of an eligible program that is more than one-half an academic year but less than a full academic year in length—

    (A) The first payment period is the period of time in which the student completes half the number of clock hours in the remaining portion of the program; and

    (B) The second payment period is the period of time in which the student completes the remainder of the program.

(iii) For any remaining portion of an eligible program that is not more than one half of an academic year, the payment period is the remainder of the program.

(d) *Number of payment periods.* Notwithstanding paragraphs (b) and (c) of this section, an institution may choose to have more than two payment periods. If an institution so chooses, the regulations in paragraphs (b) and (c) of this section are modified to reflect the increased number of payment periods. For example, if an institution chooses to have three payment periods in an academic year in a program that measures progress in credit hours but does not have academic terms, each payment period must correspond to one-third of the academic year measured in both credit hours and weeks of instruction.

(e) *Re-entry within 180 days.* If a student withdraws from a program described in paragraph (b) or (c) of this section during a payment period and then reenters the same program within 180 days, the student remains in that same payment period when he or she returns and, subject to conditions established by the Secretary or by the FFEL lender or guaranty agency, is eligible to receive any title IV, HEA program funds for which he or she was eligible prior to withdrawal, including funds that were returned by the institution or student under the provisions of Sec. 668.22.

(f) *Re-entry after 180 days or transfer.*

(1) Subject to the conditions of paragraph (f)(2) of this section, an institution calculates new payment periods for the remainder of a student's program based on paragraphs (b) through (d) of this section, for a student who withdraws from a program described in paragraph (b) or (c) of this section, and—

    (i) Reenters that program after 180 days,

    (ii) Transfers into another program at the same institution within any time period, or

    (iii) Transfers into a program at another institution within any time period.

(2) For a student described in paragraph (f)(1) of this section—

    (i) For the purpose of calculating payment periods only, the length of the program is the number of credit hours and the number of weeks, or the number of clock hours, that the student has remaining in the program he or she enters or reenters; and

    (ii) If the remaining hours, and weeks if applicable, constitute one-half of an academic year or less, the remaining hours constitute one payment period.

(Authority: 20 U.S.C. 1070 *et seq.*)

[61 Fed. Reg., Nov. 29, 1996; 67 Fed. Reg. 67071, Nov. 1, 2002]

§ 668.5 Written arrangements to provide educational programs.

(a) *Written arrangements between eligible institutions.* If an eligible institution enters into a written arrangement with another eligible institution, or with a consortium of eligible institutions,

under which the other eligible institution or consortium provides all or part of the educational program of students enrolled in the former institution, the Secretary considers that educational program to be an eligible program if it otherwise satisfies the requirements of Sec. 668.8.

(b) *Written arrangements for study-abroad.* Under a study abroad program, if an eligible institution enters into a written arrangement with a foreign institution, or an organization acting on behalf of a foreign institution, under which the foreign institution provides part of the educational program of students enrolled in the eligible institution, the Secretary considers that educational program to be an eligible program if it otherwise satisfies the requirements of paragraphs (c)(1) through (c)(3) of this section.

(c) *Written arrangements between an eligible institution and an ineligible institution or organization.* If an eligible institution enters into a written arrangement with an institution or organization that is not an eligible institution under which the ineligible institution or organization provides part of the educational program of students enrolled in the eligible institution, the Secretary considers that educational program to be an eligible program if—

(1) The ineligible institution or organization has not had its eligibility to participate in the title IV, HEA programs terminated by the Secretary, or has not voluntarily withdrawn from participation in those programs under a termination, show-cause, suspension, or similar type proceeding initiated by the institution's State licensing agency, accrediting agency, guarantor, or by the Secretary;

(2) The educational program otherwise satisfies the requirements of Sec. 668.8; and

(3)(i) The ineligible institution or organization provides not more than 25 percent of the educational program; or

    (ii)(A) The ineligible institution or organization provides more than 25 percent but not more than 50 percent of the educational program;

    (B) The eligible institution and the ineligible institution or organization are not owned or controlled by the same individual, partnership, or corporation; and

    (C) The eligible institution's accrediting agency, or if the institution is a public postsecondary vocational educational institution, the State agency listed in the Federal Register in accordance with 34 CFR part 603, has specifically determined that the institution's arrangement meets the agency's standards for the contracting out of educational services.

(d) *Administration of title IV, HEA programs.*

(1) If an institution enters into a written arrangement as described in paragraph (a), (b), or (c) of this section, except as provided in paragraph (d)(2) of this section, the institution at which the student is enrolled as a regular student must determine the student's eligibility for title IV, HEA program funds, and must calculate and disburse those funds to that student.

(2) In the case of a written arrangement between eligible institutions, the institutions may agree in writing to have any eligible institution in the written arrangement make those calculations and disbursements, and the Secretary does not consider that institution to be a third-party servicer for that arrangement.

(3) The institution that calculates and disburses a student's title IV, HEA program assistance under paragraph (d)(1) or (d)(2) of this section must—

(i) Take into account all the hours in which the student enrolls at each institution that apply to the student's degree or certificate when determining the student's enrollment status and cost of attendance; and

(ii) Maintain all records regarding the student's eligibility for and receipt of title IV, HEA program funds.

(Authority: 20 U.S.C. 1094)

[65 Fed. Reg. 65674, Nov. 1, 2000]

§ 668.6 [Reserved]

§ 668.7 [Reserved]

[60 Fed. Reg. 61809, Dec. 1995]

§ 668.8 Eligible program.

(a) *General.* An eligible program is an educational program that—

(1) Is provided by a participating institution; and

(2) Satisfies the other relevant requirements contained in this section.

(b) *Definitions.* For purposes of this section—

(1) The Secretary considers the "equivalent of an associate degree" to be—

(i) An associate degree; or

(ii) The successful completion of at least a two-year program that is acceptable for full credit toward a bachelor's degree and qualifies a student for admission into the third year of a bachelor's degree program;

(2) A week is a consecutive seven-day period; and

(3)(i) The Secretary considers that an institution provides one week of instructional time in an academic program during any week the institution provides at least one day of regularly scheduled instruction or examinations, or, after the last scheduled day of classes for a term or a payment period, at least one day of study for final examinations.

(ii) Instructional time does not include any vacation periods, homework, or periods of orientation or counseling.

(c) *Institution of higher education.* An eligible program provided by an institution of higher education must—

(1) Lead to an associate, bachelor's, professional, or graduate degree;

(2) Be at least a two-academic-year program that is acceptable for full credit toward a bachelor's degree; or

(3) Be at least a one-academic-year training program that leads to a certificate, degree, or other recognized educational credential and that prepares a student for gainful employment in a recognized occupation.

(d) *Proprietary institution of higher education and postsecondary vocational institution.* An eligible program provided by a proprietary institution of higher education or postsecondary vocational institution—

(1)(i) Must require a minimum of 15 weeks of instruction, beginning on the first day of classes and ending on the last day of classes or examinations;

(ii) Must be at least 600 clock hours, 16 semester or trimester hours, or 24 quarter hours;

(iii) Must provide undergraduate training that prepares a student for gainful employment in a recognized occupation; and

(iv) May admit as regular students persons who have not completed the equivalent of an associate degree;

(2) Must—

(i) Require a minimum of 10 weeks of instruction, beginning on the first day of classes and ending on the last day of classes or examinations;

(ii) Be at least 300 clock hours, 8 semester or trimester hours, or 12 quarter hours;

(iii) Provide training that prepares a student for gainful employment in a recognized occupation; and

(iv)(A) Be a graduate or professional program; or

(B) Admit as regular students only persons who have completed the equivalent of an associate degree; or

(3) For purposes of the FFEL and Direct Loan programs only, must—

(i) Require a minimum of 10 weeks of instruction, beginning on the first day of classes and ending on the last day of classes or examinations;

(ii) Be at least 300 clock hours but less than 600 clock hours;

(iii) Provide undergraduate training that prepares a student for gainful employment in a recognized occupation;

(iv) Admit as regular students some persons who have not completed the equivalent of an associate degree; and

(v) Satisfy the requirements of paragraph (e) of this section.

(e) *Qualitative factors.*

(1) An educational program that satisfies the requirements of paragraphs (d)(3)(i) through (iv) of this section qualifies as an eligible program only if—

(i) The program has a substantiated completion rate of at least 70 percent, as calculated under paragraph (f) of this section;

(ii) The program has a substantiated placement rate of at least 70 percent, as calculated under paragraph (g) of this section;

(iii) The number of clock hours provided in the program does not exceed by more than 50 percent the minimum number of clock hours required for training in the recognized occupation for which the program prepares students, as established by the State in which the program is offered, if the State has established such a requirement, or as established by any Federal agency; and

(iv) The program has been in existence for at least one year. The Secretary considers an educational program to have been in existence for at least one year only if an institution has been legally authorized to provide, and has continuously provided, the program during the 12 months (except for normal vacation periods and, at the discretion of the Secretary, periods when the institution closes due to a natural disaster that directly affects the institution or the institution's students) preceding the date on which the institution applied for eligibility for that program.

(2) An institution shall substantiate the calculation of its completion and placement rates by having the certified public accountant who prepares its audit report required under § 668.23 report on the institution's calculation based on performing an attestation engagement in accordance with the Statements on Standards for Attestation Engagements of the American Institute of Certified Public Accountants (AICPA).

(f) *Calculation of completion rate.* An institution shall calculate its completion rate for an educational program for any award year as follows:

(1) Determine the number of regular students who were enrolled in the program during the award year.

(2) Subtract from the number of students determined under paragraph (f)(1) of this section, the number of regular students who, during that award year, withdrew from, dropped out of, or were expelled from the program and were entitled to and actually received, in a timely manner a refund of 100 percent of their tuition and fees.

(3) Subtract from the total obtained under paragraph (f)(2) of this section the number of students who were enrolled in the program at the end of that award year.

(4) Determine the number of regular students who, during that award year, received within 150 percent of the published length of the educational program the degree, certificate, or other recognized educational credential awarded for successfully completing the program.

(5) Divide the number determined under paragraph (f)(4) of this section by the total obtained under paragraph (f)(3) of this section.

(g) *Calculation of placement rate.*

(1) An institution shall calculate its placement rate for an educational program for any award year as follows:

(i) Determine the number of students who, during the award year, received the degree, certificate, or other recognized educational credential awarded for successfully completing the program.

(ii) Of the total obtained under paragraph (g)(1)(i) of this section, determine the number of students who, within 180 days of the day they received their degree, certificate, or other recognized educational credential, obtained gainful employment in the recognized occupation for which they were trained or in a related comparable recognized occupation and, on the date of this calculation, are employed, or have been employed, for at least 13 weeks following receipt of the credential from the institution.

(iii) Divide the number of students determined under paragraph (g)(1)(ii) of this section by the total obtained under paragraph (g)(1)(i) of this section.

(2) An institution shall document that each student described in paragraph (g)(1)(ii) of this section obtained gainful employment in the recognized occupation for which he or she was trained or in a related comparable recognized occupation. Examples of satisfactory documentation of a student's gainful employment include, but are not limited to—

(i) A written statement from the student's employer;

(ii) Signed copies of State or Federal income tax forms; and

(iii) Written evidence of payments of Social Security taxes.

(h) *Eligibility for Federal Pell Grant and FSEOG programs.* In addition to satisfying other relevant provisions of this section—

(1) An educational program qualifies as an eligible program for purposes of the Federal Pell Grant Program only if the educational program is an undergraduate program or a postbaccalaureate teacher certificate or licensing program as described in 34 CFR 690.6(c); and

(2) An educational program qualifies as an eligible program for purposes of the FSEOG Program only if the educational program is an undergraduate program.

(i) *Flight training.* In addition to satisfying other relevant provisions of this section, for a program of flight training to be an eligible program, it must have a current valid certification from the Federal Aviation Administration.

(j) *English as a second language (ESL).*

(1) In addition to satisfying the relevant provisions of this section, an educational program that consists solely of instruction in ESL qualifies as an eligible program if—

(i) The institution admits to the program only students whom the institution determines need the ESL instruction to use already existing knowledge, training, or skills; and

(ii) The program leads to a degree, certificate, or other recognized educational credential.

(2) An institution shall document its determination that ESL instruction is necessary to enable each student enrolled in its ESL program to use already existing knowledge, training, or skills with regard to the students that it admits to its ESL program under paragraph (j)(1)(i) of this section.

(3) An ESL program that qualifies as an eligible program under this paragraph is eligible for purposes of the Federal Pell Grant Program only.

(k) *Undergraduate educational program in credit hours.* If an institution offers an undergraduate educational program in credit hours, the institution must use the formula contained in paragraph (l) of this section to determine whether that program satisfies the requirements contained in paragraph (c)(3) or (d) of this section, and the number of credit hours in that educational program for purposes of the Title IV, HEA programs, unless—

(1) The program is at least two academic years in length and provides an associate degree, a bachelor's degree, a professional degree, or an equivalent degree as determined by the Secretary; or

(2) Each course within the program is acceptable for full credit toward that institution's associate degree, bachelor's degree, professional degree, or equivalent degree as determined by the Secretary, provided that the institution's degree requires at least two academic years of study.

(l) *Formula.* For purposes of determining whether a program described in paragraph (k) of this section satisfies the requirements contained in paragraph (c)(3) or (d) of this section, and the number of credit hours in that educational program with regard to the Title IV, HEA programs—

(1) A semester hour must include at least 30 clock hours of instruction;

(2) A trimester hour must include at least 30 clock hours of instruction; and

(3) A quarter hour must include at least 20 hours of instruction.

(m) An otherwise eligible program that is offered in whole or in part through telecommunications is eligible for title IV, HEA program purposes if the program is offered by an institution, other than a foreign institution, that has been evaluated and is accredited for its effective delivery of distance education programs by an accrediting agency or association that—

(1) Is recognized by the Secretary under subpart 2 of part H of the HEA; and

(2) Has accreditation of distance education within the scope of its recognition.

(n) For title IV, HEA program purposes, the term eligible program includes a direct assessment program approved by the Secretary under 34 CFR 668.10.

(Approved by the Office of Management and Budget under control number 1845-0537)

(Authority: 20 U.S.C. 1070a, 1070b, 1070c-1070c-2, 1085, 1087aa–1087hh, 1088, 1091, and 1141; 42 U.S.C. 2753)

[52 Fed. Reg. 45727, Dec. 1, 1987; 53 Fed. Reg. 49147, Dec. 6, 1988; 58 Fed. Reg. 32202, June 8, 1993; 58 Fed. Reg. 39620, July 23, 1993; 58 Fed. Reg. 69594, Dec. 30, 1993; 59 Fed. Reg. 21866, April 26, 1994; 59 Fed. Reg. 22421, April 29, 1994; 59 Fed. Reg. 32656, 32657, June 24, 1994; 59 Fed. Reg. 34964, July 7, 1994; 59 Fed. Reg. 61179, Nov. 29, 1994; 60 Fed. Reg. 42408, Aug. 15, 1995; 63 Fed. Reg. 40623, July 29, 1998; 64 Fed. Reg. 58291, Oct. 28, 1999; 64 Fed. Reg. 59037, Nov. 1, 1999; 65 Fed. Reg. 65675, Nov. 1, 2000; 67 Fed. Reg. 67072, Nov. 1, 2002; 71 Fed. Reg. 45666, Sept. 8, 2006]

§ 668.9 Relationship between clock hours and semester, trimester, or quarter hours in calculating Title IV, HEA program assistance.

(a) In determining the amount of Title IV, HEA program assistance that a student who is enrolled in a program described in § 668.8(k) is eligible to receive, the institution shall apply the formula contained in § 668.8(l) to determine the number of semester, trimester, or quarter hours in that program, if the institution measures academic progress in that program in semester, trimester, or quarter hours.

(b) Notwithstanding paragraph (a) of this section, a public or private nonprofit hospital-based school of nursing that awards a diploma at the completion of the school's program of education is not required to apply the formula contained in § 668.8(l) to determine the number of semester, trimester, or quarter hours in that program for purposes of calculating Title IV, HEA program assistance.

(Authority: 20 U.S.C. 1082, 1085, 1088, 1091, 1141)

[58 Fed. Reg. 39620, July 23, 1993; 58 Fed. Reg. 69594, Dec. 30, 1993; 59 Fed. Reg. 22423, April 29, 1994; 59 Fed. Reg. 32656, 32657, June 24, 1994; 59 Fed. Reg. 61179, Nov. 29, 1994]

* * *

§ 668.11 Scope.

(a) This subpart establishes standards that an institution must meet in order to participate in any Title IV, HEA program.

(b) Noncompliance with these standards by an institution already participating in any Title IV, HEA program or with applicable standards in this subpart by a third-party servicer that contracts with the institution may subject the institution or servicer, or both, to proceedings under subpart G of this part. These proceedings may lead to any of the following actions:

(1) An emergency action.

(2) The imposition of a fine.

(3) The limitation, suspension, or termination of the participation of the institution in a Title IV, HEA program.

(4) The limitation, suspension, or termination of the eligibility of the servicer to contract with any institution to administer any aspect of the institution's participation in a Title IV, HEA program.

(Authority: 20 U.S.C. 1094)

[59 Fed. Reg. 22423, Apr. 29, 1994]

§ 668.12 [Reserved]

[52 Fed. Reg. 45727, Dec. 1, 1987, as amended by 65 Fed. Reg. 65675, Nov. 11, 2000; 59 Fed. Reg. 32657, June 24, 1994]

§ 668.13 Certification procedures.

(a) *Requirements for certification.*

(1) The Secretary certifies an institution to participate in the title IV, HEA programs if the institution qualifies as an eligible institution under 34 CFR part 600, meets the standards of this subpart and 34 CFR part 668, subpart L, and satisfies the requirements of paragraph (a)(2) of this section.

(2) Except as provided in paragraph (a)(3) of this section, if an institution wishes to participate for the first time in the title IV, HEA programs or has undergone a change in ownership that results in a change in control as described in 34 CFR 600.31, the institution must require the following individuals to complete title IV, HEA program training provided or approved by the Secretary no later than 12 months after the institution executes its program participation agreement under Sec. 668.14:

(i) The individual the institution designates under Sec. 668.16(b)(1) as its title IV, HEA program administrator.

(ii) The institution's chief administrator or a high level institutional official the chief administrator designates.

(3)(i) An institution may request the Secretary to waive the training requirement for any individual described in paragraph (a)(2) of this section.

(ii) When the Secretary receives a waiver request under paragraph (a)(3)(i) of this section, the Secretary may grant or deny the waiver, require another institutional official to take the training, or require alternative training.

(b) *Period of participation.*

(1) If the Secretary certifies that an institution meets the standards of this subpart, the Secretary also specifies the period for which the institution may participate in a Title IV, HEA program. An institution's period of participation expires six years after the date that the Secretary certifies that the institution meets the standards of this subpart, except that the Secretary may specify a shorter period.

(2) Provided that an institution has submitted an application for a renewal of certification that is materially complete at least 90 days prior to the expiration of its current period of participation, the institution's existing certification will be extended on a month-to-month basis following the expiration of the institution's period of participation until the end of the month in which the Secretary issues a decision on the application for recertification.

(c) *Provisional certification.*

(1) The Secretary may provisionally certify an institution if—

(i) The institution seeks initial participation in a Title IV, HEA program;

(ii) The institution is an eligible institution that has undergone a change in ownership that results in a change in control according to the provisions of 34 CFR part 600;

(iii) The institution is a participating institution—

(A) That is applying for a certification that the institution meets the standards of this subpart;

(B) That the Secretary determines has jeopardized its ability to perform its financial responsibilities by not meeting the factors of financial responsibility under Sec. 668.15 or the standards of administrative capability under Sec. 668.16; and

(C) Whose participation has been limited or suspended under subpart G of this part, or voluntarily enters into provisional certification;

(iv) The institution seeks a renewal of participation in a Title IV, HEA program after the expiration of a prior period of participation in that program; or

(v) The institution is a participating institution that was accredited or preaccredited by a nationally recognized accrediting agency on the day before the Secretary withdrew the Secretary's recognition of that agency according to the provisions contained in 34 CFR part 603.

(2) If the Secretary provisionally certifies an institution, the Secretary also specifies the period for which the institution may participate in a Title IV, HEA program. Except as provided in paragraphs (c)(3) and (4) of this section, a provisionally certified institution's period of participation expires—

(i) Not later than the end of the first complete award year following the date on which the Secretary provisionally certified the institution under paragraph (c)(1)(i) of this section;

(ii) Not later than the end of the third complete award year following the date on which the Secretary provisionally certified the institution under paragraphs (c)(1)(ii), (iii), (iv) or (e)(2) of this section; and

(iii) If the Secretary provisionally certified the institution under paragraph (c)(1)(v) of this section, not later than 18 months after the date that the Secretary withdrew recognition from the institutions nationally recognized accrediting agency.

(3) Notwithstanding the maximum periods of participation provided for in paragraph (c)(2) of this section, if the Secretary provisionally certifies an institution, the Secretary may specify a shorter period of participation for that institution.

(4) For the purposes of this section, "provisional certification" means that the Secretary certifies that an institution has demonstrated to the Secretary's satisfaction that the institution—

(i) Is capable of meeting the standards of this subpart within a specified period; and

(ii) Is able to meet the institution's responsibilities under its program participation agreement, including compliance with any additional conditions specified in the institution's program participation agreement that the Secretary requires the institution to meet in order for the institution to participate under provisional certification.

(d) *Revocation of provisional certification.*

(1) If, before the expiration of a provisionally certified institution's period of participation in a Title IV, HEA program, the Secretary determines that the institution is unable to meet its responsibilities under its program participation agreement, the Secretary may revoke the institution's provisional certification for participation in that program.

(2)(i) If the Secretary revokes the provisional certification of an institution under paragraph (d)(1) of this section, the Secretary sends the institution a notice by certified mail, return receipt requested. The Secretary also may transmit the notice by other, more expeditious means, if practical.

(ii) The revocation takes effect on the date that the Secretary mails the notice to the institution.

(iii) The notice states the basis for the revocation, the consequences of the revocation to the institution, and that the institution may request the Secretary to reconsider the revocation. The consequences of a revocation are described in Sec. 668.26.

(3)(i) An institution may request reconsideration of a revocation under this section by submitting to the Secretary, within 20 days of the institution's receipt of the Secretary's notice, written evidence that the revocation is unwarranted. The institution must file the request with the Secretary by hand-delivery, mail, or facsimile transmission.

(ii) The filing date of the request is the date on which the request is—

(A) Hand-delivered;

(B) Mailed; or

(C) Sent by facsimile transmission.

(iii) Documents filed by facsimile transmission must be transmitted to the Secretary in accordance with instructions provided by the Secretary in the notice of revocation. An institution filing by facsimile transmission is responsible for confirming that a complete and legible copy of the document was received by the Secretary.

(iv) The Secretary discourages the use of facsimile transmission for documents longer than five pages.

(4)(i) The designated department official making the decision concerning an institution's request for reconsideration of a revocation is different from, and not subject to supervision by, the official who initiated the revocation of the institution's provisional certification. The deciding official promptly considers an institution's request for reconsideration of a revocation and notifies the institution, by certified mail, return receipt requested, of the final decision. The Secretary also may transmit the notice by other, more expeditious means, if practical.

(ii) If the Secretary determines that the revocation is warranted, the Secretary's notice informs the institution that the institution may apply for reinstatement of participation only after the later of the expiration of—

(A) Eighteen months after the effective date of the revocation; or

(B) A debarment or suspension of the institution under Executive Order (E.O.) 12549 (3 CFR, 1986 comp., p. 189) or the Federal Acquisition Regulations, 48 CFR part 9, subpart 9.4.

(iii) If the Secretary determines that the revocation of the institution's provisional certification is unwarranted, the Secretary's notice informs the institution that the institution's provisional certification is reinstated, effective on the date that the Secretary's original revocation notice was mailed, for a specified period of time.

(5)(i) The mailing date of a notice of revocation or a request for reconsideration of a revocation is the date evidenced on the original receipt of mailing from the U.S. Postal Service.

(ii) The date on which a request for reconsideration of a revocation is submitted is—

(A) If the request was sent by a delivery service other than the U.S. Postal Service, the date evidenced on the original receipt by that service; and

(B) If the request was sent by facsimile transmission, the date that the document is recorded as received by facsimile equipment that receives the transmission.

(Approved by the Office of Management and Budget under control number 1845-0537)

(Authority: 20 U.S.C. 1099c and E.O. 12549 (3 CFR, 1989 Comp., p. 189) and E.O. 12689 (3 CFR, 1989 Comp., p. 235))

[59 Fed. Reg. 22424, Apr. 29, 1994, as amended at 59 Fed. Reg. 34964, July 7, 1994; 60 Fed. Reg. 34431, June 30, 1995; 62 Fed. Reg. 62876, Nov. 25, 1997; 63 Fed. Reg. 40623, July 29, 1998; 64 Fed. Reg. 58617, Oct. 29, 1999; 65 Fed. Reg. 65675, Nov. 1, 2000]

§ 668.14 Program participation agreement.

(a)(1) An institution may participate in any Title IV, HEA program, other than the LEAP and NEISP programs, only if the institution enters into a written program participation agreement with the Secretary, on a form approved by the Secretary. A program participation agreement conditions the initial and continued participation of an eligible institution in any Title IV, HEA program upon compliance with the provisions of this part, the individual program regulations, and any additional conditions specified in the program participation agreement that the Secretary requires the institution to meet.

(2) An institution's program participation agreement applies to each branch campus and other location of the institution that meets the applicable requirements of this part unless otherwise specified by the Secretary.

(b) By entering into a program participation agreement, an institution agrees that—

(1) It will comply with all statutory provisions of or applicable to Title IV of the HEA, all applicable regulatory provisions prescribed under that statutory authority, and all applicable special arrangements, agreements, and limitations entered into under the authority of statutes applicable to Title IV of the HEA, including the requirement that the institution will use funds it receives under any Title IV, HEA program and any interest or other earnings thereon, solely for the purposes specified in and in accordance with that program;

(2) As a fiduciary responsible for administering Federal funds, if the institution is permitted to request funds under a Title IV, HEA program advance payment method, the institution will time its requests for funds under the program to meet the institution's immediate Title IV, HEA program needs;

(3) It will not request from or charge any student a fee for processing or handling any application, form, or data required to determine a student's eligibility for, and amount of, Title IV, HEA program assistance;

(4) It will establish and maintain such administrative and fiscal procedures and records as may be necessary to ensure proper and efficient administration of funds received from the Secretary or from students under the Title IV, HEA programs, together with assurances that the institution will provide, upon request and in a timely manner, information relating to the administrative capability and financial responsibility of the institution to—

(i) The Secretary;

(ii) A guaranty agency, as defined in 34 CFR part 682, that guarantees loans made under the Federal Stafford Loan and Federal PLUS programs for attendance at the institution or any of the institution's branch campuses or other locations;

(iii) The nationally recognized accrediting agency that accredits or preaccredits the institution or any of the institution's branch campuses, other locations, or educational programs;

(iv) The State agency that legally authorizes the institution and any branch campus or other location of the institution to provide postsecondary education; and

(v) In the case of a public postsecondary vocational educational institution that is approved by a State agency recognized for the approval of public postsecondary vocational education, that State agency;

(5) It will comply with the provisions of § 668.15 relating to factors of financial responsibility;

(6) It will comply with the provisions of § 668.16 relating to standards of administrative capability;

(7) It will submit reports to the Secretary and, in the case of an institution participating in the Federal Stafford Loan, Federal PLUS, or the Federal Perkins Loan Program, to holders of loans made to the institution's students under that program at such times and containing such information as the Secretary may reasonably require to carry out the purpose of the Title IV, HEA programs;

(8) It will not provide any statement to any student or certification to any lender in the case of an FFEL Program loan, or origination record to the Secretary in the case of a Direct Loan Program loan that qualifies the student or parent for a loan or loans in excess of the amount that the student or parent is eligible to borrow in accordance with sections 425(a), 428(a)(2), 428(b)(1)(A) and (B), 428B, 428H, and 455(a) of the HEA;

(9) It will comply with the requirements of subpart D of this part concerning institutional and financial assistance information for students and prospective students;

(10) In the case of an institution that advertises job placement rates as a means of attracting students to enroll in the institution, it will make available to prospective students, at or before the time that those students apply for enrollment—

(i) The most recent available data concerning employment statistics, graduation statistics, and any other information necessary to substantiate the truthfulness of the advertisements; and

(ii) Relevant State licensing requirements of the State in which the institution is located for any job for which an educational program offered by the institution is designed to prepare those prospective students;

(11) In the case of an institution participating in the FFEL program, the institution will inform all eligible borrowers, as defined in 34 CFR part 682, enrolled in the institution about the availability and eligibility of those borrowers for State grant assistance from the State in which the institution is located, and will inform borrowers from another State of the source of further information concerning State grant assistance from that State;

(12) It will provide the certifications described in paragraph (c) of this section;

(13) In the case of an institution whose students receive financial assistance pursuant to section 484(d) of the HEA, the institution will make available to those students a program proven successful in assisting students in obtaining the recognized equivalent of a high school diploma;

(14) It will not deny any form of Federal financial aid to any eligible student solely on the grounds that the student is participating in a program of study abroad approved for credit by the institution;

(15)(i) Except as provided under paragraph (b)(15)(ii) of this section, the institution will use a default management plan approved by the Secretary with regard to its administration of the FFEL or Direct Loan programs, or both for at least the first two years of its participation in those programs, if the institution—

    (A) Is participating in the FFEL or Direct Loan programs for the first time; or

    (B) Is an institution that has undergone a change of ownership that results in a change in control and is participating in the FFEL or Direct Loan programs.

  (ii) The institution does not have to use an approved default management plan if—

    (A) The institution, including its main campus and any branch campus, does not have a cohort default rate in excess of 10 percent; and

    (B) The owner of the institution does not own and has not owned any other institution that had a cohort default rate in excess of 10 percent while that owner owned the institution.

(16) [*Reserved*]

(17) The Secretary, guaranty agencies and lenders as defined in 34 CFR part 682, nationally recognized accrediting agencies, the Secretary of Veterans Affairs, State agencies recognized under 34 CFR part 603 for the approval of public postsecondary vocational education, and State agencies that legally authorize institutions and branch campuses or other locations of institutions to provide postsecondary education, have the authority to share with each other any information pertaining to the institution's eligibility for or participation in the Title IV, HEA programs or any information on fraud and abuse;

(18) It will not knowingly—

  (i) Employ in a capacity that involves the administration of the Title IV, HEA programs or the receipt of funds under those programs, an individual who has been convicted of, or has pled nolo contendere or guilty to, a crime involving the acquisition, use, or expenditure of Federal, State, or local government funds, or has been administratively or judicially determined to have committed fraud or any other material violation of law involving Federal, State, or local government funds;

  (ii) Contract with an institution or third-party servicer that has been terminated under section 432 of the HEA for a reason involving the acquisition, use, or expenditure of Federal, State, or local government funds, or that has been administratively or judicially determined to have committed fraud or any other material violation of law involving Federal, State, or local government funds; or

  (iii) Contract with or employ any individual, agency, or organization that has been, or whose officers or employees have been—

    (A) Convicted of, or pled nolo contendere or guilty to, a crime involving the acquisition, use, or expenditure of Federal, State, or local government funds; or

    (B) Administratively or judicially determined to have committed fraud or any other material violation of law involving Federal, State, or local government funds;

(19) It will complete, in a timely manner and to the satisfaction of the Secretary, surveys conducted as a part of the Integrated Postsecondary Education Data System (IPEDS) or any other Federal collection effort, as designated by the Secretary, regarding data on postsecondary institutions;

(20) In the case of an institution that is co-educational and has an intercollegiate athletic program, it will comply with the provisions of § 668.48;

(21) It will not impose any penalty, including, but not limited to, the assessment of late fees, the denial of access to classes, libraries, or other institutional facilities, or the requirement that the student borrow additional funds for which interest or other charges are assessed, on any student because of the student's inability to meet his or her financial obligations to the institution as a result of the delayed disbursement of the proceeds of a Title IV, HEA program loan due to compliance with statutory and regulatory requirements of or applicable to the Title IV, HEA programs, or delays attributable to the institution;

(22)(i) It will not provide any commission, bonus, or other incentive payment based directly or indirectly upon success in securing enrollments or financial aid to any person or entity engaged in any student recruiting or admission activities or in making decisions regarding the awarding of title IV, HEA program funds, except that this limitation does not apply to the recruitment of foreign students residing in foreign countries who are not eligible to receive title IV, HEA program funds.

  (ii) Activities and arrangements that an institution may carry out without violating the provisions of paragraph (b)(22)(i) of this section include, but are not limited to:

  (A) The payment of fixed compensation, such as a fixed annual salary or a fixed hourly wage, as long as that compensation is not adjusted up or down more than twice during any twelve month period, and any adjustment is not based solely on the number of students recruited, admitted, enrolled, or awarded financial aid. For this purpose, an increase in fixed compensation resulting from a cost of living increase that is paid to all or substantially all full-time employees is not considered an adjustment.

  (B) Compensation to recruiters based upon their recruitment of students who enroll only in programs that are not eligible for title IV, HEA program funds.

  (C) Compensation to recruiters who arrange contracts between the institution and an employer under which the employer's employees enroll in the institution, and the employer pays, directly or by reimbursement, 50 percent or more of the tuition and fees charged to its employees; provided that the compensation is not based upon the number of employees who enroll in the institution, or the revenue they generate, and the recruiters have no contact with the employees.

  (D) Compensation paid as part of a profit-sharing or bonus plan, as long as those payments are substantially the same amount or the same percentage of salary or wages, and made to all or substantially all of the institution's full-time professional and administrative staff. Such payments can be limited to all, or substantially all of the full-time employees at one or more organizational level at the institution, except that an organizational level may not consist predominantly of recruiters, admissions staff, or financial aid staff.

  (E) Compensation that is based upon students successfully completing their educational programs, or one academic year of their educational programs, whichever is shorter.

For this purpose, successful completion of an academic year means that the student has earned at least 24 semester or trimester credit hours or 36 quarter credit hours, or has successfully completed at least 900 clock hours of instruction at the institution.

(F) Compensation paid to employees who perform clerical "pre-enrollment" activities, such as answering telephone calls, referring inquiries, or distributing institutional materials.

(G) Compensation to managerial or supervisory employees who do not directly manage or supervise employees who are directly involved in recruiting or admissions activities, or the awarding of title IV, HEA program funds.

(H) The awarding of token gifts to the institution's students or alumni, provided that the gifts are not in the form of money, no more than one gift is provided annually to an individual, and the cost of the gift is not more than $100.

(I) Profit distributions proportionately based upon an individual's ownership interest in the institution.

(J) Compensation paid for Internet-based recruitment and admission activities that provide information about the institution to prospective students, refer prospective students to the institution, or permit prospective students to apply for admission on-line.

(K) Payments to third parties, including tuition sharing arrangements, that deliver various services to the institution, provided that none of the services involve recruiting or admission activities, or the awarding of title IV, HEA program funds.

(L) Payments to third parties, including tuition sharing arrangements, that deliver various services to the institution, even if one of the services involves recruiting or admission activities or the awarding of title IV, HEA program funds, provided that the individuals performing the recruitment or admission activities, or the awarding of title IV, HEA program funds, are not compensated in a manner that would be impermissible under paragraph (b)(22) of this section.

(23) It will meet the requirements established pursuant to part H of Title IV of the HEA by the Secretary and nationally recognized accrediting agencies;

(24) It will comply with the requirements of § 668.22;

(25) It is liable for all—

(i) Improperly spent or unspent funds received under the Title IV, HEA programs, including any funds administered by a third-party servicer; and

(ii) Returns of title IV, HEA program funds that the institution or its servicer may be required to make; and

(26) If the stated objectives of an educational program of the institution are to prepare a student for gainful employment in a recognized occupation, the institution will—

(i) Demonstrate a reasonable relationship between the length of the program and entry level requirements for the recognized occupation for which the program prepares the student. The Secretary considers the relationship to be reasonable if the number of clock hours provided in the program does not exceed by more than 50 percent the minimum number of clock hours required for training in the recognized occupation for which the program prepares the student, as established by the State in which the pro-

gram is offered, if the State has established such a requirement, or as established by any Federal agency; and

(ii) Establish the need for the training for the student to obtain employment in the recognized occupation for which the program prepares the student.

(c) In order to participate in any Title IV, HEA program (other than the LEAP and NEISP programs), the institution must certify that it—

(1) Has in operation a drug abuse prevention program that the institution has determined to be accessible to any officer, employee, or student at the institution; and

(2)(i) Has established a campus security policy in accordance with section 485(f) of the HEA; and

(ii) Has complied with the disclosure requirements of § 668.47 as required by section 485(f) of the HEA.

(d)(1) The institution, if located in a State to which section 4(b) of the National Voter Registration Act (42 U.S.C. 1973gg-2(b)) does not apply, will make a good faith effort to distribute a mail voter registration form, requested and received from the State, to each student enrolled in a degree or certificate program and physically in attendance at the institution, and to make those forms widely available to students at the institution.

(2) The institution must request the forms from the State 120 days prior to the deadline for registering to vote within the State. If an institution has not received a sufficient quantity of forms to fulfill this section from the State within 60 days prior to the deadline for registering to vote in the State, the institution is not liable for not meeting the requirements of this section during that election year.

(3) This paragraph applies to elections as defined in section 301(1) of the Federal Election Campaign Act of 1971 (2 U.S.C. 431(1)), and includes the election for Governor or other chief executive within such State.

(e)(1) A program participation agreement becomes effective on the date that the Secretary signs the agreement.

(2) A new program participation agreement supersedes any prior program participation agreement between the Secretary and the institution.

(f)(1) Except as provided in paragraphs (h) and (i) of this section, the Secretary terminates a program participation agreement through the proceedings in subpart G of this part.

(2) An institution may terminate a program participation agreement.

(3) If the Secretary or the institution terminates a program participation agreement under paragraph (g) of this section, the Secretary establishes the termination date.

(g) An institution's program participation agreement automatically expires on the date that—

(1) The institution changes ownership that results in a change in control as determined by the Secretary under 34 CFR part 600; or

(2) The institution's participation ends under the provisions of § 668.26(a)(1), (2), (4), or (7).

(h) An institution's program participation agreement no longer applies to or covers a location of the institution as of the date on which that location ceases to be a part of the participating institution.

(Approved by the Office of Management and Budget under control number 1840-0537)

(Authority: 20 U.S.C. 1085, 1088, 1091, 1092, 1094, 1099a-3, 1099c, and 1141)

[54 Fed. Reg. 46538, Nov. 3, 1989; 55 Fed. Reg. 26200, June 27, 1990; 57 Fed. Reg. 57310, Dec. 3, 1992; 58 Fed. Reg. 32202, June 8, 1993; 58 Fed. Reg. 36870, July 9, 1993; 59 Fed. Reg. 21866, April 26, 1994; 59 Fed. Reg. 22423, 22425, April 29, 1994; 59 Fed. Reg. 32657, June 24, 1994; 59 Fed. Reg. 34964, July 7, 1994; 63 Fed. Reg. 40623, July 29, 1998; 64 Fed. Reg. 58617, Oct. 29, 1999; 64 Fed. Reg. 59038, Nov. 1, 1999; 65 Fed. Reg. 38729, June 22, 2000; 65 Fed. Reg. 65637, Nov. 1, 2000; 67 Fed. Reg. 67072, Nov. 1, 2002]

§ 668.15 Factors of financial responsibility.

(a) *General*. To begin and to continue to participate in any Title IV, HEA program, an institution must demonstrate to the Secretary that the institution is financially responsible under the requirements established in this section.

(b) *General standards of financial responsibility*. In general, the Secretary considers an institution to be financially responsible only if it—

(1) Is providing the services described in its official publications and statements;

(2) Is providing the administrative resources necessary to comply with the requirements of this subpart;

(3) Is meeting all of its financial obligations, including but not limited to—

(i)   Refunds that it is required to make; and

(ii) Repayments to the Secretary for liabilities and debts incurred in programs administered by the Secretary;

(4) Is current in its debt payments. The institution is not considered current in its debt payments if—

(i)   The institution is in violation of any existing loan agreement at its fiscal year end, as disclosed in a note to its audited financial statement; or

(ii) the institution fails to make a payment in accordance with existing debt obligations for more than 120 days, and at least one creditor has filed suit to recover those funds;

(5) Except as provided in paragraph (d) of this section, in accordance with procedures established by the Secretary, submits to the Secretary an irrevocable letter of credit, acceptable and payable to the Secretary equal to 25 percent of the total dollar amount of Title IV, HEA program refunds paid by the institution in the previous fiscal year;

(6) Has not had, as part of the audit report for the institution's most recently completed fiscal year—

(i)   A statement by the accountant expressing substantial doubt about the institution's ability to continue as a going concern; or

(ii) A disclaimed or adverse opinion by the accountant;

(7) For a for-profit institution—

(i)(A) Demonstrates at the end of its latest fiscal year, an acid test ratio of at least 1:1. For purposes of this section, the acid test ratio shall be calculated by adding cash and cash equivalents to current accounts receivable and dividing the sum by total current liabilities. The calculation of the acid test ratio shall exclude all unsecured or uncollateralized related party receivables;

(B) Has not had operating losses in either or both of its two latest fiscal years that in sum result in a decrease in tangible net worth in excess of 10 percent of the institution's tangible net worth at the beginning of the first year of the two-year period. The Secretary may calculate an operating loss for an institution by excluding from net income: extraordinary gains or losses; income or losses from discontinued operations; prior period adjustment; and, the cumulative effect of changes in accounting principle. For purposes of this section, the calculation of tangible net worth shall exclude all assets defined as intangible in accordance with generally accepted accounting principles; and

(C) Had, for its latest fiscal year, a positive tangible net worth. In applying this standard, a positive tangible net worth occurs when the institution's tangible assets exceed its liabilities. The calculation of tangible net worth shall exclude all assets classified as intangible in accordance with the generally accepted accounting principles; or

(ii) Demonstrates to the satisfaction of the Secretary that it has currently issued and outstanding debt obligations that are (without insurance, guarantee, or credit enhancement) listed at or above the second highest rating level of credit quality given by a nationally recognized statistical rating organization;

(8) For a nonprofit institution—

(i)(A) Prepares a classified statement of financial position in accordance with generally accepted accounting principles or provides the required information in notes to the audited financial statements;

(B) Demonstrates at the end of its latest fiscal year, an acid test ratio of at least 1:1. For purposes of this section, the acid test ratio shall be calculated by adding cash and cash equivalents to current accounts receivable and dividing the sum by total current liabilities. The calculation of the acid test ratio shall exclude all unsecured or uncollateralized related party receivables.

(C)(1) Has, at the end of its latest fiscal year, a positive unrestricted current fund balance or positive unrestricted net assets. In calculating the unrestricted current fund balance or the unrestricted net assets for an institution, the Secretary may include funds that are temporarily restricted in use by the institution's governing body that can be transferred to the current unrestricted fund or added to net unrestricted assets at the discretion of the governing body; or

(2) Has not had, an excess of current fund expenditures over current fund revenues over both of its 2 latest fiscal years that results in a decrease exceeding 10 percent in either the unrestricted current fund balance or the unrestricted net assets at the beginning of the first year of the 2-year period. The Secretary may exclude from net changes in fund balances for the operating loss calculation: Extraordinary gains or losses; income or losses from discontinued operations; prior period adjustment; and the cumulative effect of changes in accounting principle. In calculating the institution's unrestricted current fund balance or the unrestricted net assets, the Secretary may include funds that are temporarily restricted in use by the institution's governing body that can be transferred to the current unrestricted fund or added to net unrestricted assets at the discretion of the governing body; or

(ii) Demonstrates to the satisfaction of the Secretary that it has currently issued and outstanding debt obligations which are (without insurance, guarantee, or credit enhancement) listed at or above the second highest rating level of credit quality given by a nationally recognized statistical rating organization.

(9) For a public institution—

(i) Has its liabilities backed by the full faith and credit of a State, or by an equivalent governmental entity;

(ii) Has a positive current unrestricted fund balance if reporting under the Single Audit Act;

(iii) Has a positive unrestricted current fund in the State's Higher Education Fund, as presented in the general purpose financial statements;

(iv) Submits to the Secretary, a statement from the State Auditor General that the institution has, during the past year, met all of its financial obligations, and that the institution continues to have sufficient resources to meet all of its financial obligations; or

(v) Demonstrates to the satisfaction of the Secretary that it has currently issued and outstanding debt obligations which are (without insurance, guarantee, or credit enhancement) listed at or above the second highest rating level of credit quality given by a nationally recognized statistical rating organization.

(c) *Past performance of an institution or persons affiliated with an institution.* An institution is not financially responsible if—

(1) A person who exercises substantial control over the institution or any member or members of the person's family alone or together—

(i)(A) Exercises or exercised substantial control over another institution or a third-party servicer that owes a liability for a violation of a Title IV, HEA program requirement; or

(B) Owes a liability for a violation of a Title IV, HEA program requirement; and

(ii) That person, family member, institution, or servicer does not demonstrate that the liability is being repaid in accordance with an agreement with the Secretary; or

(2) The institution has—

(i) Been limited, suspended, terminated, or entered into a settlement agreement to resolve a limitation, suspension, or termination action initiated by the Secretary or a guaranty agency (as defined in 34 CFR part 682) within the preceding five years;

(ii) Had—

(A) An audit finding, during its two most recent audits of its conduct of the Title IV, HEA programs, that resulted in the institution's being required to repay an amount greater than five percent of the funds that the institution received under the Title IV, HEA programs for any award year covered by the audit; or

(B) A program review finding, during its two most recent program reviews, of its conduct of the Title IV, HEA programs that resulted in the institution's being required to repay an amount greater than five percent of the funds that the institution received under the Title IV, HEA programs for any award year covered by the program review;

(iii) Been cited during the preceding five years for failure to submit acceptable audit reports required under this part or individual Title IV, HEA program regulations in a timely fashion; or

(iv) Failed to resolve satisfactorily any compliance problems identified in program review or audit reports based upon a final decision of the Secretary issued pursuant to subpart G or subpart H of this part.

(d) *Exceptions to the general standards of financial responsibility.*

(1)(i) An institution is not required to meet the standard in paragraph (b)(5) of this section if the Secretary determines that the institution—

(A)(1) Is located in, and is legally authorized to operate within, a State that has a tuition recovery fund that is acceptable to the Secretary and ensures that the institution is able to pay all required refunds; and

(2) Contributes to that tuition recovery fund.

(B) Has its liabilities backed by the full faith and credit of the State, or by an equivalent governmental entity; or

(C) As determined under paragraph (g) of this section, demonstrates, to the satisfaction of the Secretary, that for each of the institution's two most recently completed fiscal years, it has made timely refunds to students in accordance with § 668.22(j), and that it has met or exceeded all of the financial responsibility standards in this section that were in effect for the corresponding periods during the two-year period.

(ii) In evaluating an application to approve a State tuition recovery fund to exempt its participating schools from the federal cash reserve requirements, the Secretary will consider the extent to which the State tuition recovery fund:

(A) Provides refunds to both in-state and out-of-state students;

(B) Allocates all refunds in accordance with the order delineated in § 668.22(*i*); and

(C) Provides a reliable mechanism for the State to replenish the fund should any claims arise that deplete the funds assets.

(2) The Secretary considers an institution to be financially responsible, even if the institution is not otherwise financially responsible under paragraphs (b)(1) through (4) and (b)(6) through (9) of this section, if the institution—

(i) Submits to the Secretary an irrevocable letter of credit that is acceptable and payable to the Secretary equal to not less than one-half of the Title IV, HEA program funds received by the institution during the last complete award year for which figures are available; or

(ii) Establishes to the satisfaction of the Secretary, with the support of a financial statement submitted in accordance with paragraph (e) of this section, that the institution has sufficient resources to ensure against its precipitous closure, including the ability to meet all of its financial obligations (including refunds of institutional charges and repayments to the Secretary for liabilities and debts incurred in programs administered by the Secretary). The Secretary considers the institution to have sufficient resources to ensure against precipitous closure only if—

(A) The institution formerly demonstrated financial responsibility under the standards of financial responsibility in its preceding audited financial statement (or, if no prior audited financial statement was requested by the Secretary, demonstrates in conjunction with its current audit that it would have satisfied this requirement), and that its most recent audited financial statement indicates that—

(1) All taxes owed by the institution are current;

(2) The institution's net income, or a change in total net assets, before extraordinary items and discontinued operations, has not decreased by more than 10 percent from the prior fiscal year, unless the institution demonstrates that the decreased net income shown on the current financial statement is a result of downsizing pursuant to a management-approved business plan;

(3) Loans and other advances to related parties have not increased from the prior fiscal year unless such increases were secured and collateralized, and do not exceed 10 percent of the prior fiscal year's working capital of the institution;

(4) The equity of a for-profit institution, or the total net assets of a non-profit institution, have not decreased by more than 10 percent of the prior year's total equity;

(5) Compensation for owners or other related parties (including bonuses, fringe benefits, employee stock option allowances, 401k contributions, deferred compensation allowances) has not increased from the prior year at a rate higher than for all other employees;

(6) The institution has not materially leveraged its assets or income by becoming a guarantor on any new loan or obligation on behalf of any related party;

(7) All obligations owed to the institution by related parties are current, and that the institution has demanded and is receiving payment of all funds owed from related parties that are payable upon demand. For purposes of this section, a person does not become a related party by attending an institution as a student;

(B) There have been no material findings in the institution's latest compliance audit of its administration of the Title IV HEA programs; and

(C) There are no pending administrative or legal actions being taken against the institution by the Secretary, any other Federal agency, the institution's nationally recognized accrediting agency, or any State entity.

(3) An institution is not required to meet the acid test ratio in paragraph (b)(7)(i)(A) or (b)(8)(i)(B) of this section if the institution is an institution that provides a 2-year or 4-year educational program for which the institution awards an associate or baccalaureate degree that demonstrates to the satisfaction of the Secretary that—

(i) There is no reasonable doubt as to its continued solvency and ability to deliver quality educational services;

(ii) It is current in its payment of all current liabilities, including student refunds, repayments to the Secretary, payroll, and payment of trade creditors and withholding taxes; and

(iii) It has substantial equity in institution-occupied facilities, the acquisition of which was the direct cause of its failure to meet the acid test ratio requirement.

(4) The Secretary may determine an institution to be financially responsible even if the institution is not otherwise financially responsible under paragraph (c)(1) of this section if—

(i) The institution notifies the Secretary, in accordance with 34 CFR 600.30, that the person referenced in paragraph (c)(1) of this section exercises substantial control over the institution; and

(ii)(A) The person repaid to the Secretary a portion of the applicable liability, and the portion repaid equals or exceeds the greater of—

(1) The total percentage of the ownership interest held in the institution or third-party servicer that owes the liability by that person or any member or members of that person's family, either alone or in combination with one another;

(2) The total percentage of the ownership interest held in the institution or servicer that owes the liability that the person or any member or members of the person's family, either alone or in combination with one another, represents or represented under a voting trust, power of attorney, proxy, or similar agreement; or

(3) Twenty-five percent, if the person or any member of the person's family is or was a member of the board of directors, chief executive officer, or other executive officer of the institution or servicer that owes the liability, or of an entity holding at least a 25 percent ownership interest in the institution that owes the liability;

(B) The applicable liability described in paragraph (c)(1) of this section is currently being repaid in accordance with a written agreement with the Secretary; or

(C) The institution demonstrates why—

(1) The person who exercises substantial control over the institution should nevertheless be considered to lack that control; or

(2) The person who exercises substantial control over the institution and each member of that person's family nevertheless does not or did not exercise substantial control over the institution or servicer that owes the liability.

(e) [*Reserved*]

(f) *Definitions and terms.* For the purposes of this section—

(1)(i) An "ownership interest" is a share of the legal or beneficial ownership or control of, or a right to share in the proceeds of the operation of, an institution, institution's parent corporation, a third-party servicer, or a third-party servicer's parent corporation.

(ii) The term "ownership interest" includes, but is not limited to—

(A) An interest as tenant in common, joint tenant, or tenant by the entireties;

(B) A partnership; and

(C) An interest in a trust.

(iii) The term "ownership interest" does not include any share of the ownership or control of, or any right to share in the proceeds of the operation of—

(A) A mutual fund that is regularly and publicly traded;

(B) An institutional investor; or

(C) A profit-sharing plan, provided that all employees are covered by the plan;

(2) The Secretary generally considers a person to exercise substantial control over an institution or third-party servicer, if the person—

(i) Directly or indirectly holds at least a 25 percent ownership interest in the institution or servicer;

(ii) Holds, together with other members of his or her family, at least a 25 percent ownership interest in the institution or servicer;

(iii) Represents, either alone or together with other persons, under a voting trust, power of attorney, proxy, or similar agreement one or more persons who hold, either individually or in combination with the other persons represented or the person representing them, at least a 25 percent ownership in the institution or servicer; or

(iv) Is a member of the board of directors, the chief executive officer, or other executive officer of—

(A) The institution or servicer; or

(B) An entity that holds at least a 25 percent ownership interest in the institution or servicer; and

(3) The Secretary considers a member of a person's family to be a parent, sibling, spouse, child, spouse's parent or sibling, or sibling's or child's spouse.

(g) *Two-year performance requirement.*

(1) The Secretary considers an institution to have satisfied the requirements in paragraph (d)(1)(C) of this section if the independent certified public accountant, or government auditor who conducted the institution's compliance audits for the institution's two most recently completed fiscal years, or the Secretary or a State or guaranty agency that conducted a review of the institution covering those fiscal years—

(i)(A) For either of those fiscal years, did not find in the sample of student records audited or reviewed that the institution made late refunds to 5 percent or more of the students in that sample. For purposes of determining the percentage of late refunds under this paragraph, the auditor or reviewer must include in the sample only those title IV, HEA program recipients who received or should have received a refund under § 668.22; or

(B) The Secretary considers the institution to have satisfied the conditions in paragraph (g)(1)(i)(A) of this section if the auditor or reviewer finds in the sample of student records audited or reviewed that the institution made only one late refund to a student in that sample; and

(ii) For either of those fiscal years, did not note a material weakness or a reportable condition in the institution's report on internal controls that is related to refunds.

(2) If the Secretary or a State or guaranty agency finds during a review conducted of the institution that the institution no longer qualifies for an exemption under paragraph (d)(1)(C) of this section, the institution must—

(i) Submit to the Secretary the irrevocable letter of credit required in paragraph (b)(5) of this section no later than 30 days after the Secretary or State or guaranty agency notifies the institution of that finding; and

(ii) Notify the Secretary of the guaranty agency or State that conducted the review.

(3) If the auditor who conducted the institution's compliance audit finds that the institution no longer qualifies for an exemption under paragraph (d)(1)(C) of this section, the institution must submit to the Secretary the irrevocable letter of credit required in paragraph (b)(5) of this section no later than 30 days after the date the institution's compliance audit must be submitted to the Secretary.

(h) *Foreign institutions.* The Secretary makes a determination of financial responsibility for a foreign institution on the basis of financial statements submitted under the following requirements—

(1) If the institution received less than $500,000 U.S. in title IV, HEA program funds during its most recently completed fiscal year, the institution must submit its audited financial statement for that year. For purposes of this paragraph, the audited financial statements may be prepared under the auditing standards and accounting principles used in the institution's home country; or

(2) If the institution received $500,000 U.S. or more in title IV, HEA program funds during its most recently completed fiscal year, the institution must submit its audited financial statement in accordance with the requirements of § 668.23, and satisfy the general standards of financial responsibility contained in this section, or qualify under an alternate standard of financial responsibility contained in this section.

(Approved by the Office of Management and Budget under control number 1840-0537)

(Authority: 20 U.S.C. 1094 and 1099c and Section 4 of Pub. L. 95-452, 92 Stat. 1101–1109)

[53 Fed. Reg. 49147, Dec. 6, 1988; 56 Fed. Reg. 36697, July 31, 1991; 57 Fed. Reg. 27703, June 22, 1992; 58 Fed. Reg. 32201, June 8, 1993; 59 Fed. Reg. 21866, April 26, 1994; 59 Fed. Reg. 22423, 22428, April 29, 1994; 59 Fed. Reg. 32627, June 24, 1994; 59 Fed. Reg. 34964, July 7, 1994; 59 Fed. Reg. 61179, Nov. 29, 1994; 60 Fed. Reg. 34431, June 30, 1995; 60 Fed. Reg. 42408, Aug. 15, 1995; 61 Fed. Reg. 29901, June 12, 1996; 61 Fed. Reg. 60569, Nov. 29, 1996; 62 Fed. Reg. 27128, May 16, 1997; 71 Fed. Reg. 45666, Sept. 8, 2006]

§ 668.16 Standards of administrative capability.

To begin and to continue to participate in any Title IV, HEA program, an institution shall demonstrate to the Secretary that the institution is capable of adequately administering that program under each of the standards established in this section. The Secretary considers an institution to have that administrative capability if the institution—

(a) Administers the Title IV, HEA programs in accordance with all statutory provisions of or applicable to Title IV of the HEA, all applicable regulatory provisions prescribed under that statutory authority, and all applicable special arrangements, agreements, and limitations entered into under the authority of statutes applicable to Title IV of the HEA;

(b)(1) Designates a capable individual to be responsible for administering all the Title IV, HEA programs in which it participates and for coordinating those programs with the institution's other Federal and non-Federal programs of student financial assistance. The Secretary considers an individual to be "capable" under this paragraph if the individual is certified by the State in which the institution is located, if the State requires certification of financial aid administrators. The Secretary may consider other factors in determining whether an individual is capable, including, but not limited to, the individual's successful completion of Title IV, HEA program training provided or approved by the Secretary, and previous experience and documented success in administering the Title IV, HEA programs properly;

(2) Uses an adequate number of qualified persons to administer the Title IV, HEA programs in which the institution participates.

The Secretary considers the following factors to determine whether an institution uses an adequate number of qualified persons—

   (i)   The number and types of programs in which the institution participates;

   (ii)   The number of applications evaluated;

   (iii)   The number of students who receive any student financial assistance at the institution and the amount of funds administered;

   (iv)   The financial aid delivery system used by the institution;

   (v)   The degree of office automation used by the institution in the administration of the Title IV, HEA programs;

   (vi)   The number and distribution of financial aid staff; and

   (vii)   The use of third-party servicers to aid in the administration of the Title IV, HEA programs;

(3) Communicates to the individual designated to be responsible for administering Title IV, HEA programs, all the information received by any institutional office that bears on a student's eligibility for Title IV, HEA program assistance; and

(4) Has written procedures for or written information indicating the responsibilities of the various offices with respect to the approval, disbursement, and delivery of Title IV, HEA program assistance and the preparation and submission of reports to the Secretary;

(c)(1) Administers Title IV, HEA programs with adequate checks and balances in its system of internal controls; and

(2) Divides the functions of authorizing payments and disbursing or delivering funds so that no office has responsibility for both functions with respect to any particular student aided under the programs. For example, the functions of authorizing payments and disbursing or delivering funds must be divided so that for any particular student aided under the programs, the two functions are carried out by at least two organizationally independent individuals who are not members of the same family, as defined in § 668.15, or who do not together exercise substantial control, as defined in § 668.15, over the institution;

(d) Establishes and maintains records required under this part and the individual Title IV, HEA program regulations;

(e) For purposes of determining student eligibility for assistance under a Title IV, HEA program, establishes, publishes, and applies reasonable standards for measuring whether an otherwise eligible student is maintaining satisfactory progress in his or her educational program. The Secretary considers an institution's standards to be reasonable if the standards—

(1) Are the same as or stricter than the institution's standards for a student enrolled in the same educational program who is not receiving assistance under a Title IV, HEA program;

(2) Include the following elements:

   (i)   A qualitative component which consists of grades (provided that the standards meet or exceed the requirements of § 668.34), work projects completed, or comparable factors that are measurable against a norm.

   (ii)   A quantitative component that consists of a maximum timeframe in which a student must complete his or her educational program. The timeframe must—

     (A)   For an undergraduate program, be no longer than 150 percent of the published length of the educational program measured in academic years, terms, credit hours attempted, clock hours completed, *etc.*, as appropriate;

     (B)   Be divided into increments, not to exceed the lesser of one academic year or one-half the published length of the educational program;

     (C)   Include a schedule established by the institution designating the minimum percentage or amount of work that a student must successfully complete at the end of each increment to complete his or her educational program within the maximum timeframe; and

     (D)   Include specific policies defining the effect of course incompletes, withdrawals, repetitions, and noncredit remedial courses on satisfactory progress;

(3) Provide for consistent application of standards to all students within categories of students, *e.g.*, full-time, part-time, undergraduate, and graduate students, and educational programs established by the institution;

(4) Provide for a determination at the end of each increment by the institution as to whether the student has met the qualitative and quantitative components of the standards (as provided for in paragraphs (e)(2)(i) and (ii) of this section);

(5) Provide specific procedures under which a student may appeal a determination that the student is not making satisfactory progress; and

(6) Provide specific procedures for a student to re-establish that he or she is maintaining satisfactory progress.

(f) Develops and applies an adequate system to identify and resolve discrepancies in the information that the institution receives from different sources with respect to a student's application for financial aid under Title IV, HEA programs. In determining whether the institution's system is adequate, the Secretary considers whether the institution obtains and reviews—

(1) All student aid applications, need analysis documents, Statements of Educational Purpose, Statements of Registration Status, and eligibility notification documents presented by or on behalf of each applicant;

(2) Any documents, including any copies of State and Federal income tax returns, that are normally collected by the institution to verify information received from the student or other sources; and

(3) Any other information normally available to the institution regarding a student's citizenship, previous educational experience, documentation of the student's social security number, or other factors relating to the student's eligibility for funds under the Title IV, HEA programs;

(g) Refers to the Office of Inspector General of the Department of Education for investigation—

(1) After conducting the review of an application provided for under paragraph (f) of this section, any credible information indicating that an applicant for Title IV, HEA program assistance may have engaged in fraud or other criminal misconduct in connection with his or her application. The type of information that an institution must refer is that which is relevant to the eligibility of the applicant for Title IV, HEA program assistance, or the amount of the assistance. Examples of this type of information are—

   (i)   False claims of independent student status;

   (ii)   False claims of citizenship;

   (iii)   Use of false identities;

   (iv)   Forgery of signatures or certifications; and

   (v)   False statements of income; and

(2) Any credible information indicating that any employee, third-party servicer, or other agent of the institution that acts in a capacity that involves the administration of the Title IV, HEA programs, or the receipt of funds under those programs, may have engaged in fraud, misrepresentation, conversion or breach of fidu-

ciary responsibility, or other illegal conduct involving the Title IV, HEA programs. The type of information that an institution must refer is that which is relevant to the eligibility and funding of the institution and its students through the Title IV, HEA programs;

(h) Provides adequate financial aid counseling to eligible students who apply for Title IV, HEA program assistance. In determining whether an institution provides adequate counseling, the Secretary considers whether its counseling includes information regarding—

(1) The source and amount of each type of aid offered;

(2) The method by which aid is determined and disbursed, delivered, or applied to a student's account; and

(3) The rights and responsibilities of the student with respect to enrollment at the institution and receipt of financial aid. This information includes the institution's refund policy, the requirements for the treatment of title IV, HEA program funds when a student withdraws under § 668.22, its standards of satisfactory progress, and other conditions that may alter the student's aid package;

(*i*) Has provided all program and fiscal reports and financial statements required for compliance with the provisions of this part and the individual program regulations in a timely manner;

(j) Shows no evidence of significant problems that affect, as determined by the Secretary, the institution's ability to administer a Title IV, HEA program and that are identified in—

(1) Reviews of the institution conducted by the Secretary, the Department of Education's Office of Inspector General, nationally recognized accrediting agencies, guaranty agencies as defined in 34 CFR part 682, the State agency or official by whose authority the institution is legally authorized to provide postsecondary education, or any other law enforcement agency; or

(2) Any findings made in any criminal, civil, or administrative proceeding;

(k) Is not, and does not have any principal or affiliate of the institution (as those terms are defined in 34 CFR part 85) that is—

(1) Debarred or suspended under Executive Order (E.O.) 12549 (3 CFR, 1986 Comp., p. 189) or the Federal Acquisition Regulations (FAR), 48 CFR part 9, subpart 9.4; or

(2) Engaging in any activity that is a cause under 34 CFR 85.305 or 85.405 for debarment or suspension under E.O. 12549 (3 CFR, 1986 Comp., p. 189) or the FAR, 48 CFR part 9, subpart 9.4;

(*l*) For an institution that seeks initial participation in a Title IV, HEA program, does not have more than 33 percent of its undergraduate regular students withdraw from the institution during the institution's latest completed award year. The institution must count all regular students who are enrolled during the latest completed award year, except those students who, during that period—

(1) Withdrew from, dropped out of, or were expelled from the institution; and

(2) Were entitled to and actually received in a timely manner, a refund of 100 percent of their tuition and fees;

(m)(1) Has a cohort default rate—

(i) Calculated under subpart M of this part, that is less than 25 percent for each of the three most recent fiscal years for which the Secretary has determined the institution's rate; and

(ii) As defined in 34 CFR 674.5, on loans made under the Federal Perkins Loan Program to students for attendance at that institution that does not exceed 15 percent;

(2)(i) However, if the Secretary determines that an institution's administrative capability is impaired solely because the institution fails to comply with paragraph (m)(1) of this section, the Secretary allows the institution to continue to participate in the Title IV, HEA programs but may provisionally certify the institution in accordance with § 668.13(c); and

(ii) The institution may appeal the loss of full participation in a Title IV, HEA program under paragraph (m)(1) of this section by submitting an erroneous data appeal in writing to the Secretary in accordance with and on the grounds specified in subpart M of this part;

(n) Does not otherwise appear to lack the ability to administer the Title IV, HEA programs competently; and

(*o*) Participates in the electronic processes that the Secretary—

(1) Provides at no substantial charge to the institution; and

(2) Identifies through a notice published in the Federal Register.

(Approved by the Office of Management and Budget under control number 1840-0537)

(Authority: 20 U.S.C. 1082, 1985, 1094, and 1099c)

[53 Fed. Reg. 49147, Dec. 6, 1988; 58 Fed. Reg. 32201, June 8, 1993; 59 Fed. Reg. 22423, 22431, April 29, 1994; 59 Fed. Reg. 32657, June 24, 1994; 59 Fed. Reg. 34964, July 7, 1994; 59 Fed. Reg. 61180, Nov. 29, 1994; 60 Fed. Reg. 34431, June 30, 1995; 60 Fed. Reg. 42408, Aug. 15, 1995; 61 Fed. Reg. 60603, Nov. 29, 1996; 62 Fed. Reg. 27128, May 16, 1997; 63 Fed. Reg. 40624, July 29, 1998; 64 Fed. Reg. 59038, Nov. 1, 1999; 65 Fed. Reg. 65637, Nov. 1, 2000]

§ 668.17 [Reserved]

[65 Fed. Reg. 65637, Nov. 1, 2000]

§ 668.18 [Reserved]

[59 Fed. Reg. 61718, Dec. 1, 1994]

§ 668.19 Financial aid history.

(a) Before an institution may disburse title IV, HEA program funds to a student who previously attended another eligible institution, the institution must use information it obtains from the Secretary, through the National Student Loan Data System (NSLDS) or its successor system, to determine—

(1) Whether the student is in default on any title IV, HEA program loan;

(2) Whether the student owes an overpayment on any title IV, HEA program grant or Federal Perkins Loan;

(3) For the award year for which a Federal Pell Grant is requested, the student's scheduled Federal Pell Grant and the amount of Federal Pell Grant funds disbursed to the student;

(4) The outstanding principal balance of loans made to the student under each of the title IV, HEA loan programs; and

(5) For the academic year for which title IV, HEA aid is requested, the amount of, and period of enrollment for, loans made to the student under each of the title IV, HEA loan programs.

(b)(1) If a student transfers from one institution to another institution during the same award year, the institution to which the student transfers must request from the Secretary, through NSLDS, updated information about that student so it can make the determinations required under paragraph (a) of this section; and

(2) The institution may not make a disbursement to that student for seven days following its request, unless it receives the information from NSLDS in response to its request or obtains that information directly by accessing NSLDS, and the information it receives allows it to make that disbursement.

(Approved by the Office of Management and Budget under control number 1845-0537)

(Authority: 20 U.S.C. 1091 and 1094)

[53 Fed. Reg. 33431, Aug. 30, 1988; 58 Fed. Reg. 32203, June 8, 1993; 59 Fed. Reg. 21866, April 26, 1994; 60 Fed. Reg. 61809, Dec. 1, 1995; 63 Fed. Reg. 40624, July 29, 1998; 65 Fed. Reg. 65675, Nov. 1, 2000]

§ 668.20 Limitations on remedial coursework that is eligible for Title IV, HEA program assistance.

(a) A noncredit or reduced credit remedial course is a course of study designed to increase the ability of a student to pursue a course of study leading to a certificate or degree.

(1) A noncredit remedial course is one for which no credit is given toward a certificate or degree; and

(2) A reduced credit remedial course is one for which reduced credit is given toward a certificate or degree.

(b) Except as provided in paragraphs (c) and (d) of this section, in determining a student's enrollment status and cost of attendance, an institution shall include any noncredit or reduced credit remedial course in which the student is enrolled. The institution shall attribute the number of credit or clock hours to a noncredit or reduced credit remedial course by—

(1) Calculating the number of classroom and homework hours required for that course;

(2) Comparing those hours with the hours required for nonremedial courses in a similar subject; and

(3) Giving the remedial course the same number of credit or clock hours it gives the nonremedial course with the most comparable classroom and homework requirements.

(c) In determining a student's enrollment status under the Title IV, HEA programs or a student's cost of attendance under the campus-based, FFEL, and Direct Loan programs, an institution may not take into account any noncredit or reduced credit remedial course if—

(1) That course is part of a program of instruction leading to a high school diploma or the recognized equivalent of a high school diploma, even if the course is necessary to enable the student to complete a degree or certificate program;

(2) The educational level of instruction provided in the noncredit or reduced credit remedial course is below the level needed to pursue successfully the degree or certificate program offered by that institution after one year in that remedial course; or

(3) Except for a course in English as a second language, the educational level of instruction provided in that course is below the secondary level. For purposes of this section, the Secretary considers a course to be below the secondary level if any of the following entities determine that course to be below the secondary level:

(i) The State agency that legally authorized the institution to provide postsecondary education.

(ii) In the case of an accredited or preaccredited institution, the nationally recognized accrediting agency or association that accredits or preaccredits the institution.

(iii) In the case of a public postsecondary vocational institution that is approved by a State agency recognized for the approval of public postsecondary vocational education, the State agency recognized for the approval of public postsecondary vocational education that approves the institution.

(iv) The institution.

(d) Except as set forth in paragraph (f) of this section, an institution may not take into account more than one academic year's worth of noncredit or reduced credit remedial coursework in determining—

(1) A student's enrollment status under the Title IV, HEA programs; and

(2) A student's cost of attendance under the campus-based, FFEL, and Direct Loan programs.

(e) One academic year's worth of noncredit or reduced credit remedial coursework is equivalent to—

(1) Thirty semester or 45 quarter hours; or

(2) Nine hundred clock hours.

(f) Courses in English as a second language do not count against the one-year academic limitation contained in paragraph (d) of this section.

(Authority: 20 U.S.C. 1094)

[56 Fed. Reg. 36698, July 31, 1991; 57 Fed. Reg. 27703, June 22, 1992; 58 Fed. Reg. 32203, June 8, 1993; 59 Fed. Reg. 21866, April 26, 1994; 63 Fed. Reg. 40624, July 29, 1998]

§ 668.21 Treatment of Federal Perkins Loan, FSEOG, and Federal Pell Grant program funds if the recipient withdraws, drops out, or is expelled before his or her first day of class.

(a)(1) If a student officially withdraws, drops out, or is expelled before his or her first day of class of a payment period, all funds paid to the student for that payment period for institutional or noninstitutional costs under the Federal Pell Grant, FSEOG, and Federal Perkins Loan programs are an overpayment.

(2) The institution shall return that overpayment to the respective Title IV, HEA programs in the amount that the student received from each program.

(b) For purposes of this section, the Secretary considers that a student drops out before his or her first day of class of a payment period if the institution is unable to document the student's attendance at any class during the payment period.

(Authority: 20 U.S.C. 1094)

[60 Fed. Reg. 61810, Dec. 1, 1995; 63 Fed. Reg. 40624, July 29, 1998]

§ 668.22 Treatment of Title IV funds when a student withdraws.

(a) *General.*

(1) When a recipient of title IV grant or loan assistance withdraws from an institution during a payment period or period of enrollment in which the recipient began attendance, the institution must determine the amount of title IV grant or loan assistance that

the student earned as of the student's withdrawal date in accordance with paragraph (e) of this section.

(2) For purposes of this section, "title IV grant or loan assistance" includes only assistance from the Federal Perkins Loan, Direct Loan, FFEL, Federal Pell Grant, Academic Competitiveness Grant, National SMART Grant, and FSEOG programs, not including the non-Federal share of FSEOG awards if an institution meets its FSEOG matching share by the individual recipient method or the aggregate method.

(3) If the total amount of title IV grant or loan assistance, or both, that the student earned as calculated under paragraph (e)(1) of this section is less than the amount of title IV grant or loan assistance that was disbursed to the student or on behalf of the student in the case of a PLUS loan, as of the date of the institution's determination that the student withdrew—

   (i) The difference between these amounts must be returned to the title IV programs in accordance with paragraphs (g) and (h) of this section in the order specified in paragraph (i) of this section; and

   (ii) No additional disbursements may be made to the student for the payment period or period of enrollment.

(4) If the total amount of title IV grant or loan assistance, or both, that the student earned as calculated under paragraph (e)(1) of this section is greater than the total amount of title IV grant or loan assistance, or both, that was disbursed to the student or on behalf of the student in the case of a PLUS loan, as of the date of the institution's determination that the student withdrew, the difference between these amounts must be treated as a post-withdrawal disbursement in accordance with paragraph (a)(5) of this section and § 668.164(g).

(5)(i) A post-withdrawal disbursement must be made from available grant funds before available loan funds.

   (ii)(A) If outstanding charges exist on the student's account, the institution may credit the student's account up to the amount of outstanding charges with all or a portion of any—

      (1) Grant funds that make up the post-withdrawal disbursement in accordance with § 668.164(d)(1) and (d)(2); and

      (2) Loan funds that make up the post-withdrawal disbursement in accordance with § 668.164(d)(1), (d)(2) and (d)(3) only after obtaining confirmation from the student or parent, in the case of a parent PLUS loan, that they still wish to have the loan funds disbursed in accordance with paragraph (a)(5)(iii) of this section.

   (B)(1) The institution must offer to disburse directly to a student, or parent in the case of a parent PLUS loan, any amount of a post-withdrawal disbursement that is not credited to the student's account, or for which the institution is not required to obtain confirmation to credit to the student's account, to the student, or the parent in the case of a parent PLUS loan, in accordance with paragraph (a)(5)(iii) of this section.

      (2) The institution must make a direct disbursement of any grant or loan funds that make up the post-withdrawal disbursement only after obtaining the student's, or parent's in the case of a parent PLUS loan, confirmation that they still wish to have the grant or loan funds disbursed in accordance with paragraph (a)(5)(iii).

(iii)(A) The institution must provide within 30 days of the date of the institution's determination that the student withdrew, as defined in paragraph (l)(3) of this section, a written notification to the student, or parent in the case of parent PLUS loan, that—

   (1) Requests confirmation of any post-withdrawal disbursement of loan funds that the institution wishes to credit to the student's account in accordance with paragraph (a)(5)(ii)(A)(2), identifying the type and amount of those loan funds and explaining that a student, or parent in the case of a parent PLUS loan, may accept or decline some or all of those funds;

   (2) Requests confirmation of any post-withdrawal disbursement of grant or loan funds that the student, or parent in the case of a parent PLUS loan, can receive as a direct disbursement, identifying the type and amount of these title IV funds and explaining that the student, or parent in the case of a parent PLUS loan, may accept or decline some or all of those funds;

   (3) Explains that a student, or parent in the case of a parent PLUS loan, who does not confirm that a post-withdrawal disbursement of loan funds may be credited to the student's account may not receive any of those loan funds as a direct disbursement unless the institution concurs;

   (4) Explains the obligation of the student, or parent in the case of a parent PLUS loan, to repay any loan funds he or she chooses to have disbursed; and

   (5) Advises the student, or parent in the case of a parent PLUS loan, that no post-withdrawal disbursement will be made, unless the institution chooses to make a post-withdrawal disbursement based on a late response in accordance with paragraph (a)(5)(iii)(C) of this section, if the student or parent in the case of a parent PLUS loan, does not respond within 14 days of the date that the institution sent the notification, or a later deadline set by the institution.

   (B) The deadline for a student, or parent in the case of a parent PLUS loan, to accept a post-withdrawal disbursement under paragraph (a)(5)(iii)(A)(4) must be the same for both a confirmation of a direct disbursement of the post-withdrawal disbursement and a confirmation of a post-withdrawal disbursement of loan funds to be credited to the student's account;

   (C) If the student, or parent in the case of a parent PLUS loan, submits a timely response that confirms that they wish to receive all or a portion of a direct disbursement of the post-withdrawal disbursement, or confirms that a post-withdrawal disbursement of loan funds may be credited to the student's account, the institution must disburse the funds in the manner specified by the student, or parent in the case of a parent PLUS loan, within 120 days of the date of the institution's determination that the student withdrew, as defined in paragraph (l)(3) of this section.

   (D) If a student, or parent in the case of a parent PLUS loan, submits a late response to the institution's notice requesting confirmation, the institution may make the post-withdrawal disbursement as instructed by the student, or parent in the case of a parent PLUS loan (provided the institution disburses all the funds accepted by the student, or parent in the case of a parent PLUS loan), or decline to do so.

(E) If a student, or parent in the case of a parent PLUS loan, submits a late response to the institution and the institution does not choose to make the post-withdrawal disbursement, the institution must inform the student, or parent in the case of a parent PLUS loan, electronically or in writing of the outcome of the post-withdrawal disbursement request.

(F) If the student, or parent in the case of a parent PLUS loan, does not respond to the institution's notice, no portion of the post-withdrawal disbursement of loan funds that the institution wishes to credit to the student's account, nor any portion that would be disbursed directly to the student, or parent in the case of a parent PLUS loan, may be disbursed.

(iv) An institution must document in the student's file the result of any notification made in accordance with paragraph (a)(5)(iii) of this section of the student's right to cancel all or a portion of loan funds or of the student's right to accept or decline loan funds, and the final determination made concerning the disbursement.

(b) *Withdrawal date for a student who withdraws from an institution that is required to take attendance.*

(1) For purposes of this section, for a student who ceases attendance at an institution that is required to take attendance, including a student who does not return from an approved leave of absence, as defined in paragraph (d) of this section, or a student who takes a leave of absence that does not meet the requirements of paragraph (d) of this section, the student's withdrawal date is the last date of academic attendance as determined by the institution from its attendance records.

(2) An institution must document a student's withdrawal date determined in accordance with paragraph (b)(1) of this section and maintain the documentation as of the date of the institution's determination that the student withdrew, as defined in paragraph (l)(3) of this section.

(3)(i) An institution is required to take attendance if an outside entity (such as the institution's accrediting agency or a State agency) has a requirement, as determined by the entity, that the institution take attendance.

(ii) If an outside entity requires an institution to take attendance for only some students, the institution must use its attendance records to determine a withdrawal date in accordance with paragraph (b)(1) of this section for those students.

(c) *Withdrawal date for a student who withdraws from an institution that is not required to take attendance.*

(1) For purposes of this section, for a student who ceases attendance at an institution that is not required to take attendance, the student's withdrawal date is—

(i) The date, as determined by the institution, that the student began the withdrawal process prescribed by the institution;

(ii) The date, as determined by the institution, that the student otherwise provided official notification to the institution, in writing or orally, of his or her intent to withdraw;

(iii) If the student ceases attendance without providing official notification to the institution of his or her withdrawal in accordance with paragraph (c)(1)(i) or (c)(1)(ii) of this

section, the mid-point of the payment period (or period of enrollment, if applicable);

(iv) If the institution determines that a student did not begin the institution's withdrawal process or otherwise provide official notification (including notice from an individual acting on the student's behalf) to the institution of his or her intent to withdraw because of illness, accident, grievous personal loss, or other such circumstances beyond the student's control, the date that the institution determines is related to that circumstance;

(v) If a student does not return from an approved leave of absence as defined in paragraph (d) of this section, the date that the institution determines the student began the leave of absence; or

(vi) If a student takes a leave of absence that does not meet the requirements of paragraph (d) of this section, the date that the student began the leave of absence.

(2)(i)(A) An institution may allow a student to rescind his or her official notification to withdraw under paragraph (c)(1)(i) or (ii) of this section by filing a written statement that he or she is continuing to participate in academically-related activities and intends to complete the payment period or period of enrollment.

(B) If the student subsequently ceases to attend the institution prior to the end of the payment period or period of enrollment, the student's rescission is negated and the withdrawal date is the student's original date under paragraph (c)(1)(i) or (ii) of this section, unless a later date is determined under paragraph (c)(3) of this section.

(ii) If a student both begins the withdrawal process prescribed by the institution and otherwise provides official notification of his or her intent to withdraw in accordance with paragraphs (c)(1)(i) and (c)(1)(ii) of this section respectively, the student's withdrawal date is the earlier date unless a later date is determined under paragraph (c)(3) of this section.

(3)(i) Notwithstanding paragraphs (c)(1) and (2) of this section, an institution that is not required to take attendance may use as the student's withdrawal date a student's last date of attendance at an academically-related activity provided that the institution documents that the activity is academically related and documents the student's attendance at the activity.

(ii) An "academically-related activity" includes, but is not limited to, an exam, a tutorial, computer-assisted instruction, academic counseling, academic advisement, turning in a class assignment or attending a study group that is assigned by the institution.

(4) An institution must document a student's withdrawal date determined in accordance with paragraphs (c)(1), (2), and (3) of this section and maintain the documentation as of the date of the institution's determination that the student withdrew, as defined in paragraph (l)(3) of this section.

(5)(i) "Official notification to the institution" is a notice of intent to withdraw that a student provides to an office designated by the institution.

(ii) An institution must designate one or more offices at the institution that a student may readily contact to provide official notification of withdrawal.

(d) *Approved leave of absence.*

(1) For purposes of this section (and, for a title IV, HEA program loan borrower, for purposes of terminating the student's in-school status), an institution does not have to treat a leave of absence as a withdrawal if it is an approved leave of absence. A leave of absence is an approved leave of absence if—

(i) The institution has a formal policy regarding leaves of absence;

(ii) The student followed the institution's policy in requesting the leave of absence;

(iii) The institution determines that there is a reasonable expectation that the student will return to the school;

(iv) The institution approved the student's request in accordance with the institution's policy;

(v) The leave of absence does not involve additional charges by the institution;

(vi) The number of days in the approved leave of absence, when added to the number of days in all other approved leaves of absence, does not exceed 180 days in any 12-month period;

(vii) Except for a clock hour or nonterm credit hour program, upon the student's return from the leave of absence, the student is permitted to complete the coursework he or she began prior to the leave of absence; and

(viii) If the student is a title IV, HEA program loan recipient, the institution explains to the student, prior to granting the leave of absence, the effects that the student's failure to return from a leave of absence may have on the student's loan repayment terms, including the exhaustion of some or all of the student's grace period.

(2) If a student does not resume attendance at the institution at or before the end of a leave of absence that meets the requirements of this section, the institution must treat the student as a withdrawal in accordance with the requirements of this section.

(3) For purposes of this paragraph—

(i) The number of days in a leave of absence is counted beginning with the first day of the student's initial leave of absence in a 12-month period.

(ii) A "12-month period" begins on the first day of the student's initial leave of absence.

(iii) An institution's leave of absence policy is a "formal policy" if the policy—

(A) Is in writing and publicized to students; and

(B) Requires students to provide a written, signed, and dated request, that includes the reason for the request, for a leave of absence prior to the leave of absence. However, if unforeseen circumstances prevent a student from providing a prior written request, the institution may grant the student's request for a leave of absence, if the institution documents its decision and collects the written request at a later date.

(e) *Calculation of the amount of title IV assistance earned by the student*.

(1) *General*. The amount of title IV grant or loan assistance that is earned by the student is calculated by—

(i) Determining the percentage of title IV grant or loan assistance that has been earned by the student, as described in paragraph (e)(2) of this section; and

(ii) Applying this percentage to the total amount of title IV grant or loan assistance that was disbursed (and that could have been disbursed, as defined in paragraph (l)(1) of this

section) to the student, or on the student's behalf, for the payment period or period of enrollment as of the student's withdrawal date.

(2) *Percentage earned*. The percentage of title IV grant or loan assistance that has been earned by the student is—

(i) Equal to the percentage of the payment period or period of enrollment that the student completed (as determined in accordance with paragraph (f) of this section) as of the student's withdrawal date, if this date occurs on or before—

(A) Completion of 60 percent of the payment period or period of enrollment for a program that is measured in credit hours; or

(B) Sixty percent of the clock hours scheduled to be completed for the payment period or period of enrollment for a program that is measured in clock hours; or

(ii) 100 percent, if the student's withdrawal date occurs after—

(A) Completion of 60 percent of the payment period or period of enrollment for a program that is measured in credit hours; or

(B) Sixty percent of the clock hours scheduled to be completed for the payment period or period of enrollment for a program measured in clock hours.

(3) *Percentage unearned*. The percentage of title IV grant or loan assistance that has not been earned by the student is calculated by determining the complement of the percentage of title IV grant or loan assistance earned by the student as described in paragraph (e)(2) of this section.

(4) *Total amount of unearned title IV assistance to be returned*. The unearned amount of title IV assistance to be returned is calculated by subtracting the amount of title IV assistance earned by the student as calculated under paragraph (e)(1) of this section from the amount of title IV aid that was disbursed to the student as of the date of the institution's determination that the student withdrew.

(5) *Use of payment period or period of enrollment*.

(i) The treatment of title IV grant or loan funds if a student withdraws must be determined on a payment period basis for a student who attended a standard term-based (semester, trimester, or quarter) educational program.

(ii)(A) The treatment of title IV grant or loan funds if a student withdraws may be determined on either a payment period basis or a period of enrollment basis for a student who attended a non-term based educational program or a nonstandard term-based educational program.

(B) An institution must consistently use either a payment period or period of enrollment for all purposes of this section for each of the following categories of students who withdraw from the same non-term based or nonstandard term-based educational program:

(1) Students who have attended an educational program at the institution from the beginning of the payment period or period of enrollment.

(2) Students who re-enter the institution during a payment period or period of enrollment.

(3) Students who transfer into the institution during a payment period or period of enrollment.

(f) *Percentage of payment period or period of enrollment completed*.

(1) For purposes of paragraph (e)(2)(i) of this section, the percentage of the payment period or period of enrollment completed is determined—

(i) In the case of a program that is measured in credit hours, by dividing the total number of calendar days in the payment period or period of enrollment into the number of calendar days completed in that period as of the student's withdrawal date; and

(ii)(A) In the case of a program that is measured in clock hours, by dividing the total number of clock hours in the payment period or period of enrollment into the number of clock hours scheduled to be completed as of the student's withdrawal date.

(B) The scheduled clock hours used must be those established by the institution prior to the student's beginning class date for the payment period or period of enrollment and must be consistent with the published materials describing the institution's programs, unless the schedule was modified prior to the student's withdrawal.

(C) The schedule must have been established in accordance with requirements of the accrediting agency and the State licensing agency, if such standards exist.

(2)(i) The total number of calendar days in a payment period or period of enrollment includes all days within the period, except that scheduled breaks of at least five consecutive days are excluded from the total number of calendar days in a payment period or period of enrollment and the number of calendar days completed in that period.

(ii) The total number of calendar days in a payment period or period of enrollment does not include days in which the student was on an approved leave of absence.

(g) *Return of unearned aid, responsibility of the institution.*

(1) The institution must return, in the order specified in paragraph (i) of this section, the lesser of—

(i) The total amount of unearned title IV assistance to be returned as calculated under paragraph (e)(4) of this section; or

(ii) An amount equal to the total institutional charges incurred by the student for the payment period or period of enrollment multiplied by the percentage of title IV grant or loan assistance that has not been earned by the student, as described in paragraph (e)(3) of this section.

(2) For purposes of this section, "institutional charges" are tuition, fees, room and board (if the student contracts with the institution for the room and board) and other educationally-related expenses assessed by the institution.

(3) If, for a non-term program an institution chooses to calculate the treatment of title IV assistance on a payment period basis, but the institution charges for a period that is longer than the payment period, "total institutional charges incurred by the student for the payment period" is the greater of—

(i) The prorated amount of institutional charges for the longer period; or

(ii) The amount of title IV assistance retained for institutional charges as of the student's withdrawal date.

(h) *Return of unearned aid, responsibility of the student.*

(1) After the institution has allocated the unearned funds for which it is responsible in accordance with paragraph (g) of this section, the student must return assistance for which the student is responsible in the order specified in paragraph (i) of this section.

(2) The amount of assistance that the student is responsible for returning is calculated by subtracting the amount of unearned aid that the institution is required to return under paragraph (g) of this section from the total amount of unearned title IV assistance to be returned under paragraph (e)(4) of this section.

(3) The student (or parent in the case of funds due to a parent PLUS Loan) must return or repay, as appropriate, the amount determined under paragraph (h)(1) of this section to—

(i) Any title IV loan program in accordance with the terms of the loan; and

(ii) Any title IV grant program as an overpayment of the grant; however, a student is not required to return the following—

(A) The portion of a grant overpayment amount that is equal to or less than 50 percent of the total grant assistance that was disbursed (and that could have been disbursed, as defined in paragraph (l)(1) of this section) to the student for the payment period or period of enrollment.

(B) A grant overpayment amount, as determined after application of paragraph (h)(3)(ii)(A) of this section, of 50 dollars or less that is not a remaining balance.

(4)(i) A student who owes an overpayment under this section remains eligible for title IV, HEA program funds through and beyond the earlier of 45 days from the date the institution sends a notification to the student of the overpayment, or 45 days from the date the institution was required to notify the student of the overpayment if, during those 45 days the student—

(A) Repays the overpayment in full to the institution;

(B) Enters into a repayment agreement with the institution in accordance with repayment arrangements satisfactory to the institution; or

(C) Signs a repayment agreement with the Secretary, which will include terms that permit a student to repay the overpayment while maintaining his or her eligibility for title IV, HEA program funds.

(ii) Within 30 days of the date of the institution's determination that the student withdrew, an institution must send a notice to any student who owes a title IV, HEA grant overpayment as a result of the student's withdrawal from the institution in order to recover the overpayment in accordance with paragraph (h)(4)(i) of this section.

(iii) If an institution chooses to enter into a repayment agreement in accordance with paragraph (h)(4)(i)(B) of this section with a student who owes an overpayment of title IV, HEA grant funds, it must—

(A) Provide the student with terms that permit the student to repay the overpayment while maintaining his or her eligibility for title IV, HEA program funds; and

(B) Require repayment of the full amount of the overpayment within two years of the date of the institution's determination that the student withdrew.

(iv) An institution must refer to the Secretary, in accordance with procedures required by the Secretary, an overpayment of title IV, HEA grant funds owed by a student as a result of the student's withdrawal from the institution if—

(A) The student does not repay the overpayment in full to the institution, or enter a repayment agreement with the institution or the Secretary in accordance with paragraph (h)(4)(i) of this section within the earlier of 45 days from the date the institution sends a notification to the student of the overpayment, or 45 days from the date the institution was required to notify the student of the overpayment;

(B) At any time the student fails to meet the terms of the repayment agreement with the institution entered into in accordance with paragraph (h)(4)(i)(B) of this section; or

(C) The student chooses to enter into a repayment agreement with the Secretary.

(v) A student who owes an overpayment is ineligible for title IV, HEA program funds—

(A) If the student does not meet the requirements in paragraph (h)(4)(i) of this section, on the day following the 45-day period in that paragraph; or

(B) As of the date the student fails to meet the terms of the repayment agreement with the institution or the Secretary entered into in accordance with paragraph (h)(4)(i) of this section.

(vi) A student who is ineligible under paragraph (h)(4)(v) of this section regains eligibility if the student and the Secretary enter into a repayment agreement.

(5) The Secretary may waive grant overpayment amounts that students are required to return under this section if the withdrawals on which the returns are based are withdrawals by students—

(i) Who were residing in, employed in, or attending an institution of higher education that is located in an area in which the President has declared that a major disaster exists, in accordance with section 401 of the Robert T. Stafford Disaster Relief and Emergency Assistance Act (42 U.S.C. 5170);

(ii) Whose attendance was interrupted because of the impact of the disaster on the student or institution; and

(iii) Whose withdrawal ended within the award year during which the designation occurred or during the next succeeding award year.

(i) Order of return of title IV funds.

(1) *Loans.* Unearned funds returned by the institution or the student, as appropriate, in accordance with paragraph (g) or (h) of this section respectively, must be credited to outstanding balances on title IV loans made to the student or on behalf of the student for the payment period or period of enrollment for which a return of funds is required. Those funds must be credited to outstanding balances for the payment period or period of enrollment for which a return of funds is required in the following order:

(i) Unsubsidized Federal Stafford loans.

(ii) Subsidized Federal Stafford loans.

(iii) Unsubsidized Federal Direct Stafford loans.

(iv) Subsidized Federal Direct Stafford loans.

(v) Federal Perkins loans.

(vi) Federal PLUS loans received on behalf of the student.

(vii) Federal Direct PLUS received on behalf of the student.

(2) *Remaining funds.* If unearned funds remain to be returned after repayment of all outstanding loan amounts, the remaining excess must be credited to any amount awarded for the payment period or period of enrollment for which a return of funds is required in the following order:

(i) Federal Pell Grants.

(ii) Academic Competitiveness Grants.

(iii) National SMART Grants.

(iv) FSEOG Program aid.

(j) *Timeframe for the return of title IV funds.*

(1) An institution must return the amount of title IV funds for which it is responsible under paragraph (g) of this section as soon as possible but no later than 45 days after the date of the institution's determination that the student withdrew as defined in paragraph (l)(3) of this section. The timeframe for returning funds is further described in § 668.173(b).

(2) An institution must determine the withdrawal date for a student who withdraws without providing notification to the institution no later than 30 days after the end of the earlier of the—

(i) Payment period or period of enrollment, as appropriate, in accordance with paragraph (e)(5) of this section;

(ii) Academic year in which the student withdrew; or

(iii) Educational program from which the student withdrew.

(k) *Consumer information.* An institution must provide students with information about the requirements of this section in accordance with § 668.43.

(l) *Definitions.* For purposes of this section—

(1) Title IV grant or loan funds that "could have been disbursed" are determined in accordance with the late disbursement provisions in § 668.164(g).

(2) A "period of enrollment" is the academic period established by the institution for which institutional charges are generally assessed (*i.e.*, length of the student's program or academic year).

(3) The "date of the institution's determination that the student withdrew" is—

(i) For a student who provides notification to the institution of his or her withdrawal, the student's withdrawal date as determined under paragraph (c) of this section or the date of notification of withdrawal, whichever is later;

(ii) For a student who did not provide notification of his of her withdrawal to the institution, the date that the institution becomes aware that the student ceased attendance;

(iii) For a student who does not return from an approved leave of absence, the earlier of the date of the end of the leave of absence or the date the student notifies the institution that he or she will not be returning to the institution; or

(iv) For a student whose rescission is negated under paragraph (c)(2)(i)(B) of this section, the date the institution becomes aware that the student did not, or will not, complete the payment period or period of enrollment.

(v) For a student who takes a leave of absence that is not approved in accordance with paragraph (d) of this section, the date that the student begins the leave of absence.

(4) A "recipient of title IV grant or loan assistance" is a student for whom the requirements of § 668.164(g)(2) have been met.

(Approved by the Office of Management and Budget under control number 1845-0022)

(Authority: 20 U.S.C. 1091b)

[53 Fed. Reg. 49147, Dec. 6, 1988; 58 Fed. Reg. 32202, June 8, 1993; 59 Fed. Reg. 21866, April 26, 1994; 59 Fed. Reg. 22436, April 29, 1994; 59 Fed. Reg. 32657, June 24, 1994; 59 Fed. Reg. 34964, July 7, 1994; 59 Fed. Reg. 61180, Nov. 29, 1994; 60 Fed. Reg. 34431, June 30, 1995; 60 Fed. Reg. 42408, Aug. 15, 1995; 60 Fed. Reg. 61810, Dec. 1, 1995; 61 Fed. Reg. 60396, Nov. 27, 1996; 63 Fed. Reg. 40624, July 29, 1998; 64 Fed. Reg. 59038, Nov. 1, 1999; 67 Fed. Reg. 67073, Nov. 1, 2002; 71 Fed. Reg. 45666, Sept. 8, 2006]

Department of Education Policy Guidance Letters

The Department of Education Office of Postsecondary Education periodically distributes "Dear Colleague" and "Dear Guaranty Agency" letters. These are used to communicate Department instructions and directives. This appendix contains a selection of Dear Colleague letters of particular significance for low-income borrowers. The most efficient way to obtain additional copies or to search for other Dear Colleague letters is through the Department of Education website at http://ifap.ed.gov/IFAPWebApp/currentDPCLettersPag.jsp (last accessed in June 2006). The general website is www.ed.gov. The letters are sorted on-line by publication year and by subject matter. Only letters from 1995 or later are available. The letters in this appendix can also be found on the companion CD-Rom to this manual.

C.1 Discharges

MAY 2002, GEN-02-03

This letter explains the new procedures for disability discharges, effective July 1, 2002.

Publication Date: May 2002

GEN-02-03
CB-02-08
G-02-334
L-02-228

SUBJECT: New Total and Permanent Disability Discharge Procedures for Title IV Loans— Effective July 1, 2002

SUMMARY: This letter discusses implementation of the regulatory changes for total and permanent disability discharges in the Federal Perkins Loan, Federal Family Education Loan (FFEL), and the William D. Ford Federal Direct Loan programs. The final regulations were published on November 1, 2000. While some of the provisions went into effect on July 1, 2001, most of the regulatory changes become effective July 1, 2002. This letter provides guidance to Perkins school lenders, FFEL lenders, and guaranty agencies on the new procedures for processing total and permanent disability discharge requests.

Dear Colleague:

To address weaknesses in the procedures for granting total and permanent disability discharges on federal student loans identified in a June 1999 report issued by the Department's Inspector General, the Department conducted a negotiated rulemaking process with representatives from the higher education community from January to May 2000. All members of the negotiating committee could not reach agreement on the proposed regulatory changes, and the Department published proposed regulations for public comment on August 2, 2000.

After considering the public comments received on the proposed regulations and making changes where appropriate, the Department published final regulations on November 1, 2000, that significantly revise the process for granting disability discharges. In addition, as part of those regulations, the definition of total and permanent disability was changed, removing the requirement that a borrower be unable to attend school. This revised definition became effective July 1, 2001.

Under the changed definition, a borrower is totally and permanently disabled if the borrower: "is unable to work and earn money because of an injury or illness that is expected to continue indefinitely or result in death" [34 C.F.R. §§ 674.51(s), 682.200]. The final regulations also made significant changes to the process for evaluating disability discharge applications. Those changes will go into effect on July 1, 2002.

This Dear Colleague Letter provides a general overview of the disability discharge regulations and procedures that go into effect on July 1, 2002. In addition, Attachments 1 and 2 to this letter provide guidance specific to Perkins school lenders and FFEL lenders and guarantors. Attachment 3 outlines the role of the Department in the new process.

I. Overview of Regulatory Changes

The regulatory changes revising the process for granting total and permanent disability discharges are contained in 34 C.F.R. § 674. 61(b) of the Perkins regulations, 34 C.F.R. §§ 682.402(c) and 682.402(r) of the FFEL regulations, and 34 C.F.R. § 685.213 of the Direct Loan regulations. Under the new regulations, the disability discharge procedures are as follows:

1. The borrower applies to the loan holder (i.e., the current owner of the loan) for a disability discharge. For Perkins Loans, the loan holder is the Perkins school lender. For FFEL loans, the loan holder is a lender or, if the loan has gone into default, a guaranty agency. For Direct Loans and other Title IV loans assigned to the Department, the loan holder is the U.S. Department of Education.

The loan holder must make a preliminary determination as to whether the borrower meets the criteria for a total and permanent disability discharge. For Perkins loans, the preliminary determination is made by the school. In the FFEL Program, the current loan holder makes the determination. For Direct Loans, the preliminary determination is made by Direct Loan staff. For other loans held by the Department, the preliminary determination is made by the Department's Federal Student Aid (FSA) Collections. In addition, for FFEL loans, the guaranty agency conducts an independent evaluation of the discharge request after the FFEL lender makes a preliminary determination that the borrower qualifies for the discharge, except in the case where the guaranty agency is the current loan holder and the borrower submitted the discharge request directly to the guaranty agency.

2. If during the preliminary determination a loan holder, guaranty agency or the Department determines that the borrower does not meet the criteria for a disability discharge, the discharge request is denied, the loan is returned to its prior status and, as appropriate, collection activity or regular servicing resumes on the loan.

3. For Perkins Loans, if the school determines that a borrower meets the criteria for a disability discharge, it must assign the loan to the Department's Disability Discharge Unit. For FFEL loans, the loan is assigned to the Department's Disability Discharge Unit if both the loan holder and the guaranty agency determine that a borrower meets the criteria for a total and permanent disability discharge.

4. The Department reviews all assigned loans with discharge applications to affirm that the borrower meets the criteria for a discharge. If we affirm that the borrower meets the criteria for a total and permanent disability discharge, the loan is placed in a conditional discharge status for three years. During this conditional discharge period, the borrower is not required to make payments and interest does not accrue.

5. During this conditional discharge period, we will monitor whether the borrower has been able to work and earn money or has received a new Title IV loan in order to ensure that the borrower continues to qualify for the total and permanent disability discharge. At the end of the conditional discharge period, we will make a determination that the borrower has met the definition of total and permanent disability if he or she has not had annual earnings from work during the conditional discharge period in excess of the poverty level for a family of two, and has not received any new Title IV loans during the period. If these conditions are met throughout the conditional discharge period, we will grant a final discharge.

6. In some cases, a borrower may have become totally and permanently disabled, as determined by a physician, three or more years before the loan is assigned. In these cases, the initial determination of eligibility—based on the borrower's medical documentation—and the final determination of eligibility—based on the borrower's earnings and subsequent Title IV loan activity—will be conducted at the same time and we may immediately grant a final discharge.

During the discharge process, borrowers will be given a phone number to call and speak with a representative if they have any questions about their discharge requests. Borrowers will also be told that they may contact our Student Loan Ombudsman for assistance in resolving disputes. However, as with the current total and permanent disability discharge process, there is no formal appeals process for a borrower who is denied a discharge.

II. *Application Availability and Effective Date For Use*

Currently, disability discharge requests in the FFEL and Direct Loan Program are processed using the form titled "Loan Discharge Application: Total and Permanent Disability" [OMB Number 1845-0015]. Perkins school lenders do not currently use a Department of Education form for processing disability discharge requests, although they have a comparable application process. We have developed a new total and permanent disability discharge application for use in all three of the Title IV loan programs. This form is currently under review by the Office of Management and budget. After this new total and permanent disability discharge application form is approved by OMB in the next few weeks, we will make it immediately available to the financial aid community by posting it to the Information for Financial Aid Professionals (IFAP) web site as an attachment to a Dear Colleague Letter. The new disability discharge application must be provided to all borrowers who request total and permanent disability discharges on or after July 1, 2002. However, program participants may use the previous form for borrowers who were in the discharge process prior to July 1, 2002, but must follow the new standards and procedures for all disability discharge determinations made on or after July 1, 2002.

III. *Triggering Date for Implementation of New Procedures*

The new standards and procedures for granting total and permanent disability discharges resulting from the November 1, 2000 final regulations that are discussed in this letter go into effect on July 1, 2002.

For all disability discharge requests approved on or after July 1, 2002 based on the previously approved total and permanent disability discharge form (or a school form for Perkins borrowers), the loan holder must, in the preliminary determination letter, inform the borrower that the regulations governing disability discharges have changed and explain the new total and permanent disability eligibility criteria and discharge process.

IV. *Department's Expectations for Holders' Preliminary Determinations*

We expect loan holders and guaranty agencies to conduct rigorous evaluations of disability discharge requests. If the borrower's medical documentation does not support the conclusion that the borrower is unable to work and earn money because of an injury or illness that is expected to continue indefinitely or result in death, the discharge request should be denied. Loan holders and guarantors should follow the guidance for reviewing disability claims that was provided in Dear Guaranty Agency Director Letter 99-G-324, dated November 1999. This guidance states that loan holders are expected to:

1. Require additional documentation to support a borrower's application if the information provided by the borrower is not definitive, is illegible, or is incomplete.
2. Require the physician to affirm certification of disability if the diagnosis does not appear to satisfy the standard for discharge. If it appears that the physician has used a less rigorous standard in certifying the borrower's disability, loan holders should clarify the definition of "total and permanent disability" with the physician.

Loan holders may want to seek the assistance of a qualified physician to evaluate total and permanent disability discharge requests, as appropriate. Loan holders should also report to the

Department's Office of Inspector General any questionable patterns related to physicians' certifying signatures or state licensing numbers regarding the legitimacy of the disability discharge request.

The Attachments to this letter provide more detailed information on the new eligibility criteria and procedures for granting total and permanent disability discharges.

We would like to thank the student financial aid community for its assistance in developing these new procedures and designing the new total and permanent disability discharge form. We look forward to continuing to work with you to ensure that only those borrowers who are eligible will continue to receive total and permanent disability discharges on their Title IV loans. Thank you for your cooperation in implementing these new safeguards and your continued support of the federal student financial assistance programs.

Sincerely,

Jeffrey R. Andrade
Deputy Assistant Secretary for Policy, Planning, and Innovation
Office of Postsecondary Education

Greg Woods
Chief Operating Officer
Federal Student Aid

Attachments/Enclosures

Attachment 1: Federal Perkins Loan Program
Attachment 2: FFEL Program
Attachment 3: Department of Education

[*Editor's Note: Attachments not reprinted herein.*]

NOVEMBER 1999, G-99-36

Publication Date: November 1999

GEN-99-36
99-G-324
00-L-217

Subject: Revised Procedures Related to Death and Total and Permanent Disability Discharge Requests for the Federal Family Education Loan (FFEL) Program

Dear Guaranty Agency Director:

The Department of Education's Office of Inspector General (OIG) recently completed a study of the process for granting discharges of Federal Family Education Loan (FFEL) Program loans due to death or total and permanent disability. The OIG's audit report focused on FFEL loan discharges granted from July 1, 1994 through December 31, 1996. Through a match of all borrowers receiving these discharges during this period with the Social Security Administration's master earning records, the OIG found that 23 percent of borrowers who received disability discharges during this period worked and earned money after the disability determination was made or the loan was discharged. The OIG also found that 2 percent of borrowers who received a discharge of their loan based on death were working and earning money after the loan was discharged. The OIG concluded from its review that inappropriate discharges were being provided to borrowers because of weaknesses in the current system for determining eligibility for the discharges. After reviewing the OIG report we have decided to implement the following changes to strengthen control of the process for granting death and disability discharges.

Loan Discharges Due to Death

We are concerned that documentation used to support discharges based on death may be easily forged or may not provide definitive proof of death. Section 682.402(b)(2) of the FFEL program regulations provides that the lender (or guaranty agency) may rely on a death certificate or other proof of death that is acceptable under applicable state law. If such documentation is not available, the guaranty agency is authorized to discharge a loan only if it determines that other evidence establishes that the borrower (or dependent student on whose behalf a parent has borrowed a PLUS loan) has died.

In order to strengthen the process of evaluating applications for discharge of loans based on death, we have decided that it is appropriate to interpret the regulations to require, generally, that a death cancellation may only be granted based on an *original* or *certified* copy of the death certificate. We believe this interpretation is consistent with the language of the regulation since certified death certificates are generally the ultimate proof of death under state law. In situations where the guaranty agency is unable to obtain an original or certified copy of the death certificate, it should contact our Financial Partners Channel.

We understand that stricter documentation standards for discharges based on death may lengthen the period required for securing the death certificate. The regulations in Section 682.402(b)(3) require the loan holder to suspend collection activity on a loan for 60 days after receiving a request for a death discharge while attempting to obtain the documentation needed to grant the discharge. To be sensitive to the needs of the bereaved family, the Secretary will authorize guaranty agencies to extend the suspension of collection activities an additional 60 days if extra time is needed to obtain the necessary documentation.

Loan Discharges Due to Total and Permanent Disability

Under Section 682.200, an individual is considered totally and permanently disabled for loan discharge purposes only if the individual is "unable to work and earn money or attend school because of an injury or illness that is expected to continue indefinitely or result in death." To address the issue of individuals receiving total and permanent disability discharges for conditions that do not meet this regulatory definition, we are requesting guaranty agencies to implement a more rigorous evaluation process for determining if a borrower qualifies for a total and permanent disability discharge. This process should include at a minimum:

- Requiring additional documentation to support the borrower's application for loan discharge in cases where the information provided in the initial application is not definitive, is illegible or is incomplete. Loan holders may assist borrowers who are having difficulty paying their loans while their claims are being evaluated by granting forbearance or otherwise ceasing collection activities during the evaluation period.
- Reaffirming the physician's certification if the diagnosis and prognosis do not appear to reach the standard of total and permanent disability. A disability discharge should not be granted based solely on the physician's certification if there is a question of the borrower's eligibility for the discharge. In such cases, agencies should contact the physician and review with the physician the standard that must be met to certify that a borrower is totally and permanently disabled. The guaranty agency should ensure that physicians clearly understand that the FFEL definition of total and permanent disability ("unable to work and earn money or attend school because of an injury or illness that is expected to continue indefinitely or result in death") generally is a higher standard than that used by other federal or state agencies for disability related benefits or programs. Guaranty agencies are urged to consider retaining the services of a physician to assist them in evaluating claims for which there is a question related to the disabling medical condition and the prognosis for recovery. If a guaranty agency is still not satisfied that a borrower qualifies for a total and permanent disability discharge, the guaranty agency may require the borrower to obtain a second opinion from another physician instead of simply denying the discharge claim.
- Assisting borrowers to obtain a deferment or forbearance in cases when it does not appear that the borrower is totally and permanently disabled, but there is evidence that the borrower's ability to repay has been impaired by a temporary disability. Although the temporary total disability deferment is not available to new borrowers after July 1, 1993,

these borrowers may qualify for an economic hardship deferment as a result of economic difficulties stemming from the temporary disability.

We have revised the Total and Permanent Disability Cancellation Request form to ask the physician to identify whether he or she is a doctor of medicine or a doctor of osteopathy. The revised form also requires physicians to provide their state professional license number. The revised Total and Permanent Disability Cancellation Request form is currently available on our IFAP web site at http://ifap.ed.gov and on the NCHELP web site at www.nchelp.org.

Future Activities

In consultation with guaranty agencies, lenders, and other interested parties, we expect to propose further changes to the Total and Permanent Disability Cancellation Request form to collect additional information regarding the borrower's disabling condition and prognosis for recovery that will assist agency staff in their reviews. We will also begin discussions with program constituents on other possible options for overhauling the process of granting disability discharges.

We will continue to explore strategies for ensuring that ineligible claims for loan discharges due to death or total and permanent disability are not granted. We appreciate the suggestions you shared for implementing short-term solutions. We look forward to working with you to develop and implement a process that balances the need to ensure program integrity with the need for prompt decisions and sensitivity involving a minimum of burden for borrowers and their families.

Contact Person

Should you have questions or suggestions concerning the discharge process, please contact Cameron Ishaq. Mr. Ishaq will serve as the Department's contact person for guaranty agencies on issues related to death and total and permanent disability discharges. You can e-mail Mr. Ishaq at cameron_ishaq@ed.gov, telephone him at (202) 260-5076, or send him a FAX at (202) 708-8404.

Sincerely,

Jeff Baker, Director
Program Development Division

Enclosure A

SEPTEMBER 1995, GEN-95-42

Publication Date: September 1995

GEN-95-42

SUBJECT: Loan discharges based on improper determination that a student had the ability-to-benefit (ATB) from the school's training.

REFERENCE: § 34 CFR 682.402(e) and § 685.214(a)

Dear Colleague:

Section 437(c)(1) of the Higher Education Act of 1965, as amended (HEA) provides for the discharge of a borrower's loan obligation under the Federal Family Education Loan (FFEL) Program, and § 455(a)(1) makes this relief available under the William D. Ford Federal Direct Loan Program, if the student's eligibility to borrow was falsely certified by the school. In September 1994, initial guidance concerning these loan discharges was provided in "Dear Colleague" Letter 94-L-166/G-256 issued to lenders and guaranty agencies in the FFEL Program. However, in the area of discharges based on a school's defective determination of a student's ability-to-benefit (ATB), the "Dear Colleague" Letter promised more detailed guidance concerning those discharges.

This letter addresses some common questions about discharges based on improper ATB determinations that have been asked by borrowers, lenders, guaranty agencies, and other parties. The Department intends to apply the guidance in this letter to similar false certification discharges in the William D. Ford Federal Direct Loan Program.

Thank you for ensuring that the intent of the false certification discharge provision is achieved. For further information, you may contact the Department's Customer Support Inquiry Service between the hours of 9:00 AM and 5:00 PM Eastern Time, at 1-800-433-7327. After hours calls will be accepted by an automated voice response system. Callers leaving their name and phone number will receive a return call the next business day. You may FAX your inquiry to the Customer Support Inquiry Service at any time by calling (202) 260-4199.

Sincerely,

Elizabeth M. Hicks
Deputy Assistant Secretary for Student Financial Assistance

Enclosure

Enclosure A:

SUMMARY OF ATB REQUIREMENTS[1]

For periods of enrollment beginning January 1, 1986[2] through June 30, 1987

The school could determine that the student had the ability to benefit from the school's training in accordance with the requirements of 34 CFR 668.6, as those regulations existed at that time. The school simply had to "develop and consistently apply criteria" to determine if regular students who did not have a high school diploma or GED, and who were beyond the age of compulsory attendance, had the ability to benefit from the school's training.

For periods of enrollment beginning July 1, 1987 through June 30, 1991

Schools were required to use one of the following standards for admission of students without a high school diploma or its equivalent on the basis of ATB in accordance with 34 CFR 668.7 as it was in effect at that time: (1) the student received a GED prior to the student's completion of the program or by the end of the first year of the program, whichever was earlier; (2) the student was counseled prior to admission and successfully completed the school's program of remedial or developmental education that did not exceed one academic year or its equivalent; (3) the student passed a nationally recognized, standardized, or industry-developed ATB test, subject to criteria developed by the school's accrediting association; or (4) if the student failed the ATB test, he or she successfully completed the school's program of remedial or developmental education that did not exceed one academic year or its equivalent.

For periods of enrollment beginning July 1, 1991 through July 22, 1992

A student who was not a high school graduate or did not have a GED at the time of enrollment must have passed an independently administered ATB test approved by the Department[3] before the student's receipt of Title IV aid.

For periods of enrollment beginning on or after July 23, 1992

---

1   This summary presents a brief overview of some of the major ATB requirements over time. The Department has issued several "Dear Colleague" Letters that explained ATB requirements in greater detail. The reader may find "Dear Colleague" Letters GEN-89-55 (December 1989), GEN-90-33 (September 1990), and GEN-91-20 (June 1991) to be particularly helpful.

2   Sections 437(c)(1) and 455(a)(1) of the HEA do not authorize loan discharges based on defective ATB determination for loans made before January 1, 1986.

3   Listings of approved tests were published in the Federal Register on December 19, 1990 and December 30, 1992, and in "Dear Colleague" Letter GEN-93-21 (August 1993). A comprehensive listing was published in Chapter 2 of the 1995–96 Federal Student Financial Aid Handbook.

A student who was not a high school graduate or did not have a GED at the time of enrollment must meet one of the following standards before receiving Title IV aid: (1) achieve a score specified by the Department on an independently administered ATB test approved by the Department; or (2) be considered to have the ability to benefit from the school's training in accordance with a process prescribed by the state in which the school is located.

GENERAL RULES FOR LOAN DISCHARGES BASED ON A SCHOOL'S DEFECTIVE DETERMINATION OF A STUDENT'S ATB

1. The regulations[4] require the borrower to certify, under penalty of perjury, that the school failed to determine (or improperly determined) the student's ability-to-benefit from the school's training.

2. A student may, nevertheless, be considered to have had the ability to benefit from the school's training even though the school failed to determine the student's ability or did so improperly. The regulations recognize that a student who obtains employment in the occupation for which the school's program was designed to prepare him or her has proved, on the basis of that employment, that he or she actually possessed the ability to benefit from that training, without regard to whether the school was negligent in its implementation of the Department's ATB regulations. Therefore, the borrower must further certify that the student did not secure employment in the occupation for which the school stated its program was designed to prepare the student, or if the student completed the training program, he or she either was not able to find employment in that occupation, despite a reasonable attempt, or was able to get a job in that occupation only after receiving training from another school.

3. The regulations also recognize that a student would not be regarded as having had the ability-to-benefit from the school's training, despite a school's conclusion that the student had such ability if, at the time the school certified the student's eligibility for a loan, the student would not meet the legal requirements for employment (in the student's state of residence) in the occupation for which the training program was intended because of a physical or mental condition, age, or criminal record or other reason accepted by the Secretary.[5]

QUESTIONS AND ANSWERS

No evidence

1. If a borrower asserts in a claim for discharge that the school improperly determined the student's ATB, and the borrower presents neither documentary evidence from an oversight authority nor any other information to support that claim, and the guaranty agency has no specific information about the ATB testing practices of the school the student attended, is the statement, by itself, sufficient to qualify the borrower for a false certification discharge?

In evaluating an application for discharge, a guaranty agency must consider the statements in the application together with other evidence about the testing and admission practices of the school, and inferences that can reasonably be drawn from that other evidence. Because several authorities with oversight responsibilities, including the Department, accrediting agencies, guarantors, state licensing bodies, and the school's own auditor, would typically have both the opportunity and responsibility to find and report improper ATB admission practices, the absence of any such finding in reports about a school raises an inference that no improper practices were reported because none were taking place.

A borrower's statement must be evaluated in light of such an inference and the possibility that the borrower's statement may be motivated or affected by the borrower's financial self-interest in obtaining relief from the debt. Thus, a borrower's statement that he or she (or the student, in the case of a PLUS Loan) was "falsely certified" or "improperly tested" would not ordinarily be persuasive, and would not therefore be sufficient to establish entitlement to discharge, if it is not supported by some other evidence that as a result of

---

4   34 CFR 682.402(e) for the FFEL Program, and 34 CFR 685.214(c) for the William D. Ford Federal Direct Loan Program.

5   34 CFR 682.402(e)(13)(iii)(B), published November 29, 1994, and § 685.214(a)(1)(iii), published December 1, 1994.

improper ATB admissions practices, students were admitted on the basis of ATB who should not have been admitted. That supporting evidence can include a finding by an entity or organization that had oversight responsibility over the school's SFA administration or educational programs, statements or admissions by school officials with knowledge of the school's practices, or statements made by other students who attended the school that are both sufficiently detailed and consistent with each other to appear reliable. Those statements can include statements made in other claims for discharge relief.

The Department expects a guaranty agency to obtain existing documentation available from any public or private agency that reviewed or had oversight responsibility for the school. If the guaranty agency concludes that such documentation either does not exist or does not support the borrower's assertion, it becomes the responsibility of the borrower making the claim to produce persuasive evidence that would corroborate his or her allegation of improper ATB determination.

Testing violations

2. In those instances where a school used an ATB test to determine a student's eligibility, what violations of ATB testing procedures justify discharge of a borrower's loan obligation, assuming the borrower is otherwise eligible?[6]

Discharge is warranted only in those cases where the ATB test was not "administered substantially in accordance with the requirements for use of the test."[7] For periods of enrollment beginning prior to July 1, 1991, a violation of the requirements for the use of an ATB test will be considered to have occurred if the school: (1) failed to substantially comply with the school's accrediting agency standards for ATB testing; or (2) if no such accrediting agency standards existed, the school failed to substantially comply with the test publisher's requirements for the use of the test. For periods of enrollment beginning on or after July 1, 1991, compliance with the Department's ATB requirements could only be met if the ATB test was approved by the Department and was administered substantially in accordance with the test publisher's rules for the use of the test.

The following violations of the applicable testing procedures are substantial enough to invalidate the results of the test, even though the violation may not have been knowingly committed:

— A test that was required to have been administered by an independent test administrator was not administered by such an individual.

— A school permitted a student who failed an ATB test to retake the test earlier than the minimum waiting period prescribed.

— A school permitted a student who failed an ATB test to retake the test more frequently than allowed.

— A school allowed more time for students to complete their ATB tests than was permitted.

— A school considered a student to have passed an ATB test even though the student did not achieve a minimum passing score which was permissible under the statute, regulations, and Departmental guidance in effect at the time the test was given.

— The school administered only part of a multi-part test, unless giving less than the entire test was permissible under the school's accrediting agency standards.

— For ATB tests given for periods of enrollment beginning on or after July 1, 1991, the version of the test used by the school was a version not approved by the Department.

— A school supplied answers to the ATB test, or permitted students to discuss the questions among themselves, in violation of the testing rules.

---

6 NOTE: A borrower who obtains employment in the occupation for which the school's training program was intended does not qualify for a loan discharge unless the borrower obtained employment only after receiving additional training at another school. See § 682.402(e)(3)(ii)(C) and §685.214(c)(1)(iii).

7 34 CFR 682.402(e)(13)(ii)(B)(2).

3. Even though a guaranty agency determines that a school did not completely comply with the Department's ATB regulations with respect to the use of an ATB test during periods when a test was required, are there violations of those regulations that are not sufficient to justify discharge of a borrower's loan obligation because, despite those technical regulatory violations, the test was administered substantially in accordance with the requirements for use of the test? 682.402(e)(13)(ii)(B)(2).

The Department has identified three violations of an accrediting agency's or a test publisher's requirements that, in the Department's view, do not have the effect of helping the student pass the test. These violations are not substantial enough to justify loan discharge.

— A school used photocopied versions of the ATB test.
— A school used a version of an ATB test that was obsolete by less than one year.
— A school used an ATB test that was approved by the U.S. Department of Education, but had not been approved by the school's accrediting agency.

Although some states have laws addressing the conditions under which postsecondary institutions may properly admit students who do not have a high school diploma or GED, violation of such state requirements does not make borrowers eligible for false certification loan discharge under § 437(c) of the HEA. State ATB requirements address the institution's qualification for a state license, and not whether students attending such schools are eligible for federal aid.

Section 437(c) of the HEA provides for loan discharge where a student's eligibility to borrow was falsely certified by the school. Student eligibility to borrow under the FFEL and William D. Ford Federal Direct Loan Programs is defined by the HEA and implementing regulations, and not by state laws addressing ATB admission. The regulations implementing the false certification discharge provision provide, among other things, that a borrower is eligible for false certification discharge if he or she (or the student in the case of a PLUS Loan) did not meet the requirements for admission on the basis of ability to benefit under FEDERAL law. The regulations describe FEDERAL standards for ATB admission between 1986 and the present, and explicitly refer to the FEDERAL regulatory standards in place during those periods.

Foreign language ATB test

4. A school's program was taught entirely or substantially in English. The ATB test used by the school for periods of enrollment beginning July 1, 1991 or later was given in a language other than English. The school admitted such students who passed their non-English ATB tests. Would a non-English language ATB test given to these students be considered a valid determination of their ATB?

The answer depends on whether the student was enrolled in a program with an English as a Second Language ("ESL") component, and whether the test instrument selected by the school was appropriate. The Department has approved examinations for testing students enrolled in ESL programs, programs with an ESL component, or for testing non-native speakers of English enrolling in regular academic or vocational programs taught in English. The approved examinations expect some degree of functional literacy in English. Before selecting an appropriate test, schools are encouraged to consider whether the examinations can determine the degree of English language proficiency necessary to succeed in the student's particular program of study. Whether a particular test used by a school could appropriately be used for a non-native English speaking student depends on the scope of approval of the test. For example, some tests were approved for use if Spanish is both the student's native language and the language of instruction, while others were approved for use where the student's native language is Spanish and the language of instruction is English.

Remedial Program

5. If a school admitted students for periods of enrollment beginning during the period July 1, 1987–July 1, 1991, and the school chose the ATB option of enrolling students in a program of remedial or developmental education, what rules applied to those programs?

For a school to be considered as having complied with the ATB requirements if it chose this option,[8] the school had to ensure that the students enrolled in, and successfully completed, the institutionally prescribed program of remedial or developmental education. In addition, students had to be either: (1) counselled before admission; or (2) fail an ATB test administered by the school. Those programs may not exceed one academic year or its equivalent. [NOTE: Extensive discussions concerning remedial programs were contained in "Dear Colleague" Letters GEN-89-55, issued December 1989, and GEN-91-20, June 1991.]

Student unable to get a job

6. What documentation is required to show that a student whose ATB was improperly determined was unable to get a job in the occupation for which he or she was trained?[9]

The answer depends on whether the student completed the school's training program. If the student DID NOT COMPLETE the program, the student must simply certify that he or she did not find employment in that occupation. The student's sworn statement that he or she could not get a job in that occupation will be considered proof that the school's defective (or non-existent) determination of the student's ability-to-benefit harmed the student to the extent that a discharge is permissible.

If the student COMPLETED the school's training program, it appears that, notwithstanding the school's improper ATB determination, the student's ability to successfully comprehend the subject matter was equivalent to a student who had a high school diploma or GED. The student obtained the degree or certificate that he or she desired, and for which the loan was obtained. However, the Department's regulations recognize that it is also important to consider whether the student was able to obtain employment after completing the school's program. For this reason, the loan discharge regulations permit a discharge if the student is unable to obtain employment in the occupation for which he or she was trained by the school, despite making a "reasonable attempt" to obtain employment in that occupation.

To fairly balance the interests of the student and the federal taxpayer, the Department believes that a student who COMPLETED the school's training program and who claims that he or she was unable to obtain employment in that occupation because of the school's defective determination of his or her ATB, should be expected to provide evidence that he or she made a "reasonable attempt" to obtain employment in that occupation. Ordinarily, a person who makes a reasonable attempt to obtain employment does not limit his or her job search to only one such effort. More commonly, an individual will try several times to obtain employment in a specific occupation. Therefore, if there were no unusual circumstances faced by a specific individual, it would be reasonable for a guaranty agency to consider three separate attempts by the student to find a job as a persuasive indication of the student's good-faith effort.

The type of information about a job search that most people could readily recall would include the basic facts, such as the name and address of the employer contacted, the date the employer was contacted, the position applied for, and the reason (if any) given by the employer for not hiring the person. Other information (for example, the employer's phone number or the name or title of the person contacted) may be remembered by the student, and would support his or her claim. In situations where an employer contacted by a student routinely declined to hire individuals who were trained by the school attended by the student, a generic statement from the employer to that effect would serve as evidence of the student's reasonable attempt to obtain employment with that employer.

---

8 This option was not available to schools for periods of enrollment beginning on or after July 1, 1991.
9 34 CFR 682.402(e)(3)(ii)(C) and § 685.214(c)(1)(iii).

Student's age, mental or physical condition, or criminal record

7. Are the regulatory provisions with respect to factors such as the student's age, mental or physical condition, or criminal record applicable to all students at all schools?

Those provisions[10] apply to all categories of students at all schools, including students for whom the school was not required to make ability-to-benefit determinations or for whom the school made such determinations properly.

8. What documentation is required from a borrower who requests a discharge on the basis that the student's age, mental or physical condition, criminal record, or other reason accepted by the Secretary prohibited the student from meeting the requirements for employment in the student's state of residence in the occupation for which the student was trained?

The borrower must provide evidence that the student had that disqualifying status at the time of enrollment, and evidence that a STATE PROHIBITION (in the student's state of residence) against employment in that occupation based on that status also existed at the time of enrollment. However, a loan discharge is not authorized if it can be shown that the school asked the student if he or she had such a disqualifying status, but the student did not divulge that information.

9. To whom should information be sent if it is believed that a possible "other reason" (in addition to the student's age, mental or physical condition, or criminal record) should be accepted by the Secretary?

Those parties that wish to provide such information should submit it to:

Ms. Carney McCullough
Chief, General Provisions Branch
Policy, Training, and Analysis Service
Policy Development Division
U.S. Department of Education
600 Independence Avenue, S.W.
Washington, DC 20202-5345

The submitted information must include unambiguous evidence that a STATE PROHIBITION based on that "other reason" existed at the time of the student's enrollment that would prohibit employment (in the student's state of residence) in the occupation for which the student was trained.

Group discharges

10. Does the Department regard as reasonable the approval of discharges for all borrowers who fall within a specified group, for example, ATB students who enrolled in a school with serious and well-documented ATB violations that could be considered to have affected every student admitted to the school based on ATB? If so, would those borrowers still be required to complete discharge applications?

In some cases, discharge may be authorized by the Department for borrowers who demonstrate that they fall within a particular cohort of students and who are otherwise eligible for false certification discharge. Such borrowers may receive discharge without individually presenting proof of improper determination of ATB or admission. All borrowers will, however, still be required to request a discharge and sign the sworn statement prescribed by the regulations. The Department will inform guaranty agencies when it has made such a determination, and notify them of the requirements and procedures for handling such discharges as they occur.

The Department invites interested parties to notify it of such special circumstances that may justify this approach. The type of documentation described in response to question #1 will be considered if it shows that a school committed pervasive and serious violations of the Department's regulations during the time period covered by the documentation. Those parties

---

10   34 CFR 682.402(e)(13)(iii)(B), published November 29, 1994, and § 685.214(a)(1)(iii), published December 1, 1994.

who wish to provide such documentation should submit it to Ms. Carney McCullough, at the address given in question #9.

Suspected fraud

11. What steps should a guaranty agency take if it suspects that a borrower has made false statements on a discharge request, but the agency is unable to disprove those suspected false statements?

The agency should contact the Department's Inspector General for assistance (1-800-MISUSED). Depending on the investigative strategy in a specific case, the agency will be advised whether it should grant the discharge.

Reporting school violations

12. The FFEL regulations [§ 682.402(e)(6)(i)] require a guaranty agency to notify the Department immediately whenever it becomes aware of reliable information indicating that a school may have falsely certified a student's eligibility. To what address should this notification be sent?

Guaranty agencies should notify the Guarantor and Lender Review Branch in the Department's regional office responsible for the state in which the school is located.

Former 34 CFR 668.6

13. The regulations state that for periods of enrollment beginning prior to July 1, 1987, a student's ATB was to be determined "in accordance with the requirements of 34 CFR 668.6." However, that section of the current regulations has nothing in it except the word "reserved."

The text of § 668.6 as it existed during the applicable time period follows:

§ 668.6. Ability to benefit.

(a) "Ability to benefit" means that a person admitted to an institution of higher education has the ability to benefit from the education or training he or she is to receive.

(b) (1) An institution that admits as regular students persons who do not have a high school diploma or the recognized equivalent of a high school diploma and who are beyond the age of compulsory school attendance in the State in which the institution is located, shall develop and consistently apply criteria for determining whether these students have the ability to benefit from the education or training offered.

(2) An institution must be able to demonstrate, upon request of the Secretary, that these students have the ability to benefit.

(Authority: 20 U.S.C. 1088, 1141)

SEPTEMBER 1994

Publication Date: September 1994

Summary: This letter provides guidance concerning closed school and false certification loan discharges and relief for unauthorized endorsements in the Federal Family Education Loan (FFEL) Program.

Dear Colleague:

On April 29, 1994, final regulations (effective July 1, 1994) affecting the FFEL program were published in the *Federal Register*. Sections 34 CFR 682.402(d) and (e) of those regulations prescribe the procedures for discharging the loan obligation of a borrower who received an FFEL loan on or after January 1, 1986. If the student was unable to complete his or her program of study because the school closed, or the borrower's (or the student's for whom a parent received a PLUS loan) eligibility to receive the loan was falsely certified by the school. The regulations also prescribe the procedures for providing relief for unauthorized endorsements. This letter provides guidance on implementing those regulations. Part I covers closed school loan discharges. Part II covers false certification discharges and relief for unauthorized endorsements. Part III provides guidance that applies to both types of discharges and unauthorized endorsements. Attachment A is the Department's "Cumulative List of Schools That Closed Since January 1, 1986."

The regulations give the guaranty agency initial decision-making authority on discharge claims. A formal appeal to the Department is provided under the rules only in false certification claims and unauthorized check endorsements. To review whether guarantor decisions to discharge loans comply with the regulations, the Department will use the review and audit procedures it currently uses to examine other guarantor decisions. The intent of this letter and future Department communications on this responsibility is to give guarantors an interpretation of the regulations or an explanation of the application of particular regulations to general fact patterns. In the future, more specific guidance may be given as the need arises with respect to particular schools or to specific fact patterns that come to light in litigation or otherwise.

We appreciate your assistance and cooperation as we work to implement these provisions.

Sincerely,

Leo Kornfeld
Deputy Assistant Secretary for
Student Financial Assistance Programs

Attachment

PART I. *CLOSED SCHOOL DISCHARGES*

1. How is a school's closure date determined?

For purposes of the closed school discharge authorized under the regulations, a school's closure date is the date that the school ceases to provide educational instruction in all programs, as determined by the Secretary. *See* 34 CFR 682.402(d)(1)(ii)(A).

Attachment A to this letter is the "Cumulative List of Schools That Closed Since January 1, 1986." It lists the schools known by the Secretary to have closed on or after January 1, 1986. The Secretary intends to update the Cumulative List with monthly supplements as new information and corrections become available. Guaranty agencies will be responsible for using the most current information. For example, if a school's closure date is revised, guaranty agencies will be expected to use the new closure date after receiving the monthly supplement containing that correction.

For approximately two years, the Secretary has published a quarterly cumulative list of closed schools. The Secretary intends to discontinue publishing this quarterly list and give guaranty agencies and lenders access to an electronic computer database containing the information. Guaranty agencies and lenders will be able to access the computer database by modem using the telephone system, or update their records with the printed monthly supplements. Additional details will be provided at a later date.

2. What should guaranty agencies and lenders do with the listings of closed schools published by the Department?

Guaranty agencies and lenders should review Attachment A and the subsequent lists of closed schools and notify the Department's Closed School Section immediately at (202) 401-3462 if corrections are necessary or information is missing. If the guaranty agency receives documentation that it believes will affect the Secretary's determination of a school's closure date, it should notify the Closed School Section. Evidence indicating that a school's closure date may be incorrect may include a letter from the school or state licensing agency, or a newspaper article. The Secretary will determine whether the closure date needs to be revised. In the meantime, the guaranty agency should suspend collection activity on the loan until a determination is made by the Secretary.

It is important that the Department has the correct name, address, OPE-ID number, and closure date for each school, and that all schools are listed (including unauthorized branches and locations). Unless the Department has complete and accurate information, potentially qualifying borrowers may be prevented from receiving loan discharges, and ineligible borrowers may receive discharges to which they are not entitled. Any comments, corrections, or additions to the Cumulative List, or other information regarding closed schools, should be sent to: U.S. Department of Education, Closed School Section, P.O. Box 23800, L'Enfant Plaza Station, Washington, DC 20026, telephone number (202)708-6048.

Within 30 days of receiving confirmation of the date of a school's closure by means of Attachment A or a supplemental listing of closed schools from the Department, or confirmation of a school's closure date by any other means, a guaranty agency must review its records and identify borrowers who appear to be eligible for a closed school loan discharge. After the eligible borrowers have been identified, the guaranty agency must follow the notification procedures prescribed in § 682.402(d)(6).

3. What should a guaranty agency do when it is notified of a revised school closure date by the Department?

A guaranty agency must review its records to identify any borrower who received a loan discharge from that agency based on the former closure date. If the revised closure date is less than 90 days later than the closure date on which discharge decisions were made for individuals who claimed to have been in attendance on that earlier closure date, the guarantor can deem those students to have withdrawn within the qualifying 90-day pre-closure period and need not revise those decisions or demand additional information from the borrowers to confirm the discharge previously granted. For individuals who claim to have withdrawn within that 90-day period and received discharges on that basis, the agency must redetermine the borrowers' eligibility based on the new date. Within 30 days after making a determination that a previously discharged borrower does not qualify for a discharge based on the revised closure date, the agency should notify the borrower of the reasons for that determination. The agency must advise the borrower that he or she remains obligated to repay the loan, warn the borrower of the consequences of default, and explain that the borrower will be considered to be in default on the loan unless the borrower submits a written statement to the agency within 30 days stating that the borrower acknowledges the debt and, if payments are due, will begin or resume making those payments.

The Department derives the information on which it sets or revises the closure date from the most authoritative sources available, and it is unlikely that the borrower would have more reliable information about the date of the school's closure. However, because the guarantor must explain to the borrower the reasons for any reconsideration decision denying a discharge or revoking one previously given, the borrower will be able to contest that decision before being considered to be in default. If the borrower presents evidence that the guarantor considers sufficient to warrant changing the closure date, the guarantor can defer action on the loan with respect to that debtor, and should present that evidence, with its recommendation, to the Department.

Within 30 days after receiving the borrower's written statement, if the loan had been filed as a closed school claim by a lender, the agency shall treat the loan as a repurchase by the lender and return the claim file to the lender. The amount owed by the borrower will be the sum of the claim amount previously paid to the lender plus the amount of payments refunded to the borrower by the guaranty agency when it paid the claim. The lender should be instructed to resume collection efforts if payments are due. If the borrower fails to acknowledge the debt within 30 days, the agency shall consider the borrower to be in default. If the loan had been held by the agency as a defaulted loan when it was discharged, the agency should once again treat the loan as a defaulted loan owed by the borrower (including any refunded payments) to the agency. The lender or agency shall be deemed to have exercised forbearance of payment of principal and interest from the date collection activity had been suspended, and may capitalize, in accordance with § 682.202(b), any interest accrued and not paid during that period.

If an agency discovers that a borrower may have made a false certification on an application for a loan discharge, it should follow normal procedures for reporting cases of suspected fraud by contacting the Department's Office of Inspector General.

4. Does a borrower or student who attended a branch location ineligible under the Title IV programs potentially qualify for a closed school discharge?

For purposes of closed school loan discharges, a "school" means a school's main campus or any location or branch of the main campus, regardless of whether the school or its location or branch is considered eligible. *See* § 682.402(d)(1)(ii)(C). The Secretary will list closure dates for schools or locations that received funds under Title IV of the Higher Education Act, even though the school or location may have been ineligible for any of a variety of reasons, or because the location was never approved by the Secretary. In publicizing the closure date, the Secretary will use the OPE-ID number of the funding school as the OPE-ID number for ineligible locations.

5. Does a borrower or student who claims a last day of attendance that is more than 90 days prior to the school's closure date qualify for discharge?

Unless an exception has been made (see question 6), the guaranty agency should deny the claim and state the specific reasons for the denial.

6. How can a guaranty agency obtain an extension from the Department to the 90-day limit on the pre-closure withdrawal period?

The regulations provide that the Secretary may extend the 90-day period to allow a longer time period for discharge if the Secretary determines that exceptional circumstances related to a school's closing would justify an extension. Guaranty agencies that believe that exceptional circumstances justify an extension for a particular school should request an extension by contracting the Department's Closed School Section at the address previously provided. In its request, the guaranty agency should present facts it believes would justify an extension, and make whatever recommendation it deems appropriate. The Secretary will then decide whether to extend the 90-day timeframe, and notify all guaranty agencies if he determines that an extension is warranted.

7. Does a borrower or student who did not complete the program but received a diploma or a certificate qualify for discharge?

Before closing, some schools may have issued a diploma or certificate to students who did not complete the program of study. The issuance of a diploma to a student who did not complete the training program will not disqualify the borrower for discharge if the other requirements for discharge are satisfied.

8. What is a student completed the program but the school did not issue a diploma or certificate?

If a student completed the program, the issuance of a diploma or certificate is irrelevant. A borrower is eligible for a loan discharge only if the student was unable to complete a program of study.

9. How does a guaranty agency submit a request for reinsurance and report closed school activity to the Department?

The guaranty agency files a reinsurance request and reports closed school activity to the Department by using the revised Guaranty Agency Quarterly/Annual Report (ED Form 1130) and Guaranty Agency Monthly Claims and Collections Report (ED Form 1189). For guidance on completing these forms, please refer to "Dear Guaranty Agency Director" Letters 93-G-234 (June 1993), 94-G-250 (January 1994), and 94-G-253 (June 1994).

PART II. *FALSE CERTIFICATION DISCHARGE AND RELIEF FOR UNAUTHORIZED ENDORSEMENTS*

10. If a borrower (or student) claims that he or she did not sign the application, promissory note, loan check, or electronic funds transfer authorization, how does a guaranty

agency determine if the borrower's allegation is valid?

The agency should carefully compare the contested signature(s) with the examples of signatures submitted by the borrower in accordance with § 682.402(e)(3)(iii) or (lv), and to the best of the agency's ability decide if the preponderance of evidence supports the borrower's assertion.

11. What sources of information or evidence should a guaranty agency investigate, and what actions should it take in the case of a claim for relief based on the borrower's (or student's) assertion that he or she die not sign the loan check or electronic funds transfer authorization?

If the borrower presents evidence that the guarantor finds to be credible showing that the borrower did not endorse the loan check or authorize the EFT disbursements,the guarantor must determine whether the student or borrower nevertheless received the disbursement either directly or through a credit satisfying a school charge actually due an owed by the student [*i.e.*, the tuition and other charges net of any refund owed the student]. To make that judgment, the guarantor must consider relevant evidence in its possession and other information that may be available from other sources. These sources include, in the first instance, the school records pertaining to the student's account, which may be available from State agency record custodians if not from the school itself. Where the guarantor is presented with a claim by a lender, the lender should have presented with the claim evidence to support the contention that the student received the proceeds. A guaranty agency should contact the school, the Department's regional office, the school's state licensing agency, and any other party that the guaranty agency has reason to believe would have relevant evidence and attempt to obtain documentation to show whether the student or borrower received the proceeds of the loan.

Whether the guarantor's review of evidence presented by the lender or secured by its own efforts leads it to conclude that is more probable, based on that evidence or lack of evidence, that the borrower or student did not receive the proceeds of such a disbursement, the guarantor must conclude that the loan is not enforceable, and take the actions prescribed in the regulations to give relief to the borrower and to effect the return of funds paid by the Department with respect to that loan to the lender and to the guarantor.

12. If a borrower's application for a false certification loan discharge was denied by a guaranty agency, and the borrower appeals the agency's decision to the Secretary, to what address should the guaranty agency forward the borrower's request?

Appeals should be forwarded to: U.S. Department of Education, P.O. Box 422037, San Francisco, California 94142-2037. The appeal must be clearly identified as a "false certification appeal" and must contain all the information and documentation examined by the agency when making its determination. The Department representatives in San Francisco will acknowledge receipt of the appeal to the guaranty agency and respond to the appeal request promptly. Until the appeal request is acted upon and a final decision made by the Department, the guaranty agency should cease all collections activity on the account.

13. How should guaranty agencies evaluate a borrower's claim for loan discharge based upon an alleged failure of the school to properly apply ability-to-benefit (ATB) provisions at the time the student was admitted?

Because of the complexity created by the various statutory and regulatory changes to the ATB requirements over the period covered by the false certification provisions of the regulations, the Department is still developing specific guidance which can be used by guaranty agencies to determine the validity of ATB false certification claims by borrowers seeking discharge of their FFEL loans. We will provide more detailed guidance about these ATB requirements (including guidance about what constitutes improper ATB testing) within the next few weeks.

PART III. *GENERAL*

14. Will the Department provide a standardized application form for borrowers to use to request a closed school (or false certification) discharge?

The Department is developing application forms for closed school and false certification student loan discharges for loans held by the Department. The Ad Hoc Standardization Committee, which is composed of members representing the Department and the student aid community, is developing standardized application forms for use by other entities holding FFEL Program loans eligible for discharge. The Department expects he forms to be available soon. Until forms are available, the Department encourages lenders and guaranty agencies either to develop and use their own forms, or to inform applicants of the regulatory requirements for discharge so that they can submit discharge requests without using application forms. A guaranty agency or lender may use one application for all discharges, or one application for closed school discharges and another for false certification discharges. Guaranty agencies must ensure that their discharge request/application forms require the borrower to provide the information and certifications specified in the regulations. Agencies using their own forms must submit them to the Department's FFEL Policy Section for review in accordance with 34 CFR 682.401(d).

The guaranty agency or lender must evaluate all discharge requests submitted by borrowers regardless of whether standardized forms are developed to determine if the applicants meet the regulatory requirements for discharge, and guarantors must ensure that sufficient information and supporting documents are secured to demonstrate whether the borrower qualifies for discharge.

15. What amount of a Federal Consolidation Loan is dischargeable?

The Federal Consolidation Loan is not itself dischargeable, but the Consolidation Loan proceeds used to pay off a loan that qualified for discharge are refunded to the borrower by means of a credit to the Consolidation Loan. The amount of the credit is the amount dischargeable on the FFEL Program loans paid off by the Consolidation Loan.

16. Is a payment history necessary to apply a discharge credit to a Federal Consolidation Loan?

Payment histories are necessary to determine that portion of the Consolidation Loan that was disbursed to pay off the discharged loan(s), and whether other payments were made reducing the discharged loan balance prior to the payoff from the Consolidation Loan. If the payment histories are not available from the prior lenders, the current lender must make reasonable attempts to obtain the information from other sources. If the lender is unable to obtain a payment history from other sources, the borrower will be required to submit evidence of payments made on the loan prior to the date of the Consolidation Loan. All payments made by the borrower on the old loan before that date are included in determining the discharge amount applied to the remaining balance of the Consolidation Loan. Post-consolidation interest should be calculated by the lender based on the balance of the closed school loan at the time the Consolidation Loan was made.

17. How should a discharge credit be applied to a Federal Consolidation Loan?

The total discharge credit amount shall fist be applied to reduce the outstanding balance of the Consolidation loan. If the entire outstanding Consolidation Loan balance is repaid by the discharge credit, any difference is returned to the borrower.

18. If the borrower fails to submit the written request and sworn statement within 60 days of being notified of this requirement, what action should the lender or guaranty agency take?

The lender or guaranty agency should resume collection activity on the loan. If the borrower submits the written request and sworn statement at a later date, the lender or guaranty agency must suspend collection activity and review the borrower's request. A borrowers' request for discharge may not be denied solely on the basis of failing to meet any time limits set by the lender, the guaranty agency, of the Department.

19. What should a lender do if a borrower's request for discharge is incomplete or contains information that would clearly make the borrower ineligible for the discharge?

The lender should not submit a claim to a guaranty agency, and must inform the borrower of the reasons why the borrower's request is inadequate within 30 days of the date the lender received the borrower's request. *See* § 682.208(c)(l). Some reasons will be more obvious than others, for example, the borrower's loan was disbursed before January 1, 1986. Because the eligibility requirements for a false certification discharge typically depend on information not generally known by the lender, it is likely that lenders will be unable to readily determine whether a borrower's request for a false certification discharge is insufficient unless the borrower's sworn statement is incomplete. In all cases where the borrower appears to meet the eligibility requirements described in the regulations, the lender must file a claim with the guaranty agency no later than 60 days after the lender received the borrower's written request and sworn statement or after the lender is notified by the Secretary or the Secretary's designee or by the guaranty agency to file a claim.

20. Can a loan that does not qualify for federal reinsurance be discharged?

Legally enforceable loans that have lost reinsurance, because of a violation of due diligence or other programmatic requirements by the lender or guaranty agency, are generally eligible for discharge if the borrower meets all of the requirements for a discharge. In such cases, the Secretary will use his authority pursuant to § 682.406(b) to waive his right to refuse to make a reinsurance payment on the loan.

C.2 Consolidation Loans

MAY 2006, FP-06-09

Publication Date: May 2006
DCL ID: FP-06-09

Subject: Lender options for determining Federal Consolidation Loan interest rates as of July 1, 2006

Summary: This letter provides options for lenders in the Federal Family Education Loan (FFEL) Program to use when determining Federal Consolidation Loan interest rates as of July 1, 2006 and shortly thereafter.

Posted on 05-30-2006

Dear Colleague:

Federal Consolidation Loans in the FFEL Program have fixed interest rates that are based on the weighted average of the interest rates of the loans being consolidated. Many of the loans that borrowers plan to consolidate over the next several weeks have variable interest rates that are expected to increase significantly on July 1. In response to a similar situation last year, the Department issued guidance to the student loan community in Dear Colleague Letter GEN-05-08 http://ifap.ed.gov/dpcletters/GEN0508.html to help borrowers obtain the lowest statutory weighted average interest rate, by authorizing lenders to use the lower of the weighted average of the interest rates on the loans being consolidated as of July 1 or on the date the lender received the borrower's substantially complete consolidation loan application.

We are providing the same authority to FFEL lenders again this year, and will apply the same treatment to applicants for a Direct Consolidation Loan. In exercising this authority, a lender—

1. Must apply a consistent method of determining when a substantially complete application is received.

2. Must honor a borrower's request, if possible, that his or her loan be disbursed prior to July 1st.

3. Must not hold an application received before July 1st longer than is necessary to receive and process loan verification certificates and disburse payoff amounts to the borrower's loan holders.

4. May calculate a pre-July 1 fixed interest rate for the Consolidation Loan, even if a loan verification certificate is received on or after July 1 and reflects a post-July 1 variable interest rate on the loan(s) being consolidated, provided a substantially complete application was received prior to July 1.

5. Must advise the borrower that the current holders of the variable rate loans the borrower wishes to consolidate are authorized to charge the new variable interest rate as of July 1 on those loans until they are paid off by a Consolidation Loan made by the consolidating lender, even if the borrower's substantially complete consolidation application was received by the consolidating lender prior to July 1.

Important Note: Dear Colleague Letter GEN-05-08 also included a discussion about the procedures for permitting in-school borrowers to request early conversion to repayment for the purpose of qualifying for a Consolidation Loan. A borrower's request for early repayment must be received by the holder of the underlying loan prior to July 1, 2006. An applicant whose consolidation application is received on or after July 1, 2006 must be in grace or repayment status, or in default with satisfactory repayment arrangements, on the loans the borrower requests to consolidate. See page 2 of Dear Colleague Letter GEN-06-02 http://ifap.ed.gov/dpcletters/GEN0602.html.

If you have questions concerning the guidance provided in this letter, please contact Pam Moran at (202) 502-7732 or George Harris at (202) 502-7521.

Sincerely,

James Manning
Acting Assistant Secretary

MARCH 2006, FP-06-03

Publication Date: March 2006
DCL ID: FP-06-03

Subject: Federal Family Education Loan (FFEL) Consolidation Loans

Summary: This letter reiterates and confirms the Department's position that, beginning April 1, 2006, it will enforce the single holder rule in the making of FFEL Consolidation Loans.

References: Section 428C of the Higher Education Act (HEA)
Dear Colleague Letter FP-05-09 (September 20, 2005)
Dear Colleague Letter FP-04-07 (August 26, 2004)
Dear Colleague Letter FP-04-06 (August 26, 2004)
Dear Colleague Letter FP-04-05 (April 29, 2004)

Posted on 3-17-2006:

Dear Colleague:

In the series of Dear Colleague Letters listed above, the Department reminded participants in the student loan programs under Title IV of the HEA, as amended, of the restrictions on loan consolidation in the Federal Family Education Loan (FFEL) Program and the Federal Direct Loan Program, including the single holder rule provisions in section 428C(b)(1)(A)(i) of the HEA. The single holder rule states that a FFEL lender may not make a Consolidation Loan to a borrower unless the lender holds an outstanding loan of that borrower that would be repaid by the Consolidation Loan. However, the requirement that the lender hold an outstanding loan of the borrower does not apply if the borrower has FFEL loans held by multiple FFEL lenders or if the borrower's FFEL lender either does not offer Consolidation

Loans or does not offer the borrower income-sensitive repayment terms. The Dear Colleague Letters also reminded program participants that FFEL Consolidation Loans made in violation of the single holder rule would not meet the requirements for reinsurance and other benefits under the FFEL Program.

In our earlier Dear Colleague Letters, the Department noted that Congress was considering changes to the single holder rule as part of its reauthorization of the FFEL Program. In light of that possible legislative action, the Department announced that, for a temporary period, we would not deny reinsurance on FFEL Consolidation Loans that did not comply with the single holder rule. Most recently, in Dear Colleague Letter FP-05-09 issued on September 20, 2005, the Department established a deadline of March 31, 2006, for compliance with the single holder rule.

Any FFEL Consolidation Loan made after March 31, 2006, that does not comply with the single holder rule by including at least one FFEL loan is not eligible for reinsurance and other program benefits unless the consolidating lender submitted all applicable Loan Verification Certificates (LVCs) to the holder(s) of the underlying loans on or before March 31, 2006.

Based on changes included in section 8009 of the Higher Education Reconciliation Act of 2005 (Pub. L. 109-171), a FFEL or Direct Consolidation Loan may not be made on or after July 1, 2006, to any borrower who has a Consolidation Loan in either program unless the borrower includes additional eligible loans in the new Consolidation Loan. In administering the Direct Loan Program, the Department will continue to process LVCs received from FFEL lenders through June 30, 2006, if the Direct Consolidation Loan that is the subject of the LVC resulted from a Direct Consolidation Loan application received by the Department on or before March 31, 2006. The resulting FFEL Consolidation Loan would be eligible for reinsurance and other program benefits.

Consistent with prior guidance, the Department will continue to process LVCs for borrowers with Direct Stafford and Direct Parent Loans to Undergraduate Students (PLUS) Loans.

We thank you for your cooperation in complying with this guidance. If you have any questions on this issue, please contact Pam Moran by e-mail at Pamela.Moran@ed.gov or by phone at (202) 502-7732.

Sincerely,

Sally L. Stroup Assistant Secretary for
Postsecondary Education

Theresa S. Shaw
Chief Operating Officer
Federal Student Aid

SEPTEMBER 2005, FP-05-09

Publication Date: September 2005
DCL ID: FP-05-09

Subject: Federal Family Education Loan (FFEL) Consolidation loans for borrowers with both FFEL and non-FFEL loans

Summary: This letter extends the date applicable to the guidance that was included in Dear Colleague Letter (FP-04-06) regarding FFEL Consolidation loans.

Reference: Section 428C of the Higher Education Act (HEA)
Dear Colleague Letter FP-04-06 (August 26, 2004)
Dear Colleague Letter FP-04-05 (April 29, 2004)

Posted on 09-20-2005

Dear Colleague:

In my August 26, 2004, Dear Colleague Letter (FP-04-06), I announced the Department's decision not to deny reinsurance for FFEL Consolidation loans that do not comply with the

Department's interpretation of the single-holder rule in certain circumstances described in that letter, as long as all Loan Verification Certificates were sent to loan holders by September 30, 2005 (unless the Higher Education Act was reauthorized before that date). This letter serves to notify you that the Department is extending that date to March 31, 2006.

We thank you for your cooperation. If you have any questions on the issues discussed in this letter, please contact Pamela Moran by email at Pamela.Moran@ed.gov or by phone at (202) 502-7732.

Sincerely,

Sally L. Stroup
Assistant Secretary
Office of Postsecondary Education

AUGUST 2004, FP-04-06

Publication Date: August 2004
DCL ID: FP-04-06

Federal Family Education Loan (FFEL) Consolidation loans for borrowers with both FFEL and non-FFEL loans.

Posted on 08-26-2004

Subject: Federal Family Education Loan (FFEL) Consolidation loans for borrowers with both FFEL and non-FFEL loans.

Summary: This letter expands upon guidance that was included in a prior Dear Colleague Letter (FP-04-05) regarding FFEL Consolidation loans.

Reference: Section 428C of the Higher Education Act (HEA)
Dear Colleague Letter FP-04-02 (Feb. 17, 2004)
Dear Colleague Letter FP-04-05 (Apr. 29, 2004)

Dear Colleague:

In an April 29, 2004 Dear Colleague Letter (FP-04-05), I clarified that an earlier letter from my office regarding loan consolidation in the FFEL program addressed only those instances where a borrower has both (1) a FFEL loan(s) held by a single FFEL holder, and (2) one or more non-FFEL loans.

My letter additionally provided a statement of enforcement policy in pronouncing that the Department would not deny reinsurance for FFEL Consolidation loans that do not comply with the Department's interpretation of the "single-holder rule," see section 428C(b)(1)(A) of the HEA, 20 U.S.C. 1078-3(b)(1)(A); 34 CFR 682.201(c), in the circumstances described above, as long as all Loan Verification Certificates (LVCs) were sent to the loan holders by September 1, 2004. At the time, we expected the HEA to be reauthorized by that date and to address the single-holder rule in a manner that would ameliorate the situation. Because it has become clear that HEA reauthorization will not occur by September 1, 2004, the Department will not deny reinsurance for FFEL Consolidation loans that do not comply with the Department's interpretation of the single-holder rule in the circumstances described above, as long as all LVCs are sent to the loan holders by the date the HEA is reauthorized or September 30, 2005, whichever occurs first.

In the meantime, lenders that are requested to complete LVCs in connection with borrowers who fit the situation described above and who had their non-FFEL loan(s) paid off to obtain a FFEL Consolidation loan by another lender should not refuse to make the requested certifications on the ground that the FFEL loan held by the requesting lender was made in a manner that does not comply with the Department's interpretation of the single-holder rule. That is, lenders should not "look behind" an existing FFEL Consolidation loan in determining whether to complete the requested certifications because it is the Department's responsibility, not the lenders' responsibility, to enforce the single-holder rule. This guidance in no way diminishes our view, as stated in Dear Colleague Letter FP-04-02, dated February

17, 2004, that lenders may choose to not provide the requested certification if they believe that they are the single holder of the borrower's FFEL loans, as long as the lender provides information to support that claim.

Sincerely,

Sally L. Stroup
Assistant Secretary
Office of Postsecondary Education

APRIL 2004, FP-04-05

This letter clarifies rules for FFEL Loan consolidation.

Publication Date: April 29, 2004
FP-04-05

SUBJECT: Federal Family Education Loan (FFEL) Consolidation loans for borrowers with both FFEL and non-FFEL loans.

REFERENCE: Section 428C of the Higher Education Act (HEA).

Dear Colleague:

On March 15, 2004, the Director of the Office of Postsecondary Education's Policy and Budget Development Staff wrote to the National Council of Higher Education Loan Programs (NCHELP) in response to inquiries from the lending community about the rules governing loan consolidation in the FFEL Program. That letter, a copy of which is attached, stated that in instances where a borrower had one or more FFEL loans held by a single FFEL holder and also non-FFEL loans, the borrower could obtain a FFEL Consolidation loan only from that single FFEL holder. The purpose of this letter is to provide further clarification for the entire higher education community.

The letter of March 15 addressed only those instances where a borrower has both (1) a FFEL loan(s) held by a single FFEL holder, and (2) one or more non-FFEL loans. In that situation, pursuant to section 428C(b)(1)(A) of the HEA, 20 U.S.C. 1078-3(b)(1)(A), and the FFEL Program regulations at 34 CFR 682.201(c), a borrower seeking a FFEL Consolidation loan must obtain such a loan from his or her current FFEL holder and must include at least one FFEL loan in the consolidation. However, if the borrower certifies that he or she has sought and has been unable to obtain a consolidation loan from that FFEL holder or is unable to obtain a consolidation loan from that holder with income-sensitive repayment terms, the borrower may obtain a FFEL Consolidation loan from another FFEL lender. In that case, again, the borrower must include at least one FFEL loan in the consolidation. Alternatively, a borrower may obtain a Federal Direct Consolidation Loan from the Department of Education if the borrower's non-FFEL loan(s) include a Direct Loan and the borrower selects at least one Direct Loan for consolidation.

The letter stated that we would not deny reinsurance for FFEL Consolidation loans that do not comply with the interpretation stated in that letter as long as all loan verification certificates were sent to the loan holders by May 1, 2004. It is important to note that eligibility for reinsurance is significant not only for the FFEL lender, but also for the borrower because reinsurance governs eligibility for certain borrower benefits. In light of the added clarification provided in this letter and to avoid harm to borrowers who may have recently applied or are in the process of applying for a FFEL Consolidation loan, we are extending the cutoff date noted above from May 1, 2004, to September 1, 2004.

We hope that this clarifying information is helpful.

Sincerely,

Sally L. Stroup
Assistant Secretary
Office of Postsecondary Education

JANUARY 2003, GEN-03-02

This letter addresses the time limit for FFEL loan holder response to loan consolidation verification requests.

Publication Date: January 2003
GEN-03-02
G-03-334
L-03-238

SUBJECT: Federal Family Education Loan (FFEL) Program loan holders must respond to Consolidation Loan verification requests within 10 business days.

Dear Colleague:

It has come to our attention that some FFEL loan holders may not be complying with regulatory requirements to respond to requests from another lender (FFEL or Direct Loans) for certification of loan status for a loan included on a borrower's application for a consolidation loan. Under the FFEL Consolidation Program, 34 CFR 682.209(j) states:

> (j) Certification on loans to be repaid through consolidation. Within 10 business days after receiving a written request for a certification from a lender under § 682.206(f), a holder shall either provide the requesting lender the certification or, if it is unable to certify to the matters described in that paragraph, provide the requesting lender and the guarantor on the loan at issue with a written explanation of the reasons for its inability to provide the certification.

Under the Direct Loan Consolidation Program, 34 CFR 685.220(f)(1)(i) states—

> (f) Origination of a consolidation loan. (1)(i) The holder of a loan that a borrower wishes to consolidate into a Direct Loan shall complete and return the Secretary's request for certification of the amount owed within 10 business days of receipt or, if it is unable to provide the certification, provide to the Secretary a written explanation of the reasons for its inability to provide the certification.

This is an important obligation that every loan holder must fulfill in order to ensure that a borrower's Consolidation loan is processed in a timely fashion. Loan holders must, within 10 business days after receiving a request for loan certification, provide the requesting lender with the requested certification information or a reason why it is unable to provide the information. Failure to comply with this requirement could result in a lender being subject to fines or other sanctions consistent with 34 CFR 682, Subpart G. Requesting lenders who do not receive loan certification information or responses informing them why that information is not being provided from a loan holder in a timely manner, should inform their FSA regional lender review staff, so that the Department can follow up with the loan holder.

We hope that this information helps you fully comply with the requirements of the Federal student loan programs.

Jeffrey Andrade
Deputy Assistant Secretary
Postsecondary Education

C.3 Borrower Assistance

APRIL 2005, GEN-05-06

Publication Date: April 2005
DCL ID: GEN-05-06
FP-05-04

Subject: Access To and Use of NSLDS Information

Summary: This letter reminds members of the financial aid community who have access to information contained in NSLDS that they are responsible for using their access properly and for protecting the sensitive data contained in the system.

Posted on 04-11-2005

Dear Colleague:

The U.S. Department of Education's National Student Loan Data System (NSLDS) is a comprehensive database containing personal and financial information related to an individual's receipt of Federal student financial aid authorized under Title IV of the Higher Education Act of 1965, as amended. The data contained in NSLDS is confidential and is protected by the Privacy Act of 1974, as amended and other applicable statutes and regulations. Access to NSLDS by postsecondary educational institutions, organizations that participate in the Federal Family Education Loan (FFEL) Program, and other approved entities is made available only for the general purpose of assisting with determining the eligibility of an applicant for Federal student aid and in the collection of Federal student loans and grant overpayments. NSLDS information may not be used for any other purpose, including the marketing of student loans or other products.

Failure to comply with NSLDS access and use requirements, as described in this letter, may result in the organization or individual user losing access to NSLDS and/or being subject to sanctions, including, but not limited to, the initiation of a limitation, suspension, or termination action or a debarment proceeding against the postsecondary institution or FFEL participant. Additionally, institutional sanctions may apply to any organization that, by sharing its institutional or FFEL Program identifiers, has provided other entities or individuals the capability to access to NSLDS information. We are specifically troubled by the use of FFEL lender ID's by organizations only minimally related to the lender of record. Such organizations include collection agencies and loan brokerage or marketing firms.

Access to NSLDS information is granted to individuals whose specific job responsibilities include at least one of the activities listed below. These individuals must not use their access to NSLDS information for any other purpose.

Under Federal law, the Department is required to publish a Notice identifying the routine uses of records maintained in a Federal system of records like NSLDS. The Notice for NSLDS was published on December 27, 1999, 64 Fed. Reg. 72384, 72395–72397. That notice makes it clear that the Department can properly disclose information from records in NSLDS to persons who are authorized to receive the information only for specific purposes. The system Notice explains that lenders, loan holders and servicers can have access to NSLDS information for limited purposes, which include only the following—

- Determining a specific student applicant's eligibility for Title IV student aid;
- Billing and collecting on a Title IV loan;
- Enforcing the terms of a Title IV loan;
- Billing and collecting on a Title IV grant overpayment;
- Submitting student enrollment information;
- Ensuring the accuracy of a financial aid or borrower record;
- Assisting with default aversion activities; and
- Obtaining default rate information.

Each organization whose employees are allowed access to NSLDS data is required to have a Destination Point Administrator (DPA) appointed by the organization's Chief Executive Officer (CEO) using a document that requires the signatures of both the DPA and the CEO. The DPA must not only monitor the use and access of NSLDS data by all of the organization's NSLDS users, but must also ensure users are aware of their responsibilities regarding access to NSLDS. The DPA must also de-activate a User-ID when the person to whom it was assigned is no longer with the organization or otherwise is no longer eligible to have access to NSLDS. Thus, all authorized NSLDS users in an organization, their DPA, and the organization's CEO are all personally responsible for prohibiting improper access to the NSLDS database or improper use of the data contained in and obtained from the NSLDS database.

Each NSLDS user is responsible for protecting his or her access to NSLDS and the data available. Each person who accesses NSLDS must use his or her own User-ID. That person is responsible for safeguarding the User-ID and password and must not allow any other person to use them. Access to the NSLDS Web site is limited to one borrower's record at a time by an individual user. Use of an automated tool to access borrowers' information or use of screen scraping technology for downloading data or pre-populating forms are prohibited. Further, sharing or providing data retrieved by an authorized person from NSLDS with persons or organizations who are not expressly authorized to receive that information for the purposes listed in the Systems Notice are also prohibited.

We are concerned that some organizations and individuals may not understand the requirements, as described in this letter, for access to and use of the private information contained in NSLDS. As noted above, access to NSLDS is restricted to the staff of an eligible Title IV participating postsecondary institution and to eligible FFEL lenders, lender servicers, and guaranty agencies. With exceptions not relevant here, no other persons or organizations can have access to NSLDS data. Federal laws and rules require the Department to take appropriate steps to ensure the confidentiality of records containing personal and confidential information. To meet this obligation, we regularly analyze NSLDS usage statistics to determine if security of the NSLDS system may be compromised and we have implemented an on-going daily monitoring of the system to track access usage. If, as result of these system activities or for any other reason, we believe that a user and/or an organization has violated the NSLDS access and use responsibilities we will discharge our duty under the Privacy Act by immediately, and without any advance notice or right to appeal, terminate that user's and organization's access to NSLDS. Additionally, depending upon the nature of the violation, we may initiate other sanctions against the organization, as noted above.

An eligible organization that allows unauthorized access to NSLDS will be considered to have violated its responsibilities and places itself at risk of losing access to NSLDS, to other Departmental systems and data, and to possible loss of eligibility to participate in the Title IV student aid programs. We urge all organizations to provide a copy of this letter to any of its staff who has access to NSLDS, to provide in its briefings and/or training sessions information on the importance of maintaining the privacy of NSLDS data, and to review its own policies, procedures, and agreements to ensure that it is in full compliance.

We look forward to working with our partner organizations to maintain both the usefulness of NSLDS data and the security of the information contained in NSLDS. If you have any questions on access to NSLDS information please contact NSLDS customer service at 1-800-999-8219.

Sincerely,

Matteo Fontana
General Manager, FSA Financial Partners Services

Appendix D   Student Assistance Forms

The Department of Education prints forms for the various discharge programs as well as loan and deferment applications. Most of these forms are available on the Department's website at www.ed.gov. Selected forms are reprinted below. Advocates should note that many state guaranty agencies prefer that borrowers use their discharge forms instead of the federal forms printed below. State guaranty agency forms are available from the individual agencies and are not reprinted here. The forms in this appendix and other forms can be found on the companion CD-Rom to this manual.

D.1 Applications for Loans and Federal Aid

D.1.1 The Free Application for Federal Student Aid (FAFSA)

July 1, 2006 — June 30, 2007

FREE APPLICATION FOR FEDERAL STUDENT AID

OMB # 1845-0001

Use this form to apply free for federal and state student grants, work-study and loans.

Or apply free online at www.fafsa.ed.gov.

Applying by the Deadlines

For federal aid, submit your application as early as possible, but no earlier than January 1, 2006. We must receive your application no later than July 2, 2007. Your college must have your correct, complete information by your last day of enrollment in the 2006-2007 school year.

For state or college aid, the deadline may be as early as January 2006. See the table to the right for state deadlines. You may also need to complete additional forms. Check with your high school guidance counselor or a financial aid administrator at your college about state and college sources of student aid and deadlines.

If you are filing close to one of these deadlines, we recommend you file online at **www.fafsa.ed.gov**. This is the fastest and easiest way to apply for aid.

Using Your Tax Return

If you are supposed to file a 2005 federal income tax return, we recommend that you complete it before filling out this form. If you have not yet filed your return, you can still submit your FAFSA, but you must provide income and tax information. Once you file your tax return, correct any income or tax information that is different from what you initially submitted on your FAFSA.

Filling Out the FAFSA

Your answers on this form will be read electronically. Therefore:

- use black ink and fill in ovals completely:

- print clearly in CAPITAL letters and skip a box between words:

- report dollar amounts (such as $12,356.41) like this:

Correct ● **Incorrect** ✗ ✓

| 1 | 5 | | E | L | M | | S | T |

$ | 1 | 2 | , | 3 | 5 | 6 | **no cents**

Blue is for student information and purple is for parent information.

If you or your family has unusual circumstances (such as loss of employment), complete this form to the extent you can, then submit it as instructed and consult with the financial aid office at the college you plan to attend.

For more information or help in filling out the FAFSA, call 1-800-4-FED-AID (1-800-433-3243). TTY users may call 1-800-730-8913. Or visit our Web site at **www.studentaid.ed.gov**.

Mailing Your FAFSA

After you complete this application, make a copy of pages 3 through 6 for your records. Then mail the original of only pages 3 through 6 in the attached envelope or send it to: Federal Student Aid Programs, P.O. Box 4691, Mt. Vernon, IL 62864-0059. Do not send the worksheets on page 8; keep them for your records.

If you do not receive the results of your application—a *Student Aid Report* (SAR)—within three weeks, please check online at **www.fafsa.ed.gov** or call 1-800-433-3243. If you provided your e-mail address in question 13, you will receive information about your application within a few days after we process it.

Let's Get Started!
Now go to page 3, detach the application form and begin filling it out. Refer to the notes as instructed.

STATE AID DEADLINES

File Online and File On Time
www.fafsa.ed.gov

AK April 15, 2006 *(date received)*
AR For Academic Challenge - June 1, 2006 *(date received)*
　　For Workforce Grant - Contact your financial aid administrator.
AZ June 30, 2007 *(date received)*
*^CA For initial awards - March 2, 2006
　　For additional community college awards - September 2, 2006 *(date postmarked)*
*DC June 30, 2006 *(date received by state)*
DE April 15, 2006 *(date received)*
FL May 15, 2006 *(date processed)*
^IA July 1, 2006 *(date received)*
#IL First-time applicants - September 30, 2006
　　Continuing applicants - August 15, 2006 *(date received)*
IN March 10, 2006 *(date received)*
#*KS April 1, 2006 *(date received)*
#KY March 15, 2006 *(date received)*
#^LA May 1, 2006
　　Final deadline - July 1, 2006 *(date received)*
#^MA May 1, 2006 *(date received)*
MD March 1, 2006 *(date received)*
ME May 1, 2006 *(date received)*
MI March 1, 2006 *(date received)*
MN 30 days after term starts *(date received)*
MO April 1, 2006 *(date received)*
#MT March 1, 2006 *(date received)*
NC March 15, 2006 *(date received)*
ND March 15, 2006 *(date received)*
NH May 1, 2006 *(date received)*
^NJ June 1, 2006, if you received a Tuition Aid Grant in 2005-2006
　　All other applicants
　　- October 1, 2006, fall & spring terms
　　- March 1, 2007, spring term only *(date received)*
*^NY May 1, 2007 *(date received)*
OH October 1, 2006 *(date received)*
#OK April 15, 2006
　　Final deadline - June 30, 2006 *(date received)*
#OR March 1, 2006 *(date received)*
　　Final deadline - Contact your financial aid administrator.
*PA All 2005-2006 State Grant recipients & all non-2005-2006 State Grant recipients in degree programs - May 1, 2006
　　All other applicants - August 1, 2006 *(date received)*
#RI March 1, 2006 *(date received)*
SC June 30, 2006 *(date received)*
TN For State Grant - May 1, 2006
　　For State Lottery - September 1, 2006 *(date received)*
*^WV March 1, 2006 *(date received)*

Check with your financial aid administrator for these states and territories:
AL, *AS, CO, *CT, *FM, GA, *GU, *HI, ID, *MH, *MP, MS, *NE, *NM, *NV, PR, *PW, *SD, *TX, UT, *VA, *VI, *VT, WA, WI and *WY.

\# *For priority consideration, submit application by date specified.*
^ *Applicants encouraged to obtain proof of mailing.*
* *Additional form may be required.*   ISD5472

STATE AID DEADLINES

Notes for questions **14 – 15** (page 3)

If you are an eligible noncitizen, write in your eight- or nine-digit Alien Registration Number. Generally, you are an eligible noncitizen if you are (1) a U.S. permanent resident with a Permanent Resident Card (I-551); (2) a conditional permanent resident (I-551C); or (3) the holder of an Arrival-Departure Record (I-94) from the Department of Homeland Security showing any one of the following designations: "Refugee," "Asylum Granted," "Parolee" (I-94 confirms paroled for a minimum of one year and status has not expired) or "Cuban-Haitian Entrant." If you are in the U.S. on an F1 or F2 student visa, a J1 or J2 exchange visitor visa, or a G series visa (pertaining to international organizations), you must fill in oval **c**. If you are neither a citizen nor an eligible noncitizen, you are not eligible for federal student aid. However, you may be eligible for state or college aid.

Notes for question **23** (page 3) — Enter the correct number in the box in question 23.

Enter **1** for 1st bachelor's degree.
Enter **2** for 2nd bachelor's degree.
Enter **3** for associate degree (occupational or technical program).
Enter **4** for associate degree (general education or transfer program).
Enter **5** for certificate or diploma for completing an occupational, technical, or educational program of less than two years.

Enter **6** for certificate or diploma for completing an occupational, technical, or educational program of at least two years.
Enter **7** for teaching credential program (nondegree program).
Enter **8** for graduate or professional degree.
Enter **9** for other/undecided.

Notes for question **24** (page 3) — Enter the correct number in the box in question 24.

Enter **0** for never attended college & 1st year undergraduate.
Enter **1** for attended college before & 1st year undergraduate.
Enter **2** for 2nd year undergraduate/sophomore.
Enter **3** for 3rd year undergraduate/junior.

Enter **4** for 4th year undergraduate/senior.
Enter **5** for 5th year/other undergraduate.
Enter **6** for 1st year graduate/professional.
Enter **7** for continuing graduate/professional or beyond.

Notes for questions **29 – 30** (page 3)

Some states and colleges offer aid based on the level of schooling your parents completed.

Notes for questions **33 c. and d.** (page 4) and **71 c. and d.** (page 5)

If you filed or will file a foreign tax return, or a tax return with Puerto Rico, Guam, American Samoa, the U.S. Virgin Islands, the Marshall Islands, the Federated States of Micronesia, or Palau, use the information from that return to fill out this form. If you filed a foreign return, convert all figures to U.S. dollars, using the exchange rate that is in effect today. To view the daily exchange rate, go to **www.federalreserve.gov/releases/h10/update**.

Notes for questions **34** (page 4) and **72** (page 5)

In general, a person is eligible to file a 1040A or 1040EZ if he or she makes less than $100,000, does not itemize deductions, does not receive income from his or her own business or farm, and does not receive alimony. A person is not eligible if he or she itemizes deductions, receives self-employment income or alimony, or is required to file Schedule D for capital gains. If you filed a 1040 only to claim Hope or Lifetime Learning credits, and you would have otherwise been eligible for a 1040A or 1040EZ, you should answer "Yes" to this question.

Notes for questions **37** (page 4) and **75** (page 5) — Notes for those who filed a 1040EZ

On the 1040EZ, if a person answered "Yes" on line 5, use EZ worksheet line F to determine the number of exemptions ($3,200 equals one exemption). If a person answered "No" on line 5, enter 01 if he or she is single, or 02 if he or she is married.

Notes for questions **43 – 45** (page 4) and **81 – 83** (page 5)

By applying online at **www.fafsa.ed.gov**, you may be eligible to skip some questions. If you do not apply online, you will not be penalized for completing questions 43-45 and 81-83 on the paper FAFSA.

Net worth means current value minus debt. If net worth is one million dollars or more, enter $999,999. If net worth is negative, enter 0.

Investments include real estate (do not include the home you live in), trust funds, money market funds, mutual funds, certificates of deposit, stocks, stock options, bonds, other securities, Coverdell savings accounts, college savings plans, installment and land sale contracts (including mortgages held), commodities, etc. For more information about reporting education savings plans, call 1-800-433-3243. *Investment value* includes the market value of these investments as of today. *Investment debt* means only those debts that are related to the investments.

Investments do not include the home you live in, the value of life insurance, retirement plans (pension funds, annuities, noneducation IRAs, Keogh plans, etc.), and prepaid tuition plans, or cash, savings, and checking accounts already reported in 43 and 81.

Business and/or investment farm value includes the market value of land, buildings, machinery, equipment, inventory, etc. Business and/or investment farm debt means only those debts for which the business or investment farm was used as collateral.

Notes for question **54** (page 4)

Answer "**No**" (you are not a veteran) if you (1) have never engaged in active duty in the U.S. Armed Forces, (2) are currently an ROTC student or a cadet or midshipman at a service academy, or (3) are a National Guard or Reserves enlistee activated only for training. Also answer "No" if you are currently serving in the U.S. Armed Forces and will continue to serve through June 30, 2007.

Answer "**Yes**" (you are a veteran) if you (1) have engaged in active duty in the U.S. Armed Forces (Army, Navy, Air Force, Marines or Coast Guard) or are a National Guard or Reserve enlistee who was called to active duty for purposes other than training, or were a cadet or midshipman at one of the service academies, **and** (2) were released under a condition other than dishonorable. Also answer "Yes" if you are not a veteran now but will be one by June 30, 2007.

Page 2

Notes continued on page 7.

FAFSA

July 1, 2006 — June 30, 2007
FREE APPLICATION FOR FEDERAL STUDENT AID
OMB # 1845-0001

Step One: For questions 1–30, leave blank any questions that do not apply to you (the student).

1-3. Your full name (as it appears on your Social Security card)

1. LAST NAME	2. FIRST NAME	3. MIDDLE INITIAL
FOR INFORMATION ONLY	DO NOT SUBMIT	

4-7. Your permanent mailing address

4. NUMBER AND STREET (INCLUDE APT. NUMBER)

5. CITY (AND COUNTRY IF NOT U.S.)   6. STATE   7. ZIP CODE

8. Your Social Security Number   XXX – XX – XXXX

9. Your date of birth   MMDD 19 YY

10. Your permanent telephone number   (   )   –

11-12. Your driver's license number and state (if any)

11. LICENSE NUMBER   12. STATE

13. Your e-mail address   WE WILL USE THIS E-MAIL ADDRESS TO CORRESPOND WITH YOU. YOU WILL RECEIVE YOUR FAFSA INFORMATION THROUGH A SECURE LINK ON THE INTERNET, SENT TO THE E-MAIL ADDRESS YOU PROVIDE. LEAVE BLANK TO RECEIVE INFORMATION THROUGH REGULAR MAIL. WE WILL ONLY SHARE THIS ADDRESS WITH THE SCHOOLS YOU LIST ON THE FORM AND YOUR STATE. THEY MAY USE THE E-MAIL ADDRESS TO COMMUNICATE WITH YOU.

[@   ]

14. Are you a U.S. citizen? Pick one. **See page 2.**

a. Yes, I am a U.S. citizen. **Skip to question 16.** .... ○ 1
b. No, but I am an eligible noncitizen. **Fill in question 15.** .... ○ 2
c. No, I am not a citizen or eligible noncitizen. .... ○ 3

15. ALIEN REGISTRATION NUMBER   A

16. What is your marital status as of today?

I am single, divorced or widowed ...... ○ 1
I am married/remarried .... ○ 2
I am separated .... ○ 3

17. Month and year you were married, separated, divorced or widowed   MONTH / YEAR   MMYYYY

18. What is your state of legal residence?   STATE

19. Did you become a legal resident of this state before January 1, 2001?   Yes ○ 1   No ○ 2

20. If the answer to question 19 is "**No**," give month and year you became a legal resident.   MONTH / YEAR   MMYYYY

21. Are you male? (Most male students must register with Selective Service to get federal aid.)   Yes ○ 1   No ○ 2

22. If you are male (age 18–25) and not registered, answer "Yes" and Selective Service will register you.   Yes ○ 1   No ○ 2

23. What degree or certificate will you be working on during 2006–2007 school year? **See page 2** and enter the correct number in the box.

24. What will be your grade level when you begin the 2006–2007 school year? **See page 2** and enter the correct number in the box.

25. Will you have a high school diploma or GED before you begin the 2006–2007 school year?   Yes ○ 1   No ○ 2

26. Will you have your first bachelor's degree before July 1, 2006?   Yes ○ 1   No ○ 2

27. In addition to grants, are you interested in student loans (which you must pay back)?   Yes ○ 1   No ○ 2

28. In addition to grants, are you interested in "work-study" (which you earn through work)?   Yes ○ 1   No ○ 2

29. Highest school your father completed   Middle school/Jr. High ○ 1   High School ○ 2   College or beyond ○ 3   Other/unknown ○ 4

30. Highest school your mother completed   Middle school/Jr. High ○ 1   High School ○ 2   College or beyond ○ 3   Other/unknown ○ 4

31. **Do not leave this question blank.** Have you ever been convicted of possessing or selling illegal drugs? If you have, answer "Yes," complete and submit this application, and we will send you a worksheet in the mail for you to determine if your conviction affects your eligibility for aid.

No ○ 1   Yes ○ 3   **DO NOT LEAVE QUESTION 31 BLANK**

Page 3

For Help – www.studentaid.ed.gov/completefafsa

Step Two: For questions 32–45, report your (the student's) income and assets. If you are married as of today, report your and your spouse's income and assets, even if you were not married in 2005. Ignore references to "spouse" if you are currently single, separated, divorced or widowed.

32. For 2005, have you (the student) completed your IRS income tax return or another tax return listed in question 33?

   a. I have already completed my return. ○ ₁   **b.** I will file, but I have not yet completed my return. ○ ₂   **c.** I'm not going to file. **(Skip to question 38.)** ○ ₃

33. What income tax return did you file or will you file for 2005?

   a. IRS 1040 .... ○ ₁   **d.** A tax return with Puerto Rico, Guam, American Samoa, the U.S. Virgin Islands, the Marshall Islands, the Federated States of Micronesia, or Palau. **See page 2.** .... ○ ₄

   b. IRS 1040A or 1040EZ .... ○ ₂

   c. A foreign tax return. **See page 2.** .... ○ ₃

34. If you have filed or will file a 1040, were you eligible to file a 1040A or 1040EZ? **See page 2.**   Yes ○ ₁   No ○ ₂   Don't Know ○ ₃

For questions 35–47, if the answer is zero or the question does not apply to you, enter 0.

35. What was your (and spouse's) adjusted gross income for 2005? Adjusted gross income is on IRS Form 1040—line 37; 1040A—line 21; or 1040EZ—line 4. $ ☐☐☐ , ☐☐☐

36. Enter your (and spouse's) income tax for 2005. Income tax amount is on IRS Form 1040—line 57; 1040A—line 36; or 1040EZ—line 10. $ ☐☐ , ☐☐☐

37. Enter your (and spouse's) exemptions for 2005. Exemptions are on IRS Form 1040—line 6d or on Form 1040A—line 6d. For Form 1040EZ, **see page 2.**   ☐☐

38-39. How much did you (and spouse) earn from working (wages, salaries, tips, combat pay, etc.) in 2005? Answer this question whether or not you filed a tax return. This information may be on your W-2 forms, or on IRS Form 1040—lines 7 + 12 + 18; 1040A—line 7; or 1040EZ—line 1.   **You (38)** $ ☐☐☐ , ☐☐☐

   Your Spouse (39) $ ☐☐☐ , ☐☐☐

Student (and Spouse) Worksheets (40–42)

40-42. **Go to page 8** and complete the columns on the left of Worksheets A, B, and C. Enter the student (and spouse) totals in questions 40, 41 and 42, respectively. Even though you may have few of the Worksheet items, check each line carefully.

   Worksheet A (40) $ ☐☐☐ , ☐☐☐

   Worksheet B (41) $ ☐☐☐ , ☐☐☐

   Worksheet C (42) $ ☐☐☐ , ☐☐☐

43. As of today, what is your (and spouse's) total current balance of **cash, savings, and checking accounts**? Do not include student financial aid. $ ☐☐☐ , ☐☐☐

44. As of today, what is the net worth of your (and spouse's) **investments**, including real estate (not your home)? *Net worth* means current value minus debt. **See page 2.** $ ☐☐☐ , ☐☐☐

45. As of today, what is the net worth of your (and spouse's) current **businesses and/or investment farms**? Do not include a farm that you live on and operate. **See page 2.** $ ☐☐☐ , ☐☐☐

46-47. If you receive veterans' education benefits, for how many months from July 1, 2006, through June 30, 2007, will you receive these benefits, and what amount will you receive per month? Do not include your spouse's veterans' education benefits.   **Months (46)** ☐☐

   Monthly Amount (47) $ ☐ , ☐☐☐

Step Three: Answer all seven questions in this step.

48. Were you born before January 1, 1983? . . . .   Yes ○ ₁   No ○ ₂

49. At the beginning of the 2006-2007 school year, will you be working on a master's or doctorate program (such as an MA, MBA, MD, JD, PhD, EdD, or graduate certificate, etc.)? . . . .   Yes ○ ₁   No ○ ₂

50. As of today, are you married? (Answer "Yes" if you are separated but not divorced.) . . . .   Yes ○ ₁   No ○ ₂

51. Do you have children who receive more than half of their support from you? . . . .   Yes ○ ₁   No ○ ₂

52. Do you have dependents (other than your children or spouse) who live with you and who receive more than half of their support from you, now and through June 30, 2007? . . . .   Yes ○ ₁   No ○ ₂

53. Are (a) both of your parents deceased, or (b) are you (or were you until age 18) a ward/dependent of the court? . . . .   Yes ○ ₁   No ○ ₂

54. Are you a veteran of the U.S. Armed Forces? **See page 2.** . . . .   Yes ○ ₁   No ○ ₂

If you (the student) answered "No" to every question in Step Three, go to Step Four.
If you answered "Yes" to any question in Step Three, skip Step Four and go to Step Five on page 6.

(Health Profession Students: Your school may require you to complete Step Four even if you answered "Yes" to any Step Three question.)

Step Four: Complete this step if you (the student) answered "No" to all questions in Step Three. Go to page 7 to determine who is a parent for this step.

55. What is your parents' marital status as of today?

Married/Remarried .... ○ 1   Divorced/Separated .... ○ 3

Single .... ○ 2   Widowed .... ○ 4

56. Month and year they were married, separated, divorced or widowed

MONTH YEAR
M M Y Y Y Y

57-64. What are the Social Security Numbers, names and dates of birth of the parents reporting information on this form? If your parent does not have a Social Security Number, you must enter 000-00-0000.

57. FATHER'S/STEPFATHER'S SOCIAL SECURITY NUMBER

☐☐☐ – ☐☐ – ☐☐☐☐

58. FATHER'S/STEPFATHER'S LAST NAME, AND

59. FIRST INITIAL

60. FATHER'S/STEPFATHER'S DATE OF BIRTH

M M D D 1 9 Y Y

61. MOTHER'S/STEPMOTHER'S SOCIAL SECURITY NUMBER

☐☐☐ – ☐☐ – ☐☐☐☐

62. MOTHER'S/STEPMOTHER'S LAST NAME, AND

63. FIRST INITIAL

64. MOTHER'S/STEPMOTHER'S DATE OF BIRTH

M M D D 1 9 Y Y

65. **Go to page 7** to determine how many people are in your parents' household. Enter that number here.

66. **Go to page 7** to determine how many in question 65 (exclude your parents) will be college students between July 1, 2006, and June 30, 2007. Enter that number here.

67. What is your parents' state of legal residence?

STATE

68. Did your parents become legal residents of this state before January 1, 2001?

Yes ○ 1   No ○ 2

69. If the answer to question 68 is "**No**," give month and year legal residency began for the parent who has lived in the state the longest.

MONTH YEAR
M M Y Y Y Y

70. For 2005, have your parents completed their IRS income tax return or another tax return listed in question 71?

a. My parents have already completed their return. ○ 1

b. My parents will file, but they have not yet completed their return. ○ 2

c. My parents are not going to file. **(Skip to question 76.)** ○ 3

71. What income tax return did your parents file or will they file for 2005?

a. IRS 1040 .... ○ 1

b. IRS 1040A or 1040EZ .... ○ 2

c. A foreign tax return. **See page 2.** .... ○ 3

d. A tax return with Puerto Rico, Guam, American Samoa, the U.S. Virgin Islands, the Marshall Islands, the Federated States of Micronesia, or Palau. **See page 2.** .... ○ 4

72. If your parents have filed or will file a 1040, were they eligible to file a 1040A or 1040EZ? **See page 2.**

Yes ○ 1   No ○ 2   Don't Know ○ 3

For questions 73-83, if the answer is zero or the question does not apply, enter 0.

73. What was your parents' adjusted gross income for 2005? Adjusted gross income is on IRS Form 1040—line 37; 1040A—line 21; or 1040EZ—line 4.

$ ☐☐☐ , ☐☐☐

74. Enter your parents' income tax for 2005. Income tax amount is on IRS Form 1040—line 57; 1040A—line 36; or 1040EZ—line 10.

$ ☐☐☐ , ☐☐☐

75. Enter your parents' exemptions for 2005. Exemptions are on IRS Form 1040—line 6d or on Form 1040A—line 6d. For Form 1040EZ, **see page 2.**

☐☐

76-77. How much did your parents earn from working (wages, salaries, tips, combat pay, etc.) in 2005? Answer this question whether or not your parents filed a tax return. This information may be on their W-2 forms, or on IRS Form 1040—lines 7 + 12 + 18; 1040A—line 7; or 1040EZ—line 1.

Father/ Stepfather (76) $ ☐☐☐ , ☐☐☐

Mother/ Stepmother (77) $ ☐☐☐ , ☐☐☐

Parent Worksheets (78-80)

78-80. **Go to page 8** and complete the columns on the right of Worksheets A, B, and C. Enter the parents' totals in questions 78, 79 and 80, respectively. Even though your parents may have few of the Worksheet items, check each line carefully.

Worksheet A (78) $ ☐☐☐ , ☐☐☐

Worksheet B (79) $ ☐☐☐ , ☐☐☐

Worksheet C (80) $ ☐☐☐ , ☐☐☐

81. As of today, what is your parents' total current balance of **cash, savings, and checking accounts**?

$ ☐☐☐ , ☐☐☐

82. As of today, what is the net worth of your parents' **investments**, including real estate (not your parents' home)? *Net worth* means current value minus debt. **See page 2.**

$ ☐☐☐ , ☐☐☐

83. As of today, what is the net worth of your parents' current **businesses and/or investment farms**? Do not include a farm that your parents live on and operate. **See page 2.**

$ ☐☐☐ , ☐☐☐

Now go to Step Six.

Page 5

For Help – www.studentaid.ed.gov/completefafsa

Step Five: Complete this step only if you (the student) answered "Yes" to any Step Three question.

84. **Go to page 7** to determine how many people are in your (and your spouse's) household. Enter that number here.

85. **Go to page 7** to determine how many people in question 84 will be college students, attending at least half time between July 1, 2006, and June 30, 2007. Enter that number here.

Step Six: Please tell us which schools may request your information, and indicate your enrollment status.

Enter the 6-digit federal school code and your housing plans. Look for the federal school codes at **www.fafsa.ed.gov**, at your college financial aid office, at your public library, or by asking your high school guidance counselor. If you cannot get the federal school code, write in the complete name, address, city and state of the college. For state aid, you may wish to list your preferred school first.

1st FEDERAL SCHOOL CODE
86. [ ][ ][ ][ ][ ][ ] **OR** NAME OF COLLEGE / ADDRESS AND CITY STATE [ ][ ] **HOUSING PLANS**
87. on campus ○ 1 / off campus ○ 2 / with parent ○ 3

2nd FEDERAL SCHOOL CODE
88. [ ][ ][ ][ ][ ][ ] **OR** NAME OF COLLEGE / ADDRESS AND CITY STATE [ ][ ]
89. on campus ○ 1 / off campus ○ 2 / with parent ○ 3

3rd FEDERAL SCHOOL CODE
90. [ ][ ][ ][ ][ ][ ] **OR** NAME OF COLLEGE / ADDRESS AND CITY STATE [ ][ ]
91. on campus ○ 1 / off campus ○ 2 / with parent ○ 3

4th FEDERAL SCHOOL CODE
92. [ ][ ][ ][ ][ ][ ] **OR** NAME OF COLLEGE / ADDRESS AND CITY STATE [ ][ ]
93. on campus ○ 1 / off campus ○ 2 / with parent ○ 3

5th FEDERAL SCHOOL CODE
94. [ ][ ][ ][ ][ ][ ] **OR** NAME OF COLLEGE / ADDRESS AND CITY STATE [ ][ ]
95. on campus ○ 1 / off campus ○ 2 / with parent ○ 3

6th FEDERAL SCHOOL CODE
96. [ ][ ][ ][ ][ ][ ] **OR** NAME OF COLLEGE / ADDRESS AND CITY STATE [ ][ ]
97. on campus ○ 1 / off campus ○ 2 / with parent ○ 3

98. **See page 7.** At the start of the 2006-2007 school year, mark if you will be: Full time ○ 1   3/4 time ○ 2   Half time ○ 3   Less than half time ○ 4   Not sure ○ 5

Step Seven: Read, sign and date.

If you are the student, by signing this application you certify that you (1) will use federal and/or state student financial aid only to pay the cost of attending an institution of higher education, (2) are not in default on a federal student loan or have made satisfactory arrangements to repay it, (3) do not owe money back on a federal student grant or have made satisfactory arrangements to repay it, (4) will notify your school if you default on a federal student loan and (5) will not receive a Federal Pell Grant for more than one school for the same period of time.

If you are the parent or the student, by signing this application you agree, if asked, to provide information that will verify the accuracy of your completed form. This information may include U.S. or state income tax forms that you filed or are required to file. Also, you certify that you understand that **the Secretary of Education has the authority to verify information reported on this application with the Internal Revenue Service and other federal agencies.** If you sign any document related to the federal student aid programs electronically using a Personal Identification Number (PIN), you certify that you are the person identified by the PIN and have not disclosed that PIN to anyone else. If you purposely give false or misleading information, you may be fined $20,000, sent to prison, or both.

99. Date this form was completed.

M M D D **2006** ○ **or** **2007** ○

100. **Student** (Sign below)

Parent (A parent from Step Four sign below)

If this form was filled out by someone other than you, your spouse or your parents, that person must complete this part.

Preparer's name, firm and address

101. Preparer's Social Security Number (or 102)
[ ][ ][ ] – [ ][ ] – [ ][ ][ ][ ]

102. Employer ID number (or 101)
[ ][ ] – [ ][ ][ ][ ][ ][ ]

103. Preparer's signature and date

SCHOOL USE ONLY: Federal School Code
D/O ○ 1
FAA Signature

DATA ENTRY USE ONLY: ○ P   ○ *   ○ L   ○ E

Notes for questions **55–83** (page 5) **Step Four:** Who is considered a parent in this step?

Read these notes to determine who is considered a parent on this form. **Answer all questions in Step Four about them**, even if you do not live with them. (Note that grandparents, foster parents and legal guardians are not parents.)

If your parents are living and married to each other, answer the questions about them.

If your parent is widowed or single, answer the questions about that parent. If your widowed parent is remarried as of today, answer the questions about that parent and the person whom your parent married (your stepparent).

If your parents are divorced or separated, answer the questions about the parent you lived with more during the past 12 months. (If you did not live with one parent more than the other, give answers about the parent who provided more financial support during the past 12 months, or during the most recent year that you actually received support from a parent.) If this parent is remarried as of today, answer the questions on the rest of this form about that parent and the person whom your parent married (your stepparent).

Notes for question **65** (page 5)

Include in your parents' household (see notes, above, for who is considered a parent):
* your parents and yourself, even if you don't live with your parents,
* your parents' other children if (a) your parents will provide more than half of their support from July 1, 2006, through June 30, 2007, or (b) the children could answer "no" to every question in Step Three on page 4 of this form, and
* other people if they now live with your parents, your parents provide more than half of their support, and your parents will continue to provide more than half of their support from July 1, 2006, through June 30, 2007.

Notes for questions **66** (page 5) and **85** (page 6)

Always count yourself as a college student. Do not include your parents. Include others only if they will attend, at least half time in 2006-2007, a program that leads to a college degree or certificate.

Notes for question **84** (page 6)

Include in your (and your spouse's) household:
* yourself (and your spouse, if you have one),
* your children, if you will provide more than half of their support from July 1, 2006, through June 30, 2007, and
* other people if they now live with you, you provide more than half of their support, and you will continue to provide more than half of their support from July 1, 2006, through June 30, 2007.

Notes for question **98** (page 6)

For undergraduates, "full time" generally means taking at least 12 credit hours in a term or 24 clock hours per week. "3/4 time" generally means taking at least 9 credit hours in a term or 18 clock hours per week. "Half time" generally means taking at least 6 credit hours in a term or 12 clock hours per week. Provide this information about the college you are most likely to attend.

Information on the Privacy Act and use of your Social Security Number

We use the information that you provide on this form to determine if you are eligible to receive federal student financial aid and the amount that you are eligible to receive. Sections 483 and 484 of the Higher Education Act of 1965, as amended, give us the authority to ask you and your parents these questions, and to collect the Social Security Numbers of you and your parents. We use your Social Security Number to verify your identity and retrieve your records, and we may request your Social Security Number again for those purposes.

State and institutional student financial aid programs may also use the information that you provide on this form to determine if you are eligible to receive state and institutional aid and the need that you have for such aid. Therefore, we will disclose the information that you provide on this form to each institution you list in questions 86–96, state agencies in your state of legal residence, and the state agencies of the states in which the colleges that you list in questions 86–96 are located.

If you are applying solely for federal aid, you must answer all of the following questions that apply to you: 1–9, 14–16, 18, 21–22, 25–26, 31–36, 38–45, 48–67, 70–74, 76–85 and 99–100. If you do not answer these questions, you will not receive federal aid.

Without your consent, we may disclose information that you provide to entities under a published "routine use." Under such a routine use, we may disclose information to third parties that we have authorized to assist us in administering the above programs; to other federal agencies under computer matching programs, such as those with the Internal Revenue Service, Social Security Administration, Selective Service System, Department of Homeland Security, Department of Justice and Veterans Affairs; to your parents or spouse; and to members of Congress if you ask them to help you with student aid questions.

If the federal government, the U.S. Department of Education, or an employee of the U.S. Department of Education is involved in litigation, we may send information to the Department of Justice, or a court or adjudicative body, if the disclosure is related to financial aid and certain conditions are met. In addition, we may send your information to a foreign, federal, state, or local enforcement agency if the information that you submitted indicates a violation or potential violation of law, for which that agency has jurisdiction for investigation or prosecution. Finally, we may send information regarding a claim that is determined to be valid and overdue to a consumer reporting agency. This information includes identifiers from the record; the amount, status and history of the claim; and the program under which the claim arose.

State Certification

By submitting this application, you are giving your state financial aid agency permission to verify any statement on this form and to obtain income tax information for all persons required to report income on this form.

The Paperwork Reduction Act of 1995

The Paperwork Reduction Act of 1995 says that no one is required to respond to a collection of information unless it displays a valid OMB control number, which for this form is 1845-0001. The time required to complete this form is estimated to be one hour, including time to review instructions, search data resources, gather the data needed, and complete and review the information collection. If you have comments about this estimate or suggestions for improving this form, please write to: U.S. Department of Education, Washington DC 20202-4700.

We may request additional information from you to process your application more efficiently. We will collect this additional information only as needed and on a voluntary basis.

Page 7

Notes continued from page 2.

Worksheets
Calendar Year 2005

Do not mail these worksheets in with your application.
Keep these worksheets; your school may ask to see them.

Worksheet A
Report Annual Amounts

Student/Spouse For question 40		Parents For question 78
$	Earned income credit from IRS Form 1040—line 66a; 1040A—line 41a; or 1040EZ—line 8a.	$
$	Additional child tax credit from IRS Form 1040—line 68 or 1040A—line 42	$
$	Welfare benefits, including Temporary Assistance for Needy Families (TANF). Don't include food stamps or subsidized housing.	$
$	Social Security benefits received, for all household members as reported in question 84 (or 65 for your parents), that were not taxed (such as SSI). Report benefits paid to parents in the Parents column, and benefits paid directly to student (or spouse) in the Student/Spouse column.	$
$	—Enter in question 40. Enter in question 78. —	$

Worksheet B
Report Annual Amounts

For question 41		For question 79
$	Payments to tax-deferred pension and savings plans (paid directly or withheld from earnings), including, but not limited to, amounts reported on the W-2 Form in Boxes 12a through 12d, codes D, E, F, G, H and S	$
$	IRA deductions and payments to self-employed SEP, SIMPLE, and Keogh and other qualified plans from IRS Form 1040—line 28 + line 32 or 1040A—line 17	$
$	Child support you received for all children. Don't include foster care or adoption payments.	$
$	Tax exempt interest income from IRS Form 1040—line 8b or 1040A—line 8b	$
$	Foreign income exclusion from IRS Form 2555—line 43 or 2555EZ—line 18	$
$	Untaxed portions of IRA distributions from IRS Form 1040—lines (15a minus 15b) or 1040A—lines (11a minus 11b). Exclude rollovers. If negative, enter a zero here.	$
$	Untaxed portions of pensions from IRS Form 1040—lines (16a minus 16b) or 1040A—lines (12a minus 12b). Exclude rollovers. If negative, enter a zero here.	$
$	Credit for federal tax on special fuels from IRS Form 4136—line 15 (nonfarmers only)	$
$	Housing, food and other living allowances paid to members of the military, clergy and others (including cash payments and cash value of benefits)	$
$	Veterans' noneducation benefits such as Disability, Death Pension, or Dependency & Indemnity Compensation (DIC), and/or VA Educational Work-Study allowances	$
$	Other untaxed income not reported elsewhere on Worksheets A and B (e.g., workers' compensation, untaxed portions of railroad retirement benefits, Black Lung Benefits, disability, combat pay not reported on the tax return, etc.) Don't include student aid, Workforce Investment Act educational benefits, non-tax filers' combat pay, or benefits from flexible spending arrangements, e.g., cafeteria plans.	$
$	Money received, or paid on your behalf (e.g., bills), not reported elsewhere on this form	XXXXXXXX
$	—Enter in question 41. Enter in question 79. —	$

Worksheet C
Report Annual Amounts

For question 42		For question 80
$	Education credits (Hope and Lifetime Learning tax credits) from IRS Form 1040—line 50 or 1040A—line 31	$
$	Child support you paid because of divorce or separation or as a result of a legal requirement. Don't include support for children in your (or your parents') household, as reported in question 84 (or question 65 for your parents).	$
$	Taxable earnings from need-based employment programs, such as Federal Work-Study and need-based employment portions of fellowships and assistantships	$
$	Student grant and scholarship aid reported to the IRS in your (or your parents') adjusted gross income. Includes AmeriCorps benefits (awards, living allowances and interest accrual payments), as well as grant or scholarship portions of fellowships and assistantships.	$
$	—Enter in question 42 Enter in question 80. —	$

For Help — 1-800-433-3243

385

D.1.2 Direct Consolidation Loan Application and Instructions

Direct Loans
William D. Ford Federal Direct Loan Program

Federal Direct Consolidation Loan
Instructions for Application and Promissory Note

OMB No. 1845-0053
Form Approved
Exp. Date 1/31/2005

▮▮▮▮▮▮▮▮▮

Before beginning, you will need to gather all of your loan records, account statements, and bills so that you will have on hand all the information you will need to complete the application and promissory note.

The form should be printed in blue or black ink or typewritten, and it must be signed and dated by the applicant(s). If you cross out anything and write in new information, put your initials beside the change.

Incorrect or incomplete information may delay processing.

▮▮▮▮▮▮▮▮▮▮▮▮

Items 1 and 2: Enter the information requested.

Item 3: Enter your permanent home street address. If your mailing address is an RFD, post office box, or general delivery, you must list **both** the street address and mailing address.

Items 4 - 6: Enter the information requested. Note, Items 5 and 6 are optional.

Item 7: Enter any former names under which one or more or your loans may have been made. (If none, enter "none.")

Item 8: Enter the information requested.

Item 9: First, enter in the parentheses the two letter abbreviation for the state that issued your driver's license. Then, enter your driver's license number. (If none, enter "none.")

Items 10 - 12: Enter the information requested. If none, enter "none."

Item 13: If married, check "Yes" or "No" to indicate whether you want to consolidate your loan(s) with your spouse's loan(s).

▮▮▮▮▮▮▮▮▮▮

Item 14: See instructions provided in the section.

▮▮▮▮▮▮▮▮▮▮▮

Note: Complete this section only if you are married and wish to consolidate your loans with those of your spouse. Remember, if you do this, you are both responsible for repaying the total consolidation loan, even if you become separated or divorced or if one spouse dies.

Items 15 - 17: Enter the information requested.

Item 18: First, enter in the parentheses the two letter abbreviation for the state that issued your spouse's driver's license. Then, enter your spouse's driver's license number. (If none, enter "none.")

Item 19: Enter the information requested. Note, this item is optional.

Item 20: Enter any former names under which one or more of your spouse's loans may have been made. (If none, enter "none.")

Item 21: Enter the information requested. Note, this item is optional.

Items 22 - 24: Enter the information requested. (If none, enter "none.")

▮▮▮▮▮▮▮▮▮▮▮

This section asks about your education loans. List **all** your education loans in Section D, including your Direct Loans and loans you are **not** consolidating. To find the information you will need to answer these items, there are several places you can look, such as:

- the last monthly billing statement you received,
- your quarterly interest statement or annual statement,
- your coupon book, or
- the Internet site of your loan holder or servicer.

If you are currently in school, you can contact the financial aid administrator at your school.

Item 25: Enter the information requested. You must give us at least the name, city, and state of your loan holder or servicer. Use the resources listed above to find this information. For example, on your statement, there might be two addresses: first, the address where you send your payment, and second, an address that is sometimes called the "correspondence address." For Item 25, we want you to give us the "correspondence address." If there is only one address on your documents, give us that address. If you cannot find this information on your documents, call the telephone number on the statement or use the other resources listed. For each loan, send a photocopy of the document where you found the information.

Item 26: Enter the letter that corresponds to the loan type from the chart provided. If you are not sure about the loan type, leave this item blank.

Item 27: Tell us whether the loan was made to you, to your spouse, or to both of you by entering:

B - for borrower   **S** - for spouse   **J** - for loans to both of you
You **must** complete this item, even if you are not married.

Item 28: Enter the account number for each loan (the number should be on your statement or in your payment book). If you cannot find the account number, leave this item blank.

Item 29: Enter the current balance for each loan as of your last payment. You **must** complete this item. Use the amount on your last statement or give us an approximate amount.

Item 30: Tell us whether you wish to consolidate this loan by entering "Y" in the "Yes" column or "N" in the "No" column. You **must** answer this item.

Note: If you need additional space to list all of your loans, complete the Federal Direct Consolidation Loan Additional Loan Listing Sheet and return it with your application and promissory note. Be sure to write your name and social security number in the spaces provided.

▮▮▮▮▮▮▮▮▮▮▮

Item 31: See instructions provided in the section.

▮▮▮▮▮▮▮▮▮▮

Note: Read the entire promissory note (pages 3 and 4) and the accompanying Borrower's Rights and Responsibilities before signing and dating the promissory note as indicated.

Do not make any changes to this section. Changes will void the terms and agreements of the promissory note. This is a legally binding contract.

Item 32: Sign and date the promissory note in blue or black ink. If you and your spouse are applying for a joint consolidation loan, you both must sign and date the promissory note. If you fail to do so, your application will not be processed.

Review all the information on your Direct Consolidation Loan Application and Promissory Note. When complete, make a copy for your records and mail the original to us in the envelope provided.

As soon as we receive your completed application and promissory note and supporting documents, we will begin processing. During this time, we might call you with questions. We will be sending you a notice before we pay off your loan(s).

In the meantime, if you currently are required to make payments on your loan(s), continue to do so. You will need to continue making payments until you receive written notification that your loan(s) has been successfully consolidated and it is time to start paying your Direct Consolidation Loan. If you are having difficulty making payments on your loan(s), contact the correspondence address or telephone number on your current loan statement(s) to find out ways you might be able to postpone loan payments; ask specifically about your "deferment" or "forbearance" options.

Types of Education Loans and Their Codes

Subsidized Loans	Unsubsidized Loans
A Subsidized Federal Stafford Loans	**G** Unsubsidized Federal Stafford Loans (including
B Guaranteed Student Loans (GSL)	Non-Subsidized Stafford Loans made prior to 10/1/92)
C Federal Insured Student Loans (FISL)	**H** Federal Supplemental Loans for Students (SLS)
D Federal Direct Stafford/Ford Loans	**J** Unsubsidized Federal Consolidation Loans
E Federal Direct Subsidized	**K** Federal Direct Unsubsidized Consolidation Loans
Consolidation Loans	**L** Federal Direct Unsubsidized Stafford/Ford Loans
F Federal Perkins Loans	**P** Auxiliary Loans to Assist Students (ALAS)
M National Direct Student Loans (NDSL)	**Q** Health Professions Student Loans (HPSL)
N National Defense Student Loans (NDSL)	**R** Health Education Assistance Loans (HEAL)
O Subsidized Federal Consolidation Loans	**S** Federal PLUS Loans
	T Parent Loans for Undergraduate Students (PLUS)
	U Federal Direct PLUS Loans
Note: You must consolidate at least one	**V** Federal Direct PLUS Consolidation Loans
Direct Loan or FFEL Program Loan.	**Y** Nursing Student Loans (NSL)
	Z Loans for Disadvantaged Students (LDS)
	W Other education loans ineligible for consolidation

For assistance when completing this form, call the Loan Origination Center's Consolidation Department at 1-800-557-7392.

For the hearing impaired, the TDD number is 1-800-557-7395.

Direct Loans
William D. Ford Federal Direct Loan Program

Federal Direct Consolidation Loan
Important Notices

Privacy Act Disclosure Notice

The Privacy Act of 1974 (5 U.S.C. 552a) requires that we disclose to you the following information:

The authority for collecting this information is §451 et seq. of the Higher Education Act of 1965, as amended (the HEA) (20 U.S.C. §1087a et seq.). The principal purposes for collecting this information are to determine your eligibility for a Federal Direct Consolidation Loan that is made under the William D. Ford Federal Direct Loan (Direct Loan) Program, to document your agreement to repay this loan, and to identify and locate you if it is necessary to enforce the loan.

We ask that you provide the information requested on this Federal Direct Consolidation Loan Application and Promissory Note (application and promissory note) on a voluntary basis. However, you must provide all of the requested information that is available to you so the Department may process this application and promissory note because the Department needs the information to consolidate your loans into a Federal Direct Consolidation Loan.

The information in your file may be disclosed to third parties as authorized under routine uses in the Privacy Act notices called "Title IV Program Files" (originally published on April 12, 1994, Federal

Register, Vol. 59, p. 17351) and "National Student Loan Data System" (originally published on December 20, 1994, Federal Register, Vol. 59, p. 65532). Thus, this information may be disclosed to parties that we authorize to assist us in administering the Federal student aid programs, including contractors that are required to maintain safeguards under the Privacy Act. Disclosures may also be made for verification of information, determination of eligibility, enforcement of conditions of the loan or grant, debt collection, and the prevention of fraud, waste, and abuse and these disclosures may be made through computer matching programs with other Federal agencies. Disclosures may be made to determine the feasibility of entering into computer matching agreements. We may send information to members of Congress if you ask them in writing to help you with Federal student aid questions. If we are involved in litigation, we may send information to the Department of Justice (DOJ), a court, adjudicative body, counsel, or witness if the disclosure is related to financial aid and certain other conditions are met. If this information, either alone or with other information, indicates a potential violation of law, we may send it to the appropriate authority for consideration of action

and we may disclose to DOJ to get its advice related to the Title IV, HEA programs or questions under the Freedom of Information Act. Disclosures may be made to qualified researchers under Privacy Act safeguards. In some circumstances involving employment decisions, grievances, or complaints or involving decisions regarding the letting of a contract or making of a grant, license, or other benefit, we may send information to an appropriate authority. In limited circumstances, we may disclose to a Federal labor organization recognized under 5 U.S.C. Chapter 71.

Because we request your social security number (SSN), we must inform you that we collect your SSN on a voluntary basis, but section 484(a)(4) of the HEA (20 U.S.C. 1091(a)(4)) provides that, in order to receive any grant, loan, or work assistance under Title IV of the HEA, a student must provide his or her SSN. Your SSN is used to verify your identity, and as an account number (identifier) throughout the life of your loan(s) so that data may be recorded accurately.

Financial Privacy Act Notice

Under the Right to Financial Privacy Act of 1978 (12 U.S.C. 3401-3421), ED will have access to financial records in your student loan file maintained in compliance with the administration of the Direct Loan Program.

Paperwork Reduction Notice

According to the Paperwork Reduction Act of 1995, no persons are required to respond to a collection of information unless it displays a currently valid OMB control number. The valid OMB control number for this information collection is 1845-0053. The time required to complete this information collection is estimated to average 1.0 hour (60 minutes) per response, including the time to review instructions, search existing data resources, gather and maintain the data needed, and complete and review the information collection. **If you have any comments concerning the accuracy of the time estimate(s) or suggestions for improving this form, please write to:** U.S. Department of Education, Washington, DC 20202-4651. **If you have any comments or concerns regarding the status of** *your individual submission* **of this form, write directly to:**

U.S. Department of Education
Consolidation Department
Loan Origination Center
P.O. Box 242800
Louisville, KY 40224-2800

Direct Loans
William D. Ford Federal Direct Loan Program

Federal Direct Consolidation Loan
Application and Promissory Note

WARNING: Any person who knowingly makes a false statement or misrepresentation on this form shall be subject to penalties which may include fines, imprisonment, or both, under the U.S. Criminal Code and 20 U.S.C. 1097.

OMB No. 1845-0053
Form Approved
Exp. Date 1/31/2005

Before You Begin

This form should be printed in blue or black ink or typewritten and must be signed and dated by the applicant(s). If you cross out anything and write in new information, put your initials beside the change.

Section A: Borrower Information

1. Last Name First Name Middle Initial	2. Social Security Number ___ — ___ — ___

3. Permanent Street Address (if P.O. box, see instructions)	4. Home Area Code/Telephone Number ( )

City State Zip Code	5. Fax Number (Optional) ( )	6. E-Mail Address (Optional)

7. Former Name(s)	8. Date of Birth	9. Driver's License Number (put state abbreviation first) ( )

10. Employer's Name	11. Employer's Address

12. Employer's Area Code/Telephone Number ( )	City State Zip Code

13. If you are married, does your spouse have an eligible loan(s) (see instructions) that you want to consolidate with your loan(s)?   Yes ☐   No ☐
If yes, complete Section C, include your spouse's loan(s) in Section D, and have your spouse sign and date Item 32 in Section F.

Section B: Reference Information

14. References: Enter the requested information for two relatives or acquaintances who do not live with you and who have known you for at least three years. References may not live outside the United States.

Name   1._____   2._____

Permanent Address   _____   _____

City, State, Zip Code   _____   _____

Area Code/Telephone Number (   ) _____   (   ) _____

Section C: Spouse Information   To be completed only if you responded "Yes" to Item 13.

15. Last Name First Name Middle Initial	16. Social Security Number ___ — ___ — ___

17. Date of Birth	18. Driver's License Number (put state abbreviation first) ( )	19. Fax Number (Optional) ( )

20. Former Name(s)	21. E-Mail Address (Optional)

22. Employer's Name	23. Employer's Address

24. Employer's Area Code and Telephone Number ( )	City State Zip Code

Page 1

Borrower's Name＿＿＿＿＿＿＿＿＿＿＿＿＿＿＿＿＿＿＿＿＿＿＿＿

Borrower's Social Security Number＿＿＿＿＿＿＿＿＿＿＿＿＿＿＿＿＿＿

Section D: Education Loan Indebtedness	(See instructions before completing this section.)				

25. Loan Holder/Servicer's Name, Address, and Area Code/Telephone Number	26. Loan Type	27. B=Borrower S=Spouse J=Joint	28. Account Number	29. Current Balance	30. To Be Consolidated? Yes No
( )					
( )					
( )					
( )					
( )					
( )					
( )					
( )					

Borrower's Name_____

Borrower's Social Security Number_____

Section E: Repayment Plan Selection

Carefully read the repayment plan information in "Direct Consolidation Loans" that accompanies this application and promissory note to understand your repayment plan options. Then, complete this section to select your repayment plan. Remember--

- All student loans must be repaid under the same repayment plan. Parent PLUS loans may be repaid under a different repayment plan.
- If you select the Income Contingent Repayment Plan, you must complete the "Repayment Plan Selection" and "Income Contingent Repayment Plan Consent to Disclosure of Tax Information" forms that accompany this application and promissory note. Your selection cannot be processed without these forms.
- **If you want to consolidate a defaulted student loan(s) and you have not made a satisfactory repayment arrangement with your current holder(s), you must select the Income Contingent Repayment Plan.**

31. Place an "X" in the box that corresponds to your repayment plan selection for each loan type. Note that Direct PLUS Consolidation Loans cannot be repaid under the Income Contingent Repayment Plan.

	Income Contingent	Standard	Extended	Graduated
STUDENT LOANS *Direct Subsidized and Unsubsidized Consolidation Loans*	☐	☐	☐	☐
PARENT LOANS *Direct PLUS Consolidation Loans*	Not Available	☐	☐	☐

Section F: Promissory Note (Continued on reverse side)   To be completed and signed by borrower and spouse, if applicable.

Promise to Pay:

I promise to pay to the U.S. Department of Education (ED) all sums (hereafter "loan" or "loans") disbursed under the terms of this Promissory Note (note) to discharge my prior loan obligations, plus interest, and other fees that may become due as provided in this note. If I fail to make payments on this note when due, I will also pay collection costs including but not limited to attorney's fees and court costs. If ED accepts my application, I understand that ED will on my behalf send funds to the holder(s) of the loan(s) selected for consolidation in order to pay off this loan(s). I further understand that the amount of this loan will equal the sum of the amount(s) that the holder(s) of the loan(s) verified as the payoff balance(s) on that loan(s) selected for consolidation. My signature on this note will serve as my authorization to pay off the balance(s) of the loan(s) selected for consolidation as provided by the holder(s) of such loan(s).

This amount may be more or less than the estimated total balance I have indicated in Section D. Further, I understand that if any collection costs are owed on the loans selected for consolidation, these costs may be added to the principal balance of the consolidation loan.

I understand that this is a Promissory Note. I will not sign this note before reading it, including the text on the reverse side, even if I am advised not to read the note. I am entitled to an exact copy of this note and a statement of the Borrower's Rights and Responsibilities. My signature certifies that I have read, understand, and agree, to the terms and conditions of this note, including the Borrower Certification and Authorization printed on the reverse side and the accompanying Borrower's Rights and Responsibilities.

If consolidating jointly with my spouse, we agree to the same terms and conditions contained in the Borrower Certification and Authorization. In addition, we confirm that we are legally married to each other and understand and agree that we are and will continue to be held jointly and severally liable for the entire amount of the debt represented by the Federal Direct Consolidation Loan without regard to the amounts of our individual loan obligations that are consolidated and without regard to any change that may occur in our marital status. We understand that this means that one of us may be required to pay the entire amount due if the other is unable or refuses to pay. We understand that the Federal Direct Consolidation Loan we are applying for will be cancelled only if both of us qualify for cancellation. We further understand that we may postpone repayment of the loan only if we provide ED with written requests that confirm Federal Direct Consolidation Loan Program deferment or forbearance eligibility for both of us at the same time.

I UNDERSTAND THAT THIS IS A FEDERAL LOAN THAT I MUST REPAY.

Page 3

Promissory Note (continued)

Governing Law and Notices

This Promissory Note (note) applies to Federal Direct Consolidation Loans (Direct Consolidation Loans). In this note, the Higher Education Act of 1965, as amended, 20 U.S.C. 1070 et seq., and applicable U.S. Department of Education (ED) regulations are referred to as "the Act." The terms of this note will be interpreted according to the Act and other applicable federal statutes and regulations. Applicable state law, except as preempted by federal law, may provide for certain borrower rights, remedies, and defenses in addition to those stated in this note.

Disclosure of Terms

When the loan(s) that I am consolidating is paid off, I will be sent a Disclosure Statement and Repayment Schedule (disclosure). The disclosure will identify my Direct Consolidation Loan amount and additional terms of my loan. If I have questions about the information disclosed, I will contact ED. If the information in this note conflicts with the information in the disclosure, the disclosure will be controlling.

Important additional terms of this loan are disclosed in the statement of Borrower's Rights and Responsibilities accompanying this note.

I understand that my Direct Consolidation Loan may consist of up to three separate loan identification numbers depending on the loan(s) I choose to consolidate. These loan identification numbers will represent prior subsidized loans, prior unsubsidized loans, and prior parent PLUS loans. The Borrower's Rights and Responsibilities identifies which eligible loans are included in each of these categories. Each applicable loan identification number is represented by this note.

Interest

Except for interest ED does not charge me during an in-school, grace, or deferment period, I agree to pay interest on the principal amount of my Direct Consolidation Loan from the date of disbursement until the loan is paid in full or discharged. ED may add interest that accrues but is not paid when due to the unpaid principal balance of this loan, as provided under the Act. This is called capitalization.

Interest will be calculated according to the applicable formulas provided for by the Act.

The interest rate on my Direct Consolidation Loan will be based on the weighted average of the interest rates on the loans being consolidated, rounded to the nearest higher one-eighth of one percent, but shall not exceed 8.25%. This is a fixed interest rate, which means that the rate will remain the same throughout the life of the loan.

Late Charges and Collection Costs

If I fail to make any part of an installment payment within 30 days after it becomes due, ED may collect from me a late charge that will not exceed six cents for each dollar of each late installment. If I default on the loan, I will pay reasonable collection fees and costs, plus court costs and attorney's fees associated with collection of the debt.

Grace Period

My Direct Consolidation Loan will receive a grace period if I meet all of the following conditions: (1) I have at least one William D. Ford Federal Direct Loan (Direct Loan) Program loan or attend a Direct Loan school, (2) at least one Direct Loan or Federal Family Education Loan (FFEL) Program loan that I am consolidating is in an in-school period, and (3) my application for a Direct Consolidation Loan is received by ED prior to the end of my in-school period. A six-month grace period begins the day after I cease to be enrolled at least half time at an eligible school. (If my enrollment status changes to less than half time after I apply but before the first disbursement of my Direct Consolidation Loan, I will not have to make payments on my Direct Consolidation Loan for the number of months remaining in my grace period at the time the first disbursement is made.)

Repayment

Unless my Direct Consolidation Loan is in an in-school or grace period when it is disbursed, I must select a repayment plan. If I do not select a repayment plan, ED will choose a plan for me in accordance with ED's regulations. My first payment will be due within 60 days of the first disbursement of my Direct Consolidation Loan unless it is in an in-school, grace, or deferment period. A repayment schedule will be furnished to me and will establish repayment terms, including my payment amount and the length of my repayment period. Payments will be scheduled in monthly installments. The amount of my monthly payment may be adjusted to reflect changes in the variable interest rate. ED may adjust my repayment schedule if ED learns that any of the loans listed herein is not eligible to be consolidated. My repayment period will be up to 30 years in length, depending on the amount of my student loan indebtedness and my repayment plan. Any period for which ED has granted a deferment or forbearance will not be included in determining my repayment period.

I may prepay all or any part of the unpaid balance on my loan at any time without penalty. I agree to accept written notification of such pay off in lieu of receiving the original note.

Acceleration and Default

At the option of ED, the entire unpaid balance shall become immediately due and payable when either of the following events occurs: (i) I make false representation that results in my receiving a loan for which I am not eligible, or (ii) I default on the loan.

The following events shall constitute a default on a loan: (i) I fail to pay the entire unpaid balance after ED has exercised its option under the preceding paragraph; or (ii) I fail to make installment payments when due, or fail to comply with other terms of the loan, and ED reasonably concludes I no longer intend to honor my repayment obligation. My failure must have persisted for at least 270 days. If I default, ED will capitalize all outstanding interest into a new principal balance.

If I default, this will be reported to national credit bureau organizations and will significantly and adversely affect my credit rating. I acknowledge that a default shall have additional adverse consequences to me as disclosed in the Borrower's Rights and Responsibilities.

Following default, the loan may at ED's option, be subject to income contingent repayment in accordance with the Act.

Any notice required to be given to me will be effective when mailed by first class mail to the latest address that ED has for me. I will immediately notify ED of any change of my address. Failure by ED to enforce or insist on compliance with any term on this note shall not waive any right of ED. No provision of this note may be changed or waived except in writing by ED. If any provision of this note is determined to be unenforceable, the remaining provisions shall remain in force.

Borrower Certification and Authorization

I declare under penalty of perjury that the following is true and correct:

(1) I certify that the information provided by me and my spouse, if applicable, in this note is true, complete, and correct to the best of my knowledge and belief and is made in good faith.

(2) I certify that I do not now owe a refund on a Federal Pell Grant, Basic Educational Opportunity Grant, Federal Supplemental Educational Opportunity Grant, or a State Student Incentive Grant, or if I owe a refund, I have made satisfactory arrangements with the holder to repay the amount owed. I further certify that I am not now in default on any loan I am consolidating or, if I am in default, I have either made a satisfactory repayment arrangement with the holder of that defaulted loan, or I will repay under the income contingent repayment plan. I understand that income contingent repayment is not available for the parent PLUS loan portion of my Direct Consolidation Loan.

(3) I certify that all of the loans selected have been used to finance my education, my spouse's education, or my child's education.

(4) I certify that I do not have any other application pending for a Federal Consolidation Loan with any other lender. If my student loans are in a grace or repayment period and if none of the loans I am consolidating is a Direct Loan Program loan, I further certify that I have sought and been unable to obtain a Federal Consolidation Loan from a FFEL Program lender, or a lender would not provide me with a Federal Consolidation Loan with income-sensitive repayment terms acceptable to me. If I have parent PLUS loans and none of the loans I am consolidating is a Direct Loan Program loan, I further certify that I have sought and been unable to obtain a Federal Consolidation Loan from a FFEL Program lender. If, however, I am consolidating jointly with my spouse, only one borrower, my spouse or I, must have sought a Federal Consolidation Loan from a FFEL Program lender.

(5) I understand that this loan shall, to the extent used to discharge loans that I have selected, count against the applicable aggregate loan limits under the Act.

(6) I understand that the amount of my Direct Consolidation Loan is the sum of the balance(s) of my outstanding eligible loan(s) that I have chosen to consolidate. My outstanding balance on each loan to be consolidated includes unpaid principal, unpaid accrued interest, and late charges as defined by federal regulations and as certified by each holder. Collection costs may also be included. For a Direct Loan or FFEL Program loan that is in default, ED limits collection costs that may be charged to the borrower to no more than those currently authorized under the FFEL Program and may impose reasonable limits on collection costs paid to the holder. If the amount ED advances to my holder(s) exceeds the amount needed to pay off the balance(s) of the selected loan(s), I understand that the holder will refund the excess to ED for application against the outstanding balance of this loan. If the amount that ED advances to my holder(s) is less than the amount needed to pay off the balance(s) of the loan(s) selected for consolidation, ED will include the remaining amount in this loan unless I pay the remaining balance myself.

(7) I authorize ED to contact the holder(s) identified on my application to determine the eligibility and/or payoff amount for the loan(s) I have identified. I further authorize release to ED or its agent any information required to consolidate my education loan(s) pursuant to the Act.

(8) I authorize ED to issue the proceeds of my Direct Consolidation Loan to the holder(s) of the loan(s) so selected to discharge the debt.

(9) I authorize ED to investigate my credit record and report information concerning my loan status to proper persons and organizations authorized to receive this information.

(10) I authorize the release of information pertinent to this loan: (i) by my school(s) and ED, to members of my immediate family unless I submit written direction otherwise; and (ii) by and amongst my school(s), ED, and their agents.

(11) I authorize my school(s), ED, and their agents, to verify my social security number with the Social Security Administration (SSA) and, if the number on my loan record is incorrect, then I authorize SSA to disclose my correct social security number to these parties.

Page 4

D.1.3 Income Contingent Repayment Plan, Alternative Documentation of Income

Direct Loans
William D. Ford Federal Direct Loan Program

Income Contingent Repayment Plan
Alternative Documentation of Income
William D. Ford Federal Direct Loan Program
Federal Direct Stafford/Ford Loans, Federal Direct Unsubsidized Stafford/Ford Loans,
Federal Direct Subsidized Consolidation Loans, Federal Direct Unsubsidized Consolidation Loans
WARNING: Any person who knowingly makes a false statement or misrepresentation on this form shall be subject to penalties which may include fines, imprisonment, or both, under the U.S. Criminal Code and 20 U.S.C. 1097.

OMB No. 1845-0016
Form Approved
Exp. Date 01/31/2006

Instructions

YOU ARE REQUIRED to complete this form if you are repaying your Direct Loans under the Income Contingent Repayment (ICR) Plan and:

- You are in your first year of repayment on a Direct Loan;

- You are in your second year of repayment on a Direct Loan and have been notified that alternative documentation of your income is required; or

- You have been notified that the Internal Revenue Service (IRS) is unable to provide the U.S. Department of Education (the Department) with your Adjusted Gross Income (AGI) or that of your spouse (if you are married).

YOU MAY complete this form if:

- You are repaying your Direct Loans under the ICR Plan and your AGI, as reported on your most recently filed federal tax return, or that of your spouse (if you are married) does not reasonably reflect your current income.

- Your AGI and your spouse's AGI (if you are married) does not reflect your current income and ability to repay your loan(s) in circumstances such as loss or change of employment by you or your spouse (if you are married).

In cases where alternative documentation of your income is used, the amount of your monthly payment under the ICR Plan is based on the current income information you and your spouse (if you are married) provide and is reevaluated annually. To submit alternative documentation of your income, you must attach the required documentation, complete and sign this form, and return it to the address on the back of this form. If you are married, your spouse also must complete and sign the applicable sections of this form and submit the required documentation. If you need assistance, please call 1-800-848-0979, or TDD 1-800-848-0983.

Section 1: Identifying Information (Must be completed by the borrower and the borrower's spouse, if married.)

Borrower's Name (please print clearly):

Last Name	First Name	Middle Initial

Borrower's Social Security Number:

|__|__|__|-|__|__|-|__|__|__|__|

Your Spouse's Name (please print clearly):

Last Name	First Name	Middle Initial

Your Spouse's Social Security Number:

|__|__|__|-|__|__|-|__|__|__|__|

Section 2: Income Information (Must be completed by the borrower and the borrower's spouse, if married.)

You must list all taxable income you are currently receiving (i.e., income from employment, unemployment income, dividend income, interest income, tips, alimony). Include the amount of money received, how often you receive this money, and your employer (if any) or the source of your income if you are not employed. If you are married, your spouse's income and documentation of this income also must be provided. **All income** reported under this section must have supporting documentation (i.e., pay stubs, letters from your employer containing your income, interest or bank statements, dividend statements, canceled checks, or, when these forms of documentation are unavailable, a signed statement explaining your income source(s) and giving the addresses of these sources) submitted with this application. **All supporting documentation must not be more than 90 days old**. If you have more than two sources of income, provide the information requested in this section on a separate piece of paper and mail it with this form. Do not report untaxed income such as Supplemental Security Income, child support, or TANF. If your income or the income of your spouse changes significantly after your submission of this form, you must notify the Direct Loan Servicing Center of this change.

Borrower's Income:

Amount of Income	Frequency of Payment (Please check the appropriate box.)					Employer or Source of Income
	Weekly	Bi-weekly	Semi-monthly	Monthly	Yearly	
$	☐	☐	☐	☐	☐	
$	☐	☐	☐	☐	☐	

☐ Check this box if you do not have any taxable income and receive only untaxed income such as Supplemental Security Income, child support, or TANF.

Spouse's Income:

Amount of Income	Frequency of Payment (Please check the appropriate box.)					Employer or Source of Income
	Weekly	Bi-weekly	Semi-monthly	Monthly	Yearly	
$	☐	☐	☐	☐	☐	
$	☐	☐	☐	☐	☐	

☐ Check this box if you do not have any taxable income and receive only untaxed income such as Supplemental Security Income, child support, or TANF.

Section 3: Certification and Signature (Must be completed by the borrower and the borrower's spouse, if married.)

Certification: I certify that all of the information reported to qualify for alternative documentation of income is true and complete to the best of my knowledge. I agree to provide to the U.S. Department of Education on an annual basis (or as required by the Department) alternative documentation of my income for the purpose of determining my appropriate repayment amount under the ICR Plan. I understand that if I do not provide this information the Department will base my income contingent repayment amount on my AGI, as reported by the IRS, or, in some instances, I will not be allowed to repay my loan(s) under the ICR Plan. I understand that the Department may be requesting my income information from the IRS even if alternative documentation of my income is accepted. I understand that if I am married my spouse's income information, documentation, and signature are required.

_____   _____
Borrower's Signature   Date form was signed

_____   _____
Spouse's Signature   Date form was signed

Important Notices

Return this form to:

U.S. Department of Education
Direct Loan Servicing Center
P.O. Box 4609
Utica, NY 13504-4609

If you need assistance in completing this form, call 1-800-848-0979. Individuals who use a telecommunications device for the deaf (TDD) may call 1-800-848-0983.

Privacy Act Disclosure Notice

The Privacy Act of 1974 (5 U.S.C. 552a) requires that the following notice be provided to you:

The authority for collecting the requested information from and about you is §451 et seq. of the Higher Education Act of 1965, as amended (20 U.S.C. 1087a et seq.) and the authority for collecting and using your Social Security Number (SSN) is §484(a)(4) of the HEA (20 U.S.C. 1091(a)(4)). Participating in the William D. Ford Federal Direct Loan (Direct Loan) Program and giving us your SSN are voluntary, but you must provide the requested information, including your SSN, to participate.

The principal purposes for collecting the information on this form, including your SSN, are to verify your identity, to determine your eligibility to receive a loan or a benefit on a loan (such as a deferment, forbearance, discharge, or forgiveness) under the Direct Loan Program, to permit the servicing of your loan(s), and, if it becomes necessary, to locate you and to collect on your loan(s) if your loan(s) become delinquent or in default. We also use your SSN as an account identifier and to permit you to access your account information electronically.

The information in your file may be disclosed to third parties as authorized under routine uses in the appropriate systems of records. The routine uses of this information include its disclosure to federal, state, or local agencies, to other federal agencies under computer matching programs, to agencies that we authorize to assist us in administering our loan programs, to private parties such as relatives, present and former employers, business and personal associates, to credit bureau organizations, to financial and educational institutions, to guaranty agencies, and to contractors in order to verify your identity, to determine your eligibility to receive a loan or a benefit on a loan, to permit the servicing or collection of your loan(s), to counsel you in repayment efforts, to enforce the terms of the loan(s), to investigate possible fraud and to verify compliance with federal student financial aid program regulations, or to locate you if you become delinquent in your loan payments or if you default, to provide default rate calculations, to provide financial aid history information, to assist program administrators with tracking refunds and cancellations, or to provide a standardized method for educational institutions efficiently to submit student enrollment status.

In the event of litigation, we may send records to the Department of Justice, a court, adjudicative body, counsel, party, or witness if the disclosure is relevant and necessary to the litigation. If this information, either alone or with other information, indicates a potential violation of law, we may send it to the appropriate authority for action. We may send information to members of Congress if you ask them to help you with federal student aid questions. In circumstances involving employment complaints, grievances, or disciplinary actions, we may disclose relevant records to adjudicate or investigate the issues. If provided for by a collective bargaining agreement, we may disclose records to a labor organization recognized under 5 U.S.C. Chapter 71. Disclosures may also be made to qualified researchers under Privacy Act safeguards.

Paperwork Reduction Notice. According to the Paperwork Reduction Act of 1995, no persons are required to respond to a collection of information unless it displays a currently valid OMB control number. The valid OMB control number for this information collection is 1845-0016. The time required to complete this information collection is estimated to average 0.33 hours (20 minutes) per response, including the time to review instructions, search existing data resources, gather and maintain the data needed, and complete and review the information collection. **If you have any comments concerning the accuracy of the time estimate(s) or suggestions for improving this form, please write to:** U.S. Department of Education, Washington, DC 20202-4651. *Do not send the completed form to this address.*

If you have any comments or concerns regarding the status of *your individual submission* of this form, write directly to:

U.S. Department of Education
Direct Loan Servicing Center
P.O. Box 4609
Utica, NY 13504-4609

D.2 Deferment and Forbearance Forms

D.2.1 FFEL Economic Hardship Deferment Form

ECONOMIC HARDSHIP DEFERMENT REQUEST

Federal Family Education Loan Program

HRD

Use this form only if all of your outstanding Federal Family Education Loan (FFEL) Program loans were made on or after July 1, 1993, and when your first FFEL Program loan was made on or after July 1, 1993, you had no outstanding FFEL Program loans that were made before July 1, 1993.

WARNING: Any person who knowingly makes a false statement or misrepresentation on this form or on any accompanying documents shall be subject to penalties which may include fines, imprisonment or both, under the U.S. Criminal Code and 20 U.S.C. §1097.

OMB No. 1845-0005
Form Approved
Exp. Date 01/31/2009

SECTION 1: BORROWER IDENTIFICATION

Please enter or correct the following information.

SSN |___|___|___| - |___|___| - |___|___|___|___|

Name _____

Address _____

City, State, Zip _____

Telephone - Home ( ) _____

Telephone - Other ( ) _____

E-mail Address (Optional) _____

SECTION 2: DEFERMENT REQUEST

Before answering any questions, carefully read the entire form, including the instructions and other information in Sections 4, 5, and 6.

■ I meet the qualifications stated in Section 6 for the Economic Hardship Deferment checked below and request that my loan holder defer repayment of my loan(s) beginning |___|___| - |___|___| - |___|___|___|___|. To qualify, I must meet **one** of the conditions listed below and must provide the required documentation, as described in Section 6, for only that condition. **(You must provide this date regardless of which condition you check below.)**

Check one:

(1) ❑ I have been granted an economic hardship deferment under the William D. Ford Federal Direct Loan (Direct Loan) Program or the Federal Perkins Loan Program for the same period of time for which I am requesting this deferment. **I have attached documentation of the deferment.**

(2) ❑ I am receiving or received payments under a federal or state public assistance program, such as Temporary Assistance for Needy Families (TANF), Supplemental Security Income (SSI), Food Stamps, or state general public assistance. **I have attached documentation of these payments.**

(3) ❑ I am serving as a Peace Corps volunteer. **I have attached documentation certifying my period of service in the Peace Corps.**

(4) ❑ I work full-time and my monthly income, as defined in Section 5, does not exceed the **larger of** (A) the Federal Minimum Wage Rate or (B) the Poverty Line income for a family of two for my state (regardless of my actual family size), as listed below. **I have attached documentation of this income.**

My monthly income is $ _____.

(A) Federal Minimum Wage Rate (monthly amount, based on $5.15 an hour): **$892.66**
(B) Poverty Lines for a Family of Two (monthly amounts): **$1,100.00** (48 contiguous states and the District of Columbia) **$1,375.00** (Alaska) **$1,265.00** (Hawaii)

(5) ❑ I do **not** work full-time **and** my monthly income, as defined in Section 5, does not exceed the **larger of** (A) **two times** the Federal Minimum Wage Rate, or (B) **two times** the Poverty Line income for a family of two for my state (regardless of my actual family size), as listed above under condition **(4)**. In addition, after deducting the total monthly payments that I am making on all of my federal education debts from my monthly income, the amount remaining does not exceed the **larger of** (A) the Federal Minimum Wage Rate or (B) the Poverty Line income for a family of two for my state, as listed above under condition **(4)**. If my repayment period is more than 10 years, my total monthly federal education debt payments will be adjusted to reflect a 10-year repayment period. If my repayment period is 10 years or less, my holder will use my actual scheduled monthly payment amount. **I have attached documentation of my monthly income and my federal education loan debt.**

NOTE: *A worksheet to help you determine whether you meet this condition is available from your loan holder. Completion of the worksheet is optional. Your loan holder will determine whether you qualify based on the income and education debt information that you provide below.*

My monthly income is $ _____.

For all of my federal education loans now in repayment (including loans for which I am requesting this deferment) I owe the following amounts:
• For all of my loans that have a repayment period of 10 years or less, the total amount that I pay each month is $_____.
• For all of my loans that have a repayment period of more than 10 years, the total amount I owed when the loans entered repayment is $_____.

(6) ❑ I work full-time, and the total amount of my monthly payments on all of my federal education loans in repayment is equal to or larger than 20% of my monthly income, as defined in Section 5. In addition, after deducting the total amount of my monthly payments on my federal education loans in repayment from my monthly income, the amount remaining is less than 220% of the **larger of** (A) the Federal Minimum Wage rate, or (B) the Poverty Line income for a family of two for my state (regardless of my actual family size), as listed above under condition **(4)**. If my repayment period is more than 10 years, my total monthly federal education loan payments will be adjusted, to reflect a 10-year repayment period. If my repayment period is 10 years or less, my holder will use my actual scheduled monthly payment amount. **I have attached documentation of my monthly income and my federal education loan debt.**

NOTE: *A worksheet to help you determine whether you meet this condition is available from your loan holder. Completion of the worksheet is optional. Your loan holder will determine whether you qualify based on the income and education debt information that you provide below.*

My monthly income is $ _____.

For all of my federal education loans now in repayment (including loans for which I am requesting this deferment) I owe the following amounts:
• For all of my loans that have a repayment period of 10 years or less, the total amount that I pay each month is $_____.
• For all of my loans that have a repayment period of more than 10 years, the total amount I owed when the loans entered repayment is $_____.

SECTION 3: BORROWER UNDERSTANDINGS AND CERTIFICATIONS

■ **I understand that: (1)** I am not required to make payments of loan principal during my deferment. Interest will not be charged on my subsidized loan(s) during my deferment. However, interest will be charged on my unsubsidized loan(s). **(2)** I have the option of making interest payments on my unsubsidized loan(s) during my deferment. **(3)** I may choose to make interest payments by checking the box below. My loan holder may capitalize interest that I do not pay during the deferment period.

❑ I wish to make interest payments on my unsubsidized loan(s) during my deferment.

■ **I certify that** the information I provided in Sections 1 and 2 above is true and correct, and that I have read, understand, and meet the terms and conditions and eligibility criteria of the deferment for which I have applied, as explained in Section 6.

Borrower's Signature _____ Date _____

Page 1 of 3

SECTION 4: INSTRUCTIONS FOR COMPLETING THE FORM

Type or print using dark ink. Report dates as month-day-year (MM-DD-YYYY). For example, 'January 31, 2006' = '01-31- 2006'. Include your name and social security number (SSN) on any documentation that you are required to submit with this form. If you need help completing this form, contact your loan holder.

Return the completed form and any required documentation to the address shown in Section 7.

SECTION 5: DEFINITIONS

■ **Capitalization** is the addition of unpaid interest to the principal balance of my loan. This will increase the principal and the total cost of my loan.

■ A **deferment** is a period during which I am entitled to postpone repayment of the principal balance of my loan(s). The federal government pays the interest that accrues during an eligible deferment for all subsidized Federal Stafford Loans and for Federal Consolidation Loans for which the Consolidation Loan application was received by my loan holder **(1)** on or after January 1, 1993, but before August 10, 1993, **(2)** on or after August 10, 1993, if it includes ***only*** Federal Stafford Loans that were eligible for federal interest subsidy, or **(3)** on or after November 13, 1997, for that portion of the consolidation loan that paid a subsidized FFEL Program Loan or a subsidized Federal Direct Loan. I am responsible for the interest that accrues during this period on all other FFEL Program loans.

■ Eligible **federal education loans** that may be included in determining the total amount I owed for deferment conditions (5) and (6) in Section 2 are listed below. I may include defaulted loans only if I have made repayment arrangements satisfactory to the holder of those loans.

- All Federal Family Education Loan (FFEL) Program loans (see definition)
- All William D. Ford Federal Direct Loan Program loans (see definition)
- All Federal Perkins Loan Program loans (see definition)
- Health Education Assistance Loans (HEAL)
- Health Professions Student Loans (HPSL)
- Loans for Disadvantaged Students (LDS)
- Primary Care Loans (PCL)
- Nursing Student Loans (NSL)

■ The **Federal Family Education Loan (FFEL) Program** includes Federal Stafford Loans (both subsidized and unsubsidized), Federal Supplemental Loans for Students (SLS), Federal PLUS Loans, Federal Consolidation Loans, Guaranteed Student Loans (GSL), Federal Insured Student Loans (FISL), and Auxiliary Loans to Assist Students (ALAS).

■ The **Federal Perkins Loan (Perkins Loan) Program** includes Federal Perkins Loans, National Direct Student Loans (NDSL), and National Defense Student Loans (Defense Loan).

■ **Forbearance** means permitting the temporary cessation of payments, allowing an extension of time for making payments, or temporarily accepting smaller payments than previously scheduled. I am responsible for the interest that accrues on my loan(s) during a forbearance. If I do not pay the interest that accrues, the interest may be capitalized.

■ **Full-time** employment is defined as working at least 30 hours per week in a position expected to last at least three consecutive months.

■ The **holder** of my FFEL Program loan(s) may be a lender, guaranty agency, secondary market, or the U.S. Department of Education.

■ **Monthly income is either:**

(1) the amount of my monthly income from employment and other sources before taxes and other deductions, **or**

(2) one-twelfth of the amount of my income reported as "adjusted gross income" on my most recently filed Federal Income Tax Return.

I may choose either of these income amounts for the purpose of reporting my monthly income on this deferment request.

■ **The repayment period** (for deferment conditions (5) and (6) in Section 2) refers to the total number of years that my current repayment plan allows me to repay my loan, including the years that my loan has already been in repayment. For any loan that my current repayment plan requires me to repay in a total of 10 years or less, my actual monthly payment amount will be used in determining whether I am eligible for a deferment. For any loan that my current repayment plan allows me a total of more than 10 years to repay, my payment amount will be adjusted to show the estimated monthly amount that I would owe if I were required to repay the loan in fixed installments within a 10-year repayment period.

■ The **William D. Ford Federal Direct Loan (Direct Loan) Program** includes Federal Direct Stafford/Ford (Direct Subsidized) Loans, Federal Direct Unsubsidized Stafford/Ford (Direct Unsubsidized) Loans, Federal Direct PLUS (Direct PLUS) Loans, and Federal Direct Consolidation (Direct Consolidation) Loans. These loans are known collectively as "Direct Loans."

SECTION 6: ELIGIBILITY CRITERIA / TERMS AND CONDITIONS FOR ECONOMIC HARDSHIP DEFERMENT

■ If I had no outstanding balance on a FFEL Program loan as of the date I obtained a loan **on or after July 1, 1993**, I may defer repayment of my loan(s) during the period that I meet one of the economic hardship deferment conditions described in Section 2.

■ If my economic hardship deferment eligibility is based on condition (1), as described in Section 2, I must provide my loan holder with documentation of the deferment that has been granted under the Direct Loan Program or the Federal Perkins Loan Program (for example, correspondence from my loan holder showing that I have been granted a deferment).

■ If my economic hardship deferment eligibility is based on condition (2), as described in Section 2, I must provide my loan holder with documentation confirming that I am receiving or received payments under a federal or state public assistance program.

■ If my economic hardship deferment eligibility is based on condition (3), as described in Section 2, I must provide my loan holder with documentation which certifies the beginning and anticipated ending dates of my service in the Peace Corps and which is signed and dated by an authorized Peace Corps official.

■ If my economic hardship deferment eligibility is based on conditions (4), (5) or (6), as described in Section 2, I must provide my loan holder with documentation of my monthly income as defined in Section 5. If I am reporting monthly income from employment and other sources, I must provide documentation such as pay stubs. If I am reporting one-twelfth of my adjusted gross income, I must provide a copy of my most recently filed Federal Income Tax Return.

■ If my economic hardship deferment eligibility is based on condition (5) or condition (6), as described in Section 2, I must provide my loan holder with documentation of the total amount I owed for all federal education loans that are now in repayment, such as disclosure statements or current repayment schedules. This must include the monthly payment amount, beginning loan balance, and repayment terms. If my total federal education loan debt includes defaulted loans, I must provide documentation that I have made repayment arrangements satisfactory to the holder(s) of the defaulted loans.

■ If my economic hardship deferment eligibility is based on conditions (4), (5), or (6), as described in Section 2, and I am not currently residing in the United States, I will use the Poverty Line amounts for my last state of residence in the United States.

■ I will provide additional documentation to my loan holder, as required, to support my deferment status.

Section 6 continued on Page 3

SECTION 6 (Continued)

■ I will notify my loan holder immediately when the condition that qualified me for the deferment ends.

■ My deferment will begin on the date the deferment condition began.

■ My deferment will end on the earlier of the date that the condition that establishes my deferment eligibility ends or the certified deferment end date.

■ My maximum cumulative eligibility for an economic hardship deferment is 36 months. Except for a deferment based on condition (3), as described in Section 2, I must reapply every 12 months if I continue to meet the criteria for an economic hardship deferment.

■ If my deferment does not cover all my past due payments, my loan holder may grant me a forbearance for all payments due before the begin date of my deferment. If the period for which I am eligible for a deferment has ended, my loan holder may grant me a forbearance for all payments due at the time my deferment request is processed.

■ My loan holder may grant me a forbearance on my loans for up to 60 days, if necessary, for the collection and processing of documentation related to my deferment request. Interest that accrues during this forbearance will not be capitalized.

SECTION 7: WHERE TO SEND THE COMPLETED DEFERMENT REQUEST

RETURN THE COMPLETED DEFERMENT REQUEST AND ANY REQUIRED DOCUMENTATION TO:
(IF NO ADDRESS IS SHOWN, RETURN TO YOUR LOAN HOLDER)

SECTION 8: IMPORTANT NOTICES

Privacy Act Notice

The Privacy Act of 1974 (5 U.S.C. 552a) requires that the following notice be provided to you:

The authority for collecting the requested information from and about you is §428(b)(2)(A) et seq. of the Higher Education Act (HEA) of 1965, as amended (20 U.S.C. 1078(b)(2)(A) et seq.) and the authorities for collecting and using your Social Security Number (SSN) are §484(a)(4) of the HEA (20 U.S.C. 1091(a)(4)) and 31 U.S.C. 7701(b). Participating in the Federal Family Education Loan (FFEL) Program and giving us your SSN are voluntary, but you must provide the requested information, including your SSN, to participate.

The principal purposes for collecting the information on this form, including your SSN, are to verify your identity, to determine your eligibility to receive a loan or a benefit on a loan (such as a deferment, forbearance, discharge, or forgiveness) under the FFEL Program, to permit the servicing of your loan(s), and, if it becomes necessary, to locate you and to collect and report on your loan(s) if your loan(s) become delinquent or in default. We also use your SSN as an account identifier and to permit you to access your account information electronically. The information in your file may be disclosed, on a case by case basis or under a computer matching program, to third parties as authorized under routine uses in the appropriate systems of records notices. The routine uses of this information include, but are not limited to, its disclosure to federal, state, or local agencies, to private parties such as relatives, present and former employers, business and personal associates, to consumer reporting agencies, to financial and educational institutions, and to guaranty agencies in order to verify your identity, to determine your eligibility to receive a loan or a benefit on a loan, to permit the servicing or collection of your loan(s), to enforce the terms of the loan(s), to investigate possible fraud and to verify compliance with federal student financial aid program regulations, or to locate you if you become delinquent in your loan payments or if you default. To provide default rate calculations, disclosures may be made to guaranty agencies, to financial and educational institutions, or to state agencies. To provide financial aid history information, disclosures may be made to educational institutions. To assist program administrators with tracking refunds and cancellations, disclosures may be made to guaranty agencies, to financial and educational institutions, or to federal or state agencies. To provide a standardized method for educational institutions efficiently to submit student enrollment status, disclosures may be made to guaranty agencies or to financial and educational institutions. To counsel you in repayment efforts, disclosures may be made to guaranty agencies, to financial and educational institutions, or to federal, state, or local agencies.

In the event of litigation, we may send records to the Department of Justice, a court, adjudicative body, counsel, party, or witness if the disclosure is relevant and necessary to the litigation. If this information, either alone or with other information, indicates a potential violation of law, we may send it to the appropriate authority for action. We may send information to members of Congress if you ask them to help you with federal student aid questions. In circumstances involving employment complaints, grievances, or disciplinary actions, we may disclose relevant records to adjudicate or investigate the issues. If provided for by a collective bargaining agreement, we may disclose records to a labor organization recognized under 5 U.S.C. Chapter 71. Disclosures may be made to our contractors for the purpose of performing any programmatic function that requires disclosure of records. Before making any such disclosure, we will require the contractor to maintain Privacy Act safeguards. Disclosures may also be made to qualified researchers under Privacy Act safeguards.

Paperwork Reduction Notice

According to the Paperwork Reduction Act of 1995, no persons are required to respond to a collection of information unless it displays a currently valid OMB control number. The valid OMB control number for this information collection is 1845-0005. The time required to complete this information collection is estimated to average 0.16 hours (10 minutes) per response, including the time to review instructions, search existing data resources, gather and maintain the data needed, and complete and review the information collection. *If you have any comments concerning the accuracy of the time estimate(s) or suggestions for improving this form, please write to:*

U.S. Department of Education, Washington, DC 20202-4651

If you have any comments or concerns regarding the status of your individual submission of this form, write directly to the address shown in Section 7.

ECONOMIC HARDSHIP DEFERMENT
WORKSHEET A

Use this worksheet to determine if you are eligible for an economic hardship deferment based on condition (5) in Section 2 of the Economic Hardship Deferment Request form. Completion of this worksheet is optional—if you check condition (5), your loan holder will determine your eligibility based on the income and federal education debt documentation that you provide.

DO NOT RETURN THIS WORKSHEET WITH THE DEFERMENT REQUEST—KEEP IT FOR YOUR RECORDS

STEP 1

Are you working full-time?

❐ Yes   You do not qualify for an economic hardship deferment based on condition (5). Do not continue with this worksheet. Refer to Worksheet B.

❐ No   Go to Step 2.

STEP 2

(1) Line 1. Enter the amount listed below for your state: $ _____
(2) Line 2. $ 1,785.32
(3) Line 3. Enter the **larger** of Line 1 or Line 2: $ _____
(4) Line 4. Enter your **MONTHLY INCOME**: $ _____
      (see the definition of "Monthly income" in Section 5 of the
      Economic Hardship Deferment Request)
(5) Is the amount on Line 4 **larger** than the amount on Line 3?

❐ Yes   You do not qualify for an economic hardship deferment based on condition 5. Do not continue with this worksheet.

❐ No   Go to Step 3.

Amounts for Line 1, above:

$2,200.00 (if you live in any of the 48 contiguous states or the District of Columbia) $2,750.00 (if you live in Alaska) $2,530.00 (if you live in Hawaii).

NOTE: *If you are not currently living in the United States, use the amount for your last state of residence in the United States.*

STEP 3

LOANS WITH A REPAYMENT PERIOD OF 10 YEARS OR LESS (See definition of "repayment period" in Section 5 of the deferment request form.)
Determine the total scheduled monthly payment of all your loans that are now in repayment for a period of 10 years or less (including the loans for which you are now requesting deferment). You may include defaulted loans only if you have made repayment arrangements satisfactory to the holder(s) of the defaulted loans.

Loan Type	Actual Scheduled Monthly Payment
Federal Stafford Loans (subsidized and unsubsidized)	$ _____
Direct Subsidized and Direct Unsubsidized Loans	+ $ _____
Federal PLUS Loans	+ $ _____
Direct PLUS Loans	+ $ _____
Federal SLS Loans	+ $ _____
Federal Consolidation Loans	+ $ _____
Direct Subsidized and Direct Unsubsidized Consolidation Loans	+ $ _____
Direct PLUS Consolidation Loans	+ $ _____
Federal Perkins Loans and/or National Direct Student Loans	+ $ _____
Other eligible federal education loans listed in Section 5	+ $ _____
TOTAL ACTUAL MONTHLY PAYMENT:	= $ _____

STEP 4

LOANS WITH A REPAYMENT PERIOD OF MORE THAN 10 YEARS (See definition of "repayment period" in Section 5 of the deferment request form.)
(A) Determine the total amount you owed when your loans entered repayment by adding together the amounts owed for the federal education loans listed below that are now in repayment for a period of more than 10 years (including the loans for which you are requesting deferment). You may include defaulted loans only if you have made repayment arrangements satisfactory to the holder(s) of the defaulted loans.

Loan Type	Total Amount You Owed When Your Loans Entered Repayment
Federal Stafford Loans (subsidized and unsubsidized)	$ _____
Direct Subsidized and Direct Unsubsidized Loans	+ $ _____
Federal PLUS Loans	+ $ _____
Direct PLUS Loans	+ $ _____
Federal SLS Loans	+ $ _____
Federal Consolidation Loans	+ $ _____
Direct Subsidized and Direct Unsubsidized Consolidation Loans	+ $ _____
Direct PLUS Consolidation Loans	+ $ _____
Federal Perkins Loans and/or National Direct Student Loans	+ $ _____
Other eligible federal education loans listed in Section 5	+ $ _____
TOTAL AMOUNT OWED:	= $ _____

Worksheet A
Page 1 of 2

ECONOMIC HARDSHIP DEFERMENT

WORKSHEET A (Continued)

(B) Circle the current interest rate for your FFEL Program loan(s) in the chart below. If your exact interest rate is not listed, choose the next highest interest rate. If you have loans with different interest rates, circle the rate for the loan with the highest interest rate.

Interest Rate	4.0%	4.5%	5.0%	5.5%	6.0%	6.5%	7.0%	7.5%	8.0%	8.5%	9.0%
Constant Multiplier	.0101245	.0103638	.0106066	.0108526	.0111021	.0113548	.0116108	.0118702	.0121328	.0123986	.0126676

(C) Multiply the **TOTAL AMOUNT OWED** from (A) by the constant multiplier listed directly below the interest rate that you circled in the chart above:

TOTAL AMOUNT OWED (from A)   **Constant Multiplier** (from B)   ESTIMATED MONTHLY PAYMENT*

$_____   X   _____   = $_____

*This is an estimate of the amount that you would pay each month on these federal education loans if they were scheduled to be repaid in fixed installments over a 10-year period.

STEP 5

Add the **TOTAL ACTUAL MONTHLY PAYMENT** from Step 3 with the **TOTAL ESTIMATED MONTHLY PAYMENT** from Step 4 to determine your **COMBINED TOTAL MONTHLY PAYMENT AMOUNT**.

TOTAL ACTUAL MONTHLY PAYMENT (from Step 3)   ESTIMATED MONTHLY PAYMENT (from Step 4)   COMBINED TOTAL MONTHLY PAYMENT AMOUNT

$_____   + $_____   = $_____

STEP 6

(1) Line 1. Enter your **MONTHLY INCOME** (from Step 2): $_____

(2) Line 2. Enter your **COMBINED TOTAL MONTHLY PAYMENT AMOUNT** (from Step 5): $_____

(3) Line 3. Subtract Line 2 from Line 1: $_____

(4) Line 4. Enter the amount listed below for your state: $_____

(5) Line 5. $ 892.66

(6) Line 6. Enter the **larger** of Line 4 or Line 5: $_____

(7) Line 7. Enter the amount from Line 3: $_____

(8) Is the amount on Line 7 larger than the amount on Line 6?

❐ Yes   You do not qualify for an economic hardship deferment based on condition (5).

❐ No   You meet the qualifications for an economic hardship deferment based on condition (5). Check the box for condition (5) in Section 2 of the deferment request.

Amounts for Line 4, above:

$1,100.00 (if you live in any of the 48 contiguous states or the District of Columbia)

$1,375.00 (if you live in Alaska)

$1,265.00 (if you live in Hawaii)

NOTE: If you are not currently living in the United States, use the amount for your last state of residence in the United States.

Worksheet A

Page 2 of 2

ECONOMIC HARDSHIP DEFERMENT
WORKSHEET B

Use this worksheet to determine if you are eligible for an economic hardship deferment based on condition (6) in Section 2 of the Economic Hardship Deferment Request form. Completion of this worksheet is optional—if you check condition (6), your loan holder will determine your eligibility based on the income and federal education debt documentation that you provide.

DO NOT RETURN THIS WORKSHEET WITH THE DEFERMENT REQUEST—KEEP IT FOR YOUR RECORDS

STEP 1

Are you working full-time?

- ❐ Yes   Go to Step 2.
- ❐ No   You do not qualify for an economic hardship deferment based on condition (6). Do not continue with this worksheet. Refer to Worksheet A.

STEP 2

LOANS WITH A REPAYMENT PERIOD OF 10 YEARS OR LESS (See definition of "repayment period" in Section 5 of the deferment request form.)
Determine the total scheduled monthly payment of all your loans that are now in repayment for a period of 10 years or less (including the loans for which you are requesting deferment). You may include defaulted loans only if you have made repayment arrangements satisfactory to the holder(s) of the defaulted loans.

Loan Type	Actual Scheduled Monthly Payment
Federal Stafford Loans (subsidized and unsubsidized)	$ _____
Direct Subsidized and Direct Unsubsidized Loans	+ $ _____
Federal PLUS Loans	+ $ _____
Direct PLUS Loans	+ $ _____
Federal SLS Loans	+ $ _____
Federal Consolidation Loans	+ $ _____
Direct Subsidized and Direct Unsubsidized Consolidation Loans	+ $ _____
Direct PLUS Consolidation Loans	+ $ _____
Federal Perkins Loans and/or National Direct Student Loans	+ $ _____
Other eligible federal education loans listed in Section 5	+ $ _____
TOTAL ACTUAL MONTHLY PAYMENT:	= $ _____

STEP 3

LOANS WITH A REPAYMENT PERIOD OF MORE THAN 10 YEARS (See definition of "repayment period" in Section 5 of the deferment request form.)
(A) Determine the total amount you owed when your loans entered repayment by adding together the amounts owed for the federal education loans listed below that are now in repayment for a period of more than 10 years (including the loans for which you are requesting deferment). You may include defaulted loans only if you have made repayment arrangements satisfactory to the holder(s) of the defaulted loans.

Loan Type	Total Amount You Owed When Your Loans Entered Repayment
Federal Stafford Loans (subsidized and unsubsidized)	$ _____
Direct Subsidized and Direct Unsubsidized Loans	+ $ _____
Federal PLUS Loans	+ $ _____
Direct PLUS Loans	+ $ _____
Federal SLS Loans	+ $ _____
Federal Consolidation Loans	+ $ _____
Direct Subsidized and Direct Unsubsidized Consolidation Loans	+ $ _____
Direct PLUS Consolidation Loans	+ $ _____
Federal Perkins Loans and/or National Direct Student Loans	+ $ _____
Other eligible federal education loans listed in Section 5	+ $ _____
TOTAL AMOUNT OWED:	= $ _____

ECONOMIC HARDSHIP DEFERMENT
WORKSHEET B (Continued)

(B) Circle the current interest rate for your FFEL Program loan(s) in the chart below. If your exact interest rate is not listed, choose the next highest interest rate. If you have loans with different interest rates, circle the rate for the loan with the highest interest rate.

Interest Rate	4.0%	4.5%	5.0%	5.5%	6.0%	6.5%	7.0%	7.5%	8.0%	8.5%	9.0%
Constant Multiplier	.0101245	.0103638	.0106066	.0108526	.0111021	.0113548	.0116108	.0118702	.0121328	.0123986	.0126676

(C) Multiply the **TOTAL AMOUNT OWED** from (A) by the constant multiplier listed directly below the interest rate that you circled in the chart above:

    TOTAL AMOUNT OWED (from A)   **Constant Multiplier** (from the chart above)   **ESTIMATED MONTHLY PAYMENT***

    $ _____   X   _____   = $ _____

*This is an estimate of the amount that you would pay each month on these federal education loans if they were scheduled to be repaid in fixed installments over a 10-year period.

STEP 4

Add the **TOTAL ACTUAL MONTHLY PAYMENT** from Step 2 with the **TOTAL ESTIMATED MONTHLY PAYMENT** from Step 3 to determine your **COMBINED TOTAL MONTHLY PAYMENT AMOUNT**.

    TOTAL ACTUAL MONTHLY PAYMENT (from Step 2)   **ESTIMATED MONTHLY PAYMENT** (from Step 3)   **COMBINED TOTAL MONTHLY PAYMENT AMOUNT**

    $ _____   + $ _____   = $ _____

STEP 5

(1) Line 1. Enter your monthly income: $_____

    (see the definition of "Monthly income" in Section 5 of the Economic Hardship Deferment Request)

(2) Line 2. Multiply the amount on Line 1 by .20 (= 20%): $_____

(3) Line 3. Enter your **COMBINED TOTAL MONTHLY PAYMENT**

    AMOUNT (from Step 4): $_____

(4) Is the amount on Line 3 **equal to or larger than** the amount on Line 2?

    ❑ Yes   Go to Step 6.

    ❑ No   You do not qualify for an economic hardship deferment based on condition (6). Do not continue with this worksheet.

STEP 6

(1) Line 1. Enter your monthly income: $ _____

(2) Line 2. Enter your **COMBINED TOTAL MONTHLY PAYMENT**

    AMOUNT (from Step 4): $ _____

(3) Line 3. Subtract Line 2 from Line 1: $ _____

(4) Line 4. Enter the amount listed below for your state: $ _____

(5) Line 5. $ 1,963.85

(6) Line 6. Enter the **larger** of Line 4 or Line 5: $ _____

(7) Line 7. Enter the amount from Line 3: $ _____

(8) Is the amount on Line 7 **less than** the amount on line 6?

    ❑ Yes   You meet the qualifications for an economic hardship deferment based on condition (6). Check the box for condition (6) in Section 2 of the deferment request.

    ❑ No   You do not qualify for an economic hardship deferment based on condition (6).

Amounts for Line 4, above:

    $2,420.00 (if you live in any of the 48 contiguous states or the District of Columbia)

    $3,025.00 (if you live in Alaska)

    $2,783.00 (if you live in Hawaii)

    NOTE: *If you are not currently living in the United States, use the amount for your last state of residence in the United States.*

Worksheet B
Page 2 of 2

D.2.2 Direct Unemployment Deferment Form

Direct Loans
William D. Ford Federal Direct Loan Program

UNEMPLOYMENT DEFERMENT REQUEST
William D. Ford Federal Direct Loan Program

WARNING: Any person who knowingly makes a false statement or misrepresentation on this form or on any accompanying documents will be subject to penalties which may include fines, imprisonment or both, under the U.S. Criminal Code and 20 U.S.C. 1097.

OMB No. 1845-0011
Form Approved
Exp. Date 06/30/2005

UNEM

SECTION 1: BORROWER IDENTIFICATION

Last Name	First Name	Middle Initial	Social Security Number

Street Address

Area Code/Telephone Number (home)
( )

Area Code/Telephone Number (other)
( )

City	State	Zip Code

E-mail Address (optional)

SECTION 2: DEFERMENT REQUEST

Before completing this form, carefully read the entire form, including the instructions and other information in Sections 4, 5, and 6.

■ I meet the qualifications stated in Section 6 for an Unemployment Deferment and request that the U.S. Department of Education (ED) defer repayment of my loan(s) while I am unemployed. I must reapply every 6 months. My maximum eligibility for an unemployment deferment is 36 months.

To document your eligibility for this deferment, complete the appropriate items below. *NOTE: If you are not qualifying for this deferment by providing documentation of your eligibility for unemployment benefits, you may submit your deferment request electronically at the Direct Loan Servicing Center web site: www.dl.ed.gov*

(A) ALL borrowers must complete this item:

I became unemployed or began working less than 30 hours per week on |___|___|-|___|___|-|___|___|___|___|. Except as explained in Section 3, my deferment will begin on this date, unless I request my deferment to begin on the following later date: |___|___|-|___|___|-|___|___|___|___|.

Check ONE of the boxes below:

(1) ☐ I am eligible for unemployment benefits, and I have attached documentation of my eligibility for these benefits. The documentation includes my name, address, social security number, and the effective dates of my eligibility to receive unemployment benefits.

OR

(2) ☐ I am diligently seeking but unable to find full-time employment, and I have registered with a public or private employment agency (if there is one within 50 miles of my current address).

OR

(3) ☐ I am diligently seeking but unable to find full-time employment, but I have not registered with an employment agency because there is no employment agency within 50 miles of my current address.

NOTE: For (2) and (3), school placement offices and "temporary" agencies do not qualify as public or private employment agencies.

(B) Check the box below only if: (1) you are requesting an extension of your current unemployment deferment AND (2) you are not providing documentation of your eligibility for unemployment benefits. If this is your first unemployment deferment request for your current period of unemployment, or if you are providing documentation of your eligibility for unemployment benefits, skip to Section 3.

☐ In the most recent six months, I have made at least 6 diligent attempts to find full-time employment.

SECTION 3: BORROWER UNDERSTANDINGS AND CERTIFICATIONS

■ **I understand** that the following terms and conditions apply to this deferment:

(1) I am not required to make payments of loan principal during my deferment. No interest will be charged on my subsidized loan(s) during my deferment. However, interest will be charged on my unsubsidized loan(s). For any unsubsidized loan(s), I will receive a quarterly interest statement, and I may pay the interest at any time. If I do not pay the interest that accrues on my unsubsidized loan(s), it will be capitalized at the end of my deferment period.

(2) My deferment will begin on the date I became unemployed or began working less than 30 hours per week, as shown in Section 2, Item (A), unless I request my deferment to begin on a later date. However, if this is my first unemployment deferment request for my current period of unemployment and I am not providing documentation of my eligibility for unemployment benefits, my deferment will begin no more than 6 months before the date the Direct Loan Servicing Center receives this request, even if I became unemployed or began working less than 30 hours per week more than 6 months ago.

(3) My deferment will end on the earlier of **(A)** the date I obtain full-time employment, or **(B)** the deferment end date provided to me by the Direct Loan Servicing Center. An unemployment deferment may last for no more than 6 months after the date the Direct Loan Servicing Center receives my deferment request. **I must reapply every 6 months.**

(4) If my deferment does not cover all of my past due payments, ED may grant me a forbearance for all payments that were due before the begin date of my deferment. If the period for which I am eligible for a deferment has ended, ED may grant me a forbearance for all payments that are due at the time my deferment request is processed.

(5) ED may grant me a forbearance on my loans for up to 60 days, if necessary, for the collection and processing of documentation related to my deferment request. ED will not capitalize interest that accrues during this forbearance.

■ **I certify** that:

(1) The information I have provided in Sections 1 and 2 is true and correct.

(2) I will provide additional documentation to the Direct Loan Servicing Center, as required, to support my eligibility for this deferment.

(3) I will notify the Direct Loan Servicing Center immediately if I obtain full-time employment.

(4) I have read, understand, and meet the eligibility requirements of the deferment for which I have applied.

BORROWER'S SIGNATURE _____ **DATE** _____

SECTION 4: INSTRUCTIONS FOR COMPLETING THE DEFERMENT REQUEST FORM

Type or print using dark ink. Report dates as month-day-year. For example, show "January 31, 2002" as "01-31-2002". If you are qualifying for this deferment by documenting your eligibility for unemployment benefits, attach the documentation to this form. **REMEMBER TO SIGN AND DATE THE FORM.**

Send the completed form and any required documentation to: **U.S. Department of Education** **Direct Loan Servicing Center** **P.O. Box 5609** **Greenville, TX 75403-5609**	If you need help completing this form, call **1-800-848-0979**. If you use a telecommunications device for the deaf (TDD), call **1-800-848-0983**. Direct Loan Servicing Center web site: **www.dl.ed.gov**

SECTION 5: DEFINITIONS

■ If unpaid interest is **capitalized**, this means that it is added to the principal balance of your loan(s). This will increase the principal amount and the total cost of your loan(s).

■ A **deferment** allows you to temporarily postpone making payments on your loan(s). No interest is charged during a deferment on Direct Subsidized Loans and Direct Subsidized Consolidation Loans. Interest is charged during a deferment on all other Direct Loans.

■ A **forbearance** allows you to temporarily postpone making payments on your loan(s), gives you an extension of time for making payments, or lets you temporarily make smaller payments than previously scheduled. Interest is charged during a forbearance on all types of Direct Loans.

■ **Full-time** employment means working at least 30 hours per week in a position expected to last at least 3 months.

■ The **William D. Ford Federal Direct Loan (Direct Loan) Program** includes Federal Direct Stafford/Ford (Direct Subsidized) Loans, Federal Direct Unsubsidized Stafford/Ford (Direct Unsubsidized) Loans, Federal Direct PLUS (Direct PLUS) Loans, and Federal Direct Consolidation (Direct Consolidation) Loans. These loans are known collectively as "Direct Loans".

SECTION 6: ELIGIBILITY REQUIREMENTS

■ You may defer repayment of your loans while you are unemployed. **You may receive this deferment for a maximum of 36 months.**

■ To qualify:

(1) You must be eligible for unemployment benefits and must provide the Direct Loan Servicing Center with documentation showing that you are eligible to receive unemployment benefits during the period for which you are requesting a deferment. This documentation must include your name, address, and social security number. (Check box #1 in Section 2, Item A.)

OR

(2) You must be diligently seeking but unable to find full-time employment in any field or at any salary or responsibility level and you must be registered with a public or private employment agency if there is one within 50 miles of your current address. School placement offices and "temporary agencies" do not qualify as public or private employment agencies. (Check box #2 or box #3 in Section 2, Item A.)

(3) If you are requesting an extension of your current unemployment deferment, and you are not providing documentation of your eligibility for unemployment benefits, you must check box #2 or box #3 in Section 2, Item A, **AND** you must certify that you have made at least 6 diligent attempts to find full-time employment in the most recent 6 months by checking the box in Section 2, Item B.

SECTION 7: IMPORTANT NOTICES

Privacy Act Notice. The Privacy Act of 1974 (5 U.S.C. 552a) requires that the following notice be provided to you:

The authority for collecting the requested information from and about you is §451 et seq. of the Higher Education Act of 1965, as amended (20 U.S.C. 1087a et seq.) and the authority for collecting and using your Social Security Number (SSN) is §484(a)(4) of the HEA (20 U.S.C. 1091(a)(4)). Participating in the William D. Ford Federal Direct Loan (Direct Loan) Program and giving us your SSN are voluntary, but you must provide the requested information, including your SSN, to participate.

The principal purposes for collecting the information on this form, including your SSN, are to verify your identity, to determine your eligibility to receive a loan or a benefit on a loan (such as a deferment, forbearance, discharge, or forgiveness) under the Direct Loan Program, to permit the servicing of your loan(s), and, if it becomes necessary, to locate you and to collect on your loan(s) if your loan(s) become delinquent or in default. We also use your SSN as an account identifier and to permit you to access your account information electronically.

The information in your file may be disclosed to third parties as authorized under routine uses in the appropriate systems of records. The routine uses of this information include its disclosure to federal, state, or local agencies, to other federal agencies under computer matching programs, to agencies that we authorize to assist us in administering our loan programs, to private parties such as relatives, present and former employers, business and personal associates, to credit bureau organizations, to financial and educational institutions, to guaranty agencies, and to contractors in order to verify your identity, to determine your eligibility to receive a loan or a benefit on a loan, to permit the servicing or collection of your loan(s), to counsel you in repayment efforts, to enforce the terms of the loan(s), to investigate possible fraud and to verify compliance with federal student financial aid program regulations, or to locate you if you become delinquent in your loan payments or if you default, to provide default rate calculations, to provide financial aid history information, to assist program administrators with tracking refunds and cancellations, or to provide a standardized method for educational institutions efficiently to submit student enrollment status.

In the event of litigation, we may send records to the Department of Justice, a court, adjudicative body, counsel, party, or witness if the disclosure is relevant and necessary to the litigation. If this information, either alone or with other information, indicates a potential violation of law, we may send it to the appropriate authority for action. We may send information to members of Congress if you ask them to help you with federal student aid questions. In circumstances involving employment complaints, grievances, or disciplinary actions, we may disclose relevant records to adjudicate or investigate the issues. If provided for by a collective bargaining agreement, we may disclose records to a labor organization recognized under 5 U.S.C. Chapter 71. Disclosures may also be made to qualified researchers under Privacy Act safeguards.

Paperwork Reduction Notice. According to the Paperwork Reduction Act of 1995, no persons are required to respond to a collection of information unless it displays a currently valid OMB control number. The valid OMB control number for this information collection is 1845-0011. The time required to complete this information collection is estimated to average 0.16 hours (10 minutes) per response, including the time to review instructions, search existing data resources, gather and maintain the data needed, and complete and review the information collection. **If you have comments concerning the accuracy of the time estimate(s) or suggestions for improving this form, please write to:** U.S. Department of Education, Washington, DC 20202-4651. *Do not send the completed form to this address.*

If you have questions about the status of *your individual submission of this form*, contact the Direct Loan Servicing Center (see Section 4).

D.2.3 *General Forbearance Request*

Direct Loans
William D. Ford Federal Direct Loan Program

GENERAL FORBEARANCE REQUEST
William D. Ford Federal Direct Loan Program

OMB No. 1845-0031
Form Approved
Exp. Date 06/30/2006

WARNING: Any person who knowingly makes a false statement or misrepresentation on this form or on any accompanying documents will be subject to penalties which may include fines, imprisonment, or both, under the U.S. Criminal Code and 20 U.S.C. 1097.

GFB
General

SECTION 1: BORROWER / ENDORSER IDENTIFICATION   *PLEASE PRINT LEGIBLY IN BLUE OR BLACK INK*

Last Name   First Name   Middle Initial   Social Security Number

Street Address   Area Code/Telephone Number (Home)

(   )

Area Code/Telephone Number (Other)

City   State   Zip Code   (   )

E-mail Address (optional)

SECTION 2: FORBEARANCE REQUEST

Before completing this form, carefully read the entire form, including the instructions and other information in Sections 3, 4, 5, and 6. You may complete and submit your forbearance request electronically at the Direct Loan Servicing Center's web site: *www.dl.ed.gov*.

■ I am willing but unable to make my current Direct Loan payments due to a temporary financial hardship. I am requesting this forbearance because: _____

_____

■ **If this forbearance request is approved, I want to** (check one):
☐ temporarily stop making payments; or
☐ make smaller payments of $_____ per month.

■ If this forbearance request is approved, I am requesting that the U.S. Department of Education (ED) grant a forbearance on my loan(s) beginning (MM-DD-YYYY) |____| |____|-|____| |____|-|____| |____| |____| |____| and ending (MM-DD-YYYY) |____| |____|-|____| |____|-|____| |____| |____| |____| for a period not to exceed 12 months. At the end of the forbearance, I may apply to renew the forbearance if I am still experiencing a financial hardship.

SECTION 3: BORROWER / ENDORSER UNDERSTANDINGS AND CERTIFICATIONS

■ **I understand** that the following terms and conditions apply to this forbearance request:

(1) I will continue to receive billing statements for my current payment amount which I must pay until I am notified by the Direct Loan Servicing Center that my forbearance request has been granted.

(2) ED may grant me a forbearance on my loans for up to 60 days, if necessary, for the collection and processing of documentation related to my forbearance request. ED will not capitalize interest that accrues during this forbearance.

(3) ED will not grant this forbearance request unless this form is completed and any required documentation is provided.

(4) During the forbearance period, I am not required to make payments of loan principal and interest, but interest will be charged on all of my loans.

(5) If I requested a temporary suspension of payments, I will receive a quarterly interest statement, and I may pay the interest at any time. If I do not pay the interest that accrues on my loan(s), it will be capitalized at the end of the forbearance period.

(6) If I requested a reduced payment forbearance, I will receive a monthly bill for the requested payment amount until the forbearance ends, and any unpaid interest that has accrued during the period will be capitalized at the end of the forbearance period.

■ **I certify** that:

(1) The information I have provided on this form is true and correct.

(2) I will provide additional documentation to the Direct Loan Servicing Center, as required, to support my continued forbearance status.

(3) I will notify the Direct Loan Servicing Center immediately when the condition that qualified me for the forbearance ends.

(4) I have read, understand, and meet the eligibility requirements of the forbearance for which I have applied.

(5) Upon termination of this forbearance, I will repay my loan(s) according to the terms of my promissory note and repayment schedule.

BORROWER'S OR ENDORSER'S SIGNATURE: _____   **DATE:** _____

Page 1 of 2

SECTION 4: INSTRUCTIONS FOR COMPLETING THE GENERAL FORBEARANCE REQUEST FORM

- Type or print using dark ink. Report dates as month-day-year. For example, show "January 31, 2003" as "01-31-2003". **REMEMBER TO SIGN AND DATE THE FORM.**

Send the completed form and any required documentation to: **U.S. Department of Education** **Direct Loan Servicing Center** **P.O. Box 5609** **Greenville, TX 75403-5609**	If you need help completing this form, call: **1-800-848-0979** If you use a telecommunications device for the deaf (TDD), call: **1-800-848-0983** Direct Loan Servicing Center web site: **www.dl.ed.gov**

SECTION 5: DEFINITIONS

- If unpaid interest is **capitalized**, this means that it is added to the principal balance of your loan(s). This will increase the principal amount and the total cost of your loan(s).

- An **endorser** is someone who promises to repay a PLUS loan or the PLUS portion of a consolidation loan if the parent borrower does not repay it.

- A **forbearance** allows you to temporarily postpone making payments on your loan(s), or lets you temporarily make smaller payments than previously scheduled. Interest is charged during a forbearance on all types of Direct Loans.

- The **William D. Ford Federal Direct Loan (Direct Loan) Program** includes Federal Direct Stafford/Ford (Direct Subsidized) Loans, Federal Direct Unsubsidized Stafford/Ford (Direct Unsubsidized) Loans, Federal Direct PLUS (Direct PLUS) Loans, and Federal Direct Consolidation (Direct Consolidation) Loans. These loans are known collectively as "Direct Loans".

SECTION 6: IMPORTANT NOTICES

Privacy Act Notice. The Privacy Act of 1974 (5 U.S.C. 552a) requires that the following notice be provided to you:

The authority for collecting the requested information from and about you is §451 *et seq.* of the Higher Education Act of 1965, as amended (20 U.S.C. 1087a *et seq.*) and the authority for collecting and using your Social Security Number (SSN) is §484(a)(4) of the HEA (20 U.S.C. 1091(a)(4)). Participating in the William D. Ford Federal Direct Loan (Direct Loan) Program and giving us your SSN are voluntary, but you must provide the requested information, including your SSN, to participate.

The principal purposes for collecting the information on this form, including your SSN, are to verify your identity, to determine your eligibility to receive a loan or a benefit on a loan (such as a deferment, forbearance, discharge, or forgiveness) under the Direct Loan Program, to permit the servicing of your loan(s), and, if it becomes necessary, to locate you and to collect on your loan(s) if your loan(s) become delinquent or in default. We also use your SSN as an account identifier and to permit you to access your account information electronically.

The information in your file may be disclosed to third parties as authorized under routine uses in the appropriate systems of records. The routine uses of this information include its disclosure to federal, state, or local agencies, to other federal agencies under computer matching programs, to agencies that we authorize to assist us in administering our loan programs, to private parties such as relatives, present and former employers, business and personal associates, to credit bureau organizations, to financial and educational institutions, to guaranty agencies, and to contractors in order to verify your identity, to determine your eligibility to receive a loan or a benefit on a loan, to permit the servicing or collection of your loan(s), to counsel you in repayment efforts, to enforce the terms of the loan(s), to investigate possible fraud and to verify compliance with federal student financial aid program regulations, or to locate you if you become delinquent in your loan payments or if you default, to provide default rate calculations, to provide financial aid history information, to assist program administrators with tracking refunds and cancellations, or to provide a standardized method for educational institutions efficiently to submit student enrollment status.

In the event of litigation, we may send records to the Department of Justice, a court, adjudicative body, counsel, party, or witness if the disclosure is relevant and necessary to the litigation. If this information, either alone or with other information, indicates a potential violation of law, we may send it to the appropriate authority for action. We may send information to members of Congress if you ask them to help you with federal student aid questions. In circumstances involving employment complaints, grievances, or disciplinary actions, we may disclose relevant records to adjudicate or investigate the issues. If provided for by a collective bargaining agreement, we may disclose records to a labor organization recognized under 5 U.S.C. Chapter 71. Disclosures may also be made to qualified researchers under Privacy Act safeguards.

Paperwork Reduction Notice. According to the Paperwork Reduction Act of 1995, no persons are required to respond to a collection of information unless it displays a currently valid OMB control number. The valid OMB control number for this information collection is 1845-0031. The time required to complete this information collection is estimated to average 0.2 hours (12 minutes) per response, including the time to review instructions, search existing data resources, gather and maintain the data needed, and complete and review the information collection. **If you have comments concerning the accuracy of the time estimate(s) or suggestions for improving this form, please write to:** U.S. Department of Education, Washington, DC 20202-4651. *Do not send the completed form to this address.*

If you have questions about the status of *your individual submission of this form*, contact the Direct Loan Servicing Center (see Section 4).

D.3 Discharge Forms and Letters

D.3.1 Closed School

LOAN DISCHARGE APPLICATION:
SCHOOL CLOSURE

OMB No. 1845-0015
Form Approved
Exp. Date 08/31/2008

Federal Family Education Loan Program / William D. Ford Federal Direct Loan Program / Federal Perkins Loan Program

WARNING: Any person who knowingly makes a false statement or misrepresentation on this form or on any accompanying documents will be subject to penalties which may include fines, imprisonment or both, under the U.S. Criminal Code and 20 U.S.C. 1097.

SECTION 1: BORROWER IDENTIFICATION

Please enter or correct the following information.

SSN |___|___|___|-|___|___|-|___|___|___|___|

Name

Address

City, State, Zip

Telephone – Home (   )

Telephone – Other (   )

E-mail (optional)

SECTION 2: STUDENT INFORMATION

Before completing this section, carefully read the entire form, including the instructions, definitions, and terms and conditions in Sections 4, 5, and 6 on this form. If you are a student borrower applying for loan discharge, begin with Item 3. If you are a parent borrower applying for a PLUS loan discharge, begin with Item 1.

1. Student's name (last, first, middle initial):

2. Student's SSN: |___|___|___|-|___|___|-|___|___|___|___|

3. Closed school's name:

4. Date school closed (if known): |___|___|-|___|___|-|___|___|___|___|

5. Closed school's address (street, city, state, zip):

6. Dates of attendance at the closed school: From |___|___|-|___|___|-|___|___|___|___| To |___|___|-|___|___|-|___|___|___|___|

7. Name of the program of study that you (or, for PLUS borrowers, the student) were enrolled in at the time the school closed:

8. Did you (or, for PLUS borrowers, the student) complete the program of study at the closed school? ☐ Yes ☐ No
If No, check all reasons that apply:

  ☐ The school closed while you (or, for PLUS borrowers, the student) were still enrolled.

  ☐ You (or, for PLUS borrowers, the student) withdrew from the school on: |___|___|-|___|___|-|___|___|___|___|

  ☐ You (or, for PLUS borrowers, the student) were on an approved leave of absence when the school closed:

From |___|___|-|___|___|-|___|___|___|___| To |___|___|-|___|___|-|___|___|___|___|

  ☐ Other (please explain):

9. Did you (or, for PLUS borrowers, the student) complete or are you in the process of completing the program of study or a comparable program of study at another school?
☐ Yes ☐ No   **If Yes, complete Item a) and b) below:**

  a) Did the other school give you (or, for PLUS borrowers, the student) credit for training received at the closed school by allowing transfer of credits or hours earned at the closed school, or by any other means? ☐ Yes ☐ No

  b) Were you (or, for PLUS borrowers, the student) required to start the program of study over from the beginning at the other school? ☐ Yes ☐ No

10. Did the holder of your loan receive any money back (a refund) from the school on your behalf? ☐ Yes ☐ No ☐ Don't Know
If Yes, give the amount and explain why the money was refunded:

11. Did you (or, for PLUS borrowers, the student) make any monetary claim with, or receive any payment from, the school or any third party (see definition in Section 5) in connection with enrollment or attendance at the school? ☐ Yes ☐ No ☐ Don't Know   If Yes, please provide the following information:

  (a) Name/address/telephone number of the party with whom the claim was made or from whom payment was received:

  (b) Amount/status of claim: _____   (c) Amount of payment received: $ _____
                                                   (Write "none" if no payment was received.)

SECTION 3: BORROWER CERTIFICATION

My signature below certifies that I have read and agree to the terms and conditions that apply to this loan discharge, as specified in Section 6 on the following page. Under penalty of perjury, I certify that all of the information I have provided on this form and in any accompanying documentation is true and accurate to the best of my knowledge and belief.

Borrower's Signature: _____ **Date:** _____

SECTION 4: INSTRUCTIONS FOR COMPLETING THE APPLICATION

Type or print using dark ink. For all dates, give month, day (if known), and year. Show dates as MM-DD-YYYY (for example, "January 31, 2006" = "01-31-2006"). If you need more space to answer any of the items, continue on separate sheets of paper and attach them to this form. Indicate the number of the item(s) you are answering and include your name and social security number (SSN) on all attached pages.
Sign and date the form. Then, send the completed form and any attachments to the address in Section 8.

SECTION 5: DEFINITIONS

- The **Federal Family Education Loan (FFEL) Program** includes Federal Stafford Loans (both subsidized and unsubsidized), Federal Supplemental Loans for Students (SLS), Federal PLUS Loans, and Federal Consolidation Loans.
- The **William D. Ford Federal Direct Loan (Direct Loan) Program** includes Federal Direct Stafford/Ford Loans (Direct Subsidized Loans), Federal Direct Unsubsidized Stafford/Ford Loans (Direct Unsubsidized Loans), Federal Direct PLUS Loans (Direct PLUS Loans), and Federal Direct Consolidation Loans (Direct Consolidation Loans).
- The **Federal Perkins Loan (Perkins Loan) Program** includes Federal Perkins Loans and National Direct Student Loans (NDSL).
- The **date a school closed** is the date that the school stopped providing educational instruction in **all programs**, as determined by the U.S. Department of Education (the Department).
- The **holder** of a borrower's FFEL Program loan(s) may be a lender, a guaranty agency, or the Department. The holder of a borrower's Direct Loan Program loan(s) is the Department. The holder of a borrower's Perkins Loan Program loan(s) may be the Department or a school.
- **Loan discharge** due to school closure cancels the obligation of a borrower (and endorser, if applicable) to repay the remaining balance on a FFEL Program, Direct Loan Program, or Perkins Loan Program loan, and qualifies the borrower for reimbursement of any amounts paid voluntarily or through forced collection on the loan. For consolidation loans, only the amount of the underlying loans (the loans that were consolidated) that were used to pay for the program of study listed in Item 7 will be considered for discharge. The loan holder reports the discharge to all credit reporting agencies to which the holder previously reported the status of the loan.
- The **student** refers to the student for whom a parent borrower obtained a Federal PLUS Loan or Direct PLUS Loan.
- **Dates of attendance:** The "to" date means the last date that you (or, for PLUS borrowers, the student) actually attended the closed school.
- **Program of study** means the instructional program leading to a degree or certificate in which you (or, for PLUS borrowers, the student) were enrolled.
- **Third party** refers to any entity that may provide reimbursement for a refund owed by the school, such as a tuition recovery program or performance bond.

SECTION 6: TERMS AND CONDITIONS FOR LOAN DISCHARGE BASED ON SCHOOL CLOSURE

- I received FFEL Program, Direct Loan Program, or Perkins Loan Program loan funds on or after January 1, 1986, to attend (or, if I am a PLUS borrower, for the student to attend) the school identified as "closed school" in Section 2 of this form. Those funds were either received by me directly, or applied as a credit to the amount owed to the school. I (or, if I am a PLUS borrower, the student) was enrolled at that school or on an approved leave of absence on the date that it closed, or withdrew from the school not more than 90 days before it closed (or longer if authorized by the Department). Due to the school's closure, I (or, if I am a PLUS borrower, the student) did not complete the program of study at that school. I (or, if I am a PLUS borrower, the student) did not complete and am not in the process of completing that program of study or a comparable program at another school by transferring credits or hours earned at the closed school to another school, or by any other means by which I (or, if I am a PLUS borrower, the student) benefited from the training provided by the closed school.
- I will provide, upon request, testimony, a sworn statement, or other documentation reasonably available to me that demonstrates to the satisfaction of the Department or its designee that I meet the qualifications for loan discharge based on school closure, or that supports any representation that I made on this form or on any accompanying documents.
- I agree to cooperate with the Department or its designee regarding any enforcement actions related to my request for loan discharge.
- I understand that my request for loan discharge may be denied, or my discharge may be revoked if I fail to provide testimony, a sworn statement, or documentation upon request, or if I provide testimony, a sworn statement, or documentation that does not support the material representations I have made, or if I (or, if I am a PLUS borrower, the student) completed or am in the process of completing the program of study or a comparable program at another school through transfer of credits or hours from the closed school or by any other means by which I (or, if I am a PLUS borrower, the student) benefited from the training provided by the closed school.
- I further understand that if my loan(s) are discharged based on any false, fictitious, or fraudulent statements that I knowingly made on this form or on any accompanying documents, I may be subject to civil and criminal penalties under applicable federal law.
- I hereby assign and transfer to the Department any right to a refund on the discharged loan(s) that I may have from the school identified in Section 2 of this form and/or any owners, affiliates, or assigns of the school, and from any third party that may pay claims for a refund because of the actions of the school, up to the amounts discharged on my loan(s).

SECTION 7: IMPORTANT NOTICES

Privacy Act Disclosure Notice: The Privacy Act of 1974 (5 U.S.C. 552a) requires that the following notice be provided to you:
The authorities for collecting the requested information from and about you are §428(b)(2)(A) et seq., §451 et seq. and §461 et seq. of the Higher Education Act of 1965, as amended (20 U.S.C. 1078(b)(2)(A) et seq., 20 U.S.C. 1087a et seq., and 20 U.S.C. 1087aa et seq.) and the authority for collecting and using your Social Security Number (SSN) is §484(a)(4) of the HEA (20 U.S.C. 1091(a)(4)). Participating in the Federal Family Education Loan (FFEL) Program, the William D. Ford Federal Direct Loan (Direct Loan) Program, or the Federal Perkins Loan (Perkins Loan) Program and giving us your SSN are voluntary, but you must provide the requested information, including your SSN, to participate.

The principal purposes for collecting the information on this form, including your SSN, are to verify your identity, to determine your eligibility to receive a loan or a benefit on a loan (such as a deferment, forbearance, discharge, or forgiveness) under the FFEL, Direct Loan, and/or Perkins Loan Programs, to permit the servicing of your loan(s), and, if it becomes necessary, to locate you and to collect on your loan(s) if your loan(s) become delinquent or in default. We also use your SSN as an account identifier and to permit you to access your account information electronically.

The information in your file may be disclosed to third parties as authorized under routine uses in the appropriate systems of records. The routine uses of this information include its disclosure to federal, state, or local agencies, to other federal agencies under computer matching programs, to agencies that we authorize to assist us in administering our loan programs, to private parties such as relatives, present and former employers, business and personal associates, to credit bureau organizations, to financial and educational institutions, to guaranty agencies, and to contractors in order to verify your identity, to determine your eligibility to receive a loan or a benefit on a loan, to permit the servicing or collection of your loan(s), to counsel you in repayment efforts, to enforce the terms of the loan(s), to investigate possible fraud and to verify compliance with federal student financial aid program regulations, to locate you if you become delinquent in your loan payments or if you default, to provide default rate calculations, to provide financial aid history information, to assist program administrators with tracking refunds and cancellations, or to provide a standardized method for educational institutions efficiently to submit student enrollment status.

In the event of litigation, we may send records to the Department of Justice, a court, adjudicative body, counsel, party, or witness if the disclosure is relevant and necessary to the litigation. If this information, either alone or with other information, indicates a potential violation of law, we may send it to the appropriate authority for action. We may send information to members of Congress if you ask them to help you with federal student aid questions. In circumstances involving employment complaints, grievances, or disciplinary actions, we may disclose relevant records to adjudicate or investigate the issues. If provided for by a collective bargaining agreement, we may disclose records to a labor organization recognized under 5 U.S.C. Chapter 71. Disclosures may also be made to qualified researchers under Privacy Act safeguards.

Paperwork Reduction Notice: According to the Paperwork Reduction Act of 1995, no persons are required to respond to a collection of information unless it displays a currently valid OMB control number. The valid OMB control number for this information collection is 1845-0015. The time required to complete this information collection is estimated to average 0.5 hours (30 minutes) per response, including the time to review instructions, search existing data resources, gather and maintain the data needed, and complete and review the information collection. **If you have any comments concerning the accuracy of the time estimate(s) or suggestions for improving this application, please write to:** U.S. Department of Education, Washington, DC 20202-4651.
If you have questions regarding the status of your individual submission of this application, contact your loan holder (see Section 8).

SECTION 8: WHERE TO SEND THE COMPLETED LOAN DISCHARGE APPLICATION

Send the completed loan discharge application and any attachments to: *(If no address is shown, return to your loan holder.)*	*If you need help completing this form, call:*

D.3.2 *False Certification of Ability to Benefit*

LOAN DISCHARGE APPLICATION: FALSE CERTIFICATION (ABILITY TO BENEFIT)

Federal Family Education Loan Program / William D. Ford Federal Direct Loan Program

WARNING: Any person who knowingly makes a false statement or misrepresentation on this form or on any accompanying documents will be subject to penalties which may include fines, imprisonment or both, under the U.S. Criminal Code and 20 U.S.C. 1097.

OMB No. 1845-0015
Form Approved
Exp. Date 08/31/2008

SECTION 1: BORROWER IDENTIFICATION

Please enter or correct the following information.

SSN |___|___|___|-|___|___|-|___|___|___|___|

Name _____

Address _____

City, State, Zip _____

Telephone - Home ( ) _____

Telephone - Other ( ) _____

E-mail (optional) _____

SECTION 2: STUDENT INFORMATION

Before completing this section, carefully read the entire form, including the instructions, definitions, and terms and conditions in Sections 4, 5, and 6 on this form. If you are a student borrower applying for loan discharge, begin with Item 3. If you are a parent borrower applying for a PLUS loan discharge, begin with Item 1.

1. Student's name (last, first, middle initial): _____

2. Student's SSN: |___|___|___|-|___|___|-|___|___|___|___|

3. School's name: _____

4. School's address (street, city, state, zip): _____

5. Dates of attendance at the school: From |___|___|-|___|___|-|___|___|___|___| To |___|___|-|___|___|-|___|___|___|___|

6. Name of the program of study that you (or, for PLUS borrowers, the student) were enrolled in at the school: _____

7. Did you (or, for PLUS borrowers, the student) have a high school diploma or GED at the time of enrollment at the school?
☐ Yes ☐ No   **NOTE: If Yes, you are not eligible for a loan discharge based on false certification of ability to benefit.**

8. Did you (or, for PLUS borrowers, the student) receive a GED before completing the program of study at the school?
☐ Yes ☐ No   If Yes, date GED received: |___|___|-|___|___|-|___|___|___|___|

9. Before you (or, for PLUS borrowers, the student) were admitted to the school, did the school give an entrance examination to test your (or, for PLUS borrowers, the student's) ability to benefit from the program of study listed in Item 6?
☐ Yes ☐ No ☐ Don't Know   If No or Don't Know, go to Item 10.

(a) Give the date of the test if you know it:	(b) Give the name of the test if you know it:	(c) Give the score on the test if you know it:
|___|___|-|___|___|-|___|___|___|___|		

(d) Did anything appear improper about the way the test was given or scored? ☐ Yes ☐ No
If Yes, explain in detail what appeared improper, and provide the name, telephone number and address of anyone who can support your statement (if you need more space, see the instructions in Section 4): _____

10. Did you (or, for PLUS borrowers, the student) complete a developmental or remedial program at the school?
☐ Yes ☐ No ☐ Don't Know   If Yes, list the program name, dates, courses, and grades earned: _____

11. Did the holder of your loan receive any money back (a refund) from the school on your behalf? ☐ Yes ☐ No ☐ Don't Know
If Yes, give the amount and explain why the money was refunded: _____

12. Did you (or, for PLUS borrowers, the student) make any monetary claim with, or receive any payment from, the school or any third party (see definition in Section 5) in connection with enrollment or attendance at the school? ☐ Yes ☐ No ☐ Don't know   If Yes, please provide the following information:

(a)   Name/address/telephone number of the party with whom the claim was made or from whom payment was received: _____

(b)   Amount/status of claim: _____   (c)   Amount of payment received: $ _____
(Write "none" if no payment was received.)

SECTION 3: BORROWER CERTIFICATION

My signature below certifies that I have read and agree to the terms and conditions that apply to this loan discharge, as specified in Section 6 on the following page. Under penalty of perjury, I certify that all of the information I have provided on this form and in any accompanying documentation is true and accurate to the best of my knowledge and belief.

Borrower's Signature: _____   **Date:** _____

SECTION 4: INSTRUCTIONS FOR COMPLETING THE APPLICATION

Type or print using dark ink. For all dates, give month, day (if known), and year. Show dates as MM-DD-YYYY (for example, "January 31, 2006" = "01-31-2006"). If you need more space to answer any of the items, continue on separate sheets of paper and attach them to this form. Indicate the number of the item(s) you are answering and include your name and social security number (SSN) on all attached pages.

Sign and date the form. Then, send the completed form and any attachments to the address in Section 8.

SECTION 5: DEFINITIONS

- The **Federal Family Education Loan (FFEL) Program** includes Federal Stafford Loans (both subsidized and unsubsidized), Federal Supplemental Loans for Students (SLS), Federal PLUS Loans, and Federal Consolidation Loans.

- The **William D. Ford Federal Direct Loan (Direct Loan) Program** includes Federal Direct Stafford/Ford Loans (Direct Subsidized Loans), Federal Direct Unsubsidized Stafford/Ford Loans (Direct Unsubsidized Loans), Federal Direct PLUS Loans (Direct PLUS Loans), and Federal Direct Consolidation Loans (Direct Consolidation Loans).

- The **holder** of a borrower's FFEL Program loan(s) may be a lender, a guaranty agency, or the U.S. Department of Education (the Department). The holder of a borrower's Direct Loan Program loan(s) is the Department.

- **Loan discharge** due to false certification of ability to benefit cancels the obligation of a borrower (and endorser, if applicable) to repay the remaining balance on a FFEL Program or Direct Loan Program loan, and qualifies the borrower for reimbursement of any amounts paid voluntarily or through forced collection on the loan. For consolidation loans, only the amount of the underlying loans (the loans that were consolidated) that were used to pay for the program of study listed in Item 6 will be considered for discharge. The loan holder reports the discharge to all credit reporting agencies to which the holder previously reported the status of the loan.

- The **student** refers to the student for whom a parent borrower obtained a Federal PLUS Loan or Direct PLUS Loan.

- **Program of study** means the instructional program leading to a degree or certificate in which you (or, for PLUS borrowers, the student) were enrolled.

- **Third party** refers to any entity that may provide reimbursement for a refund owed by the school, such as a tuition recovery program or performance bond.

SECTION 6: TERMS AND CONDITIONS FOR LOAN DISCHARGE BASED ON FALSE CERTIFICATION (DISQUALIFYING STATUS)

- I received FFEL Program or Direct Loan Program loan funds on or after January 1, 1986, to attend (or, if I am a PLUS borrower, for the student to attend) the school identified in Section 2 of this form. Those funds were either received by me directly, or applied as a credit to the amount owed to the school.

- I will provide, upon request, testimony, a sworn statement, or other documentation reasonably available to me that demonstrates to the satisfaction of the Department or its designee that I meet the qualifications for loan discharge based on false certification of ability to benefit, or that supports any representation that I made on this form or on any accompanying documents.

- I agree to cooperate with the Department or its designee regarding any enforcement actions related to my request for loan discharge.

- I understand that my request for loan discharge may be denied, or my discharge may be revoked, if I fail to provide testimony, a sworn statement, or documentation upon request, or if I provide testimony, a sworn statement, or documentation that does not support the material representations I have made on this form or on any accompanying documents.

- I further understand that if my loan(s) is discharged based on any false, fictitious, or fraudulent statements that I knowingly made on this form or on any accompanying documents, I may be subject to civil and criminal penalties under applicable federal law.

- I hereby assign and transfer to the Department any right to a refund on the discharged loan(s) that I may have from the school identified in Section 2 of this form and/or any owners, affiliates, or assigns of the school, and from any third party that may pay claims for a refund because of the actions of the school, up to the amounts discharged by the Department on my loan(s).

SECTION 7: IMPORTANT NOTICES

Privacy Act Disclosure Notice: The Privacy Act of 1974 (5 U.S.C. 552a) requires that the following notice be provided to you:

The authorities for collecting the requested information from and about you are 428(b)(2)(A) *et seq.* and 451 *et seq.* of the Higher Education Act of 1965, as amended (20 U.S.C. 1078(b)(2)(A) *et seq.* and 20 U.S.C. 1087a *et seq.*) and the authority for collecting and using your Social Security Number (SSN) is 484(a)(4) of the HEA (20 U.S.C. 1091(a)(4)). Participating in the Federal Family Education Loan (FFEL) Program or the William D. Ford Federal Direct Loan (Direct Loan) Program and giving us your SSN are voluntary, but you must provide the requested information, including your SSN, to participate.

The principal purposes for collecting the information on this form, including your SSN, are to verify your identity, to determine your eligibility to receive a loan or a benefit on a loan (such as a deferment, forbearance, discharge, or forgiveness) under the FFEL Program and/or Direct Loan Program, to permit the servicing of your loan(s), and, if it becomes necessary, to locate you and to collect on your loan(s) if your loan(s) becomes delinquent or in default. We also use your SSN as an account identifier and to permit you to access your account information electronically.

The information in your file may be disclosed to third parties as authorized under routine uses in the appropriate systems of records. The routine uses of this information include its disclosure to federal, state, or local agencies, to other federal agencies under computer matching programs, to agencies that we authorize to assist us in administering our loan programs, to private parties such as relatives, present and former employers, business and personal associates, to credit bureau organizations, to financial and educational institutions, to guaranty agencies, and to contractors in order to verify your identity, to determine your eligibility to receive a loan or a benefit on a loan, to permit the servicing or collection of your loan(s), to counsel you in repayment efforts, to enforce the terms of the loan(s), to investigate possible fraud and to verify compliance with federal student financial aid program regulations, to locate you if you become delinquent in your loan payments or if you default, to provide default rate calculations, to provide financial aid history information, to assist program administrators with tracking refunds and cancellations, or to provide a standardized method for educational institutions efficiently to submit student enrollment status.

In the event of litigation, we may send records to the Department of Justice, a court, adjudicative body, counsel, party, or witness if the disclosure is relevant and necessary to the litigation. If this information, either alone or with other information, indicates a potential violation of law, we may send it to the appropriate authority for action. We may send information to members of Congress if you ask them to help you with federal student aid questions. In circumstances involving employment complaints, grievances, or disciplinary actions, we may disclose relevant records to adjudicate or investigate the issues. If provided for by a collective bargaining agreement, we may disclose records to a labor organization recognized under 5 U.S.C. Chapter 71. Disclosures may also be made to qualified researchers under Privacy Act safeguards.

Paperwork Reduction Notice: According to the Paperwork Reduction Act of 1995, no persons are required to respond to a collection of information unless it displays a currently valid OMB control number. The valid OMB control number for this information collection is 1845-0015. The time required to complete this information collection is estimated to average 0.5 hours (30 minutes) per response, including the time to review instructions, search existing data resources, gather and maintain the data needed, and complete and review the information collection. **If you have any comments concerning the accuracy of the time estimate(s) or suggestions for improving this application, please write to:** U.S. Department of Education, Washington, DC 20202-4651.

If you have questions regarding the status of your individual submission of this application, contact your loan holder (see Section 8).

SECTION 8: WHERE TO SEND THE COMPLETED LOAN DISCHARGE APPLICATION

Send the completed loan discharge application and any attachments to: (If no address is shown, return to your loan holder.)	*If you need help completing this form, call:*

D.3.3 False Certification (Disqualifying Status)

LOAN DISCHARGE APPLICATION: FALSE CERTIFICATION (DISQUALIFYING STATUS)

Federal Family Education Loan Program / William D. Ford Federal Direct Loan Program

OMB No. 1845-0015
Form Approved
Exp. Date 08/31/2008

WARNING: Any person who knowingly makes a false statement or misrepresentation on this form or on any accompanying documents will be subject to penalties which may include fines, imprisonment or both, under the U.S. Criminal Code and 20 U.S.C. 1097.

SECTION 1: BORROWER IDENTIFICATION

Please enter or correct the following information.

SSN |__|__|__|-|__|__|-|__|__|__|__|

Name _____

Address _____

City, State, Zip _____

Telephone - Home ( ) _____

Telephone - Other ( ) _____

E-mail (optional) _____

SECTION 2: STUDENT INFORMATION

Before completing this section, carefully read the entire form, including the instructions, definitions, and terms and conditions in Sections 4, 5, and 6 on this form. If you are a student borrower applying for loan discharge, begin with Item 3. If you are a parent borrower applying for a PLUS loan discharge, begin with Item 1.

1. Student's name (last, first, middle initial): _____

2. Student's SSN: |__|__|__|-|__|__|-|__|__|__|__|

3. School's name: _____

4. School's address (street, city, state, zip): _____

5. Dates of attendance at the school: From |__|__|-|__|__|-|__|__|__|__| To |__|__|-|__|__|-|__|__|__|__|

6. Name of the program of study that you (or, for PLUS borrowers, the student) were enrolled in when the school certified or originated the loan that your are requesting to have discharged: _____

7. To qualify for a loan discharge based on false certification due to a disqualifying status, you (or, for PLUS borrowers, the student) must have been unable – at the time the school certified or originated your loan – to meet the **legal requirements for employment** in your state of residence (or, for PLUS borrowers, in the student's state of residence) in the occupation for which the program of study was intended because of age, a physical or mental condition, criminal record, or other reason. Indicate your disqualifying status by checking the appropriate box(es) below:

☐ Age　　☐ Physical condition　　☐ Mental condition　　☐ Criminal record　　☐ Other (please specify): _____

> **Important:** You must provide documentation to prove that you (or, for PLUS borrowers, the student) had the disqualifying status at the time the school certified or originated your loan. **Also, provide as much information as possible about the state legal requirements for employment that you (or, for PLUS borrowers, the student) could not meet. Include the title and/or section number of the specific state law or regulation, or attach a copy of the law or regulation.** You may obtain this information from the appropriate state agency, such as the consumer protection office or department of labor and employment, from a public library, or from an internet site that contains state laws and regulations.
>
> _____
>
> _____

8. (a) Before certifying or originating the loan, did the school ask you (or, for PLUS borrowers, the student) if the disqualifying status explained in Item 7 existed?
☐ Yes ☐ No ☐ Don't Know

(b) Did you (or, for PLUS borrowers, the student) inform the school of the disqualifying status before the loan was certified or originated?
☐ Yes ☐ No

9. Did the holder of your loan receive any money back (a refund) from the school on your behalf? ☐ Yes ☐ No ☐ Don't Know
If Yes, give the amount and explain why the money was refunded: _____

10. Did you (or, for PLUS borrowers, the student) make any monetary claim with, or receive any payment from, the school or any third party (see definition in Section 5) in connection with enrollment or attendance at the school? ☐ Yes ☐ No ☐ Don't Know　　If Yes, please provide the following information:

(a) Name/address/telephone number of the party with whom the claim was made or from whom payment was received: _____

Amount/status of claim: _____ (c) Amount of payment received: $ _____
(Write "none" if no payment was received.)

SECTION 3: BORROWER CERTIFICATION

My signature below certifies that I have read and agree to the terms and conditions that apply to this loan discharge, as specified in Section 6 on the following page. Under penalty of perjury, I certify that all of the information I have provided on this form and in any accompanying documentation is true and accurate to the best of my knowledge and belief.

Borrower's Signature: _____ Date: _____

SECTION 4: INSTRUCTIONS FOR COMPLETING THE APPLICATION

Type or print using dark ink. For all dates, give month, day (if known), and year. Show dates as MM-DD-YYYY (for example, "January 31, 2006" = "01-31-2006"). If you need more space to answer any of the items, continue on separate sheets of paper and attach them to this form. Indicate the number of the item(s) you are answering and include your name and social security number (SSN) on all attached pages.

Sign and date the form. Then, send the completed form and any attachments to the address in Section 8.

SECTION 5: DEFINITIONS

- The **Federal Family Education Loan (FFEL) Program** includes Federal Stafford Loans (both subsidized and unsubsidized), Federal Supplemental Loans for Students (SLS), Federal PLUS Loans, and Federal Consolidation Loans.

- The **William D. Ford Federal Direct Loan (Direct Loan) Program** includes Federal Direct Stafford/Ford Loans (Direct Subsidized Loans), Federal Direct Unsubsidized Stafford/Ford Loans (Direct Unsubsidized Loans), Federal Direct PLUS Loans (Direct PLUS Loans), and Federal Direct Consolidation Loans (Direct Consolidation Loans).

- The **holder** of a borrower's FFEL Program loan(s) may be a lender, a guaranty agency, or the U.S. Department of Education (the Department). The holder of a borrower's Direct Loan Program loan(s) is the Department.

- **Loan discharge** due to false certification (disqualifying status) cancels the obligation of a borrower (and endorser, if applicable) to repay the remaining balance on a FFEL Program or Direct Loan Program loan, and qualifies the borrower for reimbursement of any amounts paid voluntarily or through forced collection on the loan. For consolidation loans, only the amount of the underlying loans (the loans that were consolidated) that were used to pay for the program of study listed in Item 6 will be considered for discharge. The loan holder reports the discharge to all credit reporting agencies to which the holder previously reported the status of the loan.

- The **student** refers to the student for whom a parent borrower obtained a Federal PLUS loan or Direct PLUS Loan.

- **Program of study** means the instructional program leading to a degree or certificate in which you (or, for PLUS borrowers, the student) were enrolled.

- **Certification** and **origination** are steps in a school's processing of a loan. In the FFEL Program, a loan is **certified** when the school signs a loan application or submits an electronic loan record to the lender or guaranty agency after determining that the borrower meets all loan eligibility requirements. In the Direct Loan Program, a loan is **originated** when the school creates an electronic loan origination record after determining that the borrower meets all loan eligibility requirements.

- **Third party** refers to any entity that may provide reimbursement for a refund owed by the school, such as a tuition recovery program or performance bond.

SECTION 6: TERMS AND CONDITIONS FOR LOAN DISCHARGE BASED ON FALSE CERTIFICATION (ABILITY TO BENEFIT)

- I received FFEL or Direct Loan program loan funds on or after January 1, 1986, to attend (or, if I am a PLUS borrower, for the student to attend) the school identified in Section 2 of this form. Those funds were either received by me directly, or applied as a credit to the amount owed to the school.

- I will provide, upon request, testimony, a sworn statement, or other documentation reasonably available to me that demonstrates to the satisfaction of the Department or its designee that I meet the qualifications for loan discharge based on false certification (disqualifying status), or that supports any representation that I made on this form or on any accompanying documents.

- I agree to cooperate with the Department or its designee regarding any enforcement actions related to my request for loan discharge.

- I understand that my request for loan discharge may be denied, or my discharge may be revoked, if I fail to provide testimony, a sworn statement, or documentation upon request, or if I provide testimony, a sworn statement, or documentation that does not support the material representations I have made on this form or on any accompanying documents.

- I further understand that if my loan(s) is discharged based on any false, fictitious, or fraudulent statements that I knowingly made on this form or on any accompanying documents, I may be subject to civil and criminal penalties under applicable federal law.

- I hereby assign and transfer to the Department any right to a refund on the discharged loan(s) that I may have from the school identified in Section 2 of this form and/or any owners, affiliates, or assigns of the school, and from any third party that may pay claims for a refund because of the actions of the school, up to the amounts discharged by the Department on my loan(s).

SECTION 7: IMPORTANT NOTICES

Privacy Act Disclosure Notice: The Privacy Act of 1974 (5 U.S.C. 552a) requires that the following notice be provided to you:

The authorities for collecting the requested information from and about you are 428(b)(2)(A) *et seq.* and 451 *et seq.* of the Higher Education Act of 1965, as amended (20 U.S.C. 1078(b)(2)(A) *et seq.* and 20 U.S.C. 1087a *et seq.*) and the authority for collecting and using your Social Security Number (SSN) is 484(a)(4) of the HEA (20 U.S.C. 1091(a)(4)). Participating in the Federal Family Education Loan (FFEL) Program or the William D. Ford Federal Direct Loan (Direct Loan) Program and giving us your SSN are voluntary, but you must provide the requested information, including your SSN, to participate.

The principal purposes for collecting the information on this form, including your SSN, are to verify your identity, to determine your eligibility to receive a loan or a benefit on a loan (such as a deferment, forbearance, discharge, or forgiveness) under the FFEL Program and/or Direct Loan Program, to permit the servicing of your loan(s), and, if it becomes necessary, to locate you and to collect on your loan(s) if your loan(s) becomes delinquent or in default. We also use your SSN as an account identifier and to permit you to access your account information electronically.

The information in your file may be disclosed to third parties as authorized under routine uses in the appropriate systems of records. The routine uses of this information include its disclosure to federal, state, or local agencies, to other federal agencies under computer matching programs, to agencies that we authorize to assist us in administering our loan programs, to private parties such as relatives, present and former employers, business and personal associates, to credit bureau organizations, to financial and educational institutions, to guaranty agencies, and to contractors in order to verify your identity, to determine your eligibility to receive a loan or a benefit on a loan, to permit the servicing or collection of your loan(s), to counsel you in repayment efforts, to enforce the terms of the loan(s), to investigate possible fraud and to verify compliance with federal student financial aid program regulations, to locate you if you become delinquent in your loan payments or if you default, to provide default rate calculations, to provide financial aid history information, to assist program administrators with tracking refunds and cancellations, or to provide a standardized method for educational institutions efficiently to submit student enrollment status.

In the event of litigation, we may send records to the Department of Justice, a court, adjudicative body, counsel, party, or witness if the disclosure is relevant and necessary to the litigation. If this information, either alone or with other information, indicates a potential violation of law, we may send it to the appropriate authority for action. We may send information to members of Congress if you ask them to help you with federal student aid questions. In circumstances involving employment complaints, grievances, or disciplinary actions, we may disclose relevant records to adjudicate or investigate the issues. If provided for by a collective bargaining agreement, we may disclose records to a labor organization recognized under 5 U.S.C. Chapter 71. Disclosures may also be made to qualified researchers under Privacy Act safeguards.

Paperwork Reduction Notice: According to the Paperwork Reduction Act of 1995, no persons are required to respond to a collection of information unless it displays a currently valid OMB control number. The valid OMB control number for this information collection is 1845-0015. The time required to complete this information collection is estimated to average 0.5 hours (30 minutes) per response, including the time to review instructions, search existing data resources, gather and maintain the data needed, and complete and review the information collection. **If you have any comments concerning the accuracy of the time estimate(s) or suggestions for improving this application, please write to:** U.S. Department of Education, Washington, DC 20202-4651.

If you have questions regarding the status of your individual submission of this application, contact your loan holder (see Section 8).

SECTION 8: WHERE TO SEND THE COMPLETED LOAN DISCHARGE APPLICATION

Send the completed loan discharge application and any attachments to: *(If no address is shown, return to your loan holder.)*	*If you need help completing this form, call:*

D.3.4 *False Certification (Unauthorized Signature/Unauthorized Payment)*

LOAN DISCHARGE APPLICATION: FALSE CERTIFICATION (UNAUTHORIZED SIGNATURE / UNAUTHORIZED PAYMENT)
Federal Family Education Loan Program / William D. Ford Federal Direct Loan Program
WARNING: Any person who knowingly makes a false statement or misrepresentation on this form or on any accompanying documents will be subject to penalties which may include fines, imprisonment or both, under the U.S. Criminal Code and 20 U.S.C. 1097.

OMB No. 1845-0015
Form Approved
Exp. Date 08/31/2008

SECTION 1: BORROWER IDENTIFICATION

Please enter or correct the following information.

SSN |___|___|___|-|___|___|-|___|___|___|___|

Name _____

Address _____

City, State, Zip _____

Telephone - Home ( ) _____

Telephone - Other ( ) _____

E-mail (optional) _____

SECTION 2: STUDENT INFORMATION

Before completing this section, carefully read the entire form, including the instructions, definitions, and terms and conditions in Sections 4, 5, and 6 on this form. If you are a student borrower applying for loan discharge, begin with Item 3. If you are a parent borrower applying for a PLUS loan discharge, begin with Item 1.

1. Student's name (last, first, middle initial): _____

2. Student's SSN: |___|___|___|-|___|___|-|___|___|___|___|

3. School's name: _____

4. School's address (street, city, state, zip): _____

5. Dates of attendance at the school: From |___|___|-|___|___|-|___|___|___|___| To |___|___|-|___|___|-|___|___|___|___|

6. Did you sign the application, promissory note, master promissory note (MPN), or combined application/promissory note for your loan(s)? ☐ Yes ☐ No
If No, on which document(s) did someone else sign your name? ☐ Application ☐ Promissory note ☐ MPN ☐ Combined application/promissory note

7. Did you endorse each loan check or sign your name on each electronic funds transfer authorization or master check authorization?

☐ Yes ☐ No ☐ Does Not Apply

If No, on which document(s) did someone else sign your name? ☐ Loan check ☐ Electronic funds transfer authorization ☐ Master check authorization

If No, did you (or, for PLUS borrowers, the student) ever receive any money from the school, or did the school ever reduce the amount of money that you (or, for PLUS borrowers, the student) owed to the school? ☐ Yes ☐ No ☐ Don't Know   If Yes, explain (give dates, amounts, and circumstances): _____

If No or Don't Know, explain how you (or, for PLUS borrowers, the student) paid the tuition and fees owed to the school: _____

8. If you answered No to Item 6 or Item 7, do you know who signed your name on the document(s) checked in Item 6 or Item 7?
☐ Yes ☐ No   If Yes, identify the person who signed your name on the document(s).

School employee or representative (name and position): _____

Other person (name): _____

Provide any other information about the circumstances under which another person signed your name: _____

IMPORTANT: If you did not sign your name on one of the documents listed in Item 6 or Item 7, you must attach documents containing four other samples of your signature in addition to the signature on this application. At least two of these samples must clearly show that your signatures were written within one year before or after the date of the document on which someone else signed your name. Examples of documents that would include both a signature sample and the date that the signature was written include—but are not limited to—cancelled checks, tax returns, and driver's licenses. If you do not provide these signature samples, you cannot be considered for a loan discharge.

9. Did the holder of your loan receive any money back (a refund) from the school on your behalf? ☐ Yes ☐ No ☐ Don't Know
If Yes, give the amount and explain why the money was refunded: _____

10. Did you (or, for PLUS borrowers, the student) make any monetary claim with, or receive any payment from, the school or any third party (see definition in Section 5) in connection with enrollment or attendance at the school? ☐ Yes ☐ No ☐ Don't Know   If Yes, please provide the following information:

a)   Name/address/telephone number of the party with whom the claim was made or from whom payment was received: _____

b)   Amount/status of claim: _____   c)   Amount of payment received: $ _____
(Write "none" if no payment was received.)

SECTION 3: BORROWER CERTIFICATION

My signature below certifies that I have read and agree to the terms and conditions that apply to this loan discharge, as specified in Section 6 on the following page. Under penalty of perjury, I certify that all of the information I have provided on this form and in any accompanying documentation is true and accurate to the best of my knowledge and belief.

Borrower's Signature: _____   Date: _____

411

SECTION 4: INSTRUCTIONS FOR COMPLETING THE APPLICATION

Type or print using dark ink. For all dates, give month, day (if known), and year. Show dates as MM-DD-YYYY (for example, "January 31, 2006" = "01-31-2006"). If you need more space to answer any of the items, continue on separate sheets of paper and attach them to this form. Indicate the number of the item(s) you are answering and include your name and social security number (SSN) on all attached pages.

Sign and date the form. Then, send the completed form and any attachments to the address in Section 8.

SECTION 5: DEFINITIONS

■ The **Federal Family Education Loan (FFEL) Program** includes Federal Stafford Loans (both subsidized and unsubsidized), Federal Supplemental Loans for Students (SLS), Federal PLUS Loans, and Federal Consolidation Loans.

■ The **William D. Ford Federal Direct Loan (Direct Loan) Program** includes Federal Direct Stafford/Ford Loans (Direct Subsidized Loans), Federal Direct Unsubsidized Stafford/Ford Loans (Direct Unsubsidized Loans), Federal Direct PLUS Loans (Direct PLUS Loans), and Federal Direct Consolidation Loans (Direct Consolidation Loans).

■ The **holder** of a borrower's FFEL Program loan(s) may be a lender, a guaranty agency, or the U.S. Department of Education (the Department). The holder of a borrower's Direct Loan Program loan(s) is the Department.

■ **Unauthorized signature** means that the school, without the borrower's authorization, signed the borrower's name on a loan application or promissory note.

■ **Unauthorized payment** means that the school, without the borrower's authorization, endorsed the borrower's loan check or signed the borrower's authorization for electronic funds transfer or master check, and did not give the loan proceeds to the borrower or apply the loan proceeds to charges owed by the student to the school.

■ **Loan discharge** due to an unauthorized signature on a loan application or promissory note cancels the obligation of a borrower (and endorser, if applicable) to repay the remaining balance on a FFEL Program or Direct Loan Program loan, and qualifies the borrower for reimbursement of any amounts paid voluntarily or through forced collection on the loan. Discharge due to an unauthorized signature on a loan check, electronic funds transfer authorization, or master check authorization applies only to the amount of the unauthorized payment. For consolidation loans, only the loan amounts associated with the document listed in Section 2, Item 6 or Item 7, will be considered for discharge. The loan holder reports the discharge to all credit reporting agencies to which the holder previously reported the status of the loan.

■ The **student** refers to the student for whom a parent borrower obtained a Federal PLUS Loan or Direct PLUS Loan.

■ **Third party** refers to any entity that may provide reimbursement for a refund owed by the school, such as a tuition recovery program or performance bond.

SECTION 6: TERMS AND CONDITIONS FOR LOAN DISCHARGE BASED ON FALSE CERTIFICATION (UNAUTHORIZED SIGNATURE/UNAUTHORIZED PAYMENT)

■ The school identified in Section 2 of this form received FFEL Program or Direct Loan Program loan funds on or after January 1, 1986 for me to attend (or, if I am a PLUS borrower, for the student to attend) the school. I am applying for a discharge of my FFEL Program or Direct Loan Program loan(s) because the loan application, promissory note, master promissory note, combined application/promissory note, loan disbursement check, electronic funds transfer authorization, or master check authorization were not authorized for the reasons stated in this application.

■ I will provide, upon request, testimony, a sworn statement, or other documentation reasonably available to me that demonstrates to the satisfaction of the Department or its designee that I meet the qualifications for loan discharge based on unauthorized signature / unauthorized payment, or that supports any representation that I made on this form or on any accompanying documents.

■ I agree to cooperate with the Department or its designee regarding any enforcement actions related to my request for loan discharge.

■ I understand that my request for loan discharge may be denied, or my discharge may be revoked, if I fail to provide testimony, a sworn statement, or documentation upon request, or if I provide testimony, a sworn statement, or documentation that does not support the material representations I have made on this form or on any accompanying documents.

■ I further understand that if my loan(s) is discharged based on any false, fictitious, or fraudulent statements that I knowingly made on this form or on any accompanying documents, I may be subject to civil and criminal penalties under applicable federal law.

■ I hereby assign and transfer to the Department any right to a refund on the discharged loan(s) that I may have from the school identified in Section 2 of this form and/or any owners, affiliates, or assigns of the school, and from any third party that may pay claims for a refund because of the actions of the school, up to the amounts discharged by the Department on my loan(s).

SECTION 7: IMPORTANT NOTICES

Privacy Act Disclosure Notice: The Privacy Act of 1974 (5 U.S.C. 552a) requires that the following notice be provided to you:

The authorities for collecting the requested information from and about you are 428(b)(2)(A) *et seq.* and 451 *et seq.* of the Higher Education Act of 1965, as amended (20 U.S.C. 1078(b)(2)(A) *et seq.* and 20 U.S.C. 1087a *et seq.*) and the authority for collecting and using your Social Security Number (SSN) is 484(a)(4) of the HEA (20 U.S.C. 1091(a)(4)). Participating in the Federal Family Education Loan (FFEL) Program or the William D. Ford Federal Direct Loan (Direct Loan) Program and giving us your SSN are voluntary, but you must provide the requested information, including your SSN, to participate.

The principal purposes for collecting the information on this form, including your SSN, are to verify your identity, to determine your eligibility to receive a loan or a benefit on a loan (such as a deferment, forbearance, discharge, or forgiveness) under the FFEL Program and/or Direct Loan Program, to permit the servicing of your loan(s), and, if it becomes necessary, to locate you and to collect on your loan(s) if your loan(s) becomes delinquent or in default. We also use your SSN as an account identifier and to permit you to access your account information electronically.

The information in your file may be disclosed to third parties as authorized under routine uses in the appropriate systems of records. The routine uses of this information include its disclosure to federal, state, or local agencies, to other federal agencies under computer matching programs, to agencies that we authorize to assist us in administering our loan programs, to private parties such as relatives, present and former employers, business and personal associates, to credit bureau organizations, to financial and educational institutions, to guaranty agencies, and to contractors in order to verify your identity, to determine your eligibility to receive a loan or a benefit on a loan, to permit the servicing or collection of your loan(s), to counsel you in repayment efforts, to enforce the terms of the loan(s), to investigate possible fraud and to verify compliance with federal student financial aid program regulations, to locate you if you become delinquent in your loan payments or if you default, to provide default rate calculations, to provide financial aid history information, to assist program administrators with tracking refunds and cancellations, or to provide a standardized method for educational institutions efficiently to submit student enrollment status.

In the event of litigation, we may send records to the Department of Justice, a court, adjudicative body, counsel, party, or witness if the disclosure is relevant and necessary to the litigation. If this information, either alone or with other information, indicates a potential violation of law, we may send it to the appropriate authority for action. We may send information to members of Congress if you ask them to help you with federal student aid questions. In circumstances involving employment complaints, grievances, or disciplinary actions, we may disclose relevant records to adjudicate or investigate the issues. If provided for by a collective bargaining agreement, we may disclose records to a labor organization recognized under 5 U.S.C. Chapter 71. Disclosures may also be made to qualified researchers under Privacy Act safeguards.

Paperwork Reduction Notice: According to the Paperwork Reduction Act of 1995, no persons are required to respond to a collection of information unless it displays a currently valid OMB control number. The valid OMB control number for this information collection is 1845-0015. The time required to complete this information collection is estimated to average 0.5 hours (30 minutes) per response, including the time to review instructions, search existing data resources, gather and maintain the data needed, and complete and review the information collection. **If you have any comments concerning the accuracy of the time estimate(s) or suggestions for improving this application, please write to:** U.S. Department of Education, Washington, DC 20202-4651.

If you have questions regarding the status of your individual submission of this application, contact your loan holder (see Section 8).

SECTION 8: WHERE TO SEND THE COMPLETED LOAN DISCHARGE APPLICATION

Send the completed loan discharge application and any attachments to: *(If no address is shown, return to your loan holder.)*	*If you need help completing this form, call:*

Page 2 of 2

LOAN DISCHARGE APPLICATION:
TOTAL AND PERMANENT DISABILITY

OMB No. 1845-0065
Form Approved
Exp. Date 12/31/2005

Federal Family Education Loan Program / Federal Perkins Loan Program / William D. Ford Federal Direct Loan Program

WARNING: Any person who knowingly makes a false statement or misrepresentation on this form or on any accompanying documents will be subject to penalties which may include fines, imprisonment or both, under the U.S. Criminal Code and 20 U.S.C. 1097.

SECTION I: BORROWER IDENTIFICATION

Please enter or correct the following information.

SSN | | | – | | | – | | | | |

Name _____

Address _____

City, State, Zip _____

Telephone - Home ( ) _____

Telephone - Other ( ) _____

E-mail address (optional) _____

SECTION 2: BORROWER DISCHARGE REQUEST

Before signing, carefully read the entire form, including the instructions and other information on the following pages.

Borrower Request, Authorization, Understandings, and Certifications

I **request** that the U.S. Department of Education (ED) discharge my loan(s) made under the Federal Family Education Loan (FFEL) Program, the Federal Perkins Loan (Perkins Loan) Program, and/or the William D. Ford Federal Direct Loan (Direct Loan) Program.

I **authorize** any physician, hospital, or other institution having records about the disability that is the basis for my request for a loan discharge to make information from these records available to the holder(s) of my loan(s).

I **understand** that I must submit a separate discharge application to each holder of the loan(s) that I want to have discharged. I further understand that I am not eligible to receive a final discharge of my loan(s) unless I meet certain requirements during and at the end of a conditional discharge period, as explained in Sections 6 and 7. If I am a veteran, I understand that the certification by a physician on this form is only for the purposes of establishing my eligibility to receive a discharge of a FFEL Program, Perkins Loan Program, or Direct Loan Program loan and is not for purposes of determining my eligibility for or the extent of my eligibility for Department of Veterans Affairs benefits.

I **certify** that I have a total and permanent disability, as defined in Section 5. In addition, I certify that I have read and understand the information on the loan discharge process, the terms and conditions for discharge, the eligibility requirements for loan discharge, and the eligibility requirements to receive future loans as explained in Sections 6, 7 and 9.

_____ _____ _____
Signature of Borrower or Borrower's Representative   Date   Printed Name of Borrower's Representative (if applicable)

_____ _____
Address of Borrower's Representative (if applicable)   Representative's Relationship to Borrower (if applicable)

SECTION 3: PHYSICIAN'S CERTIFICATION

Instructions for Physician: The borrower identified above is applying for discharge of his/her federal education loan(s) based on total and permanent disability. You should complete and sign the certification below only if you are a doctor of medicine or osteopathy legally authorized to practice in a State (see definition in Section 5) and **if the borrower's condition meets the definition of total and permanent disability in Section 5.** Provide all requested information and attach additional pages if necessary. **Type or print in dark ink. Please return the completed form to the borrower or the borrower's representative.** The holder(s) of the borrower's loan(s) (see definition in Section 5) may contact you for additional information or documentation.

Note: The standard for determining disability for discharge of the borrower's loan(s) may be different from standards used under other programs in connection with occupational disability, or eligibility for social service or veterans benefits.

1. Diagnosis/explanation of the borrower's present medical condition (identify the borrower's condition and explain how it prevents the borrower from working and earning money in any capacity). **Do not use abbreviations or insurance codes.**

_____

_____

2. When did the borrower's medical condition begin? (MM-DD-YYYY) | | | – | | | – | | | | |

3. a. Does this medical condition prevent the borrower from being able to work and earn money in any capacity? ❏ **Yes** ❏ **No**

 b. If Yes, when did the borrower become unable to work and earn money in any capacity? (MM-DD-YYYY) | | | – | | | – | | | | |

I certify that, in my best professional judgment, the borrower identified above is unable to work and earn money because of an injury or illness that is expected to continue indefinitely or result in death. I understand that a borrower who is currently able or who is expected to be able to work and earn money, even on a limited basis, is not considered to have a total and permanent disability.

I am a doctor of (check one) ❏ medicine ❏ osteopathy legally authorized to practice in the state of _____.

My professional license no. is _____.
(Subject to verification through State records.)

_____ _____ _____
Physician's Signature (a signature stamp is not acceptable)   Date   Printed Name of Physician

_____ _____
Address   City, State, Zip

( ) _____ ( ) _____ _____
Telephone   Fax (optional)   E-mail address (optional)

SECTION 4: INSTRUCTIONS FOR COMPLETING THE FORM

Type or print in dark ink. A representative may sign on your behalf in Section 2 if you are unable to do so because of your disability. Have Section 3 completed and signed by a doctor of medicine or osteopathy. **If you are applying for discharge of more than one loan and your loans are held by more than one loan holder, you must submit a separate discharge application (original or copy) with any accompanying attachments to each holder. A "copy" means a photocopy of the original form completed by you (or your representative) and your physician. If you submit copies, each copy must include an original signature from you or your representative.**

SECTION 5: DEFINITIONS

- The **Federal Family Education Loan (FFEL) Program** includes Federal Stafford Loans (both subsidized and unsubsidized), Federal Supplemental Loans for Students (SLS), Federal PLUS Loans, and Federal Consolidation Loans.
- The **Federal Perkins Loan (Perkins Loan) Program** includes Federal Perkins Loans, National Direct Student Loans (NDSL), and National Defense Student Loans (NDSL).
- The **William D. Ford Federal Direct Loan (Direct Loan) Program** includes Federal Direct Stafford/Ford Loans (Direct Subsidized Loans), Federal Direct Unsubsidized Stafford/Ford Loans (Direct Unsubsidized Loans), Federal Direct PLUS Loans (Direct PLUS Loans), and Federal Direct Consolidation Loans (Direct Consolidation Loans).
- A **conditional discharge** due to a total and permanent disability allows you (and, if applicable, any endorser) to stop making payments on your loan(s) during the conditional discharge period (see definition) while ED evaluates your eligibility for a final discharge. A conditional discharge is granted when ED makes an initial determination that you have a total and permanent disability as defined in this section. See also Sections 6 and 7.
- The **conditional discharge period** begins on the date that you became totally and permanently disabled, as certified by the physician who completes Section 3, and lasts for up to three years. The conditional discharge period ends when ED either grants a final discharge or determines that you do not qualify for a final discharge. During the conditional discharge period, ED will monitor your eligibility for a final discharge. See also Sections 6 and 7.
- A **final discharge** due to a total and permanent disability condition cancels your obligation (and, if applicable, any endorser's obligation) to repay the remaining balance on your FFEL Program, Perkins Loan Program, and/or Direct Loan Program loan. ED grants a final discharge if you meet certain conditions during and at the end of the conditional discharge period. See Section 7.
- The **holder** of your FFEL Program loan(s) may be a lender, a guaranty agency, or the U.S. Department of Education (ED). The holder of your Perkins Loan Program loan(s) may be a school you attended or ED. The holder of your Direct Loan Program loan(s) is ED.
- **State** includes the 50 United States, the District of Columbia, American Samoa, the Commonwealth of Puerto Rico, Guam, the Virgin Islands, the Commonwealth of the Northern Mariana Islands, the Republic of the Marshall Islands, the Federated States of Micronesia, and the Republic of Palau.
- If you have a **total and permanent disability**, this means that you are unable to work and earn money because of an injury or illness that is expected to continue indefinitely or result in death. **NOTE: (1)** This standard may be different from standards used under other programs in connection with occupational disability or eligibility for social service benefits. **(2)** You cannot be considered to have a total and permanent disability if your condition existed at the time your loan(s) was made, unless your condition has substantially deteriorated so that you are now totally and permanently disabled.

SECTION 6: LOAN DISCHARGE PROCESS / TERMS AND CONDITIONS FOR LOAN DISCHARGE

1. If your loan holder (other than ED) determines, based on a review of your loan discharge application, that you appear to meet the eligibility requirements for a loan discharge based on total and permanent disability, your loan(s) will be assigned to ED. For FFEL Program loans currently held by a lender, this determination will be made by both your lender and guaranty agency. ED will be your new loan holder.
2. After receiving your loan(s), ED will review the physician's certification in Section 3 and other information relating to your application for loan discharge. Based on the results of this review, ED will make an initial determination on your application. If ED determines that you have a total and permanent disability, you will be notified that a conditional discharge has been granted for a period of up to three years from the date that you became totally and permanently disabled. If ED determines that you do not have a total and permanent disability, you will be notified of that determination and you must resume repayment of your loan(s).
3. During the conditional discharge period: **(A)** you are not required to make any payments on your loan(s); **(B)** you are not considered to be delinquent or in default on your loan(s), unless you were delinquent or in default at the time the conditional discharge was granted; **(C)** you must promptly notify ED if your annual earnings from employment exceed the poverty line amount for a family of two; **(D)** you must promptly notify ED of any changes in your address or telephone number; and **(E)** if requested, you must provide ED with additional documentation or information related to your eligibility for loan discharge. This may include, but is not limited to, documentation of your annual earnings from employment.
4. If you meet the conditions described in Section 7, Item 4, during and at the end of the conditional discharge period, ED will grant a final discharge of your loan(s) at the end of the conditional discharge period. The discharge will be reported to credit bureaus, and any payments you made after the date you became totally and permanently disabled will be returned to you.
5. If you do not meet the conditions described in Section 7, Item 4, at any time during or at the end of the conditional discharge period, the conditional discharge period will end and you will not receive a final discharge. This means that you will be responsible for repaying your loan(s) in accordance with the terms of your promissory note(s). However, you will not be required to pay interest that accrued on your loan(s) from the date ED made an initial determination that you were totally and permanently disabled until the date the conditional discharge period ended. ED will continue to be your loan holder.

SECTION 7: ELIGIBILITY REQUIREMENTS FOR LOAN DISCHARGE

1. Your condition must not have existed at the time your loan(s) was made, unless your condition has substantially deteriorated so that you are now totally and permanently disabled.
2. If you are applying for discharge of a consolidation loan, your condition must not have existed at the time any of the loan(s) you consolidated were made, unless your condition has substantially deteriorated so that you are now totally and permanently disabled. If requested, you must provide the holder of your consolidation loan(s) or ED with the disbursement dates of the loan(s) you consolidated.
3. To qualify for a **conditional discharge**, you must have a total and permanent disability, as defined in Section 5. This must be certified by a physician in Section 3.
4. To qualify for a **final discharge**, you must meet the following conditions during and at the end of the conditional discharge period described in Section 6:
   (A) your annual earnings from employment must not exceed the poverty line amount (see NOTE below) for a family of two in your state (regardless of your actual family size), and **(B)** you must not receive a new loan under the FFEL Program, the Perkins Loan Program, or the Direct Loan Program.
   NOTE: A physician cannot certify that you have a total and permanent disability if, at the time of the physician's certification, you are able to work and earn money in any capacity. However, if you attempt to work during the conditional discharge period, you may earn up to the poverty line amount each year during that period. This standard allows you to try to work without being disqualified from receiving a final discharge. The poverty line amounts are updated annually. ED will notify you of the current poverty line amounts during each year of the conditional discharge period.

SECTION 8: WHERE TO SEND THE COMPLETED LOAN DISCHARGE APPLICATION

Send the completed loan discharge application and any attachments to:
(If no address is shown, return to your loan holder.)

If you need help completing this form, call:

SECTION 9: ELIGIBILITY REQUIREMENTS TO RECEIVE FUTURE LOANS

---

1. If you are granted a final discharge due to total and permanent disability, you are not eligible to receive future loans under the FFEL, Perkins Loan, or Direct Loan programs unless: **(A)** you obtain a certification from a physician that you are able to engage in substantial gainful activity, and **(B)** you sign a statement acknowledging that the new loan you receive cannot be discharged in the future on the basis of any injury or illness present at the time the new loan is made, unless your condition substantially deteriorates so that you are again totally and permanently disabled.

2. If you are granted a conditional discharge of your loan(s), based on a total and permanent disability and you request a new FFEL, Perkins Loan, or Direct Loan program loan during the conditional discharge period, you are not eligible to receive the new loan unless: **(A)** you obtain a certification from a physician that you are able to engage in substantial gainful activity; **(B)** you sign a statement acknowledging that neither the previous conditionally discharged loan(s) nor the new loan you receive can be discharged in the future on the basis of any injury or illness present when you applied for a total and permanent disability discharge or at the time the new loan is made, unless your condition substantially deteriorates so that you are again totally and permanently disabled; **(C)** you sign a statement acknowledging that the conditionally discharged loan(s) will be removed from conditional discharge status; and **(D)** ED has removed the conditionally discharged loan(s) from conditional discharge status (see Section 6, Item 5).

SECTION 10: IMPORTANT NOTICES

Privacy Act Notice. The Privacy Act of 1974 (5 U.S.C. 552a) requires that the following notice be provided to you:

The authorities for collecting the requested information from and about you are §428(b)(2)(A) *et seq.*, §451 *et seq.* and §461 *et seq.* of the Higher Education Act of 1965, as amended (20 U.S.C. 1078(b)(2)(A) *et seq.* 20 U.S.C. 1087a *et seq.*, and 20 U.S.C. 1087aa *et seq.*) and the authority for collecting and using your Social Security Number (SSN) is §484(a)(4) of the HEA (20 U.S.C. 1091(a)(4)). Participating in the Federal Family Education Loan (FFEL) Program, the William D. Ford Federal Direct Loan (Direct Loan) Program, or the Federal Perkins Loan (Perkins Loan) Program and giving us your SSN are voluntary, but you must provide the requested information, including your SSN, to participate.

The principal purposes for collecting the information on this form, including your SSN, are to verify your identity, to determine your eligibility to receive a loan or a benefit on a loan (such as a deferment, forbearance, discharge, or forgiveness) under the FFEL, Direct Loan, and/or Perkins Loan Programs, to permit the servicing of your loan(s), and, if it becomes necessary, to locate you and to collect on your loan(s) if your loan(s) become delinquent or in default. We also use your SSN as an account identifier and to permit you to access your account information electronically.

The information in your file may be disclosed to third parties as authorized under routine uses in the appropriate systems of records. The routine uses of this information include its disclosure to federal, state, or local agencies, to other federal agencies under computer matching programs, to agencies that we authorize to assist us in administering our loan programs, to private parties such as relatives, present and former employers, business and personal associates, to credit bureau organizations, to educational institutions, and to contractors in order to verify your identity, to determine your eligibility to receive a loan or a benefit on a loan, to permit the servicing or collection of your loan(s), to counsel you in repayment efforts, to enforce the terms of the loan(s), to investigate possible fraud and to verify compliance with federal student financial aid program regulations, or to locate you if you become delinquent in your loan payments or if you default, to provide default rate calculations, to provide financial aid history information, to assist program administrators with tracking refunds and cancellations, or to provide a standardized method for educational institutions efficiently to submit student enrollment status.

In the event of litigation, we may send records to the Department of Justice, a court, adjudicative body, counsel, party, or witness if the disclosure is relevant and necessary to the litigation. If this information, either alone or with other information, indicates a potential violation of law, we may send it to the appropriate authority for action. We may send information to members of Congress if you ask them to help you with federal student aid questions. In circumstances involving employment complaints, grievances, or disciplinary actions, we may disclose relevant records to adjudicate or investigate the issues. If provided for by a collective bargaining agreement, we may disclose records to a labor organization recognized under 5 U.S.C. Chapter 71. Disclosures may also be made to qualified researchers under Privacy Act safeguards.

Paperwork Reduction Notice. According to the Paperwork Reduction Act of 1995, no persons are required to respond to a collection of information unless it displays a currently valid OMB control number. The valid OMB control number for this information collection is 1845-0065. The time required to complete this information collection is estimated to average 0.5 hours (30 minutes) per response, including the time to review instructions, search existing data resources, gather and maintain the data needed, and complete and review the information collection. **If you have comments concerning the accuracy of the time estimate(s) or suggestions for improving this form, please write to:** U.S. Department of Education, Washington, DC 20202-4651. *Do not send the completed loan discharge application to this address.*

If you have comments or concerns regarding the status of *your individual submission* of this form, contact your loan holder (see Section 8).

D.3.6 Unpaid Refund

LOAN DISCHARGE APPLICATION: UNPAID REFUND
Federal Family Education Loan Program / William D. Ford Federal Direct Loan Program

OMB No. 1845-0058
Form Approved
Exp. Date 12/31/2007

WARNING: Any person who knowingly makes a false statement or misrepresentation on this form or on any accompanying documents will be subject to penalties which may include fines, imprisonment or both, under the U.S. Criminal Code and 20 U.S.C. 1097.

SECTION 1: BORROWER IDENTIFICATION

Please enter or correct the following information:

SSN |__|__|__|-|__|__|-|__|__|__|__|

Name _____

Address _____

City, State, Zip _____

Telephone – Home (   ) _____

Telephone – Other (   ) _____

E-mail (optional) _____

SECTION 2: SCHOOL AND LOAN INFORMATION

Before responding, carefully read the entire form, including the instructions and other information on the following page. If the school that you believe owes you a refund is currently open, you should first contact the school to attempt to resolve this issue before applying for an unpaid refund loan discharge. If you are a student borrower applying for loan discharge, begin with Item 3a. If you are a parent borrower applying for a PLUS loan discharge, begin with Item 1.

1. Student's name (last, first, middle initial):

2. Student's SSN: |__|__|__|-|__|__|-|__|__|__|__|

3a. School's name:

3b. School's address (street, city, state, zip):

4. Is this school still open? ☐ Yes ☐ No ☐ Don't Know

5. If this school is closed, were you (or, for PLUS borrowers, was the student) attending the school when it closed? ☐ Yes ☐ No

6a. Do you have any other pending or approved application(s) for discharge of a loan you obtained to attend this school? ☐ Yes ☐ No

6b. Has this school or any third party (see the definition of "third party" in Section 6, on the following page) made a refund or payment for any loan for which you are requesting a discharge, or is such a refund or payment being considered? ☐ Yes ☐ No

7. If your answers to Items 6a and 6b are "No," skip to Section 3. If your answer to Item 6a or 6b is "Yes," provide the information requested in Items 7a, 7b, and 7c for each discharge, refund or payment, if known. Use a separate sheet of paper if you need to report more than one discharge, refund or payment.

7a. Reason for discharge, refund or payment:

7b. From whom did you request the discharge, refund or payment (include telephone number)?

7c. Amount you received or that you expect to receive: $ _____

SECTION 3: REFUND INFORMATION

If you have documentation from the school showing the amount of the unpaid refund, attach a copy to this form. If you believe that the amount of the refund shown in the documentation from the school is correct, skip to Section 4. If you don't believe that the amount is correct or if you don't have this documentation, complete Items 8 through 13. If you are unable to provide any of the requested information, write "Don't Know."

8. What amount do you believe the school owes you? $ _____

9. Why do you believe the school owes you this amount?

10. Your (or, for PLUS borrowers, the student's) first and last dates of attendance at the school:
|__|__|-|__|__|-|__|__|__|__| to |__|__|-|__|__|-|__|__|__|__| OR ☐ Never Attended

11. Your (or, for PLUS borrowers, the student's) program of study at the school:

12. Items 12a and 12b request information about the amount of the school's charges or the amount of the financial aid you received for the period of enrollment for which the loan was intended. For example, if you received a loan for the spring quarter only and you left school during the spring quarter, provide an amount for that quarter only. However, if you received a loan for the winter and spring quarters, provide the total amount for both quarters. If the unpaid refund is for more than one loan and the loans were for different periods of enrollment, provide the amounts requested in Item 12a or 12b for each period of enrollment separately, using a separate sheet of paper for your additional response(s).

12a. If your (or, for PLUS borrowers, the student's) last date of attendance was **before October 7, 2000**, enter the amount of the school's charges for the period of enrollment for which the loan was intended. Include tuition, fees, and other school charges. $ _____

12b. If your (or, for PLUS borrowers, the student's) last date of attendance was **on or after October 7, 2000**, enter the total amount of federal grants and loans received for any part of the period of enrollment for which the loan was intended. $ _____

13. Attach a copy of any documentation that supports your responses to Items 8 through 12. Examples of documentation may include, but are not limited to, the school's catalog, refund policy, tuition bill(s), enrollment contract, student account statement, registration forms, withdrawal form, attendance records, and any correspondence from the school that contains information about the refund you believe the school owes you.

SECTION 4: BORROWER CERTIFICATION

My signature below certifies that—

- I received each loan for which I am requesting a discharge on or after January 1, 1986. I received the loan funds directly, or they were applied as a credit to my (or, for PLUS borrowers, the student's) school account to pay the amount owed to the school.
- I (or, for PLUS borrowers, the student) did not attend the school or withdrew or was terminated from the school within the timeframe that would entitle me to a refund of some or all of my loan funds. Except as explained in Section 2, Items 6 and 7, I have not received this refund, or any benefit of a refund to which I am entitled, from the school or any third party.
- I have read and agree to the terms and conditions for loan discharge, as specified in Section 7 on the following page.
- Under penalty of perjury, all of the information I have provided on this application and in any accompanying documentation is true and accurate to the best of my knowledge and belief.

Borrower's Signature: _____   Date: _____

Page 1 of 2

SECTION 5: INSTRUCTIONS FOR COMPLETING THE FORM

Before you complete this application, you need to know the following:

- If the school is currently open, you should first contact the school and attempt to resolve the unpaid refund issue before applying for this type of discharge.

- If you (or, for PLUS borrowers, the student) are currently attending the school, you are not eligible for this type of discharge. You should contact the school about the refund that you believe you are owed.

- If you (or, for PLUS borrowers, the student) were enrolled when the school closed or withdrew from the school within 90 days before the school closed and you (or, for PLUS borrowers, the student) did not complete the program of study at another school, you may wish to apply for a closed school loan discharge rather than an unpaid refund discharge. If you are unsure about which type of loan discharge is most appropriate for you, contact your loan holder at the address shown in Section 9.

When completing this form, type or print using dark ink. For all dates, give month, day (if known), and year. Show dates as MM-DD-YYYY (for example, "July 01, 2005" = "07-01-2005"). If you need more space to answer any of the Items, continue on separate sheets of paper and attach them to this form. Indicate the number of the Item(s) you are answering and include your name and social security number (SSN) on all attached pages. If a refund is owed for more than one student or from more than one school, use separate forms for each student and school.

Return the completed form and any attachments to the address shown in Section 9.

SECTION 6: DEFINITIONS

- The **Federal Family Education Loan (FFEL) Program** includes Federal Stafford Loans (both subsidized and unsubsidized), Federal Supplemental Loans for Students (SLS), Federal PLUS Loans, and Federal Consolidation Loans.

- The **William D. Ford Federal Direct Loan (Direct Loan) Program** includes Federal Direct Stafford/Ford Loans (Direct Subsidized Loans), Federal Direct Unsubsidized Stafford/Ford Loans (Direct Unsubsidized Loans), Federal Direct PLUS Loans (Direct PLUS Loans), and Federal Direct Consolidation Loans (Direct Consolidation Loans).

- **Loan discharge** due to an unpaid refund cancels your obligation (and any endorser's obligation) to repay the portion of your loan that should have been refunded. Any accrued interest and other charges on the amount of the unpaid refund will also be discharged, and you will be reimbursed for any amount that you have repaid that exceeds the remaining balance of the loan after the discharge. Your loan holder will report the discharge to all credit reporting agencies to which the loan holder previously reported the status of the loan.

- **Program of study** means the instructional program leading to a degree or certificate in which you (or, for PLUS borrowers, the student) were enrolled.

- The **student** (as in "or, for PLUS borrowers, the student") refers to the student for whom a parent borrower obtained a Federal PLUS Loan or Direct PLUS Loan.

- **Third party** refers to any entity that may provide reimbursement for a refund owed by the school, such as a State or other entity offering a tuition recovery program or a holder of a performance bond.

SECTION 7: TERMS AND CONDITIONS FOR LOAN DISCHARGE

- I agree to cooperate with the U.S. Department of Education (the Department) or the Department's designee in any enforcement action related to this application and to provide to the Department or the Department's designee, upon request, other documentation reasonably available to me that demonstrates that I meet the qualifications for an unpaid refund discharge.

- I assign and transfer to the Department any right to recovery on the amount discharged that I may have from the school identified in Section 2 of this form and/or any owners, affiliates or assigns of the school, and from any party that may pay claims for a refund because of the actions of the school, up to the amounts discharged by the Department on my loan(s).

- I understand that this request may be denied, or my discharge may be revoked, if I fail to cooperate, provide documentation, or meet any of the other terms of my agreement on this form.

- I understand that if my loan is discharged based on any false, fictitious, or fraudulent statements that I knowingly made on this form or on any accompanying documents, I may be subject to civil and criminal penalties under applicable federal law.

SECTION 8: IMPORTANT NOTICES

Privacy Act Notice. The Privacy Act of 1974 (5 U.S.C. 552a) requires that the following notice be provided to you:

The authorities for collecting the requested information from and about you are §428(b)(2)(A) *et seq.* and §451 *et seq.* of the Higher Education Act of 1965, as amended (20 U.S.C. 1078(b)(2)(A) *et seq.* and 20 U.S.C. 1087a *et seq.*) and the authority for collecting and using your Social Security Number (SSN) is §484(a)(4) of the HEA (20 U.S.C. 1091(a)(4)). Participating in the Federal Family Education Loan (FFEL) Program or the William D. Ford Federal Direct Loan (Direct Loan) Program and giving us your SSN are voluntary, but you must provide the requested information, including your SSN, to participate.

The principal purposes for collecting the information on this form, including your SSN, are to verify your identity, to determine your eligibility to receive a loan or a benefit on a loan (such as a deferment, forbearance, discharge, or forgiveness) under the FFEL and/or Direct Loan Programs, to permit the servicing of your loan(s), and, if it becomes necessary, to locate you and to collect on your loan(s) if your loan(s) become delinquent or in default. We also use your SSN as an account identifier and to permit you to access your account information electronically.

The information in your file may be disclosed to third parties as authorized under routine uses in the appropriate systems of records. The routine uses of this information include its disclosure to federal, state, or local agencies, to other federal agencies under computer matching programs, to agencies that we authorize to assist us in administering our loan programs, to private parties such as relatives, present and former employers, business and personal associates, to credit bureau organizations, to financial and educational institutions, to guaranty agencies, and to contractors in order to verify your identity, to determine your eligibility to receive a loan or a benefit on a loan, to permit the servicing or collection of your loan(s), to counsel you in repayment efforts, to enforce the terms of the loan(s), to investigate possible fraud and to verify compliance with federal student financial aid program regulations, or to locate you if you become delinquent in your loan payments or if you default, to provide default rate calculations, to provide financial aid history information, to assist program administrators with tracking refunds and cancellations, or to provide a standardized method for educational institutions efficiently to submit student enrollment status.

In the event of litigation, we may send records to the Department of Justice, a court, adjudicative body, counsel, party, or witness if the disclosure is relevant and necessary to the litigation. If this information, either alone or with other information, indicates a potential violation of law, we may send it to the appropriate authority for action. We may send information to members of Congress if you ask them to help you with federal student aid questions. In circumstances involving employment complaints, grievances, or disciplinary actions, we may disclose relevant records to adjudicate or investigate the issues. If provided for by a collective bargaining agreement, we may disclose records to a labor organization recognized under 5 U.S.C. Chapter 71. Disclosures may also be made to qualified researchers under Privacy Act safeguards.

Paperwork Reduction Notice. According to the Paperwork Reduction Act of 1995, no persons are required to respond to a collection of information unless it displays a currently valid OMB control number. The valid OMB control number for this information collection is 1845-0058. The time required to complete this information collection is estimated to average 0.5 hours (30 minutes) per response, including the time to review instructions, search existing data resources, gather and maintain the data needed, and complete and review the information collection. **If you have comments concerning the accuracy of the time estimate(s) or suggestions for improving this form, please write to:** U.S. Department of Education, Washington, DC 20202-4651.

If you have questions regarding the status of *your individual submission of this form,* contact your loan holder (see Section 9).

SECTION 9: WHERE TO SEND THE COMPLETED LOAN DISCHARGE APPLICATION

Send the completed loan discharge application and any attachments to: *(If no address is shown, return to your loan holder.)*	*If you need help completing this form, call:*

D.3.7 *Letter from Department of Education Granting False Certification Discharge*

U. S. DEPARTMENT OF EDUCATION
STUDENT FINANCIAL ASSISTANCE

#BWNFDMC **AUTO
#50 9913W70 S68298 0#

DATE: JUNE 28, 2006

SSN: ▮▮▮▮▮▮▮▮
DEBT NO. ▮▮▮▮▮▮▮▮▮▮▮▮

DEAR BORROWER:

THIS LETTER ACKNOWLEDGES RECEIPT OF YOUR SWORN STATEMENT
REQUESTING DISCHARGE OF FEDERAL FAMILY EDUCATION LOAN(S) DUE TO
THE FALSE CERTIFICATION OF YOUR ABILITY TO BENEFIT
FROM THE TRAINING OFFERED BY THE SCHOOL ATTENDED   WITH THE LOAN.

THE U.S. DEPARTMENT OF EDUCATION HAS DETERMINED THAT YOU QUALIFY
FOR DISCHARGE OF YOUR FEDERAL FAMILY EDUCATION LOAN(S) WHICH YOU
OBTAINED TO ATTEND USA Training Academy Home Study.

AS A RESULT OF THIS DETERMINATION:

- YOU WILL BE RELIEVED OF THE OBLIGATION TO REPAY THE LOAN;

- YOU WILL BE REFUNDED ALL MONIES PAID BY YOU ON THE LOAN(S),
  WHICH OUR RECORDS INDICATE TO BE $729.52.   A CHECK HAS
  BEEN REQUESTED FROM THE U.S. TREASURY. PLEASE ALLOW 4-6
  WEEKS FOR DELIVERY;

- IF YOU WERE IN DEFAULT ON THE DISCHARGED LOAN(S), YOU WILL
  NO LONGER BE REGARDED AS IN DEFAULT ON THE LOAN(S), AND THE
  PAST REPORTING OF A DEFAULT WILL NOT PRECLUDE YOU FROM
  RECEIVING ASSISTANCE UNDER THE TITLE IV, HIGHER EDUCATION
  ACT PROGRAMS IN THE FUTURE;

- THE DEPARTMENT OF EDUCATION WILL REPORT THE DISCHARGE TO ALL
  CREDIT REPORTING AGENCIES TO WHICH IT PREVIOUSLY REPORTED SO
  THAT ANY ADVERSE CREDIT HISTORY ASSIGNED TO THE LOAN(S) MAY
  BE DELETED.

THIS DISCHARGE COVERS ONLY THE LOAN(S) HELD BY THE U.S.
DEPARTMENT OF EDUCATION, LISTED ABOVE, WHICH WERE OBTAINED
TO ATTEND USA Training Academy Home Study. THE DEPARTMENT
HAS MADE NO DETERMINATION WITH REGARD TO LOANS HELD BY
GUARANTEE AGENCIES, SERVICERS, LENDERS, OR EDUCATIONAL
INSTITUTIONS.

IF YOU HAVE FURTHER QUESTIONS REGARDING THIS MATTER, YOU CAN
CONTACT A DEPARTMENT REPRESENTATIVE BY CALLING 1-800-621-3115.

D.4 Collection Letters and Hearing Forms

D.4.1 Department of Education's Request for Administrative Wage Garnishment Hearing Form

REQUEST FOR HEARING

If you object to garnishment of your wages for the debt described in the notice, you can use this form to request a hearing. Your request must be in writing and mailed or delivered to the address below.

Your Name: _____
SSN: _____
Address:
_____
Telephone:
_____
Employer:
_____
Address: _____
Telephone: _____
Beginning Date of Current Employment: _____

() CHECK HERE if you object that garnishment in amounts equal to15% of your disposable pay would cause financial hardship to you and your dependents. (To arrange voluntary repayment, contact customer service at the number below.)

You must complete either the enclosed FINANCIAL DISCLOSURE FORM or a Financial Disclosure Form of your choosing to present your hardship claim. You must enclose copies of earnings and income records, and proof of expenses, as explained on the form. If your request for an oral hearing is granted, you will be notified of the date, time, and location of your hearing. If your request for an oral hearing is denied, ED will make its determination of the amounts you should pay based on a review of your written materials.

NOTE: You should also state below any other objections you have to garnishment to collect this debt at this time.

NOTE: IT IS IN YOUR INTEREST TO REQUEST COPIES OF ALL DOCUMENTATIONHELD BY ED BY CALLING THE CUSTOMER SERVICE NUMBER LISTED ON THE ENCLOSED NOTICE PRIOR TO COMPLETING A REQUEST FOR HEARING.

I. HEARING REQUEST (Check ONLY ONE of the following)

() I want a written records hearing of my objection(s) based on ED's review of this written statement, the documents I have enclosed, and the records in my debt file at ED.

() I want an in-person hearing at the ED hearing office to present my objection(s). I understand that I must pay my own expenses to appear for this hearing.

    I want this In-Person hearing held in: _____ Atlanta, GA, _____

Chicago. IL. _____ San Francisco, CA. (Check the location you wish for the hearing.)

( ) I want a hearing by telephone to present my objections. You must provide a daytime telephone number at which you can be contacted between the hours of 8:00 am to 4:00 pm, Monday through Friday. I can be reached at: (_____) ____-_____.

II IF YOU WANT AN IN-PERSON OR TELEPHONE HEARING, YOU MUST COMPLETETHE FOLLOWING:

The debt records and documents I submitted to support my statement in Part III, do not show all the material (important) facts about my objection to collection of this debt. I need a hearing to explain the following important facts about this debt: (EXPLAIN the additional facts that you believe make a hearing necessary on a separate sheet of paper. If you have already fully described these facts in your response in Part III, WRITE HERE the number of the objection in which you described these facts.____)

Note: If you do not request an in-person or telephone hearing, we will review your objection based on information and documents you supply with this form and on records in your loan file. We provide an oral hearing to a debtor who requests an oral hearing and shows in the request for the hearing good reason to believe that we cannot resolve the issues in dispute by review of the documentary evidence, for example, when the validity of the claim turns on the issue of credibility or veracity.

III. Check the objections that apply. EXPLAIN any further facts concerning your objection on a separate sheet of paper. ENCLOSE the documents described here (if you do not enclose documents, ED will consider your objection(s) based on the information on this form and records held by ED).

For some objections, you must submit a completed application. Obtain applications by contacting Customer Service at number below, or go to ED's website at: http://www.ed.gov/offices/OSFAP/DCS, select Forms, and then select the application described for that objection.

1   ( ) I do not owe the full amount shown because I repaid some or all of this debt. (ENCLOSE: copies of the front and back of all checks, money orders and any receipts showing payments made to the holder of the debt.)
2   ( ) I am making payments on this debt as required under the repayment agreement I reached with the holder of the debt. (ENCLOSE: copies of the repayment agreement and copies of the front and back of checks where you paid on the agreement.)
3   ( ) I filed for bankruptcy and my case is still open. (ENCLOSE: copies of any documents from the court that shows the date that you filed the name of the court, and your case number.)
4   ( ) This debt was discharged in bankruptcy. (ENCLOSE: copies of debt discharge order and the schedule of debts filed with the court.)

5   () The borrower has died (ENCLOSE: CERTIFIED Copy of Death Certificate) For Loans only.

6   () I am totally and permanently disabled - unable to work and earn money because of an impairment that is expected to continue indefinitely or result in death. Obtain and submit completed Total and Permanent Disability Cancellation Request; must be completed by physician (For loans only).

7   () I used this loan to enroll in _____(school) on or about __/__/__, and I withdrew from school on or about __/__/__. I paid the school$_____ and I believe that I am owed, but have not been paid, are fund from the school of $_____. Obtain and submit completed Loan Discharge Application: Unpaid Refund (Enclose any records you have showing your withdrawal date) for loans only.

8   () I used this loan to enroll in _____ (school) on or about ___/___/___, and I was unable to complete my education because the school closed. Obtain and submit completed Loan Discharge Application: Closed School.(ENCLOSE: any records you have showing your withdrawal date) for loans only.

9   () This is not my Social Security Number, and I do not owe this debt (ENCLOSE: a copy of your driver's license or other identification issued by a federal, state or local government agency, and a copy of your Social Security Card.)

10   () I believe that this debt is not an enforceable debt in the amount stated for the reason explained in the attached letter.(Attach a letter explaining any reason other than those listed above for your objection to collection of this debt amount by garnishment of your salary. ENCLOSE any supporting records.)

11   () I did not have a high school diploma or GED when I enrolled at the school I attended with this guaranteed student loan. The school did not properly test my ability to benefit from the training offered. Obtain and submit completed Loan Discharge Application: False Certification of Ability to Benefit. Enclose any records you have showing your withdrawal date For loans only.

12   () When I borrowed this guaranteed student loan to attend_____(school), I had a condition (physical, mental, age, criminal record) that prevented me from meeting State requirements for performing the occupation for which it trained me. Obtain and submit completed Loan Discharge Application: False Certification(Disqualifying Status) for loans only.

13   () I was involuntarily terminated from my last employment and I have been employed in my current job for less than twelve months.(Attach statement from employer showing date of hire in current job and statement from prior employer showing involuntary termination.)

14 () I believe that_____ (School) without my permission signed my name on the loan application, promissory note, loan check or electronic funds transfer (EFT) authorization. Obtain and submit completed Loan Discharge Application: Unauthorized Signature /Unauthorized Payment. (Enclose any records you have showing your withdrawal date) for loans only.

IV I state under penalty of law that the statements made on this request are true and accurate to the best of my knowledge.

DATE: _____   SIGNATURE: _____

SEND THIS REQUEST FOR HEARING FORM TO:

U.S. Department of Education
P. O. Box 617763
Chicago, Illinois 60661-7763
Telephone No: (312) 886-0939

If you wish to arrange a voluntary agreement for payments in amounts equal to 15% of your disposable pay, do not use this form. Instead, call the Customer Service Number Below. Customer Service: **(800) 621-3115**

Violation of any such agreement may result in an immediate order to your employer for garnishment of 15% of your disposable pay.

This is an attempt to collect a debt and any information obtained will be used for that purpose.

D.4.2 Department of Education Financial Disclosure Statement

U.S. Department of Education
Financial Disclosure Statement

To evaluate a hardship claim, ED compares the expenses you claim and support against averages spent for those expenses by families of the same size and income as yours. ED considers proven expenses as reasonable up to the amount of these averages. If you claim more for an expense than the average spent by families like yours, you must provide persuasive explanation why the amount you claim is necessary. These average amounts were determined by the IRS from different government studies. You can find the average expense amount that the Department uses at this IRS website: http://www.irs.gov/individuals/article/0,,id=96543,00.html then select "Administrative Wage Garnishment," and then click on "**COLLECTION FINANCIAL STANDARDS**."

> **Provide complete information about your family income, expenses, and assets**.

- **Complete all items.** Do not leave any item blank. If the answer is zero, write zero.

- **Provide documentation.** Expenses **may** not be considered if you do not provide documents supporting the amounts claimed. **You must submit proof of Childcare / Other Caregiver expenses, in order to receive full credit for claimed caregiver cost. To obtain the form, contact Customer Service at: 1-800-621-3115 or go to ED website at:** http://www.ed.gov/offices/OSFAP/DCS, **select forms then Declaration of Caregiver Services.**

- **Provide documentation of all sources of income.** You must submit two (**2**) **most** current pay stubs for yourself, spouse, and all sources of income in your household. You may submit last years W-2's and 1040 Income Tax Filing as proof of household income. Failure to provide this information may result in a denial of your claim of extreme financial hardship.

Income

Name: _____ Social Security No.: _____

Address: _____

_____ Phone: _____

_____ County: _____

Current Employer: _____ Date Employed: _____

Employer Phone: _____ Present Position: _____

Gross Income: $_____ ❑ Weekly ❑ Bi-Weekly ❑ Bi-Monthly ❑ Monthly _____
Net Income: $_____ ❑ Weekly ❑ Bi-Weekly ❑ Bi-Monthly ❑ Monthly _____

ENCLOSE A COPY OF YOUR TWO MOST RECENT PAY STUBS
ENCLOSE LAST YEARS W-2s AND 1040 INCOME TAX FILING

Number of dependents: _____ (including yourself) **Marital status:** ❑ Married ❑ Single ❑ Divorced

Spouse name: _____ Spouse SSN: _____

Gross Income: $_____ ❑ Weekly ❑ Bi-Weekly ❑ Monthly ❑ Other _____
Net Income: $_____ ❑ Weekly ❑ Bi-Weekly ❑ Monthly ❑ Other _____

ENCLOSE A COPY OF THE TWO MOST RECENT PAY STUBS
ENCLOSE LAST YEARS W-2s AND 1040 INCOME TAX FILING

Other contributing resident(s): _____ SSN: _____

Gross Income: $_____ ❑ Weekly ❑ Bi-Weekly ❑ Bi-Monthly ❑ Monthly
Net Income: $_____ ❑ Weekly ❑ Bi-Weekly ❑ Bi-Monthly ❑ Monthly

ENCLOSE A COPY OF THE TWO MOST RECENT PAY STUBS
ENCLOSE LAST YEARS W-2s AND 1040 INCOME TAX FILING

Other Income
Child support: $_____ ❑ Weekly ❑ Bi-Weekly ❑ Bi-Monthly ❑ Monthly
Alimony: $_____ ❑ Weekly ❑ Bi-Weekly ❑ Bi-Monthly ❑ Monthly
Interest: $_____ ❑ Weekly ❑ Bi-Weekly ❑ Bi-Monthly ❑ Monthly
Public assistance: $_____ ❑ Weekly ❑ Bi-Weekly ❑ Bi-Monthly ❑ Monthly
Other: $_____ Describe: _____

Please State and Explain Amounts Deducted from your pay stub

Life insurance $_____ _____
Medical & Dental Insurance $_____ _____
Retirement $_____ _____
401K $_____ _____
Garnishment $_____ _____
Child Support $_____ _____
Other (explain) $_____ _____

Monthly Expenses

Shelter (SEND COPY OF MORTGAGE OR LEASE, *INSURANCE, MAINTENANCE PAYMENTS*)
Rent/Mortgage: $_____ Paid to whom: _____
2nd home mortgage: $_____ Paid to whom: _____
Home insurance: $_____ Paid to whom: _____
Maintenance: $_____ Paid to whom: _____
Other: $_____ Describe: _____
Household Expenses
Food Expenses: $_____ (Monthly)
Housekeeping Supplies: $_____ (Monthly)
Clothing & Cleaning: $_____ (Monthly)
Personal Care Services and Expenses: $_____ (Monthly)

Utilities (SEND COPIES OF BILLS)
Electric: $_____ Gas: $_____
Water/Sewer $_____ Garbage pickup: $_____
Basic telephone: $_____ Other: $_____
Describe: _____ _____

Medical (SEND COPIES OF BILLS)
Insurance Premiums $_____ /per month *(only **list** premiums **not** deducted from paycheck)*
Bill payments $_____ /per month *(only list payments not covered by insurance)-*
Other: $_____ /per month Describe: _____

Transportation (SEND COPIES OF CAR PAYMENT AGREEMENT OR BILLS):

Number of Cars_____

1st Car payment: $_____/per month 2nd Car payment:$_____ /per month

Gas and oil: $_____/per month Public transportation:$_____/per month

Car insurance: $_____/per month **Parking:$_____/per month**

Maintenance $_____**/per month** **Registration: $_____/per year**

Other: $_____ Describe: _____

Child Care (SEND COPIES OF BILLS, COURT ORDERS, CONTRACTS, Declaration of Caregiver Services)

Child care: $_____/per month Number of children: _____

Child support: $_____/per month Number of children: _____

Other: $_____/per month Describe: ____ _____

Other Expenses: (Attach a list describing expense, monthly payment and enclose bills)
Other Insurance: **$_____/per month**
Describe: _____

Based on this Statement, I think I can afford to pay $_____per month

I declare under penalties provided by 18 U.S.C. Section 1001 that the answers and statements contained herein are to the best of my knowledge and belief true, correct, and complete.

Signature _____ Date _____

Warning: 18 U.S.C. 1001 provides that "whoever…knowingly and willfully falsifies, conceals, or covers up by any trick, scheme, or device a material fact, or makes any materially false, fictitious, or fraudulent statement or representation…shall be fined up to $10,000.00 or imprisoned up to five years, or both."

Complete, sign, and return the requested information to:
          U.S. Department of Education
          P. O. Box 617763
          Chicago, Illinois 60661-7763
          Telephone No: 312 886-0939

Privacy Act Notice

This request is authorized under 31 U.S.C. 3711, 20 U.S.C. 1078-6, and 20 U.S.C. 1095a. You are not required to provide this information. If you do not, we cannot determine your financial ability to repay your student aid debt. The information you provide will be used to evaluate your ability to pay. It may be disclosed to government agencies and their contractors, to employees, lenders, and others to enforce this debt; to third parties in audit, research, or dispute about the management of this debt; and to parties with a right to this information under the Freedom of Information Act or other federal law, or with your consent. These uses are explained in the Federal Register of June 4, 1999, Vol. 64, p.30166, revised Dec.27, 1999, Vol. 64, p. 72407. We will send a copy at your request.

This is an attempt to collect a debt and any information obtained will be used for that purpose.

D.5 Additional Forms

D.5.1 Statement of Financial Status Form

THIS IS IN RESPONSE TO YOUR REQUEST TO ESTABLISH A MONTHLY PAYMENT PLAN. IN ORDER TO DETERMINE A PAYMENT AMOUNT THAT IS BOTH AFFORDABLE FOR YOU AND REASONABLE BASED ON THE AMOUNT YOU OWE, YOU MUST COMPLETE THE FOLLOWING STATEMENT OF FINANCIAL STATUS.

INSTRUCTIONS:

1. **IMMEDIATELY BEGIN SENDING THE AMOUNT YOU PROPOSE TO PAY** EACH MONTH TO:

    U.S. DEPARTMENT OF EDUCATION
    P.O. BOX 4169
    GREENVILLE, TX 75403-4169

INCLUDE YOUR SOCIAL SECURITY NUMBER ON YOUR PAYMENT INSTRUMENT AND DO NOT SEND CASH.

2. COMPLETE EVERY FIELD ON THIS FORM. IF AN ANSWER IS ZERO, WRITE ZERO.

3. INCLUDE PROOF OF YOUR HOUSEHOLD INCOME FOR BOTH YOU AND YOUR SPOUSE (TWO MOST RECENT PAY STUBS AND FEDERAL INCOME TAX RETURNS), AND PROOF OF YOUR EXPESNSES (SUCH AS COPIES OF MONTHLY BILLS).

4. DO NOT INCLUDE MONTHLY PAYMENTS ON CREDIT CARDS IF THE ITEMS PURCHASED BY THAT CREDIT CARD FIT UNDER AN EXPENSE CATEGORY LISTED HERE. INCLUDE THOSE COSTS UNDER THAT EXPENSE CATEGORY. FOR EXAMPLE, PAYMENTS REQUIRED ON DEPARTMENT STORE CREDIT CARDS USED TO PURCHASE CLOTHING SHOULD BE LISTED UNDER CLOTHING EXPENSES.

5. IF YOU ARE PAYING SOME EXPENSES QUARTERLY OR ANNUALLY, SUCH AS AUTOMOBILE INSURANCE OR PROPERTY TAXES, CALCULATE THE AMOUNT THAT WOULD BE DUE IF THESE EXPENSES WERE PAID ON A MONTHLY BASIS AND PUT THAT AMOUNT IN THE SPACE PROVIDED.

6. RETURN THE COMPLETED FORM TO: U.S. DEPARTMENT OF EDUCATION
                                     PO BOX 5609
                                     GREENVILLE, TX 75403-5609

STATEMENT OF FINANCIAL STATUS

AMOUNT YOU ARE PROPOSING TO PAY EACH MONTH: $_____

COUNTY IN WHICH YOU LIVE: _____ SSN: _____

NAME, ADDRESS   _____
AND PHONE
NUMBER OF YOUR   _____
CURRENT
EMPLOYER(S)   _____

NUMBER OF DEPENDENTS (AS DEFINED BY IRS) INCLUDING SELF: _____
MARITAL STATUS (MARRIED, SINGLE, DIVORCED)   _____
SPOUSE'S NAME AND SSN: _____

MONTHLY INCOME:

NOTE: GROSS INCOME IS INCOME BEFORE ANY DEDUCTIONS SUCH AS TAXES. NET
INCOME IS YOUR TAKE-HOME PAY. INCLUDE A COPY OF RECENT PAY STUBS.

YOUR MONTHLY INCOME   GROSS $_____ NET $_____
YOUR SPOUSE'S MONTHLY INCOME   GROSS $_____ NET $_____
OTHER CONTRIBUTING RESIDENT(S) MONTHLY INCOME   NET $_____
OTHER (CHILD SUPPORT, ETC. DESCRIBE_____)NET $_____

MONTHLY EXPENSES:

RENT/MORTGAGE   (TO WHOM:_____)$_____
PROPERTY TAX   (TO WHOM:_____)$_____
HOME INSURANCE   (TO WHOM:_____)$_____

FOOD $_____ ELECTRICITY $_____ WATER/SEWER $_____
CLOTHING $_____ NATURAL GAS $_____ GARBAGE $_____
BASIC PHONE $_____ CAR PYMNT 1 $_____ CAR PYMNT 2 $_____
CAR INSURE $_____ PUBLIC TRAN $_____ GAS AND OIL $_____
MEDICAL INSURANCE PAYMENTS NOT DEDUCTED FROM PAYCHECK $_____
MEDICAL CO-PAYMENTS AND EXPENSES NOT COVERED BY INSURANCE $_____

CHILD CARE EXPENSES (NUMBER OF CHILDREN:_____) $_____
CHILD SUPPORT   (NUMBER OF CHILDREN:_____) $_____

LIST ANY OTHER MONTHLY EXPENSES BELOW:

1)_____ $_____
2)_____ $_____
3)_____ $_____

ASSETS:

BANK ACCOUNT 1 (BANK NAME:_____) $_____
BANK ACCOUNT 2 (BANK NAME:_____) $_____
BANK ACCOUNT 3 (BANK NAME:_____) $_____
STOCKS/BONDS   (BANK NAME:_____) $_____
HOME   VALUE $_____   OWED $_____
OTHER REAL ESTATE   VALUE $_____   OWED $_____
CAR 1 (YR,MAKE,MODEL:_____) VALUE $_____ OWED $_____
CAR 1 (YR,MAKE,MODEL:_____) VALUE $_____ OWED $_____

PLEASE SIGN THE DECLARATION BELOW:

I DECLARE UNDER PENALTIES PROVIDED BY 18 U.S.C. SECTION 1001, THAT THE
ANSWERS AND STATEMENTS CONTAINED HEREIN ARE TO THE BEST OF MY KNOWLEDGE
AND BELIEF TRUE, CORRECT AND COMPLETE.

SIGNATURE:_____ DATE:_____

WARNING:18 U.S.C. 1001 PROVIDES THAT "WHOEVER...KNOWINGLY AND WILLFULLY
FALSIFIES, CONCEALS OR COVERS UP BY ANY TRICK, SCHEME, OR DEVICE A
MATERIAL FACT, OR MAKES ANY FALSE, FICTITIOUS OR FRAUDULENT STATEMENTS
OR REPRESENTATION.., SHALL BE FINED NOT MORE THAN $10,000.00, OR
IMPRISONED NOT MORE THAN FIVE YEARS, OR BOTH".

PRIVACY ACT NOTICE

THIS REQUEST IS AUTHORIZED UNDER 31 U.S.C. 3711,20 U.S.C. 1078-6,AND
20 U.S.C. 1095A.YOU ARE NOT REQUIRED TO PROVIDE THIS INFORMATION. IF YOU
DO NOT, WE CANNOT DETERMINE YOUR FINANCIAL ABILITY TO REPAY YOUR STUDENT
AID DEBT. THE INFORMATION YOU PROVIDE WILL BE USED TO EVALUATE YOUR
ABILITY TO PAY. IT MAY BE DISCLOSED TO GOVERNMENT AGENCIES AND THEIR
CONTRACTORS, TO EMPLOYERS, LENDERS, AND OTHERS TO ENFORCE THIS DEBT; TO
THIRD PARTIES IN AUDIT, RESEARCH, OR DISPUTE ABOUT THE MANAGEMENT OF
THIS DEBT; AND TO PARTIES WITH A RIGHT TO THIS INFORMATION UNDER THE
FREEDOM OF INFORMATION ACT OR OTHER FEDERAL LAW OR WITH YOUR CONSENT.
THESE USES ARE EXPLAINED IN NOTICE IN THE STUDENT FINANCIAL ASSISTANCE
COLLECTION FILES, NO 18-11-07; WE WILL SEND A COPY AT YOUR REQUEST.

D.5.2 FFEL Compromise and Write-Off Procedures for Guaranty Agencies

National Council of Higher Education Loan Programs, Inc.

801 Pennsylvania Avenue, S.E., Suite 375

Washington, DC 20003 • (202)547-1571
FAX (202)546-8745

November 7, 1993

Clearinghouse No. 49,168
Accession No. 1095310

DEC - 8 1993

Mr. Robert W. Evans
Director of Policy and Program Development
U.S. Department of Education
Office of Student Financial Assistance
Room 4310, ROB #3
7th & D Streets, S.W.
Washington, D.C. 20202

RE: Compromise and Write-Off Procedures

Dear Bob:

Thank you for reviewing the recommendations for standardized write-off and compromise procedures submitted by the Ad Hoc Standardization Group. NCHELP has made all of the clarifications and amendments you requested.

If you have any questions regarding these revised procedures, please let me know. Your prompt approval of these revised procedures will be appreciated by the community.

Sincerely yours,

Jean S. Frohlicher
President

I hereby approve the attached Standardized Compromise and Write-Off Procedures for use by guaranty agencies in the Federal Family Education Loan Program. Agencies may use these procedures without further approval from the Department of Education. Any changes a guaranty agency wishes to make in these approved procedures must be submitted to the Department for specific approval.

Robert W. Evans   11/24/93

Robert W. Evans, Director, Division of Policy Development

cc: Woody Farber
       Art Bilski
       Fred Hasselback
       Dallas Martin

STANDARDIZED COMPROMISE AND WRITE-OFF PROCEDURES

The following guidelines are established to allow a guaranty agency to compromise amounts owing on a defaulted reinsured student loan and to write off accounts where the loan(s) is determined to be uncollectible and the agency seeks to discontinue its semi-annual reviews as required under the due diligence requirements. Write off in this context does not relate to "writing the loan off the books" but only relates to the cessation of collection activity. In all cases, the reasons for the agency's decision and actions will be documented in the borrower's file.

COMPROMISE AUTHORITY

Compromise refers to a negotiated agreement between the debtor and the guaranty agency to accept a payment of a lesser portion of the total debt as full liquidation of the entire indebtedness. A guaranty agency will be permitted in certain cases to accept a compromise amount from a debtor as full satisfaction of the debt to all parties, including the U.S. Department of Education. The authority to accept a compromise as full satisfaction of the debt is intended to maximize collections on defaulted loans. The guaranty agency may compromise a loan at any time after it pays a default claim on that loan.

A guaranty agency will be permitted to compromise under the following circumstances and in the following amounts:

1. An agency can compromise an amount up to an amount equal to all collection costs in order to obtain payment in full of all principal and interest owing on a defaulted loan(s). The agency shall consider the litigative risk of seeking a judgment on a reinsured loan, the likelihood and timing of the collection of the loan, and the borrower's current and expected financial condition.

2. An agency can compromise an amount up to 30% of all principal and interest owing in order to obtain a payment in full of the reinsured portion of a loan(s). The agency shall consider the litigative risk of seeking a judgment on a reinsured loan, the likelihood and timing of the collection of the loan, and the borrower's current and expected financial condition. Compromises of less than 70% of the total indebtedness of principal and interest do not allow the guaranty agency to waive the Secretary's right to collect the remaining balance due.

3. An agency can compromise in situations that do not meet the criteria in #1 and #2 above, provided the agency can demonstrate and document the reasons for doing so and the compromise is approved by the division/agency director.

Approval authority for compromise settlements will be determined within each guaranty agency. However, the following minimum approval authorities will exist:

1. The supervisor directly charged with collections will have the authority to compromise all collection costs and the accrued interest on the loan(s), not to exceed 30% of the principal and interest owing.

2. The next level of management will have the authority to accept compromises in #1 above and any compromise of any principal amounts, not to exceed 30% of the principal and interest owing.

3. The agency director can approve compromises described in #1 and #2 above as well as compromises which exceed the 30% threshold.

DISCRETIONARY WRITE-OFF

Write-off of a reinsured loan(s) is intended only for the purpose of the guaranty agency's ceasing required collection activity as described in 34 C.F.R. 682.410(b)(6) and (7). The write-off of the loan does not relieve the debtor of the debt. Once an agency has "written off" a loan(s), it will insure that the account is permanently assigned to the U.S. Department of Education under 34 C.F.R. 682.409 *et seq.*

Exception to the above policy will be that guaranty agencies will have the authority to write off loan(s) with principal balances of less than $100 and a total balance less than $1,000, and any loan(s) where the remaining balance represents only interest, attorney fees, court costs, or collection costs without requiring the permanent assignment of the loan(s) to the U.S. Department of Education.

In making its determination to write off a loan and to cease collection activity, an agency will consider the debtor's and, if applicable, an endorser's current and expected inability to repay the debt. Examples of this condition are:

a. Borrowers who are repeatedly unemployed and have no prospects for future employment;

b. Borrowers who are repeatedly public assistance recipients;

c. Borrowers who are chronically ill, partially disabled, or of an age that results in their inability to work;

d. Borrowers whose potential for future earnings is limited or non-existent;

e. Borrowers who have no other funds available to them from other sources, such as an inheritance.

Approval authority for the write-off of a loan(s) will be individualized within each agency. However, the following minimum guidelines will apply:

1. Balances up to $5,000 can be approved by the supervisor responsible for collection of the loan(s).

2. Balances up to $20,000 can be approved by the next level of management within the guaranty agency if the documents authorizing a write-off contain the signatures of each agency official participating or concurring in the write-off decision.

3. Balances exceeding $20,000 can be approved by the division/agency director if the documents authorizing a write-off contain the signatures of each agency official participating or concurring in the write-off decision.

In each case, upon approval of the write-off, the account will be scheduled for permanent assignment to the U.S. Department of Education under the provisions in 34 C.F.R. 682.409, *et seq.* (except those previously noted).

A debtor who benefits from a compromise or write-off must reaffirm the amount compromised or written off if he or she later wants to receive an FFEL Program loan.

D.5.3 Sample Rehabilitation Agreement

REPAYMENT AGREEMENT UNDER THE LOAN REHABILITATION PROGRAM

THIS LETTER CONFIRMS MY ACCEPTANCE INTO THE LOAN REHABILITATION PROGRAM AND MY AGREEMENT TO REPAYMENT OF MY DEFAULTED FEDERAL FAMILY EDUCATION LOAN (FFEL) PROGRAM STUDENT LOANS HELD BY THE U.S. DEPARTMENT OF EDUCATION (DEPARTMENT). I UNDERSTAND THAT COMPLIANCE WITH THIS AGREEMENT IS A PREREQUISITE TO THE SALE OF MY LOANS TO THE AUTHORIZED, DEPARTMENT-APPROVED LENDER.

PLEASE CHECK THE APPROPRIATE PARAGRAPH:

( )   I UNDERSTAND THAT I MUST MAKE AT LEAST NINE (9) MONTHLY PAYMENTS IN THE AMOUNT OF <MONTH-PAY>, BEGINNING <DUE-DATE>, WITH EACH PAYMENT DUE ON THE SAME DAY EACH MONTH THEREAFTER. I MUST MAKE THE FULL PAYMENTS IN THE AGREED AMOUNT WITHIN TWENTY (20) DAYS OF THEIR MONTHLY DUE DATES OVER A TEN MONTH PERIOD. IF I FAIL TO MAKE THE REQUIRED NUMBER OF ON-TIME PAYMENTS IN A TEN (10) MONTH PERIOD, I WILL NEED TO BEGIN A NEW SERIES OF AGREED-UPON PAYMENTS IN ORDER TO QUALIFY FOR REHABILITATION OF MY LOANS.

( )   I AM CURRENTLY MAKING MONTHLY PAYMENTS. I UNDERSTAND THAT THESE PAYMENTS, IF TIMELY, WILL BE INCLUDED IN THE CALCULATION OF THE REQUIRED MINIMUM NUMBER OF MONTHLY PAYMENTS. I WILL CONTINUE TO MEET MY ESTABLISHED MONTHLY PAYMENT DUE DATE.

I ALSO UNDERSTAND AND AGREE TO THE FOLLOWING TERMS AND CONDITIONS:

1. I UNDERSTAND THAT THIS AGREEMENT IS NULL AND VOID IF I DO NOT HONOR THE TERMS OF THIS AGREEMENT BY MAKING A FULL PAYMENT WITHIN TWENTY DAYS OF THE MONTHLY DUE DATE EVERY MONTH FOR A MINIMUM OF NINE MONTHS. SHOULD THIS OCCUR, I WILL NEED TO BEGIN A NEW SERIES OF AGREED-UPON PAYMENTS IN ORDER TO QUALIFY FOR REHABILITATION OF MY LOANS

2. I CANNOT CHANGE THE MONTHLY PAYMENT AMOUNT WITHOUT THE DEPARTMENT'S AGREEMENT OR THE AGREEMENT OF THE COLLECTION AGENCY SERVICING MY ACCOUNT.

3. I MAY HAVE TO PROVIDE A NEW FINANCIAL STATEMENT IN ORDER TO SUPPORT A REQUEST TO CHANGE MY MONTHLY REQUIRED PAYMENT AMOUNT.

4. I MUST CONTINUE TO MAKE MONTHLY PAYMENTS TO THE DEPARTMENT BEYOND THE REQUIRED MINIMUM PERIOD UNTIL I AM NOTIFIED IN WRITING BY THE DEPARTMENT OR MY NEW LENDER THAT THE SALE HAS BEEN COMPLETED AND THAT I AM TO BEGIN MAKING PAYMENTS DIRECTLY TO MY LENDER.

5. ANY INTEREST THAT I OWE AT THE TIME MY LOAN(S) IS SOLD WILL BE CAPITALIZED BY THE LENDER, THAT IS, THE LENDER WILL ADD ANY UNPAID INTEREST TO THE PRINCIPAL I OWE ON THE LOAN(S) AND THIS WILL BECOME THE NEW PRINCIPAL BALANCE ON THE LOAN(S). INTEREST WILL THEN ACCRUE ON THIS NEW HIGHER PRINCIPAL. THE DEPARTMENT AGREES TO WAIVE COLLECTION OF ANY COST THE DEPARTMENT INCURS AS A RESULT OF THE SALE OF MY LOAN(S) UNDER THIS REHABILITATION AGREEMENT UNLESS I DEFAULT ON THE LOAN(S) IN THE FUTURE AND THE DEPARTMENT TAKES ASSIGNMENT OF THE LOAN(S). THE DEPARTMENT WILL COLLECT AS PART OF THE DEBT THEN OWED, THE COLLECTION COST ORIGINALLY WAIVED UNDER THIS AGREEMENT.   THIS WILL SUBSTANTIALLY INCREASE THE AMOUNT THAT WILL THEN BE OWED TO SATISFY THE DEBT TO THE DEPARTMENT.

6. AFTER THE SALE OF MY LOAN(S), ANY PAYMENTS MADE TO THE DEPARTMENT WILL BE FORWARDED TO MY LENDER FOR CREDIT TO MY ACCOUNT. ANY INVOLUNTARY PAYMENT (TREASURY OFFSET) OR POST-DATED CHECK WILL BE REFUNDED TO ME AT THE ADDRESS ON MY BILLING STATEMENT.

7. MY NEW LENDER WILL ESTABLISH A NEW DUE DATE AND WILL CALCULATE A NEW MONTHLY PAYMENT AMOUNT BASED UPON THE BALANCE OWED AT THE TIME OF SALE. THE AMOUNT OF THE REQUIRED MONTHLY INSTALLMENT PAYMENT MAY SUBSTANTIALLY INCREASE.

I HAVE READ THE ABOVE AND AGREE TO THE TERMS AND CONDITIONS OF THE LOAN REHABILITATION PROGRAM AND THIS REPAYMENT AGREEMENT.

Signed: _____ Date: _____

D.5.4 Authorization to Release Information to a Third Party

Example
**Authorization to Release
Information to a Third Party**

Section 1: Individual Subject Information

Subject's Name: _____

Subject's Social Security Number: _____

Subject's Date of Birth: mm/dd/yy: _____

Section 2: Third Party's Information

Name(s) of individual(s) to whom the U.S. Department of Education is authorized to disclose
information about the above-named subject:

_____   _____

_____   _____

_____   _____

Company name (if applicable) and address of individuals authorized to receive information about the
above-named subject:

_____

_____

_____

Section 3: Subject's Authorization for Release

I _____, hereby certify that I am the individual named above as
the subject of these records. I understand that the knowing and willful request for, or acquisition of, a
record pertaining to an individual under false pretenses is a criminal offense under the Privacy Act
subject to a $5000 fine. I hereby authorize the U.S. Department of Education (ED) to disclose
information in my records regarding my student aid obligations held by ED to the individual(s) named in
Section 2 above.

Signature_____ Date: _____

Completed authorizations should be faxed to:

319-665-7646   or   319-665-7647

Sample Pleadings and Letters

E.1 Sample Letters and Requests for Relief

E.1.1 Request for Reasonable and Affordable Repayment Agreement

[*Date*]
[*Name*]
Administrative Assistant
Pennsylvania Higher Education Assistance Agency
1200 N. 7th St.
Harrisburg, PA 17102

Dear Ms. [*Name*]:

On behalf of my client Kristi Brown [Address], [Social Security Number], I hereby request that PHEAA establish a reasonable and affordable payment plan for her so that she can renew her eligibility for student loans and grants under Higher Education Act Section 428F(b). A statement of her income, which is entirely derived from Public Assistance and Food Stamps, is enclosed.

In light of Ms. Brown's poverty-level income, I request that her monthly payment be set at $5.00.

Ms. Brown's first payment of $5.00, for the month of November 1994, is enclosed.

Ms. Brown is a young woman with two children who is on public assistance but is working with the Single Point of Contact Program in Adams County to complete her education and develop job skills. Establishing a reasonable and affordable payment plan for her existing student loans will enable her to achieve these goals.

Thank you for your consideration of this request.

Sincerely,

[*Attorney for Student*]

STATEMENT OF INCOME AND EXPENSES

1. My name is Kristi Brown. My address is [Address]. My Social Security number is [Social Security Number].

2. My monthly income consists entirely of Public Assistance benefits: $401.50 in cash assistance under the AFDC program, and $223.00 in Food Stamps. In the past, $50 in child support paid by my husband, from whom I am separated, was passed through to me by the Department of Public Welfare, but he has not paid child support and I have not received a pass-through in a number of months.

3. I have to use all of my Food Stamps every month for food for myself and my children. My monthly expenses over and above the amount I receive in Food Stamps are as follows, totalling $402.20: $55.00, household items not covered by Food Stamps (e.g. soap, toothpaste, toilet paper); $25.00, telephone; $20.00, clothing; $74.20, storage (my furniture is in storage because I am living in the basement of my father's residence because I cannot afford my own residence); $50.00, payments on debts (credit cards); $50.00, food over and above that covered by my food stamps; $60.00, gasoline and car repairs; $60.00, laundry; $10.00, school expenses; $5.00, medical and vision care expenses not covered by Medical Assistance.

4. My two children, ages 5 and 7, live with me and are dependent upon me for support.

5. Understanding that a false statement herein would subject me to the penalties of 18 Pa.C.S. Sec. 4904, relating to unsworn falsification to authorities, I verify that the facts set forth in the foregoing statement are true and correct, to the best of my knowledge, information, and belief.

[Student]

Dated:

E.1.2 Request for Hardship Reduction

Date

U.S. Department of Education
Attn: Federal Offset Review Unit
P.O. Box 618064
Chicago, IL 60661-8064

CERTIFIED MAIL
RETURN RECEIPT REQUESTED

Dear Offset Review Unit:

I am writing to request a reduction in the amount currently being offset from my Social Security payments. [*Editor's Note*: Borrowers may also object on hardship grounds to collection of debt against other federal payments and income tax refunds. In the case of Social Security offsets only, the Department will consider a reduction or suspension of the offset due to hardship even before the offset begins. See chapter 5.]

I am 75 years old. My sole source of income is Social Security. Until recently, I was able to supplement my Social Security income with a small amount of money my husband earned from a part-time job. However, my husband passed away last year. I never worked outside my home and my sole source of income is his Social Security survivor's benefits of $900/month. This income is not enough to pay my expenses. I have included a detailed list of expenses below.

The main reason that I am writing to you now is because my situation has become very severe since my husband died. After he died last year, I needed to make some home repairs. We had not been able to afford these repairs while my husband was sick. I needed to get a loan to pay for the repairs. I used a company that came to my door and said that they would get me the best deal. It turned out that they gave me a very expensive loan and never even completed the repairs. I was not able to make the loan payments. Just a few months ago, I lost my home to foreclosure. I am now renting an apartment. It is very important to me to live near my old house because I have lived in this neighborhood for almost 50 years. I tried to find the least expensive rental situation, but it is still $550/month. This leaves me only $350 each month to pay all of my other expenses, including the prescription drugs that are not covered by Medicare, utilities, transportation food.

Based on the detailed list of income and expenses enclosed with this letter, I am requesting that you reduce the offset from $150/month to $50/month. [*Editor's Note*: Borrowers may also request a complete suspension of offset.]

Enclosed please find the following information to support this request:

1. **Treasury's Offset Notification letter**

2. **Completed financial statement, form (N33)** [*Editor's Note*: A copy of this form can be found at Appendix D.5.1. Borrowers should provide any available documentation to support the listed expenses]

3. **Proof of my annual Social Security income and most recent tax returns.**

4. **A copy of the final notice when my house was foreclosed and my current rental agreement.**

Thank you for your prompt attention to this request.

Sincerely,

E.2 Discharge-Related Pleadings

E.2.1 Group False Certification Discharge Request

Note that proof of an employment search is no longer a requirement for a false certification ability to benefit discharge. *See* § 6.3.2.2, *supra*.

[*Date*]
John Smith
Coordinator, Policy and Reports
PHEAA
1200 North Seventh Street
Harrisburg, PA 17102-1444

Re: PTC Career Institute
False Certification Discharges

Dear Mr. Smith:

I am enclosing with this letter 14 additional individual applications for false certification discharges. Attached is an alphabetical list of the sixteen individuals with social security numbers and date of their "ability to benefit" testing. These are the first applications I have submitted to you for borrowers who were administered ability to benefit (ATB) tests *after* the audit period covered by the Inspector General's report, i.e., after June 30, 1990. (By my count, this brings to 35 the total number of individual PTC false certification applications I have submitted to you.)

In contrast to the previously submitted applications—covering the period January 1, 1986 to June 30, 1990—student files are still in existence, in the custody of the Inspector General. As a result of the assistance provided by the Inspector General's office, I have been able to review these files and obtain copies of documents pertaining to the "ability to benefit" (ATB) determination made in each of these cases. Those documents are attached to the individual applications.

In addition to the individual documentation, I am enclosing copies of test instructions from the publisher of the Wonderlic test, which was utilized by PTC during 1991 and 1992; the accrediting criteria of the Accrediting Commission of Career Schools and Colleges of Technology (previously "NATTS"), the accreditor of PTC; and the following three sworn statements:

1. *Vincent Jones*. Mr. Jones was a commissioned recruiter for PTC during 1990. He describes how testing was done during that year, in particular, how admissions personnel routinely assisted students in taking the ATB tests. In his words, "[M]oney, not qualifications, was what we were about . . . [T]esting was just a formality we had to go through."

2. *Eliot Short*. Mr. Short is a vice president of Wonderlic Personnel Test, Inc., the publisher of the Wonderlic test. During the years 1991-92 PTC principally relied on the Wonderlic for its ATB determinations. Mr. Short explains in detail why the Wonderlics administered at PTC-Philadelphia are not valid tests and states that the whole PTC chain was terminated from the Wonderlic system due to "severe problems" in its testing practices.

3. *William Copley*. During the years 1991-92 Mr. Copley was employed by PTC as its "independent" ATB tester. He used a variety of ATB tests, mainly the Wonderlic, but also the PARS and CPAT. His statement makes clear that from January 1991 until it closed—i.e., during the period that PTC was required by the Education Department to use an independent tester for its ATB testing—PTC never had a truly independent tester. On the contrary, the testers were employees of the school, and, although functioning separate from the admissions department, were under constant pressure to produce passing scores, regardless of the real qualifications of student applicants. Hines was fired because his passing rate was not, in the view of his employer, high enough.

Your office has stated to me previously on several occasions that the Inspector General audit report was not sufficient evidence of ATB fraud warranting discharge of PTC loans. At least for loans disbursed during the audit period, I continue to believe that your decision is wrong and that the IG report is more than sufficient to support discharges under 20 U.S.C. § 1087(c) and the 1994 regulations. However, with these submissions, along with the various individual statements previously sent, you now have the additional evidence you asked for. This additional evidence clearly shows both that PTC continued to engage in systematic ATB fraud *after* the I.G. made his findings and that those findings concerning the earlier testing practices were indicative of an ongoing intent by PTC to defraud students and Title IV.

Moreover, in the event you investigate the PTC situation in PHEAA's own investigative files or with the Pennsylvania Board of Private Licensed Schools, I am sure that you will find ample confirmation that PTC was more in the nature of a racketeering operation than an academic institution.

I note in your letter to me dated December 19, 1994 that PHEAA believes that "criteria for evaluating improper testing has not been published." I believe you are mistaken. The Department of Education issued final regulations on April 29, 1994 which clearly set forth substantive standards for deciding false certification discharge applications and which give to guarantee agencies the responsibility of deciding these applications. In a letter to me dated February 22, 1995 your counsel, Peggy Shedden, acknowledges that the Department "does not have plans to issue any new information or instructions for guarantors regarding PTC borrowers." Since PHEAA has the obligation to decide these applications, and since no further guidance from Washington is forthcoming, it would be wrong for PHEAA to continue to deny these applications out of hand, especially in light of the additional evidence I have submitted over and above the Inspector General Report.

Applicable Standards for Measuring Whether Applicants Were Falsely Certified

The substantive standard you must apply is found at 34 C.F.R. § 682.402(e)(13). For enrollments up to July 1, 1987, you are to determine whether the school conducted ability-to-benefit determinations in accordance with 34 C.F.R. § 668.6. For those after July 1, 1987 you must determine a) whether the school was using an admissions test approved by the Department or by the school's accrediting commission; b) whether tests were administered substantially in accordance with the requirements for use of the test; and c) whether the borrower achieved a passing score.

For the period after July 1, 1987 you are to start with the school's accrediting criteria and then, after January 1, 1991, you are to look to the testing requirements imposed directly by the Secretary of Education. I have attached the accrediting criteria of NATTS, the accreditor of PTC. The pertinent criteria, at Section VIII (Admissions Policies and Practices), are as follows:

1. The school must document in writing the basis of its determination that the applicant is capable of benefitting from the training offered.
2. The school actually establishes admissions qualifications and "determines, with reasonable certainty, in advance of acceptance of the enrollment that the applicant has proper qualifications to complete the training."
3. In the case of an ATB admission, the school must maintain "documentation of the applicant's achievement of an approved score on a test or *tests that have been reviewed by a qualified independent third party for appropriateness of the instrument and specific score levels required for admission.* The acceptable score ensures that students will benefit from the training provided and a substantial number of students will complete the training and be employed in the field for which training was provided." (emphasis added)
4. Periodic studies are conducted to document the effectiveness of the admissions requirements.

For testing conducted after July 1, 1991, the specific tests and passing scores had to be taken from the approved list published by the Department, and, in addition, had to be administered by an independent test administrator, which *could not be* an employee of the school. 57 Fed. Reg. 62440 (Dec. 30, 1992). ATB test results are invalid if not independently administered, or not administered in accordance with test publisher requirements.

Established Facts

For period January 1986 to July 1, 1987 you need go no further than the Inspector General report in concluding that the PTC did not conduct ability-to-benefit determinations in accordance with 34 C.F.R. § 668.6. The rule in effect at that time required schools to "develop and consistently apply criteria for determining whether these students have the ability to benefit from the education or training offered" and required them to "be able to demonstrate, upon request of the Secretary, that these students have the ability to benefit." 1980 Final Rule, 45 Fed. Reg. 86854, 86857 (December 31, 1980). This was further refined in 1986 to require schools to maintain documentation supporting such ability-to-benefit determinations for five years. 1986 Final Rule preamble, 51 Fed. Reg. 41920 (Nov. 19, 1986). The Inspector General made a clear finding—unrebutted by any evidence you have pointed to—that such determinations were not being made at PTC and that the kind of documentation required by ATB rule did not exist. (As previously mentioned to you, a former PTC vice president, Ronald Beall, will confirm to you, if asked, that the testing practices of PTC—i.e., their reliance on the ABLE reading test analyzed by the I.G.—were in place as early as 1984. Mr. Beall can be reached at the ACT school in Upper Darby, where he is the director.)

For the period July 1, 1987 to June 30, 1990—during which, according to the false certification regulation, the relevant standard is the accrediting criteria under which PTC operated—the Inspector General report is more than adequate evidence that the NATTS accrediting criteria were not being followed at PTC. NATTS specifically required PTC to use tests and cutoff scores provided to it by an independent expert, to conduct periodic evaluations of the effectiveness of this testing, and to maintain documentation supporting its system. However, according to the I.G., none of this was occurring at PTC. PTC was using the reading test only of the ABLE test, which, according to the test publisher, was designed for adults who have not completed the eighth grade and was to be given as part of a battery of several tests. Under the NATTS criteria, it was up to PTC to establish and to maintain documentation supporting its conclusion that the ABLE reading test alone was sufficient to establish "ability to benefit" from its courses and documentation confirming the effectiveness of the results of such testing. According to the I.G., when asked how it concluded that a passing score of 48 on the ABLE reading test was an appropriate measure of "ability to benefit,"

> PTC officials indicated they talked with officials from other schools and consulted with educators. However, when asked, they were not able to present any record of their consultations. . . . It is clear from the information obtained during our audit, and from the arguments presented in its response, that PTC did not perform studies or research to establish the basis for [its use of testing

procedures different from those recommended by the test publisher]. . . . PTC was unable to produce any documentation to support the development of the cut-off scores that were used to gauge applicant success. . . .

PTC has also stated that "its ATB testing procedures] have proven to be valid predictors of ability to benefit based upon PTC's completion and placement rates during the period in which the ABLE test was in use." We strongly disagree with this statement. . . . During our audit period we attempted to verify the accuracy of PTC's completion and placement rates, only to find that no audit trail was available. Audit Report at 9, 11, 12, 16.

In your letter to me of December 19, 1994 you characterize these findings as the "*opinions of the Office of Inspector General*" (your emphasis), as opposed to being a final determination by "appropriate Education Department officials." Unless you are challenging the credibility of the Inspector General, these findings are his reports of what PTC officials stated to him in response to his requests. While the "appropriate officials" in the Department apparently chose to do little, if anything, with this information, that does not turn facts into opinions. Even in a court of law, this report, *including the conclusions contained therein,* would be regarded under the Federal Rules of Evidence as *admissible evidence* of ATB fraud at PTC. *See* Rule 803(8) (exception to hearsay rule for reports setting forth findings resulting from an investigation made pursuant to authority granted by law). Since a federal court would consider this report to be evidence, I do not understand how PHEAA can regard it as something less than evidence.

For the period of time covering the end of the audit period (July 1, 1990) to the closing of the school in January 1994, the supplemental evidence provided to you certainly is supportive of our contention that ATB fraud continued at PTC. Moreover, this evidence is relevant to the audit period as well, in so far as it shows the existence of an ongoing intent to ignore ATB requirements. Summarizing some of the additional evidence you now have before you:

— *Coaching and test fabrication by testers.* The Vincent Johnson statement provides direct evidence of systematic coaching, which supplements the I.G.'s conclusion that the ABLE test form itself was an inappropriate testing instrument. This is further confirmed by a few of the individual applications, included here or previously submitted. Yvette Prophet (SSN [Social Security Number]), whose application was submitted last week, stated that the admissions representative gave her the test in August 1987, "hurrying me along, telling me not to worry about whatever I put down, and occasionally telling me which answer to fill in." Tracey Johnson (SSN

[Social Security Number]), one of applications enclosed herein, remembers that when she was administered the CPAT test in 1993 "the tester sat beside me and helped me do it." Crystal Ball (SSN [Social Security Number]), whose application is enclosed herein, was tested in November 1990 by her admissions representative, who gave her only a "clerical test" (probably the Minnesota Clerical Test listed in her file); she was never even given the ABLE, also noted in her file, so the PARS answer sheet which appears in her file was apparently fabricated.

— *Use of invalid ATB tests.* The Eliot Long statement reveals that during 1991 PTC utilized invalid versions of the Wonderlic tests, apparently created by PTC. Moreover, contrary to the publisher's mandatory security system, individual test sheets were never submitted to the company for analysis. One so-called "independent" tester, William Hines, registered with the testing company months after he began testing, but operated totally outside the test registration system. The other tester, Art Adams, was unknown to the company, which requires all its testers to be registered. The 12-minute time limit was routinely ignored, and Hines "do[es] not recall" deducting 6 points from untimed tests as the publisher's instructions require. Also contrary to the publisher's instructions, he routinely gave retests on the exact same test form.

— *Tests administered by nonindependent testers.* As of July 1, 1991 testing had to be administered by individuals who met the Department's criteria of "independence." As the William Hines statement reveals, the testers at PTC were effectively employees of the school who administered tests chosen by the school. They were in competition with each other to see who could produce the highest pass/fail ratio, and any failure had to be specially justified to the school director. The Long statement is clear evidence that the Wonderlic testing during 1991 and 1992 certainly did not comply with the publisher's criteria for independence either. The Hines statement also makes clear that the "independence" of the tester continued to be tainted after PTC decided to switch to the CPAT in 1992, and actually the integrity of the testing worsened as sales pressures intensified. The other tester took over for him by reason of his ability to produce a higher level of "passes," a level Hines believed could not be produced by legitimate testing, especially given the fact that the qualification level of recruits was actually deteriorating.

— *Use of "approved" passing scores to mask obvious lack of qualifications.* The Hines statement explains how the tester was expected to cast a blind eye to an applicant's apparent lack of academic skills. He actually was reprimanded by the school director for going beyond the ATB test score and probing the reading capacity of an applicant who appeared to lack basic reading skills. Among those he tested and were admitted after supposedly achieving an "approved" score were Charlene Curry (SSN [Social Security Number]), a 45 year old woman who receives SSI for mental illness and who never completed *elementary* school, and Alfred Stewart, a 68 year-old, retired and disabled man who never attended high school and who was admitted into a security guard program despite putting on the application that he suffered from shortness of breath and a bad back.

— *Frequent use of retestings.* Hines also admits to routinely giving retests using the exact same test form, a practice encouraged by the school director and specifically disallowed in the Wonderlic manual. This, too, illustrates the school's intent to produce an "approved" score at all costs. The Hines reference to retesting is confirmation of the I.G. finding of a "high percentage" of retesting (40 percent tested at least twice and 24 percent tested twice during the same day). For examples of retestings, see Tracey Johnson (SSN [Social Security Number]) and Wanda Matos (SSN [Social Security Number]).

— *Unusual volume of ATB admissions.* The large volume of false certification applications from PTC is itself evidence of the fact that PTC was little more than an "ATB mill," where admissions requirements were virtually nonexistent and lack of high school credentials was more the rule than the exception. The low-skill nature of the PTC student population is confirmed by both the Hines ("the school was depending . . . on admissions of people at the bottom of the ladder, meaning those functioning at an elementary school level") and Johnson statements ("one student . . . could not read at all. There were homeless people recruited literally off the street or out of shelters.") The I.G. report itself quotes from a post-audit memorandum by PTC's Vice President of Operations which described PTC's enrollment policies as follows:

"We (PTC) have enrolled people from shelters, people who need to satisfy parole conditions, addicts, persons who cannot read, write or speak, etc. We have also enrolled people who do not qualify for Financial Aid and/or are unable to make payments. The bottom line people, is that we are enrolling just numbers—not students serious about getting job training. Why? More than likely you are doing it to keep (PTC President) and (PTC Vice President) from ripping your backsides for not making budgeted numbers. These are excuses that are unacceptable." I.G. Report at 20.

I believe that we have provided an extraordinary amount of evidence to support our request for discharges of all PTC ATB borrowers. At the very least, we have provided you with "reliable information" sufficient to warrant class-wide forbearance and notice to individual PTC borrowers of their right to apply for a discharge on account of what you know about ATB testing at PTC. I am hereby advising PHEAA that I intend to initiate federal court litigation, including a request for class-wide relief, if PHEAA continues to fail to honor this request.

I realize that the Department of Education shares considerable blame for the continued absence of action in this case. For that reason, I intend to sue the Department, as well, for its failure to discharge these loans and for the continual mixed signals it has provided to guarantee agencies in general regarding false certification and in particular regarding PTC. Accordingly, I am copying officials of the Department with this correspondence.

Sincerely,

[*Attorney for Plaintiff*]

E.2.2 Request for Discharge of All Students

REQUEST FOR DOE DETERMINATION OF ATB FRAUD BY CAMBRIDGE TECHNICAL INSTITUTE, INC. FOR USE IN STUDENT LOAN DISCHARGE APPLICATIONS

I. Introduction

This memorandum provides the basis for the U.S. Department of Education (DOE) to rule that Cambridge Technical Institute, Inc., a for-profit, proprietary vocational school formerly operating four campuses in Ohio, committed such pervasive fraud and unlawful actions in its determination of students' ability to benefit (ATB) from Cambridge's courses, that all applications for a loan discharge, based on improper ATB determination, will be granted to otherwise-eligible Cambridge students, without independent evidence of ATB fraud. This request for DOE's decision as to Cambridge's improper determination of ATB status for students is being submitted pursuant to DOE's "Dear Colleague" letter GEN-95-42, Section 10. Included herewith are: 1) previous decisions of DOE on former Cambridge students' ATB discharge applications, 2) deposition and affidavit testimony by former students and employees of Cambridge, 3) findings by the Ohio Attorney General's Office, 4) a sample of Cambridge's ATB admissions scores compared with the requirements established by DOE, the accreditation agency for Cambridge, and the ATB test publisher, 5) findings by the Ohio State Board of Proprietary School Registration, and 6) generalized evidence of the widespread fraudulent and unlawful business practices of Cambridge, as set forth in various newspaper articles over the years.

The Legal Aid Society of Cincinnati represented students in a class-action lawsuit against Cambridge in the late 1980's. That lawsuit resulted in a consent decree whereby Cambridge agreed to close its Cincinnati campus as of October, 1990. Following that, the murder of Cambridge's president, and the criminal indictment of one of Cambridge's other officers (who ultimately pleaded guilty), the other three campuses (in Middletown, Dayton, and Cleveland) were also closed or sold. As a result, Cambridge long ago closed its doors in Ohio. Nevertheless, hundreds of students who were lured into Cambridge's classrooms with a promise of a good education and a good job, are now in a worse position than they were when they first heard about Cambridge. Many of them have had their self-esteem harmed and their credit records ruined, and they continue to be dunned for thousands of dollars allegedly owed on their defaulted student loans. Many of those students never should have attended Cambridge to begin with, given their inability to benefit from what Cambridge offered them. DOE now should facilitate the loan discharge process for them by issuing an administrative decision whereby it declares Cambridge's ATB testing and admissions procedures so pervasively fraudulent as to provide across-the-board proof that any applicant for a student loan discharge, based on ATB fraud, will have his or her application granted, provided he or she is otherwise eligible.

II. Numerous Former Students Already Have Received a Discharge of Their Loans Based on Cambridge's False Certification of Their Ability to Benefit.

The U.S. Department of Education already has granted a discharge of student loans to numerous former Cambridge students, based on Cambridge's false certification of their ability to benefit. The following is a partial list of former Cambridge students who have had their loans discharged based on such false certification. See the series A exhibits, attached hereto [*not reprinted herein*].

1. Nelson Muntz: He did not possess a high school diploma or a GED. He was given a ten-question admissions test, which is not consistent with Wonderlic's (the test developer's) test manual procedures. (Wonderlic ATB tests contain 24 or 50 questions). According to Mr. Muntz, "everyone" he heard of passed the exam. After completing the Cambridge course, he could not get a job because of his extensive criminal record.

2. Selma Bouvier: She did not have a high school diploma or a GED. She took a test, but she did not answer many questions. At the time of enrollment, she was suffering from the side effects of brain surgery.

3. Martin Prince: He was not given any admissions test, even though he did not have a high school diploma or a GED.

4. Elizabeth Hoover: She was not given any admissions test, even though she had no high school diploma or GED.

5. Wendell Borton: He had three different Cambridge loans (all discharged). He did not have a high school diploma or a GED, yet was not given any admissions test. Mr. Borton was 67 years old, had a glass eye and back problems, and weighed about 100 pounds when he was enrolled for the private security course at Cambridge.

6. Maude Flanders: She stated that she took the test with a group and they all were told they had passed the test even before it was graded. She did not have a high school diploma or a GED.

7. Doris Lunchlady: She had no high school diploma or GED. She was given an admissions test in a room with several other students also taking the test. The person giving the test left the room once the test started, and there was no time limit imposed.

8. Otto Mans: He was not given an admissions test nor did he possess a high school diploma or a GED. He also had an extensive criminal record of theft and drug abuse.

9. Jessica Lovejoy: She did not have a high school diploma or a GED, and was not given an admissions test before enrolling.

10. Ned Flanders: He was not given an admissions test, nor did he have a high school diploma or a GED.

11. Lisa Simpson: She had neither a high school diploma nor a GED when she enrolled. She had only the equivalent of a fifth grade education and did not take an admissions test.

12. Jackie Bouvier: She was not given an admissions test, nor did she have a high school diploma or a GED.

See the enclosed Request for Discharge (False Certification of Ability to Benefit) applications and decisions, Exhibits A-1 through A-12 [*not reprinted herein*].

III. Sworn Testimony of Numerous Former Cambridge Students Shows a Pattern of Testing and Admissions Fraud.

In the course of litigating *Brown, et al. v. Cambridge Technical Institute, Inc., et al.*, substantial pre-trial discovery took place. Depositions were taken of former students, and affidavits were obtained from others. Although the lawsuit did not raise directly the ability-to-benefit issue, information given by former students to the attorneys shows that Cambridge's test procedures were very lax and, at times, unlawful or fraudulent. The following are summaries of the ATB problems revealed through depositions and/or affidavits given by the listed individuals. See the series B exhibits, attached hereto [*not reprinted herein*].

1. Patty Brown (a former student and named plaintiff in the lawsuit): She could not read. She could not spell much, including her address. When she took the admissions test, a lady from Cambridge had to read the questions to her. Ms. Brown was taking medication (Cogentin and Prolixin) for her nerves at that time and was being followed by a case manager at the Mental Health Services West office. Although the application form for Ms. Brown states that she went to Taft High School, she did not; she did go to West High. She did not graduate from West High School or any high school. Her last years in school were spent at Gilford School (a school for developmentally delayed students). Ms. Brown is not good at math and numbers. Ms. Brown has a guardian, but she could not remember her name. Ms. Brown does not know the difference between a positive experience and a negative experience. Of all the questions on the Wonderlic admissions test, Ms. Brown completed only six of them. She does not know who filled in the other blanks. When she handed in her test, there were only six answers given by her on her paper. She does not know what happened after that. Ms. Brown was admitted to Cambridge after the test, and enrolled for custodial maintenance, electronics, and computers. After she attended school for a few days, she stopped going.

2. Marvin Monroe (a former student and former employee of Cambridge): Mr. Monroe states: "At the Cambridge Admissions Office, I was told that I would have to take an admissions test. When I told [the Cambridge person] that I didn't have time to take the test, he said he would take it for me, and he proceeded to do that."

3. Marge Simpson (a former student): While attending Cambridge, she met another student filling out loan papers. This other student had been enrolled for private security, but had only one leg and had a deformed left hand with only two fingers on it. Ms. Simpson also heard another student boasting, in a serious way, that she had given birth last week to a baby which was going to be stuck "back up inside her like all her other babies." This person did not "seem to know where she was." Another student Ms. Simpson met seemed very slow or retarded. He would sit near the back window and stare into space. The instructors stated that he flunked every test.

4. Clancy Wiggum (a former student): Ms. Wiggum was given the admissions test. The woman at Cambridge giving the test gave Ms. Wiggum "the answers to the first five questions."

See the enclosed deposition excerpts and affidavits, Exhibits B-1 through B-4 [*not reprinted herein*].

IV. The Ohio Attorney General Found Evidence of Admissions Test Fraud by Cambridge.

The Ohio Attorney General also filed a separate lawsuit against Cambridge for its operations at the Cleveland "campus." In its investigation of Cambridge's practices at that campus, the Ohio Attorney General's office determined that serious admissions test fraud had occurred. See the series C exhibits, attached hereto [*not reprinted herein*].

In responding to civil discovery requests propounded by Cambridge's attorneys, the Ohio Attorney General stated the following in response to one of the interrogatories regarding admissions testing: "The defendants [Cambridge] administered the test without supervision to students en masse. The test was an altered and simplified version of a valid test. Students were allowed to discuss the test with each other. The test was written, but illiterate students passed the test. The test was administered without time constraint."

Additionally, in this same litigation, the Ohio Attorney General filed a memorandum with the court opposing Cambridge's motion to dismiss the lawsuit. Attached as exhibits to that memorandum were excerpts from depositions of Cambridge officials and affidavits from various other people. The depositions of the Cambridge officials discussed examples of Cambridge enrolling students who obviously could not benefit from instruction. One discussion involved the enrollment of a student when, by Cambridge's own admission, it was "obvious the student should not have been enrolled." The Cambridge official went on to testify that the student was "extremely childlike, he did not seem to be able to carry through in conversation, communication skills were very poor." The student's "mannerisms and inability to communicate and comprehend in general conversation" were acknowledged, as well as the fact that the student, when asked a question, would not respond or would talk about something that was totally different and unrelated to the conversation. Another example testified to in deposition involved a Cambridge instructor reporting a second-quarter student whom the instructor had by then determined "could not read his text books and could not read or comprehend the content of the mid-term examination."

The Attorney General also submitted affidavits executed by two former students of the Cleveland branch of Cambridge. Each details improper testing procedures, including administering the test in a crowded room of other students, giving no explanation of the exam or test procedures, and allowing students to receive assistance on the test.

See the enclosed excerpts from the Attorney General's Supplemental Answers to Defendant's Interrogatories and Appendix thereto, with attachments, and excerpts from the Attorney General's court memorandum, with attachments, and affidavits (note: the above information has been "highlighted" for easy reference), Exhibits C-1 through C-2 [*not reprinted herein*].[1]

---

1 In a separate forum, Cambridge officials of the Cleveland campus admitted that Ernest Hall, the first example of improperly admitted students cited in the deposition, took his admissions test simultaneously with several other individuals and that his sister not only attended the admissions test with him, but

V. Cambridge's Own Testing Documents Show Ability-to-Benefit Fraud and Other Irregularities.

Even a cursory review of Cambridge's admissions testing, taken from individual Cambridge files of former students, shows significant violations of the proper test procedures, scoring requirements, and remedial instruction options permitted by DOE and Cambridge's accreditation agency. See the series D exhibits, attached hereto [*not reprinted herein*].

In the 1980's, DOE promulgated regulations regarding the ability-to-benefit standards and the testing to be used by schools to determine whether prospective students actually had the ability to benefit from the school's training. The DOE summarized the ATB requirements in its September, 1995 "Dear Colleague" letter, GEN-95-42. Briefly, for enrollment periods from January 1, 1986 through June 30, 1987, a school could determine that a student had an ability to benefit in accordance with DOE regulations by using a fairly simple procedure. The school only had to:

> *develop and consistently apply criteria* to determine if regular students who did not have a high school diploma or GED, and who were beyond the age of compulsory attendance, had the ability to benefit from the school's training. [Emphasis added].

For periods of enrollment from July 1, 1987 through June 30, 1991, the DOE required more stringent evaluation of students. During this time period, a school had to use standard admissions practices for any applicants without a high school diploma or a GED. These practices required the school to determine the following:

> (1) the student received a GED prior to the student's completion of the program or by the end of the first year of the program, whichever was earlier; (2) the student was counseled prior to admission *and successfully completed the school's program of remedial or developmental education* that did not exceed one academic year or its equivalent; (3) the student passed a nationally recognized, standardized, or industry-developed ATB test, *subject to criteria developed by the school's accrediting association*; or (4) if the student failed the ATB test, he or she *successfully completed the school's program of remedial or developmental education* that did not exceed one academic year or its equivalent. [Emphasis added].

See the enclosed "Dear Colleague" letter GEN-95-42, page 2, Exhibit D-1 [*not reprinted herein*]. See also 34 C.F.R. § 668.7.

After June 30, 1987, DOE required that all ATB tests be used "subject to criteria developed by the institution's nationally recognized accrediting agency or association." 34 C.F.R. § 668.7(b)(1)(i). Cambridge was accredited by the Accrediting Council for Continuing Education and Training (ACCET), in Richmond, Virginia. ACCET standards for its accredited schools

---

actually helped him with the answers. The deposed official also conceded that the testing employee of Cambridge did not notice any of this during the exam (or, apparently, chose not to do anything about it). This is documented in Cambridge's own letter to a media reporter. See the enclosed Cambridge letter of 3/15/88, Exhibit C-3 [*not reprinted herein*].

required that the admissions policy for all students be "based on the institution's stated objectives; it must be administered for all applicants as written and published." ACCET also required each institution to document each student's ability to benefit from the training offered. Finally, the school "must determine a student's aptitude to complete successfully the . . . education *by following the applicable standards, procedures, and scores established by the publisher. . . . No deviation in scoring or testing procedures are allowed without written approval* of the test publisher and written concurrence by the ACCET Accrediting Commission." [Emphasis added]. See the enclosed 2/12/90 ACCET memorandum, with attachments of "Document 32" (June, 1989), p. 1, and "Document 32A" (February, 1990), p. 2, Exhibit D-2 [*not reprinted herein*]. Note that both of these memos state that they provide "clarification" (and thus do not change any policy); their instructions therefore are applicable back to 1986. See Exhibit D-2.

Cambridge published its admissions policy in its Policy and Procedures Manual. It eventually published the policy on a separate document. See Learning to Learn document, Exhibit D-3. This document represented Cambridge's ATB policy, written to comply with DOE's and ACCET's standards. However, the policy failed to use the cut-off scores "established by the publisher." Further, its scores did not "correspond with an appropriate grade level of the materials utilized in the instructional program" because people admitted with scores as low as Cambridge permitted do not learn well from formalized training and often need to be "explicitly taught" through an apprenticeship program rather than from "booklearning." This is explained next.

In determining the threshold scores needed to show an ability to benefit, Cambridge set scores far below the minimum suggested by the test manufacturer, Wonderlic. The following chart shows five programs offered by Cambridge, Cambridge's "conditional" passing scores on the ATB test, Cambridge's "unconditional" passing scores on the ATB test, and the test publisher's (Wonderlic's) minimum passing scores. As explained in Cambridge's admissions policy, prospective students scoring in the "conditional" range would be required to take the Learn to Learn course to gain admission. Those scoring in the "unconditional" range or higher would be admitted without conditions. However, the conditional scores fall below the scores set by Wonderlic in its testing manual:

Program	Cambridge's Conditional *Qualifying Score*	Cambridge's Unconditional *Qualifying Score*	Wonderlic's *Passing Score*
Custodial Maintenance	8	14	12
Data Entry	9	15	12
Law Enforcement/ Security	9	15	10
Nursing Assistant	9	15	11
Word Processing	9	15	15

See Exhibit D-3 and the enclosed Wonderlic ATB Test Score Registration Manual, pp. 11, 12, and 17, Exhibit D-4 [*not reprinted herein*]. Further, the test publisher recommends that schools "recruit and select students that score well above the minimum." See the enclosed Wonderlic ATB Test Score Registration Manual, p. 5, Exhibit D-5 [*not reprinted herein*].

The reason for these suggested scores and recommendations are based on Wonderlic's extensive testing and research to demonstrate its tests' validity, correlation, and reliability. Based on this research, including reviews with employers hiring people for various positions, Wonderlic explains that people in the test score ranges being used by Cambridge would not benefit from a formal training setting and would likely not find employment. Students from these ranges of scores need to be "explicitly taught," as with an apprenticeship program rather than attempting to learn through books and classroom training. See the enclosed Wonderlic User's Manual, p. 26, Exhibit D-6 [*not reprinted herein*].

As a result of Cambridge's own cut-off scores for admission, many students admitted did not have the requisite ability to benefit from the programs offered. The following examples are taken from Cambridge's own files.

1. Apu Nahasapeemapetelon: Mr. Nahasapeemapetelon was admitted in December, 1986 without having taken any admissions test. His enrollment agreement and application papers show he attended a high school, but the "Highest Grade Completed" and "Grad Date" blanks have no answers. Similar blanks for this information appear on the student's untitled data sheet containing background data with the courses, credit hours, and grades given. No high school diploma or transcript appears in the file.

2. Jo Quimby. Ms. Quimby enrolled in Cambridge in October, 1987, and received a grade of 10 on the admissions test. Accordingly, she was required to take the Learn to Learn course, but she never did take that course. A review of the file shows no indication, on any document, of her enrolling, much less completing, the remedial learning program offered by Cambridge.[2]

3. Lionel Hutz: Mr. Hutz had to take the test twice in order to achieve what appears to be a passable score to gain admittance to Cambridge's custodial maintenance program. On his

---

2 With regard to the students who were in the "conditional" range, and thus required to take the Learn to Learn course, it is evident that where a file does not note the Learn to Learn program, the student did not take that course. Included herewith are examples from other student files which do indicate that the student was enrolled in the Learn to Learn program. For example, see the enclosed Cambridge files of Patty Marie Smith and Anthony Adams, Exhibits D-7, D-8 [*not reprinted herein*]. For ease of reference, documents indicating the student was enrolled in Learn to Learn have been highlighted.

It is interesting to note, however, that even when students did take this course, many of them routinely withdrew with a failing grade. Thus, it is clear that Cambridge did not satisfy the requirement for the ability-to-benefit standard set forth in 34 C.F.R. § 668.7(b)(3): "successfully completes a remedial . . . program. . . ." Both Mr. Adams and Ms. Smith, though ostensibly receiving remedial instruction, withdrew from the Learn to Learn course. In fact, they each took the course twice, the second time after already withdrawing from it in an earlier quarter or semester. Neither, however, took a second admissions test, notwithstanding the fact that they were only conditionally eligible and had not satisfactorily completed the Learn to Learn program which they had been required to take in order to be admitted. Again, Cambridge's practices show an across-the-board disregard for DOE's ATB requirements. Even when given the chance to admit students who failed the ATB test, Cambridge played "fast and loose" with the rules.

first try, Mr. Hutz scored a 7; on his second attempt he moved up to an 8. However, serious concerns exist as to whether Mr. Hutz, himself, actually filled in all of the answers which appear on the second test. Mr. Hutz' handwriting in forming the numbers 1, 2, 3, and 4 can be gleaned from looking at the few answers he provided on the first test and most of the answers he provided on the second test. Comparing that to the two answers appearing in the second test for questions 21 and 22, it is seen that the handwriting is much lighter and the numbers are less "shaky"—those two answers appear to have been written by a person with more graceful writing. Significantly, both of those answers are correct and bring what otherwise would have been a score of 6 (failing) to an 8 (barely within the passing range). Also significant is that this appears on the second, and last, test which Mr. Hutz would be permitted to take.

Further, because the score of 8 was the absolute minimum score, and left Mr. Hutz in the "conditional" range of passing scores, he was required to take the remedial instruction program offered by Cambridge in order to qualify for admission and federal loan assistance. This remedial course, entitled "Learn to Learn," is nowhere noted in Mr. Hutz' file or on the enrollment agreement or test cover sheet. This is in contrast to the next example below, Mr. Duncan, and other student files discussed later in which the Learn to Learn program is clearly documented.

4. Julius Hubbert: Mr. Hubbert sought admittance into Cambridge's custodial maintenance program with a score of 8. This is the absolute minimum score for eligibility, and it requires that the student also take the Learn to Learn program. The Learn to Learn program is documented (as "LL"), but only for the second quarter. Inexplicably, Mr. Hubbert was not required to enroll in the Learn to Learn program for the first quarter. This violates Cambridge's own policy— promulgated to comply with DOE and ACCET mandates— which requires the student to take the instruction "in the first quarter of enrollment." The Learn to Learn program is also documented on the test cover sheet itself (as "L&L"), again, in contrast to Mr. Hutz' file.

5. Hans Moleman: Mr. Moleman was admitted in November, 1988, after scoring only a 7 on his admissions test. A score of 7 does not meet Cambridge's own admission requirements. Nevertheless, Mr. Moleman was admitted into the custodial maintenance program (and apparently required to take Learn to Learn, as documented on the Master Attendance Record appearing in his file).

6. Troy McClure: Mr. McClure scored an 11 on his admissions test, thus requiring that he take the Learn to Learn program in addition to the custodial maintenance courses he wished to attend. However, his Master Attendance Record, which notes the Learn to Learn program, indicates Mr. McClure would not have to take the remedial course until the following quarter. This violated Cambridge's own policy which requires the student to take the instruction "in the first quarter of enrollment."

7. Dewey Largo: Mr. Largo took his admissions exam in December, 1988, and scored only a 6. Nevertheless, he was admitted into the custodial maintenance program for three quarters, beginning January 2, 1989. A score of 6 does not

even meet the "conditional" eligibility minimum score set by Cambridge.

See the enclosed student files, Exhibits D-9 through D-15 [*not reprinted herein*].

VI. Cambridge Conducted its Overall Business Practices in an Unlawful and Fraudulent Manner, Resulting in Revocation of Its License by the State of Ohio.

In late 1990, the Ohio State Board of Proprietary School Registration (SBPSR), the licensing and oversight agency for proprietary, for-profit schools in Ohio, revoked the Certificate of Registration for Cambridge and imposed a civil penalty for Cambridge's violations of various sections of the Ohio Revised Code governing proprietary schools. By the time of the license revocation, Cambridge's default rate for mature student loans was an astounding 83.8%. See the enclosed SBPSR letter of 12/5/90, the SBPSR Final Resolution of 1/23/91, and the Higher Education Assistance Foundation letter of 5/12/89, Exhibits E-1 through E-3 [*not reprinted herein*].

VII. Cambridge, and Its Officers, Have Been Involved in Other Fraud and Criminal Activity.

Over the years, the Cincinnati newspapers and other media have documented numerous incidents of fraud and criminal activity by Cambridge and its employees or officers. See the series F exhibits, attached hereto [*not reprinted herein*]. Timothy Lovejoy, the former president of Cambridge, was reported by CNN as having defrauded the U.S. government out of $5 million. It was alleged that he submitted information to the DOE which falsely represented more students attending Cambridge than was true. It was further alleged that Mr. Lovejoy kept the loan monies of students who had dropped out of Cambridge instead of returning it to the banks and/or DOE. In late 1990, Mr. Lovejoy was murdered in a telephone booth at a local airport before these allegations could be brought to trial. That murder remains unsolved to this day. Pete McCallister, another officer of Cambridge, was indicted on numerous counts of bribery, conspiracy to defraud, and lying to a grand jury, to cover up student aid fraud. Mr. McCallister was tried in federal court and eventually pleaded guilty to one count of conspiracy; he was sentenced to two years in prison. Former Ohio Congressman Donald "Buz" Lukens also was indicted on various federal charges, some related to Cambridge, and was tried in federal court. He was convicted of accepting bribes from Cambridge.

The newspaper also reported that former Cambridge employees falsified student records before DOE investigators arrived at the school to check on various allegations of fraud. These employees also stated that many student records were destroyed. Additionally, numerous students complained over the years of sharp recruitment practices, unqualified teachers, problems with the school equipment, problems with attendance and books, as well as describing their experiences in job-hunting. Many, many students were told by prospective employers that their Cambridge certificates were worthless. Cambridge's high loan repayment default rate can be attributed to its poor educational quality as well as its poor administrative and business practices.

Further, physical violence was used against a former employee who went public with some of the fraudulent practices at Cambridge. Mr. Lovejoy was accused of hiring two people to physically assault Mark McClure in April, 1990 because Mr. McClure was talking to the media about Cambridge and was aiding the Legal Aid Society of Cincinnati in its litigation against the school. These two men were sentenced to jail for beating Mr. McClure. And, as was explained earlier, the lawsuit filed by the Legal Aid Society was only the first—the Attorney General's Office filed its own. Both lawsuits succeeded in having Cambridge close its doors.

See the enclosed copies of newspaper articles, Exhibits F-1 through F-8 [*not reprinted herein*].

CONCLUSION

As has been demonstrated, Cambridge's admissions practices were fraudulent across the board. The pervasive fraud and unlawful practices included all areas of the mandatory testing of students for their ability to benefit from Cambridge's purported educational programs. DOE already has seen numerous instances of Cambridge's ATB fraud from individual students and thus has granted those students a discharge of their loans. These individual cases are merely representative of Cambridge's broader approach to education, namely enrolling as many students as could be fit into classrooms, with no regard to the students' ability to learn from the programs. The Ohio State Board of Proprietary School Registration and the Ohio Attorney General found numerous instances of ATB fraud by Cambridge. Numerous former students and employees have testified to the same unlawful practices. It is time for DOE to declare Cambridge's admissions and testing practices so pervasively fraudulent and unlawful as to render their ATB certification meaningless for each and every one of its former students. DOE now should consider any application for a school loan discharge based on improper determination of the student's ability to benefit as proven, so long as that former student did not have a high school diploma or a GED at the time of attending Cambridge.

[Attorney for Plaintiff]

E.2.3 *Class Action Complaint Challenging Department of Education's False Certification Discharge Procedures*

UNITED STATES DISTRICT COURT
EASTERN DISTRICT OF NEW YORK

```
———————————————————  )
[Plaintiffs], individually and on  )
behalf of all others similarly     )
situated,                          )
                  Plaintiffs,      )
                                   )
v.                                 )
                                   )
RICHARD W. RILEY, in his           )
official capacity as Secretary of  )
the United States Department of    )
Education, and the UNITED          )
STATES DEPARTMENT OF               )
EDUCATION,                         )
                  Defendant.       )
———————————————————  )
```

COMPLAINT

PRELIMINARY STATEMENT

1. This is a class action pursuant to the Administrative Procedure Act, 5 U.S.C. § 701 *et seq.*, for declaratory and injunctive relief on behalf of individuals who have been denied discharges of their federally guaranteed student loans arbitrarily, capriciously and in violation of 20 U.S.C. § 1087(c), the Higher Education Act Amendments ("HEAA"). The statute mandates that the defendant Secretary of Education grant discharges of student loans if the schools attended by the students falsely certified that the students had the ability to benefit from the programs for which their loans were taken (hereinafter "ability-to-benefit discharge"). Instead of carefully considering the evidence of false certification presented by the plaintiffs, the defendant Secretary denied their requests for discharges arbitrarily and capriciously, on the basis of unsupported assumptions and inferences.

JURISDICTION

2. This court has jurisdiction under the Administrative Procedure Act 5 U.S.C. § 701 *et seq.*, 28 U.S.C. § 1331, § 1361, and 20 U.S.C. § 1082(a)(2).

3. Venue is proper in this district pursuant to 28 U.S.C. § 1391(e) because the named plaintiffs reside in this district.

PARTIES

4. Plaintiff 1 resides, and at all relevant times has resided, in Brooklyn, New York.

5. Plaintiff 2 resides, and at all relevant times has resided, in Brooklyn, New York

6. Defendant RICHARD W. RILEY is the Secretary of the United States Department of Education (hereafter "the Secretary" when speaking of Defendant Riley; and "U.S. ED" when referring to the Department), and as such is responsible for administration of the Federal Family Educational Loan program (hereafter "FFEL"), known until 1992 as the Guaranteed Student Loan Program (hereafter "GSLP"). Defendant Riley is sued only in his official capacity.

CLASS ACTION ALLEGATIONS

7. The named plaintiffs 1 and 2, bring this action, pursuant to Rule 23 of the Federal Rules of Civil Procedure, on behalf of themselves and as representatives of all individuals with federally guaranteed student loans obtained to attend for-profit vocational schools licensed by the New York State Department of Education, who have been or will be denied an ability-to-benefit discharge by the Secretary, without consideration of the facts in their individual cases, but rather in reliance upon an absence of findings by oversight agencies about the certification practices of the schools they attended.

8. The class is so numerous that joinder of all members is impracticable.

9. There are questions of law or fact common to the class which predominate over any questions affecting only the individual plaintiffs, including, but not limited to whether the defendant arbitrarily and capriciously relies on information provided by other agencies or on the absence of such information instead of examining the actual facts of the plaintiffs' cases.

10. The claims of the individual named plaintiff as to the legality of the defendant's practices are typical of the claims of all class

members, in that each has had her request for an ability-to-benefit discharge denied arbitrarily and capriciously, without examination by the defendant of the individual facts of her case.

11. The named plaintiffs will adequately and fairly protect the interests of all members of the class, because they have the requisite personal interest in the outcome of this action, have no interest antagonistic to others in the class, and they are represented by the Social Justice Project at BLS Legal Services Corp., counsel experienced in class action litigation generally, and specifically including the rights of people with guaranteed student loan debts.

12. The prosecution of separate actions by individual members of the class would create a risk of inconsistent or varying adjudications with respect to the practices at issue in this action. Separate actions would be, as a practical matter, dispositive of the interests of other individual members of the class and would substantially impair their abilities to protect their interests. Defendants have acted on grounds generally applicable to the class in failing to make individual determinations based on the facts in each case in determining plaintiffs' eligibility for loan discharges. A class action is superior to other available methods for the fair and efficient adjudication of this controversy.

STATUTORY SCHEME

13. The Higher Education Act, 20 U.S.C. § 1071, *et seq.*, authorizes the Secretary to administer a federal student financial aid program (formerly known as the Guaranteed Student Loan (GSL) Program, now known as the Federal Family Education Loan (FFEL) Program).

14. Under the FFEL program, lenders make loans for "eligible borrowers" to attend "eligible" post-secondary institutions; state and private guaranty agencies insure the loans; and the Secretary reinsures the agencies. 20 U.S.C. §1071 *et seq.*.

15. Through the program, a student may obtain guaranteed student loans to attend a proprietary vocational school if the school (1) admits eligible students, (2) is legally authorized to provide vocational training, (3) has been in existence for at least two years, (4) is accredited by an agency approved by the Secretary, and (5) has a cohort default rate less than the statutorily specified threshold. 20 U.S.C. §§ 1002 (b), 1085 (a).

16. To qualify for a guaranteed student loan, a student must meet various requirements, including the "ability-to-benefit" requirement. The specific requirements have changed slightly during the life of the program, but at all times relevant to this case, have required that to be considered to have the ability to benefit from the program of study, the student must have a high school diploma, or a recognized equivalent (GED), or pass a standardized test given by the school prior to admission of the student, or receive a GED prior to graduation from the course of study or before the end of the first year of study, or be enrolled in and successfully complete an institutionally prescribed program of remedial education not to exceed one year. 20 U.S.C. § 1091; 34 C.F.R. § 668.6; § 682.402(e)(13); §685.214(c).

17. The Higher Education Act Amendments and implementing regulations provide that the Secretary must discharge a student loan (including interest and collection fees) of a borrower who received a loan after January 1, 1986, if a school falsely certified the borrower as having the ability to benefit from the program of study. 20 U.S.C. § 1087(c).

18. Regulations promulgated by the Secretary require guaranty agencies to send discharge applications to all borrowers who, based on information acquired by the Secretary, may be eligible for such discharge. 34 C.F.R. § 682.402 (e) (i).

19. In evaluating the borrower's request for an ability-to-benefit discharge, the agency holding the loan must consider the information and supporting sworn statement provided by the borrower, "in light of information available from the records of the agency and from other sources, including other guaranty agencies, state authorities, and cognizant accrediting associations." 34 C.F.R. § 682.402 (e) (6) (iv).

20. If the agency determines that the borrower satisfies the requirements for an ability-to-benefit discharge, the agency must (1) pay off the loan debt; (2) notify the borrower that her liability has been suspended; (3) refund to the borrower all amounts paid by the borrower to the lender or agency with respect to the discharged amount; and (4) notify the lender that the borrower's liability with respect to the amount of the loan has been discharged. 34 C.F.R. § 682.402(e)(7)(ii).

21. If the guaranty agency decides that the borrower is not entitled to a discharge, a borrower can request a review of that decision by the Secretary. If a borrower does request a review of the guaranty agency's decision, the agency shall forward the borrower's discharge request and all relevant documentation to the Secretary. 34 C.F.R. § 682.402(e)(11)(i).

22. Discharge of a student loan under 20 U.S.C. § 1087(c), entitles the borrower to:

(a) relief from any existing or past obligation to repay the loan and any charges imposed or cost incurred by the holder with respect to the loan that the borrower is or was otherwise obligated to pay. 20 U.S.C. § 1087(c)(1).

(b) restoration of the borrower's eligibility to receive federal assistance under Title IV of the Higher Education Act Amendments. 20 U.S.C. § 1087(c)(3)–(4).

(c) correction of all adverse credit reports by reporting to all credit bureaus to which the holder previously reported the delinquent status of the loan that all adverse credit history assigned to the loan should be deleted. 20 U.S.C. § 1087(c)(5).

23. The Administrative Procedure Act ("APA"), 5 U.S.C. § 706(2)(A), specifically creates a cause of action to "hold unlawful and set aside agency action, findings, and conclusions found to be arbitrary and capricious, an abuse of discretion, or otherwise not in accordance with the law."

24. The APA also creates a cause of action to "hold unlawful and set aside agency action, findings, and conclusions found to be–in excess of statutory jurisdiction, authority, or limitations, or short of statutory rights." 5 U.S.C. § 706(2)(C).

FACTS PERTAINING TO THE CLASS

25. The Secretary denies ability-to-benefit discharges, without adequate consideration of the facts of individual students, based upon the inference that the absence of recorded findings of improper ability-to-benefit admissions practices by particular schools means the school was not engaged in improper ability-to-benefit practices.

26. The Secretary administers the guaranteed student loan program in part through giving directions to the guaranty agencies that are the first line of insurance of the federally guaranteed student

loans. These directions are sent to the guarantee agencies in the form of memoranda referred to as "Dear Colleague" letters.

27. The Secretary has issued several Dear Colleague letters about ability-to-benefit discharges.

28. In September 1995, in Dear Colleague letter Gen-95-42 (attached hereto as Exhibit A), the Secretary advised guaranty agencies about how to evaluate requests for ability-to-benefit discharges, stating that the absence of findings of improper ATB practices by authorities with oversight responsibilities "raises an inference that no improper practices were reported because none were taking place." *Id.* at 4.

29. In his own actions in administering guaranteed student loans held by U.S. ED, the Secretary follows the practices outlined in the Dear Colleague letter.

30. The Secretary supports and relies on such an inference even though Congress created the ability-to-benefit discharge specifically because agencies with oversight responsibilities have failed "to detect and or take action" regarding abuses such as failure to honestly assess students' ability to benefit from vocational programs. *Senate Permanent Subcommittee on Investigations* (hereinafter the "Committee"), *Abuses in Federal Student Aid Programs*, S. Rep. No. 102-58, (1991) (hereinafter "the Nunn Report").

31. Between 1989 and 1991, the United States Senate Permanent Subcommittee on Investigations, chaired by Senator Sam Nunn, studied the rapid increase of defaulted guaranteed student loans obtained for study at vocational schools. S. Rep. No. 102-58, at 23 (1991).

32. The Nunn Report revealed a national epidemic of fraud by proprietary trade schools, including the practice of fraudulently certifying students' ability to benefit from the schools' programs. *See id* at 12.

33. The Nunn Report found that "one of the most widely abused areas of trade school practices was admissions and recruitment, in particular the admission of students who had not finished high school under the so-called 'ability-to-benefit' or 'ATB' rule." *Id.* at 12.

34. The Nunn Report also found evidence of a failure "by state and federal authorities to detect and or take action" regarding the abuse of GSLP rules and regulations. *Id.* at 23.

35. The Nunn Report stated U.S. ED "has effectively abdicated its GSLP oversight responsibilities to private accrediting bodies, State licensing authorities, and guaranty agencies. Experience has proven that those bodies have neither the motivation nor the capabilities to effectively police the program." *Id.* at 32.

36. The mandate, in the Higher Education Act Amendments, that the Secretary discharge the loans of students who had been admitted into proprietary schools despite their lack of an ability to benefit from the programs, was a response to Congressional findings that "institutions falsely certified the eligibility of students for Federal loans. . . . students were left without the skills needed to obtain employment and consequently did not have the means to repay the loans." *Report of the House Committee on Education and Labor*, H. Rep. No. 102-447, at 116 (1992).

FACTS REGARDING NAMED PLAINTIFFS

PLAINTIFF 1

37. Plaintiff 1 was enrolled in the Robert Fiance Hair Design Institute (hereafter "RFHD") branch at [Address] (hereafter "[Address 1]").

38. RFHD is a for-profit vocational school.

39. Plaintiff 1 was enrolled in a course that was scheduled to run from March 10, 1988 to December 8, 1988.

40. Plaintiff 1 financed her studies at RFHD by taking out guaranteed student loans under the Guaranteed Student Loan Program.

41. Plaintiff 1 received the proceeds of the disbursement of her loan on March 10, 1988.

42. At the time of her application to RFHD, Plaintiff 1 did not have, and reported to RFHD that she did not have a high school diploma or a GED.

43. RFHD did not require Plaintiff 1 to take an admission test, and did not enroll her in a GED course or other program of remedial education.

44. Plaintiff 1 attended classes at [Address 1] from March 1988 to early fall 1988.

45. Plaintiff 1 did not receive the training and education for which she was contracted due to her inability to benefit from the program.

46. The guaranteed student loans obtained by Plaintiff 1 for her studies at RFHD were placed in default status by U.S. ED.

47. On December 30, 1999, Plaintiff 1 applied to the Secretary for a discharge of her guaranteed student loans based on the school's false certification of her ability to benefit from the program.

48. On April 10, 2000, the Secretary acknowledged the receipt of Plaintiff 1's loan discharge application and stated that Plaintiff 1 was not entitled to an ability-to-benefit loan discharge because authorities with oversight responsibilities had made no findings or adverse reports relating to false certification of ability-to-benefit at RFHD (Letter attached as Exhibit B [*not reprinted herein*]).

PLAINTIFF 2

49. Plaintiff 2 was enrolled at Commercial Programming Unlimited (hereafter CPU), at [Address].

50. CPU is a for profit vocational school.

51. Plaintiff 2 financed her education at CPU by taking out guaranteed student loans under the Guaranteed Student Loan Program.

52. At the time of her application to CPU, Plaintiff 2 did not have, and informed CPU that she did not have a high school diploma or a GED.

53. CPU did not require Plaintiff 2 to take an admission test and did not enroll her in a GED course or any other course of remedial education.

54. Plaintiff 2 began taking classes at CPU in August of 1988. She was enrolled in courses for computer programming.

55. Plaintiff 2 attended classes at CPU for approximately two months.

56. Plaintiff 2 discontinued her studies at CPU because of the difficulty of the course material, inadequate teaching, and overcrowded classrooms, and but she did not formally withdraw from CPU.

57. The guaranteed student loans obtained by Plaintiff 2 for her studies at CPU were placed in default status by the Secretary.

58. Plaintiff 2 applied to the Secretary for a discharge of her guaranteed student loans based on the school's false certification of her ability-to-benefit from the program.

59. In a letter dated March 8, 2000, the Secretary acknowledged the receipt of Plaintiff 2 loan discharge application and stated that Plaintiff 2 was not entitled to an ability-to-benefit discharge because authorities with oversight responsibilities had made no findings or adverse reports relating to false certification of ability-to-benefit at CPU. (Letter attached as Exhibit C [*not reprinted herein*]).

FIRST CAUSE OF ACTION

60. Defendant Secretary's adoption of the policy, stated in the September 1995 Dear Colleague letter, that the absence of findings of improper ATB practices by authorities with oversight responsibilities "raises an inference that no improper practices were reported because none were taking place," and his own reliance on that inference in denying requests for ATB discharges, without adequate consideration of the facts presented by students seeking discharges, is arbitrary and capricious and in violation of 5 U.S.C. § 706(2)(A).

SECOND CAUSE OF ACTION

61. Defendant Secretary's adoption of the policy, stated in the September 1995 Dear Colleague letter, that the absence of findings of improper ATB practices by authorities with oversight responsibilities "raises an inference that no improper practices were reported because none were taking place," and his own reliance on that inference in denying requests for ATB discharges, without adequate consideration of the facts presented by students seeking discharges, is in excess of his statutory authority, in violation of 5 U.S.C. § 706(2)(C).

PRAYER FOR RELIEF

WHEREFORE, plaintiffs respectfully request the court to:

1. Enter an order certifying this action as a class action pursuant to Rule 23(b)(2) of the Federal Rules of Civil Procedure, with the class consisting of all individuals with federally guaranteed student loans obtained to attend for-profit vocational schools licensed by the New York State Department of Education, who have been or will be denied an ability-to-benefit discharge by the Secretary, without consideration of the facts in their individual cases, in reliance upon an absence of findings by oversight agencies about the certification practices of the schools they attended.

2. Enter a judgement against the defendant
   a. declaring that the Secretary's practice of denying requests for ability-to-benefit discharges based solely on the absence of findings by oversight agencies of prior wrongdoing by a school, without consideration of the facts of a debtor's individual circumstances, is arbitrary and capricious and not in accordance with the law.
   b. directing the defendant to
      i. Review the facts of each debtor's request for an ability-to-benefit discharge;
      ii. Discontinue the practice of relying on the absence of reports by oversight agencies;

iii. Provide debtors with the supporting evidence relied upon by the Secretary in determining that they are not entitled to a loan discharge, including but not limited to a copy of the properly administered and nationally recognized ATB exam or evidence of enrollment in a remedial program of education;
      iv. discharge the loans of Plaintiffs 1 and 2;
      v. cease collection efforts on the loans of Plaintiffs 1 and 2;
      vi. correct any reports to credit agencies or eligible institutions that the loans of Plaintiffs 1 or 2 are in default or delinquent;
      vii. return all money paid voluntarily or involuntarily by Plaintiffs 1 and 2;
      viii. provide notice, within a reasonable time not to exceed 90 days from the date of a resolution favorable to the plaintiff, in a form to be agreed upon by the parties, to all student borrowers denied an a false certification of an ability-to-benefit discharge that they may be eligible for a discharge of their student loans; and providing to them all information in the possession of the Secretary relating to their eligibility for discharge, the procedures for requesting a discharge, and a form on which to request such discharge;
      ix. make determinations, and issue written decisions, on all requests for ability-to-benefit discharges, within 60 days of receipt of the requests;
   c. ordering defendant to pay the cost of this action, together with reasonable attorneys' fees pursuant to the Equal Access to Justice Act, 28 U.S.C. § 2412(d)(1)(A), as determined by the court; and
   d. granting such other and further relief as the Court may deem just and proper.

Dated:

Respectfully submitted,
[Attorney for Plaintiffs]

E.2.4 Individual Complaint Challenging Disability Discharge Denial

A preliminary injunction motion for this case as well as a similar pleading in another case can be found on the companion CD-Rom.

IN THE UNITED STATES DISTRICT COURT
FOR THE SOUTHERN DISTRICT OF GEORGIA
WAYCROSS DIVISION

————————————)	
JANE SMITH,)	
Plaintiff,)	
)	
v.)	
)	
ROD PAIGE, SECRETARY,)	
UNITED STATES)	
DEPARTMENT OF)	
EDUCATION,)	
Defendant.)	
————————————)	

COMPLAINT

INTRODUCTION

1. Plaintiff brings this action for judicial review of the United States Secretary of Education's decision denying her application for a discharge of her federally-guaranteed student loan. Plaintiff seeks declaratory and injunctive relief against the Department of Education's new ad hoc, unpublished, and unreasonable standards for evaluating requests to discharge student loans based on the borrower's permanent disability.

I. JURISDICTION

2. This court has jurisdiction under 28 U.S.C. §1331 (federal question), 20 U.S.C. §1082 (suits against Secretary of Education), and the federal Administrative Procedure Act, 5 U.S.C. §§ 701 *et seq*. With respect to Plaintiff's request for declaratory relief, this Court has jurisdiction under 28 U.S.C. §2201.

II. PARTIES

3. Plaintiff Jane Smith, an individual who resides at [Address] signed up for a federally-guaranteed student loan by the Riley Training Institute in Waycross in February 1981.

4. Defendant Rod Paige, Secretary of the United States Department of Education, is responsible for the administration of the federally-guaranteed student loan program.

5. The United States Department of Education(DOE) is an agency within the meaning of the federal Administrative Procedure Act, 5 U.S.C. §§ 701 *et seq*.

6. The Riley Training Institute in Waycross, Georgia was a proprietary trade school that was certified as an eligible institution to participate in federal financial aid programs under the Higher Education Act until it closed in May of 1991.

III. STATEMENT OF FACTS

7. Plaintiff Jane Smith is a 45-year-old single mother of one who resides in [Address], Georgia.

8. Plaintiff graduated from high school in 1975 and enrolled at Okefenokee Technical College for a six weeks nurse's aide course.

9. Plaintiff was successfully employed as a nurse's aide for a period of ten years, 1975 until 1985.

10. In 1989 Plaintiff enrolled in Riley Training Institute to study retail sales management.

11. Upon her acceptance at Riley Training Institute also located in Waycross, Georgia, Plaintiff applied for a federally guaranteed loan in February 1989.

12. Plaintiff Smith received a student loan from Florida Federal Savings in the amount of $2,625.00.

13. Plaintiff attended Riley Training Institute but did not complete her studies.

14. After being successfully gainfully employed for a period of ten years and attending school for a short while, Jane Smith suffered severe physical and mental impairments.

15. In 1995, Plaintiff applied for Social Security disability and/or Supplemental Security Income (SSI) and was determined to be permanently and totally disabled by the Social Security Administration (hereinafter "SSA").

16. Plaintiff began receiving SSI benefits in the amount of $458.00 in 1995.

17. In 1999, some four years after receipt of SSI benefits, Satilla Community Mental Health, where Ms. Smith sought assistance, recommended her for participation in the SSI work incentive subsidized/supportive employment program.

18. The subsidized work program pays benefits and wages above the amount that Ms. Smith actually earns. She is able to work because she has a job coach and accommodations are made on a daily basis in consideration of both her physical and mental disability.

19. The accommodations made on a daily basis are substantial and include the ability to leave work when necessary, to return home during the day, to work fewer hours than other employees due to fatigue and to have frequent rest periods during the day.

20. On or before December 1999, Plaintiff Smith began receiving collection notices from the Department of Education indicating that she was in arrears on her student loan payment and directing her to pay her arrearage in full to Defendant's intermediary, Pioneer Credit Recovery, Inc.

21. On or about June 29, 2000, Defendant received notice that Defendant intended to garnish her income if she did not contact Pioneer Credit Recovery, Inc. to make arrangements to pay her student loan arrearage.

22. The Department of Education has demanded from Plaintiff a loan payment in the amount of $6,004.98.

23. In response to said collection notices, Plaintiff Smith filed an application for student loan discharge due to her disability.

24. The Higher Education Act provides that an individual who is unable to work because of an injury or illness that is expected to continue indefinitely or result in death is entitled to have the federally guaranteed student loan discharged. 20 U.S.C.§ 1087(a).

25. In conjunction with her application for discharge due to a disability, Ms. Smith informed the Department of Education that she was totally and permanently disabled because she has full-blown AIDS and other complicating medical conditions.

26. Ms. Smith also informed the Agency that she received treatment for AIDS and other medical conditions from her primary care physician of many years.

27. Ms. Smith completed the Department of Education form to request a disability discharge, and, additionally, her physician completed the "Physician's Certification of Borrowers and Total Permanent Disability" listing AIDS, insulin-dependent diabetes mellitus, high blood pressure and the side-effects resulting from several AIDS medications as contributing to Plaintiff's inability to work in a genuine work place without accommodations. (*See* attached Exhibit "A" [*not reprinted herein*.])

28. In addition to notifying the Agency in July 2000 that she was disabled and making an application for a loan discharge due to disability, Plaintiff sent in a request for a hearing along with an administrative wage garnishment disclosure form.

29. Plaintiff's request for an application to cancel the school loan obligation was denied. However, a request for a hearing was granted and scheduled for February 13, 2001. The hearing was held by telephone.

30. At the outset of the hearing, Jacqueline Hughley-Leonard, a Department of Education hearing officer, stated that Plaintiff could present her argument but could not qualify for a disability discharge because she was working.

31. Ms. Hughley-Leonard refused to consider evidence of the completed application for discharge due to disability with the attached physician's certification of disability during the hearing.

32. Upon request from counsel for Plaintiff, Ms. Hughley-Leonard recused herself from the hearing because of her refusal as Hearing Officer to even consider Ms. Smith's evidence. Hearing Officer Irene Ford then joined Ms. Hughley-Leonard in the hearing and allowed Ms. Smith's counsel to present evidence of her disability.

33. On February 26, Defendant Department of Education denied Plaintiff's application for a disability discharge stating, "Receiving Social Security disability benefits does not automatically qualify a borrower for total and permanent disability cancellations." (*See* decision attached as Exhibit "B" p. 2 [*not reprinted herein.*])

34. Said February 26 opinion also stated, "A borrower is not considered totally and permanently disabled based on a condition that existed before he or she applied for the loan." (*See* Ex. "B" p.2)

35. Said recitation of fact was a factual error and despite Plaintiff's protestation to the Agency, said correction has not been made. (*See* Plaintiff's letter attached as Exhibit "C" [*not reprinted herein*]).

36. Defendant Agency also requested that Plaintiff Jane Smith provide financial evidence regarding whether or not she had sufficient funds for garnishment.

37. Said final decision (Ex. "B" p. 2) stated the intention of Defendant to garnish Ms. Smith's income. Defendant's decision stated, however, that it would stay the garnishment for six months because Ms. Smith did not have sufficient monthly income to pay the amount.

38. As a result of an additional collection activity related to this loan, Plaintiff Smith's 2000 tax return, of $262.00 and her August 2001 tax rebate in the amount of $300.00 were both intercepted.

39. Ms. Smith's income has not improved subsequent to the date of Defendant's decision, but has worsened because her tax refund and rebate were intercepted.

40. In addition to her own expenses, the Plaintiff is attempting to provide a minimum amount of income on a monthly basis to her son who is in school.

41. Garnishment of Ms. Smith's income would render her unable to moderately function on a monthly basis, and would result in her being unable to participate in her subsidized work program.

42. On June 26, 2001, Plaintiff wrote to Defendant submitting her request for reconsideration of her claim asserting that the denial appeared to be based on the mistake of fact among other issues.

43. Defendant refused to clarify or explain his decision. Defendant's decision constituted Agency action that is reviewable under the Administrative Procedure Act.

44. Defendant's decision also stated, "Our findings are conclusive and represent the Department of Education's final decision on your objections. If you disagree with this decision, you may have this decision reviewed by bringing a lawsuit in federal district court." (*See* Ex. "B" p. 1)

45. Defendant's decision denying Plaintiff's application for discharge due to disability is based on no applicable or discernible law, statute or regulation.

46. Additionally, the ad hoc decision does not contain a statement of fact or an analysis of the facts to the regulation or to the applicable law governing and controlling how a disability discharge should be resolved.

47. Defendant's refusal to discharge Plaintiff Smith's student loan is arbitrary and capricious and not in accordance with the law.

Plaintiff's application for disability discharge met all of the statutory and regulatory provisions found at 34 C.F.R. § 682.402.

48. Ms. Smith's loan balance approximates Five Thousand, Eight-Hundred Eighty dollars and 64/100 Dollars ($5,880.64).

49. Ms. Smith has no adequate remedy at law.

50. Ms. Smith, has already had her tax refund and rebate intercepted and has also been threatened with imminent garnishment against her earnings.

51. Defendant recently contacted counsel for Plaintiff requesting additional financial information so that it could move ahead to start garnishing her monthly benefit amount.

IV. DEFENDANT'S PRACTICES

52. Defendant has stated that its adverse decision dated February 26, 2001 in Plaintiff's case is "conclusive" and "final" (*See* Ex."B" p. 1), and therefore constitutes final agency action as defined by 5 U.S.C. § 704.

53. Defendant has persisted in its attempts to collect on Ms. Smith's loan, most recently seizing her year 2000 tax refund and 2001 tax rebate.

54. Defendant's actions have resulted in its applying new, more restrictive standards to Ms. Smith's request for a disability discharge.

55. On or about June 7, 1999, the Inspector General of the U.S. Department of Education issued a report entitled "Improving the Process for Forgiving Student Loans" (Hereinafter "IG Report"), which included findings that certain individuals who were allegedly not disabled, had received student loan disability discharges. (*See* attached report as Exhibit "D")

56. In response to the IG report, the Defendant began applying stricter criteria to requests for disability discharges, including but not limited to the following changes:

A. Defendant ceased its prior practice of granting a disability discharge on the basis of a properly completed physician's certification of disability submitted on the Defendant's approved form;

B. Defendant notified its employees and agents that physicians should be informed that eligibility for disability benefits under the Social Security Act would not be sufficient basis to establish eligibility for a student loan disability discharge and that the student loan discharge standard for disability was a "higher standard" than the Social Security standard; and,

C. Defendant directed its employees and agents, who have no medical training, to make an independent determination of whether a physician's certification of disability is definitive, or if the diagnosis and prognosis do not appear to reach the standard of total and permanent disability.

57. Some, but not all, of the Defendant's new policies and rules regarding disability discharges were set forth in a "Dear Colleague letter," designated GEN-99-36 (hereinafter the "Dear Colleague letter"). (*See* attached letter as Exhibit "E")

58. The Dear Colleague letter was not published in the Federal Register for notice and comment.

59. The new rules are set forth in the Dear Colleague letter as absolute requirements for eligibility for disability discharges rather than as guidelines to decision-makers.

60. The substantive changes set forth in the Dear Colleague letter are arbitrary and capricious and not in accordance with the law.

61. The Defendant's adverse decision has caused and will continue to cause substantial and irreparable harm to Ms. Smith.

V. CLAIMS FOR RELIEF

COUNT I: DEFENDANT'S DECISION VIOLATES THE DISABILITY DISCHARGE PROVISIONS FOUND IN 20 U.S.C.S. § 1087(A)

62. Plaintiff incorporates paragraphs 1 through 61 of her Complaint as if set forth fully herein.

63. The determination that Ms. Smith is permanently and totally disabled was made and certified by a medical doctor, following a personal examination.

64. Defendant's determination that Ms. Smith is not permanently and totally disabled was based solely upon nonmedical considerations.

65. Defendant's determination that Ms. Smith is not permanently and totally disabled was made by nonmedical personnel.

66. Defendant's total failure to consider Ms. Smith's documented physical disability in determining whether to grant a discharge pursuant to 20 U.S.C.S. § 1087(a) violates the Congressional mandate to provide debt relief to persons who suffer from debilitating and terminal illnesses.

COUNT II: DEFENDANT'S RELIANCE ON A MISTAKE OF FACT RESULTED IN A FINAL DECISION THAT IS ARBITRARY AND CAPRICIOUS AND VIOLATES 5 U.S.C. §706(2)(A)

67. Plaintiff incorporates paragraphs 1 through 61 of her Complaint as if set forth fully herein.

68. Ms. Smith's application seeking discharge of her student loan liability was filed under 20 U.S.C.S. § 1087(a), alleging permanent and totally disability.

69. In determining that Ms. Smith was not entitled to a discharge of her student loan obligation, Defendant failed to address any substantive considerations related to Ms. Smith's disability status.

70. Defendant relied upon a mistake of fact regarding Ms. Smith's disability onset date when it ruled against Ms. Smith.

71. Defendant has been asked to either rectify its mistake or to clarify its holding and has refused to do so, stating that its decision is final.

72. Defendant's adverse decision on Ms. Smith's application is arbitrary, capricious and not in accordance with law, and, therefore, violates 5 U.S.C. § 706(2)(a).

COUNT III: DEFENDANT FAILED TO FOLLOW ITS OWN REGULATIONS IN MAKING ITS DECISION TO DENY PLAINTIFF'S DISCHARGE APPLICATION AND, THEREFORE, THE DECISION IS UNLAWFUL UNDER 5 U.S.C. § 706.

73. Plaintiff incorporates paragraphs 1 through 61 of her Complaint as if set forth fully herein.

74. Defendant sets forth the procedures that must be followed by which a borrower becomes entitled to a disability discharge in 34 C.F.R. § 682.402.

75. Defendant's above-cited regulations require that a discharge be granted upon written certification of permanent and total disability by a physician, submitted upon a form approved by Defendant.

76. Ms. Smith submitted the required medical certification of her permanent and total disability.

77. Defendant has refused to approve Ms. Smith's discharge application in contravention of its own regulations.

COUNT IV: BY APPLYING AN UNPUBLISHED STANDARD OF REVIEW ARTICULATED IN A "DEAR COLLEAGUE" LETTER, DEFENDANT VIOLATED THE NOTICE AND COMMENT REQUIREMENTS FOUND IN 5 U.S.C. § 552.

78. Plaintiff incorporates paragraphs 1 through 61 of her Complaint as if set forth fully herein.

79. Defendant sets forth the procedures that must be followed by which a borrower becomes entitled to a disability discharge in 34 C.F.R. § 682.402.

80. Ms. Smith complied with the above-referenced procedures, and should have been entitled to a discharge.

81. In making its adverse decision, Defendant applied a different standard to Ms. Smith's application than authorized by statute or regulation.

82. Defendant ignored its formal regulations to apply different eligibility rules set forth in a Dear Colleague letter.

83. The above-mentioned letter was not submitted to a negotiated rule-making process, nor was it widely published, which violates the Administrative Procedure Act requirement, 5 U.S.C. § 552 that regulations be published in the Federal Register for notice and comment prior to being applied by federal agencies.

WHEREFORE, Plaintiff respectfully requests that the Court grant the following relief:

1. Assume jurisdiction over this case;
2. Enter an order declaring that Defendant's new more restrictive standards violate 20 U.S.C.S. § 1087(A), 34 C.F.R. § 682.402 and the requirements of the Administrative Procedure Act;
3. Grant a preliminary and permanent injunction enjoining Defendant from implementing its more restrictive disability discharge standards as set forth in unpublished rules and ordering Defendant to reevaluate any discharge requests denied under the new restrictive standard;
4. Grant a preliminary and permanent injunction enjoining Defendant and its agents from intercepting federal income tax refunds and rebates, garnishing wages or bank accounts, or otherwise collecting the balance of the Plaintiff's student loan.
5. That the Court enter an order reversing the Department's action in denying Plaintiff's discharge request;
6. That the Court enter an order directing Defendant to refund with interest all monies withheld, garnished, or unlawfully collected from Plaintiff; 7. That the Court enter an order awarding Plaintiff costs; and 8. That the Court enter an order granting any other and further relief as is just and proper.

[Dated]

Respectfully submitted,
[Attorneys for the Plaintiff]

E.3 Challenge to Student Loan Collection Letters

E.3.1 Complaint

IN THE UNITED STATES DISTRICT COURT
FOR THE MIDDLE DISTRICT OF LOUISIANA

```
————————————————   )
Mary Johnson, on behalf of      )
herself and all others similarly )
situated,                       )
                Plaintiff,      )
                                )
v.                              )
                                )
The Premier Collectors, Inc.,   )
                Defendant.      )
————————————————   )
```

CLASS ACTION COMPLAINT

Plaintiff Mary Johnson, on her own behalf and on behalf of the class defined below, complains as follows against defendant The Premier Collectors, Inc.:

INTRODUCTION

1. This action is brought to remedy defendant's violations of the federal Fair Debt Collection Practices Act, 15 U.S.C. §1692 et seq. ("FDCPA").

JURISDICTION AND VENUE

2. This Court has jurisdiction under 15 U.S.C. §1692k(d) and 28 U.S.C. §1331.

PARTIES

3. Plaintiff Mary Johnson is an individual who resides in Baton Rouge, Louisiana. She is a "consumer" as defined by the FDCPA, 15 U.S.C. §1692a(3).

4. The Premier Collectors, Inc. ("Premier Collectors") is a Delaware corporation registered to do business in the state of Louisiana. Its registered agent and address are AB Corporation Systems, 1000 Main Street, Baton Rouge, Louisiana.

5. Premier Collectors is regularly engaged for profit in the collection of debts allegedly owed by consumers. It is a "debt collector" as defined in the FDCPA, 15 U.S.C. §1692a(6).

FACTUAL ALLEGATIONS OF MS. JOHNSON

6. On or about August 11, 1993, Ms. Johnson was mailed a collection letter from Defendant for $11,417.31 allegedly owing to the U.S. Department of Education. (Attached hereto as *Exhibit A*) [*not reprinted herein*].

7. On or about April 20, 1994, Ms. Johnson was mailed a collection letter from Defendant for $10,706.14 allegedly owing to the U.S. Department of Education. (Attached hereto as *Exhibit B*) [*not reprinted herein*].

8. On or about May 5, 1994, Ms. Johnson was mailed a collection letter from Defendant for $10,732.65 allegedly owing to creditor U. S. Department of Education. (Attached hereto as *Exhibit C*) [*not reprinted herein*].

9. These collection letters were mailed in an attempt to collect alleged debts arising from transactions primarily for personal, family, or household purposes.

10. Defendant is not affiliated with the U.S. Department of Education.

11. In *Exhibits A-C*, Defendant lists the principal balance as $5650.49, interest varying from $2,242.59 to $1,744.71, and fees and costs varying from $3,524.23 to $3,310.94.

12. Defendant did not and does not determine the course of legal action taken by the U.S. Department of Justice with regard to such debts.

13. Neither Defendant, the U.S. Department of Justice, nor anyone else, has filed suit against Ms. Johnson to collect this debt.

DEFENDANT'S PRACTICES

14. Defendant regularly mails, or causes to be mailed, collection letters bearing the name of the U.S. Department of Education to Louisiana residents in an effort to collect consumer debts.

15. Defendant seeks to recover a collection fee of "42.84%", which is neither "reasonable" nor "enforceable".

16. Defendant states in the collection letters "OUR STAFF AND CLIENT WILL DETERMINE THE APPROPRIATE COURSE OF LEGAL ACTION", suggesting that The Premier Collectors, Inc. will participate in directing the initiation of litigation by the U.S. Department of Justice against the consumer.

17. Defendant states in the collection letters that The Premier Collectors, Inc. will conduct an investigation of the of the plaintiff's income, savings, employment, real estate ownership and personal assets.

18. Defendant states in the collection letter that a suit by the U.S. Department of Justice may result in garnishment, attachment and/or judgment liens without notifying the consumer of the right to be heard and the necessity of entry of judgement prior to such action.

19. Defendant's collection letter implies that it is "vouched for, bonded by, or affiliated with the United States".

20. Defendant places the validation notice and debt collection warning on the back of the collection letters without reference thereto.

DAMAGES SUFFERED

21. As a result of Defendant's practices, Plaintiff and the class are entitled to statutory damages pursuant to the Fair Debt Collection Practices Act.

VIOLATIONS OF FDCPA

22. Defendant violated the FDCPA by mailing collection letter without proper validation notice or debt collection warning, in violation of 15 U.S.C. §1692g(a)and e(11).

23. Defendant violated the FDCPA by seeking to collect fees of "42.84%", which are neither "reasonable" nor "enforceable", in violation of 15 U.S.C. §1692e(2)(A) and f(1).

24. Defendant states in the collection letters "OUR STAFF AND CLIENT WILL DETERMINE THE APPROPRIATE

COURSE OF LEGAL ACTION", suggesting that The Premier Collectors, Inc. direct the U.S. Department of Justice to file suit against the consumer in violation of 15 U.S.C. §1692e and f.

25. Defendant states in the collection letters that The Premier Collectors, Inc. will conduct an investigation of the of the consumer's income, savings, employment, real estate ownership and personal assets, in violation of 15 U.S.C. §1692e(4), (5) and (10).

26. Defendant states in the collection letter that a suit by the U.S. Department of Justice may result in garnishment, attachment and/or judgment liens without notifying the consumer of the right to be heard and the necessity of entry of judgement prior to such action in violation of 15 U.S.C. §1692e(4), (5) and (10).

27. Defendant's violated 15 U.S.C. §1692e(1) and (10) by implying that it is "vouched for, bonded by, or affiliated with the United States".

CLASS ALLEGATIONS

28. Ms. Johnson brings this action on behalf of a class of all other persons similarly situated. The class consists of all persons who satisfy the following criteria:

All Louisiana residents who received a notice from Defendant similar to *Exhibit A*, *Exhibit B*, or *Exhibit C*, regarding an alleged debt incurred for personal, family, or household purposes, subsequent to one year prior to the filing of the present litigation.

29. On information and belief, based on the fact that a large number of persons are so contacted by Defendant, the class is sufficiently numerous that joinder of all members is impractical.

30. There are questions of law and fact common to the class, which questions predominate over any questions peculiar to individual class members. The common questions include:

a. Whether Defendant is a "debt collector".

b. Whether Defendant's collection notice fails to provide a proper validation notice and debt collection warning.

c. Whether Defendant's collection notices seek to collect an amount which is not owed.

d. Whether Defendant's collection notices threaten action which is not intended to be taken or cannot legally be taken.

e. Whether Defendant's collection notices falsely represent or imply the seizure, garnishment, attachment or sale of the consumer's property which is not lawful or intended to be taken.

f. Whether Defendant's collection notices falsely represents or implies that it is vouched for, bonded by, or affiliated with the United states.

31. Ms. Johnson has the same claims as the members of the class. All of the claims are based on the same factual and legal theories.

32. Ms. Johnson will fairly and adequately represent the interest of the class members. Ms. Johnson has retained counsel experienced in prosecuting class actions and in consumer protection matters. There is no reason why Ms. Johnson and her counsel will not vigorously pursue this matter.

33. Certification of a class pursuant to Fed.R.Civ.P. 23(b)(3) is appropriate. A class action is the only appropriate means of resolving this controversy because the class members are not aware of their rights. In the absence of a class action, a failure of justice will result.

WHEREFORE, plaintiff Mary Johnson requests that the Court grant the following relief in her favor and on behalf of the class and against Defendant:

A. The maximum amount of statutory damages provided under 15 U.S.C. §1692k.

B. Attorney's fees, litigation expenses and costs.

C. Such other and further relief as is appropriate.

JURY DEMAND

Plaintiff Mary Johnson demands trial by jury.

[Attorney for Plaintiff]

E.3.2 Motion for Class Certification

IN THE UNITED STATES DISTRICT COURT
FOR THE MIDDLE DISTRICT OF LOUISIANA

Mary Johnson, on behalf of herself and all others similarly situated,	))))
Plaintiff,	)
	)
v.	)
	)
The Premier Collectors, Inc.,	)
Defendant.	)

PLAINTIFF'S MOTION FOR CLASS CERTIFICATION

Plaintiff, Mary Johnson ("Ms. Johnson"), respectfully requests that the Court enter an order certifying that this action be allowed to proceed as a class action pursuant to Fed.R.Civ.P. 23. The class is defined as all Louisiana residents who received a notice from defendant, The Premier Collectors, Inc. ("PCI"), similar to *Exhibit A*, *Exhibit B*, or *Exhibit C* [*not reprinted herein*], regarding an alleged debt incurred for personal, family or household purposes, on or after August 2, 1993.

In support of this motion, Ms. Johnson states:

1. Plaintiff filed this class action under the Fair Debt Collection Practices Act, 15 U.S.C §1692 *et seq.* ("FDCPA"). The complaint alleges that defendant PCI engaged in the following violations of the FDCPA:

a. PCI sent printed form collection letters without the "validation notice" required by 15 U.S.C. §1692g(a) or the debt collection warning required by 15 U.S.C. §1692e(11).

b. PCI added to the principal amount of the alleged debt collection fees of "42.84%", which are neither "reasonable" nor "enforceable", in violation of 15 U.S.C. §§1692e(2)(A) and 1692f(1).

c. PCI states in its printed form collection letters "OUR STAFF AND CLIENT WILL DETERMINE THE APPROPRIATE COURSE OF LEGAL ACTION". This suggests to unsophisticated consumers that PCI would direct the Government to file suit against the consumer. The suggestion is unfounded, and therefore making it violates 15 U.S.C. §§1692e and 1692f.

d. PCI states in its form collection letters that PCI will conduct an investigation of the consumer's income, savings, employment, real estate ownership and personal assets. This statement is not true, and making it violates 15 U.S.C. §1692e(4), (5) and (10).

e. PCI states in its form collection letters that nonpayment may result in garnishment, attachment and/or judgment liens. The consumer is not told that such action must be preceded by the right to be heard and the entry of judgment. By misrepresenting the imminence of garnishment, attachment and liens, PCI violates 15 U.S.C. §1692e(4), (5) and (10).

f. PCI violated 15 U.S.C. §1692e(1) and (10) by implying that it is "vouched for, bonded by, or affiliated with the United States".

2. All requirements of Rule 23 of the Federal Rules of Civil Procedure have been met.

3. The class is so numerous that joinder of all members is impractical. PCI is one of the largest collection agencies in the United States, with $800 million in annual placements. *Collection Agency Directory* (First Detroit Corporation), 1994 ed., p. 15 (*Exhibit D*) [*not reprinted herein*]. Furthermore, student loans, which were the subject of the form letters at issue, are one of four collection specialties of PCI. *Id.* It is therefore reasonable to infer that the number of members of the proposed class exceeds the 20-40 required for certification.

4. There are questions of law and fact common to the class, which predominate over any questions affecting only individual class members. The principal questions presented by this action are:

a. Whether PCI is a "debt collector".

b. Whether PCI's form collection notices fail to provide a proper validation notice and debt collection warning.

c. Whether PCI's form collection notices seek to collect an amount which is not owed.

d. Whether PCI's form collection notices threaten action which is not intended to be taken or cannot legally be taken.

e. Whether PCI's form collection notices falsely represent or imply the seizure, garnishment, attachment or sale of the consumer's property, when such action is not lawful or intended to be taken.

f. Whether PCI's form collection notices falsely represent or imply that PCI is vouched for, bonded by, or affiliated with the United States.

5. There are no individual questions, other than whether a class member was subjected to one or more of the practices complained of, which can be determined by ministerial inspection of PCI's records.

6. Ms. Johnson will fairly and adequately protect the interests of the class. She is committed to vigorously litigating this matter.

7. Plaintiff's claim is typical of the claims of the class. All arise from the same operative facts and are based on the same legal theories.

8. A class action is a superior method for the fair and efficient adjudication of this controversy in that:

a. Congress specifically contemplated FDCPA class actions as a principal means of enforcing the statute. 15 U.S.C. §1692k.

b. Most of the consumers who receive the notices undoubtedly believe that they are receiving a letter from the U.S. Department of Justice, and have no knowledge that their rights are being violated by illegal collection practices.

c. The interest of class members in individually controlling the prosecution of separate claims against defendant is small because the maximum damages in an individual action are $1,000.

d. Management of this class action is likely to present significantly fewer difficulties than those presented in many class claims, *e.g.*, for securities fraud.

These grounds are further explained and supported by the accompanying memorandum of law.

WHEREFORE, plaintiff requests that this action be certified as a class action.

[*Attorney for Plaintiff*]

E.3.3 Memorandum in Support of Class Certification

IN THE UNITED STATES DISTRICT COURT
FOR THE MIDDLE DISTRICT OF LOUISIANA

Mary Johnson, on behalf of herself and all others similarly situated,	))))
Plaintiff,	))
v.	))
The Premier Collectors, Inc.,	)
Defendant.	))

MEMORANDUM IN SUPPORT OF PLAINTIFF'S
MOTION FOR CLASS CERTIFICATION

I. NATURE OF THE CASE

Plaintiff filed this class action under the Fair Debt Collection Practices Act, 15 U.S.C. §1692 *et seq.* ("the FDCPA"). The complaint seeks redress for a number of illegal practices of defendants in connection with the collection of debts.

Specifically, the complaint alleges that The Premier Collectors, Inc. ("PCI") engages in the following practices through the use of printed form letters:

a. PCI sent printed form collection letters without the "validation notice" required by 15 U.S.C. §1692g(a) or the debt collection warning required by 15 U.S.C. §1692e(11).

b. PCI added to the principal amount of the alleged debt collection fees of "42.84%", which are neither "reasonable" nor "enforceable", in violation of 15 U.S.C. §§1692e(2)(A) and 1692f(1).

c. PCI states in its printed form collection letters "OUR STAFF AND CLIENT WILL DETERMINE THE APPROPRIATE COURSE OF LEGAL ACTION". This suggests to unsophisticated consumers that PCI would direct the Government to file suit against the consumer. The suggestion is unfounded, and therefore making it violates 15 U.S.C. §§1692e and 1692f.

d. PCI states in its form collection letters that PCI will conduct an investigation of the consumer's income, savings, employment, real estate ownership and personal assets. This statement is not true, and making it violates 15 U.S.C. §1692e(4), (5) and (10).

e. PCI states in its form collection letters that nonpayment may result in garnishment, attachment and/or judgment liens. The consumer is not told that such action must be preceded by the right to be heard and the entry of judgment. By misrepresenting the imminence of garnishment, attachment and liens, PCI violates 15 U.S.C. §1692e(4), (5) and (10).

f. PCI violated 15 U.S.C. §1692e(1) and (10) by implying that it is "vouched for, bonded by, or affiliated with the United States".

II. THE FAIR DEBT COLLECTION PRACTICES ACT

The FDCPA states that its purpose, in part, is "to eliminate abusive debt collection practices by debt collectors", 15 U.S.C. §1692(e). It is designed to protect consumers from unscrupulous collectors, whether or not there is a valid debt. *Baker v. G.C. Services Corp.*, 677 F.2d 775, 777 (9th Cir. 1982). The FDCPA broadly prohibits unfair or unconscionable collection methods; conduct which harasses, oppresses or abuses any debtor; and any false, deceptive or misleading statements, in connection with the collection of a debt. 15 U.S.C. §§1692d, 1692e, and 1692f.

Courts have generally held that whether a communication or other conduct violates the FDCPA is to be determined by analyzing it from the perspective of the "least sophisticated consumer" or "least sophisticated debtor." *Clomon v. Jackson*, 988 F.2d 1314, 1318-20 (2d Cir. 1993); *Graziano v. Harrison*, 950 F.2d 107, 111 (3d Cir. 1991); *Swanson v. Southern Oregon Credit Service, Inc.*, 869 F.2d 1222, 1225-26 (9th Cir. 1988); *Jeter v. Credit Bureau, Inc.*, 760 F.2d 1168 (11th Cir. 1985). "The basic purpose of the least-sophisticated-consumer standard is to ensure that the FDCPA protects all consumers, the gullible as well as the shrewd." *Clomon v. Jackson*, supra at 1318.

The violations alleged in this case include the following:

A. IMPROPER VALIDATION NOTICE

PCI's placement of the §1692g validation notice and §1692e(11) debt collection warning on the back of the collection letters without proper reference thereto on the front is in violation of 15 U.S.C. §§1692g(a) and 1692e(11). Among the decisions holding that similar conduct violates the FDCPA are *Rabideau v. Management Adjustment Bureau*, 805 F.Supp. 1086 (W.D.N.Y. 1992); *Riveria v. MAB Collections, Inc.*, 682 F.Supp. 174 (W.D.N.Y.1988); and *Ost v. Collection Bureau, Inc.*, 493 F.Supp. 701 (D.N.D. 1980).

B. DIRECTING THE COURSE OF LEGAL ACTION

PCI states in the collection letters "OUR STAFF AND CLIENT WILL DETERMINE The APPROPRIATE COURSE OF LEGAL ACTION," suggesting that PCI directs the filing of lawsuits against the consumer. In fact, the U.S. Department of Justice must decide to file suit against the consumer. The false statement that PCI has that authority violates 15 U.S.C. §§1692e and 1692f.

Misrepresenting the imminence of and authority to institute legal action against the consumer is a violation of the FDCPA. *Pipiles v. Credit Bureau of Lockport, Inc.*, 886 F.2d 22 (2d Cir. 1989).

C. INVESTIGATION OF THE CONSUMER'S ASSETS

PCI states in the collection letters that it will conduct an investigation of the consumer's income, savings, employment, real estate ownership and personal assets. It doesn't. The false statement is a violation of 15 U.S.C. §1692e(4), (5) and (10). *Rosa v. Gaynor*, 784 F.Supp. 1, 5 (D.Conn. 1989); *Woolfolk v. Van Ru Credit Corp.*, 783 F.Supp. 724 (D.Conn. 1990); *Cacace v. Lucas*, 775 F.Supp. 502 (D.Conn. 1990).

D. PADDING DEBTS WITH "UNREASONABLE" CHARGES

PCI, in violation of 15 U.S.C. §1692e(2)(A) and f(1), adds collection fees of "42.84%" to the principal amount of the debt. Such fees are neither "reasonable" nor "enforceable". *Jenkins v. Heintz*, 25 F.3d 536 (7th Cir. 1994); *Strange v. Wexler*, 796 F.Supp. 1117 (N.D.Ill. 1992).

E. GARNISHMENT WITHOUT NOTIFICATION OF RIGHTS

PCI states in its collection letters that a suit by the U.S. Department of Justice may result in garnishment, attachment and/or judgment liens, without notifying the consumer of the right to be heard and the necessity of entry of judgment prior to such action. This is a misrepresentation of the consequences of nonpayment, and violates 15 U.S.C. §1692e(4), (5) and (10). *Woolfolk v. Van Ru Credit Corp.*, supra; *Cacace v. Lucas*, supra; *Rosa v. Gaynor*, supra.

F. IMPLYING AFFILIATION WITH THE UNITED STATES

PCI also violated 15 U.S.C. §1692e(1) and (10) by implying that it is "vouched for, bonded by or affiliated with the United States". *Gammon v. GC Services*, 27 F.3d 1254 (7th Cir. 1994).

III. STANDARD FOR CLASS CERTIFICATION

In determining whether a class will be certified, the merits of the case are not examined and the substantive allegations of the complaint should be taken as true, except to the extent that they are contradicted by evidence. *Blackie v. Barrack*, 524 F.2d 891, 901 n. 16 (9th Cir. 1975); *Heastie v. Community Bank of Greater Peoria*, 125 F.R.D. 669, 671 n. 2 (N.D.Ill. 1989); *Riordan v. Smith Barney*, 113 F.R.D. 60, 62 (N.D.Ill. 1986). The Seventh Circuit has said that "Rule 23 must be liberally interpreted" and read to "favor maintenance of class actions". *King v. Kansas City Southern Industries*, 519 F.2d 20, 25-26 (7th Cir. 1975).

Class actions are essential to enforce laws protecting consumers. As the Illinois Appellate Court stated in *Eshaghi v. Hanley Dawson Cadillac Co.*, 214 Ill.App.3d 995, 574 N.E.2d 760 (1st Dist. 1991):

> Even without resort to the relaxed standards of proof envisioned by the Consumer Fraud Act, Illinois has been hospitable to maintenance of class actions and has been willing to recognize that common questions of law and fact predominate in a great many situations. . . . In a large and impersonal society, class actions are often the last barricade of consumer protection. . . . To consumerists, the consumer class action is an inviting procedural device to cope with frauds causing small damages to large groups. The slight loss to

the individual, when aggregated in the coffers of the wrongdoer, results in gains which are both handsome and tempting. The alternatives to the class action — private suits or governmental actions — have been so often found wanting in controlling consumer frauds that not even the ardent critics of class actions seriously contend that they are truly effective. The consumer class action, when brought by those who have no other avenue of legal redress, provides restitution to the injured, and deterrence of the wrongdoer. (574 N.E.2d at 764, 766)

Congress expressly recognized the propriety of a class action under the FDCPA by providing special damage provisions and criteria in 15 U.S.C. §§1692k(a) and (b) for FDCPA class action cases. *Brewer v. Friedman*, 152 F.R.D. 142 (N.D.Ill. 1993); *Zanni v. Lippold*, 119 F.R.D. 32, 35 (C.D.Ill. 1988); *Beasley v. Blatt* 1994 U.S.Dist. LEXIS 9383 (N.D.Ill., July 14, 1994); *West v. Costen*, 558 F.Supp. 564, 572-573 (W.D. Va. 1983) (FDCPA class certified re unauthorized charges). Plaintiff's counsel also were involved in two FDCPA class actions that were settled. *Cramer v. First of America Bank Corp.*, 93 C 3189 (N.D.Ill.) (*Exhibit E*); *Boddie v. Meyer*, 93 C 2975 (N.D.Ill.) (*Exhibit F*).

IV. THE PROPOSED CLASS MEETS THE REQUIREMENTS FOR CERTIFICATION
A. RULE 23(A)(1)— NUMEROSITY

Fed.R.Civ.P. 23(a)(1) requires that the class be "so numerous that joinder of all members is impracticable." "When the class is large, numbers alone are dispositive. . . ." *Riordan v. Smith Barney*, 113 F.R.D. 60, 62 (N.D.Ill. 1986). Where the class numbers at least 40, joinder is usually impracticable. *Cypress v. Newport News General & Nonsectarian Hosp. Ass'n*, 375 F.2d 648, 653 (4th Cir. 1967) (18 sufficient); *Swanson v. American Consumer Industries*, 415 F.2d 1326, 1333 (7th Cir. 1969) (40 sufficient); *Riordan v. Smith Barney, supra*, 113 F.R.D. 60, 62 (N.D.Ill. 1986) (10-29 sufficient); *Blatt v. Beasley, supra* (25 sufficient in FDCPA case); *Sala v. National Railroad Passenger Corp.*, 120 F.R.D. 494, 497 (E.D.Pa. 1988) (40-50 sufficient); *Scholes v. Stone, McGuire & Benjamin*, 143 F.R.D. 181, 184 (N.D.Ill. 1992) (about 70). It is not necessary that the precise number of class members be known. *McCleery Tire Service, Inc. v. Texaco, Inc.*, 1975-2 Trade Cas. (CCH) ¶60,581 (E.D.Pa. 1975). "A class action may proceed upon estimates as to the size of the proposed class." *In re Alcoholic Beverages Litigation*, 95 F.R.D. 321 (E.D.N.Y. 1982); *Lewis v. Gross*, 663 F.Supp. 1164, 1169 (E.D.N.Y. 1986).

Here, it is reasonable to infer that the numerosity requirement is satisfied because the actions complained of were carried out by one of the largest collection agencies in the United States through the use of standard, preprinted form documents. This fact alone indicates that the numerosity requirement is satisfied. *Swiggett v. Watson*, 441 F.Supp. 254, 256 (D.Del. 1977) (in action challenging transfers of title pursuant to Delaware motor vehicle repairer's lien, fact that Department of Motor Vehicles issued printed form for such transfer in and of itself sufficient to show that numerosity was satisfied). Plaintiff has propounded discovery to determine the exact number of class members (*Exhibit G*).

B. RULE 23(A)(2)—COMMONALITY

Fed.R.Civ.P. 23(a)(2) requires that there be a common question of law *or* fact. Not all factual or legal questions raised in the litigation need be common so long as at least one issue is common to all class members. *Spencer v. Central States Pension Fund*, 778 F.Supp. 985, 989 n.2 (N.D.Ill. 1991). Where a question of law involves "standardized conduct of the defendants toward members of the proposed class, a common nucleus of operative facts is typically presented, and the commonality requirement . . . is usually met." *Franklin v. City of Chicago*, 102 F.R.D. 944, 949 (N.D.Ill. 1984); *Patrykus v. Gomilla*, 121 F.R.D. 357, 361 (N.D.Ill. 1988).

There are common questions of law and fact common to the class, which questions predominate over any questions affecting only individual class members. These questions include:

a. Whether PCI is a "debt collector".
b. Whether PCI's collection notice fails to provide a proper validation notice and debt collection warning.
c. Whether PCI's collection notices seek to collect an amount which is not owed.
d. Whether PCI's collection notices threaten action which is not intended to be taken or cannot legally be taken.
e. Whether PCI's collection notices falsely represent or imply the seizure, garnishment, attachment or sale of the consumer's property which is not lawful or intended to be taken.
f. Whether PCI's collection notices falsely represents or implies that it is vouched for, bonded by, or affiliated with the United states.

Each of these questions is concerned solely with the conduct of PCI. The only individual issue is the identification of the class members affected by each practice.

C. RULE 23(A)(3)—TYPICALITY

The rule requires that the claims of the named plaintiff be typical of the claims of the class:

> A plaintiff's claim is typical if it arises from the same event or practice or course of conduct that gives rise to the claims of other class members and his or her claims are based on the same legal theory. The typicality requirement may be satisfied even if there are factual distinctions between the claims of the named plaintiffs and those of other class members. Thus, similarity of legal theory may control even in the face of differences of fact.

De La Fuente v. Stokely-Van Camp, Inc., 713 F.2d 225, 232 (7th Cir. 1983) (citation omitted); *see also, Rosario v. Livaditis*, 963 F.2d 1013, 1018 (7th Cir. 1992).

In the instant case, typicality is inherent in both of the class definitions. By definition, each of the class members was subjected to the same violations as the named plaintiff. All class members' claims arise from the same practices of PCI's which gave rise to the named plaintiff's claims.

D. RULE 23(A)(4)—ADEQUACY OF REPRESENTATION

The rule also requires that the named plaintiff provide fair and adequate protection for the interests of the class. That protection involves two factors: "(a) the plaintiff's attorney must be qualified, experienced, and generally able to conduct the proposed litigation; and (b) the plaintiff must not have interests antagonistic to those of the class." *Rosario v. Livaditis*, 963 F.2d 1013, 1018 (7th Cir. 1992).

The qualifications of plaintiff's counsel are set forth in *Exhibits H and I.* Mr. Bragg is widely experienced in FDCPA litigation and class actions. He is the co-author of National Consumer Law Center, *Fair Debt Collection* (2d ed. 1991 and Supp.). Mr. Ridge has litigated several FDCPA cases in Louisiana.

The second relevant consideration under Rule 23(a)(4) is whether the interests of the named plaintiff are coincident with the general interests of the class. Both Ms. Johnson and the class members seek money damages as the result of PCI's unlawful collection notice. Given the identity of claims between the plaintiff and the class members, there is no potential for conflicting interests in this action. There is no antagonism between the interests of the named plaintiff and those of the class.

E. RULE 23(B)(3)— COMMON QUESTIONS OF LAW OR FACT PREDOMINATE

Rule 23(b)(3) requires that the questions of law or fact common to all members of the class predominate over questions pertaining to individual members. This criterion is normally satisfied when there is an essential common factual link between all class members and the defendants for which the law provides a remedy. *Halverson v. Convenient Food Mart, Inc.*, 69 F.R.D. 331 (N.D.Ill. 1974).

In this case, the "common nucleus of operative fact," *Id.* at 335, is that all class members, by definition, were subjected to the same violations as plaintiff.

Cases dealing with the legality of standardized documents and practices, are generally appropriate for resolution by class action because the document is the focal point of the analysis. *Halverson v. Convenient Food Mart, Inc., supra; Brooks v. Midas-International Corp.*, 47 Ill.App.3d 266, 361 N.E.2d 815 (1st Dist. 1977) (claim that advertising conveyed meaning that exhaust systems would be replaced free of charge); *Spirek v. State Farm Mut. Auto. Ins. Co.*, 65 Ill.App.3d 440, 382 N.E.2d 111 (1st Dist. 1978) (propriety of insurer's practice in requiring execution of subrogation agreements before paying medical benefits); *Haynes v. Logan Furniture Mart, Inc.*, 503 F.2d 1161 (7th Cir. 1974) (propriety of disclosure documents under Truth in Lending Act); *Haroco v. American Nat'l Bk. & Tr. Co.*, 121 F.R.D. 664, 669 (N.D.Ill. 1988) (improper computation of interest); *Kleiner v. First Nat'l Bank of Atlanta*, 97 F.R.D. 683 (N.D.Ga. 1983) (same); *Heastie v. Community Bank of Greater Peoria*, 125 F.R.D. 669 (N.D.Ill. 1989) (execution of home improvement financing documents in sequence that evaded consumers' rescission rights). This is true even though the nature and amount of damages may differ among the members of the class. *Heastie v. Community Bank of Greater Peoria, supra.*

An FDCPA claim challenging the propriety of a form letter is similar to a Truth in Lending disclosure claim, which has frequently been certified as a class actions. *Haynes v. Logan Furniture Mart, Inc.*, 503 F.2d 1161 (7th Cir. 1974); *Adiel v. Chase Fed. S. & L. Ass'n*, 810 F.2d 1051 (11th Cir. 1987); *Hughes v. Cardinal Fed. S. & L. Ass'n*, 566 F.Supp. 834 (S.D.Ohio 1983); *Fetta v. Sears, Roebuck & Co.*, 77 F.R.D. 411 (D.R.I. 1977); *Bantolina v. Aloha Motors, Inc.*, 419 F.Supp. 1116, 1122 (D.Haw. 1976); *Jones*

v. Goodyear Tire & Rubber Co., 442 F.Supp. 1157 (E.D.La. 1977); *Simon v. World Omni Leasing*, 146 F.R.D. 197 (S.D.Ala. 1992); *Johnson v. Steven Sims Suburu Leasing*, 1993 U.S.Dist. LEXIS 8078 (N.D.Ill., June 9, 1993) (Magistrate Judge's recommendation).

FDCPA actions have been certified as class actions on several occasions. *Zanni v. Lippold*, 119 F.R.D. 32, 35 (C.D.Ill.1988); *Brewer v. Friedman*, 152 F.R.D. 142 (N.D.Ill. 1993); *Beasley v. Blatt*, 1994 U.S.Dist. LEXIS 9383 (N.D.Ill., July 14, 1994); *West v. Costen*, 558 F.Supp. 564, 572-73 (W.D.Va.1983).

Because of the standardized nature of the defendant's conduct, common questions predominate. The only individual issue is the identification of the consumers who received the letters, a matter capable of ministerial determination from PCI's records. This is not the kind of problem that is a barrier to class certification. *Heastie v. Community Bank of Greater Peoria*, 125 F.R.D. 669, 678 (N.D.Ill. 1989). The commonality requirement is therefore met.

F. RULE 23(B)(3) — CLASS ACTION IS SUPERIOR TO OTHER AVAILABLE METHODS TO RESOLVE THIS CONTROVERSY.

Efficiency is the primary focus in determining whether the class action is the superior method for resolving the controversy presented. *Eovaldi v. First Nat'l Bank*, 57 F.R.D. 545 (N.D.Ill. 1972). The Court is required to determine the best available method for resolving the controversy in keeping with judicial integrity, convenience, and economy. *Scholes, supra*, 143 F.R.D. at 189; *Hurwitz v. R.B. Jones Corp.*, 76 F.R.D. 149 (W.D. Mo. 1977). It is proper for a court, in deciding the "best" available method, to consider the " . . . inability of the poor or uninformed to enforce their rights, and the improbability that large numbers of class members would possess the initiative to litigate individually." *Haynes v. Logan Furniture Mart, Inc., supra*, 503 F.2d 1161 (7th Cir. 1974).

In this case there is no better method available for the adjudication of the claims which might be brought by each individual debtor subjected to PCI's practice. The special efficacy of the consumer class action has been noted by the courts and is applicable to this case:

> A class action permits a large group of claimants to have their claims adjudicated in a single lawsuit. This is particularly important where, as here, a large number of small and medium sized claimants may be involved. In light of the awesome costs of discovery and trial, many of them would not be able to secure relief if class certification were denied. . . .

In re Folding Carton Antitrust Litigation, 75 F.R.D. 727, 732 (N.D.Ill. 1977) (citations omitted). Class certification of a FDCPA damage action will provide an efficient and appropriate resolution of the controversy. *Zanni v. Lippold, supra*, 119 F.R.D. 32, 35-36 (C.D.Ill. 1988); *West v. Costen, supra*, 558 F.Supp. 564, 572-73 (W.D.Va. 1983); *Beasley v. Blatt, supra*, 1994 U.S. Dist. LEXIS 9383 (N.D.Ill., July 14, 1994); *Brewer v. Friedman*, 152 F.R.D. 142 (N.D.Ill. 1993); *Vaughn v. CSC Credit Services, Inc.*, 1994 U.S. Dist. LEXIS 2172 (N.D.Ill., March 1, 1994); *Duran v. Credit Bureau of Yuma, Inc.*, 93 F.R.D. 607 (D. Ariz. 1982); *Boddie v. Meyer, supra*, 93 C 2975 (N.D.Ill.); and *Cramer v. First of America Bank Corporation, supra*, 93 C 3189 (N.D.Ill.).

CONCLUSION

The proposed class meets the requirements of Rules 23(a) and (b)(3). Plaintiff respectfully requests that the Court certify this action as a class action.

[Attorney for Plaintiff]

E.4 Class Action Complaint Challenging Wage Garnishment Procedures

IN THE UNITED STATES DISTRICT COURT
FOR THE MIDDLE DISTRICT OF FLORIDA
FORT MYERS DIVISION

———————————)	
Pedro Martinez, Individually and)	
on behalf of all others similarly)	
situated,)	
Plaintiff,)	
)	
v.)	
)	
Payco General American)	
Credits, Inc., Great Lakes)	
Higher Education Guaranty)	
Corporation, and Richard W.)	
Riley, Secretary of the United)	
States Department of Education)	
Defendants.)	
———————————)	

SECOND AMENDED COMPLAINT—CLASS ACTION

TO THE HONORABLE JUDGE OF THE COURT:

Plaintiff Pedro Martinez ("Plaintiff" or "Martinez") complains of Payco General American Credits, Inc. ("Payco"), Great Lakes Higher Education Guaranty Corporation ("Great Lakes") [jointly called "Private Defendants"], and Richard W. Riley, Secretary of the United States Department of Education ("Secretary"), by way of a class action, and shows the Court the following:

INTRODUCTION

This is a class action for damages and injunctive relief for the Private Defendants' violations of the federal Fair Debt Collection Practices Act, 15 U.S.C. § 1692 *et seq.* ("FDCPA") and the Florida Consumer Collection Practices Act, Florida Statutes § 559.55 *et seq.* ("Florida Act"). This action also seeks to enjoin violations of 20 U.S.C. § 1095a *et seq.* and to challenge the constitutionality of that statute, along with interpretive regulations issued by the Secretary.

Martinez brings this class action on behalf of himself and on behalf of all other consumers who have been subjected to similar practices, seeking declaratory relief, damages, restitution, and a permanent injunction forcing the Private Defendants to stop their illegal efforts to collect student loans. Martinez seeks limited declaratory and injunctive relief against the Secretary.

Payco is one of the largest collection agencies in the country. Its success is in large part founded on its willingness to violate both state and federal laws regulating the conduct of debt collectors, by engaging in a variety of abusive and deceptive practices. This case is an example of its wrongful practices. This suit seeks damages and injunctive relief against Payco.

Great Lakes serves the dual role of guaranteeing student loans and acting as a collection agency for some of those loans. Under 20 U.S.C. § 1095a *et seq.*, it is authorized to garnish wages under certain circumstances. In violation of the constitutional guarantees of due process of law, it has unlawfully delegated its authority to private collection agencies such as Payco. This suit seeks damages and injunctive relief against Great Lakes.

The Secretary has failed to insure that collections of student loan debts through garnishment meet minimal constitutional due process requirements. The Secretary is sued in his official capacity seeking declaratory and injunctive relief only.

JURISDICTION AND VENUE

Jurisdiction of this Court arises under 15 U.S.C. § 1692k(d) and 28 U.S.C. § 1331. Supplemental jurisdiction exists for the state law claims pursuant to 28 U.S.C. § 1367(a).

Venue is proper in the Middle District of Florida, under 28 U.S.C. § 1391(b), (c) & (e).

PARTIES

Plaintiff Pedro Martinez is a natural person who resides in Naples, Florida. Martinez and each of the other members of the classes are "consumers" as defined in FDCPA and the Florida Act.

Defendant Payco is a for-profit Delaware corporation that regularly does business in this judicial district and elsewhere in this state. Payco regularly collects or attempts to collect debts owed or due or asserted to be owed or due another. Payco is a "debt collector" as defined by FDCPA and the Florida Act. Payco has appeared in this action.

Defendant Great Lakes is a non-profit Wisconsin corporation. Great Lakes is engaged in the practice of guaranteeing and collecting student loans in this judicial district and elsewhere in this state. It regularly collects or attempts to collect debts owed or due or asserted to be owed or due another. Great Lakes is a "debt collector" as defined by FDCPA and the Florida Act. Great Lakes has appeared in this action.

Richard W. Riley, sued in his official capacity as Secretary of the United States Department of Education, has appeared in this action.

CLASS ACTION ALLEGATIONS

Martinez sues on his own behalf and, as class representative, sues on behalf of two classes of people, defined as follows:

Class I

Consumers residing in Florida who have been the victims of the illegal acts of Payco and/or Great Lakes in violation of the Florida Act, as detailed below, beginning four years prior to the date the original Complaint was filed.

Class II

Consumers residing in any of the United States, including Florida, who have been the victims of the illegal acts of the Secretary, Payco and/or Great Lakes in violation of the FDCPA and/or the United States Constitution, as detailed below, beginning one year prior to the date the original Complaint was filed.

Whenever this Complaint simply refers to the "class" or "classes" it includes both Class I and Class II.

Martinez brings this lawsuit as a class action because (1) the classes are so numerous that joinder of all members is impracticable, (2) there are questions of law and fact common to the classes, (3) Martinez's claims are typical of the claims of the classes, and (4) Martinez can and will fairly and adequately protect the interests of the classes. Questions of whether, and to what extent, the Private Defendants engaged in the practices described herein, whether they did so intentionally or knowingly, and whether they thereby violated the law will be common to all members of the classes.

It is appropriate to maintain this lawsuit as a class action for injunctive relief pursuant to Federal Rule of Civil Procedure 23(b)(2) because all defendants acted on grounds generally applicable to the classes, thereby making injunctive and declaratory relief appropriate with respect to each class as a whole.

It is also appropriate to maintain this lawsuit as a class action for damages pursuant to Federal Rule of Civil Procedure 23(b)(3) because questions of law and fact common to the members of the classes predominate over questions affecting only individual members and because a class action is superior to other available methods for the fair and efficient adjudication of the controversy.

Martinez's claims are typical of the claims of both classes as a whole. He can and will fairly and adequately protect the interests of the classes, because he has retained experienced counsel to represent the classes, he has no conflict of interest with the classes, and he brings this lawsuit specifically for the protection of consumers who have been and will be harmed by these practices, and not solely to recover his personal damages. Acts of Agents

Whenever in this Complaint it is alleged that a defendant did any act, it is meant that the defendant performed or participated in the act, or the officers, agents, or employees of the defendant performed or participated in the act on behalf of and under the actual, vicarious, or apparent authority of the defendant.

Conditions Precedent

All conditions precedent to the filing of this case have been performed, have occurred, or have been satisfied.

FACTS

Pedro Martinez accumulated approximately $29,000.00 in several student loans during his seven years of college and law school. In 1988, he consolidated those loans through a federal consolidation program run by the Student Loan Marketing Association ("Sallie Mae") on which Great Lakes was a guarantor. Sallie Mae is a financial services corporation that specializes in funding education. It currently funds approximately 40% of all insured student loans, by purchasing loans from lenders to replenish their funds. Sallie Mae is headquartered in Reston, Virginia, and maintains education loan servicing centers around the country.

After consolidation, Martinez received periodic offers from Sallie Mae to defer his loan for up to six months. In the fall of 1995,

Martinez accepted an offer of deferral in order to finance his upcoming wedding. Sallie Mae told him that no additional documentation was required for this deferment and that he would be notified by mail when to resume payments.

Instead of a notice to resume payments, the next notice Martinez received from anyone relating to his student loan was a notice of default from Great Lakes. When he contacted Great Lakes by telephone to attempt to clear up the misunderstanding, Great Lakes refused to discuss his loan and insisted that he contact Payco.

Martinez telephoned Payco, which advised him that his only option was to enter into a rehabilitation program. Since he was told that this was his only option, Martinez took it.

Payco included in the repayment amount, without Martinez's authorization, approximately $5,000.00 in collection fees. When Martinez tried to contest these fees, he was rebuffed.

In October, 1997, Martinez received a communication ostensibly from Great Lakes, but possibly generated by Payco, styled "NOTICE PRIOR TO WAGE WITHHOLDING," that was "issued" on October 22, 1997 ("Notice"). The Notice represented that Martinez currently owed $35,935.61 and told Martinez that unless he established a new written repayment agreement with Payco on or before November 21, 1997, Martinez's employer would be ordered to begin garnishment of Martinez's wages.

The Notice advised Martinez that he could request a hearing concerning *only* (1) the existence of the debt, (2) the amount of the debt, or (3) the terms of his repayment schedule. Although federal law provides for other bases for cancelling or deferring a debt, the Notice did not advise Martinez of those rights. By stating only these three limited grounds for requesting a hearing, the Notice misrepresented Martinez's rights under the law.

Martinez timely sought a telephone hearing before garnishment, by completing and returning to Payco a form provided with the Notice. In that form, he stated that he wished to be heard regarding the terms of his repayment schedule and that he contested the amount of the debt because of the inclusion of the collection fees.

Despite the fact that Martinez timely sought a pre-garnishment hearing, Payco sent Martinez a letter dated December 16, 1997, which "denied" Martinez's request for a hearing without explanation and further represented to Martinez that nonpayment of the alleged debt would result in an "Administrative Wage Garnishment" without further opportunity for a hearing unless he made other arrangements. This letter stated that the amount of the debt was now $36,326.48 and was going up daily. This amount included $4,981.24, which the letter represented was *required* by federal regulation. This representation is false.

This letter did not advise Martinez of his rights pursuant to FDCPA § 1692g to dispute the debt and receive verification of the debt. On information and belief, Martinez never received the notice advising him of those rights.

On or about January 20, 1998, Payco issued an "ORDER OF WITHHOLDING FROM EARNINGS" ("Order") and served it on Martinez's employer. The Order directed the employer to garnish Martinez's wages and to send the money direct to Payco.

Martinez's employer began withholding his wages in the amount of $110.00 per week in February 1998, pursuant to the garnishment Order. The weekly garnishment continues to this day.

The Order deceptively advises the employer to withhold "10% of debtor's disposable pay" or an amount permitted by 15 U.S.C. § 1673. This method of withholding conflicts with federal law, and will result in overwithholding in many instances. Congress enacted limitations on wage garnishment, providing that the maximum amount of disposable earnings "subjected to garnishment may not exceed . . . (2) the amount by which his disposable earnings for that week exceed thirty times the Federal minimum hourly wage prescribed by section 206(a)(1) of Title 29 in effect at the time the earnings are payable . . . ." 15 U.S.C. § 1673. The effect of this law is to reduce the permissible amount withheld below the 10% required by Payco, for many debtors. For example, although 10% of Martinez's weekly disposable pay (and the amount currently being withheld weekly pursuant to the Garnishment Order) is $110.00, which is within the limits of 29 U.S.C. § 206, on information and belief many other members of the classes will have excessive amounts of their earnings subject to garnishment.

The practices of Payco and Great Lakes violated the the the due process guarantees of the United States Constitution; the protections against wrongful garnishment provided by the Higher Education Act of 1965, 20 U.S.C. 1095a; various provisions of the Fair Debt Collection Practices Act, 15 USC 1692 *et seq.*; and various provisions of the Florida Consumer Collection Practices Act, Florida Statutes § 559.55 *et seq.* By enactment of policies that encourage and permit these practices, the Secretary has exceeded his lawful authority and has contributed to the denial of due process.

On information and belief, the practices of Payco and Great Lakes in collecting Martinez's debt are typical of their student loan garnishment practices in general.

FIRST CAUSE OF ACTION

Request For Relief Pursuant To Florida Consumer Collection Practices Act

By the actions set forth above, Payco and Great Lakes violated the Florida Act Section 559.72(9), which was the proximate or producing cause of damages to Martinez and the other members of Class I.

As a result of the above violations of the Florida Act, Payco and Great Lakes are liable to Martinez for his actual damages, statutory damages, and costs and reasonable attorneys' fees.

On behalf of himself and of each Class I member, Martinez seeks statutory damages of $500.00 for each violation of the Florida Act by Payco and Great Lakes.

On behalf of himself and of each Class I member, Martinez seeks orders, for which he hereby prays, enjoining future violations of the Florida Act by Payco and Great Lakes.

SECOND CAUSE OF ACTION

Request For Relief Pursuant To FDCPA

By the actions set forth above, Payco and Great Lakes violated the FDCPA, which was the proximate or producing cause of damages to Martinez and the other Class II members. These violations include, but are not limited to:

a. Violating FDCPA Section 1692(e)(2) by falsely representing the character, amount or legal status of a debt or the compensation which may be lawfully received by the debt collector.

b. Violating FDCPA Section 1692e(4) by the representation or implication that nonpayment of a debt will result in the gar-

nishment of wages when such action is not lawful or the debt collector does not intend to take such action.

c. Violating FDCPA Section 1692e(5) by threatening to take action that cannot legally be taken or that is not intended to be taken.

d. Violating FDCPA Section 1692e(10) by using false representations and deceptive means to collect and to attempt to collect a debt or to obtain information concerning a consumer.

e. Violating FDCPA Section 1692e(11) by failing to disclose clearly in the initial communication made to collect a debt or to obtain information about a consumer that the debt collector is attempting to collect a debt and that any information will be used for that purpose.

f. Violating FDCPA Section 1692f(1) by collecting amounts that are not expressly authorized by the agreement creating the debt or permitted by law.

g. Violating FDCPA Section 1692g by failing to give the notices and to take the actions required by that Section.

h. Violating FDCPA Section 1692i by bringing legal action (including a garnishment) on a debt in a judicial district or similar legal entity that is neither the one in which the consumer signed the contract sued upon or in which the consumer resides at the time of commencement of the action.

As a result of the above violations of the FDCPA, Payco and Great Lakes are liable to Martinez for his actual damages, statutory damages, and costs and reasonable attorneys' fees.

On behalf of himself and of each Class II member, Martinez seeks an order of the Court directing Payco and Great Lakes to restore to him and all other Class II members all money obtained by Payco or Great Lakes through garnishment or the threat of garnishment.

In addition, Martinez seeks on behalf of all other Class II members, without regard to minimum individual recovery, an award in the amount of the lesser of $500,000.00 or 1% of the separate net worths of Payco and Great Lakes.

SUMMARY OF RELIEF SOUGHT

Martinez individually seeks to recover his actual damages sustained as the result of Private Defendants' illegal acts, as well as statutory civil penalties, for which he hereby prays. Martinez also seeks equitable relief.

On behalf of himself and the class members, Martinez seeks statutory damages, restitution, and equitable relief from the Private Defendants.

On behalf of himself and the class members, Martinez seeks a declaratory judgment from this Court pursuant to 28 U.S.C. §§ 2201 & 2202, declaring that, as to Payco: (1) Payco regularly engages in the practices described herein, and (2) Payco's practices violate the FDCPA and the Florida Act.

On behalf of himself and the class members, Martinez seeks a declaratory judgment from this Court pursuant to 28 U.S.C. §§ 2201 and 2202, declaring that, as to Great Lakes, (1) Great Lakes regularly engages in the practices described herein; (2) Great Lakes' practices violate the FDCPA and the Florida Act, and (3) Great Lakes unlawfully delegated its administrative wage garnishment authority and violated 20 U.S.C. § 1095a *et seq.*, thereby violating the Fifth Amendment's requirement of due process of law.

On behalf of himself and the class members, Martinez seeks a declaratory judgment from this Court pursuant to 28 U.S.C. §§ 2201 and 2202, declaring that the federal statute codified at 20 U.S.C. § 1095a *et seq.* is unconstitutional on its face and as applied under the circumstances of this case, because it violates procedural due process requirements of the Fifth Amendment.

On behalf of himself and the class members, Martinez seeks an injunction directing the Secretary to retract all policies and procedures that fail to meet the procedural due process requirements of the Fifth Amendment and to refrain in the future from conduct that encourages or permits violations of the law by Payco, Great Lakes, or any other debt collector or guaranty agency.

Martinez seeks attorneys' fees for himself and the classes that are reasonable in relation to the amount of work expended, and his costs.

PRAYER

THEREFORE, plaintiff respectfully prays that this Court:

a. Upon notice and hearing, but at the earliest possible date, certify this action as a class action.

b. Upon final trial of this cause, enter a Declaratory Judgment declaring that the practices complained of herein are illegal and a Permanent Injunction as sought herein.

c. Upon final trial of this cause, award plaintiff and the members of the classes judgment for their damages and statutory civil penalties as set forth herein. Plaintiff further prays that these damages be multiplied pursuant to the provisions of the law.

d. Award punitive damages in an amount necessary to punish the Private Defendants for their conduct, in amount not less than $1,000,000.00.

e. Award plaintiff and the class attorneys' fees and costs of court.

f. Award pre-judgment and post-judgment interest at the maximum rate permitted at law or at equity.

g. Grant plaintiff and the classes all other relief to which they may show themselves and the classes entitled.

DEMAND FOR JURY TRIAL

Please take notice that Plaintiff demands trial by jury in this action for all claims against the Private Defendants, but not as to the claims against the Secretary.

Respectfully submitted,

[Attorney for Plaintiff]

E.5 Cases Challenging Trade School Abuses

E.5.1 Individual Student's State Court Complaint Against School

COURT OF COMMON PLEAS
PHILADELPHIA COUNTY

SARAH WILLIAMS	)
	)
v.	)
	)
NATIONAL SCHOOL OF	)
HEALTH TECHNOLOGY,	)
INC.	)

COMPLAINT

1. This is a damage action against a for-profit trade school by a former student of the school for breach of contract, for misrepresentation, conversion and fraud, as well as for treble damages and other appropriate relief under the Pennsylvania Unfair Trade Practices and Consumer Protection Law, 73 P.S. § 201-9.2.

2. Plaintiff Sarah Williams is a 44-year old individual who resides at [*Address*] but who is preparing to move to [*Address*]. She has an 11th-grade education and for several days in 1989 was a student at National Health Technology, Inc.

3. Defendant National Health Technology, Inc. (hereinafter "NSHT") is a corporation doing business at 801 Arch Street, Philadelphia, PA as a trade school licensed by the Pennsylvania Board of Private Licensed Schools to conduct vocational training courses in a variety of medical fields.

4. During the early part of 1989 defendant advertised its on television in the Philadelphia area, including in such advertising representations (a) linking completion of defendant's course with eventual employment in the medical industry and (b) the availability of government grants and loans to pay for the course.

5. Plaintiff, who had some prior work history as a nurse's aide and who was interested in obtaining a state certification to enable her to return to that line of work, saw the said commercial. Because her prior employment as a nurse's aide was at or near the minimum wage, she was particularly swayed by the impression communicated in the ad that those graduating from defendant's program were earning wages significantly greater than the minimum wage.

6. Plaintiff called the telephone number listed in the said television ad and, as a result of her call, was contacted by a representative of NSHT and was given an appointment to visit the school. At that initial meeting with defendant's sales representative, she informed him of her interest to return to work as a nurse's aide. He represented to her, among other things,

a. that completion of the course would entitle her to jobs earning in excess of $9.00/hour;

b. that she would gain such employment through the placement assistance offered to graduates as part of the service offered by NSHT and,

c. that, due to the professional reputation of NSHT, a graduation certificate from NSHT would provide plaintiff with enhanced job opportunities.

7. The salesman gave her an admissions test, which she failed, and invited her to return in several days to retake the same test. Plaintiff could not complete a substantial portion of the test, especially the part that involved mathematics. Nonetheless, on her second attempt plaintiff was told that she had passed the test with a nearly a perfect score and could enroll in the school.

8. On or about February 4, 1989 plaintiff entered into an enrollment agreement with defendant for enrollment in a twenty-six (26) week program, divided into two thirteen (13) week terms. A copy of the enrollment agreement is attached hereto as Exhibit A.

9. The enrollment agreement provided for a total cost to plaintiff of $3,228.35, payable entirely from a federal grant and from a guaranteed student loan. Thus, the total cost for each of the two terms was approximately $1,614. Defendant arranged for the entire financial aid package.

10. During the orientation session plaintiff attended during the first week of classes, the employees conducting the session repeatedly represented to the students that a good performance in the course would enable a graduate to obtain employment far in excess of the minimum wage. There were, in addition, repeated references to the placement services provided to students upon graduation.

11. Plaintiff attended classes for only one full week. Having not attended academic classes for approximately 25 years, she had considerable difficulty with the material covered. Prior to beginning her classes at the beginning of the second week, she was summoned to meet with an executive committee of the school which informed her that, due to her unacceptable academic performance, she would have to withdraw from her class and would have to repeat the first week with the next group of students.

12. Plaintiff returned to defendant's school several weeks later and repeated the first two days of the course. During the second day she was called from the school to deal with an emergency in her home and she did not resume attendance. On the third day of her absence she was told by defendant not to return.

13. Concerned about her loan and grants—checks from which defendant had already had her endorse—plaintiff contacted the school and was assured that she would incur no financial liability under the enrollment agreement. Several months later, after she began receiving a bank bill for a student loan obligation, she contacted the school again and this time was informed that she was responsible for the loan.

14. Plaintiff believes and therefore avers that defendant received grant and loan proceeds on plaintiff's behalf in an amount equal to or in excess of the $3,228 total cost referred to in paragraph 7, *supra*. She is currently being dunned for a student loan debt of $2,700 arising out of her brief enrollment in defendant's school. She does not know how much defendant retained in government grants received on her behalf.

15. Under the enrollment agreement and under state law, *see* 22 Pa. Code § 73.134, defendant was required to refund to plaintiff at least 75% of the first term's portion of the tuition and lab fees. Defendant was entitled to retain at most (a) the remaining 25%, or $375, plus (b) an enrollment fee of $150, for a total of $525. Moreover, as to this maximum allowable retention, the agreement provides that in the event a student is subject to "circumstances that make it impractical for the student to complete the program,

the shall make a settlement that is reasonable and fair to the student."

16. Despite plaintiff's demand, defendant has refused to refund her anything and has, on the contrary, retained all monies received on her behalf.

17. Contrary to the representations made by defendant,

a. most students enrolling in defendant's program do not obtain employment as nurse's aides nor in other related fields;

b. those that do find employment as nurse's aides earn wages at or near the minimum wage;

c. defendant offers little, if any, placement assistance and

d. a graduation certificate issued by defendant provides job applicants with little, if any, enhancement in job opportunities.

18. Contrary to the representations made by defendant to plaintiff, defendant does not provide a legitimate and useful educational service to students who are unskilled and who lack a high school diploma or its equivalent. For such students, the "school" is little more than a business stratagem to obtain student grant and loan proceeds by inducing low-income, unemployed and unskilled individuals to sign enrollment agreements like the one signed by plaintiff.

19. Defendant lures prospective students with express and implied promises of future employment at levels significantly above those they are living at (a) with little or no concern for the academic skills of the prospective students and through the use of meaningless and deceptive admissions standards; (b) with minimal contacts and/or credibility among relevant employers and with insignificant success in placing graduates in relevant work and (c) with the knowledge that relevant wage levels for nurse's aides (or equivalent positions) are at or near the minimum wage and that those lucky enough to find work in this field will be unlikely to have the ability to afford the student loan debt they have incurred.

Count I
(Contract)

20. All previous allegations are realleged and are incorporated by this reference.

21. By retaining all funds received on plaintiff's behalf, defendant has breached the enrollment agreement including, but not limited to,

a. the terms at page 2, paragraphs C(1) and (2), which required defendant to return all but 25% of one term's portion of tuition and lab fees;

b. the terms at page 2, paragraph C(3), which required defendant to "make a settlement that is reasonable and fair to the student" and

c. the terms at page 3 which required defendant to refund the money within thirty (30) days of plaintiff's separation from the school.

22. Plaintiff is entitled to recover an amount equal to all funds obtained by defendant on her behalf, less the $150 enrollment fee, plus interest.

Count II
(Unfair or Deceptive Acts or Practices)

23. All previous allegations are realleged and are incorporated by this reference.

24. Defendant's conduct constituted unfair or deceptive acts or practices within the meaning of the Pennsylvania Unfair and Deceptive Practices and Consumer Protection Law, 73 P.S. § 201-1 et seq. including, but not limited to, the following:

  a. Making misleading and deceptive representations as to the efficacy of its training course, as to the economic value of an NSHT certificate, as to the school's professional reputation in the community and as to endorsements from former students and from employers;

  b. Making misleading and deceptive representations concerning the nature and extent of employment placement assistance offered to graduates and of defendant's success rate in this regard;

  c. Making misleading and deceptive representations concerning the wage levels which course graduates are likely to earn;

  d. Failing to endeavor to establish the qualifications which a prospective student should have in order to assimilate successfully the subject matter of the course, failing to inform prospective students of such qualifications and enrolling prospective students whether or not they are so qualified;

  e. Employing unfair, misleading and deceptive admissions tests and procedures which are designed to encourage prospective students to sign enrollment agreements regardless of their academic abilities and regardless of other factors relevant to success in defendant's course;

  f. Employing unfair, misleading, deceptive and fraudulent representations and practices regarding the prices charged students for tuition, books, lab fees and other charges and regarding the total ultimate cost to the student;

  g. Failing to supply prospective students with written, detailed and accurate disclosures concerning

    1. defendant's policy and regulations relative to make-up work and to delinquency in meeting course requirements,

    2. the standards required of the student for achieving satisfactory progress, including class attendance,

    3. the extent, nature and success rate of defendant's placement service and

    4. other materials facts concerning the school and the program of instruction which are reasonably likely to affect the decision of the student to enroll therein;

  h. Utilizing stricter academic and other standards after NSHT has received the proceeds of a student's financial aid package than it does before receiving them;

  i. Failing to provide academic remediation to those students who are admitted despite failing to meet industry-accepted admissions requirements and

  j. Failing to make prompt and accurate refunds to students who withdraw or who are terminated in accordance with defendant's contractual and regulatory obligations.

25. Plaintiff is entitled to damages equalling three times her economic loss, plus "other appropriate relief," 73 P.S. § 201-9.2, including attorney's fees.

Count III
(Misrepresentation, Fraud and Conversion)

26. All previous allegations are realleged and are incorporated by this reference.

27. Defendant having obtained plaintiff's grants and loan proceeds through knowingly false pretenses and representations upon which plaintiff relied, and having retained said funds without legal right despite her demand, defendant has committed the intentional torts of misrepresentation and conversion.

28. In addition to the lost tuition and lab fees, plaintiff incurred additional economic loss as a result of defendant's conduct, including, but not limited to the following:

  a. The enrollment fee;

  b. Book costs and

  c. Uniform costs.

29. In addition to said economic loss defendant caused plaintiff to suffer severe humiliation and emotional distress.

30. Plaintiff is entitled to compensatory and punitive damages. WHEREFORE, plaintiff seeks the following relief:

  a. Compensatory, treble and punitive damages not in excess of $20,000 and

  b. A reasonable attorney's fee to her attorney.

[Attorney for Plaintiff]

E.5.2 Class Actions

E.5.2.1 Class Action Complaint Against Department of Education

UNITED STATES DISTRICT COURT
EASTERN DISTRICT OF PENNSYLVANIA

HOMER SIMPSON,
MONTGOMERY BURNS,
PATTY BOUVIER and
WAYLON SMITHERS, on
behalf of themselves and all
others similarly situated,
　　　　　Plaintiffs,

v.

MOE SZYSLAK, Secretary,
United States Department of
Education,
　　　　　Defendant.

AMENDED COMPLAINT—CLASS ACTION

PRELIMINARY STATEMENT

1. Plaintiffs Homer Simpson, Montgomery Burns, Patty Bouvier and Waylon Smithers bring this class action on behalf of several classes of student loan borrowers who were victimized by a fraudulent truck-driving-by-correspondence school and who have been wrongfully denied relief mandated by federal law. Congress expressly mandated that the Secretary of Education "shall discharge" the loan obligations of all borrowers whose eligibility for financial aid was "falsely certified" by schools participating in the financial aid system. 20 U.S.C. § 1087(c). Plaintiffs are eligible for a false certification discharge because, among other things, Andover falsely certified their "ability to benefit" from the particular course of study. Plaintiffs seek declaratory and injunctive relief to

enforce the said statutory mandate, including, a reversal of the Secretary's denial of their applications for loan discharges, notification to class members that may be entitled to discharges and an order remedying his inaction on applications already submitted but not acted upon.

JURISDICTION AND VENUE

2. This court has jurisdiction under 28 U.S.C. § 1331 (federal question) and 20 U.S.C. § 1082 (suits against Secretary of Education). Venue is proper because a) this is a civil action in which the defendant is an officer of the United States, b) a substantial part of the events or omissions giving rise to the claims occurred in this judicial district and c) the plaintiffs reside in this district. 28 U.S.C. § 1391(e).

PARTIES

3. Plaintiff Homer Simpson is an individual residing at [Address]. He currently owes a student loan obligation that purportedly was used to pay the costs for participating in a commercial truck driving program run by a now-defunct trade school known as Andover Tractor Trailer School (hereinafter "Andover"). He never attended the school or participated in any such studies.

4. Plaintiff Montgomery Burns is an individual residing at [Address]. He currently owes a student loan obligation that purportedly was used to pay the costs for participating in a commercial truck driving program run by Andover. He never attended the school or participated in any such studies.

5. Plaintiff Patty Bouvier is an individual residing at [Address]. She currently owes a student loan obligation that purportedly was used to pay the costs for participating in a commercial truck driving program run by Andover. She never attended the school or participated in any such studies.

6. Plaintiff Waylon Smithers is an individual residing at [Address]. He currently owes a student loan obligation that purportedly was used to pay the costs for participating in a commercial truck driving program run by Andover. He never attended the school or participated in any such studies.

7. Defendant Moe Szyslak, the Secretary of the United States Department of Education (hereinafter "the Secretary"), is responsible as the chief executive of the Department of Education (hereinafter "the Department") for the administration of the student financial aid programs established by Title IV of the Higher Education Act, 20 U.S.C. § 1070 *et seq.*, including the Federal Family Education Loan ("FFEL") program (formerly "Guaranteed Student Loan Program," or "GSL"). Among other things, he and his predecessors were responsible for, among other things, approving and monitoring the Title IV eligibility of the so-called "school" that perpetrated the underlying fraud, for enforcing the eligibility requirements for student borrowers, and for administering the loan discharge program enacted by Congress for the purpose of extending relief to FFEL borrowers victimized by fraudulent schools.

CLASS ACTION ALLEGATIONS

8. Plaintiffs bring this action on behalf of the following four classes of similarly situated individuals:

a. *Class A*: All individuals who incurred FFEL obligations to attend Andover Tractor Trailer School and who did not, at the time of their enrollment, have a high school or high school equivalency diploma;

b. *Class B*: All individuals who incurred FFEL obligations to attend Andover Tractor Trailer School and who did not, at the time of their enrollment, have a valid driver's license;

c. *Class C*: All student loan borrowers who incurred FFEL obligations to attend correspondence courses accredited by the National Home Study Council (now known as the Distance Education and Training Council) and who did not, at the time of their enrollment, have a high school or high school equivalency diploma;

d. *Class D*: All FFEL borrowers who have submitted applications for false certification loan discharges or requests for review of denials of such applications to the United States Department of Education and who have not obtained a decision from the Department within ninety (90) days of such submission.

9. As to each of the above-specified classes, and for the reasons set forth below:

a. The class is so numerous that joinder is impracticable. Plaintiffs believe there are thousands of individuals in Classes A and B and tens of thousands of individuals in Classes C and D.

b. There are questions of law and fact common to the class, as more fully set forth below.

c. The claims of the named plaintiffs are typical of the claims of the class in that they all carry student loan obligations purportedly the result of attending the bogus truck driving program at Andover. Two of them (Simpson and Smithers) did not have high school credentials at the time they were admitted; all four were not licensed drivers; three (Simpson, Bouvier and Burns) were denied false certification discharges by the U.S. Department of Education and one of them (Smithers) filed an application for such a discharge but never got a decision rendered on the application.

d. Plaintiffs will fairly and adequately assert and protect the interests of the class, in that:

i. The attorney for Plaintiffs is an experienced litigator, an expert in the federal student loan program and has successfully managed consumer class actions before;

ii. Neither plaintiff nor counsel have any conflict of interest in the maintenance of the class action

iii. Plaintiffs and their counsel have adequate financial resources available to ensure competent and aggressive representation of the class, namely the resources of Community Legal Services, Inc., a well-established, public-interest legal services organization with an annual operating budget of approximately $5.5 million.

FACTUAL ALLEGATIONS OF THE NAMED PLAINTIFFS

Homer Simpson

10. Sometime during the summer of 1989, Plaintiff Homer Simpson, who was at the time homeless and addicted to drugs, signed what he now believes were enrollment and financial aid documents and course test sheets for a combined correspondence and resident commercial truck driving program supposedly being

offered by a Massachusetts trade school named Andover Tractor Trailer School ("Andover"). He received $35 from an Andover recruiter in return for his signatures.

11. Mr. Simpson did not have a high school or GED diploma at the time he signed the various papers at the Andover recruiting office. His formal schooling ended during the tenth grade. He also did not have a driver's license at the time so could not have legally participated in a truck driving course.

12. Plaintiff assumes and therefore avers that Andover received proceeds from a FFEL loan made on his behalf, despite the fact that he never attended Andover and never participated in any home study program.

13. Andover falsely certified Mr. Simpson's eligibility for the student loans based on his "ability to benefit" from a postsecondary course in commercial truck driving. Among the reasons this certification was false was that it implied his having passed a valid admission test or having completed a remedial course, federal requirements for obtaining financial aid on behalf of a student who does not have a high school or equivalency diploma. He was not administered a test and did not complete any remedial course. In addition, the enrollment ignored the fact that he was not a licensed driver and, therefore, could not legally get behind the wheel of a truck.

14. Andover also falsely certified on the guaranteed student loan application that Mr. Simpson was in attendance at the school and was making satisfactory progress in his studies. This certification is a material part of the certification process since it is an eligibility requirement under Title IV that the student borrower be in attendance at a school and that he be making satisfactory progress. 20 U.S.C. § 1091(a)(2).

15. Years later, after he had recovered and was gainfully employed, Mr. Simpson began receiving student loan collection notices from a FFEL guaranty agency, American Student Assistance ("ASA") and, in 1995, $2,284 owed to him for a tax refund was taken and applied to the student loan obligation.

16. On March 3, 1995, Mr. Simpson submitted a sworn statement requesting a discharge of the student loan to ASA under 11 U.S.C. § 1087(c).

17. While his application was pending before ASA, Mr. Simpson also began a correspondence with the Department regarding his request for discharge. In particular, on November 6, 1995, he wrote to the official designated by the Secretary to accept requests for "group discharges" requesting that she consider granting a false certification discharge to all student loan borrowers whose loans originated from Andover's fraudulent Philadelphia recruiting office.

18. On March 11, 1996, after receiving no response from ASA and then, after learning that ASA could not locate his request for discharge, Mr. Simpson submitted the request again, this time on a form supplied by ASA. He asserted four separate grounds for discharge: 1) the absence of an ability-to-benefit admissions test; 2) his lack of a driver's license; 3) the school's false certification of his enrollment status; and 4) likely forgery of the loan proceeds check.

19. On March 21, 1996 ASA advised Mr. Simpson that his loan had been assigned to the Defendant Secretary and that the request for discharge had also been referred to the Secretary.

20. In the months that followed, Mr. Simpson contacted the Department various times in order to try to get some action on the pending discharge request. As part of one of these contacts, he submitted proof on August 1, 1996 that Andover's accrediting agency, the National Home Study Council ("NHSC"), required its accredited schools to obtain advance approval of admissions tests or remedial programs they intended to use to admit students without high school credentials, and that Andover had never obtained such approval. He also followed up on the earlier request for group discharge, submitting in October and November 1996 investigative material from the criminal investigation surrounding Andover, audits and reviews by ASA and additional declarations of other student loan borrowers who also had incurred their obligations under circumstances similar to those described by Mr. Simpson.

21. On or about May 20, 1997, in response to the materials submitted by Mr. Simpson, the Secretary notified him that he had indeed proved that Andover had engaged in "serious and well-documented violations" of the Department's "ability-to-benefit" regulations, but, for reasons not stated, the Secretary also concluded that these violations occurred only during the time period June 1, 1986 to April 30, 1989.

22. On or about October 22, 1997, the Secretary issued a decision that Mr. Simpson is not eligible for a false certification discharge and that he is responsible for paying any outstanding balance on the loan. The Secretary's stated reason for denying the discharge request was that the loan was issued in July 1989, i.e., after the April 30, 1989 cut-off referred to in the May 20, 1997 letter, and that, in the absence of any official reports or audits pertaining to activities after such date, "[i]t is reasonable to conclude that . . . the school met the ability to benefit requirements for the enrollment period in question." The decision made no mention of the evidence submitted showing that Andover's accrediting agency had failed to approve any ability-to-benefit admissions by Andover.

23. In addition, the Secretary stated that lack of a driver's license was not a relevant "ability to benefit" factor. He made no decision on the additional false certification claims based on the false certification of his enrollment status or on the likely forgery of the check. (A copy of the October 22, 1997 decision letter is attached hereto as Exhibit A. [*not reprinted herein*])

24. In the October 22, 1997 decision, the Secretary invited Mr. Simpson to contest the decision by submitting corroboration in the form of "statements made by other students who attended the school that are both sufficiently detailed and consistent with each other to appear reliable."

25. On August 18, 1998 Mr. Simpson submitted to the Secretary nine separate statements by individuals who were victimized during the summer of 1989 by the fraudulent recruiting office operated by Andover in North Philadelphia during that period.

26. The Secretary's adverse decision has caused and will continue to cause substantial harm to Mr. Simpson. He had his income tax refunds seized and is threatened by seizure of future refunds and earned income tax credits. In addition, because of his default he has adverse credit history barring him access to credit and is ineligible for further financial aid to pursue legitimate education or job training.

Montgomery Burns

27. Like Mr. Simpson, Plaintiff Burns was, during 1989, a homeless addict and he, too, was induced by the same fraudulent

recruiting operation to sign papers pertaining to an enrollment into Andover's commercial truck driving program. He was paid $25 to sign the papers.

28. At the time, he did have a high school diploma. However, he did not have a driver's license.

29. Mr. Burns assumes and therefore avers that Andover received proceeds from a FFEL loan made on his behalf, despite the fact that he never attended Andover and never participated in any home study program.

30. Andover falsely certified Mr. Burns's eligibility for the student loans based on his "ability to benefit" from a postsecondary course in commercial truck driving in that it ignored the fact that he was not a licensed driver and therefore could not legally get behind the wheel of a truck.

31. Andover also falsely certified on the guaranteed student loan application that Mr. Burns was in attendance at the school and was making satisfactory progress in his studies. This certification is a material part of the certification process since it is an eligibility requirement under Title IV that the student borrower be in attendance at a school and that he be making satisfactory progress. 20 U.S.C. § 1091(a)(2).

32. Mr. Burns is now recovered and is being dunned by ASA on a account of student loan obligation. He is also now gainfully employed and, therefore, faces the prospect of wage garnishments and tax refund intercepts to enforce that obligation.

33. On December 20, 1996, Mr. Burns submitted a sworn statement to ASA, requesting a discharge of the student loan under 11 U.S.C. § 1087(c).

34. On January 21, 1997 ASA denied the loan discharge request on the grounds that, according to the Secretary, a false certification discharge application could not be based solely on the absence of a driver's license. (A copy of that decision is attached hereto as Exhibit B [*not reprinted herein*].)

35. On January 27, 1997 Mr. Burns submitted a request for review of ASA's decision to the Secretary.

36. On May 23, 1997 the Secretary issued a written decision, denying Mr. Burns' request for a loan discharge, on the grounds that the lacking of a valid driver's license could not be the basis for a false certification discharge. While acknowledging that a borrower would be eligible for a false certification discharge if he "would not meet the requirements for employment . . . in the occupation for which the training program supported by the loan was intended because of a physical or mental condition, age, or criminal record *or other reason accepted by the Secretary*," 34 C.F.R. § 682.402(e)(13)(iii)(B) (emphasis added), the Secretary decided that not having a driver's license before enrolling in a commercial truck driving course was not an acceptable reason. (A copy of the May 23, 1997 decision is attached hereto [*not reprinted herein*].)

37. The Secretary's adverse decision has caused and will continue to cause substantial harm to Mr. Burns. He faces the threat of wage garnishments and tax refund intercepts and, because of his default, has an adverse credit history that bars him access to credit and renders him ineligible for further financial aid to pursue legitimate education or job training.

Patty Bouvier

38. Like Mr. Simpson, Plaintiff Bouvier was, during 1989, a homeless addict and she, too, was induced by the same fraudulent

recruiting operation to sign papers pertaining to an enrollment into Andover's commercial truck driving program. She was paid $25 to sign the papers.

39. At the time, she did have a high school diploma. However, she did not have a driver's license.

40. Ms. Bouvier assumes and therefore avers that Andover received proceeds from a FFEL loan made on her behalf, despite the fact that she never attended Andover and never participated in any home study program.

41. Andover falsely certified Ms. Bouvier's eligibility for the student loans based on her "ability to benefit" from a postsecondary course in commercial truck driving in that it ignored the fact that she was not a licensed driver and therefore could not legally get behind the wheel of a truck.

42. Andover also falsely certified on the guaranteed student loan application that Ms. Bouvier was in attendance at the school and was making satisfactory progress in her studies. This certification is a material part of the certification process since it is an eligibility requirement under Title IV that the student borrower be in attendance at a school and that she be making satisfactory progress. 20 U.S.C. § 1091(a)(2).

43. Years later, after she had recovered and was gainfully employed, Ms. Bouvier began receiving student loan collection notices from a student loan guaranty agency, American Student Assistance ("ASA") and, in 1996 her tax refunds began getting seized and being applied to the student loan obligation. Over the last three years, she estimates that at least $5,000 has been paid on account of this loan obligation from tax refunds owing to her. She believes that a balance still exists on the loan obligation and that, therefore, she continues to face seizure of future tax refunds.

44. On March 26, 1997, Ms. Bouvier submitted a sworn statement to ASA, requesting a discharge of the student loan under 11 U.S.C. § 1087(c).

45. On September 11, 1997 ASA denied the loan discharge request on the grounds that, according to the Secretary, a false certification discharge application could not be based solely on the absence of a driver's license. (A copy of that decision is attached hereto as Exhibit C [*not reprinted herein*].)

46. Ms. Bouvier did not request the Secretary to review her case, since such a request for review would have been fruitless, given that the Secretary had already decided that Andover borrowers who had high school diplomas could not obtain false certification discharges based on their lacking valid driver's licenses.

47. The Secretary's final decision regarding Andover borrowers has caused and will continue to cause substantial harm to Ms. Bouvier. She had her income tax refunds seized and is threatened by seizure of future refunds and earned income tax credits, as well as wage garnishments. In addition, because of her default, she has adverse credit history barring her access to credit and is ineligible for further financial aid to pursue legitimate education or job training.

Waylon Smithers

48. Like Mr. Simpson, Plaintiff Smithers was, during 1989, a homeless addict and he, too, was induced by the same fraudulent recruiting operation to sign papers pertaining to an enrollment into Andover's commercial truck driving program. He was paid about $20 to sign the papers.

49. At the time, he did not have a high school diploma or a G.E.D., nor did he have a driver's license.

50. Mr. Smithers assumes and therefore avers that Andover received proceeds from a FFEL loan made on his behalf, despite the fact that he never attended Andover and never participated in any home study program.

51. Andover falsely certified Mr. Field's eligibility for the student loan based on his "ability to benefit" from a postsecondary course in commercial truck driving. Among the reasons this certification was false was that it implied his having passed a valid admission test or having completed a remedial course, federal requirements for obtaining financial aid on behalf of a student who does not have a high school or equivalency diploma. He was not administered a test and did not complete any remedial course. In addition, the enrollment ignored the fact that he was not a licensed driver and, therefore, could not legally get behind the wheel of a truck.

52. Andover also falsely certified on the guaranteed student loan application that Mr. Smithers was in attendance at the school and was making satisfactory progress in his studies. This certification is a material part of the certification process since it is an eligibility requirement under Title IV that the student borrower be in attendance at a school and that he be making satisfactory progress. 20 U.S.C. § 1091(a)(2).

53. Mr. Smithers is now recovering and is being billed by an agent of either the Secretary or ASA regarding a FFEL obligation. He has already lost the benefit of a substantial tax refund was seized several years ago on account of the student loan. He faces the prospect of wage garnishments and tax refund intercepts to enforce the balance of that obligation.

54. During 1998 he learned from Plaintiff Simpson about the false certification discharge program and about his efforts to get the Secretary to discharge the loans of Andover borrowers. Upon information and belief, Plaintiff avers that the Secretary did not attempt to notify him of the fact that his loan, because it was originated by Andover, was potentially dischargeable.

55. On August 17, 1998, Mr. Smithers submitted a sworn statement to the Secretary on his own behalf, requesting a discharge of the student loan under 11 U.S.C. § 1087(c). By this time the Secretary should have either acted on his request, or, if the loan is held by ASA rather than the Secretary, should have been forwarded to ASA for its action. Upon Plaintiff's information and belief, the Secretary has done neither.

FACTUAL ALLEGATIONS PERTAINING TO THE CLASS

A. The Title IV System

56. Title IV of the Higher Education Act, 20 U.S.C. § 1070 et. seq., created a comprehensive program of educational grants and loans in which the Secretary, who is empowered to prescribe such regulations as may be necessary to carry out the Congressional purpose, 20 U.S.C. § 1082, coordinates the extension of Title IV grants and loans to certain eligible students for education at certain eligible institutions, and also coordinates the collection of such loan obligations.

57. Under Title IV of the HEA, financial assistance in the form of loans and grants is made available to students who enroll in a recognized "institution of higher education," 20 U.S.C. § 1091(a). Originally designed to provide student aid to those attending the

nation's colleges and universities, Title IV was amended several times during the 1970's and 1980's so as to include within the definition of eligible institutions proprietary vocational and trade schools (hereinafter "trade schools") offering training programs often less than a year in duration.

58. Title IV grants ("Pell" and "SEOG" grants) are generally issued directly from the federal treasury to the approved educational institution. FFEL program loans, on the other hand, are generally issued by eligible lenders, guaranteed by approved guaranty agencies such as ASA, and then reinsured by the Secretary. Lenders receive direct interest subsidies from the Secretary and, in the event of default, receive repayment of the loans from the guaranty agencies, who, in turn, can by repaid by the Secretary.

59. The Secretary has contracted with ASA and the other guaranty agencies to administer the FFEL program, including the collection of defaulted loans, the handling of inquiries from participants in the program and the conducting of program reviews of participating schools.

60. Under Title IV "eligible students" are students with high school diplomas or General Education Development certificates (GEDs). A student failing to meet this requirement may nonetheless qualify to receive a FFEL loan to attend an eligible vocational institution if that institution certifies that the student has the "ability to benefit" from the school's training. 20 U.S.C. §§ 1085(c) (1990) and 1091(d) (1997). In 1989, when Plaintiffs incurred their education loans, institutions determined "ability to benefit" based on the student's performance on a test, or based on the student's successful completion of a remedial education program provided by the institution. 34 C.F.R. §§ 668.7(b). ("Ability to benefit" will occasionally be referred to hereafter as "ATB.")

61. An additional student eligibility requirement is that the student actually be in attendance at an eligible school and that he be making satisfactory progress in a program of study. 20 U.S.C. § 1091(a)(2).

62. Around 1990, Congress began investigating widespread allegations of fraud and abuse by vocational institutions that wrongfully obtained Title IV funds by enrolling ineligible students who were not capable of benefitting from the training. *See* United States Senate, Permanent Subcommittee on Investigations of the Senate Committee on Governmental Affairs, "Abuses in Federal Student Aid Programs," Senate Rep. No. 58, 102d Congress, 1st Session (1991) ("Victimized by unscrupulous profiteers and their fraudulent schools, students have received neither the training nor the skills they hoped to acquire and, instead, have been left burdened with debts they cannot repay.").

63. Congress responded to this problem in the 1992 reauthorization of the Higher Education Act. The 1992 amendments mandated that the Secretary of Education discharge liability on a FFEL loan received on or after January 1, 1986 if the "student's eligibility to borrow . . . was falsely certified by the eligible institution." 20 U.S.C. § 1087(c)(1).

64. In April 1994, the Secretary published regulations implementing the new false certification loan discharge provision. 34 C.F.R § 682.402(e). Among those borrowers identified in the regulation as being eligible for the new discharge were those whose "ability to benefit" from the educational program was falsely certified by the school they attended.

65. The Secretary's "false certification" regulation provides that borrowers a) who were admitted without a high school diploma or G.E.D. and without a proper determination of ability to benefit, and

b) those who would not meet the requirements for employment in the occupation for which the training program supported by the loan was intended because of a condition or legal status approved by the Secretary, are entitled to have their student loans discharged upon submission of a sworn statement establishing their eligibility. 34 C.F.R. § 682.402(e)(3), (13).

66. Under the regulation, a student borrower who was enrolled during the relevant time period in Title-IV-funded education based on his having the requisite "ability to benefit" would meet the definition of "false certification" if he was admitted without a) passing an admissions test approved by the school's accrediting agency, or b) successfully completing a program of developmental or remedial education provided by the school. 34 C.F.R. § 682.402(e)(13)(ii).

67. The regulation does not deal separately with a situation where a school enrolls individuals with the intent of not teaching them and signs FFEL certifications that the student is making satisfactory progress in an educational program. Accordingly, under the regulation, only such students who did not have high school credentials could obtain a false certification discharge even where the school falsely certified the fact that a high school graduate was in attendance making satisfactory progress in his studies.

68. Under the Secretary's regulations, in order to qualify for discharge of a "falsely certified" student loan, a borrower is required to submit to the holder of the loan a written request that sets forth, under penalty of perjury, the factual basis for the request. 34 C.F.R. § 682.402(e)(3). Within 90 days, a decision must be rendered on the request for discharge, § 682.402(e)(6)(iv).

69. Where a loan is held by a guaranty agency, a discharge request is submitted to such agency which has the power to make the eligibility determination in the first instance. In the event the guaranty agency denies the request, the borrower can seek a *de novo* review by the Secretary. 34 C.F.R. § 682.402(e)(9), (11).

70. Under his regulation, the Secretary has an independent obligation to gather information about groups of borrowers who might be eligible for a loan discharge and to notify such borrowers where reliable information suggests a pattern of false certification. *See* 34 C.F.R. § 682.402(e)(6)(I)–(ii).

71. In September 1995, as part of a "Dear Colleague" letter to participants in the Title IV system, the Secretary announced the designation of a Department official who would accept and decide requests for group discharges for borrowers who are members of a cohort of students that were signed up by a school "with serious and well-documented ATB violations that could be considered to have affected every student admitted to the school based on ATB." Borrowers covered by such group discharges do not have to submit any additional evidence that the school was falsely certifying students and, assuming they provide a sworn statement that conforms to the other requirements of the regulation, are entitled to a discharge of their loan.

B. The Andover Correspondence Course in Commercial Truck Driving

72. Andover Tractor Trailer School, Inc. was one of the most blatant and extensive trade school frauds perpetrated on the Title IV system. When it closed in 1990, it was taking in over $3 million annually in Title IV grants and loans, for the most part, for "students" who were not participating in any educational program.

Most, if not all of the FFEL loans arranged by Andover were guaranteed by the Massachusetts guaranty agency, ASA.

73. The essence of the Andover scheme was to recruit "students" by paying commissions to recruiters and to the "students" themselves, for a Commercial Tractor Trailer Driving course supposedly consisting of a correspondence segment and a residential on-the-road driving segment at the school's facility in Methuen, Massachusetts and supposedly designed to enable graduates to sit for the commercial truck driving exam. The owners did not intend for more than 10% of the "students" to show up in Massachusetts and purposely targeted their recruitment efforts to disadvantaged, vulnerable individuals who had no intention of enrolling in a course of study. Employees were trained, among other things, in falsifying driver's license information, forging financial aid documentation and completing correspondence lessons on behalf of the "students."

74. A 1990 audit by the Inspector General of the Department of Education determined that the academic content of the correspondence segment was bogus. While Title IV requires such courses to involve at least 440 clock hours of study, the IG determined that the course material would take a student only 50 hours to complete. The audit also determined that 86% of sampled students withdrew before completing the course.

75. A 1990 program review by ASA noted that of an estimated 942 individuals scheduled to complete the Tractor Trailer Driving course, at most 87 graduated, and four allegedly found jobs, although the agency found no evidence that any of these four individuals were in fact employed as truck drivers. In this review the agency also found that Andover did not determine the ability-to-benefit of students enrolled without high school credentials.

76. In 1992 a federal grand jury in Boston indicted five former employees of Andover. *U.S. v. Cotter et al.*, Crim. Act. 92-10297K (D.Mass.). The grand jury included, as part of the indictment, the following charge:

> 39. It was further part of the conspiracy to ignore student eligibility requirements for federal financial aid, including, but not limited to, whether a student possessed a valid motor vehicle license; whether a student possessed a high school diploma or GED equivalent and whether a student could successfully complete an "ability to benefit" examination.

The indictment further charged the defendants with fabricating driver's license numbers as part of the enrollment process. The defendants ultimately plead guilty and were sentenced.

77. During 1990–91 Andover lost its eligibility to participate in Title IV, ceased operations and filed for bankruptcy.

78. Andover's Commercial Tractor Trailer Driving course was accredited by a national accrediting commission called the National Home Study Council ("NHSC") (now "Distance Education and Training Council"). During the relevant time period, the NHSC prohibited its accredited schools from admitting "ability-to-benefit" students, i.e., those lacking high school credentials, unless the school received prior approval for an admissions test or for a remedial course. No such approval was ever given to any school accredited by the NHSC.

C. The Department's Actions regarding Plaintiffs' Applications for Relief

79. On October 9, 1996 counsel for Plaintiffs submitted to the appropriate agent of the Secretary documentation supporting a request that Andover be designated as a "group discharge" school. This documentation consisted for the most part of documents already in the possession of the Secretary, including the Massachusetts indictment, investigative memos from the Inspector General, and excerpts from the IG audit and the ASA program reviews mentioned above.

80. Counsel also submitted individual false certification discharge requests to ASA or to the Secretary (depending on who was holding the particular loan) in addition to the above-mentioned applications submitted by the named Plaintiffs. Some were, like Plaintiffs, denied. One (Seymour Skinner) was approved in November 1996 and another (Milhouse Van Houten) has been awaiting a decision from the Secretary since October 1996. In total, the Secretary has at least nine sworn statements of Andover borrowers from Philadelphia who described circumstances surrounding their incurring of a FFEL obligation similar to those described by the Plaintiffs.

81. In August 1996 counsel also advised the Secretary of the facts surrounding ability-to-benefit admissions by correspondence programs accredited by NHSC, namely, that, according to the NHSC, it had never provided the required advance approval for either a testing or remedial program for ATB admissions to any of its schools and, therefore, that any ATB admission in a NHSC-accredited program was by definition a "false certification" within the meaning of the Secretary's regulation.

82. On February 6, 1997 the Secretary's representative in charge of group discharges wrote to counsel for Plaintiffs, advising him that the Department was conducting a mass mailing directed to all FFEL borrowers "who received loans from Andover Tractor Trailer School between January 1986 and August 1990," to inform them about the existence of the false certification discharge program and to provide them with an application form. "In addition," she advised, "we are examining the information you provided" in support of a request for a group discharge. (A copy of this letter is attached as Exhibit D [*not reprinted herein*].)

83. Plaintiffs believe and therefore aver that this mass mailing was mailed to only a fraction of the borrowers who should have received it. More specifically, they believe that the Secretary did not notify any borrowers whose loans are held by guaranty agencies, such as ASA.

84. On May 20, 1997 the Secretary's representative issued a decision on the group discharge request. (A copy of this letter is also attached as Exhibit E [*not reprinted herein*].) First, she approved the group discharge of borrowers enrolled as ATB students, on the grounds that the submitted documentation did support a finding of widespread ATB fraud by Andover, but she limited the scope of the discharge to cover only borrowers enrolled by Andover between June 1, 1986 and April 30, 1989. Since Plaintiff Simpson and the other known victims of Andover's Philadelphia recruiting operation were enrolled after April 30, 1989, the decision effectively denied them the benefit of the Secretary's group discharge approval. The decision did not reveal the significance of the mentioned dates, nor did it refer to any evidence supporting an inference that Andover changed its practices after April 30, 1989.

85. The May 20, 1997 decision also rejected one of the additional claims asserted in support of the request for a group discharge, namely, the argument that it constituted a false certification of financial aid eligibility to fabricate driver's licenses for individuals lacking valid licenses and to enroll them into a commercial truck driving program that assumed students were already licensed drivers. The Secretary's representative determined that the lack of a driver's license of a student enrolling in a commercial truck driving course is not a "reason accepted by the Secretary" to discharge a loan under 34 C.F.R. § 682.402(e)(13)(iii)(B).

86. The Secretary has yet to render any decision regarding the additional claim that NHSC-accredited correspondence schools were not authorized to admit ATB students and that, therefore, ATB enrollments at such schools constitute false certifications within the meaning of the Department's regulation, nor did he consider the additional argument that Andover falsely certified that its students were in attendance making satisfactory progress.

87. Plaintiffs believe and therefore aver that even the inexplicably limited discharge approval, for enrollments between June 1, 1986 and April 30, 1989, has not been implemented in terms of actually notifying borrowers and discharging individual loans.

88. Thousands of FFEL borrowers, who, like the Plaintiffs, went to fraudulent trade schools have applied to the Secretary for a false certification discharge or have requested the Secretary review a discharge denial by a guaranty agency.

89. Despite the statutory mandate that falsely certified loans be discharged and despite the Department's own regulation that imposes a 90-day decision period, the Secretary has not assigned adequate staff to administer the program, resulting in a backlog of over 10,000 undecided applications that have been pending, in some cases, for years.

90. The discharge regulations provide that FFEL borrowers who are eligible for a loan discharge are entitled to a refund of any payments made on the loan, including those made by enforced collection action, and to rehabilitation of their credit record. 34 C.F.R. § 682.402(e)(2). The Secretary's adverse decision and/or his inaction has deprived Plaintiffs and class members of these important rights.

CLAIMS FOR RELIEF

COUNT I
(*Failure to Grant Discharge to Andover ATB Students—Class A*)

91. Plaintiffs reaver all previous allegations and incorporate them by this reference.

92. The Secretary's duty to discharge "falsely certified" loans is a mandatory and clear statutory duty.

93. Class members are suffering ongoing harm and the real threat of future harm by the Secretary's actions and inaction in complying with this duty. Since the targets of trade school fraud, in general, and in the Andover fraud, in particular, tend to be those living at the bottom of the economic scale, this harm is having substantial impact on the health and welfare of class members. Such harm includes having to pay student loan obligations they no longer owe out of their meager incomes; the continued threat of collection actions against them, including wage garnishments and the seizure of their tax refunds and earned income credits; bad credit reports; and an inability to obtain further Higher Education Act assistance, often critical to self-improvement efforts to move out of poverty.

94. The Secretary's failure to act for the benefit of plaintiff and the class constitutes reviewable, final agency action within the meaning of the Administrative Procedures Act ("APA"), 5 U.S.C. § 704. Plaintiff and class members can compel agency action wrongfully withheld via an action under the APA or, alternatively, under the Mandamus Act, 28 U.S.C. § 1361.

95. The Secretary's adverse decision on Plaintiff Simpson's application for a false certification discharge of his loan was arbitrary, capricious, and not in accordance with law, and/or un-supported by substantial evidence and should be reversed under the Administrative Procedure Act, 5 U.S.C. §§ 702 and 706.

96. The Secretary's adverse decision on Plaintiffs' request for a group discharge covering all of Andover's ATB enrollments, was arbitrary, capricious, and not in accordance with law, and/or un-supported by substantial evidence and should therefore be reversed under the Administrative Procedure Act, 5 U.S.C. § 706(2). Al-ternatively, the Secretary's failure to implement a group discharge for Andover borrowers should be compelled as being unlawfully withheld or unreasonably delayed, under § 706(1).

COUNT II
(Failure to Grant Discharge to Andover Students Who Lacked Driver's License—Class B)

97. Plaintiffs reaver all previous allegations and incorporate them by this reference.

98. The Secretary's adverse decision on Plaintiff's applications for a false certification discharge, based on their being enrolled into a truck driving course and the school fabricating a driver's license to justify the enrollment, was arbitrary, capricious, and not in accordance with law, and should be reversed under the Adminis-trative Procedure Act, 5 U.S.C. §§ 702 and 706.

99. The Secretary's adverse decision on Plaintiffs' request for a group discharge covering all of Andover's students who lacked driver's licenses, was arbitrary, capricious, and not in accordance with law, and should be reversed under the Administrative Proce-dure Act, 5 U.S.C. §§ 702 and 706. Alternatively, the Secretary's failure to implement a group discharge for Andover borrowers should be compelled as being unlawfully withheld or unreasonably delayed, under § 706(1).

COUNT III
(Failure to Treat Andover's False Certification that Borrowers Were Actually in Attendance and Making Satisfactory Progress as Sufficient to Trigger a Right to Discharge—Classes A and B)

100. Plaintiffs reaver all previous allegations and incorporate them by this reference.

101. In pursuit of their criminal scheme, the employees of Andover repeatedly and systematically certified that FFEL appli-cants were participating in an educational program in which said applicants were making satisfactory progress. These certifications were false when made.

102. The Secretary's determination that such a false certification does not trigger his obligation to discharge falsely certified loans is arbitrary, capricious, and not in accordance with the law. Alterna-tively, his failure to consider such a claim is unlawful and unrea-sonable.

COUNT IV
(Failure to Grant Discharge to ATB Borrowers that Enrolled in Correspondence Programs—Class C)

103. Plaintiffs reaver all previous allegations and incorporate them by this reference.

104. The Secretary's failure to take any action to extend the benefits of his obligation to discharge falsely certified loans to ATB borrowers whose loans are attributable to correspondence pro-grams accredited by the National Home Study Council is unlawful and unreasonable.

COUNT V
(Failure to Act on Submitted Applications for Discharge—Class D)

105. Plaintiffs reaver all previous allegations and incorporate them by this reference.

106. The Secretary's failure to act on submitted applications for discharge is unlawful and unreasonable.

PRAYER FOR RELIEF

WHEREFORE, Plaintiffs request that this Honorable Court grant the following relief for themselves and for the class:
   A. Take jurisdiction and certify the four classes;
   B. Declaratory and injunctive relief, (i) requiring the Secretary to grant discharges and/or provide appropriate notices, (ii) imposing a deadline for the Secretary to act on pending discharge requests, and/or (iii) granting interim relief to class members so as to protect them from further harm pending the action by the Secretary on their request for discharges;
   C. An award of attorney's fees and costs pursuant to the Equal Access for Justice Act; and
   D. Such other appropriate relief the Court deems necessary and proper.

[Attorney for Plaintiff]

E.5.2.2 Memorandum of Law Supporting Summary Judgment

UNITED STATES DISTRICT COURT
EASTERN DISTRICT OF PENNSYLVANIA

——————————————)	
EDNA KRABAPPLE,)	
Plaintiff)	
)	
v.)	
)	
MOE SZYSLAK, Secretary,)	
United States Department of)	
Education,)	
Defendant.)	
——————————————)	

MEMORANDUM OF LAW IN SUPPORT OF
PLAINTIFF'S MOTION FOR SUMMARY JUDGMENT

Plaintiff Edna Krabapple brought this action for a discharge of her federally-guaranteed student loans, pursuant to 20 U.S.C. § 1087(c), because the trade school she attended falsely certified her as eligible for the loans. Ms. Krabapple did not have a high school diploma or G.E.D. when she enrolled in a Nurse Assistant training program at the American Institute of Design ("AID"), a for-profit trade school that at the time did business in Philadelphia. She thus was ineligible under the Higher Education Act and regulations of the defendant Secretary of Education ("the Department") to participate in the financial aid program unless AID determined through proper testing that she had the "ability to benefit" from the training program. The test that AID administered to Ms. Krabapple to make this determination was a simple alphabetizing and number-comparison test that was completely unrelated to her Nurse Assistant training. This test was not administered in accordance with the test publisher's instructions, nor in accordance with the requirements of AID's accrediting agency. According to the Department's regulations, therefore, AID's falsely certified Ms. Krabapple's ability to benefit from its training. Hence, the Department's denial of Ms. Krabapple's request for a discharge of her student loans pursuant to the 1992 amendments to the Higher Education Act was arbitrary, capricious, and contrary to law. Ms. Krabapple seeks a judgment that she is entitled to a discharge of her student loans.

I. REGULATORY BACKGROUND AND
FACTS OF THE CASE

A. HOW TRADE SCHOOLS PARTICIPATING IN THE FEDERAL FINANCIAL AID PROGRAM CAN ADMIT STUDENTS WHO LACK HIGH SCHOOL CREDENTIALS

Title IV of the Higher Education Act of 1965 ("HEA" or "Title IV"), as amended, 20 U.S.C. § 1070 *et seq.*, creates various educational grant and loan programs designed to assist students in paying the cost of postsecondary education. The guaranteed student loan ("GSL") program, now known as the Federal Family Education Loan Program ("FFEL"), is one of those Title IV programs, providing loans for students to attend postsecondary institutions, including colleges, universities, and vocational training schools. The loans are issued by banks and other lenders, guaranteed in most cases by a state or nonprofit guarantee agency such as the Pennsylvania Higher Education Assistance Agency ("PHEAA") or United Student Aid Funds ("USAF," now USA-Group Guarantee Services, Inc.) and ultimately reinsured by the federal government. If a student does not repay the loan, the United States eventually pays the holder of the loan, and then attempts to collect the unpaid amount from the student, often using the guarantee agencies as collection agents. 20 U.S.C.A. §§ 1078, 1080 (1998).

To qualify for a GSL, the student must be an eligible student, *id.* § 1091; 34 C.F.R. §§ 668.31–668.39 (1997) (formerly § 668.7), and the school must be an eligible institution, 34 C.F.R. §§ 600.1–600.11 (1997), under the Department's regulations. Ordinarily, one would expect students to obtain a high school diploma or its equivalent before enrolling in postsecondary education. However, many proprietary trade schools, and some community

colleges, admit students without high school diplomas or the equivalent. In the late 1970s and early 1980s the Higher Education Act was amended to allow more students without a high school diploma or G.E.D., and the schools that admit them, to qualify for financial aid by showing that the students had the "ability to benefit" ("ATB") from postsecondary education or training. 20 U.S.C. § 1091(d). The "ability to benefit" rules for financial aid eligibility have gotten progressively more strict, but they have generally allowed schools to use standardized ATB tests to determine whether a prospective student without high school credentials had the requisite "ability to benefit." In July 1988, when plaintiff Edna Krabapple enrolled at AID, the statute required that the student first be

> administered a nationally recognized, standardized or industry developed test, subject to criteria developed by the appropriate accrediting association, measuring the applicant's aptitude to complete successfully the program to which the applicant has applied. . . .

20 U.S.C.A. § 1091(d)(3)(A) (1990).[3]

Thus, during the time period at issue in this case, a trade school seeking to obtain financial aid for students lacking high school credentials was required to use entrance testing procedures that complied with two general requirements. First, the school's choice of tests was limited to only "nationally recognized, standardized or industry-developed" ATB tests. And second, to the extent the school's accrediting criteria imposed additional requirements, those requirements, too, had to be followed.

AID, the school involved in this case, was accredited by the National Association of Trade and Technical Schools ("NATTS").[4] As of July 1988, the NATTS accrediting criteria pertaining to ATB testing provided as follows:

> If the school enrolls a person who does not have a high school diploma or a GED, but admits the individual based on "ability to benefit," the school must document the basis on which ability is determined. The documentation is left to the discretion of the institution and may use one or more of the following: standardized test, practicum examination, interview, prior work experience, or other measurement indicators. *Periodic studies are to be conducted to document the reli-*

---

3 In 1988, ATB students could also pass the eligibility threshold under two alternative methods: a student was eligible if she completed a program of remedial education from her school or if she obtained a G.E.D. before completing the program. 20 U.S.C.A. § 1091(d)(1), (2) (1990). It is undisputed that AID used testing, rather than one of these alternative mechanisms, to determine "ability to benefit."

4 This organization is currently named the Accrediting Commission of Career Schools of Colleges of Technology ("ACCSCT"). A.R. 1. It is one of seven accrediting entities that accredit the vast majority of trade schools receiving federally-guaranteed loan funds. *See* United States Senate, Permanent Subcommittee on Investigations of the Committee on Governmental Affairs, *Abuses in Federal Student Aid Programs*, S. Rep. 102-58, at 4 (1991) ("Nunn Report") (attached hereto as Exhibit 1).

ability of the entrance requirements for all stu-dents.

Accrediting Commission, National Association of Trade and Technical Schools, Standards for Accreditation, Document C, Section VI (A)(7) (Jan. 28, 1997) (emphasis added). Administrative Record ("A.R.") 32 (as referenced at A.R. 7).[5] Adding these criteria to the federal financial aid requirement that mandated the use of an established ATB test, AID was operating within a relatively clear regime for its ATB determinations. First, it had to follow the instructions accompanying the "nationally recognized, standardized or industry developed" test itself. Second, it had to conduct "periodic studies . . . to document the reliability" of the test as an effective measure of students' ability to benefit from the school's training programs, i.e., it had to study the extent to which the individuals it admitted ultimately were able to complete the program and obtain employment in their field of training. As will be demonstrated, AID failed to comply with each of these requirements.

B. CONGRESSIONAL ENACTMENT OF THE "FALSE CERTIFICATION" DISCHARGE PROGRAM AS A RESPONSE TO WIDESPREAD ADMISSIONS ABUSES BY TRADE SCHOOLS

From 1989 to 1991, the U.S. Senate Subcommittee on Investigations of the Committee on Governmental Affairs, chaired by Senator Sam Nunn, studied the rapid escalation of loan default costs in the GSL program in the 1980s. United States Senate, Permanent Subcommittee on Investigations of the Committee on Governmental Affairs, *Abuses in Federal Student Aid Programs*, S. Rep. 102-58 (1991) ("Nunn Report") (attached hereto as Exhibit 1).[6] The Subcommittee focused on fraud and abuse by the for-profit trade schools, which accounted for a disproportionate share of GSL default dollars. The Subcommittee's report identified several trade school practices that contributed to fraud, abuse, and waste of GSL funds, including fraudulent admission of "ability to benefit" students. Nunn Report at 13.

The Subcommittee concluded that "the mechanism on which [Guaranteed Student Loan Program] oversight of schools depends—the Triad of licensure, accreditation, and certification/eligibility—provides little or no assurance that schools are educating students efficiently and effectively." *Id.* at 33. Among the Subcommittee's recommendations were the following:

> (2) Congress and the Administration must hold the U.S. Department of Education accountable for the regulation and oversight of the [Guaranteed

Student Loan Program]. In the past, the Department has effectively abdicated its GSLP oversight responsibilities to private accrediting bodies, State licensing authorities, and guaranty agencies. Experience has proven that those bodies have neither the motivation nor the capabilities to effectively police the program.

   . . . .

> (15) The Department of Education must develop ways to assist those students who continue to be victimized by fraud and abuse within the GSLP. Because the Department's oversight systems have failed, students who have not received the education promised have been left responsible for loans that they cannot repay and, therefore, on which they all too often default. The Department must not only increase efforts to prevent this type of abuse in the future, but also work with students to ease financial burdens imposed as a result of past abuse.

Id. at 34, 37.

In response to the growing evidence of ATB fraud, as noted by the Nunn Committee and similar findings of the General Accounting Office and the Education Department's Inspector General,[7] Congress began tightening the ATB eligibility rules in the early 1990s, mandating that admissions tests be administered by an independent tester. Congress also took review of ATB testing out of the hands of the accrediting agencies and mandated that the Department itself approve the tests and the cutoff scores to be used. 20 U.S.C.A. § 1091(d)(1) (1998). As required, the Department has since published lists of tests it has approved for determining a student's ability to benefit from training. 55 Fed. Reg. 52160 (Dec. 19, 1990); 57 Fed. Reg. 62440 (Dec. 30, 1992); 61 Fed. Reg. 55542 (Oct. 25, 1996).[8]

In 1992 Congress also acted on the Nunn Report's recommendation regarding help for victims of admissions fraud by enacting the false certification loan discharge provision. Higher Education Act Amendments of 1992, Pub. L. 102-325, § 428, 106 Stat. 551 (1992). The law as amended in 1993 provides that:

> If a borrower who received, on or after January 1, 1986, a loan made, insured, or guaranteed under this part and the student borrower, or the student on whose behalf a parent borrowed, is unable to complete the program in which such student is enrolled due to the closure of the institution or *if such student's eligibility to borrow under this part was falsely certified by the eligible institution*, then the Secretary *shall discharge* the borrower's liability on the loan (including interest and collection fees) by repaying the amount owed on the loan and shall subsequently pursue any claim

---

5   As can be seen by these criteria, NATTS did not itself require ATB testing, and instead listed testing as one of several allowable methods for making entrance decisions regarding ATB students, including, apparently, a bare interview. It did, however, require ongoing assessment by the school that measured whether the particular method used was effectively admitting only those individuals who had the "ability to benefit." Of course, if a NATTS school wanted to obtain federal financial aid on the student's behalf, its choice of methods was limited to those allowed by Title IV rules.

6   The court may take judicial notice of this report. *Overfield v. Pennroad Corp.*, 146 F.2d 889, 898 (3d Cir. 1944); *see also, e.g., Carolene Products Co. v. United States*, 323 U.S. 18, 21 (1944).

7   *See, e.g.,* United States General Accounting Office, GAO/HRD-91-82BR, *Student Loans: Characteristics of Defaulted Borrowers in the Stafford Student Loan Program* (1991); Office of Inspector General (United States Education Department) Audit Report 03-00001 (1991) (audit of PTC Career Institute).

8   Not surprisingly, the "Roeder" test—the test involved in this case—was not among the tests approved by the Department.

available to such borrower against the institution and its affiliates and principals or settle the loan obligation pursuant to the financial responsibility authority under subpart 3 of part G.

20 U.S.C.A. § 1087(c)(1) (1998) (emphasis added). The law also provides that students entitled to this discharge "shall not be precluded from receiving additional grants, loans, or work assistance . . . for which the borrower would be otherwise eligible (but for the default on such discharged loan)," and requires the Secretary to report the discharges to credit bureaus. *Id.* § 1087(c)(4), (5).

In 1994, the Department issued regulations implementing the "false certification" provision of section 1087(c). These regulations provide that

> [t]he Secretary reimburses the holder of a loan received by a borrower on or after January 1, 1986, and discharges a current or former borrower's obligation with respect to the loan . . . if the borrower's . . . eligibility to receive the loan was falsely certified by an eligible school. . . . A student's eligibility to borrow shall be considered to have been falsely certified by the school if the school
>
> (A) Certified the student's eligibility for a FFEL Program loan on the basis of ability to benefit from its training and the student did not meet the applicable requirements described in 34 CFR Part 668 and section 484(d) of the Act, as applicable and as described in paragraph (e)(13) of this section. . . .

34 C.F.R. § 682.402(e)(1)(i) (1997). Paragraph (e)(13) of section 682.402 then sets forth the relevant requirements for eligibility for federally-guaranteed student loans based on "ability to benefit" from training. Students such as the plaintiff in this case, who enrolled in training after July 1, 1987, are considered to have had the ability to benefit from training if they

> achieved a passing grade on a test—
>
> (1) Approved by the Secretary, for periods of enrollment beginning on or after July 1, 1991, or by the accrediting agency for other periods; and
>
> (2) Administered substantially in accordance with the requirements for use of the test. . . .

Id. § 682.402(e)(13)(ii)(B). Under the Department's regulation, requests for false certification discharges must be directed at the first step to the guarantee agency holding the applicant's loan. In the event the application is denied, the borrower can request a *de novo* review by the Department. *Id.* § 682.402(e)(9).

C. PLAINTIFF'S ADMISSION INTO A NURSE ASSISTANT PROGRAM BASED ON HER PERFORMANCE ON A CLERICAL APTITUDE TEST

Plaintiff Edna Krabapple enrolled in a 6-month Nurse Assistant program at AID on July 22, 1988. A.R. 137–38. According to the school catalogue, the purpose of the program was to prepare students to work as a nurse assistant or home health care aide for a hospital or other health care facility. A.R. 126. At the time she enrolled, she was 17 years old, had only an eighth grade education, and was dependent on public assistance for her income. A.R. 183, 440. She was attracted to the school by a flyer inviting people without high school degrees to apply. A.R. 183, 214. When she applied she was administered a brief test (described by AID as "an aptitude evaluation," A.R. 189), ostensibly for the purpose of determining her ability to benefit from the Nurse Assistant course. A.R. 183. She correctly answered 57 of 64 questions on this test. A.R. 190–93. Based on plaintiff's performance on this test, the school enrolled her, arranged a financial aid package, and, as a result, obtained approximately $5,000 in Title IV funds. A.R. 397, 449. The financial aid package included two GSLs, one guaranteed by PHEAA and one guaranteed by United Student Aid Funds (now USAGroup Guarantee Services, Inc.). (A.R. 231, 419, 421, 426).[9]

The "aptitude evaluation" used by AID was part of a commercially purchased series of tests called the Aptitude Tests for Occupations devised by Wesley S. Roeder (the "Roeder tests"). A.R. 190. These tests were not designed by their author as ATB tests; instead, they were "devised as aids in the vocational counseling of high school students, college students, and adults." A.R. 197. The overall test consisted of six parts, each part measuring a distinct area of aptitude: "personal-social," "mechanical," "general sales," "clerical routine," "computational," and "scientific" aptitude. A.R. 198. The manual for using the Roeder tests lists patterns of occupations related to each of the six areas of aptitude, and to combinations of aptitudes. A.R. 201–03. The manual instructs that the test user to consider the occupations listed under each area of aptitude, or the combination of aptitudes, on which examinee scores the highest. A.R. 204.

AID administered only the "clerical routine" portion of the Roeder tests to Ms. Krabapple. A.R. 37. This test measures four types of skills: name-checking, number-checking, alphabetizing, and spelling. A.R. 198. Not surprisingly, the occupations listed in the test manual as being related to this form of aptitude are entirely clerical; none is related in any way to nursing or to health care. A.R. 201–02. Although the occupational patterns list does not include Nurse Assistant, it does include the similar occupations of Dentist's Assistant, Doctor's Assistant, and Nurse; each of these occupations is listed as related to "personal-social" or "scientific" aptitudes, or to both. *Id.*

Ms. Krabapple completed her training, which involved the study of geriatrics, nursing procedures, anatomy, and physiology. A.R. 270, 126. However, she had difficulty in understanding and performing clinical tasks involving measuring because of her weakness in basic math skills. A.R. 183. In searching for a job after completing the AID program, she discovered that prospective employers were not interested in hiring a 17-year-old without a high school education. AID referred her to a nursing home for a try-out, but she was unable to remain at that position because the nursing home expected her to do things she did not know how to do, such as taking blood pressure. A.R. 183–84. Later testing

---

9 In 1992 alone, nearly $2.3 million in Title IV loans and grants were paid to AID. More than 47 percent of the school's students defaulted on their loans that year, giving the school the dubious distinction of having the 5th highest default rate among career

revealed that Ms. Krabapple's grade equivalent in "number operations" was 7.9, meaning she had less than an eighth grade ability in this area. A.R. 184, 194.

D. THE DEPARTMENT'S DENIAL OF PLAINTIFF'S REQUEST FOR A FALSE CERTIFICATION DISCHARGE

On June 29, 1995, Ms. Krabapple applied for a false certification discharge to the two guarantee agencies holding her loans, USA-Group Guarantee Services, Inc. (formerly United Student Aid Funds) and the Pennsylvania Higher Education Assistance Authority. A.R. 176, 301. In support of her applications, she submitted, among other things, a declaration concerning her admission, a copy of the Roeder test that was administered to her and her answer sheet, correspondence with AID, a news articles concerning AID, copies of NATTS accrediting material, and an explanatory letter by her counsel. A.R. 176–220, 301–344. Both of these agencies denied her application, A.R. 70, 291. Ms. Krabapple appealed both denials to the Department. A.R. 1, 76. On January 17, 1997, the Department issued a final decision denying Ms. Krabapple's application for a false certification discharge. A.R. 1 (also attached as Exhibit A to the Complaint).

The Department gave several reasons for its denial. It concluded that NATTS did not impose any requirements on AID regarding its use of the Roeder tests, and that the Roeder manual itself allows one of the six test batteries to be used without using others. It also relied on the facts that Ms. Krabapple ultimately completed the program and, upon completion, seemed satisfied with her experience at AID. Finally, after obtaining copies of reviews of AID conducted by NATTS and by PHEAA, the Department stated that it "is aware of no reviews conducted in 1988 which made adverse findings about the ATB testing at AID," apparently relying on this fact as evidence that AID was in fact complying with Title IV ATB requirements.[10] As a result of this decision, the Department advised Ms. Krabapple that she will continue to be responsible for repayment of her loans. This appeal followed.

II. ARGUMENT

THE DEPARTMENT'S ACTION, IN DENYING PLAINTIFF'S REQUEST FOR A FALSE CERTIFICATION DISCHARGE, WAS ARBITRARY AND CAPRICIOUS AND CONTRARY TO LAW BECAUSE THE DEPARTMENT DID NOT PROPERLY APPLY ITS OWN FALSE CERTIFICATION REGULATION AND BECAUSE THE DEPARTMENT RELIED ON IMPERMISSIBLE CONSIDERATIONS.

Judicial review of informal agency adjudication, such as the Department's decision to deny Ms. Krabapple's request for a false certification discharge, is governed by the Administrative Procedure Act. The pertinent section provides that the court shall

> hold unlawful and set aside agency action, findings, and conclusions found to be—
> (A) arbitrary, capricious, an abuse of discretion, or otherwise not in accordance with law. . . .

5 U.S.C.A. § 706(2)(A) (1998).

Section 706 "require[s] the reviewing court to engage in a substantial inquiry." *Citizens to Preserve Overton Park, Inc. v. Volpe*, 401 U.S. 402, 415 (1971); *C.K. v. New Jersey Dep't of Health & Human Services*, 92 F.3d 171, 182 (3d Cir. 1996). In determining whether an agency's action was unlawful under § 706(2)(A), the court must "consider whether the decision was based on a consideration of the relevant factors and whether there has been a clear error in judgment." *Overton Park,* 401 U.S. at 416 (citations omitted); *C.K.,* 92 F.3d at 182.

> If the court determines that the agency relied on factors Congress did not intend for it to consider, or has failed to consider an important aspect of the problem, then the action should be set aside as arbitrary and capricious.

Frisby v. U.S. Dep't of Housing and Urban Development, 755 F.2d 1052, 1055 (3d Cir. 1985) (citing *Motor Vehicle Mfrs. Ass'n v. State Farm Mut. Auto. Ins. Co.*, 463 U.S. 29, 43 (1983)).

An agency is bound by its own regulations. *See United States v. Nixon*, 418 U.S. 683, 696 (1974). If an agency's action does not comport with its regulations, the action is contrary to law and should be reversed by a reviewing court. *See Frisby,* 755 F.2d at 1055–56; *Kelly v. Railroad Retirement Board,* 625 F.2d 486, 491–92 (3d Cir. 1980).

The governing standard for evaluating plaintiff's request for a false certification discharge under 20 U.S.C. § 1087(c) is found at 34 C.F.R. § 682.402(e)(13)(ii)(B) (1997). For the time period corresponding to AID's enrollment of Plaintiff, the ATB test used to measure her "ability to benefit" must have been (1) "[a]pproved . . . by the accrediting agency," and it must have been (2) "[a]dministered substantially in accordance with the requirements for use of the test." *Id.* If the ATB test administered to her failed to meet either of these criteria, then, under the Department's regulation, AID falsely certified her eligibility for Title IV funding, and she is entitled to a discharge.

In denying plaintiff's application for a false certification discharge, the Department acted arbitrarily and capriciously and contrary to law by failing to follow its own regulation. It ignored the regulation's plain language and, instead, used an analysis that rendered the regulation meaningless. The Department's analysis also departed from the statutory directions and intent concerning ATB admissions practices and concerning the consideration of false certification discharge applications. That this was an arbitrary and capricious departure from governing law is demonstrable in several ways. First, the Department collapsed the required inquiry into compliance with the standardized test publisher's instructions into the totally separate inquiry into accrediting agency approval, effectively rendering the former inquiry meaningless. Second, the Department failed to analyze the accrediting agency's ATB requirements and so ignored AID's failure to comply with the NATTS requirement that schools conduct periodic studies documenting the reliability of their entrance testing practices. Finally, the Department improperly considered factors that were irrelevant to the criteria set forth in the regulation entitling students to a discharge.

---

10 The Department also rejected an additional argument made by plaintiff regarding AID's failure to follow the time requirements for administering the Roeder test. This aspect of the Department's decision is not being appealed.

1. The Department Made a Clear Error in Judgment in Determining That the Roeder Test Was "Administered Substantially in Accordance with the Requirements for the Use of the Test."

Ms. Krabapple is entitled to a false certification discharge if AID did not administer the Roeder test to her "substantially in accordance with the requirements for the use of the test." 34 C.F.R. §§ 682.402(e)(1)(i)(A), (e)(13)(ii)(B)(2) (1997).[11] As she demonstrated in her application, AID used a commercial test that on its face was not designed as an ATB test, and then ignored the test publisher's explicit instructions regarding which parts of the test measure aptitude for which kinds of jobs. For a training program designed to prepare unskilled people for work as nurse assistants in nursing homes or hospitals, the school used only the "Clerical Routine" part of the Roeder test, testing such "aptitudes" as the ability to recognize which listed name or number matches a given name or number, A.R. 191, and the ability to alphabetize four listed names, A.R. 192. AID chose not to use the "Scientific" and "Personal-Social" parts of the Roeder test, despite these being the parts that the test publisher stated were appropriate for measuring aptitude for jobs in health care fields. AID was seemingly more interested in making sure ATB applicants were admitted into the school—and in collecting students' financial aid awards—than in conducting any sort of serious evaluation of their capabilities. As a result, Ms. Krabapple enrolled in the six month course, incurring $5,000 in student loan debt, only to learn upon graduating that health care facilities were not interested in hiring a teenage high school dropout who, among other things, could not take simple measurements on medical equipment.

The Department's explanation for denying Ms. Krabapple's claim for a discharge on the basis that AID did not administer its ATB test "substantially in accordance with the requirements for use of the test" was as follows:

> You also argue that your loans should be discharged because AID did not comply with the test publisher's requirements for use of the test as the school used the Roeder Clerical test to test students for admission on the basis of ATB. You suggest the school should have used the Personal Social and Scientific tests rather than the clerical test. . . . NATTS did not mandate how a school used the test instruments it selected in July, 1988. The manual for the Aptitude Test for Occupations submitted with your discharge application provides that the tests, [*sic*] can be used as a basis for aiding the selection of subjects in high school and colleges. While the Aptitude Test for Occupations can be used as a battery of six tests, the manual states that "[a]ny one test or a combination of test [*sic*] may be administered." Test Manual at 3.
>
> . . . .
>
> Based on a review of the accrediting agency standards and the materials submitted with your

application, the Department cannot conclude that you were not tested substantially in accordance with the requirements for use of the test.

A.R. 2.

Thus, the Department gave two reasons for concluding that AID had substantially complied with the requirements of the Roeder test. The first was that "NATTS did not mandate how a school used the test instruments it selected in July, 1988." The second was that the Roeder manual stated that it was possible to use one of the parts of the test or a combination of parts. Both of these reasons are patently capricious and contrary to law.

As to the first reason articulated, the Department's analysis collapses into the inquiry regarding compliance with the requirements for the use of the test a second inquiry of whether the accrediting agency disapproved the test. Having found no accrediting agency disapproval, the Department apparently concluded that AID was essentially free to do what whatever it wanted. Under the Department's interpretation, a school could administer an untimed typing test, despite requirements built into the test that it be timed, as long as the accrediting agency never explicitly told the school not to. However, the structure of the regulation itself makes the accrediting agency's approval or disapproval a separate question from whether the test requirements were followed.

The Department's own regulations make clear that a test is not properly administered if it is not administered in accordance with the test publisher's requirements. The current regulation governing ATB testing requires that tests be "properly administered," 34 C.F.R. § 668.151(a)(2) (1997), and define that term as follows:

> [t]he Secretary considers that a test is properly administered if the test administrator—
>
> . . .
>
> (2) Administers the test in accordance with instructions provided by the test publisher, and in a manner that ensures the integrity and security of the test. . . .

Id. § 668.151(d).

Thus, it is the Roeder manual itself, not the action or inaction of NATTS, that provides the source material for determining whether or not AID administered the Roeder test "substantially in accordance with the requirements of the test." Contrary to the Department's out-of-context quotation from the manual, the Roeder test instructions provide no basis for using the "clerical routine" test to assess a student's ability to benefit from training to be a Nurse Assistant. The design of the Roeder test is to test students for various aptitudes, so that students may consider occupations in the areas of their strengths. The publisher's manual instructs examiners to convert the student's raw scores into percentile ranks. A.R. 204. Then,

> [i]f an examinee has only one high percentile rank, the vocations in that particular field should be considered. If, for instance, he ranks high in Test 3, the occupational patterns listed under the number 3, on page 6 should be considered.
>
> If an examinee has two high percentile ranks, the numbers of the two fields in which he ranked highest should be combined, placing the smaller number first. For instance, if he is high in the

---

11 Under the regulation, proper ATB testing in July 1988 was contingent on *both* the "approval" of the accrediting agency *and* on using the test in a manner "substantially in accordance" with the test requirements. Thus, if AID fell short regarding either of these factors, Ms. Krabapple is entitled to a discharge.

Clerical Routine and Computational fields (numbers 4 and 5), the numbers of these two fields should be combined into the number 4–5. Therefore, the occupational patterns listed under 4, 5, and 4–5 should be used by the counselor.

Id. The instructions conclude that "Regardless of where an individual's profile falls, the jobs of the occupational pattern list in which he has the highest aptitude should be considered." *Id.*

The jobs in the occupational pattern listed as related to the clerical routine aptitude for which Ms. Krabapple was tested are, of course, clerical jobs with no relationship to the training in geriatrics, anatomy, physiology, and nursing procedures that AID provided. Although the occupation of Nurse Assistant does not appear on Roeder's list of occupational patterns, the closely-related occupations of Nurse, Dentist's Assistant, and Doctor's Assistant appear under "scientific" or "personal-social" aptitude, or a combination of these aptitudes. A.R. 201–02. If any of the Roeder tests—tests not designed to measure ability to benefit from training at all, but rather designed for vocational counseling—were to be used to measure ability to benefit from Nurse Assistant training, it should have been the tests measuring these wholly different aptitudes.

Although, as the Department notes, the manual does state that "[a]ny one test or any combination of tests may be administered," the manual gives no suggestion that examiners could use one test to measure aptitude for unrelated occupations. Certainly, if a student shows an interest in a particular occupation, an examiner might choose to administer only one test to determine whether the student shows aptitude in the area of her interest. However, that one test tells nothing about the student's aptitude for other occupations. The Department's logic would yield absurd results: if the score on one test used in isolation can demonstrate ability to benefit from training in an unrelated field, then a school could use the "general sales" portion of the Roeder test to measure ability to benefit from training as an "aeronautical engineer," or could use the "mechanical" aptitude test for to show ability to benefit from training to be a "taxation accountant."

Because the "requirements for the use" of the Roeder test instruct that each test only be used to measure aptitude for the related list of occupations, and because the occupation of Nurse Assistant is unrelated to "clerical routine" aptitude, the test given Ms. Krabapple was not "administered substantially in accordance with the requirements for use of the test." The test therefore did not meet the requirements of 34 C.F.R. § 682.402(e)(13)(ii)(B)(2). By focusing only on the single statement in the manual that "any one test . . . may be administered," the Department essentially ignored the manual's clear directions regarding which single test parts or combination of parts were relevant to measuring aptitude for which jobs. The conclusion that the Roeder publisher endorsed the practice of giving a simple clerical test to applicants for a health care training program was without any reasonable basis whatsoever, and, as such, was "capricious" and contrary to law.

2. The Department Made a Clear Error in Judgment in Determining that the Clerical Routine Portion of the Roeder Tests Was Approved by AID's Accrediting Agency.

The false certification regulation provides that a student is not considered to have had the requisite ability to benefit unless she "achieved a passing grade on a test . . . [a]pproved . . . by the accrediting agency." 34 C.F.R. § 682.402(e)(13)(ii)(B)(1) (1997). In this case, as of July 1988, AID's accrediting agency had neither approved nor disapproved the school's use of the Roeder "clerical routine" as an appropriate instrument for measuring ability to benefit. The meaning of this accrediting "approval" consideration, however, comes from the ability-to-benefit rule that was in effect at the time of Plaintiff's admission to AID. The relevant statutory language limited ATB enrollments to those individuals passing "a nationally recognized, standardized or industry developed test, *subject to criteria developed by the appropriate accrediting association.*" 20 U.S.C.A. § 1091(d)(3)(A) (1988) (emphasis added). The false certification regulation, by requiring separate reviews of the test publisher's instructions and of the accrediting commission "approval," corresponds to the statute's two-part requirement for schools' use of testing to admit ATB students, that the test be an established test (and administered in accordance with the requirements that accompany the test) and that it be used in a way that conforms to applicable accrediting criteria.

In its denial of Ms. Krabapple's application, the Department implicitly agreed that the analysis of whether the accrediting agency "approved" the use of a particular ATB test involves a determination of whether the school complied with applicable accrediting criteria regarding ATB testing. However, rather than actually applying the appropriate criteria to this case, the Department did little more than refute what plaintiff believed, at the time of her application, to be the relevant accrediting criteria. A proper analysis of the actual NATTS standards shows that AID did not comply with even the lenient accrediting criteria in effect when it admitted Ms. Krabapple into the school.

The Department, AID, and plaintiff's counsel have had some difficulty identifying NATTS's ATB requirements at the time of Ms. Krabapple's application. After Ms. Krabapple applied for a false certification discharge, the Department obtained a chronology from NATTS of its ATB requirements. This chronology provides the following "summary" of the ATB requirements at the relevant time:

> Document C, Section VI(A)(7) of the Accrediting Standards describes the criteria the Commission uses to determine a school's compliance with accrediting standards. The Commission does not wish to be prescriptive in either the method or materials that a school may use and encourages all accredited schools to carefully study and select the most appropriate process for its students.

A.R. 7. The referenced Section VI(A)(7)—not provided to the Department by NATTS but included in an AID submission to the Department—provides:

> If the school enrolls a person who does not have a high school diploma or a GED, but admits the individual based on "ability to benefit," the school must document the basis on which ability is determined. The documentation is left to the discretion of the institution and may use one or more of the following: standardized test, practicum examination, interview, prior work experience, or other measurement indicators. Periodic

studies are to be conducted to document the reliability of the entrance requirements for all students.

A.R. 32. Thus, at the time of Ms. Krabapple's enrollment at AID, NATTS required schools seeking accreditation to conduct "periodic studies . . . to document the reliability of the entrance requirements for all students." *See also* A.R. 6–7 (another statement of NATTS's ATB criteria, including the requirement to conduct periodic studies).[12]

The Department's response to Ms. Krabapple's application for a discharge on the grounds that NATTS did not approve AID's use of the Roeder test was as follows:

> During July, 1988 NATTS did not require schools it accredited to have ATB tests or scores reviewed by an independent third party. NATTS standards in effect at the time did not mandate the use of a particular test, and did not mandate that standardized or industry developed tests be used in a particular way. NATTS stated that it "does not wish to be prescriptive in either the method or materials that a school may use and encourages all accredited schools to carefully study and select the most appropriate process for its students." The requirement cited in your discharge application that the school have its test reviewed by a third party was not adopted until after you enrolled. Therefore, the fact that the third party validations used by the school were dated after you enrolled is not a basis to determine that the school failed to comply with accrediting agency requirements.

A.R. 2. This analysis does not actually address the accrediting criteria that were in effect at the time Ms. Krabapple enrolled at AID. In particular, the Department does not address the requirement that schools conduct periodic studies to document the reliability of their entrance requirements. The Department's only reference to NATTS's ATB requirements is a reference to a statement in the "summary" that the Department quotes as supporting its position that AID complied with NATTS's accrediting criteria. However, even this quoted statement encourages schools to "carefully study and select the most appropriate process" for testing

their students. The record contains no evidence that AID ever studied the reliability of the Roeder test to measure ability to benefit.

Although given a full opportunity to do so, AID did not produce any documentation demonstrating that it conducted any periodic studies regarding the reliability of its use of the Roeder "clerical routine" as its ATB test. Both the Department and plaintiff's counsel solicited documentation from AID that it had complied with the applicable accrediting criteria. A.R. 49, 186. The Department also solicited such information from NATTS. A.R. 48. The only reasonable inference from NATTS's and AID's failure to provide such documentation is that AID did not conduct the required studies. The absence of any documentation that AID complied with the requirement to conduct periodic studies of the reliability of its entrance requirements is compelling evidence that AID was not in compliance with NATTS's criteria for use of the ATB tests. Consequently, the test was not "approved" by the accrediting agency, and AID did not satisfy the requirements of 34 C.F.R. § 682.402(e)(13)(ii)(B)(1).

Rather than inferring from this absence of evidence of reliability studies that AID failed to comply with the NATTS criteria, the Department came to precisely the opposite conclusion: it essentially treated the absence of an explicit finding by NATTS that AID was in violation of its ATB requirements as NATTS "approval" of AID's ATB testing. In other words, the Department failed to conduct its own independent analysis of whether AID was complying with its accrediting criteria, and, instead looked to the absence of some affirmative disapproval by NATTS as the critical fact. This was a clear departure from the kind of inquiry that the false certification regulation contemplates and, therefore, constituted an error of law.

As will now be discussed, this complete reliance on the assumed integrity of oversight by the accrediting agencies is also unreasonable given the legislative context that gave rise to the false certification discharge in the first place. Specifically, Congress's adoption of the false certification discharge to provide relief to victimized students stemmed in part from the conclusion of the Nunn Report that accrediting commissions had turned blind eyes to ATB abuses by trade schools.

3. The Department Relied on Irrelevant Factors in Denying Plaintiff's Application for a False Certification Discharge.

In addition to its errors in judgment in considering the regulatory factors governing its decision whether to grant a false certification discharge, the Department also considered factors that are irrelevant to its decision. Its reliance on irrelevant factors constitutes separate grounds for setting aside its action as arbitrary and capricious. *Frisby v. U.S. Dep't of Housing and Urban Development*, 755 F.3d 1052, 1055 (3d Cir. 1985).

Section 1087(c)(1) entitles students whose eligibility for student loans was falsely certified by their schools to a discharge of their loans. 20 U.S.C.A. § 1087(c)(1) (1998). The Department's implementing regulations interpret this entitlement to apply to students whose eligibility for student loans was based on purported ability to benefit from training, and who were administered a test that either (1) was not approved by the school's accrediting agency or (2) was not administered substantially in accordance with the requirements for use of the test. 34 C.F.R. § 682.402(e)(1)(i)(A), (e)(13)(ii)(B) (1997). These criteria, addressing only whether the

---

12   In January 1989, NATTS amended its accreditation criteria to require that ATB tests be "reviewed by a qualified third-party, such as an expert in tests and measurements, for both the appropriateness of the test and the specific score levels required for admission into each program." A.R. 34. When in 1993 plaintiff's counsel requested documentation from AID that its testing of Ms. Krabapple had complied with accrediting agency requirements, A.R. 186, AID stated that "Ability to Benefit prior to the current regulations allowed schools to use a test which had been evaluated by an independent third party." A.R. 187. AID also provided what now appears to be the January 1989 NATTS revision to its accrediting criteria, along with two letters purporting to satisfy the third-party evaluation requirement. A.R. 212, 213. Plaintiff's application to the Department for a false certification discharge assumed that AID had accurately described the applicable accrediting criteria.

test given the student was appropriately selected and administered, are the only factors that the statutory and regulatory scheme makes relevant to a decision whether to discharge a student's loans.[13]

The Department's decision denying Ms. Krabapple's application for a false certification discharge states that

> I also note that you did well at the school and graduated. In an evaluation of the school in your academic file you answered "yes" to the questions "If you had it to do over again would you enroll in the same program?" and "Are the text books easy to understand?"

A.R. 2. Ms. Krabapple's completion of the nurse assistant program and her stated satisfaction—before she started her job search and discovered that her training was not sufficient to get work as a nurse assistant—have no bearing on whether the test administered to Ms. Krabapple was proper.[14] Indeed, the false certification regulation itself considers actual employment, not but graduation from the program, to undercut a claim of improper ATB admission. See 34 C.F.R. § 682.402(3)(3)(ii)(C) (borrower who completes program and makes a reasonable, but unsuccessful, attempt to obtain employment is still eligible for discharge if ATB testing was improper). The Department should not have relied on these irrelevant comments as a basis for denying Ms. Krabapple's application.

The Department's denial letter also states that

> [b]ecause entities with oversight responsibility would typically have both the opportunity and responsibility to find and report improper ATB admission practices, the absence of such findings raises an inference that improper practices were not reported because none were taking place.

Id. In other words, the fact that the Department did not turn up any reference to improper ATB practices in the program reviews of AID that it obtained from NATTS, PHEAA, and its own files was determined to outweigh the actual evidence of improper practices contained in plaintiff's submissions.

This is a remarkable inference. The actual text of the Department's program reviews, which the Department cites as evidence of an absence of ATB fraud at AID, reject any inference that its failure to identify particular forms of abuse means that such abuses did not occur:

Although the review was thorough, it cannot be assumed to be all-inclusive. The absence of statements in the report concerning the institution's specific practices and procedures must not be construed as acceptance, approval or endorsement of those specific practices and procedures. Furthermore, it does not relieve the institution of its obligation to comply with all of the statutory or regulatory provisions governing the Title IV programs.

A.R. 462, 493; *see also* A.R. 453, 475, 481 (similar disclaimers in PHEAA reviews). Moreover, the Department's assumption that program reviews were comprehensive and can be relied on to have uncovered any wrongdoing represents a complete inversion of the facts as Congress found them to be at the time the false certification discharge program was enacted. As stated in the Nunn Report,

> the mechanism on which [Guaranteed Student Loan Program] oversight of schools depends—the Triad of licensure, accreditation, and certification/eligibility—provides little or no assurance that schools are educating students efficiently and effectively. Similarly, the investigation disclosed that the lure of fast and easy program profits, coupled with no effective government oversight, had already had devastating effects on the program's financial intermediaries, with similar problems likely in the future. Lastly, the Subcommittee found that through gross mismanagement, ineptitude, and neglect in carrying out its regulatory and oversight functions, the Department of Education had all but abdicated its responsibility to the students it is supposed to service and the taxpayers whose interests it is charged with protecting.

Nunn Report at 33.[15] As a direct result of this collapse in regulatory oversight, Congress felt compelled to extend relief to some of the student victims who were left with worthless educations and loans they could not afford to repay. It would be a miscarriage of legislative intent if the failure of oversight agencies to notice that AID was ignoring Title IV ATB rules was used to defeat plaintiff's convincing case for a false certification discharge. If the court does not order the Department to discharge Ms. Krabapple's student loans pursuant to 34 C.F.R. § 682.402(e)(1)(i)(A) and § 682.402(e)(13)(ii)(B), the court should nonetheless remand this matter to the Department for redetermination without considering these irrelevant factors.

III. CONCLUSION

For the foregoing reasons, Ms. Krabapple is entitled to a judgment that the Department's action was arbitrary and capricious and not in accordance with law. The court should therefore set the defendant's action aside as unlawful pursuant to 5 U.S.C. §

---

13 The Department's regulations also authorize discharges for other false certifications besides false certification of ability to benefit, but these other forms of false certification are not at issue in Ms. Krabapple's case. 34 C.F.R. § 682.402(e)(1)(i)(B), (ii) (1997).

14 The Department reliance on Ms. Krabapple's statements in her student evaluation was highly selective: in response to other questions, Ms. Krabapple stated that she found the school to be "sort of" as it was represented to her when she enrolled, and that "maybe" she would recommend the school to her friends. A.R. 147. The Department also neglected the context in which Ms. Krabapple's comments were given: Ms. Krabapple was jobless and was relying on AID to find her a job; she consequently would have been reluctant to offend the school.

15 The Nunn Report specifically questioned the validity of Departmental and accrediting agency program reviews, noting testimony that both agency and NATTS review staff allowed schools to provide them with student files. This practice permitted schools to alter the student records or to hide problem cases. Nunn Report at 19, 32.

706(2)(A). This matter should be remanded to the Department for a discharge of her student loans and a refund of any payments made, with interest.

[Attorney for Plaintiff]

E.6 Raising School's Fraud in Bankruptcy Proceeding

E.6.1 Dischargeability Complaint Raising School's Fraud

UNITED STATES BANKRUPTCY COURT
EASTERN DISTRICT OF PENNSYLVANIA

```
————————————————— )
In re: MAE N. WEST,            )
                   Debtor )
MAE N. WEST,                   )
                   Plaintiff )
                               )
v.                             )
                               )
PENNSYLVANIA HIGHER            )
EDUCATION ASSISTANCE           )
AGENCY, PHILADELPHIA           )
SAVINGS FUND SOCIETY           )
and LAMAR ALEXANDER,           )
Secretary, United States       )
Department of Education,       )
                   Defendants )
Stephen Raslavich,             )
                   Interim Trustee )
————————————————— )
```

DEBTOR'S COMPLAINT TO DETERMINE DISCHARGEABILITY OF STUDENT LOAN

PRELIMINARY STATEMENT

1. This is an adversary proceeding brought under the Bankruptcy Code, 11 U.S.C. § 523(a)(8), to determine the dischargeability of an educational loan made, insured or guaranteed by a governmental unit. The debtor also raises various claims under applicable nonbankruptcy law against the defendants.

JURISDICTION

2. Jurisdiction of the bankruptcy court in this matter is provided by 28 U.S.C. §§ 1334 and 157 and the Order of the United States District Court for this district dated July 25, 1984.

3. This is a core proceeding.

PARTIES

4. Plaintiff is an adult individual who resides at [Address]. She is the debtor in above-captioned chapter 7 case.

5. Defendant Pennsylvania Higher Education Assistance Agency ("PHEAA") is an instrumentality of the Commonwealth of Pennsylvania, doing business at [Address].

6. Defendant Philadelphia Savings Fund Society ("PSFS") is a Pennsylvania corporate financial institution whose local student loan operations are located at [Address].

7. Defendant Lamar Alexander is the Secretary of the Department of Education ("ED") and as such is the chief executive official of an agency of the United States (hereinafter "the Secretary.")

8. Stephen Reynolds is the interim trustee in this bankruptcy case and is a nominal party to this action.

FACTUAL ALLEGATIONS

9. In November, 1988 plaintiff enrolled in a data entry course at a proprietary trade school in Philadelphia named Commercial Programming Unlimited. Plaintiff, who had never graduated high school, was at the time 55 years old. She was induced to enroll by sales representatives of the school who promised her a) that she would obtain job training and a GED diploma at the school, b) that upon graduation she would receive job placement assistance and c) that the entire cost of this service would be financed by federal financial aid programs.

10. The school arranged a financial aid package for plaintiff which totalled $6,225 for a nine-month course. Included in this package were approximately $5,500 in loans provided by PSFS, guaranteed by PHEAA and insured by ED under the Guaranteed Student Loan (GSL) and Supplemental Loan (SLS) programs established by Subchapter IV of the Higher Education Act, 20 U.S.C. § 1077 et seq.

11. Plaintiff attended classes at the school for approximately one month, at which time, due to dissatisfaction with the quality of the teaching, she transferred to another trade school in the next building, the Palmer Business School. As with the first school, Palmer representatives assured her of a GED, job training and placement and a financial aid package covering all costs. The second package, like the first, was arranged by the school through PSFS and was guaranteed and insured, respectively, by PHEAA and ED.

12. In the case of all the above-mentioned student loans, plaintiff did not obtain the loans by herself, nor did she have any direct dealings whatsoever with PSFS. On the contrary, PSFS had the schools, among other things, verify plaintiff's identity, complete all the forms ordinarily completed by the lender, explain the transaction to plaintiff, and obtain her signature on all documents relating to the loans.

13. Plaintiff graduated from Palmer in the summer of 1989. She did not receive a GED, and, on the contrary, learned that she had to contact the School District of Philadelphia in order to take the test and to receive whatever additional GED training she needed. At the one job interview Palmer arranged for plaintiff, she discovered that a GED was a requirement for the job. Soon after this interview Palmer went out of business.

14. Plaintiff's present indebtedness on her student loans is approximately $5,524.

CAUSES OF ACTION

Count I—Undue Hardship

15. Plaintiff-debtor's present income consists of approximately $600/month earned from a small beauty shop she rents. This amount is not even adequate for her to afford the basic necessities of life.

16. She lacks the resources to repay the student loans and any payments she would make would be at a great hardship. Excepting the loans from discharge would impose an undue hardship on her.

17. The above-described student loan debts are dischargeable under 11 U.S.C. § 523(a)(8)(B).

Count II—Breach of Contract

18. The purpose of the above-described loans, which the two schools arranged, was to finance the costs of a GED course, job training and job placement services purportedly provided by the school. Thus, plaintiff agreed to repay her indebtedness in consideration for the schools' agreement to provide her with the said services.

19. The schools never provided her the said services and, as a result, failed to perform in accordance with the above-described contract and breached said contract.

20. Plaintiff has been injured by this breach by the indebtedness involved in this case.

21. PSFS had an "origination relationship," *see* 34 C.F.R. §682.200, with each of the two schools plaintiff attended. Therefore, PSFS, PHEAA and the Secretary are subject to plaintiff's claims and defenses.

Count III—Fraud, Misrepresentation and/or Unfair Trade Practices

22. Both of the trade schools induced plaintiff to enroll and to continue in these so-called academic programs through a number of misleading, deceptive or fraudulent representations, including but not limited to representations concerning the quality, value and usefulness of the offered training, concerning the qualifications needed to benefit from the training and to obtain employment, concerning the ability to earn a GED after successful completion of the course, concerning the nature and wage levels of possible employment, and concerning the success rate of students completing the training.

23. The debtor relied on these representations, enrolled in the schools and then maintained herself in good standing until graduation.

24. The defendants are subject to plaintiff's claims and defenses as a result of the "origination relationship" that existed between the schools and PSFS.

Count IV—Violation of Higher Education Act

25. The underlying student loans are void and unenforceable in that, in addition to defrauding students as described above, the schools also violated numerous federal regulatory requirements, including but not limited to, enrolling plaintiff into the program when she did not have the "ability to benefit" from the training as defined by federal law and failing to maintain standards and procedures for determining whether any applicants for admission had such an "ability to benefit."

WHEREFORE, plaintiff-debtor requests the this Court:

1. Assume jurisdiction of this case;
2. Declare the subject student loans dischargeable under 11 U.S.C. § 523(a)(8);
3. Declare the loan void;
4. Award the debtor damages;

5. Award the debtor's counsel reasonable attorney's fees and
6. Grant the debtor any other appropriate relief.

[Attorney for Plaintiff]

E.6.2 Complaint to Enjoin Discriminatory Denial of Guaranteed Student Loan

UNITED STATES BANKRUPTCY COURT
EASTERN DISTRICT OF PENNSYLVANIA

IN RE: [Debtor]	)
Debtor	)
[Debtor],	)
Plaintiff	)
	)
v.	)
	)
[Director, Higher Education	)
Assistance Agency]	)
Defendant	)

COMPLAINT

I. PRELIMINARY STATEMENT

1. This is an action brought by Plaintiff [*debtor*], a bankruptcy debtor who has received his discharge, seeking declaratory and injunctive relief to invalidate certain policies of and regulations promulgated by the Higher Education Assistance Agency ("HEAA") as violative of federal bankruptcy law, 11 U.S.C. § 525(c), 42 U.S.C. § 1983 and the Supremacy Clause of the United States Constitution.

II. JURISDICTION

2. Jurisdiction for this action is conferred by 28 U.S.C. § 1334. This proceeding is a core proceeding.

III. PARTIES

3. [*Debtor*] is an individual residing at [*address*].

4. Defendant HEAA is a public corporation and government instrumentality of the Commonwealth of [*state*] whose corporate purpose is to improve the higher education opportunities of [*state*] residents by granting scholarships and guaranteeing loans to such persons to assist them in meeting their expenses of higher education. [*cite provision(s) of state law*].

5. Defendant [*defendant—director*] is the Executive Director of HEAA and is responsible for the overall operations of HEAA, including the enforcement of HEAA regulations codified at [*cite provision(s) of state law*].

6. Defendant [*defendant—deputy director*] is the Deputy Director of HEAA and is responsible for the operation of HEAA's guaranteed student loan program, including the enforcement of HEAA regulations codified at [*cite provision(s) of state law*].

IV. FACTS

7. Plaintiff attended undergraduate school at the University of [*name*] from the fall term of 1988 to the spring term of 1990.

8. During this period, Plaintiff received student loans guaranteed by HEAA in the total amount of approximately $5,874,00.

9. After leaving school, Plaintiff was financially unable to repay his student loans.

10. On March 12, 1996, Plaintiff filed a voluntary petition in bankruptcy under chapter 13 of the Bankruptcy Code, Bkr. No. [*number*].

11. By Order dated June 29, 1999, the Bankruptcy Court ordered Plaintiff released from all his dischargeable debts, including his obligation to HEAA.

12. During the spring term of 1999 Plaintiff returned to the University of [*name*] to complete the twelve credits he needed for his undergraduate degree.

13. To finance his education, Plaintiff applied for an HEAA higher education grant.

14. HEAA denied Plaintiff's grant application based upon section [*number*] of its regulations, [*cite provision of state law*].

15. In 1999, Plaintiff also applied for an HEAA guaranteed student loan.

16. Plaintiff graduated from the University of [*name*] in May 2000, with a B.A. in political science and philosophy.

17. When this action was filed, Plaintiff had been accepted for admission into several law schools commencing the fall term of 2000.

18. On or about June 21, 2000, Plaintiff filed an application through [*name*] Bank, [*address*], for an HEAA guaranteed student loan to assist the financing of his law school education at University of [*name*] Law School. The application has been approved by [*name*] Bank and is pending before HEAA.

19. On August 11, 2000, Plaintiff was accepted for admission into the University of [*name*] Law School.

20. Plaintiff has applied for financial aid from the University of [*name*] Law School.

21. The University of [*name*] Law School will provide $4,000.00 assistance in loans and grants and requires that Plaintiff obtain a guaranteed student loan of at least $4,700.00.

22. Plaintiff is in the process of applying for an HEAA student loan for the University of [*name*] Law School and expects that the application will be received by HEAA by August 31, 2000.

23. Pursuant to [*cite provision(s) of state law*], Plaintiff is ineligible for an HEAA guaranteed student loan due to his debt on the prior loans, even though his obligation has been discharged in bankruptcy.

24. Unless Plaintiff obtains a guaranteed student loan he will be unable to attend law school and he will suffer irreparable harm.

V. STATEMENT OF CLAIMS

A. First Claim

25. Defendants' policy of denying guaranteed student loans to individuals who have discharged in bankruptcy prior student loans which were in default constitutes discrimination against Plaintiff because he was a debtor under the Bankruptcy Code or because Plaintiff has not paid a debt that was discharged under the Bankruptcy Code, in violation of 11 U.S.C. § 525(c).

B. Second Claim

26. Defendants' policy of denying guaranteed student loans to individuals who have discharged in bankruptcy prior student loans which were in default violates 11 U.S.C. § 524 in that it fails to give Plaintiff a "fresh start" and it fails to treat Plaintiff as if he had never had a liability arising from that debt. Therefore, the policy violates the Supremacy Clause of the United States Constitution, Article VI, Clause 2.

27. By denying Plaintiff his rights guaranteed by federal law, i.e., the Bankruptcy Code and the United States Constitution, Defendants acting under color of law, have violated 42 U.S.C. § 1983.

VI. PRAYER FOR RELIEF

WHEREFORE, Plaintiff requests that this Court:

a. Take jurisdiction of this case;

b. Enter judgment and grant relief declaring that [*cite provision(s) of state law*] and Defendants' practice of denying guaranteed student loans to individuals who have discharged prior student loans in bankruptcy violates:

i. 11 U.S.C. § 525(c);

ii. 42 U.S.C. § 1983;

iii. 11 U.S.C. § 524; and

iv. The Supremacy Clause of the United States Constitution.

c. Enjoin Defendants from continuing the practice of denying Plaintiff guaranteed student loans, pursuant to [*cite provision(s) of state laws*], due to his prior loans which have been discharged in bankruptcy;

d. Order Defendants to process Plaintiff's application for a guaranteed student loan without consideration of or discrimination based upon Plaintiff's prior loans which have been discharged in bankruptcy;

e. Award Plaintiff's counsel a reasonable attorney's fee; and

f. Grant Plaintiff all such other relief as shall be just and proper.

Date: [Attorney for Plaintiff]

DECLARATION

I, [*debtor*], the Plaintiff in the above-captioned action, certify under penalty of perjury that the foregoing is true and correct to the best of my knowledge, information and belief.

Date: [Debtor]

E.6.3 Trial Memorandum to Support Borrower's Claim for Discharge of Student Loan Based on Undue Hardship

UNITED STATES BANKRUPTCY COURT
DISTRICT OF MASSACHUSETTS
(EASTERN DIVISION)

In re [CONSUMER],	)
Debtor	)
[CONSUMER],	)
Plaintiff	)
	) Chapter 7
v.	) Case No. 04-14943-jnf
	) Adv. No. 04-1224
EDUCATIONAL CREDIT	)
MANAGEMENT CORPORA-	)
TION,	)
Defendant	)
	)

PLAINTIFF'S TRIAL MEMORANDUM

The Plaintiff respectfully submits this trial memorandum for the consideration of the court in ruling on her request that her student loan debt to Educational Credit Management Corporation (ECMC) should be discharged in the associated bankruptcy case because repayment would create undue hardship for herself and her dependents within the meaning of 11 U.S.C. § 523(a)(8).

QUESTIONS PRESENTED

1. What is the appropriate legal standard for evaluating whether repayment of student loan debt would create "undue hardship" for a debtor and her dependents?

2. Does the availability of an income contingent repayment plan, such as the William D. Ford Direct Loan repayment program (hereinafter the "Ford Program"), mean that repayment of the Debtor's student loan debt would not cause undue hardship for herself and her dependents?

3. Would repayment of all or part of this Debtor's student loan debt cause undue hardship for herself and her dependents?

4. May the court discharge just a portion of the Debtor's student loan debt to the Defendant?

SUMMARY OF ARGUMENT

This court should consider all of the circumstances surrounding the Debtor's case in deciding whether she can repay her student loan debt without undue hardship. The Debtor respectfully submits that neither previous-repayment-attempts nor dominant-purpose tests are appropriate in the analysis.

The existence of an income contingent repayment plan (ICRP) is relevant in this proceeding only insofar as it provides information about the minimum payments that the Debtor would have to make should her loans not be discharged. Congress never intended an ICRP to meet all hardship situations or to replace a bankruptcy discharge. This court may not abdicate its responsibility to apply the Bankruptcy Code as written simply because an administrative alternative exists. Furthermore, an ICRP denies a debtor the fresh start promised by the Bankruptcy Code.

The Debtor cannot now afford to make the minimum payments for even one of her loans. Her limited English-language skills and child-care responsibilities make it impossible for her to seek or hold higher-paying jobs. Her job prospects are unlikely to change in the foreseeable future. Her living standard is already below an acceptable minimum because she cannot afford medical insurance, a car to replace the one she is now driving, or any sort of recreation. Her children lack opportunities for enrichment. Any foreseeable increase in her earnings should be devoted to curing these shortfalls in her living standard rather than to repaying loans for an education that has not yielded the expected benefits.

While this court may discharge some of the Debtor's notes and not others, doing so in this case would not make sense because the Debtor and her dependents would still suffer undue hardship in repaying even the smallest of the loans.

ARGUMENT

I. UNDUE HARDSHIP SHOULD BE MEASURED BY ALL THE CIRCUMSTANCES OF THE CASE, NOT INCLUDING DOMINANT PURPOSE OR PREVIOUS ATTEMPTS TO REPAY

This court has previously stated its preference to weigh all of a debtor's circumstances in deciding whether repayment of student loans would create undue hardship for purposes of § 523(a)(8). *See Burkhead v. United States,* 304 B.R. 560, 564 (Bankr. D. Mass. 2004); *Anelli v. Sallie Mae Serv. Corp.,* 262 B.R. 1, 8 (Bankr. D. Mass. 2000). As this court noted in *Anelli,* courts tend to apply the same factors to dischargeability determinations regardless of whether they claim to be following *Brunner*[1] or a more flexible "totality of circumstances" approach. 262 B.R. at 8. *See also ECMC v. Polleys,* 356 F.3d 1302, 1309 (10th Cir. 2004) ("We do not read *Brunner* to rule out consideration of all the facts and circumstances"). As was true in *Burkhead* and *Anelli,* this case does not require the court to engage in metaphysical speculation concerning how many angels can dance on the head of a doctrinal pin. Rather, it requires the court to identify and weigh the relevant factors bearing on the degree of hardship this Debtor would suffer were she to be forced to attempt repayment of her $50,000 loan debt.

As District Judge O'Toole recently said, in an opinion affirming the judgment of this court in another case, the court's job is to "evaluate the evidence before [it] in a methodical and thorough way to see if [the Debtor has] satisfactorily established that her case [is] exceptional enough to warrant suspension of the usual rule of nondischargeability for her student loans." *Nash v. Connecticut Student Loan Foundation (In re Nash),* No. 04-11745, slip op. at 7 (D. Mass. Aug. 17, 2005). Or, as recently stated by the First Circuit Bankruptcy Appellate Panel,

> Under "totality of the circumstances" analysis, a debtor seeking discharge of student loans must prove by a preponderance of evidence that (1) her past, present, and reasonably reliable future financial resources; (2) her and her dependents' reasonably necessary living expenses, and; (3) other relevant facts or circumstances unique to the case prevent her from paying the student loans in

---

1 *Brunner v. New York State Higher Educ. Servs. Corp.,* 831 F.2d 395 (2d Cir. 1987).

question while still maintaining a minimal standard of living, even when aided by a discharge of other pre-petition debts.

ECMC v. Savage (In re Savage), 311 B.R. 835, 839 (B.A.P. 1st Cir. 2004). *Accord, ECMC v. Kelly (In re Kelly),* 312 B.R. 200, 205 (B.A.P. 1st Cir. 2004).

The Debtor submits, however, that "dominant purpose" and "good faith" tests, as they have sometimes been applied, are inappropriate measures of undue hardship. It is true that bankruptcy relief aids the "honest but unfortunate debtor". *Local Loan Co. v. Hunt,* 292 U.S. 234, 244 (1934). Consequently, bankruptcy courts traditionally apply equitable principles in measuring the conduct of debtors. *Cf., e.g., In re Ringham,* 294 B.R. 204, 209–210 (Bankr. D. Mass. 2003) (homestead exemption disallowed even after undoing arguably bad-faith pre-petition transfer). Courts—including this one—have sometimes regarded with suspicion bankruptcy filings whose dominant purpose was the discharge of student loan debt, and they have expanded the notion of "good faith" to encompass bona fide attempts to repay student loans. *See, e.g., Pennsylvania Higher Ed. Assist. Agency v. Johnson,* 1979 U.S. Dist. LEXIS 11428, slip op. at 41 & 61 (Bankr. E.D. Pa. 1979).

Denying discharge when a greater or lesser fraction of a debtor's obligations are for student loans invites line drawing that has no basis in the Code. Furthermore, "avoiding the consequences of debts is normally the reason for filing for bankruptcy and the fact that the Debtor seeks to discharge almost exclusively student loan obligations in his bankruptcy should be irrelevant." *In re Bryant,* 72 B.R. 913, 915 (Bankr. E.D. Pa. 1987); *accord, Kopf v. Department of Education (In re Kopf),* 245 B.R. 731, 742 (Bankr. D. Me. 2000).

The notion that a debtor should demonstrate previous attempts to repay student loans before seeking bankruptcy protection has historical roots. Prior to 1998, § 523(a)(8) distinguished between student loan debts older than seven years, which were fully dischargeable, and younger debts, which were dischargeable only on a showing of undue hardship. *See* Pub. L. No. 95-598, § 101, 92 Stat. 2591 (1978) (original version of § 523(a)(8), allowing discharge after five years); Pub. L. No. 101-647, § 3621, 104 Stat. 4964–65 (1990) (changing five years to seven). The apparent purpose of the pre-1998 rule was to close a perceived loophole that allowed discharges to enter "on the eve of lucrative careers". *Johnson v. Missouri Baptist College (In re Johnson),* 218 B.R. 449, 451 (B.A.P. 8th Cir. 1998). *Accord, Limkemann v. United States Dep't of Educ. (In re Limkemann),* 314 B.R. 190, 197 (Bankr. N.D. Iowa 2004) (persons on the eve of lucrative careers were the class targeted by § 523(a)(8)). Phrased with less of a moral overtone, debtors who sought discharge within the five- or seven-year period "might not yet have given repayment efforts a chance." *Kopf, supra,* 245 B.R. at 741.

Undue hardship in the pre-1998 regime was, then, an escape valve intended to ameliorate a rule that might prove too rigid in exceptional cases. Courts therefore phrased their rules of decision in very narrow terms. *See, e.g., Texas Instruments Fed. Credit Union v. DelBonis,* 72 F.3d 921, 927 (1st Cir. 1995) ("[t]he hardship alleged, however, must be undue and attributable to truly exceptional circumstances, such as illness or the existence of an unusually large number of dependents"). After 1998, however, courts must interpret "undue hardship" in a new way to avoid harsh and unjust results. *See Kopf, supra.* The underpinnings of *Johnson* and *Brunner* have washed away, and the receding water

has undermined the precedential value of those cases as well. *Cf. Patterson v. McLean Credit Union,* 491 U.S. 164, 173 (1989) (departure from *stare decisis* appropriate in statutory realm "where the later law has rendered the decision irreconcilable with competing legal doctrines or policies").

The policy favoring a fresh start for honest but unfortunate debtors is a competing policy that compels abandonment of previous repayment attempts as a factor in weighing undue hardship. On the other hand, a debtor who "willfully contrives a hardship", *Polleys, supra,* 356 F.3d at 1310, or who is "deliberately underemployed" or (for example) takes in foster children to avoid having the means to repay her student loans, *Kelly, supra,* 312 B.R. at 207–208, might be denied a discharge.[2] So too might a debtor who visits casinos instead of looking for work, and then refuses to use any of her winnings to pay down her student loans. *Cf. Nash v. Connecticut Student Loan Foundation,* Adv. No. 02-1466, slip op. at 18 (Bankr. D. Mass. June 18, 2004). Saying that such a debtor acts in bad faith is a shorthand way of saying that the debtor might, merely by removing a self-imposed impediment, have sufficient excess of income over expenses to be able to repay his loans. *See Allen v. Am. Educ. Servs. (In re Allen),* 324 B.R. 278, 282 (Bankr. W.D. Pa. 2005) ("undue hardship encompasses a notion that the debtor may not willfully or negligently cause his own default"). This case presents no such circumstance, however.

This court intimated in *Burkhead* that refusal to participate in the ICRP option of the Ford Program might evidence bad faith weighing against discharge. 304 B.R. at 566. It cited *Swinney v. Academic Fin. Servs. (In re Swinney),* 266 B.R. 800, 806–807 (Bankr. N.D. Ohio 2001). *Swinney* rather frankly cast the question as one of clean hands, saying that a debtor who seeks an equitable adjustment of student loan debt must first do equity by exploring other alternatives. Yet, the debtor's fault or lack of fault should have no place in analyzing a student-loan discharge case. *See Rutanen v. Baylis (In re Baylis),* 313 F.3d 9, 19 (1st Cir. 2002). Furthermore, "there is no per se requirement that the debtor pay a certain percentage or minimum amount of the student loans in order to be found in good faith, and the failure to make a payment, standing alone, does not establish a lack of good faith. Instead, the debtor's good faith is interpreted in light of [her] ability to pay and a failure to pay does not prevent a finding of good faith if the debtor never had the resources to make payments." *McMullin v. United States Dep't of Educ. (In re McMullin),* 316 B.R. 70, 81 (Bankr. E.D. La. 2004) (citations and internal quotations omitted). The Debtor expects the evidence to show that she never had the wherewithal to make more than token payments on her student loans and should therefore not be penalized for failure to do more.

Bankruptcy courts have more recently treated eligibility for an ICRP as being simply one more factor bearing on ability to pay. The Debtor argues in the next section of this memorandum that, far from being the panacea that *Swinney* might imply, an ICRP in fact traps a debtor in yet another perpetual cycle of debt and despair. Factually, the Ford Program's ICRP would lead to negative amortization of her loan debt, such that she could never even cover the interest charges on an ever-increasing principal balance. Consequently, the fact that she did not leap onto the Ford Program bandwagon when ECMC offered the opportunity earlier in this proceeding should not be a factor at all.

---

2   The debtor in *Kelly* was not guilty of either sin, as the court was at pains to note.

II. ELIGIBILITY FOR AN ICRP UNDER THE FORD PROGRAM DOES NOT NEGATE UNDUE HARDSHIP

Regulations codified at 34 C.F.R. § 685.209 govern the income contingent option under the Ford Program. According to these regulations and to ECMC's letter to the Debtor, payments under this ICRP would start at $188.33 per month and would be adjusted annually to reflect changes in her income relative to the federal poverty level. (Ex. D-2). The plan would last at most 25 years, but the time limit would be tolled pursuant to § 685.209(c)(4)(ii) during periods of deferment or forbearance. The Debtor's loans are subject to a variable interest rate that presently equals 6.10% (Ex. P-6), and she presently owes $54,188.01 (Id.). The monthly interest on this principal amount is therefore $275.46. It is apparent that payments of just $188.33 will lead to negative amortization of the loan unless interest rates decline.

ECMC may argue that the Debtor's eligibility for an ICRP under the Ford Program automatically establishes that she can repay her loan obligation without undue hardship. ECMC has made just this argument in several cases in other courts within the past few years, and the courts have soundly rejected it. *See generally, Durrani v. ECMC (In re Durrani),* 311 B.R. 496, 506–509 (Bankr. N.D. Ill. 2004) (collecting cases and summarizing arguments), *aff'd,* 320 B.R. 357 (N.D. Ill. 2005). ECMC is bound by those holdings in this proceeding under the *Parklane Hosiery* doctrine. *See Parklane Hosiery Co. v. Shore,* 439 U.S. 322 (1979) (collateral estoppel may be used offensively by someone not a party in previous case). "Once a court of competent jurisdiction has decided an issue of fact or law necessary to its judgment, that decision can—and should—preclude relitigation of the issue in a suit on a different cause of action involving a party to the first case." *Fiumara v. Fireman's Fund Ins. Cos.,* 746 F.2d 87, 91–92 (1st Cir. 1984).

Congress plainly never said that eligibility for an ICRP equates to absence of undue hardship. *See, e.g., Nanton-Marie v. Department of Education (In re Nanton-Marie),* 303 B.R. 228, 235 (Bankr. S.D. Fla. 2003);[3] *Johnson v. ECMC (In re Johnson),* 299 B.R. 676, 683 (Bankr. M.D. Ga. 2003); *Porrazzo v. ECMC (In re Porrazzo),* 307 B.R. 345, 351 (Bankr. D. Conn. 2004). For a court to defer to an administrative determination of hardship would be an abdication of judicial responsibility. *See, e.g., Furrow v. Department of Education (In re Furrow),* 2004 Bankr. LEXIS 1482 (Bankr. W.D. Mo. 2004). "If Congress had intended the question of dischargeability of student loans to be delegated to a nonjudicial entity, no matter how fair its formulas and intentions may appear, it could have provided for such." *Johnson, supra,* 299 B.R. at 682. "A debtor's failure to participate in an ICRP does not necessarily imply a lack of good faith, particularly where, as here, doing so would appear futile in light of the debtor's particular circumstances." *Curiston v. Conn. Student Loan Found. (In re Curiston),* 2004 Bankr. LEXIS 2322 (Bankr. D. Conn. 2004).[4]

An ICRP is also contrary to the fresh-start policy of the Bankruptcy Code. *Cf., e.g., Grogan v. Garner,* 498 U.S. 279, 286–287 (1991). Signing up for an ICRP can "doom[] a debtor to perpetual indebtedness." *Berscheid v. ECMC (In re Berscheid),* 309 B.R. 5, 13 (Bankr. D. Minn. 2002). Indeed, requiring a debtor to enter into an extended repayment plan that significantly exceeds the debtor's working life may itself constitute undue hardship. *See Fahrer v. Sallie Mae Serv. Corp. (In re Fahrer),* 308 B.R. 27, 35 (Bankr.

W.D. Mo. 2004). The loan debt will continue to haunt the debtor, harming her creditworthiness. *See Korhonen v. ECMC (In re Korhonen),* 296 B.R. 492, 497 (Bankr. D. Minn. 2003); *Rutherford v. William D. Ford Direct Loan Program (In re Rutherford),* 317 B.R. 865, 881 (Bankr. N.D. Ala. 2004). In this case, the Debtor would be 59 years old and a grandmother at the end of the ICRP. Her children will have lived their entire childhoods in the shadow of a massive and insurmountable debt. This bankruptcy would not have given the debtor or her children any sort of fresh start.

At least two courts have considered the psychological impact of continued loan liability under the Ford Program. In *Fahrer,* the debtor introduced evidence concerning the emotional toll of dealing with family and financial problems, and the court inferred that the toll would be exacerbated if she remained responsible for $180,000 in student loan debt. 308 B.R. at 36. In *Durrani,* the court noted that the debtor would be "burdened by a huge and growing obligation" that would arguably condemn her to remaining in an unsafe neighborhood. 311 B.R. at 508. This Debtor is expected to testify to weight gain and to feelings of hopelessness and frustration arising from the stress caused by her debt obligations. Given that ECMC has managed to except itself from the fair debt collection standards that govern other debt collectors, *Pelfrey v. ECMC,* 71 F. Supp. 2d 1161, 1180 (N.D. Ala. 1999), *aff'd,* 208 F.3d 945 (11th Cir. 2000), this Debtor has nothing but constant dunning to look forward to if her debts are not discharged.

The court should also consider the tax consequences of the ICRP. *See, e.g., Thomsen v. Department of Education (In re Thomsen),* 234 B.R. 506, 514 (Bankr. D. Mont. 1999); *Parker v. Gen. Revenue Corp. (In re Parker),* 322 B.R. 856, 862 (Bankr. E.D. Ark. 2005) (citing *Thomsen* and other cases). At the end of the 25-year repayment plan, the Debtor would realize ordinary income in an amount equal to the unpaid principal and accumulated interest. *See* I.R.C. § 108(a). The relief afforded by the ICRP would therefore be illusory to the extent of the tax assessed on that amount. ECMC may argue that the Debtor's tax liability would be forgiven because she would be insolvent at the time, but there is no way from this vantage to foretell insolvency. The Bankruptcy Code does not require the debtor to trade one debt (on her student loan) for a future debt (for income taxes) that would itself be nondischargeable in bankruptcy for a period of time in the future.

Finally, before finding that eligibility for an ICRP is a relevant factor in a discharge case, the court should find that it would meaningfully reduce the debt. *See Strand v. Sallie Mae Servicing Corp. (In re Strand),* 298 B.R. 367, 377 (Bankr. D. Minn. 2003) (repayment without undue hardship does not mean "nonpayment, or zero payment, or payment toward accumulating interest only");[5] *Stockstill v. A.C.S. (In re Stockstill),* 2005 Bankr. LEXIS 626 (Bankr. D. Kan. 2005) (failure to participate in ICRP that would lead to negative amortization not evidence of bad faith).[6] Expert actuarial testimony is required to establish this factor: assumptions about interest rates, inflation, income tax rates, and the time value of money to someone like the Debtor who has no funds to invest would all have to be combined using an appropriate mathematical model to yield present-value sums that could be meaningfully compared to the $54,000 presently owed. An impossibly naive calculation suggests that the Debtor would make 300 payments totaling $56,499, whereupon she would be hit with an income tax

---

3 ECMC was a party in the *Nanton-Marie* litigation.
4 ECMC was a party in the *Curiston* litigation.

5 ECMC was a party in the *Strand* litigation.
6 ECMC was a party in the *Stockstill* litigation.

bill of $22,491 (28% of the unpaid balance, which will have grown to over $80,000 due to the negative amortization described earlier). This calculation is not evidence, however. The court should require ECMC to show the efficacy of the Ford Program, but ECMC has not adduced the expert testimony required to make that showing. As Judge Rosenthal said,

> barring abuse of the bankruptcy courts and the Code, all debtors deserve at least a chance at a fresh start. This assertion is further supported by the notion that is now axiomatic, at least in this circuit, that discharge for the debtor, absent debtor abuse, should be the norm, and that exceptions to that rule, e.g., § 523(a)(8), should be narrowly construed with all doubts resolved in favor of the debtor.

Coutts v. Mass. Higher Educ. Corp. (In re Coutts), 263 B.R. 394, 399–400 (Bankr. D. Mass. 2001) (citations omitted). Without expert actuarial testimony, there is no basis to conclude that the ICRP would make any meaningful contribution to repayment, whereas it is reasonably foreseeable given present circumstances that the ICRP would keep this Debtor harnessed to a millstone for nearly all of her working life.

The court should therefore reject any argument by ECMC that eligibility for the Ford Program's ICRP defeats this Debtor's claim of undue hardship. A court, not an administrative agency, must make that determination. Requiring [Consumer] to enter into a fruitless 25-year repayment plan that would retire an unknown, but assuredly small, portion of the debt cannot comport with Congressional intent. "[B]ankruptcy relief is designed to give the honest but unfortunate debtor a fresh start, and although government guaranteed student loans are meant to be more difficult to discharge than general unsecured debts, they are not meant to be impossible to discharge." *Korhonen, supra*, 296 B.R. at 497.

III. THE DEBTOR AND HER DEPENDENTS WOULD SUFFER UNDUE HARDSHIP BY BEING REQUIRED TO REPAY ANY PORTION OF HER STUDENT LOAN DEBT

The Debtor expects the evidence to show the following, leading to the conclusion that she cannot repay her indebtedness for any or all of the loans now owned by ECMC.

The Debtor's financial resources. The Debtor is currently employed as a home health aide scheduler for a home care and hospice agency. She earns $15 per hour. Her take-home pay is $930 every two weeks, or $2,015 per month. Aged 34, she has three children aged three, six, and eleven. The fathers of her children provide no support. She receives WIC vouchers exchangeable in kind for grocery items for her three-year-old, but that benefit will cease when the child reaches five years of age. She does not receive food stamps or other government benefits.

The Debtor immigrated to the United States from Haiti in 1990, when she was twenty. She is a U.S. citizen. She obtained a high school diploma in 1991 after attending Hyde Park High School. She attended Suffolk University from 1991 until 1997. She obtained a Bachelor's Degree in General Studies and a Master's Degree in Public Administration. She believed that obtaining an advanced degree would fit her for a managerial job paying $40,000 or more per year. Her unofficial transcript (Ex. P-1) discloses an undergraduate grade point average of 2.4 out of 4. She spent her first two semesters exclusively studying written and spoken English, with one introductory math course. Her grades show considerable variation, such as an A in Calculus I, a D in Calculus II, and an F in Calculus III. In general, her undergraduate performance was better in introductory courses than in more advanced ones. Her graduate coursework, by contrast, was nearly all A's and B's, with an overall GPA of 3.3.

The Debtor speaks English with a moderate Creole accent. The Debtor is expected to offer into evidence a short letter that she wrote to her high school to request release of personal information to her attorney. (Ex. P-2) The letter contains many grammatical and diction errors. Deborah J. Veatch, a vocational rehabilitation expert retained by the Debtor, is expected to testify that the Debtor did not understand the term "cover letter" or how to submit a professional resume to a prospective employer.

The Debtor has held many jobs since graduation from Suffolk University. The following table summarizes her job experience since 2000. (Ex. D-3, ¶ 3)

Year	Employer	Description	Pay rate	Total earnings
2000	Boston Globe	"Department Coordinator", but mostly performed data entry	$10/hour	$ 3,000
2000	Temporary Services, Inc.	Data entry clerk	$10/hour	$ 2,400
2000	Beth Israel Deaconess	Asst. Mgr. in dept. of transport, maintenance & housekeeping	$15/hour	$ 7,000
2000	Quest Diagnostics	Lab technician (night shift)	$12/hour	$13,600
2001	Prostaff	Data entry clerk	$10/hour	$ 1,000
2001	Boston Globe	Data entry clerk	$10/hour	$ 8,900
2001	Epix I, Inc.	Data entry clerk	$12/hour	$ 1,200
2002	Horace Mann	Mental health asst.	$15/hour	$ 5,000
2002	Sunrise Asstd Living	Home health aide	$10.50/hour	$ 4,000
2002	Hammond Pointe Nursing Home	Weekend activities asst.	$10/hour	$ 1,300
2002	Dobbs Temporary Services		$10/hour	$ 300
2002	Judge Rotenberg Ed. Center	Mental health asst.	$11/hour	$ 2,000
2002	Epix I, Inc.	Data entry clerk	$12/hour	$ 900

Year	Employer	Description	Pay rate	Total earnings
2003	Horace Mann	Mental health asst.	$15/hour	$ 1,200
2003	Chestnut Hill Nursing Home			$ 28
2003	Parmenter VNA	Home health coordinator	$15/hour	$28,000
2004	Parmenter VNA	Home health coordinator	$15/hour	$30,137

The Debtor attempted to secure employment by consulting with the career placement office at Suffolk University, attending career fairs at Suffolk, and answering advertisements in the newspaper. She was pleased to land the job at Beth Israel in 2000, but staff cutbacks resulted in her being laid off. She left her job with the Boston Globe when her third child was born in September of 2001. Some of her jobs included health benefits.

The Debtor has had a desire to work as a physician or dentist. At one point in the fall of 2000, she actually enrolled in a medical school in Mexico. She found that she could not tolerate being away from her children, who had to remain in Massachusetts for financial reasons. She therefore withdrew after just one week. It should also be noted that she received low grades in biology during her undergraduate training. (Ex. P-1) Thus, her goal to work as a medical professional is probably unrealistic.

In short, the Debtor lacks the business and linguistic skills needed to obtain or hold professional employment. Her Master's Degree is of little value to her. In the opinion of Ms. Veatch, the Debtor lacks the skills, time, experience, attire, or computer resources to independently seek professional level employment, and she lacks the financial resources to pay for individualized career counseling or additional training. According to Ms. Veatch, the Debtor is presently working at her full capacity and to the best of her ability.[7] Furthermore, and also according to Ms. Veatch, the Debtor cannot financially or emotionally subsidize a search for a better job in the foreseeable future. Under these circumstances, the Debtor has carried her burden of showing that "her prospects for increasing her income in the future are too limited to afford her sufficient resources to repay the student loans and provide herself and her dependents with a minimal (but fair) standard of living." *Smith v. ECMC (In re Smith)*, 2005 Bankr. LEXIS 973 (B.A.P. 1st Cir. 2005).

The Debtor's schedules disclosed tangible assets worth approximately $3,700 at the time she filed her petition. The Debtor drives a 15-year-old car that is in such poor condition that it was returned after having been seized on execution by a judgment creditor.[8] The Debtor's job requires her to commute 32 miles round trip by car,

and the commute takes 45 minutes each way. She cannot afford to buy a new car.[9] The car breaks down frequently, and she must pay to have it repaired.

The Debtor listed cash and bank accounts totaling $143, but the amount of cash she actually has fluctuates from a monthly low of as little as zero (or negative) immediately before she receives a paycheck to a little over $900 immediately afterward. The debtor sometimes overdraws her checking account, and therefore has a negative account balance during brief periods.[10]

The Debtor listed a personal injury claim on her petition, which she valued at $2,500 after deducting medical expenses and attorney's fees that she expected to be withheld. She has now abandoned that claim after being told by her personal injury lawyer that the prospective defendant is not liable.

The Debtor received a $25,000 settlement earlier this year as a result of an adversary proceeding brought against a debt collector to redress alleged fair-debt-collection and stay violations.[11] She purchased a certificate of deposit with the proceeds and continues to hold the entire sum, with accrued interest, on the date of trial. The debt collector in question (Delta Management Associates, Inc., hereinafter Delta) was acting as the agent of ECMC's own predecessor in interest (American Student Assistance, hereinafter ASA) while attempting to collect the very debts that are in issue in this proceeding. The Debtor therefore submits that it would be inequitable in the extreme to force her to turn this sum over to ECMC.

ASA was bound by Delta's misconduct in furtherance of the purpose of the agency. *See Konick v. Berke, Moore Co.*, 355 Mass. 463, 468 (1969); *Kansallis Finance Ltd. v. Fern*, 421 Mass. 659,

---

7 This Debtor, who is represented *pro bono* by counsel, was able to secure the assistance of a qualified vocational expert, who also agreed to serve *pro bono*. Most debtors seeking discharge of student loan debt are not so lucky and will be unable to satisfy this court's desire for an expert evaluation of prospective earning capacity. *Cf. Burkhead, supra*, 304 B.R. at 565–66. The Debtor urges the court to consider, for its impact on future cases, the opinion in *Mosley v. Gen. Revenue Corp. (In re Mosley)*, 2005 Bankr. LEXIS 1640 (Bankr. D. Ga. 2005), wherein Bankruptcy Judge Mullins suggests methods (such as judicial notice, court appointment of experts pursuant to Fed. R. Evid. 706, and a pragmatic application of evidentiary rules) for tempering the need for prognostication in *pro se* or *pro bono* cases.

8 The circumstances of the execution sale exemplify the sort of judicial problems that afflict this Debtor. An identity thief opened an account in her name at a local discount store. The Debtor could not afford to hire a lawyer to defend her in a lawsuit by the store,

which refused to believe her explanation. In the end, the store's judgment went unsatisfied because the Debtor had no valuable assets. The FTC later charged the store with violations of the FTC Act because of lax controls that led to millions of dollars in fraudulent purchases. *See http://www.ftc.gov/opa/2005/06/bjswholesale.htm.* (Press Release dated June 16, 2005).

9 The Debtor in fact purchased another car in July of 2000, but it was stolen and stripped in March of 2004. The insurer declined coverage after an investigation by an individual who exhibited bias and inability to understand the Debtor's accent and that of another witness. The Debtor could not afford to hire an attorney to take action against the insurer.

10 On one occasion in October of 2004, she sent a $20 check to someone. The payee's son gave the account information to Verizon, which charged the Debtor's account $337 to pay the son's phone bill. The resulting charge against the Debtor's checking account caused multiple overdraft charges that were eventually reversed. A subprime credit card lender was making unauthorized monthly withdrawals of $39.95 from her checking account; these withdrawals, since they were unexpected, also led to overdraft charges.

11 The adversary proceeding was *Paul v. Delta Management Associates, Inc.*, No. 04-1213 (Bankr. D. Mass.). This court approved the settlement on January 26, 2005.

665 (1996). The Debtor could have estopped ASA to rely on the settlement as evidence of her ability to pay had ASA attempted to collect the Notes. Since the Notes are not negotiable,[12] the common law of contract assignments controls the extent to which the Debtor may assert defenses against ECMC that she had against ASA. *Cf.* Mass. Gen. L. c. 106, § 3-102(a) (UCC Article 3 applies only to negotiable instruments). The Debtor's adversary proceeding against the collector was filed one day before ECMC took title to the loans by assignment. Under the common law, since the Debtor had no notice of the assignment from ASA to ECMC until after her defense against ASA arose, ECMC is subject to the same defense. RESTATEMENT (SECOND) OF CONTRACTS, § 336; *Quincy Trust Co. v. Pembroke,* 346 Mass. 730, 732 (1964). The parties' stipulation concerning defenses on the instruments do not govern this equitable defense to ECMC's claim that the Debtor can repay the loans without undue hardship.[13]

The Debtor owed no federal income tax for calendar year 2004. She received federal and state income tax refunds totaling $7,028 earlier this year. Of this amount, $2,836 represents child tax credits and the earned income credit. The remainder represents a return of sums withheld from her paycheck.

The Debtor's living expenses. The Debtor's schedules, as clarified by her testimony at trial, are expected to reveal that she and her three minor children have a life-style that can most charitably be called "frugal". She lives with her three children, her parents, and a 16-year-old sister in a 4-bedroom apartment on the first floor of a 3-decker owned by one of her brothers. The brother occupies a second unit, and an unrelated stranger the third. She contributes $1,000 per month of the total $1,500 rent for the unit. Her parents are responsible for paying for gas and electricity, but she contributes something towards these expenses when she is able. She spends about $64 per month for telephone service; $400 per month for food; an average of $158 per month for gasoline, oil, car maintenance and auto insurance; and $61 per month for clothing and laundry. She spends $90 every two weeks for day care, or an average of $194 per month. In the last eight months, she has paid a total of $204 for medical care for herself. On the average, these regular expenses add up to $1,902 per month.

The Debtor purchases dental insurance through her employer at a cost of $11 every two weeks, but she cannot afford to pay $250 every two weeks to purchase health insurance for herself. She does not usually have the money to purchase MassHealth insurance for her children, so she usually takes them to the emergency room at Boston City Hospital. She does not smoke. She had been in the habit of making occasional $10 payments to a gospel group, but she has stopped doing so after learning that the charity may have been a scam. In previous years, she spent $50 for an annual trip to Canobie Lake Park for herself and her children, but she was unable to afford that trip this year.

Of the $7,028 total tax refund she has received, she has spent the following sums not accounted for in the preceding narrative: three months of MassHealth coverage for her children, $324; auto excise tax, $27.50; AAA membership, $48.00; summer clothing for the children, $250; electricity and gas, which were about to be cutoff because her parents had not paid the bills, $300; car parts and labor, $584.28; and a bunk bed so her two oldest children (a son and a daughter, aged 6 and 11, respectively) would no longer have to share a twin bed, $800. These extra expenses total $2,333.78. On the Saturday preceding this trial, she was holding (uncashed) a U.S. Treasury check in the amount of $3,890.25 issued in partial payment for her refund.

The Debtor's budget does not provide for many of the expenses that are part of a "minimal" lifestyle in Boston. While a debtor cannot expect her creditors to subsidize her children's education, *Savage, supra* at 841 n. 9, the Congressional mandate to focus on "undue hardship on the debtor and the debtor's dependents," 11 U.S.C. § 523(a)(8), necessarily implies some allowance for an upbringing that will fit the debtor's children for life in twenty-first century America. That allowance should embrace a modicum of culture in addition to mundane employment skills. This Debtor cannot afford to take her children to movies or other cultural events that are not free. She does not own a VCR or DVD player and can therefore not rent movies to enrich or entertain herself and her children. She cannot afford cable TV and can therefore not expose her children to educational programs on channels like History, Discovery, or even CNN. She has never taken her children to an art museum or the New England Aquarium. She and her children once toured the lobby of the Science Museum and browsed the gift shop without buying anything, but they did not go inside the museum.[14] Although one of her neighbors has a computer, neither she nor her children has regular access to a computer to learn computer skills or to access the vast educational and cultural content available on the Internet.[15]

Most importantly, the Debtor cannot afford health insurance or a new car, and she cannot afford to pay market rent for housing. A medical or mechanical emergency would financially devastate her

---

12 The seven notes at issue in this proceeding are identical except for date, amount, and certain other, insignificant, details. Each of them contains the following promise to pay: "I promise to pay to the lender, or a subsequent holder of this Promissory Note, all sums disbursed (hereinafter "loan" or "loans") under the terms of this Note, plus interest and other fees which may become due as provided in this Note." This is not a promise to pay to bearer or to order, and it is not a promise to pay a sum certain in money. The notes are therefore not negotiable instruments within the purview of the UCC, as it was amended in 1990. *See* Mass. Gen. L. c. 106, §§ 3-102(a), 3-104.

13 The Joint Pretrial Memorandum (docket # 48) in this proceeding recites [¶ (G)(6)] that "[t]he Notes are the valid, subsisting obligations of the Plaintiff and are not subject to any defense other than that the Plaintiff claims that repayment of the same would cause undue hardship for herself and her dependents."

14 The Debtor did not realize that she could also tour the southeast lobby of the museum, including the musical stairs, without paying an admission charge.

15 Policy makers have highlighted the existence of a "digital divide" between those who have Internet access and those who have not. "The consequences to American society of this race gap in Internet use are expected to be severe. Just as A. J. Liebling observed for the freedom of the press, the Internet may provide for equal economic opportunity and democratic communication, but only for those with access. The United States economy may also be at risk if a significant segment of our society, lacking equal access to the Internet, wants for the technological skills to keep American firms competitive." Hoffman, Novak & Schlosser, "The Evolution of the Digital Divide: How Gaps in Internet Access May Impact Electronic Commerce", 2000 Journal of Computer-Mediated Communication, *reprinted at www.ascusc.org/jcmc/vol5/issue3/hoffman.html* (citations omitted).

family. The Debtor believes that $1,600 per month is typical rent for one floor of a 3-decker, but the Debtor pays just $1,000 and makes no regular payments for energy.

Were reasonable but presently unfunded expenses to be included in the Debtor's budget, the Debtor would need to spend $5,900 immediately and to have monthly take-home pay of $3,896 to cover recurring monthly expenses. She is in urgent need of a replacement car and should purchase a computer for her children. Her second-oldest needs uniforms for the school year that has just started. These expenses would be $5,000, $700, and $200, respectively. Her additional monthly expenses include an extra $600 for market-rate housing, $649 for health insurance for herself and her children, $200 for energy (assuming she can find superbly insulated housing), $50 for cable TV, $15 for Internet access, and $30 for one trip to the movies (without popcorn or other concessions). For purposes of this proceeding, the court should consider that she presently has a $1,881 monthly shortfall before she can even achieve the "minimal" lifestyle described in *Kelly* and *Savage*.

Summary. Through no fault of her own, the Debtor has been unable to make effective use of her education to obtain adequate employment. She has been leading a Joe Btfsplk[16] sort of existence as a result of naiveté concerning financial and legal matters. Her reasonable expenses, could she but fund them, would exceed her take-home income by about $1,900 per month. Life for her and her dependents is already an undue hardship; there is no practical possibility that she will ever be able to pay any portion of her student loan debt. Accordingly, the court should rule her debt to ECMC to be fully dischargeable.

IV. ALTHOUGH THE COURT MIGHT DISCHARGE SOME OF THE DEBTOR'S NOTES BUT NOT OTHERS, SUCH A PARTIAL DISCHARGE WOULD STILL CAUSE UNDUE HARDSHIP.

ECMC may argue that this court should discharge just a portion of the student loan debt. The Debtor submits, however, that a partial discharge would still lead to undue hardship.

Cases in this district support the use of a hybrid partial discharge approach, wherein the court grants a discharge on certain student loan notes but not on others. *See ECMC v. Kelly, supra,* 312 B.R. at 208. *See also, e.g., Lamanna v. EFS Servs. (In re Lamanna),* 285 B.R. 347, 353 (Bankr. D.R.I. 2002); *Grigas v. Sallie Mae Servicing Corp. (In re Grigas),* 252 B.R. 866, 874 (Bankr. D.N.H. 2000).

Some courts in other districts have conceived that § 105(a) permits them to reform student loan contracts in various ways. *See generally Tennessee Student Assistance Corp. v. Hornsby (In re Hornsby),* 144 F.3d 433, 438–440 (6th Cir. 1998). In *Miller v. Department of Education (In re Miller),* 254 B.R. 200, 206–207 (Bankr. N.D. Ohio 2000), for example, a bankruptcy judge discharged the interest, but not the principal, due on a student loan. He did so, moreover, only on condition that the Debtor adhere to a payment schedule. In *Barron v. Texas Guaranteed Student Loan Corp. (In re Barron),* 264 B.R. 833, 846–847 (Bankr. E.D. Tex. 2001), the court discharged interest that had accrued after a state court judgment. Finally, in *Saxman v. ECMC (In re Saxman),* 325 F.3d 1168, 1175 (9th Cir. 2003), the panel affirmed a district court

order that the bankruptcy court consider what portion of a single debt might be discharged without undue hardship.[17]

Still other courts, following a "strict" approach to the question of partial discharge, have held that either all of a debtor's student loans must be discharged or none of them. *See, e.g., United Student Aid Funds v. Taylor (In re Taylor),* 223 B.R. 747, 753 (B.A.P. 9th Cir. 1998).[18]

Despite the Solomonic appeal of the "flexible" approach articulated in *Hornsby* and *Saxman,* there is no textual support in the Bankruptcy Code for it. *See Grigas, supra,* 252 B.R. at 872. "[B]ankruptcy judges do not have a roving commission [under § 105(a)] to do equity in a fashion inconsistent with other provisions of the Code." *Lamanna, supra,* 285 B.R. at 352. Moreover, fashioning a customized remedy in every case invites subjective and unpredictable line drawing—the sort of judicial subjectivity that led seventeenth century lawyer John Selden to remark that "[e]quity is a roguish thing."[19] A customized remedy may also involve the court in ongoing supervision for many years. The Debtor therefore urges this court to reject the *Hornsby/Saxman* "flexible" approach.

While the Debtor acknowledges that the great weight of authority permits a partial discharge, she submits that repaying even the smallest of the notes would still create an undue hardship, and she cites the familiar cliché of loading straw onto a camel. In its Supplemental Response of ECMC to Plaintiff's Interrogatories (Ex. P-4), ECMC stated that it "does not allow for an 'interest only' payment." ECMC provided a table of minimum payments for repayment periods lasting 15, 20, and 25 years. (Ex. P-6) The payments are obviously smaller the longer the repayment period lasts. Using the figures in the table for 25 years, and placing the loans in increasing order by amount, the metaphorical load on the Debtor's back would stack up like this:

Loans Numbered	Monthly Payments
2	26.87
2 & 3	55.33
2, 3, & 4	84.56
2, 3, 4 & 1	124.28
2, 3, 4, 1, & 6	181.19
2, 3, 4, 1, 6, & 5	265.87
2, 3, 4, 1, 6, 5, & 7	352.46

---

16 From the character in the Li'l Abner cartoon series, who has been characterized as "world's most loving friend and worst jinx who always travels with a dark cloud over his head". *See, e.g., http://www.lil-abner.com/other.html.*

17 The loans held by ECMC in *Saxman* had been consolidated into a single obligation. The "hybrid" approach to partial discharge mandates an undue hardship analysis of each separate obligation. *See, e.g., Coutts, supra.*

18 *Taylor* was effectively overruled by the Ninth Circuit Court of Appeals in *Saxman.*

19 J. Selden, Table Talk, 61 (Reynolds ed. 1892). Selden continued, "For law we have a measure, know what to trust to; equity is according to the conscience of him that is chancellor, and as that is larger or narrower, so is equity. 'Tis all one as if they should make the standard for the measure we call a foot, a chancellor's foot. What an uncertain measure would this be. One chancellor has a long foot, another a short foot, a third an indifferent foot; 'tis the same thing in the chancellor's conscience." Many years later, Lord Chancellor Eldon retorted that "[n]othing would inflict on me greater pain, in quitting this place, than the recollection that I had done any thing to justify the reproach that the equity of this Court varies like the Chancellor's foot." *Gee v. Pritchard,* 36 Eng. Rep. 670, 674 (1818).

If it were possible to reliably forecast the Debtor's income and expenses for twenty-five years with sufficient precision, the court could easily divine the point at which the total of payments would exceed ability. Such precision is not possible, however. This Debtor can't afford the luxury of a budget: she is forced by circumstances to react to each new financial crisis as it occurs. She might have the ability in any single month to pay, say $27. In another month, she might have just $10.00 left over after paying her necessary household expenses. She cannot easily shift excess funds from one month to the next because she is perpetually on the verge of collapsing under the weight of her expenses.

Thus, without forcing the Debtor into an ICRP, it makes little sense to discharge less than all of the separate loan debts. Nor can the court apply the partial discharge concept to the Ford Program ICRP. The relevant regulations state that

> The amount the borrower would repay is based upon the borrower's Direct Loan debt when the borrower's first loan enters repayment, and this basis for calculation does not change unless the borrower obtains another Direct Loan or the borrower and the borrower's spouse obtain approval to repay their loans jointly under paragraph (b)(2) of this section. If the borrower obtains another Direct Loan, the amount the borrower would repay is based on the combined amounts of the loans when the last loan enters repayment.

34 C.F.R. § 685.209(a). The reference to "combined amounts" would not seem to give the court discretion to fashion a partial discharge remedy even in this case, when the loans haven't been officially consolidated. Even if permission for a partial discharge lurks in the interstices of the complex Ford Program regulations, the fresh start policy of the Bankruptcy Code and the analysis given in Part II of this argument militate against the ICRP altogether.

The court should therefore discharge all of the Debtor's student loan debt because a preponderance of the evidence shows that the Debtor cannot afford to make minimum payments on even the smallest of the loans.

CONCLUSION

A preponderance of the evidence will show that the Debtor cannot now repay any portion of her student loan debt without suffering undue hardship and forcing her three minor children to endure undue hardship. Despite her formal education, she is unlikely to improve her lot in life in the future. Her budget leaves her and her children well below a "minimal" lifestyle. For these reasons, her entire student loan debt should be discharged.

Dated: September 18, 2005

[CONSUMER], by her attorney,

[Attorney for Consumer]

E.7 Private Student Loan Cases

E.7.1 Class Action Complaint Against Private Student Loan Servicer, Lender, and Bank

IN THE UNITED STATES DISTRICT COURT
FOR THE EASTERN DISTRICT OF VIRGINIA
Richmond Division

[CONSUMER 1] and	)
[CONSUMER 2],	)
[CONSUMER 3],	)
[CONSUMER 4] and	)
[CONSUMER 5],	)
Plaintiffs, vs.	)
	) Civil Action
SLM FINANCIAL	) No._____
CORPORATION, SALLIE	)
MAE, INC., and STERLING	)
BANK,	)
Defendants.	)
	)

COMPLAINT AND DEMAND FOR JURY TRIAL
INTRODUCTION

1. Plaintiffs bring this action for damages to redress the many violations of law made by a loan broker and a bank regarding an educational loan. Plaintiffs obtained an educational loan arranged by a school but the students were not able to complete their courses because the school closed. The school was never licensed to operate as a school and the loan disclosures were not accurate. Even though the terms of the loans require the Defendants to honor all claims and defenses that Plaintiffs have against the school, the Defendants have not cancelled the loan. This Complaint is filed and these proceedings are instituted under the Truth in Lending Act ("the Act"), 15 U.S.C. § 1601, for statutory, actual, and punitive damages, reasonable attorney fees and costs to redress Defendants' violation of this federal consumer protection statute, their violations of the Virginia Consumer Protection Act and the Virginia Credit Service Businesses Act, and their common law conspiracy.

PARTIES

2. The Plaintiffs [Consumer 1] and [Consumer 2] are natural persons and residents of Midlothian, Virginia.

3. The Plaintiff, [Consumer 3] is a natural person and resident of Chester, Virginia.

4. The Plaintiffs [Consumer 4] and [Consumer 5] are natural persons. [Consumer 4] is a resident of Maryland and [Consumer 5] is a resident of New Jersey; they obtained the loan for classes in Virginia.

5. Defendant, SLM Financial Corporation (SLM), is a Virginia corporation and has, as its registered agent, Commonwealth Legal Services Corporation, at [Agent's address].

6. Defendant, Sallie Mae, Inc., (Sallie Mae) is a Delaware corporation doing business in Virginia and has, as its registered agent, Commonwealth Legal Services Corporation, at [Agent's address].

7. Defendant Sterling Bank is a New Jersey Bank conducting business in Virginia.

8. At all times relevant hereto, in the ordinary course of its business, Sterling Bank regularly extended or offered to extend consumer credit for which a finance charge is or may be imposed or which, by written agreement, is payable in more than four installments, making Defendant a creditor within the meaning of the Act, 15 U.S.C. § 1602(f) and Regulation Z, 12 C.F.R. § 226.2(a)(17).

JURISDICTION

9. This Court has jurisdiction over this action pursuant to 15 U.S.C. § 1640(e) and 28 U.S.C. § 1331 and has supplemental jurisdiction of the state law claims regarding the same transaction and events under 28 U.S.C § 1367(a).

FACTS

[CONSUMERS 1 AND 2] TRANSACTION

10. In September 2001, Plaintiff [Consumer 1] wanted to take classes with Solid Computer Decisions, Inc. (Solid Computer).

11. Solid Computer acted as a representative of SLM to obtain an extension of credit to pay for those classes.

12. Solid Computer was not licensed or certified to conduct business as a proprietary school in Virginia as required by Va. Code § 22.1-331 and 332.

13. In addition to providing assistance regarding obtaining an extension of credit, Solid Computer guaranteed employment to [Consumer 1] on the condition that he complete the educational program; this promise violated 8VAC20-350-310 of the Virginia Administrative Code.

14. SLM and Solid Computer and Sterling Bank had agreed that Solid Computer would solicit business for SLM and Sterling Bank.

15. As part of that agreement, Solid Computer interacted with consumers on behalf of SLM, including presenting and explaining documents.

16. As part of their agreement, SLM arranged for Sterling Bank to act as the lender for these extensions of credit and SLM would act as servicer.

17. On September 24, 2001, [Consumer 1] and [Consumer 2] agreed to accept credit from Sterling Bank to pay for tuition at Solid Computer.

18. Solid Computer presented [Consumer 1] with loan documents that these Plaintiffs signed.

19. On behalf of Sterling Bank, SLM and Solid Computer presented these Plaintiffs with Truth in Lending disclosures for the credit. (A true and accurate copy is attached as Exhibit A). [*Editor's note: Exhibit A not reproduced herein.*]

THE [CONSUMER 3] TRANSACTION

20. On or about January 10, 2002, [Consumer 3] was contacted by a representative of Solid Computer.

21. [Consumer 3] was informed about employment opportunities at Solid Computer and agreed to come to interview.

22. On January 14, 2002, [Consumer 3] interviewed at Solid Computer in Glen Allen, Virginia, and was informed that once he completed the training program he was guaranteed employment.

23. [Consumer 3] stated that he only wanted to take certain classes rather than the full training component.

24. The Solid Computer representative, [Employee 1], informed him that, because of the arrangement between SLM and Solid Computer, he would be required to take additional classes to meet SLM's funding requirements.

25. On behalf of SLM and Solid Computer, [Employee 1] represented that SLM was the lender and that SLM required that he take $11,000.00 of classes.

26. The allegations of Paragraphs 11 through 16 apply equally to [Consumer 3]'s transaction as to [Consumer 1].

27. To obtain a loan to cover the courses, [Consumer 3] agreed to take $11,000.00 of classes from Solid Computer and filled out an application to obtain the student loan.

28. On January 22, 2002, [Consumer 3] agreed to accept credit from Sterling Bank to pay for tuition at Solid Computer.

29. Solid Computer presented [Consumer 3] with loan documents that he signed.

30. On behalf of Sterling Bank, SLM and Solid Computer presented [Consumer 3] with Truth in Lending disclosures for the credit. (A true and accurate copy is attached as Exhibit B). [*Editor's note: Exhibit B not reproduced herein.*]

THE [CONSUMER 4] TRANSACTION

31. Like [Consumer 1] and [Consumer 3], [Consumer 4] signed up for a loan to cover courses at Solid Computer Decisions.

32. [Consumer 4] was induced to agree to pay the tuition because of the guarantee of employment that was provided by Solid Computer.

33. The allegations of Paragraphs 11 through 16 apply equally to [Consumer 4's] transaction as to [Consumer 1].

34. On October 29, 2001, [Consumer 4] agreed to accept credit from Sterling Bank to pay for tuition at Solid Computer.

35. Solid Computer presented him with loan documents that he signed.

36. On behalf of Sterling Bank, SLM and Solid Computer presented [Consumer 4] with Truth in Lending disclosures for the credit. (A true and accurate copy is attached as Exhibit C). [*Editor's note: Exhibit C not reproduced herein.*]

THE PLAINTIFFS RECEIVE NO BENEFIT FOR THE LOANS THEY SIGNED

37. In each transaction, SLM acted as a credit services business, and was required to comply with Virginia's Credit Services Business Act, Va. Code § 59.1-335.1 *et seq.*

38. In each transaction, Solid Computer acted as a credit services business, and was required to comply with Virginia's Credit Services Business Act, Va. Code § 59.1-335.1 *et seq.*

39. Because Solid Computer was not licensed or certified to operate in Virginia, the contracts it created with any students are void and unenforceable under the common law of Virginia and unenforceable under Va. Code § 22.1-335.

40. Neither Solid Computer nor SLM complied with the requirements of Virginia's Credit Services Business Act.

41. Because of the violations of Virginia's Credit Services Business Act, any contract with Solid Computer or with SLM is unenforceable.

42. As part of Sallie Mae, SLM had been previously informed by the Proprietary Schools Unit of the Virginia Department of Education not to create loans for students of unlicensed or uncertified schools.

43. SLM was specifically informed by the Proprietary Schools Unit of the Virginia Department of Education not to create loans for students of Solid Computer because it was not certified to operate.

44. Even after being specifically informed by the Proprietary Schools Unit of the Virginia Department of Education not to create loans for students of Solid Computer, SLM continued to create loans through its arrangement with Sterling Bank and Solid Computer.

45. Solid Computer never obtained any license or certification to operate in Virginia and simply closed down after signing up hundreds of students.

46. The actions of Defendants towards Plaintiffs were not an isolated instance because Solid Computer signed up approximately 160 students in Northern Virginia and 85 in Richmond.

47. Plaintiffs are informed and believe that Sallie Mae purchased the Plaintiffs' loan contracts from Sterling and that SLM Financial and Sallie Mae currently seek repayment of each loan.

48. Sallie Mae, SLM, and Sterling refuse to abide by the terms of the loan contracts that allow each student to raise against a demand for payment all of their claims and defenses against Solid Computer. (A true and accurate copy of [Consumer 3's] Promissory Note is attached as Exhibit D, and each of the Plaintiffs' Notes are the similar form; the pertinent paragraph is in all capitals on the third page.) [*Editor's note: Exhibit D is not reproduced herein.*]

49. Sallie Mae, SLM, and Sterling never intended to abide by the terms of the loan contracts that allow each student to raise against a demand for payment all of their claims and defenses against Solid Computer.

50. As part of the intent to not honor all the claims and defenses, SLM and Sterling Bank placed a term in the Plaintiffs' notes that seeks to waive each Plaintiffs' right to assert these claims and defenses. (See Exhibit D, Paragraph 10 near the top of the third page.)

51. Sallie Mae and SLM continue to use that term to contradict consumers' rights to assert against such loan contracts their claims and defenses against Solid Computer Decisions. (See letter from SLM dated August 7, 2002, Exhibit E.) [*Editor's note: Exhibit E is not reproduced herein.*]

52. Plaintiffs were harmed by the Defendants' conduct and each have been saddled with a loan in excess of $11,000.00, for which no benefit was received.

53. The Defendants' actions were in intentional or reckless disregard of Plaintiffs' rights sufficient to justify an award of punitive damages.

54. Each and every term in each loan contract, including any limitation and waiver, is unenforceable and void against the Plaintiffs.

55. The Promissory Note signed by each of the Plaintiffs is not actually an agreement to extend credit but is more in the nature of an application for credit. (See Paragraph 1 of Section XII on the second page.)

56. Pursuant to the terms of the Notes, the Amount Financed shown on Exhibit A, B, and C, is merely an estimate of the amount of the credit that may be provided at some time in the future.

57. For each transaction, the disclosure of the Annual Percentage Rate, the Amount Financed, the Finance Charge, the Total of Payments, and the Schedule of Payments are not accurate.

CLASS ACTION ALLEGATIONS

58. Plaintiffs bring this action on behalf of themselves and on behalf of a class of similarly situated persons pursuant to F.R. Civ.P. 23. The Class is defined as follows:

> Persons who obtained a loan arranged by SLM Financial to pay for courses at Solid Computer Decisions in Virginia where Sterling was identified as the lender.

59. Members of the class are so numerous that joinder of them is impractical.

60. There are numerous questions of law and fact common to the Class. Such common questions include, but are not limited to:

(a) The acts and practices of the defendants in the scheme described in the paragraphs above;

(b) The violation of the Federal Truth in Lending Act by the defendants in a uniform fraudulent and illegal scheme;

(c) The violation of state statutory and common law provisions by the defendants in a uniform fraudulent and illegal scheme; and

(d) Whether exemplary damages should be awarded and the amount of such damages which should be awarded.

61. Plaintiffs are members of the Class, and their claims are typical of other class members' claims in that, like the other class members, the named plaintiffs obtained a loan arranged by SLM with Sterling as the lender for courses at Solid Computer; that Solid Computer was never licensed to offer classes in Virginia; that Sallie Mae and SLM knew that SLM was not licensed; that each loan will contain similar Truth In Lending Act violations; that each loan is unenforceable; and that Sallie Mae and SLM continue to want repayment of each loan.

62. Plaintiffs are adequate representatives of the Class's interests in that they will vigorously pursue this action on behalf of the entire Class, have no conflicts with the Class, and retained experienced counsel to represent them.

63. Questions of law and fact common to the Class, including the legal and factual issues relating to operation of the scheme described herein by the defendants, and the liability and the nature of the relationships among the defendants, predominate over any questions affecting only individual members.

64. A class action is superior to other available methods for the fair and efficient adjudication of this controversy; the Class is readily definable and can easily be identified by examination of the defendants' records; prosecution of this case as a class action will eliminate the possibility of repetitious litigation and duplicative punitive damage awards against the defendants and will provide redress for claims for individuals who otherwise might not be able to retain counsel to pursue their claims; there are no problems which would make this case difficult to manage as a class action.

CLAIMS FOR RELIEF

FIRST CAUSE OF ACTION

Violations of the Truth in Lending Act

65. In each transaction and for each member of the class, Sterling Bank violated the Truth in Lending Act and Regulation Z by failing to deliver accurate disclosures as required by the Truth in Lending Act and Regulation Z, including the following:

a. by failing to disclose accurately the "finance charge" in violation of 15 U.S.C. § 1638(a)(3), and Regulation Z, 12 C.F.R. § 226.18(d) and 226.4;

b. by failing to disclose accurately the "amount financed" in violation of 15 U.S.C. § 1638(a)(2) and Regulation Z, 12 C.F.R. § 226.18(b); and

c. by failing to disclose accurately the "annual percentage" in violation of 15 U.S.C. § 1638(a)(4) and Regulation Z, 12 C.F.R. § 226.18(e).

66. The violations of this Act are apparent on the loan documents assigned to Sallie Mae and on the face of each loan document for the class such that Sallie Mae, and any other assignee, is liable for the Truth in Lending Act violation.

SECOND CAUSE OF ACTION

Violations of the Virginia Consumer Protection Act

67. Each transaction and each transaction in the class was a consumer transaction for the purchase of goods or services, and SLM was a supplier as defined by the Virginia Consumer Protection Act ("the VCPA") Va. Code § 59.1-196, *et. seq.*, at § 59.1-198.

68. In each transaction and in each transaction in the class, SLM violated the prohibitions contained in § 59.1-200(A)(8) against refusing to provide goods on the terms offered and in § 59.1-200(A)(14) against using any other deception, fraud, false pretense, false promise, or misrepresentation in connection with a consumer transaction.

69. In each transaction and in each transaction in the class, SLM's violations of the Credit Services Business Act were also violations of the VCPA.

70. Plaintiffs and each member of the class suffered a loss as a result of the Defendant's violations.

71. Plaintiffs and each member of the class are entitled to recover three times their actual damages, or at minimum $1,000.00, pursuant to Va. Code § 59.1-204, because Defendant's violations were willful.

THIRD CAUSE OF ACTION

Violations of the Virginia Credit Services Business Act

72. In each transaction and in each transaction in the class, SLM engaged in the activities of a "credit services business" under Va. Code § 59.1-335.2, and Plaintiffs were consumers protected by the Virginia Credit Services Business Act.

73. In each transaction and in each transaction in the class, SLM willfully failed to comply with the requirements of the Virginia Credit Services Business Act.

74. Plaintiffs and each member of the class sustained actual damages as a result of those violations.

75. In the alternative of willful failures to comply, SLM was negligent in failing to comply with this Act.

FOURTH CAUSE OF ACTION

Conspiracy

76. SLM and Sterling and Solid Computer conspired together to accomplish the legal objective of financing education through illegal means.

77. SLM and Sterling and Solid Computer conspired together to accomplish the illegal objectives of funding an unlicensed school and of avoiding the requirements of the state and federal laws regulating the transaction.

78. Sallie Mae joined the conspiracy by purchasing the Plaintiffs' loan and by seeking to enforce them with knowledge that each was unenforceable.

79. Plaintiffs and each member of the class were harmed by the Defendants' actions.

WHEREFORE, Plaintiffs respectfully pray that this Court:

1. Assume jurisdiction of this case;

2. Award statutory damages to each set Plaintiffs and each member of the class against Sterling Bank and Sallie Mae of twice the actual finance charge, pursuant to 15 U.S.C. § 1640(a)(2)(A)(i) for the extension of credit;

3. Award to Plaintiffs and each member of the class against SLM three times actual damages, or $1,000.00, whichever is greater, for each of the willful violations of the Virginia Consumer Protection Act pursuant to Va. Code § 59.1-204;

4. Award Plaintiffs and each member of the class one award of actual damages pursuant to their actual damages claims under the Truth in Lending Act, Virginia Consumer Protection Act, Virginia Credit Services Business Act, and conspiracy claims;

5. Assess punitive damages against each Defendant under the conspiracy claim and against SLM under the Credit Services Business Act claim;

6. Declare that the Plaintiffs' loan agreements and each member of the class's loan agreements with Sterling Bank are unenforceable, and require Defendants to remove any negative credit references regarding this transaction from all credit reports;

7. Award Plaintiffs their costs, expenses, and reasonable attorney fees pursuant to the Truth in Lending Act, at 15 U.S.C. § 1640(a)(3), and the Virginia Consumer Protection Act, at Va. Code § 59.1-204; and

8. Award Plaintiffs such other relief as the court deems appropriate.

TRIAL BY JURY IS DEMANDED

Respectfully submitted,

[Consumer 1]
[Consumer 2]
[Consumer 3]
[Consumer 4]
[Consumer 5]
By Counsel

E.7.2 Private Student Loan Borrower's Complaint Against Proprietary School and Lender

[Attorneys for Plaintiff]
[Attorneys' Address and Phone Number]

THIS IS AN ARBITRATION MATTER. ASSESSMENT OF DAMAGES IS REQUIRED.

```
——————————————————  )
[CONSUMER]                       )
[Consumer's Address]             )
                      Plaintiff  )
                                 )
v.                               )
                                 )
CAREER VISION OF                 )
PENNSYLVANIA, INC.               )
[Defendant's Address]            )
                                 )
KEY BANK USA, NA                 )
[Defendant's Address]            )
                     Defendants  )
——————————————————  )
```

COMPLAINT—CIVIL ACTION

I. INTRODUCTION

1. Plaintiff brings this suit against a for-profit trade school and the bank providing financing for its students, seeking declaratory and equitable relief and damages for Defendants' illegal, unfair, and deceptive business practices. Defendant Career Vision canceled the computer networking course in which plaintiff enrolled several months before completion, and refused to refund his tuition, while Defendant Key Bank refused to acknowledge is liability or responsibility for the actions of its business partner.

II. PARTIES

2. Plaintiff [Consumer] resides at [Consumer's Address].

3. Defendant, Career Vision of Pennsylvania, Inc., d/b/a Career Vision, is a Pennsylvania corporation with a place of business at 1617 John F. Kennedy Boulevard, Philadelphia, Pennsylvania, 19103, and a place of business at 120 Wood Avenue, Suite 509, Iselin New Jersey, 08830.

4. Defendant Key Bank, USA, NA is a corporation and federally-chartered bank with its principal place of business at m127 Public Square, Cleveland Ohio, 44114.

III. FACTS

5. Defendant Career Vision owns and operates a for-profit trade school licensed by the Pennsylvania Board of Private Licensed Schools, offering courses in computer technology.

6. In May or June of 2003 [Consumer] saw a newspaper advertisement placed by Career Vision offering classes in computer networking, with financial aid available for qualified students.

7. [Consumer] visited the school in response to the advertisement, and was greeted by a female sales and admissions representative employed by Career Vision.

8. The Career Vision representative told [Consumer] that he could enroll in a nine month computer networking course that would qualify him for jobs earning as much as $70,000 per year.

9. The Career Vision representative also assured [Consumer] of the high quality of the networking course, mentioning among other things that the school was licensed by the Pennsylvania Education Department, and accredited.

10. The representations regarding the quality of the training and the salary of its graduates were false and misleading.

11. Relying on these representations [Consumer] signed a written enrollment agreement for a nine month Networking course for a tuition of $12,000, and paid a $100 registration fee. A copy of the agreement is attached as Exhibit "A".

12. Career Vision's employees presented [Consumer] with various documents to sign in order to apply for financial aid. Although represented to him as financial aid documents, the forms were in reality nothing more than an application and promissory Note to borrow $12,000 plus a $600 loan fee from Defendant Key Bank. [Consumer] was also required to obtain a cosigner. A copy of the Note is attached as Exhibit "B".

13. Career Vision and Key Bank had a close business relationship according to which Career Vision employees assisted its customers in applying for Key Bank loans and Key Bank directed the loan proceeds to Career Vision in payment of tuition and fees. In particular and without limitation, Career Vision employees regularly and systematically provided loan application forms from Key Bank to [Consumer] and its other students, forwarded the applications to Key Bank, assisted students in completing any additional steps to obtain the loans, and arranged for the loan proceeds to be paid directly from Key Bank to Career Vision.

14. The loan provided by Key Bank to fund the training course was *not* guaranteed or insured by any federal or state government program. As a result, [Consumer] would not be eligible for deferments, forbearance, loan discharges, consolidation and other programs commonly available to student loan borrowers with government-backed student loans. This aspect of the loan was not disclosed or explained to [Consumer].

15. The courses provided to [Consumer] were all taught by a single instructor. After about three months, the instructor began arriving late to class, leaving early, and teaching only one to two hours of a scheduled three hour class.

16. By early November the instructor ceased all instruction. Career Vision employees told [Consumer] and the other students that they would be notified when they could return to continue their studies. [Consumer] was never contacted after that point and was never offered satisfactory arrangements to complete his course.

17. The Career Vision course did not provide [Consumer] with any transferable credits usable by him at any other training or educational institution.

18. [Consumer] received no benefit from the aborted and partial training course provided by Career Vision.

19. [Consumer] filed a complaint with the Pennsylvania Board of Private Licensed Schools, which eventually found Career Vision in violation of its regulations for failure to make tuition refunds.

20. Career Vision never refunded [Consumer] any of his tuition or fees.

21. [Consumer] notified Key Bank of the failure of Career Vision to perform its contractual obligations. Nevertheless, Key Bank has continued to insist that he repay the loan used to fund his aborted training course.

22. [Consumer] has made payments to Key Bank of $117.08 monthly for principal and interest from June 2003 to the present. Key Bank continues to assert that he remains liable for the remaining balance of the $12,600 loan.

COUNT I: VIOLATION OF PENNSYLVANIA UNFAIR TRADE PRACTICES AND CONSUMER PROTECTION LAW (CPL)73 P.S. § 201-1 ET. SEQ.

23. Plaintiff realleges and incorporate by reference all preceding allegations of law and fact.

24. Plaintiff obtained the student loans at issue primarily for personal, family or household purposes.

25. Career Vision represented to [Consumer] that its services had benefits and characteristics that they did not have, including the quality of the instruction and the potential salary of graduates.

26. Career Vision failed to disclose to [Consumer] the drawbacks and lack of benefits that resulted from obtaining a private student loan not guaranteed or provided by any government agency. This information would have been highly material to him.

27. Career Vision's failure to provide the services promised, and its continuing representations that it was not required to refund [Consumer's] tuition despite its complete failure to provide him the training course, was unfair and deceptive conduct within the meaning of the CPL.

28. The representation by Key Bank that Career Vision's failure to deliver the training services promised does not affect [Consumer's] liability on the loan was unfair and deceptive within the meaning of the CPL.

29. The loan from Key Bank to Plaintiff was a "purchase money loan" within the meaning of the Federal Trade Commission's regulation on preservation of claims and defenses, 16 C.F.R. 433.

30. Key Bank failed to include in its promissory Note the Notice required by 16 C.F.R. § 433.2, stating that the loan holder is subject to the consumer's claims arising from the sale of services funded by the loan, i.e., the trade school course.

31. Defendants' violation of the FTC Rule and Pennsylvania law constitutes a *per se* unfair or deceptive act or practice, in violation of the CPL.

32. In addition, Defendants' acts described above are unfair acts or deceptive acts or practices, as defined by 73 P.S. § 201-2(4) and 73 P.S. § 201-3, in that the Defendants have:

a. Caused a likelihood of confusion or misunderstanding as to the source of the loans, and the relationship between the Defendants and the legal consequences thereof, in violation of 73 P.S. § 201-2(4)(ii) and (iii),

b. Represented that the training services and the loan services had characteristics or benefits that they did not have, in violation of 73 P.S. § 201-2(4)(v),

c. Represented that services are of a particular quality when they are of another, in violation of 73 P.S. § 201-2(4)(vii),

d. Failing to comply with the terms of a written guarantee or warranty, namely the enrollment agreement's guarantee of a full refund in the event a program is canceled, in violation of 73 P.S. § 201-2(4)(xiv) and

e. Engaged in other deceptive conduct which created a likelihood of confusion or of misunderstanding, as defined by 73 P.S. § 201-2(4)(xxi).

33. In addition to the fact that the above-described illegality constitutes *per se* unfair or deceptive trade practices, Plaintiff has relied to his detriment on Defendant's implied misrepresentations concerning the legality of the contract terms and he has suffered an ascertainable loss of money as a result of these unfair or deceptive acts or practices.

34. Defendants' acts were made knowingly, deliberately, and repeatedly, warranting the imposition of an award of treble damages under 73 P.S. § 201-9.2(a).

COUNT II: BREACH OF CONTRACT

35. Plaintiffs reallege and incorporate by reference all preceding allegations of law and fact.

36. Career Vision breached its contract with Plaintiff.

37. The breach was material and complete, in that the partial and incomplete services offered to the Plaintiff were of no value in the absence of a means to complete the course or transfer credits elsewhere.

38. The enrollment agreement and promissory Note constituted a single and unified contract for the purchase and financing of educational services.

39. Due to Career Vision's material breach, Plaintiff is not obligated to pay the price of the educational services that were never provided, or to pay the loan to Key Bank.

40. Due to Career Vision's material breach, Plaintiff is entitled to a refund of all payments made to Career Vision and Key Bank.

COUNT III: DECLARATION OF CONTRACTUAL UNCONSCIONABILITY

41. Plaintiffs reallege and incorporate by reference all preceding allegations of law and fact.

42. As part of Defendant's scheme to evade U.S. and Pennsylvania law, they implemented a plan to try to increase the likelihood that they could escape accountability for their illegal actions by including in their form loan contracts several provisions intended to limit the legal remedies available to borrowers who might wish to challenge the legality of Defendants' practices.

43. In accordance with this plan, all Key Bank USA contracts during the relevant time period failed to include the mandatory Notice of preservation of consumer claims and defenses required by the FTC Rule, and contained provisions that claim to make the contracts governed by Ohio law, and (c) require borrowers to bring any legal action under the contract in Ohio.

44. These provisions are procedurally unconscionable in that Key Bank loan contracts are essentially adhesion contracts. Borrowers lack the bargaining power to negotiate any material changes to the terms imposed by Defendants.

45. These contract provisions are substantively unconscionable in that they function, as a practical matter, as exculpatory clauses that insulate Defendants from legal accountability and deny consumers access to reasonable and appropriate remedies. As a result Key Bank unreasonably and illegally attempts to shift significant risks associated with the trade school contract to the consumer.

46. It would unfair and unconscionable for Defendant Key Bank to be able to insulate itself from the misconduct of its trade school business partner.

47. Because the contractual clauses and absence of the required FTC Rule provisions are procedurally and substantively unconscionable, Plaintiff is entitled to a declaratory judgment that as to these provisions, the contract is unenforceable because it violates public policy.

WHEREFORE, Plaintiff requests judgment in his favor and against defendant, for actual and treble damages, attorney's fees and costs, voiding or reformation of the contract(s), and any other and further relief as the court deems just and proper.

_____

[Attorney for Plaintiff]

[Attorneys for Plaintiff]
[Attorneys' Address and Phone Number]

_____	)
[CONSUMER]	)
[Consumer's Address]	)
Plaintiff	)
	)
v.	)
	)
CAREER VISION OF	)
PENNSYLVANIA, INC.	)
[Defendant's Address]	)
	)
KEY BANK USA, NA	)
[Defendant's Address]	)
Defendants	)
_____	)

VERIFICATION

I, [Consumer], verify under the penalties of 18 Pa. C. S. A. § 4904 relating to unsworn falsification to authorities that I am the plaintiff in this case and that the facts set forth in this pleading are true and correct to the best of my knowledge, information and belief.

Date: _____

[Consumer]

Sample Discovery and Freedom of Information Act Requests

F.1 Discovery in Student Loan Collection Cases

IN THE UNITED STATES DISTRICT COURT
FOR THE MIDDLE DISTRICT OF LOUISIANA

```
                                    )
Mary Johnson, on behalf of          )
herself and all others similarly    )
situated,                           )
                       Plaintiff,   )
                                    )
v.                                  )
                                    )
The Premier Collectors, Inc.,       )
                       Defendant.   )
                                    )
```

PLAINTIFF'S FIRST DISCOVERY REQUEST

Plaintiff hereby requests that defendant respond to the following requests for admission, interrogatories and document requests. Throughout this request:

A. If defendant's response to any of the requests for admissions submitted herewith is anything other than an unqualified admission, describe in detail the basis for the inability to make such admission.

B. If any document requested in the document requests submitted herewith was but no longer is in defendant's possession, custody or control, state: the date of its disposition; the manner of its disposition (e.g., lost, destroyed, transferred to a third party); and the circumstances surrounding the disposition of the document including the identity of the person who disposed of it, the reason for its disposal, the identity of anyone who may have copies of it, the identity of anyone ordering or requesting its disposal, and whether its disposal was in compliance with defendant's document destruction policies.

C. Unless otherwise specified in a particular paragraph, the "relevant time period" covered by this request is August 1, 1993 to the present.

D. PCI means The Premier Collectors, Inc.

E. These requests are subject to the instructions and definitions attached hereto as *Exhibit 1 [reprinted at the end this section].*

REQUESTS FOR ADMISSION

PLEASE TAKE NOTICE THAT, pursuant to Federal Rules of Civil Procedure 26 and 36, plaintiff hereby requests that defendant admit or deny the truth of the following matters in writing within 30 days after service of this request.

1. The Premier Collectors, Inc. ("PCI") is regularly engaged for profit in the collection of debts allegedly owed by consumers.
RESPONSE:

2. PCI is a "debt collector" as defined in the Fair Debt Collection Practices Act, 15 U.S.C. §1692a(6).
RESPONSE:

3. On or about August 11, 1993, PCI mailed to plaintiff a collection letter demanding $11,417.31 allegedly owing to the U.S. Department of Education. *Exhibit A* is a copy of the letter [*not reprinted infra*].
RESPONSE:

4. On or about April 20, 1994, PCI mailed to plaintiff a collection letter demanding $10,706.14 allegedly owing to the U.S. Department of Education. *Exhibit B* is a copy of the letter [*not reprinted infra*].
RESPONSE:

5. On or about May 5, 1994, PCI mailed to plaintiff a collection letter demanding $10,732.65 allegedly owing to the U.S. Department of Education. *Exhibit C* is a copy of the letter [*not reprinted infra*].
RESPONSE:

6. *Exhibit A-C* were mailed in an attempt to collect alleged debts arising from transactions primarily for personal, family, or household purposes, namely, an alleged student loan.
RESPONSE:

7. Defendant is not affiliated with U.S. Department of Education.
RESPONSE:

8. Defendant did not and does not determine the course of legal action, if any, taken by the United States Government with respect to student loans.
RESPONSE:

9. Neither PCI, the U.S. Department of Justice, nor anyone else, has filed suit against plaintiff to collect the alleged debt referred to in *Exhibits A-C.*
RESPONSE:

10. PCI regularly mails, or causes to be mailed, collection letters

bearing the name of the U.S. Department of Education to Louisiana residents in an effort to collect consumer debts.

RESPONSE:

11. Between August 1, 1993 and the present, PCI mailed more than 20 letters prepared on the same form as *Exhibit A* to Louisiana residents in an effort to collect student loans.

RESPONSE:

12. Between August 1, 1993 and the present, PCI mailed more than 20 letters prepared on the same form as *Exhibit B* to Louisiana residents in an effort to collect student loans.

RESPONSE:

13. Between August 1, 1993 and the present, PCI mailed more than 20 letters prepared on the same form as *Exhibit C* to Louisiana residents in an effort to collect student loans.

RESPONSE:

14. Between August 1, 1993 and the present, PCI sought to recover collection fees exceeding 20% of the principal debt from more than 20 Louisiana residents who allegedly owed money on student loans.

RESPONSE:

15. PCI does not in fact conduct an investigation of the income, savings, employment, real estate ownership and personal assets of each person to whom *Exhibit B* is sent.

RESPONSE:

16. PCI has not in fact conducted an investigation of the income, savings, employment, real estate ownership and personal assets of any person to whom *Exhibit B* was sent. [not reprinted *infra*]

RESPONSE:

17. A suit by the U.S. Department of Justice on a student loan may not result in garnishment, attachment or judgment liens until the consumer is heard in court and a judgment entered against the consumer.

RESPONSE:

INTERROGATORIES

PLEASE TAKE NOTICE THAT, pursuant to Federal Rules of Civil Procedure 26 and 33, plaintiff propounds the following Interrogatories to be answered by defendant under oath, within 30 days of service hereof.

1a. Describe the method, procedure, or general approach which defendant presently uses in the preparation and mailing of collection notices which are eventually sent to persons who allegedly owe money on student loans. Include in your answer a description of all letters or any series of letters that PCI sends to such persons.

ANSWER:

b. State when the method, procedure or general approach described in response to (a) was adopted;

ANSWER:

c. Describe all other methods, procedures or general approaches defendant uses in the preparation of and mailing of collection letters eventually sent to such persons.

ANSWER:

2a. How many notices, using the same form as *Exhibit A*, were sent to Louisiana residents between August 1, 1993 and the present [not reprinted *infra*].

ANSWER:

b. State the names and addresses of each such person.

ANSWER:

3a. How many notices, using the same form as *Exhibit B*, were sent to Louisiana residents between August 1, 1993 and the present [not reprinted *infra*].

ANSWER:

b. State the names and addresses of each such person.

ANSWER:

4a. How many notices, using the same form as *Exhibit C*, were sent to Louisiana residents between August 1, 1993 and the present [not reprinted *infra*].

ANSWER:

b. State the names and addresses of each such person.

ANSWER:

5. Describe all reports, recommendations for action, or other advice provided by PCI to the United States Government with respect to alleged student loan debts which PCI is unable to collect.

ANSWER:

6. Identify all instances in which PCI has filed suit or caused suit to be filed to collect an alleged student loan debt owed to the U. S. Department of Education.

ANSWER:

7. Describe any basis which PCI has in contract, regulation, or otherwise for demanding a 42.84% collection fee from plaintiff, and how the amount of such fee was determined.

ANSWER:

8. State whether any person to whom PCI has ever (before or during the class period) sent a letter using the same form as *Exhibit B* has had their salary garnished, equity or bank accounts attached, or liens placed against their real estate without a judgment being first entered against that person by a court.

ANSWER:

9. Describe all investigations of income, bank accounts, business and employment information, real estate ownership, automobile ownership and personal assets which PCI has conducted of persons who were sent letters using the same form as *Exhibit B*, identifying each person who was investigated:

ANSWER:

REQUESTS FOR PRODUCTION OF DOCUMENTS

PLEASE TAKE NOTICE THAT, pursuant to Federal Rules of Civil Procedure 26 and 34, plaintiff hereby requests that defendant produce to plaintiff's counsel for examination, inspection and copying all of the documents specified herein in its possession, custody or control, within 30 days of service of this request.

1. All documents showing the number of Louisiana residents to whom PCI sent collection letters using the same forms as *Exhibit A-C* during any portion of the period between August 1, 1993 and the present [not reprinted *infra*]. If no documents showing the number of Louisiana residents exists, produce all documents showing the number of persons to whom PCI sent such letters during such period, without regard to residence.

RESPONSE:

2. All documents showing the names and addresses of Louisiana residents who were sent a collection letter prepared using the same forms as *Exhibit A-C*, during any portion of the period between August 1, 1993 and the present.

RESPONSE:

3. A copy of each form collection letter sent to Louisiana residents by PCI on or after August 1, 1993.

RESPONSE:

4. All documents purporting to authorize or justify the 42.84%

collection fee referred to in *Exhibit C*.

RESPONSE:

5. All reports, recommendations for action, or other advice provided by PCI to the United States Government with respect to alleged student loan debts which PCI is unable to collect.

RESPONSE:

6. All documents relating to any instance in which PCI has filed suit or caused suit to be filed to collect an alleged student loan debt owed to the U. S. Department of Education.

RESPONSE:

7. All documents relating to any instance (before or during the class period) in which a person to whom PCI sent a letter using the same form as *Exhibit B* has had their salary garnished, equity or bank accounts attached, or liens placed against their real estate without a judgment being first entered against that person by a court.

RESPONSE:

8. All documents relating to investigations of income, bank accounts, business and employment information, real estate ownership, automobile ownership and personal assets which PCI has conducted of persons who were sent letters using the same form as *Exhibit B*.

RESPONSE:

9. All documents relied on by PCI in answering any of the accompanying interrogatories or in responding to any of the accompanying requests for admission.

RESPONSE:

[*Attorney for Plaintiff*]

EXHIBIT 1

INSTRUCTIONS AND DEFINITIONS

Instructions

1. All documents within your possession, custody, or control or that of your agents, employees, or attorneys shall be produced. Without limitation of the term "control" as used in the preceding sentence, a document is deemed to be in your control if you have the right to secure the document or a copy thereof from another person having actual possession thereof.

2. To the extent any paragraph is objected to, set forth all reasons for your objection.

3. If you prefer, you may provide legible copies of documents that reflect all markings, notations and highlighting on the originals.

4. Documents to be produced shall be either (1) organized as they are kept in the ordinary course of business or (2) organized and labelled to correspond with the paragraphs of the request for production or interrogatory to which they are responsive.

5. The singular includes the plural number and vice versa. The masculine includes the feminine and neuter genders. The past tense includes the present tense where the clear meaning is not distorted by change of tense.

6. To the extent that any document cannot be furnished, such documents as are available shall be supplied, together with a description of the documents not furnished and the reason for not furnishing them.

7. "And" as well as "or" are used either disjunctively or conjunctively as necessary to bring information within the scope of the request that might otherwise be outside the scope of the request.

8. Plaintiff requests that documents be produced as they become ready and that defendant does not wait until all documents are ready to start production.

Definitions

1. The term "document" is used in the broadest sense permitted and includes, by way of illustration only and not by way of limitation, the following, whether printed or reproduced by any process, or written or produced by hand: ledgers; notes; correspondence; communications of any nature; telegrams; memoranda; notebooks of any character; summaries or records of personal conversations; diaries; reports; publications; photographs; microfilm, microfiche and similar media; minutes and records of meetings; transcripts of oral testimony and statements; reports and summaries of interviews; reports and summaries of investigations; court papers; brochures; pamphlets; press releases; drafts of, revisions of drafts of and translations of any document; tape recordings; dictation belts; invoices; bills; accounting records; telephone toll records; and disks, tapes and other magnetic or electronic information storage media. Any document or reproduction of a document bearing on any sheet or side thereof any marks, including by way of illustration only and not by way of limitation initials, stamped indicia or any comment or any notation of any character and not a part of the original text, is to be considered a separate document. Where it is uncertain whether something is a document, this definition shall be construed to include it.

2. References to "you" or any named entity or individual include agents, employees and attorneys of that person, whether or not acting within the scope of their authority; all other persons acting on behalf of the person referred to; and in the case of an entity its merged or acquired predecessors.

3. "Person" includes any individual, corporation, partnership, joint venture, firm, association, proprietorship, governmental agency, board, authority, commission and other entity.

4. "Communication" includes every manner or means of disclosure, transfer or exchange of information, whether orally or by document or whether face-to-face, by telephone, mail, personal delivery or otherwise.

5. "Relates," "refers," and "reflects" include constitutes, describes, contains, discusses, reflects, refers to, and logically pertains to.

6. "Identify" or "identification," when used with respect to a document, means to state the general nature of the document (*i.e.*, letter, memorandum, etc.); the name of the author or originator; each addressee; all individuals designated on the document to receive a copy or otherwise known to have received a copy; the date, title and general subject matter of the document; the present custodian of each copy thereof and the last known address of each such custodian; and the date of the making of the document.

7. "Identify" or "identification," when used with respect to a communication, means to state the date of the communication; the type of communication (*i.e.*, telephone conversation, meeting, etc.); the place where the communication took place; the identification of the person who made the communication; the identification of each person who received the communication and of each person present when it was made; and the subject matter discussed.

8. "Identify" or "identification," when used with respect to a person, means state the name, last known business and home addresses and telephone numbers, occupation, job titles and Social Security Number of the person being identified.

F.2 Discovery Directed to Trade Schools

F.2.1 First Interrogatories and Requests for Production of Documents from a School

COURT OF COMMON PLEAS PHILADELPHIA COUNTY

————————————)	
PAULA WILLIAMS)	
)	
v.)	
)	
NATIONAL SCHOOL OF)	
HEALTH TECHNOLOGY, INC.)	
————————————)	

PLAINTIFF'S FIRST SET OF INTERROGATORIES AND REQUESTS FOR PRODUCTION DIRECTED TO DEFENDANT

Pursuant to Rules 4005, 4006 and 4009, Pa. Rules of Civil Procedure, defendant demands response within thirty (30) days to the following interrogatories and requests for production of documents:

DEFINITIONS

a. "Defendant" or "the school" shall refer to National School of Health Technology, its agents, officers, or employees.

b. "Plaintiff" shall refer to Paula Williams.

c. "Document" is used in the broadest possible sense permissible under the rules of civil procedure. Such term shall refer to any mechanism of preserving or transmitting any information, whether it be written, printed, photographed, electronically recorded, or otherwise made and maintained. It shall include all tangible items of any nature, both originals and copies, and all attachments and appendices thereto, and all drafts thereof, including but not limited to, agreements, contracts, communications, correspondence, letters, telegrams, faxes, memoranda, records, reports, books, summaries or other records of meetings and conferences, summaries or other records of negotiations, diaries, calendars, statistical data or statements, work papers, charts, accounts, brochures, circulars, press releases, marginal notations, bills, invoices, journals, lists, files and file jackets, printouts, compilations, minutes, checks, envelopes or folders or similar containers, vouchers, transcripts, articles, tape or disc recordings, photographs and including any information contained in a computer, although not yet printed out, within the possession, custody or control of defendant.

d. "Trial" includes arbitration hearings.

e. "State board" means the Pennsylvania Board of Private Licensed Schools.

f. "And" as well as "or" shall be construed either disjunctively or conjunctively as necessary to bring within the scope of the following interrogatories and requests information and documents that might otherwise be construed to be outside their scope; and as used herein the singular shall include the plural and the plural shall include the singular except as the context may otherwise dictate.

INTERROGATORIES

1. State the date of defendant's incorporation, the state(s) in which it is incorporated and the name of the incorporators.
Answer:

2. State the number of outstanding shares of stock and identify the owners of said stock, including the numbers of shares owned by each person.
Answer:

3. Identify by name, home address and occupation all members of defendant's board of directors on a) January 1, 1985, b) January 1, 1987, c) January 1, 1989 and d) January 1, 1991.
Answer:

4. Identify by name, home address and occupation the officers of defendant corporation as of a) January 1, 1985, b) January 1, 1987, c) January 1, 1989 and d) January 1, 1991.
Answer:

5. Identify by name and home address all individuals who have served as the chief administrator of the school between January 1, 1985 and the present, stating for each the time period during which they served and their salaries during that period.
Answer:

6. a. Is defendant the subsidiary of any other corporation?
   b. Does defendant own any subsidiaries?
   c. If the answer to either a. or b. is affirmative, identify and explain.
Answer:

7. Has defendant undergone any ownership changes since 1980? If so, explain such changes and identify the dates and the parties involved.
Answer:

8a. When did the school at 801 Arch Street open its doors?
   b. When did the (i) Nurse's Aide and (ii) Medical Assistant programs begin?
   c. Is the school at 801 Arch Street a branch of some other school? If so, identify the branching institution.
   d. Describe the relationship, if any, between the school at 801 Arch Street and school of the same name in Northeast Philadelphia.
Answer:

9. Identify all institutional accreditations and all program accreditations pertaining to the Nurse's Aide or Medical Assistant programs which defendant has received since 1980, including the commencement and expiration dates and the accrediting agency.
Answer:

10. Have any past or present employees, directors or officers of defendant served on or been associated with an accreditation commission or agency? If so, identify the person, his/her relationship to defendant, the accrediting institution, position held at the accrediting institution and relevant dates.
Answer:

11. List the fee schedules for a) the Nurse's Aide and b) the Medical Assistant programs for each year since 1985, including all

components of that schedule, and for each component explain what it is and, where applicable, the reason for increases.

Answer:

12. List the names, home addresses and positions of all employees or representatives of defendant who, during the time period 1988 to the present worked in the marketing, admissions or financial aid component of defendant's organization, and for each specify the particular job responsibilities held and, as to each position held, the time period applicable and the name and position of the individual's immediate supervisor. In addition, identify which, if any, individuals are still associated with defendant.

Answer:

13. State the names, home addresses, and positions of all officials or employees of defendant which had any policy-making responsibility concerning the standards and procedures employed by admissions personnel at the school during the time period 1988 to the present, and as to each, state what, if any, other positions the individual has had in defendant's organization and the relevant dates of such positions.

Answer:

14. State the names and home addresses of all individuals who made decisions or who participated in making decisions during the time period 1988 to the present to admit prospective students under the school's "ability-to-benefit" standards.

Answer:

15. List all academic instructors who taught courses in either the Nurse's Aide or Medical Assistant program during the years 1988 to the present and for each specify:

a. The courses taught and the applicable time period;

b. The individual's degrees, certifications and prior teaching experience;

c. His/her last known address and telephone number.

Answer:

16. State the names, and, if not previously listed, their last known addresses and phone numbers, of all individuals who participated in the development of the curriculum of either the Nurse's Aide or Medical Assistant program and, in addition, as to each of them:

a. List their academic and professional credentials;

b. Describe the nature of the participation; and

c. Specify all positions, with applicable dates, that they have held in defendant's organization.

Answer:

17. Regarding defendant's pleading that "admissions representatives . . . disclose to applicants the range of hourly rates earned by past graduates based upon the school's placement data," *Answer* ¶ 6(a),

a. Specify the range of rates which were disclosed to applicants in the Nurse's Aide and Medical Assistant programs during the period 1988 to the present and

b. Identify the data and the source of such data upon which the said disclosures were based.

Answer:

18. Identify the name and position of all representatives of defendant who interviewed plaintiff prior to her first day of class and specify the dates and purposes of such interviews.

19a. Describe defendant's policy(ies) in effect during the years 1987-89 regarding the payment of commissions to sales representatives, financial aid employees or students?

b. Was any individual paid a commission as a result of plaintiff's enrollment, financial aid award or attendance? If so, identify the person by name and relationship to defendant and explain the terms and amount of such commission.

c. What documents were examined for purpose of answering "b?".

Answer:

20a. State the dates in which plaintiff actually attended classes at the school.

b. State the date plaintiff was terminated from the school.

c. If the date of termination is different from the last date of attendance, explain how defendant determined the date of termination.

Answer:

21a. State the amount defendant refunded to plaintiff.

b. State the date paid and the method of payment.

c. Explain how the amount refunded was calculated.

Answer:

22a. Specify the amounts of all financial aid which defendant received on plaintiff's behalf, including the specific aid program under which funds were received, the payor of such funds and the date received.

b. Specify the amounts of all financial aid funds received on plaintiff's behalf which defendant refunded to a lender, guarantee agency, or the United States government and as to each refund specify the program, the payee and the date payment was sent.

Answer:

23. State the names, positions and, if not previously stated, the home addresses of all individuals who were responsible to assist prospective or enrolled students in obtaining information concerning the matters covered in document request # 17, *infra*, with the relevant dates.

Answer:

24. For years ending December 31, 1986, 1988 and 1990, identify by name and itemized dollar figures the four highest paid employees or officers of defendant, including salary, fees, commissions or any other form of direct compensation and also including any payments for expenses such as automobiles or travel.

Answer:

DOCUMENT REQUESTS

1. Organizational charts for defendant's organization which exhibit the chain of authority and responsibility.

2. Any and all advertisements, mailings and marketing literature employed by defendant during the period 1988 to the present which was targeted either to prospective students or to prospective employees, including the scripts of all television commercials broadcast during said period.

3. All internal memoranda, training manuals, scripts, documents or writings of any kind which pertain to the standards, procedures

or marketing tips or strategies employed by the school's admissions personnel or which instruct, advise, set policy, train or otherwise advise, educate or set guidelines for agents, representatives, officers or employees of defendant, which were in use or which applied to the time period 1987 to the present.

4. All documents involved in, referring to or relating to studies or surveys pertaining to or used in connection with defendant's recruitment of new students.

5. Any and all admissions tests administered by defendant for admission into its Nurse's Aide and Medical Assistant programs during the time period 1988 to the present, and as to each:

    a. Identify the source for the test and

    b. Produce copies of all applicable written criteria or correspondence from the school's accrediting commission pertaining to the school's use of the particular test.

6. The entire contents of plaintiff's admission file, including file jacket and all documents, notes, and other writings contained therein, including, but not limited to, admissions tests, enrollment agreements, "How Our Students Are Doing" disclosures, interview notes, financial aid inquiries and internal memoranda concerning the plaintiff's application or admission and defendant's decision to admit her.

7. The entire contents of plaintiff's academic and disciplinary files including the file jacket and all documents, notes, and other writings contained therein, including, but not limited to, transcripts, evaluations, internal memoranda, letters and notes of conversations.

8. Any and all account cards, ledger sheets or other documents showing debits, credits, and/or a running balance, pertaining to charges, payments, refunds and other financial transactions involving plaintiff.

9. Any and all documents, not covered by another section of this request, that are signed by plaintiff or that relate to the transaction in question.

    10a. Course outlines and reading lists for any remedial courses offered by defendant for "ability to benefit" students during the period 1988 to the present.

    b. Names and addresses of all individuals who taught such courses and relevant time periods that they did so.

11. Any and all applications and supporting documents sent to a third-party accrediting agency or commission and all accrediting documents received regarding the defendant's school in general or regarding in particular the Nurse's Aide or Medical Assistant programs.

12. The raw data, regardless of the form in which it is kept, from which defendant reported to the state board its Nurse's Aide or Medical Assistant enrollments, completions, withdrawals and the employment of graduates for years ending June 30, 1987 to the present.

13. Any and all application forms and all supporting documents submitted by defendant to the United States Department of Education and all eligibility notifications received by defendant concerning a) the school's status as an "eligible institution" to participate in federal financial aid program, and b) the school's designation as a participant in individual programs administered by the Department of Education.

14. All applications and supporting documents submitted by defendant to the state board pertaining to the licensing of its Nurse's Aide and Medical Assistant programs and all documents received from the state board pertaining to same.

15. All site visit and monitoring reports concerning any aspect of defendant's operation which was performed by the state board, by an accrediting institution or by the United States Department of Education since 1985.

16. All written policies and all documents pertaining to such policies in effect during the period 1988 to the present regarding the school's definition of satisfactory academic progress and regarding student appeal rights concerning determinations of unsatisfactory progress and for each identify a) all persons (and their positions) who were responsible for developing these policies and b) their effective dates.

17. All written policies and all documents pertaining to such policies in effect at the school during the time period 1988 to the present regarding student refunds and regarding the application of such refunds to appropriate financial aid accounts.

18. All written materials which defendant disseminated to prospective and enrolled students in the Nurse's Aide or Medical Assistant program during the period 1988 to the present regarding a) financial aid eligibility criteria and the criteria and methods employed for making award determinations, b) itemized course costs, c) the refund policy, d) standards for progress, attendance and other student regulations, e) the academic content of and faculty for each program, f) the extent, nature and success rate of the placement service, g) the pass rates of former students, h) the rate of employment by former students, i) completion rates by former students and j) information regarding starting salaries and job availability in relevant fields.

19. For each document produced in response to request #18, identify a) the source for the document, b) the source of all data which would be contained in a form designed to be filled out, d) all individuals who participated in preparing the document and their positions, e) the time period during which it was used and f) all individuals who would have provided any data contained in a completed form.

20. All documents from which the data referred to in interrogatory #17, *supra*, were obtained.

21. Defendant's annual, audited financial reports for years ending December 31, 1986-1990.

22. Any and all professional articles written by present or past employees or officers of defendant.

23. All documents referring or relating to defendant's document retention policy.

24. All court pleadings pertaining to litigation between defendant and a former student or former employee which were filed on behalf of the former student or employee.

25. Any and all documents defendant intends to introduce at trial.

[Attorney for Plaintiff]

F.2.2 Additional Interrogatories and Request for Production of Documents from a School

UNITED STATES DISTRICT COURT
EASTERN DISTRICT OF PENNSYLVANIA

```
—————————————————  )
PAULA WILLIAMS, on behalf   )
of herself and of others    )
similarly situated,         )
                Plaintiffs, )
                            )
v.                          )
                            )
NATIONAL SCHOOL OF          )
HEALTH TECHNOLOGY,          )
INC., UNITED STUDENT AID    )
FUNDS and MERITOR           )
SAVINGS BANK/PSFS, on       )
behalf of themselves and of )
others similarly situated, and )
LAMAR ALEXANDER,            )
SECRETARY OF THE            )
UNITED STATES               )
DEPARTMENT OF               )
EDUCATION,                  )
                Defendants  )
—————————————————  )
```

PLAINTIFF'S FIRST SET OF INTERROGATORIES AND REQUESTS FOR PRODUCTION TO DEFENDANTS FRANCE AND ROBERTS

Plaintiff Sarah Williams, by her undersigned counsel, propounds the following Interrogatories and Requests for Production of Documents to defendants Diane France and Elizabeth Roberts pursuant to Fed.R.Civ.P. 26, 33 and 34. Each Interrogatory must be answered separately and full in writing under oath, and the answers must be signed by the person making them. A copy of defendants' answers, together with any objections, must be served upon plaintiffs no later than thirty (30) days after the service of these Interrogatories and Document Requests. Defendants are requested to produce for inspection and copying, within thirty (30) days from the date of service hereof, at the offices of below-signed counsel, any and all documents described in the Document Requests below.

INSTRUCTIONS

1. In answering, defendants are requested to identify separately and in a manner suitable for use in a subpoena all sources of information (whether human, documentary or other) and all records maintained by them, by National School of Health Technology or any by any other person, entity or organization on which defendants rely in answering the Interrogatories or which pertain or relate to the information called for by the Interrogatories.

2. The Interrogatories and Document Requests are to be considered continuing, and supplemental answers and documents must be filed by defendants upon discovering or becoming aware of additional responsive documents or of information rendering prior answers or any part thereof inaccurate, incomplete or untrue.

3. If any information called for by any Interrogatory is not available in the full detail requested, such Interrogatory shall be deemed to require the setting forth of the information related to the subject matter of the request in such detailed manner as is available.

4. If defendants withhold any requested information or identification and production of any document on the basis of privilege, please so state, and for each such document provide:

   (a) The nature of the privilege(s) claimed;
   (b) The type of document;
   (c) The general subject matter of the document;
   (d) The date of the document; and
   (e) Such other information as is sufficient to identify the document for a subpoena duces tecum including, where appropriate, the author of the document, the addressee of the document, any other recipients of the document and, where not apparent, the relationship of the author addressee and any recipients to one another.

5. If any requested document has been misplaced, destroyed or discarded, or otherwise disposed of, please so state, and for each such document provide:

   (a) Its date;
   (b) The identity of the person(s) who prepared the document;
   (c) The identity of all persons who participated in preparing the document, to whom the document was sent or who have otherwise seen the document;
   (d) The length of the document;
   (e) The subject matter of the document;
   (f) If misplaced, the last time and place it was seen and a description of efforts made to locate the document;
   (g) If disposed of, the date of and reason for disposal, the identity of the person(s) who authorized disposal and the identity of the person who disposed of the document.

6. If defendants are currently without information necessary to respond to any Interrogatory or Document Request, such Interrogatory or Document Request shall be deemed to require a reasonable investigation and any response thereto shall set forth the facts surrounding such investigation, including the identity of other individuals with knowledge.

7. Unless otherwise noted, the time period for the Interrogatories is 1987 through the present.

DEFINITIONS

1. The terms "you" or "your" shall include Diane Holland, Ilse Lobel and all individuals who were employees, officers or agents of National School of Health and Technology. Reference to "the school" means National School of Health and Technology.

2. The term "document" is used in the broadest possible sense and means, without limitation, any written, printed, typed, photostated, photographic, computerized, recorded or otherwise reproduced communication or representation, whether comprised of letters, words, numbers, pictures, sounds or symbols, or any combination thereof. This definition includes copies or duplicates of documents contemporaneously or subsequently created that have

any non-nonconforming notes or other markings. Without limiting the generality of the foregoing, the term "document" includes, but is not limited to, correspondence, memoranda, notes, records, letters, envelopes, file folders, telegrams, messages, studies, reports, analyses, contracts, agreements, forms, working papers, summaries, statistical statements, financial statements or work papers, accounts, analytical records, trade letters, press releases, comparisons, books, calendars, diaries, logs, articles, magazines, newspapers, booklets, brochures, pamphlets, circulars, bulletins, notices, drawing, diagrams, instructions, notes or minutes of meetings, reports and/or summaries of investigations, or other communications of any type, including inter and intra-office communications, questionnaires, surveys, charts, graphs, recordings, films, tapes, computer and word processor disks, data cells, drums, print-outs, all other data compilations from which information can be obtained (translated, if necessary, into usable forms), and any preliminary versions, drafts or revisions of any of the foregoing.

3. The term "identify" when used in connection with a natural person means to state his or her:

    (a) Full name and any aliases;

    (b) Last known address and phone number;

    (c) Last known business address and phone number;

    (d) Employment, title, and job description during the time of their employment at the school; and

    (e) Present employment and job description.

4. The term "identify" or "identity" when used in connection with a "document" or "documents" means to state the following:

    (a) Its date;

    (b) The identity of its author;

    (c) The identity of its sender;

    (d) The identity of the person to whom it was addressed;

    (e) The identity of the recipient;

    (f) Its format;

    (g) Its title;

    (h) The number of pages or other measure of length or size; and

    (i) The identity of each person known or believed to have possession, custody, control of or access to any copy of the document having writings, notations, corrections or markings unique to such copy.

5. The phrase "identify the factual basis" for a denial or an Interrogatory answer means to state:

    (a) Each and every fact which you believe supports the denial or Interrogatory answer;

    (b) The identity of each and every person having knowledge of facts which you believe supports the denial or Interrogatory answer, along with a summary of such facts which that person knows; and

    (c) The identity of each and every document which you believe supports the denial or Interrogatory answer.

INTERROGATORIES

1. Do you contend that plaintiff Williams had the "ability to benefit" from the school's Medical Assistant course, within the meaning of federal financial aid regulations? If the answer is "yes," identify the factual basis for this contention.

2. Identify all former students of the school who were admitted without a high school or equivalency diploma and on whose behalf the school obtained any federal grants or loans and, for each, also provide the following information:

    a. The date of the enrollment agreement;

    b. The course of study;

    c. Whether or not the student completed the course;

    d. The relevant dates the student withdrew or graduated;

    e. All grants obtained (not counting refunds);

    f. All grant refunds made to the Government;

    g. All loan proceeds obtained (not counting refunds);

    h. All loan refunds made to a lender or guarantee agency; and

    i. If the student was placed in a job related to the course of study, identify the employer and the starting salary paid.

3. As to the individuals identified in response to Interrogatory #1, do you contend that these individuals had "the ability to benefit" from the course you enrolled them in? If the answer is "yes," identify the factual basis for this contention.

4. Identify all "ability to benefit" tests which the school administered to admissions applicants who lacked a high school or GED diploma from 1986 until the closing. As to each test, also provide the following information, and, if different tests or scores were used for different courses of study, provide all relevant information for each:

    a. The dates during which the test was used;

    b. The author of the test (if purchased from a third party, the name of the entity that produced the test);

    c. The cutoff scores used to determine whether an applicant was qualified for admission;

    d. How such cutoff scores were established, including a description of the methodology and identification of those individuals or entities who participated in making the decision to set a particular cutoff;

    e. The name, address and telephone number of every person who was authorized to administer the test, including the relevant time period for each.

5. Did the school ever study or analyze the relationship between performance on an admission test or "ability to benefit test," on the one hand, and academic success and job placement, on the other? If the answer is "yes," describe the method used to study or analyze the relationship, as well as the system employed for maintaining data on this relationship, and identify all documents which pertain to such studies, analyses and data.

6. Identify all individuals who administered "ability to benefit" tests and the relevant time periods for each.

7. For the years ending December 31, 1986, 1988 and 1990, identify the four highest paid employees or officers of the school, and for each itemize the relevant figures for salary, fees, commissions and other form of compensation, including payments for automobiles or other expenses.

8. For the years 1986-92 identify all payments made by the school to Ilse Lobel, including for each year a description of the factual basis for such payments.

9. For the years 1986-92 identify all automobiles owned or leased by the school including for each:

    a. The year, make and model;

    b. The date of acquisition;

    c. The identity of the person who primarily used the vehicle;

    d. The purchase price or monthly lease payment;

e. A description of any customization which was done and the cost of such customization; and

f. A description of the disposition of the vehicle including the date and the reason the school lost possession of the vehicle.

10. During the years 1987-91 did the School arrange loans through guarantee agencies and lenders other than United Student Aid Funds and Meritor Savings Bank? If so, identify the entities and the approximate volume of such dealings.

11. Regarding the averment in defendant Holland's answer to the original complaint (at ¶ 17) that "students were told about the school's placement rate and the range of salaries that recent graduates received,"

a. Describe in detail the system that existed at the school for ensuring that this information was communicated accurately, including, but not limited to, identification of the roles of the various individuals involved, the methods of communication used between school departments and between the school and students, and any procedures used to ensure and monitor the accuracy of the information.

b. Identify what, if any, statistics or other information the school maintained concerning placement and salary levels of graduates, including, but not limited to identification of the roles of the various individuals involved, the methods used to obtain and record this information and the manner of maintaining such records.

c. Identify what, if any statistics or other information the school provided to prospective students and which substantiated the accuracy and truthfulness of such claims, including, but not limited to identification of the roles of the various individuals involved and a description of the form, manner and timing of such disclosures.

REQUESTS FOR PRODUCTION OF DOCUMENTS

1. All documents pertaining to the transfer of ownership and control in the School in December, 1986 from Ilse Lobel to Diane Holland and James Lupfer.

2. The most current resumes or personnel data sheets in your possession for the following individuals:

a. Diane Holland;

b. Ilse Lobel;

c. James Lupfer;

d. William Lorman;

e. Theodore Kaczorowski;

f. Joseph Paprzycki;

f. Phil Sherr;

g. Marge Ross and

h. Kim Wilcox.

3. All "ability to benefit" tests which the school administered to admissions applicants who lacked a high school or GED diploma from 1986 until the closing and all instruction books for each test.

4. All documents pertaining to the selection of particular tests, the procedures used in administering the tests, and the selection by the school of particular cutoff scores used to determine success or failure on the test.

5. All invoices, purchase orders, cancelled checks or other documents pertaining to the purchase of "ability to benefit" tests from vendors or testing companies.

6. All data or records pertaining to the relationship between performance on admission tests and academic/employment success, including, if they exist, summary reports produced by the testing companies.

7. All annual reports to accrediting commissions, including both NATTS and ABHES, for the years 1985-91.

8. All correspondence between the school and its accrediting commissions during the years 1986-1992.

9. Copies of site visit reports, reviews, show-cause orders or audits pertaining to the school, covering the years 1987-91, which were prepared by either an accrediting commission, the State Board of Private Licensed Schools, or the United States Department of Education, and copies of any responses thereto.

10. Copies of the accrediting criteria of NATTS and of ABHES, which were applicable to the accreditation of the school and/or to the school's Medical Assistant course.

11. The school's annual, audited financial reports for the years 1986-90.

[Attorney for Plaintiff]

F.3 Discovery in Bankruptcy Proceeding to Determine Dischargeability of Student Loan

UNITED STATES BANKRUPTCY COURT
DISTRICT OF NEW JERSEY, CAMDEN VICINAGE

IN RE: [Debtor]	)
Debtor	)
[Debtor],	)
Plaintiff	)
	)
v.	)
	)
United States Department of	)
Education	)
Defendant	)
	)

PLAINTIFF'S INTERROGATORIES TO DEFENDANT U.S. DEPARTMENT OF EDUCATION

To: Defendant U.S. Department Of Education

By and through its attorney of record

A. Defendant is hereby required to answer in writing, under oath in accordance with Rule 7033 of the Rules of this court, the interrogatories attached hereto.

B. In answering these interrogatories, furnish all information in the possession of Defendant, its officers, agents and employees and its attorneys and investigators for its attorneys.

C. If Defendant cannot answer the following interrogatories in full after exercising due diligence to secure the information to do so, state the answer to the extent possible specifying your inability to answer the remainder, and state whatever information or knowledge Defendant has concerning the unanswered portion.

D. Each interrogatory is considered continuing, and if Defendant obtains information which renders its answers or one of them, incomplete or inaccurate, Defendant is obligated to serve amended answers on the undersigned.

E. Insofar as may be applicable, and except as otherwise indicated, the term "document" or "documents" shall refer to any and all writings and recorded materials, of any kind whatsoever, that is or has been in the possession, control or custody of Defendant or of which Defendant has knowledge, whether originals or copies, including but not limited to contracts, documents, notes, rough drafts, interoffice memoranda, memoranda for the files, letters, research materials, correspondence, logs, diaries, forms, bank statements, tax returns, card files, books of account, journals, ledgers, invoices, blueprints, diagrams, drawings, computer print-outs or tapes, reports, surveys, statistical computations, studies, pictures, maps, graphs, charts, minutes, manuals, pamphlets, or books of any nature or kind whatsoever; and all other materials handwritten, printed, typed, mimeographed, photocopied or otherwise reproduced; and slides or motion pictures, television tapes; all tape recordings (whether for computer, audio or visual replay) or other written, printed or recorded matter or tangible things on which words, phrases, symbols or information are affixed.

F. A request to "identify" a document is a request to state (insofar as may be applicable):

1. The date of such document.
2. The type of document or written communication it is.
3. The names and present addresses of the person or persons who prepared such document and of the signers, addressors and addressees of such document.
4. The name of any principal whom or which the signers, addressors and preparers of such document were thereby representing.
5. The present location of such document.
6. The name and present address of the person now having custody of the document.
7. Whether you possess or control the original or a copy thereof and if so, the location and name of the custodian of such original or copy.
8. A brief description of the contents of such document.

G. A request to "describe" any oral statement or communication is a request to state:

1. The name and present address of each individual making such statement or communication.
2. The name of any principal or employer whom or which such individual was thereby representing and the position in which such individual was then employed or engaged by such principal or employee.
3. The name and present address of the individual or individuals to whom the oral statement or communication was made, and the name of any principal or employer whom such person or persons were representing at the time of and in connection with such oral statement or communication, as well as the employment position in which they were then employed or engaged.
4. The names and present addresses of any other individuals present when such oral statement or communication was made or who heard or acknowledged hearing the same.
5. The place where such oral statement or communication was made.
6. A brief description of the contents of such oral statement or communication.

H. A request to "cite" portions or provisions of any document is a request to state, insofar as applicable with reference to such portion or provision, the title, date, division, page, sheet, charge order number, and such other information as may be necessary to accurately locate the portion or provision referenced.

I. The term "person" shall include a natural person, partnership, corporation, association, or other group however organized.

J. Whenever a request is made to "identify" a natural person, it shall mean to supply all of the following information:

1. His/her full name.
2. His/her employer and position at the time.
3. The name of any person or entity (natural or artificial) whom she/he is claimed to have represented in connection with the matter to which the interrogatory relates.
4. His/her last known address, telephone number, and employer.
5. His/her present employer.

K. A request to "explain fully" any answer, denial or claim is a request (insofar as may be applicable) to:

1. State fully and specifically each fact and/or contention in support of your answer, denial or claim; and
2. For each such fact or contention, to identify each person who has knowledge relative to that fact or contention, each document that tends to support that fact or contention; and each document that tends to dispute that fact or contention.

L. A request in any of the enclosed interrogatories to "identify" any document is a request to attach said document to answers to these interrogatories. If documents are attached to answers to these interrogatories, they must be marked to identify which interrogatory they refer to. In identifying documents you

(a) how many hours each loan agent spent under such instruction;
(b) whether such instruction was mandatory or voluntary;
(c) the subject matter of the instruction.

INTERROGATORIES

IMPORTANT: All questions containing the terms "document," "documents," "identify," "describe," "cite," "person" or "explain fully" must be answered in accordance with the definitions of those terms contained in the attached instructions.

1. Please identify the person answering each of these interrogatories.

2. Identify each person Defendant may call as a witness in this case.

3. Identify each document which Defendant may introduce into evidence in this case.

4. State the total amount Defendant alleges to be owing as of the date of the filing of this lawsuit.

5. Itemize the total amount Defendant alleges to be owing by unpaid amounts financed, accrued finance charge, and other charges, as applicable.

6. Please identify any and all persons known to Defendant who have personal knowledge concerning the instant loans. Please specify which of these people are agents of Defendant or were agents of Defendant at the time of the instant transaction.

7. State the total amount of dollars in cash that Plaintiff has paid to Defendant. Identify each payment individually and state the date of payment.

8. List separately all persons to whom and charges, fees, or any other amounts were paid in connection with these loans, including the name and address of the payee, the amount disbursed to each, the date of dispersal, and the check number for each dispersal.

9. State whether you received any requests for deferment of loans from Plaintiff. If so, please specify when each request was made.

10. If you identified any requests in interrogatory 9, please provide your response to Plaintiff's requests.

11. State whether you received any requests for forbearance of loans from Plaintiff. If so, please specify when each request was made.

12. If you identified any requests in interrogatory 11, please provide your response to Plaintiff's requests.

13. Identify your procedures for granting of deferment and forbearance of loans at all relevant times.

14. State any policies and/or programs, outside of traditional deferment and forbearance of loans policies, in which plaintiff may have been qualified to participate.

15. If you identified any such policies and/or programs in interrogatory 14, please provide any information relating to Plaintiff's participation.

16. Please state each and every fact which is the basis for your contention in the Second Affirmative Defense of your Answer and Affirmative Defenses that "Debtor has not made a good faith effort to repay the loan and would not qualify for a discharge on the basis of undue hardship," and for each and every fact, please list the name, address, and telephone number of all witnesses with the knowledge relevant to the fact and all documents, giving the document description, date, and custodian, which touches upon or relates to that fact.

17. Please specify all amounts received from Plaintiff, and when such amounts were received, from the total sum identified in your Ninth Affirmative Defense of your Answer and Affirmative Defenses.

18. Please identify all policies relating to deferment and forbearance of loans, utilized by loan guarantors, the [Guaranty Agency].

19. Identify all documents containing information about the instant loans. State which, if any, of the above documents were given to Plaintiff, including where and when each document was given to Plaintiff.

20. Identify each telephone contact made to Plaintiff by Defendant or Defendant's agent regarding the loans. Describe the substance of each such telephone conversation.

21. Identify each document, including each notice, that Defendant mailed or otherwise delivered to Plaintiff concerning the instant loans. For each document, state the address it was mailed to and whether it was received by Plaintiff.

PLEASE TAKE NOTICE that a copy of the answers to the attached interrogatories and the requested documents must be served upon the undersigned within the time allowed by Rule 7033 of the Rules of this Court.

[Attorney for Plaintiff]

F.4 Freedom of Information Act Sample Requests

[Date]

Office of the Inspector General
U. S. Department of Education
400 Maryland Avenue, S.W.
Washington, D.C. 20202-1510

Attn: FOIA Request Officer—Inspector General's Office

Dear Sir or Madam:

This is a request for copies of public records under the Freedom of Information Act, 5 U.S.C. § 552 *et seq.* As you know, this Act requires public bodies to make available for inspection and copying all public records, except certain exempt records, within ten working days of receipt of a written request.

Please provide copies of any and all records, reports, forms, writings, letters, memoranda, books, papers, maps, photographs, microfilms, cards, tapes, recordings, electronic data processing records, recorded information and all other documentary material, regardless of physical form or characteristics, having been prepared or having been or being used, received, possessed or under control of the U.S. Department of Education pertaining to **any and all investigations, inquiries, audits, inspections, findings, administrative actions, or other determinations from *1985 to the present* regarding violations of local, state, or federal law, regulations, or guidelines involving** *"ability to benefit" determinations, testing, admissions or the false certification of student eligibility* **for the following school:**

[School]
[Address]

If you determine that any of the information requested is exempt from release, please delete the material which you determine to be exempt and send me copies of the remaining nonexempt material within ten working days. If you do withhold any part of the requested material, please advise me as to which exemption(s) you believe to be applicable.

I am requesting a fee waiver regarding this material. In support of a waiver, I am advising you of the following:

1. The subject of this request concerns the operations or activities of the government, namely, the administration of Title IV by the Department, and in particular the determination of eligibility of institutions which received Title IV funds.

2. The disclosure is likely to contribute to an understanding of the above-mentioned governmental operations and activities both by us and by the indigent clients we represent.

3. The disclosure is likely to contribute to a public understanding of these matters through our work as public interest lawyers for the poor.

4. Neither I nor my office has any commercial interest which would be furthered by disclosure. On the contrary, we are salaried employees of a government-funded program which provides free legal assistance to the poor.

5. The information we obtain will be disseminated and shared with other members of the public. We continue to provide information to other legal aid and community service agencies, as well as to the general media, on problem schools participating in Title IV financial aid programs. We expect to make some of the materials obtained available through the National Center on Poverty Law, publishers of the Clearinghouse Review, which makes such documents available at no charge to subscribing legal services agencies around the country, as well as to other individuals and organizations, in both paper and computer-readable forms.

If you have any questions concerning this request, I may be reached at (312) 347-8307.

Sincerely,

[Attorney for Plaintiff]

[Date]

Freedom of Information Act Officer

U.S. Department of Education
Washington, D.C. 20002

> Re: *Freedom of Information Act Request*
> School Name: [School]
> OPE-ID: [Number]

Dear Sir or Madam:

This is a request pursuant to the Freedom of Information Act, 5 U.S.C. §552 ("FOIA"). I would like to receive a copy of the following documents (including any original, reproduction or copy of any kind, whether recorded, drafted, printed, written or documentary matters, including without limitation, correspondence, memoranda, reports, records, studies, computer tapes or other computer storage mediums, compilations, and/or summaries of data and other information) and any other written or printed material evidencing, relating to, or commenting upon the following matters at Tri-State Beauty College, referred to hereinafter as the "College," from January 1, 1985 through the present:

1. Pre-admission testing of students who did not have a high school diploma or GED, including efforts to comply with ability-to-benefit requirements promulgated by DOE;

2. Assessments and decisions made regarding students' ability to benefit ("ATB") from the courses and programs offered by the College;

3. Complaints made by any person or organization to DOE, other organization, or the College itself regarding any aspect of the College's admission's process;

4. All inspections, audits, assessments, evaluations, and findings made by any person or organization as to any aspect of the College operations;

5. All litigation or administrative proceedings brought by or against the College;

6. All information regarding College closure dates established by DOE for each branch of the College, including all materials that relate to how each such date was determined;

7. As to student loan closed school discharge applications filed with DOE, the number:
a) granted
b) denied
c) pending

8. As to student loan ability to benefit false certification discharge applications filed with DOE, the number:
a) granted
b) denied
c) pending

9. Default rates of former students and any default reduction plans, programs, and agreements;

10. All applications and documentation submitted by any former student of the College receiving a discharge of a student loan based on false ATB certification by the College; and

11. Any and all "Emergency Action" memoranda relating to the College.

To the extent that you determine that the release of certain requested documents or records would constitute a clearly unwarranted invasion of the personal privacy of third parties, I ask that you proceed according to 5 U.S.C. §552(b). For each such document or record, please delete or redact the names, addresses, and SSNs of applicants, loan recipients, students and other persons before producing it so as to remove any risk of invading someone's privacy. *See, Norwood v. Federal Aviation Administration*, 993 F.2d 570, 574-576 (Sixth Cir. 1993) (requiring disclosure after names, SSNs, and other information which, by itself, would identify an individual, had been redacted.)

I request a waiver of fees in connection with this request. Disclosure of these records is in the public interest because it will contribute significantly to public understanding of the activities of this proprietary voc-ed College which received federal monies and federally guaranteed loan monies. I will receive no business, commercial, or financial benefit from this request. Release of this information will serve the public interest because it pertains to the operations of the College and the possible discharge of certain student loans. Disclosure of this information also will benefit a large segment of the population, namely those persons in Ohio who attended the College and who have applied or may apply in the future for discharge of their student loans.

The Legal Aid Society of Greater Cincinnati is a federally funded legal services office. As such, it is a non-profit organization that exists to represent low income people both locally and, when appropriate, state-wide in matters such as federally supported education programs. By law, this office represents only clients who cannot afford to pay for legal assistance; they also cannot afford the cost associated with this request. I intend to use the requested information to assist clients.

I look forward to your response within the time frame described in the FOIA. Please contact me at the above number if you have any questions. Thank you for your assistance.

Yours truly,

[Attorney for Plaintiff]

Appendix G   Directory of Guaranty Agencies

The following information may be found at the U.S. Department of Education website at http://wdcrobcolp01.ed.gov/Programs/EROD/org_list.cfm under "State Guaranty Agency" (last accessed on June 16, 2006). The list in this appendix can also be found on the companion CD-Rom to this manual.

STATES

Alabama
Kentucky Higher Education Assistance Authority
P.O. Box 798
Frankfort, KY 40602-0798
Phone: (502) 696-7200
Toll-Free: (800) 928-8926
Fax: (502) 696-7496
E-mail: webmaster@kheaa.com or rpotts@kheaa.com
Website: www.kheaa.com
States Served: Alabama, Kentucky

Alaska
No records found.

Arizona
USA Funds
P.O. Box 6028
Indianapolis, IN 46206-6028
Phone: (317) 806-1283
Toll-Free: (888) 272-5543
Fax: (317) 806-1203
TTY: (800) 331-2357
E-mail: contact@usafunds.org
Website: www.usafunds.org
States Served: Arizona, Guam, Hawaii, Indiana, Kansas, Maryland, Mississippi, Nevada, Wyoming

Arkansas
Student Loan Guarantee Foundation of Arkansas
219 South Victory
Little Rock, AR 72201-1884
Phone: (501) 372-1491
Toll-Free: (800) 622-3446
Fax: (501) 688-7675
E-mail: slgfa@slgfa.org
Website: www.slgfa.org

California
EDFUND
P.O. Box 419045
Rancho Cordova, CA 95741-9045
Phone: (916) 526-7900
Toll-Free: (877) 2EDFUND (233-3863)
E-mail: webmaster@edfund.org
Website: www.edfund.org

Colorado
College Access Network
Suite 425
999 18th Street
Denver, CO 80202-2471
Phone: (303) 305-3000
Toll-Free: (800) 727-9834
Fax: (303) 294-5076
TTY: (800) 727-5343
E-mail: cbergquist@college-access.net
Website: www.college-access.net

Connecticut
Connecticut Student Loan Foundation
525 Brook Street
P.O. Box 1009
Rocky Hill, CT 06067
Phone: (860) 257-4001
Toll-Free: (800) 237-9721
Fax: (860) 563-3247
E-mail: mvalent@mail.cslf.org
Website: www.cslf.com

Delaware
American Education Services/PHEAA
1200 North Seventh Street
Harrisburg, PA 17102-1444
Phone: (717) 720-2860
Toll-Free: (800) 692-7392
Fax: (717) 720-3903
TTY: (800) 654-5988
E-mail: loanhelp@aessuccess.org or mlafer@aessuccess.org
Website: www.aessuccess.org
States Served: Delaware, Pennsylvania, West Virginia

District of Columbia
American Student Assistance
100 Cambridge Street
Boston, MA 02114
Toll-Free: (800) 999-9080
Fax: (617) 521 6154
TTY: (800) 999-0923
E-mail: webmaster@amsa.com
Website: www.amsa.com
States Served: District of Columbia, Massachusetts

Florida
Office of Student Financial Assistance (Florida)
Department of Education
Suite 70
1940 North Monroe Street
Tallahassee, FL 32303-4759
Phone: (850) 410-5200
Toll-Free: (800) 366-3475
Fax: (850) 488-3612
E-mail: osfa@fldoe.org or Janie.Westberry@fldoe.org
Website: www.floridastudentfinancialaid.org/osfahomepg.htm

Georgia
Georgia Higher Education Assistance Corporation
Suite 220
2082 East Exchange Place
Tucker, GA 30084
Phone: (770) 724-9003
Toll-Free: (800) 505-GSFC (4732)
Fax: (770) 724-9004
E-mail: TimC@gsfc.org or davidb@gsfc.org
Website: www.gsfc.org

Hawaii
USA Funds
P.O. Box 6028
Indianapolis, IN 46206-6028
Phone: (317) 806-1283
Toll-Free: (888) 272-5543
Fax: (317) 806-1203
TTY: (800) 331-2357
E-mail: contact@usafunds.org
Website: www.usafunds.org
States Served: Arizona, Guam, Hawaii, Indiana, Kansas, Maryland, Mississippi, Nevada, Wyoming

Idaho
Northwest Education Loan Association
Suite 300
190 Queen Anne Avenue, North
Seattle, WA 98109
Phone: (206) 461-5300
Toll-Free: (800) 562-3001
Fax: (206) 461-5449
E-mail: cheryll@nela.net

Website: www.nela.net
States Served: Idaho, Washington

Illinois
Illinois Student Assistance Commission
1755 Lake Cook Road
Deerfield, IL 60015-5209
Phone: (847) 948-8500
Toll-Free: (800) 899-4722
Fax: (847) 831-8549
TTY: (800) 526-0857
E-mail: collegezone@isac.org
Website: www.collegezone.com

Indiana
USA Funds
P.O. Box 6028
Indianapolis, IN 46206-6028
Phone: (317) 806-1283
Toll-Free: (888) 272-5543
Fax: (317) 806-1203
TTY: (800) 331-2357
E-mail: contact@usafunds.org
Website: www.usafunds.org
States Served: Arizona, Guam, Hawaii, Indiana, Kansas, Maryland, Mississippi, Nevada, Wyoming

Iowa
Iowa College Student Aid Commission
Fourth Floor
200 10th Street
Des Moines, IA 50309-3609
Phone: (515) 242-3344
Toll-Free: (800) 383-4222
Toll-Free Restrictions: IA residents only
Fax: (515) 242-3388
E-mail: info@iowacollegeaid.org or
keith.greiner@iowa.gov
Website: www.iowacollegeaid.org

Kansas
USA Funds
P.O. Box 6028
Indianapolis, IN 46206-6028
Phone: (317) 806-1283
Toll-Free: (888) 272-5543
Fax: (317) 806-1203
TTY: (800) 331-2357
E-mail: contact@usafunds.org
Website: www.usafunds.org
States Served: Arizona, Guam, Hawaii, Indiana, Kansas, Maryland, Mississippi, Nevada, Wyoming

Kentucky
Kentucky Higher Education Assistance Authority
P.O. Box 798
Frankfort, KY 40602-0798
Phone: (502) 696-7200
Toll-Free: (800) 928-8926
Fax: (502) 696-7496
E-mail: webmaster@kheaa.com or
rpotts@kheaa.com
Website: www.kheaa.com
States Served: Alabama, Kentucky

Louisiana
Louisiana Office of Student Financial Assistance
P.O. Box 91202
Baton Rouge, LA 70821-9202
Phone: (225) 922-1012
Toll-Free: (800) 259-5626
Fax: (225) 922-0790
E-mail: gwales@osfa.state.la.us
Website: www.osfa.state.la.us

Maine
Education Assistance Division (Maine)
Finance Authority of Maine
5 Community Drive
P.O. Box 949
Augusta, ME 04332-0949
Phone: (207) 623-3263
Toll-Free: (800) 228-3734
Fax: (207) 623-0095
TTY: (207) 626-2717
E-mail: info@famemaine.com
Website: www.famemaine.com

Maryland
USA Funds
P.O. Box 6028
Indianapolis, IN 46206-6028
Phone: (317) 806-1283
Toll-Free: (888) 272-5543
Fax: (317) 806-1203
TTY: (800) 331-2357
E-mail: contact@usafunds.org
Website: www.usafunds.org
States Served: Arizona, Guam, Hawaii, Indiana, Kansas, Maryland, Mississippi, Nevada, Wyoming

Massachusetts
American Student Assistance
100 Cambridge Street
Boston, MA 02114
Toll-Free: (800) 999-9080
Fax: (617) 521 6154
TTY: (800) 999-0923
E-mail: webmaster@amsa.com
Website: www.amsa.com
States Served: District of Columbia, Massachusetts

Michigan
Michigan Higher Education Assistance Authority
Office of Michigan Guaranty Agency
P. O. Box 30047
Lansing, MI 48909-7547
Phone: (517) 373-2439
Toll-Free: (800) 642-5626
Fax: (517) 241-0155
E-mail: mga@michigan.gov
Website: www.MGALOAN.com

Minnesota
Great Lakes Higher Education Corporation
P.O. Box 7658
2401 International Lane
Madison, WI 53704
Phone: (608) 246-1800
Toll-Free: (800) 236-5900

E-mail: service@glhec.org
Website: www.mygreatlakes.com
States Served: Minnesota, Ohio, Puerto Rico, Virgin Islands, Wisconsin

Student Loans of North Dakota-Guarantor
Bank of North Dakota
P.O. Box 5524
700 East Main Avenue
Bismarck, ND 58506-5524
Phone: (701) 328-5654
Toll-Free: (800) 472-2166
Fax: (701) 328-5716
TTY: (800) 643-3916
E-mail: werhardt@nd.gov or slndga@nd.gov
Website: http://mystudentloanonline.com
States Served: Minnesota, Montana, North Dakota, South Dakota, Wyoming

Mississippi
USA Funds
P.O. Box 6028
Indianapolis, IN 46206-6028
Phone: (317) 806-1283
Toll-Free: (888) 272-5543
Fax: (317) 806-1203
TTY: (800) 331-2357
E-mail: contact@usafunds.org
Website: www.usafunds.org
States Served: Arizona, Guam, Hawaii, Indiana, Kansas, Maryland, Mississippi, Nevada, Wyoming

Missouri
Missouri Department of Higher Education
3515 Amazonas Drive
Jefferson City, MO 65109
Phone: (573) 751-2361
Toll-Free: (800) 473-6757
Fax: (573) 751-6635
TTY: (800) 735-2966
E-mail: info@dhe.mo.gov
Website: www.dhe.mo.gov

Montana
Montana Guaranteed Student Loan Program
P.O. Box 203101
Helena, MT 59620-3101
Phone: (406) 444-6594
Toll-Free: (800) 537-7508
Fax: (406) 444-1869
E-mail: custserv@mgslp.state.mt.us or
scholars@mgslp.state.mt.us
Website: www.mgslp.org

Student Loans of North Dakota-Guarantor
Bank of North Dakota
P.O. Box 5524
700 East Main Avenue
Bismarck, ND 58506-5524
Phone: (701) 328-5654
Toll-Free: (800) 472-2166
Fax: (701) 328-5716
TTY: (800) 643-3916
E-mail: werhardt@nd.gov or slndga@nd.gov
Website: http://mystudentloanonline.com
States Served: Minnesota, Montana, North Dakota, South Dakota, Wyoming

Nebraska
National Student Loan Program (Nebraska)
P.O. Box 82507
Lincoln, NE 68501-2507
Phone: (402) 475-8686
Toll-Free: (800) 735-8778
Fax: (402) 479-6658
TTY: (800) 735-8778
E-mail: Randyh@nslp.org or Jillh@nslp.org
Website: www.nslp.org

Nevada
USA Funds
P.O. Box 6028
Indianapolis, IN 46206-6028
Phone: (317) 806-1283
Toll-Free: (888) 272-5543
Fax: (317) 806-1203
TTY: (800) 331-2357
E-mail: contact@usafunds.org
Website: www.usafunds.org
States Served: Arizona, Guam, Hawaii, Indiana, Kansas, Maryland, Mississippi, Nevada, Wyoming

New Hampshire
New Hampshire Higher Education Assistance Foundation
P.O. Box 2087
4 Barrell Court
Concord, NH 03302-2087
Phone: (603) 225-6612
Toll-Free: (800) 525-2577
Fax: (603) 224-2581
E-mail: info@gsmr.org or collegeplanning@gsmr.org
Website: www.nhheaf.org

New Jersey
Higher Education Student Assistance Authority (New Jersey)
P.O. Box 540
Trenton, NJ 08625-0540
Phone: (609) 588-3214
Toll-Free: (800) 792-8670
Fax: (609) 588-7389
TTY: (609) 588-2526
E-mail: clewis@hesaa.org
Website: www.hesaa.org/intro.asp

New Jersey After 3, Inc.
391 George Street
Second floor
New Brunswick, NJ 08901
Phone: (732) 246-7933
E-mail: info@njafter3.org
Website: www.njafter3.org

New Mexico
New Mexico Student Loan Guarantee Corporation
7400 Tiburon
Albuquerque, NM 87190
Phone: (505) 345-8821
Toll-Free: (800) 279-3070
Fax: (505) 344-3631
E-mail: guarantee@nmslgc.org
Website: www.nmstudentloan.org

New York
New York State Higher Education Services Corporation
99 Washington Avenue
Albany, NY 12255
Phone: (518) 473-7087
Toll-Free: (888) 697-4372
Fax: (518) 474-2839
TTY: (800) 445-5234
E-mail: webmail@hesc.org
Website: www.hesc.org

North Carolina
North Carolina State Education Assistance Authority
P.O. Box 13663
Research Triangle Park, NC 27709
Phone: (919) 549-8614
Toll-Free: (800) 700-1775
Fax: (919) 549-8481
E-mail: information@ncseaa.edu
Website: www.ncseaa.edu

North Dakota
Student Loans of North Dakota-Guarantor
Bank of North Dakota
P.O. Box 5524
700 East Main Avenue
Bismarck, ND 58506-5524
Phone: (701) 328-5654
Toll-Free: (800) 472-2166
Fax: (701) 328-5716
TTY: (800) 643-3916
E-mail: werhardt@nd.gov or slndga@nd.gov
Website: http://mystudentloanonline.com
States Served: Minnesota, Montana, North Dakota, South Dakota, Wyoming

Ohio
Great Lakes Higher Education Corporation
P.O. Box 7658
2401 International Lane
Madison, WI 53704
Phone: (608) 246-1800
Toll-Free: (800) 236-5900
E-mail: service@glhec.org
Website: www.mygreatlakes.com
States Served: Minnesota, Ohio, Puerto Rico, Virgin Islands, Wisconsin

Oklahoma
Oklahoma Guaranteed Student Loan Program
P.O. Box 3000
Oklahoma City, OK 73101-3000
Phone: (405) 234-4300
Toll-Free: (800) 442-8642
Fax: (405) 234-4390
TTY: (405) 234-4511
E-mail: info@ogslp.org
Website: www.ogslp.org

Oregon
Educational Credit Management Corporation (Oregon)
Suite 190
1500 Valley River Drive
Eugene, OR 97401
Phone: (541) 984-2450

Toll-Free: (888) 323-3262
Fax: (541) 984-2468
TTY: (541) 984-2496
E-mail: response@ecmc.org
Website: www.ecmc.org

Pennsylvania
American Education Services/PHEAA
1200 North Seventh Street
Harrisburg, PA 17102-1444
Phone: (717) 720-2860
Toll-Free: (800) 692-7392
Fax: (717) 720-3903
TTY: (800) 654-5988
E-mail: loanhelp@aessuccess.org or mlafer@aessuccess.org
Website: www.aessuccess.org
States Served: Delaware, Pennsylvania, West Virginia

Rhode Island
Rhode Island Higher Education Assistance Authority
560 Jefferson Boulevard
Warwick, RI 02886-1320
Phone: (401) 736-1100
Toll-Free: (800) 922-9855
Fax: (401) 732-3541
TTY: (401) 222-6195
E-mail: gjsilva@riheaa.org
Website: www.riheaa.org

South Carolina
South Carolina Student Loan Corporation
P.O. Box 210219
Suite 210, Interstate Center
Columbia, SC 29221
Phone: (803) 798-0916
Toll-Free: (800) 347-2752
Fax: (803) 772-9410
E-mail: mfox@slc.sc.edu
Website: www.scstudentloan.org

South Dakota
Education Assistance Corporation (South Dakota)
115 First Avenue SW
Aberdeen, SD 57401
Phone: (605) 225-6423
Toll-Free: (800) 592-1802
Fax: (800) 354-7070
TTY: (800) 752-3949
E-mail: EAC@eac-easci.org
Website: www2.eac-easci.org/welcome.shtml

Student Loans of North Dakota-Guarantor
Bank of North Dakota
P.O. Box 5524
700 East Main Avenue
Bismarck, ND 58506-5524
Phone: (701) 328-5654
Toll-Free: (800) 472-2166
Fax: (701) 328-5716
TTY: (800) 643-3916
E-mail: werhardt@nd.gov or slndga@nd.gov
Website: http://mystudentloanonline.com
States Served: Minnesota, Montana, North Dakota, South Dakota, Wyoming

Tennessee
Tennessee Student Assistance Corporation
Suite 1950, Parkway Towers
404 James Robertson Parkway
Nashville, TN 37243-0820
Phone: (615) 741-1346
Toll-Free: (800) 342-1663
Fax: (615) 741-6101
E-mail: stephanie.aylor@state.tn.us or
TSAC.aidinfo@state.tn.us
Website: www.state.tn.us/tsac

Texas
TG
P.O. Box 83100
Round Rock, TX 78683-3100
Phone: (512) 219-5700
Toll-Free: (800) 845-6267
Fax: (512) 219-4633
TTY: (512) 219-4560
E-mail: cust.assist@tgslc.org
Website: www.tgslc.org

Utah
Utah Higher Education Assistance Authority
60 South 400 West
Salt Lake City, UT 84101-1284
Phone: (801) 321-7200
Toll-Free: (800) 418-8757
Fax: (801) 321-7299
TTY: (801) 321-7130
E-mail: uheaa@utahsbr.edu
Website: www.uheaa.org

Vermont
Vermont Student Assistance Corporation
P.O. Box 2000
10 East Allen Street
Winooski, VT 05404-2601
Phone: (802) 655-9602
Toll-Free: (800) 642-3177
Fax: (802) 654-3765
TTY: (802) 654-3766
E-mail: info@vsac.org
Website: www.vsac.org

Virginia
Educational Credit Management Corporation
(Virginia)
Boulders, Building VII
Suite 200
7325 Beaufont Springs Drive
Richmond, VA 23225
Phone: (804) 267-7100
Toll-Free: (888) 775-3262
Fax: (804) 267-7159
TTY: (804) 267-7104
E-mail: response@ecmc.org
Website: www.ecmc.org

Washington
Northwest Education Loan Association
Suite 300
190 Queen Anne Avenue, North
Seattle, WA 98109
Phone: (206) 461-5300
Toll-Free: (800) 562-3001
Fax: (206) 461-5449
E-mail: cheryll@nela.net
Website: www.nela.net
States Served: Idaho, Washington

West Virginia
American Education Services/PHEAA
1200 North Seventh Street
Harrisburg, PA 17102-1444
Phone: (717) 720-2860
Toll-Free: (800) 692-7392
Fax: (717) 720-3903
TTY: (800) 654-5988
E-mail: loanhelp@aessuccess.org or
mlafer@aessuccess.org
Website: www.aessuccess.org
States Served: Delaware, Pennsylvania, West
Virginia

Wisconsin
Great Lakes Higher Education Corporation
P.O. Box 7658
2401 International Lane
Madison, WI 53704
Phone: (608) 246-1800
Toll-Free: (800) 236-5900
E-mail: service@glhec.org
Website: www.mygreatlakes.com
States Served: Minnesota, Ohio, Puerto Rico,
Virgin Islands, Wisconsin

Wyoming
Student Loans of North Dakota-Guarantor
Bank of North Dakota
P.O. Box 5524
700 East Main Avenue
Bismarck, ND 58506-5524
Phone: (701) 328-5654
Toll-Free: (800) 472-2166
Fax: (701) 328-5716
TTY: (800) 643-3916
E-mail: werhardt@nd.gov or slndga@nd.gov
Website: http://mystudentloanonline.com
States Served: Minnesota, Montana, North Da-
kota, South Dakota, Wyoming

USA Funds
P.O. Box 6028
Indianapolis, IN 46206-6028
Phone: (317) 806-1283
Toll-Free: (888) 272-5543
Fax: (317) 806-1203
TTY: (800) 331-2357

E-mail: contact@usafunds.org
Website: www.usafunds.org
States Served: Arizona, Guam, Hawaii, Indiana,
Kansas, Maryland, Mississippi, Nevada, Wyo-
ming

TERRITORIES

American Samoa
No records found.

**Commonwealth of the Northern Mariana
Islands**
No records found.

Federated States of Micronesia
No records found.

Guam
USA Funds
P.O. Box 6028
Indianapolis, IN 46206-6028
Phone: (317) 806-1283
Toll-Free: (888) 272-5543
Fax: (317) 806-1203
TTY: (800) 331-2357
E-mail: contact@usafunds.org
Website: www.usafunds.org
States Served: Arizona, Guam, Hawaii, Indiana,
Kansas, Maryland, Mississippi, Nevada, Wyo-
ming

Puerto Rico
Great Lakes Higher Education Corporation
P.O. Box 7658
2401 International Lane
Madison, WI 53704
Phone: (608) 246-1800
Toll-Free: (800) 236-5900
E-mail: service@glhec.org
Website: www.mygreatlakes.com
States Served: Minnesota, Ohio, Puerto Rico,
Virgin Islands, Wisconsin

Republic of Palau
No records found.

Republic of the Marshall Islands
No records found.

Virgin Islands
Great Lakes Higher Education Corporation
P.O. Box 7658
2401 International Lane
Madison, WI 53704
Phone: (608) 246-1800
Toll-Free: (800) 236-5900
E-mail: service@glhec.org
Website: www.mygreatlakes.com
States Served: Minnesota, Ohio, Puerto Rico,
Virgin Islands, Wisconsin

Appendix H   Student Loan Collection Agencies

The Department of Education contracts with collection agencies to administer certain collection activities. According to the Department, only those accounts which fail to establish and adhere to a repayment arrangement are subject to assignment to a collection agency. The list of collection agencies is posted on the Department's website and reprinted below. It is current as of June 2006. Future supplements will include any changes that are posted on the Department's website. Advocates may also check the site on their own at www.ed.gov/ offices/OSFAP/DCS/collection.agencies.html. This list can also be found on the companion CD-Rom to this manual.

Progressive Financial Services
P.O. Box 24098
Tempe, AZ 85285
(800) 253-8167

Collecto, Onc. Dba Collection Company of America
P.O. Box 5369
Norwell, MA 02061-5369
(800) 896-0282

Allied Interstate, Inc.
P.O. Box 26190
Minneapolis, MN 55426
(800) 715-0395

Pioneer Credit Recovery, Inc.
P.O. Box 99
Arcade, NY 14009
(888) 287-0571

NCO
P.O. Box 41420
Philadelphia, PA 19101-1420
(888) 475-6741

The CBE Group, Inc.
P.O. Box 930
Waterloo IA 50704-0930
(800) 410-8089

Diversified Collection Services, Inc.
P.O. Box 9049
Pleasanton, CA 94566-9049
(888) 335-6267

Allied International Credit Corp
P.O. Box 813220
Smyrna, GA 30081
(800) 464-2076

CollectCorp
P.O. Box 960
Phoenix, Arizona 85001
(877) 719-7015

Premiere Credit of North America, LLC
P.O. Box 19289
Indianapolis, IN 46219
(866) 808-7286

Account Control Technology, Inc.
P.O. Box 11750
Bakersfield, CA 93380-1750
(866) 887-2800

GC Services
P.O. Box 27323
Knoxville, TN 37927
(866) 846-9964

Financial Management Systems
P.O. Box 1423
Elk Grove Village, IL 60009-1423
(800) 889-6321

West Asset Management, Inc.
P.O. Box 725169
Atlanta, GA 31139
(800) 270-1022

Financial Asset Management Systems, INC. (FAMS)
P.O. Box 81401
Atlanta, GA 30341
(888) 668-6925

ConServe
P.O. Box 190
Fairport, NY 14450-0190
(866) 804-1700

Van Ru Credit Corporation
P.O. Box 1027
Skokie, IL 60076-8027
(888) 337-8331

Nationwide Credit, Inc.
P.O. Box 290276
Nashville, TN 37229
(866) 381-5530

Maximus
P.O. Box 9265
Oak Brook, IL 60522-9265
(800) 863-9025

Aman Collection Service
P.O. Box 1149
Aberdeen, SD 57402-1149
(800) 874-8969

Collection Technology, Inc.
P.O. Box 7888
Burbank, CA 91510-7888
(800) 620-4284

Federal Student Financial Assistance: Frequently Asked Questions

This appendix contains frequently asked questions regarding federal student financial assistance. The questions and answers are provided by NCLC. For more information, call the Federal Student Aid Information Center at 1-800-4-FED-AID or visit http://studentaid.ed.gov. The questions and answers reproduced in this appendix can also be found in Word and PDF formats on the companion CD-Rom to this manual.

1. Is Everyone Eligible for Federal Student Assistance?

No. There are a number of requirements to get federal aid. The first requirement is that you must be a student pursuing higher education. You must also be enrolled in a degree, certificate, or other approved program at an eligible higher education school. You must be a U.S. citizen or eligible non-citizen. In addition, you must have a valid Social Security number and register with the Selective Service if required. Also, your eligibility for federal student aid is suspended if you have a conviction for sale or possession of illegal drugs. The period of ineligibility based on drug conviction varies. You will become ineligible only if the conviction is for conduct that occurred during a period of enrollment for which you were receiving government student assistance.

2. Must I Have a High School Diploma?

No. You are eligible for financial aid even if you don't have a high school diploma, but the school must certify that you can benefit from the instruction by giving you a valid "ability-to-benefit" (ATB) test. You must pass this test if you don't have a high school diploma or equivalency at the time of admission.

3. Is Assistance Based on Financial Need?

In most cases, yes. Most federal financial aid is awarded on the basis of financial need. There are a couple of important exceptions. You can get an unsubsidized Stafford loan without having to demonstrate financial need. Loans for parents (PLUS) loans are also unsubsidized and not dependent on financial need. Interest is charged on unsubsidized loans from the time the loan is disbursed until it's paid in full. In contrast, interest on subsidized loans is not charged until repayment begins.

4. Can Parents Borrow to Finance Their Children's Education?

Yes. Parents can apply for the PLUS loan program to help pay education expenses for dependent undergraduate students. Parents have to pass a credit check to qualify. (PLUS loans are now available for graduate and professional students as well.)

5. What Are the Different Types of Student Loans and What's the Difference Between Them?

Federal Stafford loans are made through the Direct Loan Program and the Federal Family Education Loan (FFEL) program. The major difference between the Direct Loan and the FFEL Program is that Direct Loans are originated by the government and FFEL loans by private lenders. There are also some differences in repayment options. Stafford loans may be either subsidized or unsubsidized. (See question # 3 above.)

Perkins loans are low-interest loans for both undergraduate and graduate students with exceptional financial need. Perkins loans are originated and serviced by participating schools and repaid to the schools.

PLUS loans allow parents to borrow to pay for the education of dependent undergraduate children enrolled in school at least half time.

These are the main federal financial loan programs. There are also federal grant programs such as Pell grants as well as many state financial assistance programs. In addition, there are a growing number of private lenders that offer student loans.

6. What Happens After I Finish School? Do I Have to Pay My Loans Back Right Away?

In most cases, no. The repayment date varies depending on the type of loan you have. Stafford loan repayment generally begins six months after graduation. The time before you have to start repaying is called a grace period. You don't have to pay any principal on the loan and you won't be charged interest during the grace period if you have a subsidized loan. During the grace period on an unsubsidized loan, you don't have to pay any principal, but you will be charged interest. You can choose to pay the interest during the grace period. Perkins loan repayment usually begins nine months after graduation. Parent PLUS loans must be paid back within sixty days after the final loan disbursement for the period of enrollment for which the parent borrowed. There is no grace period for these loans.

7. What Happens If I Drop Out? Do I Still Have to Pay Back My Loans?

You may cancel all or a portion of your loan if you inform the school within fourteen days after the school sends you notice that it is crediting your account. If you withdraw later than that, there is a formula that schools must use to determine the amount of assistance you have earned up until your withdrawal date. If you received more assistance than you earned, the excess funds must be returned. If you received excess funds, your school should help explain what portion needs to be returned.

The amount of financial assistance you've earned is calculated on a pro-rata basis. For example, if you completed 30% of the payment period or period of enrollment, you earned 30% of the assistance you were originally scheduled to receive. Once you've completed more than 60% of the payment period or period of enrollment, you earn all of your assistance. You are generally responsible for paying back the assistance you have earned.

8. Do I Have to Pay Back My Loans If the School Didn't Provide Quality Instruction?

Probably. However, you may have some options particularly if the school deceived you by promising something that it didn't deliver. You may be able to raise deception or fraud as a defense if you are later sued for collection. The problem is that it is very difficult to get the lender on the hook for problems caused by the school. You should be eligible to cancel your loan if the school closed while you were in attendance or within ninety days of when you withdrew (see # 11 below). Be sure to send complaints about the school to both the state and federal departments of education. The sooner you complain, the more likely you can get help.

9. What Can I Do If I Can't Pay Back My Loans?

The answer depends first on whether you are already in default. You have a lot more options if you haven't yet defaulted. In general, you will be in default if you haven't made your payments for nine months.

One way to stay out of trouble before default is to change your payment plan to a more affordable plan. Although the options vary depending on the type of loan you have, every program gives you choices beyond the standard repayment plan. Both the FFEL and Direct Loan programs have payment plan options for low-income borrowers. The Direct Loan program offers an income-contingent repayment plan (ICRP) and the FFEL program has an income-sensitive repayment plan (ISRP). Under these plans, your monthly loan payment is based on your annual income, family size, and loan amount.

You can also postpone (or defer) your payments if you are not yet in default (see #10 below). Additionally, you can apply for forbearance whether you are in default or not. Forbearance is a temporary stoppage of payments, extension of time to make payments, or acceptance of smaller payments. Unlike deferments, interest continues to accrue while you are in a forbearance period.

10. What Types of Deferments Are Available?

The deferments are somewhat different depending on the type of loan you have. The following deferments are available for most loans disbursed after July 1993:

- student deferments for at least half-time study,
- graduate fellowship deferments,
- rehabilitation training program deferments,
- unemployment deferments not to exceed three years, or
- economic hardship deferments, granted one year at a time for a maximum of three years.

11. What Types of Cancellations Are Available?

Cancellations vary by type of loan. In particular, the Perkins loan program has many more options than other loan programs. The key cancellation options for all federal loan programs are:

- closed school (the school closed while you were enrolled or close to the time you withdrew),
- false certification (the school falsely certified your eligibility, usually because you were not a high school graduate and there was a problem with the ability-to-benefit test. There are other grounds for false certification cancellations, including if your loan was forged or if you were a victim of identity theft),
- borrower's permanent and total disability,
- borrower's death,
- unpaid refund (partial or full cancellation if the school failed to pay a refund owed), or
- limited cancellations for teachers working in certain designated low-income areas or teaching high-need subjects such as math and science.

You should always check first to see whether you are eligible for a cancellation. This is the most complete way to get out of trouble. If you apply and qualify, your loan will be cancelled, any money you paid voluntarily or involuntarily should be returned, and your credit report should be cleared up.

12. How Do I Apply for a Cancellation?

You usually have to apply in writing. There are different forms for different types of cancellations. The forms are available on the Department of Education website (www.ed.gov) or by calling the Federal Student Aid Line, 1-800-4-FED-AID. They are also reprinted in the National Consumer Law Center's publication, *Student Loan Law* (3d ed. 2006).

13. What Can the Government Do to Collect from Me If I Can't Repay My Loans?

The government has collection powers far beyond those of most private creditors. Once you are in default, they can try to collect from you in the following ways:

- Seizing your tax return,
- Garnishing a portion of your wages,
- Taking a portion of certain federal benefits such as Social Security retirement, or
- Suing you in court.

Like most creditors, the government will also report delinquencies and defaults to credit reporting bureaus. Even before you are in default, if you stop paying back your loans, you will begin to receive collection letters and phone calls informing you of the various powers the government can use to collect from you.

14. Doesn't the Government Have to Sue Me First Before Garnishing My Wages, Seizing My Tax Return, or Taking My Federal Benefits?

No.

15. Does the Government Have a Time Limit When They Have to Stop Collecting from Me?

In general, there is no statute of limitations for student loan collections.

16. Can I Go Back to School If I Already Have an Outstanding Student Loan?

You can go back to school, but you are not eligible for new financial assistance if you are in default on previous loans. You can become eligible again if you can get out of default.

17. Can I Discharge My Student Loan in Bankruptcy?

Only in very limited circumstances. You must show that repaying your student loan will cause "undue hardship." You can find out more about this standard in the National Consumer Law Center's publication *Student Loan Law* (3d ed. 2006).

18. What Is Loan Consolidation?

Loan consolidation generally allows you to lower monthly payments by combining several loans into one packaged loan and extending your repayment period. It is similar to refinancing a mortgage loan. You can even consolidate just one loan. There are two main types of consolidation loans. Direct Consolidation loans are available through the Department of

Education. FFEL Consolidation loans are available from participating lenders. There are some important differences between the two programs.

To find out more about FFEL loan consolidation, you will need to contact private lenders. You can find out about the Department of Education's Direct Loan consolidation program by calling 1-800-557-7392 or going on-line at www.ed.gov/offices/OPE/DirectLoan.

19. What Are the Best Ways to Get Out of Default?

The most complete solution is to cancel your loan (see # 11 above). The problem is that cancellations are available only in very limited circumstances.

You can renew eligibility, but not necessarily get out of default, by requesting a "reasonable and affordable payment plan" and making six on-time consecutive payments under this plan. It is critical not to enter into a repayment plan that you can't afford. If you stop making payments after renewing eligibility through a reasonable and affordable repayment plan, you won't automatically have this option again.

If you make nine consecutive on-time payments in a ten-month period and jump through a few other hoops, you will be eligible to "rehabilitate" your loan. Successful rehabilitation will get you out of default. Loan consolidation (see # 18 above) is another option. Consolidation eliminates the old loans on which you were in default in favor of a new consolidation loan, with new terms and a new payment schedule. However, not all lenders will consolidate defaulted loans. There are limits in both the FFEL and Direct Consolidation loan programs.

In some cases, you can also get out of default by paying a lump sum to the Department of Education or requesting the Department to compromise your loan.

20. Where Can I Go for More Information?

You can find a lot of information on the Department of Education website at www.ed.gov. You can also call the Department of Education toll-free at the Federal Student Aid Information Center, 1-800-4-FED-AID (1-800-433-3243). The number for TTY users is 1-800-730-8913. You can get information about the Direct Consolidation Loan program by calling 1-800-557-7392 (TTY: 1-800-557-7395). If you already have a student loan and are having a problem, you should consider contacting the Student Loan Ombudsman toll-free at 1-877-557-2575 or on-line at www.fsahelp.ed.gov/ombudsman/index.html. You should first try to resolve the problem on your own before calling the Ombudsman.

The Department of Education publishes very useful guides, including "Funding Education Beyond High School" and "Repaying Your Student Loans" (http://studentaid.ed.gov/PORTALSWebApp/students/english/publications.jsp). The National Consumer Law Center publishes *Student Loan Law* (3d ed. 2006), a guide for advocates representing clients with student loan problems. See www.consumerlaw.org or call National Consumer Law Center Publications 617-542-9595, ext. 1, for more information.

Index

ASSISTANCE FOR BORROWERS (*cont.*)
for-profit counselors, 1.9.2
frequently asked questions, Appx. I
FSAIC, *see* FEDERAL STUDENT AID INFORMATION
    CENTER
NSLDS, *see* NATIONAL STUDENT LOAN DATA SYSTEM
    (NSLDS)
Student Loan Ombudsman, *see* STUDENT LOAN OMBUDS-
    MAN

ATB
see ABILITY-TO-BENEFIT (ATB) CERTIFICATION

ATTORNEY FEES AND COSTS
see also ATTORNEYS; COLLECTION FEES
collection fees, inclusion, 4.4.2

ATTORNEYS
see also ATTORNEY FEES AND COSTS
FDCPA, application, 4.5.3.2
public service attorneys, cancellation of loans, 6.8

BANKRUPT SCHOOLS
claims against, 9.4.1.4

BANKRUPTCY DISCHARGE
availability, 7.2
Bankruptcy Abuse Prevention, Consumer Protection Act, 7.2.2
chapter 13 advantages when loan not dischargeable, 7.4
    co-debtor stay, 7.4.2
    raising defenses, 7.4.3
    separate classification, 7.4.1
dischargeability determination, 7.3
    adversary proceedings, 7.3.1, 7.3.2
    change in circumstances, effect, 7.3.1
    chapter 13 plan provisions, 7.3.2
    deferral by court, 7.2.4.2
    older standards, use, 7.3.4
    procedure, 7.3.1
    sample complaint, Appx. E.6.1
    sample discovery, Appx. F.3
    state agencies, involving, 7.3.3
    subsequent to bankruptcy proceeding, 7.3.1, 7.3.4
effect, 7.5
    credit record, on, 4.3.4.2.3
filing of proceedings
    considerations, 7.1
    forbearances, 3.3.2
    tax refund intercepts, effect, 5.2.4
guaranteed-loan status lost, 9.6.4
HEALs, 7.2.4.7
ICRPs, effect, 7.2.4.6
old loans, 7.2.3
    undue hardship claims, 7.2.4.4
overview, 7.1
partial discharges, 7.2.4.5
post-petition interest, 7.3.2
raising school's fraud, Appx. E.6
reopening bankruptcy cases, 7.3.1
restrictions, 7.2.1, 7.2.2
rights after discharge, 7.5
    enjoining discriminatory denial of loan, Appx. E.6.2
seven-year rule, 7.2.3
undue hardship requirement, 7.2.1, 7.2.2, 7.2.4

BANKS
guaranteed loans, *see* FFELs

private loans, *see* PRIVATE STUDENT LOANS
school-related defenses, application, 9.7

BASIC EDUCATIONAL OPPORTUNITY GRANTS
    (BEOG)
see also GRANTS
overpayments, 1.4.2.4
    bankruptcy discharge, 7.2.1, 7.2.2
overview, 1.4.2.4
repayment, 1.4.2.4

BORROWER ASSISTANCE
see ASSISTANCE FOR BORROWERS

BUSINESS SCHOOLS
see VOCATIONAL SCHOOLS

CANCELLATION OF LOAN
see also COMPROMISES; FORBEARANCES; STATUTORY
    DISCHARGES
checklist, 1.8.1
Direct Loans, 6.8
FFELs, 6.8
government loans, 2.6
    after disclosures, 2.4.1
    return of funds, 2.6
overview, 6.1
Perkins Loans, 6.8
tax issues, 6.9

CHECKLISTS
loan cancellation, 1.8.1
repayment, 1.8.3
steps where cancellation unavailable, 1.8.2

CHECKS
student loan funds, endorsement, 9.5.3.1

CHILD CARE PROVIDERS
cancellation of loans, 6.8

CIVIL RIGHTS CLAIMS
collection practices, 4.5.5.1

CLASS ACTIONS
advantages and disadvantages, 9.4.2
sample pleadings
    collection procedures, Appx. E.3
    DOE discharge procedures, Appx. E.2.3
    DOE for trade school fraud, Appx. E.5.2
    private student loans, Appx. E.7.1
    wage garnishment challenges, Appx. E.4
trade school abuses, 9.4.2, Appx. E.5.2

CLEARINGHOUSE NUMBERS
see also SARGENT SHRIVER NATIONAL CENTER ON
    POVERTY LAW
documents, 1.3.2

CLOSED SCHOOL DISCHARGE
see also STATUTORY DISCHARGES
application, 6.2.1
effect, 6.2.3
FISLs, 6.2.5
form, Appx. D.3.1
guaranteed-loan status lost, 9.6.4
obtaining, 6.2.4
    appeals, 6.2.4.4, 6.10
    generally, 6.2.4.1

SCHOOL-RELATED CLAIMS AND DEFENSES (*cont.*)
affirmative litigation
class actions, 9.4.2
common law claims, 9.3.4
declaratory relief, 9.4.1.1, 9.5.1
developing the case, 9.4.3
federal claims, 9.3.3
injunctive relief, 9.4.1.1
potential defendants, 9.4.1
proving damages, 9.4.4
state claims, 9.3.2
affirmative vs. defensive claims, 9.3.1
bankrupt schools, 9.4.1.4
chapter 13 bankruptcy, raising, 7.4.3
class actions, *see* CLASS ACTIONS
closed schools, 9.4.1.4
common law claims, 9.3.4
consolidation loans, raising after, 8.2.4, 9.6.5
contract claims and defenses, 9.3.4.2, 9.5.3
credit reports, correcting, 4.3.4.2.3
defending collection actions, 9.5, 9.6
consolidated loans, 9.6.5
contract defenses, 9.5.3
Direct loans, 9.6.2.2
FFELs, 9.6.2.4, 9.6.3, 9.6.4
FISLs, 9.6.2.3
generally, 9.6.2.1
Perkins loans, 9.6.2.1
procedural issues, 9.5.1
servicemembers, 9.5.4
Direct Loans, 9.6.2.2
DOE, claims against, 9.3.3.3, 9.4.1.1
evidence, obtaining, 9.4.3
false certification, 6.3
federal claims, 9.3.3
False Claims Act, 9.3.3.2
HEA, 9.3.3.1
other claims, 9.3.3.3
RICO, 9.3.3.1
FFELs, 9.6.2.4, 9.6.3, 9.6.4
FISLs, 9.6.2.3
guaranteed status lost, effect, 9.6.4
ineligible schools, 9.6.3.6, 9.6.4
insolvent schools, 9.4.1.4
joinder, 9.5.1
legal theories and strategies
agency, 9.6.3.2
common law claims, 9.3.4
contract claims and defenses, 9.3.4.2, 9.5.3
education laws, 9.3.2.2, 9.3.3.1
False Claims Act, 9.3.3.2
federal claims, 9.3.3
fraud claims, 9.3.4.1
misrepresentation, 9.6.3.2
negligence claims, 9.3.3.3, 9.3.4.1
RICO, 9.3.2.3, 9.3.3.1
state claims, 9.3.2
UDAP claims, 9.3.2.1
lender liability for
agency theories, 9.6.3.2
DOE, 9.6.2.2, 9.6.2.3
FTC Holder Notice, 9.6.2.4, 9.6.3.4
origination theories, 9.6.3.5
non-guaranteed loans, 9.6.4

private loans, 9.7
school as lender, 9.6.2.1
state law, 9.6.3.3
overview of trade school abuses, 9.1
Perkins Loans, 9.6.2.1
private loans, 9.7
raising, 9.3.1, 9.6.1
recoupment claims, 9.4.1.4
sample discovery, Appx. F.2
sample pleadings, Appx. E.5
school closure, 6.2.5
state claims, 9.3.2
education laws, 9.3.2.2
UDAP theories, 9.3.2.1
state licensing agencies, claims against, 9.4.1.3
statutory discharges
alternative, 9.5.3.1
interrelationship, 9.5.3.2
tuition recovery funds, 9.8
types of school misconduct, 6.3.1, 9.1
UDAP claims, *see* UDAP CLAIMS

SCHOOLS
bankrupt or insolvent schools, 9.4.1.4
claims against, *see* SCHOOL-RELATED CLAIMS AND DEFENSES
closed-school discharge, 6.2
correspondence schools, *see* CORRESPONDENCE SCHOOLS
default rate sanctions, 9.2.5
appeals, 9.2.5.3
direct loans from
collection fees, 4.4.1
Perkins Loans, 1.4.2.2
"school as lender" program, 1.4.2.1.2
DOE files on, obtaining, 6.3.2.2.2
"eligible institutions," 1.4.4, 7.2.2, 9.2
regulations, selected text, Appx. B.5.1
falsification discharge, 6.3
FDCPA, application, 4.5.3.4
federal student aid
percentage restrictions, 9.2.2
regulations, selected text, Appx. B.5
files and records, obtaining, 6.3.2.2.3
origination relationships, 9.6.3.5
proprietary schools, *see* PROPRIETARY INSTITUTIONS
recruiters, *see* RECRUITERS
trade school abuses, *see* SCHOOL-RELATED CLAIMS AND DEFENSES
transcripts, *see* TRANSCRIPTS
unpaid refunds, 6.4
vocational schools, *see* VOCATIONAL SCHOOLS

SECONDARY MARKET LENDERS
see also LENDERS
FDCPA, application, 4.5.3.4
Sallie Mae, *see* STUDENT LOAN MARKETING ASSOCIATION (SALLIE MAE)

SECRETARY OF EDUCATION
see DEPARTMENT OF EDUCATION (DOE)

SEIZURE OF ASSETS
federal benefits, *see* ADMINISTRATIVE OFFSETS
generally, 5.1
tax refunds, *see* TAX REFUND INTERCEPTS
wage garnishments, *see* WAGE GARNISHMENTS

SERVICEMEMBER CIVIL RELIEF ACT
see also MILITARY SERVICE
protections, 9.5.4.1

SERVICING AGENCIES
FDCPA, application, 4.5.3.4
function, 1.4.1
reporting to credit bureaus, 4.3.4.2.1
Sallie Mae, *see* STUDENT LOAN MARKETING ASSOCIA-
TION (SALLIE MAE)

SLSs
see SUPPLEMENTAL LOANS FOR STUDENTS (SLSs)

SOCIAL SECURITY BENEFITS
deferment eligibility, 3.2.4.2.1
offsets, *see* ADMINISTRATIVE OFFSETS

SOVEREIGN IMMUNITY
laches doctrine, application, 4.2.3.1
state agencies, bankruptcy dischargeability proceedings and,
7.3.3

SPOUSES
consolidation of loans, 8.2.2.2
ICRP payments, 8.2.2.5
repayment plans, income considerations, 8.3.3
temporary disability, FFEL deferment, 3.2.5
tax refund intercepts, rights, 5.2.5

STAFFORD LOANS (GSLs)
see also DIRECT LOANS; FFELs
bankruptcy discharge, 7.2.1, 7.2.2
closed-school discharge, 6.2.5
consolidation loans, 8.2.2.2
death discharge, 6.7
disbursement of funds, 2.6
disclosures prior to repayment, 2.7.1
DOE collection, 4.3.2
history of, 1.4.1
interest rates, 2.1.1
loan limits, 2.2
origination fees, 2.3
overview, 1.4.2.1.1
repayment prior to default, 2.7
    disclosures, 2.7.1
    grace period, 2.7.2
unpaid-refund discharge, 6.4

STATE AGENCIES
bankruptcy dischargeability proceedings, 7.3.3
complaints to re collection abuses, 4.5.5.2
FOIA requests, 9.4.3
guaranty agencies, *see* GUARANTY AGENCIES
licensing agencies, *see* LICENSING AGENCIES (STATE)

STATE LAW
collection laws, application to student loans, 4.5.4
    garnishment restrictions, 5.3.1
    personal exemptions, 5.2.2.7
lender liability statutes, 9.6.3.3
loan enforceability, application, 9.5.3.1
preemption, *see* FEDERAL PREEMPTION
private student loans, application, 9.7
professional license suspension for default, 5.5
trade school abuses, 9.3.2
    education statutes, 9.3.2.2
    RICO claims, 9.3.2.3

UDAP claims, *see* UDAP CLAIMS
usury limits, 2.1.2

STATE LICENSING AGENCIES
see LICENSING AGENCIES

STATE TUITION RECOVERY FUNDS (STRFs)
see STUDENT TUITION RECOVERY FUNDS (STRFs)

STATUTE OF LIMITATIONS
appeals of agency decisions, 6.10
federal benefits offsets, 5.4.3.3
federal student loans, elimination, 4.2.1, 9.5.2
    DCIA, application, 5.4.3.3
    equitable defenses, application, 4.2.3.1
    scope, 4.2.2
private student loans, 4.2.2

STATUTORY DISCHARGES
appeals, 6.10
closed-school discharge, 6.2
contract defenses
    alternative, 9.5.3.1
    interrelationship, 9.5.3.2
credit record, cleaning up, 4.3.4.2.3
death discharge, 6.7
disability discharge, 6.6
DOE policy guidance letters, Appx. C.1
effect on future loans
    bankruptcy discharge, 7.5
    closed-school discharge, 6.2.3
    disability discharge, 6.6.4.3, 6.6.6, 6.6.7
    false-certification discharge, 6.3.6
false-certification discharge, 6.3
forbearances pending, 3.3.2
forms, Appx. D.3
guaranteed status lost loans, 9.6.4
interrelationship, 6.5
judicial review, 6.10
multiple discharges, 6.5
overview, 6.1
paid-in-full loans, refunds, 6.2.3, 6.6.3
sample pleadings, Appx. E.2
STRFs, interrelationship, 9.8.2
tax issues, 6.9
unpaid-refund discharge, 6.4

STUDENT AID REPORT (SAR)
expected family contribution, 1.4.3

STUDENT GUIDES
DOE publications, 1.9.1.2

**STUDENT LOAN MARKETING ASSOCIATION (SALLIE
MAE)**
FDCPA, application, 4.5.3.4
function, 1.4.1

STUDENT LOAN OMBUDSMAN
contacting, 1.9.1.1
    collection abuse complaints, 4.5.5.2
    information on loan collections, 4.3.2
function, 1.9.1.1

STUDENT LOANS
assistance for borrowers, *see* ASSISTANCE FOR BORROW-
ERS
bankruptcy discharge, *see* BANKRUPTCY DISCHARGE

References are to sections

Quick Reference to the Consumer Credit and Sales Legal Practice Series

References are to sections in *all* manuals in NCLC's Consumer Credit and Sales Legal Practice Series. References followed by "S" appear only in a Supplement.

Readers should also consider another search option available at ***www.consumerlaw.org/keyword***. There, users can search all seventeen NCLC manuals for a case name, party name, statutory or regulatory citation, or *any* other word, phrase, or combination of terms. The search engine provides the title, page number and context of every occurrence of that word or phrase within each of the NCLC manuals. Further search instructions and tips are provided on the web site.

The Quick Reference to the Consumer Credit and Sales Legal Practice Series pinpoints where to find specific topics analyzed in the NCLC manuals. References are to individual manual or supplement sections. For more information on these volumes, see *What Your Library Should Contain* at the beginning of this volume, or go to www.consumerlaw.org.

This Quick Reference is a speedy means to locate key terms in the appropriate NCLC manual. More detailed indexes are found at the end of the individual NCLC volumes. Both the detailed contents pages and the detailed indexes for each manual are also available on NCLC's web site, www.consumerlaw.org.

NCLC *strongly recommends*, when searching for PLEADINGS on a particular subject, that users refer to the *Index Guide* accompanying *Consumer Law Pleadings on CD-Rom*, and *not* to this *Quick Reference*. Another option is to search for pleadings directly on the *Consumer Law Pleadings* CD-Rom or on the *Consumer Law in a Box* CD-Rom, using the finding tools that are provided on the CD-Roms themselves.

The finding tools found on *Consumer Law in a Box* are also an effective means to find statutes, regulations, agency interpretations, legislative history, and other primary source material found on NCLC's CD-Roms. Other search options are detailed in *Finding Aids and Search Tips, supra.*

Abbreviations

AUS	=	Access to Utility Service (3d ed. 2004 and 2006 Supp.)
Auto	=	Automobile Fraud (2d ed. 2003 and 2006 Supp.)
Arbit	=	Consumer Arbitration Agreements (4th ed. 2004 and 2006 Supp.)
CBPL	=	Consumer Banking and Payments Law (3d ed. 2005 and 2006 Supp.)
Bankr	=	Consumer Bankruptcy Law and Practice (8th ed. 2006)
CCA	=	Consumer Class Actions (6th ed. 2006)
CLP	=	Consumer Law Pleadings, Numbers One Through Twelve (2006)
COC	=	The Cost of Credit (3d ed. 2005 and 2006 Supp.)
CD	=	Credit Discrimination (4th ed. 2005 and 2006 Supp.)
FCR	=	Fair Credit Reporting (6th ed. 2006)
FDC	=	Fair Debt Collection (5th ed. 2004 and 2006 Supp.)
Fore	=	Foreclosures (2005 and 2006 Supp.)
Repo	=	Repossessions (6th ed. 2005 and 2006 Supp.)
Stud	=	Student Loan Law (3d ed. 2006)
TIL	=	Truth in Lending (5th ed. 2003 and 2006 Supp.)
UDAP	=	Unfair and Deceptive Acts and Practices (6th ed. 2004 and 2006 Supp.)
Warr	=	Consumer Warranty Law (3d ed. 2006)

References are to sections in *all* manuals in NCLC's Consumer Credit and Sales Legal Practice Series

References are to sections in *all* manuals in NCLC's Consumer Credit and Sales Legal Practice Series

References are to sections in *all* manuals in NCLC's Consumer Credit and Sales Legal Practice Series

References are to sections in *all* manuals in NCLC's Consumer Credit and Sales Legal Practice Series

About the Companion CD-Rom

CD-Rom Supersedes All Prior CD-Roms

This CD-Rom supersedes the CD-Roms accompanying *Student Loan Law* (2d ed. 2002) and its supplements. Discard all prior CDs. The 2006 CD contains everything found on prior CDs and much additional material.

What Is on the CD-Rom

For a detailed listing of the CD's contents, see the CD-Rom Contents section on page xxi of this book. Highlights and new additions include:

- Key federal student loan statutes and regulations, all up-to-date for 2006, and Department of Education policy guidance letters, including new letters regarding the Higher Education Reconciliation Act;
- Department of Education forms to apply for deferment, forbearance, loan discharges, and consolidation loans, many newly updated for 2006;
- Sample letters seeking reasonable repayment plan, group false certification discharge, and legal pleadings regarding collection abuse, garnishment, and trade school fraud as a defense;
- Complaints and discovery in student loan collection abuse cases;
- Directory of guaranty agencies;
- GAO, Department of Education, and other reports on student loans, including a new NCLC report on the urgent need for student loan reform; and
- Several guides for students regarding student loans, including the 2006–2007 Department of Education Student Financial Aid Guide in English and Spanish.

How to Use the CD-Rom

The CD's pop-up menu quickly allows you to use the CD—just place the CD into its drive and click on the "Start NCLC CD" button that will pop up in the middle of the screen. You can also access the CD by clicking on a desktop icon that you can create using the pop-up menu.[1] For detailed installation instructions, see *One-Time Installation* below.

All the CD-Rom's information is available in PDF (Acrobat) format, making the information:

- Highly readable (identical to the printed pages in the book);
- Easily navigated (with bookmarks, "buttons," and Internet-style forward and backward searches);
- Easy to locate with keyword searches and other quick-search techniques across the whole CD-Rom; and
- Easy to paste into a word processor.

While much of the material is also found on the CD-Rom in word processing format, we strongly recommend you use the material in PDF format—not only because it is easiest to use, contains the most features, and includes more material, but also because you can easily switch back to a word processing format when you prefer.

Acrobat Reader 5.0.5 and 7.0.7 come free of charge with the CD-Rom. **We strongly recommend that new Acrobat users read the Acrobat tutorial on the Home Page. It takes two minutes and will really pay off.**

How to Find Documents in Word Processing Format

Most pleadings and other practice aids are also available in Microsoft Word format to make them more easily adaptable for individual use. (Current versions of WordPerfect are able to convert the Word documents upon opening them.) The CD-Rom offers several ways to find those word processing documents. One option is simply to browse to the folder on the CD-Rom containing all the word processing files and open the desired document from your standard word processing program, such as Word or WordPerfect. All word processing documents are in the D:\WP_Files folder, if "D:" is the CD-Rom drive,[2] and are further organized by book title. Documents that appear in the book are named after the corresponding appendix; other documents have descriptive file names.

---

1 Alternatively, click on the D:\Start.pdf file on "My Computer"

or open that file in Acrobat—always assuming "D:" is the CD-Rom drive on your computer.

2 The CD-Rom drive could be any letter following "D:" depending on your computer's configuration.

Another option is to navigate the CD in PDF format, and, when a particular document is on the screen, click on the corresponding bookmark for the "Word version of . . ." This will automatically run Word, WordPerfect for Windows, or *any other word processor* that is associated with the ".DOC" extension, and then open the word processing file that corresponds to the Acrobat document.[3]

Important Information Before Opening the CD-Rom Package

Before opening the CD-Rom package, please read this information. Opening the package constitutes acceptance of the following described terms. In addition, the *book* is not returnable once the seal to the *CD-Rom* has been broken.

The CD-Rom is copyrighted and all rights are reserved by the National Consumer Law Center, Inc. No copyright is claimed to the text of statutes, regulations, excerpts from court opinions, or any part of an original work prepared by a United States Government employee.

You may not commercially distribute the CD-Rom or otherwise reproduce, publish, distribute or use the disk in any manner that may infringe on any copyright or other proprietary right of the National Consumer Law Center. Nor may you otherwise transfer the CD-Rom or this agreement to any other party unless that party agrees to accept the terms and conditions of this agreement. You may use the CD-Rom on only one computer and by one user at a time.

The CD-Rom is warranted to be free of defects in materials and faulty workmanship under normal use for a period of ninety days after purchase. If a defect is discovered in the CD-Rom during this warranty period, a replacement disk can be obtained at no charge by sending the defective disk, postage prepaid, with information identifying the purchaser, to National Consumer Law Center, Publications Department, 77 Summer Street, 10th Floor, Boston, MA 02110. After the ninety-day period, a replacement will be available on the same terms, but will also require a $20 prepayment.

The National Consumer Law Center makes no other warranty or representation, either express or implied, with

---

3 For instructions on how to associate WordPerfect to the ".DOC" extension, go to the CD-Rom's home page and click on "How to Use/Help," then "Word Files."

respect to this disk, its quality, performance, merchantability, or fitness for a particular purpose. In no event will the National Consumer Law Center be liable for direct, indirect, special, incidental, or consequential damages arising out of the use or inability to use the disk. The exclusion of implied warranties is not effective in some states, and thus this exclusion may not apply to you.

System Requirements

Use of this CD-Rom requires a Windows-based PC with a CD-Rom drive. (Macintosh users report success using NCLC CDs, but the CD has been tested only on Windows-based PCs.) The CD-Rom's features are optimized with Acrobat Reader 5 or later. Acrobat Reader versions 5.0.5 and 7.0.7 are included free on this CD-Rom, and either will work with this CD-Rom as long as it is compatible with your version of Windows. Acrobat Reader 5 is compatible with Windows 95/98/Me/NT/2000/XP, while Acrobat Reader 7.0.7 is compatible with Windows 98SE/Me/NT/2000/XP. If you already have Acrobat Reader 6.0, we *highly* recommend you download and install the 6.0.1 update from Adobe's web site at www.adobe.com because a bug in version 6.0 interferes with optimum use of this CD-Rom. See the *Acrobat 6 Problem* button on the home page for details. The Microsoft Word versions of pleadings and practice aids can be used with any reasonably current word processor (1995 or later).

One-Time Installation

When the CD-Rom is inserted in its drive, a menu will pop up automatically. (Please be patient if you have a slow CD-Rom drive; this will only take a few moments.) If you do not already have Acrobat Reader 5.0.5 or later, first click the "Install Acrobat Reader" button. Do not reboot, but then click on the "Make Shortcut Icon" button. (You need not make another shortcut icon if you already have done so for another NCLC CD.) Then reboot and follow the *How to Use the CD-Rom* instructions above.

[*Note*: If the pop-up menu fails to appear, go to "My Computer," right-click "D:" if that is the CD-Rom drive, and select "Open." Then double-click on "Read_Me.txt" for alternate installation and use instructions.]